The Age of Belief

Jesus of Nazareth, c4 B.C.–A.D. 30

Paul's missionary journeys,
cA.D. 32–60

Barbarian invasions of Rome,
3rd–5th centuries

Roman Empire reunified under
Constantine; Christianity
spreading there, 324

Goths depose last Emperor of
Western Empire, 476

Justinian Byzantium Emperor,
527–65

Muhammad, 570–632

Charlemagne crowned Holy
Roman Emperor, 800

Battle of Hastings, 1066

Crusades, 1096–1291

Franciscan and Dominican orders founded, 1210, 1215

Magna Carta, 1215

Black Death, 14th century

Hundred Years' War, 1337–1453

Printing press invented, 1440

Ottoman Turks capture
Constantinople, 1453

Spanish Inquisition, 1478–1834

Jews expelled from Spain, 1492

Christopher Columbus's first
voyage to America, 1492

Martin Luther's ninety-five
theses, 1517

Ferdinand Magellan circum-
navigates globe, 1519

Henry VIII severs ties with
Rome, 1534

English destroy Spain's
Invincible Armada, 1588

Augustine, 354–430
  On Free Choice of the Will, 395
  Confessions, c397
  The Nature of the Good, 404
  On the Trinity, 417
  The City of God, 426

Boethius, c480–524
  The Consolation of Philosophy,
  c523

Plato's Academy closed, 529

Al-Kindi, c800–870

John Scotus Erigena, c810–77

Al-Farabi, c873–950

Avicenna, 980–1037

Anselm, 1033–1109

Al-Ghazzali, 1058–1111

Averroes, 1126–98

Moses Maimonides, 1135–1204

Albert the Great, 1193–1280

Roger Bacon, 1214–94

Bonaventure, 1221–74

Thomas Aquinas, 1224/5–74
  On Being and Essence, c1252–55
  Disputed Questions on Truth,
  c1256–59
  Summa contra Gentiles, 1259–65
  Disputed Questions on Evil,
  c1269–72
  Summa Theologica, c1266–74

Duns Scotus, c1270–1308

William of Ockham, 1280–1349

Desiderius Erasmus, 1466–1536

Niccolo Machiavelli, 1469–1527
  The Prince, 1532

Michel de Montaigne, 1533–92
  Apology for Raymond Sebond,
  1580

Writing of Gospels,
1st century A.D.

Christian apologetic writings,
2nd century

Christian homiletic and theological writings, 3rd century

Writings of Greek and Latin
Fathers, 4th–6th centuries

Nicene Creed, 325

Library at Alexandria destroyed
by fire, 391

Bede, father of English literature
and history, 673–735

Beowulf, English epic poem, early
8th century

Revival of learning under
Charlemagne launched, 782

Development of Gothic
polyphony, late 12th century

Dante, poet, 1265–1321

Giotto, painter, c1266–1337

Petrarch, poet, 1304–74

Geoffrey Chaucer, author,
c1340–1400

Leonardo da Vinci, painter,
sculptor, 1452–1519

Michelangelo, sculptor, painter,
1475–1564

Titian, painter, c1487/90–1576

Raphael, painter, 1483–1520

Benvenuto Cellini, sculptor,
author, 1500–1571

John Calvin, theologian,
1509–64

El Greco, painter, 1541–1614

Nicolaus Copernicus proposes
heliocentric theory, 1543

The Age of Reason

Stuarts replace Tudors on
English throne, 1603

Jamestown founded, 1607

Thirty Years' War, 1618–48

Pierre Charron, 1541–1603

Francis Bacon, 1561–1626

Jean-Pierre Camus, 1584–
1654

Miguel de Cervantes, author,
1547–1616

William Shakespeare, dramatist,
poet, 1564–1616

THE WESTERN WORLD	PHILOSOPHY	OTHER DISCIPLINES
African slaves to Virginia, 1619	Thomas Hobbes, 1588–1679	Galileo, physicist, astronomer, 1564–1642
Mayflower compact, 1620	*De Cive*, 1642	
Purchase of Manhattan by Dutch, 1624	*The Elements of Law*, 1650	Johannes Kepler, astronomer, 1571–1630
	Leviathan, 1651	
The Long Parliament, 1640	*De Corpore*, 1655	John Donne, poet, clergyman, 1572–1631
English Civil War, 1642–46	*De Homine*, 1658	
Louis XIV, King of France, 1643–1715	Pierre Gassendi, 1592–1655	Peter Paul Rubens, painter, 1577–1640
	Rene Descartes, 1596–1650	
Charles I of England executed, 1649	*Discourse on Method*, 1637	William Harvey, physician, anatomist, 1578–1657
	Meditations on First Philosophy, 1641	
The Commonwealth (England), 1649–60	*Principles of Philosophy*, 1644	Giovanni Bernini, sculptor, architect, 1598–1680
	The Passions of the Soul, 1649	
Restoration of the Stuarts, under Charles II, 1660	*Rules for the Direction of the Mind*, 1701	Rembrandt, painter, 1606–69
		John Milton, poet, 1608–1674
English seize New Amsterdam, 1664	Blaise Pascal, 1623–62	King James Bible, 1611
	Baruch Spinoza, 1632–77	Molière, dramatist, actor, 1622–1673
Great Plague kills 15% of London population, 1665	*Ethics*, 1677	
	John Locke, 1632–1704	Sir Christopher Wren, architect, 1632–1723
Habeus Corpus Act passed in England, 1679	*An Essay concerning Human Understanding*, 1690	
		Harvard University, 1636
Glorious Revolution, 1688–89	Joseph Glanvill, 1636–80	Sir Isaac Newton, physicist, mathematician, 1642–1727
Salem witch trials, 1692	Nicolas Malebranche, 1638–1715	
London stock exchange formed, 1698	Gottfried Wilhelm Leibniz, 1646–1716	Henry Purcell, composer, 1659–95
	Theodicy, 1710	

The Age of Enlightenment

Peter the Great, Czar of Russia, 1682–1725	Pierre Bayle, 1647–1706	Edmund Halley, astronomer, 1656–1742
	Giambattista Vico, 1668–1744	
War of the Spanish Succession, 1701–13	Christian Wolff, 1679–1754	Alessandro Scarlatti, composer, 1660–1725
	George Berkeley, 1685–1753	
Union of England and Scotland, 1707	Baron de Montesquieu, 1689–1755	Daniel Defoe, novelist, journalist, c1660–1731
Hanoverians replace Stuarts on English throne, 1714	Joseph Butler, 1692–1752	Jonathan Swift, satirist, 1667–1745
	Voltaire, 1694–1778	
War of the Austrian Succession, 1740–48	Johathan Edwards, 1703–58	Antonio Vivaldi, composer, violinist, 1678–1741
Frederick II (the Great), "the Enlightenment King" of Prussia, 1740–86	Julien Offray de La Mettrie, 1709–51	Johann Sebastian Bach, composer, organist, 1685–1750
	Thomas Reid, 1710–96	George Frideric Handel, composer, 1685–1759
Seven Years' War (French and Indian War, in America), 1756–63	David Hume, 1711–76	
	A Treatise of Human Nature, 1739–40	Alexander Pope, poet, 1688–1744
George III, King of England, 1760–1820	*Essays Moral and Political*, 1741–42	Benjamin Franklin, statesman, inventor, 1706–90

(continued in back of book)

TWELVE GREAT PHILOSOPHERS

« « « « « « « « « « « « « « « « « « » » » » » » » » » » » » » » » » » » »

Twelve Great Philosophers

A Historical Introduction
To Human Nature

Wayne P. Pomerleau

GONZAGA UNIVERSITY

ARDSLEY HOUSE PUBLISHERS, INC., NEW YORK

Address orders and editorial
correspondence to:
Ardsley House, Publishers, Inc.
320 Central Park West
New York, NY 10025

ISBN: 1-880157-54-3

Printed in the United States of America

10 9 8 7 6 5 4 3 2 1

Lovingly dedicated
to my parents,
Joseph and Blanche Pomerleau,
who first taught me
about human nature
and
who enabled me
to pursue the life
of academic philosophy
I find so fulfilling

Contents

«‹«‹«‹«‹«‹«‹«‹«‹«‹«‹«‹«‹«‹«‹«‹«‹«‹«»›»›»›»›»›»›»›»›»›»›»›»›»›»›»›»›»›»

II   *The Age of Belief*   55

HISTORICAL BACKGROUND 56

III   *The Age of Reason* 117

HISTORICAL BACKGROUND *118*

IV The Age of Enlightenment *181*

HISTORICAL BACKGROUND *182*

VI   The Age of Analysis   367

HISTORICAL BACKGROUND 368

Preface

« » » » » » » » » » » » » » » » » » » »

ith which noble tradition do you identify? The assumptions in this ancient greeting, used when meeting someone for the first time, are interesting. Our self-image is tied up with how we relate to various traditions; indeed, this is what it means to have a cultural identity. Among the most important influences on human thought and action are the systems of ideas and ideals with which we identify. But so many traditional systems of views and values compete, in a sense, for our allegiance. In order to choose among them in a rational and responsible way, we must be exposed to them, become familiar with them, understand them, and critically reflect on them. Of course, this is easier said than done and requires time and effort on our part. We normally want some assurance that the time and effort we expend will pay off for us. This is as true for the introductory study of philosophy as for anything else. Why should we believe that pursuing it will be worth our while?

The study of philosophy is no more risk-free than most human activities. What we study could turn out to be trivial, and its presentation could be miserable. People who write and teach philosophy believe it is significant and that progress can be made by pursuing it, that Henry B. Adams was wrong in joking that it is just unintelligible answers to insoluble problems. Philosophical issues are ancient, extending back through two and a half millennia of recorded history. They include such questions as

1. What is reality, both physical and mental, and how are those two dimensions related?
2. How does a human know anything, and what are the limits of human knowledge?
3. Are we genuinely free in (at least some of) our actions, or is that merely a comfortable illusion?
4. What moral, social, and religious values should we adopt and try to follow?
5. Is there any reason to hope that the human personality can survive the death of the body, and what constitutes the fulfillment of human nature?

The philosophical systems we have inherited from the great thinkers of the past attempt to answer these questions in an intelligible, coherent, and comprehensive manner. Philosophers support their theories with reasons. A theory is not just a cluster of alleged facts to be scientifically proved or disproved. Its goal is to *explain* the facts of experience. To the extent that a theory seems valuable, we want to avoid uncritically swallowing it. After we have come to understand it and its supporting reasoning and have seen how its component parts hang together, we need to evaluate it. If a theory fails to make sense, we are not likely to pursue it. If it does make sense but fails to connect with our own experience of the world, we will find it irrelevant. If it both makes sense and connects with our experience of the world, we may consider how persuasive is the explanation it offers. Then it is helpful to be able to compare and contrast this theory with others that offer alternative explanations. If we are lucky, we may find a theory that works for us and seems generally correct. More likely, we will find that different theories present various elements that work for us, and then we will embark on the journey of trying to synthesize those elements. Or, if we are unlucky, we may conclude that every theory we have studied is fatally flawed and that we need to create our own more adequate alternative.

But what if it is not merely a matter of luck? What if there is a way of figuring out, before investing time and effort in studying them, which theories are more likely to pay off, in terms of offering us at least elements of explanations that we can use (either positively or negatively)? Would it not be smart to hedge our bets by studying those theories? And, if there are any such theories, from all those generated over twenty-five centuries, how could we identify them before committing ourselves to considering them?

When we study literature or music, there is a body of great works called "the classics." When we wish to learn about fine paintings, there's a group of artists called the "old masters." These represent achievements that have stood the test of time. They are part of our heritage, a legacy from the past. Of course, there is no guarantee that we will like Shakespeare's sonnets or the symphonies of Beethoven or Rembrandt's paintings; we may hate them and decide, "I'm not interested in *that sort* of literature or music or art at all!" But the fact that serious people, for generations or even centuries, have appreciated them should indicate that they are of some value, even if we don't personally appreciate them. By being exposed to them, we can become better connected with our own cultural traditions and begin to formulate (if only by contrast) alternative approaches that might work better for us (e.g., modern free verse or rap music or pop art).

PAIRS OF ALTERNATIVE VIEWS.   Likewise, some philosophical theories have stood the test of time and are great in the sense of influencing (for better or for worse) the way we think about ourselves, our fellow humans, and our world. There may be few real Platonists walking on our planet today; nevertheless, Plato's philosophy has had a profound impact on our ideas. I am not an Aristotelian myself; yet I know I cannot help being affected by Aristotle's contributions to the Western civilization of which I am part. Although these ancient thinkers died more than twenty-three centuries ago, their theories live and both intrigue and challenge us today. We are also influenced by medieval culture, which has a philosophical history rooted in the dialectical relationship between Augustine (a Christian Platonist) and Aquinas (a Christian Aristotelian). And we are perhaps affected even more immediately by the alternatives of modern theories: Descartes's dualism vs. Hobbes's materialism in the seventeenth century, Hume's scepticism vs. Kant's transcendentalism in the eighteenth, Hegel's idealism vs. Mill's utilitarianism in the nineteenth, and James's pragmatism vs. Sartre's existentialism closer to our times. These twelve are among the classic thinkers, the "old masters," of philosophy. By studying their theories, we can improve our chances of finding something worthwhile, even though, as with masterpieces of literature, music, and pictorial art, we may not like what we find. **We shall analyze these philosophers in pairs** (in every case but one, their lives overlap in time), **to present a kind of debate of ideas in each of these six historical periods, between a theory that tends to be rationalistic and one that is at least broadly empirical.** The choices here reflect pairings of great philosophers, whose systems of thought contrast strongly. Thus, for example, Hobbes was selected for "The Age of Reason" chapter, rather than Locke (who is at least as great a thinker), because the former represents the stronger contrast with Descartes, the father of modern philosophy. For "The Age of Ideology" chapter, Mill seemed the greatest philosopher (Marx being more a great political economist, for example) whose thought represents a powerful ideological contrast to that of Hegel, the giant of the nineteenth century. The most challenging and perhaps most controversial choices were those for "The Age of Analysis" chapter, since most twentieth-century philosophers are too recent to have stood the test of time; James died early in the twentieth century and Sartre finished his most important contributions by midcentury—thus, they have had the time to achieve the greatness of classic thinkers. The other choices—Plato and Aristotle for "The Age of Synthesis," Augustine and Aquinas for "The Age of Belief," Hume and Kant for "The Age of Enlightenment"—seem far more obvious.

A SELECTION FROM GREAT PHILOSOPHERS' WORKS.   This book attempts to solve several practical problems. First, every one of these twelve thinkers presents a philosophical system comprising many hundreds or even thousands of pages of crucial material. Even a professional philosopher or philosophy teacher cannot be expected to have studied it all. How can a beginning student of philosophy hope to cover it? **This book is an attempt to process that mass of material so that it can be absorbed, understood, and critically considered** in the relatively brief span of a semester or even an academic quarter. In the case of all twelve thinkers, we shall concentrate on their masterpieces, while also considering key ideas from their less famous works.

HUMAN NATURE.   A second problem is that each of these twelve philosophical systems is complex in terms of issues analyzed; furthermore, although the issues overlap, not all the great thinkers discuss all the same topics. So, how can we avoid a supermarket approach, with few or no connections relating one theory to another and making comparative analysis possible? **This book focuses on one big issue confronted by each of these twelve philosophers: what is the nature of the human person, essentially relating him or her to all other humans and essentially distinguishing him or her from all nonhuman beings?** In other words, what conditions are both necessary and sufficient to qualify something as human? For example, it seems that all of the more than five billion humans currently inhabiting our planet have hair follicles; but if we met someone who, because of a genetic abnormality, did not, we could still acknowledge him or her as truly human. On the other hand, we would be reluctant to acknowledge as human a being devoid of DNA or any trace of (or potential for) a central nervous system. Even if having hair follicles is a universal quality of humans, it does not seem essential; having DNA and a central nervous system, by contrast, seems a necessary condition for being human. An "essential" characteristic of anything is a necessary condition, without which it would not be that sort of thing. However, this does not mean that it is a sufficient condition for being that sort of thing. Thus, having DNA and a central nervous system is not, by itself, sufficient to qualify something as human; for, though this is necessary, *more* than this is required. The basic issue pursued with these twelve theories, then, is what they view as essential to human nature. As Alexander Pope wrote in his *Essay on Man* (1733–34), "The proper study of mankind is man."

TEN DIMENSIONS.   A third problem is how such a big issue can be approached, especially since most of these philosophers did not make it the explicit focus of their work. **We shall study ten topics addressed by each of these twelve thinkers and constituting dimensions of a theory of human nature.**

1. Human beings can only be understood as part of **reality**; a thinker's conception of reality has a powerful bearing on the way he or she analyzes human nature.

2. Humans either are or have **bodies**; a theory of human nature must account for the importance of bodies in our lives.

3. Humans essentially are or normally have the capacity to become persons; **personality** here refers to that fundamental feature variously identified as soul or mind or consciousness (and not merely to our popular sense of character traits).

4. Humans have a potential for **knowledge** of themselves, others, and their world; exploring how this knowledge is possible reveals something important about what we are.

5. Human beings tend to believe that they have the **freedom** to choose at least some of their actions, rather than to have these actions always determined by external forces; if this is correct, this capacity contributes to our special dignity.

6. Humans throughout recorded history have emphasized **morality** in a way in which no other animals apparently can; the sense of moral responsibility for becoming good people and performing right actions also seems distinctive.

7. Human beings normally develop and live in **society**; our communities crucially affect our views and values.

8. Human beings tend to take **religion** seriously; our thoughts and actions tend to be influenced by its doctrines and teachings.

9. Humans are unique not only in knowing they will die but also in contemplating the possibility of **immortality**; the idea of an afterlife can shape our sense of identity and significance.

10. Human beings have a self-aware sense of **fulfillment** that guides our choices and our conduct; this is often interpreted in terms of some combination of happiness, virtue, and individual self-realization.

Each of these twelve thinkers discusses all ten of these topics to some extent in developing a theory of what is essential to human nature.

A SYSTEMS APPROACH WITH QUOTATIONS.   A fourth problem is how to strike a balance between letting great thinkers speak for themselves and offering a single interpretive narrative. Introductory philosophy books typically go to one of these extremes or the other. Anthologies of readings emphasize the first approach, often presenting a "bits and pieces" set of selections with little or no continuity among them or coherent focus. On the other hand, ordinary textbooks tend to ignore or downplay the contributions of the philosophical giants of the past to present the author's own point of view. Both of these approaches tend to lack impressive depth, the anthologies skimming the surface of others' famous thoughts and the ordinary textbook presenting merely the author's own ideas. **This book** tries to strike a balance between these extremes; it **is committed to studying the systems** (rather than miscellaneous ideas) **of twelve great thinkers in some depth. It focuses on their actual writings, which are presented in short, carefully documented quotations that are connected by means of an ongoing interpretive narrative. Coherent focus is provided by the one common issue of human nature, analyzed from the perspectives of the ten topics mentioned in the preceding paragraph.** Although there is a lot of quoted material, each quotation is brief in order to make the material easier to understand and to show more clearly how it all connects. The model for this way of using quoted material is *A History of Philosophy,* by Frederick Copleston, S.J., a very different sort of book from this one, but one by which I have been quite influenced for almost three decades now.

THE CONTEXT OF EACH THEORY; ALTERNATIVE THEORIES.   A fifth problem is one of context. **Each chapter begins with a brief background on the historical period, and the discussion of each philosopher's theory is preceded by a biography.** No theory emerges or should be critically considered in a vacuum. Historical background and biography inevitably influence a thinker's work, and it is a mistake to ignore them. This does not mean that a theory's truth or adequacy is simply relative to those considerations. Certainly, we must judge that for ourselves in the light of our own experience. But understanding the problems a theory is trying to solve and appreciating its solutions require context. Besides, we are products of this cultural history as surely as the great philosophers were, so that it affects our thinking as well as theirs. Despite the stereotype of philosophers as leading bland and boring lives, I hope you will find that these famous thinkers defy that generalization. **Further context is provided in each chapter by a brief discussion of three other views, which play off the two theories emphasized.** These alternative perspectives show that there are important thinkers beyond the ones on whom we are concentrating. Of course, there is no suggestion here that these are the only important alternatives for a philosophical period or even that these are the most important ones. Important thinkers were sometimes omitted in favor of their more provocative followers (e.g., Schopenhauer in favor of Nietzsche) or because they are too difficult for an introductory text (e.g., Heidegger) or because their work is too wide-ranging to be summarized briefly (e.g., Bertrand Russell).

REFLECTIONS AND CHALLENGES.   A final problem is how you might begin philosophizing for yourself. The ancient Greeks used the word "philosophy" to mean (literally) the love of wisdom. Yet that should involve the development of one's own ideas, rather than merely the passive absorption of others' ideas. What can you do with a theory once you understand it? You should be able to appropriate it critically, discriminating between its strengths and its weaknesses, and determining which aspects of it (if any) you might adopt. My own definition of philosophy is critical reflection on basic concepts, assumptions, and principles; this can relate to diverse aspects of experience, generating different areas of philosophy—ultimate reality (metaphysics), knowledge and belief (epistemology), moral values (ethics), art and beauty (aesthetics), religious faith (philosophical theology), civic relations (political philosophy), the essence of the human person (philosophy of human nature), and so forth. **The "Reflections" sections following the analysis of each theory not only provide summaries of key points already discussed but also try to provoke you to work out your own ideas.** They indicate my sense of the relative strengths and weaknesses of each theory, as approached by way of our ten topics. You will find that I am more sympathetic towards some of these theories and more critical of others. (You may even discern that I tend to be a follower of one of these twelve philosophers.) Yet I want the emphasis to be on urging you to work out your own point of view rather than on developing mine, since that is what the study of philosophy should provoke you to do. This is why I shall highlight the great achievements of even the theories to which I am most opposed and point out problems in even those with which I most agree. They all offer us penetrating insights we should be able to incorporate into our own perspective; yet none is so perfect that we should accept it uncritically. **The questions near the end of each chapter serve to focus on salient points and to challenge you to use your own critical thinking skills in reflecting on key aspects of the material just covered.**

Still, you may wonder, don't I have my own view of human nature, and am I unwilling to divulge what that is? The answers are, respectively, yes and no. Some ancient Greeks regarded a human being as a "rational animal." I think that analysis is on the right track but that the adjective is too narrow. I prefer to say that a human being is a "personal animal." By an animal I mean a physical organism living in and biologically dependent on a material environment. By a person I mean a being that has or normally and naturally would have the capacities for rational thought, social emotions, and moral freedom. Thus, not all animals are persons, and there could be persons who are not animals. But in you and me, as human beings, these two categories overlap. Now no theory we are about to study here puts it quite this way. This is rather my own composite, which synthesizes contributions from most (if not all) the thinkers on whom we shall focus. My hope for you is that you might adopt a theory that works for you or put together your own synthesis. Understanding these great views should provide you with materials with which to work. But there is no substitute for your own critical reflection on these materials.

For the most part, this book is arranged in chronological order. However, those using it may not wish (or may not have time) to cover all of its contents. Some might choose to focus on certain historical periods (such as the Age of Synthesis or the Age of Belief) to the exclusion of others (e.g., not both the Age of Reason and the Age of Enlightenment). Some might choose to cover each of the six periods but to represent each with a single philosopher covered in depth, rather than both covered hurriedly. Some might wish to trace lines of influence among thinkers (e.g., from Plato through Augustine to Descartes and then to Sartre). The historical background sections of each chapter and the biographies have been designed so that their inclusion is optional, in the sense that the body of each chapter can be understood without necessarily referring to them, although they are meant to provide context for it. For those who prefer an issues or problems approach to the historical one, the ten topics considered in relation to all twelve theories emphasized can facilitate that. For example, a more theoretical course could move from a general conception of reality to a view of bodies to a theory of the human personality to human knowledge to religion and then immortality; a more practical course might move from human personality to freedom to morality to society and then to fulfillment. Thus, options are manifold, and one need not read the book as it is presented, straight through, from beginning to end. Course instructors can design their courses as seems most appropriate, using some combination of these materials, and perhaps varying the selections from semester to semester.

GLOSSARY AND CHRONOLOGY.   The glossary is provided to help you with technical terms. The first time in each chapter that a term appears, it is printed in boldface. The very first time a term appears in the body of the book, a definition is also given at the bottom of that page. In the Appendix, at the first appearance of each term the definition is given *within a logical context* at the bottom of the page. When a term occurs in a quotation, it is printed in boldface, even though the original quotation was in lightface.

This book also contains a fairly detailed chronology establishing parallels among famous philosophers and some of their works, historical events, and other cultural achievements. The philosophers are listed in the order of their births, with five works being mentioned for each of our twelve main thinkers and one work each for alternative philosophers. Dates for ancient and medieval writings are quite problematic, sometimes amounting to guesses as to when they were composed or transcribed; from the Renaissance on (after Gutenberg), we can precisely cite years of publication for works considered here.

INSTRUCTOR'S MANUAL.   An Instructor's Manual (ISBN: 1-880157-57-8) is available for teachers of courses for which the text might be appropriate. It contains:

1. A chapter-by-chapter guide to the material in the book —
   ■ key ideas;
   ■ the most important primary-source texts;
   ■ a distinction between essential and less crucial aspects of the exposition;
   ■ highlights of the relatively difficult passages; and
   ■ a brief concluding overview of each chapter.
2. Suggested topics for class discussion and writing assignments.
3. Sample quiz questions and examination topics.

PRIMARY-SOURCE TEXTS.   Regarding primary-source texts, you will find that the list of those used here is enormous, and bibliographies are included at the end of each chapter. Some sources (those of Hume, Mill, and James) tend to be relatively clear reading; some (those of Kant and Hegel) are quite challenging; and others are somewhere in between. I tend to make references to relatively inexpensive paperback editions of classic texts (rather than to the multivolumed Collected Works you can find in libraries), in hopes that you will obtain and read some of these yourself. I particularly recommend to you the following works for our twelve thinkers:

■ Plato's *Phaedo* and *Republic*;
■ Aristotle's *Nicomachean Ethics* and *De Anima*;
■ Augustine's *On Free Choice of the Will*;
■ Aquinas on "Man" (*Summa Theologica*, I, Questions 75-89);
■ Descartes's *Discourse on Method* and *Meditations*;

- Hobbes's *Human Nature* or *Leviathan,* Part I;
- Hume's *Enquiry concerning Human Understanding*;
- Kant's *Grounding for the Metaphysics of Morals* and (the more difficult) *Prolegomena to Any Future Metaphysics*;
- Hegel's (difficult) *Phenomenology of Spirit,* Introduction and sections on Consciousness and Self-Consciousness;
- Mill's *Utilitarianism* and *On Liberty*;
- James's *Will to Believe and Other Essays* and *Pragmatism*; and
- Sartre's "Existentialism Is a Humanism."

This textbook, ideally used in conjunction with some of these great works, will help you make your way through the philosophical perspectives on human nature that they represent. May it enable you to appropriate a "noble tradition" with which you can identify!

ACKNOWLEDGMENTS. I am grateful for the corrections and helpful suggestions proffered by the following reviewers, all of whom read through the entire manuscript:

JOHN H. BROWN
University of Maryland at College Park

JOHN CARVALHO
Villanova University (PA)

THEODORE GULESERIAN
Arizona State University

TRACY LOUNSBURY
Loyola University of Chicago (IL)

DON SMITH
Lakeland Community College (OH)

JUDITH CHELIUS STARK
Seton Hall University (NJ)

I also greatly appreciate the various suggestions made by:

PETER P. CVEK
Saint Peter's College (NJ)

MICHAEL J. DEGNAN
University of Saint Thomas (MN)

JAMES MAHONEY
Saint Anselm College (NH)

ROBERT J. MULVANEY
University of South Carolina

ELIZABETH STICH
The College of Saint Scholastica (MN)

I thank Gonzaga University for granting me a sabbatical leave, during which I was able to do the research and writing for half of this book. Three departmental colleagues, David Calhoun, William Ryan, S.J., and John Wagner, gave me constructive criticisms for the glossary. Catherine Ann Pomerleau, of the History Department of the University of Arizona, gave me valuable ideas for my historical background sections. My wife, Martha Pomerleau, helped me with word processing, creating the index, and proofreading the endnotes for each chapter. Finally, I thank the staff at Ardsley House for their consistently clear and kind instructions.

TWELVE GREAT PHILOSOPHERS

«« «« «« «« «« «« «« «« «« «« «« «« «« «« «« «« «»»» »» »» »» »» »» »» »» »» »» »» »» »»

Historical Background

《《《《《《《《《《《《《《《《《《《《《《《《《《》》》》》》》》》》》》》》》》》》》》》》》》》》

he fifth and fourth centuries B.C. were a turbulent time in ancient Greece. Conflicts among the city-states (poleis; singular, **polis**) (including, especially, Athens, Sparta, and Corinth), commonplace except when all were threatened by foreign powers, culminated in the devastating Great Peloponnesian War that united Sparta and Corinth (and their allies) against Athens (and her allies) and lasted for twenty-seven years (431–404 B.C.). Whereas Corinth was a commercial state ruled by the rich (a **plutocracy**) and Sparta was a militant society ruled by a warrior nobility, Athens experimented with **democracy** under Pericles. This was not a representative democracy of the sort with which we are familiar, but rather a pure democracy limited to the roughly ten percent of the population who were adult male citizens; for citizenship was restricted to children of free-born parents (which excluded all foreigners and slaves and most laborers). Athenian women were not able to vote, enjoyed few property rights, and had little educational opportunity. In Sparta women as well as men could be educated and were trained, in effect, to become mothers of warriors. The **Sophists**, who were itinerant teachers, tended to limit their teaching to men. Later, Plato not only advocated the radical idea of equal educational opportunities for women but also accepted some as students in his own Academy.

Pericles led Athens at the outset of the Peloponnesian War. The Athenian historian Thucydides reports on his stirring Funeral Oration, celebrating the Athenian democracy and culture as worth dying for and describing his people as lovers of beauty and of wisdom. Greek sculpture was exquisite, as was the architecture, such as the Athenian Parthenon, the temple of Athena, which housed a colossal bronze statue of the goddess, created by the gifted sculptor Phidias. Greek literature was also magnificent at this time, ranging from the satirical comedies of Aristophanes (such as *Clouds*, which pokes fun at Socrates) to the great dramas of Sophocles (such as *Oedipus Rex*, which focuses on tragic destiny, and *Antigone*, which features the conflict between civil

---

Polis.   A city-state, as in ancient Greece

Plutocracy (from the Greek *ploutokratia*, meaning rule of the rich).   A special sort of oligarchy, in which wealthy people govern

Democracy (from the Greek *demokratia*, meaning rule of the common people).   Government by the people, either directly (pure democracy) or through elected officials (representative democracy)

Sophists (from the Greek *sophos*, meaning wise).   Itinerant teachers of ancient Greece (such as Protagoras and Gorgias), who trained young men for political life but were often regarded as eloquent charlatans, propounding relativism and scepticism; we speak of a sophism as a specious, deceptive argument and condemn sophistry, or disputation pursued merely for its own sake

authority and family obligation). Also active at this time was the Greek physician Hippocrates, the father of medicine, whose professional ideals are embodied in the Hippocratic Oath.

When Pericles died in 429 B.C., there was no great leader to replace him; demagogues emerged, ingratiating themselves with the rabble and clutching for power. In 415, the Athenians, under Alcibiades, an ambitious, untrustworthy politician who had been a follower of Socrates and who ended up betraying Athens (by giving the Spartans military advice), blundered into launching an expedition against Sicily. A couple of years later, the Athenian expedition was destroyed. Yet even after this miserable fiasco, the war dragged on for another decade. When Athens finally submitted to an unconditional surrender, the Corinthians advised demolishing the city, killing its adult males, and casting its women and children into slavery. Instead, Sparta set up an **oligarchical** group, sometimes called the Thirty Tyrants, to rule the conquered Athens; among its leaders were Plato's uncle and great-uncle.

The earliest **philosophers** (starting with Thales in the sixth century B.C.) sought scientific understanding of our world and of our place within it, as opposed to the mythological accounts of poets such as Hesiod and Homer, who explained events by reference to the gods and goddesses of Greek polytheism. These **cosmological** speculators sought a common universal **substance** underlying all reality.

Thales claimed it is water, which, when sufficiently cooled, changes from a liquid to a solid state, and, when sufficiently heated, passes into a gaseous state. Pythagoras founded a religious society which was fascinated with mathematics (we still use the Pythagorean Theorem in geometry) and its application to cosmological speculation; Pythagorean thought was **dualistic** in resolving reality into the two basic principles of the Limited and the Unlimited, believed in the transmigration of **souls**, and advocated practical moderation. Whereas Heraclitus saw all reality as involved in a never-ending, changing flux (he said you cannot step twice into the same river), Parmenides held the **monistic** view that all reality is one and claimed that all being is stable and that all becoming and change are illusory. Zeno of Elea created **paradoxes** designed to illustrate the point. Empedocles was a **pluralist** who maintained that the four eternal roots of all reality are earth, air, fire, and water; against Parmenides, he argued that reality must be manifold since there is change and that Love and Strife are the two physical forces **causing** the changes of combination and separation. Anaxagoras (under whom Pericles studied) tried to account for both the one and the many of the world, in response to Empedocles, by substituting an infinite variety of particles or "seeds" for the four roots (diversity) and by replacing Love and Strife with the one principle of **Mind** or *Nous* (unity), although he seems to

---

Oligarchy (from the Greek *oligarkhia*, meaning the rule of the few).   Government by a small group of people; when these people must be wealthy, it is a plutocracy

Philosophy (from the Greek *philosophos*, meaning loving wisdom).   The most general systematic rational inquiry; philosophers disagree about its proper definition, but the one used here is critical reflection on basic concepts, assumptions, and principles related to any areas of experience and/or reality

Cosmology.   That area of inquiry that theorizes about the cosmos, or universe as an organized whole; for Kant, rational cosmology (along with rational psychology and rational theology) is one of the three branches of metaphysical speculation

Substance (from the Latin *substare*, meaning to stand under).   An independently existing entity, supporting, or providing the foundation for, its phenomenal appearances and properties

Dualism.   The view that there are two irreducible sorts of reality, often physical and spiritual, or two irreducible components of human nature, such as body and soul

Soul.   Broadly, the principle of life in a living thing; more commonly, a spiritual substance that is or can be the subject of conscious thought

Monism (from the Greek *monos*, meaning alone or single).   The view that ultimately only one type of substance or only one numerical being is real; in the first sense, Hobbes's materialism is monistic, whereas Hegel's idealism is monistic in the second sense

Paradox (from the Greek paradoxos, meaning contrary to opinion).   A seemingly absurd or self-contradictory view, often based on apparently sound reasoning from plausible assumptions (an ancient example was the saying of the Cretan Epimenides that all Cretans always lie)

Pluralism.   The view (as in James) that reality comprises many distinct substances or kinds of substance (vs. dualism and monism)

Cause.   That which explains something, especially in terms of its origin or source of change; the sufficient condition(s) of something to be explained; Aristotle's four principles of explanation are material, formal, efficient, and final causes; Kant identifies causality as one of the twelve categories or concepts of the understanding

Mind.   Individual (or cosmic) consciousness; a psychological self or soul (or an intellectual aspect of the self or soul)

have conceived of the latter **materialistically**. The last step to complete mechanistic materialism was taken by the **atomists**, such as Democritus, who reduced all reality to an **infinite** number of invisible and indivisible particles, called atoms, moving in the void and colliding with each other in such a way as sometimes to combine and then to separate.

By the second half of the fifth century B.C., in addition to the political conflicts among city-states and the military collisions of the Peloponnesian Wars, there was an intellectual challenging of traditional views and values by the Sophists, who (for pay) taught **aristocratic** young men skills of rhetoric and argumentation that would be valuable instruments for the achieving, wielding, and maintaining of political power. The Sophists tended to be **relativists** and/or **sceptics**. Protagoras, one of the earliest and greatest of them, best expresses their relativism with his famous saying, "Man is the measure of all things, of things that are that they are and of things that are not that they are not." A later Sophist, Gorgias, represents their scepticism with his three-fold claim that nothing exists, that even if anything did exist, it would be unknowable to man, and that even if anything knowable to man existed, it would be impossible to articulate and communicate it to others. The Sophists have gotten a bad name (thanks largely to Plato's dialogues) as superficial tricksters more concerned with appearances and influence than with objective reality and truth. But, like the cosmological speculators, they pursued alternatives to thinking that is based on authority, tradition, and

mythology, paving the way for the two greatest ancient Greek philosophers whose writings are available to us, Plato and Aristotle.

As Plato was Socrates' greatest student and Aristotle was Plato's, Aristotle's most famous pupil was not a philosopher at all, but a successful conqueror and ruler. Philip II had become king of Macedonia and expanded the kingdom to dominate the Greek city-states. He invited Aristotle to tutor his bright teenaged son, who would later be called Alexander the Great. As an adult, Alexander first invaded Asia Minor, beating the Persians, and advanced eastward across the Indus River into the Ganges valley. Contrary to the antiforeign prejudices of his culture, Alexander wore Persian dress and encouraged his men to intermarry with the peoples they conquered, he himself marrying Roxana, a Bactrian princess. He controlled Egypt and founded cities modeled on the Greek *polis*, the most famous of which was Alexandria, an important port on the Mediterranean. But when Alexander died in 323 B.C., his empire became divided into separate kingdoms. At this point the **Hellenistic** period, in which Greek influence was grafted onto other cultures, replaced the earlier **Hellenic** period, which was purely Greek. The great library at Alexandria contributed to that city's becoming a prominent center of Hellenistic learning. The famous mathematician Euclid, renowned for his *Elements*, which treated geometry, taught at Alexandria.

Meanwhile, in the Italian peninsula, the Roman **republic** was expanding, conquering several Greek

---

Materialism.   The theory (e.g., of Hobbes) that all reality is ultimately physical and that whatever we may regard as mental or spiritual is actually only an expression of some fundamentally material being

Atomism (from the Greek *atomos*, meaning indivisible).   The view that reality is composed of tiny, indivisible physical particles; more generally, the tendency to analyze things in terms of basic, independent constituent elements

Infinite (from the Latin *infinitus*, meaning unlimited).   Unbounded, without any limits (often said of God)

Aristocracy (from the Greek *aristokratia*, meaning rule of the best).   A government by the superior people, favored by philosophers prior to the rise of modern representative governments

Relativism.   The view that truths and values vary among different individuals and/or cultures rather than being absolutely binding; thus, Protagoras the Sophist espoused relativism in proclaiming that "man is the measure of all things"

Scepticism (or **skepticism**) (from the Greek *skeptesthai*, meaning to consider or examine).   The doctrine that knowledge is unobtainable, in some or even all areas of inquiry; many of the greatest philosophers (e.g., Plato, Augustine, Descartes, and Kant) try to refute scepticism

Hellenistic (from the Greek *Hellen*, meaning a Greek).   Pertaining to the ancient Greeks and their culture, following the death of Alexander the Great in 323 B.C., and to Greek influences which were adopted by, and grafted onto, other cultures, such as that of Rome

Hellenic (from the Greek *Hellen*, meaning a Greek).   Pertaining to the ancient Greeks and their culture in a pure, undiluted form, prior to the death of Alexander the Great in 323 B.C., as opposed to Hellenistic

Republic (from the Latin *respublica*, meaning public affairs or commonwealth).   Any nonautocratic political order; a constitutional government, especially a democratic one

colonies in southern Italy. By about 275 B.C., Rome controlled all of the peninsula south of the Po valley. Rome then engaged Carthage, a city in northern Africa, in the three Punic Wars, beginning in 264 and covering more than a century. During the second of these, the great Carthaginian general Hannibal led his men and a few dozen elephants across the Pyrenees and the Alps into Italy itself. But by the end of the third one, Roman troops had stormed, taken, and utterly devastated the great city of Carthage in accord with Cato the Elder's appeal to the Senate, "Carthage must be destroyed" (*Carthago delenda est.*) By 148, Romans had conquered Macedonia, which became a Roman province; within a few years, Rome was appropriating Greek culture, adopting Greek religious divinities and imitating Greek art, as in its sculpture and in architecture, such as the Colosseum and Pantheon. The Roman Senate later sent Gnaeus Pompey east to quell an uprising against Roman power in Greece; Pompey was successful, securing the eastern territories under Roman rule.

Soon thereafter, Julius Caesar, governor of Spain, began winning significant military victories. In 60 B.C., Pompey and Caesar, along with Marcus Licinius Crassus, formed a triumvirate to rule Rome. After Caesar was appointed governor of Gaul, a region in western Europe, he conquered the northern Gallic territories and launched an invasion of Britain. In 52, Pompey was appointed sole Roman consul (Crassus had died the preceding year). Caesar completed his conquest of Gaul and wrote his famous *De Bello Gallico* (whose often quoted opening line is, "All Gaul is divided into three parts"). Pompey's supporters tried to block Caesar's return to the consulship. In 49, the Senate ordered Caesar to relinquish his Gallic command; instead, he defied the Senate by leading troops across the Rubicon river into Italy, precipitating a civil war. Pompey fled to Greece, pursued by Caesar's troops, and was defeated at Pharsalia.

In 51 B.C., Cleopatra VII assumed the throne of Egypt with her brother Ptolemy XIII. She ordered the murder of the defeated Pompey. Caesar conquered her enemies, and she became his mistress,

bore him a son, Caesarion, and lived with Caesar until his death. (Like the Greeks, the Egyptians and Romans maintained the practice of enslaving their conquered foes.) Caesar later returned to Rome with Cleopatra and became Roman dictator, introducing the Julian calendar and adopting his nephew Gaius Octavian as his heir. On March 15 ("the ides of March"), 44 B.C., Caesar was assassinated by conspirators led by Marcus Junius Brutus and Cassius Longinus (as dramatized in the famous play by Shakespeare). Rome sank into another civil war. In 42, the forces of Octavian and Mark Antony, at the Battle of Philippi, defeated Brutus and Cassius, who both committed suicide.

Cleopatra soon seduced Antony and bore him twins. Antony, already married to Octavian's sister Octavia, married Cleopatra in Egypt; when he formally divorced Octavia, Octavian declared war on Antony and Cleopatra, his fleet defeating theirs in the Battle of Actium. In 30, Mark Antony and Cleopatra committed suicide, and Octavian declared Egypt a Roman province. Three years later, Octavian was granted supreme power by the Senate, along with the title of "Augustus," although he preserved the trappings of republican government. (The Roman **Empire** dates from 31 B.C., when Octavian established his government after defeating Antony and Cleopatra at the Battle of Actium.) His long reign endured until A.D. 14, extending the boundaries of the Empire to the upper Danube, inaugurating reforms, and beginning the two centuries of relative peace within the Empire, called the *Pax Romana*, which assured safe travel on the impressive system of roads the Romans constructed as well as protection for all citizens in the Empire under the carefully crafted Roman law. During Augustus's reign, the great Latin poets Virgil and Ovid flourished, the former producing his epic *Aeneid* and the latter writing love poems. After the death of Augustus there was a peaceful transition of power to his adopted son Tiberius, who ruled for almost a quarter of a century and improved the financial standing of the Empire. Some early emperors, such as the infamous Caligula (37–41) and Nero (54–68), exhibited irrational

---

Empire (from the Latin *imperium*, meaning realm or dominion). An extensive territory, often including many nations, under the supreme authority of one person (the emperor or empress) or one sovereign state

behaviors, and Claudius I (41–54) was regarded as a driveling imbecile.

In the Roman world, as in the previous Greek civilization, the socially respectable roles for women were those of daughter, wife, mother, and widow, while those of slave, concubine, and prostitute were regarded as dishonorable. However, Boadicea, a warrior queen in Britain, led a rebellion against Roman rule before being defeated and killed in 62.

In Judea, Jesus of Nazareth, proclaimed by some as the Messiah, attracted a group of followers, subsequently known as Christians (from the Greek Khristos, meaning "the anointed one," a reference to the Messiah), and was crucified in about 30, by order of Pontius Pilate, procurator of Judea. (Early Christianity will be treated in the historical background for Chapter 2.) In 66, Jews revolted against poor government by Roman procurators, and Vespatian was dispatched to Judea to quell the rebellion; when he was recalled to Rome to become Emperor (69–79), his son Titus, later Emperor (79–81), captured and destroyed Jerusalem in 70, stifling the Jewish revolt, with Masada, the last stronghold of Jewish zealots, falling three years later. This led to the gradual dispersion of the Jews throughout the Empire. After Trajan, commanding general in lower Germany, became Emperor (98–117), he extended the Empire to its largest size (ringing the Mediterranean, which the Romans called *mare nostrum* or "our sea") and fiercely quashed a Jewish rebellion in Africa, Palestine, and Cyprus in 115. Prior to the persecution of the Christians, who refused formal obeisance to the Emperor as a god on the grounds that it was idolatrous, the Romans, while encouraging Hellenistic practices, generally tolerated the religious beliefs and practices of conquered peoples, so long as they obediently submitted to Roman authority. The year before he died, Trajan created the new provinces of Mesopotamia and Assyria. By the end of the rule of Marcus Aurelius (161–80), Roman power was clearly in decline. Indeed, the third century is characterized by a general collapse of government and economics throughout the Mediterranean.

This historical background indicates the instability and discord of the ancient Greco-Roman civilizations. Moral and religious values had been challenged, and mythology was being replaced by the earliest attempts at scientific **knowledge**. The relativism and scepticism represented by the Sophists in the fifth and fourth centuries B.C. had to be met. Various pre-Socratic philosophers had offered bits and pieces of insights, several dealing with the problem of the One and the Many, how to relate the unity of reality to its diverse appearances. What was needed was the genius to pull these strands together coherently. This was done first by the **rationalist** Plato and subsequently by the more **empirical** Aristotle in what we might call the Age of **Synthesis**. After the death of Alexander, the collapse of Greek dominance, and the hegemony of Roman rule, new theories would be sought to accommodate the turmoil and alienation of those later times.

There are many strands of this Hellenistic philosophy, which was Greek in its roots, and they can viewed as various reactions to the loss of Greek political power. Plato's Academy continued to function (until A.D. 529), but its thought tended to swing from the extreme of scepticism to the opposite extreme of **dogmatism**. After Alexander died, Pyrrho of Elis founded a school of scepticism. At the end of

---

Knowledge.   Belief that is both true and justifiably held to be true (although some philosophers criticize and deny this traditional analysis)

Rationalism.   The philosophical theory that some synthetic or existential knowledge is derived from reason rather than from sense experience, as opposed to empiricism

Empiricism (from the Greek *empeiria*, meaning experience).   The theory that all synthetic or existential knowledge is derived ultimately from sense experience, as opposed to rationalism

Synthetic.   Combining elements together to form a greater whole; a synthetic judgment (since Kant) is one whose predicate term adds new information not even implicitly contained in its subject (e.g., "All bachelors are frivolous"), as opposed to an analytic one; in dialectical reasoning (as in Hegel), synthesis is the higher unity of opposed antitheses

Dogmatism (from the Greek *dogma*, meaning opinion).   Unwarranted certainty in asserting any doctrine; since Kant, the word more specifically refers to metaphysical claims not grounded in a prior critique of the cognitive powers of reason

the fourth century B.C. his younger contemporary Epicurus founded his own school (**Epicureanism**) in Athens. Less than a decade later, Zeno of Citium founded the school of **Stocism**. All three of these schools had enormous influence throughout the Hellenistic period following the political eclipse of the Greeks by the Romans. Marcus Tullius Cicero, in the first century B.C., a famous **eclectic** who studied with Epicureans, Stoics, and an **Academician**, tried to come to terms with scepticism in certain areas of his thought. Among the most famous Epicureans was the Roman poet Lucretius, who wrote *On the Nature of Things* (*De Rerum Natura*) in the first century B.C. Among the most famous Stoics were Epictetus, a Greek slave of the Romans in the first century A.D., and Marcus Aurelius, the Roman Emperor of the following century. Our main source for the doctrines of ancient Scepticism is the early third century *Outlines of Pyrrhonism*, by Sextus Empiricus. Another important Hellenistic philosophy is the **Neoplatonism** of the third century. Its greatest proponent was Plotinus, who founded a school in Rome and taught a mystical monism, viewing all reality as emanating from the divine One.

Epicureanism.   The view of followers of Epicurus, that the hedonistic pursuit of pleasure and avoidance of pain aims at the ultimate good

Stoicism (from the Greek *stoa*, meaning a portico or covered porch).   An ancient (Greek and Roman) philosophical movement, emphasizing rational will, mastery of one's passions, doing one's duty, and detachment from external things over which one has no ultimate control

Eclecticism.   The selecting and combining of ideas or doctrines from diverse schools of thought

Academician.   A member of Plato's Athenian Academy, lasting from about 387 B.C. to A.D. 529; often (as in Augustine) identified with scepticism, because of the later Academy's sceptical tendency

Neoplatonism.   A philosophical movement in which Plotinus was prominent, based on Platonic ideas, beginning in Alexandria in the second century A.D. and extending to at least the fifth century

Plato

*The
unexamined
life is not
worth
living
for man.*

APOLOGY

BIOGRAPHY

Plato, born in Athens around 427 B.C. (which was during the Great Peloponnesian War; biographical dates for early figures tend to be inexact), was an aristocrat on both sides of his family. After his father's death, his mother married a friend of Pericles. So, Plato was politically connected to both the oligarchy and democracy. (Some reports indicate that his real name was Aristocles, "Plato" being a nickname meaning broad and referring to his stocky figure.) He may have fought near the end of the Peloponnesian War. After the war ended, his mother's brother and uncle tried to persuade him to join them in the oligarchical rule of Athens.

But by this time Plato had already followed his older brothers, Glaucon and Adeimantus, in becoming a pupil of Socrates, who engaged his contemporaries in dialogue and challenged them to examine their ideas and beliefs critically, annoying and antagonizing many in the process. Socrates seems to have adopted as his own the motto of the Delphic Oracle, "Know thyself"; and, while trying to dissociate himself from the Sophists' brand of instruction for hire, he taught his followers that "it is the greatest good for a man to discuss **virtue** every day and those other things about which you hear me conversing and testing myself and

others, for the unexamined life is not worth living."[1] He was an opponent of the relativism and scepticism of the Sophists; but, like them (and unlike other pre-Socratic philosophers), he focused on values rather than on physical science. Aristotle credits Socrates with emphasizing moral questions and precise definitions; and Plato surely absorbed these lessons.

Socrates was no friend of the Thirty Tyrants, who unsuccessfully attempted to get him involved in their ruthless intrigues. Their reign (of 404–403 B.C.) lasted for a brief but bloody eight months, after which Athenian democracy was restored. But Socrates did not get along well with its leaders either, alienating them by his method of critical interrogation. In 399 B.C., he was brought to trial, accused of the (terribly ironic) capital charges of religious impiety and corruption of youth, convicted, and sentenced to death. Plato attended the trial and reports on it in one of his earliest writings, the *Apology* (which comprises Socrates' speech in his own defense, then his addressing the issue of whether an alternative sentence might be more appropriate than death, and finally his farewell remarks to the 501 citizens composing the court), which we assume to be an accurate record of the trial. Plato was among the friends who offered to help pay a fine for him if that were acceptable as an alternative to the death penalty. Plato also tells us in the *Phaedo* that he was sick and thus absent when Socrates died.

As Plato reports in his Seventh Letter, after Socrates' death, he became disenchanted with all existing political regimes and convinced that the only salvation would require that "either true and genuine philosophers attain political power or the rulers of states by some dispensation of providence become genuine philosophers." Eleven years later (388/387 B.C.), when he was about forty years old, Plato visited Sicily. He was invited to the court of Dionysius, the tyrant of Syracuse, and befriended his brother-in-law, Dion. His Seventh Letter expresses his disgust for the profligate, self-indulgent lifestyle of the Syracusans.[2] His objections seem to have aroused the **tyrant's** anger; and there is a story (not confirmed in Plato's own writings) that he had Plato sold into slavery, from which he was

---

Virtue (from the Latin *virtus*, meaning excellence or manliness).   A morally excellent or good habit or quality of character, as opposed to a vice

Tyranny (from the Greek *turannos*, meaning tyrant).   The rule of one who assumes absolute political power

fortunately ransomed by a friend who happened to spot him and helped him get back to Athens.

About 387 B.C., Plato founded a school in Athens, in a grove sacred to the demigod Academus, called the Academy (from which our word "academic" is derived). It was, in effect, a university of higher studies, including physical science, astronomy, and mathematics, as well as philosophy. The school (which was to survive for more than nine centuries!) attracted students from far and wide. In addition to presiding over the Academy and directing research, Plato delivered lectures, which, unlike his famous dialogues, were never published.

In 367 B.C., Dionysius died and was succeeded by his teenage son, Dionysius II, whose uncle, Dion, Plato's friend and admirer, invited Plato to come to direct the boy's education. This seemed a unique opportunity to achieve his dream of helping to produce a philosopher-king, so Plato embarked on a second voyage to Sicily. But things went badly. Shortly after Plato's arrival, ill will developed between Dionysius II and Dion, and the young tyrant exiled his uncle. Without the assistance of his friend, Plato was unable to convert the boy to philosophy and returned to Athens, where Dion also established residence.

Plato continued to correspond with the younger Dionysius and attempted to reconcile him with his uncle. In 361 B.C., Dionysius II lured Plato back to Syracuse with the suggestion that he would patch things up with Dion and commit himself to serious philosophical study. But it was apparently a ruse. The tyrant was not sincere about his commitments to philosophy; and, far from recalling the banished Dion, whose beneficial influence on the boy might have helped Plato's cause, he confiscated Dion's property. Plato was not allowed to leave Syracuse until 360, at which time he returned to Athens and resumed his functions as president of the Academy until about 347, when he died at about the age of eighty.

It is customary to divide Plato's published writings into three periods, although this is an approximation, since they are not dated and their chronology is disputable. The early works seem to have been written between Socrates' death in 399 B.C. and the first

Sicilian voyage eleven years later; these works—including the *Apology*, the *Crito*, the *Euthyphro*, the *Protagoras*, and possibly Book I of the *Republic*—are often called "Socratic" because they are thought accurately to reflect the tendency of the historical Socrates to emphasize critical inquiry over conclusive doctrine. The middle dialogues seem to have been written during the twenty years between the first and second of Plato's Sicilian voyages; these works—including the *Phaedo*, at least the last nine books of the *Republic*, the *Symposium*, the *Phaedrus*, the *Parmenides*, and the *Theaetetus*—show Plato moving away from mainly reporting ideas of Socrates to beginning to build his own system on their basis. Because of their style, one may assume that the dialogues *Meno* and *Gorgias* were written at the end of Plato's early period, although they may have been among the earliest works of his middle period. The latest writings were done after the second Sicilian voyage; these works—including the *Sophist*, the *Philebus*, the *Timaeus*, and the *Laws*—tend to reflect the attempts of the mature Plato to complete his own philosophical system, Socrates (to the extent that he is still prominent at all) serving merely as a mouthpiece. In the middle and late dialogues we cannot assume that Socrates always speaks for Plato.

Plato's philosophy can be regarded as a synthesis of the method of critical inquiry learned from Socrates, the Socratic ideas he appropriated, and the system he developed in practicing that method and building on those ideas. Although it might be more accurate to speak of the Socratic-Platonic philosophy, we have no works written by Socrates himself, and the Socratic views we shall use have been filtered through the writings of his best student.

Reality

Some of Plato's middle dialogues develop a two-tiered **metaphysics** (or theory of ultimate reality), which ingeniously tries to solve what may be the oldest problem in the history of philosophy, that of the One and the Many. We experience an enormous welter of objects; yet they appear to constitute some sort

---

Metaphysics (from the Greek *meta*, meaning after, and *phusika*, meaning physics; we think the word derives from the editorial placement of Aristotle's works on this subject after his writings on physics; we can think of it as "beyond the physical"). That area of philosophy that studies the nature of ultimate reality and the fundamental structures of being

of unity. Is reality, then, ultimately one or ultimately many things? Pre-Socratic cosmological speculators (starting with Thales, the father of Western philosophy) theorized both ways. Some (like Heraclitus) saw reality as **essentially** a multiplicity of constantly changing, temporal things; others (like Parmenides) viewed it as essentially one, eternal, and immutable. There seems to be some truth on each side of this disagreement. Plato saw a possible way to synthesize the two apparently opposed positions.

PARTICULAR THINGS AND FORMS.   His theory sees reality in terms of two different orders or realms. Elms, oaks, maples, pines, and so forth must have something in common, whereby they are all legitimately called trees; likewise, individual humans must share some quality or qualities accounting for their common humanity. Thus, there is the world of particular things, such as this tree or that human being; and there is a world of universal Ideas or **Forms**, which are independent of us, such as the Idea of a tree in general or the Form of humanity. We experience the former world by means of our bodily senses because it is in time and physical space; but we can only experience the latter world through intellectual **reason** because it is timeless and spiritual. For Plato, the world of Ideas is not merely as real as, but somehow more real than, that of particular things; for that which is eternal, immutable, and self-sufficient is of a higher order of reality than that which is time-bound, changing, and dependent for its very being.

Plato's famous dialogue, the *Phaedo*, seems to assume this two-tiered theory of reality. Here Socrates reminds us that we comfortably speak of "the Just itself, . . . the Beautiful, and the Good," which we cannot experience by means of our physical senses, but

"with thought alone." Consider the Ideas of Equality and Inequality. Although "equal stones and sticks sometimes" can be experienced as equal while at other times appearing unequal, Equality itself can never appear unequal. Therefore, equal things, like sticks and stones, cannot be identical to Equality itself. Nevertheless, there must be some sort of relationship between the equal things we perceive with our senses and Equality itself, which we conceive through reason. Does the perception of things as equal lead the mind to a knowledge of Equality itself or does such perception presuppose such knowledge? Perhaps both are somehow the case. Experience helps us to grasp such Ideas, but only they can render the experience intelligible. And this argument applies not only to the Idea of Equality but to "the Beautiful itself, the Good itself, the Just," and all Ideas "to which we can attach the word 'itself,' " so that we are speaking of **universals** (general Forms, whose extramental reality is independent of both the particulars of sense and any individual human minds). The narrator, Phaedo, later adds that the argument demonstrates not only the reality of the Forms but also "that other things acquired their name by having a share in them." The example he uses is "that Simmias is taller than Socrates but shorter than Phaedo" because he somehow participates in the Forms of both the Tall and the Short.[3] We shall return to this tricky notion of participation shortly.

Plato's greatest dialogue, the *Republic* (most of which was written after his first voyage to Sicily), also uses the theory of Forms or eternal, immutable Ideas, whose reality is external to the mind and the physical world. Socrates points out, "We are accustomed to assuming one Form in each case for the many particulars to which we give the same name." Thus, for example, we call all beagles, collies,

---

Essence.   The set of properties that characterize something as the type of thing it uniquely is and that is necessary for it to be that sort of thing, as opposed to its accidents

Form.   In Plato, an immaterial, immutable, independently existing, eternal entity, in which particular things of our world may participate, thus deriving their natures; in Aristotle, form is the essential principle in matter making it the sort of thing it is; in Kant, the *a priori* element in experience whereby the data of sensible intuition are structurally organized by the mind

Reason.   Generally, the intellect, the capacity for abstract thought, logical inference, and comprehension; in Kant, reason is the intellectual faculty that engages in metaphysical speculation, as opposed to understanding, which is the intellectual faculty capable of knowledge; philosophers (such as Aristotle and Kant) distinguish between theoretical reason, which pursues knowledge, and practical reason, whose deliberations are oriented to action

Universal.   As an adjective, pertaining to an entire class or all-encompassing rather than partial or particular; as a noun, a general concept (such as "tree") common to a number of particulars (such as pines, maples, oaks, etc.) or an abstract idea (such as justice, truth, or beauty); for Platonists, the Forms are universal entities

hounds, mastiffs, terriers, and so forth by the common name "dog" because we suppose they all share a single essential Form, despite their particular differences. Whenever artisans make beds and tables, they "look to the Form" as an ideal prototype which the finished product should resemble. "The Form, itself," however, is not man-made, "for how could it be?" The true philosopher had been defined as one who can grasp the Forms of this higher realm of Ideas.[4]

Plato presents the arresting **analogy** of the Sun as a literary illumination of his two-worlds theory. Of all the Forms, that of the Good or Goodness is portrayed as comparable to what the Sun is in the physical world. In the realm of sensible things the bodily eye can achieve physical sight of colors only in the medium of light, which ultimately emanates from the star we call the Sun; likewise, in the realm of Ideas the mind can achieve rational insight into the truth only in the medium of Ideas, which ultimately emanate from the highest and brightest of them, that of the Good. As the Sun is the ultimate source of both light and life in our physical environment, so is the Good the ultimate source of all intellectual light and all spiritual life in the world of Ideas, since,

> as for the objects of knowledge, not only is their being known due to the Good, but also their being, though the Good is not being but superior to and beyond being in dignity and power.[5]

THE ALLEGORY OF THE CAVE. But the most haunting passage of all is the memorable allegory of the cave. Here the physical world is compared to a subterranean cave in which we humans are trapped from the beginning of our earthly lives, shackled in such a way that we must remain stationary, unable even to turn our heads. In this condition we can perceive only shadows and echoes, inevitably mistaking such illusions for realities. Without any explanation, one of us is liberated from his fetters and is encouraged to turn towards the entrance to the cave. The revelation is confusing and painful. Then he is pulled towards the upper world, struggling and dragging his heels, because approaching the natural light of day hurts his unaccustomed eyes and threatens the security of the only life

he knows. The world of daylight, of course, represents the realm of Ideas, where the liberated prisoner experiences things as they are, rather than merely their shadows and echoes. His eyes gradually adjust to the light until, finally, he can look upon the Sun itself and start to understand how it is the ultimate source of all light and life in the upper world. This, of course, is symbolic of the Idea of the Good in the realm of Forms. The gradual process of adjustment is a metaphor for the process of education, which is often a difficult and unpleasant experience we would prefer to forgo. But when we start comprehending reality and its interconnections, how satisfying it is! And how dismal it is to contemplate returning to our former life of ignorance and blindness! Yet the lesson of Plato's story is that the one who has been so fortunate as to become enlightened now has a moral responsibility to return to the world of ordinary experience to try to share what he has learned with others who have not been so fortunate. Plato is quite realistic in admitting that the benighted, uneducated masses—far from welcoming his efforts—will resent them, to the point where (like Socrates) he will find that his very life might be threatened:

> As for the man who tried to free them and lead them upward, if they could somehow lay their hands on him and kill him, they would do so.[6]

RELATING THE TWO WORLDS. Plato seems to have recognized that the key difficulty with his theory of reality (as with any dualistic theory) has to do with relating the two worlds. We have already seen that he tries to explain this relationship in terms of the particular things of the physical world that participate in the universal Forms of the world of Ideas. But this presents a problem. How exactly can a particular, temporal, changing, physical object participate in universal, eternal, immutable, nonphysical Forms?

To his credit, Plato tackles the problem head-on in the *Parmenides*, where (for a change) Socrates is portrayed as a young man put on the defensive by the more experienced Parmenides, who points out that if "there exist certain Forms, of which these other things come to partake and so to be called after their names," then

---

Analogy. A resemblance or set of similarities between different things, sometimes used as a basis for an inductive inference; some theists, like Aquinas, regard analogy as the correct way to think and speak of God

the things must participate in either the whole or some part(s) of the Forms. But if the whole Form is in a particular thing, the Form would be "separate from itself," alienated from the world of Ideas into the physical world. And if a thing shares in only part of the Form, then the Form will be divided, not unitary. Both alternatives are unacceptable. Thus, it seems unintelligible how particular things can participate in Forms. Parmenides asks,

> Well then, Socrates, how are the other things going to partake of your Forms, if they can partake of them neither in part nor as wholes? [Socrates can only admit that] it seems no easy matter to determine in any way.[7]

Parmenides argues further that the theory of participation involves other related problems. If we say that large things are like other large things by participating in the "certain single character" of Largeness, then don't we have to conclude that all large things somehow resemble Largeness itself? But how can we explain this resemblance or likeness except in terms of still another Form related to Largeness? The relationship between this other Form and Largeness will then require explanation, and so on, leading to an infinite regress. (This is sometimes referred to as the "third man" argument.) Also, how can we know these Forms, since we only directly experience things of our physical world where Forms are not to be found? But if we cannot know the Forms, how can they render anything else knowable by us? Parmenides concludes that

> these difficulties and many more besides are inevitably involved in the Forms, if these characters of things really exist and one is going to distinguish each Form as a thing just by itself;

thus, the theory, far from explaining things well, leads to perplexity and scepticism.[8]

Plato's two-tiered theory of reality is fundamental to his philosophy of human nature. On this view, man properly exists in two worlds rather than merely in one. Indeed, as we shall see, we more properly belong in the world of Ideas than in the physical world because of the kind of beings we essentially are. It is only our bodies that are legitimately at home in the realm of physical objects, and they are not central to our nature as persons. It is the purpose of philosophy to educate us to our spiritual reality, to wean us from our attachment to the things of the body, and to orient our values towards eternal Ideas—in short, to liberate us from the illusions of the cave.

Bodies

In the *Timaeus* Plato analyzes the makeup of the bodily world. Unlike spiritual realities, which are eternal, bodies must come into being through some process of composition. Indeed, whatever comes to be must be "corporeal, visible and tangible." The physical world comprises combinations of the four corporeal elements of pre-Socratic thought (i.e., of Empedocles)—fire, earth, water, and air. It is formed in "a rounded spherical shape," at the core of which is the world-soul, its principle of life. This soul is prior to the physical elements "both in time and value," so that it is fit to be their "dominating and controlling partner." All that is physical in the universe was adapted to this world-soul. Since no physical creature can be eternal, all bodies must exist in time, which is described as the "moving image" of eternity. Finally, the four elements of bodies require a medium in which they can be situated and interrelated. This "receptacle" of becoming is space, the matrix of all bodies.[9]

As we have seen, the allegory of the cave identifies the world of bodies as a realm of darkness and illusion. In the *Phaedo* Plato holds that the human body distorts the truth and deceives the soul, distracting it from the acquisition of knowledge.

> And indeed the soul reasons best when none of these senses troubles it, neither hearing nor sight, nor pain nor pleasure, but when it is most by itself, taking leave of the body and as far as possible having no contact or association with it in its search for reality.

The soul's unfortunate relationship to the body is compared to that of a prisoner to his prison-cell (a particularly appropriate metaphor in this dialogue, which presents Socrates' final discussion, while imprisoned, on the last day of his life). Philosophical reflection reveals that the soul "is imprisoned in and clinging to the body, and that it is forced to examine other things through it as through a cage." But, as if this is not bad enough, by submitting to the desires of the body, "the prisoner himself is contributing to his own incarceration." We are told that

> every pleasure and every pain provides, as it were, another nail to rivet the soul to the body and to weld them together.[10]

This graphic imagery helps Plato argue that the best service philosophy can render to human nature is to liberate the soul from its attachment to its cave-like bodily prison.

Personality

SOUL AND BODY. A key assumption here is that the body is not the essence (or even part of the essence) of the human person (this word "person" itself comes from subsequent Roman philosophy). Can this crucial **presupposition** be philosophically justified? There is a fine **argument** purporting to do so in *Alcibiades I*, a dialogue which may or may not have been written by Plato himself. (It was published anonymously and could have been the work of one of Plato's immediate disciples at the Academy; this is the only Platonic work used here whose authenticity as a work of Plato himself is in serious doubt.) It is a **process-of-elimination argument** predicated on three possibilities: that the human person is essentially a soul or a body or a combination of body and soul. (As with any such argument, its success hinges, in part, on the question of whether the analysis exhausts all conceivable possibilities.) Whatever rules and governs the body is essential to the human person. But the body does not rule itself. Because a human person uses and rules his own body, he cannot essentially be his body, since "the user and the thing he uses are different." And if the body does not rule itself, then it cannot be joined with the soul as part of a ruling coalition, "for if one of the two does not share in the rule, it is quite inconceivable that the combination of the two can be ruling." Hence, by a process of elimination, the soul must rule the body and be the essence of the human person.[11]

Notice that all this assumes that there is such a reality as a soul, which we have not seen Plato trying to prove. A plausible argument, though, might go thus: there is an obvious difference between living and nonliving things; and whatever is the principle of life in living things is what is called "soul." As Socrates says in the *Republic*, its two-fold function must be to give life and to rule with deliberation. This natural function also constitutes the "excellence of the soul."[12]

THE NATURE AND MAKEUP OF THE SOUL. If the soul is to be considered the essence of the human person, it is important that we should understand its nature and makeup. In the *Phaedo* Socrates is challenged by Simmias and Cebes to show that the soul has an independent, substantial reality, rather than being merely an **epiphenomenal** (or derivative and dependent) by-product of the functioning of the body. Cebes and Simmias use three metaphors to express the view of epiphenomenalism that they want Socrates to refute: first, that the soul is like breath or a puff of smoke that dissipates when the body dies; second, that it is like a musical harmony which will cease to be when the bodily musical instrument is destroyed by death; and, third, that the soul is like a weaver who weaves, wears, and wears out many cloak-like bodies, but finally dies, leaving behind the last body, which ceases to function and soon deteriorates. Socrates chooses to confront the harmony analogy directly. If the soul were a harmony, that harmony would consist of goodness and virtue, whereas spiritual disharmony would consist of evil and **vice**. Yet the good and virtuous soul is no more a soul than the evil, vicious soul, nor the latter less of a soul than the former; despite their opposed moral conditions (or the extent to which they are "harmonized"), they are equally souls. Now some souls are good and others evil. Yet, "according to correct reasoning, no soul, if it is a harmony, will have any share of wickedness, for harmony . . . would never share in disharmony." Thus, the harmony theory of soul must be incorrect. Whereas a harmony is merely a passive interrelationship of component parts, we experience the soul as actively "ruling over all the elements of which one says it is composed,"[13] restraining its appetites, controlling its emotions, exercising its reason. It must be a substantial reality

---

Presupposition. An assumption, especially of an argument

Argument. A logical reasoning process designed to infer one proposition (the conclusion) from one or more other propositions (the premises), which collectively are supposed to support it; more loosely, any dispute

Process-of-elimination argument. An argument of the form, "if both *p* or *q* and not *p*, then *q*.

Epiphenomenalism. The view that mental events are merely by-products of physical ones rather than the results of actions of spiritual substances such as souls

Vice. A morally reprehensible or evil habit or quality of character, as opposed to a virtue

since only thus could it function as an independent agent.

In the *Republic* Plato argues that the soul (*psyche*) is composed of three parts. (These are not, of course, physical parts that could possibly be separated from each other, and it might be better to think of them as dimensions or aspects or **faculties** of the soul, though Plato uses the word "parts.") The argument is based on a fundamental principle:

> It is clear that one thing cannot act in opposite ways or be in opposite states at the same time and in the same part of itself in relation to the same other thing.

Although you can simultaneously move your body in several different directions, that is because you are moving different parts of it; but you can only move the last joint of the little finger on your left hand in one direction at a time. Now let us see how the principle applies. A thirsty person deliberately holds back from drinking when doing so would quench his thirst because the only available drink is thought to be poisoned. Here it seems obvious that the rational part of the soul, which restrains him from drinking, is conflicting with the appetitive part, which desires that he drink. But there is also a "spirited part" of the soul, which is competitive, experiences anger and shame, and is related to aggressive behavior. The question remains whether it is reducible either to reason or to the appetites. Plato tells the story of Leontius, who was both morbidly curious to look at some corpses of executed men and queasy at the prospect of doing so, until, finally, angry and disgusted with himself, he forced himself to look, showing "that anger sometimes wars against the appetites as one thing against another," so that they cannot be identical. But neither is spirit (*thumos*) reducible to reason, since the latter can conflict with and prevail over the former's anger, ambition, and tendencies towards aggressive action and since spiritedness is evident in little children who have not yet developed the capacity for reason.[14]

Thus, reason, spirit, and the appetites must be three different—though inseparable—parts of the soul. In the *Timaeus*, where Plato identifies the human soul with the world-soul, he repeats his commitment to this psychological trichotomy. But he also associates the three parts of the soul with distinct parts of the body, locating reason in the head, spirit in the chest, and the appetites below the waist, so that spirit, the "part of the soul which is the seat of courage, passion and ambition," is in direct communication with "the commands of reason" to which it should submit and can "combine with it in forcibly restraining the appetites when they refuse to obey the word of command from the citadel"[15] of reason. Plato clearly holds that there is a proper ordering of the three parts of the soul such that reason should rule and spirit should be its ally in controlling the dangerous, self-indulgent inclinations and desires of the appetites.

THE ALLEGORY OF THE CHARIOT. This brings us to one of the most beautiful images in all of Plato's writings, the allegory of the chariot, a symbolic depiction of the tripartite analysis of the soul found in the *Phaedrus*. The chariot (of the personality) is drawn by two horses. "One of the horses, we say, is good and one not." The good horse, representing spirit, is noble, well-formed, handsome, very responsive to discipline, and tending to behave magnificently. "The other horse," representing the appetites, "is crooked, lumbering, ill-made; stiff-necked, short-throated," with bloodshot eyes; "wantonness and boastfulness are his companions, and he is hairy-eared and deaf, hardly controllable even with whip and goad."[16] The charioteer, whose job it is to determine the proper direction and speed, to drive the chariot, and to coordinate the activities of both his horses, is symbolic of reason.

Thus, we see that Plato's philosophy of human nature involves not only external conflict between body and soul but also internal conflict among the parts of the soul itself. All such conflict is a distraction from the soul's proper activity, which includes the pursuit of knowledge. If reason is to rule wisely, its command must be informed by knowledge.

Knowledge

THE MYTH OF RECOLLECTION. In the *Meno* the title character (who has been frustrated by his own inability to provide a definition of virtue that will withstand critical analysis) throws an old sophistic puzzle at Socrates, who paraphrases the dilemma thus: how can

---

Faculty. An ability, capacity, or power, as of the mind, or of the soul, or of the body

anyone ever profitably "search either for what he knows or for what he does not know? He cannot search for what he knows—since he knows it, there is no need to search—nor for what he does not know, for he does not know what to look for." Socrates breaks Meno's paradox by reference to the myth of recollection:

> As the soul is immortal, has been born often and has seen all things here and in the underworld, there is nothing which it has not learned.

If our souls are eternal and knew things from before this natural life (this will require argumentation later to render the supposition philosophically respectable) but forgot them in the traumatic passage into the physical world, then we could profitably search for what we once knew and might recognize on rediscovery—"for searching and learning are, as a whole, recollection." Socrates attempts to demonstrate this process of recollection with one of Meno's slave boys, who knows basic arithmetic but has never (in this life) learned any geometry. By asking him a series of questions, Socrates leads the boy to "recollect" the solution to a geometrical problem.[17] Thus, we allegedly learn in this life by remembering knowledge originally acquired in a previous life.

THE ROAD TO LARISSA. Later in the *Meno* Socrates argues that knowledge, whatever it is, must be different from correct opinion.

> A man who knew the way to Larissa, or anywhere else you like, and went there and guided others would surely lead them well and correctly;

but so would someone who merely has a correct opinion concerning the right road to Larissa. In terms of the result alone—that is, getting to Larissa—correct opinion would be as effective as knowledge (even if the person who knows has a greater sense of security and confidence about the trip than the one who merely believes correctly, while the two are in transit). The key difference, though, is that even true beliefs are unstable so long as we cannot provide an adequate explanation of why they should be believed. But true beliefs seem to become knowledge when a person thus "ties them down by (giving) an account of the reason why."

> It is recollection of Forms that provides this explanatory, justificatory account. That is why knowledge is prized higher than correct opinion, and knowledge differs from correct opinion in being tied down,[18]

even in such a mundane example as that of the road to Larissa.

THE NATURE OF KNOWLEDGE. Plato's most sustained and systematic analysis of knowledge (*episteme*) is in the *Theaetetus*, where he has Socrates confess,

> Well, now we're at the heart of what puzzles me and I cannot satisfactorily grasp on my own . . . what knowledge in fact is.

Theaetetus offers three analyses of knowledge, all of which Plato has Socrates reject. The first is that "knowledge and perception are the same." But knowledge must be an infallible apprehension of reality; and our perceptions are of the appearances of reality and far from infallible. Plato proves a master of the **counterexample** technique of **refutation**. We can perceive without knowing, as when we see written or hear spoken a foreign language we have not learned. Also, we can know without perceiving; for example, I can know I drank sweetened tea yesterday morning, although, of course, I do not now perceive myself doing so and only remember having done so. But if we can perceive without knowing and know without perceiving, then knowledge cannot be identical to perception.[19]

Theaetetus' second attempt maintains that "perhaps true belief is knowledge." Again, Plato provides a brilliant counterexample to demolish this theory. When a jury becomes convinced a defendant is guilty on the basis of the prosecuting attorney's glib rhetoric, rather than of any solid evidence, it cannot be said to "know" that the accused is guilty even if, in fact, he is; here the jury's true judgment falls short of being knowledge, for it lacks something essential— but what? Theaetetus' third effort to define knowledge aims at supplying that missing something (in the way that Socrates himself had done in the *Meno*), when he says that

---

Counterexample. An instance that refutes a universal claim; for example, Europeans once believed that "all swans are white," until the counterexample of a black swan was discovered

Refutation. The disproof of an argument or the demonstration that a position is false or erroneous

true belief accompanied by a rational account is knowledge, whereas true belief unaccompanied by a rational account is distinct from knowledge.

Socrates appreciates this good suggestion. The problem, however, revolves around the ambiguity of the word "account" (*logos*). Three possible interpretations are considered, all of which are deemed inadequate. They are

1. A verbal formulation, expressing "one's thought in words and phrases by means of speech";
2. An analysis of the object believed in by enumerating its "elements"; and
3. An identification of some unique, defining characteristic or "mark which differentiates the object in question from everything else."[20]

So, poor Theaetetus has struck out, taking three swings at an adequate definition of knowledge but failing to connect.

A couple of observations are in order. First, although this is a magnificent example of negative **epistemology**, brilliantly attacking apparently inadequate theories of knowledge, it fails positively to answer the question of what knowledge is. Second, it is noteworthy that the discussion does not involve any explicit use of the theory of Forms. Plato's point may be that we cannot even understand what knowledge is—let alone achieve it—except by employing the Forms. Remember that knowledge must be infallible, and its object must be reality. The ultimate reality is that of the Forms and never the shadowy physical appearances of the cave. Infallible apprehension must be of that which does not change and is eternal; and this is nothing perceived in the physical world, but only in the spiritual reality of the world of Ideas.

THE DIVIDED LINE SIMILE. Perhaps Plato's best known treatment of knowledge is his divided-line simile in the *Republic*. The range of awareness is "like a line divided into two unequal parts," the lower, shorter one representing opinion and the higher, longer one symbolizing knowledge. These two major divisions, we can see, correspond, respectively, to the appearances of the cave-like physical world and the ultimate reality of the world of Ideas. Then each of these two major parts of the line must be subdivided again. The lower portion of the realm of opinion is imaginative conjecture (*eikasia*) based on no evidence at all. We all must operate at this primitive level near the beginning of our lives, and some of our ideas continue to function thus; for example, you may have an opinion, in this sense of imaginative conjecture, that there is intelligent extraterrestrial life without having a shred of evidence to support this notion. The higher portion of the realm of opinion is sensible belief (*pistis*) based on common experience. As we process the data of experience, many of our opinions move up into this area; thus, for example, you believe that your mother loves you, based on her verbal and behavioral evidence over the last couple of decades. Notice that both types of opinion have sensible, changing, time-bound things for objects. By contrast, the objects of genuine knowledge must be ideal, immutable, and eternal—that is, they must involve the Forms. The lower level of knowledge is scientific reasoning (*dianoia*), which understands truths in terms of universal principles. Formal education in our culture, as in Plato's Academy, exposes us to mathematics and science, which provide this sort of specific, compartmentalized knowledge; thus, for example, a mathematician knows the Pythagorean theorem in that she understands the principles of Euclidean geometry by which it can be proved to be universally and necessarily true. (The word "know" here is used to refer to true belief or correct judgment justified by adequate evidence.) The higher level of knowledge is an intuitive understanding (*noesis*) of everything in relation to "the intelligible reality" of the Forms. It is allegedly "by the power of **dialectic**" (inquiry into and discovery of the essentially real) that the philosopher comes to achieve this highest, most comprehensive level of knowledge;[21] unlike the knowledge of scientific reasoning, which always presupposes hypothetical assumptions (such as the postulates of geometry), the knowledge of intuitive understanding is allegedly unconditioned or absolute.

Epistemology (from the Greek *episteme*, meaning knowledge and *logos*, meaning on account).   That area of philosophy dealing with the nature, conditions, and limits of human knowledge

Dialectic (from the Greek *dialektikos*, meaning discourse).   A process of thought, whereby one thesis, or line of inquiry, leads to its opposite, or antithesis; Plato regards dialectic as the science of first principles; Kant considers antithetical conflict an indication of metaphysical illusion, whereas Hegel sees it as an opportunity to advance rationally to a higher unity, or synthesis

Freedom

If the fulfillment of human nature requires the enlightenment of knowledge, which ought to be pursued, we must be free to choose to do so. Unfortunately, Plato assumes human freedom, rather than systematically discussing it. For example, in the *Apology* Socrates is depicted as free to stop annoying his fellow Athenians by ceasing to carry on philosophical discussions, although he chooses to continue serving Athens by playing the philosophical "gadfly," as he feels morally obliged to do.[22] Again, in the *Crito* Plato portrays Socrates as free to accept Crito's offer to escape from prison, flee to another part of the Greek world such as Thessaly, and save himself from imminent death, although he chooses to stay and abide by the order of the Athenian court.[23]

THE MYTH OF ER. Likewise the myth of Er, a judgment tale at the end of the *Republic*, degenerates into a foolish fairy tale unless free choice be assumed. Each soul is "to choose a life which will of **necessity** be his. . . . The responsibility is his who makes the choice." Yet things are complicated by another consideration, which seems to limit or condition freedom: "For the most part their choice depended upon the character of their previous life."[24] If a soul's "choice" of a life is largely **determined** by the character of a previous life, the "choice" of which was, in turn, largely determined by the character of a life before that, and so forth, then the question of how free that soul ever ultimately is must arise. However, Plato does not confront it.

CHOOSING TO DO WRONG. Still another feature of Platonic philosophy which compromises the assumption of freedom is the doctrine of certain **ethical** dialogues that no one can ever knowingly and willingly choose to do wrong. In the *Protagoras* Socrates holds that moral knowledge can so rule a person's actions "that if he can distinguish good from evil, nothing

will force him to act otherwise than as knowledge dictates," and he clearly rejects the notion that people ever "recognize the best but are unwilling to act on it."[25] Again, in the *Gorgias* Socrates avers that the person who has learned of justice will necessarily be just and that "no one does what's unjust because he wants to, but that all who do so do it unwillingly."[26]

Plato does not help us understand how these limiting factors of moral knowledge and the character of previous lives can be reconciled with human freedom. Rejecting the bogus conception of freedom as license, or the capacity to do anything one pleases, he would presumably argue that those limiting factors are compatible with genuine freedom, or the ability to do what we truly want because we consider it to be good. In that case, true freedom turns out to be inseparable from the knowledge of moral value.

Morality

Like most ancient Greek philosophers starting with Socrates, Plato is fundamentally interested in understanding the nature of the good life for human beings. This inevitably involves an analysis of private and public morality, which these thinkers saw as interconnected. Thus Plato's masterpiece, the *Republic*, is both a great work of ethical theory and a seminal text in political philosophy (a distinction that is more important to us than it would have been to him). Most of Plato's greatest dialogues deal with morality; and we shall have to be selective in deciding on which to focus here. Let us consider one or more from each of the three different periods of his career.

NEVER DOING WRONG. One of the earliest dialogues, the *Crito*, is **existentially** gripping because it shows Socrates in a situation in which he will die if he continues to practice the morality he has preached. Recall that he has been sentenced to death, is in prison awaiting the date of his execution, and is being tempted by his dear old friend Crito to escape and

---

Necessity. That which could not be otherwise than it is, as opposed to contingency

Determinism. The doctrine that every event in the universe, including every human action, is causally necessitated by antecedent conditions, to the exclusion of free will

Ethics (from the Greek *ethos*, meaning custom). Moral philosophy, that area of philosophy that studies value judgments regarding "good" and "evil," "right" and "wrong," and obligation

Existential (from the Latin *existere*, meaning to stand out). Having to do with what exists; existentialists relate what exists to the dynamic reality of consciousness

save himself. Socrates argues from analogy for moral standards: as a person pursuing physical fitness should follow the advice of his "doctor or trainer" and will only "suffer harm" through following the instructions of the ignorant, so a person seeking to maintain a healthy soul should be instructed by the wise rather than by the foolish, lest his soul suffer the extreme harm of vice and wrongdoing. Socrates insists on acting in accordance with principle rather than out of self-interest, as he makes clear with an argument: since "the most important thing is not life, but the good life," which consists in acting rightly, "the only **valid** consideration . . . is whether we should be acting rightly" in following Crito's advice. But acting rightly, Socrates has taught, requires that "one must never do wrong" or even, "when wronged, inflict wrong in return, as the majority believe." This is a revolutionary ethical principle, as Socrates admits: "For I know that only a few people hold this view or will hold it, and there is no common ground between those who hold this view and those who do not, but they inevitably despise each other's views."[27] Socrates proceeds to show how the principle applies to the moral decision he must make (to be discussed in our next section). But our focus here is on Socrates' commitment to an absolute moral principle which is independent of our thoughts, feelings, desires, and so forth, as opposed to the relativism of the Sophists.

THE INDEPENDENCE OF MORALITY FROM RELIGIOUS VIEWS. Another early dialogue, the *Euthyphro*, tries to show that the principles of morality are independent of religious beliefs. As the dialogue begins, both Socrates and the title character are on their way to court when they meet, the former having been indicted by his accusers and the latter bringing a charge of murder against his own father. Witnessing Socrates' expressions of astonishment, Euthyphro claims to know that it is a pious, righteous thing he is doing. Socrates asks what is his criterion of righteousness and piety. Euthyphro responds,

> Well then, what is dear to the gods is pious, what is not is impious.

This is sometimes called a "divine command" theory of morality and needs to be repudiated if morality is to be absolute and independent, rather than relative to

and contingent on the will of the gods. Socrates points out that the gods are reputed to disagree among themselves; and there is nothing about which disagreement is more likely to arise, among both gods and humans, than questions of value—

> the just and the unjust, the beautiful and the ugly, the good and the bad. Are these not the subjects of difference about which, when we are unable to come to a satisfactory decision, you and I and other men become hostile to each other whenever we do?

Thus, the same sort of action may be dear to some gods and condemned by others. But on Euthyphro's criterion this would make it both pious and impious, which seems absurd. So, at the very least, a modification is needed. That which is tried maintains that

> what all the gods hate is impious, and what they all love is pious, and that what some gods love and others hate is neither or both.

But why should the gods love the pious and hate the impious? If divine affections are not to be arbitrary on so important a matter as morality, the gods must have good reason for what they love and hate. But why should the gods love the pious except because it is pious?

> It is loved then because it is pious, but it is not pious because it is loved.[28]

(Notice that Socrates is not denying that there is a correlation between morality and divine preference, but is merely asserting that the former is the independent and the latter the dependent variable.)

THE GOOD, THE BAD, AND THE MORALLY NEUTRAL. The *Gorgias* is Plato's great work of negative ethical theory, as the *Theaetetus* is his great work of negative epistemology. We should distinguish among three moral categories—that which is good, that which is bad, and that which is morally neutral. Of the third category Socrates says,

> And by things which are *neither good nor bad* you mean things which sometimes partake of what's good, sometimes of what's bad, and sometimes of neither, such as sitting or walking, running or making sea voyages, or stones and sticks and the like.

(We see the language of participation emerging here.) This threefold distinction is important for Socrates'

Validity.   Technically, the quality of a deductive argument, such that its conclusion necessarily follows from its premises; loosely, cogency

refutation of the view of Callicles, that the good life requires that "the superior rule the inferior" and consists in "wantonness, lack of discipline," and a reckless, self-indulgent pursuit of pleasure and satisfaction of desire. The sort of superiority Callicles adulates is a relative quality, neither **intrinsically** good nor bad, and difficult to define. Further, Socrates pushes Callicles to say that "the pleasant and the good are the same"—that is, to embrace the position of **hedonism**. Socrates refutes this identification by showing that we can simultaneously experience the pain of desire and the pleasure of satisfying that desire (for example, when we are drinking while very thirsty); yet the same thing cannot be both good and bad, so that the basic tenet of hedonism must be mistaken. It is more reasonable to say that "some pleasures are good while others are bad" and likewise with pains. But then there must be some other criterion of good and bad than that of hedonism, if pleasures and pains can be either good or bad. We ought to choose the good pleasures and pains because they are good and avoid the bad ones because they are bad, pleasures and pains themselves being morally neutral in the sense just explained. Socrates draws his antihedonistic **conclusion**, that we should pursue pleasant things, when we ought to do so at all, because they are good, rather than pursuing good things merely because they happen to be pleasant. Finally, the life of uncontrolled self-indulgence is foolish as well as wrong, since the well-being of the soul requires order, a **necessary condition** of which is self-control. Only the disciplined person can be completely good and happy.[29] This is an important critique of hedonistic immoderation.

THE NATURE OF JUSTICE. In the *Republic* Socrates refutes three inadequate moral theories. The one attributed to Cephalus is a simplistic, rule-bound theory, which holds, for example, "that justice or right is simply to speak the truth and to pay back any debt one may have contracted." Socrates can dispatch this with a counterexample: if a friend has lent you weapons which you are to return when he asks for them and subsequently comes demanding them when he is raving mad, you should not return them or even tell him the truth as to where they are, since it is predictable that he will use them to do terrible harm. Second, Polemarchus, the son of Cephalus, asserts the conventional view that justice requires that we give all people their due, which he thinks means "to benefit one's friends and harm one's enemies." But, apart from the difficulty of knowing who our real friends and enemies are and the fact that most people in the world are neither, a far more relevant criterion is whether those friends and enemies are good or bad people. It doesn't seem right that we should help bad people merely because they happen to be friends or hurt good people merely because they are enemies. But, beyond this, there is the question of whether we should ever deliberately harm anyone—even the person who is both bad and an enemy. Socrates (four centuries before Christ) argues that "it is never just to harm anyone" deliberately, since doing so is only likely to make him worse. Third, Thrasymachus tries to define justice (*dikaiosyne*) in terms of "the advantage of the stronger." After some preliminary skirmishing, Socrates points out that, no matter how we define "the stronger," they are people and thus fallible. When they mistakenly order what is really to their disadvantage, should we obey them or not? However we sort this out, justice often requires that the interests of the weaker should be served: the just practice of medicine serves the interests of the patients, and a ship's captain, although he is boss aboard his own vessel, must serve the interests of the sailors working under him, providing for their welfare while they are under his charge. Finally, Socrates argues that the life of justice—in his sense of the word, rather than that of Cephalus, Polemarchus, or Thrasymachus—is "more profitable" than that of injustice, in that it is wiser, more secure, and happier.[30]

Plato's brothers, Glaucon and Adeimantus, who

Intrinsic. In itself, for its own sake, rather than as a means to something else, or instrumental; a different meaning is inherent or essential, as opposed to extrinsic or accidental

Hedonism (from the Greek *hedone*, meaning pleasure). The theory that pleasure is in fact (psychological hedonism) and/or should be in principle (ethical hedonism) our ultimate good

Conclusion. In an argument, a proposition that is supported by one or more other propositions (the premises)

Necessary condition. That without which something else could not be or occur; for example, the presence of oxygen is a necessary condition for human respiration

are the main interlocutors (other characters discussing ideas with Socrates) of most of the dialogue, express dissatisfaction with the previous argument. Although Thrasymachus has been silenced, they are not rationally convinced. Glaucon invokes a threefold distinction of types of goods: some things, such as joy and harmless pleasures, are intrinsically good, valued for their own sake without leading to any further significant consequences; others, such as money and medicines, are instrumental goods, merely valued as means to other ends; and then there are those goods, such as knowledge and health, which are both intrinsically and instrumentally valuable. He asks Socrates, "Under which of these headings do you put justice?" Socrates wants to hold that justice belongs "in the finest class," as both intrinsically and instrumentally good, "that which is to be welcomed both for itself and for its consequences." But Glaucon and Adeimantus object that the argumentation of the preceding paragraph, to the extent that it works at all, only shows that justice is instrumentally "more profitable" and, playing devil's advocates, resurrect Thrasymachus' position, articulating it more powerfully than he ever did. In the process of challenging the value of justice, Glaucon tells the fabulous story of a shepherd who accidentally discovers a magical ring which allows him to become invisible and commit any sort of evil with impunity. The question is why we should not, like the shepherd, enjoy all kinds of wrongdoing if there were not bad extrinsic consequences to worry about.[31] Socrates must provide his own analysis of justice, in order to show that it is intrinsically valuable, regardless of external rewards and punishments.

Socrates observes that anything that is "completely good" must have all four of the "**cardinal virtues**" of conventional ancient Greek morality, so that "it is wise, brave, moderate, and just." (The word "cardinal" comes from the Latin word for a "hinge"; so the metaphor suggests that these are the four hinges on which the entire door of morality swings.) His strategy is to use a process-of-elimination analysis to determine the nature of justice: articulate what the virtues of wisdom, courage, and moderation are; then whatever is left over as essential to that which is "completely good" will be justice. Later, after the argumentation for the three parts of the soul, Socrates says that courage or bravery is that virtue (i.e., a morally desirable quality or excellence; the Greek word for virtue, *arete*, also means excellence) which "preserves in the midst of pain and pleasure" a person's rational convictions "as to what he should fear and what he should not." Wisdom allows a person to know what is ultimately beneficial to the soul as a whole. Moderation (*sophrosune*) is a harmonious agreement among all the parts of the soul "that reason should rule." So, whatever remains as essential to a "completely good" person but has not yet been specified will allegedly be justice. It consists in each part of the soul performing its own proper job and not meddling with the legitimate functioning of any other parts. This virtue especially unifies and integrates the personality. By contrast, a bad soul is disintegrated and suffers "a kind of civil war between the three parts"; and a thoroughly wicked soul might be characterized by the four cardinal vices of "injustice and license and cowardice and ignorance." Given this analysis of the nature of moral virtue, Glaucon and Adeimantus are convinced that this sort of morality, in general, and justice, in particular, provide the "health and beauty and well-being of the soul," so that they are intrinsically good, valuable in themselves, whether other people are aware of them or not and regardless of their external consequences.[32] The moral life, on this view, is essential for spiritual health and the fulfillment of human nature.

PLEASURES IN PROPER PERSPECTIVE. Plato's *Philebus* argues that the good life is a structured mixture of elements including certain types of pleasures. This is important to counterbalance the impression that may have been given thus far that Plato is **categorically** opposed to pleasure. Here he holds that the good cannot be equated with pleasure, no matter how much of it we may enjoy, for without intelligence we could not

---

Cardinal virtues (from the Latin *cardo*, meaning hinge, as if all excellence pivots on them). The most important or basic ideals of excellence—often four in number: wisdom or prudence, courage or fortitude, moderation or temperance, and justice

Categorical. Unconditional or without exception; having to do with definite concepts or structures of understanding; in Kant, a categorical imperative is unconditionally obligatory, as opposed to a hypothetical imperative, which only applies conditionally

be aware of, remember, or know anything of pleasure. But it is also true that a life of intelligence utterly devoid of pleasure would also be undesirable. So, neither pleasure without intelligence nor intelligence devoid of pleasure is sufficient for the good life, which must contain some mixture of the two. Every sort of knowledge is allowed into the mixture but not every sort of pleasure. Pure pleasures of the mind, the necessary pleasures related to sound health and steady temperance, and pleasures associated with the exercising of virtue are all to be included. But the wildest, most intense sensual pleasures are rejected as dangerous threats to the rule of reason and the equilibrium of the soul. There are bad pleasures, associated with "self-indulgence and other forms of vice," which have no proper place in the good life. In the mixture of intelligence and pleasure, finally, the former has the greater share because it partakes more of "beauty, proportion and truth," three essential characteristics of the Good.[33] So the pursuit of the Good that morality requires of human nature allows for the enjoyment of pleasures of the right sort, so long as they are kept in proper perspective.

OVERCOMING SELFISHNESS. In what may have been Plato's last book, the *Laws*, he warns us against selfishness, or "excessive love of ourselves," which he calls the "most serious vice **innate** in most men's souls" and "the cause of each and every crime we commit." Although everyone ought primarily to value "acts of justice, not only when they are his own, but especially when they happen to be done by someone else," the egocentric "vice of selfishness" all too often prevents us from achieving this ideal. Because we are "men, not gods," we cannot consistently achieve the ideal in this life.

Human nature involves, above all, pleasures, pains, and desires, and no mortal animal can help being hung up dangling in the air (so to speak) in total dependence on these powerful influences.

But the trick is to convince people to desire the moral life and to pursue virtuous, legitimate pleasures.[34] There lies our hope for overcoming natural selfishness and orienting people towards the Good in general, as well as towards the welfare of society.

Society

DUTY TO SOCIETY. In the *Crito* Plato reveals Socrates as taking seriously his commitments to society. As he had held in the *Apology* that he has a duty to society to play the philosophical gadfly, so here he argues that he has a moral obligation not to damage the fabric of social law and order deliberately. When he applies his ethical principle that we should never intentionally harm anyone, even in retaliation for harm done to us, he sees that disobeying the lawful order of the court for the sake of self-interest would be wrong. Because Crito has trouble accepting his decision, Socrates resorts to a kind of fairy tale, asking that we imagine him doing what Crito advises, escaping from Athens, and meeting a personification of the Athenian laws on the way, who would argue that he is doing something wrong for two reasons. First, because he was born, raised, married, and lived virtually all his life in Athens, so that everything he has achieved and come to be has been influenced by that culture, he has a debt of obligation to his society; what a wretched ingrate he would be to repay all he owes his society by deliberately flouting its laws for his own selfish purposes. Second, although he was free to leave Athens throughout most of the seventy years of his life, he never chose to leave except in military service to Athens itself, so that he has made an implied agreement to abide by and respect its laws so long as they do not violate his moral principles.[35] Both reasons concern our political obligations as members of society; justice requires that we return good (rather than harm) to society for the blessings of citizenship we have received and that we honor even the implicit commitments we have made so long as we can do so in good conscience.

Let us reflect for a moment on what Socrates does not do in discussing his relation to society—he does not merely tell people what he knows very well they want to hear; during his trial he refuses to flatter the court and ingratiate himself with its members, and in the *Crito* he refuses the advice that most people would consider to be for his own good. This is why he proclaims (perhaps immodestly) in the *Gorgias* that

---

Innate (from the Latin *innatus*, meaning inborn). Inborn, not derived from sense experience; Plato and Descartes believe we have some innate ideas, whereas empiricists deny them

he is one of the few Athenians "to take up the true political craft and practice the true politics," despite the fact that he has never been a professional politician. To grasp this point we must consider his distinction between the genuine arts of politics (namely, legislation and judicial administration) and their spurious counterfeits (namely, sophistry and oratory), which are mere forms of flattery; the real arts are concerned with "whatever is best," whereas the counterfeits aim to please people by telling them what they want to hear. Even the famous Pericles is taken to task for pandering to the public, rather than standing staunchly for the public morality[36]—a flaw of which Socrates certainly cannot be accused.

RULERS, AUXILIARIES, AND PRODUCERS. The alleged correlation between society and human nature is such that Plato asserts, in the *Republic*, that the organized society of the *polis* presents a macroscopic view of the human individual, who, in turn, can be regarded as an analogue of the *polis* on a microscopic scale. The *polis* comes into being "because not one of us is self-sufficient." The good life, if not survival itself, requires social cooperation. Efficiency calls for a division of labor in which there is coordinated activity in producing the means of livelihood. Socrates seems quite willing to settle for such a simple society as would be constituted by a cooperating association of producers; but Glaucon, Plato's older brother, objects that this would be merely "a city of pigs," providing only for survival and the most primitive animal needs, but not providing for higher culture and the fruits of civilization. So, Socrates reluctantly agrees to elaborate a more sophisticated society, which he derisively calls "the feverish city," to provide the wherewithal for luxury, creature-comforts, and so forth. But then it will require protection, so that a guardian class must arise, whose responsibilities are distinct from those of the producers. It turns out that there will be two levels of guardians—those who fight for the protection and security of the *polis*, on the one hand, and the lovers of wisdom (literally "philosophers") who can rule the city well, on the other.[37]

It is the higher order of guardians whose job it is to rule and whose orders are to be carried out by the others, their auxiliaries. It is through the filtering of the education process that society will determine who "is to be made a ruler as well as a guardian." Plato develops a myth of metals, as a kind of propaganda ploy, to convince people that everyone has his or her proper station in society—it being appropriate that the people of "gold" should rule, with those of "silver" serving as their auxiliaries, and those of "iron and bronze" being producers. This is not exactly a caste system because it is not strictly hereditary, in that, for example, "a silver child will occasionally be born from a golden parent, and vice versa." But once the education system has determined the "metallic" nature of a member of society, no social mobility is possible for him or her.[38]

Plato has Socrates call for a system of communal life for the guardian classes, who are to own no private property, who must be provided with common quarters and dining facilities, and who will not be allowed any luxuries, lest they be tempted to abuse their positions for their own profit. Adeimantus, Plato's brother, protests that it is unfair that the guardians, who bear the responsibility of power, should be deprived of the most desirable material goods, which producers will be able to enjoy. Socrates' response is twofold: if the guardians have been well trained and inculcated with the right values, they will be "very happy" to serve society thus, sacrificing lower goods for higher ones; and, even if they are not, the common good of "the whole city" is more important than individual satisfaction or the happiness of "any one group." There is a suggestion, to be developed later, that the guardians' spouses and children "must be held in common," rather than having the sort of private families that producers will be allowed. As the four cardinal virtues are associated with the three parts of the soul, so they are also with the three classes of society. If the ideal republic, whose blueprint we are reviewing, is "completely good," it must comprise all four of the cardinal virtues. The rulers especially need wisdom, "sound judgment" and "the knowledge of guardianship." The auxiliaries particularly require courage, the capacity to maintain and fight for the welfare of the *polis* in the face of danger and potential pain. All three classes require moderation, which is "a kind of harmony" arising from agreement as to who should rule. Justice also applies to all three classes and has both a positive and a negative side; for "justice is to perform one's own task and not to meddle with that of others."[39] A society so structured and characterized would allegedly be ideal or "completely good."

OBJECTIONS TO THE IDEAL SOCIETY. Socrates must face three potential "waves of objections" that can be aimed at radical features of his theory. The first has to do with equal opportunity for women, who are to be educated to their ability along with the men and allowed to rise to the ruling class if they are sufficiently capable. (Why should Plato not advocate this extremely revolutionary view, given his theory that the body is not essential to human nature and that the soul has no gender, especially if equality might be for the greater benefit of society?) Second, as mentioned earlier, there is to be an extension of family ties among the guardian classes, so that all guardians regard all others of their class as their parents, their brothers and sisters, their children, rather than sentimentally playing favorites in a way that might jeopardize a sweeping sense of solidarity within a class. (By the way, slavery is mentioned as a noncontroversial feature of the ideal society, on the condition that only "barbarians"—i.e., non-Greeks—should be enslaved and that those of "the Greek race" should not.) And, third, "the greatest wave" of all would require philosophical leadership in the *polis*:

> Cities will have no respite from evil, my dear Glaucon, nor will the human race, I think, unless philosophers rule as kings in the cities, or those whom we now call kings and rulers genuinely and adequately study philosophy, until, that is, political power and philosophy coalesce.

(Remember that Plato tried and failed to educate Dionysius II, the tyrant of Syracuse, in a philosophical "love of wisdom" or commitment to ideas.) All of this is presented as part of an ideal "model," such that it is allegedly irrelevant whether, and to what extent, "the things we have described in theory can exist precisely in practice."[40]

ALTERNATIVE SOCIETIES, LAW, AND GOVERNMENT. Unfortunately, the ideal is rarely (if ever) met, and Plato discusses the four decadent societies that fall short of the ideal of meritocratic aristocracy (literally, the rule of the best). The second best form of society is a **timocracy**, the rule of the most honorable; this might be a military regime, perhaps like ancient Sparta, in which spirit, rather than reason, tends to dominate. Third, there is an oligarchy, the rule of the few, such as the rich; here the most orderly of the baser appetites, namely that for money, prevails over both reason and spirit. The next to worst society is a democracy, which is a chaotic rule of the rabble, in which all of the appetites have an equal influence on public policy and license (a perverted sort of "freedom") is an ultimate value. Worst of all is a dictatorship of the cruelest, most selfish appetites of all, exploiting and savaging the rest of society for its own despotic pleasure and mania for power.

In his *Statesman* Plato avers that practical politics, which inevitably "falls short of the ideal," requires a rigorous maintaining of law and order with violators severely punished. The "rule of the few" is seen as a middle ground between a government of one and a government of many. The rule of the many is the weakest sort of society because power is so dissipated. This dispersal is for the best in an unprincipled society; but in one that is "lawful and ordered" democracy is the least desirable and **monarchy** the best.[41] (Here we are talking about governments that actually exist, rather than about the ideal republic.)

By the time Plato writes the *Laws* (after the fiasco of his final voyage to Sicily), he seems more dogmatic than ever, more distant from his earlier abstract **idealism**, and more concerned with theorizing about the "nuts and bolts" of jurisprudence and practical public administration. The law should be supreme in a good state. But "laws which are not established for the good of the whole state are bogus laws"; when they are designed to serve class interests, rather than the common good, they are illegitimate, and it becomes fruitless to insist that they be obeyed. In a good society, "law is the master of government," rather than the other way around. The purpose of the laws is to "explain the duties we owe" other members of society. They fulfill this function partly by "persuasion and partly" by "compulsion and chastisement." The simpler form of law consists of two parts: commands (e.g., "A man must marry between the ages of thirty and thirty-five") and sanctions (e.g., "If he does not,

---

Timocracy. In Plato, government by those most honored, as for courage and military prowess

Monarchy (from the Greek *monarkia*, meaning the rule of one). Government by a single person, such as an emperor or a queen

Idealism. The philosophical theory that reality is ultimately mental or spiritual in its nature and/or its origins (metaphysical idealism) or that we can only know minds and their ideas (epistemological idealism)

he must be punished by fines and disgrace"). The longer form of law includes persuasive explanations as to why the commands and sanctions are appropriate.[42] We must establish and maintain a good society—if not an ideal one—as a context for human flourishing, since our natures as persons are essentially social.

Religion

THE NATURE OF PIETY. It is ironic that Socrates, who was accused of religious impiety, refused to give up the practice of philosophy because he considered it his god-given mission; in the *Apology* he speaks of a divine voice which, since childhood, has warned him against doing things that are wrong.[43] (It is also ironic that the other accusation was of corrupting the young, given that for about twenty-four centuries now Socrates has served as a model inspiring us to better ourselves through critical reflection.) In the *Euthyphro*, after the relationship between piety and the will of the gods has been explored, the nature of piety is discussed. Although, like many of the early Socratic dialogues, this one is inconclusive, Socrates resists the view that the "honour, reverence, and . . . gratitude" involved in the attitude of piety can "benefit" the gods in any way; so, it seems that piety is a religious duty incumbent on us, although the gods have nothing to gain from our fulfilling it.[44] Piety is presented as a religious virtue that is important for the excellence of human nature.

RELIGIOUS CENSORSHIP. In the *Republic*, Plato advocates censoring "any story," such as those told "by Hesiod and Homer and the other poets," which "gives a bad image of the nature of the gods," portraying them as petty, devious, or "warring and plotting and fighting against each other." For children, especially, are vulnerable to such blasphemies and need to be protected from them by society. The gods should only be represented as causing good and never as responsible for evil-doing, since it is the nature of divinity to be good. Nor should the gods be portrayed as changing, since any change in divinity "must be for the worse." Thus, no god would cause himself to change;[45] nor could anything else cause any change in divinity, which must be perfect and, therefore, not susceptible to being changed.

CREATION. In the *Timaeus* Plato discusses the creation of the universe by a divinity. Our universe is a world of change, a process of "coming to be and ceasing to be, but never fully real," and therefore cannot be self-sufficient but must have been created. He warns us, however, that we cannot achieve precise, communicable knowledge of the creator, because we are limited mortals, so that we should accept what follows as merely a probable tale. Being divine, the creator must be good and devoid of selfishness. Therefore, "he wished all things to be as like himself as possible." So, the world was created to share in the being and goodness of its creator, who brought order out of the pre-existing chaos (this is not a creation from nothing, as in traditional Christianity). Since the divinity is good, he desired that which is best, so the entire created order is governed "through god's providence." The things of this world were fashioned on the models of the Forms.[46] Thus, this universe of becoming has been made in the image of the ultimate realities by its creator, the causal link between Plato's two worlds.

THE NATURE OF THE GODS. The *Laws* contains considerable material about religion. Its major character, the Athenian, says, against the Sophist followers of Protagoras, "In our view it is God who is preeminently the 'measure of all things,' much more so than any 'man,' as they say." Worship of the gods (notice that on the very same page Plato vacillates indiscriminately between speaking of "God" and "the gods") and religious practices are recommended as "the best and noblest policy" man can adopt. There must be a first cause of all movement, which generates its own motion, and is spiritual and divine. Second, because the gods are good, wise, and provident, we must acknowledge that they care for humans as part of the created order. But, third, because they are righteous and need nothing from us, they cannot be bribed by sacrifices and flattery to deviate from the universal moral order. The Athenian concludes that he has provided argumentation for "three theses—that the gods exist, that they are concerned for us, and that they are absolutely above being corrupted into flouting justice." On this view, an attitude of religious piety is a legitimate dimension of human nature; indeed, it is to be required by law, with stiff penalties up to and including capital punishment.[47] Religion establishes a relationship between reverential humans and concerned gods.

Immortality

IMMORTALITY OF THE SOUL. As we have seen, in the *Phaedo* Socrates tries to meet the epiphenomenalist challenge of Simmias and Cebes and show that the human soul is an independent substance, rather than a by-product of the body. If this is so, then there is no reason to presume that the soul will die when and because the body does so. But Plato tries to go beyond this by providing four proofs of **immortality** to demonstrate that the soul will not die. The first is based on a principle of opposites. As only what was larger can become smaller (and vice versa), the weaker can only come to be from the stronger (and vice versa), and something can get worse only from having been better (and vice versa), we may draw the **inductive generalization** "that all things come to be in this way, opposites from opposites." But life and death are opposites, so that death must give rise to new life. The second proof recalls the attempt of the *Meno* to demonstrate recollection. If there are matters, such as universal truths, which we have never been taught in this life but can be led to remember, they could only have been learned prior to this life—in which case it follows that the life of the soul does not merely extend from womb to tomb. But Simmias acutely objects that life before birth is not equivalent to life after death, which is what Socrates was to prove. Socrates' response to this is that we must therefore combine these two arguments: as the nonphysical life of the soul preceded its physical incarnation (which is terminated by physical death), that, in turn, is followed by nonphysical life again, and so forth.[48] So, it turns out that the second proof also involves the interplay of opposites.

In a way, the third does too. We are asked to recognize that there are two types of reality: visible things are "compound by nature" and therefore dissoluble, changing, physical, multiform, unintelligible, and mortal; by contrast, invisible realities are spiritual, "most like the divine, deathless, intelligible, uniform, indissoluble, always the same." The human body seems clearly to belong to the first category, and the soul to the second; but if the soul is noncomposite and therefore indissoluble, it must be immortal. So, two sets of opposite qualities are set up to prove immortality. The fourth argument presents a new use of opposites. Here we are urged to agree that opposites always retreat from their opposites and resist becoming like them. Thus, fire and snow repel each other, neither ever becoming the other because they have opposite essential qualities (i.e., heat and cold); or again, it is the essence of the number three to be an odd number, and it can never become even without ceasing to be three. But the soul essentially brings life, the opposite of which is death. Therefore, the soul will retreat from and resist death at all costs—in which case it must be immortal.[49]

REINCARNATION. Death is defined as "the separation of the soul from the body"; but it is not the end of the soul, on this theory. Plato believes in **metempsychosis**, the transmigration of souls from one living thing to another, and in **reincarnation**, the rebirth of the soul in new—and even different kinds of—bodies. In the *Phaedo* Plato gives us another myth of judgment, comparable to the myth of Er near the end of the *Republic*, according to which, after the death of their bodies, it will be determined whether souls are worthy of punishment or reward. Those that have been purified by the philosophical pursuit of knowledge and virtue can be liberated from the cycle of reincarnation.[50]

The *Phaedrus* offers a new proof of the soul's immortality, of which we have seen a later version in the *Laws*, purporting to prove the existence of gods from self-generating motion. We are told, "All soul is immortal; for what is always in motion is immortal."

Immortality. The unending existence of a soul or spirit, once it has begun to be

Induction. Reasoning that takes the form of a probability argument, deriving a conclusion from the premise(s) as more or less likely, rather than as certain, as opposed to deduction

Generalization. An inductive inference that what is true (or false) of some observed individuals is probably also true (or false) of others that have not yet been observed

Metempsychosis (or **reincarnation**) (from the Greek *meta*, meaning changed, *en*, meaning in, and *psukhe*, meaning soul). The passage of a soul, after bodily death, into a different body

Reincarnation. *See* Metempsychosis

This **premise** seems self-evident because of the meaning of "always." But how do we know the soul is "always in motion"? Being "in motion" here means undergoing change. It is allegedly the nature of soul to initiate its own changes, to be self-moving, rather than merely extrinsically moved; but then it could never cease to be self-moving "without being false to its own nature." On this view, something that is essentially self-moving "can neither be destroyed nor come into being"; it is an independent and eternal reality. Types of personalities the soul can take on, from "a seeker after wisdom" to that of "a tyrant," are outlined. We are told that "the lot which befalls a man between two incarnations corresponds to the goodness or badness of his previous life." And, in the process of reincarnations, the human soul may be required to enter into the body of a beast, if its previous life has rendered it unfit "to enter into our human shape." Only the soul of the philosophical lover of knowledge and virtue is worthy of soaring beyond the process of rebirth to its ultimate fulfillment.[51]

Fulfillment

THIS LIFE AND THE AFTERLIFE. It might be helpful to distinguish between our relative happiness in this life and that ultimate fulfillment in the afterlife, even if Plato does not explicitly do so. In a minor Socratic dialogue called *Euthydemus* it is agreed that everyone obviously wants to succeed at being happy, so that it is appropriate to consider what makes this possible. It requires the possession of "plenty of good things"; but this is not enough. It is rash and wrong to assume "that if we had plenty of good things, we would be happy and successful." For the "mere possession and use of good things" are insufficient to constitute happiness because we must know how they are "to be used correctly."[52] Thus, a philosophical understanding of ethics is required.

The *Gorgias* contains a more mature discussion of the happiness possible in this life. Socrates, after refusing to assume that the rich and powerful king of Persia is happy, maintains "that the admirable and good person, man or woman, is happy, but that the one who's unjust and wicked is miserable." Therefore, it is most important for us to strive to know what is good, "and most shameful not to" do so. If we are

physically ill, it is better that the illness be detected and treated; but best of all is never to have contracted illness in the first place. Likewise, spiritual sickness, if contracted, is better treated by detection and punishment; but it is best that it not be contracted at all.

> The happiest man, then, is the one who doesn't have evil in his soul, now that this has been shown to be the most serious kind of evil.[53]

HAPPINESS AND LOVE. This conception of happiness should be connected with love, and Plato does this in the *Symposium*. The lover of the good aims his love at the possession of the good, which, in turn, is oriented towards happiness, which requires no further explanation, so that "the inquiry is at an end; there is no need to ask the further question 'Why does a man desire to be happy?' " In other words, happiness is an intrinsic good. We are not talking here of earthly love, which "is physical rather than spiritual," erratic and haphazard, "and quite as often bad as good." Even the love of other persons that is sometimes called Platonic love must be for the noble and virtuous, "even though they may be inferior in looks," or physical appearances, if it is to be "held in the highest esteem." Erotic love, which is oriented towards sexual relationships, is merely physical; and Plato spins out a myth to explain that Zeus once cut us into two parts, so that sexual desire expresses one's search for his other half. But the love pursued by the philosopher as essential to happiness is divine and never either "inflicts wrong upon" or "suffers it from" gods or men; and love

> is richly endowed with self-control. Everyone admits that self-control is mastery over pleasures and desires, and that no pleasure is stronger than Love.[54]

The higher love of knowledge or wisdom drives our striving for the good, which must be grasped (to the extent possible) so that happiness can be achieved.

BECOMING AS GOOD AND WISE AS POSSIBLE. In the *Phaedo* Plato portrays Socrates as maintaining that death can be a blessing rather than a curse for the person who has led a good life committed to the pursuit of knowledge and virtue, in that the soul will be freed from all bodily association, liberated from the distortions and distractions of the cave, and enabled to achieve its ultimate fulfillment. This will presumably consist of the soul's enjoying "pure knowledge" in

---

Premise. In an argument, a proposition or statement that is used to provide support for the conclusion

the world of Forms, in company with the gods and other virtuous human souls. We prepare for and render ourselves worthy of such bliss by valuing knowledge and virtue in this life and achieving them to the limited degree that we can. This is through the practice of philosophy, and it explains what Plato means by the ironic phrase that philosophy is a training or rehearsal for dying and death, for it weans us from our servile attachment to the body and the physical world of the cave, reorienting our souls to the world of Ideas. Far from considering his own imminent death as "a misfortune," Socrates poignantly compares himself to dying swans that "sing of the blessings" of the afterlife. From this perspective, our hope for "salvation" lies in our "becoming as good and wise as possible." Philosophical understanding and detachment from selfish physical desires purify the soul. "The well-ordered and wise soul," which "has had a pure and moderate life," earns its liberation from the cycle of reincarnation and "dwells in a place suited to it,"[55] where the ultimate fulfillment of human nature is to be attained.

REFLECTIONS

Plato's theory is idealistic in that it identifies ultimate reality and the ultimate good with the realm of Ideas and eternal, immutable ideals. There is an excellent illustration of this in the *Republic*, where Glaucon, Plato's older brother, describes the ideal society under consideration as "our city of words." Socrates' response is telling. He replies that "it is a model laid up in heaven, for him who wishes to look upon, and as he looks, set up the government of his soul. It makes no difference whether it exists anywhere or will exist."[56] It is our responsibility to grasp the ideal intellectually and to do our best to achieve it through our choices, commitments, and actions. It may be a limit that can only be approached asymptotically and never fully reached, as when a curve approaches a line. But that, we are told, "makes no difference" to what we must strive to do. This is the core of Plato's idealism.

REALITY. This focus on the spiritual dimension of the human person, on what we are able to become as transcending what we find ourselves to be, attests to the **dignity** of human nature. But this pivot point of Plato's entire philosophy is also where it is most vulnerable to criticism. Although the fact that few people who have studied it are convinced that there is an eternal, immutable realm of Ideas that are real independently of any and all minds (whether human or divine) does not disprove his theory, it should lead us, as critical thinkers, to be hesitant about accepting it. Our access to and utilization of universal ideas like equality and justice seem to derive from the ability of the human mind to generalize and abstract from the particular features of concrete experience. Even if we grant Plato his world of Forms, there is the enormous problem, which he himself had the perspicacity to recognize, of how, precisely, they could be related to the things of this world of time and space. The metaphor of participation is too vague and elusive to provide an adequate account.

BODIES. Second, regarding the status of bodies in Plato's world-view, we should be suspicious of its implications for the proper attitude towards the physical world, including especially our own bodies. Is it healthy or constructive to regard them in so negative a manner as to long for liberation from them? This one-sided denial of an aspect of our being which, for now at least, is inescapable seems to alienate us from a sense of wholeness and to produce a kind of metaphysical schizophrenia.

PERSONALITY. On the third topic, of personality, the engaging argument from *Alcibiades I* requires that we accept the premise that a person uses and rules his own body. But this assumes the very dualism that must be proved—namely, that a person is something distinct from (so that she can use and rule) her body. In logic this is called the **fallacy** of **circular reasoning**. Another key presupposition, that there is such a *thing* or *reality* as soul, should not pass unchallenged. The principle of life in living things might be an activity or function of biochemical processes rather than an independent substance, taking us back to epiphenomenalism;

Dignity (from the Latin *dignitas*, meaning worthiness). The intrinsic worth of persons
Fallacy. An error in reasoning, such that the conclusion of an argument does not logically follow from its premises; a formal fallacy renders deductive arguments invalid, while an informal fallacy is psychologically tricky because of irrelevance, ambiguity, emotional appeals, etc.
Circular reasoning (or **begging the question**). The fallacy of assuming the conclusion of an argument in its premises

and Plato's battering of the harmony simile does not eliminate this crucial alternative theory. Regarding the three parts of the soul, can we make any sense of how a nonphysical thing can be comprised of parts? What does it mean for reason to be a "part" of the soul that is different from and in conflict with the appetitive "part"? And doesn't this theory render psychological stability and integration fleeting and precarious?

KNOWLEDGE. Regarding the fourth topic, knowledge, what Plato calls "recollection" strikes most of us as learning—and sometimes being led—to figure things out. Socrates' leading questions to Meno's slave boy reveal a master teacher at work; but it is quite implausible that the boy is remembering the correct answers known from a previous life. Plato's discussion of the relation between knowledge and correct opinion or true judgment, in the *Meno* and the *Theaetetus*, is superb; but it is troubling that we never get a definitive analysis of so pivotal a concept as that of knowledge. The divided-line simile is memorable; but its highest rung is murky, ill-defined, and difficult for most of us to grasp.

FREEDOM. Plato gives perhaps his least impressive coverage of our fifth topic of freedom. He does not seem to realize to what extent he is simply taking freedom for granted without any argumentation. Worse than that, although it is clear that it is not the perverted license that he associates with democracy, he is not very helpful in revealing what it is. And, beyond that, he seems oblivious to the problem of how to reconcile human freedom with the determining influence of moral knowledge and the necessary relationship between our present situations and the character of our previous lives.

MORALITY. Plato is, perhaps, at his best on the treatment of morality, our sixth topic. Socrates' fidelity to universal principles at risk of his own life is inspiring. The detachment of morality from religious beliefs in the *Euthyphro* is among the permanently valuable legacies of ancient Greek thought. The *Gorgias* is terrific for its conceptual distinctions of the good, the bad, and the morally neutral, as well as for its refutation of a crude form of hedonism. Socrates' critique of the three inadequate theories of justice in the *Republic* is monumental, as is the challenge against the intrinsic value of justice, made by Glaucon and Adeimantus. Plato's own derivation of the nature of justice is unconvincing, however, because the notion of what is "completely good" is too simplistic. A person might have all four of the cardinal virtues but be devoid of any interpersonal love (discussed so eloquently in the *Symposium*), in which case few of us would consider him "completely good." Plato's notion of justice assumes a parts-of-the-whole structure, with each part having its own stringently delineated function; and we have not been given sufficient reason to accept such a cut-and-dried analysis. The idea of the *Philebus* that the good life requires an ordered mixture, including intelligence and the right sort of pleasures, seems sound enough. But the trick is to separate cleanly the good from the bad pleasures; we should beware, for example, of assuming that all unnecessary physical pleasures are illegitimate.

SOCIETY. Seventh, Plato's discussion of society is as exciting and dangerous as a hornet's nest. Socrates' conviction that we have debts of obligation to and implicit agreements with the societies of which we are members seems well-founded, especially given the conditions he attaches of our being free to leave and not being bound to obey against the moral dictates of conscience. However, the parallel between society, with its three rigidly demarcated classes, and the human soul, with its three functioning "parts," is a **false analogy**. The soul, by its nature, either does or does not have the **constitutive** makeup attributed to it by Plato; by contrast, we can establish society to serve our needs and interests as we deem best. Remember that Socrates himself wanted a simple society comprising only a single class of mutually cooperating producers. What seems most dangerous is the uncompromising lack of social mobility and the elitist authoritarian social engineering of Plato's ideal republic, which would deprive all but a few members

---

False analogy.   A fallacy that can arise when similarities that are observed are tangential rather than essential and/or when crucial dissimilarities are overlooked or ignored

Constitutive.   Forming a part of, helping to make up a whole; in Kant, ideas have a constitutive (as opposed to a regulative) function when they can lead to knowledge

of society—the philosophers!—of political **autonomy**. Although we cannot legitimately blame Plato for being unaware of the possibility of representative democracy a couple of millennia before it was invented, we who have lived with it and enjoyed its benefits need not swallow his blueprint for political organization. Plato's glib, uncritical assumption of the general legitimacy of slavery is indicative of his lack of a universal perspective of all persons as spiritually equal. On the other hand, how exciting that Plato, over two thousand years before any other great philosopher, calls for equal opportunity for women, even if his motive is the welfare of society, rather than a respect for their natural human rights!

RELIGION. On the eighth topic, of religion, Plato makes at least three valuable contributions: his divorcing of ethics from religious beliefs and his admittedly inconclusive analysis of piety in the *Euthyphro*, as well as the seed of what later came to be known as **cosmological argumentation** for divine existence in the *Laws*. On the other hand, it is ironic, given the trial, conviction, and execution of his beloved Socrates, that Plato should be so mercilessly intolerant as to call for censorship standards against impious treatments of divinity and for draconian legal measures, including the death penalty, against religious dissenters.

IMMORTALITY. Ninth, the four arguments for immortality in the *Phaedo* all involve different forms of a doctrine of opposites, none of which seems particularly compelling. It is a rash generalization (both hasty and unrepresentative) to conclude that all things, including the nonphysical life of the soul, are derived from their opposites merely because a handful of physical states or qualities seem to be so derived. But, if so, this undercuts both the first and second proofs, the latter of which also requires the dubious claim that all learning is actually recollection. The third argument assumes uncritically that the two categories of realities constitute a **mutually exclusive** and **exhaustive** set of **alternatives**, such that nothing can be subsumed (in part) under both categories and that no third category is conceivable; against Plato,

we might object that the soul seems to belong to a third, mixed category, being invisible and spiritual, but changing and multiform (remember its three parts), with the issue unresolved as to whether it is dissoluble or immortal. Even if the fourth argument convinces us that all opposites resist and try to retreat from each other, we know that intense fire sometimes destroys snow and that a sufficient quantity of snow can extinguish fire, so that it remains an open question whether the soul, whose essential principle is life, will always overcome death or will sometimes succumb to it. The proof for immortality in the *Phaedrus* is particularly subtle and different (not utilizing any doctrine of opposites), but it requires that we accept the dubious premise that a self-moving reality, such as the soul allegedly is, could never cease to be self-moving, so that it must be eternal.

FULFILLMENT. On the tenth topic, Plato's diagnosis of human happiness, to the extent that it is possible in this life, is a powerful profile of the good life and the importance of virtue and selfless love as its prerequisites. But his view of our ultimate fulfillment in the afterlife is highly speculative (usually presented in the context of a myth) and unsupported by much argumentation or evidence.

* * *

In conclusion, Plato does offer us a coherent, comprehensive, systematic theory of human nature, which incorporates and takes seriously all ten of the dimensions on which we are focusing. It is a philosophical theory in that its component features arise as a result of critical reflection on the foundations of experience and are interrelated by means of argumentation. Its idealism is both its strength and its weakness; it is uplifting and accentuates the unique dignity of the human spirit while downgrading and dismissing our bodies, our animality, and our physical environment. The historical influence of this theory on Western Civilization has been so enormous that British philosopher Alfred North Whitehead's famous remark that the tradition of European philosophy comprises a series of footnotes to Plato is only a slight exaggeration.

Autonomy (from the Greek *autonomos*, meaning self-legislating).   Self-determination, the capacity and/or right to determine one's own views, values, and actions (in Kant, contrasted with heteronomy)

Cosmological argument.   An argument purporting to prove the existence of God as the necessary, ultimate First Cause of the universe or cosmos, whose reality (by contrast) is regarded as contingent

Mutually exclusive alternatives.   Two possibilities that cannot simultaneously hold true (e.g., either frail or robust)

Exhaustive alternatives.   Two possibilities that are so related that no third alternative is possible (e.g., either living or dead)

Aristotle

All men
by nature
desire
to know.

METAPHYSICS

BIOGRAPHY

To the extent that we take seriously Whitehead's remark that European philosophy is a series of footnotes to Plato, it seems fair to say that the most important of these footnotes are those of his greatest student, Aristotle, who was born in 384 B.C. (fifteen years after the death of Socrates) in Stagira (so that he is sometimes called the Stagirite), a city in Thrace. Aristotle's father was physician to the king of Macedonia. In 368 or 367 B.C., when he was seventeen years old, Aristotle went south to Athens, to complete his education at the Academy. He was there, first as a student, later as researcher and teacher, for roughly the last twenty years of Plato's life; it is said that Plato referred to him as "the mind" (*nous*) of the Academy. He seems to have adopted and developed Platonic ideas while there and to have expressed them in dialogue form, although we have only fragments of these surviving today. Near the end of this time, Aristotle may have differed with Plato over the latter's growing emphasis on mathematics and his mystical attachment to numbers.

In his will Plato bequeathed the presidency of the Academy to his nephew Speusippus rather than to his gifted student Aristotle. We can only speculate as to why. It may have simply been an act of nepotism on Plato's part. It may have represented a response to flattery, since Speusippus taught that Plato's real father was the god Apollo rather than the human

Ariston. It may have reflected traces of xenophobia, since Aristotle was a resident alien from the Thracian land mass. It may have had to do with doctrinal agreement; Speusippus extended his uncle's enthusiasm for mathematics and fascination for numbers to an extreme, for which Aristotle had little use. At any rate, Aristotle left Athens with Xenocrates, another disciple of Plato's, to go to Assos, in Asia Minor, where he established a branch campus of the Academy. There he met Hermias, another former student of Plato, who had become king of Assos, southeast of Troy. Aristotle married Pythias, Hermias' niece and adopted daughter, who died ten years later. During these years in Assos, it appears that Aristotle was starting to break from Platonism and to develop his own ideas.

Hermias was a friend and ally of King Philip of Macedonia, who wanted to unite the Greeks against Persia. The Persian general Mentor, in violation of a safe-conduct pass, captured Hermias and tortured him for information, which he did not divulge. It is said that he died asking that his friends be told that he did nothing to disgrace philosophy. It is probably thanks to Hermias that Philip invited Aristotle to Pella, the capital of Macedonia in 343 or 342 B.C., to tutor his thirteen-year-old son, Alexander.

In 359 B.C., when Aristotle was in his mid-twenties and still working at the Academy, Philip had become king of Macedonia, expanding the kingdom to include Stagira and other Thracian cities at the northern edge of the Greek world. He developed a powerful army and was legendary for his own personal courage. His dream was to unify and strengthen all the Greek world and lead it in conquest over the Persians. In 340, Philip set off to subdue the Greek city-states that opposed him, naming the sixteen-year-old Alexander regent in his absence, in effect ending Aristotle's instruction of the boy. Within a few years, Philip had prevailed over armed opposition within Greece and started planning the assault on Persia, when he was murdered, in 336, with the complicity of Alexander's mother, his first wife, whom he had divorced.

Alexander, now twenty years old, became king, gathered and mobilized Philip's great army, quashed some uprisings in Greece, and began the conquests that would make him Alexander "the Great" and establish the Macedonian Empire, which ultimately extended into Persia, Egypt, and Phoenicia. Meanwhile, Aristotle went home to Stagira for a while. He did not altogether agree with his former student's plans, preferring the government of the city-state to the hegemony of empire and opposing Alexander's goal of uniting Greeks and "barbarians" (i.e., non-Greeks) through intermarriage. Still, whatever their disagreements, we are told that Alexander rebuilt his former teacher's hometown of Stagira and assigned some of his men, while on military expeditions, to gather flora and fauna to send to Aristotle as specimens for scientific study.

In 335 B.C., Aristotle returned to Athens. Speusippus had died, but again Aristotle was passed over as head of the Academy, the position going, instead, to his one-time colleague Xenocrates. So, Aristotle founded his own school, the Lyceum, named after Apollo Lyceus, the second great school of ancient Greece, also known as "the Peripatetic school" because of the covered walk (*peripatos* in Greek) where people discussed ideas while walking. The Lyceum, like the Academy, was a university of higher learning and a research institution; it placed less emphasis on mathematics than did the Academy and more on natural sciences such as biology, on psychology, and on systematic logic. Most of the great works of Aristotle that survive and identify his philosophy were once notes for and from his lectures at the Lyceum. These include some of his works on logic; most of his *Metaphysics*; much of his *Physics*; the *De Anima,* his great work on psychology; his *Nicomachean Ethics*; parts of his *Politics*; and his *Poetics*, of which only a portion has survived.

In 323 B.C., twelve years after the founding of the Lyceum, Alexander the Great died. There was no leader strong enough to replace him effectively, and the empire began to crumble. In Greece resentment against the Macedonian hegemony seethed and anti-Macedonian riots broke out. Aristotle was accused of impiety (one of the two charges that had been brought against Socrates), and his life was in serious jeopardy. So he left Athens, allegedly commenting that he was thus preventing the Athenians from sinning a second time against philosophy, and went to his late mother's estate at Chalcis on the island of Euboea, near a Macedonian garrison. He died there the next year, 322, of a stomach ailment. After the death of his first wife, he had married Herpyllis, a woman from his hometown of Stagira; and he provided generously for her and their son, Nicomachus, in his will. Nevertheless, he asked to be buried in the tomb of his first wife, Pythias.

Reality

Like Plato's, Aristotle's philosophy is anti-Sophist in that it attempts to develop a theory of the good life based on the foundations of our knowledge of the stable nature of reality. But whereas Plato is a rationalist, viewing our knowledge of reality as derived from intuitive reason, and an idealist, locating ultimate reality in an eternal, immutable world of Ideas, Aristotle is an empiricist, anchoring all knowledge of reality in perceptual experience, and a **realist**, identifying reality with the concrete spatio-temporal objects of this world. The **Renaissance** painter Raphael captures this difference beautifully in the central portion of his famous painting "The School of Athens," which portrays an elderly Plato with his hand pointing up to the Heavens and the younger Aristotle gesturing towards the Earth.

PRIMARY SUBSTANCES. Aristotle's *Metaphysics* is an abstract, difficult book dealing with the nature of reality. The work received its title from a later editorial decision to place it "after the Physics" (which is what the word literally means) in the corpus of his writings; to this extent, the title is not descriptively meaningful, but we might usefully interpret it as dealing with ultimate reality or that which goes "beyond the physical." Aristotle describes metaphysics as the science dealing with "the theory of being as being and of what 'to be' means." He distinguishes it from all those "sciences whose subjects are defined as special aspects of being," such as astronomy, which deals with stars, or geology, which is concerned with the Earth. As with any science, metaphysics strives to know its object (being as such or in general, rather than the particular being of individual things) through first principles.

Realism.   Generally, the view that some condition or sort of entity exists independently of the human mind; common-sense realism (condemned by its critics as "naive realism") holds that perception normally grasps external objects directly or reveals them to us as they really are

Renaissance (from the French *renaistre*, meaning to be born again).   That period of Western Civilization, especially in fifteenth- and sixteenth-century Europe, marked by a "rebirth" of ideas and humanistic learning

Although " 'being' has several meanings," referring to substances or "primary beings," their modifications, their processes of coming to be or ceasing to be, or their qualities, for example, the fundamental meaning relates to substances as the primary beings, so that metaphysics will deal with "the first principles and primary factors of primary beings."[57]

Aristotle's *Categories* discusses substances, distinguishing between the individual things that are "primary substances," such as this man or that horse, and the classes of things to which individuals belong (he uses the biologist's terminology of genus and species), such as humanity or animality, which are "secondary substances." That particular man named Socrates is a primary substance, belonging to the species of humanity in the genus of animals. A genus and a species are real, but only "in a secondary sense," depending on the more fundamental realities of the individuals classified under them. Primary substances signify this or that particular thing, whereas secondary substances signify what sorts of things they are. Thus, Socrates and Plato are two distinct primary substances, who happen to share the same genus and species. Substances have no opposites, yet only substances can have opposite qualities and be subject to change.[58] So, there is no opposite to a tree, but the same tree can be soft in its roots and hard in the trunk or change from being resilient and strong to being fragile and weak.

Much of Aristotle's *Physics* is concerned with the study of reality that modern and contemporary philosophers consider metaphysical. There is a distinction between natural substances, such as animals, plants, and the four elements ("earth, fire, air, and water"), and artificial objects, such as "beds and clothes," that are "products of art." Aristotle reminds us that some pre-Socratic materialists tried to reduce nature to its material elements, whereas the **Platonists** attempt to analyze it in terms of ideal forms. But we ought to conceive of primary substances as combinations of matter (*hule*) and form (*eidos*).[59] Aristotle rejects Plato's two-tiered theory of reality, maintaining that all that is real is part of one world. Rather than being consigned to some abstract world of Ideas, forms are defining principles embedded in the particular

things he calls primary substances. There is no Form of Tree apart from this world; but the maples, oaks, birches, aspens, and so forth of this world all contain the form of a tree; each tree, as a primary substance, is formed matter; in this world we never experience pure form or pure matter. The form of a thing (primary substance) establishes its essential nature in terms of genus and species (or secondary substances); so that oak has the form of plant life we call a tree.

CAUSAL EXPLANATION.   We come to understand reality in terms of causal explanation, which involves some combination of four causes: there is, first, the material cause, "the material constituent from which a thing comes" into being; second, its formal cause, the "pattern of a thing, that is, the reason (and the kind of reason) which explains what it was to be that thing," in terms of its genus and species, and makes it that sort of thing; third, the efficient cause or "agent whereby a change or a state of rest is first produced" in the thing; and, fourth, the final cause is "the end or the where-for" of the thing or its purpose. Consider, for example, the reality of the original sculptured work of art we call Rodin's "Thinker": it is made of bronze material in the form of a man in a sitting position by the artist, Rodin, for the purpose of providing aesthetic satisfaction. We may not always understand a thing in terms of all four causes, especially when dealing with natural substances such as a mosquito, as opposed to artificial objects, such as a chair. But to the extent that we can use the four causes in relation to any substantial reality, our efforts to explain "why" can be "in terms of each type of explanatory factor: the material, the form, the agent, the 'where-for.' "[60]

In *Metaphysics* Aristotle (the first important historian of philosophy) observes that many of the earliest ancient Greek philosophers tried to explain reality merely in terms of material elements, such as air, water, fire, and earth. Then later philosophers added explanations in terms of such efficient causes of reality as Love and Strife and Mind. With Plato explanation in terms of formal causes, or participation in Ideas, developed. Finally, there has come to emerge a vague sense of final causality, though

---

Platonism.   The idealistic and dualistic philosophy associated with Plato, especially as it affirms the transcendent reality of eternal, ideal forms, accessible to reason alone, and regards the phenomena of the spatio-temporal, sensible world as derivative and transitory

philosophers before Aristotle himself "fail to use it accurately in the way it naturally functions."[61] Here we see Aristotle's methodology, analyzing and building on the views of his predecessors as a foundation for developing his own. He is a **teleological** thinker in that he is committed to the view that everything in nature occurs for an end (a *telos* is a goal or end).

POTENTIALITY AND ACTUALITY. Aristotle distinguishes between what any reality already is and what it has the "power" to become. A thing may be legitimately analyzed in terms of what it **potentially** is as well as its actuality.

> For there is a passive power residing in anything acted upon which is the source of its underlying change through the action of some other thing or through its own activity upon itself.

For example, a wooden chair is potentially firewood to be burned; or you, who are now actually seated, have the capacity to stand and walk around. In all such examples, "it is evident that actuality is prior to potentiality," in that only an actual being is able to become or do anything. Matter is associated with potentiality, while form is related to actuality.[62] Thus, the matter of a block of wood is potentially a table or a bench; but once it has been carved in the form of a bed frame, that is what it actually is. This theory allows Aristotle to account for the reality of change, contrary to Parmenides' claim that all change is purely illusory.

ARISTOTLE VS. PLATO. Notice that Aristotle's incorporation of form into the primary substances of this world of experience makes for a simpler theory of reality than Plato's two-tiered model. It would also seem to allow him to avoid the problem of how to relate an alien concept to physical objects, which Plato tried to solve with the vague notion of participation. And, as we are about to see, it has an impact on his treatment of bodies.

Bodies

Because there is only one world for Aristotle and because all its primary substances that we can experience are formed matter, it follows that all objects of perception either are bodies or are related to bodies. Thus, Aristotle must take the physical world much more seriously than his teacher did. As we have seen, he distinguishes between natural bodies, such as horses and trees, which he thinks contain within themselves the source of their own change and stability, on the one hand, and artificial objects, such as tables and chairs, on the other. Both sorts of physical beings have the potentiality to be moved. **Animate** bodies, such as horses and trees, naturally move themselves, whereas inanimate objects "are moved by something else" either naturally (as when the water in a stream flows downhill) or violently (as when molten rock is ejected from the mouth of a volcano). Inanimate bodies, without being able to initiate or sustain movement, are at least "amenable to movement." Major types of bodily movement are generation, destruction, and the changes of "quality and quantity and place."[63] Thus, a pond can form, become siltier and more polluted, double in size and shift location due to cataclysmic earthquake activity, then drain off and cease to be.

This movement of bodies must occur in time and place. Aristotle says that "time is not sheer process" or movement or change, but rather its "numerable aspect"; he defines time as "the number of precessions and successions in process." So, it has to do with measurable changes of priority (and simultaneity) within a continuous process. In order for time to be measured or numbered, there must be "a living or rational being to do the counting," although its foundation as a successive process of change would continue to exist even without any mind to measure it. The formed matter of bodies always exists in some place or other. Aristotle defines "*the place of anything*" as "*the first unmoved boundary of what surrounds it.*" This limit immediately surrounding a body does not itself move, though, of course, the body can move through it.[64]

It should not be difficult to discern the impact of Aristotle's theory of reality and bodies on his conception of human nature. If all reality as we know it is

---

Teleology (from the Greek *telos*, meaning end). The study of reality as oriented towards natural ends or, in rational beings, as having purposes; Aristotle and Aquinas are teleological thinkers

Potentiality. The capacity of a thing to undergo change or become different; in Aristotle, opposed to actuality

Animate (from the Latin *anima*, meaning soul), Living, having a soul

consigned to the world of perceptual experience, if its fundamental constituents are those particular, individual beings called primary substances, and if all the primary substances to which we have access, including ourselves, are combinations of matter and form, then we are essentially bodies. This is not to eliminate or denigrate the crucially important role of soul in human nature, as we are about to see. But Aristotle cannot agree with his teacher that our bodies are incidental or **accidental** to our essential nature or that our physical world is an alien environment. For Aristotle (but not for Plato) man is essentially an animal of a unique sort—one with a rational soul and, therefore, personality.

Personality

THE RATIONAL SOUL. If a human being's genus is animal, we should understand what specific difference distinguishes humans from all other animals. In his *Posterior Analytics*, Aristotle describes the **analytic** process by which we divide kinds of beings to establish an essence, working gradually from broadest down to progressively narrower classifications:

> Thus to the question "What is the essential nature of man?" the divider replies "Animal, mortal, footed, biped, wingless," etc.

Aristotle's notion of a thing's essential definition requires an identification of both the general sort of thing it is (genus) and its unique specific difference within that general class of reality.[65] The specific difference that makes humans unique among the animals is the intellect or rational soul.

Aristotle's work *De Anima* (literally "On the Soul") is arguably the greatest psychology written in ancient times. It begins by pointing out that all knowledge is valuable but that knowledge of the soul is especially so.

> For the soul is, so to speak, the first principle of living things.

After critically reviewing earlier psychological theories (including "the thesis that the soul is a kind of harmony"), he investigates the nature and types of soul. He reminds us that we can think of substance as matter, as form, or as a combination of the two, that "matter is potentiality, and form is actuality," and that natural bodies, as formed matter, are the substances that are most obvious in ordinary experience. "Now of natural bodies some have life and some do not," with all animate (the word in Latin means having a soul) things normally capable of nutrition, "growth, and decay. So every natural body that partakes of life would be a substance, and a substance in the way that a composite is." The soul of a natural body, thanks to which it is alive, is not its matter but the form that actualizes its potentiality for life. But if a soul is, by definition, the form of a living natural body, it would seem "that the soul is not separable from the body"[66] (more of this later in our section on Immortality).

We have begun with the observation "that the ensouled is distinguished from the unsouled by its being alive." We can identify living things by the presence of "intellect or perception or spatial movement and rest or indeed movement connected with nourishment and growth and decay." A living body is an "ensouled thing," its body being matter with the potentiality for life and its soul being the form which actualizes that potentiality.

> And for this reason they have supposed well who have believed that the soul is neither without body nor a kind of body. For it is not a body but belongs to a body, and for this reason is present in a body . . . of the appropriate kind

—for example, not a rock, which has no potentiality for life. Now we can distinguish types of souls by their special faculties, which are "nutritive, perceptive, desiderative, locomotive, and intellective, plants having only the nutritive," animals also having the faculties of perception and desire, some animals also having the ability to change their own location, and man also having "the thinking faculty and intellect."[67] Thus, there is a hierarchy here among the five types of faculties, from lowest and most common (nutritive) up to highest and least common (intellectual), such

---

Accident. An attribute or property of a thing that is not essential to its nature; more popularly, an unintended event

Analytic. Using or pertaining to the resolution of something complex into simpler elements (as in Descartes); an analytic judgment (since Kant) is one whose predicate term is already implicitly contained in its subject (e.g., "All bachelors are unmarried"), as opposed to a synthetic judgment

that a living thing that has any of them will naturally have all lower ones as well.

MORE PRIMITIVE SOULS.   It may seem strange to us, but because Aristotle believes all living things have souls and because plants are obviously living things, on this view they must have souls. But these are the most primitive sorts of souls, having only the nutritive faculty, providing for the nourishment, growth, and reproduction of the plant. Animals also have the capacity for sense perception, being aware of their environment through the bodily senses. There are five animal senses oriented towards special sorts of perceptual objects; and there are "common objects" which are "not special to any one sense but common to all," such as "movement, rest, number, shape and size." Of the five special senses, the object of sight is visible color; that of hearing is sound; that of smell is odor; that of taste is flavor (e.g., sweet, bitter, salty, sour); that of touch is the tangible (e.g., "hot and cold, dry and wet, rough and smooth"). What the senses receive or take in from perceived objects are their "forms without their matter, as the wax" absorbs the impression of a signet ring's shape without absorbing the material, gold, of which the ring is made.[68]

IMAGINATION, INTELLECT, AND MOTIVATION.   Aristotle analyzes imagination, intellect, and motivation. He seems to see imagination as a bridge between sense perception and intellect and does not explicitly relate imagination to memory. He argues "that perceiving and understanding are *not* the same. For although all animals have a share of the former, only a few have a share of the latter." Imagination requires perception as a foundation and can, but need not, lead to understanding. Imagination is that faculty of soul "in virtue of which we say that an image occurs to us." For example, someone has an image in her mind of what her dead grandfather looked and sounded like, based on her past sense perceptions of him when he was alive. Aristotle argues that imagination cannot be reduced to any combination of "perception, belief, knowledge and intellect." It cannot be the same as belief because that, unlike imagination, which many nonhuman

animals have, "is followed by conviction," which only human animals have. Nor can it be "one of those faculties that are always correct, such as knowledge or intellect; for imagination can also be false."[69] So, imagination seems to be a distinct faculty of the soul which employs images derived from sense perception and is useful, but which can also be deceptive (as, for example, in nightmares).

Intellect is another distinct faculty of the soul which only the human animal has. Because intellect is not associated with any external sense organ and is neither limited in the scope of its objects nor inclined to take on the qualities of its objects, as do the senses, it seems "unreasonable that it be mixed with the body" at all. Aristotle distinguishes between the passive intellect, which receives images derived from experience and is "characterized by the capacity to become all things," on the one hand, and the active intellect, which abstracts intellectual concepts from those images and is "characterized by that [capacity] to bring all things about."[70] His wording here is obscure. But the passive intellect, which is a blank slate (or *tabula rasa*) prior to experience, can passively absorb and reflect the images of any sort of object, whereas the active intellect creatively constructs conceptual relationships. As we shall see, the active intellect is the only aspect of soul that Aristotle thinks might be sufficiently independent of the body to be immortal.

We distinguish the activity of animal souls (including the human soul) in terms of "two capacities, that of discernment, which is the function of thinking and perceiving, and that of producing locomotion." We have considered the first and now turn to the second. Aristotle expresses his reservations about the Platonists' manner of "distinguishing the reasoning, spirited and desiderative parts" of soul; for such an analysis of "parts" leads us to distinguish a "nutritive part" and an "imaginative part" as well. But he does want to consider what motivates the soul's activities of locomotion. He does not believe that thought by itself, whether imaginative thinking or intellectual knowledge, can suffice to motivate action. You can imagine how good a peppermint ice cream cone would taste,

I could argue this claim

Tabula rasa (literally, in Latin, scraped or shaved tablet, or, more loosely, a blank slate).   A metaphor for the human mind as devoid of ideas prior to sense experience, as opposed to the doctrine of innate ideas

or even know how much you would enjoy it, without being motivated to go get one. What is required is sufficient desire, for "it is the sort of capacity of the soul that is called desire that produces movement." This desire assumes imagination without being identical with it, as imagination itself presupposes sense perception without being reducible to that. Both "rational and perceptive imagination" can generate motivational desire. We are the only animals having the former type of imagination; "the latter is enjoyed no less by the other animals than by man."[71]

*   *   *

We might note that this is a more integrated psychological theory than Plato's. Not only is the soul essentially defined in relation to the body; but it is also not analyzed in terms of conflicting "parts." Aristotle manages to show both our continuity with and difference from other living things in the natural world. Furthermore, in his theory of knowledge, to which we now turn, he substitutes scientific classification and analysis for poetic analogy and symbolism.

Knowledge

EXPERIENCE VS. ART.   One of the most famous claims in the history of philosophy, made in the first sentence of Aristotle's *Metaphysics*, holds that all men naturally desire knowledge. Because we have rational souls, this "impulse" to know is embedded in our human nature. He explains that the reason we "prefer sight to any of the other senses" is that it is the one most fit for providing knowledge. As animals, we naturally have the power of sensation, and we are among those animals that also have the ability to remember sense perceptions. This allows us to acquire cumulative experience and makes learning possible, enabling us to achieve "scientific knowledge and art." Through experience we know particular objects; but through art, understood as skilled practice (rather than as aesthetic production), we gain general knowledge.

> Men of experience discern the fact "that," but not the reason "why," whereas experts know the reason why and explanation.

Thus, for example, you know that Tom, Dick, and Harry all happen to be taking genetics this semester; as their advisor, your biology professor knows they

are doing so because they are junior-level biology majors or pre-med students. Aristotle says another indication "that art is more scientific than experience" is that artists, or expert practitioners, can teach what they know, whereas those who are "only experienced cannot." Also, as experienced people are "wiser than those who merely sense things," so is "the artist than men of experience." The knowledge of the wise involves the causal explanation of what is known: "wisdom is rational knowledge concerning certain basic factors and principles" going beyond the mere compilation of factual data to their general causes. Such knowledge is comprehensive and "forms a systematic whole,"[72] rather than being piecemeal. (This reflects a distinction between the two levels of knowledge in Plato's divided-line analogy.)

INTELLECTUAL CURIOSITY.   In the *Theaetetus* Plato had said that the sense of wonder or intellectual curiosity is the distinguishing mark of the philosopher and the origin of philosophy itself. Here in the *Metaphysics* Aristotle agrees with his teacher. "For it was their curiosity that first led men to philosophize and that still leads them." Like Socrates, the true philosopher is acutely aware of the limits of his own knowledge, for "whoever is perplexed and wonders thinks himself ignorant." Philosophers, trying to overcome ignorance, pursue knowledge for its own sake, and not merely for its practical utility. They seek to know reality—that is, the nature of substances as they exist, their qualities or constitutive makeup, their derivation, and the order of their activity or development. But this necessarily involves the use of the four types of explanatory causes. To the extent that we understand a thing's essential nature (formal cause), physical constitution (material cause), how it came to be (efficient cause), and the teleological end of its changing (final cause), we can be said to know it scientifically.[73]

LOGIC AS A TOOL.   Aristotle, the father of formal **logic**, points out the importance of logic as a tool in the quest for knowledge, when he says that "the philosopher, who examines the most general features of primary being must investigate also the principles of reasoning." Otherwise, we are liable to err in

---

Logic (from the Greek *logos*, meaning reasoning).   The systematic study of reasoning and argumentation, often divided into deductive (or formal) logic vs. inductive (or informal) logic

drawing conclusions from experience. For example, the **principle of noncontradiction,**

> It is impossible for the same thing at the same time to belong and not to belong to the same thing and in the same respect,

which Aristotle calls "the most certain of all principles" of thought, can protect us against logical **inconsistency**. All thinking oriented towards knowledge is of three possible kinds, "practical or artistic or theoretical."[74] Thus, for example, ethics and politics are practical sciences aimed at knowledge oriented to human action; **aesthetics** is an artistic science concerned with what we produce; and physics and metaphysics are theoretical sciences designed to provide speculative knowledge of reality.

GENERALITIES TO PARTICULARITIES. In the *Physics* Aristotle describes the process of coming to know, which, as we might expect, has nothing do with Platonic recollection. Rather, our concrete experiences require "interpretation in terms of their principles, basic factors, or elements." Initially what we experience "is a confused situation to be analyzed." We proceed from generalities about the object of our experience "to their particular aspects." So we move from being "acquainted with the situation which we 'sense' as a whole" to analyzing it in terms of its constituent elements. But these and their interrelationships as a whole must be explained or accounted for in terms of "one or more than one *principle*."[75] As we have seen, this requires the four causes.

Freedom

POTENTIALITY VS. ACTUALITY. In the *Metaphysics* Aristotle condemns those who deny that inactive substances nevertheless have the power to act and who hold "that there is no power apart from its operation." Here we see his metaphysical distinction between potentiality and actuality leading into a doctrine of freedom. Because you lack the ability to run a mile when handcuffed to a stationary pole, you cannot actually do so; but, if freed of physical impediments, you

normally become capable of doing so. "A thing is 'capable,' therefore, when there results no impossibility from its actually doing what it is said to have the power to do."[76] This is not yet a doctrine of human freedom, as it can apply even to inanimate things, such as rocks, which have the power to fall towards the center of the Earth when unsupported.

VOLUNTARY CHOICE. In the *Nicomachean Ethics*, named after his son Nicomachus, Aristotle does apply this to the power of **voluntary** choice in relation to moral responsibility. As he points out, we can only legitimately assign "praise or blame" to voluntary actions, so that we need to be able to distinguish between "the voluntary and the involuntary." An action is usually considered involuntary when it "comes about by force or because of ignorance." If you are pushed into the room or brainwashed into hitting someone, your action is the result of physical or psychological compulsion and, to that extent, involuntary. Fear can be a more difficult sort of compulsion. If you do something wrong in order to save your kidnapped family or if a ship's captain starts "throwing cargo overboard" during a storm at sea because it seems the only way to save his ship, his crew, his passengers, and himself, we have "mixed" cases of duress; the actions are done "willingly" in those regrettable circumstances imposed upon the agent, who would not choose such actions were it not for those circumstances. In such cases there are mitigating circumstances; but, strictly speaking, such "mixed" actions are not compelled, since "something is forced unconditionally whenever its cause is external and the agent contributes nothing." Still less does the desire for pleasure or honor compel our actions, because we normally have the power to resist such desires.[77]

Aristotle distinguishes between actions "caused by ignorance" and those "done in ignorance." Actions of the first kind are always "non-voluntary," since the agents did not sufficiently know what they were doing, but only "involuntary" if the agents experience "pain and regret" for them once the ignorance is

---

Noncontradiction, law or **principle of**.   The Aristotelian law of thought that no proposition (or statement) and its negation (or denial) can both be true of the same thing(s) at the same time in the same respect

Inconsistency.   A logical conflict between two statements, such that one of them must be false if the other is true

Aesthetics (from the Greek *aisthetikos*, meaning pertaining to sense perception).   The branch of philosophy dealing with art and beauty; in Kant, the aesthetic examines the *a priori* conditions of sense experience

Voluntary.   Resulting from free choice rather than constrained or extrinsically determined, as opposed to both involuntary and nonvoluntary

overcome. For example, if you do not know that the animal you are shooting at in the forest is your own (human) enemy, your action is nonvoluntary, in that you are not choosing to shoot her. But once you realize what you have done, feelings of "pain and regret" are prerequisites for that action also being involuntary (i.e. now that you know, you are sorry you did it). An "action done in ignorance" is not necessarily involuntary. If you shoot your enemy when you are "drunk or angry," your action is caused by your "drunkenness or anger" rather than (directly) by ignorance, "though it is done in ignorance" brought on by the alcohol or your fury. But you are responsible for getting drunk and for controlling your anger. Aristotle considers six particulars of an action of which an agent might conceivably be ignorant. They are:

1. Who is doing it;
2. What he is doing;
3. About what or to what he is doing it;
4. Sometimes also what he is doing it with, e.g., the instrument;
5. For what result, e.g., safety; and
6. In what way, e.g., gently or hard.

Nobody in his right mind can "be ignorant of *all* of these" particulars, especially the first. But we can be in ignorance of many of them, which could mitigate our responsibility for our actions. In such cases, whether the action is involuntary depends on whether its agent will "feel pain and regret" after he is no longer ignorant. In conclusion, a voluntary action is one that "has its origin in the agent himself when he knows the particulars" involved.[78] This is a free action for which the agent is responsible.

VIRTUE AND VICE.   Later, Aristotle considers whether virtue and vice are always within our power. Whatever object of desire motivates our action, we are free to "deliberate and decide about what promotes it" as means to an end. We have it within our power to choose fine or shameful actions; to that extent, each of us is free to become "a good or bad person." Plato's notion "that no one is willingly bad or unwillingly blessed," says Aristotle, is "partly true but partly false." Although everyone wants to be "blessed," it is nevertheless true that "vice is voluntary." If a person commits a vicious act while incapacitated by alcohol, he is normally responsible for his drunkenness. Sometimes we are responsible for our ignorance,

when we easily could and should have known better. Nor is carelessness always an excuse since we ought to be careful in what we do. Nor can we excuse our actions as being caused by our own bad characters since we are largely responsible for the characters we develop; however, Aristotle admits that once a person develops a bad character, reform is difficult. Against the Platonist, who holds that everyone does what he thinks is good and therefore vice is caused by ignorance, rather than by free choice, Aristotle objects that because we are responsible for our virtues, we must likewise be responsible for our vices, given that both are consequences of "the sort of character" we have developed.[79] Character is the product of free choice and is at the heart of Aristotle's discussion of morality.

Morality

THE GOOD LIFE.   For Aristotle ethics is a practical discipline fundamentally aimed at action rather than at speculation. Like Plato, he conceives of it as a study of the nature and conditions of the good life in both its personal and its social dimensions. The famous first sentence of his *Nicomachean Ethics* applies his teleological, or goal-oriented, approach to this subject-matter:

> Every craft and every investigation, and likewise every action and decision, seems to aim at some good; hence the good has been well described as that at which everything aims.

Like Plato, he distinguishes between an intrinsic good, "which we wish for because of itself," and instrumental goods desired as means to such an end. And, like Plato, he conceives of ethics as an inquiry into the ultimate intrinsic good—"i.e. the best good." He sees ethics as a branch of political science because morally significant human action occurs in a social context. Like Plato, he maintains that "the good is the same for a city as for an individual," but that whenever individual good seems to conflict with political good, "it is finer and more divine to acquire and preserve it for a people and for cities" than for individuals. He issues two general warnings concerning the study of politics—that we should not expect the level of precision and demonstration that would be appropriate, say, to mathematics and that it is not profitably studied by the very young who lack the experience and character development to appreciate it.[80]

HAPPINESS. With these "preliminary points" behind him, Aristotle proceeds to analyze the ultimate intrinsic good at which political science aims. People generally agree that it is happiness (the Greek word is *eudaimonia*, which literally means "good spirit" and might also be translated as well-being) but disagree about its nature and conditions. Many try to reduce happiness to "pleasure, wealth or honour" or virtue. We should take these beliefs seriously but critically examine them. Aristotle rejects the hedonists' reduction of the good to pleasure and "the life of gratification" as "completely slavish, since the life they decide on is a life for grazing animals"; nevertheless, it does seem that pleasure is an element of the good life. Second, those who are politically ambitious "conceive the good as honour," but Aristotle rejects this as "too superficial" to be the ultimate good "since it seems to depend more on those who honour than on the one honoured," rendering it too **contingent**; yet, again, honor seems a legitimate component of the good life. Third, even virtue seems "too incomplete" to constitute the good life since one can have virtue without exercising it or be virtuous but miserable; nevertheless, we shall see that virtue is a necessary component of the good life. Fourth, "wealth is not the good we are seeking, since it is [merely] useful" as an instrumental value[81]; yet it too will contribute to the good life.

If none of these **reductionistic** conceptions is adequate, what of Plato's Idea of the Good as an eternal, immutable Form? Aristotle approaches this view hesitantly, saying "those who introduced the Forms were friends of ours." As philosophers, we must sometimes criticize our friends in the defense of truth; "for though we love both the truth and our friends, piety requires us to honour the truth first." Against Plato, Aristotle argues that there are too many categories of good for some essence of good "that is universal and single" to underlie them all and that since there is no "single science of all goods," there must not be any "single Idea" of the Good that could be scientifically studied. Also, it is perpetually vague what is meant by the Forms, so that we cannot help but "be puzzled about what [the believers in Ideas] really mean in

speaking of The So-and-So Itself." Further, the alleged eternity of the Good seems irrelevant to the understanding of what it is. Then there is the thorny problem of how other goods participate in the Form of the Good; if "nothing except the Idea is good in itself," how can that be used to "explain the goodness of anything" else that is good? But most damaging of all is the objection that the Form of the Good is, at best, an Idea of speculative reason divorced from "the sort of good a human being can pursue in action or possess." It is hard to imagine what in the world "the weaver or carpenter will gain for his own craft from knowing this Good Itself, or how anyone will be better at medicine or generalship from having gazed on the Idea Itself."[82] This is one of the earliest examples in Western Civilization of one first-rate philosopher systematically criticizing the theory of another.

Well, if happiness is not reducible to such particular objects of desire as pleasure, honor, virtue, or wealth and is not to be defined by reference to some eternal Platonic Form, how are we to determine what it is? The ultimate good that constitutes genuine happiness must meet certain criteria: first, it must be a final end or intrinsically valuable as "that for the sake of which the other things are done" which seem worth doing; second, it must be "the most complete" or comprehensive good; third, it must be "self-sufficient," requiring nothing else beyond itself; and, fourth, it must be the most desirable or "most choice-worthy of all goods." These are not four radically different criteria so much as different ways of emphasizing aspects of what would count as the ultimate good. Money is not a final end but merely a means to an end; virtue, though genuinely good, is not complete; pleasure without virtue is not sufficient to constitute happiness; and honor, though desirable, is not the most desirable good of all. Happiness meets all the criteria; the most desirable of all goods, it is "something complete and self-sufficient, since it is the end of the things pursued in action." But so far, so vague; we still must seek a more precise definition of happiness.[83]

In order to do this, Aristotle suggests that we consider "the function of a human being." Why should

---

Contingency.   That which could be otherwise (as opposed to necessity)

Reductionism.   The view that all reality and/or value can (and should) be resolved into one sort of thing; the materialist Hobbes, for example, reduces all mental activity to physical processes

we not be able to identify this function (*ergon*) as a result of our study of human nature? For

> just as eye, hand, foot and, in general, every [bodily] part apparently has its functions, may we likewise ascribe to a human being some function besides all of theirs?

This should be what is unique to the human person and exercised in action in such a way as to express virtue (the Greek *arete* also means excellence)— namely, the rational activity of the human soul in accordance with virtue.

> And if there are more virtues than one, the good will express the best and most complete virtue.

Furthermore, this must be over the course of a complete lifetime.

> For one swallow does not make a spring, nor does one day; nor, similarly, does one day or a short time make us blessed and happy.

This must include a measure of external goods, including "friends, wealth and political power," as well as "good birth, good children, beauty," not to mention health. Thus, Aristotle defines the good life by saying that

> the happy person is one who expresses complete virtue in his activities, with an adequate supply of external goods, not just for any time but for a complete life.

What still needs to be explored is the nature of virtue, so central to this definition. Since the soul has nonrational and rational dimensions (for example, appetites and the intellect), there should be virtues corresponding to each—moral "virtues of character" and intellectual "virtues of thought."[84] Each of these major types of virtues must be analyzed for an adequate understanding of happiness or the good life.

MORAL VIRTUES. The *Nicomachean Ethics* further deals with the moral virtues of character, which are seen as the products of habits of action, rather than as innately given. Against Plato, Aristotle emphasizes the practical over the theoretical when he says that

> the purpose of our examination is not to know what virtue is, but to become good.

He observes that virtuous states of character "naturally tend to be ruined by excess and deficiency." We must try to perform those actions that avoid such extremes. Pleasure and pain are valuable marks of virtue. If we find it satisfying to exercise a virtue, we have developed it as a well-cultivated habit; on the other hand, if the practice is painful, we have not yet done so. Aristotle specifies three conditions of a moral action: first, the agent must know what he is doing; second, he must choose the action for its own sake; and, third, that choice must proceed from a stable disposition of character.[85]

We still must find a general definition of virtue. Since it is some sort of condition of the soul, of which "feelings, capacities and states" are the three possible types, it must be one of these. But it cannot be a feeling because we are not good or bad, praiseworthy or blameworthy, merely on account of our feelings. Nor is it merely a capacity since these terms of moral appraisal do not merely reflect on the capacities with which nature has endowed us. Thus, by a process of elimination, it must be a state or disposition of the soul. But then (pursuing the quest for an Aristotelian definition) we still need to determine the specific difference between a moral virtue and all other sorts of states of character or dispositions of soul. We have already seen that the extremes of "excess and deficiency" are dangerous to moral virtue, which provides a clue. Moral virtue must aim at "the intermediate" position that "is equidistant from each extremity." It is all too easy to miss the **mean** in our "feelings and actions," but virtue requires that they be expressed "at the right times, about the right things, towards the right people, for the right end, and in the right way"—and this is not easily achieved. Now, finally, we are ready for a definition of moral virtue: it is a disposition or state of soul that enables us to make decisions in accordance with "the mean relative to us," as "defined by reference to reason," as is appropriate to "the intelligent person." However, we should realize that some feelings (such as spite and envy) and some actions (such as adultery and murder) do not morally admit of mean conditions, but they are always intrinsically evil.[86]

Mean.   An intermediate point between undesirable extremes of excess and deficiency, to be determined by reason; Aristotle identifies moral virtue with such a desirable middle ground

Aristotle provides a list of particular moral virtues with their relative extremes:

1. Courage is a mean between extremes of rashness and cowardice;
2. Temperance between insensibility and a profligate intemperance;
3. Generosity or liberality between prodigality and stinginess;
4. Magnificence between ostentatious vulgarity and shabbiness;
5. Magnanimity or proper pride between vanity and pusillanimity;
6. Honor between ambition and the lack of it;
7. Mildness or gentleness between spiritlessness and irascibility;
8. Truthfulness between boastfulness and self-deprecation;
9. Wittiness between buffoonery and boorishness;
10. Friendliness between obsequiousness and surliness; and
11. Proper indignation between envy and spite.

Aristotle promises to deal with the virtue of justice later.[87]

After his discussion of the difference between voluntary and involuntary actions Aristotle analyzes these moral virtues much more closely than we can afford to do here. Then he fulfills his promise by offering a detailed analysis of justice (*dikaiosyne*). Justice is associated with obedience to law and with fairness:

> Hence what is just will be both what is lawful and what is fair, and what is unjust will be both what is lawless and what is unfair.

He distinguishes between distributive justice, which concerns "the distribution of honours or wealth or anything else that can be divided among members of a community who share in a political system" and corrective justice, which "concerns rectification in transactions" that fall short of fairness. As a moral virtue, justice is a mean between committing injustice and suffering it, though, unlike other moral virtues, justice is related to two extremes that have a common name (injustice).

And doing injustice is awarding to oneself too many of the things that, [considered] unconditionally, are good, and too few of the things that, [considered] unconditionally, are bad.[88]

For Aristotle, justice is the most important social virtue.

INTELLECTUAL VIRTUES. Aristotle deals with the intellectual virtues, which we might regard as outside the bounds of morality. However, for Aristotle, ethics essentially concerns the pursuit of the good life; and if the intellectual virtues are its necessary conditions, due to the makeup of human nature, then we are morally required to cultivate them. Morally significant action, as we have seen, must be the product of decision-making, which is rooted in "desire together with reason"; so choice is the result of a combination of rational thought and moral character. There are five intellectual virtues, which fulfill the rational dimension of the soul (as the moral virtues do its non-rational dimension): "craft, scientific knowledge, intelligence, wisdom and understanding"; all of these, by their nature, grasp the truth, unlike "belief and supposition," which are not included in the list because they can be false.[89]

INCONTINENCE. Aristotle considers the moral **phenomenon** of **incontinence** (*akrasia*, which can also be translated as weakness of the will) the failure to contain oneself morally. Unlike Plato, he holds that a person may know what is right and yet not do it or, knowing that something is wrong, choose it anyway. Such a person still acts for a good, but sacrifices a greater, more long-term good for a lesser short-term satisfaction because of a lack of practical wisdom. Such incontinence can be due either to impetuosity or to weakness. Remember that intelligence is one of the five intellectual virtues. It is incompatible with incontinence since no one can "be at once both intelligent and incontinent," given that incontinence is a character flaw whereas "an intelligent person must also at the same time be excellent in character." However, mere knowledge is not intelligence. The intelligent person acts in proper accordance with moral knowledge,

---

Phenomenon.   Generally, an object of experience; more specifically, an appearance or object of perception; in Kant, opposed to noumenon
Incontinence (from the Latin *incontinens*, meaning unrestrained).   A lack of moral self-restraint (identified by Aristotle with weakness of will)

which is precisely what the incontinent person fails to do.[90]

FRIENDSHIP. Aristotle discusses friendship (*philia*), which he says "is a virtue, or involves virtue, and besides is most necessary" for the good life. Friendship is oriented towards what is "good or pleasant or useful." Friendship requires the conscious awareness of mutual goodwill arising in one or another of three ways. First, there is a friendship of utility, in which people are associated for the sake of mutual advantage. Second, a friendship of pleasure is motivated by the agreeableness of the relationship for both parties involved.

> But complete friendship is the friendship of good people similar in virtue . . . who wish goods to their friend for the friend's own sake.

This third sort of friendship is enduring but rare, requiring time and care.[91]

PLEASURE, CONTEMPLATION, AND HAPPINESS. So, the good life requires exercising moral and intellectual virtue, a certain measure of external goods, and friendship. But Aristotle is also interested in the relationship between happiness, on the one hand, and pleasure and contemplation, on the other. He wants to avoid both the hedonistic view that "pleasure is the good" and the opposite extreme, that "it is altogether base"; this latter view apparently had become current in the Academy after Plato's death. Aristotle's middle view is that, while pleasure is not the good and "not every pleasure is choiceworthy," some pleasures are good and contribute to happiness. Since living involves activity motivated by desire, pleasure naturally accompanies successful activity. Yet happiness is not mere amusement; rather, amusement, like relaxation, is a means to productive activity, not an end in itself. The most pleasant activity is held to be that of contemplation or theoretical study. It is the most continuous, most self-sufficient, aims at nothing beyond itself, and actualizes the "divine element" in our human nature.[92] Thus, human happiness should involve contemplative activity as well as virtue and some external goods, including healthy interpersonal relationships.

Society

COMMUNITIES. As we have seen, Aristotle views ethics as a branch of politics, and it is only for our own organizational purposes that we distinguish his treatment of morality from his discussion of society. His *Politics* discusses the conditions for the social fulfillment of human nature. The good life is only possible in the context of community. Like the *Nicomachean Ethics*, the *Politics* begins with a consideration of purpose—in this case, the good purpose of community in general and "the most sovereign of all goods," that of the *polis* or political community in particular:

> Observation tells us that every state is an association, and that every association is formed with a view to some good purpose. I say "good" because in all their actions all men do in fact aim at what they think good.

Aristotle recommends an analytical and empirical study of communities as they develop. Man forms a basic community by taking a woman as wife and raising their children with the help of slaves. "Thus it was out of the association formed by men with these two, women and slaves, that a household was first formed," which is described as the "association of persons, established according to nature for the satisfaction of daily needs." Then when several families unite, the community formed to serve their mutual interests is a village, the most natural form of which is a colony made up of extended family. "The final association, formed of several villages, is the state." This is the practical completion of the process of social evolution. For "while the state came about as a means of securing life itself, it continues in being to secure the good life." The formation of the state is natural, since "man is by nature a political animal." The Sophists' idea of man as a more or less self-sufficient individual is a mere abstraction. Aristotle goes so far as to add that the person who cannot participate in society or who "has no need to" because he "is perfectly self-sufficient" must be either a beast or a god. Justice is important as the social virtue that binds human beings together in political community.[93]

ON SLAVERY AND WOMEN. Unlike Plato, who uncritically assumed the institution of slavery, with the proviso that Greeks should not be enslaved, Aristotle considers and defends it. The state "consists of households," and these incorporate the three basic relationships of "master and slave, husband and wife, father and children." (We cannot help noticing that all of these are defined with reference to the citizen of the *polis*, who had to be a free, adult male.) Every household requires property, and "a slave is a sort of living piece of property," an instrument whose function it is to serve the interests of the master. Aristotle considers the question of whether slavery is natural or "contrary to nature" and opts for the former alternative, saying that humans are naturally marked "from birth, some to rule, some to be ruled." Just as it is fit that males, who are naturally superior to females, should rule over them, so it is for masters and slaves. Nature has allegedly ordained that some of us, who are intellectually and morally superior, should rule.

> It is clear then that by nature some are free, others slaves, and that for these it is both just and expedient that they should serve as slaves.

We can distinguish between natural and legal slavery. Some societies adopt the convention of enslaving those they conquer in war. But this is an inadequate justification and creates moral problems if the conquerors have waged an unjust war or enslaved people who are not fit for slavery. Aristotle agrees with Plato that only barbarians, that is, non-Greeks, are natural slaves. Whereas Aristotle denies that barbarians have any "deliberative faculty" at all, he adds that "in a female it is present but ineffective." Likewise, a woman can have moral virtue, but it will be naturally inferior to a man's. Since intellect and character are criteria for legitimate social superiority, the authority of "male over female" is allegedly as appropriate as that of master over slave.[94]

FORMS OF GOVERNMENT. Aristotle distinguishes between "correct" forms of government, which serve "the common good" according to principles of justice, on the one hand, and "all deviations" or perverted forms, which despotically "aim only at the good of the rulers," on the other. There are three main examples of each in a *polis* or city-state, depending on whether we have government by one, by a few, or by the many. A monarchy could be a fine form of government by one if that person "is pre-eminent in virtue." But such an excellent natural leader is rare, and the tyrannical perversion of this form of government is the worst possible. The rule of law is preferable to the dangers of an individual's selfish abuse of power. All people are subject to their passions,

"whereas a law has none." The rule of a few, when they are the best sort of people, is an aristocracy, a good form of government when exercised for the welfare of the entire *polis*. But, again, it is difficult to find such excellent men who will not abuse their power and degenerate into an oligarchy, which usually turns out to be a rule of the rich, who exploit the others for their own selfish purposes. Democracy is the best perverted form of government because it so diffuses political power; it emphasizes the values of equality, liberty, and majority rule. The problem is that it invests decision making in the poor, who tend to be a rabble without property and susceptible to the blandishments of demagogues. Finally, there is the "**polity**" (of which democracy is the perverted form), which is the type of government most appropriate in nonideal, practical circumstances:

> What is the best constitution and what is the best life for the majority of states and the majority of men? We have in mind men whose virtue does not rise above that of ordinary people

and who are not ideally blessed. Aristotle appeals to his own ethical doctrine of the mean and says that every state has an extremely rich class of people, who "do not know how to be ruled" and will rule despotically, and a very poor class that does "not know how to rule, but only how to be ruled as a slave is." The mean between these extremes is the middle class, in which "you find least reluctance to hold office as well as least eagerness to do so"; its members constitute the most stable social class, neither coveting their neighbors' goods like the poor nor being the objects of envy like the rich.

> It is clear then both that the best partnership in a state is the one which operates through the middle people, and also that those states in which the middle element is large, and stronger if possible than the other two together, or at any rate stronger than either of them alone, have every chance of having a well-run constitution.

That is, it is the best in ordinary, nonideal circumstances. Still, we must also add that the mixed form of polity needs to abide by the rule of law, which "is preferable" to that of any individual[95] or group of individuals, for the sake of justice and stability.

Polity (from the Greek *politeia*, meaning government or constitution). Government ordained to the common good and administered by many citizens; Aristotle identifies it with the rule of the middle class and sees democracy as its perverted form

Aristotle does not include empire, such as he witnessed Philip and Alexander of Macedonia building, in his list of political societies because, like Plato, he prefers the small size of the city-state.

FUNCTIONS OF THE STATE.   Aristotle maintains, "A state's purpose is not merely to provide a living but to make a life that is good"; otherwise, he comments, "it might be made up of slaves or animals other than man," which is absurd since they lack sufficient deliberative intellect and free choice. Protection, security, and mere companionship are not the be-all and end-all of political community. For a state is not a mere society of convenience but "an association" based on civic friendship, designed to promote "noble actions" and "living happily." Like Plato, Aristotle sees a parallel between what is best for individual members of a political community and what is best for the state, and he holds that a wise legislator "must instil" such common goods "into the souls of men." Therefore, "there should be laws laid down about education," which "itself must be made a public concern"; public education should develop both intellectual and moral virtue.[96] Effective education is a pillar of the kind of society that facilitates the good life.

Religion

THE SUPREMACY OF THEOLOGY.   As far as we can tell, Aristotle is further than Plato from subscribing to conventional religious views, though he gives theology (literally, the study of God) the highest place in the rank of possible studies. If we think of religion as a relationship between humans and the divine with implications for human behavior, what we have of Aristotle's philosophy is virtually devoid of any traces of religion. His "God" is the Unmoved Mover, a metaphysical principle, the causal source of our world, not personally related to it and caring nothing for us as individuals or for our worship.

In the *Metaphysics* Aristotle speaks of theology as "the most divine knowledge" and the "most worthy of honor." It is a "divine" science in a two-fold sense: its object is God and that is the most appropriate object of thought for God. He criticizes the anthropomorphic tendencies "of those who assert that there are gods but that they are like men. For such theologians merely establish eternal men," which is a sort of mythological superstition. He classifies theology as one of the "three theoretical branches of philosophy," along with mathematics and physics, calling it the "supreme" area of philosophy because it deals with "the supreme kind of being."[97] So, we should consider what sort of knowledge he thinks it can give us.

THE UNMOVED MOVER.   Since there is eternal motion (or change) in our world, there must be an eternal cause of motion, which is "an unmoved mover, being eternal, primary, and in act," rather than having any unactualized potentiality. Such an Unmoved Mover causes change in other things without itself undergoing change. Unmoved motion must originate in desire or intellect, the former aiming at "what appears good" and the latter at "what is good." But, as Plato suggested in the *Euthyphro*, "an end is desired because it seems good; it does not seem good because it is desired. So the starting-point is the activity of knowing," since desire requires knowing at least what appears to be good. Thus, the activity appropriate to the Unmoved Mover is thought. (Aristotle is ambiguous about whether there might be more than one transcendent unmoved mover, at one point suggesting there may be fifty-five or forty-seven, corresponding to the number of celestial spheres that must be moved.) The Unmoved Mover, then, is a divine mind. But it must think about something, and what might that be? "Either itself or something else. If something else, either always the same thing or different things." But the only object worthy of divine thought is that which is itself divine, eternal, and unchanging. And this is only to be found in the divine nature itself.

> Accordingly, a divine mind knows itself, since it is the supreme excellence; and its intelligence is the intelligence of intellect.[98]

So, although it is the efficient (and final) cause of our world, the Unmoved Mover has no concern for us

---

Theology (from the Greek *theos*, meaning God, and *logos*, meaning an account).   The study of God; we can distinguish between rational theology, which is part of philosophy, and revealed theology, which is not, because it is based on revelation

Anthropomorphism (from the Greek, *anthropos*, meaning human form and *morphe*, meaning form).   The attribution of human characteristics to something, such as God, which is nonhuman

at all. This is different from Plato's view that the Divine cares for man and that an attitude of religious piety on our part is appropriate. For Aristotle, the full actualization of human nature requires the theoretical knowledge of God; but this does not entail that any expression of that knowledge in religious practice need follow.

Immortality

Whereas Plato understood the soul to be an independent substance essentially distinct from all bodies, we recall that Aristotle defines the soul as the animating form of a living body. This definition might logically suggest that the soul could not possibly exist apart from the body and might rule out (by definition) the possibility of immortality.

He admits that most of the soul's affections, such as anger, desire, and perception, depend on the body and are inconceivable except in relation to it. On the other hand, he leaves open the possibility that thinking might be an activity of soul that is independent of the body, in which case part of the soul might be capable of separable existence. Aristotle struggles with the issue of how the mind could degenerate. We know that the bodily brain and our physical means of expressing thought age and decay; but it does not follow that the intellectual aspect of the soul does as well. Most of the activities of soul are functions arising out of bodily states—e.g., nutrition, locomotion, sense perception, and desire.

> It is quite clear then that the soul is not separable from the body, or that some parts of it are not, if it is its nature to have parts.

It is problematic how the soul can have separable parts; yet here we see Plato's student backing off from an outright rejection of immortality. Even though the intellect requires the input of sensory data through the body, its capacity to transcend the physical in abstract thought gives it a sort of independence. This is, of course, the active intellect;

> and it is this alone that is immortal and eternal, though we have no memory, as the separate intellect is unaffected, while the intellect that is affected is perishable.[99]

This last is a murky passage; but it seems to suggest that if the intellectual aspect of soul is immortal, it is impersonal. Personality requires memory, a faculty for

which the passive intellect depends on the body and which therefore cannot survive. The active intellect, which might survive as an independent agent, cannot be affected by anything, including memory. Thus, what survives the death of the body, if anything does, is devoid of personality. But this would not seem to be the sort of immortality in which most people would be vitally interested.

Fulfillment

Whereas for Plato it seems quite appropriate to distinguish between the limited measure of happiness that is possible in this life and ultimate fulfillment in the afterlife, such a distinction would appear groundless for Aristotle, for whom any afterlife would be impersonal. For this reason, it is difficult to speak of any Aristotelian conception of fulfillment that goes beyond his treatment of this world's happiness. Unlike Plato, he does not have a two-world theory of reality to deal with; and even though his Unmoved Mover is a God, no personal relationship between it and human nature is indicated.

We have seen that the last book of Aristotle's *Nicomachean Ethics* maintains that contemplation or theoretical study is that activity which best realizes the unique potentiality of human nature and is essential to our happiness:

> Hence a human being's complete happiness will be this activity, if it receives a complete span of life.

Because intellect is the "divine element" in human nature, "so also will the life that expresses understanding be divine." This is as close as we can get to the ultimate fulfillment of human nature that Aristotle calls "blessedness." He assures us that the "gods more than anyone are blessed" in their activities. But the only activity worthy of the divine is contemplation.

> Hence the gods' activity that is superior in blessedness will be an activity of study.

Because of the "divine element" of intellect, we can emulate such contemplative thought and then reap its rewards.

> For the whole life of the gods is blessed, and human life is blessed to the extent that it has something resembling this sort of activity.

Among the animals only humans have this capacity.[100] Thus, the potentiality for blessedness attests to the special dignity of human nature.

REFLECTIONS

It is a commonplace notion that thinkers in the history of philosophy tend to be either Platonists or Aristotelians. Though this old chestnut should be taken with a grain of salt appropriate to all such sweeping generalizations, there is considerable truth in the truism. A thinker, following Plato, can do philosophy with a literary flair, deriving ideas from abstract reason, engaging in theoretical speculation that is clearly designed to transcend the realm of natural experience. Or, like Aristotle, a philosopher can adopt a quasi-scientific approach, inductively inferring ideas from concrete experience, emphasizing their practical application to our natural lives. Although there are some synthetic philosophers (like Kant) who defy this dichotomy, broadly speaking, most important philosophers can be located on one side of this line or the other. Having considered strengths and weaknesses of the Platonic perspective, let us now assess Aristotle's treatment of each of the ten topics discussed above.

REALITY.   His conception of reality, our first topic, is simpler than Plato's dualistic model. This would seem to be an advantage, if it can adequately account for everything that the more complex theory will cover. (There is an old principle of parsimony known as "**Ockham's Razor**," which holds that explanatory principles should not be multiplied unnecessarily.) Aristotle's substance-based metaphysics has become so entrenched in the thinking of Western Civilization that there was virtually no alternative to it until Hegel planted the seeds of **process thought** at the beginning of the nineteenth century. Indeed, the very structure of our language, in terms of qualities and actions predicated of subjects, reflects this substance-based metaphysics. Aristotle's incorporation of the forms in the primary substances of this world, rather than leaving them exiled in Plato's world of Ideas, is a brilliant move.

Also, it is easier to understand how the things we experience must have internal forms than how they can be related to the Forms of some external other world. Aristotle's four principles of causal explanation have also stood the test of time, although his common-sense conception of causality is subject to the sort of critique that Hume and Kant would develop in the **Enlightenment** age of modern science.

BODIES.   Second, Aristotle's analysis of bodies might seem preferable to Plato's for two reasons. He takes the world of physical objects more seriously than his teacher does, dealing with it on its own terms, rather than regarding it as some shadowy reflection of ideal reality. He also approaches it from the perspective of a natural scientist, rather than viewing it through the eyes of a poet.

PERSONALITY.   Third, as has been noted already, Aristotle's discussion of human personality is probably the most acute work of psychology written in ancient times. Its analytical power remains impressive after more than two millennia. His conception of the soul as the animating form of a living body allows for a more integrated theory of human nature than Plato's. Nevertheless, is it not obscure how the forms of some bodies (e.g., those of horses and humans) can give them life, while those of others (e.g., rocks and rivers) cannot do so? This theory of soul as the form that gives life to the matter of body (the theory of "**hylomorphism**," as it is called) cries out for clearer explanation. By contrast, the idea that certain superior psychological faculties, such as desire and thought, presuppose and build upon inferior ones, such as nutrition and sense perception, seems both intelligible and plausible.

KNOWLEDGE.   On the fourth topic, namely, knowledge, Aristotle's notion of the four explanatory principles represents an advance from Plato on the difference between true belief, based on experience, and scientific knowledge. His systematic development of logic as a tool for gaining knowledge is also a distinct advantage.

Ockham's razor (principle of parsimony).   The principle that, other things being equal, a simpler explanation is preferable to one that is more complex, that explanatory entities should not be multiplied needlessly

Process thought/philosophy/theology.   A contemporary theory analyzing reality in terms of dynamically changing events rather than static substances; Hegel seems to anticipate this movement

Enlightenment.   An intellectual movement, especially of eighteenth-century Europe and America, advocating the ideals of reason, science, liberty, and progress

Hylomorphism (from the Greek *hule*, meaning matter, and *morphe*, meaning form).   The theory (e.g., of Aristotle and Aquinas) that everything in our world is composed of matter and form united together

Moreover, his analysis of the process of coming to know is far more in line with our experience than is Plato's doctrine of recollection. On the other hand, Aristotle's theory of knowledge is marred by the realists' assumption, which is never radically criticized (leading some opponents to refer to it as "naive realism"), that things are as ordinary experience reveals them to be.

Freedom. Fifth, his discussion of the difference between voluntary and nonvoluntary action is a positive contribution to an understanding of human freedom. But it is not particularly well anchored in his faculty psychology, as it could and should have been. It seems evident that it is rational souls that are free and capable of voluntary choice. But why and how? What has yet to be developed here is an adequate concept of the human will.

Morality. Sixth, Aristotle's theory of morality lives on in the sense that many serious, thoughtful people today subscribe to Aristotelian ethics. It is a richly complete theory that offers an integrated perspective on moral agency in a social context as well as sophisticated insights into moral and intellectual virtues. Nevertheless, those of us who cannot accept his sort of moral teleology are sceptical that the idea of what is morally right can or should be based on some prior notion of excellent character, which will inevitably be biased by its author's contingent socio-cultural perspective, or that human happiness is ultimately the linchpin of morality. What is missing in this ethical theory is a sufficiently universal conception of morals as grounded in the very nature of human personality (such as we shall see developed by Kant). Even linking morality to "the function of a human" is too vague and presumes too much to be adequate.

Society. This lack of a universal perspective is reflected in Aristotle's discussion of society, our seventh topic. His model of political community is the *polis* in which he preferred to live. The sort of empire that his own student was putting together and expanding does not even have a place in his political taxonomy. His notion of "good" community reflects the biased interests of a male Greek citizen of the *polis*. His view of women as naturally inferior betokens the sexist bias of his own culture; yet, as Plato's student, he cannot be excused as unaware of any reasonable alternative. Aristotle's defense of the institution of slavery is also a mere rationalization of the *status quo*; it is remarkable that he, as a resident alien in Athens, deprived of its rights of citizenship, is so insensitive to the denial of equal opportunity to others. Here his empirical ethical theory seems to obscure the ideals of universality and moral necessity which might undergird a more adequate view of society. Even if he is merely guilty of erroneous judgments as to how to apply his own principles regarding humanity, the theory itself fails to protect against such bias. On the other hand, his call for government by a middle class is noteworthy in light of the political evolution of recent times.

Religion. Regarding our eighth topic, as we have seen, Aristotle develops a philosophical theology, which, for better or for worse, is devoid of any practical religious implications. His reservations about anthropomorphism are in order and might motivate his noncommittal attitude towards religion. What, then, of his philosophical theology itself? To the extent that it works at all, it only leads to an abstract metaphysical principle, his Unmoved Mover, a supernatural mind that has no ongoing relation to us or our world. As we have seen, Aristotle is conspicuously ambiguous about whether there is a single Unmoved Mover or not, as well as about how many there might be if more than one. And what of his argument for an Unmoved Mover? Even granting its fundamental premise that there is eternal motion in our world (which Aristotle surely cannot establish empirically), does it follow that its (efficient and final) cause must itself be eternal, as well as pure actuality with no unrealized potentiality, a divine mind? Considerably more careful work (such as Aquinas would attempt to produce some fifteen centuries later) is needed to demonstrate these dimensions of his conclusion. Furthermore, notice how the conclusion itself compromises the integrity of Aristotle's one-world, **naturalistic** conception of reality. The primary substances of our world are all composed of formed matter,

---

Naturalism.   The view that everything can, at least in theory, be explained in terms of natural realities, their actions, and their interrelationships, as opposed to supernaturalism

whereas the Unmoved Mover is not. How *could* they be related, except causally? For that matter, how could they be even *causally* related? After ceremoniously booting Plato's two-world theory out the front door of philosophy, Aristotle seems to be surreptitiously sneaking it in through its back door.

IMMORTALITY.   There is a similar muddle on the issue of human immortality, our ninth topic. Given that the soul is, by definition, the animating form of a living body, it ought to follow that it is not a primary substance capable of existing (let alone of functioning) independently of the body. However, though indecisive in this matter, Aristotle backs off from this conclusion, which would be thoroughly consistent with his naturalism, veering towards his teacher's doctrine of immortality. Yet how can any sort of "immortality," stripped of personal memory and psychological continuity, hold any practical interest for us?

FULFILLMENT.   Tenth, on human fulfillment, Aristotle's naturalism, coupled with his half-hearted, stripped-down view of possible immortality, leaves little room for a "blessedness" that will transcend the happiness of this life. His notion of the "divine element" in human nature that allegedly allows for a "blessedness" like that of the gods is nothing more than a poetic analogy, far removed from the scientific empiricism that typically distinguishes his theory from the abstract speculations of Plato. The fulfillment of human nature found in the exercise of moral and intellectual virtue, friendship, fortunate circumstances, and so forth should constitute our natural happiness or well-being, in his view.

* * *

In conclusion, we can observe that, like Plato, Aristotle develops a comprehensive philosophical system that can be analyzed in terms of all ten of our dimensions of human nature and which has proved enormously influential in the intellectual history of Western Civilization. In every area both thinkers offer us challenging ideas that call for, and are worthy of, our careful critical consideration. As Plato's theory is a creative synthesis of pre-Socratic and Socratic philosophy, Aristotle's synthesis is a critical appropriation of what he learned from Plato. These two thinkers reflect both the glory and the limitations of the culture of the golden age of the ancient Greek era.

QUESTIONS

1. *Does Plato exhibit a consistent attitude towards bodies and the physical world? If so, what is it? If not, why not?*

2. *How does Plato argue that the human person is essentially a soul? Why do you find this argument convincing or unconvincing?*

3. *What is the relation between knowledge and opinion for Plato? Why do you think him correct or incorrect here?*

4. *Explain Aristotle's four causes in your own words. Apply them to a single example of your own.*

5. *What is the relation between body and soul in human nature for Aristotle? Why do you agree or disagree with him here?*

6. *What factors do (and do not) compromise voluntary action for Aristotle? Think up your own illustrations.*

7. *How does Aristotle's theory of reality differ from Plato's? Which one seems to you to be closer to being correct, and why?*

8. *How do Plato and Aristotle analyze the powers of the soul? What do you suppose to be the basis and the significance of their different views here?*

9. *How does Aristotle reinterpret the status of form? Can his empiricism handle the problems Plato's theory of recollection was designed to solve? If so, how? If not, why not?*

10. *How do Plato and Aristotle differ in their analyses of the good life? Why do both regard virtue as essential to it? How could someone reasonably criticize this demand?*

11. *Why does Aristotle disagree with Plato's model of an ideal society? How would he prefer that political society be organized? Which view do you think more correct, and why?*

12. *Evaluate any of Plato's arguments for the immortality of the soul. What do you think of Aristotle's approach to this issue? How do their positions arise out of their general worldviews?*

ALTERNATIVES

After the death of Alexander the Great in 323 B.C. the military and political power of the Greek world started to deteriorate and sank into turmoil. New philosophies were needed to fit the changing cultural circumstances. The three most popular Hellenistic philosophies were Epicureanism, Stoicism, and Neoplatonism. Let us briefly consider Epicurus, the founder of the first of these schools, Epictetus, one of the most famous proponents of the second, and Plotinus, the most important representative of the third.

EPICURUS

Epicurus (342/1–270 B.C.) was born (at about the time Aristotle became Alexander's tutor) of Athenian parents on the island of Samos. As a youth he heard a teacher try to explain everything as coming from Chaos; the boy asked where the Chaos came from (and was supposedly told that no one knows the answer). He wanted to understand and later attended lectures by a disciple of Plato and a follower of Democritus (an important pre-Socratic materialist who explained everything in terms of atoms). At the age of eighteen Epicurus went to Athens to fulfill his military obligations; this was around the time of Alexander's death (and Aristotle's flight from Athens in the wake of anti-Macedonian hostility). Epicurus' family, being Athenian, was evicted from Samos by the Macedonians and fled to Colophon, in Asia Minor. Epicurus rejoined them in 321 B.C. and spent a decade there studying under a noted atomist. He began teaching about 310, moved back to Athens in 307 or 306, and set up a school of philosophy there in his own garden, where he taught until his death in 270; this third great school of ancient Athens (after Plato's Academy and Aristotle's Lyceum) was called "the Garden" and was co-educational and open to all classes of students (including slaves). Epicurus was a prolific writer, purportedly producing about three hundred works, though only a few fragments survive. Much of what we know about his thought comes from the Roman epic poem by Lucretius, called *De Rerum Natura* (*On the Nature of Things*). But we do have a couple of his important letters and his *Principal Doctrines*.

As an atomist, Epicurus believes that all reality is comprised of eternal material atoms that tend to move in a downward direction, except for occasional chance swervings that cause them to collide with other atoms, temporarily combine, and later separate. The world as we experience it is undergoing a period of relative stability, although it cannot last indefinitely. The world could not have come from Chaos, since Chaos is nothing, and nothing comes from nothing. All the universe is made up of bodies moving in space, those bodies either being or being comprised of seedlike atoms. The atoms of the soul are exceedingly fine; and those making up the gods are even finer still.

In his ethical views Epicurus is a hedonist, who advocates the moderate enjoyment of pleasure, the avoidance of pain, and the maintenance of an attitude of contentment (*ataraxia*, the tranquil imperturbability of mind). It is a cruel irony of history that his name is associated with gourmet dining and the indulgent lust for sensuous pleasures, since he lived simply and urged restraint. He tries to help us deal with the twin terrors that threaten our peace of mind, the fear of the gods and the fear of death. The gods are immortal and blessed, unperturbed by any regard for us (like the Unmoved Mover of Aristotle), disposed neither to punish us in anger nor to reward us because of our flattery. Likewise, death should be nothing to us since all good and evil consist in sensation and death annihilates all possibility of sensation. Pleasure is our ultimate good, and no pleasure is intrinsically bad; nevertheless, the means used to secure pleasure can be bad and cause greater pain. Some of our desires are artificial and vain, while others are natural; of the natural ones, some are necessary (i.e., for happiness or for physical repose or for life itself), while others are not. But among our best desires and greatest pleasures, for Epicurus (as for Plato and Aristotle), are those of friendship and philosophical understanding.

EPICTETUS

Moving ahead more than three centuries, we find that not much is known about Epictetus' (A.D. c50–130) life because he was born to an obscure slave woman and lived a significant portion of his life in slavery. He was born (during the reign of the Roman Emperor Claudius I) at Hierapolis, in Phrygia, was taken prisoner during a Roman invasion, and sold as a slave to an officer of Emperor Nero's bodyguard. While he was in slavery, it is believed, Epictetus was crippled by his cruel master; according to one anecdote, he warned his angry master, who was twisting his leg, that it would break if he continued doing so, adding an "I told you so," after it did snap. But he was allowed to attend the lectures of a Stoic teacher in Rome. Stoicism, the fourth great philosophical school of ancient Athens, had been founded by Zeno of Citium, a younger contemporary of Epicurus, who lectured from his *Stoa* (or porch); later, after Rome appropriated Greek culture, Stoicism was well received in the Roman world. At any rate, after his master's death, Epictetus was freed and remained in Rome to teach philosophy. Around A.D. 89, the Emperor Domitian expelled all philosophers from Rome, and Epictetus went to Nicopolis, in Epirus, where he founded his own school of Stoic philosophy and where he taught until his death. None of his original writings have survived, although we have transcripts of his *Discourses* and *Enchiridion* (or *Manual*) from one of his disciples, as well as some extant fragments.

Unlike early Greek Stoics, such as Zeno, who equally emphasized logic, physics, and ethics, Epictetus (and other later Roman Stoics) focused on ethics. He sees the proper purpose of philosophy as a practical guide to achieving the good life rather than as a theoretical pursuit of scientific understanding. Even though he was suspicious of Epicureanism, he, like Epicurus, considers inner tranquillity (*ataraxia*) to be the key to the good life. In order to achieve it, we must use reason, the distinctive faculty of human nature, to see our place in the cosmic order, to discern our duty so that we may act accordingly, and to master our own desires. We must accurately distinguish between what is within our power (our thoughts, actions, and reactions) and what is not (physical occurrences and things, what others say and do, and the events of our environment), focusing our attention and effort on the former and accepting the latter. An old slogan associated with Stoicism is "bear and forbear" (*suspine et abstine*).

Through the exercise of reason, our governing principle, we allegedly can come to understand and follow Nature, rather than foolishly ignoring or resisting it. Epictetus advocates the cosmopolitan view that we are all citizens of the world and, as such, have duties towards all other persons. He holds up Socrates as a model of a man of reason who did his duty against selfish inclinations, focusing on the things of the soul rather than on goods of the body and nobly resigned to his fate. Virtue and vice lie within the power of a rational will, and we are morally responsible for them. Like Epicurus, Epictetus tries to help us rise above fear of the gods and fear of death. He sees the human soul as intimately joined to God and a part of the divine essence. Death is inevitable, and all our anxiety regarding it will only contaminate our lives rather than enabling us to avoid death. The love of pleasure is a dangerous trap to be resisted, lest it enslave us, since the attaining of pleasure is, to such a great extent, beyond our control; so he disagrees with the hedonism of the Epicureans. What philosophy should teach us is to control our desires and aversions, to pursue our duty and avoid wrongdoing, and to maintain integrity of mind through rational judgment.

PLOTINUS

The Hellenistic reaction against the unstable vicissitudes of this world takes a more mystical turn in the Neoplatonic philosophy of Plotinus (204/5–c270). He was born (some seventy-five years after Epictetus died) somewhere in Egypt. He found lectures of various teachers in Alexandria disappointing until he became a student of Ammonius Saccas, at about the age of twenty-eight. More than a decade later, in the year 242, Plotinus joined Emperor Gordian's expeditionary march to Persia, wanting to become more familiar with Eastern thought. But when Gordian was assassinated in Mesopotamia, Plotinus fled to Antioch and then on to Rome, arriving there at about the age of forty. He opened a school in Rome, where his teachings became well received. He had become a follower of Plato's philosophy and hoped to found a new city, to be called Platonopolis and to be governed according to the ideas of the *Republic*; but the Emperor withdrew his support for the project, and it never materialized. Around the year 265, Porphyry of Tyre became Plotinus' pupil and disciple. Plotinus seems to have been kind and gentle, to have been ashamed of the physical aspects of this life, and to have been profoundly spiritual, allegedly experiencing mystical union with the Divine on at least four different occasions. When Plotinus died (probably of leprosy), his last words to his physician were, "The divine spirit within me departs to unite with the universal divine spirit." After his death, his writings were edited by Porphyry into fifty-four treatises, arranged in six groups of nine chapters each, called *Enneads* (the Greek word for nine).

Plato's teaching that ultimate reality transcends this physical world had enormous appeal for Plotinus, who uses religious philosophy to approach that which is beyond being and beyond all rational knowledge. Plotinus is one of the greatest of monists, viewing all reality as one. He speaks of the divine source of all being as the One. It is pure, active energy and is the Good spoken of in Plato's *Republic*. It neither thinks nor wills, both of which actions require a subject-object distinction that is inappropriate here. There can be no creation since nothing can be other than or apart from the immutable One. Rather, reality eternally and necessarily flows from the One like rays of light emanating from the Sun. The initial emanation is that of Mind (or *Nous*), which intuitively apprehends both the One and itself and which contains the Ideas. Soul, in turn, emanates from Mind (and corresponds to Plato's world-soul) and contains within itself all souls, including human ones. The One, Mind, and Soul are all utterly incorporeal and constitute a sort of divine Trinity. As light emanating from the Sun gets dimmer and increasingly diffuse the further it travels from its source, so reality becomes diminished with each emanation. Soul gives rise to the phenomenal world of nature, which involves formed matter (as in Aristotle). In itself, matter is utter darkness, the privation of all light; but, as combined with intelligible forms, matter is partially illuminated in the realm of nature. In itself, matter is the principle of evil, the privation of all good.

The double movement of reality is such that this emanation from the One must lead to a reabsorption of all back into the One. We humans, in particular, yearn to return to the divine source of our being. To do so, we must purify our souls by converting them towards the Good and turning them away from the base desires of the body. This process can occur slowly through a series of reincarnations or more quickly through mystical union with the One. Salvation requires a detachment from the realm of material things, which, in turn, requires spiritual discipline. The soul must first liberate itself from its servitude to the body and must habitually practice the cardinal virtues; then it must transcend the life of sense perception and turn towards the higher orders of science and philosophy; then it must overcome discursive rational thought to achieve union with Mind; and, finally, it must abolish all subject-object separation. These views of Plotinus constitute the form of Neoplatonism that would so powerfully influence Augustine.

*   *   *

The three Hellenistic philosophies of Epicureanism, Stoicism, and Neoplatonism represent different intellectual reactions to the disturbances of a culture in geopolitical flux. They recommend various methods of rationally coping with the fickle, unpredictable ways of the world. They are the three philosophical systems that dominated Western Civilization between the collapse of Greek power and the development of Christian philosophy by Augustine.

Notes

1. Plato, "Apology," in *Five Dialogues*, trans. G. M. A. Grube (Indianapolis: Hackett Publishing Co., 1981), pp. 37, 41. This work is henceforth called "*Five Dialogues*."

2. Plato, *Phaedrus and the Seventh and Eighth Letters*, trans. Walter Hamilton (Harmondsworth, England: Penguin Books, 1973), pp. 114, 116. This work is henceforth called "*Phaedrus and the Seventh and Eighth Letters*."

3. *Five Dialogues*, pp. 102, 112–14, 140–41.

4. Plato, *Plato's Republic*, trans. G. M. A. Grube (Indianapolis: Hackett Publishing Co., 1974), pp. 240, 142. This work is henceforth called "*Plato's Republic*."

5. Ibid., pp. 161–63.

6. Ibid., pp. 168–72.

7. Plato, *Plato and Parmenides*, trans. Francis MacDonald Cornford (Indianapolis: Bobbs-Merrill, no date), pp. 84–86.

8. Ibid., pp. 87–88, 93, 97–98, 100.

9. Plato, *Timaeus and Critias*, trans. Desmond Lee (London: Penguin Books, 1977), pp. 43–51, 70–71. This work is henceforth called "*Timaeus and Critias*."

10. *Five Dialogues*, pp. 101–2, 120–22.

11. *Plato*, Vol. VIII, trans. W. R. M. Lamb (London: William Heinemann, 1955), pp. 197–201.

12. *Plato's Republic*, p. 26.

13. *Five Dialogues*, pp. 106, 124–26, 132–33.

14. *Plato's Republic*, pp. 100, 103–5.

15. *Timaeus and Critias*, pp. 58, 97–98.

16. *Phaedrus and the Seventh and Eighth Letters*, pp. 61–63.

17. *Five Dialogues*, pp. 69–75.

18. Ibid., pp. 85–86.

19. Plato, *Theaetetus*, trans. Robin A. H. Waterfield (London: Penguin Books, 1987), pp. 20, 30–31, 50–52.

20. Ibid., pp. 91, 115, 124, 127.

21. *Plato's Republic*, pp. 164–66.

22. *Five Dialogues*, pp. 34–35.

23. Ibid., pp. 47–48.

24. *Plato's Republic*, pp. 257–63.

25. Plato, *Protagoras and Meno*, trans. W. K. C. Guthrie (Harmondsworth, England: Penguin Books, 1956), p. 89.

26. Plato, *Gorgias*, trans. Donald J. Zeyl (Indianapolis: Hackett Publishing Co., 1987), pp. 19, 90; earlier (p. 12), Socrates offers a neat argument showing that knowledge cannot be identical to conviction, since the latter can be either true or false, whereas the former can only be true. This work is henceforth called "*Gorgias*."

27. *Five Dialogues*, pp. 49–52.

28. Ibid., pp. 11–12, 14–16.

29. *Gorgias*, pp. 29, 54, 59–62, 65, 67–68, 70–71, 76–77, 85–88.

30. *Plato's Republic*, pp. 5–10, 13–14, 16, 21–27.

31. Ibid., pp. 30–38.

32. Ibid., pp. 93, 106–8.

33. Plato, *Philebus*, trans. Robin A. H. Waterfield (London: Penguin Books, 1982), pp. 67–69, 139–47. It is on p. 116 that we find a reference to the Delphic motto, "know thyself," which Socrates adopted as his own.

34. Plato, *The Laws*, trans. Trevor J. Saunders (London: Penguin Books, 1975), pp. 196–98. This work is henceforth called "*The Laws*."

35. *Five Dialogues*, pp. 52–54. Notice that Socrates could justify acts of civil disobedience, when the orders of political authorities violate moral conscience, as a couple of incidents he mentions in his trial make clear (pp. 36–37).

36. *Gorgias*, pp. 105, 24–25, 102.

37. *Plato's Republic*, pp. 39–46.

38. Ibid., pp. 80–83.

39. Ibid., pp. 84–86, 89, 93–99.

40. Ibid., pp. 114–19, 129–33.

41. Plato, *The Collected Dialogues of Plato*, ed. Edith Hamilton and Huntington Cairns (New York: Pantheon Books, 1966), pp. 1067, 1073–74.

42. *The Laws*, pp. 173–74, 178, 182–83.

43. *Five Dialogues*, p. 36.

44. Ibid., p. 21.

45. *Plato's Republic*, pp. 47–49, 51.

46. *Timaeus and Critias*, pp. 40–43.

47. *The Laws*, pp. 175, 425, 435–37, 440–42, 444–45.

48. *Five Dialogues*, pp. 107–16.

49. Ibid., pp. 117–19, 143–46.

50. Ibid., pp. 100, 120–21, 151–52.

51. *Phaedrus and the Seventh and Eighth Letters*, pp. 49, 54–55.

52. Plato, *Early Socratic Dialogues*, ed. Trevor J. Saunders (London: Penguin Books, 1987), pp. 327, 329–30.

53. *Gorgias*, pp. 34, 36, 47.

54. Plato, *The Symposium*, trans. Walter Hamilton (Harmondsworth, England: Penguin Books, 1951), pp. 84, 46, 49, 60–62, 69–70.

55. *Five Dialogues*, pp. 99–104, 123–24, 146–47.

56. *Plato's Republic*, p. 238.

57. Aristotle, *Metaphysics*, trans. Richard Hope (Ann Arbor: Univ. of Michigan Press, 1960), pp. 61–62. This work is henceforth called "*Metaphysics*."

58. Aristotle, *The Basic Works of Aristotle*, ed. Richard McKeon (New York: Random House, 1968), pp. 9–14. This work is henceforth called "McKeon."

59. Aristotle, *Aristotle's Physics*, trans. Richard Hope (Lincoln: Univ. of Nebraska Press, 1961), pp. 23–27. The work is henceforth called "*Aristotle's Physics*."

60. Ibid., pp. 28, 35.

61. *Metaphysics*, pp. 10–22.

62. Ibid., pp. 181–82, 192–93.

63. *Aristotle's Physics*, pp. 152, 155, 93–94.

64. Ibid., pp. 80, 87, 66.

65. McKeon, pp. 164, 176–77.

66. Aristotle, *De Anima*, trans. Hugh Lawson-Tancred (London: Penguin Books, 1986), pp. 126, 156–58. This work is henceforth called "*De Anima*."

67. Ibid., pp. 159, 161–63.

68. Ibid., pp. 165–66, 172–73, 176, 180, 182–84, 187.

69. Ibid., pp. 197–99.

70. Ibid., pp. 202, 204–5.

71. Ibid., pp. 211–12, 214–16.

72. *Metaphysics*, pp. 3, 6.

73. Ibid., pp. 7–9.

74. Ibid., pp. 67–68, 124.

75. *Aristotle's Physics*, pp. 3–4.

76. *Metaphysics*, pp. 184–85.

77. Aristotle, *Nicomachean Ethics*, trans. Terence Irwin (Indianapolis: Hackett Publishing Co., 1985), pp. 53–56. This work is henceforth called "*Nichomachean Ethics*."

78. Ibid., pp. 56–58.

79. Ibid., pp. 66–70.

80. Ibid., pp. 1–4.

81. Ibid., pp. 5–8.

82. Ibid., pp. 8–13.

83. Ibid., pp. 13–15.

84. Ibid., pp. 16–17, 21, 26–27, 30, 32–33.

85. Ibid., pp. 33–37, 40. *See also* Aristotle, *Eudemian Ethics*, 2nd ed., trans. Michael Woods (Oxford, England: Oxford Univ. Press, 1992), p. 6. This work is henceforth called "*Eudemian Ethics.*"

86. *Nicomachean Ethics*, pp. 41–45.

87. Ibid., pp. 46–49.

88. Ibid., pp. 117, 122, 131–32.

89. Ibid., pp. 150–51.

90. Ibid., pp. 192, 196–97.

91. Ibid., pp. 207, 209–13.

92. Ibid., pp. 266, 273, 277, 283–86.

93. Aristotle, *The Politics*, rev. Trevor J. Saunders, trans. T. A. Sinclair (London: Penguin Books, 1981), pp. 54–61.

94. Ibid., pp. 62–72, 95.

95. Ibid., pp. 189, 215, 221, 252–56, 249–51, 265–67, 226.

96. Ibid., pp. 196–98, 435, 453. On pp. 429–30, Aristotle argues that people become good through a confluence of "nature, habit, and reason."

97. *Metaphysics*, pp. 8, 46, 125.

98. Ibid., pp. 258, 264–66. In *Eudemian Ethics*, Aristotle does mention the value of "the service and speculation of the god" (p. 42), indicating a religious attitude not called for in the passages we are emphasizing.

99. *De Anima*, pp. 128, 146, 158, 205.

100. *Nicomachean Ethics*, pp. 286, 289.

Bibliography

GENERAL

Copleston, Frederick, S.J. *A History of Philosophy*, Vol. I. Garden City, NY: Image Books, 1962.

Irwin, Terence. *Classical Thought*. Oxford, England: Oxford Univ. Press, 1989.

Jones, W. T. *The Classical Mind*, 2nd ed. New York: Harcourt, Brace & World, Inc., 1969.

PLATO   **Primary Sources**

The Collected Dialogues of Plato. Ed. Edith Hamilton and Huntington Cairns. New York: Pantheon Books, 1966.

Early Socratic Dialogues. Ed. Trevor J. Saunders. London: Penguin Books, 1987.

Five Dialogues. Trans. G. M. A. Grube. Indianapolis: Hackett Publishing Co., 1981.

Gorgias. Trans. Donald J. Zeyl. Indianapolis: Hackett Publishing Co., 1987.

Great Dialogues of Plato. Ed. Eric H. Warmington and Philip G. Rouse. Trans. W. H. D. Rouse. New York: Menor Books, 1984.

The Laws. Trans. Trevor J. Saunders. London: Penguin Books, 1975.

Phaedrus and the Seventh and Eighth Letters. Trans. Walter Hamilton. Harmondsworth, England: Penguin Books, 1973.

Philebus. Trans. Robin A. H. Waterfield. London: Penguin Books, 1982.

Plato and Parmenides. Trans. Francis MacDonald Cornford. Indianapolis: Bobbs-Merrill, no date.

Plato's Republic. Trans. G. M. A. Grube. Indianapolis: Hackett Publishing Co., 1974.

Protagoras and Meno. Trans. W. K. C. Guthrie. Harmondsworth, England: Penguin Books, 1956.

The Symposium. Trans. Walter Hamilton. Harmondsworth, England: Penguin Books, 1951.

Theaetetus. Trans. Robin A. H. Waterfield. London: Penguin Books, 1987.

Timaeus and Critias. Trans. Desmond Lee. London: Penguin Books, 1977.

Secondary Sources

Field, G. C. *The Philosophy of Plato*, 2nd ed. London: Oxford Univ. Press, 1969.

Grube, G. M. A. *Plato's Thought*. Boston: Beacon Press, 1958.

Kraut, Richard, Ed. *The Cambridge Companion to Plato*. New York: Cambridge Univ. Press, 1992.

Raven, J. E. *Plato's Thought in the Making*. Cambridge, England: Cambridge Univ. Press, 1965.

Ross, Sir David. *Plato's Theory of Ideas*. London: Oxford Univ. Press, 1953.

Shorey, Paul. *What Plato Said*. Chicago: Univ. of Chicago Press, 1933.

Taylor, A. E. *Plato: The Man and His Work*. London: Methuen & Co., 1966.

Vlastos, Gregory, ed. *Plato: A Collection of Critical Essays*, Vols. I, II. Garden City, NY: Doubleday & Co., 1971.

ARISTOTLE   *Primary Sources*

Aristotle: Selected Works. Trans. Hippocrates G. Apostle and Lloyd P. Gerson. Grinnell, IA: The Peripatetic Press, 1986.

Aristotle's Physics. Trans. Richard Hope. Lincoln: Univ. of Nebraska Press, 1961.

The Basic Works of Aristotle Ed. Richard McKeon. New York: Random House, 1968.

De Anima. Trans. Hugh Lawson-Tancred. London: Penguin Books, 1986.

Eudemian Ethics, 2nd ed. Trans. Michael Woods. Oxford, England: Oxford Univ. Press, 1992.

Metaphysics. Trans. Richard Hope. Ann Arbor: Univ. of Michigan Press, 1960.

A New Aristotle Reader. Ed. J. L. Akrill. Princeton: Princeton Univ. Press, 1987.

Nicomachean Ethics. Trans. Terence Irwin. Indianapolis: Hackett Publishing Co., 1985.

The Philosophy of Aristotle. Ed. Renford Bambrough. Trans. A. E. Wardman and J. L. Creed. New York: Mentor Books, 1963.

The Politics. Rev. Trevor J. Saunders. Trans. T. A. Sinclair. London: Penguin Books, 1981.

Secondary Sources

Allan, D. J. *The Philosophy of Aristotle*, 2nd ed. London: Oxford Univ. Press, 1970.

Barnes, Jonathan. *Aristotle*. Oxford, England: Oxford Univ. Press, 1982.

————, Ed. *The Cambridge Companion to Aristotle*. New York: Cambridge Univ. Press, 1995.

Lloyd, G. E. R. *Aristotle: The Growth and Structure of His Thought*. Cambridge, England: Cambridge Univ. Press, 1968.

Moravsik, J. M. E., Ed. *Aristotle: A Collection of Critical Essays*. Garden City, NY: Doubleday & Co., 1967.

Mure, G. R. C. *Aristotle*. New York: Oxford Univ. Press, 1964.

Ross, Sir David. *Aristotle*. London: Methuen & Co., 1968.

Taylor, A. E. *Aristotle*. New York: Dover Publications, 1955.

Veatch, Henry B., *Aristotle*. Bloomington: Indiana Univ. Press, 1974.

Historical Background

《《《《《《《《《《《《《《《《《《《《《《《《》》》》》》》》》》》》》》》》》》》》》

he Age of Belief constitutes the long but ill-defined period between **antiquity** and **modernity**. It is marked by the deliberate effort to render thought not only in conformity with the doctrines of religious faith, but supportive of them. During this period scriptural revelation and ecclesiastical teachings were regarded as ultimate authorities, to which all thought should be subordinate. The **Renaissance**, which is often considered a separate period, was less deferential to religious authority than were the "**Middle Ages**," or **medieval** period. This historical background will review the extensive period from the decline of the Roman **Empire** to the end of the sixteenth century, in an attempt to provide a context for Augustine and Aquinas, the two **philosophical** giants of the Age of Belief. Though living several hundred years apart, both were medieval figures, as was Boethius, the last classical thinker; the Renaissance period produced no first-rate philosophers, although Machiavelli and Montaigne provide two good examples of the Renaissance transition to modernism.

Christianity emerged as a new religion, splitting off from Judaism. Around A.D. 32, a couple of years after the crucifixion of Jesus, Saul, a rabbinical student and a Roman citizen who had helped persecute Christians, converted to Christianity because of a religious experience he had on the road to Damascus and took the name of Paul. He undertook many missionary journeys throughout the Empire to convert non-Jews to Christianity and struggled to cement the bonds between the Jewish Christian and the growing gentile Christian communities. The four Christian Gospels, all written in the first century, after the deaths of Paul and Peter (the first head of the Christian Church), were those of Mark, Matthew, Luke, and John. These and other New Testament books, including the Epistles of Paul, were most important for the early development of Christian thought. The twenty-seven books of the New Testament were transmitted in *koine* Greek, making them more accessible throughout the Empire. The Christian doctrine of a savior who died for all humanity, combined with the Gospel (which literally means "good news") message of universal love, came to have great

---

Antiquity.   Ancient times, before the Middle Ages, including the Hellenic and Hellenistic periods—for our purposes, until the late fourth or early fifth century A.D.

Modernity (or **modernism**).   That period of Western history extending from the beginning of the seventeenth century; when contrasted with contemporary times, modernity ends early in the twentieth century

Middle Ages.   That period of Western history between antiquity and the Renaissance—i.e., from the late fourth or early fifth century A.D. to the end of the fourteenth century

Medieval (from the Latin *medium aevum*, meaning the middle age).   Of or pertaining to the Middle Ages

popular appeal, despite the fact that Christians were persecuted and martyred until the fourth century. For almost three hundred years after the death of Jesus, the focus of Christians seems to have been on sacramental liturgies and preaching conducted secretly, as, for example, in subterranean catacombs. Writings from the period, called patristic literature, focused on apologetics, designed to make converts. Attempts to interpret Christian beliefs in pagan terms (as by the **Gnostics**) or to assimilate their beliefs to other religions (for example, by the **Manicheans**) had to be resisted during this time; and heretics within Christianity (the Marcionites, the Montanists, the Arians, and the Nestorians) were condemned during the three centuries following Jesus' death. Church clergy were organized under the authority of bishops, who were viewed as successors of the original followers of Jesus (his "apostles"), with special honor being granted to the bishop of Rome as the successor of Peter.

Near the middle of the third century, the Roman Empire was in decline, and the Germanic Goths managed to sack Athens, Corinth, and Sparta. The Emperor Diocletian (284–305), thinking the Empire too large to be ruled effectively by one person, split it into eastern and western portions, ruling the eastern section himself from Nicomedia in Asia Minor, with Maximian governing the west from Milan. During most of his reign, Diocletian continued the policy of his predecessors of tacit toleration of Christianity; however, he ordered a general persecution of Christians throughout the Empire in 303. Two years later, when Diocletian and Maximian both abdicated, a power struggle for succession was generated. In 306, Constantine (306–37) was proclaimed emperor by the troops of his recently deceased father, who had ruled the Western Empire for a while; the next year, he declared himself emperor, although he was effectively in charge of only Gaul and Britain at the time. Constantine began marching on Rome; he claimed to have had a vision of a cross in the sky and to have

heard the words, "In this sign you will conquer" (*In hoc signo vinces*), on the outskirts of the city during a pivotal battle which he won. Some time later, he converted to Christianity. He became absolute ruler of the Western Empire in 312; the following year, he issued a proclamation, often called the Edict of Milan, granting toleration to Christians throughout both halves of the Empire. In 324, Constantine reunified the Empire, where Christianity flourished. This created an opportunity for the development of a distinctively Christian philosophy, such as would be articulated by Augustine within the next century. Constantine summoned the Council of Nicaea, the great council of the Christian church which promulgated the Nicene Creed (325), affirming the divinity of Christ and declaring as orthodox the doctrine of the Trinity. In 330, Constantine dedicated the new city of Constantinople, built on the site of the old Byzantium, as capital of the Roman Empire; he was baptized a Christian on his deathbed. When he died in 337, the Empire was divided among his three sons; one of them, Constantius II, later ordered the closing of all pagan temples throughout the Roman Empire.

While Christianity was being thus established within the Empire, the peoples outside the Empire, whom the Romans considered uncivilized "barbarians," were on the move. The Huns, nomadic Mongols from Asia, were invading Europe, conquering the Ostrogoths, eastern Germanic peoples, and massacring the Visigoths, from western Germany. The Visigoths got permission to cross the Danube River and enter the Roman Empire collectively. But this led to fighting with the Romans; the Visigoths defeated and killed Valens, Emperor of the Eastern Empire (364–78) at Adrianople, and Theodosius was summoned to replace him, subsequently becoming Emperor of the Eastern Empire (379–95). In 391, a fire destroyed the great library at Alexandria, which contained many irreplaceable manuscripts; that same year, Theodosius ordered the destruction of non-Christian works. Theodosius

---

Gnosticism (from the Greek *gnosis*, meaning knowledge).   A movement, originating in Hellenistic times, that became popular among early Christian heretical sects, associating the material world with evil, claiming that Christ was noncorporeal, and viewing salvation as attainable through esoteric knowledge of spiritual truth rather than through ordinary faith

Manicheanism.   The teaching of Mani, a third-century A.D. religious leader who tried to synthesize Christianity and Zoroastrianism, of the dualistic gnostic doctrine that there is a God of light and goodness and an equally powerful principle of darkness and evil, which are at war in human nature

briefly reunited the Roman Empire in 394, but it split into two parts again when he died at Milan the following year.

In the early years of the fifth century, the barbarians were closing in, the Visigoths penetrating northern Italy. The last Roman troops in Britain had to withdraw to defend Rome, which came under siege. Under the command of Alaric, the Visigoths sacked Rome in 410, leaving no doubt that the old Roman Empire was a thing of the past. The Visigoth army invaded Gaul and Spain, driving the Vandals, under Gaiseric, into North Africa, where they established a kingdom that would last for over a century. In 430, the Vandals, another Germanic people, besieged Hippo, the city of Augustine, and Gaiseric captured Carthage nine years later. The Goths deposed the last Emperor of the Western Empire in 476, bringing it to a dead end. Twenty years later, Clovis, King of the Franks, converted to Christianity; in 507, the Franks conquered the Visigoths in southern France.

The Eastern Empire, now called the Byzantine Empire, survived the fall of the western half. Justinian became the Byzantine Emperor (527–65). In 529, he codified the Empire's laws and closed Plato's Athenian Academy because of suspected unchristian activities there. Some regard this as the termination of classical ancient thought and the inception of the Middle Ages. Another reason some view 529 as the beginning of medievalism is that **monasticism** then became solidified with the founding of the Benedictine monastery at Monte Cassino by Benedict, an Italian monk. Thus, in a period of about three centuries, Christianity had become established, the Roman Empire had fallen in the West, and antiquity had expired. Byzantine forces then conquered the Vandals, ending their control of North Africa, and reconquered Italy before Justinian died in 565.

During the fourth and fifth centuries, Church councils combated the threat of heresy, often regarding the doctrines of the divine Trinity (the Father, the Son, and the Holy Spirit as the three persons of the one God) and the divine and human natures of Christ (as God incarnate in the human person of Jesus). A century after the Council of Nicaea condemned the Arians (who denied that Christ coexisted with the Father from all eternity), the Council of Ephesus (431) condemned the Nestorians (who claimed that the divine and human personalities were separate in Christ and that Mary was only the mother of his human personality), and the Council of Chalcedon (451) condemned the Monophysites (who held that Christ had only one nature combining the human and the divine). Christian writers whose work was considered orthodox and influential came to be called Fathers of the Church; one convenient grouping distinguishes four who wrote in Greek (Basil the Great, Athanasius, Gregory Nazianzen, and John Chrysostom) and four who wrote in Latin (Ambrose, Jerome, Augustine, and Gregory the Great); all eight are regarded as Christian saints. During this time the prestige and ecclesiastical authority of the bishop of Rome, the "Pope," were growing, especially from the time of Leo the Great (440–61) to that of Gregory the Great (590–604).

The early Christian Church did not distinguish between the educating of men and of women; but by the fourth century, with the institutionalization of the Church, opportunities for women became more restricted. There were some cases of women scholars, such as Hypatia, who taught mathematics and philosophy at a university in Alexandria, invented some scientific instruments, and produced writings on astronomy and mathematics; in 415, the Christian patriarch of Alexandria provoked a mob, which attacked and killed her, subsequently burning her body and her books. At about that time, Augustine, the Bishop of Hippo, encouraged women to establish religious communities around Carthage; his sister, Perpetua, founded an order for women in his diocese. In medieval times, privileged Christian women in Europe joined religious orders, giving up any property claims they might have and taking vows to remain cloistered and celibate for the duration of their lives. The women worked within these communities, which were to remain self-sufficient. But, apart from the life of the nun, the socially acceptable roles for women then, as in ancient times, were those of daughter, wife, mother, and widow.

Monasticism. A movement in which people withdrew from the secular world to live in religious communities, under vows, such as those of obedience, chastity, and poverty

In 570, five years after the death of Justinian, Muhammad, the founder of Islam, was born at Mecca. He dictated the Qur'an (or Koran) and captured Mecca before he died in 632. Six years later, Muslims captured Jerusalem; a few years after that, they conquered Egypt. They besieged Constantinople twice, though without success. Meanwhile, the Moors (Arabs and Berber Muslims from North Africa) had invaded the Iberian Peninsula and controlled most of Spain and Portugal by 711. For several centuries under Moorish rule, Spain was characterized by economic wealth and relative tolerance, resulting in a rich Muslim and Jewish cultural development. In 732, Charles Martel of the Franks defeated the Moors at Tours (in France).

His grandson, Charlemagne ("Charles the Great"), became sole King of the Franks in 771. He took the side of the Pope in a war between the papacy and the Lombards, defeating the latter and assuming their crown. In 782, Charlemagne launched a revival of learning when he invited the English churchman Alcuin (who had been educated at York by a follower of Bede, the author of *Ecclesiastical History of the English People*) to set up a school at his court; thanks to his influence, the seven liberal arts (consisting of the *quadrivium*—arithmetic, geometry, astronomy, and music—and the *trivium*—grammar, rhetoric, and logic) became the core of the curriculum of Western Europe in the Middle Ages. Charlemagne was crowned Holy Roman Emperor by Pope Leo III (795–816), whom he had supported in another power struggle, in Rome in 800. He successfully fought against the pagan Saxons, forcing many to convert to Christianity. The end of his reign was troubled by the raids of Viking invaders. These raids of the Vikings or Norsemen bedeviled the French coast and the Saxon kingdoms in England throughout the ninth century. Even Charles the Fat, the French King, had to pay tribute to the Vikings; and King Charles the Simple agreed to let the Norsemen keep that part of the northern Frankish coastal territory that became Normandy. Meanwhile, Saxon England remained politically unstable, and, thus, a tempting target. Philosophers living in the ninth century included John Scotus Erigena, a Christian, and Al-Kindi and Al-Farabi, Islamic thinkers.

In 1066, Duke William of Normandy conquered England by defeating the Saxon King Harold at the Battle of Hastings; he was crowned King William I of England in Westminster Abbey on Christmas Day of that year and ruled for more than twenty years. William subdued the northern part of England in 1069, and three years later, he invaded Scotland. William's reign brought Britain more solidly under the influence of Christianity. In 1077, Holy Roman Emperor Henry IV stood barefoot in the snow for three days at Canossa as penance for trying to depose Pope Gregory VII (1073–85), for which the Pope absolved Henry and withdrew his declaration of excommunication against the emperor.

Between the end of the eleventh century and the latter half of the thirteenth, Christian Europe launched nine Crusades meant to win parts of the Holy Land back from Islamic conquerors. The First Crusade began in 1096, after Pope Urban II (1088–99) appealed to the knights of Christendom to liberate that sacred area; crusaders defeated Muslim Saracens at Antioch and captured Jerusalem. Three more Crusades followed in the twelfth century and the first decade of the thirteenth, ending with the Christians capturing and sacking Constantinople. In 1212, there occurred a pathetic expedition, called the "Children's Crusade," of tens of thousands of French and German children marching to the Holy Land to try to win it back peacefully; but the German children were diverted from their goal, and others were sold into slavery. More Crusades followed in the thirteenth century, with the holy city of Jerusalem being won and lost by the Christians. The unsuccessful Ninth Crusade, led by Prince Edward of England, was the final one, and in 1291, Saracens captured the last Christian stronghold in Palestine. So, for almost two centuries, these expeditions generated ongoing battles with the Muslims, but no lasting territorial gains for the Christians. The Crusades strongly influenced trade by increasing awareness of, and demand for, such Eastern products as spices and textiles.

During the twelfth and thirteenth centuries institutions of learning evolved as universities at such places as Bologna and Naples in Italy, Paris in France, and Oxford in England; by 1500, there were about eighty universities in Europe. The curriculum centered on the seven liberal arts, which were also taught in medieval monasteries and cathedral schools. In addition to studying these liberal arts and the classics, universities also included faculties of law, medicine, and **scholastic theology**. By the fourteenth and fifteenth centuries, Italian universities (e.g., those at Bologna and Salerno) were granting medical degrees to women, enabling them to become physicians; European women practiced surgery for the duration of the Middle Ages in Italy, France, England, Germany, and Switzerland.

At this time great cathedrals were being constructed, such as Notre Dame de Paris, a striking example of Gothic architecture, with its flying buttresses and lofty towers. Among the masterworks of Gothic art are the sculpture of the father and son, Nicola and Giovanni Pisano, and the frescoes and murals of Giotto. Gregorian chant, which dated back several centuries, was evolving into polyphonic religious music during the late Middle Ages. In 1210, Francis of Assisi founded the Franciscan Order of Friars Minor, which ministered to the poor, did missionary work, and produced scholars. Five years later, Dominic founded the Dominican Order of Preachers at Toulouse; they would do outstanding work as missionaries, teachers, and scholars. That same year, English barons forced King John of England to sign the Magna Carta (or "Great Charter") at Runnymede, acknowledging their rights; this guarantee was significant in foreshadowing the later protections of constitutional law. In the eleventh and twelfth centuries, important religious thinkers emerged in all three of the great monotheistic faiths: Anselm, the Christian; Moses Maimonides, the Jew; and Avicenna, Al-Ghazzali, and Averroes, among the Muslims. In the thirteenth century, Albert the Great, Roger Bacon, and Bonaventure made important intellectual contributions, in addition to Thomas Aquinas. Prominent philosophers of the fourteenth century include Duns Scotus and William of Ockham.

The fourteenth century brought forth literary giants: the Italian poets Dante, most famous for his *Divine Comedy*; Petrarch, who wrote exquisite sonnets; Giovanni Boccaccio, acclaimed for his *Decameron*; and the English poet Geoffrey Chaucer, most renowned for his *Canterbury Tales*. In Germany in 1440, Johannes Gutenberg invented a process of printing from movable type, which would be most important for the explosion of learning in Renaissance and modern times.

The Hundred Years' War, which ended in 1453, had actually begun in 1337 and was a series of wars precipitated by English claims to the throne of France and territorial disputes. During this period of more than a century, the English had made significant, but temporary, military gains. Around 1429, Joan of Arc, a humble peasant girl, inspired the French by commanding their army; but she was captured by the Burgundians and turned over to the English in 1430, and the following year she was tried by a local court of the Inquisition in Normandy and burned as a relapsed heretic. By the end of the Hundred Years' War, England's only possession in France was the port city of Calais, across the English Channel from Dover. In 1453, the Ottoman Turks, under Sultan Mohammed II, captured Constantinople, which became the center of the Muslim Ottoman Empire that replaced the Christian Byzantine Empire; this may be regarded as the end of the Middle Ages. Many scholars fled from Constantinople towards the West, promoting the revival of learning called the Renaissance.

A renewal of interest in ancient classics, a spirit fostering broader critical inquiry less restricted by traditional submission to authority, and a heightened passion for and appreciation of aesthetic achievement characterized the Renaissance (French for "rebirth"), which was more **humanistic** (and less **theocentric**) than the Middle Ages. In the fifteenth and sixteenth centuries, especially in Italy, Renaissance art flourished at the hands of such geniuses as Leonardo da Vinci, renowned for his painting of the "Last Supper" and the "Mona Lisa," Michelangelo, who sculpted "David" and painted the ceiling of the Sistine Chapel, and Raphael, who painted "The School of

---

Scholasticism (from the Greek *skholastikos*, meaning learned). The educational tradition (both philosophical and theological) of medieval universities, often as influenced by Aristotle, its masters being scholastics or "schoolmen"

Humanism. Any view (e.g., in James or Sartre) emphasizing the value and dignity of human individuals

Theocentrism. The view that reality is God-centered; medieval thought is distinctly theocentric, as Enlightenment thought is not

Athens." Other magnificent Renaissance painters include Fra Angelico, Sandro Botticelli, Giovanni Bellini, Titian, and El Greco, and, in the North, Albrecht Dürer, Hans Holbein, Lucas Cranach, and Pieter Breughel; among the great sculptors are Donatello, Lorenzo Ghiberti, and Benvenuto Cellini. By the sixteenth century, science was also developing. In 1543, Nicolaus Copernicus, a Polish Catholic priest, proposed a **heliocentric** theory of our planetary system as a simpler alternative to Ptolemy's **geocentric** model of the universe, which had been maintained by Aristotle and scholastic thought. Because the Copernican theory dislodged man and his planet from the center of the universe, it was unwelcome and failed to gain acceptance until the following century.

During the Renaissance, educational emphases shifted: in the fifteenth century, humanistic education stressed literature and art; in the sixteenth century, **ethics** and social thought were emphasized (Michel de Montaigne, for example, advocated the teaching of **virtue** as a primary focus). Throughout this time, European societies remained male-dominated. A striking phenomenon of the sixteenth and seventeenth centuries was the ongoing custom of witch trials, as a result of which more than 100,000 European and American women were killed as witches by Christian zealots. Under the authority of the Spanish Inquisition, sometimes up to one hundred people a day were burned. The Spanish Inquisition, which had begun under Ferdinand and Isabella and had been organized by Tomás de Torquemada in the late fifteenth century, was designed to expose and punish Jews and Muslims who, under severe social, political, and economic pressure, had insincerely converted to Christianity. In 1492, the Jews were expelled from Spain and, five years later, from Portugal; many of these exiles died, while others fled to asylum in Turkish possessions and Italy. The Inquisition became most virulent during the era of Spain's greatest influence, under Charles I and Philip II, the first

two Hapsburg kings, who consolidated the power of absolute **monarchy**, flexed Spain's military muscles at home and abroad, and developed a great naval fleet. Philip II even tried to impose the Inquisition on the Netherlands, though its officials would not cooperate, and this interference helped trigger the Dutch struggle for independence.

In 1517, Martin Luther nailed his ninety-five theses on the church door at Wittenberg, in hopes of stimulating discussion concerning the controversial policy of selling indulgences; though not initially intending to break from the Church, he thus precipitated the Protestant Reformation, which fractured Roman Catholicism's control of ideas in Europe. In England King Henry VIII, who had been educated in Renaissance learning and whom the Pope had named "Defender of the Faith" for a treatise against Luther, wanting to divorce his first wife, Catherine of Aragon (the youngest daughter of Ferdinand and Isabella of Spain), severed ties with Roman ecclesiastical authority and in 1534 established the Church of England with the king as its supreme head. Desiderius Erasmus, a Dutch Catholic priest, ridiculed scholastic philosophers and protested clerical abuse and lay ignorance, but he never questioned the essence and principles of the Roman Catholic Church; he attacked Luther's views on predestination in his *On the Freedom of the Will*. John Calvin, who had studied law in France, wrote his *Institutes of the Christian Religion*, a seminal work of Protestant theology, and established the Reformation at Geneva. As part of a Catholic Reformation, new religious orders arose, the greatest of these being the Society of Jesus, founded by Ignatius Loyola in 1534 and formally approved by Pope Paul III (1534–49) six years later; the Jesuits, as the members of Loyola's order came to be called, distinguished themselves as preachers, intellectuals, missionaries, explorers, and the schoolmasters of Europe.

This was also a time of exciting geographical discoveries, revealing a world much larger and more diverse than had been imagined. In 1492, under the

Heliocentrism (from the Greek *helios*, meaning Sun, and *kentrikos*, meaning of the center).   The theory of Copernicus that the Sun is the center of our planetary system with the Earth revolving around it, as opposed to geocentrism

Geocentrism (from the Greek *geo*, meaning Earth, and *kentrikos*, meaning of the center).   The theory of Ptolemy that our Earth is the fixed center of the universe with all other heavenly bodies, including the Sun, moving around it, as opposed to heliocentrism

patronage of Queen Isabella of Spain, the Italian Christopher Columbus crossed the Atlantic Ocean with three ships under his command, discovering land which he mistakenly believed to be the East Indies (and therefore calling the natives "Indians"). He subsequently made three more voyages to the New World, establishing a permanent Spanish settlement at Santo Domingo in 1496. In 1512, Ponce de Leon discovered Florida, and the following year, Balboa crossed the Isthmus of Panama, seeing the Pacific Ocean. In 1519, Ferdinand Magellan set out from Spain with five ships, one of which would become the first ever to circumnavigate our planet. That same year, Hernando Cortez landed on the Mexican coast, remarkably conquering the rich and powerful Aztec empire in a few months with only six or seven hundred men, eighteen horses, and a few cannon; a few years later, Francisco Pizarro conquered the Incas in South America. These great explorers represented Spain, which had become the premier naval power in the world. In 1588, Spain launched its Invincible Armada of one hundred thirty ships to invade England; but the expedition was a fiasco, and only about half the fleet survived to return home. After this, England became more prominent in exploration, establishing colonies in North America early in the next century.

This long historical review prominently involves the crumbling of the Roman Empire, the rising influence of the Christian religion in Western Europe, and the achievements of the Renaissance. The medieval era, dominated by the demands of religious faith and a fundamental acceptance of doctrines based on scriptural revelation, is rightly considered the Age of Belief. Augustine, Aquinas, and other thinkers of this period attempt to support teachings of Christianity by means of the philosophical systems available to them; for the **rationalist** Augustine this was **Platonism**, while for Aquinas it was Aristotelian **empiricism** (which is more moderate than the more modern version, starting with Hobbes, we shall study later). The philosophical activity of this era is well described (by Anselm) as that of "faith seeking understanding" (*fides quaerens intellectum*). It represents the need to think through our beliefs critically, to systematize them, and to determine whether, and to what extent, rational **knowledge** of them is possible.

Augustine

This is
our freedom,
when we are
subject to
the truth;
and the truth
is God
himself.

On Free Choice of the Will

BIOGRAPHY

Aurelius Augustinus was born on November 13, 354 (seventeen years after Constantine died), in the Numidian town of Thagaste in Roman North Africa (located in present-day Algeria). His parents were Roman citizens of modest means; his father, Patricius, was a pagan, and his mother, Monica, a Christian. It was in his mother's religion that Augustine was raised. The first nine (of the thirteen) books of his *Confessions* are autobiographical, dramatically recounting the first third of a century of his life from his birth to his second birth by baptism, in 387. The *Confessions* is largely a narrative, addressed to God, of his painful, troubled search for spiritual fulfillment. As he writes on its very first page,

> Thou hast made us for Thyself and our hearts are restless till they rest in Thee.

After studying Latin, some Greek (which he says he hated), and arithmetic with a schoolmaster in Thagaste, around the year 365 (many of the dates in this chapter—as in our last one, and unlike those in subsequent chapters—are necessarily approximations) he went to a school in the pagan town of Madauros (some twenty miles away). He is self-critical in confessing his own disobedience, frivolity, and competitiveness as a child. He begged to be

baptized when, in childhood, he "fell gravely ill with some abdominal trouble and was close to death"; but he suddenly recovered, and the baptism was postponed.[1]

Augustine describes his adolescence in terms of "my past wickedness and the carnal corruptions of my **soul**." When he was almost sixteen years old, his studies were interrupted while "the money was being got together" to send him to Carthage. During this interim, he says, he "lived idly at home" with his family and was pricked by the "briars of unclean lusts." He tells a memorable story of how he and several other mischievous boys stole "an immense load of pears" late one night, "not to eat—for we barely tasted them before throwing them to the hogs. Our only pleasure in doing it was that it was forbidden." In 370, the year his father died (shortly after converting to Christianity), Augustine was sent to study rhetoric at Carthage (in present-day Tunisia). As he writes,

> I came to Carthage, where a cauldron of illicit loves leapt and boiled about me. I was not yet in love, but I was in love with love.

Around 371, he took a concubine and "did fall in love, simply from wanting to." He had a son by her, named Adeodatus (literally meaning "given by God"), about 372. Meanwhile, he was preparing for "the study of law" and figured, "the less honest I was, the more famous I should be." But in 373, he read the Roman **eclectic Stoic** Marcus Tullius Cicero's *Hortensius*, which "changed the direction" of his interests and kindled a passion for philosophy and its quest for truth. He compared the "simplicity" of "the Sacred Scriptures" unfavorably "with the majesty of Cicero." He turned from orthodox Christianity to the Manichean sect. Mani, a third-century Babylonian of the **Hellenistic** period, taught the **dualistic** doctrine that two eternal, original principles of our world, Ormuzd, a god of light and goodness, and Ahriman, a source of darkness and evil, were staging a struggle within human nature itself between man's good soul and evil body. Later, looking back on his attraction to the Manicheans, Augustine dismisses them as "talking high-sounding nonsense" and writes, "The snares of the devil were in their mouths, to trap souls." It seems that, for a while, he was trapped by their open **materialism** and easy solution to the **problem of evil**. Around 374, Augustine conducted

---

Evil, problem of. The puzzle as to how a perfect (e.g., omnipotent, omniscient, and infinitely good) God can be compatible with the reality of evil in the world

a school of rhetoric at Thagaste. He writes that, throughout the "nine-year period, from my nineteenth year to my twenty-eighth, I was led astray myself and led others astray." During this time he remained faithful to his concubine, bonded by "a lustful love," and cared for their son.[2]

In the autumn of 376, he returned to Carthage, where he founded a school. Around 380, he wrote his first published work, "*De Pulchro et Apto*—on the Beautiful and the Fitting." Meanwhile, he was experiencing growing doubts about Manichean teachings. Local leaders of the sect could not adequately answer his questions but promised that he would be satisfied by the explanations of Faustus, a prominent Manichean bishop, when he came to visit Carthage. Augustine found Faustus "a pleasant man of pleasant speech" but was sorely disappointed by his facile, shallow responses. This "somewhat blunted" Augustine's enthusiasm for Manichean doctrines. As he writes, "Thus Faustus, who had been a snare that brought death to many, did without his knowledge or will begin to unbind the snare that held me." In 383, Augustine left Carthage for Rome, for he "had heard that youths there pursued their studies more quietly and were kept within a stricter limit of discipline" than was the case with the rowdy, impertinent schoolboys of Carthage. He opened a school of rhetoric in Rome, and became attracted to the **scepticism** of the later **Academy**. He found out that his Roman students were too clever at finding ways to avoid paying their tuition fees; with the support of Manicheans he secured a professorship of rhetoric in Milan (the capital of the Empire) in 384. There he heard Bishop Ambrose preach. At first, Augustine was interested only in his eloquent style rather than in the content of his sermons. But gradually, he writes, Ambrose made him

> see that the Catholic faith, for which I had thought nothing could be said in the face of the Manichean objections, could be maintained on reasonable grounds: this especially after I had heard explained figuratively several passages of the Old Testament which had been a **cause** of death for me when taken literally.[3]

At about this time, he started studying Latin translations of **Neoplatonic** works, presumably including Plotinus' **monistic** *Enneads,* which helped him overcome his tendencies to materialism and scepticism.

In 385, his mother, Monica, came to Milan from North Africa, finding her son "in a perilous state" as a result of his "deep despair of ever discovering the truth." She became devoted to Ambrose and his preaching. She pushed her son to give up his concubine and to marry someone respectable. Marriage plans were made; the mistress was sent back to Africa, leaving Adeodatus behind with Augustine. Augustine could not wait for the marriage and took another mistress. Meanwhile his reading of Latin translations of **Platonic** works was intellectually turning him towards spiritual ideas, eternal truth, and God. He writes, "Being admonished by all this to return to myself, I entered into my depths." He was becoming more intensely focused on spiritual reflection. But in 386, sexual passion still restrained him from committing to Christianity.

> I in my great worthlessness [he writes to God] had begged You for chastity, saying: "Grant me chastity and continence, but not yet." For I was afraid that You would hear my prayer too soon, and too soon would heal me from the disease of lust which I wanted satisfied rather than extinguished.

He was unhappily wondering how long it would take before his intellectual conversion would be accompanied by a moral one, when suddenly a child's voice, in "a sort of sing-song, repeated again and again, 'Take and read, take and read.'" He interpreted this as a message from God and opened up the Bible to read the first passage he saw. It was from Paul's *Epistle to the Romans* 13:13–14:

> Not in rioting and drunkenness, not in chambering and impurities, not in contention and envy, but put ye on the Lord Jesus Christ and make not provision for the flesh in its concupiscences.

He says that as soon as he finished the sentence, he felt as if "all the darkness of uncertainty vanished away." Now his **will** as well as his **mind** was converted to God. He resigned his chair as professor of rhetoric at Milan. In 387, at Eastertime, he and his son were baptized by Ambrose. He, Monica, and Adeodatus left Milan later that year to return to Africa. But Monica contracted a fever and died on the way, leaving him and his son grief-stricken.[4] They stayed in Rome for a while, where he worked on some writings, including *On Free Choice of the Will* and *On the **Immortality** of the Soul.*

In 388, Augustine and his son returned to Thagaste. He formed a small monastic community on his father's old farm and published his first dialogues

(*Against the Academicians, The Soliloquies, The Happy Life,* and *De Ordine*). About 389, Adeodatus died at Thagaste at the age of seventeen. Augustine so admired the intelligence of his son that he wrote *Concerning the Teacher* that year as a dialogue between the two of them; in it he says that "all the ideas which are put into the mouth" of the boy there "were truly his, though he was but sixteen." In 391, Augustine visited Hippo (a seaport in present-day Algeria) to hear Bishop Valerius speak. The people there offered the reluctant Augustine up for ordination. Valerius ordained him as a priest, and Augustine established a monastery there. The next year, he publicly debated a prominent Manichean named Fortunatus. Two years later, he engaged in polemics against the Donatists, who taught the heresy that the validity of the sacraments could be nullified by the moral unworthiness of the clergymen performing them. In 395, he was appointed auxiliary to the aging Valerius; when the latter died soon thereafter, Augustine became Bishop of Hippo. Around 412, he began a controversy with the Pelagians, heretics who denied both the doctrine of **original sin** and the one proclaiming that man is utterly dependent on God's grace for salvation. The next year, he began writing *The City of God* (against those who blamed Christianity for the sacking of Rome and the general crumbling of the Empire), which was completed about 426. His writings also include: *Of True Religion* (c390), *On the Advantage of Believing* (c391), *On Free Choice of the Will* (395), *Confessions* (c397), *On Christian Doctrine* (c397), *On Faith in Things Unseen* (c400), *The Nature of the Good* (404), *On the Trinity* (begun about 400 and completed in 417), and *Enchiridion on Faith, Hope and Love* (421). In 427, he published his *Retractations,* which critically discuss his previous works, pointing out errors and views he had abandoned. On August 28, 430, while the Vandals were besieging Hippo, he died, while reciting the Psalms. When the Vandals subsequently conquered Hippo, they burned the city, though, out of respect for Augustine, they left his cathedral and his library unscathed.

In many ways the story of Augustine's life is crystallized in his conversion from the licentious life of self-gratification to the pursuit and service of Truth. As he writes so movingly to his God,

> Late have I loved Thee.... For behold Thou wert within me, and I outside; and I sought Thee outside and in my unloveliness fell upon those lovely things which Thou hast made. Thou wert with me and I was not with Thee.[5]

His is among the most dramatic of biographies presented in this book; and his philosophy of human nature reflects the spiritual destination of his life's striking odyssey.

Reality

GOD, SOULS, AND BODIES. For the Christian Augustine the three types of reality are God (the Creator), souls, and bodies (as creatures). All of them are good, to the extent that they exhibit "measure, form and order," as he explains near the beginning of *The Nature of the Good.*[6] We might observe that there is no separate world of Forms here, as for Plato; eternal ideas are rather located in the mind of God. Against the Manicheans, he asserts that even matter, having the capacity to be formed, must be good. In a letter to Caelestinus he uses spatio-temporal change as a framework for explaining the three types of realities:

> There is a nature, which is subject to the changes of both time and space, as the body; and there is a nature which is not subject to space but only to time, as the soul; and there is a nature which is subject to neither space nor time, and that is God,[7]

who is spiritual and eternal.

A HIERARCHY OF BEINGS. In *The City of God* Augustine maintains that the world of God's creation comprises a hierarchy of being, with **animate** creatures "ranked above" inanimate ones; "among the things that have life, the sentient are higher than those which have no sensation"; in the category of "the sentient, the intelligent are above those that have not intelligence"; finally, "among the intelligent, the immortal" rank "above the mortal." Thus, to illustrate these natural "gradations," a flower is above a rock because it is alive; a bird ranks above a flower because it is sentient; a human being is higher than a

---

Original sin. In theology, the tendency to commit evil supposedly innate in all humans, as inherited from Adam, the first man, who deliberately disobeyed the manifest will of God

bird because of intelligence; and an angel is **ontologically** superior to a human being because it is immortal. He also assures us that God must have had good reason for setting the world in the part of space it occupies, even if we cannot comprehend that reason. And, since time is a measure of movement and change, which are part of the world rather than of God, time and the world must have originated simultaneously.[8]

THE NATURE OF TIME.   In his *Confessions* Augustine presents a memorable meditation on the nature of time, the measure of movement and change in all creatures:

> What *is* this time? If no one asks me, I know; if I want to explain it to a questioner, I do not know.

He is certain that past time requires that movement and change have already occurred, that the present time measures ongoing movement and change, and that future time anticipates future movement and change. Yet he is puzzled about the nature of each of these three temporal dimensions: "But the two times, past and future, how can they *be*, since the past is no more and the future is not yet?" And "if the present," not being static like eternity, constantly "flows away into the past, how can we say that it *is*?" It seems that "neither future nor past actually exists" at any given moment. Only the present exists; and, because it is constantly becoming the past, its reality is problematic. Yet all "three exist in the mind" as present, he remarks (anticipating the more sophisticated analysis of Kant by almost fourteen centuries);

> the present of things past is memory, the present of things present is sight, the present of things future is expectation.

What the mind expects can pass into sensible experience; and what it attends to in sensible experience, in turn, passes into what it can remember.[9]

NATURAL SUBORDINATION.   In *On Music* Augustine specifies that the natural hierarchy of being entails proper relationships of subordination:

> For the soul must be ruled by the superior, and rule the inferior. But God alone is superior to it, and only body is inferior to it, if you mean the soul whole and entire.

This neat expression of Christian Platonism is followed by a warning that when this proper order is destroyed and the soul "is seduced by" the blandishments of "carnal concupiscence," the soul is diminished in its excellence.[10]

*   *   *

To summarize the preceding, Augustine holds that reality includes God, the unchanging Creator, and the world of changing creatures, both spiritual and physical. God has created the physical world in space. Both bodies and souls change in time, though the nature of time itself is elusive. There is a hierarchy of being, such that God, the Supreme Being, should rule all souls, which, in turn, are superior to and should rule over bodies.

Bodies

THE NATURE OF BODIES.   In *On Free Choice of the Will* Augustine analyzes bodies as complex, divisible objects of "the bodily senses. Anything that is perceived by such a sense is clearly not one but many, for it is a material object and therefore has countless parts," of which it is comprised. There can be no ultimate unity to bodies,

> for any material object, however small, surely has a right and a left, a top and a bottom, a near side and a farther side, ends and a middle. We must admit that these parts are present in any material object, however tiny, and so we must concede that no material object is truly and simply one.[11]

This is as true of the human body as of other physical creatures and helps to differentiate it from the soul (which we shall discuss in the following section).

Unlike the Manicheans and even Plato, who sometimes suggests that bodies are evil, Augustine, as a Christian, must affirm that they are good since they are creatures of an all-good God. In *The City of God* he indicates that all creatures have a valuable place in the hierarchy of reality and contribute to its overarching beauty. Moreover, he says, "it is ridiculous to condemn the faults of beasts and trees," which, by their nature, cannot measure up to the perfection of higher beings. From our own narrow, limited, biased perspectives we blame things in the

---

Ontology (from the Greek *onta*, meaning really existing things, and *logos*, meaning the study of).   The study of being; that branch of metaphysics which speculates about the essential characteristics of being as such, as opposed to the study of particular beings

physical world for not always suiting our own purposes. Relative "to our convenience or discomfort," he avers, we "may find fault with the sun itself," for being too bright or too hot. However, all bodies, being created by the perfect God, "inasmuch as they are, and have therefore a rank and species of their own, and a kind of internal harmony, are certainly good," however they may affect us subjectively.[12]

In his *Confessions* Augustine holds that God "created the world out of formless matter," which, being formless, is invisible and imperceptible. Matter is passive in its "capacity for all the **forms** into which mutable things can be changed." It is difficult for Augustine to analyze what formless matter is apart from this capacity (as it was for Aristotle); and he is tempted to say "that it is a nothing which is in some way something, or that it is and yet is not." Everything that is a thing has form; being formless, matter can only be the stuff of which bodies can be formed. This "formless matter" that is "almost-nothing" and of which all bodies are made was itself created out of nothing (*ex nihilo*) by God.[13]

SEMINAL REASONS. A vague idea of Augustine's that might be mentioned here is his notion of "seminal reasons" (*rationes seminales*), which are the imperceptible germs or "seeds" of all physical things, causally accounting for their changes and development. In *The Trinity* he writes that "certain seeds of all the things which are generated in a corporeal and visible fashion lie hidden in the corporeal elements of this world." For example, "the smallest shoot," which can become a tree "when properly planted in the earth," is itself derived from the visible seed drawn from "some grain of the same species"; but because all bodies are divisible, "we can conjecture" that the smallest visible seeds are the products of smaller, invisible ones, which give them the capacity for growth and development. Through these "seminal reasons," God, "the Creator of the invisible seeds," endows bodies with "the first beginnings" of all their **potentialities**,[14] determining how they should change in time. They seem more **substantial** and active than Aristotle's principle of potentiality, but more **teleologically** directed than ancient

thinkers conceived atoms as being. It is not quite clear how to interpret them, but through these "seeds" God can direct the future activities of bodies. Although the physical world was created all at once, aspects of it existed merely in embryonic form and needed time to become what they would eventually become.

Personality

As a Christian, Augustine is committed to the belief that God created the human soul. As he writes in *The City of God*,

> God, then, made man in His own image. For He created for him a soul endowed with **reason** and intelligence, so that he might excel all the creatures of earth, air, and sea.

The first man was created "upright" but was free to choose; his abuse of that freedom in choosing evil allegedly corrupted not only his character but humanity as it descended from him; for

> the seminal nature was there from which we were to be propagated; and this being vitiated by sin, and bound by the chain of death, and justly condemned, man could not be born of man in any other state.

This is a reference to the theological doctrine of original sin, which Augustine accepts on faith. Yet even in its fallen state, the human soul is distinguished by the "spark of reason," which is "the image of God" in humans and which renders them "more excellent than all other animals of the earth." Thanks to reason, the human soul can understand truth, love goodness, and develop the **cardinal** (from the Latin word *cardo*, meaning hinge) **virtues** of "prudence, fortitude, temperance, and righteousness" or justice. Even in their physical appearance and bodily demeanor, Augustine claims, humans are distinguished from other terrestrial creatures, standing erect, looking up to heaven, and having physical features designed to express the glory of the soul. Certain characteristics of the body, such as a manly beard, seem to exist solely as ornamentation, not being truly functional,[15] testifying to our being created in God's image.

THE ESSENCE OF THE HUMAN PERSON. Augustine's *On Free Choice of the Will* contains considerable material analyzing the nature of the human person. He admits that other animals surpass us in strength and other physical abilities, but avers that our superiority consists in our having a rational soul or a mind, which should rule the other dimensions of human nature if we are to be well-ordered. Some attributes, "for example, joking and laughing," seem distinctively human. "Anyone with a proper understanding of human nature," however, will recognize that these are derived from our rational minds and are therefore less **essential**. Of all the aspects of human nature, only the mind or rational soul can think in a characteristically human manner. As the soul is superior to the body, the mind is more powerful than physical desire and should govern it. Although the body, as created by God, is good, it is allegedly "the least valuable part of a human being."[16]

AN ANALYSIS OF HUMAN EXISTENCE.   Augustine systematically develops an analysis of human existence and its hierarchical powers. First, in order to think of ourselves as existing, as we do, we would have to exist actually, be alive, and have some understanding. Understanding **presupposes** life and is superior to it, as life presupposes mere existence and is superior to it. Our understanding, limited and fallible as it is, distinguishes us from brute animals and is our most valuable characteristic. We have the five external senses of "sight, hearing, smell, taste, and touch," with their appropriate objects (of color, sound, odor, flavor, and texture). But an "inner sense" is needed to judge the objects of these external senses; even brute animals have such an inner sense, allowing them to relate what is seen with what is smelled, for example; thus, the inner sense is not the same as reason, which is distinctly human and because of which we understand. Whereas the senses enable an animal to be aware of its environment, reason is self-aware. Whereas the external senses perceive their own objects, the inner sense can correlate these objects and judge them appropriate for avoidance or pursuit. But reason judges both external and inner senses, as the inner sense judges the objects of external senses. Thus, reason is superior to even the inner sense because "the judge is superior to the thing judged." Augustine asks his friend Evodius whether "anything that is part of our human nature" can be conceived to be "more excellent than understanding" or reason; and since the answer is "nothing at all," they agree that if anything is discovered to be superior to human

reason, it will point to something higher than human nature itself and, ultimately, to God. Even the souls that abuse their free will to sin are superior to all physical realities, including the human body, on account of reason, which constitutes "the **dignity** of their nature." Nevertheless, the rational soul, for all its glory, must struggle with "ignorance and difficulty" as punishment for the sin into which we are born:

Because of ignorance, error warps our actions; because of difficulty, our lives are a torment and an affliction.

Furthermore, Augustine insists, it is just that we should experience the punishments of "ignorance, difficulty, and mortality" as a result of our inherited corruption, even though original sin is not our own fault.[17]

THE NATURE OF THE SOUL.   Augustine's dialogue *The Magnitude of the Soul* is also important. Evodius poses six questions about the soul for Augustine to consider:

1. What is the origin of the soul?
2. What is its nature?
3. What is its magnitude?
4. What is the reason for its union with the body?
5. What is the effect of this union?
6. What is the effect of its separation from the body?

In answer to the first question, Augustine holds that the soul is a spiritual substance (not composed of any combination "of earth or water or air or fire," the four elements of physical things) created by God. Second, it is immortal and Godlike in its spiritual nature (being rational and free). Third, the question of the soul's "magnitude" inquires about its "greatness," which cannot be physically measured, since the soul is not bodily, but which is nevertheless real; its greatness is to be measured in terms of its powers or capacities, such as that of memory. Putting these ideas together, Augustine can now define the soul (*anima*) as "a certain kind of substance, sharing in reason, fitted to rule the body" (*substantia quaedam rationis particeps, regendo corpori accommodata*). Augustine works out seven degrees or levels of the soul's powers, ranked "from the lowest to the highest" as

first, Animation; the second, Sensation; the third, Art; the fourth, Virtue; the fifth, Tranquillity; the sixth, Approach; the seventh, Contemplation.

He explains that the first three of these are powers the soul has regarding the body, the next two are powers it has regarding itself, and the last two are powers it has regarding God; it can give life, sensation, and artful movement to the body, secure virtue and tranquillity for itself, and spiritually approach and contemplate God. Augustine briefly answers Evodius' final three questions. Fourth, then, the soul is united to the body so that it may move and control it. Fifth, the effect of the soul's union with "this mortal and frail body" is that they must someday separate with the death of the body. And, sixth, the effect of this separation on the soul depends on whether the soul is to be punished for sins or rewarded for virtue.[18]

THE RATIONAL SOUL AS ESSENTIAL. We can now consider one of Augustine's attempts to define the human person:

Man, then, . . . is a rational soul with a mortal and earthly body in its service.[19]

This is a very Platonic analysis, viewing the soul, and not the body, as essential. Nevertheless, he elsewhere accepts the more Aristotelian definition:

Man is an animal, rational and mortal.

He comments that animality represents our genus and that, of the two characteristics essential to our species, rationality distinguishes us "from brute animals," whereas mortality distinguishes us from God.[20] On this second definition, it would seem, the disembodied soul would merely be an aspect of a human, as is later the case for Aquinas.

In *On the Immortality of the Soul* Augustine holds that reason, which is essential to human nature, either "is the aspect of the mind which perceives the true *per se* and not through the body; or it is the contemplation of the true, not through the body; or it is the true itself which is contemplated." In any case, the mind or rational soul is independent of the body (which will provide a basis for arguing that it does not die with the body). We might try to specify where the soul is located in relation to the body, if we mistakenly think of it in physical terms.

But the soul is present as a whole not only in the entire mass of a body, but also in every least part of the body at the same time

—not as a physical thing but as an aware, animating, motivating principle.[21]

SENSATION, MEMORY, UNDERSTANDING, AND WILL. The soul is the source of sensation, memory, understanding, and will in human nature, each of which we shall now briefly consider (setting up the next two sections on "Knowledge" and "Freedom"). In *On Music* Augustine analyzes sensation as an activity of the soul that can produce feelings of pleasure or pain in the body. Such feelings enable the soul to act for the good of the body. "And by such actions it willingly associates proper things and resists improper ones," without itself being essentially affected, or changed in its very nature, by the passions of the body.[22] In his *Confessions* he extols the great power of the human memory to retain images drawn from past sensation and to recombine them freely. It can even transcend sense images by dealing with abstract ideas and principles, such as those of mathematics. Third, it can retrieve feelings no longer being experienced. As he writes,

For I remember that in the past I was cheerful, but I am not cheerful now; and I remember past sadness yet am not sad. I remember past fears without fear, and past desires without desire.

It is not clear to him, however, whether or not this is done through images. This wonderfully great power of memory is identified with the mind in human nature, rather than with the body.[23] In *The Trinity* he analyzes understanding and will, as well as memory. Memory is seen as an aid to understanding. Mental ability refers to a person's capacities of memory, understanding, and will; learning refers to the contents of memory and understanding; and mental usefulness refers to the capacity of the will to dispose of the contents of memory and understanding. He says that

these three, the memory, the understanding, and the will, are . . . not three minds but one mind, . . . not three substances, but one substance.

They are interrelated in being able to refer to each other.

For I remember that I have memory, understanding, and will; and I understand that I understand, will, and remember; and I will that I will, remember, and understand.

Knowledge requires memory, is identified with understanding, and can activate the will.[24] In *The Happy Life* Augustine asks whether the soul requires its own form of nourishment as the body requires food. His mother, Monica, replies that "the soul has no other nourishment than the knowledge and understanding of things." Augustine concurs that, as a body deprived of food is malnourished, feeble, and prone to illness, so is the human soul, when starved of knowledge.[25]

Knowledge

DIVINE ILLUMINATION. For Augustine, philosophy and religion are two interrelated paths to knowledge. In *Of True Religion* he maintains that "philosophy, i.e., the pursuit of wisdom, cannot be quite divorced from religion." Reason and religious authority are the twin foundations of knowledge, the first leading to understanding and the second to the conviction of belief. In its quest for knowledge, reason makes judgments regarding both the workings of the senses and their objects: "It knows why the oar dipped in water must appear crooked though it is really straight, and why the eyes must see it that way."[26] What we want to know through reason is the truth; but for the Christian Augustine that is ultimately identified with God. Thus, he prays in his *Soliloquies,* "Thee I invoke, O God, the Truth, in, by and through whom all truths are true" (*Te invoco, Deus Veritas, in quo et a quo et per quem vera sunt, quae vera sunt omnia*). He sees God as a source of spiritual light, which must flood our minds if they are to attain knowledge—"the Intelligible Light, in, by and through whom all intelligible things are illumined." This theory of divine illumination is reminiscent of Plato's **analogy** of the Sun. But what are the most worthy objects of knowledge to be illumined? Augustine answers, "I desire to know God and the soul" (*Deum et animam scire cupio*). Nothing else is so deserving of knowledge, and he regrets not yet understanding both of them: "But I love nothing but God and the soul, and I know neither" (*Nunc autem nihil aliud amo quam Deum et animam, quorum neutrum scio*). So, he strives to understand God and the soul. But, as he cannot see the visible things of the Earth without their being illuminated by the Sun, so he cannot know these intelligible realities without divine illumination of the truth. He adopts a version of the **correspondence theory** of truth when he writes,

> Truth is that which is as it seems to him who knows it, if he will and can know it.[27]

LEARNING, BELIEF, AND TRUTH. In *On Free Choice of the Will* Augustine argues that all true learning is good and that we can never come to know evil things, such as how to commit a crime, through true learning:

> Well then, if all understanding is good, and no one who does not understand learns, then everyone who learns is doing good. For everyone who learns, understands; and everyone who understands is doing good.

On this view, every genuine teacher must be good:

> If he is evil, he is no teacher; and if he is a teacher, he is not evil.

While distinguishing between learning through faith and learning through reason, Augustine maintains that we must first believe as a basis for rational knowledge, and he endorses the scriptural text, "Unless you believe, you will not understand" (*Isaiah* 7:9). The object of reason common to all knowing minds is eternal, immutable truth, such as that found in mathematics. The "fixed, secure, and unchangeable" order of numbers is perceivable by the mind through "an inner light of which the bodily sense knows nothing." Although it is temporally, **contingently**, and privately true that you did or did not have breakfast yesterday, it is eternally, necessarily, and commonly true that seven plus three equals ten. Other common truths are nonmathematical—for example, "one ought to live justly; inferior things should be subjected to superior things; like should be compared with like; everyone should be given what is rightly his." These are all held to be "true and unchangeable rules of wisdom." Both mathematical truths and these rules of wisdom should be regarded as eternal and immutable, as well as common. Now this sort of truth must be related to our knowing minds in one of three **logically** possible ways: "Is it more excellent than our minds, or equal to them, or even inferior to them?" It cannot be inferior to our minds, since we judge "*in accordance with* it" rather than judging "*about*" its truth; and it cannot be equal

---

Correspondence theory. The traditional view that a belief or judgment is true if it conforms to reality, subscribed to by almost all Western philosophers before Kant; Kant's revolutionary proposal is that objects must conform to the requirements of the mind rather than the other way around; after Kant, coherence and pragmatic usefulness become alternative criteria of truth

to our minds since it is unchangeable, while they are changing. By a **process of elimination,** we **deductively** draw the correct **inference**:

> Therefore, since the truth is neither inferior nor equal to our minds, we can conclude that it is superior to them and more excellent than they are.[28]

(Later, we shall see that this inference that truth is higher than our reason provides a basis for arguing that God must exist, since God is the ultimate Truth.)

THE OVERCOMING OF SCEPTICISM. Remembering that Augustine, as a young man, was tempted by the scepticism of the New Academy, we should not be surprised that he tries to conquer such scepticism in one of his earliest writings, *Against the Academicians*. "The Academicians are of the opinion that knowledge cannot be attained by man in so far as those things are concerned which pertain to philosophy," and their "**conclusion** is that the wise man should not assent to anything." According to this sceptical view, "everything is uncertain." This need not deny that there is truth but only that we have any certain access to it, as it seems to be "obscured because of the darkness of our nature." But Augustine uses logic to attack such scepticism. We can be "certain either that there is or is not one world; and if there is not one, there are either a finite or an **infinite** number of worlds"; likewise, any world either is or is not eternal. "For those **disjunctions** are true nor can anyone confuse them with any likeness to what is false." They are matters of certain knowledge and not of mere uncertain opinion. Likewise, mathematical truths resist the challenges of scepticism; "for that three threes are nine and represent the square of intelligible numbers is necessary," regardless of human fallibility. And what of the alleged untrustworthiness of sense experience? To use a previous example, is it true that the straight oar that is partially submerged in water looks bent?

> It certainly is true. For when the reason is added for its appearing thus, if the oar dipped in the water seemed

straight, I should rather blame my eyes for the false report. For they did not see what should have been seen, given the phenomenon of the refraction of light. As long as we carefully judge that it *looks* bent rather than rashly asserting that it *is* bent, we are invulnerable to the sceptical **refutations** of the Academicians. Augustine is confident that the authority of the Scriptures and the philosophical **argumentation** of Plato, Plotinus, and other Platonists will continue to expose the specious errors of scepticism.[29]

Is there any **existential** claim, relating to matters of fact independent of the mind, that we can certainly know as **categorically** true or false? We experience such claims every day of our lives. And, as Augustine says in *Concerning the Teacher*,

> Whenever we say anything, either the hearer does not know whether what is said is false or true, or he knows that it is false, or he knows that it is true.

The sceptic claims that only the first option proves genuine, the second and third options being bogus. Augustine continues,

> In the first mode he will either believe (or accept in good confidence), or he will form an opinion, or he will hesitate; in the second mode he will resist the statement and reject it; in the third he merely confirms.[30]

What we seek now is an existential claim that can either be confirmed as certainly true or rejected as certainly false, to the detriment of scepticism.

In a well-known passage in *The City of God* Augustine presents three truths of which we can have absolutely certain knowledge:

> For we both are, and know that we are, and delight in our being, and our knowledge of it.

The first of these, at least, is an existential fact of the sort we are seeking. But how can this existential truth-claim be proved by argumentation? He explains,

> I am not at all afraid of the arguments of the Academicians, who say, What if you are deceived? For if I am deceived, I am. For he who is not, cannot be deceived; and if I am deceived, by this same token I am.

This insight that "if I am deceived, I am" (*si fallor, sum*) precedes Descartes's celebrated "I think,

---

Deduction.   Reasoning in which the truth of all the premises of an argument supposedly necessitates the truth of its conclusion as certain, as opposed to induction

Inference.   A process of deductive or inductive reasoning from one or more statements, called premises, to another, called the conclusion

Disjunction (from the Latin *disjunctio*, meaning a separation).   The act of separating or the fact of things being separated or disjoined; in logic, this refers to a uniting of propositions, as expressed with the word "or" in the inclusive sense; in order for a logical disjunction to be true, at least one of its disjuncts must be true.

therefore I am" (***cogito, ergo sum***) passage by more than twelve centuries. Augustine continues,

> And since I am if I am deceived, how am I deceived in believing that I am? for it is certain that I am if I am deceived. Since, therefore, I, the person deceived, should be, even if I were deceived, certainly I am not deceived in this knowledge that I am.[31]

And the self thus known to exist is known as a mind or rational soul, rather than as a body, since it is only as such that it can believe and be deceived. Thus, Augustine has confirmed an existential truth against the sceptics. He has simultaneously achieved knowledge of the soul, one of the two most worthy objects of understanding; later, we shall see (in the section on "Religion") how he strives to establish knowledge of God, the other one, as well.

Freedom

FREE WILL VS. DIVINE FOREKNOWLEDGE. As the rational soul is characterized by understanding, which is oriented towards knowledge, it is also characterized by will, which is oriented towards free choice. In *The City of God* Augustine considers Cicero's reasoning against God's **foreknowledge**, presenting it as a "chain" or **hypothetical argument**:

> If there is free will, all things do not happen according to fate; if all things do not happen according to fate, there is not a certain order of causes; and if there is not a certain order of causes, neither is there a certain order of things foreknown by God.

Against this argument, Augustine maintains both human freedom of the will and divine foreknowledge of all future events. But where is the flaw in the reasoning, the weak link in the chain? It is with the second **premise**. Even if there is free will and an absence of any all-encompassing **deterministic** fate, there can still be "for God a certain order of all causes," among which causes are our freely choosing wills. Even

Cicero "confesses that whatever happens must be preceded by a cause." We must recognize that there are "**voluntary** causes," as well as physical ones, all of which are foreknown by the omniscient God. Whatever is utterly beyond our power of choice constitutes "*our* **necessity**," as, for example, is the fact of our mortality. But "our wills by which we live uprightly or wickedly are not under such a necessity; for we do many things which, if we were not willing, we should certainly not do." God's foreknowledge of what we shall choose does not **negate** the freedom of our wills.

> Therefore we are by no means compelled, either, retaining the prescience of God, to take away the freedom of the will, or, retaining the freedom of the will, to deny that He is prescient of future things.

If the two are, indeed, logically compatible, then the challenge to choose between them is a **false dilemma**. In order "that we may live well," we must affirm freedom of choice. Otherwise, it would be "in vain that laws are enacted, and that reproaches, exhortations, praises, and vituperations are had recourse to,"[32] and moral responsibility would be compromised.

THE NECESSITY OF FREE WILL. As the title suggests, Augustine's *On Free Choice of the Will* deals with this very topic. Evodius asks "why God gave human beings free choice of the will," given that it enables us to sin. Augustine's answer is that it is a **necessary condition** for virtuous action: "The fact that human beings could not live rightly without it was sufficient reason for God to give it." All moral accountability, for better and for worse, requires it:

> No action would be either a sin or a good deed if it were not performed by the will, and so both punishment and reward would be unjust if human beings had no free will.

Then Evodius raises the question of whether free will, which we can misuse to sin, should be regarded as good. Augustine replies that some goods of the body,

---

Cogito (from the Latin, *cogito, ergo sum,* meaning I think, therefore I am). Descartes's insight that I know I must mentally exist insofar as I experience any sort of thinking

Foreknowledge. Knowledge, traditionally attributed to God, of that which is yet to be

Hypothetical argument. A valid form of inference derived from at least one hypothetical, or conditional (e.g., if-then), premise

Negation. Generally, a denial; in logic, the claim or assertion that a proposition is false, so that a given proposition and its negation have the opposite truth values

False dilemma (bifurcation). The fallacy of presuming that an either-or distinction is exhaustive (and/or mutually exclusive) when other alternatives exist

which is itself a lesser good than the soul, can be misused; though, for example, sight, the highest of the external senses, can be used to intrude on others' privacy, it is nevertheless a good power of the body. Evodius presses Augustine further "to prove that free will is a good thing," to which the reply is that it must be, since it is the necessary means to the good end of "living rightly." Yet it is "an intermediate good," in that it can be used wrongly, lower than virtue, which can never be used wrongly, but superior to all physical goods. Evodius next asks how God's omniscient foreknowledge does not necessitate sin and annihilate freedom (and thus also responsibility). Augustine himself poses the problem in logical form:

> if God foreknows that someone is going to sin, then it is necessary that he sin. But if it is necessary, the will has no choice about whether to sin; there is an inescapable and fixed necessity.

He points out that this argument is based on the false presupposition that God's foreknowledge encompasses only natural necessity and not also voluntary causation. But if God's foreknowledge is all-encompassing, it must include our human will, which "could not be a will unless it were in our power. Therefore, he also foreknows this power" and cannot destroy it through foreknowledge. But Evodius does not yet understand how the will, as foreknown by God, can be free rather than extrinsically determined. Augustine asks whether we could not know that someone else was about to sin freely. Evodius answers that if we "foreknew something with certainty," rather than making a reasonable guess, it would happen necessarily. But Augustine replies that, as our knowing that something will occur does not necessarily cause it to occur, so "God's foreknowledge" of our choices is not coercive.[33]

Morality

GOOD WILL AND EVIL WILL. *On Free Choice of the Will* is also seriously concerned with good and evil, virtue and **vice**. Augustine analyzes the root of evil in an act such as adultery as consisting in "inordinate desire" (*libido*). Whereas "cupidity desires its object," fear drives us to avoid its object. Good and wicked people alike "desire to live without fear." But this desire motivates good people to "turn their love away from things that cannot be possessed without the fear of losing them," such as physical beauty, money, and earthly power. "The wicked, on the other hand, try to get rid of anything that prevents them from enjoying such things securely." It is evil to sacrifice higher (e.g., spiritual) goods out of cupidity for lower (e.g., material) ones. Augustine defines "a **good will**" as one "by which we desire to live upright and honorable lives and to attain the highest wisdom." (Unlike Kant, who would make famous the moral ideal of good will almost fourteen centuries later, Augustine does not specify the necessary motive for such desire.) He regards the good will as more valuable than all earthly goods and as leading to the exercise of the four cardinal virtues of prudence, "the knowledge of what is to be desired and what is to be avoided," fortitude, the quality through which "we have no fear of misfortune or of the loss of things that are not in our power," temperance, "the disposition that checks and restrains the desire for things that it is wicked to desire," and justice, the habit whereby we will that "all people are given their due." These cardinal virtues are the four virtues on which the entire door of natural morality revolves. They will be exhibited by a person of good will and render a life morally praiseworthy, deserving of happiness, and actually happy, insofar as that is possible in the natural world.[34]

By contrast, an evil will lusts after such uncontrollable lower goods as "wealth, honors, pleasures, physical beauty, and everything else that one cannot get or keep simply by willing." There is an eternal, immutable law derived from God, by which people of good will try to live; and there is a temporal law, rooted in the transient reality of the natural world, to which the unhappy people of ill will remain subject. The eternal law is superior to the temporal law and should supersede it. In a statement of extreme Platonism, Augustine says, "So the eternal law demands that we purify our love by turning it away from temporal things and toward what is eternal." This either-or bifurcation seems to require a rejection of five sorts of temporal goods:

Good will.   Generally (as in Augustine), the desire to live virtuous lives; but, more specifically (as in Kant, who considers good will to be the only intrinsic, unqualified good), the will to do our duty out of a rational sense of duty

1. The goods of the body, "such as health, keen senses, strength, beauty," and so forth;
2. The bogus sort of freedom that consists of an absence of restraints;
3. Other people we care about, such as "parents, brothers and sisters, a spouse, children, neighbors, relatives, friends, and anyone who is bound to us by some need";
4. The political organization of the state; and
5. Physical "property, which includes anything over which the law gives us control and which we have a recognized right to sell or give away."

Yet it would seem that we must love at least other people, to the extent that that love does not divert us from God and the goods of the soul. Indeed, all these temporal goods can be used well or badly, depending on our attitude. The virtuous person of good will is "ready to possess and make use of them when there is need, and even readier to lose them and do without them"; by contrast, the vicious person of ill will is so slavishly desirous of them as to neglect eternal, spiritual values for their sake. Sin consists in the will's freely turning away from unchangeable, eternal goods towards the inferior temporal goods. This is a defective, but voluntary, movement of the will, caused by us rather than by God, and bound to lead to unhappiness.[35]

SUICIDE. For example, the person who "is driven by his unbearable troubles to desire death with all his heart" can jeopardize the well-being of his eternal soul and his own true happiness because of his inordinate and misguided desire for peace and respite from the suffering of this life. This moral problem of suicide is pursued more carefully in *The City of God*. The scriptural injunction, "Thou shalt not kill" (*Exodus* 20:13), Augustine claims, "prohibits suicide," since it applies to all rational creatures, including ourselves. He admires "the saintly Job, who endured dreadful evils," more than pagans like Cato, who killed himself to escape his troubles. Because suicide is "a detestable and damnable wickedness," it cannot be justified even by the wish to avoid another future sin, such as that of adultery. As Augustine rhetorically asks, "Is it not better to commit a wickedness which penitence may heal, than a crime which leaves no place for healing contrition?" The only exception to this general proscription would be if God clearly commanded our self-destruction, as "was the

case with Samson" in the Old Testament. But we would need to be absolutely certain that we have correctly understood that it is God's command; otherwise, we shall foolishly "escape the ills of time by plunging into those of eternity."[36]

TWO WAYS OF LIFE. Because of the original sin of our first ancestors, "human nature was altered for the worse," which fallen state "was transmitted also to their posterity," leaving us with two alternative ways of living our lives. These correspond to the realms of the "two cities," the earthly city and the city of God. "The one consists of those who wish to live after the flesh, the other of those who wish to live after the spirit"; each approach pursues its own distinctive kind of peace. The person of good will "resolves to love God, and to love his neighbours as himself," in accordance with the commandments of the New Testament (*Matthew* 22:36–40; *Mark* 12:30–31). The good will is motivated by "well-directed love." Proper love must be directed to three objects—God, oneself, and other people; and it involves negative and positive courses of action—"that a man, in the first place, injure no one, and, in the second, do good to every one he can reach." Love that is "well-directed" will move us to practice the four cardinal virtues of prudence, fortitude, temperance, and justice, in obedience to God's eternal law.[37]

SIN. In *The Nature of the Good* Augustine argues that all things are good to the extent that they are "measured, formed, and ordered," evil being "nothing but the corruption of natural measure, form or order." Nothing is purely evil, and evil is nothing but "a diminishing of good." Something deprived of all its good would cease to be.[38] This is as true of an evil will as of anything else; the most wicked soul imaginable must remain good to some minuscule extent in order to continue to be. As he writes in *Of True Religion*, "the sum-total of evil" consists of wrongful choices and their penalties. We mistakenly assume that something is entirely evil if we consider it out of the context of the whole of which it is a part. "The colour black in a picture," by analogy, "may very well be beautiful if you take the picture as a whole." So an evil soul, though blameworthy and regrettable in its evil, may contribute to the larger pattern of creation. But, properly regarded, "there is no evil except sin and sin's penalty, that is, a voluntary abandonment of highest being, and toil among inferior beings which is not voluntary" but punishment for ill will.[39]

What exactly is the sin to which voluntary wrong-doing leads?

> Sin, then, is any transgression in deed, or word, or desire, of the eternal law. The eternal law is the divine order or will of God

(*lex est ratio divina et voluntas Dei*). Sin always involves an inversion of the "natural order in man," whereby "the soul is superior to the body" and, within the soul, "reason is superior" to all the other parts, and theoretical reason, oriented to contemplation, is superior to practical reason, oriented to action. The ultimate object of contemplation and good will is God.[40]

LYING.   Another example of sin (in addition to suicide, which we have considered) is lying. In the *Enchiridion* Augustine acknowledges that some people hold that there can be circumstances in which it is "the duty of a good man to lie," and not merely morally permissible to do so. He writes, "To me, however, it seems certain that every lie is a sin, though it makes a great difference with what intention and on what subject one lies." Lying to help another is less grievous than a lie intended to cause harm. Lying requires the will to deceive, so that the person who says what is false while honestly believing it to be true is not lying; **conversely**, the person who speaks the truth while thinking it false is lying. Some lies, because of their subject matter, do little or no harm; by contrast, it is most harmful when a person "does not believe what leads to eternal life, or believes what leads to eternal death," because of a lie. However, every lie, "considered in itself, is an evil: a great evil if it concern a great matter, a small evil if it concern a small matter, but yet always an evil."[41] This Christian moral rigorism can be contrasted with Socrates' view that it is sometimes right or even required that we not tell the truth, lest it seriously harm innocent persons.

Society

Human choices and interpersonal relations must be ordered by law, and it is crucial that society be governed by just laws. Indeed, in *On Free Choice of the Will* Augustine maintains

> that an unjust law is no law at all,

since justice is a necessary condition of genuine, legitimate law. As we have seen, he distinguishes between the temporal law, which is changeable, and the eternal law, which comes from God and is immutable. Now he adds that

> nothing is just and legitimate in the temporal law except that which human beings have derived from the eternal law.[42]

Thus, God's eternal law is the source of all just laws passed by humans; to the extent that the laws of society are in conflict with the eternal laws, they are not genuine laws at all.

SOCIAL JUSTICE AND WAR.   *The City of God* is perhaps our best resource for Augustine's theory of society, in general, and his views on social justice, in particular. He not only rejects the cynical view that a "**republic** cannot be governed without injustice" but agrees with Cicero that, in fact, "it cannot be governed without the most absolute justice." He goes further to assert that "Rome never was a republic, because true justice had never a place in it." Indeed, he thinks, only a Christian society can be founded on true justice. The just person is spiritually free even if enslaved by an unjust society; conversely, the unjust person, "even if he reigns, is a slave" of his own vices. The evils imposed on just persons "by unjust rulers are not the punishment of crime" but should be regarded as "the test of virtue." The unjust person is attached to the earthly city "by the love of self, even to the contempt of God"; by contrast, the just person is attached to the heavenly city "by the love of God, even to the contempt of self." This is in contrast to the Greek view (i.e., of Aristotle) that the virtue of magnanimity requires a healthy, proper self-love and is incompatible with a "pusillanimous" humility. Augustine also distinguishes between just and unjust wars; though war may be necessary and morally justifiable, it should never be motivated by hatred or the lust for conquest. "For it is the wrong-doing of the opposing party which compels the wise man to wage just wars." And, even when warfare is justified, Augustine maintains,

> it is obvious that peace is the end sought for by war. For every man seeks peace by waging war, but no man seeks war by making peace.[43]

Converse.   Loosely, a reversal of ideas or an opposite assumption

THE STATUS OF WOMEN.   Another significant topic of social relations discussed in *The City of God* is the status of women. There Augustine endorses the scriptural view that God created humans "male and female—in other words, two sexes manifestly distinct" for purposes of reproduction. They are naturally related by both "the matrimonial union," which God has ordained, and "the origin of the woman, who was created from the side of the man," as reported in *Genesis*. He holds that women are as surely God's creatures as are men, but that "her creation from man" indicates woman's natural union with the male. He even considers whether the **resurrected** bodies of women will be male rather than female, since the resurrected body is to be perfected; but he concludes that women's resurrected bodies will remain female, since "the sex of woman is not a vice, but nature."[44] In *Confessions* Augustine writes that man was made in God's "image and likeness," due to man's "power of reason and understanding" fit to dominate all brute animals, but that

> woman has been created corporeally for man: for though she has indeed a nature like that of man in her mind and rational intelligence, yet by her bodily sex she is subjected to the sex of her husband.[45]

This androcentric view of women tends to regard them as naturally subordinate to men, rather than as independent and **autonomous**.

Religion

FAITH VS. REASON.   *The Advantage of Believing* was composed soon after Augustine's ordination in 391. Against the Manicheans, he defends the temporal priority of faith over reason. Faith submits to the authority of the Scriptures, which is transmitted in four ways: "according to history, according to aetiology, according to analogy, and according to allegory." Historical tradition tells us what has been said or done; aetiological tradition explains the causal reasons for things being said or done; analogical tradition establishes comparisons, as, for example, between the Old and New Testaments; and allegorical tradition shows how certain writings are to be understood figuratively rather than literally. Thus, even faith requires an element of rational interpretation. Still, faith is essentially a submission to authority without understanding, and the question arises as to whether that is legitimate regarding religion. Augustine questions whether religion should be the prerogative of those who are blessed with great powers of understanding. Also, he maintains, the open receptivity of faith renders the mind more fit to receive the truth at the level of rational understanding. The two sorts of people who are "praiseworthy" regarding religion are those who have already discovered the truth and those who are doing their best to do so. Three other sorts of persons are "worthy of censure": those with incorrect opinions, who "think that they know what they do not know"; those who "realize that they do not know, but do not seek in such a way as to find"; and those who "neither think they know nor wish to seek" in any way at all.[46]

Augustine distinguishes among understanding, which is "always without fault," belief, which is "at times faulty," and mere opinion, which is "never without fault." Belief is "blameworthy," according to him, when it is "too readily held" or when it attributes to God what "is unworthy of Him." Otherwise, belief is without fault, so long as it is held with the honest realization that it is not rational knowledge. Mere opinion is objectionable because it stifles the incentive to gain knowledge and involves the rashness of acceptance without foundation. True understanding, by contrast, must be of the truth and on adequate grounds.

> What we understand, accordingly, we owe to reason; what we believe, to authority; and what we have an opinion on, to error. But everyone who understands also believes, and everyone who has an opinion believes, too; but not everyone who believes understands, and no one who merely has an opinion understands.

Fideists (who oppose knowledge while supporting faith) and sceptics (who deny both knowledge and faith) are both enemies of truth. Those (like the gnostics) who attack faith without understanding would undermine parental authority since children must believe and obey their parents, even before understanding why they rule as they do. The utility of belief is that it gives the soul access to truth prior to rational knowledge and prepares it to attain understanding.[47]

Resurrection (from the Latin *resurrectus*, meaning risen again).   Returning to life after being dead

Fideism (from the Latin *fides*, meaning faith).   The view that religious truth must be accepted purely on faith rather than justified by reason

In *On Faith in Things Unseen* Augustine defends Christianity against those who ridicule it as too credulous. He observes (as William James would do fifteen centuries later) that we all normally believe all sorts of things for which we have no tangible proof:

> Tell me, I ask you, with what eyes do you see your friend's will toward you? For, no will can be seen with bodily eyes. Or, indeed, do you also see in your mind that which is taking place in the mind of another?

It would be foolish to forswear friendship because it cannot be sensibly demonstrated. The gnostics who ridicule Christianity themselves must believe in some things for which they have no adequate evidence; otherwise, they could not function as normal humans in everyday life. The interpersonal relationships of human society require faith in what cannot be seen. Often, we believe on the basis of "certain manifestations" experienced, as of friendly behavior patterns. Likewise, religious faith is based on "certain manifestations," such as the fulfillment of prophecies and "the unexpected illumination of the human race by divine brightness" in the wake of Christ's life on Earth.[48] Thus, Christians do not render themselves ridiculous by believing in religious doctrines that cannot be proved, such as the **mystery** of the Incarnation.

THE NATURE AND EXISTENCE OF GOD.   On the topics of God and religious faith, as on so many other topics, *On Free Choice of the Will* is a valuable resource for the views of this thinker, who would become a Christian saint. Augustine maintains that God, being all-good, never does evil. On the other hand, God does cause some people to suffer evil as punishment for their own wrongdoing. We should conceive of God as supreme, omnipotent, the immutable Creator, the most excellent of all beings, and the just Ruler of all creation. But how do we know that anything exists corresponding to such an idea? Remember we have seen that Augustine argues that reason is the highest "part of our human nature" and thus superior to anything else of this Earth. He asks Evodius if he would be willing to call "God" anything shown to exist that "is more excellent than our reason." Evodius cautiously responds that he would do so only if "nothing is superior" to what is shown to be higher than reason.

Also, recall that we have shown how Augustine establishes that there is eternal, immutable truth, such as that of mathematics and the rules of wisdom, superior to human reason itself. But whether this truth is itself the highest reality (and therefore God) or subordinate to God, God's existence can be established as rationally certain.

> For if there is something more excellent than the truth, then that is God; if not, the truth itself is God. So in either case you cannot deny that God exists.[49]

THE PROBLEM OF EVIL.   But how can we explain the evil of the world, given an all-good and perfect God who created all aspects of our world? Augustine argues that everything real is good insofar as it is real:

> For every nature is either corruptible or incorruptible. If it is an incorruptible nature, it is better than a corruptible nature; and if it is a corruptible nature, it is undoubtedly good, since corruption makes it less good. Therefore, every nature is good.

When we condemn something as "evil," it is because of "a flaw," an imperfection contrary to its nature. However, this implies that its unflawed nature is good. And it is only voluntary defects that are morally blameworthy.[50]

Augustine also discusses this problem of evil in the *Enchiridion,* where he holds that God made all things good, though not equally good. If abstracted from the context of all creation, some good things appear evil. "Taken as a whole, however, they are very good, because their *ensemble* constitutes the universe in all its wonderful order and beauty." That which we call evil is really "but the absence of good" and allegedly contributes to our appreciation of the whole of reality—"for we enjoy and value the good more when we compare it with the evil." Only God is perfectly good; the goodness of creatures, being imperfect, is subject to corruption. Evil is the corruption of good; and, since all being or reality must be good to some extent, evil is parasitic on good and cannot exist by itself. Augustine himself acknowledges the **paradox** (or apparent **contradiction**) of this position:

> From all this we arrive at the curious result: that since every being, so far as it is a being, is good, we just seem

---

Mystery.   A doctrine, usually associated with religious truth, that defies complete rational understanding

Contradiction (from the Latin *contradictio,* meaning a speaking against or refutation).   Loosely, a denial or the act of opposing; in logic, the relationship between two propositions, such that one must be true and the other false

to say that what is good is evil, and that nothing but what is good can be evil, seeing that every being is good, and that no evil can exist except in a being.

Thus, a human being "is a good thing," and a wicked human is, to that extent, "an evil good." Augustine also tellingly admits that this constitutes an exception to the law of **noncontradiction**:

Accordingly, in the case of these **contraries** which we call good and evil, the rule of the logicians, that two contraries cannot be predicated at the same time of the same thing, does not hold.

The notion that there can be exceptions to the laws of logic might amaze Aristotle. But, for Augustine, the paradox attached to evil is that, though it is the contrary of good, it "cannot exist without good or in anything that is not good." So, God is the ultimate source of all other realities, which are imperfectly good in their natures, subject to corruption, and thus the root of evil. Augustine is sure that God's divine providence is such that the permitting of evil will ultimately be justified: "For He judged it better to bring good out of evil, than not to permit any evil to exist."[51] But we do not yet understand how this will come to pass.

HUMAN UNDERSTANDING OF GOD. Our understanding of God is inevitably imperfect. But in *The Trinity* Augustine advises us to conceive of God

as good without quality, as great without quantity, as the Creator who lacks nothing, who rules but from no position, and who contains all things without an external form, as being whole everywhere without limitation of space, as eternal without time, as making mutable things without any change in Himself, and as a Being without passion.

Thus, our attempts to conceive of God positively tend to require qualification.

But God is without doubt a substance, or perhaps essence would be a better term, which the Greeks call *ousia*.

For God is that Being that is not "susceptible of **accidents**" or change, the necessary and immutable Being. We speak of the Trinity in terms of "one essence or substance, three persons"; in other words, the single divine substance is shared by the three persons of the Trinity—the Father, the Son, and the Holy Spirit. But ultimately, we must admit that we cannot understand how three persons can share the same substance, that it is a mystery which "**transcends** all the limits of our wonted manner of speaking."[52] There are insuperable limits to what we can understand regarding God and the doctrines of religion, and even what we can understand must be cultivated on the basis of faith. As Augustine writes,

Do you want to understand? Believe. For God said through the prophet, "Unless you believe, you will not understand"

(*Isaiah* 7:9).[53] This Augustinian doctrine of "faith seeking understanding" (as Anselm later called it) would dominate Christian philosophy throughout medieval times.

Immortality

As a Christian, Augustine is committed to the immortality of the rational soul; as a Platonist, he believes he can demonstrate it. In his *Soliloquies* he imagines himself involved in a dialogue with Reason, in which he admits that he does not yet know that he is immortal but would most dearly wish to know it. He agrees that falsity is eternal. But Reason observes that falsity is impossible without a living soul in which it subsists. "Therefore the soul lives eternally." But if there were no falsity, there would only be truth. Again, truth can only subsist in a living soul. Thus, again, it seems that the soul must always be alive. However, Augustine realizes that the loophole in the argument is that there could be an endless succession of mortal souls perceiving truth and falsity, rather than any that are truly immortal. But Reason still insists that all learning subsists in the mind as truth.

If a thing, *A*, existing in another thing, *B*, lasts for ever, *B* must last for ever.

But truth is eternal.

Therefore, if learning is eternal, the mind must also be eternal.[54]

However, what if this argument establishes only the eternity of the divine Mind and not the immortality of the human soul? It seems more work is required.

In *On the Immortality of the Soul*, written around the time of his baptism, Augustine pursues a similar line of argumentation. Science (in the sense of a systematic

---

Contrary (from the Latin *contra*, meaning opposite or against). Loosely, what is opposed or the opposite; in logic, contraries are two propsitions such that it is impossible for both to be true, although they could both be false

Transcendence. That which is higher than or beyond the realm of natural experience, as opposed to immanence—e.g., the God of deism is transcendent; for Kantians, that which is transcendent is necessarily unknowable

body of knowledge) exists in the human mind; for, otherwise, it could not exercise reason as it does.

> If science [*disciplina*] exists anywhere, and cannot exist except in that which lives; and if it is eternal, and nothing in which an eternal thing exists can be non-eternal; then that in which science exists lives eternally.

But science must be eternal because its reality is not susceptible to change.

> Therefore the human mind always lives.

A second argument, following a different line of thought, shows that because reason is better than body, which is a substance, it must likewise be a substance. Whereas the body is mutable, reason, which understands immutable truth, is immutable, which is better. But, being an immutable substance, reason "is not a harmony of the body" or essentially affected by the body's changes, such as death. Thus, reason, which "either is the mind or is in the mind," is immortal. A third line of argumentation maintains that mind is essentially spiritual life animating the body. "Hence the mind cannot die. For if anything can lack life, this thing is not mind which animates, but a thing which has been animated," such as the body. When the mind or rational soul separates from the body, the latter dies and becomes a corpse rather than a living body.

> Moreover, this life which deserts the things which die is itself the mind, and it does not abandon itself; hence the mind does not die.[55]

But if we can be thus convinced of the immortality of our souls, we must look to the afterlife for an adequate understanding of our ultimate good.

Fulfillment

OUR TRUE HAPPINESS. In *On Free Choice of the Will,* after distinguishing between persons of good will who pursue virtue and persons of ill will who are governed by inordinate desire, Augustine affirms that the former deserve and enjoy happiness, whereas the latter do not. We all want happiness; yet some fail to attain it because they do not lead virtuous lives. Our ultimate and final happiness is God.[56] But those who reject God and spiritual values for the sake of inferior, earthly goods cannot be truly happy in this life and are damaging their chances for that final happiness in the afterlife.

UNHAPPINESS AND THE ACHIEVEMENT OF HAPPINESS. In *Of the Morals of the Catholic Church* Augustine analyzes three sorts of unhappy people:

1. Those who love and seek what they cannot obtain;
2. Those who obtain what is not truly desirable and cannot be loved; and
3. Those who obtain what is desirable but fail to love it.

By contrast, happiness is achieved "when that which is man's chief good is both loved and possessed." Our chief good should be superior to us and better than any other, but also obtainable. The chief good of the body, he says, is the soul, which gives life to the body. But what is the chief good of the soul? It is virtue that perfects the soul and is a great good, in that it cannot be misused or lost against our will. Yet God is a greater good than virtue, for all its goodness: "The perfection of all our good things and our perfect good is God." To desire happiness is always, at least implicitly, to desire God; "to reach God is happiness itself." Even death cannot separate the immortal soul from God.

> For that with which we love God cannot die, except in not loving God; for death is not to love God, and that is when we prefer anything to Him in affection and pursuit.

Love of God both unites us with Him and subjects us to His will. This love will be expressed in a life of virtue and particularly issues in the practice of the four cardinal virtues.[57]

ETERNAL FELICITY. In *The City of God* Augustine shows how philosophy is motivated by a desire for happiness and should, therefore, lead us to our "supreme good," which is an eternal life with God. Despite the **alienation** of original sin, he maintains, this blessedness has been made possible for us by the redemptive self-sacrifice of Christ, the God-man. And that blessedness will consist of a **beatific vision** of

---

Alienation (from the Latin *alius*, meaning other).   The sense of estrangement from or foreignness to consciousness, especially as discussed by Hegel, Marx, and existential thinkers

Beatific vision (from the Latin *beatus*, meaning blessed).   In Christian theology, the direct knowledge and love of God that produces happiness for the blessed in the afterlife

God, which cannot be understood or explained by us now. This "eternal felicity" will admit of degrees, yet none shall envy any others. We shall enjoy perpetual peace and union with God in heaven.

> There we shall rest and see, see and love, love and praise. This is what shall be in the end without end. For what other end do we propose to ourselves than to attain to the kingdom of which there is no end?[58]

In *The Happy Life* Augustine's mother, Monica, says that a person is happy who "wants and possesses good things," whereas a person will be unhappy "if he wants evil things, although he possesses them," and Augustine agrees. They work together to detect the **fallacy** in an argument that holds that "whoever seeks God has God favorably inclined toward him, and everyone who has God favorably inclined toward him is happy; hence, he who is seeking is happy," even though he does not yet possess what he seeks. This leads to the implausible conclusion that "he who does not have what he wants" can be happy, and they realize that the second premise is false, that "not everyone who has God favorably inclined toward him is happy." This leads to a threefold distinction among:

1. Those who have found God and are truly happy;
2. Those who seek God but have not yet found Him, to whom God is favorably inclined but who are not yet truly happy; and
3. Those who alienate themselves from God, who are unhappy, towards whom God is not favorably inclined.

Thus, the soul's possession of God is true happiness; we achieve it by means of "a well-founded faith, joyful hope, and ardent love,"[59] and it constitutes the ultimate fulfillment of our human nature.

REFLECTIONS

Augustine, the greatest philosophical example of Christian Platonism of all time, wrestled vigorously with the problem of interrelating his religious faith and rational thought. He admirably blends the lofty **idealism** of Platonic philosophy with the theocentric focus of Christian thought, straddling the end of antiquity and the beginning of Europe's Middle Ages. He is a good enough philosopher to try to support his views with rational argumentation, checking the excesses of religious **dogmatism**, and a fervent enough Christian to strain the Platonism he has inherited through his religious filters. Yet his system curiously suffers from both sorts of commitment. The fixed hierarchical thinking and ambivalent attitude towards the body and its natural inclinations constitute a troubling Platonic legacy; his theocentric Christian perspective is only as strong, philosophically, as its supporting arguments are rationally convincing.

REALITY. His theory of reality, our first topic, reflects that Platonic hierarchy of being very clearly. Even if we are sympathetic to the idea that the animate is superior to the inanimate, the sentient to the insentient, the intelligent to the unintelligent, and the immortal to the mortal, we should recognize that these alleged "gradations" might reflect our own **subjective** interests without necessarily being descriptive of reality in itself. His analysis of the problem of time is hauntingly memorable and marvelously expressed, but he fails to offer us a cogent solution (such as Kant would provide fourteen centuries later).

BODIES. Second, as a Christian, he must admit that all bodies are good in themselves since they were created by the infinitely perfect God. Yet there is a tension between this and his Platonic suspicion and distrust of the human body, which seems to be perpetually threatening to seduce the soul to wrongdoing. His view of formless matter as an ultimate constituent of bodies is no clearer or more compelling than the same idea as it appeared in Aristotle. His notion of "seminal reasons" in bodies, though equally vague, at least provides possibilities for explaining how God's divine providence governs all purely physical action.

PERSONALITY. Augustine's view of the human personality, our third topic, as rooted in a rational soul, which animates and directs an animal body, is attractive to those of us who are not upset by dualism. Within human nature we allegedly find a hierarchy of powers, whose objective reality can again be questioned; but, to the extent that "higher" powers are based on and transcend lower ones, the hierarchy at

---

Subjectivism. The theory that all knowledge and/or value is relative to an individual subject's mental states or experiences, as opposed to objectivism

least seems plausible. His definition of human nature not only accentuates his dualism, but it also wavers between a Platonism that subordinates body to soul and an Aristotelianism that sees personality as specifically distinguishing us within the general class of animals. His dogmatic assumption that reason grasps truth independently of the body threatens the cogency of his argument that soul and body are ontologically distinct (which will also affect his argumentation for immortality).

KNOWLEDGE.   Regarding our fourth topic, his theory of knowledge rashly maintains that all understanding is good and that no genuine teacher, as such, can be evil. This seems to hold, for Augustine, by definition, so that understanding how to do evil may not be true understanding and a person teaching evildoing to others does not qualify as a genuine teacher. Augustine is correct that the human mind is capable of **universal and necessary** knowledge, such as that of mathematics. However, it does not logically follow from this fact that the truth thus known is "more excellent" than our knowing minds, this providing yet another example of the perilous assumption of Platonic hierarchical thinking. On the other hand, his refutation of scepticism is brilliant, especially the argument for the certain existence of the thinking mind (which foreshadows Descartes).

FREEDOM.   Fifth, Augustine is the first notable Christian philosopher to wrestle with the problem of reconciling genuine human freedom with infallible divine foreknowledge. His distinction between voluntary causes and physical causes is valuable. But can we really understand how there can be a certain order of causes known by God from all eternity without this constituting the sort of deterministic necessity that compromises genuine freedom? It might be better to admit (with Descartes) that we cannot or to give up (with Hobbes) on indeterminism or to modify (with James) our commitment to divine knowledge. Augustine's friend Evodius may be correct that certain foreknowledge seems logically **inconsistent** with indeterminism. On the other hand, Augustine seems correct in regarding free will as a good, despite its possible misuse, since it is a necessary condition of moral action and responsibility.

MORALITY.   Sixth, his theory of morality focuses adroitly on the central importance of good will

(which Kant would later make famous). However, this notion is rendered problematic to the extent that it presupposes that the goods of this physical realm are always to be subordinate to those of the spiritual order—another instance of a fixed Platonic hierarchy—and it expresses a negative attitude towards temporal things. By contrast, his Neoplatonic privation theory of evil provides an extremely clever and profoundly influential explanation of how everything real can be good, to some extent, no matter how evil it may be.

SOCIETY.   On the seventh topic, Augustine's views on society may be too theocentric and nonprogressive for contemporary comfort. His use of God's eternal law as a standard for judging the legitimacy of all human laws must presuppose a confident knowledge of the former, which is difficult (if not impossible) to justify rationally and which tends to rely on religious authority commanding faith. The claim that only a Christian society can be truly just sounds narrow-minded relative to present-day **pluralism**. His doctrine of a just war as having to meet certain moral conditions, by contrast, has stood the test of time quite well. His stereotypical conception of women as naturally subordinate to men and created for matrimonial union and reproduction relies far more on scriptural doctrine and customary thinking than on scientific evidence and rational argumentation; it is hard to accept this today as anything more than an easy endorsement of the *status quo*.

RELIGION.   Eighth, Augustine may be correct that religion properly starts at the level of faith, which can provide a basis for seeking rational understanding. His threefold analysis of understanding, belief, and mere opinion improves on Plato's divided-line image of human awareness and foreshadows Kant's trichotomy (of knowledge, rational faith, and opinion). Augustine (like James after him) is correct that it is appropriate for us to believe many things without tangible proof and that to live otherwise would be unnatural and dangerous. On the other hand, even if we admit that if anything supernatural exists that is superior to human reason, then there is a God, still, his argument for the supreme Creator does not work. There is a problem of the "existence" of eternal, immutable truth apart from minds in which it subsists; it is problematic to characterize it as "superior" to the mind that grasps it; finally, there is a large leap between a **metaphysical** principle identified with truth and the personal, infinitely perfect God of **monotheism**. Nor is Augustine's **theodicy**, his solution to the problem of evil, for all its longlasting influence, philosophically satisfying, requiring our faith that God has some morally sufficient reason for allowing the evil that is or stems from sin; as Hume will argue, even though an infinitely perfect God might be logically compatible with evil, it is hard to understand how we can know the former while admitting the latter.

IMMORTALITY.   Ninth, Augustine's arguments for immortality presuppose too much. He assumes an eternal reality of truth, which is problematic. Even if we grant him that, how can it prove human immortality, rather than merely the existence of God as eternal Knower? He also assumes that the mind or rational soul knows eternal, immutable truth independently of the body, reason itself being immutable and eternal, and thus not vitally affected by the body's changes, including death. Finally, he assumes that the mind is a spiritual substance whose essence is to live and provide life, so that it cannot possibly lose its essence and die.

FULFILLMENT.   Tenth, his views on the fulfillment of human nature are nicely consistent with and, in a sense, the culmination of, the rest of his Christian theory. If the rational soul was, indeed, created by God for union with God, the beatific vision of the afterlife should be its goal. Meanwhile, the happiness of this life should consist in the practice of virtue and the love of God, which he sees as necessary means to that ultimate end.

*   *   *

Augustine is a great philosopher not merely because of his monumental influence throughout the Middle Ages and, to some extent, up to the present day; he is also justly renowned (as are all the thinkers on which this book focuses) for developing a rich and comprehensive system. He has something significant to say about every topic we are considering here, and the various aspects of his system tend to reinforce one another. Although the problems with his

system arise from dubious assumptions drawn from his dual allegiances to Platonism and Christianity, they should not conceal the value of his views as representative of an era and should invite us to come to grips with them critically on our own terms. He offers us a brilliant expression (probably the best ever) of Christian Platonism, as Aquinas does of Christian Aristotelianism.

Aquinas

Person signifies what is most perfect in all nature— that is, a subsistent individual of a rational nature.

SUMMA THEOLOGICA

BIOGRAPHY

Thomas Aquinas was born in his family's castle at Roccasecca, near Aquino (close to Naples), around the end of 1224 or in early 1225 (during the period of the Crusades). He was the seventh (and youngest) son of Landulfo, a knight, and his wife, Theodora, a noblewoman from Naples. Landulfo was a relative of Frederick II, Emperor of the Kingdom of Sicily, and served in his army. About 1230, Thomas's parents presented him as an oblate to the Benedictine Abbey at Monte Cassino; this meant that he was offered up for religious life by his family,

---

Monotheism (from the Greek *monos*, meaning single, and *theos*, meaning God).   The belief or doctrine that one God exists, as opposed to polytheism

Theodicy (from the Greek *theos*, meaning God, and *dike*, meaning justice or right).   The attempt to justify the goodness and justice of God in light of the reality of evil, to solve the problem of evil rationally

if he chose to pursue it later on. Thomas's uncle was abbot at the monastery, where the boy stayed until 1239, when conditions became politically dangerous due to a quarrel between Frederick II and the Pope. Thomas then returned to Roccasecca for a few months, until the autumn of that year, when he went to study the liberal arts at the University of Naples (which Frederick II had founded some fifteen years earlier). Here he was probably first exposed to the newly available ideas of Aristotle and met members of the recently founded Dominican Order of Preachers, who had opened a school of theology at the University. His father died at Christmastime in 1243; a few months later, in the spring of 1244, Thomas joined the Dominican Order at Naples.

His family was displeased that he would choose a poor, new order over the more prestigious and well-established Benedictines. This led to one of the few dramatic incidents in his life. For the following month, when he was accompanying the Dominican General on a journey to Paris, some of Thomas's brothers abducted him and took the young novice back to Roccasecca and his mother, where he was held prisoner for about a year. One story indicates that some of his brothers sent an attractive woman to his cell in the tower to seduce him but that he chased her away, brandishing a burning stick he had pulled out of the fireplace. In the summer of 1245, Thomas's family released him from his captivity; he returned to the Dominican order and completed his interrupted journey to Paris to take up studies there as a novice for three years.

In 1248, he accompanied the famous Dominican scholar Albert the Great to Cologne, where Albert was to establish a house of studies for their order. Albert valued the writings of Aristotle and passed on that enthusiasm to his young assistant. Aquinas was physically large and quiet. Some of his peers made fun of him, calling him "the dumb ox," to which Albert once reputedly predicted that some day the entire world would be listening to the bellowing of this "dumb ox." Near the end of 1250 or early in 1251, Aquinas was ordained a priest at Cologne. The next year, he returned to Paris to continue his studies. He probably wrote his *On Being and Essence* in the early 1250s, as a student. In the spring of 1256, he received his licentiate in theology and became a master

(or professor) of theology, being appointed to one of the teaching chairs granted the Dominicans at the University of Paris. He seems to have been a popular, capable teacher.

Between 1256 and 1259, Aquinas served as regent master of theology at Paris; and during this period he wrote his *Disputed Questions on Truth*. In 1259, he began writing the *Summa contra Gentiles* and then returned to Italy, where he was appointed Preacher General the following year. He was attached to the papal court of Urban IV at Orvieto from 1261 to 1265, during which period he completed the *Summa contra Gentiles* and (perhaps) wrote his treatise *On Kingship*. In 1265, he was sent to Rome to serve as regent master, and the following year he began his *Summa Theologica*. For more than a year, between 1267 and 1268, he was assigned to Viterbo, where Pope Clement IV was staying.

In November of 1268, Aquinas returned to the University of Paris, assigned to one of its Dominican chairs of theology, where he taught from January of 1269 to the spring of 1272. During this time he continued work on his *Summa Theologica* and wrote his *Disputed Questions on Evil* (*de Malo*). Classes were suspended at the university in early 1272 due to disputes between the secular clergy and mendicant orders. In the spring of 1272, Aquinas went to Florence and then returned to Naples to organize a Dominican house of studies. In December of 1273, he had a mystical experience, while saying Mass, which convinced him that all he had written was insignificant, and he ceased writing.

Early in 1274 he was summoned by Pope Gregory X to the Council of Lyons in France. He fell ill on the way, stopped at his sister's house, and then was taken on a donkey to the Cistercian monastery at Fossanuova, between Naples and Rome. There he died on March 7, 1274. Exactly three years after he died, the Bishop of Paris condemned 219 propositions, including some of Aquinas's (though he was not mentioned by name). A few days later, the Dominican Archbishop of Canterbury issued a similar condemnation at Oxford. In 1278, a General Chapter of Dominicans upheld Aquinas's views, though four years later, a General Chapter of Franciscans discouraged the study of the *Summa Theologica* in Franciscan schools. Early in the fourteenth century, canonization inquiries were conducted at Naples and Fossanuova; and on July 18, 1323 Aquinas was canonized by Pope John XXII (1316–34) at Avignon. Soon, the Archbishop of Paris revoked the condemnation of Aquinas's teachings. In 1567, Pope Pius V (1566–72) proclaimed Aquinas "the Angelic Doctor." Near the end of the nineteenth century, in his encyclical *Aeterni Patris*, Pope Leo XIII (1878–1903) recommended Thomistic thought for Catholic study. Aquinas is still influential today, and Neo-Thomists continue to develop his thought.

Reality

THE HIERARCHY OF REALITY. Like Augustine, the greatest medieval Christian Platonist, Aquinas, the greatest medieval Christian Aristotelian, presents a hierarchical view of reality, starting with God, the Creator, and working down through levels of perfection in creatures. Or, working from the bottom up (which may be more appropriate for an empiricist), he affirms three general sorts of reality:

> For some things have being only in this individual matter; such are all bodies. There are other beings whose natures are themselves subsisting, not residing in matter at all, which, however, are not their own being, but receive it.

These are created spirits, such as angels, who do not exist by their very nature, despite their independence from physical reality, but depend on God's creative activity for their being. And, third, "to God alone does it belong to be His own subsistent being," in that God's existence is necessary and inseparable from the divine nature, so that God must exist (as uncreated being) from all eternity. Because of the psychophysical character of human nature, we necessarily know reality in a different manner than would a pure spirit, whether angelic or divine. Through sense experience we know individual objects in our physical environment; but "we can understand these things in a universal way" by abstracting from their particularity. By contrast, angelic intellects naturally know immaterial reality in a nonsensible manner of which we are incapable in this natural world. But knowledge of "self-subsistent being is natural to the divine intellect

alone," so that no created intellect is naturally capable of knowing God's essence.[60]

TYPES OF BEINGS. In his *Principles of Nature,* Aquinas also draws Aristotelian distinctions between things that exist potentially but not actually and things that actually exist, and between things that actually exist "*essentially* or *substantially* (as when a man exists)" and those that actually exist but "*accidentally*" (as the whiteness of a man's beard). In *On Being and Essence* Aquinas follows Aristotle (whom he calls "the Philosopher") in an attempt to elucidate fundamental metaphysical concepts. As an empiricist, Aquinas holds that we must acquire our "knowledge of simple things" from our experience of the complex and that "a knowledge of prior things must be acquired from those that are posterior." Thus, he will first pursue "the meaning of *being* and then take up the meaning of essence," for being (*ens*) is "complex," in that it includes both essence and existence, and therefore naturally "posterior" to its component constituents. As Aristotle maintains, being can be understood "in two ways," either in terms of the categories of substance and (the nine) accidents or in terms of true **propositions**. In the first way we can only speak "of something which exists in reality," e.g., of a man who is white, wrinkled, bearded, and sitting in the corner; in the second way we can speak of blindness, even though "it posits nothing in reality," as when we say that Homer's blindness was incurable. It is being in the first sense that involves essence as a component; and "being is asserted absolutely and primarily of substances" but only derivatively of accidents. Simple beings, like God, which are not compounded of parts, and complex beings, like pencils, which are, both have essence; although the essences of the former have a sort of priority, they "are more hidden from us," so that we need to start with a study of the latter. A composite substance contains matter and form, neither of which, by itself, represents its essence, "which is signified by the definition of a thing." The essence of a tree includes both its woody and leafy matter and the animating form of its botanical structure. So, "in the case of all composite substances, the term 'essence'

Proposition (from the Latin *propositio,* meaning what is put forward or proposed).   A statement or what is expressed by a declarative sentence relating a subject term to a predicate term in such a way that the proposition as a whole can be regarded as true or false; an example of a proposition is provided by the sentence, "The book is on the table."

signifies the composite of matter and form." Yet, as we have seen, there are three ways in which substances can possess an essence:

1. God's essence is to exist, so that there is no distinction in God between essence and existence.

2. Created intellectual beings do not exist by their very essence but receive their existence and are essentially immaterial substances (thus, though the individuation of the human soul begins with the body, it does "not necessarily cease" with the death of the body).

3. Physical things are essentially "substances composed of matter and form," whose existence is received and inseparable from matter.[61]

We shall consider the first of these substances (God) in the "Religion" section and the second (the human soul) in sections on "Personality" and "Immortality." But let us turn to the third one immediately.

Bodies

A CAUSAL ANALYSIS OF BODIES. In his *Principles of Nature* Aquinas holds that "matter, form, and privation" are the three natural structures of all physical reality, the first two being essential principles and the third being accidental. All matter is formed; and, since matter always assumes some form and is thus deprived of other possible forms, privation is its necessary accident. In being generated and in undergoing change (from potency to act), bodies are also susceptible to analysis by means of the four (Aristotelian) causal principles; in addition to its "form and matter," a body must be brought into being by some "*efficient* or *moving cause*" and acts for some "end," whether deliberately or not.

> From what has been said it is evident that there are four causes, namely, material, efficient, formal, and final,

for Aquinas as for Aristotle. Matter and form are "**intrinsic**" causes, "inasmuch as they are **constitutive** parts of a thing, whereas the efficient and the final causes are called extrinsic, since they are external to the thing." A sapling is essentially woody and leafy matter animated by its botanical form, having begun from a seed and oriented towards the end of being a full-grown tree.[62]

THE NATURE OF BODIES. In *On Being and Essence* Aquinas defines a "body" as a substance whose nature is "such that three dimensions can be designated in it," namely, those of length, width, and depth. Body is "an integral and material part" of every animal, distinct from its animating soul. The animal body not only has the sort of form allowing us to designate its physical dimensions but is also capable of life. The "definition or species" of an animate or inanimate body must include both its "determinate matter, designated by the term 'genus,' and determinate form, designated by the term 'difference.'" Thus, to say that "a man is a rational animal" is to designate animality as his genus and to assert that what differentiates his species from other things in that genus is rationality. A man is "composed of body and soul after the manner of a third thing that is constituted of two things, and identical with neither of them."[63] So, a man is neither merely his body nor merely his soul, but he is essentially a composite of the two, as every body is formed matter.

In his *Summa contra Gentiles* Aquinas points out that the matter of a body is not the whole of its substance but "only part of the substance" along with its form. What has being is the composite of matter and form. It is true that "the form can be called *that by which it is*," say, a rock, "inasmuch as it is the principle of being; the whole substance itself, however," e.g., of the rock, "is *that which is*." In this respect bodies are, of course, different from intellectual substances or pure spirits, which are immaterial substantial forms;[64] if there are angels, for example, they are immaterial substances. Although Aquinas believes that the world was created by God, he does not think we can demonstratively prove that it "did not always exist." But he does argue that there is only one created world, comprising bodies and spirits, on the basis of "the unity of order" of creatures to one another and to God as Creator.[65] This world, of course, is the matrix within which human nature, as we know it, is found.

Personality

This background on Aquinas's theory of reality and bodies provides an apt context for his view of the human person. Man is an animal body (material cause), animated by a rational soul (formal cause), created by God (efficient cause) for a particular intelligible purpose (final cause). Aquinas adopts Aristotle's conception of man as a psychophysical unity, whose material component is the body and whose animating form is the soul; this theory is often called "**hylomorphism**," from Greek words meaning "matter" and "form." Let us begin this section by considering Aquinas's views on the nature of the human soul and its relation to the body.

THE SOUL AS THE FIRST PRINCIPLE OF LIFE. In *Summa Theologica* Aquinas defines the soul as "the first principle of life in those things in our world which live." Self-initiated movement and cognitive activities distinguish animate from inanimate things. Although it is the soul that gives life to animate bodies, the soul cannot itself be a body, because, if it were the nature of a body to be a principle (or metaphysical causal source) of life, then every body would be alive. Rather, some bodies have the potentiality for life, and the soul, "the first principle of life," actualizes that potentiality in a living body. Although only bodies can move other bodies through physical contact, a soul has a nonphysical power to move the body it animates. In addition to being incorporeal, however, the human soul must, second, be subsistent because it intellectually knows physical things without itself being physical. Indeed, "the intellectual principle, which we call the mind or the intellect, has essentially an operation in which the body does not share," namely the act of knowing universals. "Now only that which subsists in itself can have an operation in itself," since it is only substances that act. "We must conclude, therefore, that the human soul, which is called intellect or mind, is something incorporeal and subsistent." Third, it must be shown, against Plato, that "the human soul is a part of human nature" rather than all it essentially is and that Aristotle and Augustine are correct in analyzing us as combinations of body and soul. "Plato, through supposing that sensation was proper to the soul, could maintain man to be *a soul making use of a body*." Aquinas agrees that humans are essentially whatever perform human operations. Nevertheless, experience convinces him "that sensation is not the operation of the soul alone," but of body and soul in collaboration. His conclusion is that "man is not only a soul, but something composed of soul and body." Fourth, Aquinas argues that the rational soul is the form of the body, using Aristotle's insight that it is the form of a thing that constitutes its essential difference. "But the difference which" distinguishes man from all other earthly

creatures is reason, which is predicated "of man because of his intellectual principle. Therefore the intellectual principle is the form of man." A thing acts by virtue of its form. But our "soul is the primary principle of our nourishment, sensation, and local movement; and likewise of our understanding." Hence, the soul must be united to the body as its form. But the body is also essential to human nature as constituting the matter informed by the soul. Plato mistakenly held that a human person simply is his intellectual soul and that his body is nonessential. Aquinas continues: "But one cannot sense without a body, and therefore the body must be some part of man" essentially. Fifth, it is important to emphasize that the intellectual soul is the only one in a human being, providing for the powers of nutrition and sensation, as well as for the rational powers, without the need for other (i.e., nutritive and sensitive) souls. For a multiplicity of souls would entail a multiplicity of essential forms, which would compromise the unity of human nature. Also, the fact that an intense operation of the soul tends to impede other operations is evidence that there is a single principle involved.

> We must therefore conclude that the sensitive soul, the intellectual soul and the nutritive soul are in man numerically one and the same soul.

But man's intellectual soul, in addition to providing the powers distinctive to the rational mind, also "contains virtually whatever belongs to the sensitive soul of brute animals, and to the nutritive soul of plants." So, there is no substantial form in human nature other than the intellectual soul.[66]

THE RELATION BETWEEN SOUL AND BODY. In the *Summa contra Gentiles* Aquinas also considers the rational soul in its relation to the human body. He makes it clear that "an intellectual substance cannot be united to a body *by way of mixture*," because this would require the passive receptivity of matter, yet the soul is immaterial. It would also require physical contact between them, which is impossible, since the soul is not physical; as we have seen, there is only a "contact of power" between body and soul, and not any "bodily contact." Yet the relation between body and soul is not merely one of a "contact of power," as "Plato and his followers" taught, when they maintained "that the soul is in the body 'as a sailor in a ship.'" The fact that human beings "are sensible and natural realities" requires that their bodies be part of their essence, rather than their being merely souls using bodies. In sensation the soul is passively moved by objects of external sense, rather than merely actively moving bodies. So, the soul is not merely the mover of the body, as Plato holds. Rather, it is the form animating the body and actualizing its potential, as is shown by the following argument: Whatever internal principle moves a being from potentiality to act is its form; but the soul is the internal principle that moves a potentially living body to act. "Therefore, the soul is the form of the animated body." Although we normally enjoy the powers of the nutritive and sensitive soul as well as those of the rational soul, there is only one soul per human being, providing all these powers in a natural hierarchy:

> For the sensitive is subordinate to the intellective and the nutritive to the sensitive, as potency is subordinate to act, since in the order of generation the intellective comes after the sensitive and the sensitive after the nutritive.

Thus, the hierarchical rank of psychological powers follows the temporal order of development. It is the hylomorphic theory of the soul as a form actualizing the potentiality of the body that allegedly allows Aquinas (and other Aristotelians) to have it both ways—to say that the soul and body are two distinct substances and to insist that they nevertheless, in their union, constitute a dynamic unity. It is the soul that unites the body, "a sign of which is the fact that, when the soul departs, the body is dissolved." But if there were more than one soul—for example, a rational, a sensitive, and a nutritive one—something else would be needed to unite them; and that something else would need to be related to them by another something, a process that could not intelligibly go on infinitely. "Therefore, there must be but one soul in one man or in one animal,"[67] despite the diversity of types of psychological powers, which we shall now discuss.

A HIERARCHY OF LIVING CREATURES. Like Aristotle, Aquinas avers that there are five types of psychological powers—"*the vegetative, the sensitive, the appetitive, the locomotive, and the intellectual*"—and that the first, second, and fifth of these correspond to kinds of souls. The "*rational soul*" naturally has powers of intellect and will. The "*sensitive soul*" naturally has powers of external and internal sensation. The "*vegetative soul*" naturally has powers of nutrition, growth, and reproduction. The hierarchy of these three types of souls corresponds to the generality or universality of their objects. The object of the vegetative soul is the body it animates; other sensible bodies are natural objects of the sensitive soul; and being, truth, and value are objects of the rational soul. We can also consider the natural hierarchy of living earthly creatures, from dandelion plants, which have only vegetative powers, to immobile shellfish, which also have "the sensitive, but not the locomotive, power," to chipmunks, which also have the locomotive power of moving themselves about, to humans, who also have the rational powers of intellect and will. "But the appetitive power does not constitute a degree of living things; because *wherever there is sense there is also appetite,*" as Aristotle taught. The three powers of the vegetative soul are "the *generative* power" of reproduction, "the *augmentative* power" of growth, and "the *nutritive* power" of feeding. The sensitive soul enjoys powers of external and internal sensation. The five external senses can be ordered hierarchically from "the most spiritual" one of sight, whose objects can be very removed from the sense organ and are not physically altered by being seen, to hearing and smell, whose objects must be closer to the sense organs and are somewhat physically altered by the perceptual experience, to touch and taste, "the most material of all" external senses, whose objects must be in physical contact with the sense organs and are physically altered by being touched and tasted. There are also internal sensitive powers of memory, which allows a dog to remember where it buried a bone, of estimation, which allows the sheep to sense that the wolf is "a natural enemy," of common sense, which allows an animal to refer objects of various external senses to a common object, and imagination (or phantasy), which allows animals to recall and entertain images derived from past sense experience. Thus, there are "four interior powers of the sensitive part—namely, the common sense, the imagination, and the estimative and memorative powers." Finally, the rational soul has powers of intellect and will.

> But the human intellect, which is the lowest in the order of intellects and most remote from the perfection of the divine intellect, is in potentiality with regard to things intelligible, and is at first *like a clean tablet on which nothing is written*, as the Philosopher says.[68]

This is Aristotle's **tabula rasa** theory and is related to Aquinas's view of the passive intellect, which must be moved from potentiality to act by external objects.

The Agent Intellect and the Will.   Yet there is also an agent intellect as a power of the human soul, without whose activity the potentially intelligible could not be rendered "actually intelligible." The action performed by the active intellect is that of abstracting the general forms of its objects from the "phantasms" or mental images providing their particular material conditions. The human intellect is both speculative and practical, as Aristotle taught, without these being two distinct powers. The other power of the rational soul, in addition to intellect, is the will, which can control "the irascible and the concupiscible" appetites of the sensitive soul, which incline us, respectively, to anger and physical desire, but are "subject to reason," can resist it, and should obey it. Aquinas considers whether the will desires anything necessarily and agrees with Augustine that it does so desire happiness. Yet this is not "the necessity of coercion," such as would negate freedom of choice, but a "natural necessity" whereby the will seeks its appropriate ultimate fulfillment. "The will does not desire of necessity whatsoever it desires," since it desires some objects that are not necessarily connected to happiness. Even those things that are necessarily connected to man's ultimate fulfillment (in God) do not prove coercive for us in this life, to the extent that we fail to understand that necessary connection. The will is only inclined to an object to the extent that it seems good; but because, in this life, we are attracted to so many goods, some of which conflict with others, none of them proves coercive and destructive of free choice. These powers of intellect and will, along with nutritive, sensitive, appetitive, and locomotive powers, are ours as a result of our rational souls. The intellect, naturally oriented towards truth, requires the intellectual virtues of "*wisdom, science, and understanding*" for its fulfillment, as the will, naturally oriented towards the good, requires the habits of moral virtues.[69]

Individuality.   Of all earthly creatures, humans are unique in having rational souls, with these powers of intellect and will. These rational souls distinguish us as persons, unique in that respect among all animals. Aquinas (adopting Boethius's definition) writes, "*Person* signifies what is most perfect in all nature—that is, a subsistent individual of a rational nature." We have just analyzed that idea of a rational nature; and, before that, we saw that human beings are substantial beings. But now we notice an emphasis on individuality. Every person is a unique self-aware individual and not merely another member of its species, a fact associated with personal dignity. The word *persona* seems to have originated in the theater, where people of "high dignity" were portrayed "in comedies and tragedies." Then the name was used to refer to high-ranking Church officials. "And because subsistence in a rational nature is of high dignity, therefore every individual of the rational nature is called a *person*."[70] Although this discussion is pursued in the context of an analysis of the personal nature of God, it clearly applies to human nature as well.

Knowledge

Truth and Knowledge.   Given that the rational soul is an immaterial substance related to the human body as animating form to matter, that one of its essential characteristic powers is that of intellect, and that intellect is oriented towards knowledge of truth, consideration of Aquinas's **epistemology** is now appropriate. In *Truth* he adopts the standard definition of truth as "the 'conformity of things and intellect.' But since this conformity can be only in the intellect, truth is only in the intellect" primarily and merely secondarily in things. Truth is not relative to the knowing of human minds because the conformity is also in the divine intellect. Yet the human mind can achieve knowledge of the truth through the intellectual processes of "composition and division." By **synthetic** and **analytic** judgments the mind comes to know the truth. But this also requires self-reflection by the mind:

> And truth is known by the intellect in view of the fact that the intellect reflects upon its own act—not merely as knowing its own act, but as knowing the proportion of its act to the thing.

Without this awareness of self-consciousness a full knowledge of truth is impossible. "Just as truth consists in an equation of thing and intellect, so falsity consists in an inequality between them," and human judgments can be false when they fail to conform to reality. We sometimes refer to a thing as false (for example, a mirage) "because its natural appearance is likely to cause a false apprehension" by the mind. For the empirical Aquinas, all human knowing must be rooted in images derived from our experience of reality:

> Our knowledge, taking its start from things, proceeds in this order. First, it begins in sense; second, it is completed in the intellect. As a consequence, sense is found to be in some way intermediary between the intellect and things.

Intellectual knowledge transcends the superficial awareness of which other animals are capable;

> for to understand (*intelligere*) means to read what is inside a thing (*intus legere*). Sense and imagination know only external accidents, but the intellect alone penetrates to the interior and to the essence of a thing.[71]

In *Summa Theologica* Aquinas analyzes how the human mind knows. Before Plato, some philosophers, like Heraclitus (who is famous for having asserted that we can never step into the same stream twice), became sceptical of the possibility of human knowledge because they were convinced that all reality is in a constant state of flux. Plato tried "to save the certitude of our knowledge of truth through the intellect" by **postulating** his world of stable, eternal ideas (in which the things of the physical world allegedly participate), which are the true objects of knowledge. But Aquinas criticizes this theory on two grounds: first, it excludes all "knowledge of movement and matter" from the realm of science; and, second, "it seems ridiculous" to introduce utterly different sorts of beings from those we experience in order to account for the "things which are to us manifest." So Plato's theory was mistaken, and we must find some way to establish "that the soul knows bodies through the intellect by a knowledge which is immaterial, universal and necessary." In other words, some view other than Plato's must be developed to refute those pre-Platonic sceptics.[72]

KNOWLEDGE THROUGH SENSE EXPERIENCE. Unlike God, the human soul cannot understand physical things through its essence, in an act of pure intellectual intuition, but it must proceed through sense experience. As we have seen, Aquinas (rejecting Plato's theory of **innate** ideas known through recollection) adopts Aristotle's *tabula rasa* model of the human intellect as "like *a tablet on which nothing is written*" prior to sense experience. A human being is born "a potential knower" and is moved from that potentiality "through the action of sensible objects on his senses, to the act of sensation; by instruction or discovery, to the act of understanding." Without such concrete experience we cannot actually know. "For instance, a man who is born blind can have no knowledge of colors. This would not be the case if the soul had innate likenesses of all intelligible things," as Plato taught. Here, of course, Aquinas generally follows Aristotle. Indeed, we might say of his relation to Aristotle something parallel to what Aquinas himself says of Augustine—namely, "whenever Augustine, who was imbued with the doctrines of the Platonists, found in their teaching anything consistent with faith, he adopted it; and those things which he found contrary to the faith he amended." Aquinas gives us a quick history of philosophers' views on whether human knowledge is derived from the senses: materialistic pre-Socratics such as the **atomist** Democritus failed to "distinguish between intellect and sense" and imputed all knowledge to physical sensation; Plato went to the other extreme, severing all knowledge from the body and sensible things. "Aristotle chose a middle course. For with Plato he agreed that intellect and sense are different. But he held that the sense has not its proper operation without the cooperation of the body; so that *to sense is not an act of the soul alone*, but of the *composite*" of body and soul, agreeing with Democritus that sense knowledge is caused by the impressions of sensible things on our bodily sense organs.[73]

SENSE KNOWLEDGE AND INTELLECTUAL KNOWLEDGE. Sense knowledge provides us with mental images (or "phantasms") from which the mind abstracts ideas which serve as materials for intellectual knowledge. We have sense knowledge of that short-haired yellow dog barking and wagging its tail when we see and hear it; this provides us with mental

---

Postulate (from the Latin *postulare*, meaning to demand). An indemonstrable rational hypothesis used as a fundamental assumption of a system of thought; in Kant, freedom, God, and immortality are the three postulates of practical reason demanded by morality

images that can be related to mental images drawn from other experiences, from which we abstract ideas regarding dogs' behavior on being reunited with their masters.

> Therefore we must needs say that our intellect understands material things by abstracting from phantasms; and that through material things thus considered we acquire some knowledge of immaterial things,

such as our own souls and God. Aquinas attacks the theory of certain pre-Socratics (such as Heraclitus and the **Sophist** Protagoras) that we can only know our own impressions and not things themselves, on the grounds that it would undermine science and introduce an invincible epistemological **relativism**, whereby *"whatever seems, is true."* Sense knowledge, whose objects are particular things, must precede and somehow cause intellectual knowledge, whose objects are universal ideas. "The human intellect must of necessity understand by composition and division." In understanding an object we distinguish between its essence (or "its quiddity," its whatness), on the one hand, and its "properties, accidents, and various dispositions," on the other, recognizing all the while that these aspects of the thing comprise a whole. Thus, the human mind "necessarily relates one thing with another by composition or division; and from one composition and division it necessarily proceeds to another, and this is *reasoning*." By contrast, Aquinas avers, pure intellects, such as those of angels and God, intuitively grasp their objects all at once, rather than being thus discursive. When we know that Socrates, as a man, is a rational animal, we understand how various distinguishable objects of experience are interrelated.

> For *animal* signifies that which has a sensitive nature; *rational*, that which has an intellectual nature; *man*, that which has both; and *Socrates*, that which has all these things together with individual matter.

Of course, effective reasoning requires talent and time, so that some people understand things better than others. But through discursive reasoning we can attain not only knowledge of sensible things but even of the soul itself, by reflecting on its activities.[74] Thus,

for example, we can know that the human will exercises free choice.

Freedom

THE HUMAN CAPACITY FOR FREE CHOICE. As intellect is that power of the rational soul oriented towards knowledge of truth, so will is that power oriented towards free choice of what appears good. We have already analyzed that power in general but now must focus on the human capacity for free choice. In the *Summa Theologica* Aquinas, following Augustine's lead, writes,

> Man has free choice, or otherwise counsels, exhortations, prohibitions, rewards and punishments would be in vain.

This is an **enthymeme** (a deductive argument, part of which is implied rather than explicitly stated), which we might unpack in terms of the following **syllogism**: If humans did not have free choice, then counsels, exhortations, commands, prohibitions, rewards, and punishments would be in vain; but they are not in vain; therefore humans must have free choice. This **valid** hypothetical syllogism contains plausible premises. Experience does indicate that advice, threats, and so forth do influence human actions; and we might well wonder how this would be possible if people could not choose whether to comply with them or not. By contrast, "brute animals" act from instinct, as when "the sheep, seeing the wolf, judges it a thing to be shunned" and flees, this being a sensitive judgment of estimation or "natural instinct," rather than a rational judgment of deliberation. As we have seen, man has "a natural desire" for happiness, which "is not subject to free choice," yet remains free to choose the means to that natural end. Even our inclinations, though natural, "are subject to the judgment of reason," unlike those of the sheep. According to Aquinas, "free choice is an appetitive power" of the rational soul, whose proper action is that of "election, for we say that we have a free choice because we can take one thing while refusing another; and this is to elect." It involves a collaboration of **cognition** and

---

Enthymeme (from the Greek *enthumeisthai*, meaning to have in mind or consider). A syllogism in which one premise, or even the conclusion, is merely implied rather than explicitly stated

Syllogism (from the Greek *syllogismos*, meaning a reckoning together). A deductive argument with two premises and a **conclusion**

Cognition (from the Latin *cognitio*, meaning learning, acquiring knowledge). The act or faculty of knowing

appetite. "On the part of the cognitive power, counsel is required, by which we judge one thing to be preferred to another; on the part of the appetitive power, it is required that the appetite should accept the judgment of counsel." But free choice is fundamentally "an appetitive power."[75]

The same power of the rational soul wills and elects. "And on this account will and the free choice are not two powers, but one." Actions compelled by external force are not freely chosen by the will. "Violence is directly opposed to the voluntary" and nullifies free choice. Aquinas agrees with "the Philosopher" that actions "done through fear *are of a mixed character,* being partly voluntary and partly involuntary," and he even employs Aristotle's example of throwing cargo overboard during a storm at sea for fear of the ship's capsizing. Aquinas denies that the lustful desires of concupiscence render an act involuntary; but, like Aristotle, he must make distinctions in determining the relation between ignorance and voluntary action. We are ignorant *concomitantly* when the act done in ignorance would have been done even if the ignorance had been lifted; this sort of ignorance renders an action nonvoluntary. Second, ignorance can be "*consequent* to the act of the will" either because we want to remain ignorant or because we neglect to acquire knowledge we ought to have; in this case, action remains voluntary. Third, ignorance can be merely "*antecedent* to the act of the will when it is not voluntary, and yet is the cause of man's willing what he would not will otherwise"; this kind of ignorance does render an act involuntary. So, some conditions nullify or mitigate voluntary action, whereas others are merely unjustified excuses. Although free choice follows the deliberation of the intellect, it is essentially an "appetitive power" of the will.[76]

THE NECESSITY OF FREE CHOICE. The twenty-fourth of Aquinas's *Disputed Questions on Truth* is "On Free Choice." He offers a religious argument here that is reminiscent of Augustine:

> Without doubt it must be said that man has free choice. Faith demands that we hold this position, since without free choice one could not merit or demerit, or be justly rewarded or punished.

The Christian doctrines of heaven and hell and of a just God require human accountability, which presupposes free choice. Humans act freely "and are moved by a judgment of reason, for they deliberate about courses of action." By contrast, the actions of all "brute animals" are motivated by the "natural judgment" of instinct or estimation. This is why human actions are so much more diverse than those of other animals. Aquinas analyzes free action in terms of three elements—"namely, knowledge, appetite, and the operation itself." A free act requires that the appetitive power of will be under the control of the agent, which, in turn, requires that the cognitive judgment of reason be in his power. "The root of all liberty, therefore, is found in reason"; but since humans are the only rational animals, they are the only ones with free choice. It is not a habit of action (as a virtue is) but the rational will's power of acting. Aquinas agrees with Aristotle that free choice is a rational soul's "desire for that about which previous deliberation has been made." The will is rational appetite; and free choice is that will "in relation to one of its acts," namely, that of election. As truth is the natural object of the intellect, so the good is the natural object of the will. We must distinguish between natural "good which is proportioned to human nature" and transcendent good "which exceeds the **faculty** of human nature." Man's natural powers allow him to achieve the first sort of good, whereas the second can only be achieved with the assistance of divine grace.[77] Nevertheless, the rational will gives human nature the power of free choice, which is a condition of moral responsibility.

Morality

EVIL AND VICE. Like other medieval Christians, Aquinas is extremely concerned about moral good and evil. He agrees with Augustine that "the very nature of evil consists in the privation of good" and that all things are good as God created them. Not every negation of good is evil, but only the privation of a good that naturally should belong to a thing. Otherwise, he observes, "a man would be evil because he did not have the swiftness of a roe," which does not properly belong to human nature. By contrast, "the privation of sight" in a human is a natural evil. So "evil is the absence of the good which is natural and due to a thing." Aquinas agrees with Augustine's paradoxical view that only the good can be the causal source of evil, since all things are naturally good. Aquinas also concurs with Augustine's claim that God cannot be the cause of moral evil and argues the point: the evil that is a defect of action must be caused by a defective agent; however, "in God there is no defect, but the highest perfection"; thus, God cannot cause the moral "evil which consists in defect of action." But natural evil, "which consists in the corruption of some things," can be caused by God, as is the evil of the just punishment of sinners. "And so God is the author of the evil which is penalty, but not of the evil which is fault." The universe of God's creation is allegedly fuller, richer, and, hence, more perfect, for including corruptible, as well as incorruptible, beings; but thus there must be "some which can fail in goodness, and thence it follows that sometimes they do fail." Even the seven deadly or "capital vices"— pride, gluttony, lust, avarice, sloth, envy, and anger— are related to the three categories of human goods: "namely, the good of the soul, the good of the body, and the good of external things."[78] But let us now turn from this discussion of evil and vice to Aquinas's analysis of how we should morally evaluate actions as well as his analysis of virtue.

MORALLY EVALUATING ACTIONS.   In morally evaluating actions we should consider them objectively; an action may be objectively good, evil, or morally indifferent, depending on its *genus*; for example, "*to take what belongs to another*" tends to be objectively wrong because of the general sort of action it is— namely, one contrary to the requirements of justice. Second, we should analyze what specific type of action it is within that general category; for example, it matters whether we take another's property with or without her permission. Third, we should also consider the circumstances in which an act is performed.

> For the fullness of its goodness does not consist wholly in its species, but also in certain additions which accrue to it by reason of . . . its due circumstances.

For example, ordinarily giving money to someone who is needy is a good action; but if such a gift would deprive the giver's family of the money necessary to pay the rent and lead to their eviction from their home, this would compromise that goodness. Also relevant to the morality of an action is the end, purpose, or intention for which it is done. For instance, if you give money to poor people, under appropriate circumstances, for the purpose of corrupting them, that would be evil. "Accordingly," Aquinas concludes,

> a fourfold goodness may be considered in a human action. First, that goodness which, as an action, it derives from its genus

—for example, giving money to another person is the general sort of action.

> Secondly, it has goodness according to its species, which is derived from its befitting object

—for example, giving money to a needier person.

> Thirdly, it has goodness from its circumstances

—for example, a person who is sufficiently well off giving to a needier person, believing the gift will be properly used.

> Fourthly, it has goodness from its end

—for example, that same situation, where the giver's purpose is to pay for a nutritious meal. These four factors are all relevant to our evaluation of the morality of an action, which, in general, is a function of the extent to which it "is suitable or unsuitable to reason"; that which is good is reasonable, while evil action is unreasonable. Also, the goodness or evil of the will to act can be increased by the fulfillment of that will in action, due to the intensity or perseverance required to achieve that action.[79]

VIRTUES.   A pattern of choosing actions generates habits, which can be good or bad, depending on whether they are suitable or unsuitable to our rational nature. Morally good habits are virtues, and bad ones are vices.

> Thus, acts of virtue are suitable to human nature, since they are according to reason, whereas acts of vice are opposed to human nature, since they are against reason.

Aquinas adopts and analyzes Augustine's definition of virtue as "*a good quality*" (formal cause), "*of the mind*" (material cause), "*by which we live righteously*" (final cause), "*of which no one can make bad use, which God works in us without us*" (efficient cause). Like so many moralists, Aquinas maintains that "there are four cardinal virtues" of natural morality: "*prudence*," which perfects reason, "*justice*," which perfects the will, "*temperance*," which perfects the concupiscible appetite, and "*fortitude*," which perfects the irascible appetite. In addition to such natural moral virtues, there are others called "*theological virtues,*" because they relate to God, are granted us by

God's grace, and are only revealed to us "in Holy Scripture." The object of the theological virtues is God, who surpasses our rational comprehension. But, since the objects of moral and intellectual virtues are "comprehensible to human reason," we can conclude that "the theological virtues are distinguished specifically from the moral and intellectual virtues." The three theological virtues are *"faith,"* which is belief in God, *"hope,"* which is trust in God, and *"charity,"* which is love of God. Finally, like Aristotle, Aquinas maintains that natural virtue consists of a rational **mean** "between excess and deficiency."[80] In the following section, on "Society," we shall examine his treatment of law in detail. But for now, we can observe that morality is a matter of **natural law**, which is reason's manner of relating to God's eternal law. To the extent that actions are natural and rational, they conform to God's law, are good, and contribute to virtue; to the extent that they are unnatural and contrary to reason, they violate God's law, are wicked, and contribute to vice.

SIN.   Although we should not stray too far from the philosophical into the theological portions of Aquinas's thought, something should be said of his notion of sin because it has a bearing on moral issues still to be discussed. He accepts Augustine's conception of sin as *"a word, deed, or desire, contrary to the eternal law"* of God. But what is contrary to God's eternal law also violates natural reason.

> The theologian considers sin chiefly as an offense against God; and the moral philosopher, as something contrary to reason.

Sin can be analyzed as a voluntary act on the part of the sinner, an act that is inordinate with reference to God's eternal law. But then a sin can be more or less inordinate, accounting for "the difference between venial and mortal sin." A mortal sin is so grave a repudiation of God as to warrant eternal punishment, whereas a venial sin is less grievous. We can sin in doing something wrong ("a sin of commission") or in failing to do what we ought ("a sin of omission"). Likewise, we can distinguish between "sins of excess," which go too far beyond what is reasonable, and "sins by deficiency," which fall short of what is

reasonable; this latter distinction, of course, connects with Aristotle's doctrine of the mean, which, as we have seen, Aquinas embraces. To call a sin "mortal" (from the Latin word for "deadly") is to indicate a naturally irreparable corruption comparable to a fatal disease. We do not have the power to "cure" the damage done by our mortally sinning, but we must rely on God's supernatural grace for a "cure," if any is to come. By contrast, a sin that is venial (from the Latin word for "pardon") is one whose damage is reparable by our natural efforts.[81] This brief incursion into Aquinas's moral theology is designed to provide background for moral analyses of the following sins of injustice: killing, lying, and lust.

INJUSTICE AND KILLING.   Justice is a virtue that perfects the will in its interpersonal relationships and that "denotes a kind of equality" among people, determining how they are rightly treated. Aquinas distinguishes between *"natural right,"* based on the very nature of things, and *"positive right,"* based on the agreement or consent of the persons involved. Killing an innocent person is an unjust violation of natural right, regardless of commitments made; by contrast, breaking a promise is an unjust violation of positive right, dependent on a prior commitment. Aquinas defines justice as *"a habit whereby a man renders to each one his due by a constant and perpetual will."* Thus, strictly speaking, sins of injustice always involve "our dealings with others," and we cannot do ourselves an injustice, except in an extended, metaphorical sense. Murdering another person is a special sin of injustice because it involves deliberately depriving him of his natural right to life. But not all acts of homicide are murder, and it is sometimes just to kill another person voluntarily. For example, it is just to kill in self-defense. Capital punishment is justifiable and even commendable, because

> if a man be dangerous and infectious to the community, on account of some sin, it is praiseworthy and advantageous that he be killed in order to safeguard the common good.[82]

Suicide, the deliberate killing of oneself, is a mortal sin and is morally wrong "for three reasons": because it violates the natural law requirement of

---

Natural law   The theory (found in ancient Stoics and commonly associated with Aquinas and scholasticism) that the nature of things (often seen as grounded in the will of God) determines an objective set of rationally intelligible principles, governing all legitimate action

self-preservation, because it represents an injury to the community of which each of us is a part, and because it arrogates the power of life and death that rightly "belongs to God alone." The only exception to this proscription against suicide would be in rare cases, such as that of Samson in the Old Testament, in which it is commanded by God; but it is not permissible, for example, to commit suicide in order to keep oneself pure and untainted by other sins "because *evil must not be done that good may come* (*Rom*. iii.8) or that evil may be avoided" (this is often called the **Pauline principle**). Committing a moral evil is never permissible, even as a means to a desirable end. Likewise, one may never legitimately kill innocent persons. Killing in self-defense can be legitimate to the extent that it seems necessary to preserve one's own (relatively innocent) life against unjust aggression. But a great deal depends on one's intention, which should be "to save one's own life" rather than "the slaying of the aggressor," although, in fact, the same act of self-defense may have both effects. (This is often called the **principle of double effect**.) It is unlawful to use more than the force necessary to stop aggression, even in cases of legitimate self-defense. If someone attacks you with a knife, you ought to try to protect yourself; if you can disarm him without killing him, you should; but if the only way you can save yourself is to kill him, that is legitimate so long as the effect you intend is that of self-preservation rather than that of destroying human life.[83]

LYING AS INJUSTICE. Justice also requires that we be truthful in our communications with others. Lying to others unjustly deprives them of the truth; the sinfulness essentially consists in "the will to deceive," even in cases in which what one says, believing it false, turns out to be true. There are three types of lies: "an officious lie" aims at someone's convenience; "a jocose lie" is told in fun; and "a mischievous lie" is motivated by malice. How grievous a lie is depends on the intention behind it. To lie in order to spare someone's feelings or to amuse another is not as serious as maliciously depriving another of important truth she needs to know. Yet Aquinas agrees with Augustine that "every lie is a sin"; even though "jocose and officious lies are not mortal sins," mischievous lies can be.[84]

LUST AS INJUSTICE. Finally, sins of lust, like those of killing and lying, can be injustices. Aquinas says that "the sin of lust consists in seeking venereal pleasure not in accordance with right reason," either because the type of action is wrong or because the circumstances are illicit. Aquinas believes that procreation, "the begetting of children," is the natural end of the sex act. So a sex act that does not allow for that purpose (e.g., masturbation, homosexual sex, or bestiality) is wrong; but even a sex act between humans of opposite genders is wrong if performed outside of the marital relationship because it fails to assure that possible offspring will be raised by both parents. Thus, Aquinas writes, "fornication and all intercourse with other than one's wife is a mortal sin." He even offers a deductive argument: "nothing but mortal sin debars a man from God's kingdom. But fornication debars him" from God's kingdom. "Therefore a simple fornication is a mortal sin." Natural law requires a careful nurturing of our children. "Now it is evident that the upbringing of a human child requires not only the mother's care for his nourishment, but much more the care of his father as

---

Pauline principle. In moral theology, the principle, associated with the apostle Paul (*Romans* 3:8), that no end, regardless how good it may be, can justify an evil means

Principle of double effect. The view (often associated with Aquinas) that an act which produces both good and bad results can be morally permissible if such conditions as the following are met:

1. The action is not intrinsically evil.
2. The good effect and not the bad effect is intended.
3. The action causes both results (rather than either causing the other).
4. The good effect cannot be achieved without the bad.
5. The good effect provides a sufficient reason to permit the bad one.

For example, when a surgeon amputates her patient's gangrenous arm it is permissible because:

1. There is nothing intrinsically wrong in the surgical act.
2. She intends to save his life rather than to leave him disabled.
3. The act of amputation both saves his life and leaves him disabled.
4. She cannot save his life (in those circumstances) without disabling him.
5. The good of saving his life proportionately outweighs the bad effect of leaving him disabled.

guide and guardian." But this cannot be assured outside the bounds of the stable relationship of marriage.

> Hence human nature rebels against an indeterminate union of the sexes and demands that a man should be united to a determinate woman and should abide with her a long time or even for a whole lifetime.

Even though we might find sexual promiscuity tempting, "human nature rebels" against it in the sense that reason allegedly requires the commitment of marriage as a condition of legitimate sexual relations. Fornication, or sexual intercourse between unmarried people, defies this requirement and risks conception outside the context of a permanent marital commitment. Even though it is a mortal sin, "fornication is the least of the sins comprised under lust." Even actions inclining us to sexual intercourse outside of marriage can be mortally sinful. "A lustful look is less than a touch, a caress or a kiss." Yet all of these can be lascivious and constitute mortal sin. Worse than fornication is adultery, which is "*sexual intercourse with another man or woman in contravention of the marriage compact.*" It is wrong because it involves the injustice of violating the marriage contract, as well as because it leaves unprotected any children resulting from the union (the reason for fornication being immoral).[85]

*　　*　　*

Thus, sins of killing, of lying, and of lust can all be mortal and can all be violations of justice. It is our nature as moral agents, having free choice and being responsible for our conduct, that we can understand and should follow such proscriptions.

Society

LAW IN GENERAL AND GOD'S ETERNAL LAW. Aquinas regards humans as naturally social and related to other human beings as well as to God. These natural relationships are not arbitrary but are governed by law. "Law is a rule and measure of acts, whereby man is induced to act or is restrained from acting," and it is reason which legitimately provides this "rule and measure of human acts." Second, law must be "ordained to the common good," rather than being merely conducive to the benefit of any individual or narrowly defined group of individuals (making the law, for example). Third, the lawmaker must have authority

derived from a care for the welfare of all. And, fourth, law must be promulgated, or communicated to those required to obey it, if it is to be properly binding. Putting these four analytical elements together, Aquinas gives us his definition of law in general:

> Law is nothing else than an ordinance of reason for the common good, promulgated by him who has the care of the community.

Next, he considers the various kinds of law, and we learn that the most comprehensive is God's eternal law, which governs not only humans but all of creation. For, "granted that the world is ruled by divine providence," it follows that "the whole community of the universe is governed by the divine reason," which, as Augustine has written, must be unchangeable and eternal. The law of gravity, for instance, is a part of God's eternal law, which affects apples falling from trees as well as people falling off chairs.[86]

NATURAL LAW. Second, there is the special way in which persons share in God's eternal law, "and this participation of the eternal law in the rational creature is called the natural law." Because persons are blessed with "the light of natural reason," they can understand God's law and freely choose to submit to or resist it; and "the natural law is nothing else than the rational creature's participation of the eternal law." Aquinas holds that all human beings, in all places, at all times, under all cultural circumstances know "at least the common principles of the natural law," if not all its particular details. He also maintains that all laws that are legitimate, rational, and just "are derived from the eternal law. Hence Augustine says that *in temporal law there is nothing just and lawful but what man has drawn from the eternal law*" of God. To the extent that any human law "deviates from reason, it is called an unjust law, and has the nature, not of law, but of violence." Aquinas writes that "the first precept" of natural law is that "*good is to be done and promoted, and evil is to be avoided.*" This ultimate principle, commanding us to do good and avoid evil, is so general that it would be helpful for us to hear what sorts of actions are good and what kinds are evil. So he provides helpful illustrations. Self-preservation and the preservation of all (innocent) human life is good and obligatory; thus, suicide and murder are violations of natural law. Second, the licit procreation of our species and the careful education of offspring are good; sexual intercourse outside of marriage and the neglect of one's children are contrary to natural law. Third, the pursuit of knowledge of the truth (including, especially, that concerned with God) and living congenially in society are good and required by natural law; so it would be wrong smugly to wallow in ignorance or unnecessarily to offend other members of one's community. The natural law may change "by way of addition," but it "is altogether unchangeable in its first principles," at least, "by way of subtraction." For example, it could never become permissible for a human arbitrarily to murder another person; but the development of nuclear weapons of mass destruction that make it impossible to discriminate between combatants and noncombatants may have added to the natural law requirements regarding means of deterring and waging war. The "common principles" of natural law, according to Aquinas, can never be abolished from human reason, though their applications and "secondary and more particular precepts . . . can be blotted out from men's hearts."[87] For example, although all people should know that murder is wrong, some people might not consider the killing of an innocent man from another society murder or the torturing of a rival in order to extract information from him to be wrong.

HUMAN LAWS.   In addition to God's eternal law and the natural law, there are, third, human laws. If all people were reasonable in constantly obeying natural law, human laws might be superfluous.

> But since some are found to be dissolute and prone to vice, and not easily amenable to words, it was necessary for such to be restrained from evil by force and fear, in order that, at least, they might desist from evil-doing, and leave others in peace, and that they themselves, by being habituated in this way, might be brought to do willingly what hitherto they did from fear, and thus become virtuous.

Hence, it is useful for us to have human laws enforced with penal sanctions. Human law, in order to be legitimate and binding, should be in conformity with the natural law. "But if in any point it departs from the law of nature, it is no longer a law but a perversion of law," as Augustine taught.[88] So, members of society are bound by just human laws as well as being subject to God's eternal law and the natural law of morality.

WOMEN.   Aquinas is a Christian Aristotelian and a traditionalist in his views on women and political government. In the *Summa Theologica* he quotes Aristotle's opinion that "the *female is a misbegotten male*" (*femina est mas occasionatus*). Since God cannot make mistakes, Aquinas must argue that the creation of woman was

> necessary . . . as *a helper* to man; not, indeed, as a helpmate in other works, as some say, since man can be more efficiently helped by another man in other works; but as a helper in the work of generation.

So, in relation to "human nature in general, woman is not misbegotten," but part of God's intelligent plan for the procreation and nurturing of offspring. "As regards the individual nature" relative to males, however, Aquinas asserts, "woman is defective and misbegotten." Aquinas considers it good that woman was made from man because this promotes their love and union in "domestic life, in which each has his or her particular duty, and in which the man is the head of the woman." Aquinas also thinks it appropriate that God created woman from man's rib, "to signify the social union of man and woman"; she was not made from his head since she should not exercise any "*authority over man,*" but neither was she made from his feet since it is wrong "for her to be subject to man's contempt as his slave."[89]

POLITICAL GOVERNMENT.   In his treatise *On Kingship* Aquinas writes that, because "it is natural for man, more than any other animal, to be a social and political animal, to live in a group," the good of social order forbids that each person can "be a king unto himself, under God." Individual human beings are not self-sufficient. "It is therefore natural that man should live in the society of many." But then the unity and order of society requires political power "which watches over the common good of all members." As in human nature the soul should rule over the body and within the soul reason should govern the irascible and concupiscible appetites, so a society of free men should be ruled for the common good.

> If, on the other hand, a rulership aims, not at the common good of the multitude, but at the private good of the ruler, it will be an unjust and perverted rulership.

Such an unjust government by a single man is **tyranny**; that by a small group of men is an **oligarchy**; and that by the whole multitude is **democracy**. Likewise, we can analyze just political governments into three sorts: that administered by many men is a **polity**; that administered by a few virtuous men is an **aristocracy**; and that administered by one man is a monarchy. This analysis, of course, is taken from the writings of Aristotle. Aquinas describes a king as "one man who is chief" and compares him to "a shepherd seeking the common good of the multitude and not his own." Finally, the kingdom ruled should be united as a single city or state.[90]

TOLERANCE, WAR, AND SEDITION.   Let us conclude this section with a brief examination of Aquinas's discussion of five social issues—tolerance, war, sedition, slavery, and property rights. He does not believe that heretics should be tolerated but maintains that "they deserve not only to be separated from the Church by excommunication, but also to be severed from the world by death." His reason is that heretics are far more dangerous and harmful than "forgers of money," who are rightly condemned to death. On the other hand, he does hold that the Church should be sufficiently merciful towards heretics as to admonish them in hopes they might recant; but, if that attempt at mercy fails, they should be handed over to civil authorities for execution. Second, Aquinas subscribes to Augustine's theory of a just war, laying down three conditions for its legitimation: first, it must be declared by someone with proper political authority and not by any private individual(s); second, it must be waged for the sake of "a just cause"; and, third, those making war should maintain "a rightful intention, so that they intend the advancement of good, or the avoidance of evil." Aquinas points out that a legitimate authority can declare war for a just cause, such as self-defense against an aggressor, but that war is "rendered unlawful through a wicked intention," such as a vengeful lust for destruction. A third social issue is that of sedition, which threatens the social order of a state. Aquinas regards it as "a mortal sin" because it opposes "the unity of law and common good: whence it follows manifestly that sedition is opposed to justice." Nevertheless, rebellion against "tyrannical government" need not be sedition and may be just.[91]

SLAVERY AND PROPERTY RIGHTS.   Fourth, Aquinas occasionally discusses slavery, though not in any comprehensive, systematic manner, apparently accepting it as part of the social order. He approvingly quotes Aristotle's notorious dictum that "a slave belongs to his master, because he is his instrument." He denies that the "*dominative*" relationship between master and slave can be one of simple justice any more than the "*paternal*" one between father and son can be. By contrast, he says, "there is more scope for justice between husband and wife," because matrimony represents a kind of social relationship, despite the fact that "she is something belonging to the husband"—this being "*domestic justice* rather than *civic*." Aquinas does not agree with Aristotle that some people are naturally superior to others; as a Christian, he believes that "by nature all men are equal" as persons created by God. Still, he does hold that a slave is bound to obey "his master in matters touching the execution of the duties of his service." He also maintains that the Church can require a Jew to free one of his slaves who has become a Christian and that this is no injustice to the Jew, even though no compensation be paid, because "unbelievers" should not have such sovereign authority over the "children of God." Fifth, Aquinas defends property rights on the grounds that "man has a natural dominion over external things" and should be "able to use them for his own profit." Private property is useful to man for three reasons: because people work harder for what will belong to them than for what will be held in common, because society is more orderly if individuals look after their own possessions than if everyone had to care for everything, and because private property contributes to personal contentment that is conducive to "a more peaceful state." Natural law neither requires nor forbids the division of common goods into private possessions, and the ownership of private property is "an addition" to the natural law "devised by human reason." Given the development of property rights, "theft is a means of doing harm to our neighbor in his belongings" and can be a mortal sin. A person in sufficient need can "either openly or secretly" take from another who has more than is needed without this being "theft or robbery," since the natural right of self-preservation has priority over the human right to property. Theft and robbery are both unjust and sinful; but robbery is even worse than theft, which is secretive, because it is done through "violence and coercion," which are injurious to the victim in his person and not merely in his possessions.[92]

* * *

It is because of the social character of human nature that the various issues discussed here arise and must be addressed.

Religion

THEOLOGY AND GOD'S EXISTENCE. Aquinas's philosophy of human nature, like Augustine's, is particularly dependent on a rational case being made for the God of Christianity, since it depicts man as essentially a personal creature of God. Aquinas considers theology (the study of God) a science (in the sense of a systematic body of knowledge), though not one derived "from principles known by the natural light of the intellect, such as arithmetic and geometry" are. Rather, it proceeds from divine revelation. It is a single science, "partly speculative" (concerned with God) and "partly practical" (regarding human action); indeed, it is the noblest of all sciences because it speculates about the highest reality and orients us practically towards our most final end of "eternal beatitude." In the science of theology "all things are treated under the aspect of God, either because they are God Himself, or because they refer to God as to their beginning and end." Some might claim that it is useless to try to prove God's existence because it is "**self-evident**." Indeed, Anselm and his followers seem to maintain that "the proposition *God exists* is self-evident" insofar as God essentially is that "than which nothing greater can be conceived" and it is greater to exist "actually and mentally" than "only mentally." Aquinas answers that God's existence is "self-evident in itself, though not to us." In order for Anselm's argument (which Kant later calls "**ontological**") to work, God's essence would have to be self-evident to us, as it naturally is not in this life. So, it is not possible for us to argue from mere ideas to actual existence. Given that God's existence is not self-evident to us, it is meaningful to try to prove it. But can it possibly be demonstrated? If it were "an article of faith," it would seem to be beyond demonstration; but Aquinas includes it among "preambles to the articles" of faith "which can be known by natural reason," although they can also be simply believed. He says there are two types of demonstration. The first, "called *propter quid*" (literally, because of which), argues from the cause to its effects. In this sense we cannot demonstrate God's existence, since God, the very object of our demonstration, is the cause and is not naturally experienced or known by us in this life. The other approach, "called a demonstration *quia*" (literally, since), argues from effects back to their causes. This approach can work for us, since we naturally experience and know the effects of God's creation. Now it is true that no combination of God's created effects is proportionate to God as its cause, so it cannot provide us with any "perfect knowledge of that cause"; nevertheless, it does provide us with a clear way of demonstrating divine existence.[93]

THE "FIVE WAYS." In introducing his own demonstrations (and five of the most famous paragraphs he ever wrote), Aquinas says, "The existence of God can be proved in five ways" (*Dicendum quod Deum est quinque viis probari potest*). "The first and more manifest way" (*Prima autem et manifestior via*) for an Aristotelian like Aquinas is from motion (*motus*). Through sense experience we encounter things being "moved" to change "from potentiality to actuality." But the mover must already be in a state of actuality or itself be "moved" by another. "But this cannot go on to infinity, because then" there would be nothing initiating the entire process, or chain reaction, of change.

> Therefore it is necessary to arrive at a first mover, moved by no other; and this everyone understands to be God

(*Ergo necesse est devenire ad aliquod primum movens quod a nullo movetur, et hoc omnes intelligunt Deum*). "The second way is from the nature of efficient cause" (*Secunda via est ex ratione causae efficientis*). We experience and come to understand "an order of efficient causes" among the objects of sense experience. Nothing can possibly be its own efficient cause since this would require that it "be prior to itself, which is impossible." But again, there cannot be an infinite regress from effect back to cause, back to cause of that cause, and so forth, for then nothing would be causally produced in the first place.

> Therefore it is necessary to admit a first efficient cause, to which everyone gives the name of God

---

Self-evident. So obviously true (or false) as to require no justification (or refutation)

Ontological argument. An *a priori* argument purporting to deduce the necessary existence of God from the very idea of God as an infinitely perfect Being; though Kant gave it this name, the argument originated in the Middle Ages and was used by Descartes

(*Ergo necesse est ponere aliquam causam efficientem primam, quam omnes Deum nominant*). "The third way is taken from possibility and necessity" (*Tertia via est sumpta ex possibili et necessario*), starting with objects of our experience that contingently exist; in other words, though they are, they could conceivably not have been.

> But it is impossible for these always to exist, for that which can not-be at some time is not. Therefore, if everything can not-be, then at one time there was nothing in existence.

However, since nothing comes from nothing, then nothing would now exist, which is **absurdly** contrary to experience.

> Therefore, not all beings are merely possible, but there must exist something the existence of which is necessary.

That necessary being either derives its necessity from another or it does not. If it does, that process of derivation cannot "go on to infinity," since then the chain would never be causally begun.

> Therefore we cannot but admit the existence of some being having of itself its own necessity, and not receiving it from another

(*Ergo necesse est ponere aliquid quod est per se necessarium non habens causam suae necessitatis aliunde*).

> This all men speak of as God

(*omnes dicunt Deum*).[94]

"The fourth way is taken from the gradation to be found in things" (*Quarta via sumitur ex gradibus qui in rebus inveniuntur*). We experience objects as representing degrees of qualities—"some more and some less good, true, noble, and the like." But such qualitative degrees of comparison presuppose some maximum standard—whereby something is best, truest, noblest, and so forth. "Now the maximum in any genus is the cause of all in that genus," as fire, allegedly the hottest of things, is the causal source of all other heat. Some one being must be "greatest in being" and have all desirable qualities to the maximum extent.

> Therefore there must also be something which is to all beings the cause of their being, goodness, and every other perfection; and this we call God

(*Ergo est aliquid quod est causa esse et bonitatis et cujuslibet perfectionis in omnibus rebus, et hoc dicimus Deum*). "The fifth way is taken from the governance of the world" (*Quinta via sumitur ex gubernatione rerum*). We experience things that lack understanding regularly acting for intelligible ends. But this could not so consistently occur by mere chance. Whatever lacks understanding, if it is not moved by mere chance, must be "directed by some being endowed with knowledge and intelligence"; thus, for example, an arrow flies towards the target because of an archer's aim.

> Therefore some intelligent being exists by whom all natural things are directed to their end; and this being we call God

(*Ergo est aliquis intelligens a quo omnes res naturales ordinantur ad finem, et hoc dicimus Deum*). Aquinas also briefly considers the problem of evil as an obstacle to the existence of a perfect God; but he adopts Augustine's explanation that God allows evil from which greater good will be produced.[95]

Thus far, Aquinas has purportedly demonstrated a Supreme Being that is the unmoved Mover and first efficient Cause of everything else, the absolutely necessary, greatest Source of all perfection, and intelligent Governor of the world.

THE DIVINE ESSENCE. We now briefly consider some of what Aquinas writes regarding the divine essence (what God is as opposed to whether God is). First, God is simple, in the sense of not being composed of parts. God is pure form, not "composed of matter and form," as we are, for God is an immaterial Being. There is no unrealized potentiality in God (since no matter), so that God's essence is to be—thus the Old Testament God says, "I am Who I am" (*Exodus* 3:14); in God essence and existence are identical and only distinguishable in our way of thinking of them. Second, Aquinas's "God is the highest good absolutely" and not merely relatively good. Third, God is infinite, or unlimited, and, indeed, unique in being the only "absolutely infinite" perfect Being; even angels, which are immaterial creatures, are only relatively infinite in that they receive their being from God. Fourth, because God is simple and

---

Absurd. Loosely, contrary to reason or to the rules of logic; more precisely, for such existentialists as Sartre, lacking any ultimate rational explanation

uniquely infinite, there can only be one God, not many, as the ancient pagans surmised; the unity of God is also indicated by the unity, or coherent **design**, of the world. Fifth, God is omniscient or "knows all things," both those that actually have been and are and those that are merely "future contingent things" to us humans. Sixth, God's omnipotent will governs all creation, and "all things are subject to divine providence," which imposes necessity on some creatures, while respecting the freedom of others like us.[96]

ANALOGY AND OUR COMPREHENSION OF GOD. No creature, including the human person, can comprehend, or perfectly know, God's nature; for every creature, as such, is finite or limited, whereas God, as we have seen, is absolutely infinite. In this life our natural knowledge must be grounded in our experience of sensible things. Our intellect, through the rational powers of abstraction, can transcend those sensible things—for example, to establish truths concerning the human soul and God's existence. But our intellect lacks the power to comprehend the divine essence. In this life we can naturally know God only in "His relationship with creatures," although God's grace and divine revelation provide us with "a more perfect knowledge" than we can achieve "by natural reason" alone. The concepts we use to think of God and the names we use to speak of God are not "predicated univocally of God and of creatures"—that is, they do not have identical meanings; for example, though God and Aristotle are both knowledgeable, God's knowledge is neither discursive nor limited, as human knowledge always is. But neither are our concepts and "names applied to God and creatures in a purely equivocal sense"—that is, their meanings are not utterly unrelated; for example, Aristotle's knowledge bears some comparison to God's. Rather than being univocal or equivocal, our concepts and "names are said of God and creatures in an *analogous* sense," bringing out a telling similarity that is yet not an identity of meaning. Analogy, then, provides a middle ground or "mean between pure equivocation and simple univocation. For in analogies the idea is not, as it is in univocals, one and the same; yet it is not totally diverse as in equivocals." Theological language, used analogously, allows us to form true affirmative propositions about God,[97] as when we say that God justly deals with personal creatures, so that we are neither restricted to negative statements nor condemned to silence concerning God.

RELIGIOUS FAITH AND MIRACLES. Let us conclude this section by examining what Aquinas says about religious faith and then by applying it to belief in miracles. In a rare use of first-person singular pronouns, he writes, in the *Summa contra Gentiles*, "I have set myself the task of making known, as far as my limited powers will allow, the truth that the Catholic faith professes, and of setting aside the errors that are opposed to it." Some religious truths, such as the mystery of the Trinity, "exceed all the ability of the human reason" and must either be accepted in faith or not. Others, such as the existence and unity of God, can be demonstrated by reason, as well as accepted by faith. Even these latter religious truths are appropriately given to us for our belief; for, if they were merely limited to rational inquiry, only those few persons capable of philosophical argumentation would possess them, and even they would grasp them only after much effort and time and with the inescapable risk of error. But it is also appropriate that religious truths above reason be given to us for our belief because we should strive for that which transcends the goods of this life and because it helps us in "the curbing of presumption, which is the mother of error." It is not foolish, but proper, that we should assent to truths of faith that exceed all possible human understanding. "Since, therefore, only the false is opposed to the true," there can be no logical opposition between "the truth of the Christian faith" and truths that can be established by human reason.[98] So, truths of faith that are above reason can never be contrary to the truths of reason, even though we may not be able to understand how they are compatible.

In *Truth* Aquinas embraces and analyzes Paul's characterization of faith as "the substance of things hoped for, the evidence [*argumentum*] of things that appear not" (*Hebrews* 11:1). Because it deals with "things that appear not," religious faith is

---

Design, argument from.   An argument (also called teleological) for the existence of God as the Designer responsible for the combination of order and complexity characteristic of our world

distinguished from all scientific knowledge and understanding; the word "evidence" distinguishes it from ordinary opinion and doubt; and the phrase "substance of things hoped for" distinguishes religious faith from the broader belief whereby we take someone's word for something. For Aquinas, "faith consists essentially in knowledge," rather than being opposed to it. It is not, of course, the knowledge of first-hand experience and understanding. "But, in so far as there is certainty of assent, faith is knowledge"; for in faith we assent with certainty to doctrines revealed by God and taught by the Church. Once we understand a truth, we cease merely to believe it. "Hence, it is impossible to have faith and scientific knowledge about the same thing" by the same person at the same time.[99]

Miracles provide a convenient example of matters of faith not rationally understood. God has created the things of this world in such a way that they have their own natural operations, which are scientifically understandable. However, as Augustine observed, God sometimes intervenes in such a way that things depart from their natural operations. Aquinas quotes with approval Augustine's description of a miracle as "*something difficult, which seldom occurs, surpassing the faculty of nature, and going so far beyond our hopes as to compel our astonishment.*" Aquinas himself observes that the word "miracle" is "derived from admiration, which arises when an effect is manifest, whereas its cause is hidden." We are filled with wonder at the idea, for example, that sick people could "be healed by the shadow of Peter" passing over them (*Acts* 5:15) because the cause of the cure is allegedly divine power, which we cannot directly experience or understand. "Wherefore those things which God does outside those causes which we know, are called miracles."[100] Christian believers purportedly have certain knowledge of such miracles, based on faith assenting to the authority of scriptural revelation, although this faith is, by definition, not subject to our rational understanding.

Immortality

In the *Summa Theologica* Aquinas tries to show us that the immortality of the rational soul is not merely a matter of religious faith but can be philosophically demonstrated by reason. He argues that the only two ways in which things can be corrupted are in themselves and by accident. But no subsistent thing can be accidentally corrupted, and the rational soul, as he has already argued, is subsistent. So, it could only be corrupted in itself, if at all. But, he claims, no substance that is pure form can be corrupted in itself. "For it is clear that what belongs to a thing by virtue of the thing itself is inseparable from it." But being belongs to a pure form essentially; "and therefore it is impossible for a subsistent form to cease to exist." Another argument holds that corruption can only occur where there is contrariety; but the rational soul contains no internal contrariety, and, thus, the rational soul is incorruptible. A third argument maintains that "everything that has an intellect naturally desires always to exist." The rational soul of a human being has an intellect and, hence, naturally desires always to exist. "But a natural desire cannot be in vain. Therefore, every intellectual substance is incorruptible," including the human soul.[101]

The *Summa contra Gentiles* contains these and other arguments. Aquinas reasons there that "all corruption occurs through the separation of form from matter." The human soul is an intellectual substance. But "no intellectual substance is composed of matter and form," being pure form, so that no such separation is possible. "Therefore, no intellectual substance is corruptible." Another intriguing argument goes like this: the proper perfection of man is his "understanding, since it is in this that he differs from brutes, plants, and inanimate things." The uniquely characteristic activity of human understanding is "to apprehend objects universal and incorruptible as such." But there must be a proper proportion between the perfection of human understanding, which grasps the incorruptible, and the soul it perfects. "Therefore, the human soul is incorruptible." A final argument holds that any form is corruptible "by three things only: the action of its contrary, the corruption of its subject, the failure of its cause." But the human soul, as subsistent form, has no contrary, no underlying subject on which it is ontologically dependent (as the power of sight requires an eye as its subject), and no cause other than God, who created it and cannot fail. "Therefore, in no way can the human soul be corrupted."[102]

Other arguments for the immortality of the human soul are also offered, but for our purposes this will suffice. As a medieval theologian, Aquinas has powerful reasons for wanting us to subscribe to this doctrine; and, as a Christian philosopher, he considers it important to make his case through logical reasoning. Hence, he offers us such a vast array of arguments. And this issue of human immortality, of course, has a direct bearing on Aquinas's theory regarding the ultimate end and final goal of human nature.

Fulfillment

FULFILLMENT IN GOD.   In the *Summa contra Gentiles* Aquinas mounts an involved and sophisticated argument to show that our ultimate fulfillment can only be found in God and not in any combination of the goods of this world.

Every agent acts either by nature or by intellect. Intellectual agents act for ends and can know and intend those ends as purposes. But even natural agents, though they cannot know and intend their ends as purposes, do act for ends.

Therefore every agent acts for an end,

and nothing acts in a purely random, chaotic manner in the world. We may not always know the ends for which action occurs; for example, a man scratching his beard may not be consciously aware of the itching sensation or nervousness causing him to do so. All agents, both intellectual and natural, act for ends that are, in some sense, good or avoid evil. The end for which anything acts is the object of appetite; but, as Aristotle and other philosophers have shown, the object of appetite is good.

Therefore the end of everything is a good.

But if every end is in some sense good, then "that which is the supreme good is supremely the end of all." Now God is the only supreme good.

Therefore all things are directed to the highest good, namely God, as their end.

Another argument goes like this. Every creator is also the ultimate end of what he produces.

Now God is the producing cause of all things,

being the Creator of the entire world.

Therefore He is the end of all things.

So God is both the first cause and the final cause of all creation. God, being perfect and without any unrealized potentiality, can never benefit from action but acts only to bestow benefits on others. All God's "creatures are made like unto God" in sharing in being and goodness, in their own manner, rather than fully and perfectly. Intellectual creatures like us relate to God in a special way, through understanding; and their ultimate end is to know God. Thus, their highest faculty is fulfilled. Though this also involves an act of the will of the intellectual creature, desiring and loving God, its fulfillment is essentially in the intellectual act of knowing.[103]

EARTHLY GOODS.   But how can we show that ultimate human happiness cannot be achieved through any earthly goods? In order to do this, we can categorize the objects of earthly desire and show that none of them is ultimately fulfilling to human nature. The pleasures of the flesh are desirable, but not the ultimate ends of the operations giving rise to them; for example, the pleasures of eating and drinking are ordained to the end of preserving bodily life, and those of "sexual intercourse to the generation of offspring." Besides, we share such bodily pleasures in common with "brute animals," which, surely, "cannot be deemed happy, unless we stretch the meaning of the term." Therefore, the ultimate happiness of felicity cannot consist in such pleasures. Also, the ultimate end of a thing should be related to its noblest feature, which, in human nature, is intellectual understanding, rather than sense pleasures. Second, human felicity cannot consist in honors since they are too dependent on those extending the honors; also, honor is good and desirable because of virtuous qualities and meritorious actions rendering someone worthy of honor rather than in itself. Third, human felicity cannot consist in glory since it is "sought for the sake of honor" and thus is a means to an end which is not itself ultimate, as we have seen. Besides, glory consists in being known. But it is distinctly nobler to know than to be known since "only the more noble things know, but the lowest things are known." Also, our highest good should be "most enduring," whereas "glory, in the sense of fame, is the least permanent of things," being a function of fickle, transient human opinion. Fourth, human felicity cannot consist in a wealth of riches since they are merely desirable as means to other ends that they can purchase. "Now, that which is the highest good is desired for its own sake and not for the sake of something else. Therefore, riches are not the highest good for man." Besides, our highest good should be superior to us, whereas riches are inferior to us and are subordinate to our uses for them. Fifth, our felicity cannot consist in worldly power, which, like riches, is so very subject to chance and thus unstable. Also, worldly power can be used either well and wisely or badly and foolishly, whereas that which can only be used well and wisely (like virtue) is better. But, it seems, we have exhausted the list of external goods of this world, "the ones that are called 'goods of fortune,'"[104] and found that human felicity is to be found in none of them.

Let us, then, consider the goods of the body as candidates. But similar considerations will suffice to show that "goods of the body, such as health, beauty, and strength" cannot constitute man's highest good either. "For these things are possessed in common by both good and bad men; they are also unstable; moreover, they are not subject to the will" of the person possessing them. If you are healthy, good looking, and particularly strong, an accident can rob you of all these benefits in a moment. Also, these goods are common to humans and other animals, whereas true happiness is the prerogative of humans alone, in the animal kingdom. Indeed, some other animals even surpass man in certain goods of the body, yet without being capable of genuine happiness. Besides, since the human soul is superior to the human body, its goods, such as understanding and virtue, must surpass the goods of the body. But "neither does man's supreme good consist in goods of his sensitive faculty," for they too are common to man and lower animals. Besides, man's intellect is superior to all his faculties of sensation, so that its good must surpass theirs. Well, then, might human felicity consist in the goods of the soul? Virtues and moral actions are ordered to something beyond themselves, such as being and doing good. But "human felicity is incapable of being ordered to a further end, if it is ultimate." Therefore, it cannot consist in these spiritual goods. Besides, as was intimated earlier, "the ultimate end of all things is to become like unto God." So whatever most brings this about in man will constitute his true felicity. But virtues and moral actions "cannot be attributed to God, except metaphorically" and therefore cannot represent man's ultimate end. Nor does prudent action constitute human felicity because it is merely concerned "with contingent problems of action" and is shared in by some irrational animals. Nor does the intellectual virtue of art, in the sense of skilled practice, represent our highest end since it gives us practical knowledge ordered to some other extrinsic ends having to do with mere artifacts.[105] So, human felicity is not a function of any external goods, goods of the body, or goods of the soul we have analyzed.

THE CONTEMPLATION OF GOD. Now that all these possible candidates have been eliminated, where does that leave us? It seems we must "conclude that man's ultimate happiness consists in the contemplation of truth," which, in the last resort, is God. "For this operation alone is proper to man," among all the animals. Also, only this "is not directed to anything further as to its end since the contemplation of the truth is sought for its own sake." Further, it is in this pursuit that humans are least dependent on external things and contingent circumstances. Now, this contemplation of the truth is not necessarily a matter of scientifically knowing first principles, which is always imperfect for us. It rather "consists in wisdom, based on the consideration of divine things" or on the contemplation of God. This is not the common, confused sense of God that most people generally possess, for that is defective and susceptible to error. But, at the other extreme, neither is it the demonstrative knowledge of God sought by philosophers, since too few people can ever achieve this and it too "is subject to the admixture of many errors." Nor is it merely a relation of a believer to God through faith alone, for this is too imperfect in its failure to understand and is chiefly an act of will rather than of intellect. In this life we are so limited by our bodies, "the corporeal senses," and our physical environment that we can never see the divine essence. Since man's ultimate happiness requires that he see the divine essence, rather than any of the approaches to God that are possible for us in this life, "man's ultimate happiness" cannot be attained in this life. The kind of knowledge and understanding possible in this life leaves us yearning for more, rather than achieving the "stability and rest" characteristic of true felicity. Also, we can never be free of evils in this life, including that of the fear of death, and this fact is an insurmountable obstacle to genuine happiness in this life. If we ever achieved our final end, all natural desire would be stilled, which is impossible in this life. We have a natural desire for final happiness.

Natural desire cannot be empty, since *nature does nothing in vain.*

Thus, it must be possible for this natural desire to be fulfilled. But, Aquinas has argued, this cannot ever be in this life.

Therefore man's ultimate happiness is after this life.

This is the beatific "vision of God" which "is promised to us in Holy Scripture" (I *Cor.* 13:12), whereby we shall experience God directly, know God, "become most like God," and share most fully in the divine blessedness. We cannot achieve this by our own natural power, but only by divine grace. But God's grace, combined with our own virtuous living in this world, can bring to pass that "eternal life" after our natural death which constitutes the final fulfillment of human nature.[106]

REFLECTIONS

Aquinas constructed a philosophical world-view of Christian Aristotelianism to rival that of Christian Platonism developed by Augustine (although Platonic themes, such as those developed by Augustine himself, also figure into Aquinas's thought). As befits a follower of Aristotle, Aquinas may be the most impressive employer of logical argumentation of all the thinkers considered here. Indeed, his entire system can be viewed as a **coherent**, intricate body of deductive arguments, staggering in its comprehensive scope, acutely critical, and routinely valid. But, just as the problems with Augustine's system stem from assumptions derived from Platonic philosophy and Christian faith, so, generally, those affecting Aquinas's system can be tracked back to his Aristotelian presuppositions and Christian assumptions. Again, however, these views are representative of the era and present us with ample material for our own critical reflection.

REALITY.   His theory of reality, our first topic, is built on a hierarchical view of being which fits neatly into the molds of both ancient Greek philosophy and the Christian conception of an orderly creation. His idea of levels of perfection—extending from God, the perfect Creator, at one extreme, down to the lowest, most basic inanimate creature, at the other—presumes both a **realistic** epistemology and some equivalence between ontology and perfection. The realistic epistemology, allowing us to know things as they actually are in themselves rather than merely as they appear to us humans, will be severely challenged by the great **Enlightenment** philosophers we shall study, Hume and Kant. The equivalence between ontology and perfection, the presumption that the excellence of a thing is directly proportionate to how independent and spiritual a being it is, is sufficiently dubious to require rational support.

BODIES.   Second, his Aristotelian analysis of bodies exhibits strengths and weaknesses similar to those of Aristotle. The idea of bodies as formed matter, with form actualizing the potentiality of matter and the four causes providing a theoretical explanation of it all, has a neatness to it and invites scientific study. On the other hand, here as in Aristotle, how the hylomorphism works is problematic, namely, what are the matter and form in themselves, and how does the latter actualize the potentiality of the former? Although the doctrine of the four causes is famous and fascinating, it assumes a teleological view of reality that is more a postulate than a scientific finding, and it is subject to the critique we shall see modern thinkers develop.

PERSONALITY.   Third, Aquinas offers us a conception of human personality that though remarkably complex, nevertheless holds together quite well. His rich conception of the soul, though problematic in its hylomorphic characterization as the animating form of a body, allows him to explain a vast array of activities as operations derived from various powers of different kinds of souls. It also allows him to say that all animate things have souls, or principles of life, while maintaining the unique nature, activities, and capacities of the human soul. But it is most crucial for Aquinas's purposes, both here and later, that he convince us that the soul is an immaterial substance. Rather than accepting his view of the soul as an incorporeal thing (mysteriously connected to the corporeal body), why should we not say, as some later thinkers will, that it is a word we use to refer to the life and activities of which some bodies are capable because of their biological nature? On this view, some kinds of bodies have the capacity for life and vital

---

Coherence.   A relation between experiences, beliefs, or propositions such that they are logically compatible or consistent

activities on account of their physiology, combined with favorable environmental conditions, "soul" being merely what we call this capacity. Likewise, one might object, the human faculty of knowing might not be an immaterial substance at all but rather, the human brain, which is part of this wonderful organism we call the human body. This view might make it easier to see how we can know physical reality since the principle of knowing is itself physical. Nor does it seem plausible that we need an immaterial substance to account for abstract, universal knowledge. Aquinas wants to have it both ways—to maintain that all human knowledge is anchored in sense experience and to hold that some human knowledge transcends all sense experience—without explaining clearly and cogently how such a combination is possible. The human mind might abstract from sense particulars as a physical process of the brain, rather than needing to be a faculty of a spiritual substance to do so.

KNOWLEDGE. Aquinas's theory of knowledge, fourth, assumes that we know things as they really are rather than only ideas of things as they appear to us. But why should we grant him that Aristotelian assumption (derogatorily called that of "naive realism")? As modern thinkers from Descartes to Kant (and even more recent ones) argue, the direct, immediate objects of the mind's experience are its ideas of things. You experience this book only through its appearances—the way it feels in your hands, looks to your eyes, and smells in your nostrils—as they are filtered through your ideas of it. What good reason could you possibly have to suppose that it is, in itself, as you experience it to be? This introduces a second major problem with Thomistic epistemology: if we only directly experience our own ideas, through which all our experience of things must be filtered, then how could we ever establish the truth as a conformity between the one and the other? Our knowledge of any correspondence between our ideas and external reality requires that we have access to things as they are in themselves, independent of our experience, which access is dubious.

FREEDOM. Aquinas's discussion of human freedom, to move to our fifth topic, may be familiarly comfortable to most of us, reinforcing what we would like to believe about ourselves. Yet there are two possible problems with it, one of proof and the other of compatibility. Against his philosophical argumentation, the determinist will say that advice, threats, appeals, and so forth do affect human action, not because we freely choose whether to comply with them or not, but because they become parts of a stimulus-response process that determines behavior. But then there is also the issue of how human freedom is compatible with an infinite God who created humans while infallibly knowing how they would behave and who rules over them and their world with all-encompassing power. It might be more tenable to consider human freedom a rational postulate, as Kant and James will, than to imagine it to be logically demonstrable.

MORALITY. Sixth, Aquinas's treatment of morality provides a particularly striking example of his deft synthesizing of Aristotle's philosophy and Christian teachings. Augustine's privation theory of evil, Aristotle's moral teleology, and medieval Christian ethics blend neatly in Aquinas's thought. He can portray the human soul as naturally perfected by intellectual and moral virtue, while—through God's grace—also being supernaturally perfected by the theological virtues. His ethical theory can even be more universal than Aristotle's because of its foundation in the eternal, immutable, all-encompassing will of God. But this also presents a serious problem with it, that it presupposes a commitment to a God whose divine commands dictate moral values. To his credit, Aquinas tries to argue rationally for his God as Sovereign of all creation; but, we shall observe, that entire line of reasoning is uncertain. Also, as Mill later points out, we should be quite suspicious of claims that the natural is equivalent to the right. It is too tempting to identify actions of which we wish to approve as "natural" and arbitrarily to condemn acts of which we disapprove as "unnatural"; indeed, morality often seems to allow, or even require, us to intervene in or resist natural processes, rather than always permitting nature to run its course.

SOCIETY. Aquinas's model of society, to consider our seventh topic, may well be that dimension of his system that will be least appealing to most of us today. What is attractive about it is its strong sense of lawful community and social order. But we tend to recoil at its illiberal, intolerant, nondemocratic, sexist acceptance of a *status quo* in order to conserve those desirable values. There is not much more emphasis on personal autonomy and individual liberty in Aquinas than in his predecessors. His intolerance of heretics strikes many of us as odious and indicative of a smug, dogmatic arrogance that he and his Church have a monopoly on religious truth. His affinity for the political kingship of his own age seems an obsolete vestige of an era predating the evolution of representative democracy. His treatment of women as designed to serve man and bear and rear his children is offensive and calls for the excuse that it reflects the limited perspective of his culture. And his uncritical acceptance of slavery seems to condone a great social evil of his day. Even his idea that human laws must conform to the requirements of natural law, which ultimately relates to God's eternal law, is troubling in its cozy conjunction of Church and state. Overall, there is much here of which we should be suspicious.

RELIGION.   Eighth, Aquinas's position on God and religion is impressive, yet unconvincing. Theology is valuable as a systematic body of doctrinal beliefs about God; but whether it can be shown to be a science, as Aquinas maintains it is, depends on the doubtful prospects of our being able to establish such beliefs as knowledge. The most basic of these, of course, is the very existence of God. Aquinas's arguments for this are classic exercises in logic, all requiring that we accept dubious premises. The "first and more manifest way" of proving God's existence assumes as self-evident that the process of things moving others to change could not have gone on infinitely; but, in fact, reality might be so complex that there have always been many actual beings, none of which is infinitely perfect, which moved others from potentiality to actuality without themselves being moved into being. The second way assumes that cause-effect relationships, which apply to things in the world of our experience, apply similarly to the production of the world as a whole. The third way supposes, without justification, that, if everything exists contingently, then everything at some time or other will not exist and that, thus, there would have been some one time when nothing existed; but a contingent thing could just happen to be forever, and the temporarily existing things could temporally overlap in their existence, even if none of them existed forever, so that there never would be a time when

nothing existed. These first three proofs are often regarded as variations on the **cosmological argument**. The fourth of Aquinas's "five ways" imagines that the maximum of any sort must productively cause everything else of that kind and that the maxima of all perfections must be united in a single causal source. The fifth way, which assumes that the order we see in the world is there objectively, rather than being merely our way of organizing experience, conveniently ignores the disorder of reality, and imagines that no naturalistic explanation of order can be adequate. Even if we accept any combination of these arguments, what they give us is a metaphysical principle, and not necessarily the infinitely perfect personal God of religion. But the one, absolutely simple, purely actualized highest Good, who is uniquely infinitely perfect, omniscient, and omnipotently ruling the whole world of creation, though it does correspond to the God of monotheism, transcends all our natural experience and thus would not appear to be available as an object of scientific knowledge. Aquinas's view of theological language as analogical is a lasting legacy. But his notion of religious faith as a kind of knowledge, as illustrated by belief in miracles, seems to stretch the concept of knowledge too far.

IMMORTALITY.   Aquinas's arguments for immortality of the human soul, to consider our ninth topic, are ingenious examples of logical reasoning. But they presuppose that we are already convinced that the soul is an immaterial substance, which we have already questioned. Without this presupposition his best arguments for immortality collapse. His most questionable assumptions are probably the one concerning our alleged desire to live forever and the confident assertion that no natural desire can be in vain. It is at least questionable whether we all desire to live forever. But, granting that for the sake of argument, it seems a mere leap of faith to think that the naturalness of such a desire requires that it be actually fulfilled; it might not be in vain if it merely motivated us to strive to stay alive. It is at least rationally possible that God could have created human souls that, despite their desire for immortality, would have a limited temporal duration before ceasing to be. It would seem that it is Christian theology, rather than logical argumentation, that definitively rules out this idea.

FULFILLMENT. Finally, Aquinas offers us the most sustained and rigorous position on human fulfillment, our tenth topic, of any philosopher we are considering. His reasoning here is intricate and brilliant. If we grant his teleological view that human nature must have a final, ultimate end which is uniquely fulfilling to it, and that it must consist in our transcending what we naturally are, then it does seem that Aquinas's conception of it is powerful, given his analyses of the human soul and God. But, of course, that requires us to concede many planks of his platform already questioned. If we do not grant those conditions, might we not reasonably question the identity of God as the supreme Good of all and that which is achievable as best fulfilling our human nature?

* * *

Even apart from his achievements as a theologian, Aquinas is a first-rate philosopher—perhaps the greatest during the nineteen centuries between Aristotle and Descartes. He constructed a remarkable system in which every one of our ten topics is handled impressively. Although he died more than seven centuries ago, he is a living philosopher in the sense that professional philosophers today accept and build on his thought. To the extent that his Aristotelianism is more acceptable than Augustine's Platonism, he has an advantage over his Christian predecessor. Both are apt representatives of the medieval spirit of "faith seeking understanding." But, as Augustine relies too uncritically on the authority of Plato, so does Aquinas on that of Aristotle. Famous thinkers of the Renaissance would challenge this easy, comfortable acceptance of the authority of others, setting the stage for the revolution of modern philosophy that would occur in the seventeenth century, with such thinkers as Descartes and Hobbes. This revolution will develop epistemology, or the theory of knowledge, as the foundational area of philosophy that it never was in the ancient and medieval eras. This would better enable us to test the extent to which philosophy, in general, and the philosophy of human nature, in particular, can be treated as demonstrative sciences.

QUESTIONS

1. *How does Augustine distinguish among three general types of reality, and why are they all essentially good? How do the things that exist allegedly constitute a hierarchy of being?*

2. *What is the problem of evil, and how does Augustine try to solve it? What are one advantage and one disadvantage of his view?*

3. *How does Augustine argue for the immortality of the human soul? What do you consider the weakest premise in his reasoning, and how could he most convincingly support it?*

4. *How is Aquinas's theory of bodies influenced by Aristotle, and how are matter and form supposedly related in a living body? How do you find the doctrine of the four causes helpful (or why do you think it worthless) in explaining any particular body?*

5. *What are the powers of the human soul for Aquinas, and how do they represent a hierarchy? To what extent does this theory help us to understand the human person's relationship to other animals?*

6. *How does Aquinas argue that nothing in this life can be man's final end and ultimate happiness? How would you evaluate the reasoning he uses to show that only our beatific vision of God in the afterlife will truly fulfill our human nature?*

7. *How do Augustine and Aquinas agree in their understanding of the human person? What are their significant disagreements? With which side are you more sympathetic, and why?*

8. *How does Augustine's theory of knowledge exhibit the influence of Platonism? How does Aquinas's epistemology borrow from Aristotle? Which approach do you consider more promising, and why?*

9. *Why is free choice good even though it leads to evil and sin, according to Augustine? How does Aquinas argue for free choice? How can they answer the objection that human beings cannot be truly free, given God's infallible foreknowledge?*

10. *What are moral virtues, for Augustine and Aquinas? Which ones do they emphasize, and why? What are strengths and weaknesses of the view that morality must correspond to God's eternal will?*

11. *Why do Augustine and Aquinas both put so much emphasis on law and order as essential to a good society? What problems might stem from such an emphasis? Does our own society sufficiently respect these values?*

12. *How does Augustine argue for the existence of God? Summarize the one of Aquinas's "five ways" of proving God's existence you think most convincing. Why do you (or do you not) find either of these arguments logically persuasive?*

ALTERNATIVES

BOETHIUS

Approximately half a century after Augustine's death, Anicius Manlius Severinus Boethius (c480–524) was born into an ancient aristocratic Roman family which had converted to Christianity in the previous century. His father had been a Roman consul but died when Boethius was very young. The boy was adopted by Symmachus, a wealthy Roman senator, received a fine education in the liberal arts and philosophy, and learned Greek. He married his guardian's daughter Rusticiana and pursued the life of a scholar, translating Aristotle's logical *Organon* into Latin, which rendered it accessible to scholastic thinkers throughout the rest of the Middle Ages. He wrote works on arithmetic, music, and geometry, three of the seven liberal arts of medieval times; he also composed a theological book, *On the Trinity,* which significantly follows Augustine. When Boethius was a teenager, Theodoric, King of the Ostrogoths, became Governor of Rome, though technically under the authority of the Eastern Emperor. Theodoric belonged to the heretical Arian sect of Christianity, which considered Jesus the highest of created beings, rather than of "one substance" with God, the Creator. Theodoric maintained the Roman Senate and administrative system of consuls, but he energetically and ably supervised the government so that he, himself, retained ultimate power. In 510, Boethius was appointed Roman consul, and later Theodoric appointed him head of the entire civil service system. Boethius greatly admired Plato's *Republic* and subscribed to its ideal of philosophical political leadership. In 522, his two sons became joint consuls. Then fortune sharply turned against him. He was accused of treason (he had disapproved of Theodoric's undermining the power of the Senate), arrested, exiled, tortured, and executed by bludgeoning around 524. While he was in prison he wrote one of the most popular medieval works, *The Consolation of Philosophy.* He is both the last important Roman philosopher and the taproot of medieval scholasticism, which includes Aquinas.

The Consolation is a dialogue, set in prison at Pavia, between Boethius and Lady Philosophy. At its outset the author is feeling sorry for himself for being betrayed by fickle fortune and complains of the injustice of his plight. The personification of Philosophy offers him rational consolation and reminds him that Socrates courageously faced an undeserved death for her sake. Philosophers often have to cope with injustices committed against them because their opposition to wickedness arouses hostility from evildoers. When Philosophy asks Boethius to define human nature, he gives the traditional response that man is a rational, mortal animal; but he fails to remember the final end proper to all creatures, without which he cannot achieve an adequate understanding of his nature or situation. We are told that the only permanent quality of fortune, ironically, is its constant mutability and that we should expect and accept its changes, not allowing ourselves to become overly attached to its blessings, over which we have little control. No human can ever be completely happy in this life because of the anxiety that inevitably attends this lack of control. As the Stoics taught, we must learn to subordinate our concern for the things of fortune to an attachment to higher values that we can control. This is, of course, reminiscent of Augustine's distinctions between temporal and eternal goods and between material and spiritual values.

We are warned against identifying the final good of human nature with any of the earthly goods of wealth, social position, political power, fame, or physical pleasure. If we have a lot of money, we need help protecting it and must fear its loss. People in exalted social positions are either worthy or not: if not, their position is shameful; but if they are worthy, it is because of their virtue, which can be corrupted by high office. Political power is a transient good, too dependent on other people and external circumstances. Fame is either deserved or not: if not, it is embarrassing; if deserved, it adds nothing to the excellence of good character. Physical pleasure is fleeting and often brings remorse in its wake, since it subjects us to the animal part of our nature. So, the argument (which anticipates the reasoning of Aquinas) concludes that genuine happiness, the fulfillment of human nature, must lie elsewhere. Philosophy then presents a poetic, Neoplatonic analysis of God as the perfect Good and, like Augustine, describes God as the greatest conceivable Being. Ultimate happiness must be oriented towards the highest good, which is God, the final end of all creatures, including humans. Since God is all-good and created all things, no creature can be intrinsically evil; and Philosophy invokes the Neoplatonic and Augustinian privation theory of evil.

The problem of evil is explicitly posed—how can evil exist and go unpunished in a world created and governed by an all-good God? Philosophy observes that we all want what is good for us. But evil men become the slaves of their own selfish passions, losing their power to achieve the good, which is a natural punishment that inevitably accompanies cupidity. Likewise, good will naturally carries with it the power to achieve the good, which is the reward of happiness. Since goodness and happiness are correlative, the good person will gain happiness by virtue of being good. Like Plato, Philosophy argues that the wicked are happier if they are caught, punished, and corrected than if their wickedness goes undetected and that the unjust are less happy than their innocent victims, regardless of surface appearances, because they corrupt their souls and make themselves deserving of punishment.

Boethius worries that human freedom might be incompatible with divine foreknowledge. Philosophy points out, in a passage somewhat reminiscent of Plato's divided-line analysis, that there is a hierarchy of four levels of awareness: sense perception, imagination, reason, and intelligence. The senses discern particular forms in matter, whereas the imagination considers those forms without matter; yet neither the senses nor the imagination grasps the universal. Reason does so by reflecting on the species inherent in individual objects. Finally, intelligence transcends even

the universal considerations of genus and species to apprehend simple forms through pure insight. Different sorts of living beings are capable of different sorts of awareness. Animals that are incapable of self-movement have only the most primitive sensation; self-moving animals also have imagination; humans have the power of reason; and God enjoys pure intelligence. Our rational way of discerning the future does not correspond to the divine foreknowledge of pure intelligence. Divine intelligence is eternal and not limited, as is human reason, by the structures of past, present, and future time. Yet even our temporal, rational awareness of things does not render them necessary. We must distinguish between simple necessity and conditional necessity. It is simply necessary, by virtue of human nature itself, that all men should die; but the necessity of someone's walking is merely conditioned by my knowledge that she is walking. There is nothing in the nature of a human that dictates that she be walking at any particular moment; and my rational awareness that she is walking, though it requires that she actually be walking now, is not the efficient cause of her walking. Likewise, God's eternal foreknowledge that you would be reading now conditionally requires that you be doing so; yet it is not a simple necessity of your nature that dictates the fact, nor is God's foreknowledge its efficient cause in any sense that would preclude your free choice and responsibility. Because the will of a rational creature is free of simple necessity, he or she must choose to cultivate virtue and avoid vice in order to achieve the final good of true happiness that is the genuine fulfillment of human nature. This remains within our power, regardless of fickle fortune and adverse circumstances.

* * *

Between the medieval era and the rise of modernism there is a period in the history of Western Civilization called the Renaissance, from the French word for rebirth; it is quite remarkable, though it produced no philosophers of the first order (comparable to any of the dozen being considered in depth in this book). Although the fall of Constantinople to the Turks in 1453 led to the greatest influx of Greek manuscripts and scholars that broadly scattered this rebirth of learning throughout Europe, the humanistic revival of interest in the classics had begun earlier in Italy. In order to make a transition between medievalism and the early modernism covered in our next chapter, let us briefly examine two sixteenth-century philosophers, Machiavelli and Montaigne.

MACHIAVELLI

Niccolo Machiavelli (1469–1527), a contemporary of da Vinci and Michelangelo, was born in Florence (in present-day Italy), the son of a jurist, and apparently received a humanistic education, though not much is known of his youth. He became active in the political life of the Florentine Republic, serving as its defense secretary and as a diplomat, until the Republic collapsed and the Medici family was restored to power in 1512, dismissing him from public office. The following year he was imprisoned and tortured on the rack on unproved accusations of having conspired against the Medici. When he was released, he was banished from Florence and retired to his country estate, where he wrote his most important works. These included *The Prince,* the *Discourses,* and the comic play, *Mandragola.* Because he humbled himself before the Medici in hopes of regaining favor, he was distrusted by his countrymen when the Republic was briefly restored in 1527, and he died an embittered man.

The Prince, dedicated to Lorenzo de' Medici, was published in 1532, five years after Machiavelli's death; but it had been circulated in manuscript form, did little to win him favor with the Medici family, and only served to antagonize others. It is a revolutionary little handbook that is cynically and provocatively detached from the religious idealism of the medieval era and is often considered a pioneering work of realistic political science. It describes and analyzes the way an ideal prince (presumably modeled on Cesare Borgia, whom he twice met) achieves and maintains political power.

Machiavelli categorizes governments as either republics or monarchies and focuses on the latter in *The Prince* (in his *Discourses* he expresses republican sympathies). A monarch who inherits political power tends to be more fortunate than one who must win it for himself, Machiavelli maintains, because he will likely make fewer enemies and need not make as many commitments. Sometimes, a prince must resort to cruelty in order to secure and retain power; when that is the case, he should execute that cruelty as quickly and ruthlessly as possible, rather than dragging it out or seeming softhearted and apologetic about it. An effective prince must be well-versed in and constantly ready for war and not be hampered by moral scruples. Although a prince should try to be both feared and loved, the former is more valuable and secure than the latter. He should rule by law when he can and by force when he must, imitating a combination of the clever, wily fox and the fearless, powerful lion. He need not keep his word when doing so would run counter to his own interests. A prince should assign the most unpopular duties to others, lest he personally suffer the people's hatred on account of them.

A successful prince must be prepared to do evil in order to maintain power, for he must deal with other people, who are selfish and bad. It is better for him to appear virtuous than actually to be virtuous, since the former endears him to the people, whereas the latter can cost him his power. Like other Renaissance thinkers, Machiavelli is concerned about the unpredictable role Fortune plays in human affairs. Even the shrewdest man cannot anticipate all the twists and turns of Fortune, leading to unforeseen consequences and limiting our free will. The effective prince will boldly exploit the benefits and fiercely combat the adversities of Fortune, which can only be conquered by force.

What is striking about this view, especially in contrast to the great medieval theories, is its cynical detachment of realistic politics from idealistic morality. More than a century before Hobbes, Machiavelli eschews religious pieties, refuses to appeal to conventional authorities, and presents a boldly secular humanism. He seems to regard human nature as frail, fickle, devious, selfish, and untrustworthy. In this portrait, power—the lust for power and subjection to it—assumes a central role that it never played in the great philosophies of ancient and medieval times.

MONTAIGNE

Michel de Montaigne (1533–92), born six years after Machiavelli's death, is most renowned as the French pioneer of the modern essay. He was learning Latin and some Greek before the age of six, attended college in Bordeaux, and then began studying law at the age of thirteen. From 1557 to 1570, he served as a councilor of the Bordeaux parliament. His first literary work, published in 1569, was a translation of the *Natural Theology* of Raymond Sebond, who argued that human reason can naturally comprehend the universe and establish the existence and nature of God. In the 1570s, Montaigne was temporarily retired from political life, writing essays on the estates he had inherited from his father. The longest of his essays, *Apology for Raymond Sebond*, was written about 1576, while Montaigne was studying Greek scepticism and succumbing to its influence; he adopted the slogan "*Que sais-je?*" ("What do I know?") as his personal motto. After the first two books of his *Essays* (including the *Apology*) were published in 1580, he went to Paris to present copies of them to the king and then proceeded to travel through Germany, Switzerland, and Italy. While he was gone, he found out that he had been elected mayor of Bordeaux; he cut short his visit to Italy to assume his official functions and served two terms, from 1581 to 1585. He composed a third volume of *Essays*, publishing the complete edition in Paris in 1588, four years before he died.

The *Apology,* surely one of the finest examples of Renaissance scepticism, is a "defense" of Raymond Sebond's natural theology only in the extended sense of contending that all human reasoning is unsound, that Sebond's is no worse than anyone else's attempts at it, and that the Christian religion should be founded on faith alone. Montaigne expresses his belief that Sebond's reasoning is largely drawn from Aquinas. Against the entire enterprise of natural theology, Montaigne holds that human reason is naturally incapable of establishing religious truth, though it can aid in strengthening the faith we have already acquired through God's grace. He characterizes human beings as naturally wretched and puny creatures, vainly puffing themselves up with a foolish conceit and exclaims, quoting Cicero, over the narrow limits of man's mind.

He holds that our alleged superiority over other animals, which we have seen extolled by Augustine and Aquinas, as well as by their ancient predecessors, is only a presumption based on pride. Other animals communicate with members of their own species as surely as we do. Other animals exhibit intelligence and social order as well. The brutes exercise certain natural capacities, in fact, which exceed our own, though, on balance, we are on a level comparable to theirs. It is by virtue of our free-ranging imagination that we are remarkable in relation to the other animals; but, unfortunately, this is also the root source of our problems—sin, sickness, confusion, and despair. Our fertile imagination leads us to suffer illusory ills and to fear future misfortunes, which would be better endured in ignorance. Our true welfare consists in freedom from pain and suffering.

Montaigne divides philosophers into three types: those who claim to have found the truth, those who claim it can never be found, and those who are still seeking it. Sceptics reject the presumption of the first two groups, accepting the imaginative and appetitive functions of the soul, while declining to utilize its consenting function, preferring to suspend judgment. This is especially so in relation to God, who transcends our experience and eludes our analogical notions. Philosophy, by its very nature, is so speculative that Montaigne describes it as no more than sophisticated poetry. Even the reality of our own human nature, in its combination of body and soul, is beyond all certain understanding, as even the rationalist Augustine admits. All objects of natural human reasoning are doubtful, and the only certain truth is revealed by God and accepted in faith. All alleged natural knowledge must be derived from sense experience, all of which is unreliable and subject to distortion. The dreams of sleep often seem more solid than our reasonings based on waking experience. The doctrine of a set of firm, eternal, immutable, knowable natural laws is merely an amusing invention of philosophers. Everything in our lives is constantly changing, so that all experience is relative and natural knowledge is impossible. What we lack is a criterion for judging the reliability of our experiences. Given the uncertainty of the senses, reason must be the judge; but reasoning itself could only be justified by a prior reasoning, and so on, *ad infinitum*, so that no final criterion can ever be justified. We naturally experience only the appearances of things; for us to try to grasp their reality, Montaigne insists, is like trying to clutch water in our hands.

* * *

As Machiavelli's *Prince* represents a sharp break from the Christian idealism of the medieval period and foreshadows the more realistic perspective of Hobbes, Montaigne's *Apology* forswears the confidence in rational knowledge exhibited by Augustine and Aquinas and extends an epistemological challenge Descartes would take up in the following century. Machiavelli and Montaigne invoke classical authors without appealing to literary or religious authorities to justify their positions; they develop their own perspectives, no matter how iconoclastic those might seem. Finally, both of them suggest a view of human nature that is less grand and more humbling than that embraced by philosophers of the medieval era.

Notes

1. Augustine, *Confessions*, trans. F. J. Sheed (Indianapolis: Hackett Publishing Co., 1993), pp. 3, 10–13. This work is henceforth called "*Confessions*."

2. Ibid., pp. 23–27, 35, 37–39, 51–52.

3. Ibid., pp. 57, 61, 73, 75–76, 79, 81–82.

4. Ibid., pp. 87, 103, 116–17, 123, 135, 139, 146, 157–58, 160, 165–66.

5. Ibid., pp. 158, 192.

6. Augustine, "The Nature of the Good," in *Augustine: Earlier Writings*, ed. and trans. John H. S. Burleigh (The Library of Christian Classics, Vol. VI) (London: SCM Press, Ltd., 1953), pp. 327, 331. This work is henceforth called "*Good*."

7. Augustine, *Letters*, trans. Sister Wilfrid Parsons (The Fathers of the Church, ed. Roy Joseph Deferrari) (New York: Fathers of the Church, 1951), Vol. I, p. 44. This work is henceforth called "*Letters*."

8. Augustine, *The City of God*, trans. Marcus Dods (New York: Modern Library, 1950), pp. 360, 350. This work is henceforth called "*City*."

9. *Confessions*, pp. 219, 223, 229–30.

10. Augustine, "On Music," trans. Robert Catesby Taliaferro, in *Writings of Saint Augustine*, Vol. 2, ed. Ludwig Schopp (New York: CIMA Publishing Co., 1947), p. 338. This work is henceforth called "*On Music*." Cf. Augustine, *Of True Religion*, trans. J. H. S. Burleigh (Chicago: Henry Regnery Co., 1959), pp. 3–4. This work is henceforth called "*Religion*."

11. Augustine, *On Free Choice of the Will*, trans. Thomas Williams (Indianapolis: Hackett Publishing Co., 1993), p. 45. This work is henceforth called "*Will*."

12. *City*, pp. 383–84.

13. *Confessions*, pp. 236–38.

14. Augustine, *The Trinity*, trans. Stephen McKenna (The Fathers of the Church, Vol. 45, ed. Roy Joseph Deferrari) (Washington, D.C.: The Catholic Univ. of America Press, 1963), pp. 108–9. This work is henceforth called "*Trinity*."

15. *City*, pp. 407, 422–23, 851–54. Cf. Augustine, *On the Literal Interpretation of Genesis: An Unfinished Book*, trans. Roland J. Teske, S.J. (The Fathers of the Church, Vol. 84, ed. Thomas P. Halton) (Washington, D.C.: The Catholic Univ. of America Press, 1991), p. 186.

16. *Will*, pp. 12–16, 27.

17. Ibid., pp. 33–40, 81–82, 107–10. On p. 111, Augustine considers four theories of the soul's origin, including the traditional Christian one that it is individually created "for each person who is born," but refrains from pursuing the matter philosophically, deferring to "divine authority" in the matter.

18. Augustine, "The Magnitude of the Soul," trans. John J. McMahon, S.J., in *Writings of Saint Augustine*, Vol. 2, ed. Ludwig Schopp (New York: CIMA Publishing Co., 1947), pp. 59–65, 67, 83, 147, 149.

19. Augustine, "Of the Morals of the Catholic Church," in *Writings in Connection with the Manichaean Heresy*, trans. Richard Stothert (*The Works of Aurelius Augustine*, Vol. 5, ed.

Marcus Dods) (Edinburgh: T. & T. Clark, 1872), p. 33. This work is henceforth called "*Morals*."

20. Augustine, "Divine Providence and the Problem of Evil" ("*De Ordine*"), trans. Robert P. Russell, in *Writings of Saint Augustine*, Vol. 1, ed. Ludwig Schopp (New York: CIMA Publishing Co., 1948), p. 309. This work is henceforth called "*De Ordine*." Likewise Augustine, in *Concerning the Teacher*, trans. George G. Leckie (New York: Appleton-Century-Crofts, 1938), p. 34, defines man as "a rational, mortal animal." This work is henceforth called "*Teacher*."

21. Augustine, *On the Immortality of the Soul*, trans. George G. Leckie (New York: Appleton-Century-Crofts, 1938), pp. 67–69, 83–84. This work is henceforth called "*Immortality*."

22. *On Music*, pp. 335–36.

23. *Confessions*, pp. 180–84, 186.

24. *Trinity*, pp. 310–12.

25. Augustine, "The Happy Life," in *Augustine of Hippo: Selected Writings*, trans. Mary T. Clark (New York: Paulist Press, 1984), pp. 172–73. This work is henceforth called "*Happy*."

26. *Religion*, pp. 10, 19–20, 41, 49–50; in *De Ordine* (p. 303), Augustine writes that we approach "the acquiring of knowledge . . . in a twofold manner: by authority and by reason," the former occurring as temporally prior and the latter being epistemologically superior.

27. Augustine, "The Soliloquies," in *Augustine: Earlier Writings*, ed. and trans. John H. S. Burleigh (The Library of Christian Classics, Vol. VI) (London: SCM Press, 1953), pp. 24, 26–27, 32, 45. This work is henceforth called "*Soliloquies*." For another example of the analogy between God and the Sun, regarding illumination, see *Happy*, p. 192. In Augustine, *The Enchiridion on Faith, Hope and Love*, trans. J. F. Shaw (Chicago: Henry Regnery Co., 1961), p. 19, he holds that error is the opposite of truth, "that to err is just to take the false for the true, and the true for the false, or to hold what is certain as uncertain, and what is uncertain as certain." This work is henceforth called "*Enchiridion*."

28. *Will*, pp. 2–3, 32, 44–46, 50, 52, 54–55.

29. Augustine, *Against the Academicians*, trans. Sister Mary Patricia Garvey (Milwaukee: Marquette Univ. Press, 1957), pp. 38–39, 66–68, 81–82. In Augustine, *The Retractations*, trans. Sister Mary Inez Bogan (The Fathers of the Church, Vol. 60, ed. Roy Joseph Deferrari) (Washington, DC: The Catholic Univ. of America Press, 1968), p. 10, he expresses regret for the excessive praise he lavished on Plato and other "irreligious men," meaning non-Christians. This work is henceforth called "*Retractations*." For further endorsements of Platonism, however, *see City*, pp. 247–50.

30. *Teacher*, p. 51.

31. *City*, p. 370; cf. *Trinity*, pp. 480–81.

32. *City*, pp. 154–57.

33. *Will*, pp. 29–30, 57, 64–67, 73–74, 77–78.

34. Ibid., pp. 5–8, 19–22.

35. Ibid., pp. 24–27, 68–69, 72.

36. Ibid., p. 87; *City*, pp. 26, 29–31.

37. Ibid., pp. 441, 448–49, 692–93, 678, 706–7; for more on the original sin affecting humanity, *see* pp. 550–51, 782–83, 811, 850. In connection with the commandments of love, we should consider one of the most famous and most easily misunderstood of Augustine's sayings: In Augustine, *Tractates on the First Epistle of John*, trans. John W. Rettig (The Fathers of the Church, Vol. 92, ed. Thomas P. Halton) (Washington, DC: The Catholic Univ. of America Press, 1995), p. 223, he writes, "Love and do what you will" (*Dilige et quod vis fac*), which should be interpreted as an assurance that proper love will always choose the good rather than serve as a license to behave anyway we may please. In addition to the natural virtues, a good soul that is properly oriented towards God should exercise the three theological virtues of faith, hope, and love (*Soliloquies*, pp. 31–32).

38. *Good*, pp. 327, 330–31.

39. *Religion*, pp. 34, 73–74.

40. Augustine, *Writings in Connection with the Manichaean Heresy*, trans. Richard Stothert (*The Works of Aurelius Augustine*, Vol. 5, ed. Marcus Dods) (Edinburgh: T. & T. Clark, 1872), p. 424.

41. *Enchiridion*, pp. 20–24.

42. *Will*, pp. 8, 11–12.

43. *City*, pp. 61, 63, 112, 477, 123, 683, 687. For more on the notion of a just war, see the selection from "Against Faustus the Manichaean," in Augustine, *Political Writings*, ed. Ernest L. Fortin and Douglas Kries and trans. Michael W. Tkacz and Douglas Kries (Indianapolis: Hackett Publishing Co., 1994), pp. 220–29. This work is henceforth called *"Political."*

44. *City*, pp. 469–70, 839–40; cf. the selection from *On the Literal Interpretation of Genesis*, in *Political*, pp. 250–53.

45. *Confessions*, p. 283. For more on the alleged natural subordination of women, see *Trinity*, pp. 351–55.

46. Augustine, "The Advantage of Believing," trans. Luanne Meagher, in *Writings of Saint Augustine*, Vol. 2, ed. Ludwig Schopp (New York: CIMA Publishing Co., 1947), pp. 392, 396–97, 419–24. This work is henceforth called *"Believing."*

47. Ibid., pp. 424–27, 440. Cf. *Teacher*, p. 47.

48. Augustine, "On Faith in Things Unseen," trans. Roy J. Deferrari and Mary Francis McDonald in *Writings of Saint Augustine*, Vol. 2, ed. Ludwig Schopp (New York: CIMA Publishing Co., 1947), pp. 451–56, 460, 464–65, 467.

49. *Will*, pp. 1, 3–4, 40–41, 58. For more on the idea that God is "above the rational mind," see *Religion*, pp. 53–54. For more on the view that God is the Supreme Being, *see* Augustine, *On Christian Doctrine*, trans. D. W. Robertson, Jr. (Indianapolis: Bobbs-Merrill, 1958), pp. 11–12.

50. *Will*, pp. 96–100.

51. *Enchiridion*, pp. 10–16, 33; cf. *City*, pp. 354, 365, 383–84, and *Confessions*, pp. 111, 118–19, for more on the problem of evil.

52. *Trinity*, pp. 176–77, 229; cf. letter to Consentius, in *Letters*, Vol. II, pp. 310–11, and Saint Augustine, *Sermons on the Liturgical Seasons*, trans. Sister Mary Sarah Muldowney (The Fathers of the Church, Vol. 38, ed. Roy Joseph Deferrari) (New York: Fathers of the Church, 1959), p. 119. This last work is henceforth called *"Sermons."*

53. Augustine, *Tractates on the Gospel of John*, trans. John W. Rettig (The Fathers of the Church, Vol. 88, ed. Thomas P.

54. *Soliloquies*, pp. 41, 43–44, 55; cf. *Believing*, p. 409.

55. *Immortality*, pp. 59–61, 63, 74. In his *Retractations*, p. 20, Augustine criticizes this early work as "so obscure" that he seems to regret its publication.

56. *Will*, pp. 22–23, 60; cf. *Confessions*, p. 190, and *De Ordine*, p. 324.

57. *Morals*, pp. 3–7, 9, 13–17.

58. *City*, pp. 671–72, 676, 786, 859, 864–65, 867.

59. *Happy*, pp. 174, 183–84, 192–93.

60. Thomas Aquinas, *Introduction to St. Thomas Aquinas*, ed. Anton C. Pegis (New York: Modern Library, 1948), pp. 77–78. This anthology is henceforth called "Pegis" and will be used where possible, quotes from other works being used to supplement its contents.

61. Thomas Aquinas, *Selected Writings of St. Thomas Aquinas*, trans. Robert P. Goodwin (Indianapolis: Bobbs-Merrill, 1965), pp. 7, 33–34, 36–37, 58–60, 62. This collection is henceforth called "Goodwin."

62. Ibid., pp. 10, 15–16.

63. Ibid., pp. 40–43.

64. Thomas Aquinas, *On the Truth of the Catholic Faith: Summa contra Gentiles*, trans. Anton C. Pegis, James F. Anderson, Vernon J. Bourke, and Charles J. O'Neil (Garden City, NY: Image Books, 1955–57), Book Two, p. 157. This series is henceforth called *"Gentiles."*

65. Pegis, pp. 254, 265.

66. Ibid., pp. 281–87, 292–93, 304–6, 308. For comparable material from *On Being and Essence*, see Goodwin, pp. 36–37, 45, 47–49, 53, 57. For even more detailed argumentation, see Thomas Aquinas, *Questions on the Soul*, trans. James H. Robb (Milwaukee: Marquette Univ. Press, 1984), Questions One, Two, and Eleven. This book is henceforth called *"Soul."*

67. *Gentiles*, Book Two, pp. 164–66, 169–76.

68. Pegis, pp. 322–26, 329, 332–34, 339.

69. Ibid., pp. 341–42, 348, 356–64, 569–70, 581–82. For an interesting comparative analysis of intellect and will, *see* Thomas Aquinas, *On Evil*, trans. Jean Oesterle (Notre Dame, IN: Univ. of Notre Dame Press, 1995), p. 244. This book is henceforth called *"Evil."*

70. Thomas Aquinas, *Summa Theologica*, trans. Fathers of the English Dominican Province (New York: Benziger Brothers, 1947), Vol. One, p. 158. This work is henceforth called *"Theologica."*

71. Thomas Aquinas, *Truth*, trans. Robert W. Mulligan, S.J., James V. McGlynn, S.J., and Robert W. Schmidt, S.J. (Indianapolis: Hackett Publishing Co., 1994), Vol. I, pp. 10–11, 13, 41, 44–45, 48, 50. See also Pegis, pp. 171 and 181, for the definition of truth as *adaequatio intellectus et rei*. In *Evil*, p. 513, Aquinas writes, "As long as we are in this life an image is always necessary for us in using knowledge, no matter how spiritual the knowledge is because even God is known to us through an image of His effect."

72. Pegis, pp. 377–79.

73. Ibid., pp. 382, 384–85, 390, 393–94.

74. Pegis, pp. 402, 406, 409, 415–16, 419, 427.

75. Ibid., pp. 369–70, 373; cf. *Gentiles*, Book Two, pp. 142, 146.

76. Pegis, pp. 375, 486–90, 492–94.

77. Goodwin, pp. 121–24, 128, 131–33, 151–52. *See also Evil*, pp. 238–43.

78. Pegis, pp. 146, 268, 272, 275–76; *Theologica*, Vol. One, p. 249; *Evil*, p. 313. *See also Evil*, pp. 4–6, 104–7, 110, and *Gentiles*, Book Three, I, p. 44.

79. Pegis, pp. 523, 525–26, 528, 542.

80. Ibid., pp. 558, 562–64, 588–89, 591–92, 594, 606. For further valuable discussion of "the Virtues in General," see Goodwin, especially pp. 93, 96, 101–2, 110–11.

81. *Theologica*, Vol. One, pp. 901–2, 906–8, 980–81.

82. *Theologica*, Vol. Two, pp. 1431–32, 1435–36, 1467.

83. Ibid., pp. 1469–71.

84. Ibid., pp. 1664–68.

85. Ibid., pp. 1815–19, 1823.

86. Pegis, pp. 610, 612, 614–17.

87. Ibid., pp. 618, 631, 633, 637–38, 641–45.

88. Ibid., pp. 647, 649.

89. *Theologica*, Vol. One, pp. 466–68.

90. Thomas Aquinas, *On Kingship*, trans. Gerald B. Phelan (Toronto: Pontifical Institute of Medieval Studies, 1949), pp. 3–10.

91. *Theologica*, Vol. Two, pp. 1226, 1359–60, 1366.

92. Ibid., pp. 1434, 1645, 1221, 1476–77, 1480–82.

93. Pegis, pp. 5–9, 12–13, 21–24.

94. Ibid., pp. 25–26; *see also Gentiles*, Book One, pp. 86–96, and Goodwin, pp. 55–56.

95. Pegis, pp. 26–27.

96. Ibid., pp. 29, 31–32, 48, 54–56, 67, 152, 218, 223, 230–31; *see also Gentiles*, Book One, pp. 156–72, and Goodwin, p. 59. For a critique of Aquinas's theory of divine infinity, see Wayne P. Pomerleau, "Does Reason Demand That God Be Infinite?" *Sophia*, 24, No. 2 (1985), 18–27.

97. Pegis, pp. 83–84, 93–95, 107–8, 124–25; *see also Gentiles*, Book One, pp. 138–48, and Goodwin, pp. 26–27.

98. *Gentiles*, Book One, pp. 62–64, 66–72, 74.

99. *Truth*, II, pp. 213, 217, 220–21, 250.

100. *Theologica*, Vol. One, pp. 518–20.

101. Pegis, pp. 288–89.

102. *Gentiles*, Book Two, pp. 158–60, 162–63, 254–56; *see also Soul*, Question Fourteen, especially pp. 176–78.

103. Pegis, pp. 431–39, 442–43, 447–48; cf. *Theologica*, Vol. One, pp. 583–89.

104. *Gentiles*, Book Three, I, pp. 111, 114–18; cf. *Theologica*, Vol. One, pp. 589–94.

105. *Gentiles*, Book Three, I, pp. 119–23.

106. Pegis, pp. 453–60, 463–66, 469, 471, 660.

Bibliography

GENERAL

Copleston, Frederick, S.J., *A History of Philosophy*, Vols. II, III. Garden City, NY: Image Books, 1962–63.

Fremantle, Anne. *The Age of Belief*. New York: Mentor Books, 1954.

Jones, W. T. *The Medieval Mind*, 2d ed. New York: Harcourt, Brace & World, 1969.

AUGUSTINE *Primary Sources*

"The Advantage of Believing." Trans. Luanne Meagher. In *Writings of Saint Augustine*, Vol. 2. Ed. Ludwig Schopp. New York: CIMA Publishing Co., 1947.

Against the Academicians. Trans. Sister Mary Patricia Garvey. Milwaukee: Marquette Univ. Press, 1957.

Augustine: Earlier Writings. Ed. and trans. John H. S. Burleigh (The Library of Christian Classics, Vol VI). London: SCM Press, 1953.

Augustine of Hippo: Selected Writings. Trans. Mary T. Clark. New York: Paulist Press, 1984.

An Augustine Reader. Ed. John J. O'Meara. Garden City, NY: Image Books, 1973.

The City of God. Trans. Marcus Dods. New York: Modern Library, 1950.

Concerning the Teacher and *On the Immortality of the Soul*. Trans. George G. Leckie. New York: Appleton-Century-Crofts, 1938.

Confessions. Trans. F. J. Sheed. Indianapolis: Hackett Publishing Co., 1993.

The Enchiridion on Faith, Hope and Love. Trans. J. F. Shaw. Chicago: Henry Regnery Co., 1961.

The Essential Augustine. Ed. Vernon J. Bourke. New York: Mentor Books, 1964.

"The Magnitude of the Soul." Trans. John J. McMahon, S.J. In *Writings of Saint Augustine*, Vol. 2. Ed. Ludwig Schopp. New York: CIMA Publishing Co., 1947.

"Of the Morals of the Catholic Church." In *Writings in Connection with the Manichaean Heresy*. Trans. Richard Stothert (*The Works of Aurelius Augustine*, Vol. V. Ed. Marcus Dods). Edinburgh: T. & T. Clark, 1872.

Of True Religion. Trans. John H. S. Burleigh. Chicago: Henry Regnery Co., 1959.

On Christian Doctrine. Trans. D. W. Robertson, Jr. Indianapolis: Bobbs-Merrill, 1958.

On Free Choice of the Will. Trans. Thomas Williams. Indianapolis: Hackett Publishing Co., 1993.

Political Writings. Ed. Ernest L. Fortin and Douglas Kries. Trans. Michael W. Tkacz and Douglas Kries. Indianapolis: Hackett Publishing Co., 1994.

Selected Writings of Saint Augustine. Ed. Roger Hazleton. Cleveland: The World Publishing Co., 1962.

The Trinity. Trans. Stephen McKenna (The Fathers of the Church, Vol. 25. Ed. Roy Joseph Deferrari). Washington, DC: Catholic Univ. of America Press, 1963.

Writings in Connection with the Manichaean Heresy. Trans. Richard Stothert (*The Works of Aurelius Augustine*, Vol. V. Ed. Marcus Dods). Edinburgh: T. & T. Clark, 1872.

Writings of Saint Augustine, Vol. 2. Ed. Ludwig Schopp, New York: CIMA Publishing Co., 1947.

Secondary Sources

Bourke, Vernon J. *Augustine's Quest of Wisdom*. Milwaukee: Bruce Publishing Co., 1945.

Chadwick, Henry. *Augustine*. Oxford, England: Oxford Univ. Press, 1986.

Markus, R. A., ed. *Augustine: A Collection of Critical Essays*. Garden City, NY: Doubleday & Co., 1972.

Marron, Henri. *Saint Augustine*. Trans. Patrick Hepburne-Scott. London: Longmans, Green and Co., 1957.

Meagher, Robert. *Augustine: An Introduction*. New York: Harper & Row, 1979.

Pope, Hugh. *St. Augustine of Hippo*. Garden City, NY: Image Books, 1961.

Van der Meer, F. *Augustine the Bishop*. Trans. Brian Battershaw and G. R. Lamb. New York: Harper & Row, 1965.

AQUINAS   Primary Sources

An Aquinas Reader. Ed. Mary T. Clark. Garden City, NY: Image Books, 1972.

Basic Writings of Saint Thomas Aquinas, 2 vols. Ed. Anton C. Pegis. New York: Random House, 1945.

Introduction to Saint Thomas Aquinas. Ed. Anton C. Pegis. New York: Modern Library, 1948.

On Evil. Trans. Jean Oesterle. Notre Dame, IN: Univ. of Notre Dame Press, 1995.

On Kingship. Trans. Gerald B. Phelan. Toronto: Pontifical Institute of Medieval Studies, 1949.

On Law, Morality, and Politics. Ed. William P. Baumgarth and Richard J. Regan, S.J. Indianapolis: Hackett Publishing Co., 1988.

On the Truth of the Catholic Faith: Summa contra Gentiles. Trans. Anton C. Pegis, James F. Anderson, Vernon J. Bourke, and Charles J. O'Neil. Garden City, NY: Image Books, 1955–57.

Philosophical Texts. Ed. and trans. Thomas Gilby. New York: Oxford Univ. Press, 1967.

The Pocket Aquinas. Ed. by Vernon J. Bourke. New York: Pocket Books, 1960.

Questions on the Soul. Trans. James H. Robb. Milwaukee: Marquette Univ. Press, 1984.

Selected Philosophical Writings. Ed. and trans. Timothy McDermott. New York: Oxford Univ. Press, 1993.

Selected Writings of St. Thomas Aquinas. Trans. Robert P. Goodwin. Indianapolis: Bobbs-Merrill, 1965.

Summa Theologica. Trans. Fathers of the English Dominican Province. New York: Benziger Brothers, 1947.

Truth. Trans. Robert W. Mulligan, S.J., James V. McGlynn, S.J., and Robert W. Schmidt, S. J. Indianapolis: Hackett Publishing Co., 1994.

Secondary Sources

Copleston, Frederick, S.J. *Aquinas*. Baltimore: Penguin Books, 1955.

D'Arcy, M. C., S.J. *St. Thomas Aquinas*. Westminster, MD: The Newman Press, 1954.

de Wulf, Maurice. *The System of Thomas Aquinas*. Trans. Ernest Messenger. New York: Dover Publications, 1959.

Kenny, Anthony, ed. *Aquinas: A Collection of Critical Essays*. Garden City, NY: Doubleday & Co., 1969.

Kretzmann, Norman, and Eleonore Stump, eds. *The Cambridge Companion to Aquinas*. New York: Cambridge Univ. Press, 1993.

Maritain, Jacques. *St. Thomas Aquinas*. Trans. Joseph W. Evans and Peter O'Reilly. New York: Meridian Books, 1958.

McInerny, Ralph. *St. Thomas Aquinas*. Notre Dame, IN: Univ. of Notre Dame Press, 1982.

Pieper, Josef. *Guide to Thomas Aquinas*. Trans. Richard and Clara Winston. New York: New American Library, 1964.

«‹»›»›»›»›»›»›»›»›»›»›»›»›»›»›»›»›»›»›»

Historical Background

«« «« «« «« «« «« «« «« «« «« «« «« «« «« «« «« «« «»» »» »» »» »» »» »» »» »» »» »» »» »» »» »»

y the beginning of the seventeenth century, England, Spain, France, and Germany, which had established their cultural identities during the **Middle Ages**, were emerging as **modern** nation-states. In 1603, Queen Elizabeth I of England, the younger daughter of Henry VIII, ended her reign of almost half a century and the Tudor dynasty of over a century, and was succeeded by the Stuart **monarch** James I, a Scot. Following the destruction of the Spanish Armada, England had become a preeminent naval power and was spreading its empire overseas. In 1607, the English established the Jamestown Colony in Virginia (named in honor of Elizabeth, who never married and was known as "the Virgin Queen"). Thirteen years later, Pilgrims, emigrating from England, by way of the Netherlands, because of laws punishing dissent from the Anglican religion, founded the Plymouth Colony in Massachusetts and signed the Mayflower compact, pledging allegiance to King James but agreeing to govern themselves by majority rule. Spain, the great power of the preceding century, was in decline following the death of Philip II in 1598. Throughout the seventeenth century, it was ruled by three of his Hapsburg successors, who tried to maintain the empire of its colonies abroad but lost its control over Portugal. In France political absolutism was achieved under the Bourbon kings, Louis XIII and Louis XIV, and their chief ministers, Cardinal Richelieu and Cardinal Mazarin, who exhibited their power by denying the Huguenots (the Calvinist Protestants of France) all political influence, while assuring them religious toleration, but then revoking the policy of tolerance and attempting to crush them altogether. The reign of Louis XIV (1643–1715), who was known as the "Sun King," was characterized by the pursuit of the king's glory: these years witnessed a reform of internal administration, a growth of industry, an encouragement of writers and artists, and a passion for architecture, with the building of the Versailles palace and Les Invalides and the completion of the Louvre's magnificent colonnade. Louis XIV's egocentrism is epitomized by his haughty boast, "I am the state" (*L'état, c'est moi*). The French began colonizing Canada near the beginning of the seventeenth century, although there was not much emigration or elaborate colonial administration there. The Holy Roman Empire, under the Hapsburgs, was losing power, and the German states were politically fragmented, lacking any effective central authority, and torn by religious enmity between Protestants and Catholics. This weakness afforded England, Spain, and France opportunities to exploit German instability and dissension for their own gain. Meanwhile, Holland was becoming an important power, with Amsterdam a burgeoning financial center and with a national economy boosted by talented, industrious immigrants (such as Jews from the Iberian Peninsula) attracted there by a policy of tolerance, and buoyed by prosperous trading by the Dutch East India Company and the Dutch West India Company.

In the realm of ideas, the aftermath of the **Renaissance** featured a **humanistic** (rather than **theocentric**) intellectual climate conducive to the beginning of the Age of **Reason**, in which developed the **phenomenon** of a scientific revolution that would so inspire the rise of modern **philosophy**. In the early seventeenth century, Francis Bacon developed the **inductive** method of modern science as an alternative to the *a priori* methodology of **medieval scholasticism**. Near the start of the seventeenth century, Johannes Kepler, using the careful astronomical observations of Tycho Brahe, published his three mathematical laws of elliptical planetary motion around the Sun. William Harvey, an English physician, helped lay the foundations of modern medicine by his discovery of the function of the heart and circulation of blood in animals. In Italy Galileo lectured at the University of Padua on the Copernican system, which the Catholic Inquisition had condemned; he was warned by the Church not to advocate this new astronomy, but his *Dialogues Concerning the Two Chief World Systems* (1632) led to his being tried by the Inquisition, found guilty of defending **heliocentrism**, called upon to abjure it, and punished with house arrest, in which confinement he worked until his death. Clearly, the importance of method and the achievements of modern science were becoming firmly established and provided a model for the intellectual efforts of the Age of Reason.

The first half of the seventeenth century in Europe was marked by the Thirty Years' War (1618–48), which started as a conflict between Catholics and Protestants in Germany but soon became a general European war, devastatingly conducted, mainly in Germany, in a series of phases featuring shifting alliances. This war was concluded by the Peace of Westphalia, which granted religious freedom to the German states and reduced the imperial power of the Hapsburgs. Swiss and Dutch independence were acknowledged, and France gained some of the western territories of the still surviving German Empire. The old Holy Roman Empire was moribund.

Meanwhile, England was occupied with its own internal problems. Under James I and his son, Charles I, Parliament started asserting its rights against the throne; inflation was rampant, aggravated by wasteful spending by the Stuart court, leading to the raising of taxes and customs duties. Unlike the Tudor Elizabeth, the Stuart kings were conciliatory towards Catholics, despite the anti-Catholic sentiments of the people. James increased public disaffection by attempting to befriend Catholic Spain. Charles married a French Catholic princess (the sister of Louis XIII), treated the Puritans harshly, and tried to force nonconformist Protestant sects to conform to "high church" Anglicanism. Parliament condemned the king's taxing without its consent, as well as his efforts to enforce religious conformity. Charles dissolved Parliament and governed without it for eleven years. But in 1640, he had to reconvene Parliament to raise funds for the recruiting of troops to force Scottish Presbyterian conformity to Anglicanism. The Long Parliament annulled the king's authority to dissolve it and required that it meet regularly whether or not it was convened by the king. Charles tried to exploit an internal Parliamentary division between extremists and moderates by taking up arms against Parliament, civil war erupting in 1642. In general, the Anglicans and the remaining Catholics supported the king, while Parliament was supported by the Puritans, Presbyterians, and Congregationalists. Charles was beaten, fled to Scotland, was captured and handed over to parliamentary forces, tried and found guilty of treason, and finally executed in 1649. Oliver Cromwell took charge of the government, assuming almost absolute powers, and Charles's family and retinue found refuge in France. Two years after Cromwell's death in 1658 and an ensuing dispute pitting Cromwell's son and successor against the army, the Stuarts returned to power, with Charles II, "the merrie monarch," assuming the throne. The Restoration

---

A priori (literally, in Latin, from the previous). Knowledge prior to, or independently of, any particular sense experience, as opposed to *a posteriori*

period, as it is known, was an era of social gaiety and intellectual pursuit, in marked contrast with the austerity of the Cromwell years. When Charles died in 1685, he was succeeded by his Catholic brother James II, who reclaimed some of the power that Parliament had appropriated. Anti-Catholic sentiment, combined with the birth of James's son, led to anxiety about protracted Catholic sovereignty. The Glorious Revolution of 1688–89 led to the exile of James to France and the installation of his Protestant daughter, Mary, and her husband, William of Orange, the governor of Holland, on the throne at the invitation of Parliament and subject to its conditions.

Despite the turmoil, this was an exciting time for literary and pictorial art. In the first few years of the seventeenth century, William Shakespeare was producing his great tragedies, *Hamlet, Othello, King Lear*, and *Macbeth*. The English **metaphysical** poet John Donne wrote sonnets, both secular and sacred; John Milton wrote *Areopagitica*, arguing for freedom of the press, and his epic poem, *Paradise Lost*; and John Bunyan wrote his Calvinist narrative, *The Pilgrim's Progress*. In Spain, Miguel de Cervantes wrote his great satire on chivalry, *Don Quixote*. In France Pierre Corneille, the tragic dramatist, wrote *Le Cid*; Molière wrote great comedies, such as *Tartuffe, The Misanthrope, The Miser*, and *The Imaginary Invalid*; and Jean Racine wrote the tragic play, *Phèdre*. In fine arts the robust style and bright colors of the Flemish Peter Paul Rubens, who painted *The Three Graces, Adoration of the Magi*, and *The Judgment of Paris*, gave way to the more serious and dramatic works of the Dutch Rembrandt, who painted *The Night Watch* and *Aristotle Contemplating the Bust of Homer*, and the portraits of the Flemish Anthony Van Dyck, who was summoned to England by James I and was the court painter of Charles I. Finally, the Italian Giovanni Bernini gained fame for his magnificent sculpture and architecture.

The seventeenth century is often called the Age of Reason. It exhibits enormous confidence in the power of human reason to establish **knowledge** and to help us meet the **ethical** obligations of moral **virtue**. The philosophy of this period tends to avoid resting claims on appeals to authority, is generally disrespectful of Aristotelian scholasticism, uses mathematics as a model of scientific knowledge, and struggles against **epistemological** and moral **scepticism**. During the first quarter of the century, French sceptics, such as Pierre Charron, Jean-Pierre Camus, and Pierre Gassendi, followed the trail blazed by Montaigne. Although an opponent of scepticism, Bacon does deny that our unaided senses can give us reliable knowledge and advocates a provisional suspension of judgment until our senses can be aided by the methods of scientific inquiry; later in the century, Englishman Joseph Glanvill, a chaplain of Charles II, adopted a limited scepticism by denying that humans can ever achieve infallibly **certain** knowledge and advocating a scientific methodology that settles for certainty beyond reasonable doubt. The scientific apotheosis of the Age of Reason was Sir Isaac Newton (1642–1727), the English physicist and mathematician at Cambridge University, whose *Mathematical Principles of Natural Philosophy* (1687) established the three laws of motion that govern all bodies in the physical universe. His law of universal gravitation holds that every body exerts a force of attraction on every other body in direct proportion to the product of their masses and inversely proportional to the square of the distance between them. Along with Gottfried Wilhelm Leibniz, he discovered the basic principles of calculus. He saw God's function (after the creation) as that of keeping the stars from collapsing into one another under the influence of gravitational force and maintaining the stability of the solar system. The central philosophical problem of the Age of Reason is whether an accurate worldview must rest on some abstract **rational** ideas and principles or can only be based on perceptions of concrete experience. Two prominent participants in this controversy are René Descartes, the father of modern rationalism, and Thomas Hobbes, the founder of modern **empiricism**. Other prominent philosophers from the Age of Reason in addition to these two thinkers include Blaise Pascal, Baruch Spinoza, John Locke, Nicolas Malebranche, and Leibniz.

Certainty. The assurance that a belief is wholly reliable or that a proposition is indubitably known

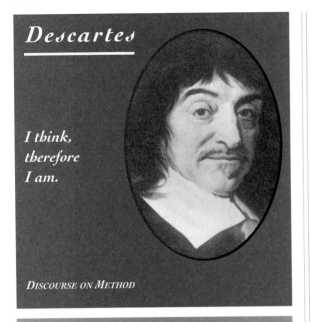

Descartes

I think,
therefore
I am.

DISCOURSE ON METHOD

BIOGRAPHY

René Descartes was born on March 31, 1596 (four years after Montaigne died) in a village in Touraine, France, which is now called La Haye-Descartes. His mother died when he was thirteen months old, although a rare mention of her in his correspondence mistakenly fixes her death at "a few days after my birth"; she died of a lung disease, and he claims to have inherited from her the frail health that marked his first twenty years and that led to the expectation that he "would die young."[1] His father, Joachim Descartes, the son and grandson of physicians, was a councilor of the Parliament of Brittany and thus was away from home quite frequently; René does not seem to have been close to his father, who remarried a few years after the boy's mother died. About 1606, René entered the Jesuit college of La Flèche, which had just opened and where a relative of his, Father Charlet, a **theologian**, would watch out for him. In a letter of 1645, Descartes told Charlet twice that he considered him "like a father to me";[2] Charlet later became rector of the school and, after that, head of the Jesuits in France. Because of his delicate health, Descartes was allowed to spend mornings in bed, meditating, reading, and writing—a habit he maintained for most of his life.

Despite the criticisms found in his autobiographical *Discourse on Method*, his correspondence makes it clear that he appreciated the education the college afforded him; to a man about to send his son off to college, Descartes wrote that "nowhere on earth is philosophy taught better than at La Flèche,"[3] although it is probably safe to say that Descartes would not have chosen the content of Aristotelian-Thomistic scholasticism taught there. In the *Discourse* he says that his education at La Flèche left him "embarrassed with so many doubts and errors," rather than filled with the certain knowledge he craved, despite the fact that it was "one of the most celebrated Schools in Europe." He respected theology but saw it as a matter of faith "above our intelligence"; he was especially "delighted with Mathematics because of the certainty of its demonstrations and the evidence of its reasoning," but could not yet see any practical use for it; he criticizes the philosophy that was taught for containing nothing "which is not dubious" and the sciences for being based on such shaky philosophical foundations. Thus, he chose to leave La Flèche after about nine years. "And resolving to seek no other science than that which could be found in myself, or at least in the great book of the world, I employed the rest of my youth in travel."[4] He studied at the University of Poitiers in 1615–16, earning a bachelor's degree and a licentiate in law there.

After amusing himself for a while in Paris, at the age of twenty-two, he went to Holland and joined the army of Prince Maurice of Nassau. The next year, he transferred to the army of Maximilian, Duke of Bavaria; his correspondence from that period discusses his constant travels.[5] But on the night of November 10, 1619, "in a stove-heated room" in Germany, during the Thirty Years' War,[6] he had a series of three dreams, which he interpreted as expressive of God's will that he devote the rest of his life to the rational quest for certain truth. After ending his **voluntary** military service, Descartes returned to Paris and, indeed, seems to have committed himself thereafter to that vocation. While there, he worked on developing a mathematical method. In 1627, he was encouraged by Cardinal Berulle, the founder of the French Oratory, to undertake a reform of philosophy. About this time Descartes wrote his *Rules for the Direction of the **Mind***, which he never finished and which was not published until 1701, more than half a century after his death.

The social life in Paris was too distracting, so that

he found it prudent to move to Holland in 1628. He liked it there, enjoying peaceful sleep, solitude, "complete freedom," and "all the conveniences of life and all the curiosities you could hope to see."[7] Holland was probably the most intellectually tolerant country in Europe at that time, which would render it attractive to a thinker who was trying to develop new ideas. He lived in Holland until 1649, although frequently changing his address and asking his good friend and former schoolmate at La Flèche, Father Marin Mersenne, a noted musician and mathematician, to keep his address a secret.[8] During his time in Holland, he avoided reading any scholastic texts, though he wrote Mersenne, who worried that he did not have enough books there, "I have here a *Summa* of St. Thomas and a Bible which I brought from France."[9]

In 1629, Descartes started writing his treatise on *The World*; four years later, he abandoned his plans to publish it after hearing of the Inquisition's condemnation of Galileo for writing about the Earth moving around the Sun. His letters to Mersenne indicate his alarm at the implications of Galileo's fate for his own work. Descartes admits that if the view that the Earth moves "is false, so too are the entire foundations of my philosophy, for it can be demonstrated from them quite clearly. And it is so closely interwoven in every part of my treatise that I could not remove it without rendering the whole work defective." Yet he did not wish to publish material condemned by the Church or to become embroiled in controversy. Far from desiring publicity, he adopted as his own Ovid's "motto 'to live well you must live unseen.'" He borrowed a copy of Galileo's book and examined it, concluding "that he philosophizes well enough on motion, though there is very little he has to say about it that I find entirely true." He also read and quoted from the text of Galileo's condemnation. Descartes made it clear that he never met or communicated with Galileo.[10]

From our fortunate perspective, Descartes's decision to suppress *The World* (published posthumously in 1677) may seem somewhat cowardly. But, in addition to the censuring of Galileo, thinkers (e.g., Giordano Bruno at Rome, Giulio Cesare Vanini at Toulouse, and Fontanier of Montpellier in Paris) were burned to death for their lack of orthodoxy. It is at least reasonable to suppose that he was practicing what he later preached, in his *Passions of the Soul*,

that it is unwise to lose one's life when it can be saved without dishonour, and that if a match is very unequal it is better to beat an honourable retreat or ask quarter than stupidly to expose oneself to a certain death.[11]

Descartes never married, but his daughter Francine was born in 1635. In 1637, he anonymously published his *Discourse on Method,* which was written in French so clearly that it might "be intelligible in part, even to women while providing matter for thought for the finest minds."[12] Near the end of the *Discourse*, Descartes invites objections from fellow thinkers, promising to publish them along with his replies. He explains that he is writing in the vernacular "language of my country, rather than in Latin which is that of my teachers" in hopes of reaching an audience of literate lay persons, "who unite good sense with study" and who (we might suppose), less prejudiced by academic scholasticism, might be open to new ideas:

> I hope that those who avail themselves only of their natural reason in its purity may be better judges of my opinions than those who believe only in the writings of the ancients.[13]

In late 1640, Descartes's daughter and father both died; his grief over both deaths was expressed in his correspondence a few months later.[14]

Descartes's most famous philosophical application of the method is to be found in his *Meditations on First Philosophy*, published in Latin in 1641. Here he tries to fulfill the dream of more than a decade earlier, "to prove metaphysical truths in a manner which is more evident than the proofs of geometry.[15] (He was himself a great mathematician and the founder of analytic geometry; the "Cartesian coordinate system" is named after him, the Latin version of his name being Cartesius.) Through Mersenne, he invited scholars and intellectuals to respond to his work; six sets of their objections, along with Descartes's replies, were published with the first edition of the *Meditations*: the first by Johannes Caterus, a Dutch priest and Catholic theologian, the second attributed to various "theologians and philosophers," many doubtlessly composed by Mersenne himself, the third by the "celebrated English philosopher," Thomas Hobbes, who had gone into exile in France in 1640 for political reasons, the fourth by the Augustinian theologian and **logician** Antoine Arnauld, the fifth by an anti-Aristotelian philosopher-priest Pierre Gassendi, and the sixth by several unnamed theologians and philosophers, compiled by Mersenne. Descartes also asked Mersenne to submit his work to the theology faculty at Paris in hopes of winning their approval. A second edition, published in 1642, included a seventh set of objections by the Jesuit Pierre Bourdin, Descartes's replies to them, and a letter to Father Dinet, Bourdin's Jesuit superior.

Descartes's philosophy became famous during this last decade of his life. Regius, a professor of science and medicine at the University of Utrecht, advocated it. In 1643, it was condemned by Voetius, the rector at Utrecht, to whom Descartes sent a scathing letter. Descartes was later accused of heresy at the University of Leyden and wrote a letter of self-defense to its trustees in 1647.[16] He feared that he might be arrested and that his work might be officially condemned, as had happened a decade earlier to Galileo.

But Descartes also had influential admirers and followers. He was invited to join the courts of King Charles I of England and King Louis XIII of France but declined the invitations in hopes of staying out of the public eye. In 1643, he began a correspondence with Princess Elizabeth of Bohemia, the daughter of Frederick the Elector, who had briefly been King of Bohemia, and the niece of Charles I of England. Descartes had enormous respect for her "outstanding intelligence" and grasp of philosophical issues. As he wrote to a friend, "I set more store by her judgement than by that of those learned doctors whose rule is to accept the truth of Aristotle's views rather than the evidence of reason." In 1644, Descartes published his *Principles of Philosophy* in Latin, dedicated to her; three years later he invited her to suggest any different wording she deemed appropriate in the dedicatory letter for the French version of it that was about to be published. In 1649, he wrote her a letter attempting to console her in her grief over the execution of her uncle, Charles I, in London, a few days earlier.[17]

Descartes was granted a pension by the King of France in 1647. The following year, he was interviewed by Frans Burman, who took notes on their conversation, of which we have a transcript. About this time, he was writing *The Passions of the Soul*. Through a friend Descartes began a correspondence with Queen Christina of Sweden, to whom he sent a manuscript copy of this book. She invited him to come to her court to instruct her in philosophy.

Despite his cautious reluctance, Descartes accepted her invitation. She sent an admiral with a warship to carry him to Sweden; after arranging for the publication of *The Passions of the Soul*, Descartes left for Stockholm in September of 1649. It may have been the costliest mistake of his life. Descartes, who had enjoyed the habit of spending his mornings in bed, was expected to be in her library at five A.M. His last letters testify to his unhappiness and longing to recapture "my solitude, away from which it is difficult for me to make any advances in the search for truth."[18] The bitterly cold Swedish winter, combined with what he regarded as an abnormally early schedule, presumably led to his getting pneumonia in just a few months after his arrival and dying on February 11, 1650. He was buried in Stockholm, but his body was taken back to France in 1666 and buried in Paris. Despite his careful allegiance to Catholicism, the Church put his works on its Index of Forbidden Books in 1663. His *Treatise on Man* was posthumously published in 1664; and an uncompleted dialogue, *The Search for Truth*, was published in 1701.

Reality

Although Descartes is a revolutionary philosopher who tries to avoid employing other thinkers' principles and concepts, he could not help being influenced by the Aristotelian scholasticism he had been taught at La Flèche. However, the discoveries of Copernicus, Kepler, and Galileo cast into scientific doubt the old world-view locating the Earth at the center of the universe, identifying planetary orbits as perfectly circular, and maintaining that all celestial bodies are perfect spheres. If the traditional theory inherited from the Middle Ages was so mistaken, why should any old assumed beliefs be trusted? On the other hand, like all great Western philosophers after Aristotle and before Hegel, Descartes adopts a **substance**-based view of reality. Like the thinkers of medieval times, he sees God as the ultimate efficient **cause** of all reality. Yet in the spirit of modern science, he tends to avoid final causality in favor of a mechanical analysis of physical reality.

SUBSTANCE. Since Descartes identifies reality with substance, it is appropriate that we consider his use of that concept. In the *Meditations*, he writes that no finite substances can come to be "without being created by God"; also, using a stone as his example, he says that a substance is "a thing capable of existing of itself."[19] This may appear to be a **contradiction**, but he explains more carefully in his *Principles of Philosophy*:

> By substance, we can understand nothing else than a thing which so exists that it needs no other thing in order to exist.

He immediately adds that, strictly speaking, only God fits this definition, but that other things can be regarded as substances in the looser sense of being realities independent of everything else except God for their existence. Whereas substances exist independently, attributes are **necessarily** of some substance(s). Every substance must have some **essential** attribute, of which its other qualities are modifications or "modes." Thus, God is essentially the **infinite** Substance, minds are essentially thinking substances, and bodies are essentially **extended** substances. All reality consists of these three types of substances and their interrelationships; Descartes is confident that we can have clear and distinct ideas of all three, such that knowledge of them is possible.[20] So, a pencil is a body, physically extended (or stretched out) in space, a substance in the sense of a reality existing independently of everything else except God; its color and other qualities are modifications of its essential attribute of extension; whatever it does or is done to it can only be understood of it with reference to its substantive reality.

Descartes is a metaphysical **dualist** in the sense that he analyzes all reality in terms of two irreducible categories of substances. In the *Principles of Philosophy* he denies that we can

> observe more than two ultimate classes of real things— the one is intellectual things, or those of the intelligence, that is, pertaining to the mind or to thinking substance, the other is material things, or that pertaining to extended substance, i.e., to body.

We have clear and distinct ideas of thought and extension, the essential attributes of minds and bodies, respectively, in terms of which we can know the substances themselves. But Descartes admits that it is difficult to know substance in the abstract, apart from its attributes, qualities, and so forth.[21]

God, being infinite, is the supremely real Substance. And any substance has a higher degree of reality or more being than its essential attribute or any of its modifications. As though intentionally adopting a medieval view, Descartes writes,

> There are various degrees of reality or being: a substance has more reality than an **accident** or a mode; an infinite substance has more reality than a finite substance.[22]

Thus, he holds a **Neoplatonic** sense of a hierarchy of reality. God is the ultimate efficient Cause of all created substances. But Descartes warns against our seeking for the final causes of things, since "all the purposes of God are hidden from us, and it is rash to want to plunge into them." Here he tries to distance himself from his predecessors:

> Indeed, this constant practice of arguing from ends is Aristotle's greatest fault.[23]

It is typical of modern science and modern philosophy to view causality as efficient and to be suspicious of explanations of natural things in terms of final causes.

PHILOSOPHY AS A TREE. The very function of philosophy, for Descartes, is to enable us to understand reality, as he explains to Abbé Claude Picot, who translated his *Principles of Philosophy* into French, in a letter which was published as a preface to that translation. Descartes says it is this understanding of reality alone that "distinguishes us from savages and barbarians" and that "the civilization and refinement of each nation is proportionate to the superiority of its philosophy." He offers a memorable simile to illustrate the organic interconnectedness of all philosophical sciences:

> Thus philosophy as a whole is like a tree whose roots are metaphysics, whose trunk is physics, and whose branches, which issue from this trunk, are all the other sciences. These reduce themselves to three principal ones, viz. medicine, mechanics and morals.

The four fruits of the tree, which we can expect to enjoy as a result of cultivating philosophy, are both theoretical and practical: first, the satisfaction derived from the discovery of certain truths; second, the acquisition of better judgment; third, the minimizing of otherwise irresolvable disputes; and, fourth, the

---

Extension.   The essential attribute of all bodies whereby they occupy some expanse of physical space (no matter how small)

knowledge of the whole of reality that constitutes wisdom.[24]

Bodies

EXTENSION.   Most of the substantial realities we experience are physical, and Descartes analyzes bodies in his *Rules*, *Discourse*, *Meditations*, and *Principles*. He points out that the external senses passively perceive the qualities of bodies, such as their "figure, hardness, roughness, etc." We have simple ideas of bodies, such as "figure, extension, motion, etc.," and complex ideas which are "in some way compounded out of these." He acknowledges that a person deprived from birth of one type of sense experience will be unable to "perceive the true ideas" derived from that sense alone. As we have seen, he considers extension to be the essential attribute of bodies.

> By extension we understand whatever has length, breadth, and depth.

Every body, as a physical substance, has theoretically quantifiable dimensions.

> Thus it is not merely the case that length, breadth, and depth are dimensions; but weight also is a dimension in terms of which the heaviness of objects is estimated. So, too, speed is a dimension of motion.

This ties in nicely with the modern scientific view of physical reality as mathematically measurable. In the *Discourse* Descartes says we do not have strict certainty regarding bodies but rather "a moral assurance,"[25] which is theoretically fallible, yet supported by experimental evidence.

THE "PIECE OF WAX" ANALOGY.   In the *Meditations* he offers a definition:

> By the body I understand all that which can be defined by a certain figure: something which can be confined in a certain place, and which can fill a given space in such a way that every other body will be excluded from it; which can be perceived either by touch, or by sight, or by hearing, or by taste, or by smell: which can be moved in many ways

—by external forces, if not by itself. He uses the example of a "piece of wax" to illustrate. What we initially perceive are its sense qualities—its color, odor, figure, size, texture, coldness, the noise it makes when thumped, and so forth. But now suppose we place it a little too close to the fire. We find that those sense qualities all change—it loses its color, it smells a bit burnt, its figure melts, its size expands, it becomes liquified and hot, "and when one strikes it, no sound is emitted." Yet it is the same wax, despite all these changes. Hence such sensible qualities cannot constitute the essence of the wax. But, if none of these, what is essential to the wax both before and after the fire experiment? "Certainly nothing remains excepting a certain extended thing which is flexible and movable." Yet this essential attribute of bodies, extension (and the attendant qualities of flexibility and mobility), can only be the object of "an intuition of the mind." Thus, Descartes draws his startling rationalistic **conclusion**,

> that even bodies are not properly speaking known by the senses or by the **faculty** of imagination, but by the understanding only.[26]

Even if sense experience and memory be necessary to our gaining essential knowledge of bodies, that knowledge can only be achieved through rational intuition.

THE REALITY OF BODIES.   In the *Meditations* he observes that we experience bodies without necessarily wishing to do so. We are bombarded by sights, sounds, smells, tastes, and feelings all our lives. Furthermore, the ideas derived from such experience are typically "much more lively, more clear, and even, in their own way, more distinct" than those derived from memory or imagination or abstract reason. Yet we have all been deceived by our senses to the point that we are reasonably sceptical of their findings. So how can we know that bodies are real? Descartes provides an **argument** for the reality of the physical world based on the perfect character of the Judeo-Christian God he thinks he has already proved exists. Although it is theoretically possible that God could cause or allow him to believe in bodies when there is neither any foundation for nor prevention of such ideas, "since God is no deceiver" (deception being incompatible with divine perfection), this possibility is ruled out.

> For since He has given me no faculty to recognize that this is the case, but on the other hand, a very great inclination to believe that they are conveyed to me by corporeal objects, I do not see how He could be defended from the accusation of deceit if these ideas were produced by causes other than corporeal objects. Hence we must allow that corporeal things exist.[27]

Descartes's argument can be reconstructed thus: If I cannot help believing in a physical world, then either God is a deceiver or a physical world really exists. I cannot help believing in a physical world. But

God (being perfect) cannot be a deceiver. Therefore, a physical world must really exist. This is a formally **valid deductive** argument, although, of course, we might dispute its **premises**. At any rate, among the bodies comprising the physical world, one is particularly interesting and important to any person— namely, his own body. Descartes speaks of "the machine of the human body," saying, "I consider the body of a man as being a sort of machine" that is "built up and composed of nerves, muscles, veins, blood and skin." Like all bodies, ours are divisible into parts and subject to the mechanical laws of science. For example, he writes,

> the nature of body is such that none of its parts can be moved by another part a little way off which cannot also be moved in the same way by each of the parts which are between the two, although this more remote part does not act at all.[28]

BODIES IN SPACE AND MOTION.   In *The Principles of Philosophy* Descartes observes that whatever other qualities we may perceive as belonging to physical reality, "the nature of matter or of body in its **universal** aspect, does not consist in its being hard, or heavy, or coloured, or one that affects our senses in some other way, but solely in the fact that it is a substance extended in length, breadth and depth." Being extended, it occupies space. Since bodies are essentially extended and thus, by their very nature, divisible, there can be no material atoms which are theoretically indivisible. The physical universe is "extended without limit," and there is only one material world. The motion of bodies "in the vulgar sense, is nothing more than the *action by which any body passes from one place to another.*" But this common-sense understanding of motion as a body's passing from one part of space to another gives way to a more precise analysis of motion as "the *transference of one part of matter or one body from the vicinity of those bodies that are in immediate contact with it . . . into the vicinity of others.*"[29] A human being, as is obvious, either is or has a body living in a material environment.

Personality

MIND.   In addition to being or having a living body, it seems obvious to Descartes that a human being is a person and that man's personality, which is unique in the animal realm, is rooted in the "cognitive power,"

which is the source of his understanding, imagination, memory, and sensation.

> It is properly called mind when it either forms new ideas in the fancy, or attends to those already formed.

This, of course, is the rational faculty in human nature. Descartes declares his break from the scholastic tradition of identifying this faculty as soul because that concept has been so watered down as to be applied to the principle of life in any living thing, however exalted or base its capacities may be:

> I say that, when soul is taken to mean *the primary actuality* or *chief essence of man*, it must be understood to apply only to the principle by which we think, and I have called it by the name *mind* as often as possible in order to avoid ambiguity; for I consider the mind not as part of the soul but as the whole of that soul which thinks.[30]

Unlike Plato and other philosophers who identify mind as the rational part of the soul, Descartes views the rational soul as indivisible and calls it "mind,"

THE *COGITO*.   In his *Discourse* and in the *Meditations* Descartes offers reasoning designed to justify his belief in the mind. The method of systematic doubt he is employing requires that he not assume anything that can be reasonably doubted and that he build his philosophical system only on ideas so clearly and distinctly understood as to be indubitable. Given this methodology, the existence of the mind is the first certain truth he discovers. In the very process of testing and contesting all his previous beliefs, he is determined

> to reject as absolutely false everything as to which I could imagine the least ground of doubt, in order to see if afterwards there remained anything in my belief that was entirely certain.

Since Descartes's system requires epistemological foundations that are indubitable, doubtful beliefs are of no more theoretical use to him here than outright falsehoods:

> But immediately afterwards I noticed that whilst I thus wished to think all things false, it was absolutely essential that the "I" who thought this should be somewhat, and remarking that this truth "I think, therefore I am" was so certain and so assured that all the most extravagant suppositions brought forward by the sceptics were incapable of shaking it, I came to the conclusion that I could receive it without scruple as the first principle of the Philosophy for which I was seeking.[31]

These words,

> I think, therefore I am

(*cogito ergo sum* in Latin), may be the most celebrated in the history of philosophy; we may call this passage (and the corresponding one in the *Meditations*) the **cogito**.

His presentation in the *Meditations* is even more dramatic. Having radically employed the method of systematic doubt, Descartes goes so far as to suppose that, instead of the perfectly good God of Christianity,

> some evil genius not less powerful than deceitful, has employed his whole energies in deceiving me.

This hypothesis of an evil genius (*malin génie*) leaves him drowning in a sea of doubt,

> just as if I had all of a sudden fallen into very deep water, I am so disconcerted that I can neither make certain of setting my feet on the bottom, nor can I swim and so support myself on the surface.

At this point it looks as if his quest for certain truth has backfired, leaving him with only the thesis of scepticism, "that there is nothing in the world that is certain." Then comes the breakthrough. No matter the extent to which the evil genius deceives him and despite all doubts about everything conceivable, his doubting and the very possibility of his being deceived logically require his real existence. As he writes,

> Then without doubt I exist also if he deceives me, and let him deceive me as much as he will, he can never cause me to be nothing so long as I think that I am something.[32]

The *cogito* is not an original insight on Descartes's part. As Arnauld observes, Augustine develops a similar principle in his *On Free Choice of the Will*. In response to this observation Descartes resorts (perhaps sarcastically) to "thanking my distinguished critic for bringing to my aid the authority of St Augustine."[33] He does not seem to be embarrassed to have borrowed another's ideas without attributing credit to the source. At any rate, the *cogito* has proved to be one of the sturdiest principles in the history of philosophy. Until David Hume did so about a century later, hardly anyone seriously challenged Descartes's contention that the very act of thinking (including doubting and believing) constitutes certain evidence for the reality of an enduring thinker. The *cogito* is important to Descartes because it provides him with not merely an initial certain truth, but also a model of clarity and distinctness that he can use for testing the certainty of other truths to come.

Another controversial issue concerns the nature of the *cogito* reasoning. Descartes's epistemology requires that all certainty be grounded in rational intuition or logical demonstration based on intuition. The language of the *cogito* (in both the *Discourse* and the *Meditations*) gives the impression that it is a logical deduction. The valid form such an argument might take is this: Since everything that thinks exists and I think, therefore I must exist. Yet this would require a universal premise which Descartes has not justified, undermining his method of systematic doubt. So, he denies that the *cogito* functions as a demonstration at all:

> This is evident from the fact that if it were **syllogistically** deduced, the major premise, *that everything that thinks is, or exists*, would have to be known previously.

But if it is not a logical demonstration, Descartes's method requires that the *cogito* be a rational intuition,

> a primitive act of knowledge derived from no syllogistic reasoning. He who says, "*I think, hence I am, or exist,*" does not deduce existence from thought by a syllogism, but by a simple act of mental vision, recognizes it as if it were a thing that is known *per se*.[34]

In the *Discourse* Descartes concludes from the *cogito* that I, in the activity of thinking, must be a thinking, nonmaterial reality:

> From that I knew that I was a substance the whole essence or nature of which is to think, and that for its existence there is no need of any place, nor does it depend on any material thing; so that this "me," that is to say, the soul by which I am what I am, is entirely distinct from body.

Descartes has been criticized for this hasty **inference**. In the *Meditations* he explains that the passage only means to make the epistemological claim that the first thing I could know for certain is "that I was a thing that thinks, or a thing that has in itself the faculty of thinking," promising to try to justify the **ontological** claim that my essence is spiritual or mental. The *Meditations* immediately moves from the *cogito* to the nature of the mind. Given *that* I am, the next issue is "what I am." I am accustomed to thinking of myself as "a man" in the Aristotelian sense of "a reasonable animal," but this conception makes too many assumptions that cannot yet be justified. It is thinking that emerges from the *cogito* as the essential attribute of mind:

I am not more than a thing which thinks, that is to say a mind or a soul, or an understanding, or a reason. . . . I am, however, a real thing and really exist; but what thing? I have answered: a thing which thinks.

Next comes a functional analysis of a thinking thing (*res cogitans* in Latin) as one "which doubts, understands [conceives], affirms, denies, wills, refuses, which also imagines and feels." These are the natural functions of a thinking thing, none of which seems to require the assistance of body. An evil genius might deceive me into thinking that I have a body which functions in a material environment; but, since I am certain that I exist so long as I think, it follows that I cannot be identical or reducible to my body. The *Meditations* later argues that my inability to find "that any other thing necessarily pertains to my nature or essence, excepting that I am a thinking thing" suffices to show "that my essence consists solely in the fact that I am a thinking thing."[35]

Thomas Hobbes cuts to the core of the issue, conceding that "I am a thing that thinks" but denying that this requires that my essential nature be spiritual, and argues that "it is possible for a thing that thinks . . . to be something corporeal," chastising Descartes for merely assuming the opposite. Hobbes observes that it is just as presumptuous to conclude that I am essentially a thinker from the fact that I am thinking as it would be to infer that I am essentially a walker from the fact that I am walking. In response, Descartes attacks the **analogy**, maintaining that although walking is nothing but a physical activity, the idea of thinking applies to an activity of mind, to the mental faculty that makes that activity possible, and to the substantial reality in which that faculty exists. Descartes denies merely assuming that the thinking thing must be noncorporeal, claiming that it is proved in Meditation VI and maintaining that "there are certain activities, which we call *corporeal*" and that "there are other activities, which we call *thinking* activities," each set belonging to its own proper substance—namely, body and mind, respectively; Descartes insists that it is a mistake to "confound" the two orders of reality.[36] This exchange conveniently crystallizes the contrast between the dualism of Descartes and the **materialistic monism** of Hobbes.

THE SUPREMACY OF THE HUMAN MIND. It is our mind or rational soul, with these faculties of understanding and will, that separates us from all other earthly creatures. In the *Discourse* Descartes imagines that we might construct "machines, possessing the organs and outward form of a monkey or some other animal without reason" so intricately and ingeniously designed that "we should not have had any means of ascertaining that they were not of the same nature as those animals," but that it would be impossible to construct such a perfect replica of a human being. No matter how well-designed the automaton might be, he says, "we should always have two very certain tests by which to recognize that, for all that, they were not real men." These are the use of abstract language and deliberate action. He concedes that an artificial machine could be programmed to utter words.

> But it never happens that it arranges its speech in various ways, in order to reply appropriately to everything that may be said in its presence, as even the lowest type of man can do.

Though machines might perform certain behaviors "as well as or perhaps better than any of us can do," they never "act from knowledge, but only from the disposition of their organs"; in other words, their actions are programmed rather than deliberately chosen. Descartes is convinced that these two capacities of the human mind make us unique among the animals. He admits that certain birds, such as "magpies and parrots," are "able to utter words just like ourselves, and yet they cannot speak as we do, that is, so as to give evidence that they think of what they say." We act from reason rather than merely from instinct, and we use language in creative, inventive ways rather than mechanically like other animals.

> And this does not merely show that the brutes have less reason than men, but that they have none at all.[37]

Thus, the special **dignity** of human nature is rooted in our mental capacities.

THE MIND-BODY PROBLEM. We must now consider a problem in Descartes's writings that is central to his understanding of human nature. If our bodies are machines and thus not radically different from those of brutes such as chimpanzees or gorillas, and if it is our minds that make us unique among the animals, it is obvious that bodies and minds are different—the former being physical substances, the latter spiritual ones. But how are the human mind and the human body related in one living person? This has come to be called the **mind-body problem**. The classic text here is Descartes's *Meditations*. He emphasizes his dualism by defining them as opposite sorts of substances, saying that mind is "a thinking and unextended thing," whereas body is "an extended and unthinking thing." Also, as we have seen, "there is a great difference between mind and body, inasmuch as body is by nature always divisible, and the mind is entirely indivisible." Yet natural experience throughout our lives reveals to us that they somehow **interact**, as when we feel pain, hunger, and thirst, to such an extent that we cannot reasonably doubt this.

> Nature also teaches me by these sensations of pain, hunger, thirst, etc., that I am not only lodged in my body as a pilot in a vessel, but that I am very closely united to it, and so to speak so intermingled with it that I seem to compose with it one whole.

Against the Platonists (with whom he is aligned in some respects), Descartes points out that we do not dispassionately observe wounds in our own bodies, "as the sailor perceives by sight when something is damaged in his vessel." We do not merely feel that our bodies are hurt but that *we* are hurt, which indicates a "union and apparent intermingling of mind and body." Yet this passage also indicates something of Descartes's ambiguity regarding the relation of one's body to oneself. It is an "apparent intermingling"; regarding my body, I am "so to speak so intermingled with it that I seem to compose with it one whole." He is cautious about breaking down his dualism. He obviously is committed to some sort of "union" of mind and body; but the precise nature of that unity is not specified. Clearly, there is interaction, such that mind affects body and vice versa in human nature. Physical experiences motivate the mind "to flee from things which cause the sensation of pain, and seek after the things which communicate to me the sentiment of pleasure." The mind is interactively related to parts of the body from head to toe: "yet if a foot, or an arm, or some other part, is separated from my body, I am aware that nothing has been taken

away from my mind" itself. Thus, the mind is independent of most body parts for its functioning. Finally, Descartes observes, "the mind does not receive the impressions from all parts of the body immediately, but only from the brain, or perhaps even from one of its smallest parts." So, we have a position of dualistic interactionism, with some part of the brain identified as the meeting place of mind and body. Yet, as Descartes makes clear, the "mind can act independently of the brain; for certainly the brain can be of no use in pure thought: its only use is for imagining and perceiving."[38] Thus, the mind, though identified with the brain, is not identical to it, and dualism is preserved.

UNDERSTANDING, WILL, AND ERROR.   In trying to account for human error in a way that does not put the blame for it on God the Creator, Descartes presents a twofold analysis of the mind of a person, in terms of "the faculty of knowledge" and "the power of choice or of free will." (In the next two sections we shall examine human knowledge and human freedom in detail.) In themselves, both understanding and will are good dimensions of human nature, as created by God. The problem is that human understanding is quite limited in its capacities, whereas human will is so unlimited as to constitute that respect in which we most obviously "bear the image and similitude of God." It is our fault, rather than God's, when we abuse or misuse the gift of free will to make judgments about matters we fail to understand clearly and distinctly. Descartes's philosophy presumably provides a discipline that will help us to restrict our judgments to those that are justified.[39]

EMOTIONS.   Beyond understanding and will, human personality has an affective dimension of feelings or emotions, to which Descartes devotes his last important writing, *The Passions of the Soul*. He begins by expressing his opinion that what the ancients have said about human emotions is worse than worthless and better dismissed altogether than discussed. He analyzes our thoughts into two types:

Mind-body problem.   A philosophical puzzle as to how the physical body and the nonphysical mind are related in human nature; this problem was dramatically delineated by Descartes

Interactionism.   The theory (e.g., of Descartes) that physical bodies and nonphysical minds causally affect each other in human nature, despite their essential differences

actions or desires and passions or perceptions. Our desires can be either spiritual or physical, and our perceptions can be either mentally or physically caused. Physical perceptions, such as seeing a light or hearing a bell, affect the brain in mechanical ways, whereas mental perceptions, such as the feelings of joy and anger, do not prove so mechanical; physical perceptions are usually more lively than spiritual ones. Descartes defines "the passions of the soul" in general as "the perceptions, feelings, or emotions of the soul." They are neither active desires nor clear **cognitions** but feelings or emotions which affect the soul. They "particularly relate to the soul" itself, rather than to either the body (as do feelings of pain, hunger, and thirst) or external objects (as do sights, sounds, and smells). In this consideration of emotions we are drawn back to the relationship between the mind and the body, which, Descartes says again, are "really joined" in "a certain very small gland which is situated in the middle of" the brain, called the pineal gland. This "small gland which is the main seat of the soul is so suspended" between the two hemispheres of the brain that it can be "diversely moved by the soul" in such a way as to affect "the machine of the body." He gives an example of seeing an animal approaching in such a menacing manner that the soul becomes apprehensive or terrified and disposes the body to run away. Here we see obvious interaction between body and soul. Although human "passions cannot be directly excited or removed by the action of our will," the soul can indirectly control its own passions "by the representation of things which are usually united to the passions which we desire to have, and which are **contrary** to those which we desire to set aside." And, indeed, it is this ability indirectly to control one's own passions that distinguishes "the strongest souls" from "the most feeble souls."[40]

* * *

So, human personality, for Descartes, is rooted in the mind or rational soul, which is a spiritual substance. It is distinct from but related to the body. Its essential attribute is thought, in a broad sense of that term, and its association with the body is primarily in the pineal gland of the brain. The mind has a cognitive faculty of understanding, which is oriented towards knowledge, a volitional faculty of will, which is oriented towards free choice, and an affective dimension oriented towards feelings or emotions. Let us now examine the mind's capacity for knowledge.

Knowledge

Descartes believes that the mind naturally seeks knowledge, and he is confident that its capacity to achieve it is great. His methodology, systematically developed in his *Rules* and *Discourse* and applied in his *Meditations*, revolutionized philosophy by establishing epistemology (the theory of knowledge) as its foundation.

DESCARTES'S EPISTEMOLOGY. In his *Rules* Descartes advocates the interconnectedness of all the sciences as discerning aspects of the truth. He urges us not to settle for mere probabilities but to pursue certain truth, such as that achieved in the mathematical sciences of "Arithmetic and Geometry." Of the "two ways by which we arrive at the knowledge of facts, viz. by experience and by deduction," he points out that deduction leads to certain knowledge, "while our inferences from experience are frequently fallacious." He maintains that we should base our inquiries on our own clear and distinct ideas and certain deductions, rather than on conjecture or the authority of others. Descartes says, for example, that "though we have mastered all the arguments of Plato and Aristotle, if yet we have not the capacity for passing a solid judgment on these matters," we would have only historical knowledge and not true philosophical understanding. The only two "mental operations by which we are able, wholly without fear of illusion, to arrive at the knowledge of things," he says, are intuition and deduction. Intuition, as Descartes uses the word, is not some vague hunch, nor is it derived from the senses or the imagination in any way. Rather,

> *intuition* is the undoubting conception of an unclouded and attentive mind, and springs from the light of reason alone; it is more certain than deduction itself in that it is simpler.

By contrast, "*deduction*" is a mental process "by which we understand all necessary inference from other facts that are known with certainty," to the extent that the recommended method is being followed. Intuitions provide the ultimate grounds for logical deductions. Ultimate first principles must be known through intuition, while deduction logically derives conclusions from them. "These two methods are the most certain routes to knowledge, and the mind should admit no others."[41]

Descartes tells us of the need to employ a systematic method in order to achieve certain and comprehensive truth; by a method Descartes means particular simple rules such as those we are considering here. He is so committed to a scientific approach that he holds that "it were far better never to think of investigating truth at all, than to do so without a method"; though we might thus accidentally stumble on the truth, our "unregulated inquiries and confused reflections" would only tend to "confound the natural light and blind our mental powers" (the phrase "the natural light" is a favorite metaphor of his for reason). He assures us that we are provided with the basic building blocks of knowledge, in the form of "certain primary germs of truth implanted by nature in human minds," ideas available as objects of rational intuition (and comparable to Plato's **innate** ideas). He urges us to reduce complex and obscure **propositions** to clear and simple constituent parts so that we can begin by understanding them and gradually work our way up to increasingly complex truths. We have access to a "few pure and simple essences, which either our experiences or some sort of light innate in us enable us to behold as primary and existing *per se*, not as depending on others."[42] These ideas are appropriate starting points.

He maintains that complete scientific knowledge requires that our thought processes should be continuous, adequate, and methodical. Then he warns us that we should stop our examination whenever we reach steps we fail to comprehend, rather than charging on to the next step; nevertheless, we should strive to determine what is knowable by the human mind. Epistemological investigation is especially valuable "to determine the nature and scope of human knowledge," which, Descartes claims, "should be undertaken once at least in his life by anyone who has the slightest regard for truth." Without such prior investigation we run the risk of embarking on useless, groundless flights of fancy. Although the understanding is the only faculty of the mind that can achieve knowledge, it can be "either helped or hindered by three other faculties, namely imagination, sense, and memory." Descartes points out that even small, easily understood facts can be worthy of contemplation, exercising our intuitive powers and providing models

of certainty. He observes the advantage of understanding how other people have conducted mental investigations and systematically solved problems. Descartes attaches two requirements to true mental intuition: "Firstly the proposition intuited must be clear and distinct; secondly it must be grasped in its totality at the same time and not successively," as in deduction. Finally, he urges us to use "imagination, sense and memory" as aids to the understanding in its quest for truth.[43] Thus, *Rules* represents a general procedure for training the mind to pursue knowledge scientifically.

Descartes's *Discourse* begins with the affirmation,

> Good sense is of all things in the world the most equally distributed;

yet equally good mental powers are not equally well applied by all people. Some are lazy in their use of reason, while others are haphazard in their thinking. He reports that he has developed a method of thinking which he has found valuable but which he is reluctant to say that "everyone should follow in order to promote the good conduct of his Reason." Then he says that he has found it useful to sweep away (at least temporarily) all of his old opinions, which fall short of certain knowledge, "so that they might later on be replaced, either by others which were better, or by the same, when I had made them conform to the uniformity of a rational scheme." He reduces his epistemological method to four principles.

> The first of these was to accept nothing as true . . . more than what was presented to my mind so clearly and distinctly that I could have no occasion to doubt it;

let us call this the *principle of clarity and distinctness*.

> The second was to divide up each of the difficulties which I examined into as many parts as possible;

let us call this his *analytic* principle of division.

> The third was to carry on my reflections in due order, commencing with objects that were the most simple and easy to understand, in order to rise little by little, or by degrees, to knowledge of the most complex;

let us refer to this as his *synthetic* principle of order.

> The last was in all cases to make enumerations so complete and reviews so general that I should be certain of having omitted nothing;

let us speak of this as his *principle of review*. He holds up the mathematical sciences of "Geometrical Analysis and Algebra" as methodological models. Because the object of scientific inquiry is certain knowledge, he recommends a process of systematic doubt, whereby each sort of belief is critically scrutinized before it can be accepted. We can only safely commit ourselves to believing in ideas that are supported "by the evidence of our Reason." This method is similar to, but simpler than, that represented in his *Rules*. Descartes continues here by expressing his confidence that the use of such a method will have beneficial consequences; unlike "that speculative philosophy which is taught in the Schools," this will generate "a practical philosophy" contributing to "the general good of all mankind," producing "knowledge which is very useful in life," and ultimately helping us to "render ourselves the masters and possessors of nature."[44] He is confident because he sees all scientific knowledge as integrated and rooted in metaphysics, which can only be understood through the use of a rational methodology.

REASON VS. SENSATION AND IMAGINATION. In the *Meditations* Descartes, using his method of systematic doubt, suspends belief in the senses and everything derived from sense experience, at least for his theoretical purposes of philosophizing, because he realizes "that these senses are deceptive" sometimes, as when we see a straight stick that is half submerged in water and looks bent at the water line. He is also concerned about our inability to distinguish dream experiences from waking reality because he has experienced dreams that seem quite real. As we have seen, it is reason that discovers his first indubitable truth, concerning the existence of the self as a thinking thing, by means of the *cogito*. This yields an idea so clearly and distinctly conceived by the mind that it could not be false; thus, it provides a model for other certainties. As he writes, "I can establish as a general rule that all things which I perceive very clearly and distinctly are true." He then proceeds to use the principle of division to analyze possible ideas into three sorts: "some appear to me to be innate, some **adventitious**, and others to be formed [or invented] by myself." The idea of truth is innate in the sense of being somehow inborn, as is the idea of oneself as a thinking thing. Second, the idea of the Sun or that of a book is adventitious, in the sense of coming to us from

outside ourselves through experience. And, third, the idea of mythological creatures, such as centaurs, leprechauns, "sirens, hippogryphs, and the like," are "fictitious" or made up by us. We might note that these three types of ideas are derived, respectively, from reason, sensation, and imagination and that all of them can be recalled by memory. Descartes thinks some principles are rationally **self-evident**, such as the causal principle, which will be a foundation for proving God's existence: "Now it is manifest by the natural light that there must at least be as much reality in the efficient and total cause as in its effect."[45]

Descartes illustrates the difference between imagination and reason. Not only do we understand that a triangle is a three-sided, rectilinear geometrical figure, but we have a mental image of what one looks like; by contrast, although we can understand the concept of a geometrical "figure composed of a thousand sides," we "cannot in any way imagine the thousand sides of a chiliagon." As the senses proved unreliable in establishing the essence of the piece of wax, so imagination is limited and inferior to the understanding. Finally, once Descartes has argued for the reality of a world of bodies and thus for the *general* reliability of sense experience, he can use **coherence** as a criterion for distinguishing dreams from waking perceptions. He ends the *Meditations* with a warning that "the life of man is very frequently subject to error in respect to individual objects," despite all our caution in making judgments, "because the exigencies of action often oblige us to make up our minds before having leisure to examine matters carefully" enough. Although our minds are oriented towards certain knowledge and philosophical method should help us achieve it, "we must in the end acknowledge the infirmity of our nature."[46] Human reason, though powerful, remains fallible.

DESCARTES VS. HOBBES. This rationalistic epistemology is implausible to empiricists. Thomas Hobbes challenges Descartes's claim to have ideas of things, such as God, of which we have never had any experience. In response, Descartes chastises Hobbes for reducing "the term idea" to "images depicted in the corporeal imagination," which is, indeed, what the empirical Hobbes does. By contrast, Descartes

---

Adventitious. Coming from without, as from objects outside the mind (for Descartes); more commonly, accidental or casual

insists, "I take the term idea to stand for whatever the mind directly perceives" as its objects, whether or not those be mental images. Because he doubts the legitimacy of this broader use of the term "idea," Hobbes denies that we can have any idea "of God or of the soul" or, for that matter, "of substance." But the two thinkers remain at an impasse, Descartes denying that all ideas are mental images and affirming that we do have such ideas of pure reason, which Hobbes rejects. Descartes does admit that we do not know substances themselves stripped of all attributes and qualities.[47]

CLARITY AND DISTINCTNESS. Descartes's innate ideas can allegedly be conceived clearly and distinctly by the mind. But what does he mean by clarity and distinctness? In his *Principles of Philosophy* he explains: "I term that clear which is present and apparent to an attentive mind. . . . But the distinct is that which is so precise and different from all other objects that it contains within itself nothing but what is clear." Thus, distinctness **presupposes** clarity, but not vice versa; for example, the perception of "a severe pain" may be all too clear, though we be confused about its nature and causal source. And what about those alleged innate ideas, which have remained the central bone of contention between Descartes and all empiricists? In a letter to Princess Elizabeth he writes, "I hold that there are in us certain primitive notions, which are like the models on whose pattern we form all other knowledge. There are very few of these notions," but they include the ideas of "being, number, duration," as well as "the notion of extension" and "the notion of thought." He goes on to say that knowledge consists "in distinguishing these notions clearly and in attributing each of them correctly to the thing to which it applies."[48] On this rationalistic view, human knowledge presupposes such allegedly clear and distinct innate ideas.

Freedom

As understanding naturally seeks knowledge, the human will is naturally free. The most important passage in which Descartes discusses free will is from *Meditations*. As we have seen, he regards the freedom of the human will "or liberty of choice . . . to be so great" that it is the respect in which we most resemble divine infinity. His initial analysis of human freedom—as "our having the power of choosing to do a

thing or choosing not to do it (that is, to affirm or deny, to pursue or to shun it)"—seems ordinary enough. But then he immediately presents a more complicated definition when he says that "it consists alone in the fact that in order to affirm or deny, pursue or shun those things placed before us by the understanding, we act so that we are unconscious that any outside force constrains us in doing so." He indicates that this addition is designed to rule out any identification of freedom with indifference of the will; we can be inclined towards an object without our freedom in choosing it being compromised. We can freely choose things to which we are inclined, for example, because we know them to be good or because divine grace so inclines us. As we have seen, when the will makes judgments beyond the scope of understanding, "it easily falls into error and sin, and chooses the evil for the good, or the false for the true." But the responsibility for this is mine, rather than God's, since, in such cases, "I no longer make use as I should of my free will." And then, even when I make fortunately correct judgments, "this comes about only by chance, and I do not escape the blame of misusing my freedom." Descartes admits that it is conceivable that God could have created us both free and not liable to error by giving us a clear and distinct understanding of all matters concerning which we would ever make judgments or by impressing on us more deeply the resolution never to judge what we fail to understand. He reflects, though,

> I cannot deny that in some sense it is a greater perfection in the whole universe that certain parts should not be exempt from error as others are than that all parts should be exactly similar.[49]

This expresses a version of Augustine's aesthetic theme that the capacity for evil contributes to the diversity, and thus to the greatness, of God's creation.

Hobbes's objection here is worth noting, that in *Meditations*, "the freedom of the will has been assumed without proof." Descartes curtly replies that "universal experience" renders human freedom "most evident."[50] This is typical of his disrespect for Hobbes (and, indeed, for materialists in general). In letters to his friend Mersenne, written in April, 1641, Descartes dismisses something "the Englishman" wrote as "childish and ridiculous," calls his latest arguments "as bad as all the others I have seen from him," and chooses to be brief in replying to his objections, lest he seem to attach "too much importance" to them.[51]

The *Principles* also contains some important sections on free will. Descartes observes that "desiring, holding in aversion, affirming, denying, doubting, all these are the different modes of willing." He holds that the power of free will "is the greatest perfection in man," through the exercise of which we become "masters of our actions and thereby merit praise or blame." He maintains that free will is so "self-evident" that it "may be counted as one of the first and most ordinary notions that are found innate in us," the proof of which emerges in the very acts of doubting and suspending judgment. He avers that we must believe that everything in the universe of God's creation is divinely "pre-ordained" and that we must beware of trying to comprehend how God's "pre-ordinances harmonize with the freedom of our will." He claims that we have sufficient intelligence to know clearly and distinctly both that divine preordination is comprehensive and that the human will is free but not enough to comprehend how those two facts are compatible. After all, God's omnipotence is infinite, whereas our understanding is finite.[52]

Although the passages are far less known, Descartes's correspondence includes several interesting discussions of human freedom. He writes Mersenne that his third moral **maxim** in the *Discourse* (which we shall consider in the following section) was intended to hold that only our own freely chosen thoughts could ever be "absolutely in our power" and was not intended to suggest that "all our thoughts are in our power." He also says that he meant to suggest there "that our free will has no absolute jurisdiction over any corporeal thing." In another letter to Mersenne he affirms that he does, indeed, regard the idea of free will as a "primary notion." In a letter to Denis Mesland, a Jesuit priest, Descartes maintains that "the fewer reasons" a person "knows which impel him to choose one side rather than another" in any set of alternatives, the "more indifferent" is his will. By contrast, as long as we are consciously aware that something is good for us, we cannot be indifferent towards it and cannot help desiring it to some extent. Yet, as we have seen, such an inclination does not destroy "free" or "voluntary" choice. Descartes agrees that the human will has the "positive power" of

self-determination and denies that any "animals that lack reason" can be free in the sense of having "this positive power to determine themselves." In another letter to Mesland Descartes says that he considers arbitrary choices of "things to which we are indifferent" to be "the lowest degree of freedom," inferior to self-determination of action where we see that good and evil are at stake. Likewise, freedom is compromised by actions "which others command us to do, and which we would not otherwise do spontaneously."[53]

In a letter to Princess Elizabeth, Descartes writes that we cannot help thinking of ourselves as independent apart from God, but that when we think of ourselves in relation to "the infinite power of God," on which all creatures depend, we must admit "that our free will is not exempt from this dependence." Our independence in making free choices of will is compatible with our dependence on God's creative and sustaining omnipotence. He later tells her a story of a king who "has forbidden duels" but who orders a subject to go to a town where the subject's archenemy lives, knowing that they cannot help but meet, renew their mutual hostility, and engage in a duel against the king's prohibition. Although the king knows what will occur and could prevent it, the king is allegedly not to blame for their dueling; despite the fact that he has arranged the circumstances leading to it, they freely choose to break the law and can be "justly punished for disobeying the prohibition." Finally, in a letter to Queen Christina, Descartes writes that free will is our "noblest" faculty, "since it makes us in a way equal to God" as self-determining agents, and that "its correct use is the greatest of all the goods we possess" and leads to "our greatest happiness."[54] Because we are free in and responsible for some of our actions, morality is an important dimension of human action.

Morality

It is commonplace in the history of philosophy to recognize that free choice is a **necessary condition** of morality; as we have indicated, Descartes does so. We might reasonably expect him to develop "a code of morals sufficient to regulate the actions" of a good life, especially since he says in the *Principles* that "we ought above all other things to live well." Yet he does not carefully explore this "branch" of the "tree"

Maxim.   In Kant, a subjective principle of will that can motivate action; more loosely, a general truth or rule of conduct

of philosophy called ethics, "the highest and most perfect moral science which, presupposing a complete knowledge of the other sciences, is the last degree of wisdom."[55] In a letter to Hector-Pierre Chanut, a French diplomat, he admits "that normally I refuse to write down my thoughts concerning morality," explaining that his reluctance is based on two reasons. First, it is a "subject in which malicious people can so readily find pretexts for vilifying me"; and, second, only political rulers, or their authorized representatives, should "concern themselves with regulating the morals of other people."[56]

A CODE OF MORALS.   Descartes's most famous discussion of morality occurs in the *Discourse*, where he presents "a code of morals" consisting of "three or four maxims." These are not philosophically argued for in such a way as to constitute a system of ethical principles but are merely offered as a provisional set of practical guidelines to be observed while applying the method of philosophical doubt in other areas.

> The first was to obey the laws and customs of my country, adhering constantly to the religion in which by God's grace I had been instructed since my childhood, and in all other things directing my conduct by opinion the most moderate in nature.

Here we see a policy of cautious conservatism, very different from his revolutionary theoretical inquiry, and an Aristotelian distrust of extreme views.

> My second maxim was that of being as firm and resolute in my actions as I could be, and not to follow less faithfully opinions the most dubious, when my mind was once made up regarding them, than if these had been beyond doubt.

Again, we can easily see the variance between this practical rule and his theoretical principle of clarity and distinctness.

> My third maxim was to try always to conquer myself rather than fortune, and to alter my desires rather than change the order of the world, and generally to accustom myself to believe that there is nothing entirely within our power but our own thought,

so that we are not to blame when things go wrong as long as "we have done our best." Here we see a **Stoical** distinction between that within ourselves which can be controlled and "things that are without us" and largely beyond our control.

> And last of all, to conclude this moral code, I felt it incumbent on me to make a review of the various occupations of men in this life in order to try to choose the best.

Without casting any criticism on other lifestyles, Descartes concludes that his own occupation of cultivating his reason and using his method to develop knowledge of the truth is best for him.[57]

THE VIRTUOUS LIFE.   In *The Passions of the Soul* Descartes holds that "the chief utility of morality" consists in the control of our passionate desires. Such

> desire is always good when it conforms to true knowledge; likewise it cannot fail to be bad when based on some error. And it seems to me that the error we commit most commonly in respect to desires is failure to distinguish adequately the things which depend wholly on us from those which do not depend on us at all.

A morally desirable life, on this view, requires "the pursuit of virtue," which "consists in doing the good things that depend on us." Like Aristotle, he defines virtues as "habits of the soul" but gives that definition a characteristically rationalistic twist by adding that virtuous habits are those which "dispose" the soul "to have certain thoughts." Finally, he maintains a softened Platonic view that "**vice** usually proceeds from ignorance,"[58] which is, again, quite compatible with his rationalism. In general, he seems to discuss morality more in terms of practical rules for controlling one's desires, improving one's character, and conducting one's life than in those of systematically argued ethical theory.

Society

LOVE, FRIENDSHIP, AND GENEROSITY.   If anything, Descartes's comments on society are even fewer, briefer, and more scattered than those on morality. Love is an emotion that he discusses in *Passions of the Soul* "which impels the soul to join itself willingly to objects that appear to be agreeable to it." He distinguishes among "simple affection," which is for objects we esteem less than we do ourselves, "friendship," which is for those we esteem "equally with ourselves," and "devotion," which is for what we esteem more than we do ourselves. Things, such as "a flower, a bird, or a horse," are properly objects of affection; but unless our mind is very disordered, we can have friendship only for persons, while we should have devotion towards God, "our sovereign, our country, our town, and even for a particular person when we have much more esteem for him than for ourselves." Love, in general, and friendship, in particular, draw us to other members of society. Another important social inclination is that of generosity, which Descartes associates with humility (and dissociates from contempt for others). As we have seen, the morally good person tries to do "whatever he judges to be best." The generous person regards others as likewise well-intentioned people of **good will**.

> Although they often see that others do wrong in ways that show up their weakness, they are nevertheless more inclined to excuse than to blame them and to regard such wrong-doing as due rather to lack of knowledge than to lack of a virtuous will.

So, they try to assume the best of others, rather than having contempt for their personal shortcomings. Likewise, the generous person is humble in not presuming that he is morally superior to others. Generous people, typically committed to "doing good to others and disregarding their own self-interest," tend to be "courteous, gracious and obliging to everyone" else in society.[59] Consequently, generosity, like love and friendship, contributes to beneficial social relationships.

Some of Descartes's letters contain fragmentary reflections on social relationships. In a letter to Chanut, Descartes writes that reciprocal "friendship between human beings" tends to close social gaps between them and to render them "in some way equal to each other," whereas love, in general, "is a passion which makes us join ourselves willingly to some object, no matter whether the object is equal to or greater or less than us." Love disposes us to identify ourselves and "the object loved as a single whole . . . and to transfer the care one previously took of oneself to the preservation of the whole." Friendship, in particular, according to Descartes, inclines us to value another more than ourselves and to be willing to sacrifice ourselves for her welfare. In another letter to Chanut he provides a rare glimpse into his own childhood, writing that he once "loved a little girl of my own age who had a slight squint" and later, for a while, associated this defect with a lovable attraction. "So, when we are inclined to love someone without knowing the reason, we may believe that this is because he has some similarity to something in an earlier object of our love, though we may not be able to identify it." Descartes says that "the chief good of life is friendship," if it is for persons in whom we see mental worth.[60]

SELFISH INTERESTS AND THE COMMON GOOD. In a letter to Princess Elizabeth he writes that "if someone considers himself a part of the community, he delights in doing good to everyone, and does not hesitate even to risk his life in service of others when the occasion demands." In another letter written to her Descartes admits that it is difficult to draw a precise line between looking out for one's own interests and devotion to the common good. "For God has so established the order of things, and has joined men together in so close a community, that even if everyone were to relate everything to himself and had no charity for others, he would still commonly work for them." In other words, our selfish interests tend to be extremely tied up with the well-being of our communities.[61]

ADVICE TO A MONARCH. Finally, in another letter to Princess Elizabeth, Descartes says he has read Machiavelli's *Prince* and approves of some of its "many maxims"; he also advises her on how to deal with subjects, allies, and enemies. He thinks a monarch "has a virtual license to do anything" to enemies, whom he defines as "all those who are neither friends nor allies," short of deceiving them into believing that they are friends.

> Friendship is too sacred a thing to be abused in this way; and someone who has once feigned love for someone in order to betray him deserves to be disbelieved and hated by those whom he afterwards genuinely wishes to love.

A prince should maintain his commitments to allies, "even when it is to his own disadvantage," for the sake of his own reputation, except where keeping his word would lead to his being "altogether ruined." A monarch should strive to be "on friendly terms" with most of his neighbors but should beware of alliances with more powerful sovereigns who might easily get away with betrayal. Descartes categorizes subjects into two types: "great people," who are powerful enough to "form parties against the prince," and the "common people," who lack such power. A monarch must be sure of the fidelity of great people or bring them down if they threaten "to rock the ship of state," which makes them, in effect, enemies within the realm. "As for his other subjects, he should above all avoid their hatred and contempt" by just administration and execution of the law. "Altogether, the common people will put up with whatever they can be persuaded is just, and they are offended by whatever they imagine to be unjust."[62]

*   *   *

Considering these tidbits collectively, it seems that Descartes values good social relations and a stable political order, even if he never wrote any systematic analysis of society.

Religion

PROVING GOD'S EXISTENCE. By contrast with the topics of morality and society, Descartes offers us extensive material on God in several of his published works. In the *Discourse* he praises "the constitution of the true Religion whose ordinances are of God alone"; after presenting his provisional moral code, he writes that he also continues to adhere to "the truths of religion which have always taken the first place in my creed." And after presenting the *cogito,* he adumbrates his arguments for God. He says that he has an "idea of a Being more perfect than my own," which must have originated from some causal source more perfect than his mind and "which even had within itself all the perfections of which I could form any idea—that is to say, to put it in a word, which was God." He also recognizes that his own existence is not self-sufficient; otherwise, he would have all the perfections of which he can conceive, but which he knows he lacks—"infinite, eternal, immutable, omniscient, all-powerful"; thus, there must be "some other more perfect Being on which I depended," which does have these qualities. Unlike us, who are composed of mind and body, God could not be "composed of these two natures," because all composition is indicative of dependence, which "is manifestly an imperfection"—so that God must be pure Spirit. In analyzing his idea of "a Perfect Being," Descartes concludes that existence "is implied in it in the same manner in which the equality of its three angles to two right angles is implied in the idea of a triangle," so that God's existence proves to be "at least as certain . . . as any demonstration of geometry can possibly be."[63] These arguments are more carefully developed in the *Meditations*.

In his dedicatory letter to the theology faculty at the Sorbonne, Descartes writes that God's existence "ought to be demonstrated by philosophical rather than theological argument" lest "impious persons" use the lack of rational proof as a pretext for disbelief. He admits that he has been criticized for assuming that his idea of a perfect Being is more perfect than he is and for purporting to prove, on the basis of that assumption, that a Being outside his mind exists corresponding to that idea in his mind. In reply, he says that the word "idea" is equivocal: when it is "taken materially," as the object of understanding, it is not more perfect than the one who thinks it, since it is dependent on that person as a thinking substance; but, when "taken objectively, as the thing which is represented by this act," it discloses an ideal essence which can, indeed, surpass the person thinking it. He promises to show how God's existence follows from a person's having an idea which is more perfect than he is. In the Synopsis of his *Meditations*, Descartes says that "the principal argument" he uses "to prove the existence of God" is in Meditation III, although Meditation V adds "a new proof" in which "certain difficulties" may appear, though he is confident that those are dealt with adequately in his Replies to Objections.[64]

We have already seen that, in *Meditations*, Descartes analyzes all ideas into innate, adventitious, and fictitious ones and presents his allegedly self-evident causal principle. By this point he has allegedly shown that he exists as a mind but must find a way to transcend **solipsism** by arguing that something else is real outside his own mind; in fact, he wants to do far more than this, showing that something exists which somehow guarantees the reality of the world around us. If he is to be true to his principle of clarity and distinctness, he can only proceed to argue on the basis of what has been established as indubitably real—namely, his own self as a mental substance and the ideas that are in his mind. Using his principle of analysis, he concludes that he can account for all but one of the various sorts of his ideas without presupposing the reality of any substance outside himself. That one is his idea of God,

> a substance that is infinite [eternal, immutable], independent, all-knowing, all-powerful, and by which . . .

Solipsism (from the Latin *solus ipse*, meaning oneself alone). The theory that all that is real is one's own mind and its states of consciousness (metaphysical solipsism) or that the only things one can know to exist are one's own mind and its states of consciousness (epistemological solipsism)

everything else, if anything else does exist, [must] have been created.

Though he be a substance, the very act of doubting assures him that he is imperfect and has none of these perfections. But then the causal principle applies in such a way that he, being finite, could not acquire the idea of an infinite substance "if it had not proceeded from some substance which was veritably infinite. We might formulate the argument thus: By the causal principle, "there must at least be as much reality in the efficient and total cause as in its effect." But since Descartes is finite, he has less reality or perfection than "the idea of an infinite substance." Therefore, he could not be the ultimate cause of that idea, which could only have "proceeded from some substance which was veritably infinite," which would be God. So "we must conclude that God necessarily exists."[65]

Descartes immediately considers and answers two objections. First, an empiricist might argue that our alleged notion of "the infinite" is not "a true idea" but merely indirectly derived "by the **negation** of the finite"; but Descartes replies that the idea of the infinite has priority over that of finiteness to such an extent that without the former as a standard, we could not even recognize the deficiencies of the latter. And, secondly, it might be maintained that he is more perfect than he realizes "and perhaps all those perfections" which he attributes to God are in some way **potentially** in him, "although they do not yet disclose themselves, or issue in action"; but, against this, Descartes observes, though he be actualizing his potential, he has no reason to think that he will ever achieve the infinite, the need to develop potential itself being indicative of imperfection.[66]

From Human Existence to God's Existence. This has been a causal argument from the idea of infinite Substance to the necessary existence of God. Descartes immediately proceeds "to inquire whether I, who have this idea, can exist if no such being exists." It is difficult to say whether what follows is a different causal argument or merely a second phase of the same one; but it does not matter much for our purposes. Granted my knowledge that I exist as a thinking thing, "I ask, from whom do I then derive my existence?" Several theoretically possible answers come to mind. "Perhaps from myself or from my parents, or from some other source less perfect than God." But if I were self-sufficient, "I should have bestowed on myself every perfection of which I possessed any idea and should thus be God"; for it seems more difficult to be the source of my own existence than to improve upon my known perfections; and, further, I realize that I lack the power to assure my own continued existence in the future, which is a lesser power than being the causal source of my own existence in the first place. Second, it will not suffice to say that "I am created either by my parents or by some cause less perfect than God," because the causal principle requires that the ultimate source of my idea of perfection must itself be perfect; and since my parents are finite humans and any other cause than God is less than perfect, we would have to inquire then into the source of their existence, with "no regression into infinity" satisfactory as a causal explanation.

> Nor can we suppose that several causes may have concurred in my production, and that from one I have received the idea of one of the perfections which I attribute to God, and from another the idea of some other, so that all these perfections indeed exist somewhere in the universe, but not as complete in one unity which is God;

for I find that an essential characteristic of my idea of infinite Substance is "the unity, the simplicity or the inseparability" of all perfections. Again, the argument can be formalized thus: Either I ultimately derive my existence "from myself or from my parents, or from some other source less perfect than God" or from "several causes" inferior to God or God exists. But my existence could not be ultimately derived "from myself or from my parents, or from some other source less perfect than God" or from "several causes" inferior to God. Therefore, God must exist. Again Descartes adds two observations. First, if the idea of God is neither received "through the senses" nor "a fiction of my mind," by a **process of elimination**, it must be "innate in me," stamped on my mind by my Creator, "like the mark of the workman imprinted on his work." Second, since the God thus argued for is perfect, the hyperbolical doubt concerning an "evil genius" deity can now be eliminated; "it is manifest that He cannot be a deceiver since the light of nature teaches us that fraud and deception necessarily proceed from some defect."[67] As we have seen, Descartes uses this divine perfection as a logical steppingstone to arguing for the reality of the physical world.

THE ONTOLOGICAL ARGUMENT. In the *Meditations*, Descartes presents another argument for God's existence, which Kant later names the **ontological argument** and which, unlike Descartes's earlier argumentation, does not rely on the causal principle. This argument also starts with "the idea of God" as "the idea of a supremely perfect Being." But "a supremely perfect Being," by definition, "possesses every sort of perfection," including that of existence, "since existence is one of these." If I separate existence from the idea of God, by definition I am no longer thinking of God. "For it is not within my power to think of God without existence (that is of a supremely perfect Being devoid of a supreme perfection)." The idea of God necessarily includes existence. "And this necessity suffices to make me conclude (after having recognized that existence is a perfection) that this first and sovereign Being really exists." We can formulate the argument thus: Our "idea of God" is "the idea of a supremely perfect Being." Any "supremely perfect Being" conceivable "possesses every sort of perfection." But "existence is a perfection." Hence, God "really exists." Descartes claims that the demonstration of a perfect, nondeceiving God provides us with a warrant for all truths which I can "recollect having formally demonstrated" or clearly and distinctly conceived.

> And so I very clearly recognize that the certainty and truth of all knowledge depends alone on the knowledge of the true God, insomuch that, before I knew Him, I could not have a perfect knowledge of any other thing.[68]

SOME OBJECTIONS AND REPLIES. Let us briefly consider some of the Objections and Replies before turning to a few passages in the *Principles*. In his replies to Caterus, Descartes tries to distinguish his own version of the ontological argument from the medieval one criticized by Aquinas, agreeing with the latter that "the existence of God is in itself" not "obvious to each single individual." He admits that his own argument does raise "no little difficulty" in its claim that "we clearly and distinctly understand" existence to be a divine perfection inseparable from God's nature. But he insists that careful analysis reveals that "necessary existence ... belongs to the true and immutable nature" of a supremely perfect Being. He worries that this argument might be dismissed as "a sophism" except by the person "who considers the matter attentively" and admits that, for that reason, he considered omitting it altogether. "But since there are two ways only of proving the existence of God, one by means of the effects due to him, the other by his essence or nature," having used the former approach previously in *Meditations*, he wants to proceed to offer the latter for the sake of completeness. Descartes is accused of **circular reasoning** in denying that we can have any certain knowledge of anything else prior to our knowledge of God's existence, when he has allegedly justified his arguments for God by intuitions of himself as a thinking thing and of his idea of an infinitely perfect Being (this problem is sometimes called the **Cartesian circle**). But Descartes insists that God's existence provides a necessary warrant only for "such conclusions *as can recur in memory without attending further to the proofs which led me to make them*" and not to presently intuited "first principles" or deductions currently perceived.[69]

Hobbes raises some powerful criticisms. He questions whether reality admits of degrees, as Descartes's causal principle requires. But Descartes merely repeats that "an infinite and independent substance" must be more real "than a substance that is finite and dependent" and that "substance is greater than" any mode in its reality, adding that "all this is quite self-evident," needing no further explanation. Second, Hobbes criticizes Descartes's analysis of the idea of God, saying that it is merely the idea of an incomprehensible substance "of which we have no image" in our minds. "Thus any idea of God is ruled out." Also, the idea of God could not truly be innate unless it were always present to the mind; yet how could it be present to "the minds of those who are in a profound and dreamless sleep"? In reply, Descartes points out that our idea of God, unlike mental images, cannot "come from external objects as a copy proceeds from its exemplar, because we conceive that in God there is nothing similar to what is found in external things, i.e. in corporeal objects." Rather, "we form the idea" of God by reflecting on our own perfection, such as it is, and "extending this indefinitely." Nor must an innate idea be "always present to us," for then

---

Cartesian circle A problem in Descartes's philosophy, arising from his claim that the reliability of all clear and distinct ideas depends on our knowledge of God, although that knowledge, in turn, is allegedly based on our grasp of clear and distinct ideas

there would be none; we need only "possess the faculty of summoning up" an idea at any time for it to be innate. Third, Hobbes challenges Descartes's claim that all certain knowledge depends on our knowledge of God by asking whether an **atheist** cannot know that he is awake. Descartes replies that an atheist can conclude from connections with past experience that he is awake but cannot certainly know it without a knowledge that there is a nondeceiving God that is the epistemological warrant of memory. Later, Gassendi maintains that "existence is a perfection neither in God nor in anything else; it is rather that in the absence of which there is no perfection" at all. Thus, Descartes can be said "to beg the question" by including existence among the perfections inseparable from God. In reply, Descartes exclaims,

> I do not see to what class of reality you wish to assign existence, nor do I see why it may not be said to be a property as well as omnipotence, taking the word property as equivalent to any attribute or anything which can be predicated of a thing.[70]

REASON AND RELIGIOUS FAITH. In his *Principles of Philosophy* Descartes more carefully says that we can be certain of truths, even apart from our knowledge of God, "so long as the premises from which they are derived are attended to." But the conclusions of our inferences are rendered uncertain when we are not focusing on their premises, unless we have that knowledge of God to guarantee the reliability of memory. Thus, he breaks the alleged circle of reasoning of which he is accused. He later denies that existence "is necessarily contained" in our "idea of any other thing" than God, so that the ontological argument cannot be used to prove the reality of any **contingent** being. He writes that we must have faith in all revealed truths, "such as the **mysteries** of the incarnation and the Trinity," despite their being "beyond the range of our comprehension," and that "we ought to submit to the Divine authority rather than to our own judgment" on matters of revelation, being ruled by reason in all other areas.[71]

This discussion of God, so heavily emphasizing logical arguments for divine existence, allows Descartes to conceive of human nature as created by God, though few conclusions are evident regarding what may be religiously appropriate. Room is left for faith in religious doctrines, but the pivotal issue of the existence and nature of God is rendered a matter of rational knowledge.

Immortality

Although he clearly believes that the human soul is **immortal** and will survive the death of the body, Descartes rarely discusses immortality in his published works, and he never does so in any sustained, systematic manner. In *The Passions of the Soul*, he speaks of death as a phenomenon of the body, rather than of the soul. As earlier he had compared the living body to a machine, he now speaks of it as "a watch or other automaton (i.e. a machine that moves of itself), when it is wound up and contains in itself the corporeal principle of those movements for which it is designed along with all that is requisite for its action," whereas a corpse is like "the same watch or other machine when it is broken and when the principle of its movement ceases to act." In his *Discourse* Descartes expresses the hope that his radical dualistic distinction between the body and "the rational soul" will help "to prove that our soul is in its nature entirely independent of body, and in consequence that it is not liable to die with it. And then, inasmuch as we observe no other causes capable of destroying it, we are naturally inclined to judge that it is immortal." It would seem that this falls short of a strict demonstration but lends support to immortality as a rational belief. In the Synopsis of his *Meditations*, Descartes warns us against expecting these thoughts to provide "reasons establishing the immortality of the soul." He suggests that he has not discovered "very exact demonstrations" of this but has provided some support of it by showing that the mind or soul is "entirely distinct from all the conceptions which we may have of body." The dualistic distinction between mental and physical substance "is sufficient to show clearly enough that the extinction of the mind does not follow from the corruption of the body," he thinks, even if it does not strictly demonstrate immortality. He also suggests that "a complete system of Physics" would show that all substances, once created by God, are naturally incorruptible, unless God annihilates them; the human body, being composed of parts, is subject

---

Atheism (from the Greek *atheos*, meaning godless).   Disbelief in or denial of the existence of God or any gods

to decomposition, but the simple substance of mind is not, since it allegedly comprises no parts.

> From this it follows that the human body may indeed easily enough perish, but the mind [or soul of man (I make no distinction between them)] is owing to its nature immortal.[72]

But, of course, such a proof would require that the "complete system of Physics" he has mentioned should be firmly established.

There are occasional references to immortality in Descartes's correspondence. As early as November of 1630, he writes Mersenne that he hopes to "some day complete a little treatise of Metaphysics" in which he proves the independence of souls from body, "from which their immortality follows." He later responds to Mersenne's complaint that the *Meditations* does not establish "the immortality of the soul" by saying,

> You should not be surprised. I could not prove that God could not annihilate the soul, but only that it is by nature entirely distinct from the body, and consequently it is not bound by nature to die with it.

He writes Mersenne again, suggesting that a subtitle be added to the title of Meditation II, "The Nature of the Human Mind," in order "that people will not think that I was intending to prove its immortality in that place." Finally, in a letter to Princess Elizabeth, Descartes expresses his fear "that knowledge of the immortality of the soul," coupled with awareness "of the felicity of which it will be capable after this life, might give occasion to those who are tired of this life to leave it" by means of suicide. "But no reason guarantees this,"[73] he proceeds to assure her.

Fulfillment

Descartes rarely discusses that "felicity" or ultimate human fulfillment in his published works. In the preface to his *Principles*, he does say that "men, in whom the principal part is the mind, ought to make their principal care the search after wisdom, which is its true source of nutriment." In *The Passions of the Soul*, Descartes claims that "the pursuit of virtue" is such a worthy goal that it "cannot fail to have a happy outcome for us, since it depends on us alone, and so we always receive from it all the satisfaction we expected from it," as opposed to our pursuits of external goods, whose achievement lies beyond our power. In order to be happy, a person must live "in such a way that his conscience cannot reproach him for ever failing to do

something he judges to be the best (which is what I here call 'pursuing virtue')." A person living such a life, Descartes is confident, will derive "a satisfaction which has such power to make him happy that the most violent assaults of the passions will never have sufficient power to disturb the tranquillity of his soul."[74] We might notice here that he is speaking of fulfillment to be achieved in this life, rather than in the hereafter.

Again, we can find further references in his correspondence, especially in his letters to Princess Elizabeth. He promises to tell her about "that supreme felicity which common souls vainly expect from fortune, but which can be acquired only from ourselves" and recommends that she read *On the Happy Life*, by the Stoic Seneca. He later writes that "two classes" of things contribute to our "supreme contentment" or happiness: "those which depend on us, like virtue and wisdom, and those which do not, like honours, riches and health." He then reviews for her the practical maxims of the moral code he presented in the *Discourse*, as parameters within which happiness might be achieved. He says that happiness is compatible with theoretical error and that "virtue by itself is sufficient to make us content in this life," although "virtue unenlightened by intellect can be false." Thus, "the right use of reason" should guide our pursuit of virtue if we are to achieve "the greatest felicity of man." In a later letter he writes her that "happiness is not the supreme good, but presupposes it, being the contentment or satisfaction of the mind which results from possessing" virtue. He tells her that we prefer the pleasures of the mind to those of the body, which "are minor" and not essential to happiness. "However, I do not think that they should be altogether despised, or even that one should free oneself altogether from the passions. It is enough to subject one's passions to reason." He tells her, "I make a distinction between the supreme good—which consists in the exercise of virtue, or, what comes to the same, the possession of all those goods whose acquisition depends upon our free will—and the satisfaction of mind which results from that acquisition" and which he calls happiness. Like Augustine, he is distinguishing between a virtuous will, oriented towards higher goods within our control rather than lower goods that are beyond our control, and the actual enjoyment of happiness. The exercise of virtue is independent of pleasant circumstances. Nevertheless, he does admit that "the pleasure of the soul which constitutes happiness is not inseparable from cheerfulness and bodily comfort." In a letter to Queen Christina, he writes that "the greatest and most solid contentment in life" is produced by "a firm and constant resolution" to judge what is best and to do it. "So I conclude that it is this which constitutes the supreme good" for human nature.[75]

REFLECTIONS

The value of Descartes's theory of human nature is partially due to the fact that it is developed in the context of a broader philosophical system, which is different from earlier ones in being obviously grounded in an epistemology that was explicitly worked out and conscientiously followed. That system is not as comprehensive as were those of some earlier thinkers, lacking both a rigorous ethical theory and a carefully articulated social philosophy. His rationalism is well adapted to the quasi-mathematical model of precision and certainty; yet it employs dubious presumptions which sometimes fly in the face of his method and lead him to embrace unconvincing argumentation. His allegiance to the intellectual climate of his own era pushes him to adopt a scientific perspective on human nature; but he maintains a commitment to certain core beliefs—in freedom and immortality, for example—which transcend the bounds of any scientific method, so that his treatment of them lacks cogency. But let us, more specifically, assess his discussion of the ten topics on which we have focused our study of Descartes's philosophy.

REALITY. His theory of reality, our first topic, may prove attractive to those who embrace a traditional Judeo-Christian world-view that conceives of the universe as comprising a vast number of finite things and as ultimately created by the infinite God, its ultimate efficient cause. But his method requires that all building blocks of his system be justified; and it is not clear that Descartes realizes that he is uncritically adopting the substance-based view of reality we have inherited from Aristotle. It is true that no other way of conceiving reality emerges until Hegel; but Descartes should have argued on its behalf or tried to convince us that it is so intuitively self-evident as to render all attempts at argumentation superfluous. Next, his definition of substance creates a minor problem: it must include

such mundane things as sticks and stones; yet, as he realizes, only God strictly meets the requirement of independence embedded in his definition. Finally, does he adopt too blithely the scientific prejudice of his time, repudiating all explanations in terms of final causes and reducing causality to the efficient sort that a mechanistic science can accommodate?

BODIES. Second, his analysis of bodies has an intuitive appeal. We do think of physical things as stretched out in space, as having multiple qualities which are perceptible by the senses, and as interacting with other bodies. But again, this presupposes physical substance as determinably quantifiable. His argument for the existence of the physical world, though quite valid, can be disputed by challenging either the premise that we cannot help believing in it (there are, after all, philosophies, such as Plato's, which help us to see the physical world as less than substantially real) or the premise that holds that a perfect, nondeceiving God exists (we shall see that all his arguments for this are dubious). Finally, is there something **reductionistic** and inadequate about his metaphor of "the machine of the human body," since the human body is organic, rather than mechanical?

PERSONALITY. Descartes's view of human personality, our third topic, may be satisfying, in that it accentuates our unique dignity among all creatures in the physical universe. It features a neat simplicity in reducing all aspects of personality to the multidimensional reality of mind. On the other hand, Hobbes rightly questions whether Descartes succeeds in showing that personality is a spiritual substance essentially independent of the body and of all physical processes. Although the reasoning of the *cogito* is close to a sacrosanct achievement in the history of philosophy, it may assume too much to satisfy Descartes's stringent principle of clarity and distinctness. As Hume later suggests, it would be more accurate to say that I experience thought or thinking than that I experience my self thinking. Descartes's two criteria allegedly distinguishing humans from all other earthly creatures seem less convincing today than they probably did in the seventeenth century, because behavioral psychology has shown that other primates, such as chimpanzees and gorillas, can learn rather complex uses of computer and sign language, even becoming creative in adapting it, and because artificial intelligence seems to be blurring the distinction between programmed reactions and deliberate action. The most controversial feature of his theory of personality has to do with its dualistic interactionism. In a sense, he has done such an impressively thorough job of distinguishing mind and body as opposite created substances that it is difficult to see how they could naturally interact. It also seems inconceivable that they could come together or intermingle in a particular gland of the brain, since the mind, being defined as incorporeal, should not occupy space or be able to move even the most flexible and impressionable physical object. Descartes has rendered us the service of highlighting the intractable mind-body problem, to which no obviously satisfactory solution is yet available. Finally, although he does not exhibit the Platonists' contempt for the body, he does reflect their conviction that reason and the passions are locked in ongoing conflict, rather than being mutually supportive.

KNOWLEDGE.   As for our fourth topic, his theory of knowledge revolutionizes philosophy by making the quest for epistemological certainty a pivotal goal and by insisting that methodology must be foundational to any system-building. His preference for reason over sense experience and his recognition of intuition and deduction as the only ultimately reliable bases for knowledge may seem peculiar in this early age of modern science. Such a rationalistic program requires a compelling case for innate ideas if it is to succeed. Here is the most vulnerable part of his epistemology. It is not as obvious as it should be that crucial ideas, such as those of substance, self, God, causality, and freedom, are innate. Empiricists such as Hobbes and Hume will deny that any ideas are innate and call into doubt or radically reinterpret the key ideas just mentioned. The principle of clarity and distinctness, admirable though it be as an ideal, is a notoriously slippery criterion, since what is evident to the "natural light" of one person's reason is often questionable or false to that of another's. Without innate ideas hardly any factual reasoning will lead to the sort of indubitable certainty that Descartes demands.

FREEDOM.   Fifth, his discussion of human freedom is a case in point. It is so evident to him, in the course of his attempts at systematic doubt, that the human mind is free that it seems superfluous to argue the point. The problem is that **determinists** will argue that all actions, including those of the human will, are determined by forces which ultimately escape free choice. Even if they are mistaken, human freedom is not so evident that they could accept it without argument. Hobbes seems correct that Descartes has assumed it without proof. Descartes's failure to show how human freedom can be compatible with divine preordination is also disappointing because the latter can reasonably be thought to render the former impossible. Yet, in a sense, he is correct that most of us intuitively feel that we are free in at least some of our actions; and this feeling can be so powerful as to seem self-evident.

MORALITY.   Descartes's treatment of morality, our sixth topic, is thin. In general, the maxims of his provisional moral code seem sensible. But does the third one, that we should change ourselves, rather than trying to change the world, encourage too much passive acceptance of external reality and undermine our conviction that we have the power to effect genuine change in the world? His identification of the morally desirable life with the pursuit of virtue is plausible but in need of a precise criterion of ethical judgment. And his view of vice as usually the result of ignorance, far from being argued convincingly, ignores or downplays the significance of ill will.

SOCIETY.   Seventh, his discussion of society may be the weakest dimension of his theory. His distinctions among affection, friendship, and devotion seem spurious to the extent that the three are blended in our feelings towards certain fellow members of our own society—for example, a man's feelings towards his beloved wife. His analysis of generosity is a good account of how it affects one's thinking of others, if not of how it should affect one's external behavior towards them. Descartes is correct that, as members of society, we find our interests so identified with the welfare of our communities that it is often difficult to discriminate between them; they overlap, though they are not identical. Finally, his advice to Princess Elizabeth on how a ruler should relate to subjects, allies, and enemies may be too oriented towards power politics and insufficiently rooted in universal ethical principles.

RELIGION. Descartes's views on religion, our eighth topic, are mainly focused on his argumentation for God. The causal arguments require his causal principle for support. Unfortunately, this is another case where he sees no need to support it, since he finds it evident to the "natural light" of reason. Further, though, Hobbes's criticism is apt, that the very notion of degrees of reality is dubious. Hobbes also cuts to the core of all Descartes's arguments for God by challenging whether we have, or ever can have, any real idea of God. Descartes admits it is not derived from sense experience or the imagination; hence, its legitimacy is made to depend on the questionable claim that it is innate, a claim which does not seem to have been adequately established. The ontological argument is also subject to Gassendi's criticism that Descartes has mistakenly assumed that existence is a predicate, in effect defining God into existence in a question-begging way. It does seem that Descartes, in his Replies and *Principles*, if not in his *Meditations*, is successful in breaking the "Cartesian circle." Nevertheless, all the arguments for God are problematic; and Descartes has set up his system in such a way that, without a cogent proof for a nondeceiving God, it cannot transcend solipsism.

IMMORTALITY. Ninth, he probably does the best his stringent methodology allows with human immortality, trying to support it as a reasonable belief rather than demonstrating it. As Hobbes observes, it is doubtful that he adequately shows that mind is a spiritual substance distinct from the body and not dependent on it for all mental functions. But, even if we grant that tenet of Cartesian dualism, why should we agree that substances created by God are naturally incorruptible, unless they be annihilated by God? This is a major assumption underlying Descartes's attempts to provide rational support for the mind or soul surviving the death of the body. Without this assumption perhaps all Descartes can say is that the possibility of immortality is supported by the substantial distinctness of soul and body.

FULFILLMENT. Finally, Descartes presents a reasonable view of human fulfillment focused entirely on this life. Though it is **idealistic** in its confidence that happiness will follow from the pursuit of virtue, it acknowledges the importance of bodily comfort as well. It calls for the control of the passions by reason without denying the passions altogether. His conception of fulfillment coheres well with the dualism and rationalism of his general view of human nature. But what is striking about it is how oriented it is to this world, how nonreligious it is, and how disconnected it is from faith statements regarding eternal beatitude. It resembles Aristotle's views more than the theories of Christian thinkers like Aquinas.

*　　*　　*

The various dimensions of Descartes's theory generally hang together well. But he sets such high standards of rigor and certainty that it should not be too surprising that he sometimes falls short of meeting them. It is a complex theory in that it must relate God and man, mind and body, freedom of the will and the determinism of physical nature, the rational knowledge based on innate ideas and the common opinions derived from sense experience. To his credit, he invited and tried to answer the argued objections of his critics, including the empiricist and materialist Thomas Hobbes, who would go on to develop his own simpler theory of human nature. Whereas Descartes views everything in the universe as physical except for mind, Hobbes makes no such exception.

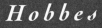

Hobbes

[In the state of nature,] the life of man [is] solitary, poor, nasty, brutish, and short.

LEVIATHAN

BIOGRAPHY

Thomas Hobbes, born on Good Friday, April 5, 1588 (during Queen Elizabeth's reign), in Malmesbury, England, was the second son of the vicar of Westport (adjoining Malmesbury), who was also named Thomas Hobbes. In his autobiography, written eighty-four years later, he jokes that his premature birth was brought on by the terror instilled by the approaching invasion of the ill-fated Spanish Armada:

> For the rumour ran, spreading alarm through our towns, that the Armada was bringing the day of doom to our race. Thus my mother was big with such fear that she brought twins to birth, my self and fear at the same time.

Not much more is known about his mother.

> From my father, who was minister, I received baptism, and the name he gave me was his own.

Shortly thereafter, his father, a hot-tempered man, when provoked by a parson at the door of his church, hit the fellow, had to run off into hiding, and subsequently died in obscurity. When he was four, the boy was sent to school at the Westport church; at eight years of age he went to a little private school in Malmesbury. As he writes,

> I was four years learning to speak, and four more years learning to read, count, and shape my letters indifferently well. Then for six years I applied myself to the

Greek and Latin tongues, and in my fourteenth year was sent to Oxford.[76]

Indeed his skill at classical languages was such that he translated Euripides' *Medea* from Greek into Latin verse before leaving Malmesbury. Because of his black hair and serious nature, his schoolmates called him "the Crow."

His uncle, a childless and prosperous glover and alderman of Malmesbury, provided for his education, and the boy was admitted into Magdalen Hall, Oxford, which was under Puritan administration. He studied Aristotelian syllogisms, which he seems to have despised. As he writes, "These I was slow to learn, but I did learn them, and reject them and get leave to prove everything in my own way." He was promoted to the study of Aristotelian scholastic physics, but he was unimpressed with its accounts of forms, sensible species, and sympathy and antipathy. Instead, his interests turned to the study of "maps celestial and maps terrestrial" and of ocean voyages in which "Drake and Cavendish had cast a girdle round Neptune's waist and the different regions they had visited."[77] After five years at Oxford, he received his bachelor's degree, in February of 1608, shortly before turning twenty.

His rector at Magdalen Hall recommended him for service to William Cavendish, who ten years later would become the first Earl of Devonshire. That same year he became employed by the Cavendish family, with which he would be associated off and on for the rest of his life. He was assigned to serve as companion and tutor for young William Cavendish, who was only a couple of years younger than Hobbes himself. As he writes, "Him I served for twice ten years without a break. He was not so much a master as a friend, and this was by far the sweetest portion of my life."[78] This position gave him access to influential people and a fine library, and it afforded him opportunities to travel abroad, all of which contributed significantly to his development as a thinker.

Each of Hobbes's three trips to the Continent proved relevant to that development. In 1610, he made the grand tour of France, Germany, and Italy with young William Cavendish. He came to realize that the scholastic Aristotelianism he found so tedious and worthless when he was at Oxford was being spurned by intellectuals of his day. A new science was emerging. Kepler had recently published the first two of his laws of planetary motion, and Galileo had used his telescope to discover satellites of Jupiter. Hobbes also encountered political turmoil; that same year, the French King Henry IV was assassinated with a knife at the hands of an insane Jesuit named François Ravaillac. After returning to England, Hobbes became associated with Francis Bacon, the Lord Chancellor of England, who enjoyed talking with Hobbes and had Hobbes translate some of his essays into Latin. Bacon was another scholar who had repudiated Aristotelian scholasticism in favor of a new scientific method. In 1626, the first Earl of Devonshire died; the younger William Cavendish became the second Earl, but he died in June of 1628.

While employed by the Cavendish family, Hobbes says,

> I applied myself to histories in our own tongue, in Greek, and in Latin. . . . but my special favourite was Thucydides. He taught me how stupid democracy is and how much one man is wiser than an assembly.

He decided to translate Thucydides' *History of the Grecian War*. As he says, "I made it my business that this author should speak to the English in their own tongue and warn them against the temptation" posed by democratic demagogues. He agrees with the Greek author that "the principal and proper work of history," as he puts it, is "to instruct and enable men, by the knowledge of actions past, to bear themselves prudently in the present and providently towards the future."[79] When Hobbes published his translation in 1628, Charles I had been king of England for three years and was having trouble with Parliament.

The same year his master died, Hobbes took a position as tutor and traveling companion to the son of Sir Gervase Clinton, a gentleman of Nottinghamshire. He accompanied him to France and Italy. While in Paris, during this second journey to the Continent, Hobbes saw a proposition in Euclid's *Elements*, which he (literally) swore was impossible. But in reading the demonstration, which referred him back to earlier propositions, he found it convincingly proved and fell in love with the deductive method of geometry.

In 1631, Hobbes was recalled from Paris by the widow of the second Earl of Devonshire to take charge of their son, who had inherited his father's title. Hobbes taught the boy Latin, rhetoric, geography, and other subjects "for seven busy years. His apprehension was quick and his memory retentive." They

visited France and Italy from 1634 to 1637. This third voyage to the Continent provided the stimulation that would make Hobbes an original thinker. He visited Galileo near Florence in 1636, where the scientist was under house arrest after being tried by the Inquisition. Like other anti-Aristotelians and critics of scholastic **realism**, Hobbes became convinced that things are not as they appear in sense experience and that the natural state of physical reality is one of motion, rather than of rest. We experience merely the phenomenal appearances of things, as he says, "the only inner reality of which is motion." After leaving Italy, they returned to Paris, where the Franciscan friar, Marin Mersenne, was living in a monastery. As Hobbes writes, "Here I got to know Mersenne, and I communicated to him my meditations on the motion of things. He approved and recommended me to many others. From that time I began to be numbered among the philosophers." Mersenne, who was about his own age, put him in contact with Descartes and helped him meet Pierre Gassendi. Hobbes later describes this intermediary between intellectuals in warm terms as "a man learned, wise, and supremely good. His cell was to be preferred to all the schools in the circuit of the whole round world." Like a professional editor today, this man helped authors get their ideas published. Hobbes writes, "Mersenne was the Pole round which revolved every star in the world of science."[80]

Hobbes returned to England in 1637 with his pupil, who was still a year away from coming of age. He tells us that he was starting "to think of connecting into a whole the knowledge I had gained, so that the conclusions might shine bright in the light of the first principles and the whole argument might have the permanence of a strong chain." This was the year in which Descartes published his *Discourse*, and Hobbes shared his dream of a deductively constructed universal philosophical system, except that his would be purely materialistic and organized in three component parts—"for three things comprise the whole of philosophy, namely, Body, Man, and the Citizen."[81] He prepared to write three books on those topics but was interrupted by the prospect of civil war between the royalists and the Puritan-led Parliament. By his fiftieth birthday he had not yet produced any original works that would make him famous and was only on the verge of putting together the system represented by the many writings that would burst into print in the 1640s and 1650s. In April of 1640, England was at war with Scotland, and King Charles had to call Parliament into session in order to raise the funds to wage that war. Parliament would not even discuss the matter until the king answered certain charges against the Crown, so that Charles dissolved the session on May 5th. During that short session, Hobbes had written *The Elements of Law*, arguing, on the basis of human psychology, for the necessity of undivided sovereignty, such as was then invested in the king and being threatened by Parliament. "Of this treatise, though not printed, many gentlemen had copies, which occasioned much talk of the author; and had not his Majesty dissolved the Parliament, it had brought him into danger of his life." He goes on to describe himself as "the first that had ventured to write in the King's defence" and one of the few who remained "perfectly loyal," without any ulterior motives based on self-interest. (*The Elements of Law* was published ten years later in two parts on *Human Nature* and *De Corpore Politico*.) Parliament was again called into session in November of 1640, with bitter animosity against the king. The political atmosphere was so charged with the hostility of Parliamentarians towards Royalists that Hobbes, "doubting how they would use him, went over into France, the first of all that fled, and there continued eleven years."[82]

He was warmly welcomed to Paris by Mersenne, who, at Descartes's request, was soliciting critical objections to the *Meditations*. At Mersenne's invitation, Hobbes wrote up the third set of *Objections*, which was published anonymously with the *Meditations* and Descartes's replies. Descartes did not appreciate Hobbes's direct attacks or his materialistic metaphysics; Hobbes had more respect for Descartes, though despising his Catholic theological view (the two cordially dined together with Gassendi in Paris in 1648). In 1642, Hobbes published in Latin his political book *De Cive* (i.e., *On the Citizen*). In 1645, Charles, the Prince of Wales, "the heir to the throne, came to Paris, accompanied by a large retinue of men renowned for arms or nobility, to wait the passage of the evil days and the subsidence of the people's rage" back home in England. Hobbes had prepared his materials for the writing of his "*De Corpore*, but was obliged to put it off" to become mathematics tutor to the prince. In 1647, Hobbes became ill with a fever that put his life in grave danger. As he writes, "for six months I was prostrated by illness; I was preparing myself for the approach of Death. But *I* stood my ground and *she* fled."[83] Father Mersenne visited him on his sickbed and gingerly tested Hobbes's willingness to convert to Catholicism; but Hobbes cut him off, asking for news of their mutual friend, Gassendi. Mersenne got the message and changed the subject. A bit later, Hobbes did receive the Anglican sacrament of last rites—an event Hobbes later invoked as proof that he was not an irreligious atheist.

After Hobbes's recovery, the beheading of Charles I occurred; as Hobbes writes in a posthumously published dialogue, Parliament "murdered their King (a King that sought no greater glory upon earth, but to be indulgent to his people, and a pious defender of the Church of England)."[84] In Hobbes's view, as he says in his autobiography, this made Charles II "the rightful King." He expresses his contempt for the political situation in England at that time:

> The rebel mob seized power and governed the people without law. Few though they were, they assumed the name of Parliament and glutted themselves with the blood of nobility.

In 1650, the two parts of Hobbes's earlier *Elements of Law, Human Nature* and *De Corpore Politico,* were published in London. Hobbes's English translation of his own *De Cive* was published in 1651 (under the title of *Philosophical Rudiments concerning Government and Society*), as was his masterpiece, *Leviathan*, written in English, a book which, he says, "now fights for all kings and for those under any title who exercise the rights of kings." Hobbes had antagonized the French clergy with his attacks on the papacy. His clerical friend Mersenne had died in 1648. *Leviathan* was viewed by royalists as undermining the traditional divine-right-of-kings doctrine. Hobbes, in effect, found himself isolated and on the defensive. He was virtually accused of treason. As he says, "I was accounted of the enemy party. I was bidden for ever to absent myself from the King's court." Nor did he blame Charles for being temporarily poisoned against him by malicious advisors.

> So I returned to my native land, not well assured of safety, but because there was nowhere else I could be safer. It was cold, the snow was deep, I was old, the wind was biting and fierce, my horse restive, and the road full of pot-holes.

This return home from his final trip abroad was in the winter of 1651–52. He writes,

> When I reached London, I had to make terms with the Council of State to avoid the suspicion of a secret return. This done I was pardoned and withdrew, and, as of old, applied myself again to my studies.[85]

Hobbes settled into private life and returned to the previously abandoned project of writing *De Corpore*. But, while working on that, he found himself ensnared in a controversy over human freedom. While in France he had argued against free will with a Bishop Bramhall; and in 1654, his writing *Of Liberty and Necessity* was published without his consent. Despite this distraction, Hobbes finally published *De Corpore* (literally, *On the Body*) in 1655, followed by an English version the next year. Hobbes had already tangled with the universities (over his criticisms of them in *Leviathan*) and now found himself tangled in disputes with mathematicians (over his attempt to square the circle). In 1658, his *De Homine* (literally, *On Man*) was published in London. In 1660, the monarchy was restored, Charles returning to England as King Charles II. Hobbes was accused of having written *Leviathan* to ingratiate himself with Oliver Cromwell, even though it was published years before Cromwell became Protector.[86] When the Royal Society was founded in 1662, Hobbes was disappointed at not being invited to join, having antagonized some of its leading members.

Despite the attacks of his enemies, Hobbes was invited to the court of Charles II, who appreciated his old tutor's wit and granted him a pension of one hundred pounds a year; there is a letter in which Hobbes petitions the king for payment.[87] The king called Hobbes "the Bear" on account of his large size and robust build, and Charles was amused at the efforts of courtiers to bait him. In 1665–66, London was devastated by the Great Plague and the Great Fire; some of Hobbes's enemies said these were signs of God's wrath over Hobbes's ideas. Some bishops reportedly demanded that the old philosopher be burnt as a heretic. A bill came before Parliament to suppress atheism, and a committee was formed to investigate *Leviathan*. The dangerous bill passed in the House of Commons but then collapsed, perhaps under pressure from the king. Even so, Charles forbade Hobbes to publish his *Behemoth*, written in 1668, because it

seemed inflammatory; like his dialogue on the common law, written about 1673, it was only published posthumously.

Hobbes liked to walk every day and played tennis into his seventies. In 1672, he wrote a brief autobiography in Latin verse. At the age of eighty-six, for lack of anything better to do, he produced verse translations of Homer's *Iliad* and *Odyssey*, published in 1675. In late 1679, he suffered an attack of paralysis; he died on December 4th, at the age of ninety-one. His last four decades were committed to producing the work for which he is now famous, including his theory of political obligation. As he says near the end of his autobiography,

> My life and my writings are of one pattern. Justice I teach, justice I practise.[88]

In 1683, *De Cive* and *Leviathan* were condemned and burned at Oxford.

Reality

Like Descartes's, Hobbes's conception of reality is substance-based. But unlike the dualist, who views mind and body as two distinct, irreducible substances, Hobbes presents a monistic view of all reality as physical:

> For the *universe*, being the aggregate of all bodies, there is no real part thereof that is not also *body*, nor anything properly a *body* that is not also part of (that aggregate of all *bodies*) the *universe*.

This passage from *Leviathan* goes on to identify all substantial reality as material:

> And according to this acceptation of the word, *substance* and *body* signify the same thing; and therefore, *substance incorporeal* are words which, when they are joined together, destroy one another, as if a man should say, an *incorporeal body*.

With this one sentence Hobbes rejects the traditional idea of a soul, endorsed by Descartes—a move which will have serious ramifications for his view of human nature. Later, Hobbes reiterates his materialistic metaphysics:

> The world (I mean not the Earth only . . . but the *universe*, that is, the whole mass of all things that are) is corporeal (that is to say, body) and hath the dimensions of magnitude (namely, length, breadth, and depth).

A bit later, he proceeds to say that "every part of the universe is body, and that which is not body is no part of the universe. And because the universe is all, that which is no part of it is nothing." He explains that this assertion need not entail a denial of spirits, but only an analysis of them as bodily.[89]

De Corpore contains a fuller treatment of the world as the aggregate of parts, all of which are physical, which is essentially subject to our quantitative measurement:

> Of the whole world we may inquire what is its magnitude, what its duration, and how many there be, but nothing else.

Qualitative descriptions of the world, in terms of colors, sounds, smells, and so forth, are merely phantasms of sense in us as perceivers. There is no empty space in the universe, according to Hobbes; its parts are "contiguous to one another, in such a manner as not to admit of the least empty space between," so that "all space is full."[90] Thus, there is no problem of a scientifically inexplicable vacuum here.

Bodies

BODIES AND SCIENTIFIC LAWS.   If reality is comprised of bodies, what can be said about them? They are subject to scientific laws. For example, in *Leviathan* Hobbes writes,

> When a body is once in motion, it moveth (unless something else hinder it) eternally; and whatsoever hindreth it, cannot in an instant, but in time and by degrees, quite extinguish it.

In living bodies, or animals, there are two sorts of motions: vital ones, necessary for the maintenance of life, "such as are the *course* of the *blood*, the *pulse*, the *breathing*," and so forth, for which "there needs no help of imagination," and voluntary motions, arising from the will, "as to *go*, to *speak*, to *move* any of our limbs, in such a manner as is first fancied in our minds." Theoretically, both types of animal motions are as scientifically explicable as are the movements of inanimate bodies. He defines a body as "that which filleth or occupieth some certain room or imagined place, and dependeth not on the imagination, but is a real part of that we call the *universe*." So, like Descartes, he conceives of bodies as extended objects of sensation. Being an animal, "*a man is a living body*."[91] In the next section we shall see

how this materialistic view of human nature leads to an attempt to analyze all human activities in mechanistic terms.

CAUSALITY, BODIES, AND MOTION.   Again, *De Corpore* offers us more in the way of details. The cause of all changes in bodies "consists in motion." Hobbes defines "*a cause*" as

> the sum or aggregate of all such accidents, both in the agents and the patient, as concur to the producing of the effect propounded; all which existing together, it cannot be understood but that the effect existeth with them; or that it can possibly exist if any one of them be absent.

In other words, a cause is a **condition** of an event that is both **sufficient** and necessary for its occurring. We experience bodies as in time and space, though these are phantasms, or mere images in our minds.

> The definition, therefore, of *body* may be this, *a body is that, which having no dependence upon our thought, is coincident or coextended with some part of space.*

Bodies are experienced in terms of their qualities or accidents; for Hobbes, "an *accident*" is defined as "*the manner by which any body is conceived*; which is all one as if they should say, *an accident is that faculty of any body, by which it works in us a conception of itself*." The enduring accidents of any body are its extension and figure; all others, "as *to be at rest, to be moved, color, hardness*, and the like, do perish continually, and are succeeded by others." Hobbes says that a body's "*extension*" is its "*magnitude*" or occupation of space. A body's "*place*" in space is merely a phantasm of our thinking, but its magnitude is independently real; as he puts it, "*place* is nothing out of the mind, or *magnitude* any thing within it. . . . *place* is feigned extension, but *magnitude* true extension." Against the Aristotelians, Hobbes thinks the natural state of bodies is one of motion, rather than of rest. "Motion *is a continual relinquishing of one place, and acquiring of another*." A body is "*at rest, which, during any time, is in one place*"; while a body is "*moved*" when it "*was formerly in another place than that which it is now in*." Bodies at rest remain so unless and until they are moved by other bodies, and moving bodies will continue to move unless and until arrested by other bodies. When one body acts upon

---

Sufficient condition.   That which is adequate to bring about something else, so that whenever the first occurs, the second will as well; for example, a pet's being a dog is a sufficient condition for its also being a mammal

another, the agent body causally produces effects in the body acted upon. (Later in the seventeenth century, Sir Isaac Newton would more carefully develop this idea in his laws of motion.) Of the four Aristotelian causes, Hobbes takes seriously efficient and material causality, the former being in an "agent" body and the latter in the "patient" body acted upon; he repudiates formal and final causality as separate, reducing them to "efficient causes."[92]

Since no two bodies can be in the same place at the same time, they must "*differ* from one another," in the sense that "something may be said of one of them, which cannot be said of the other at the same time." Hobbes wrestles with the problem of the identity of bodies—

> namely, in what sense it may be conceived that a body is at one time the same, at another time not the same as it was formerly. For example, whether a man grown old be the same man he was whilst he was young, or another man.

His answer is that it is the same person legally and psychologically, but not physically the same; if the body has changed, then so has its physical identity, while "if the matter be the same, the thing also is *individually* the same." One body may physically impede or resist the motion of another. Hobbes writes,

> I define resistance *to be the endeavor of one moved body either wholly or in part contrary to the endeavor of another moved body, which toucheth the same.*

And the force of a moving body is defined as its "impetus or *quickness of motion*" whereby it "*works more or less upon the body that resists it.*" The science that studies bodies in motion is physics, whose objects are natural phenomena appearing in sense experience.

> But you will say, by what sense shall we take notice of sense? I answer, by sense itself, namely, by the memory which for some time remains in us of things sensible, though they themselves pass away.[93]

Yet how do we persons, as living bodies, perform such functions as are required for the achievement of physical science?

Personality

THE CLOCK ANALOGY. The very first paragraph of *Leviathan* emphasizes the materialistic quality of Hobbes's view of human nature—

> life is but a motion of limbs. . . . For what is the *heart*, but a *spring*; and the *nerves*, but so many *strings*; and

the *joints*, but so many *wheels*, giving motion to the whole body?

This analogy between a living body and an operating clock sets up the subsequent mechanistic analysis of all human functions. He maintains that human actions and passions are essentially common to all of us, though their objects may vary. Voluntary (as opposed to vital) motions are caused by imperceptible forces in the living organism. "These small beginnings of motion within the body of man, before they appear in walking, speaking, striking, and other visible actions, are commonly called ENDEAVOUR."[94]

OBJECTS OF HUMAN ENDEAVOR, DELIBERATION, AND WILL. Using physical language, he distinguishes two basic types of endeavors: appetites or desires, which attract us towards objects, and aversions, which repel us away from them. On this analysis, love becomes an appetite for something and hatred an aversion to something; when we are neither pulled towards nor away from an object, he says we experience a kind of "immobility" called "contempt" for it. Our concepts of "good" and "evil" get reduced to these terms—the former what we call the objects of our desire, the latter what we call the objects of our hatred—rather than signifying any objective, absolute values. He offers a long catalogue of other more specific passions. For example, pleasure is a sense of good and displeasure a sense of evil. "Grief" is a displeasure over expected consequences. He likewise says, "*Desire* of good to another" is what we call "Benevolence, Good Will, Charity." Similarly, "*Love* of persons for society" is "Kindness." He defines "Religion" as "*Fear* of power invisible, feigned by the mind, or imagined from tales publicly allowed," which he holds may be either superstitious or true. "*Grief* for the calamity of another is pity" or compassion or fellow feeling. When our endeavors are tugging us in different directions, we are said to deliberate, a phenomenon apparent in other animals as well as in us—"and therefore beasts also deliberate." Unlike Descartes, Hobbes does not think deliberate action unique to man among the animals. "In *deliberation*, the last appetite or aversion immediately adhering to the action, or to the omission thereof, is that we call the will"; and, since beasts allegedly deliberate, they "must necessarily also have *will*." He repudiates the scholastic definition of will as "rational appetite" because it eliminates the possibility of irrational voluntary acts; as he says, "a *voluntary act*" is any that proceeds from the will, whether it be in accordance with reason or not. "*Will* therefore *is the last appetite in deliberating.*"[95]

POWER.   Like Aristotle, Hobbes analyzes such desirable qualities or "abilities of the mind as men praise, value, and desire should be in themselves," which are intellectual virtues. These include wit, good judgment, discretion, and prudence. He defines a person's power as "his present means to obtain some future apparent good," so that it is relative to our desires. Natural human power is relative to that possessed by other persons and is defined as "the eminence of the faculties of body or mind, as extraordinary strength, form, prudence, arts, eloquence," and so forth. So even here there is the suggestion of natural competition among us. Acquired powers, such "as riches, reputation, friends, and the secret working of God, which men call good luck," are valued as "means and instruments to acquire more" of what we desire. But the greatest of all human powers, he observes, is political. Human "*value* or Worth," is measured in terms of what "would be given for the use" of a person's power. This esteem can be established by other individuals or by society at large.

> The public worth of a man, which is the value set on him by the commonwealth, is that which men commonly call Dignity.[96]

It is natural for us to value power as a means of satisfying our desires; and, since our power is relative to that of other persons, this generates conflict.

> Competition of riches, honour, command, or other power, inclineth to contention, enmity, and war; because the way of one competitor to the attaining of his desire is to kill, subdue, supplant, or repel the other.

This competitive consequence of our natural inclinations will have profound implications for Hobbes's theory of society. But another complicating factor is the virtual natural equality of all humans.

> Nature hath made men so equal in the faculties of body and mind as that, though there be found one man sometimes manifestly stronger in body or of quicker mind than another, yet when all is reckoned together the difference between man and man is not so considerable as that one man can thereupon claim to himself any benefit to which another may not pretend as well as he.

As Hobbes bluntly observes, even the naturally weakest person has ability "enough to kill the strongest, either by secret machination, or by confederacy with others." So, on the one hand, we are naturally competing with other persons for the satisfaction of desires; and, on the other hand, no one is naturally so vastly superior to others as to discourage the pursuit of such competition.[97]

AT WAR WITH ONE ANOTHER.   This leads to what Hobbes calls "diffidence," or the distrust of others. "And from this diffidence of one another, there is no way for any man to secure himself so reasonable as anticipation, that is, by force or wiles to master the persons of all men he can, so long till he see no other power great enough to endanger him." And, Hobbes adds, this natural orientation to dominate others is quite appropriate because it is conducive to self-preservation. But, given this attitude towards other persons, we are naturally antisocial rather than sociable; as he says,

> men have no pleasure, but on the contrary a great deal of grief, in keeping company where there is no power able to over-awe them all,

—that is, outside the artificial constructs of society. Indeed, this natural condition of mankind is one of

> war as is of every man against every man.

Hobbes even anticipates our twentieth-century idea of a "cold war" by saying that war, in his sense of the term, extends beyond the period of "actual fighting" to "the known disposition thereto" and the apparent "will to contend" with others.[98]

In *De Cive*, Hobbes considers the Aristotelian claim that "man is a creature born fit for society," a *zoon politikon*, or political animal, and denies it as "an error proceeding from our too slight contemplation of human nature." We are not naturally sociable but must work to become socialized and do so merely as an instrumental means to selfish ends: "We do not therefore by nature seek society for its own sake, but that we may receive some honour or profit from it; these we desire primarily, that secondarily." What each of us naturally desires is his own good, especially his own self-preservation; what each person naturally avoids is what he regards as evil, "but chiefly the chiefest of natural evils, which is death." We have a natural right to protect ourselves and avail ourselves of whatever is required for self-preservation; and in the **state of nature** (that is, outside the conventions of society) each person must judge such matters for himself. Even when deliberation leads us to limit our natural rights, this is **egoistically** motivated, "because whatsoever is voluntarily done, is done for some good to him that wills it." Indeed, all voluntary motions are actions proceeding from the will, as motivated by "hope and fear." Unlike Aristotle, Hobbes says that men are uniquely political among the animals, in the sense of needing to subordinate their individual wills to constitute one united will; and, as we will see, he lists six key differences that prevent us from being naturally sociable as are some other animals.[99]

EGOISM. We usually think of Hobbes as the greatest example in the history of Western philosophy of psychological egoism, the view that all human motivation is ultimately rooted in self-interest. In explaining the will to curtail our natural rights in order to enter into society, he writes, in *Leviathian,*

> Whensoever a man transferreth his right or renounceth it, it is either in consideration of some right reciprocally transferred to himself or for some other good he hopeth for thereby. For it is a voluntary act, and of the voluntary acts of every man the object is some *good to himself.*

This can be formulated as a valid deductive argument: every abridgement of natural rights is a voluntary act, and every voluntary act is motivated by self-interest; therefore, every abridgement of natural rights is motivated by self-interest. It is the second premise that lies at the heart of psychological egoism. In discussing gifts inspired by a feeling of gratitude, Hobbes says,

> For no man giveth but with intention of good to himself, because gift is voluntary, and of all voluntary acts the object is to every man his own good.[100]

This is basically the same syllogism, containing the same controversial second premise, expressing psychological egoism.

A human being, both naturally and socially, functions as a person.

> A person is he *whose words or actions are considered either as his own, or as representing the words or actions of another man, or of any other thing to whom they are attributed.*

Thus, when one speaks or acts on his own behalf or on behalf of his spouse, child, or king, he is functioning as a person. In a political context, a group of humans, such as a congress, a committee, or a jury, can exercise the authority of a single person: "A multitude of men are made *one* person, when they are by one man, or one person, represented" with the consent of all, as when the speaker, chairperson, or foreman has the authority to represent congress, committee, or jury. Hobbes disputes Aristotle's contention that the human person is naturally social like bees and ants, pointing out six crucial differences that prevent us from easily living at peace with one another:

1. We naturally compete for intangibles such as "honour and dignity."
2. We distinguish between "the common good" and our own private benefit.
3. Reason allows us to blame others and view ourselves as superior.
4. Our language allows us to "represent to others that which is good in the likeness of evil, and evil in the likeness of good," deceiving others "and troubling their peace."
5. Unlike all "irrational creatures," we differentiate between damage or harm, on the one hand, and injury, or the violation of rights, on the other, taking offense at the latter.
6. Our agreement with our fellows is artificial rather than natural, "by covenant only."[101]

In examining these contrasts between human persons and other animals, we might notice that Hobbes does not regard all the relative advantages as being on our side but attributes some of our problems to indicated differences.

In the dedicatory letter to his patron, William Cavendish, attached to *De Cive,* Hobbes points to a tension between "the *concupiscible* part" and "the *rational*" part of human nature. In his preface he shows that it is natural for human beings to "distrust and dread each other" and to apply their resources for

---

State of nature. The hypothetical condition of humans had they not entered into society by means of a social contract; Hobbes describes it graphically as a war of all against all, in which life would be "solitary, poor, nasty, brutish, and short"; Rawls's "original position" is its analogue in contemporary theory

Egoism. The view that everyone does in fact (psychological egoism) and/or should in principle (ethical egoism) act ultimately to further his or her own interests, as opposed to altruism

purposes of self-preservation. But he denies that this tendency to antisocial egoism means "that men are evil by nature." Though human beings naturally "have this disposition, that immediately as much as in them lies they desire to do whatsoever is best pleasing to them, . . . yet are they not for this reason to be accounted wicked." As he argues, natural "affections of the mind" are not, in themselves, evil, any more than the natural peevishness of small children. In *De Cive*, he writes, "The faculties of human nature may be reduced unto four kinds: bodily strength, experience, reason, passion."[102] The first is obviously physical, and we have seen his materialistic account of the last; in the next section, we shall see that his analysis of reason and experience is also rooted in our corporeal sensation.

HUMANS AND BRUTE ANIMALS. In *De Homine* Hobbes maintains, somewhat like Descartes, that speech and understanding distinguish humans from brute animals. "Speech or language is the connexion of names constituted by the will of men to stand for the series of conceptions of the things about which we think." Beasts can utter significant sounds and be taught to respond to ours but "do not know that words are constituted by the will of men for the purpose of signification." Lacking reason, they cannot grasp the links among words, thoughts, and will. "Therefore other animals also lack understanding. For understanding is a kind of imagination, but one that ariseth from the signification constituted by words." It is worth noting that Hobbes keeps comparing humans to "brute animals," saying we are more rapacious and cruel than "wolves, bears, and snakes" and that without artificial social covenants, justice is no more to be found among men than "among beasts." He says that the causes of our appetites and aversions are objects of sense experience and that "will itself is an appetite." However free our actions may be, our appetites and aversions are determined, as are those of other animals; "one can, in truth, be free to *act*; one cannot, however, be free to *desire*." Human nature is such that "all desire good for themselves" and that "the greatest of goods for each is his own preservation." This includes a natural desire for "life, health, and . . . security." Hobbes admits that, in extreme circumstances, life can be so hopelessly painful as to "lead men to

number death among the goods," thus undoing the natural desire for self-preservation. But, normally, power is desirable for purposes of self-preservation, self-protection, and security; even friendship is an artificial power tending to those good consequences. And our egoism is such, for Hobbes, that we are pleased at another's misfortunes because they are not our own and displeased at another's good fortune because it is not ours to enjoy.[103]

HUMAN EMOTIONS AND DISPOSITIONS. We are driven by our endeavors. Hobbes writes,

> Emotions or *perturbations* of the mind are species of appetite and aversion, their differences having been taken from the diversity and circumstances of the objects that we desire or shun. They are called *perturbations* because they frequently obstruct right reasoning.

Emotion is analyzed in terms of "various motions of the blood," caused by "phantasms concerning good and evil excited in the mind by objects." We still need to see (in the following section) how ideas in the mind ("phantasms") are themselves materialistically explained; but this theory of human emotions is thoroughly physical and mechanistic. He goes on to analyze particular emotions, such as joy, hate, hope, fear, and anger. He analyzes six sources of our personal dispositions or inclinations:

1. Our own bodily constitutions;
2. The habits into which our past actions have led us;
3. Our experience of the things in our external environment;
4. Various accidents of fortune, such as "riches, nobility of birth, and civil power," we have been granted;
5. Our own self-image; and
6. The influences of authorities, such as parents and teachers.

All of these affect the ways in which our personalities are disposed to act and respond. Hobbes reiterates his definition of a "person" as one "*to whom the words and actions of men are attributed, either his own or another's*"; a "*natural*" person is one to whom his own words and actions are attributed, while an "*artificial*" person is one to whom the words and actions of another are attributed. He repeats that one person can represent many,[104] as a political ruler does his many subjects.

HUMAN FACULTIES AND MOTIVATION. In *Human Nature* Hobbes writes, "Man's *nature* is the *sum of his natural faculties and powers*, as the faculties of *nutrition, motion, generation, sense, reason, &c.*" Our natural physical faculties include "power *nutritive*, power *motive*, and power *generative*," while our mental faculties are of "two sorts, *cognitive, imaginative*, or *conceptive* and *motive*." We notice here both physical and mental sources of motivation. Ultimately, all ideas in the mind are derived from sense experience. Past sense experiences leave traces in the mind in the form of images that tend to become gradually less clear and distinct with time, imagination being defined in terms of "*conception remaining, and by little and little decaying from and after the act of sense.*" In addition to the five external senses, all of which are identified with particular organs of the body, memory is an internal "*sixth sense.*" It is memory, the accurate retention of images derived from sensation, that makes possible what we call *experience*. We are motivated by a desire for "*pleasure*, which is nothing really but motion about the heart, as conception is nothing but motion in the head," as well as by our natural aversion to pain. It is worth noting how **consistent** Hobbes is in explaining all the functions of persons in terms of bodily motions. Even the passion of sympathy for others is an emotion physiologically based in self-interest:

> *Pity* is *imagination* or *fiction* of *future* calamity to *ourselves*, proceeding from the sense of *another* man's calamity.

Hobbes likewise speaks of "*good will* or *charity*" as the enjoyment a man has "of his own power...to assist other men" in accomplishing their desires. Thus, he does not so much deny what others regard as benevolent action as provide an egoistic interpretation of it. He also distinguishes between dull personalities, which tend to enjoy only "the appetite of sensual or bodily delight," and witty personalities, which have sufficient "agility of spirits" and curiosity to enjoy "both *fancy* and *judgment*" as well as the pleasures of the body.[105]

* * *

In conclusion, as Hobbes says in *De Corpore Politico*, he tries in his "treatise of human nature" to "set forth the whole nature of man, consisting in the powers natural of his body and mind," which are basically "four, *strength of body, experience, reason, and passion*."[106] As we shall see now, his analysis of experience and reason, as of everything pertaining to human knowledge, is as consistently materialistic as are his discussions of bodies and the passions of the human personality.

Knowledge

SENSATION AS THE ULTIMATE SOURCE OF THOUGHT. As images derived from sensation provide the basis for human emotions, according to Hobbes, they are also considered the grounds of human knowledge. Near the beginning of *Leviathan* he says that every human thought is "a *representation* or *appearance*, of some quality or other accident, of a body without us, which is commonly called an *object*." The objects of experience affect our sense organs so as to produce the representations or appearances of thought. This representational theory requires that sensation be the ultimate original source of all thought.

> For there is no conception in a man's mind which hath not at first, totally or by parts, been begotten upon the organs of sense.

Sensation occurs as a result of an external body or object pressing against the appropriate sense organ. When we have touched table tops or seen mountains, pressure has been exerted by the object or light on our hands or eyeballs, "which pressure, by the mediation of nerves and other strings and membranes of the body, continued inwards to the brain," causing there "a resistance, or counter-pressure," taking the form of images. "And this *seeming*, or *fancy*, is that which men call *sense*." Though it is caused by bodies outside us, "sense in all cases, is nothing else but original fancy" within us; in other words, we perceive the images in us rather than bodies outside us. Thus, not only does Hobbes reject the Aristotelian-scholastic explanation of sensation in terms of visible species, audible species, tangible species, and so forth; but, more radically, he repudiates its very assumption of common-sense realism. If our experience were limited to present sensation, it would be pathetically slight. But imagination provides us with the means to

---

Consistency. The compatibility of things, actions, beliefs, or logical propositions, such that they can coexist, or be done or held without contradiction, or be simultaneously true

transcend that narrow range. "For after the object is removed, or the eye shut, we still retain an image of the thing seen, though more obscure than when we see it." Such images, stored in the brain, are dwindling after-effects of sense experience. "Imagination therefore is nothing but *decaying sense*, and is found in men and many other living creatures, as well sleeping as waking." Touching the tabletop or seeing the distant mountains makes an impression on the brain which persists after the touching or seeing has ceased, though it tends to become less vivid and distinct as time separates it from the prior sensation. "This *decaying sense*" is called imagination when we wish to emphasize the images in the brain derived from sensation; but that same "decaying sense" is called memory when we want to emphasize the fact that the images are fading with time. "So that *imagination* and *memory* are but one thing, which for diverse considerations hath diverse names." Unlike Descartes, Hobbes has no innate ideas, sensation and imagination being his only sources of thought. "Much memory, or memory of many things, is called *experience*,"[107] which will provide the foundation for all reasoning.

IMAGES IN THE MIND.   Though Hobbes never doubts the reality of things outside his mind, as Descartes did, in *De Corpore*, he holds that the direct, immediate objects of perception are phantasms or images in the mind itself. Our five external senses give rise to such images. As he points out, "The proper phantasm of sight is light" rather than the object seen. "The phantasm, which is made by hearing, is sound; by smell, odor; by taste, savor; and by touch, hardness and softness, heat and cold, wetness, oiliness," and so forth. Objects outside the mind causally work on the sense organs (and central nervous system) to produce these phantasms in the brain.[108] This presents a kind of scepticism about the objectivity of thought and knowledge that makes Hobbes revolutionary relative to earlier great thinkers.

THE GREAT DECEPTION OF SENSE.   He boldly spells this out in *Human Nature*, writing that

> *whatsoever accidents* or qualities our senses make us think there be in the *world*, they be *not* there, but are

seeming and *apparitions* only: the things that really are in the world without us, are those *motions* by which these seemings are caused.

Hobbes calls this "*the great deception of sense*," adding that it must "be by sense *corrected*." But Descartes might challenge whether the senses can be *self*-correcting; and, if they cannot, an epistemology so empirically anchored in sensation as is Hobbes's seems destined to be thoroughly sceptical in its conception of knowledge. To the extent that knowledge must be universal, this scepticism is heightened by his **nominalistic** repudiation of all who "so seriously contend, that besides Peter and John, and all the rest of the men that are, have been, or shall be in the world, there is yet something else that we call *man*, and *man in general*, deceiving themselves, by taking the universal, or general appellation, for the thing it signifieth."[109] What Hobbes does not do, curiously enough, is push this epistemological position to the point of questioning whether there can be any universal human nature at all.

THE TRAIN OF THOUGHTS.   In *Leviathan*, Hobbes discusses the train of thoughts, called mental discourse, based on experience. The brain associates some ideas with certain other ideas based on past experience, so that the processing of images is neither entirely random nor chronologically determined: "Not every thought to every thought succeeds indifferently." The flexibility with which the brain associates images is a function of previous sense experience. "This train of thoughts, or mental discourse, is of two sorts. The first is *unguided, without design*, and inconstant." Such is freely associated stream of consciousness, in which our "thoughts are said to wander," somewhat as they do in dreams. "The second is more constant, as being *regulated* by some desire, and design," as when we are trying to understand a new theory. Regulated thought is causally guided, moving from imagined effects back to productive causes ("this is common to man and beast") or from imagined objects or actions forward to the possible effects they might produce (a direction apparently occurring "in man only").[110]

SPEECH.   He discusses speech, "the most noble and profitable invention" of mankind, "consisting of

---

Nominalism (from the Latin *nominalis*, meaning of a name).   The theory (as in Hobbes) that only particulars exist and that the only universals are names, the products of human language

names or *appellations*, and their connexion, whereby men register their thoughts, recall them when they are past, and also declare them one to another for mutual utility and conversation, without which there had been amongst men, neither commonwealth, nor society, nor contract, nor peace, no more than amongst lions, bears, and wolves." The fundamental function of speech "is to transfer our mental discourse into verbal, or the train of our thoughts into a train of words." This function serves two primary useful purposes—to record notes of our thoughts and to communicate them to others. But speech can also be abused in four dangerous ways—to record our thoughts erroneously, to deceive others with metaphorical language, to speak insincerely, and to cause others grief.[111]

HOBBES'S NOMINALISM. Hobbes is a nominalist in the sense that he believes all things and all images to be particulars and acknowledges only names as universal—"there being nothing in the world universal but names; for the things named are every one of them individual and singular." This puts him at odds with all Platonists, who believe in a world of universal Ideas independent of our minds. "One universal name is imposed on many things for their similitude in some quality or other accident; and whereas a proper name bringeth to mind one thing only, universals recall any one of those many." For example, we experience cars, carriages, trucks, trains, airplanes, ships, and so forth as similar (in that they convey people from one place to another) and therefore apply the universal name "vehicle" to all of them. Truthful speech consists "in the right ordering of names in our affirmations," whereas incorrect ordering of language is false. "For *true* and *false* are attributes of speech, not of Things. And where speech is not, there is neither *truth* nor *falsehood*." Unlike Descartes, who identifies truth and falsehood with the judgments of will, Hobbes attributes them to speech alone. He emphasizes the importance of precise definitions for the achievement of truth and avoidance of error and warns that the person who uses language in a careless, slipshod manner "will find himself entangled in words, as a bird in lime twigs." The mastery of language is a necessary condition of wisdom, and its abuse is the gateway to folly. "For words are wise men's counters, they do but reckon by them; but they are the money of fools." Language can devolve to

dangerously misleading "insignificant sounds" when it either is newly coined and undefined or combines "contradictory and **inconsistent**" names, such as "an *incorporeal body*, or (which is all one) an *incorporeal substance*"; both misuses are allegedly perpetuated by scholastic professors and puzzled philosophers. When one hears significant speech and then has the thoughts its words were meant to communicate, "he is said to understand it, *understanding* being nothing else but conception caused by speech." Thus, Hobbes concludes, to the extent that speech is unique to humans, so must be understanding.[112]

REASONING THROUGH LOGIC. Reason is conceived of as a quasi-mathematical calculation, using names instead of numbers. Logical syllogisms are convenient examples of reasoning in this sense. When we say all humans are rational animals and all Greek citizens are humans, we "add" together names to infer that all Greek citizens are rational animals. Likewise, when we say that all English philosophers are humans and that no humans are pure spirits, by "subtraction" we can conclude that no English philosophers are pure spirits. "For REASON, in this sense, is nothing but *reckoning* (that is, adding and subtracting) of the consequences of general names agreed upon." Hobbes warns us of seven causes of absurd conclusions in reasoning, from a failure methodically to use precise definitions to the use of insignificant names "taken up and learned by rote from the schools, as *hypostatical, transubstantiate, consubstantiate, eternal-now*, and the like canting of schoolmen." He warns that good reasoning is the product of hard work and defines science as the "knowledge of all the consequences of names appertaining to the subject in hand."[113] So, science is a function of reason, which is a function of speech, which is a function of mental experience, which depends on images, which are ultimately derived from sense.

ABSOLUTE FACTUAL KNOWLEDGE VS. CONDITIONAL KNOWLEDGE. As deliberation normally terminates in will, so mental discourse is oriented towards judgment, which is the opinion on which the mind settles (at least provisionally); until judgment is made, we are said to doubt. All absolute knowledge of fact is derived from sense and memory, and never from rational discourse, which can only lead to the conditional judgments of science.

No man can know by discourse that this or that is, has been, or will be, which is to know absolutely, but only that if this be, that is, if this has been, that has been, if this shall be, that shall be, which is to know conditionally; and that not the consequence of one thing to another, but of one name of a thing to another name of the same thing.

Thus, science gives us only "conditional knowledge," telling us, for example, that if this is what we call water, then it comprises what we call hydrogen and what we call oxygen molecules in a ratio of two to one, has a boiling point of 212 degrees Fahrenheit, normally freezes below 32 degrees Fahrenheit, and so forth. For mental discourse to be scientific, it must be based on precise definitions. Otherwise, it is based on a person's own impressions and is "called opinion" or on the authority of another person, in which case we call it faith or belief—"*faith, in* the man; *belief*, both *of* the man, and *of* the truth of what he says." Absolute factual knowledge, derived from sense and memory, is the sort required of a witness in a court of law, whereas the conditional knowledge of science is the sort expected of a philosopher. Hobbes says that history is the register of factual knowledge and distinguishes between natural and civil history; by contrast, scientific books, including those of philosophy, are the registers of our conditional knowledge derived from reasoning.[114]

SCIENTIFIC REASONING.   A consequence of Hobbes's empirical epistemology is that we cannot have any images of the Infinite, "of God, nor of the soul of man, nor of spirits, but only of bodies visible" or objects of actual sense experience. Likewise, genuine philosophy must involve scientific reasoning concerning objects of experience. It cannot be based on "supernatural revelation" or mere faith in "the authority of books." He expresses his disdain for all appeals to ancient thinkers, writing, in particular, that

> scarce anything can be more absurdly said in natural philosophy than that which now is called *Aristotle's Metaphysics*; nor more repugnant to government than much of that he hath said in his *Politics*; nor more ignorantly than a great part of his *Ethics*.

Hobbes attacks the universities for subordinating philosophy to "the authority of Aristotle," for treating it as a mere handmaid to religion, for leaving it to wander in the barren wilderness of abstract jargon, and for allowing it to serve the parochial interests of Roman Catholicism. Elsewhere, like Descartes, he speaks of "the tree of philosophy," which branches into the science of figures called geometry, the science of motion called physics, and the science of natural right called morals.[115] Like Descartes's, Hobbes's epistemology demands rigor, precision and the systematic use of a deductive method with no appeals to external authority; but, unlike Descartes, Hobbes is empirical in basing everything on the images derived from sense and eschewing all use of allegedly innate ideas.

PHILOSOPHY AS CAUSAL REASONING.   Hobbes defines philosophy as

> such knowledge of effects or appearances, as we acquire by true ratiocination from the knowledge we have first of their causes or generation: And again, of such causes or generations as may be from knowing first their effects.[116]

Thus, by its very nature, philosophy involves **causal** reasoning (from effects back to causes or from causes forward to their effects).

LOGICAL INFERENCES.   In *De Corpore* Hobbes defines a "proposition" as

> a speech consisting of two names copulated, by which he that speaketh signifies he conceives the latter name to be the name of the same thing whereof the former is the name; or (which is all one) that the former name is comprehended by the latter.

In his example, "*man is a living creature*," the predicate term (living creature) includes or is identical with the subject term (man), since the proposition is true. "A *true* proposition" is one "whose predicate contains, or comprehends its subject" or whose predicate also names that "of which the subject is the name." Since truth is strictly a function of language, which is a man-made invention, Hobbes concludes, "the first truths were arbitrarily made by those that first of all imposed names upon things, or received them from the imposition of others." As a nominalist and an empiricist, he acknowledges no transcendent truth independent of persons. He shows how two propositions, called *premises*, can be logically combined so that a third, called the *conclusion*, can be validly inferred— the set of propositions forming a deductive argument called a *syllogism*.

> For example, this speech, *every man is a living creature, every living creature is a body*, therefore, *every man is a body*, is a *syllogism*, because the third proposition follows from the two first; that is, if those be granted to be true, this must also be granted to be true.

Hobbes rejects the scholastic doctrine "that *the definition is the essence of a thing*," saying it is a form of "speech signifying what we conceive of the essence thereof,"[117] rather than what the object itself is.

After repeating his own definition of philosophy in terms of causal reasoning, he focuses on method, as Descartes had done a couple of decades earlier, though his is a predictably different approach.

> Method, therefore, in the study of philosophy, *is the shortest way of finding out effects by their known causes, or of causes by their known effects.*

Rather than Descartes's method of systematic doubting and the pursuit of clear and distinct ideas, Hobbes adopts Galileo's scientific one of "*composition* and *division* or *resolution*. There is therefore no method, by which we find out the causes of things, but is either *compositive* or *resolutive*, or *partly compositive*, and *partly resolutive*. And the resolutive is commonly called *analytical* method, as the compositive is called *synthetical*." We use the inductive or analytical method of resolution to reason from particular truths to general ones; and we use the deductive or synthetic method of composition to reason from universal claims to particular ones. In either case, we try to "proceed from known things to unknown" conclusions. A definition analyzes or resolves a

> name into its most universal parts. As when we define man, saying *man is a body animated, sentient, rational*, those names, *body animated*, &c. are parts of that whole name *man*; so that definitions of this kind always consist of *genus* and *difference*; the former names being all, till the last, *general*; and the last of all, *difference*.[118]

This perspective on definitions is quite Aristotelian.

Like Descartes, Hobbes thinks that philosophy should be conducive to practical effects regarding "the commodity of human life." Like Francis Bacon, he writes, "The end of knowledge is power." The "utility" of natural philosophy is that it affords us the benefits of a civilized life. "But the utility of moral and civil philosophy is to be estimated, not so much by the commodities we have by knowing these sciences, as by the calamities we receive from not knowing them," such as the violation of rights and horrors of civil war.

> The *subject* of Philosophy, or the matter it treats of, is every body of which we can conceive any generation, and which we may, by any consideration thereof, compare with other bodies, or which is capable of composition and

resolution; that is to say, every body of whose generation or properties we can have any knowledge.

As Hobbes immediately observes, this definition "excludes *Theology*" from the domain of philosophical science, since it is "the doctrine of God, eternal, ingenerable, incomprehensible, and in whom there is nothing neither to divide nor compound, nor any generation to be conceived." Hobbes divides philosophy into three main parts: natural philosophy, dealing with bodies in motion, ethics, dealing with the dispositions and manners of human beings, and civil philosophy, dealing with commonwealths and subjects' political duties.[119]

Freedom

A DENIAL OF FREE WILL. Hobbes's determinism is as radical as are his materialism and empiricism. He brusquely dismisses the believer in "*free will*" in *Leviathan*, saying, "I should not say he were in an error, but that his words were without meaning, that is to say, absurd." For only substances can be free, all substances are bodies, and will is not a body. He defines natural liberty as "the absence of external impediments" and writes,

> Liberty, or Freedom, signifieth (properly) the absence of opposition (by opposition, I mean external impediments of motion) and may be applied no less to irrational and inanimate creatures than to rational.

For example, water that is dammed up is not at liberty to move, whereas when the dam is broken or removed, it flows freely. Likewise, a

> Free-man *is he that in those things which by his strength and wit he is able to do is not hindered to do what he has a will to.* But when the words *free* and *liberty* are applied to anything but *bodies*, they are abused; for that which is not subject to motion is not subject to impediment.

When we speak of a person's free will, we really mean the freedom of the person to act as he will; it is not as if the will is a substantial faculty that can be free or otherwise. To illustrate the compatibility of freedom and fear, Hobbes uses Aristotle's example: "when a man throweth his goods into the sea for *fear* the ship should sink, he doth it nevertheless very willingly, and may refuse to do it if he will." More importantly, he argues, "*Liberty* and *necessity* are consistent: as in the water, that hath not only *liberty*, but a *necessity* of descending by the channel" unless and until it be blocked from its natural flow. Likewise, a human action is free if it proceeds from the person's will without external restraint. Yet, since all events are caused, "every act of man's will and every desire and inclination proceedeth from some cause, and that from another cause," which causes "in a continual chain . . . proceed from *necessity*." Thus, if we, like God, "could see the connexion of those causes, the *necessity* of all men's voluntary actions would appear manifest."[120] It is only due to our ignorance of those causal connections that we are inclined to doubt the necessity of the human actions which we correctly identify as voluntary.

In *De Homine* Hobbes observes that the will to act is always a prerequisite of personal liberty:

> Whenever we say that someone hath free-will to do this or that, or not to do it, it must always be understood with this necessary condition: *if he wills*. For to talk of having free-will to do this or that whether one wills or not is absurd.

Freedom should not be confused with license or arbitrary, accidental whimsy. In *De Cive*, he defines liberty as "*an absence of the lets and hindrances of motion*; as water shut up in a vessel is therefore not at liberty, because the vessel hinders it from running out; which, the vessel being broken, is made *free*." Human freedom is relative; "the more ways a man may move himself, the more *liberty* he hath." Likewise, "civil *liberty*" may be more or less extensive; but, even under the most oppressive regimes, it must include at least a person's natural right to "make use of all means necessary to the preservation of his life and health."[121]

In *De Corpore* Hobbes proposes the deterministic principle "that all the effects that have been, or shall be produced, have their necessity in things antecedent." He raises the question of whether even future events which we call contingent are necessary. His answer is that all events "have their necessary causes," but that we call some events contingent when we cannot discern their necessary causes.

> Wherefore, all propositions concerning future things, contingent or not contingent, as this, *it will rain*

tomorrow, or this, *tomorrow the sun will rise*, are either necessarily true, or necessarily false; but we call them contingent, because we do not yet know whether they be true or false; whereas their verity depends not upon our knowledge, but upon the foregoing of their causes.

This would apply to all propositions concerning human acts of will as well as to those about other natural events, and this is a position of determinism. It views free actions as determined by the will; presenting freedom and determinism as compatible, it is now called **compatibilism**. Hobbes denies that humans have any greater natural freedom than other animals, saying that

> such a liberty as is free from necessity, is not to be found in the will either of men or beasts. But if by liberty we understand the faculty or power, not of willing, but of doing what they will, then certainly that liberty is to be allowed to both, and both may equally have it, whensoever it is to be had."[122]

Here again, as in his materialistic monism and sensation-based empiricism, Hobbes is challenging any radical qualitative difference of kind between humans and other animals.

DETERMINATION BY INTRINSIC FORCES. Hobbes's most important work on this topic is to be found in *Of Liberty and Necessity*, which originated in his dispute with Bishop Bramhall. Here again, freedom is analyzed as the ability "to do a thing" a person has the will to do and to avoid doing whatever he has the will to forbear doing. "And yet if there be a *necessity* that he shall have the *will* to do it, the action is necessarily to follow: and if there be a *necessity* that he shall have the *will* to forbear, the forbearing also will be necessary." So, the crucial issue is whether the human will is always necessarily determined by extrinsic forces. Every voluntary action is spontaneous or willed, whether or not it is necessarily determined; but not every spontaneous action is voluntary, "for *voluntary* presupposes some precedent *deliberation*," and some spontaneous acts are performed without prior deliberation, as when we "in anger *strike* or *revile*." The judgment resulting from deliberation is the last part of the cause that necessarily moves the will; it is not the entire cause but concludes a cumulative process, just

---

Compatibilism. The view (held, for example, by Hobbes, Hume, and Mill) that some human actions are free, in the sense that they do not result from external compulsion, despite the fact that all actions are causally determined "as the last feather may be said to break a horse's back, when there were so many laid on before as there wanted but that one to do it."[123]

Hobbes responds to several objections raised against his deterministic position. To the objection that it would render unjust all laws prohibiting action, he answers that injustice only arises from "the *will* to break the *law*" and that laws sanctioned by punishment can contribute to justice by deterring such ill will. To the objection that Hobbes's view would render all consultations and admonitions useless, he answers, on the contrary, that consultations and admonitions can be effective causal determinants of future action. To the charge (raised by Aquinas, among others) that praise, condemnation, rewards, and punishments would be in vain on his view, he responds that all of these are instruments that can be used to "conform the will to good and evil." And the same response is offered to the objection that books, teaching, and courses of study would seem superfluous. He also denies that his view annihilates sin, since sin consists in illegal voluntary action, regardless of whether the will was necessitated in its actions. When we understand the forces that motivate action, "we acknowledge *necessity*; but when we see not, or mark not the force that moves us, we then think there is none, and that it is not *causes* but *liberty* that produceth the action," though such an assumption is merely a testament to our ignorance. He summarizes his view in eight points:

1. Free action without deliberation necessarily follows the agent's perception "of the *good* or *evil* consequence thereof to himself."

2. Deliberation prior to action involves the imagining of good and evil future consequences.

3. In all deliberation, the last prevailing appetite is what is called the agent's will and precipitates action.

4. Actions arising out of deliberation "are said to be *voluntary*."

5. "*Liberty*" is "rightly defined" as "*the absence of all the impediments to action that are not contained in the nature and **intrinsical** quality of the agent.*"

6. All (even voluntary) actions have necessary causes, and nothing (including the human will) can be self-caused.

7. All voluntary actions have been produced by sufficient causal forces and are consequently necessitated.

8. The "ordinary *definition* of a *free agent*" as one which can choose not to act when conditions are present sufficient to produce such action "implies a contradiction, and is nonsense."

Hobbes tries to support each of these eight points.[124]

Morality

A MORAL RELATIVISM.   As human freedom is a function of those voluntary motions called desires or appetites, for Hobbes, so is morality. In *Leviathan*, he writes that "whatsoever is the object of any man's appetite or desire that is it which he for his part calleth *good*; and the object of his hate and aversion, *evil*." He adds that these basic moral concepts only have meaning in "relation to the person that useth them, there being nothing simply and absolutely so, nor any common rule of good and evil to be taken from the nature of the objects themselves." This represents a moral **relativism** not prominent in the history of Western philosophy after Plato's repudiation of the Sophists. Our mental deliberations lead us to act on the basis of the apparent balance of "*seeming good*" and "*seeming evil*." Our natural desires and the actions to which they give rise, he says, are not intrinsically moral or immoral, no matter how selfish and rapacious they may be. In the state of nature (outside the man-made conventions of society), which is a state of war, there is no objective morality.

> The notions of right and wrong, justice and injustice, have there no place. Where there is no common power, there is no law; where no law, no injustice. Force and fraud are in war the two **cardinal virtues.**

There are, indeed, natural laws, for Hobbes; yet they are merely prudential rules for the agent's own advantage, rather than (as for Aquinas) morally binding commands. He defines a natural law as "a precept or general rule, found out by reason, by which a man is forbidden to do that which is destructive of his life or taketh away the means of preserving the same, and to omit that by which he thinketh it may be best preserved." The most basic law of nature comprises two parts: that we should do whatever we can to achieve peace and that, where this attempt is unsuccessful, we should do whatever is necessary to defend ourselves. The second law of nature holds that we should be willing—as long as others are equally willing—to limit our natural liberty in order to promote peace. He writes that the science of natural laws is "moral philosophy" and explains that laws of nature "are not properly laws, but qualities that dispose men to peace."[125] These "laws" are both descriptive and **prescriptive**, universally describing human motivations and prescribing rational principles of conduct.

In *De Homine* Hobbes maintains that "politics and ethics" can be demonstrative sciences precisely because "we ourselves make the principles" that underlie them. He maintains his moral relativism, saying that "*good*" is the appropriate name for "all things that are desired, insofar as they are desired," and "*evil*" the name for "all things we shun." However, he adds, "since different men desire and shun different things, there must needs be many things that are *good* to some and *evil* to others." One person likes to read Shakespearean sonnets and despises football games, while another has the contrary preferences. Or, for that matter, a single person's desires can radically change with time and shifting circumstances. Though we share the language of moral evaluation, "this way of speaking is relative; therefore one cannot speak of something as being *simply good*; since whatever is good, is good for someone or other." Nevertheless, all humans are driven by egoistic concerns, so that "the greatest of goods for each is his own preservation. For nature is so arranged that all desire good for themselves. Insofar as it is within their capacities, it is necessary to desire life, health, and further, insofar as it can be done, security of future time." This is why death is normally regarded as "the greatest of all evils," because it terminates all possibility of satisfying desires; yet even this is relative to circumstances, since "the pains of life can be so great that, unless their quick end is foreseen, they may lead men to number death among the goods." He speaks of virtues and vices as manners, with the laws and customs of civil life providing "a common standard for virtues and vices," advancing us beyond **subjectivism**. The two primary virtues are justice, which is a function of civil laws, and charity, which is a function of natural laws. "Furthermore, all moral virtue is contained in

these two," the other three traditional cardinal virtues (prudence, courage, and temperance) being primarily valuable to the persons having them rather than to others or to society.[126]

Natural, Civil, and Religious Duties.   In *De Cive* Hobbes distinguishes among natural duties, civil duties, and religious duties; as humans, we are obligated "first, as men; then as subjects; lastly, as Christians." He says that, outside of civil society, each person would have to judge for himself what ought to be done for self-preservation, with no extrinsic limits on permissible action.

> Nature hath given to *every one a right to all*; that is, it was lawful for every man, in the bare state of nature, or before such time as men engaged themselves by any covenants or bonds, to do what he would, and against whom he thought fit, and to possess, use, and enjoy all what he would, or could get.

Man is naturally at liberty, unbound by any objective moral rules; "in the state of nature, to have all, and do all, is lawful for all." This reduces morality to sheer pragmatic advantage— "in the state of nature profit is the measure of right." The problem, though, is that we cannot enjoy this absolute liberty from all moral restraints because everyone else in the natural state has a similar liberty, which makes for massive insecurity for all. He points out the destabilizing lack of a consistent criterion without objective law, since "men condemn the same things in others, which they approve in themselves." Yet we share that "part of human nature" called reason, which will provide the touchstone for distinguishing objective right and wrong, in terms of the laws of nature, which lead us to the formation of society and civil law. He writes that "the natural law is the same with the moral" law; but, prior to the **social contract**, subjective relativism is an insurmountable obstacle, since "what this man commends, that is to say, calls *good*, the other undervalues, as being evil." Through reason we come to identify actions as good when they are conducive to peace and evil when they tend to discord. At this point we become aware of the laws of nature that constitute moral philosophy and that also "are delivered by God in holy Scriptures," so that reason and revelation are

---

Prescriptive.   Having to do with what ought to be, as opposed to descriptive, which concerns what actually is

Social contract.   An original agreement whereby individuals allegedly united to form society and to constitute the state; some philosophers (e.g., Hobbes) subscribe to this manner of justifying political obligation, whereas others (e.g., Hume and Mill) reject it

dual approaches to them. He writes that sin "comprehends every *deed, word* and *thought* against right reason," violating the laws of nature, which are ultimately derived from God. Wicked people not only violate God's natural laws by their actions, but they even set their minds against them; by contrast, those who generally want to obey God's laws but "sin only through infirmity, are *good men* even when they sin."[127] (This is similar to Aristotle's concept of **incontinence**.)

We notice here that ethics and political obligation, though related for Hobbes, are separable. And, indeed, he says, in *De Corpore*, "Civil and *moral philosophy* do not so adhere to one another, but that they may be severed." In *Human Nature* he makes the moral concepts of good and evil relative to what pleases and displeases us, respectively. In *De Corpore Politico* he suggests that we use the Golden Rule to discipline our egoistic tendencies rationally and to free ourselves from subjective bias when judging

> whether the action I be to do, be against the law of nature, or not. And it is but this: *That a man imagine himself in the place of the party with whom he hath to do, and reciprocally him in his.*

Yet later (more in line with his egoism), Hobbes seems to reduce "virtue in general" to prudence. (He also criticizes Aristotle's moral doctrine of the **mean**, which maintains "that virtue consisteth in mediocrity.") Far from there being any conflict between the natural laws of morality and God's divine law, human nature is such that our God-given reason shows us what we ought to do for our own benefit;[128] and this inevitably involves learning to get along with others in society.

Society

THE STATE OF NATURE AND THE STATE OF CIVIL SOCIETY. In his dedication of *Leviathan* Hobbes writes of the dangerous extremes of "too great liberty" and "too much authority" in political society and how difficult it is to pass unscathed between them. Yet we should try to avoid both extremes in creating political society, "which is but an artificial man, though of greater stature and strength than the natural, for whose protection and defence it was intended; and in which the *sovereignty* is an artificial *soul*, as giving

life and motion to the whole body" of the state. Since Hobbes's state of nature is conceived as a state of war, although human liberty is maximal there, so are human insecurity and terror, rendering (in his most famous phrase)

the life of man, solitary, poor, nasty, brutish, and short.

It is "solitary" in that man is naturally egoistic and antisocial, having no reason to trust others or enjoy their company. It is "poor" in the sense that no one can accumulate many resources without their being plundered by others. It is "nasty" because constantly marred by vile, rapacious attacks, the threat of future ones by others, and preparations for ones we ourselves might make. It is "brutish" in that this way of life reduces us to the level of brute beasts. The descriptive adjective "short" should be self-explanatory. Human reason, motivated by self-interest and acknowledging the two basic laws of nature, comes to recognize that some liberty must be given up in exchange for greater security than we can provide for ourselves. We can mutually renounce certain rights (e.g., to kill others, to hurt one another arbitrarily, to take others' physical goods, to violate the liberty of others) in order to gain greater assurance that other rights (e.g., not to be killed ourselves, not to be hurt arbitrarily, not to be deprived of our physical goods, not to have our liberty violated) may be enjoyed. Notice that a person's motive for renouncing rights (or transferring them to others) is purely self-interested. "For it is a voluntary act, and of the voluntary acts of every man the object is some *good to himself.*" There need be no **altruism** at work here; everything Hobbes is saying here is quite consistent with his psychological egoism. "The mutual transferring of right is that which men call Contract." It is by means of the social contract that we pass out of the state of nature and constitute the state of civil society. Such a contract may be either express, as when we explicitly make promises, or tacitly understood, implied by our actions. People can be freed of their contractual obligations by performing them or being excused from having to do so. Contracts or covenants extorted by fear are still binding. A covenant can be rendered null and void by a prior contract that does not leave a party free to contract further. And there are limits to what can be legitimately contracted—for example, a

---

Altruism (from the Latin *alter*, meaning other).   A selfless concern for the welfare of other people, as opposed to egoism

person's covenant not to defend himself or to incriminate himself is null and void.[129]

Hobbes presents seventeen more laws of nature beyond the basic two (discussed in the preceding section). The third is the principle of justice, *"that men perform their covenants made."* Once we have committed ourselves to contractual agreements, justice and injustice come to be; "and the definition of injustice is no other than *the not performance of covenant. And whatsoever is not unjust, is just.*" In order for a covenant to be valid, given our natural egoism and distrust of others, there must be sufficient coercive power to assure its being honored. But such coercive power can only be provided by political society, never by mere individuals; "therefore where there is no commonwealth, there nothing is unjust." The coercive power of the state is necessary to ensure that covenants will be validly binding; in turn, valid covenants are the necessary conditions of justice, injustice, and property rights. Distributive justice, for Hobbes (as for Aristotle), requires "the distribution of equal benefit to men of equal merit"; for in society people are not necessarily as equal as they were in the state of nature. The fourth law of nature requires gratitude to others for what they give us. The fifth requires that each member of society try to get along with others. The sixth holds that we should forgive the past offenses of others who repent of them. The seventh maintains that revenge can only be justified by future good consequences and never by past evils done. The eighth forbids the declaration of hatred or contempt of others, as the ninth forbids pride and requires that we acknowledge others as our natural equals. The tenth forbids arrogance, or the claiming of rights for ourselves, which we are unwilling to respect in others. The eleventh requires equity or distributive justice for all members of society; and the twelfth calls for equal access to the use of those goods that cannot be divided but must be shared in common. The thirteenth holds that goods which can neither be divided nor enjoyed by all in common should be distributed by lot; while the fourteenth says that distribution by lot may be either arbitrary (for example, a lottery) or natural (for example, by order of birth). The fifteenth requires that mediators for peace should be allowed safe conduct. The sixteenth requires that citizens should be willing to submit disputes to arbitration; the seventeenth holds that no person can act as judge in his own case. The eighteenth says no one can act as judge in a case in which he has a vested interest; and the nineteenth requires respect for the evidence of witnesses. The last sixteen laws are designed to help hold society together and to minimize friction. Hobbes thinks the laws of nature boil down to the Golden Rule, which he states negatively, *"Do not that to another, which thou wouldst not have done to thyself"*; and he says they always "oblige *in foro interno*" (that is, in conscience), though *"in foro externo"* (in external effect) they are binding only where there is the security of social sanctions.[130]

In the dedicatory letter for *De Homine* Hobbes maintains that man is both a *natural* body and a part of the body *politic*. He points out that human language presents both social advantages (e.g., allowing us to teach, communicate knowledge, command, and understand) and disadvantages (e.g., allowing us to deceive others as well as ourselves). He discusses various emotional attitudes we can exhibit towards others, including love, compassion, and envy, emphasizing the importance of the social virtues of justice and charity towards others.[131] As members of society, we learn to manage egoism and identify our interests with the public welfare.

In the preface of *De Cive* Hobbes says that his purpose is to show "that the state of men without civil society, which state we may properly call the state of nature, is nothing else but a mere war of all against all," that we naturally desire to escape its miseries, that such escape is impossible "except by compact," that the sovereignty of civil government must be established, and that there need be no conflict between political power and God's sovereignty. He admits that his arguments in favor of monarchy fall short of conclusive demonstrations. He maintains that the basis "of all great and lasting societies consisted not in the mutual good will men had towards each other, but in the mutual fear they had of each other," saying this fear is grounded "partly in the natural equality of men" and "partly in their mutual will of hurting" one another. As we have seen, these are fundamental characteristics of "men in the state of nature." We compete with others for the satisfaction of desires; this natural competition leads to antagonism and mortal danger. "For every man is desirous of what is good for him, and shuns what is evil, but chiefly the chiefest of natural evils, which is death." Our natural liberty is such that "in the state of nature, to have all, and to do all, is lawful for all"—that is, in accordance with the laws of nature, since at this point there are no civil laws. Thus, "in the state of nature profit is the measure of right," though in such hostile circumstances there can be little genuine benefit since no one is likely to enjoy much for long. There is no natural sense of selfless community, so that all fellowship is based on some combination of force and mutual agreement. In such an insecure condition, reason requires that we seek a peaceful society. The means to such an escape is the social contract. When two or more people reach agreement, "mutually conveying their rights," this is "called a *contract*"; and a contract in which credit is given, by either party to the other or mutually, "is called a *covenant*." Any contract involves a voluntary limitation on liberty and the subsequent generation of obligation. "For where liberty ceaseth, there beginneth obligation."[132]

In *De Corpore Politico*, which deals with many of the same topics we have been analyzing in *Leviathan* and *De Cive*, Hobbes gives an argument to support his claim that there are no limits to what a person may rightly do to protect himself in the state of nature. He has a natural right to self-preservation.

> And because where a man hath right to the end, and the end cannot be attained without the means, that is, without such things as are necessary to the end, it is consequent that it is not against reason, and therefore right, for a man to use all means, and do whatsoever action is necessary for the preservation of his body.

But this puts us at odds with one another in a natural "state of war." In this condition "might is right," so that, if we subdue another, prudence dictates that we take whatever precautions are possible that he never be able to recover sufficiently to get the better of us. Hobbes discusses the basic law of nature and initiation of contract that we have already analyzed, as well as the ideas of justice and injustice. He considers how our natural desire for security leads us to establish political union and to consolidate sovereign power.[133]

THE RIGHTS AND DUTIES OF SOVEREIGNS. In *Leviathan* Hobbes reminds us that our goal in limiting our own liberty and accepting the structures of society is the prospect of our "own preservation, and of a more contented life thereby." But the motivation of others is as selfish as our own. So what will restrain us from violating the social contract when it seems beneficial to

do so? Some mechanism must be erected to prevent such self-indulgence, and this is provided by the coercive power of the state. This is why Hobbes says that "covenants without the sword are but words, and of no strength to secure a man at all." He tells us how people can come together to generate a commonwealth and offers a sample formula they could use:

> I authorise and give up my right of governing myself to this man, or to this assembly of men, on this condition, that thou give up thy right to him, and authorise all his actions in like manner.

A commonwealth, then, is people united by mutual covenants in one sovereign power, in whom they have invested their support and whom they authorize to act as seems best for the maintenance of peace and the securing of a common defence. The person or group of persons in whom this power is invested is the sovereign, and all other members of society are the subjects. Sovereign power can be attained through natural force ("commonwealth by *acquisition*") or by popular consent ("commonwealth by *institution*").[134]

Hobbes discusses the rights of sovereigns by institution (and the corresponding limits on the rights of their subjects). First, the subjects cannot take it upon themselves to change the form of government; second, the sovereign makes no covenant with his subjects and thus cannot forfeit his sovereignty; third, a dissenter in society has no legitimate grounds for protest; fourth, a sovereign cannot injure his subjects, in the strict sense of doing them an injustice, though he might harm them; fifth, no sovereign can ever be legitimately punished by his subjects; sixth, the sovereign is the proper judge of what is necessary for the peace and defense of his subjects, as well as of the doctrines they may be taught; seventh, it is the sovereign's prerogative to prescribe the rules regulating property rights; eighth, the right to judge and decide all disputes in society is the sovereign's; ninth, so is the right of waging war and making peace; tenth, the sovereign has the right to select his own counselors and ministers; eleventh, the sovereign has the ultimate authority for rewarding and punishing members of society; and, twelfth, titles of honor and assignments of social status are to be awarded by the sovereign. If this seems to grant too much privilege to the sovereign so that his subjects seem left in a "very miserable" position, Hobbes responds that they are better off than if burdened by "the miseries, and horrible calamities that accompany a civil war."[135] Indeed, the purpose of his deliberately graphic portrait of the nastiness of the state of nature is to help us realize how fortunate we are to have even a poor society.

Hobbes sets forth six dangerous opinions that can undermine sovereignty:

1. That a sovereign can be satisfied with less than absolute power;
2. That private individuals can judge independently about good and evil;
3. That anything a person does contrary to conscience is sinful;
4. That the sovereign is himself subject to civil laws;
5. That subjects have absolute property rights against their sovereign; and
6. That the sovereign power can be divided.

He says that the duty of the sovereign is to provide for "*the safety of the people*," which includes their contentment as well as their preservation. This will involve the protection of a subject's property from the unjust appropriation of other subjects. A person's property includes, especially, his life, physical integrity, family relations, money, and means of livelihood. Subjects must be taught to respect the property rights of other subjects; so, attitudes as well as actions are important.[136]

In *De Corpore Politico*, he discusses the need for the sovereign to wield both "the sword of justice" and "the sword of war." He explains how humans can have dominion over other humans, as masters over servants (as well as how it is natural for man to have dominion over beasts). Hobbes analyzes the three sources of sedition as discontent with one's condition in society, the pretense of having rights against the government, and the hope of success in rebellion. He maintains that "the duty of a sovereign consisteth in the good government of the people," meaning the provision for their safety and welfare. This should involve leaving them as much liberty and property as possible, educating them politically, and avoiding unnecessary wars.[137]

TYPES OF COMMONWEALTHS. In *Leviathan* Hobbes discusses the three types of commonwealths in categories comparable (though not identical) with those of Aristotle. Any political society governed by one person is a monarchy, the negative name for which is **tyranny**; a political society ruled by an assembly of some part of it, like a congress or a parliament, is called an **aristocracy**, the harmful form of which is **oligarchy**, which is often the rule of the rich; and a political society governed by the group of all its members is a **democracy**, which, when criticized, is called **anarchy**. Hobbes favors monarchy over the other two forms because it better identifies public and private interest, because a monarch has easier access to everyone desirable for advice, because of its greatest likely stability, and because it minimizes dissension. He admits that two inconveniences of monarchy are that it leaves individual subjects vulnerable without recourse to the whims of the monarch and its sovereign power may be inherited by an infant or one less fit to rule. But other forms of government have problems, and overall monarchy seems most secure.[138]

He considers a commonwealth by acquisition, that is, one that "is acquired by force." Whereas "fear of one another" leads people to submit to sovereignty by institution, fear of the sovereign motivates subjects to submit to sovereignty by acquisition, as, for example, when they are a conquered people. But, says Hobbes, the rights of the sovereign "are the same in both" types of rule. In addition to conquest, the other way in which dominion is acquired is through parental authority over children. Though this is often called paternal power, Hobbes does not think that men are always superior to women in power. Indeed, in the state of nature, where there are no contracts to govern family relationships, maternal dominion over the children seems obvious. Hobbes also (anticipating Hegel's analysis of the master-slave relationship) discusses the despotic dominion a conqueror can acquire over the vanquished, who, in order "to avoid the present stroke of death," can consent to serve the victor. "It is not . . . the victory that giveth the right of dominion over the vanquished, but his own covenant." In this relation, the conqueror also acquires mastery over everything the servant has. At any rate, Hobbes would maximize the power of sovereignty, warning that the alternative, of "perpetual war of every man

---

Anarchy (from the Greek *anarkhos,* meaning without a ruler). The absence of effective governmental authority, typically resulting in political disorder

against his neighbour," is very dangerous. And he claims that the formation and maintenance of commonwealths should be governed by "certain rules, as doth arithmetic and geometry, not (as tennis-play) on practice only."[139] There is a science of politics that should be conscientiously followed if a state is to be well-established and well-administered.

In *De Cive* Hobbes tells us that if sovereign authority is to be absolute, there must be no division of powers, executive, legislative, and judicial authority being united. The sovereign does not contract with the subjects, is not bound by the civil laws, and cannot be rightly punished. The three types of government—democracy, aristocracy, and monarchy—are analyzed, as in *Leviathan*. Hobbes sees the people as functioning democratically at the time of the initial social contract, with aristocracy normally emerging, this in turn often evolving into monarchy. Since monarchs make no contract with political subjects, "it necessarily follows, that they can do no *injury* to the subjects," strictly speaking. However, a monarch can violate laws of nature, "as by cruelty, iniquity, contumely, and other like vices," which would be sinful and answerable to God. Subjects can be freed from political obligation if the sovereign abdicates or if the kingdom falls into the hands of an enemy or (in a monarchy) if there is no legitimate successor. Hobbes compares the three types of government, arguing that monarchy has the most conveniences and the fewest inconveniences. He holds that its inconveniences are normally due to the personal character of the monarch rather than to the unity of this form of government. He attacks democracy as an arrangement in which too many demagogues and their hangers-on tend to feed at the public trough. Nor does he admit that there is necessarily less liberty under monarchy than under democracy. The decision-making process in democracies is particularly inefficient, getting bogged down in rhetorical long-windedness, being derailed by divisive factions and plagued with incessant leaks of matters that should remain confidential. "These inconveniences," says Hobbes, "evince *monarchy* to be better than *democracy*,"[140] though we recall that he does not pretend to prove the point conclusively.

CIVIL LAW AND MORAL LAW.   Once a political society has been formed by the contractual agreements of the people, Hobbes writes in *Leviathan*, they also

find themselves bound by those "artificial chains, called *civil laws*, which they themselves by mutual covenants have fastened at one end to the lips of that man or assembly to whom they have given the sovereign power, and at the other end to their own ears. These bonds, in their own nature but weak, may nevertheless be made to hold by the danger (though not by the difficulty) of breaking them." As we have seen, there are limits to what the civil law can legitimately require of subjects: they always retain their liberty to defend themselves, even against lawful authorities; they cannot be obliged to kill or harm themselves, to refrain from vital necessities, or to engage in self-incrimination. If drafted into a war, they can find substitutes, though if they have joined up voluntarily, they are obliged to serve. Even rebellion against the state is legitimate if deemed necessary for self-preservation. "As for other liberties, they depend on the silence of the law. In cases where the sovereign has prescribed no rule, there the subject hath the liberty to do or forbear, according to his own discretion." We are bound to obey the sovereign as long as he exercises the power needed to protect us, since that was the original purpose of the contract. If a subject be captured as a prisoner of war, if his sovereign abdicates, if he is banished into exile, or if the sovereign submits to another, that power of protection is broken and political obligation to obey ceases.[141]

Hobbes defines civil law as that set of rules binding on a political subject, "*which the commonwealth hath commanded him (by word, writing, or other sufficient sign of the will) to make use of, for the distinction of right and wrong.*" So, in political society there is a connection between civil law and morality. Subjects are always bound to obey all civil laws that are not contrary to the laws of nature. Hobbes denies that ignorance of the law of nature ever excuses a person or that ignorance of the sovereign or of the sanctions of civil law ever excuses a subject, although ignorance of the civil law itself sometimes does excuse a subject. Civil laws cannot bind retroactively. He defines punishment as "*an evil inflicted by public authority on him that hath done or omitted that which is judged by the same authority to be a transgression of the law, to the end that the will of men may thereby the better be disposed to obedience.*" Thus, the purpose of punishment is deterrence. He goes on to lay down several parameters within which punishment is legitimate. Laws that are good for society must be necessary, easily understood, and conducive to the public welfare.[142]

Hobbes, in *De Cive*, discusses law, which he defines as "*the command of that person, whether man or court, whose precept contains in it the reason of obedience.*" He distinguishes (in a manner reminiscent of Aquinas) between divine law and civil law, the former comprising the "*natural* or *moral*" law, on the one hand, and the "positive" law "which God hath revealed to us," on the other. Civil law is man-made (or human), may be either sacred (pertaining to religious worship) or secular, and has sanctions or penalties attached to it. Civil law can help define moral law. "For though the law of nature forbid theft, adultery, &c.; yet if the civil law command us to invade anything, that invasion is not theft, adultery, &c." For example, the ancient Spartans permitted the deliberate taking of others' goods in cases that our society would classify as theft; likewise, what counts as adultery can vary from one society to another. Finally (as Aquinas also observed), the law must be promulgated to the people who are to be subject to it in order that it be binding.[143]

JUSTICE AND INJUSTICE.   Injury and injustice are defined in terms of violations of contract. But the justice and injustice of people (as opposed to actions) is a matter of attitude, signifying "to be delighted in just dealing" and "to neglect righteous dealing, or to think it is to be measured not according to my contract, but some present benefit." Hobbes acknowledges that

> innumerable actions of a just man may be unjust, and of an unjust man, just. But that man is to be accounted just, who doth just things because the law commands it, unjust things only by reason of his infirmity; and he is properly said to be unjust, who doth righteousness for fear of the punishment annexed unto the law, and unrighteousness by reason of the iniquity of his mind.[144]

This focus on motivation as crucial is remarkably **deontological** (i.e., duty-based, as opposed to being oriented merely towards consequences), though for Hobbes this focus is only appropriate in the context of social commitments.

Hobbes admits that human psychology is such that people's wills are selfishly motivated by "hope and fear, insomuch as when they shall see a greater good

or less evil likely to happen to them by the breach than observation of the laws, they will wittingly violate them." Thus, the laws of nature and our capacity for justice do not suffice. What is needed is the fearful restraint of injustice such as can be put in place by a large number of people pooling their power collectively to oppose outlaws. But this kind of political union is civil society and establishes the dominion of sovereign power. Hobbes writes about how civil society can be constituted as one body, in which the citizens covenant with one another to obey the laws and to support the sovereign power's enforcement of the laws. Through their covenants, they confer on the sovereign both "*the sword of justice*" and "*the sword of war*,"[145] giving up the right to wield either "sword" independently themselves.

*   *   *

Although Hobbes does not regard human nature as naturally social, rational self-interest allegedly leads us to acknowledge the practical value of the law and order of political society.

Religion

Hobbes's materialism and empiricism lead him to adopt a highly unorthodox conception of God, and his comprehensive social theory leads to a highly political view of religion. In *Leviathan* he observes that most popular religions are based on superstitious fear, the abolition of which would probably raise the level of civil obedience. With characteristic antischolastic disgust, he adds, "And this ought to be the work of the schools; but they rather nourish such doctrine."[146]

THE EXISTENCE AND NATURE OF GOD.   Since all our mental images are grounded in sense perception, which can only be of finite objects, he says, "Whatsoever we imagine is *finite*. Therefore there is no idea or conception of anything we call *infinite*." This is a direct rejection of the rationalistic theory of Descartes, for whose innate ideas Hobbes has no respect. Why, then, do we speak of God as infinite? Hobbes answers, "When we say anything is infinite, we signify only that we are not able to conceive the ends and bounds of the thing named, having no conception of

---

Deontology (from the Greek *deon*, meaning that which is obligatory, and *logos*, meaning an account).   The view (e.g., of Kantians) that moral duty must be determined rationally rather than empirically and is independent of the consequences of acts, as opposed to ethical consequentialism

the thing, but of our own inability. And therefore the name of *God* is used, not to make us conceive him (for he is *incomprehensible*, and his greatness and power are unconceivable), but that we may honour him." He defines religion as "*Fear* of power invisible," distinguishing between "True Religion," in which such fear is legitimate, and "Superstition," in which it is not, but without providing a criterion for our reliably telling which is which. He uses a simple version of the **argument from design** when he writes that "by the visible things of this world and their admirable order, a man may conceive there is a cause of them, which men call God, and yet not have an idea or image of him in his mind." He holds that our inquisitive natures lead us to speculate about the causal origin of our world but that this contributes to our anxiety about the future. We fear the power of invisible beings whom we imagine to be causally responsible for our world. Hobbes offers a version of the **cosmological argument**:

> For he that from any effect he seeth come to pass should reason to the next and immediate cause thereof, and from thence to the cause of that cause, and plunge himself profoundly into the pursuit of causes, shall at last come to this: that there must be (as even the heathen philosophers confessed) one first mover, that is, a first and an eternal cause of all things, which is that which men mean by the name of God.

Yet people should admit that the God to which this argument leads is "incomprehensible, and above their understanding," rather than trying to define its nature by such self-contradictory language as incorporeal spirit. Transcending careful philosophical reason, popular religion seems to be grounded "in these four things, opinion of ghosts, ignorance of second causes, devotion towards what men fear, and taking of things casual for prognostics," all of which are conducive to superstition. Our best access to true religion is through faith in God's "supernatural revelation."[147] We should not claim to "conceive and imagine (or have an *idea* of) him in our mind; for whatsoever we conceive is finite." If we ascribe understanding and will to God, we should not identify those with human faculties, since it would be unworthy of God to be limited by discursive thought and conflicting appetites as we are. When we think and speak of God, we should do so in ways that do not pretend to understand the divine nature—through "such negative attributes (as *infinite, eternal, incomprehensible*) or

superlatives (as *most high, most great*, and the like) or indefinite (as *good, just, holy, creator*)." Using a medieval distinction, Hobbes insists that we can only understand God's existence and not God's essence:

> For the nature of God is incomprehensible; that is to say, we understand nothing of *what he is*, but only *that he is*; and therefore, the attributes we give him are not to tell one another *what he is*, nor to signify our opinion of his nature, but our desire to honour him with such names as we conceive most honourable amongst ourselves.[148]

In *De Cive* Hobbes reminds us that the natural law and the moral law are identical and derived from the divine will. He invokes scriptural passages, from the Old Testament and the New, to show that God's will that we follow the natural law of morality has been revealed to us. He describes himself as "an enemy to atheists," who are "enemies of God" and justly punished by both God and the state. He reminds us that all men can know "by natural reason *that there is a God*," even apart from revelation, although he admits that those who reason poorly, those who are too concerned with external distractions, and fools will fail to achieve this knowledge. We should think of God as existing and the cause of the world, with attributes of unlimited greatness and power. We cannot understand the infinite and use the term merely to signify our own lack of understanding. Nor can we have any genuine idea of God in our minds since all our ideas are of finite things. We should not think of God as confined to any place, as either moving or at rest, as either happy or sad; nor should we conceive of the divine will as subject to rational desires as is our will.[149] In short, we should avoid **anthropomorphically** reducing God to finite terms.

In *Human Nature* Hobbes writes, since God "is *incomprehensible*, it followeth, that we can have *no* conception or *image* of the *Deity*, and consequently, all *his attributes* signify our *inability* and defect of power to *conceive* anything concerning his nature, and not any conception of the same, excepting only this, that *there is a God*." He goes on to show how this theological minimalism can be justified by the causal reasoning of the cosmological argument, through which, as we have seen, we "may know *that* God is, though not *what* he is." We may speak of God as a spirit but should remember that all reality is material. "By the name of *spirit*, we understand a *body natural*, but of such *subtlety*, that it worketh not upon the senses." Hobbes rejects the concept of supernatural spirits as a contradiction in terms. Since spirits are not perceptible by sense, we can have no natural knowledge of them, but only *"faith* from supernatural revelation given to the holy writers of the Scriptures."[150]

A more obscure work is Hobbes's response to Bramhall's critique of *Leviathan*, in which the Bishop accused Hobbes of "atheism, blasphemy, impiety, subversion of religion," and so forth. Here Hobbes says that God is *"corporeal* and *infinite."* He continues to deny any incorporeal substance "and nevertheless maintain God's existence, and that he is a most pure, and most corporeal spirit." He does not deny the Holy Trinity but insists that God is "one pure, simple, and eternal corporeal spirit." Hobbes condemns anthropomorphites who think of the persons of the Trinity as individual parts of God. "Spirit is thin, fluid, transparent, invisible body"; this must be the nature of God. *"Pure* and *simple* body, is body of one and the same kind, in every part throughout," as opposed to the composite bodies of our world. This is Hobbes's God, "a most pure, simple, invisible spirit corporeal." Finally, Hobbes holds that it is political authority that warrants that the Scriptures are, indeed, God's law.[151] Our rational nature is such that we can demonstrate God's existence but should admit that the divine nature is incomprehensible, accepting the interpretation of scriptural revelation furnished by the state.

FAITH AND OUR DUTY TO GOD. In *Leviathan*, Hobbes claims that all humans, whether they realize it and admit it or not, are forever subject to God's divine power. "By denying the existence or providence of God, men may shake off their ease, but not their yoke." We honor God, in our thoughts, by conceiving of divine power and goodness as highly as possible; and the external signs of such honor "appearing in the words and actions of men are called *worship."* Some forms of worship, such as *"prayers, thanks,* and *obedience,"* are natural, whereas others, such as particular gestures, are arbitrary. Worship can be either public or private. In honoring God, "it is manifest, we ought to attribute to him *existence.* For no man can have the will to honour that which he thinks not to have any being." Second, we should not identify the world with God, its cause, as **pantheists** do. Third,

we should not suppose the world to be eternal, because then there would be no causal need for God.[152]

Certain teachings concerning the role of Jesus are central doctrines of Christian faith. Hobbes finds scriptural support for his analysis of Christ's threefold office in the true religion: "the first of a *Redeemer,* or *Saviour*; the second of a *pastor, counsellor,* or *teacher* (that is, of a prophet sent from God, to convert such as God hath elected to salvation); the third of a *king,* an *eternal king,* but under his Father." Hobbes believes that God revealed moral law to man in the Ten Commandments. He writes that the two conditions "Necessary *to salvation"* are *"faith in Christ"* and *"obedience to laws"* of reason established by God. Thus, the only article of faith necessary for salvation is that "Jesus is the Christ" whom God promised, through "the prophets of the Old Testament, to send into the world to reign" and provide the possibility of eternal life. This faith must be supplemented by obedience, that is, "the will to obey the law of God."[153]

In *De Homine* Hobbes describes "natural piety," the belief in invisible powers, from which "all goods are to be hoped and all evils are to be feared," as "the first foundation of all religions." He analyzes religion as "the external worship (*cultus*) of men who sincerely honour God." Piety requires that we "love and fear God," which leads to religious worship. Religious faith, "because it concerns things that are placed beyond the grasp of human nature, is opinion which ariseth from the authority of the speakers," such as prophets and religious leaders. The three virtues associated with the Christian religion are *"faith, hope,* and *charity,"* but Hobbes is convinced that the Golden Rule is a rational precept summarizing the duties of "universal justice." He claims "the will of God is not known save through the state."[154]

Immortality

As we might suppose from his materialism and radical empiricism, Hobbes does not have a great deal to say about immortality, though he does briefly discuss it. In *Human Nature* he accepts the doctrine of immortality on faith:

Pantheism (from the Greek *pan,* meaning all, and *theos,* meaning God). The view that God and the world are simply identical, with individual things being mere modifications, moments, or phenomenal appearances of God and God being absolutely immanent without transcending the world in any respect

We that are Christians *acknowledge* that there be angels good and evil, and that there are spirits, and that the soul of a man is a spirit, and that those spirits are immortal: *but*, to *know* it, that is to say, to have natural evidence of the same, it is *impossible*.

His reason is that all evidence must ultimately rest in sense experience, and spirits, by their very nature, cannot be objects of sense. Hence, we have no natural knowledge of immortality, but only faith.[155]

In *Leviathan* Hobbes writes that

there is no natural knowledge of man's estate after death, much less of the reward that is then to be given to breach of faith, but only a belief grounded upon other men's saying that they know it supernaturally, or that they know those that knew them that knew others that knew it supernaturally.

In a chapter dealing with eternal life, salvation, and redemption, Hobbes says that, since eternal life represents a greater reward than our present natural life (and eternal torment a greater punishment than natural death), we should try to consider what sorts of actions (and offenses) might lead to consequences hereafter. Hobbes expresses his belief in the Biblical doctrine that mankind lost eternal life through the sin of Adam, but he holds that "the faithful Christian hath recovered eternal life by Christ's passion, though he die a natural death, and remain dead for a time (namely, till the **resurrection**)." This indicates that the human person does die and cease to be—ruling out what is traditionally called immortality—but is subsequently resurrected to eternal life by the power of God, though Hobbes adds that he cannot find any conclusive evidence for faith in our future heavenly existence either in reason or in the texts of Scripture. Hobbes interprets the religious teaching of immortality in terms of the body's resurrection after death, rather than of continued, uninterrupted spiritual existence essential to human nature.

That the soul of man is in its own nature eternal, and a living creature independent on the body, or that any mere man is immortal otherwise than by the resurrection in the last day . . . is a doctrine not apparent in Scripture.

Thus, man's eternal life, which can be called immortality, in Hobbes's unorthodox sense, "beginneth not in man till the resurrection and day of judgment, and hath for cause, not his specifical nature," but the action of divine power. He admits that this interpretation "will appear to most men a novelty," and he submits his unusual theory to the political authority of the sovereign.

The joys of life eternal are in Scripture comprehended all under the name of Salvation, or being saved. To be saved is to be secured, either respectively, against special evils, or absolutely, against all evil (comprehending want, sickness, and death itself).

Since humanity forfeited natural "happiness by the sin of Adam," the redemptive act of Christ was necessary for our salvation. Christ's death for us provided a redemptive penalty acceptable to God for human salvation. Hobbes reminds us that none of this is philosophically provable from an analysis of human nature, stating his view as a matter of faith—"supposing eternal life by grace only, there is no life but the life of the body, and no immortality till the resurrection."[156] This theory is clearly more compatible with Hobbes's materialism than the traditional Christian interpretation (for example, of Aquinas) would be.

Fulfillment

In discussing Hobbes's analysis of human fulfillment, we should distinguish between the happiness of this life and the ultimate satisfaction of eternal life, though he seems to use the word "felicity" for both. In *Leviathan* he writes,

Continual success in obtaining those things which a man from time to time desireth, that is to say, continual prospering, is that men call Felicity; I mean the felicity of this life.

Since all life as we know it is motion fueled by desire, there can be no complete tranquillity this side of death. As for our ultimate fulfillment, he rejects the medieval scholastic notion of the **beatific vision** as "unintelligible." Even though he accepts the prospect of man's eternal fulfillment on faith, he is **agnostic** about its proper description: "What kind of felicity God hath ordained to them that devoutly honour Him, a man shall no sooner know than enjoy," since it is "incomprehensible" to us now. Hobbes denies that there can be any "***Summum Bonum***" or ultimate good in this life or that our desires can be permanently satisfied here and now. "Felicity is a continual

---

Agnosticism. The view that something, especially the existence of God, cannot be known

Summum Bonum. Literally, in Latin, the greatest good

progress of the desire, from one object to another, the attaining of the former being still but the way to the latter." Though our voluntary actions be oriented to contentment, it remains an elusive ideal. This is in contrast to the unimaginable condition of what he calls the "perpetual felicity of heaven" and our "eternal felicity after death,"[157] which is a matter of faith.

In *De Homine* he writes,

> The greatest good, or as it is called, felicity and the final end, cannot be attained in the present life. For if the end be final, there would be nothing to long for, nothing to desire; whence it follows not only that nothing would itself be a good from that time on, but also that man would not even feel.

Hobbes does not believe that we ever, while alive and functioning, cease to desire more goods. "For of goods, the greatest is always progressing towards ever further ends with the least hindrance."[158]

In this life the dynamic pursuit of happiness is more satisfying than any static contentment. As he says in *Human Nature*, "*Felicity*, therefore, by which we mean continual delight, consisteth *not* in *having* prospered, but in *prospering*." And he compares "the life of man to a race," admitting that the analogy is imperfect. "But this *race* we must suppose to have no other *goal*, nor other *garland*, but being foremost." Thus, fulfillment in this life is intrinsically competitive, human nature being what it is. He says, "Continually to out-go the next before, is *felicity*."[159] Presumably, the fulfillment of eternal life will not be so competitive, but philosophical reason can give us no adequate knowledge of what it will involve.

REFLECTIONS

There is a point-counterpoint contrast between Hobbes's philosophy of human nature and that of Descartes on so many key aspects of their theories, which is the main reason for this chapter's focus on Hobbes (rather than on Locke or Leibniz, who are more in agreement with Descartes than is Hobbes). Although both conceive of reality in terms of substance, Descartes's metaphysics is dualistic, whereas Hobbes's is materialistic. Where Descartes adopts a rationalistic epistemology based on a commitment to innate ideas, Hobbes is an empiricist, viewing all ideas as mental images ultimately derived from sensation. Whereas Descartes claims to have a

self-evident innate idea of human freedom, Hobbes reduces it to the necessitated desires of will. Hobbes has a far more relativistic theory of morality than does Descartes and consequently must place far greater emphasis on the contractual agreements of society. Both maintain that philosophical reason can prove the existence of God, although Hobbes's conception of God is far less orthodox than Descartes's, and the former is far less committed to knowledge of the divine nature than is the latter. And although both believe in eternal life and neither can assemble a conclusive demonstration on its behalf, Hobbes replaces Descartes's notion of the continuous survival of soul with that of the dead body being resurrected by God. Yet each tries to construct his philosophy of human nature in the spirit of the modern science of their day, using its mathematical model of deductive reasoning. We have already considered strengths and weaknesses of Descartes's theory; let us now assess the perspective of Hobbes on each of the ten topics we have analyzed.

REALITY. His conception of reality, the first of our ten topics, supplies the foundation for his entire system, his thoroughgoing materialism providing the basis for everything else. Some might find his hardheaded scientific repudiation of abstract spiritual beings a welcome relief from the imperceptible objects of medieval speculation, still represented by the soul and God in Descartes's philosophy. On the other hand, Hobbes's materialism is **dogmatic**, axiomatically assumed rather than rationally argued. For example, why should we grant his assertion that all substance is physical? Since he does not prove his materialism, its justification or collapse must rest on its theoretical explanatory power rather than on the strength or weakness of evidence offered on its behalf.

BODIES. Second, Hobbes is at his best in dealing with physical reality, his mechanistic view of bodies as substances in motion providing an advance on the static analysis of Aristotelian scholasticism. His scientifically streamlined conception of causality was typical of modern thought and would continue to function adequately until challenged by the blistering critique of Hume. His supplementing Descartes's emphasis on extension with a focus on physical force provides a valuable dimension for physics.

PERSONALITY. Regarding our third topic, his characterization of personality reduces human nature to mechanistic physical motions. On this view, we are merely complex organisms driven by (often conflicting) desires. There is nothing particularly noble about our emotions or will here, no radical qualitative difference of kind between us and the beasts, though our rational and linguistic skills have developed in ways that provide a quantitative difference of degree (of competition, cooperation, and sociability). To his credit, Hobbes recognizes the important role of power in human psychology, as few of his predecessors did; but he may exaggerate its centrality, reducing even human dignity to its terms. Thus, he presents a pessimistic view of man as insatiably craving power over and dominance of others and as egoistically committed to self-interest above all else. It must strain to explain away altruistic cases of deliberate sacrifice of life, limb, health, and welfare for other people, causes, or principles; indeed, even before we study the critique of egoism offered by such successors as Hume, the stand strikes us as unconvincingly one-sided. Hobbes's view is a strong example of **atomistic** individualism, leaving too little room for any natural tendency to community. For all these reasons, it seems to erode a sense of the intrinsic dignity of the human person.

KNOWLEDGE. Fourth, his epistemology is admirable for its forthright and consistent empiricism. There is something refreshing about his analysis of all thought as a subjective representation of the appearances of objects. His mechanistic account of sense awareness as physical pressures transmitted to the brain, where reactions are generated, seems on the right track. In visual sensation, for example, we know that waves or particles of light pass through the cornea of the eye and are focused by the lens onto the retina, the layer of cells lining the interior of the eyeball, which contains receptors known as rods and cones, transmitting impulses to the brain via the optic nerve, those impulses being interpreted in the brain as visual images. But to root all knowledge in subjective sense-based images seems to militate against the possibility of universal and necessary objectivity and to promote a kind of scepticism that Hobbes probably does not intend. Finally, his mechanistic account of human reason as merely a "reckoning" calculation of names

disconnects reasoning from extra-mental reality, overreacting too dramatically against the Cartesian notion of a direct apprehension of reality itself through abstract ideas.

FREEDOM. For our fifth issue, Hobbes's analysis of human freedom as a necessity of the will, though unproved, could be correct. Yet it is too negative a conception of liberty, reducing it to merely a freedom from restraint, rather than including a spontaneous capacity to choose independently of all external influences. As the much later radical empiricist William James observes, this does not feel right to most of us and would seem to undermine moral responsibility and to promote a sort of practical paralysis.

MORALITY. Sixth, Hobbes's theory of morality is flawed by its underlying egoistic relativism, natural law being reduced to mere prudential guidelines for survival and the satisfaction of selfish desire. It leaves no room, short of the artificial conventions of society, for any genuine altruism or universal, objective duty. The most admirable element of his ethics, that we should try to consider actions from the point of view of others who will be affected by them, does not seem plausible, given his profile of human nature, unless and until we become socially conditioned to do so.

SOCIETY. Hobbes's view of political society, our seventh topic, is that part of his philosophy that has remained most famous. It is a powerful, arresting analysis. To his credit, he avoids both the divine-right-of-kings theory so traditional in his day and any acceptance of an arbitrary rule of the rabble, balancing a foundation of consensual liberty with an insistence on stable authority. His critique of democracy is surely worth our serious consideration. Yet it is doubtful whether people in general are as intensely security-minded as he is, to the point of being willing to give up as much liberty as Hobbes would relinquish. Also, he downplays the problem of the abuse of power by the political sovereign, a problem which is all the more frightening, given Hobbes's pessimistic profile of human nature as selfishly driven by desires for power and dominance, combined with his view that the sovereign makes no contract with political subjects, who consequently have no legal recourse against abuses by the sovereign power. A better balance of stable authority and consensual liberty can be struck by combining constitutional government with continuing popular elections of officials.

RELIGION. Eighth, Hobbes's controversial theory of God and religion is also quite problematic. His use of the old cosmological argument, combined with an argument from design, adds nothing new to their employment in medieval times and is subject to the critique of causal and analogous reasoning which Hume will develop. Further, it might seem strange that Hobbes should claim to prove the existence of a Being whose essence is utterly incomprehensible, reducing God to an unknown and unknowable source of the world of our experience. He is too eager to make religion an instrument of the state, in order to minimize possible social conflicts. He does not seem to have been the atheist he was accused of being. But his theological minimalism and religious reductionism seem calculated to help him avoid doctrinal commitments. Even his support of Christianity seems merely a function of his own fidelity to the authority figures of his Christian society.

IMMORTALITY. As for our ninth topic, Hobbes's treatment of immortality neatly synthesizes the implications of his materialism and the religious teachings of his culture. Apart from the latter, the former should lead him to characterize all life as annihilated forever by the death of the body. And, apart from the former, the latter should lead him to opt for spiritual survival after physical death. His ingenious but contrived compromise has human life terminate with physical death until God (miraculously) resurrects the dead body. He accurately speaks of the "novelty" of this position.

FULFILLMENT. Finally, his discussion of human fulfillment is at least consistent with the rest of his theory. But if he is mistaken about our egoistic drive to satisfy our own desires at all costs and/or about natural morality as being strictly relative to such self-interest, then his analysis of the felicity of this life may well seem shallow. Do we not fulfill our human nature more effectively by serving others as well as ourselves and by trying to act in accordance with disinterested moral duty? If so, life need not be pictured as so competitive a matter as his race analogy inevitably suggests. But he is probably correct that the felicity of eternal life is a matter of faith and speculation, not knowable through natural reason.

*　*　*

In conclusion, Hobbes, like Descartes, gives us a consistent, comprehensive, and controversial theory of human nature. The simplicity of his theory, as opposed to that of Descartes, is both a great advantage and a great flaw. His dogmatic materialism and strict empiricism cohere well and lead to his egoism, determinism, moral relativism, political absolutism, and theological minimalism. Yet his thought in all these areas seems one-sided, failing to do justice to spirituality, abstract ideas, altruism, free initiative, universal ethics, self-government, and a personal God. Its greatness consists in its uncompromising pursuit of the implications of the modern scientific perspective for a philosophy of human nature.

QUESTIONS

1. *How does Descartes argue for the reality of the physical world? What does he think essential to all bodies, and why?*

2. *How does Descartes relate mind to body in human nature? What are the advantages and disadvantages of this theory?*

3. *What do you think of the maxims of Descartes's moral code? Should they have been exempt from doubt and critical scrutiny? Why or why not?*

4. *How does Hobbes analyze bodies? Why does this analysis square well (or poorly) with our understanding of them today?*

5. *What connections are there between Hobbes's egoism and his view of morality? Are his ideas here alarming or merely realistic?*

6. *Is Hobbes's profile of the state of nature convincing? How does it lead him to the need for a social contract and a strong social order?*

7. *How does Hobbes's monism significantly differ from Descartes's dualistic theory of reality? Which seems preferable, and why?*

8. *What is the essence of the human person, for Descartes, and what is it, for Hobbes? What do you think of their views here?*

9. *How does Hobbes's theory of knowledge fundamentally differ from Descartes's? What is really at stake in this disagreement?*

10. *How does Hobbes's view on human freedom differ from that of Descartes? Is either closer to being correct, and why?*

11. *Compare and contrast any of Descartes's arguments for God's existence with one from Hobbes. Which thinker is more convincing here, and why?*

12. *Why do Descartes and Hobbes each have difficulty dealing with human immortality? Why do they even bother trying to do so?*

ALTERNATIVES

SPINOZA

An important seventeenth-century philosopher after Descartes and Hobbes, Baruch Spinoza, a Dutch Jew, was born in 1632 (when Descartes was living in Holland). Spinoza was excommunicated from the Amsterdam synagogue in 1656 for his heterodox religious views. Four years later, with his first name changed to Benedict, he went to live near Leyden; and three years after that he took up residence near The Hague. He supported himself by grinding lenses for optical instruments. Though offered a teaching position in philosophy by the University of Heidelberg in 1673, he turned it down in order to maintain his peaceful freedom as a scholar. Only two of his works were published in his lifetime, the first (in 1663) being on Descartes's *Principles of Philosophy* and the other (1670) being his *Theological-Political Treatise*, whose most important sixteenth chapter is remarkably Hobbesian. Spinoza's masterpiece, *The Ethics*, published in Latin soon after his death from consumption in 1677, uses a geometrical method, deductively demonstrating propositions on the basis of previously stipulated definitions and axioms.

The Ethics purports to establish the monistic world-view that all reality is one. Where Descartes maintained three types of substances and Hobbes thought that there is an immense number of substances, all of which are material, Spinoza argues that there is only a single substance, which encompasses all that is real. From a scientific point of view this substance is called Nature; from a theological perspective it is God. This substance, being infinite, comprises an infinite number of attributes, two of which, Thought and Extension, are known to us. Individual minds are seen as modes (or modifications) of Thought, and individual bodies are viewed as modes of Extension. Whereas Descartes has difficulties

relating mind and body, because they are distinct and opposite sorts of created substances, and Hobbes has no such problem at all, due to his not accepting spiritual substance, Spinoza maintains that mind and body are merely different perspectives on the same reality (a "dual-aspect" theory), neither being a substance at all. He also adopts a position of determinism, in the sense that all bodies and minds are determined in their behavior by the divine nature; only Substance or God is free, and that only in the sense of being determined by the necessity of its own nature, rather than being extrinsically determined.

For Spinoza, as for Hobbes, we are driven by appetite. Good is what we consider things we find useful for our own purposes; and we think evil anything that frustrates our appetites. For Spinoza, virtue and power are synonymous, and the highest mental virtue is the intellectual love of God, which increases the adequacy of our ideas and, thus, our power of action. To the extent that we are guided by emotions, we tend to disagree and contend with one another; to the extent that we are rational, we tend to agree and cooperate with one another. We can gain knowledge of the many causal forces that affect us and, thus, learn to accept what happens to us and our oneness with the rest of reality. This is ultimate virtue and constitutes human fulfillment. Because it is difficult, it is rarely achieved, as should be reasonably expected of genuine excellence.

LOCKE

Another great philosopher of the seventeenth century is the Englishman John Locke, who (like Spinoza) was born in 1632 and who died in 1704. He had a Puritan upbringing and (like Hobbes) studied at Oxford University, getting a medical degree in 1674. While at Oxford he discovered the writings of Descartes; like Spinoza, he found them a refreshing alternative to his day's Aristotelian scholasticism. He became attached to the Earl of Shaftesbury, who was subsequently arrested, imprisoned, and tried for his political intrigues. After King Charles II died and was succeeded by his Catholic brother, James II, in 1685, Locke was suspected of being involved in the failed rebellion of the Duke of Monmouth, an illegitimate son of Charles II. Locke had already gone into hiding in Holland, living under the pseudonym of Dr. Van der Linden. There he met and befriended Prince William and Princess Mary of Orange, who would soon become King and Queen of England, following the bloodless "Glorious Revolution" of 1688. Locke then returned to England, where he spent his remaining years, suffering from asthma and failing in health.

His two greatest works, *An Essay concerning Human Understanding* and *The Second Treatise of Government*, were both published in 1690. The former begins with a critique of innate ideas, of the sort associated with Descartes's epistemology. As an empiricist, Locke argues that the mind is initially like a **tabula rasa** or blank tablet, devoid of characters until they are acquired through sensation and reflection, which are our only sources of ideas. Simple ideas (of sensation and reflection) are the basic building blocks of all complex ideas and, hence, of all knowledge. We only experience the qualities and relations of things, substance itself being inferred rather than directly experienced. We sense the primary qualities of bodies (like their solidity and their shapes), which are inseparable from them and which correspond to the way they really are, and their secondary qualities (like their colors and odors), which are perceived sensations in us rather than in the objects themselves. We form general ideas by abstracting the special features of our ideas, which are representations of particular objects. Thanks to our general ideas knowledge is possible. It consists of our mental perceptions of the agreement and/or disagreement of our own ideas. For Locke (as for Descartes), the two degrees of certain knowledge are intuition and demonstration, although he also accepts sensitive knowledge as practically certain; we have intuitive knowledge of our own existence, demonstrative knowledge of God's existence, and sensitive knowledge of other things, such as this page of paper. Locke adopts a **correspondence theory** of knowledge, calling knowledge "real" when our ideas conform to the reality of things. But, since

we only directly experience our own ideas and have no access to things except through the filters of our perceptions, he wonders how we can ever establish such correspondence, but he does not provide a compelling answer (setting the stage for the critiques of Hume and Kant, which we shall consider in the next chapter). For Locke (as for Descartes), a person or self is an intelligent, thinking being; Locke identifies personal identity with continuity of consciousness. Like Descartes (and unlike Spinoza), Locke believes that God, finite minds, and bodies are three distinct types of substances and that mind and body somehow interact in human nature.

Locke's *Second Treatise of Government* presents a social contract theory that is comparable to, but different from, that of Hobbes. Locke also writes of a state of nature, which is one of liberty and equality, though it is not necessarily a state of war, for we are all bound by natural law, which comes from God. As an orthodox Anglican, Locke maintains that we should refrain from harming anyone's life, health, liberty, or possessions. Although the resources of the Earth were given by God to humans in common, a person can acquire property of his own by investing his labor in it. Some people will selfishly violate natural law, infringing the liberties and property rights of others, who are left with no recourse but their own judgment and retaliatory force. The solution to this liability is a contract, whereby men give up some of their liberty, by mutual consent, to enter into political society in order to establish a common good and public safety. Unlike Hobbes, Locke opposes absolute monarchy as incompatible with civil society, since the latter is a withdrawal from the state of nature, whereas the former establishes a state of nature between the ruler and his subjects. Locke distinguishes three basic powers of government, the legislative (making the laws), the executive (assuring that they are enforced), and the federative (waging war and making peace), with the legislative being supreme. Whenever government becomes tyrannical, violating citizens' liberties and property rights, it breaches the social contract, and its citizens may legitimately dissolve that government; it is the people themselves who must judge whether such action is appropriate. In these ideas of legitimate government being based on the consent of the governed, of a separation of powers of government, and of the people retaining the right to dissolve a government that has become oppressive, we see the intellectual seeds of the American Declaration of Independence and of the establishment of a new constitutional nation.

LEIBNIZ

As Locke represents a famous empirical link between Hobbes and Hume (one of the two greatest philosophers of the eighteenth century), the most important rationalistic link between Descartes and Kant (the other) is Gottfried Wilhelm Leibniz, who was born in Leipzig (in present-day Germany) in 1646 (fourteen years after Spinoza and Locke were born). His father was a professor of moral philosophy at the University of Leipzig, and his maternal grandfather had been a law professor there as well. Leibniz was precocious, learning Latin at the age of eight, studying Greek as a child, and avidly reading philosophy before becoming a teenager. He entered the university at the age of fifteen, studying the works of Galileo, Descartes, and Hobbes, among others. He went on to study law and was granted a Doctorate of Law by the University of Altdorf in 1667. He declined the offer of a professor's chair, choosing instead to enter into diplomatic service, which led to his traveling widely. (While in London, he hoped to visit Hobbes, but the meeting was not arranged.) He discovered the infinitesimal calculus independently of Newton. In 1676, he was appointed librarian and historian for the court of Hanover and visited with Spinoza. His *Discourse on Metaphysics* was written in 1686. His *New Essays on the Human Understanding*, a critique of Locke's *Essay*, was written about the time of Locke's death in 1704. Leibniz's ***Theodicy*** was published in 1710, and his famous essay "The Monadology" was written in 1714. He was sadly neglected in the last couple of years of his life, and his death in 1716 passed almost unnoticed.

Although he denies being a follower of Descartes, Leibniz is a rationalist and defends innate ideas against the *tabula rasa* theory of Locke and the empiricists. Like Descartes (and Spinoza), Leibniz favors ontological argumentation for God. Like Descartes, Hobbes, Spinoza, and Locke, he adopts a substance-based metaphysics. All composite things must be made up of parts, which ultimately resolve into simple substances. Leibniz is a **pluralist**, who believes that reality comprises many irreducible simple substances, which he calls "monads," the ultimate elements of all things. Each monad is unique and has its own perspective on reality. He describes monads as "windowless" in the sense that they are impervious to any natural principles of change outside themselves. The two main activities of monads are perception, through which objects are represented, and **apperception**, whereby there is consciousness or reflective knowledge of perception. Souls and bodies are related through the preestablished harmony set up by God. Intelligent souls, or spirits, are capable of self-knowledge, are moral agents, and were created as immortal. The two kinds of truths are those of reason, governed by the principle of **noncontradiction**, and those of fact, governed by the principle of sufficient reason, which specifies that there is a cause adequate to explain every matter of fact, the ultimate "sufficient reason" for reality being God. Of the infinite number of universes possible, God chose to create this one because it is the best of all possible worlds, in the sense of combining the greatest variety compatible with the greatest order.

Leibniz's great work *Theodicy* defends the conformity of religious faith and philosophical reason. No two truths can possibly contradict each other; therefore, the truths of faith must be compatible with those of reason. Nevertheless, there are mysteries we humans cannot comprehend. But how, in particular, can we reconcile the fact of evil in the world with the truth of an all-powerful, all-knowing, and all-good God? Leibniz's distinctly Augustinian response is that evil is merely a privation of being, that the alternative of evil enhances the appreciation of the good, and that the freedom of God's personal creatures allows them to lead moral lives that provide a sufficient reason for God's allowing them to misuse that freedom to do evil. Leibniz distinguishes three sorts of evil: metaphysical evil is merely imperfection, which is inseparable from being a creature; the physical evil of pain and suffering is a consequence of the misuse of freedom by personal creatures that constitutes the

---

Apperception.   Self-awareness, the mind's consciousness of its own inner states; in Kantian thought, it is the ego's awareness of a unity of self-consciousness

third sort, moral evil, which God allows but never wills. Divine **foreknowledge**, Leibniz is confident, does not amount to the sort of predestination that would negate human freedom. He is the last great seventeenth-century philosopher, extending his work into the beginning of the eighteenth century. In many ways he is the paradigmatic example of Hume's target, as well as the philosopher Kant followed prior to being dissuaded by Hume. It is to their theories we shall turn in our next chapter.

Notes

1. René Descartes, *The Philosophical Writings of Descartes,* Vol. III, trans. John Cottingham, Robert Stoothoff, Dugald Murdoch, and Anthony Kenny (Cambridge, England: Cambridge Univ. Press, 1991), pp. 250–51. This book is henceforth called "*Writings,* III."

2. Ibid., pp. 240–41.

3. Ibid., pp. 123–24, 236.

4. René Descartes, *The Essential Descartes,* ed. Margaret D. Wilson, trans. Elizabeth S. Haldane and G. R. T. Ross (New York: New American Library, 1969), pp. 109–12. This book is henceforth called "Wilson."

5. *Writings,* III, pp. 4–5.

6. Wilson, p. 113. *See also* René Descartes, *The Philosophical Writings of Descartes*, Vol. I, trans. John Cottingham, Robert Stoothoff, and Dugald Murdoch (Cambridge, England: Cambridge Univ. Press, 1985), p. 4. This book is henceforth called "*Writings,* I."

7. *Writings,* III, pp. 30–32.

8. Ibid., pp. 20–21.

9. Ibid., p. 142.

10. Ibid., pp. 40–45, 124, 127–28; *see also* Wilson, pp. 140–41, 145.

11. *Writings,* I, p. 404.

12. *Writings,* III, p. 86.

13. Wilson, pp. 151–52.

14. *Writings,* III, p. 167.

15. Ibid., p. 22.

16. Ibid., pp. 220–21, 316–17.

17. Ibid., pp. 214–15, 324, 367.

18. Ibid., pp. 383–84.

19. Wilson, pp. 163, 187; *see also* p. 274.

20. Ibid., pp. 323–25. *See also* "Replies to the Second Set of Objections," in René Descartes, *The Philosophical Writings of Descartes,* Vol. II, trans. John Cottingham, Robert Stoothoff, and Dugald Murdoch (Cambridge, England: Cambridge Univ. Press, 1984), p. 114. This book is henceforth called "*Writings,* II."

21. Wilson, pp. 322, 329.

22. *Writings,* II, p. 117.

23. Wilson, pp. 315–16; *see also Writings,* III, p. 341.

24. Wilson, pp. 301–2, 305, 307–8.

25. Ibid., pp. 74, 79, 94, 97, 101, 131.

26. Ibid., pp. 172, 175–78.

27. Ibid., pp. 211–13, 215.

28. Ibid., pp. 218–20; cf. pp. 298–99.

29. Ibid., pp. 333, 337–41, 344–46.

30. Ibid., pp. 77, 279.

31. Ibid., pp. 127–28; cf. *Writings,* II, pp. 409–10, 417.

32. Wilson, pp. 169–71; *see also* p. 310.

33. Ibid., pp. 264–65, 270.

34. Ibid., p. 238; *see also Writings,* III, p. 333.

35. Wilson, pp. 128, 159, 171–74, 213–14; cf. p. 311.

36. Ibid., pp. 246–50.

37. Ibid., pp. 138–39.

38. Ibid., pp. 214–20, 281–82; cf. pp. 337, 347; *see also* "Treatise on Man," in *Writings,* I, pp. 100, 106.

39. Wilson, pp. 196–201.

40. Ibid., pp. 353, 358–67.

41. Ibid., pp. 37–43.

42. Ibid., pp. 44–45, 47, 50, 52.

43. Ibid., pp. 55, 59, 62–67, 73.

44. Ibid., pp. 107–8, 115, 118–19, 127, 132, 142.

45. Ibid., pp. 166–67, 179–80, 182, 184.

46. Ibid., pp. 209, 223.

47. Ibid., pp. 252–53, 255–57, 272.

48. Ibid., pp. 320–21, 374–75; cf. *Writings,* III, p. 336.

49. Wilson, pp. 197–201.

50. Ibid., p. 261.

51. *Writings,* III, pp. 178, 180.

52. Wilson, pp. 317–19; cf. *Writings,* I, pp. 343, 384, 386–87; *see also Writings,* II, pp. 259–60, 291–92.

53. *Writings,* III, pp. 160–61, 233–34, 245.

54. Ibid., pp. 277, 282, 326; *see also* "Conversation with Burman," in *Writings,* III, p. 342.

55. Wilson, pp. 305–6.

56. *Writings,* III, p. 326; *see also* pp. 352–53.

57. Wilson, pp. 121–24; *see also Writings,* III, pp. 257–58.

58. *Writings,* I, pp. 379, 387; cf. *Writings,* III, p. 234.

59. *Writings,* I, pp. 356–57, 384–85.

60. *Writings,* III, pp. 310–11, 322–23.

61. Ibid., pp. 266, 273.

62. Ibid., pp. 292–95.

63. Wilson, pp. 114, 125, 129–30.

64. Ibid., pp. 154–55, 159–60, 163–64.

65. Ibid., pp. 184–88.

66. Ibid., pp. 188–89.

67. Ibid., pp. 190–93.

68. Ibid., pp. 204–5, 207–8.

69. Ibid., pp. 227–31, 238, 277.

70. Ibid., pp. 257–59, 264, 289–90.

71. Ibid., pp. 313–14, 336.

72. Ibid., pp. 355, 140, 162–63.

73. *Writings*, III, pp. 29, 163, 172, 272; *see also* pp. 189, 208.

74. Wilson, p. 303; *Writings*, I, pp. 379, 382.

75. *Writings*, III, pp. 256–58, 261–62, 264–65, 268, 270, 325.

76. Thomas Hobbes, "The Autobiography of Thomas Hobbes," trans. Benjamin Farrington, *The Rationalist Annual* (1958), pp. 23–24. This work is henceforth called "Autobiography."

77. Ibid., p. 24.

78. Ibid., pp. 24–25.

79. Ibid., p. 25. The last sentence quoted is from Thomas Hobbes, *The English Works of Thomas Hobbes of Malmesbury*, ed. Sir William Molesworth (London: John Bohn, 1839–45), Vol. VIII, p. vii. This multivolumed collection is henceforth called "*Works*."

80. Autobiography, pp. 25–27.

81. Ibid., p. 26.

82. *Works*, Vol. IV, p. 414.

83. Autobiography, p. 27; *see also Works*, Vol. IV, p. 415.

84. Thomas Hobbes, *Body, Man, and Citizen*, ed. Richard S. Peters (New York: Collier Books, 1962), p. 402. This book is henceforth called "*Body*."

85. Autobiography, pp. 27–28.

86. *Works*, Vol. IV, pp. 413, 415.

87. *Works*, Vol. VII, pp. 471–72.

88. Autobiography, p. 31.

89. Thomas Hobbes, *Leviathan*, ed. Edwin Curley (Indianapolis: Hackett Publishing Co., 1994), pp. 261–62, 459. This work is henceforth called "*Leviathan*."

90. *Works*, Vol. I, pp. 410–11, 414–15.

91. *Leviathan*, pp. 8, 27, 261, 460.

92. *Body*, pp. 75, 80, 95–96, 101–3, 106–7, 111, 115–16, 124; cf. pp. 163–64, 175 (from Hobbes's "Little Treatise").

93. Ibid., pp. 125, 127–29, 135–36, 146.

94. *Leviathan*, pp. 3, 28.

95. Ibid., pp. 28–33.

96. Ibid., pp. 38–40, 50–52.

97. Ibid., pp. 58, 74.

98. Ibid., pp. 75–76.

99. Thomas Hobbes, *Man and Citizen*, ed. Bernard Gert (Indianapolis: Hackett Publishing Co., 1991), pp. 110–11, 115–16, 125, 165, 167–69. This book is henceforth called "*Man*."

100. *Leviathan*, pp. 82, 95.

101. Ibid., pp. 101, 104, 108–9.

102. *Man*, pp. 93, 99–100, 109. In his Introduction (pp. 5ff.), Bernard Gert denies that Hobbes is a psychological egoist, in the sense of claiming "that *all* actions of *all* men are motivated entirely by self-interest"; the interpretation adopted here holds that self-interest is always a fundamental motivation, underlying, for example, any concern for others or sense of moral obligation.

103. Ibid., pp. 37–38, 40, 43, 45–46, 48–49, 51.

104. Ibid., pp. 55–56, 63–67, 83–84.

105. *Body*, pp. 182–84, 189, 191, 194–95, 207, 210, 218, 221, 226–27.

106. Ibid., p. 277.

107. *Leviathan*, pp. 6–9.

108. *Body*, pp. 156–58.

109. Ibid., pp. 188, 199; cf. pp. 198–201, 203–4, 376–77.

110. *Leviathan*, pp. 12–13.

111. Ibid., pp. 16–17.

112. Ibid., pp. 17–19, 21.

113. Ibid., pp. 22–25.

114. Ibid., pp. 35–36, 47.

115. Ibid., pp. 444, 453–54, 457–58, 480; *Man*, pp. 90–91.

116. *Body*, p. 24.

117. Ibid., pp. 44, 48–49, 56, 68; see pp. 34–37 for his analysis of names.

118. Ibid., pp. 72–75, 83–85.

119. Ibid., pp. 27–31.

120. *Leviathan*, pp. 24, 79, 136–37.

121. *Man*, pp. 46, 216.

122. *Body*, pp. 117, 123, 161; *see also* pp. 237–39.

123. Ibid., pp. 245–46, 248–49, 251.

124. Ibid., pp. 254–57, 260, 264, 269–74.

125. *Leviathan*, pp. 28–29, 34, 77–80, 100, 174.

126. *Man*, pp. 42–43, 47–49, 68–70.

127. Ibid., pp. 95, 116–17, 122–23, 150–52, 282–84.

128. *Body*, pp. 77–78, 207, 298–301, 304–5.

129. *Leviathan*, pp. 1, 3, 76, 81–82, 86–87.

130. Ibid., pp. 89, 94–99.

131. *Man*, pp. 35, 39–41, 60–61, 69–70.

132. Ibid., pp. 101–2, 104, 113–15, 117–19, 124–27.

133. *Body*, pp. 278–80, 282–87, 289–90, 306–10.

134. *Leviathan*, pp. 106, 109–10.

135. Ibid., pp. 110–15, 117.

136. Ibid., pp. 211–14, 219, 224.

137. *Body*, pp. 315, 330, 333, 369, 379–80, 383; cf. pp. 395–96, 398, 406, 408, 410.

138. *Leviathan*, pp. 118–21.

139. Ibid., pp. 127–31, 135.

140. *Man*, pp. 178–85, 192–99, 203–4, 221–32.

141. *Leviathan*, pp. 138, 142–45.

142. Ibid., pp. 173, 188, 191–93, 203–6, 229.

143. *Man*, pp. 272, 274–79.

144. Ibid., pp. 136–39.

145. Ibid., pp. 165–67, 170–71, 174–77.

146. *Leviathan*, pp. 10–11.

147. Ibid., pp. 15, 31, 62–66, 71; for another use of the cosmological argument, *see Works*, I, p. 412.

148. *Leviathan*, pp. 239–40, 263.

149. *Man*, pp. 153–54, 284–85n, 298–99.

150. *Body*, pp. 230–33.

151. *Works*, Vol. IV, pp. 281, 306–7, 309, 313, 339.

152. *Leviathan*, pp. 234, 237–39.

153. Ibid., pp. 326–27, 351–52, 398, 402, 407; *see also Body*, pp. 349–50, 353–54, 356.

154. *Man*, pp. 58, 71–73, 85; *see also Body*, p. 400.

155. *Body*, pp. 231–33.

156. *Leviathan*, pp. 92–93, 301, 303–5, 310, 313–14, 424, 429.

157. Ibid., pp. 34–35, 57, 92; cf. p. 309.

158. *Man*, pp. 53–54.

159. *Body*, pp. 209, 224–25.

Bibliography

GENERAL

Copleston, Frederick, S.J. *A History of Philosophy*, Vols. IV, V, Part I. Garden City, NY: Image Books, 1963–64.

Hampshire, Stuart. *The Age of Reason*. New York: Mentor Books, 1956.

Jones, W. T. *Hobbes to Hume*, 2d ed. New York: Harcourt, Brace & World, 1969.

DESCARTES   Primary Sources

Descartes: Philosophical Writings. Ed. and trans. Norman Kemp Smith. New York: Modern Library, 1958.

Discourse on Method and *Meditations on First Philosophy*, 3rd ed. Trans. Donald A. Cress. Indianapolis: Hackett Publishing Co., 1993.

Discourse on Method and *The Meditations*. Trans. F. E. Sutcliffe. London: Penguin Books, 1968.

The Essential Descartes. Ed. Margaret D. Wilson. Trans. Elizabeth S. Haldane and G. R. T. Ross. New York: New American Library, 1969.

The Passions of the Soul. Trans. Stephen H. Voss. Indianapolis: Hackett Publishing Co., 1989.

Philosophical Essays. Trans. by Laurence J. Lafleur. Indianapolis: Bobbs-Merrill, 1964.

The Philosophical Works of Descartes, 2 vols. Trans. Elizabeth S. Haldane and G. R. T. Ross. New York: Cambridge Univ. Press, 1968 & 1970.

The Philosophical Writings of Descartes, 3 vols. Trans. John Cottingham, Robert Stoothoff, Dugald Murdoch, and Anthony Kenny. Cambridge, England: Cambridge Univ. Press, 1984, 1985, 1991.

Selected Philosophical Writings. Trans. John Cottingham, Robert Stoothoff, and Dugald Murdoch. Cambridge, England: Cambridge Univ. Press, 1988.

Secondary Sources

Cottingham, John, ed. *The Cambridge Companion to Descartes*. New York: Cambridge Univ. Press, 1992.

Dicker, Georges. *Descartes: An Analytical and Historical Introduction*. New York: Oxford Univ. Press, 1993.

Doney, Willis, ed. *Descartes: A Collection of Critical Essays*. Garden City, NY: Doubleday & Co., 1967.

Grene, Marjorie. *Descartes*. Minneapolis: Univ. of Minnesota Press, 1985.

Keeling, S. V. *Descartes*, 2nd ed. London: Oxford Univ. Press, 1968.

Kenny, Anthony. *Descartes: A Study of His Philosophy*. New York: Random House, 1968.

Sorell, Tom. *Descartes*. Oxford, England: Oxford Univ. Press, 1987.

Williams, Bernard. *Descartes: The Project of Pure Enquiry*. London: Penguin Books, 1978.

Wilson, Margaret D. *Descartes*. London: Routledge & Kegan Paul, 1978.

HOBBES   Primary Sources

Body, Man, and Citizen. Ed. Richard S. Peters. New York: Collier Books, 1962.

The English Works of Thomas Hobbes of Malmesbury, 11 vols. Ed. Sir William Molesworth. London: John Bohn, 1839–45.

Hobbes Selections. Ed. Frederick J. E. Woodbridge. New York: Charles Scribner's Sons, 1958.

Human Nature and *De Corpore Politico*. Ed. J. C. A. Gaskin. Oxford, England: Oxford Univ. Press, 1994.

Leviathan. Ed. by Edwin Curley. Indianapolis: Hackett Publishing Co., 1994.

Man and Citizen. Ed. Bernard Gert. Indianapolis: Hackett Publishing Co., 1991.

The Metaphysical System of Hobbes. Ed. Mary Whiton Calkins. La Salle, IL: Open Court, 1948.

Secondary Sources

Cranston, Maurice, and Richard S. Peters, eds. *Hobbes and Rousseau: A Collection of Critical Essays.* Garden City, NY: Doubleday & Co., 1972.

Goldsmith, M. M. *Hobbes's Science of Politics.* New York: Columbia Univ. Press, 1966.

Peters, Richard S. *Hobbes.* Baltimore: Penguin Books, 1967.

Ross, Ralph, Herbert W. Schneider, and Theodore Waldman, eds. *Thomas Hobbes in His Time.* Minneapolis: Univ. of Minnesota Press, 1974.

Stephen, Sir Leslie. *Hobbes.* Ann Arbor: Univ. of Michigan Press, 1961.

Strauss, Leo. *The Political Philosophy of Hobbes.* Trans. Elsa M. Sinclair. Chicago: The Univ. of Chicago Press, 1963.

Tuck, Richard. *Hobbes.* Oxford, England: Oxford Univ. Press, 1989.

Historical Background

«« «« «« «« «« «« «« «« «« «« «« «« «« «« «« «« «« «»»» »» »» »» »» »» »» »» »» »» »» »» »» »» »»

he eighteenth century is "the Age of **Enlightenment**" (*Aufklärung* in German and *l'âge de lumière* in French), which is an extension of the Age of **Reason**. Its roots can be found in the writings of two English thinkers of the late seventeenth century, Sir Isaac Newton, who published his scientific work on gravity in 1687, and John Locke, whose great works in **epistemology** and political **philosophy** appeared three years later. From these roots grew a cultural confidence that disciplined thought could be applied to contribute to the well-being of humanity. Enlightenment thinkers are committed to certain central guiding ideas, including those of reason, experience, science, nature, liberty, education, progress, and happiness. These ideals came to typify intellectual culture on both sides of the Atlantic. Many of the founding fathers of the United States (including Thomas Paine, Benjamin Franklin, and Thomas Jefferson) were Enlightenment thinkers. The movement was particularly strong in France, Scotland, and Prussia. In France Baron de Montesquieu, Voltaire, and Jean-Jacques Rousseau, in their own various ways, contributed to its development, as did Pierre Bayle, Marquis de Condorcet, and the **philosophes** responsible for the great *Encyclopedia*, edited by Denis Diderot and Jean d'Alembert from 1751 on; intellectual discussions of its ideas were common in French *salons*. In Scotland the Enlightenment featured Edward Gibbon in history, Adam Smith in economic theory and philosophy, and David Hume in philosophy. In Prussia the writings of Gotthold Ephraim Lessing and the philosophy of Immanuel Kant proved influential. Enlightenment thought, among other things, challenged traditional views on religion, sometimes leading to **deism** (as in Hume) or even to atheism (as in Baron d'Holbach). The Protestant revival movement of Methodism, founded by the British John Wesley, may be regarded as countering such trends. Other prominent thinkers of the eighteenth century include Giambattista Vico, Christian Wolff, George Berkeley, Joseph Butler, Jonathan Edwards, Julien Offray de la Mettrie, Thomas Reid, Moses Mendelssohn, William Paley, and Johann Gottfried von Herder.

The eighteenth century was also marked by shifting political arrangements and revolutionary changes of government. The Peace of Westphalia, which

---

Philosophes (literally, in French, philosophers).   The eighteenth-century philosophical thinkers of the French Enlightenment, including Voltaire, Condorcet, and the editors of the great *Encyclopedia* (Diderot and d'Alembert)

Deism (from the Latin *Deus*, meaning God).   The belief in a transcendent God who created or designed our world but does not intervene in it ended the Thirty Years' War in 1648, made France a dominant political power on the European continent. Expansionist policies and a growing French army threatened European neighbors, leading to various alliances and wars against France, until the Peace of Utrecht in 1713, which benefited Austria, England, Prussia, and Holland, while leaving the defeated France still a great power. This period included the Seven Years' War (called the French and Indian War, in America), which ended in 1763 with the Treaty of Paris, with France surrendering parts of its overseas colonies and Britain acquiring all of Canada and virtually all of the present-day United States east of the Mississippi River.

In England William and Mary were succeeded by Queen Anne, who generally also respected the prerogatives of Parliament; during her reign (1702–14) political union with Scotland was achieved, with Scotsmen given seats in Parliament. The Stuarts failed to retain the throne; Parliament saw to it that the German elector of Hanover became George I and was succeeded by his son George II, who reigned until 1760. These two Hanoverian kings were more concerned with foreign than with domestic affairs, but Parliament governed the latter rather effectively. The great political parties of the Whigs (advocating representative government) and the Tories (supporting Royalist interests) had formed even before the Glorious Revolution of the preceding century and had solidified over the years. Foreign policy was often designed to counter the perceived threats of the French, with England developing (and taxing) its American Colonies.

In Prussia Frederick II became king in 1740. Commanding a fine army, he greatly increased his territory and made Prussia an important power on the Continent. He came to be called "Frederick the Great" and "the Enlightenment King" due to his fostering of learning and tolerant policies towards the free discussion of ideas. He admired French culture and literature, bringing Voltaire to his court, as well as studying the philosophies of Locke and Leibniz. He practiced religious toleration, offering refuge to Jews and to Jesuits (who were temporarily suppressed by a papal decree). Under Frederick's benevolent autocracy, agriculture was developed,

the condition of the serfs improved, and immigration was encouraged. By the time he died in 1786, succeeded by his illiberal, anti-Enlightenment nephew, Frederick William II, Prussia had become a great nation-state. Meanwhile, the Enlightenment had been introduced into Russia early in the eighteenth century during the reign of the energetic Peter the Great; but its influence declined at his death in 1725, only to be renewed under Catherine the Great, who ruled from 1762 to 1796.

The last quarter of the eighteenth century was a period of political revolution in America and then in France. The American Colonists had reluctantly helped England defeat France in the French and Indian War but yearned for independence from Colonial rule. George III, the grandson of George II, ruled Great Britain autocratically from 1760 into the nineteenth century. The American Colonists protested against the British Stamp Act of 1765. But after it was repealed the next year, the British government continued to impose taxation on the Colonists without the consent of their elected representatives, fueling the fires of rebellion. A Continental Congress was formed in 1774, followed by a Colonial army in the following year. In July of 1776, Colonial representatives assembled in Philadelphia and issued a Declaration of Independence, mostly written by Thomas Jefferson. Under the leadership of George Washington, the Colonial army defeated the British troops, leading to the surrender of General Charles Cornwallis at Yorktown in 1781, and the peace treaty of Paris two years later successfully concluded the revolution and established the Thirteen Colonies as independent; a constitutional convention later brought into being the United States of America.

Popular discontent was also rampant in France under the rule of Louis XVI and his Austrian wife, Marie Antoinette. There were problems with employment, inflationary prices, shortages of food, and oppressive tax burdens on the poor. On July 14, 1789, a mob stormed the Bastille, the Parisian fortress used as a prison. The people acquired arms and agitated for change. The next month, the *Declaration of the Rights of Man and Citizen* inspired the call for liberty, equality, and fraternity for all. A mob marched on the king's palace at Versailles and drove him to relocate his court at Paris. In 1791, the king was caught trying to flee from France. He was subsequently humiliated, imprisoned, tried for treason, and then guillotined in early 1793 along with Marie Antoinette. Then "the Terror" prevailed under the lawyer Maximilien Robespierre (a follower of Jean-Jacques Rousseau). In 1794, Robespierre was toppled from power and himself guillotined; the following year, a new constitution was set in place, ending monarchical absolutism in France, protecting the rights of its citizens, and establishing a "Directory" of five leaders and two houses of political representatives, elected by property owners. In 1795, Prussia and Spain concluded a peace treaty with France at Basel, but the French continued to fight against Austria and England. The French won victories in Italy under the command of a young Corsican named Napoleon Bonaparte, leading to the surrender of Austria and the gaining of territory through the Peace of Campoformio in 1797. The next year, Napoleon launched an unsuccessful campaign against the English in Egypt, abandoning his troops there and fleeing to Paris.

The Age of Enlightenment was also a period of important musical composers, pictorial artists, and literary authors. The German Johann Sebastian Bach wrote *The Well-Tempered Clavier* and his six Brandenburg Concertos. The German-born George Frideric Handel went to Britain, where his employer, the elector of Hanover, soon became King George I; there Handel wrote his famous *Messiah*. Later in the century, Austrian Wolfgang Amadeus Mozart composed a staggering array of symphonies, concertos, and operas in his short lifetime, and fellow Austrian Franz Joseph Haydn composed over one hundred symphonies. In Italy, Antonio Vivaldi, a priest, who is best known for *The Four Seasons*, wrote many operas, sonatas, and concertos. Three of the great pictorial artists of the period were English: William Hogarth, a painter and engraver, who did *The Rake's Progress*, Thomas Gainsborough, the portrait and landscape painter who did *The Blue Boy*, and Sir Joshua Reynolds, another portraitist. In literature, in France, Voltaire wrote *Candide*, poking fun at the optimistic **rationalism** of Leibnizians. Great British authors of the period included Daniel Defoe (who wrote *Robinson Crusoe* and *Moll*

Flanders), Jonathan Swift (author of the satirical *Gulliver's Travels* and *A Modest Proposal*), poets Alexander Pope (who wrote *The Rape of the Lock* and *An Essay on Man*) and William Blake (who was also a noted engraver and illustrator), and novelist Henry Fielding (author of *Joseph Andrews* and *Tom Jones*). During this period, the Scottish engineer James Watt invented the modern steam engine and the French scientist Antoine Lavoisier laid the foundations of modern chemistry.

We might also briefly consider the state of education and the reexamination of women's roles in society at this time. From the middle of the sixteenth century to the middle of the eighteenth, education in France was undertaken by Jesuits and other religious orders; in 1763, the Jesuit order was suppressed, and its schools were closed, leading to the subsequent development of a system of public schools. In England around the beginning of the eighteenth century, a great system of charity schools, providing basic education for poor children in London and its neighboring towns, was undertaken by the Society for the Promotion of Christian Knowledge. In Prussia education was dominated by the Lutheran State Church until 1787, when schools were brought under direct state control. In America colleges were opening up: Harvard in 1636, William and Mary in 1693, Yale in 1701, and Princeton in 1746. The college curriculum here comprised classics, **theology**, rhetoric, **ethics**, logic, mathematics, and history, with science added in the eighteenth century. The first state universities in America were the University of Georgia (1785) and the University of North Carolina (1789); the Jesuits founded their first college in the United States, Georgetown, in 1789. By the end of the century the limited place of women in society was being challenged. In 1790, Condorcet advocated greater equality and the political emancipation of women. (But the Napoleonic Code of 1804 later blocked this and reinforced the political impotence of women in France.) In England Mary Wollstonecraft's *Vindication of the Rights of Women* of 1792 promoted equal rights for women.

The intellectual currents during this Age of Enlightenment challenged the comfortable tenets of earlier rationalism in philosophy, in religion, and in politics. By the early eighteenth century, the doctrine of **innate** ideas was becoming unfashionable, thinkers were becoming increasingly **sceptical** of the old logical **arguments** for God's existence, and a move towards greater social equality and representative government was underway. It is in this context that Hume and Kant develop their great systems. After we study these, we shall consider Rousseau, Jeremy Bentham, and Johann Gottlieb Fichte as philosophical alternatives from this period.

Hume

Be a philosopher; but, amidst all your philosophy, be still a man.

ENQUIRY CONCERNING HUMAN UNDERSTANDING

BIOGRAPHY

The Scottish thinker David Hume was born in Edinburgh, on April 26, 1711 (four years after the union of England and Scotland), the youngest child of Joseph Home (pronounced Hume), a lawyer who died two years later, and Katherine Falconer, the daughter of a president of the College of Justice. The family owned the estate at Ninewells, where she raised her three children, John, Katherine, and David, after her husband's death. In his autobiographical "My Own Life," Hume writes, "My family, however, was not rich, and being myself a younger brother, my patrimony, according to the mode of my country, was of course very slender." He lovingly describes his mother as "a woman of singular merit, who, though young and handsome, devoted herself entirely to the rearing and educating of her children."[1] The family belonged to the Calvinist Presbyterian Church, and David appears to have been a pious child.

A letter Hume wrote shortly before his twenty-third birthday contains what he called "a kind of History of my Life" up to that time. There he reports that "from my earliest Infancy, I found alwise a strong Inclination to Books & Letters." Before his twelfth birthday he was sent to Edinburgh University to study with his brother John (who was two years older). He writes,

> As our College Education in Scotland, extending little further than the Languages, ends commonly when we are about 14 or 15 Years of Age, I was after that left to my own Choice in my Reading, & found it encline me almost equally to Books of Reasoning & Philosophy, & to Poetry.

Yet he seems to have realized, even as a teenager, that "there is nothing yet establisht in either" philosophy or literary criticism and that "they contain little more than endless Disputes, even in the most fundamental Articles."[2] He was probably introduced to the works of Newton and Locke while at Edinburgh, and he may have begun losing his Calvinist faith during that time as well.

Although he received no academic degree from the university, he writes,

> I passed through the ordinary course of education with success, and was seized very early with a passion for Literature, which has been the ruling passion of my life, and the great source of my enjoyments.

Because of his sober temperament and disciplined habits, his family pushed him towards the legal profession.[3] But, he says,

> The Law, which was the Business I design'd to follow, appear'd nauseous to me, & I cou'd think of no other way of pushing my Fortune in the World, but that of a Scholar & Philosopher.

He pursued this course "with an Ardor natural to young men" and was "infinitely happy" for a while. In the earliest letter of Hume's we have, written when he was sixteen, he reports, "just now I am entirely confind to my self & Library for Diversion." Of his studies he says, "I take no more of them than I please, for I hate task-reading, & I diversify them at my Pleasure; sometimes a Philosopher, sometimes a Poet. . . . I live like a King pretty much by myself"—this being at Ninewells after he had left the university. He describes philosophy, in particular, as "a Subject I think much on & could talk all day long" about.[4]

Then, at the age of eighteen, he temporarily lost his enthusiasm. He reports that in early September, 1729, "all my Ardor seem'd in a moment to be extinguisht, & I cou'd no longer raise my **mind** to that pitch, which formerly gave me such excessive Pleasure." He blamed this listlessness on his own "Laziness of Temper, which must be overcome by redoubling my Application. In this Condition I remain'd for nine Months, very uneasy to myself." He also came down with scurvy and other ailments, getting medical attention and taking antihysteric pills and claret wine. His health and energy gradually returned. He writes, "I began to consider seriously, how I shou'd proceed in my Philosophical Enquiries." He was already rejecting those handed down from the past as "being entirely Hypothetical, & depending more upon Invention than Experience" and for being **dogmatically** constructed "without regarding human Nature." By the spring of 1734, Hume had decided upon a temporary change. As he writes, "I resolved to seek out a more active Life, & tho' I cou'd not quit my Pretensions in Learning, but with my last Breath, to lay them aside for some time, in order the more effectually to resume them." He opted for the life of a merchant over that of a traveling tutor and went to work for a businessman in Bristol.[5] (Soon after leaving Scotland, Hume was accused of fathering an illegitimate child; but he did not appear to defend himself against the mother's accusation, and there was insufficient evidence to find against him.) While in Bristol, he changed the spelling of his surname from "Home" to "Hume" to conform to the way it was pronounced. He quarreled with his supervisor and found his clerical work unpleasant. After a few months, he had "found that scene totally unsuitable" for himself and decided to abandon the world of commerce. In the summer of 1734, the twenty-three-year-old Hume "went over to France" to pursue his "studies in a country retreat," mainly at the Jesuit college of La Flèche, where Descartes had studied in the previous century. Hume spent "three years very agreeably" there, composing his *Treatise of Human Nature*, before returning to London in 1737.[6]

He was in London from the end of that year to early 1739, revising his *Treatise* and attempting to arrange for its publication. As he reports in a letter at that time,

> I began to feel some Passages weaker for the Style & Diction than I cou'd have wisht. The Nearness & Greatness of the Event rouz'd my Attention, & made me more difficult to please than when I was alone in perfect Tranquillity in France.

Enclosed with that letter were "some Reasonings concerning Miracles," which he feared would "give too much Offence" if published with the *Treatise*. He asks his correspondent to read them, to tell him what he thinks of them, but to show them to no one else before burning them. Hume acknowledges that his discarding such controversial passages of what he wrote in France is tantamount to

> castrating my Work, that is, cutting off its noble Parts, that is, endeavouring it shall give as little Offence as possible. This is a Piece of Cowardice, for which I blame myself; tho I believe none of my Friends will blame me. But I was resolv'd not to be an Enthusiast, in Philosophy, while I was blaming other Enthusiasms.[7]

At the end of 1738, Hume did arrange for the publication of his *Treatise,* the first two books of which appeared in early 1739; the third book required more revisions and was only published near the end of 1740. In 1740, Hume anonymously published an *Abstract* of the *Treatise*, which effectively crystallizes some of its key points. Reviews of the book were unfavorable. Hume comments in his autobiography,

> Never literary attempt was more unfortunate than my Treatise of Human Nature. It fell *dead-born from the press,* without reaching such distinction, as even to excite a murmur among the zealots.

Though this is a bit of an exaggeration of the book's poor reception, it poignantly indicates his disappointment over the response to a book on which he had worked so hard (and which today is recognized as his masterpiece and one of the greatest philosophy books ever written in the English language). Nevertheless, he goes on to say, "being naturally of a cheerful and sanguine temper, I very soon recovered the blow, and prosecuted with great ardour my studies in the country." He spent the next several years (1739–45) at Ninewells and in Edinburgh. He produced his *Essays Moral and Political*, which were published anonymously in Edinburgh in two volumes in 1741–42. Unlike his *Treatise,* they were a success. As he comments, "the work was favourably received, and soon made me entirely forget my former disappointment."[8] In June of 1742, he brags in a letter,

> The Essays are all sold in London. . . . There is a Demand for them; & . . . Innys the great Bookseller in Paul's Church Yard wonders there is not a new Edition, for that he cannot find Copies for his Customers.

He even expresses his hope that this success might help to "bring forward the rest of my Philosophy."[9]

In 1744, Hume applied for a vacant chair in ethics and spiritual philosophy at the University of Edinburgh. The person filling the position would be required to instruct students in Christian doctrine. He was accused "of Heresy, Deism, Scepticism,

Atheism," and so forth. As a result of the "popular Clamour" raised against him, he was denied the position. So, in 1745, he accepted a well paid job in England as "a travelling Tutor" to the Marquis of Annandale,[10] who proved to be insane, exhibiting erratic and occasionally violent behavior. While he was away, Hume was further distressed to hear of the death of his beloved mother, which event, he writes in a letter at that time, "leaves such an immense void in our Family."[11]

In 1746, Hume left the service of the Marquis and went to work as a private secretary to General James St. Clair, a distant relative planning an invasion of French Canada. As Hume indicates in a letter, he was prepared to accompany the general to America on this "Romantic Adventure"; but the expedition was aborted. The general had Hume commissioned as a judge-advocate and prepared his forces "to seek Adventures on the Coast of France"; but their assault on Brittany was ill-fated and failed.[12] In 1747, Hume visited "the courts of Vienna and Turin" on a secret mission with the general, wearing "the uniform of an officer." He says that these years of working with the general "were almost the only interruptions which my studies have received during the course of my life: I passed them agreeably and in good company; and my appointments, with my frugality, had made me reach a fortune" of nearly a thousand pounds.[13]

Hume was about six feet tall and, as a result of eating well during these years, had grown obese before leaving his job with the general. Lord Charlemont, who met him in Turin, left us this vivid description:

> Nature, I believe, never formed any man more unlike his real character than David Hume. . . . His face was broad and fat, his mouth wide, and without any other expression than that of imbecility. His eyes vacant and spiritless, and the corpulence of his whole person was far better fitted to communicate the idea of a turtle-eating alderman than of a refined philosopher.[14]

Hume decided to rework the material in Book I of his *Treatise*. As he said much later, "I had always entertained a notion, that my want of success in publishing the Treatise of Human Nature, had proceeded more from the manner than the matter"; so he "cast the first part of that work anew" to constitute his *Enquiry concerning Human Understanding,* which was published in 1748, while he was in Turin. But, as he observes, "this piece was at first little more

successful" than his *Treatise.* In 1749, he returned to Ninewells to live with his brother for a couple of years. He heard from his bookseller that his "former publications (all but the unfortunate Treatise) were beginning to be the subject of conversation; that the sale of them was gradually encreasing, and that new editions were demanded." In 1751, when his brother married, he moved to Edinburgh, where his sister lived, "the true scene for a man of letters." That same year, he published his *Enquiry concerning the Principles of Morals,* a revision of Book III of the *Treatise,* considered by Hume himself the best of all his writings; but, like his two earlier efforts at serious philosophy, it "came unnoticed and unobserved into the world." The following year, he published his *Political Discourses,* which he called "the only work of mine that was successful on the first publication. It was well received abroad and at home."[15] Hume's works were now receiving favorable reviews and were being published in collections, as well as being translated into French and German.

About this time, he was elected secretary of Edinburgh's Philosophical Society. He unsuccessfully applied for the Chair of Logic at Glasgow University in 1752, but was appointed Keeper of the Advocates' Library in Edinburgh. This latter position, which he held until resigning in 1757, placed thousands of printed materials at his disposal which could be used for the writing of his *History of England,* which was published in six volumes between 1754 and 1762. At first, this history was coolly received, but it became quite popular later in Hume's lifetime. He was assailed for being partial to the Stuart kings; as he wryly comments:

> English, Scotch, and Irish; Whig and Tory, churchman and sectary, free-thinker and religionist; patriot and courtier, united in their rage against the man, who had presumed to shed a generous tear for the fate of Charles I.

He confesses to being so discouraged as to consider retiring "to some provincial town," and changing his name. Yet he continued his work, becoming less sensitive about the attacks of critics. In 1757, he also published his *Four Dissertations*, one on "The Passions," adapted from Book II of his *Treatise,* including the controversial *Natural History of Religion,* which inspired a hostile pamphlet written "against it, with all the illiberal petulance, arrogance, and scurrility" typical of religious enthusiasts. He sardonically writes, "This pamphlet gave me some consolation for the otherwise indifferent reception" it had encountered.[16] He also was reviled for his first *Enquiry*, which he had published against the advice of friends, to one of whom he writes, "I won't justify the prudence of this step, any other way than by expressing my indifference about all the consequences that may follow."[17]

In 1763, after completing his *History of England*, Hume accompanied the Earl of Hertford, the British ambassador to France, to Paris, as personal secretary. It was as if Hume's reputation was purified. As he says in a letter that year, "I was now a Person clean & white as the driven Snow."[18] He still seems astonished by the warm welcome he received as he comments, in his autobiography, "Those who have not seen the strange effects of modes, will never imagine the reception I met with at Paris, from men and women of all ranks and stations." This popularity lasted for the entire twenty-six months he was in France, rather than proving to be a passing fancy. Hume (affectionately called *"le bon David"*) established warm friendships with d'Alembert and Diderot, the *philosophes* who edited the *Encyclopedia*. In the summer of 1765, Hume was officially "appointed secretary to the embassy" in Paris.[19]

While he was in France, Hume fell in love with a Madame de Boufflers, who was estranged from her husband and the mistress of the widowed Prince de Conti. At the time of their first meeting, Hume was fifty-two and she was thirty-eight. His letters from this period indicate that he was suffering "the inquietudes of the most unfortunate passion." He swears never to sever his devotion to her. His friend Gilbert Elliot visited him in France and wrote him subsequently, warning him "in friendship" that he was wavering "upon the very brink of a precipice" in this affair. But the infatuation only waned after her husband died and she became obviously obsessed with the goal of marrying the prince, with so little regard for Hume as to use him as her go-between. Yet Hume's caring loyalty towards her lasted for the rest of his life; indeed, five days before he died, he wrote her a letter of condolence for the death of the prince earlier that month.[20]

At the beginning of 1766, Hume left Paris for London, taking with him Jean-Jacques Rousseau, who was being persecuted for his recently published *Social Contract* and *Émile*. Although Hume had been warned about Rousseau's irascible character, he kindly helped him get settled in England. The paranoid Rousseau recklessly accused Hume of hypocritically plotting against him. Hume tried to defend himself in print against these public accusations and finally broke off all connections with the man. At the end of that year, in a letter to Madame de Boufflers, Hume writes, "Thanks to God, my affair with Rousseau is now finally and totally at an end, at least on my part: for I never surely shall publish another line on that subject."[21]

In 1767, Hume accepted an invitation to become under-secretary of state, despite his reluctance to continue living in England. Shortly before receiving that appointment, he describes London as "very little tempting to one, who believes he is there hated as a Scotsman and despised as a Man of Letters."[22] His political sympathies were for the Whigs, for republicanism, and for the American Colonies in their grievances against England. (In letters of 1775, he writes, "I am an American in my Principles, and wish we would let them alone to govern or misgovern themselves as they think proper" and that "the Republican Form of [Government] is by far the best."[23]) Still, he remained in office in London until August of 1769, when he retired to Edinburgh, "very opulent (for I possessed a Revenue of 1,000 £ a year), healthy, and though somewhat stricken in years, with the prospect of enjoying long my ease, and of seeing the increase of my reputation." He briefly considered marrying but cautiously refrained. He had a house built in St. Andrews Square in Edinburgh, where his (unmarried) sister lived with him. (The American Benjamin Franklin was among his first house-guests.) Hume maintained warm feelings for the large family of his brother John, living at Ninewells, being especially fond of his namesake nephew, David, and paying for his education at Glasgow. Towards the end of his autobiography he says, "In spring 1775, I was struck with a disorder in my bowels, which at first gave me no alarm, but has since, as I apprehend it, become mortal and incurable." Nevertheless, he maintained his good spirits and enthusiasm for his work.[24]

He was particularly anxious to complete his *Dialogues concerning Natural Religion*, which he had been writing, off and on, since the 1750s. A few months before his death, he writes of his intention to get it printed, saying, "Some of my Friends flatter me, that it is the best thing I ever wrote. I have hitherto forborne to publish it, because I was of late desirous to live quietly, and keep remote from all Clamour." He asked his friend Adam Smith to help get the *Dialogues* published, but the famous economist refused. In a codicil to his will, Hume provides for their eventual printing as well as for that of his autobiography: "I also ordain that if my dialogues from whatever cause, be not published within two years and a half of my death, as also the account of my life, the property shall return to my Nephew, David, whose duty in publishing them as the last request of his uncle, must be approved of by all the World." And he made certain that three different copies of the *Dialogues* were in the possession of his nephew, his publisher, William Strahan, and Adam Smith to ensure their eventual printing.[25]

Hume died on August 25, 1776 in Edinburgh. When he was buried four days later, a great crowd assembled in the rain and watched his coffin pass. In the final paragraph of his autobiography, he provides a self-assessment which rings true:

> I was, I say, a man of mild dispositions, of command of temper, of an open, social, and cheerful humour, capable of attachment, but little susceptible of enmity, and of great moderation in all my passions. Even my love of literary fame, my ruling passion, never soured my humour, notwithstanding my frequent disappointments.[26]

In a letter to Strahan, written several weeks later, Smith touchingly says of Hume,

> His temper, indeed, seemed to be more happily balanced, if I may be allowed such an expression, than that perhaps of any other man I have ever known. . . . The extreme gentleness of his nature never weakened either the firmness of his mind, or the steadiness of his resolutions. . . . Upon the whole, I have always considered him, both in his lifetime, and since his death, as approaching as nearly to the idea of a perfectly wise and **virtuous** man, as perhaps the nature of human frailty will admit.[27]

His autobiography was published the year after his death, as were two essays he had previously suppressed, "On Suicide" and "On the **Immortality** of the **Soul**"; but his cherished *Dialogues* were not published until 1779.

Reality

Hume is a **phenomenalist**, in the sense that he holds that we can only know **phenomena** as they appear in our experience and insofar as he is therefore sceptical of the possibility of our ever knowing the ultimate nature of anything in itself. Nevertheless, he never denies the reality of the external world, which is a **presupposition** of normal thought and action. As he writes in his first *Enquiry*, "The experienced train of events is the great standard, by which we all regulate our conduct."[28] But what things are included and which are excluded from our systems of reality, as well as our analysis of it in terms of **substance**, inhering properties, independent existence, and interconnectedness, are issues that do come under critical scrutiny in his philosophy.

Like most of us and like almost all significant Western philosophers from Aristotle to the end of the eighteenth century, Hume tends to conceive of reality in terms of substances and their modifications. But the very idea of substance is critically suspect. As we shall see, Hume's **empirical** thesis maintains that all legitimate ideas (and thus all genuine **knowledge**) must ultimately be derived from impressions of sensation and reflection. This leads him in his *Treatise* to demand the source of the alleged idea of substance. It does not seem to be derived directly from any combination of the senses since we cannot see, hear, smell, touch, or taste any substances but directly experience only their qualities. "The idea of substance must therefore be deriv'd from an impression of reflexion, if it really exist." But impressions of reflection are grounded in "our passions and emotions," which could only react to substances, rather than communicating them directly to the mind. "We have therefore no idea of substance, distinct from that of a collection of particular qualities." This brief but penetrating sceptical argument follows nicely from Hume's rigorously empirical epistemology, which we shall consider later. When we experience an apple, we see its red skin and white meat, feel its firm texture, smell its faint odor, taste its sweetness and hear the crunch made by our biting it; but we have no experience of

---

Phenomenalism. The view (as in Hume) that we can only be aware of appearances or sense data and never of things-in-themselves; this leads some phenomenalists (like Mill) to conceive of physical objects, such as sticks and stones, as mere sets of appearances or enduring possibilities of sensation

what its underlying substance is, independent of our ideas of such qualities. "The idea of a substance as well as that of a mode, is nothing but a collection of simple ideas, that are united by the imagination, and have a particular name assigned to them," whereby perceived qualities are "commonly refer'd to an unknown *something*, in which they are supposed to inhere." Nor are there any abstract realities, such as triangles in general or humanity in general, as the **Platonists** hold, since, as he writes later, "Every thing in nature is individual." We relate all our experiences to real existence in some way. However, "tho' every impression and idea we remember be consider'd as existent, the idea of existence is not deriv'd from any particular impression."[29] All we directly experience are our perceptions, and there is no difference between the idea of anything and the idea of that thing as existent, apart from our attitudinal feelings towards it.

Unlike Descartes, who considers existence a perfection, Hume says, "That idea, when conjoin'd with the idea of any object, makes no addition to it." We think of reality as interconnected, but again this does not conform to the findings of direct experience:

> Objects have no discoverable connexion together; nor is it from any other principle but custom operating upon the imagination, that we can draw any **inference** from the appearance of one to the existence of another.

Our views of reality are relative to our patterns of experience. Hume makes it clear that this critique of the possible knowability of substance, existence, and **intrinsic** interconnectedness applies to both physical and mental reality. Since an impression is different from an independently existing substance, it cannot exactly resemble it and therefore cannot adequately represent or copy it. As he argues,

> We have no perfect idea of any thing but of a perception. A substance is entirely different from a perception. We have, therefore, no idea of a substance.[30]

Since this **syllogism** is **valid**, it could only be disputed by means of a **refutation** of its **premises**. But we should notice that none of this denies that reality *may be* substantial, independently existent, and intrinsically interconnected. Hume's critique is epistemological, merely challenging any knowledge claims regarding the nature of reality in itself.

Bodies

The objects represented by our sense impressions are physical. As Hume writes in his *Treatise*,

> Upon opening my eyes, and turning them to the surrounding objects, I perceive many visible bodies; and upon shutting them again, and considering the distance betwixt these bodies, I acquire the idea of **extension**.

But what is this extension, which Descartes thought the very **essence** of physical reality? Hume is true to his empiricism in reducing it to that in the external object of experience which corresponds to our perceptions. For example, when we see a table, we experience "impressions of colour'd points, dispos'd in a certain manner." Thus, relative to visual perception, "the idea of extension is nothing but a copy of these colour'd points, and of the manner of their appearance" in experience. We think of bodies as extended in space as a result of "the disposition of visible and tangible objects" in our perceptual field. It is only through reflection on visual and tangible experience that we derive the idea of space; we never perceive it independently of bodies and their parts. We can analyze and critically assess our beliefs about bodies, as philosophy pushes us to do. However, according to Hume, " 'tis in vain to ask, *Whether there be body or not*? That is a point, which we must take for granted in all our reasonings," because it is a condition of sense experience itself. We cannot conceive of anything that is utterly divorced from all our perceptions. Yet we think of bodies as having a continuing existence distinct from our perceptions of them and may well ask "whether it be the *senses, reason,* or the *imagination,* that produces the opinion of a *continu'd* or of a *distinct* existence." Our senses cannot perform this role because they give us perceptions of the sensible qualities of bodies, which we directly experience, rather than the bodies themselves. The "three different kinds of impressions convey'd by the senses" are primary qualities, such as "the figure, bulk, motion and solidity of bodies," secondary qualities, such as "colours, tastes, smells, sounds, heat and cold," and feelings of "pains and pleasures" arising from their physical contact with our own bodies. These various appearances need not correspond to the intrinsic reality of bodies. Second, "we can attribute a distinct continu'd existence to objects without ever consulting reason, or weighing our opinions by any philosophical principles," as even little children and the most ignorant people do. Thus, reason is not the source of our normal "assurance of the continu'd and distinct existence of body." At this point, Hume is prepared to draw the **conclusion** of his **process-of-elimination argument**. If that assurance comes from "the *senses, reason,* or the *imagination,*" and if we have eliminated the first two, then we are left with the third. "That opinion must be entirely owing to the imagination." Our sense experiences "have a certain **coherence**," even when sporadic and interrupted. This coherence is rendered intelligible by our imagining an even "greater and more uniform" coherence in the objects perceived. Our imagination connects sense impressions and attributes a corresponding identity to the bodies perceived. "The smooth passage of the imagination along the ideas of the resembling perceptions makes us ascribe to them a perfect identity." We mistakenly assume that, through sensation, the experienced object, "which is intimately present to the mind, is the real body or material existence," rather than merely our perceptions, which are the only things immediately "present to the mind." In order to reconcile the conflict between imagination's perspective on our perceptions as having "a continu'd and uninterrupted existence" and reflection's analysis of all perceptions as individual and continuously interrupted, we resort to a distinction, ascribing "the *interruption* to perceptions, and the *continuance* to objects," even while supposing those "external objects to resemble internal perceptions" somehow.[31] But this is itself a fiction of the imagination, explaining but not proving our idea of bodies as having continuous, distinct existence.

Hume deals with bodies more briefly in his first *Enquiry*. He observes that physical reality behaves **deterministically**:

> It is universally allowed, that matter, in all its operations, is actuated by a necessary force, and that every natural effect is so precisely determined by the energy of its **cause**, that no other effect, in such particular circumstances, could possibly have resulted from it.

The deterministic behavior of matter in motion is so thoroughgoing that our very idea of **necessity** is most clearly related "to the operation of bodies." This is true even "in the human body," which is such "a mighty complicated machine" that we cannot always understand the many physical forces determining its behavior; but mystified as we may be by the workings of the body, we should not imagine "that the laws of nature are not observed with the greatest regularity in its internal operations and government." Hume reasserts his thesis concerning the unknowability of bodies apart from their experienced appearances:

> Bereave matter of all its intelligible qualities, both primary and secondary, you in a manner annihilate it, and leave only a certain unknown, inexplicable *something,* as the cause of our perceptions.[32]

Again, this is an epistemological, rather than an **ontological**, point that is sceptical about what we can know of bodies, without presuming to deny their reality. As it is practically beneficial for us to think of reality, in general, as substantial, existent, and inherently interconnected, so it works for us to conceive of bodies, the objects of our sense perceptions, as continuously and independently extended in themselves. But these are pragmatically justified beliefs rather than matters of certain knowledge.

Personality

A SCIENCE OF HUMAN NATURE. Human nature is rooted in the body and its experiences, but it must also encompass the development and functioning of personality. Hume wants to contribute to the construction of a "science of human nature," which, he says in his first *Enquiry*, can be approached in two different ways. "The one considers man chiefly as born for action; and as influenced in his measures by taste and sentiment; pursuing one object, and avoiding another, according to the values which these objects seem to possess"; this is the approach he takes in his second *Enquiry* and in the *Treatise*. Or, alternatively, philosophers can "consider man in the light of a reasonable rather than an active being, and endeavour to form his understanding more than cultivate his manners"; this is the approach he takes in the *Treatise* and here in the first *Enquiry*. Since man is both a reasonable and an active being, both the more theoretical and the more practical approaches are legitimate. Indeed, Hume recognizes at least three dimensions of human nature: a human is not only "a reasonable being" and "an active being," but "a sociable" one as well; and Hume's political essays will emphasize this facet of our nature. He warns that we must try to maintain a balanced point of view and not lose ourselves in abstruse profundities:

> Be a philosopher; but, amidst all your philosophy, be still a man.

Although admitting that "these reasonings concerning human nature" will sometimes strike the reader as "abstract" and "difficult," he says this should not be surprising, since "so many wise and profound philosophers" have failed to produce them in the past and the effort should prove worthwhile, given the immense importance of self-understanding. Later he adds that humans are motivated by their desires, which they naturally seek to satisfy:

> As Man is a reasonable Being and is continually in Pursuit of Happiness, which he hopes to find in the Gratification of some Passion or Affection, he seldom acts or speaks or thinks without a Purpose and Intention." He also warns us that the relationship between our bodies and the human personality is ultimately "**mysterious**."[33]

In the *Abstract* Hume expresses his goal of trying to determine "if the science of *man* will not admit of the same accuracy which several parts of natural philosophy are found susceptible of." He comments, "There seems to be all the reason in the world to imagine that it may be carried to the greatest degree of exactness." If this prospect is confirmed as realistic, the achievement should be momentous, since "almost all the sciences are comprehended in the science of human nature, and are dependent on it." But he warns us that this science will be empirical and lead to "very sceptical" conclusions regarding our **transcending** experienced phenomena and comprehending knowledge of things in themselves. Specifically, the idea of a knowable spiritual substance is rejected by such a science, for which "the soul, as far as we can conceive it, is nothing but a system or train of different perceptions, those of heat and cold, love and anger, thoughts and sensations; all united together, but without any simplicity or identity," such as was imagined by Descartes and earlier **metaphysicians**. As Hume avers,

> We have no idea of substance of any kind, since we have no idea but what is derived from some impression, and we have no impression of any substance either material or spiritual.[34]

This valid syllogism is grounded in a radically empirical epistemology, which, as we shall see, rules out metaphysical knowledge.

THE SCIENCES AND HUMAN NATURE.   In the introduction to his *Treatise*, Hume writes, " 'Tis evident that all the sciences have a relation, greater or less, to human nature." Since the judgments of mathematics, natural philosophy (or physics), and natural religion are only intelligible in the light of human "powers and **faculties**," even they presuppose "the knowledge of man." The connection is closer still in the case of logic, which rests on operations of human reasoning, morals and criticism, rooted in human "tastes and sentiments," and politics, which deals with humans as social and interdependent. Indeed, says Hume, "There is no question of importance, whose decision is not compriz'd in the science of man; and there is none, which can be decided with any certainty, before we become acquainted with that science." And as this science is "the only solid foundation for the other sciences," so its only adequate foundation must be "experience and observation," rather than abstract speculation. This may lead us to accept unwelcome and humbling conclusions—for example, that "the essence of the mind" is "equally unknown to us with that of external bodies" and that any *a priori* "hypothesis, that pretends to discover the ultimate original qualities of human nature, ought at first to be rejected as presumptuous and chimerical."[35] This empirical declaration of independence is a deliberate repudiation of the rationalistic approach of such thinkers as Plato and Descartes.

HUMANS AND ANIMALS.   Imagination plays a pivotal role in human thought and action for Hume (as also for Hobbes). In a footnote Hume explains that he sometimes uses the term in both a broader sense, to refer to the mind dealing with its mental images, and a narrower sense distinguished from the mental faculties of memory and reason: "When I oppose the imagination to the memory, I mean the faculty, by which we form our fainter ideas. When I oppose it to reason, I mean the same faculty, excluding only our demonstrative and probable reasonings." Other philosophers, like Descartes, try to claim that it is reason (or our rational soul) that radically distinguishes us from other animals. Yet we perceive other animals also "adapting means to ends" in their behavior. "A dog, that avoids fire and precipices, that shuns strangers, and caresses his master, affords us an instance" of behavioral patterns which "proceed from a reasoning, that is not in itself different, nor founded on different principles, from that which appears in human nature." We may protest that other animals "never perceive any real connexion among objects" and act only on the basis of custom stemming from experience. But, as we shall see in the next section, Hume argues that the same is true of humans. To object that we act on reason while other animals are merely driven by instinct is to fall back on a dubious distinction. Indeed, Hume writes, "To consider the matter aright, reason is nothing but a wonderful and unintelligible instinct in our souls,"[36] to the extent that we cannot fully understand or explain it.

He compares human nature to that of other animals, observing that humans and other animals alike derive expectations by inference from past experience and that this inference is based on psychological custom rather than on logical reason. As other animals are driven by instincts, so are we; indeed, Hume urges us to acknowledge "that the experimental reasoning itself, which we possess in common with beasts, and on which the whole conduct of life depends, is nothing but a species of instinct or mechanical power, that acts in us unknown to ourselves." On this view, traditional philosophers before Hobbes seem mistaken in supposing that reason sets us apart from other animals as radically different. In a long footnote Hume explains that nine ways in which humans "surpass animals in reasoning" are also sources of different degrees of human understanding.[37] So, distinctions between humans and other animals, like those among humans themselves, are quantitative and experientially explicable.

THE SOUL AS A BUNDLE OF PERCEPTIONS. Like Hobbes (and unlike Plato, Augustine, and Descartes), Hume seems not to believe in any soul as a spiritual substance that might exist and function independently of body and to prefer to speak of the mind or self. Yet in the *Treatise* he analyzes even that in phenomenalistic terms, saying that

> what we call a *mind,* is nothing but a heap or collection of different perceptions, united together by certain relations, and suppos'd, tho' falsely, to be endow'd with a perfect simplicity and identity.

Traditional philosophers from Plato through Descartes can object that our perceptions inhere in an immaterial substance called soul, which has an identity of its own, independent of body. But, as we have seen, Hume denies that we have any adequate idea of substance, whether material or immaterial. But then how can we comprehend the notion of perceptions inhering in something so unknowable? What does this do to our idea of the personal identity of a self? It reduces it to perceptions, which are the only immediate objects of our experience. Hume expresses the point quite personally:

> For my part, when I enter most intimately into what I call *myself,* I always stumble on some particular perception or other, of heat or cold, light or shade, love or hatred, pain or pleasure. I never can catch *myself* at any time without a perception, and never can observe any thing but the perception.

He admits that some philosophers, like Descartes, fancy they have introspective experience of the mind itself and that he does not know how to disprove their claims. "But setting aside some metaphysicians of this kind, I may venture to affirm of the rest of mankind, that they are nothing but a bundle or collection of different perceptions, which succeed each other with an inconceivable rapidity, and are in a perpetual flux and movement."[38]

THE THEATER OF THE MIND. This suggests another metaphor, and Hume compares the mind to "a kind of theatre, where several perceptions successively make their appearances"; yet he warns that the analogy is limited, in the sense that we cannot experience the theater itself or its constituent elements, but only the perpetually changing mental actions on the stage. In trying to account for the unity and coherence of our perceptions, we "feign" or imagine "the notion of a *soul,* and *self,* and *substance*" underlying them. "The identity, which we ascribe to the mind of man, is only a fictitious one," then, for all we know. And it is memory of the succession of perceptions that supports that fiction by discovering their connections. Yet even here imagination is fundamental to the workings of the mind, which requires the materials of images to process.

> The memory, senses, and understanding are, therefore, all of them founded on the imagination, or the vivacity of our ideas.

In the appendix to his *Treatise,* Hume acknowledges problems with this phenomenalistic account of the self, but he can see no escape from its underlying logic. As he expresses it syllogistically,

Every idea is deriv'd from preceding impressions; and we have no impression of self or substance, as something simple and individual. We have, therefore, no idea of them in that sense.

The first premise of this valid argument is rooted in his epistemology, which we shall consider in the following section. The second is based on his view that our impressions are only of phenomenal appearances. There is an **inconsistency** in this theory of the self, of which Hume himself is well aware. As he says,

> I am sensible, that my account is very defective, and that nothing but the seeming evidence of the precedent reasonings cou'd have induced me to receive it.

What ties our perceptions together in a "bundle"? What constitutes the unity of the play of images in the "theatre" of the mind?

> If perceptions are distinct existences, they form a whole only by being connected together. But no connexions among distinct existences are ever discoverable by human understanding. We only *feel* a connexion or determination of the thought, to pass from one object to another.

Hume honestly admits that he can find no way "to explain the principles, that unite our successive perceptions in our thought or consciousness." If we could experience either a persisting substance in which our perceptions inhere or "some real connexion among them," the apparent inconsistency would evaporate. But both of these options are ruled out by Hume's rigorous empiricism, and he seems to throw up his hands, exclaiming, "For my part, I must plead the privilege of a sceptic, and confess, that this difficulty is too hard for my understanding." But, with characteristic good humor, he immediately adds that he does not declare it absolutely insoluble and hopes that he or someone else will some day solve it.[39]

PASSIONS. Let us turn from Hume's phenomenalistic analysis of the mind to his account of human emotions or passions, discussed in his *Treatise*. The connecting link between these two topics is our perceptions, the only immediate objects of experience. All perceptions are either impressions or ideas, the latter being derived from the former (more on that in the following section). Our impressions are either *"original,"* derived from sensation, or *"secondary,"* derived from reflection on original perceptions or on the objects of original perceptions. Our passions or emotions, as immediately experienced, for example, are secondary impressions of reflection. These "reflective impressions" can be *"calm,"* as is "the sense of beauty and deformity," or *"violent,"* as are "the passions of love and hatred, grief and joy, pride and humility," although Hume admits that this is a rough distinction. He also distinguishes between "direct passions," such as "desire, aversion, grief, joy, hope, fear, despair, and security," which immediately arise from our perceptions of good and evil or pleasure and pain, and "indirect passions," such as "pride, humility, ambition, vanity, love, hatred, envy, pity, malice, generosity," and so forth, which arise from the same perceptions, "but by the conjunction of other qualities" as well, rather than simply and immediately. Pride and humility, for example, are conditioned by our self-image. "According as our idea of ourself is more or less advantageous, we feel either of those opposite affections, and are elated by pride, or dejected with humility." But, though the object of each is the same, "pride is a pleasant sensation, and humility a painful" one. By contrast, we may consider examples of calm emotions; *"beauty* of all kinds gives us a peculiar delight and satisfaction; as *deformity* produces pain" in **aesthetic** experience. The sources of these reactions are varied, since "beauty is such an order and construction of parts, as either by the *primary constitution* of our nature, by *custom,* or by *caprice,* is fitted to give a pleasure and satisfaction to the soul."[40] At any rate, for whatever reason, what we experience as beautiful arouses a calm pleasing emotion in us.

More important for Hume's purposes is our natural capacity for sympathy:

> No quality of human nature is more remarkable, both in itself and in its consequences, than that propensity we have to sympathize with others.

For this provides a basis for morals and social relations. This capacity does not extinguish our sense of self, which, Hume observes, "is always intimately present with us." Indeed, the more strongly we identify any object of experience with ourselves, the more passionately we tend to feel about it.

> As the immediate *object* of pride and humility is self or that identical person, of whose thoughts, actions, and sensations we are intimately conscious; so the *object* of love and hatred is some other person, of whose thoughts, actions, and sensations we are not conscious.

(Thus, for example, "self-love" and love of inanimate objects are "love" in an extended sense.) We can love or hate others for a wide variety of reasons. The sensation of love is pleasant, while that of hatred is normally unpleasant.

> Love is always follow'd by a desire of the happiness of the person belov'd, and an aversion to his misery: As hatred produces a desire of the misery and an aversion to the happiness of the person hated.

Our sympathy for fellow humans makes us capable of relating to their ill-fortune, rendering us susceptible to pity and malice, even when they bear no personal relationship to us.

> *Pity* is a concern for, and *malice* a joy in the misery of others, without any friendship or enmity to occasion this concern or joy.

Normally, benevolence accompanies love, and malevolence accompanies hatred; likewise, to a lesser extent, benevolence can be associated with pity, and malevolence with malice. Benevolence is normally experienced as pleasurable and malevolence as more or less unpleasant.[41]

The direct passions of desire and aversion involve the human will in an obvious way, although the will is not, strictly speaking, one of the passions. Hume defines it as *"the internal impression we feel and are conscious of, when we knowingly give rise to any new motion of our body, or new perception of our mind."* So it is a conscious feeling attached to our own activity. Some desires are quite calm, such as "the general appetite to good, and aversion to evil." Yet even when they are so calm that they "cause no disorder in the soul" and can be mistaken "for the determinations of reason," as passions, they can motivate the will. The same object, under different circumstances, can provoke either violent or calm passions in us. We usually think of passions as being violent emotions, and those are the sort most readily distinguished from reason. Some of our direct passions, such as "hunger, lust, and a few other bodily appetites," seem to "arise from a natural impulse or instinct." We are also motivated by the passions of hope and fear, whose objects play on the imagination, whether they be conceived of as probable or possible or even as certain or impossible.[42]

Hume disagrees with Hobbes's **egoistic** theory of personality, writing in the *Treatise*,

> So far from thinking, that men have no affection for any thing beyond themselves, I am of opinion, that tho' it be rare to meet with one, who loves any single person better than himself; yet 'tis as rare to meet with one, in whom all the kind affections, taken together, do not over-balance all the selfish.

We value "three different species of goods"—namely, "the internal satisfaction of our minds, the external advantages of our body, and the enjoyment of such possessions as we have acquir'd by our industry and good fortune." A satisfying life would include friends and loved ones in that third category. Human nature is such that sympathy is common. "The minds of all men are similar in their feelings and operations, nor can any one be actuated by any affection, of which all others are not, in some degree, susceptible." Of course, we cannot directly experience another person's emotional state. "We are only sensible of its causes or effects. From *these* we infer the passion: And consequently *these* give rise to our sympathy" for the person.[43]

* * *

Hume's "science of human nature," which is a philosophical psychology, is based on a careful analysis of the character and workings of our perceptions, which are allegedly the only immediate objects of our experience and observation and, therefore, the only adequate foundations of our knowledge claims.

Knowledge

THE PERCEPTIONS OF THE MIND. In his first *Enquiry* Hume expresses his hope that the "true metaphysics" of epistemology will "destroy the false and adulterate" metaphysics of the past and liberate us from senseless abstract speculation:

> The only method of freeing learning, at once, from these abstruse questions, is to enquire seriously into the nature of human understanding, and shew, from an exact analysis of its powers and capacity, that it is by no means fitted for such remote and abstruse subjects.

He is confident that there is truth to be discerned and comprehended regarding the powers and operations of the knowing mind. He observes the "considerable difference" between perceptions that are vividly experienced and those either recalled in memory or anticipated in imagination. For example, he says, "A man in a fit of anger, is actuated in a very different manner from one who only thinks of that emotion." He analyzes "the perceptions of the mind into two classes or species": impressions, which are "our more lively perceptions," such as are attained "when we hear, or see, or feel, or love, or hate, or desire, or will," on the one hand, and ideas, which are "less forcible and lively," such as our memories of past impressions or anticipations of future ones, on the other hand. What we regard as the "creative power of the mind amounts to no more than the faculty of compounding, transposing, augmenting, or diminishing the materials afforded us by the senses and experience"—namely, our perceptions. For example, the idea of "a golden mountain" is attained by the imaginative joining together of "two **consistent** ideas, *gold* and *mountain,* with which we were formerly acquainted" through sensation. But what is the relationship between our impressions and our ideas? A rough answer is that "all our ideas or more feeble perceptions are copies of our impressions or more lively ones."[44] But this breaks down even with the example we just considered of a golden mountain since we have never had an impression of any such thing.

At this point we must distinguish between simple and complex perceptions, as Hume emphasizes in his *Treatise*:

> Simple perceptions or impressions and ideas are such as admit of no distinction nor separation. The complex are the **contrary** of these and may be distinguished into parts.

It is a rash **generalization** to assert that all ideas correspond to, resemble, or copy impressions because some complex ideas, such as that of the golden mountain or of "the *New Jerusalem,* whose pavement is gold and walls are rubies," obviously do not. So, a more careful statement of the relation is that "every simple idea has a simple impression, which resembles it" and from which it is derived and that every complex idea is made up of such simple perceptions joined together. Thus, Hume's general rule regarding perceptions holds that

> *all our simple ideas in their first appearance are deriv'd from simple impressions, which are correspondent to them, and which they exactly represent.*

This means that we can be deprived of ideas by virtue of not experiencing certain sorts of impressions, "as when one is born blind or deaf." But almost immediately, Hume self-critically recognizes a **counterexample** to this general rule, imagining a person who, over a period of several decades, has perceived impressions of "colours of all kinds, excepting one particular shade of blue" and now arranges all the colors, from the darkest end of the spectrum over to the lightest extreme. Couldn't that person, "from his own imagination," Hume wonders, "raise up to himself the idea of that particular shade" of blue as intermediary between the next darkest shade and the next lightest shade, of both of which he has experienced impressions? Hume answers honestly, "I believe there are few but will be of opinion that he can; and this may serve as a proof, that the simple ideas are not always derived from the correspondent impressions." But then, unfortunately, he dismisses the significance of his own missing-shade-of-blue counterexample in a single clause, exclaiming that "the instance is so particular and singular, that 'tis scarce worth our observing, and does not merit that for it alone we should alter our general **maxim**." The impressions from which ideas can be derived themselves "may be divided into two kinds, those of Sensation and those of Reflexion." Through impressions of sensation one can see and hear one person hitting another, which provokes the idea of a drunken bully beating up an innocent victim. This idea, in turn, can evoke the impression of anger towards the aggressor, which impression of reflection can conjure up the reflective idea of a suitable punishment that might be inflicted on him. "So that the impressions of reflexion are only antecedent to their correspondent ideas; but posterior to those of sensation, and derived from them."[45] This indicates a complicated dynamic among our perceptions—simple versus complex impressions and ideas of sensation or reflection.

IDEAS DERIVED FROM IMPRESSIONS. Hume's radically empirical epistemology has no room for the sort of *a priori* ideas that Descartes called "innate." In an important footnote in his first *Enquiry,* Hume says that the word might be meaningfully used in various senses:

1. "If innate be equivalent to natural," then all our perceptions (impressions and ideas alike) can be regarded as such.
2. "If by innate be meant, contemporary to our birth," then none of our perceptions (neither any impressions nor any ideas) qualify.
3. If innate means "what is original or copied from no precedent perception," then we may say that "all our impressions are innate," but none of our ideas.

So, all ideas are derived from impressions, the ultimate source of all of which is concrete experience. He also proposes what we might call "Hume's empirical test" of ideas:

When we entertain, therefore, any suspicion, that a philosophical term is employed without any meaning or idea (as is but too frequent), we need but enquire, *from what impression is that supposed idea derived*? And if it be impossible to assign any, this will serve to confirm our suspicion,[46]

justifying our dismissing the notion as a senseless abstraction. Indeed, we have already (in the previous section) seen him applying this test to the idea of an enduring substantial self; and in subsequent sections we shall see him applying it to the ideas of freedom, virtue, God, and immortality.

RESEMBLANCE, CONTIGUITY, AND CAUSE AND EFFECT. But having ideas is not enough to establish even the possibility of knowledge, as bricks without mortar do not suffice to construct a stable wall. As Hume writes,

It is evident that there is a principle of connexion between the different thoughts or ideas in the mind, and that, in their appearance to the memory or imagination, they introduce each other with a certain degree of method and regularity.

Indeed, it turns out that there are three such principles used by the human mind to associate its ideas— "namely, *Resemblance, Contiguity* in time or place, and *Cause* or *Effect*." Hume provides a brief example of each of these three in turn:

A picture, naturally leads our thoughts to the original: The mention of one apartment in a building naturally introduces an enquiry or discourse concerning the others: And if we think of a wound, we scarcely forbear reflecting on the pain which follows it.

The first two of these, resemblance and spatio-temporal contiguity, are intuited through sensation or reflection; by contrast, as we shall see, causation is far more difficult to explain. Hume analyzes the objects of human reasoning into two types: "*Relations of Ideas*," such as the truths of mathematics, which are "either intuitively or demonstratively certain," on the one hand, and "Matters of Fact," such as the claims of science and common sense, which are highly likely or extremely probable, at best, on the other hand. We can discern the indubitable truth of an abstract relation of ideas like the Pythagorean Theorem merely by analyzing the conceptual interrelationships among its constituent terms. By contrast, the truth concerning matters of fact can only be established by means of concrete experience and can never be rendered absolutely certain. As Hume puts it,

The contrary of every matter of fact is still possible; because it can never imply a **contradiction**.

Loosely speaking, we might claim to know that the Sun will rise tomorrow, on the basis of our **inductive** generalization from past experience that it does so every day. Yet it is theoretically possible that it will explode tonight and never "rise" again.

That the sun will not rise to-morrow is no less intelligible a proposition, and implies no more contradiction, than the affirmation, *that it will rise*. We should in vain, therefore, attempt to demonstrate its falsehood,[47]

as we reasonably could do in the case of $2 + 3 = 9$. So, matters of fact have to do with **existential** reality but can only be rationally established as more or less probable; whereas relations of ideas can be rationally established as certain but only deal with concepts of the mind.

THE PROBLEM OF CAUSAL CONNECTIONS.

All reasonings concerning matter of fact seem to be founded on the relation of *Cause and Effect*. By means of that relation alone we can go beyond the evidence of our memory and senses.

Thus, the question of what we can know of causal connections is critical to any factual knowledge which is rationally established (that is not derived directly from sensation and memory). Hume holds that our awareness of the causal relation is never "attained by reasonings a priori; but arises entirely from experience." Let us consider his example of a billiard ball colliding with another ball which was previously stationary.

Motion in the second Billiard-ball is a quite distinct event from motion in the first; nor is there any thing in the one to suggest the smallest hint of the other.

Because of familiar past experiences, we customarily "know" what to expect when the balls collide. But many other possible outcomes could result, all of which are theoretically as "consistent and conceivable" as the one we, in fact, prefer in our anticipations. "All our reasonings a priori will never be able to shew us any foundation for this preference."[48]

We may consider three questions, the first two of which Hume thinks easily answered, while the third is not: First, "*What is the nature of all reasonings concerning matter of fact?*" He has already said that they are all based on the relationship between cause and effect. Second, "*What is the foundation of all our reasonings and conclusions concerning that relation?*"

He answers, in a single word, "experience." But, third, *What is the foundation of all conclusions from experience?* This, he responds, is a question "of more difficult solution and explication." We may know what we have experienced in the past. But how can we justify conclusions about the present or future inferred from the findings of past experience, no matter how certain those findings may be? This is the problem of induction. Hume's example is as good as any:

> The bread, which I formerly eat, nourished me; that is, a body of such sensible qualities, was, at that time, endued with such secret powers: But does it follow, that other bread must also nourish me at another time, and that like sensible qualities must always be attended with like secret powers?

We would need to be able to justify this move from past experience to future results in order to substantiate a general knowledge claim such as "bread is nutritious." He asks us to notice the difference between a report on past experience, such as *"I have found that such an object has always been attended with such an effect,"* and a prediction about future experience, such as *"I foresee, that other objects, which are, in appearance, similar, will be attended with similar effects."* Granted that we reasonably infer the second statement from the first, by what argument might that inference be justified? An appeal to the uniformity of nature does not help us here since it is **circular reasoning**. Our inductive inferences from experience do, indeed, presuppose "that the future will resemble the past" in key relevant respects; but our investigation is exposing the theoretical possibility "that the course of nature may change, and that the past may be no rule for the future," which would render prior experience inferentially useless.

> It is impossible, therefore, that any arguments from experience can prove this resemblance of the past to the future; since all these arguments are founded on the supposition of that resemblance.

Yet the uniformity of nature is not a **self-evident** *a priori* truth. Nor does it help us solve the problem to object that we do successfully act as if the uniformity of nature is in place as a principle justifying the causal inference. Hume writes,

> My practice, you say, refutes my doubts. But you mistake the purport of my question. As an agent, I am quite satisfied in the point; but as a philosopher, who has some

share of curiosity, I will not say scepticism, I want to learn the foundation of this inference.[49]

CUSTOM AND BELIEF. Indeed a sceptical view is emerging here. Yet Hume wryly assures us that it is practically "harmless and innocent" and poses no threat to the thoughts and actions of ordinary life.

> Nature will always maintain her rights, and prevail in the end over any abstract reasoning whatsoever.

But let us return to the problem of establishing the basis of causal reasoning. Hume invites us to engage in a brief thought-experiment. Imagine a person, who is as smart as we are but who is deprived of any experience of physical objects interacting as billiard balls do on a pool table, being suddenly dropped into our world and immediately having such an experience. "He would not, at first, by any reasoning, be able to reach the idea of cause and effect; since the particular powers, by which all natural operations are performed, never appear to the senses." Unless and until he acquires further experience, he will be simply bewildered by what he perceives. But imagine that he continues to live in our world so that, after a while, "he has acquired more experience" of such events. Now he does draw causal inferences. Yet he has still not perceived any power whereby causes produce effects. These inferences, if not purely arbitrary, must be determined by some principle. But what is it? Hume answers,

> This principle is custom or habit. For wherever the repetition of any particular act or operation produces a propensity to renew the same act or operation, without being impelled by any reasoning or process of the understanding; we always say, that this propensity is the effect of *Custom*.

Like Aristotle and Aquinas and unlike Plato and Descartes, Hume sees habit or custom as a pivotal element of human thought and action.

> Custom, then, is the great guide of human life. It is that principle alone, which renders our experience useful to us, and makes us expect, for the future, a similar train of events with those which have appeared in the past.

Apart from its influence, our factual knowledge would be confined to objects "immediately present to the memory and senses." Planning would be rendered impossible. "There would be an end at once of all action, as well as of the chief part of speculation." But custom must always be anchored in past experience.[50]

Custom establishes beliefs, which guide our thoughts and actions in ways that imaginative fictions do not. But what is "the difference between such a fiction and belief?" It is not their objects, which may be identical.

> It follows, therefore, that the difference between *fiction* and *belief* lies in some sentiment or feeling, which is annexed to the latter, not to the former, and which depends not on the will, nor can be commanded at pleasure.

It is this feeling or sentiment that renders belief "a more vivid, lively, forcible, firm, steady conception of an object, than what the imagination alone is ever able to attain." This feeling is established by the customary conjunctions of past experience, rendering "the sentiment of belief" a more settled conviction than any "mere fictions of the imagination." The child who believes in Santa Claus may have the same conception of him as the adult who regards him as fictitious; but the child has an "intense and steady" feeling about him which the adult has not, because of the "customary conjunction" between that conception and the pattern of fulfilled anticipations experienced by the child (but broken for the adult).[51]

CAUSAL CONNECTIONS EXPLAINED. Our belief in causal connections is fundamental to our thought and action. As Hume writes, there is "no such thing as *Chance* in the world." What sort of argument might justify our belief in causal connection and elimination of chance? A footnote distinguishes three types of arguments as "*demonstrations*," based on abstract relations of ideas, "**proofs**," based on experience but certain enough to "leave no room for doubt or opposition," and "*probabilities*," based on the calculation of likelihood falling short of certainty.[52] The first of these is clearly out of the question here; so any argument in this case will have to be either an empirical proof or a **probability argument**. Can we prove or establish as probable that our idea of necessary connection applies to events in the world which we identify as causes and effects?

Later, Hume reminds us of his empirical test:

> It seems a proposition, which will not admit of much dispute, that all our ideas are nothing but copies of our impressions, or, in other words, that it is impossible for us to *think* of anything, which we have not antecedently *felt*, either by our external or internal senses.

So, let us seek the impression or set of impressions that will provide an adequate source for our idea of necessary connection. But we find no such impression in the physical world of "external objects" of sensation. We only perceive a contiguity in time and space between causes and effects (their physical proximity at a certain time) and the temporal priority of the cause to the effect (the causal event occurring before its effect). But if we cannot find this impression in our sensation of external objects, perhaps we should consider "whether this idea be derived from reflection on the operations of our own minds, and be copied from any internal impression." Indeed, when we desire to raise our hands, we normally feel that we have the power to cause such an action to occur: "An act of volition produces motion in our limbs, or raises a new idea in our imagination. This influence of the will we know by consciousness"—and so we might suppose that we arrive at the idea of necessary connection as one derived from reflection, "since it arises from reflecting on the operations of our own mind, and on the command which is exercised by will, both over the organs of the body and faculties of the soul." But, as we "proceed to examine this pretension," we find that it is illusory. In fact, we find no impression of the necessary connection between an act of will and movements in bodily organs or mental activities. Again, all we directly perceive is the conjunction between the act of will and the subsequent physical movement or mental activity and nothing necessarily connecting the two. For all we know, as some of Descartes's followers fancifully suppose, the former may be merely an occasion for God's causing the latter. So, it appears, "we have sought in vain for an idea of power or necessary connexion, in all the sources from which we could suppose it to be derived." We perceive spatio-temporal contiguity between causes and effects and the temporal priority of the former over the latter, but never any necessary connection between them; the most we directly experience is their constant conjunction. In a now famous passage, Hume says,

> All events seem entirely loose and separate. One event follows another; but we never can observe any tye between them. They seem *conjoined*, but never *connected*.

Proof. Evidence establishing a fact or an argument establishing a conclusion; often identified with a demonstration, as leading to certainty (though Hume distinguishes a proof as an argument from experience)

Probability argument. Any argument (such as an inductive one) designed to establish its conclusion as more or less likely or probable, rather than as certain

This leads him to an *apparent* conclusion (but notice in what follows how he emphasizes "seems"):

> And as we can have no idea of any thing, which never appeared to our outward sense or inward sentiment, the necessary conclusion *seems* to be, that we have no idea of connexion or power at all, and that these words are absolutely without any meaning, when employed either in philosophical reasonings, or common life.[53]

We have been unable to detect either an external impression of sensation or an internal impression of reflection that will satisfy Hume's empirical test and seem driven to an extremely sceptical conclusion regarding the legitimacy of the fundamental idea of causal connection. "But," says Hume, "there still remains one method of avoiding this conclusion, and one source which we have not yet examined." What if the answer lies, not in our observation of any individual conjunction of events, but in our reaction to an experienced pattern of such conjunctions? Here lies Hume's solution to the problem of the experiential source of our idea of causal connection—in the felt sentiment or belief of the mind that reflects on the observation of such conjunctions.

> This connexion, therefore, which we *feel* in the mind, this customary transition of the imagination from one object to its usual attendant, is the sentiment or impression, from which we form the idea of power or necessary connexion.

The necessary connection for which we have been searching, then, reduces to a feeling in the mind rather than being any object of observation. "When we say, therefore, that one object is connected with another, we mean only, that they have acquired a connexion in our thought." Hume admits that this conclusion is "somewhat extraordinary," but it does provide an experiential basis for this fundamental idea. Yet because this connection seems arbitrary and **contingent** on circumstances, it looks more like a probability argument than the sort of proof that involves **certainty** and necessity. This leads Hume to a definition of a cause as "*an object, followed by another, and where all the objects, similar to the first, are followed by objects similar to the second*"; this definition focuses on the conjunction between types of objects of experience. But, because this conjunction establishes a connection in the mind, a second definition of cause is offered, as "*an object followed by another, and whose appearance always conveys*

the thought to that other"; this shifts the focus from the conjunction of objects of experience to the connection in the mind. We have no more than probable knowledge of the relationship between causes and effects. We must first experience patterns of conjunctions between them.

> We then *feel* a new sentiment or impression, to wit, a customary connexion in the thought or imagination between one object and its usual attendant; and this sentiment is the original of that idea which we seek for.

Since all reasonings regarding matters of fact are based on causal connections, it would seem that they too can only be probable, never yielding absolutely certain conclusions. As Hume adds, another basis for claiming that such reasonings can never be more than probable is that they are inevitably "founded on a species of **analogy**,"[54] which must be inductive and probabilistic.

SCEPTICISM. This is a very sceptical conclusion, to which Hume has been led by following the logic of his extremely empirical epistemology, which bases all knowledge on ideas, all of which must be derived from the impressions of concrete experience. All we can know with certainty are relations of ideas and matters of fact presently perceived through sensation or memory. But, as Hume points out, there are at least three different types of scepticism; and it is appropriate to realize that he rejects two of them in favor of the third. First, what he calls "*antecedent*" scepticism is represented by Descartes and is a preliminary unwillingness to accept any beliefs unless and until they are established as indubitable; although a "moderate" amount of such caution can be a healthy antidote to personal bias, the practice of "universal doubt" would be "entirely incurable" except for the fact that it is practically impossible. Second, there is "*consequent*" scepticism, whereby philosophy allegedly leads people to the view that "their mental faculties" are so deceptive or impotent as to be incapable of reaching any reliable conclusions; but this is a stultifying position that would lead to paralysis, except that it is naturally undone by the practical need for "action, and employment, and the occupations of common life." Third, there is "a more *mitigated* scepticism," which requires "a degree of doubt, and caution, and modesty" about our knowledge claims, as well as "the limitation of our enquiries to such subjects as are best adapted to the narrow capacity of human understanding"; Hume is a "mitigated" sceptic in this sense. But what gets chopped off the block in his mitigated scepticism is the area of traditional metaphysics, including philosophical theology, as he makes clear in the famous final paragraph of his first *Enquiry*. There he recommends that whenever we pick up any book "of divinity or school metaphysics," we should ask two questions about it. "*Does it contain any abstract reasoning concerning quantity or number?*" Since, unlike a book of mathematics, it is not dealing merely with abstract conceptual relations, the answer will be, "No. *Does it contain any experimental reasoning concerning matter of fact and existence?*" Since it does not purport to be a work of empirical science, the answer again will be, "No." Hume immediately draws his inflammatory conclusion: "Commit it then to the flames: For it can contain nothing but **sophistry** and illusion."[55]

As the *Treatise* makes clear, reason never can establish any factual knowledge as certain. This is what Hume means when he says that "all knowledge degenerates into probability; and this probability is greater or less," relative to our experience and the circumstances. It is in relation to our reasoning concerning matters of fact that he writes that "all knowledge resolves itself into probability, and becomes at last of the same nature with that evidence, which we employ in common life." In other words, it is neither demonstrative nor empirically proved, and thus never certain. This is a scepticism that can assume the form of "clouds" of "melancholy," which Hume says are dispelled by the practical distractions and necessities of nature and society:

> I dine, I play a game of back-gammon, I converse, and am merry with my friends; and when after three or four hours' amusement, I wou'd return to these speculations, they appear so cold, and strain'd, and ridiculous, that I cannot find in my heart to enter into them any farther. I find myself absolutely and necessarily determin'd to live, and talk, and act like other people in the common affairs of life.

Yet, after a while, he tires of such distractions and amusements and finds himself drawn back to his philosophical reasonings by intellectual curiosity and the hope of justifying his beliefs and distinguishing those that can from those that cannot be known.[56]

Freedom

CASUAL NECESSITY AND DETERMINISM. Like Hobbes, Hume is led to a position of determinism by his rigorous empiricism, adopting a sceptical attitude towards the view that any actions are free of causal determination. We have already seen Hume's assertion that there is "no such thing as *Chance* in the world." Logically, this should imply that whatever we do, there is no chance or possibility that we could have done otherwise, given that set of conditions antecedent to our acting. Hume's best discussion of human freedom is the section of his first *Enquiry*, "Of Liberty and Necessity," where he claims that this "long disputed question" has gone without a conclusive answer because of a lack of conceptual clarity surrounding it and that "a few intelligible definitions would immediately put an end to the whole controversy." He reminds us of the conclusions drawn from his empirical analysis of causal necessity:

> Our idea, therefore, of necessity and causation arises entirely from the uniformity, observable in the operations of nature; where similar objects are constantly conjoined together, and the mind is determined by custom to infer the one from the appearance of the other.

On this view causal necessity comprises a combination of two factors. "Beyond the constant **conjunction** of similar objects, and the consequent *inference* from one to the other, we have no notion of any necessity, or connexion." So, the question before us is whether, and to what extent, such necessity pertains to human actions.

> It is universally acknowledged, that there is a great uniformity among the actions of men, in all nations and ages, and that human nature remains still the same, in its principles and operations. The same motives always produce the same actions.

Consequently, there does appear to be a high degree of constant conjunction experienced. Indeed, this is the basis for the powerful value of history, that it reveals

---

Conjunction (from the Latin *conjunctio*, meaning a joining together or combination). The act of joining together or the fact of things being combined

the constant and **universal** principles of human nature, by shewing men in all varieties of circumstances and situations, and furnishing us with materials, from which we may form our observations, and become acquainted with the regular springs of human action and behaviour.

It is because of the uniformity of human behavior—that is, the constant conjunction between circumstances (including character and motivation) and action—that history provides us with useful, applicable lessons. In support of his point Hume asks us to imagine "a traveler, returning from a far country" with tales of humans whose behavior is "wholly different" from any with which we are familiar, who, for example, are completely devoid of "avarice, ambition, or revenge; who knew no pleasure but friendship, generosity, and public spirit"; Hume observes that we would not believe such stories because they are so diametrically opposed to the entire course of our experience, which it would be foolish to dismiss.

> By means of this guide, we mount up to the knowledge of men's inclinations and motives, from their actions, expressions, and even gestures; and again, descend to the interpretation of their actions from our knowledge of their motives and inclinations.[57]

The capacity for such understanding is of great practical value to us and would be nullified if human behavior were not uniform.

On the other hand, our behavior does not appear completely predictable, as does that of falling rocks. As Hume admits, "We must not, however, expect that this uniformity of human actions should be carried to such a length, as that all men, in the same circumstances, will always act precisely in the same manner, without making any allowance for the diversity of characters, prejudices, and opinions. Such a uniformity in every particular, is found in no part of nature." Our behavior is far more complex, and thus less readily predictable, than that of rocks because of personality and the intricate network of psychological influences upon it. Hume goes even further in his acknowledgment of the difficulty:

> I grant it possible to find some actions, which seem to have no regular connexion with any known motives, and are exceptions to all measures of conduct, which have ever been established for the government of men.

Random, self-destructive acts of violence not apparently brought on by physical disease or psychological disorder or emotional distress may appear devoid of any causal explanation. But, Hume responds, we should remember that our awareness and understanding are limited and that there are many determining causes of which we remain ignorant, particularly regarding human personalities and motives.

> The most irregular and unexpected resolutions of men may frequently be accounted for by those, who know every particular circumstance of their character and situation.

Indeed, Hume is confident that, to the extent that we understand people's characters, "the conjunction between motives and **voluntary** actions is as regular and uniform, as that between the cause and effect in any part of nature" and is popularly assumed as a matter of course.[58]

Not only do we have probable reason to accept the customary conjunction between the determinations of character, motives, and circumstances, on the one hand, and the subsequent patterns of action, on the other hand, but this also provides the basis for our common *"inferences* concerning them," which, we recall, is the other ingredient in Hume's analysis of causal necessity. Both our theoretical and our practical commitments presuppose this "doctrine of necessity, and this *inference* from motives to voluntary actions; from characters to conduct" in human life. Hume gives an example of a prisoner condemned to capital punishment; he knows that the actions of the prison guards and executioner are predictable and as causally determinative of his impending death as are "the walls and bars" that now detain him and "the ax" that will soon dispatch him. All of these factors combined determine his future with overwhelming probability. "Here is a connected chain of natural causes and voluntary actions; but the mind feels no difference between them, in passing from one link to another" while drawing its inferences. In case we find it difficult to relate to the capital criminal, Hume provides another example that might more readily hit home for most of us.

> Were a man, whom I know to be honest and opulent, and with whom I live in intimate friendship, to come into my house where I am surrounded with my servants, I rest assured, that he is not to stab me before he leaves it, in order to rob me of my silver.

Because I know him, his character, his values, his habits, and his circumstances, I can be and am confident of his behavior. A critic might object, "*But he may have been seized with a sudden and unknown frenzy.*—So may a sudden earthquake arise, and shake and tumble my house about my ears," Hume responds. In other words, of course, it is theoretically possible that any of our predictions concerning human behavior will prove to be mistaken, but the same is true of our anticipations regarding physical events. Thus, we do not achieve strict certainty here but can encounter extremely high degrees of probability, "proportioned to our experience of the usual conduct of mankind in such particular situations."[59]

People are far more willing to accept the causal necessity of physical events than that of human acts of the will because they feel a connection between physical causes and physical effects.

> But being once convinced, that we know nothing farther of causation of any kind, than merely the *constant conjunction* of objects, and the consequent *inference* of the mind from one to another, and finding, that these two circumstances are universally allowed to have place in voluntary actions; we may be more easily led to own the same necessity common to all causes.

Hume's argument here is fairly straightforward; if there are two conditions sufficient to establish necessity and both apply to acts of the human will, then those actions must occur necessarily. Likewise, the challenge for traditional defenders of free will in their theories is clear: let them

> try whether they can there form any idea of causation and necessity, except that of a constant conjunction of objects, and subsequent inference of the mind from one to another. If these circumstances form, in reality, the whole of that necessity, which we conceive in matter, and if these circumstances be also universally acknowledged to take place in the operations of the mind, the dispute is at an end.

Nor need we give up the concepts of freedom or liberty, so long as we recognize that they are a species of determinism or necessity (nowadays this is called **compatibilism**). What we should avoid is the illusions that there is no uniform conjunction between causal influences and voluntary actions and that the former provide no adequate grounds for inferring the latter.

> By liberty, then, we can only mean *a power of acting or not acting, according to the determinations of the will.*

All actions are necessarily determined; but what we call voluntary actions are necessarily determined from within, by the will. Hume does not pursue the question of what, in turn, determines the will; but its actions too must be caused, and every cause involves, by "definition, a *necessary connexion* with its effect."

Hume utterly repudiates the traditional identification of freedom with the absence of necessary connections (between causal influences and the will) as "the same thing with chance; which is universally allowed to have no existence" at all.[60]

Hume proceeds to explore some of the implications of this deterministic theory.

> All laws being founded on rewards and punishments, it is supposed as a fundamental principle, that these motives have a regular and uniform influence on the mind, and both produce the good and prevent the evil actions.

The laws, backed up by political sanctions, determine that we shall voluntarily act in prescribed ways, exerting causal influence on our behavior. Second, personal responsibility requires that human actions should have been determined by the will. Whenever actions do not proceed "from some *cause* in the character and disposition of the person who performed them, they can neither redound to his honour, if good; nor infamy, if evil." A person is only responsible for the actions determined by his will, which is why we excuse insane behavior. If action is not determined by the will, which, in turn, is necessitated by a combination of character, motives, and circumstances, then

> a man is as pure and untainted, after having committed the most horrid crime, as at the first moment of his birth, nor is his character any wise concerned in his actions; since they are not derived from it, and the wickedness of the one can never be used as a proof of the depravity of the other.

So, Hume insists that liberty, as he has defined it, is "essential to morality, and that no human actions, where it is wanting, are susceptible of any moral qualities, or can be the objects either of approbation or dislike."[61]

AN ATTACK ON FREE WILL.   In his *Treatise* Hume attacks

> the **scholastic** doctrine of *free-will*, which, indeed, enters very little into common life, and has but small influence on our vulgar and popular ways of thinking. According to that doctrine, motives deprive us not of free-will, nor take away our power of performing or forbearing any action.

It is this denial of necessary determination in our voluntary actions that Hume regards as unjustified. He points out that even the most ardent supporters of free will "acknowledge the force of *moral evidence*, and both in speculation and practice proceed upon it, as upon a reasonable foundation." But all moral evidence, purporting to show that people are saints or scoundrels, having virtuous or **vicious** characters, "is nothing but a conclusion concerning the actions of men, deriv'd from the consideration of their motives, temper and situation." We cannot read people's souls, yet we routinely make moral judgments about them. This presupposes that actions which we do observe are causally determined by characters which we cannot observe. " 'Tis only from experience and the observation of their constant union, that we are able to form this inference." Second, we may be reluctant to accept that our wills are necessarily determined because we are often not aware of the causal influences motivating them. "We feel that our actions are subject to our will on most occasions, and imagine we feel that the will itself is subject to nothing" or free of all necessity. But our ignorance of determining factors does not render them inoperative.

> We may imagine we feel a liberty within ourselves; but a spectator can commonly infer our actions from our motives and character; and even where he cannot, he concludes in general, that he might, were he perfectly acquainted with every circumstance of our situation and temper, and the most secret springs of our complexion and disposition.

Third, Hume argues that reason by itself can neither motivate the will nor effectively oppose the passions that do motivate it. After all, as we have seen, the function of reason is to make judgments. "The understanding exerts itself after two different ways, as it judges from demonstration or probability; as it regards the abstract relations of our ideas, or those relations of objects, of which experience only gives us information"—namely, matters of fact. But even when such judgments guide actions, they cannot motivate them and must depend on the impulses of our passions and desires.

> Since reason alone can never produce any action, or give rise to volition, I infer, that the same faculty is as incapable of preventing volition, or of disputing the preference with any passion or emotion.[62]

If reason, by itself, is incapable of generating impulses of will or causing voluntary actions, then, it seems, it must also be incapable of opposing such impulses or blocking such actions. In one of the most famous sentences he ever wrote, Hume says,

> Reason is, and ought only to be the slave of the passions, and can never pretend to any other office than to serve and obey them.

However, passions can be legitimately considered "unreasonable" when they are either "founded on the supposition of the existence of objects, which really do not exist" or moving us to employ means which are inadequate to achieve the desired end. Apart from such mistaken judgments, there can be no conflict between reason and the passions that motivate the will. As Hume flamboyantly expresses the point,

> 'Tis not contrary to reason to prefer the destruction of the whole world to the scratching of my finger. 'Tis not contrary to reason for me to chuse my total ruin, to prevent the least uneasiness of an *Indian* or person wholly unknown to me.

If I think the destruction of the world will do me less damage than the scratching of my finger, then I am mistaken; and if I superstitiously believe that my self-destructive behavior will magically secure bliss for someone who has nothing to do with me, I am in error.

> In short, a passion must be accompany'd with some false judgment, in order to its being unreasonable; and even then 'tis not the passion, properly speaking, which is unreasonable, but the judgment.[63]

As we are about to see, this view has a direct bearing on Hume's theory of morality.

Morality

THE ISSUE OF MORALITY'S SOURCE. Hume is certain that our wills can be sufficiently influenced by moral values that we shall choose to develop virtuous characters and to adopt right actions. Indeed, despite his well-deserved reputation for scepticism, in his second *Enquiry*, he takes it for granted that we do make moral distinctions and can rely on experience to realize that others do as well. He is interested in the question of whether these are ultimately derived "from reason, or from sentiment; whether we attain the knowledge of them by a chain of argument and induction, or by an immediate feeling and finer internal sense." Are morals objective and universal, or are they **subjective** and relative? He points out that arguments can be presented on both sides. On behalf of rational objectivism it can be said that we only dispute matters of objective, rational truth, not matters of subjective, emotive taste, and that we clearly do dispute about morality. On behalf of emotive **relativism** it can be said that the purpose of morality is to motivate us to do our duty and to pursue virtue, but that (as we have seen) reason is impotent to motivate action, as only the passions or feelings can do. Hume finds "arguments on each side" of the controversy to be "so plausible" that he wonders if morality might be the joint product of "*reason* and *sentiment*" combined, but he says that he is not ready to decide the issue until he has completed an empirical study of moral values, grounded in "fact and observation" and beginning with an analysis of two "social virtues, benevolence and justice."[64]

PUBLIC UTILITY AND VIRTUES. Using language as a guide to our feelings, we notice that the words associated with benevolence connote approval.

> The epithets *sociable, good-natured, humane, merciful, grateful, friendly, generous, beneficent,* or their equivalents, are known in all languages, and universally express the highest merit, which *human nature* is capable of attaining.

Why do we so universally approve of this quality in people, whatever we call it? We see it as generally conducive to "the happiness and satisfaction" of human beings and normally cannot help relating to and approving of that. Thus,

> the utility, resulting from the social virtues, forms, at least, a *part* of their merit, and is one source of that approbation and regard so universally paid to them.

This element of "public utility" is at least a significant part of the reason we regard benevolence as a moral virtue and approve of it. The moral virtue of justice, by contrast, is entirely founded on beneficial consequences, so that

> public utility is the *sole* origin of justice, and that reflections on the beneficial consequences of this virtue are the *sole* foundation of its merit.

Hume realizes that this **consequentialist** thesis is controversial and, therefore, provides an argument based on four hypothetical scenarios to render it more plausible. He asks us, first, to imagine a paradise situation, in which

> nature has bestowed on the human race such profuse *abundance* of all *external* conveniences, that, without any uncertainty in the event, without any care or industry on our part, every individual finds himself fully provided with whatever his voracious appetites can want, or luxurious imagination wish or desire.

What need would there be for a virtue of justice here? It would be "totally USELESS," he replies. Second,

imagine that human nature were such that all of us were totally **altruistic**, perpetually subordinating our own self-interest to a regard for the well-being of others. Again, the rules of justice would be superfluous. Third, imagine a natural environment of utter deprivation, a world in which there are scarcely enough resources for any to survive, let alone thrive. Here self-preservation would be the paramount consideration, and we could not afford the luxury of justice. Fourth, imagine that we found ourselves surrounded by people so totally egoistic as to be cruel and thoroughly insensitive to others, who were no more than the victims of their brutality. Here the practitioner of justice would be a foolish, helpless target of their exploitation. Hume's point is that justice, as we know and value it, would be a virtue in *none* of these four hypothetical situations. He draws the conclusion for us as explicitly as possible:

> Thus, the rules of equity or justice depend entirely on the particular state and condition, in which men are placed, and owe their origin and existence to that UTIL-ITY, which results to the public from their strict and regular observance.

A key word here is the adverb which says that justice is "entirely" relative to public utility. As Hume observes, the real world in which we actually live is intermediate among the four extremes of his fictitious scenarios: the natural resources of our environment are such that "by art, labour, and industry, we can extract them in great abundance," though they are limited and require work on our part; and human nature is such that, though we are "partial to ourselves, and to our friends," we are normally moved by sympathy for others, to some extent.[65]

This conception of justice is closer to that of the ancient Sophists and Hobbes than to ones proposed by Plato or Aristotle, Augustine or Aquinas. We should also notice that this view reduces the rules of justice to regulations and enforcement of property rights. Next, he repudiates the idea of building equality into our conception of justice, calling it "impracticable," in the sense that it could not be enforced, because human talents and efforts are naturally unequal, and "pernicious," in the sense that the attempts to enforce it would violate liberty and privacy and destroy the incentive to excel. A just "regulation of

---

Consequentialism. Any theory that judges morality in terms of the consequences of actions; utilitarianism is, perhaps, its most common type today

property" requires an understanding of "the nature and situation of man" and an eye to public utility. Hume is quite conservative about wanting to maintain current property relations; yet even this can be subject to **utilitarian** considerations. He asks rhetorically, "Does any one scruple, in extraordinary cases, to violate all regard to the private property of individuals, and sacrifice to public interest a distinction, which had been established for the sake of that interest?" He defines a person's property as anything "which it is lawful for him, and for him alone, to use."[66] This would presumably include his life, liberty, bodily capacities, and physical possessions.

ALTRUISM.   Hume makes it clear that he is an ethical naturalist, who believes that human nature provides a large part of the foundation of morals, but not a pure conventionalist, like some of the ancient Sophists, since he denies that all moral values are thoroughly adaptable by "precept and education." Not all the moral virtues are strictly relative to circumstances, as is justice; but some of them "have a natural beauty and amiableness" prior to any social conditioning and are rooted in our being as humans. Nor is this strictly a matter of pleasurable and painful self-interest, as Hobbes might suppose.

> We frequently bestow praise on virtuous actions, performed in very distant ages and remote countries; where the utmost subtilty of imagination would not discover any appearance of self-interest, or find any connexion of our present happiness and security with events so widely separated from us.

Indeed, as he goes on to observe, we can even approve of and admire actions of our own adversaries, whose consequences militate *against* our own interests. Experience provides too many examples of people deliberately and coolly sacrificing their own interests, their welfare, and even their lives for the apparent (or possible) benefit of others for psychological egoism to ring true. "Compelled by these instances, we must renounce the theory, which accounts for every moral sentiment by the principle of self-love," although the latter is undeniably "a principle in human nature of such extensive energy" that it normally has a significant influence on our behavior.[67]

Hume is confident that even the most selfish of people will have some regard for the well-being of others, wherever his own interests are not at stake. He rhetorically asks, "Would any man, who is walking along, tread as willingly on another's gouty toes, whom he has no quarrel with, as on the hard flint and pavement?" All of us have some degree of fellow feeling, which affects our behavior sometimes. "And if the principles of humanity are capable, in many instances, of influencing our actions, they must, at all times, have *some* authority over our sentiments, and give us a general approbation of what is useful to society, and blame of what is dangerous or pernicious." This sanguine belief in our altruistic feelings sets Hume apart from Hobbes, though he is careful not to exaggerate the extent of such feelings:

> Sympathy, we shall allow, is much fainter than our concern for ourselves, and sympathy with persons remote from us, much fainter than that with persons near and contiguous; but for this very reason, it is necessary for us, in our calm judgments and discourse concerning the characters of men, to neglect all these differences, and render our sentiments more public and social.[68]

Some moral virtues (like benevolence) are desirable at least in part because they promote and fulfill our (admittedly limited) natural human sympathy for other persons.

A CLASSIFICATION OF VIRTUES.   At this point Hume begins his four-fold classification system of the virtues, one of the most original facets of his ethical theory. We all approve of public utility and praise what promotes it, he says; but "it is the *sole* source" of some virtues, such as "justice, fidelity, honour, allegiance, and chastity"—in other words, these qualities are only considered virtues because they have proved to be useful to others in society. Second, there are those qualities that we value as virtues primarily because experience has shown them to be useful to ourselves; these include "*discretion, caution, enterprise, industry, assiduity, frugality, economy, good-sense, prudence*," and others. "*Temperance, sobriety, patience, constancy, perseverance, forethought*," and so forth, might be added to this second category. Third, there are qualities that are considered virtues primarily because they are agreeable to ourselves, such as cheerfulness, self-esteem, courage, and tranquillity

---

Utilitarianism.   The ethical theory (started by Bentham and popularized by Mill) that moral value is a function of good and bad consequences for the people who will be affected by an action; for hedonistic utilitarians (e.g., Bentham and Mill), happiness and unhappiness are measured in terms of pleasure and pain

(for which Hume praises Socrates). We recall that utility was recognized as constituting part of the reason benevolence is a virtue; now we find out that the other part is that it is naturally agreeable, the sentiment and its expressions proving to be "delightful in themselves," even apart from any utilitarian consequences. Fourth, there are qualities we regard as virtues primarily because they are immediately agreeable to other people; these include good manners or politeness, wit and ingenuity, modesty, decency, cleanliness, and other (what Hume calls) "*companionable* qualities*." Thus, Hume classifies all virtues into these four types. In a footnote he defines virtue in general as "*a quality of the mind agreeable to or approved of by every one, who considers or contemplates it,*" adding that we approve of some qualities, whether or not they are immediately agreeable, because of their utility.[69]

Hume suggests that this is a complete taxonomy of the virtues and that any quality which is neither agreeable nor useful to oneself or to other members of society must fail to qualify. "Celibacy, fasting, penance, mortification, self-denial, humility, silence, solitude, and the whole train of monkish virtues" are commonly rejected by normal people as serving no valuable purposes. Indeed, since they seem both disagreeable and detrimental to both their practitioners and society at large, Hume prefers to "place them in the catalogue of vices." With caustic sarcasm, he adds,

> A gloomy, hare-brained enthusiast, after his death, may have a place in the calendar; but will scarcely ever be admitted, when alive, into intimacy and society, except by those who are as delirious and dismal as himself.

Trying to draw this analysis to a close, Hume writes that "every quality of the mind, which is *useful* or *agreeable* to the *person himself* or to *others*, communicates a pleasure to the spectator, engages his esteem, and is admitted under the honourable denomination of virtue or merit." With a touch of self-effacing humor, he admits that it seems "unphilosophical" to be as "positive or dogmatical on any subject" as he is about this classification scheme for the virtues but that he does not, "*at present,*" see any flaw in it. Still, when he considers how long philosophers have been arguing about moral virtue, he must "fall back into diffidence and scepticism, and suspect, that an hypothesis, so obvious, had it been a true one, would, long ere now, have been received by the unanimous suffrage and consent of mankind." He also confronts the problem of the "sensible knave," or clever rascal, who wants the rules of morality to be observed and enforced, but would make himself the exception to those rules.

> That *honesty is the best policy*, may be a good general rule; but is liable to many exceptions: And he, it may, perhaps, be thought, conducts himself with most wisdom, who observes the general rule, and takes advantage of all the exceptions.

The reason the "sensible knave" is a problem for Hume is that his entire system of morality fundamentally rests on feelings rather than on reason, so that we cannot reason a moral rebel into having virtuous feelings of which he is devoid. Hume honestly responds,

> I must confess, that, if a man think, that this reasoning much requires an answer, it will be a little difficult to find any, which will to him appear satisfactory and convincing. If his heart rebel not against such pernicious maxims, . . . he has indeed lost a considerable motive to virtue.[70]

Hume's ethical **emotivism** must presuppose moral sentiments as imbedded in human nature and as at least generally operative.

MORALS DERIVED FROM FEELINGS.   In an appendix to this second *Enquiry* Hume returns to the question of whether moral distinctions are ultimately derived from reason or from feelings. We should not be surprised, by now, that he opts for the latter alternative. Yet he reminds us that reason is important for determining the utility of actions. "But though reason . . . instruct us in the pernicious or useful tendency of qualities and actions; it is not alone sufficient to produce any moral blame or approbation." We must have a feeling or conviction that utility is valuable and that what is detrimental should be avoided.

> It is requisite a *sentiment* should here display itself, in order to give a preference to the useful above the pernicious tendencies. This sentiment can be no other than a feeling for the happiness of mankind, and a resentment of their misery.

Emotivism.   The view in ethics (associated with Hume) that moral values are ultimately derived from emotions rather than from reason, as opposed to ethical rationalism

Without being aligned with some feelings, reason is impotent to motivate action. Hume considers, as an illustration, "the crime of ingratitude." Can reason, by itself, show that it is wrong? His answer is, no. "Reason judges either of *matter of fact* or of *relations*" of ideas, as we have seen. But he denies that the evil involved in an act of ingratitude can be shown to be either a matter of fact or any relation of ideas. On this view the vice is not analyzable in terms of reason's judgments alone but must involve feelings. His ethical theory breaks with the rationalisms of the past and, he says, "maintains, that morality is determined by sentiment. It defines virtue to be *whatever mental action or quality gives to a spectator the pleasing sentiment of approbation*; and vice the contrary."[71]

This ethical emotivism holds that moral approval or disapproval "cannot be the work of the judgment, but of the heart; and is not a speculative proposition or affirmation, but an active feeling or sentiment." He even compares moral evaluation with aesthetic experience, indicating that each is a matter of taste. Our values, he holds, are ultimately not rationally justifiable, "but recommend themselves entirely to the sentiments and affections of mankind." For example, if we ask a person why he engages in regular physical exercise, he might reply that it is to maintain his health. If we ask why he wants that, he can answer that illness is a painful nuisance. If we ask why he dislikes pain, there seems no rational response. Or if, in answer to the question why he values his health, he says to continue doing his work, we might ask why that matters, to which he might respond that he wants his salary. If we ask why, he can reply that the money is a means to purchases that give him pleasure. But if we ask why he desires pleasure, again there seems to be no rational response. We have a natural desire for pleasure and aversion to pain which are more basic than reason and in terms of which other goods and ills can be rationally explained as means to ends. Reason deals with facts and truth; but morality is a matter of value and (pleasurable and painful) taste, which can only be based on feelings, which motivate action, as reason allegedly never can do by itself.[72]

A Critique of Egoism. Hume criticizes the "depraved" principle of psychological egoism, which threatens to undermine any ethical theory based on sympathetic feelings for others, mentioning Hobbes by name as a proponent of this "selfish system of morals." He appeals to our experience as the basis for repudiating it.

> The most obvious objection to the selfish hypothesis, is, that, as it is contrary to common feeling and our most unprejudiced notions, there is required the highest stretch of philosophy to establish so extraordinary a **paradox**. To the most careless observer, there appear to be such dispositions as benevolence and generosity; such affections as love, friendship, compassion, gratitude.

We experience both "*general*" benevolence for people merely because they are fellow persons and "*particular*" benevolence for those to whom we have some special relation. "Both these sentiments must be allowed real in human nature," rather than learned ways of camouflaging self-interest. Hume invokes the example of a mother who knowingly sacrifices her health and endangers her very life to care for her sick child, whom she loves, and who later "languishes and dies of grief, when freed, by its death, from the slavery of that attendance." He observes that "a thousand other instances" could be produced to establish the reality of "benevolence in human nature."[73]

A Rule-Utilitarian View of Justice. Hume further discusses the virtue of justice and adopts a position which, in the twentieth century, has come to be called **rule utilitarianism**. It is not each individual act of justice that promotes utility. The public welfare is rather served by "the whole scheme or system, concurred in by the whole, or the greater part of the society." For example, the enforcement of just property relations might actually cause "particular hardships" in some individual cases. Yet that is legitimate, "if the whole plan or scheme be necessary to the support of civil society, and if the balance of good, in the main, do thereby preponderate much above that of evil." Hume does defend a conventional theory of justice, in the sense that he views it in terms of social

---

Rule utilitarianism. An ethical theory that morally evaluates actions in terms of the extent to which they conform to rules that are justified by the principle of utility, as opposed to *act utilitarianism*, which evaluates actions in terms of the extent to which their own consequences are justified by the principle of utility and which views rules merely as normative guidelines

commitments anchored in "a sense of common interest," although these commitments need never be formulated in terms of any explicit promises. "Thus two men pull the oars of a boat by common convention, for common interest, without any promise or contract," if that is what it takes to get back to dry land and save themselves. In a footnote, Hume briefly considers the "merely verbal" dispute as to whether justice is a "natural" virtue: it is natural in the sense of normal and as opposed to the "*unusual*"; second, it is natural, as opposed to supernatural or "*miraculous*"; but, third, it is "*artificial*," rather than natural, in that it is the product of human design and conventions. Finally, Hume acknowledges that we have moral duties to ourselves as well as those we bear in relation to other people.[74]

MORALS AS RELATIVE.   In his "Dissertation on the Passions," he defines good and evil in relation to "an agreeable sensation" and a "disagreeable sensation" we can experience. To a great extent, this is a matter of a natural fit between our passions and objects that prove to be "naturally conformable or contrary" to them.[75] But in his essay, "Of Civil Liberty," he indicates that moral good and evil are, to a great extent, relative to social conditioning when he says,

> It is not fully known what degree of refinement, either in virtue or vice, human nature is susceptible of, nor what may be expected of mankind from any great revolution in their education, customs, or principles.[76]

Thus, if we ask whether morality is a product of "nature or nurture," Hume's answer is that it is both of them combined.

In the *Treatise*, Hume provides a well-focused argument in opposition to moral rationalism:

> Since morals, therefore, have an influence on the actions and affections, it follows, that they cannot be deriv'd from reason; and that because reason alone, as we have already prov'd, can never have any such influence.

This valid argument hinges on Hume's claim that the role of reason is limited to making judgments.

> Morals excite passions, and produce or prevent actions. Reason of itself is utterly impotent in this particular. The rules of morality, therefore, are not conclusions of our reason.

There is a famous example in which he draws an analogy between a sapling that grows until it finally "overtops and destroys the parent tree," on the one hand, and a human parricide, who deliberately murders a parent, on the other; Hume defies us to show, on grounds of reason alone, why the first action has no moral quality attached to it, while the second is immoral. Then he gives a second example of incest among nonhuman animals, which we all agree is morally innocent, and incest among humans, against which there is a universal moral taboo. In another famous passage, he asks us to notice the difference between descriptive language about what "*is*, and *is not*" the case and **prescriptive** language, dealing with "an *ought*, or an *ought not*." So often, he observes, moralists slide from the former use of language to drawing prescriptive conclusions in terms of the latter, with no attempt to show how the latter logically follow from the former. Against **natural law** theorists like Aquinas, Hume writes that "nothing can be more unphilosophical than those systems, which assert, that virtue is the same with what is natural and vice with what is unnatural." For both "vice and virtue are equally natural," as opposed to being supernatural; second, virtue is often unnatural, in the sense of unusual; and, third, both virtue and vice are largely artificial conventions, rather than purely innate. " 'Tis impossible, therefore, that the character of natural and unnatural can ever, in any sense, mark the boundaries of vice and virtue."[77] They are rather distinguished by our feelings of approval and disapproval, as we have seen.

SUICIDE.   Finally, Hume's essay "On Suicide" is valuable as an application of his relativistic ethical emotivism to a practical moral problem. In contrast to the Christian natural law theory of Aquinas, which argues that suicide is morally wrong because it violates our obligations "to God, our neighbor, or ourselves," Hume tries to show otherwise. He argues that it is not necessarily an interference with God's law. After all, God gave us the "bodily and mental powers" to act thus and allows us to do so. Besides, we also change the course of nature when we act to save life from destruction. Hume says, "It would be no crime in me to divert the Nile or Danube from its course, were I able to effect such purposes. Where then is the crime of turning a few ounces of blood from their natural channel?" Why should God's will be thwarted by any human action, unless it "be a breach of our duty to our *neighbor* and to *society*"? Second, then, by killing himself, a man may do harm if he has social obligations that he could otherwise meet, to the benefit of others. But there may be circumstances in which he has no such obligations and, far from being able to benefit society, is a grave social burden. Third, a person is the best judge of what are his duties to himself. Hume is confident "that no man ever threw away life while it was worth keeping" but that "age, sickness, or misfortune" can render it worse than death, so that our duty may be to end it.[78] In short, none of the three sorts of considerations necessarily suffices to show that suicide is universally immoral.

Society

Although both adopt an empirical approach to society, Hume's theory will predictably differ from that of Hobbes because the former, unlike his predecessor, sees man as naturally sociable, rather than egoistic. Thus, Hume can write, for example, that "friendship is the chief joy of human life." We might also note, by way of introduction, that he includes politics among the "sciences, which treat of general facts," rather than classifying it with morality and criticism, which "are not so properly objects of the understanding as of taste and sentiment."[79]

A CRITIQUE OF THE SOCIAL CONTRACT THEORY. Hume's essay "Of the Original Contract" may be the best known critique of the **social contract** theory of Hobbes and others in the history of political philosophy. There Hume is also critical of the divine-right-of-kings theory, holding that all lawful authority "acts by a divine commission" but that popular consent is the source of legitimate political authority. This idea of a need for the consent of the governed is the germ of truth in the social contract theory. But Hume denies that there ever normally is an explicit "compact or agreement" that is "expressly formed for general submission" to government. In fact, what are empirically common, says Hume of eighteenth-century society, are rulers who claim authority independently of popular consent and their "subjects who acknowledge this right in their prince and suppose themselves born under obligations of obedience to a certain sovereign." If it is claimed that the "*original contract*" was made by our ancestors prior to all recorded history, "it cannot now be supposed to retain any authority" on us

who have not ratified it ourselves. In fact, Hume the historian observes,

> Almost all the governments which exist at present, or of which there remains any record in story, have been founded originally on usurpation or conquest or both, without any pretense of a fair consent or voluntary subjection of the people.

Even the case of the "Glorious Revolution," which set William and Mary on the throne of Great Britain, only affected the issue of succession "in the regal part of the government" (not Parliament) and was ratified by "only the majority of seven hundred, who determined that change for near ten millions" of subjects. Even granting that the latter might have agreed to the decision, they, in fact, had no choice in the matter. During the days of the ancient Athenian democracy,

> if we make the requisite allowances for the women, the slaves, and the strangers, we shall find, that that establishment was not at first made, nor any law ever voted, by a tenth part of those who were bound to pay obedience to it.

Indeed, in Hume's day, truly representative government was hardly to be found on any large scale anywhere. Nevertheless, he does maintain that government based on popular consent is "the best and most sacred of any." But his critical point here is that "Reason, history, and experience show us that all political societies" are otherwise established. Nor does the notion of "a *tacit* consent" given merely "by living under the dominion of a prince" prove compelling, since, in reality, people are practically quite limited in their geographical mobility.[80]

Thus far, Hume's critique has been mainly historical; but now he shifts to "a more philosophical" one. He reminds us that there are two types of moral duties: "those to which men are impelled by a natural instinct or immediate propensity," such as love of our children, gratitude towards our benefactors, and pity for the unfortunate; and those that are based on "the necessities of human society and the impossibility of supporting it if these duties were neglected," such as duties of justice, respect for the property of others, and the keeping of our promises. Then, "the political or civil duty of *allegiance*" is clearly of the second type, being based entirely on public utility.[81]

As the duty of political allegiance is founded on public utility, so, Hume writes, in his essay "Of Passive Obedience," it can reasonably "be suspended and give place to public utility in such extraordinary and such pressing emergencies" as those of brutal oppression and tyranny.

> The maxim *fiat Justitia, ruat Coelum*, 'let justice be performed though the universe be destroyed,' is apparently false, and by sacrificing the end to the means shows a preposterous idea of the subordination of duties.

In other words, if justice is merely valuable as a means to the end of public welfare and has no intrinsic worth, then the sort of fanatical rule-worship that damages the common good for the sake of upholding the abstraction is foolishly wrong. Therefore, resistance against oppression can be justified on this view, the practical question then being how much oppression is necessary to justify it. Hume provides his own conservative response:

> And here I must confess that I shall always incline to their side who draw the bond of allegiance very close and consider an infringement of it as the last refuge in desperate cases, when the public is in the highest danger from violence and tyranny.

Even when we submit to political authority, we retain the right to fair treatment under just laws.

> But as a right without a remedy would be an absurdity, the remedy in this case is the extraordinary one of resistance, when affairs come to that extremity that the constitution can be defended by it alone.[82]

In his *History of England*, as a case in point, Hume considers the "tragical death of Charles" I, towards whom he is sympathetic, arguing that there should be "a wide interval" maintained "between resisting a prince and dethroning him" and "another very wide interval" beyond that "between dethroning a prince and punishing him. We should be most reluctant ever to execute a deposed monarch."[83]

In his second *Enquiry* Hume challenges "the *philosophical* fiction of the **state of nature**," from which social contract theorists say society emerges and which they describe as one of "a perpetual war of all against all," resulting from the "untamed selfishness and barbarity" of human nature. (In a footnote, he correctly observes, "This fiction of a state of nature, as a state of war, was not first started by Mr. Hobbes, as is commonly imagined. Plato endeavours to refute an hypothesis very like it" in his *Republic*.) Hume doubts that such a state ever was or could long endure. "Men are necessarily born in a family-society, at least; and are trained up by their parents to

some rule of conduct and behaviour." So, we are not only born with a natural propensity for sympathy for others, but we also necessarily develop in a social context. Hume points out that government would be superfluous and would therefore cease to exist if we all had sufficient wisdom to practice the virtue of justice, since

> the SOLE foundation of the duty of ALLEGIANCE is the *advantage*, which it procures to society, by preserving peace and order among mankind.

To some extent, the rules of justice govern international relations, in the form of alliances and treaty commitments; but they are essential to our well-being in society.

> Human nature cannot, by any means, subsist, without the association of individuals; and that association never could have place, were no regard paid to the laws of equity and justice.

By contrast, Hume thinks that different nations could ignore one another. In any case, he holds, the rules themselves are derived from and subordinate to public utility, so that

> REASONS OF STATE may, in particular emergencies, dispense with the rules of justice, and invalidate any treaty or alliance, where the strict observance of it would be prejudicial, in a considerable degree, to either of the contracting parties,

though he adds that only "the most extreme necessity" can ever warrant deliberately violating our commitments.[84]

POLITICS.   In the introduction to his *Treatise* Hume includes politics in the science of human nature. Later, he points out that a human individual, in isolation, has limited power, limited ability, and limited security and that, among its many practical advantages, "Society provides a remedy for these *three* inconveniences." As we grow up in society, we normally come to appreciate these advantages. He again dismisses the nonsocial "*state of nature*" as "a mere philosophical fiction, which never had, and never cou'd have any reality." The rules of justice are viewed as artificial contrivances for maintaining peaceful social relations and are based on a combination of self-interest and concern for the common good. Against Hobbes, he maintains that we are capable "of society without government," and cites the native "*American* tribes, where men live in concord and amity among themselves without any establish'd government," as an example. Bands of families coexisting and cooperating without government nevertheless do need a common code of justice, including "three fundamental laws concerning the stability of possession, its translation by consent, and the performance of promises," to hold them together peacefully. Once political society has been established, according to Hume, "the obligation of submission to government is not deriv'd from any promise of the subjects" or contract but from utility. For that matter, the ultimate basis of our obligation to honor our promises is also utility. But utility can also reveal cases in which there are exceptions to our duties of allegiance and promise-keeping. Hume does assert that legitimate government "arises from the voluntary conventions of men," as do obligations of political allegiance. He lists five ways in which governments, in fact, become recognized as legitimate:

1. when there has been "*long*," continuous possession of power;
2. through its "*present* possession";
3. by "right of *conquest*";
4. through "the right of *succession*"; and
5. in accordance with "positive laws" already established.

Utility also supports rules of international law, such as safeguard "the persons of ambassadors," require that war be declared before attacks are made, and prohibit the use of poisonous weapons. National leaders are expected to abide by the rules of international justice, "so that no one of ever so corrupt morals will approve of a prince, who voluntarily, and of his own accord, breaks his word, or violates any treaty"; however, Hume allows that we do normally grant more leeway to the discretionary judgment of a leader in such cases than we would to a private individual.[85]

In "That Politics May Be Reduc'd to a Science," Hume observes that, whereas autocratic, "absolute governments" require efficient executive administration for their survival, "a *republican* and free government" will be guided by constitutional "checks and controls," which make it beneficial for all citizens "to act for the public good." He goes so far as to exclaim that the conclusions of political science might be **deduced** with "almost" as much certainty as we find in

"the mathematical sciences." He says that the best form of **monarchy** is "*an hereditary prince*," the best form of **aristocracy** is "*a nobility without vassals*," and the best form of **democracy** is "*a people voting by their representatives*." In "Of the First Principles of Government," he says that wherever "the many are governed by the few," as in a monarchy, or aristocracy, the rulers must rely on the opinions that the government serves the general welfare, that its power is legitimate, and that the ruler is properly entitled to his authority. In "Of the Origin of Government," Hume writes,

> Man, born in a family, is compelled to maintain society, from necessity, from natural inclination, and from habit. The same creature, in his farther progress, is engaged to establish political society, in order to administer justice; without which there can be no peace among them, nor safety, nor mutual intercourse.

In order to protect ourselves from "the frailty or perverseness of our nature," we need public officials to enforce the rules of justice and to whom we owe allegiance. "In a word, OBEDIENCE is a new duty which must be invented to support that of JUSTICE; and the types of equity must be corroborated by those of allegiance." Every political society represents a more or less successful attempt to strike a balance "between AUTHORITY and LIBERTY; and neither of them can ever absolutely prevail," except to the detriment of public utility.[86]

In his "Idea of a Perfect Commonwealth," Hume emphasizes the "infinite advantage" tradition offers any established government, "the bulk of mankind being governed by authority, not reason." A wise ruler will recognize this and conservatively avoid unnecessarily breaking from tradition;

> and though he may attempt some improvements for the public good, yet will he adjust his innovations, as much as possible to the ancient fabric, and preserve entire the chief pillars and supports of the constitution.

The form of government he seems to advocate is a "limited monarchy" including a balance of power with elected representatives, who will bear the executive and legislative authority of the commonwealth. Although he admits that it is "difficult to form a republican government" of this sort at the level of a nation-state, he is confident that, once established, it will be stable and best promote public utility.[87]

Religion

We might expect Hume to apply his empirical test to the idea of God, as he did to those of the self and human freedom. In his first *Enquiry*, he writes,

> The idea of God, as meaning an infinitely intelligent, wise, and good Being, arises from reflecting on the operations of our own mind, and augmenting, without limit, those qualities of goodness and wisdom.[88]

So, we imaginatively extrapolate beyond the qualities of which we have impressions of reflection from within ourselves.

MIRACLES.   Hume critically examines the alleged evidence for such a Supreme Being based on miracles, claiming that he has "discovered an argument" which "will, with the wise and learned, be an everlasting check to all kinds of superstitious delusion." He reminds us that concrete experience must "be our only guide in reasoning concerning matters of fact" and that it can only lead us to more or less probable conclusions. "A wise man, therefore, proportions his belief to the evidence," being more guarded about his beliefs to the extent that the evidence supporting them is doubtful. As a historian, he must admit "that there is no species of reasoning more common, more useful, and even necessary to human life, than that which is derived from the testimony of men, and the reports of eye-witnesses and spectators." This is the basis of the belief most religious people invest in miracle stories. We must assess the probability of such stories in the light of "the conjunction between any particular kind of report" and our experience of reality. But we must critically beware of accepting dubious evidence.

> We entertain a suspicion concerning any matter of fact, when the witnesses contradict each other; when they are but few, or of a doubtful character; when they have an interest in what they affirm; when they deliver their testimony with hesitation, or on the contrary, with too violent asseverations.

These are only four possible grounds for regarding alleged witnesses as unreliable. Usually, we try to accept the word of others as honest and accurate. But when we perceive a conflict between their reports and reality as we have experienced it, we do well to doubt them. Sometimes, our scepticism is misplaced, though reasonable, as in the case of the prince in India who refused to believe that rivers can freeze over, because he had never experienced anything of this sort.

The idea must have struck him as astonishing, though perhaps not miraculous.[89]

Hume defines a miracle as "*a transgression of a law of nature by a particular volition of the Deity, or by the interposition of some invisible agent.*" This definition requires that an act must violate a law of nature; and in order for something to count as a law of nature, it must be supported by "a uniform experience" thus far.

> And as a uniform experience amounts to a proof, there is here a direct and full *proof*, from the nature of the fact, against the existence of any miracle.

On this view, it is unreasonable to believe in miracle stories, because their supporting evidence, at best, can only be relatively probable, whereas the laws of nature supposedly violated are supported by the sort of empirical evidence that constitutes an empirical proof. But can we even accept testimony on behalf of miracles as relatively probable? It seems there are at least four obstacles to our doing so, four problems with the credibility of miracle stories (remember that Hume speaks as a critical historian here): first, we never find a sufficient number of intelligible, trustworthy witnesses testifying to the same facts, interpreted in the same way; second, we derive too much satisfaction in telling the sort of tall tales that will engender in our audience the passions of surprise and wonder; third, miracle stories arise among primitive, ignorant people, who do not understand the workings of nature; and, fourth, since the doctrines of one religion conflict with those of another, their underlying, allegedly supportive evidences must likewise be opposed and, in effect, cancel each other out as credible. Hume is prepared to draw his conclusion: "Upon the whole, then, it appears, that no testimony for any kind of miracle has ever amounted to a probability, much less to a proof" and that it is inevitably outweighed by the empirical proof supporting the law of nature allegedly violated; "therefore we may establish it as a maxim, that no human testimony can have such force as to prove a miracle, and make it a just foundation for any system of religion." This is not quite tantamount to a denial of the theoretical possibility of a miracle, which could overturn what previously was a law of nature. But it challenges the reasonableness of accepting the testimony of miracle stories as a proof of religious truth. In a very famous (and sarcastic) sentence, he adds,

Our most holy religion is founded on *Faith*, not on reason; and it is a sure method of exposing it to put it to such a trial as it is, by no means, fitted to endure.

He makes it clear that this critique of miracles can also "be applied, without any variation, to prophesies" as an allegedly reasonable basis for religion. The truth of "the *Christian Religion*," in particular, is not rationally confirmable. "And whoever is moved by *Faith* to assent to it, is conscious of a continued miracle in his own person, which subverts all the principles of his understanding, and gives him a determination to believe what is contrary to custom and experience."[90]

THE ARGUMENT FROM DESIGN. Hume critically examines the **argument from design**, which he regards as the best philosophical basis for religion; but he resorts to the literary device of casting it in the form of a dialogue, with "a friend who loves sceptical paradoxes," and it is the sceptical friend who attacks the argument. (This device presumably protects Hume from being identified as irreligious, though it seems inconsistent with his straightforward assault on miracles.) Proponents of the argument

> paint, in the most magnificent colours, the order, beauty, and wise arrangement of the universe; and then ask, if such a glorious display of intelligence could proceed from the fortuitous concourse of atoms, or if chance could produce what the greatest genius can never sufficiently admire.

This argument "from the order of nature" is causal, "an argument drawn from effects" allegedly experienced to causes inductively inferred. But in any such argument, the cause inferred must be proportional to the effects experienced, and we "can never be allowed to ascribe to the cause any qualities, but what are exactly sufficient to produce the effect" experienced, without rushing beyond reasoning to arbitrary conjecture. Wherever our only access to the cause is through its effects, we should never "ascribe to it any qualities, beyond what are precisely requisite" for producing those effects. "Nor can we, by any rules of just reasoning, return back from the cause, and infer other effects from it, beyond those by which alone it is known to us," to the extent that it is known at all.

Thus, insofar as the argument from design works at all, the phenomena of our world can only point to a God with "that precise degree of power, intelligence, and benevolence, which appears in their workmanship; but nothing farther can ever be proved, except we call in the assistance of exaggeration and flattery to supply the defects of argument and reasoning." On this view, an imperfect world cannot prove a perfect God. Even if a powerful, intelligent, and benevolent God must be inferred as the cause of our world, it is "mere hypothesis" to suppose that that cause is omnipotent, omniscient, and all-good. But, worse, this entire approach to justifying religion "is both uncertain and useless. It is uncertain; because the subject lies entirely beyond the reach of human experience." It is "useless" because the argument from design, even if accepted within legitimate logical limits, can never "establish any new principles of conduct and behaviour," so that it has no practical import.[91]

This sort of causal argument is "uncertain" to the extent that it departs from actual experience. Hume provides two legitimate cases: if we saw "a half-finished building, surrounded with heaps of brick and stone and mortar, and all the instruments of masonry," we could reasonably infer that humans were constructing a house, because we have experienced that sort of phenomenon many times in the past; likewise, if we "saw upon the sea-shore the print of one human foot," we could "conclude, that a man had passed that way, and that he had also left the traces of the other foot," although they have been effaced by the rolling in of tidal waves, again because we have had such experience before. But we have no such experiential basis for the argument from design, since we have no experience of the Designer, who is uniquely unlike any cause we have ever experienced. We can only conceive of God "by **analogy**" to creatures that are radically different. The examples of the "half-finished building" and the set of single footprints on the sand indicate that **argumentation from analogy** can be rather persuasive.

> But this method of reasoning can never have place with regard to a Being, so remote and incomprehensible, who bears much less analogy to any other being in the universe than the sun to a waxen taper, and who discovers

---

Argument from analogy   A relatively weak inductive argument alleging similarities on the basis of comparisons previously encountered rather than on that of experience

himself only by some faint traces or outlines, beyond which we have no authority to ascribe to him any attribute or perfection.

So, the argument is theoretically unconvincing in its efforts to prove God. And, as has been indicated, it is also practically useless: "No new fact can ever be inferred from the religious hypothesis; no event foreseen or foretold; no reward or punishment expected or dreaded, beyond what is already known by practice and observation" independently of the argument. In a sense, the uniqueness of God damages the rational force of the argument since we can only infer causes from effects in cases where "two *species* of objects are found to be constantly conjoined"; but since God is "entirely singular, and could not be comprehended under any known *species*," this approach by way of "experience and observation and analogy" seems doomed to frustration and failure. Later, Hume also makes it clear that causal reasoning is the only philosophical approach to God that could be legitimate. Reasoning *a priori*, as in the **ontological argument** used by Descartes, is hopeless, since all matters of fact and existence are "incapable of demonstration. Whatever *is* may *not be*. No **negation** of a fact can involve a contradiction. The non-existence of any being, without exception, is as clear and distinct an idea as its existence."[92] Consequently, the very idea of necessary existence, in God or anything else, is utterly undermined.

DEMEA, CLEANTHES, AND PHILO IN DIALOGUE. Hume's *Dialogues* involve an interplay of three main characters: Demea, a kind of rationalistic theist, who gets branded a "mystic" because he thinks the nature of God is absolutely unknowable; Cleanthes, a kind of empirical theist, who is accused of **anthropomorphism** because he thinks and speaks of God in human terms; and Philo, the sceptical deist, who best represents Hume himself most of the time. It is worth noting, at the outset, that "the BEING of a God" is taken for granted here and that the dispute in which the three engage is only "concerning the NATURE of that divine being." Even Philo, whom Cleanthes justly accuses of trying "to erect religious faith on philosophical scepticism," agrees that there is some Supreme Being: "Nothing exists without a cause; and the

original cause of this universe (whatever it be) we call GOD; and piously ascribe to him every species of perfection." So, the key question is what, if anything, reason can establish about the divine nature. Philo throws down the gauntlet before Cleanthes, who shares his empirical approach:

> Our ideas reach no farther than our experience: We have no experience of divine attributes and operations: I need not conclude my syllogism: You can draw the inference yourself.[93]

The conclusion that validly follows is that we have no ideas of divine attributes and operations, so that knowledge here is purportedly out of the question. But Cleanthes invokes the argument from design to defy the second premise.

He appeals to common experience as his starting point: "Look round the world: contemplate the whole and every part of it: You will find it to be nothing but one great machine, subdivided into an infinite number of lesser machines," all of which are intricately designed so that the whole universe "resembles exactly, though it much exceeds, the productions of human contrivance; of human designs, thought, wisdom, and intelligence." But because the effects (of universe and man-made mechanisms) are so similar,

> we are led to infer, by all the rules of analogy, that the causes also resemble; and that the Author of Nature is somewhat similar to the mind of man; though possessed of much larger faculties, proportioned to the grandeur of the work, which he has executed.

Demea immediately protests that this *a posteriori* (empirical) argument from analogy is not an *a priori* demonstration and thus fails to reach beyond the level of "experience and probability." Philo objects that the argument is based on "a very weak analogy" because of a lack of experience of similar cases. We reasonably conclude that a house had a builder because of our experience of many instances. "But surely you will not affirm, that the universe bears such a resemblance to a house, that we can with the same certainty infer a similar cause, or that the analogy is here entire and perfect." Nor is it obvious, in general, that "order, arrangement, or the adjustment of final causes" is intrinsically and necessarily "any proof of design"; it is at least conceivable that "matter may contain the source or spring of order originally, within itself."

Granting that intelligent design, such as we find in our own activities, is one of the principles of reality, it does not follow that it is the only one or the ultimate one. Our experience is far too limited to provide an ultimate explanation of all reality: "A very small part of this great system, during a very short time, is very imperfectly discovered to us; and do we then pronounce decisively concerning the origin of the whole?" Philo goes on to explain that this sort of reasoning only works where "two *species* of objects have always been observed to be conjoined together" but must fail in a case such as this one, where the cause inferred is unique and not quite like anything we have experienced and where we know nothing "of the origin of worlds." Philo challenges Cleanthes to defend his analogy between a man-made artifact and the universe and to cite its experiential basis.[94]

Philo presses the logic of Cleanthes' anthropomorphic empiricism and arguments from analogy, saying that "the liker the effects are, which are seen, and the liker the causes, which are inferred, the stronger is the argument. Every departure on either side diminishes the probability, and renders the experiment less conclusive." But then what follows is that, to the extent that it is a strong argument, it should establish that the divine mind is extremely similar to (if not identical with) the human, destroying any basis for ascribing to it infinity or perfection. Also, human construction is the result of trial and error; thus, we might reasonably infer,

> Many worlds might have been botched and bungled, throughout an eternity, ere this system was struck out.

Also, human construction is so often the result of collaborative effort; so, why not suppose a committee of "several deities" working together to produce our world, suggesting polytheism rather than monotheism? Humans are mortal and corporeal; why not infer that the same is true of the Designer of the universe, if the analogy is to be truly tight? Cleanthes protests against these extravagant suppositions but expresses satisfaction in the fact that they all assume "the hypothesis of design in the universe," which, he maintains, is "a sufficient foundation for religion."[95]

Demea gets his chance to propose the alternative *a priori* approach, since it seems that the argument from design, to the extent that it works at all, is merely probable and can establish neither God's infinite perfection nor unity. So he presents a version of the **cosmological argument**, similar to the reasoning in the first three of Aquinas's five ways: Everything that exists "must have a cause or reason of its existence," and nothing can be self-caused. The chain "from effects to causes" cannot regress infinitely "without any ultimate cause at all"; so there must be "some ultimate cause, that is *necessarily* existent" and the source of all other reality.

> We must, therefore, have recourse to a necessarily-existent Being, who carries the REASON of his existence in himself; and who cannot be supposed not to exist without an express contradiction;

and this is God. Cleanthes attacks the argument with a counterargument: if anything is truly demonstrable, its contrary would **imply** a contradiction; but nothing conceivable implies a contradiction; anything we conceive as existent, we can at least conceive of as nonexistent; thus, no being's nonexistence implies a contradiction; and, therefore, "there is no being, whose existence is demonstrable." There cannot be any "necessarily-existent being" whose nonexistence is conceivable; yet we can at least conceive of the nonexistence of every being, including even God. "The words, therefore, *necessary existence*, have no meaning; or, which is the same thing, none that is consistent." But, adds Cleanthes, if we wish to think in those terms, "why may not the material universe be the necessarily-existent Being" of Demea's argument requiring no ultimate cause outside itself?[96] Not only have we no experiential grounds for the alleged idea of necessary existence; but we also have none for anything transcending our universe.

The three characters turn from disputing about arguments for God to discussing the **problem of evil**. Philo and Demea set the stage for this by emphasizing "the misery and wickedness of men," our unhappiness, and "the general corruptions of our nature." Demea seems to mock the words Cleanthes used to introduce the argument from design, when he

---

Implication. That which necessarily follows from something else

exclaims, "Look round this library of Cleanthes," indicating that most of the authors represented communicate "the sense of human misery." They go on in this vein, establishing a challenge to the anthropomorphic assumption holding "the moral attributes of the Deity, his justice, benevolence, mercy, and rectitude, to be of the same nature with these virtues in human creatures." Philo crystallizes the problem astutely, asking of God,

> Is he willing to prevent evil, but not able? then is he impotent. Is he able, but not willing? then is he malevolent. Is he both able and willing? whence then is evil?

Demea adopts the traditional Christian solution of Augustine when he defends the compatibility of divine perfection and evil in our world by saying that the world of our experience here and now is only a minute part of reality and that the "present evil phenomena" we experience "are rectified in other regions, and in some future period of existence," in the larger scheme of divine providence. Cleanthes protests against these "arbitrary suppositions" based on no experienced evidence. His own solution attempts "to deny absolutely the misery and wickedness of man," although he slips, almost immediately, into the concession that there is some evil, though it is outweighed by happiness and goodness. Philo points out that this misses the point. Cleanthes is too faithful an empiricist to deny evil altogether, and his concession that there is any at all leaves the problem unsolved.

> For this is not, by any means, what we expect from infinite power, infinite wisdom, and infinite goodness. Why is there any misery at all in the world? Not by chance surely.[97]

Cleanthes acknowledges that his empirical position, accepting that there is at least some evil in the world, does not allow for, let alone prove, a God "with infinite attributes." So, he holds "the Author of Nature to be finitely perfect, though far exceeding mankind." But this leaves open the question of what, if anything, we can conclude about God's moral attributes. In still another take-off on Cleanthes' "Look round the world" speech, Philo says, "Look round this universe," pointing out how "hostile and destructive to each other" various life forms are. It is enough to lead us to wonder if "the **Manichean** system," of a good God and an evil deity **dualistically** coexisting, might be the "proper hypothesis." But the "uniformity and agreement of the parts of the universe" militate against such a division of its originating cause, leading him to conjecture, "The true conclusion is, that the original Source of all things is entirely indifferent" to moral principles. He points out that "*four* hypotheses" are logically possible "concerning the first causes of the universe; *that* they are endowed with perfect goodness, *that* they have perfect malice, *that* they are opposite and have both goodness and malice, *that* they have neither goodness nor malice." The fact that we experience both good and evil phenomena in our world argues against the first two hypotheses, either the perfect God of monotheism or an evil genius; "the uniformity and steadiness of general laws" in the world opposes the third hypothesis of good and evil ultimate causes. "The fourth, therefore, seems by far the most probable."[98]

After the pious Demea has left the discussion in disgust, Philo admits that "the works of Nature bear a great analogy to the productions of art" and that "their causes have a proportional analogy." It does seem appropriate to attribute intelligence and power to the Cause of the universe, if not moral qualities. The final disagreement between Cleanthes and Philo is over the value versus the dangers of religion. Cleanthes maintains that religion has a salutary effect on us: "The proper object of religion is to regulate the heart of men, humanize their conduct, infuse the spirit of temperance, order, and obedience," motivating moral and just behavior. By contrast, Philo says that only "the philosophical and rational kind of religion" has such good effects but that popular religion leads to persecution, oppression, and hostility. "True religion," he admits, does not lead to such bad consequences; but it—as opposed to the fanaticism of "vulgar superstition"—is not widely practiced. It is "philosophical Sceptics" who best practice true religion. In what were probably Hume's last words on the subject, Philo reduces the rational truth of philosophical religion to a single cautiously worded assertion,

> *that the cause or causes of order in the universe probably bear some remote analogy to human intelligence.*

Our faith may carry us beyond this extremely limited finding of reason; and certainly we can hope that divine revelation might tell us more. But, our experience thus far being what it has been, Philo concludes,

"To be a philosophical Sceptic is, in a man of letters, the first and most essential step towards being a sound, believing Christian."[99]

POPULAR RELIGION VS. NATURAL RELIGION.   In both of his essays "The **Stoic**" and "The Platonist," Hume repeats his commitment to the experience of design in the universe as a rational basis for belief in a Supreme Being. His essay "Of Superstition and Enthusiasm" explores some of those dangerous errors of popular religion. "Weakness, fear, melancholy, together with ignorance, are" the roots of religious superstition. "Hope, pride, presumption, a warm imagination, together with ignorance, are" the roots of religious enthusiasm or fanaticism. Whereas religious superstition tends to make believers despise themselves as being unworthy, enthusiasm tends to render them arrogant, as if specially chosen by God. Second, whereas religions rooted in enthusiastic fanaticism are initially "*more furious and violent*" than those rooted in superstition, after a while they "*become more gentle and moderate*," whereas superstitions become more fiercely entrenched. Third, although superstition tends to oppose civil liberty, under the prodding of priests, who wish to dictate to others, enthusiasm, which erodes ecclesiastical power, tends to support civil liberty, in order to promote authentic devotion.[100]

Hume's *Natural History of Religion* reinforces his commitment to the argument from design:

> The whole frame of nature bespeaks an intelligent author; and no rational enquirer can, after serious reflection, suspend his belief a moment with regard to the primary principles of genuine Theism and Religion.

This argument should lead us to believe in "one single being, who bestowed existence and order on this vast machine, and adjusted all its parts, according to one regular plan or connected system," since a single, integrated design pervades the universe. But primitive peoples tend to believe in a polytheistic pantheon of gods and goddesses, who turn out "to be nothing but a species of human creatures," as imagined and described. Humans throughout history have only seemed to agree on one general theological tenet, "that there is invisible, intelligent power in the world"; how this belief gets articulated leads to the profusion of religious faiths in our world. Popular religion, whether polytheistic or monotheistic, does not naturally and originally tend to be based on philosophical reason at all.

> *A little philosophy*, says lord Bacon, *makes men atheists: A great deal reconciles them to religion.*

Hume agrees that philosophy, superficially explored, tends to undermine religion; but when it is seriously pursued, it lends some rational support to it. Monotheism tends to evolve out of polytheism. Religious superstition, whether polytheistic or monotheistic, tends to be obsessed with private terrors, to perpetrate crimes intolerantly against others, and to spread misery through its environment. Natural religion does indicate a Deity:

> A purpose, an intention, a design is evident in every thing; and when our comprehension is so far enlarged as to contemplate the first rise of this visible system, we must adopt, with the strongest conviction, the idea of some intelligent cause or author.

But good and evil phenomena, "happiness and misery, wisdom and folly, virtue and vice," are so mixed in our world that it is difficult to draw many reliable conclusions regarding the nature of the Deity. There is also often a terrible disparity between the morals advocated by organized religion and its corrupt practices. Hume's conclusion here is as sceptical as is most of his philosophy:

> The whole is a riddle, an aenigma, an inexplicable mystery. Doubt, uncertainty, suspence of judgment appear the only result of our most accurate scrutiny, concerning this subject.[101]

Immortality

Hume's rigorously empirical epistemology leads him to draw an equally sceptical conclusion regarding our chances of surviving the death of the body. In the *Treatise* he writes, "A future state is so far remov'd from our comprehension, and we have so obscure an idea of the manner, in which we shall exist after the dissolution of the body, that all the reasons we can invent" can never "bestow a sufficient authority and force on the idea.[102] So, we invent reasons to support our belief in **immortality** but, in fact, have no experiential basis for even understanding the notion.

METAPHYSICAL ARGUMENTS.   Hume writes in his essay "On the Immortality of the Soul" that we invent three types of arguments to try to lend support to this belief. First, metaphysical arguments, the sort used by philosophers from Plato on, suppose that the soul is an immaterial substance distinct from the body, and therefore, not essentially affected by what happens to the body, including its death. But, as we have seen, Hume maintains that "the notion of substance is wholly confused and imperfect; and that we have no other idea of any substance, than as an aggregate of particular qualities inhering in an unknown something." Also, since experience is the only legitimate basis for reasoning about matters of fact and we do not experience the body in itself, we have no way of conclusively determining "whether matter, by its structure or arrangement, may not be the cause of thought" (as Hobbes claimed it is). If despite such epistemological reservations, one wishes to pursue such metaphysical reasoning, why may not an argument be equally framed to show that souls are eternal, as Plato maintained, and not merely immortal? The argument would say that whatever is incorruptible must also be ingenerable; so, if the soul is immortal, and thus incorruptible, it must have always existed before our physical birth. And to the extent that we do not care about life before birth, there is no reason to suppose that we should be concerned about life after death. Further, if the metaphysical argument works to establish the immortality of our souls, why not also, as Plato supposed, the souls of other animals, which are presumably also immaterial? Yet Christians (like Aquinas) want to restrict the application of the argument to human souls (among all earthly creatures) and to show only their immortality, not their eternity (since they were allegedly created by God).[103]

Moral Arguments. Second, "the moral arguments" appeal to "the justice of God, which is supposed to be further interested in the future punishment of the vicious and reward of the virtuous." (We shall see something like this approach adopted by Kant.) "But these arguments are grounded on the supposition that God has attributes beyond what he has exerted in this universe, with which alone we are acquainted." As we have seen, our experience provides us with only minimal evidence for certain natural attributes of God (including, especially, power and intelligence), according to Hume, and none for any moral attributes (such as divine justice). If we do, nevertheless, take this tack,

how in the world can we know by what criteria divine rewards and punishments might be allotted? Also, what good could eternal punishment possibly do, anyhow? Hume repudiates the black-and-white dichotomy presupposed by the notions of eternal rewards and eternal damnation: "Heaven and hell suppose two distinct species of men, the good and the bad; but the greatest part of mankind float betwixt vice and virtue," in shades of gray moral mediocrity. Also, as we have seen, all moral ideas allegedly arise from reflection on natural human feelings and personal and interpersonal interests (some of which are artificial). Hume asks rhetorically, "Ought these interests, so short, so frivolous, to be guarded by punishments eternal and infinite?" It seems disproportionate to damn a single soul to eternal punishment for any actions we can perform here and now.[104]

Physical Arguments. Third, the "physical arguments from the analogy of nature" often compare death to a sleep, from which we ultimately wake up. But Hume points out that it is a poor analogy; sleep only partially and temporarily disables the body in order to restore its vigor, whereas death does so totally and permanently with no restorative physical consequences. In fact, physical analogies should point to mortality, rather than to immortality:

> Nothing in this world is perpetual; every thing, however seemingly firm, is in continual flux and change: the world itself gives symptoms of frailty and dissolution.

Hence, by analogy, we should conclude that the same attributes probably pertain to souls. Hume both begins and ends the essay by maintaining that this issue is properly a matter of faith and revelation rather than of rational argumentation.[105]

Fulfillment

If we have no reason to expect fulfillment in the hereafter, the happiness to be enjoyed in this life seems all the more precious. In his second *Enquiry*, Hume writes that

> wherever we go, whatever we reflect on or converse about, every thing still presents us with the view of human happiness or misery, and excites in our breast a sympathetic movement of pleasure or uneasiness.

The prospect of happiness motivates our actions; and our natural sympathy for others leads us to value theirs as well. He claims that the "sole purpose" of virtue is to make its practitioners and, through them, "all mankind, during every instant of their existence, if possible, cheerful and happy"; he denies that virtue ever forbids people "any pleasure but in hopes of ample compensation in some other period of their lives." So, virtue, far from being its own reward, is **hedonistically** justified. And what does his conception of happiness comprise?

> Inward peace of mind, consciousness of integrity, a satisfactory review of our own conduct; these are circumstances very requisite to happiness,[106]

he replies.

Hume discusses the topic further in scattered passages from his literary essays. In "Of the Delicacy of Taste and Passion," he observes that emotionally delicate people are particularly susceptible to being robbed of happiness by misfortune, becoming deprived "of all relish in the common occurrences of life, the right enjoyment of which forms the chief part of our happiness." Delicacy of taste can make us more sensitive to both pleasures and pains, "which escape the rest of mankind." Hume thinks that "delicacy of passion is to be lamented, and to be remedied, if possible," since it renders us too vulnerable to **accidents** beyond our control. By contrast, "delicacy of taste" is greatly "to be desired and cultivated," since it sensitizes us to a greater range of satisfying stimuli. "When a man is possessed of that talent, he is more happy by what pleases his taste, than by what gratifies his appetites, and receives more enjoyment from a poem, or a piece of reasoning, than the most expensive luxury can afford." In "Of Refinement in the Arts," Hume identifies "*industry, knowledge*, and *humanity*" as normal conditions of the fulfillment of human nature.[107]

In "The **Epicurean**" he urges us to try to "enjoy the present" time and not to waste any "part of so perishable an existence"; we should embrace "love and jollity, and remove all the scruples of a vain superstition." In "The Stoic" he warns against the "eager pursuit of pleasure" that primarily depends on "fortune and accidents" and the access to "external objects, which chance may, in a moment, ravish from you"; happiness, he says, requires security, and the security of external goods is always too threatened by fortune. In "The Platonist" he denies that any rational soul can ever find complete "tranquillity or satisfaction, while detained in the ignoble pursuits of sensual pleasure or popular applause." We are capable of both aesthetic and moral appreciation. "The most perfect happiness

surely must arise from the contemplation of the most perfect object. But what more perfect than beauty and virtue?" However, in "The Sceptic" he warns us that "such is the disorder and confusion of human affairs, that no perfect or regular distribution of happiness and misery is ever in this life to be expected." Unfortunately, life is not completely fair; and even "the most worthy character" does not necessarily or always enjoy "the highest felicity." In some people a "gloomy and melancholy disposition" is joined with a high level of moral "honor and great integrity"; another person, though "a selfish villain," may enjoy an undeserved *"gaiety of heart."*[108] Each of these last four perspectives seems at least partly correct, in Hume's opinion: the Epicurean is right in urging us to enjoy the present moment; the Stoic is right in warning us against the insecurity of external pleasures; the Platonist is right in promoting the aesthetic and moral joys of the mind; and the sceptic is right in denying that there is any perfect proportion in this life between virtue and apparent happiness. Still, philosophical reflection provides us with useful guidelines in our efforts to fulfill our own human nature.

REFLECTIONS

Hume is probably the most provocative and influential philosopher ever to write in the English language. Much of his greatness consists in his facility for challenging the easy assumptions of the previous two millennia of philosophical thought. There is so much that is comforting in the theories of Plato, Aristotle, Augustine, Aquinas, and Descartes, all of whom place great confidence in the powers of human reason to know so very much about ourselves and our world, all of whom emphasize the spiritual dimension of human life, all of whom try rationally to establish a transcendent, supernatural realm, and all of whom are committed to objective, rationally determinable moral values. Many of us approach philosophy inclined to believe (and wanting to believe) in such matters; and these traditional philosophers seem to hand us a satisfying theoretical warrant for doing so. Then along comes Hume, who (like Hobbes) is not easy to accept, because his rigorous empiricism leads to so many sceptical conclusions that threaten our cherished beliefs. Let us briefly assess some of his views on the ten topics we have been discussing.

REALITY.   There seems to be something right and something wrong with his phenomenalistic theory of reality. If all ideas must be derived from the impressions of experience, it does seem that the **realism** of philosophers before Hobbes is presumptuous and that we are not capable of access to reality in itself unfiltered by our subjective experiences. But it is the very subjectivity of his theory that strains credulity. We experience the same world in sufficiently similar ways to allow us to communicate about it rather effectively. In some sense, for example, we are sure that this book is an existing thing with perceptible attributes. Yet Hume's theory calls into question the meaningfulness of the very ideas of existence and substance because it cannot account for them on its own epistemological principles. To the extent that this undermines our basic experience of (admittedly limited) factual objectivity, it can strike us as objectionably implausible.

BODIES.   Second, it is also peculiar that an empiricist should reduce bodies to the unknowable, inexplicable objects of our experience. Since our experiences are our only access to reality, this would seem to condemn us to **solipsism**. But, again, in some sense we know this book as an enduring object. And it strains credulity to say that this is merely a belief rooted in our imagination. Why do we happen to agree in exercising our imaginations in so fixed a fashion? Why does this collective habit of the imagination happily work so well for us?

PERSONALITY.   Hume's recognition that rational thought, practical action, and social relationships are all significant dimensions of human personality (to refer to our third topic) seems healthy; and, to his credit, he analyzes all three with earnest commitment. Like Hobbes, Hume takes human imagination more seriously and gives it a more prominent place than any other great philosopher up to the time of Descartes, not subordinating it to reason, for example, but acknowledging its ultimate importance. But his "bundle" theory of the self—yet another example of his phenomenalistic scepticism—is as odd and counterintuitive as he himself admits. There must be some psychological thread binding together a person's perceptions to constitute that particular "bundle" and to distinguish it from every other "bundle." However, Hume's theory is incapable of accounting

for any such source of unity and coherence. Nor is memory an adequate explanation here, insofar as there seems to be no agent to do the remembering. On the other hand, Hume seems importantly correct in defending our natural capacity for (at least limited) sympathy for others, against the egoism of, say, Hobbes; his theory of the passions is otherwise as empirical as was that of Hobbes; but this gives it greater range than can be found in an egoistic one.

KNOWLEDGE.   Fourth, an advantage of Hume's theory of knowledge is its clear building-blocks approach; his insight into the psychological connections established by his three principles of associating ideas has proved to be a valuable lasting legacy of his epistemology. His empirical test of suspicious ideas is important; but to the extent that it is unable to deal with fundamental ideas (such as substance and existence) or downgrades the knowledge of others (such as causality and the self), it seems misguided. As an empiricist, Hume does well to reject all *a priori* innate ideas; the problem is that he has nothing to offer to replace them as a basis for reasoning to certain knowledge about matters of fact. His critical analysis of causality is a bold step that had not been taken by any previous great thinker in the history of Western philosophy (including even Hobbes); but it is most disturbing for its implications regarding the possibility of scientific certainty, as it reduces the idea of necessary connection to merely a feeling of the imagination, which need be neither universal nor necessary.

FREEDOM.   Regarding our fifth topic, Hume's theory of human freedom is essentially one of what William James later calls "soft determinism." It reduces all human actions to necessity in Hume's limited sense of that word, while attempting to retain the language of freedom and liberty for those voluntary ones that are causally determined from within by the will. If we ask what determines the will in such cases, the answer is that it is a complex of character, motives, circumstances, and so forth—all of which, themselves, will ultimately be extrinsically determined. Thus, it seems, freedom in any ultimately meaningful sense evaporates. But this poses a threat to the possibility of moral responsibility. And the thesis that, in even our "voluntary" actions, reason is no more than a "slave of the passions," on this deterministic view, seems dangerous, indeed, since our passions often push us in unfortunate directions and require restraint that goes beyond mere channeling.

MORALITY. Sixth, his moral theory poses a valuable challenge to the rationalistic views of ancient and medieval ethics, in that it urges us to consider whether, and to what extent, human feelings play a fundamental role in the determination of values. Yet his corrective may be too extreme, ruling out reason as a source of morality altogether and establishing too rigid a dichotomy between facts and values. His conception of justice, for example, as a merely artificial, utilitarian virtue, loses any plausibility it might have if justice is not reducible to legitimate property relations; those of us who believe that justice also requires equal respect for the **dignity** of all persons must feel that something significant has been omitted. His four-fold classification of the virtues, ingenious though it is, seems to collapse any distinction between what we happen to appreciate and what is intrinsically good—which, strangely enough, violates his own dichotomy between what is and what ought to be the case; granting that we approve of some qualities and disapprove of others, the ethical question is whether we should do so (and why). His relativism may be consistent with his empiricism; but the problem of the "sensible knave" indicates the inadequacy of his ethics ever to show why things should be other than they are.

SOCIETY. On our seventh topic, society, Hume's critique of the social contract theory misses the point a bit; there is no need to interpret it in terms of historically verifiable facts (although, even here, the Mayflower Compact signed by the Pilgrims when they reached Massachusetts and the American Constitution might provide such evidence). Even if there be no obligation of fidelity inherited from our ancestors, our remaining in a society and continuing to derive benefits from so doing, when we could do otherwise, can provide a basis for the doctrine of tacit consent (as Hume begrudgingly recognizes was the case with Socrates). Otherwise, his theory of society does well to observe that human nature is inclined to sociable relationships and that we only grow and develop in a social context. His sympathies for mixed republican government, characterized by a balance of powers, seems politically healthy by today's standards.

RELIGION. Eighth, to the extent that Hume's theory of religion renders it more a matter of faith than of rational proof, his perspective is valuable. Miracle stories (and prophecies) handed down in traditional revelation require faith in both their content and their divine sources and thus are not themselves objective evidence corroborating the fundamentals of religious belief. No human being has ever developed a more masterful critique of the argument from design than Hume; and it is striking that he seems, nevertheless, to have had some confidence in its limited psychological force. His treatment of the problem of evil is honest and revolutionary, showing that it is not provable that the infinitely perfect God of monotheism can coexist with evil. And, though it may be offensive to say so, much of popular religion has fostered superstition and fanaticism, as he tries to show.

IMMORTALITY. As for our ninth topic, the critical reservations Hume presents regarding any rational justification of beliefs in immortality also appear well taken. One need not be an extreme empiricist to find the arguments traditionally mounted on its behalf logically flawed exercises in wishful thinking. Here too, we seem to be in the arena of faith rather than in that of rational knowledge.

FULFILLMENT. Finally, Hume's naturalistic theory of happiness, though attractive, seems too hedonistic. There is more to the fulfillment of human nature than even his rather broad conception of satisfaction allows. There is the complex actualization of one's many **potentialities**, in general; and, more particularly, there is the need to achieve a life of **good will** and to do one's duty.

* * *

Throughout his philosophical system, Hume remains a splendid example of Enlightenment thought and representative of its ideals (of experience, science, utility, progress, and so forth). He defies appeals to authority and challenges us to think things through for ourselves. His errors—if, indeed, they are such— are the logical outcome of the extreme empiricism that is their foundation. And most of the criticisms of his thought suggested here inevitably push us towards that of the other great Enlightenment philosopher, his younger contemporary, Immanuel Kant.

Kant

Philosophy can never be learned, save only in historical fashion.

CRITIQUE OF PURE REASON

BIOGRAPHY

Immanuel Kant was born on April 22, 1724 (thirteen years after Hume was born), the son of Johann Georg Kant, a harness maker, and Anna Regina Reuter; he was the fourth of their nine children, but, in addition to him, only one older sister, two younger sisters, and a younger brother survived childhood. His parents were Pietists in Königsberg (now called Kaliningrad), the capital city of East Prussia. In this city of about 54,000 people Kant was born, grew up, spent almost his entire life, and died; indeed, he never traveled more than seventy miles from the city (and never out of East Prussia). Despite its remote location on the outskirts of Prussia, Kant admired the city, from which he had no great wish to roam, as he makes clear in a footnote to one of his last books:

> A large city like Königsberg on the river Pregel, the capital of a state, where the representative National Assembly of the government resides, a city with a university (for the cultivation of the sciences), a city also favored by its location for maritime commerce, and which, by way of rivers, has the advantages of commerce both with the interior of the country as well as with neighboring countries of different languages and customs, can well be taken as an appropriate place for enlarging one's knowledge of people as well as of the world at large, where such knowledge can be acquired even without travel.[109]

In 1732, at the age of eight, the boy was sent to the Collegium Fredericianum (Friedrich's College), a Pietist school directed by Franz Albert Schultz, the Kant family's pastor, who subscribed to the philosophy of the Leibnizian rationalist, Christian Wolff. We do not know much about Kant's schooling there, except that he was well trained in Latin. It seems that discipline was quite strict. And a couple of sentences from *Education* make it doubtful that his childhood was much fun:

> Many people imagine that the years of their youth are the pleasantest and best of their lives; but it is not really so. They are the most troublesome; for we are then under strict discipline, can seldom choose our own friends, and still more seldom can we have our freedom.[110]

When he was thirteen, his mother died suddenly of rheumatic fever, which she had caught while ministering to a sick friend.

When he was sixteen years old, Kant entered the Albertus University of Königsberg (founded almost two centuries earlier by Albert I, the Duke of Prussia)—the same year, 1740, that Frederick II, called "Frederick the Great" and "the Enlightenment King," became King of Prussia. (In his essay, "What Is Enlightenment?" Kant later writes that "this is the age of enlightenment, or the century of Frederick," and extols the king as an enlightenment monarch who fosters a spirit of free critical argumentation.[111]) Contrary to normal practice, Kant did not enroll as a student of law, medicine, or theology, choosing to study philosophy, in the broad sense of the arts and sciences, in general. He was particularly influenced by Martin Knutzen, the extraordinary professor of logic and metaphysics there, who, like Pastor Schultz, was a Pietist and a disciple of the philosophy of Leibnizian rationalism, as systematized by Wolff. Knutzen brought the young Kant into this school of philosophy, introduced him to the scientific writings of Newton, and made his own extensive library available to his avid student. Despite Schultz's hopes that he would enter the ministry, Kant was more obviously drawn to pursue Knutzen's vocation, as is indicated by his first publication, *Thoughts on the True Estimation of Living Forces*, which was dated 1746 and which concerned modern philosophical and scientific theory, focusing on the thought of Descartes and Leibniz. That was also the year Kant's father died, having suffered a palsy stroke more than a year earlier. Kant was now without financial support and in need of employment.

He left Königsberg to take up a position as family

tutor in the household of a pastor of the Reformed Church, about sixty miles east of Königsberg, where he stayed for about three years. Then for about a year and a half, he served as tutor for a second family about sixty miles southwest of Königsberg. And finally, he lived as family tutor in the household of Count Kayserling, near Königsberg. He did not consider himself well-suited for tutoring children. During his nine years of tutoring, Kant developed a taste for refined fashion, dress, and manners. (He was a small man, who never grew to more than five feet, two inches, nor weighed more than a hundred pounds; he was narrow in the chest, frail, and with one of his shoulders higher than the other.) He was also able to pursue his studies during these years; and in 1755, he returned to Königsberg and presented a scientific dissertation, *On Fire* (*De Igne*), for his graduate degree. That year, he also qualified for an appointment as a *Privatdozent* (or licensed private lecturer at the university) with his treatise, *A New Exposition of the First Principles of Metaphysical Knowledge* (the *Nova Dilucidatio*). Also in 1755, he published his *Universal Natural History and Theory of the Heavens*, written from a Newtonian perspective, proposing a nebular theory of the formation of the solar system and dedicated to Frederick the Great.

Now Kant was qualified to begin his life's work. Between 1755 and 1770, he taught as a *Privatdozent*, receiving no salary and no compensation at all for his public lectures, but being paid by the fees generated from the students who chose to hear his private lectures. Kant was fortunate to have been an engaging lecturer; his lectures were so well attended that, after a while, students often found they had to arrive early to get seats. Still, his livelihood was extremely modest through most of these fifteen years. He had a single coat, which became so shabby that some friends offered to buy him a new one; but, not wanting to be beholden to anyone, he declined. His lectures initially dealt with mathematics and physics; then those on logic and metaphysics were added; a bit later, ethics, natural theology, pedagogy, geography, and anthropology were included in his repertoire. As a member of the philosophical faculty, he was free to range considerably. As a *Privatdozent*, he lectured between sixteen and twenty-eight hours per week. During this period there were about thirty-eight professors at the University of Königsberg.

In 1756, after Knutzen died, Kant applied for that professorial chair, but it was left unfilled for lack of funding due to the Seven Years' War, which was underway. A couple of years later, he applied for a chair in logic and metaphysics, but a more senior *Privatdozent*, named Buck, got the position. Königsberg, which was near the Russian border, was occupied by the Russians from 1758 to 1762; they allowed the university to operate as usual during this time. In 1764, Kant was considered for a chair in poetry, which he prudently chose not to pursue.

In the 1760s, while still a *Privatdozent*, Kant was studying Rousseau and Hume and shifting the focus of his writings from science to pure philosophy. In 1763, his *Enquiry concerning the Clarity of the Principles of Natural Theology and Ethics* and his *One Possible Basis for a Demonstration of the Existence of God* were published. The next year, he published *Observations on the Feeling of the Beautiful and Sublime*, which was followed in 1766 by his *Dreams of a Spirit Seer*. He was establishing a reputation that opened up new opportunities for him. Also, in 1766, he was appointed second librarian of the Royal Library, a government position with a salary attached to it. Three years later, he considered accepting a professorship in logic and metaphysics at Erlangen; the following year he was encouraged to take a philosophy chair at Jena. Meanwhile, a chair in mathematics became vacant at Königsberg. It was arranged that Dr. Buck would shift into that position and that Kant would fill the chair in logic and metaphysics, which he had unsuccessfully sought twelve years earlier. Finally Kant had a stable, salaried professorship in his own beloved university.

In August of 1770, he read his dissertation, in Latin, *On the Form and Principles of the Sensible and Intelligible World*. This is the pivotal work that separates all of Kant's precritical philosophical writings from those that were to constitute his critical philosophy, which is based on a critique of the powers of the mind. The next ten years of Kant's life are sometimes called his silent decade because he published no important philosophical works during that interval. Having the benefit of a fixed salary, he cut back his teaching to two lectures a day, six days a week, usually from seven to nine in the morning, leaving the rest of the day free for his writings. His public lectures were to audiences of up to one hundred, while his private lectures were normally to no more than twenty students. Rather than trying to make professional philosophers of his students, Kant tried to teach them correct opinions and sound principles. In addition to strictly philosophical subjects, he deliberately continued to give lecture series on the popular subjects of anthropology and physical geography, trying to communicate a "knowledge of the world."[112] In letters of 1778 to Marcus Herz, a physician, friend, and disciple of Kant, he complains that "it is a matter of luck whether one has attentive and capable students during a certain period of time" and that the students "who are most thorough in note-taking are seldom capable of distinguishing the important from the unimportant."[113]

Still, he was proud of his ability to benefit average students, believing that anyone can teach the geniuses, whereas the dunces can be taught by no one. He tried to challenge his students actively to use their critical skills rather than merely cramming information. One of his pupils who went on to become a distinguished philosopher and man of letters in his own right, Johann Gottfried von Herder, later wrote of Kant:

> His broad forehead, built for thought, was the seat of an imperturbable cheerfulness and joy. Speech, the richest in thought, flowed from his lips. Playfulness, wit, and humor were at his command. His lectures were the most entertaining talks.

Then, after exclaiming about his teacher's extraordinary range of knowledge, Herder continues:

> No cabal, no sect, no prejudice, no desire for fame, could ever tempt him in the slightest away from broadening and illuminating the truth. He incited and gently forced others to think for themselves; despotism was foreign to his mind.[114]

It may be difficult for the reader of his more abstract philosophical treatises to believe, but he appears to have been an excellent teacher.

Kant was a careful, reflective, thrifty, conscientious man of great integrity. As he wrote to an intellectual who expressed concerns about the ironic tone of Kant's *Dreams of a Spirit Seer*,

> I shall certainly never become a fickle or fraudulent person. . . . Losing the self-respect that stems from a sense of honesty would therefore be the greatest evil that could, but most certainly shall not, befall me. Although I am absolutely convinced of many things that I shall never have the courage to say, I shall never say anything I do not believe.[115]

Though rarely sick until his later years, Kant seems to have been continually obsessed with his own health. He complains of his "sensitive nerves," his intolerance of "all medicines," his "irregular pulse," his "heartburn," digestive problems, and a "clouded brain."[116]

He was also fanatical about his daily schedule. Every morning, a few minutes before five, Martin Lampe, his servant from 1762 to 1802, would awaken him, saying, "It is time." For the next hour, Kant would drink tea and smoke a single bowl of tobacco in his pipe. The remainder of his morning was devoted to his lectures. He had dinner at one in the afternoon, usually with at least two, but no more than five, guests. The dinner usually lasted two or three hours and featured lively conversation, frequently about politics. After dining, Kant walked for an hour, eight times back and forth on the avenue that came to be known as the Philosopher's Walk. He supposedly failed to make his daily walk twice over the years—once, when he was absorbed in Rousseau's *Émile* and the other time, when awaiting news of the French Revolution. After 1785, he would only walk by himself so that he would not need to talk at the same time (he feared it might be unhealthy to breathe outdoors air in through his mouth). It has been said that the routine of his walk was so predictable that some housewives used to set their clocks by it. (His own most valued physical possession, by the way, was his watch.) After completing his walk, he would devote the rest of his day to reading and thinking until retiring at ten in the evening.

He never married but apparently thought about proposing marriage twice after he became financially comfortable. One woman was a young widow who married someone else before he could make up his mind; the other was a noble lady's pretty traveling companion, who left Königsberg before he could propose.

Kant seems to have been rather cool towards his siblings and their children. In a brief letter of 1792 to his brother, Johann Heinrich (who was eleven years younger, had attended Kant's lectures at the university, become a village pastor, and was to die eight years later), he writes: "Despite my apparent indifference, I have thought of you often and fraternally—not only for the time we are both living but also for after my death."[117] Thus, he was informing his brother of his intentions to provide for him and his family in his will. But Kant allowed many years to pass without contacting his brother at all and, it seems, may never have even met his sister-in-law.

The main thing Kant was doing in his silent decade, besides his teaching, was working out his own critical philosophy. A letter he wrote in 1765 indicates that even then he was thinking of moving in that direction: "What I am working on is mainly a book on the proper method of metaphysics (and thereby also the proper method of the whole of philosophy)." A few months later, he wrote a fellow philosopher,

> I think I have reached some important . . . insights that will establish the proper procedure for metaphysics. . . . To the extent that my other distractions permit, I am gradually preparing to submit these ideas to public scrutiny.

Those "other distractions" were, no doubt, the toil for low pay of his teaching as a *Privatdozent*, combined with his other writings that were helping him to become known in Prussia. Less than two weeks after assuming his professorial chair, he writes,

> For perhaps a year now, I believe I have arrived at a position that, I flatter myself, I shall never have to change, even though extensions will be needed, a position from which all sorts of metaphysical questions can be examined according to wholly certain and easy criteria.

In a famous letter of 1772 to his former student Dr. Marcus Herz, Kant describes his "plans for a work that might perhaps have the title, 'The Limits of Sense and Reason,'" comprising a theoretical portion of "two sections, (1) general **phenomenology** and (2) metaphysics," and a practical portion of "two sections, (1) the universal principles of feeling, taste, and sensuous desire and (2) the basic principles of morality." This may be viewed as a one-sentence synopsis of the entire philosophical system Kant was to develop over the next three decades. He goes on to say that "the pure concepts of the understanding must not be abstracted from sense perceptions," as British empiricists (like Hobbes and Hume) try to do, and that "sensuous representations present things as they appear," rather than "as they are," contrary to the views of realists (like Aristotle and Aquinas). Here already are the germs of what would become Kant's critical **idealism**; he claims to have systematically classified categories of the understanding on which he will be able to construct a "**transcendental** philosophy" and to be "in a position to bring out a 'Critique of Pure Reason.'" But the job would prove more laborious and challenging than Kant imagined. Five-and-a-half years later, he writes Herz,

> There is an obstacle to the completion of my 'Critique of Pure Reason'. . . . The thing that detains me is the problem of presenting these ideas with total clarity.

This is a problem Kant never entirely solved, and several more years of effort lay ahead before the monumental book was published in 1781 in Halle, dedicated to Baron von Zedlitz, Frederick the Great's liberal minister of justice and education. A couple of years later, Kant writes to Christian Garve, who had published a critical review of it,

> I must admit that I have not counted on an immediately favorable reception of my work. That could not be, since the expression of my ideas—ideas that I had been working out painstakingly for twelve years in succession— was not worked out sufficiently to be generally understandable. To achieve that I would have needed a few more years instead of the four or five months I took to complete the book.[118]

The book was little read, understood, or appreciated at first, largely because of the combination of its great length (almost seven hundred pages) and forbidding style. His assessment, in the preface to his own *Prolegomena*, is brutally honest, saying that "the work is dry, obscure, opposed to all ordinary notions, and moreover long-winded."[119] Nevertheless, it has proved to be a revolutionary book in the history of philosophy.

If the decade prior to the publication of his first *Critique* was Kant's silent decade, that immediately following it was prodigiously prolific. While continuing to meet the responsibilities of his full-time professorial position, he developed his philosophical system in work after remarkable work. In response to the unenthusiastic reception of the first *Critique*, he wrote the much shorter and easier, condensed version of its

---

Phenomenology.   Broadly, the study of appearances providing the content for all empirical knowledge; in Hegel, it is the study of the mind by way of the hierarchy of phenomena it considers; in the twentieth century, it is a philosophical movement (from Husserl and including Sartre) which uses introspective analysis to describe in depth the various forms of intentional consciousness

Transcendental.   In Kant, having to do with the *a priori* necessary conditions of organized experience (e.g., time and space), of knowledge (e.g., the concepts of the understanding), of metaphysical speculation (the ideas of pure reason), and so forth

key ideas, published in 1783 as the *Prolegomena to Any Future Metaphysics*. The following year, his essays, "What Is Enlightenment?" and "Idea for a Universal History from a Cosmopolitan Point of View," appeared in print. In 1785, his famous *Grounding for the Metaphysics of Morals* was published. The year after that, "Conjectural Beginning of Human History," his essay "What Is Orientation in Thinking?" and his *Metaphysical Foundations of Natural Science* appeared. In 1787, the second edition of his extensively revised first *Critique* was published. The following year, the *Critique of Practical Reason* appeared in print; and in 1790, the *Critique of Judgment* was published. Kant's fame was spreading throughout Prussia; by the middle of the 1790s, his philosophy was taught outside East Prussia by younger professors, some of whom were Kant's former students. The minister of education, Baron von Zedlitz, had already tried and failed to lure Kant to a more visible and prestigious professorship at Halle. Opportunities were opening up to him, but they threatened to infringe on the precious time, as Kant put it, "which I must rather use to complete my project"; and, indeed, this was his top priority, since he had already begun to "feel the infirmities of age"[120] advancing on him.

In 1786, the enlightened Frederick the Great died after ruling for four and a half decades. His illiberal nephew, Frederick William II, succeeded to the throne, being ceremoniously crowned in Königsberg when Kant was serving as rector (or vice-chancellor) of the university. The intellectual atmosphere quickly chilled. Near the end of that year, Kant learned from one of his disciples that a "Cabinets Order" had been issued temporarily forbidding any lecturing on the Kantian philosophy at Marburg; the following year, that injunction was removed, though such lectures were to be limited to advanced students. To make matters even worse, in mid-1788, the liberal von Zedlitz was replaced by an anti-Enlightenment former preacher, Johann Christoff Wollner, whom Frederick the Great had earlier called "a deceitful, scheming priest and nothing more." Less than a week after his appointment, Wollner issued a religious edict, requiring strictly orthodox adherence to Biblical doctrines. Less than half a year later, another censorship edict was announced mandating prepublication approval by official state censors of all works

dealing with religion. Wollner planted a spy at the lectures on the Kantian philosophy given by one of Kant's followers, even while feigning a friendly attitude towards Kant himself. This was the unpleasant climate surrounding what would be Kant's distressing confrontation with established authority. By the turn of the decade, Kant was in his late sixties and no longer as prolific as he had been. Yet he continued to write, including on religious matters. "On the Failure of All Attempted Philosophical **Theodicies**" was published in 1791, and his essay on "The End of Things" appeared in 1794. Meanwhile, he was working on the book that would embroil him in conflict, *Religion within the Limits of Reason Alone*. In 1791, a friend had warned him that Wollner was untrustworthy, that the king was acting like a religious fanatic, and that a "new edict on religion" was expected, requiring subjects "to go to church and Holy Communion."[121] While maintaining a private sense of religious reverence, Kant did not attend services or participate in public religious practices as an adult and appeared to regard external displays of piety as distasteful.

In 1792, Kant published "On the Radical Evil in Human Nature" with the permission of one of Wollner's censors in Berlin (it would later become Book One of his *Religion*). But Berlin denied Kant authorization to publish the next part (later Book Two), which was considered in conflict with Biblical teachings. This placed Kant in a difficult situation. As an Enlightenment thinker, he had defended the right of scholars to publish even controversial ideas. In "What Is Enlightenment?" he had urged, *"Sapere aude!* 'Have courage to use your own reason!'—that is the motto of enlightenment." He maintained that a person's use of reason "as a scholar before the reading public" should not be censored, but "must always be free."[122] Yet he was not himself the most courageous of men; furthermore, he felt a sincere respect for political authority. In what must have been a difficult decision for him, he ignored the Berlin censor and got permission to publish the last three books of *Religion* from the philosophy faculty at Jena (which did have the authority to grant it); all four books of his *Religion* were published together at Königsberg, in 1793. (That same year, he also published "On the Common Saying: 'This may be True in Theory, but it does not Apply in Practice.'") From Kant's point of view, as he explained to a professor of theology (to whom he later dedicated his *Conflict of the Faculties*), in sending him a copy of his *Religion*, this work was a necessary part of the Kantian system, which was established to solve certain problems:

> (1) What can I know? (metaphysics). (2) What ought I to do? (moral philosophy). (3) What may I hope? (philosophy of religion). A fourth question ought to follow, finally: What is man? (anthropology, a subject on which I have lectured for over twenty years). With the enclosed work, *Religion within the Limits* [*of Reason Alone*], I have tried to complete the third part of my plan.[123]

In October of 1794, Wollner wrote and signed a document censuring Kant for his "misuse of philosophy in distorting and depreciating many of the basic teachings of Holy Scripture and of Christianity," particularly in his *Religion*, demanding that Kant produce a "conscientious vindication" of his actions, and ordering him, with the threat of unspecified unpleasant consequences, "not to repeat this sort of offense in the future." Kant wrote a reply to the king, denying that he had done anything to challenge or compromise "the state religion" in any of his writings and maintaining that that book, in particular, far from ever "depreciating Christianity," in fact, "contains no assessment of any actual revealed religion." He continues,

> My true respect for Christianity is demonstrated by my extolling the Bible as the best available guide for the grounding and support of a truly moral state religion, perennially suitable for public instruction in religion.

Nevertheless, Kant tells his king,

> as Your Majesty's loyal subject, in order not to fall under suspicion, it will be the surest course for me to abstain entirely from all public lectures on religious topics, whether on natural or revealed religion, and not only from lectures but also from publications. I hereby promise this.

That same year, Kant received a letter regretting this commitment and admonishing,

> You thereby prepare a great triumph for the enemies of the Enlightenment, and the good cause suffers a great loss. It seems to me that you did not need to make this promise.

Kant later said that he included the phrase "as Your Majesty's loyal subject" for the express purpose of qualifying the commitment so that it would last only so long as Kant was a subject of Frederick William II.[174]

From the end of 1794 until the king's death in 1797, Kant kept his promise, publishing only on non-religious subjects: *Perpetual Peace* in 1795, both parts of *Metaphysics of Morals* (*The Metaphysical Elements of Justice* and *The Metaphysical Principles of Virtue*) in 1797, and his essay "On a Supposed Right to Lie from Altruistic Motives," also in 1797. The new king, Frederick William III, dismissed Wollner and abolished the censorship regime. Then, in 1798, Kant published *The Conflict of the Faculties*, which does deal with religion and includes the essay, "An Old Question Raised Again: Is the Human Race Constantly Progressing?" as well as his *Anthropology from a Pragmatic Point of View*. By this decade, other intellectuals were writing books on Kant's critical philosophy, and his ideas had spread to England, France, and the Netherlands. We have letters from two Benedictine professors at the Catholic University at Wurtzburg, in 1796, applauding the popularity of Kant's philosophy there. Meanwhile, however, the old professor was becoming feeble. In 1795, he reduced his teaching to the daily public lectures on logic and metaphysics; and two years later, he stopped teaching completely. In late 1798, he writes a letter, complaining that he feels "mentally paralyzed" and that his lifestyle seems reduced to "not that of a scholar but of a vegetable—eating, seeing, sleeping."[125]

By the turn of the century, he was losing both his memory and his vision. During the few years between his retirement and his death, Kant was working on restating his philosophy; but all we have is a series of unorganized, fragmentary notes now called his *Opus Postumum*, a work so impressionistic that one can only conjecture as to what to make of it and how to relate it to the published writings for which he is famous. By late 1803, it was unsafe for Kant to be alone, and his youngest sister, who had been widowed, moved in to care for him. On February 12, 1804, he died, his final spoken words being, "It is good" (*Es ist gut*). For more than two weeks, crowds gathered to pay their respects; his funeral, held on February 28, was well-attended. On April 23rd (the day after what would have been his eightieth birthday), a convocation solemnly assembled at the university to hear a memorial address in honor of the professor who had made remote little Königsberg a philosophical magnet attracting students from far and wide. Beginning in 1805, a Kant Club annually convened to celebrate his birthday; and in 1864, a statue of Kant was erected in Königsburg, depicting him walking.

Reality

As a dualist, Kant believes that the reality of the phenomenal world, which operates by mechanistic laws, is grounded in the **supersensible** reality of **things-in-themselves**, which functions according to **teleological** (or purposive) principles.[126] But only the realm of phenomenal reality is knowable, supersensible reality remaining merely a metaphysical realm of rational faith. For more than two millennia before Hume, philosophers had assumed the possibility of metaphysical knowledge—an assumption that Hume's thought radically calls into question. Although it is doubtful that Kant read English, in 1755 (the year he became a *Privatdozent*) Hume's first *Enquiry* was translated into German; the following year, Kant recommended it to one of his classes. So, his previously rationalistic views must have been challenged by Hume's works prior to the development of Kant's own critical philosophy.

CHALLENGING METAPHYSICS AS A SCIENCE. Metaphysics is that area of philosophy that deals with the nature of reality. The entire preface of Kant's *Prolegomena to Any Future Metaphysics* questions its very possibility. Metaphysics pretends to be a science; yet Kant is struck by the lack of any "universal and permanent recognition" of any of its conclusions. With a trace of sarcasm, he writes,

> It seems almost ridiculous, while every other science is continually advancing, that in this, which pretends to be wisdom incarnate, for whose oracle every one inquires, we should constantly move round the same spot, without gaining a single step.

He maintains that in the entire history of metaphysics nothing "more decisive to its fate" has occurred "than the attack made upon it by David Hume," who undermined the idea of causal necessity as rationally *a priori* and reduced it to "nothing but a bastard of imagination, impregnated by experience," depriving reason of all universality and necessity in the realm of factual reality and apparently gutting the very

possibility of metaphysics as traditionally conceived. Kant adds,

> I openly confess that my remembering David Hume was the very thing which many years ago first interrupted my dogmatic slumber and gave my investigations in the field of speculative philosophy a quite new direction.

This was, of course, the direction of a critical examination of the powers of human reason, involving a deduction of certain *a priori* structures of the mind as universal in and necessary for all human knowledge; as Kant observes, this is a task which Hume, as a rigorous empiricist, thought impossible and which "had never even occurred to any one else." For too long metaphysicians had dogmatically assumed such concepts as those of substance, reality, and causality with no prior critical reflection on their objective validity. Against such dogmatism Kant affirms

> that critique must exist as a science, systematic and complete as to its smallest parts, before we can think of letting metaphysics appear on the scene.

Indeed, this is the very meaning of his title, *Prolegomena* [i.e., Introductory Remarks] *to Any Future Metaphysics*. Any philosophical theory of reality must ultimately transcend the objects of experience to reach their foundations, thus striving for not only "physical but metaphysical knowledge, i.e., knowledge lying beyond experience."[127] But now Kant's question is whether—and, if so, how—such knowledge can even be possible.

In a famous sentence from his first *Critique*, Kant articulates the perplexity intrinsic to all metaphysical speculation:

> Human reason has this peculiar fate that in one species of its knowledge it is burdened by questions which, as prescribed by the very nature of reason itself, it is not able to ignore, but which, as transcending all its powers, it is also not able to answer.

Reason cannot help speculating about the nature of reality. We think and speak of the whole world as "the absolute *totality* of all existing things" and of nature as the dynamic "sum-total of all appearances" in the world.[128]

ANTINOMIES REGARDING THE COSMOS. Our attempts to get below the surface, so to speak, of nature lead us to the metaphysical idea of the cosmos, the world as

---

Supersensible.   In Kant, beyond the physical realm of possible sense experiences

Things-in-themselves.   Independent realities transcending the realm of phenomenal appearances; for Kant, they are humanly unknowable, though we have (noumenal) ideas of them

an ordered whole. But our attempts to reflect on this idea land us in the quicksand of rational **antinomies**, that is, mutual contradictions of **antithetical** principles resting on arguments of apparently equal validity. Kant analyzes four such antinomies regarding the cosmos: the first contains, as a **thesis**, the claim that reality as a whole has a temporal beginning and spatial limits, while its antithesis holds that reality as a whole is spatio-temporally infinite; the second has a thesis maintaining that everything real is resolvable into simple parts, while its antithesis denies that anything in the world is ultimately simple or indivisible; the third contains a thesis that there is free causality in the world as well as naturally determined causality, while its antithesis denies freedom, reducing all action to that which is naturally determined; and the fourth has a thesis that the world involves an absolutely necessary Being, as either a part of it or its cause, while the antithesis denies that there is any such absolutely necessary Being.[129]

Kant is convinced that equally plausible arguments can be mounted for both the thesis and the antithesis of each antinomy, so that something must be logically wrong with any such **cosmological** reasoning. He calls the inevitable error involved in this sort of cosmological thinking about the whole of reality "the **dialectical** illusion of pure reason": it is an "illusion" because it indicates the possibility of knowledge where logic shows us only self-contradiction; it is "dialectical" in the sense that it emerges from the mutual contradictions of thesis and antithesis in each of the four antinomies; and it is a matter of "pure reason," divorced from the findings of any possible concrete experience. What Kant thinks this shows is that our very attempt to apply concepts such as limitation (first antinomy), plurality (second), causality (third), and necessity (fourth) to reality as a whole, which is never a possible object of human experience, is illegitimate. He regards both the thesis and the antithesis of the first two antinomies as false: neither limitation

nor its negation applies to reality as a whole; likewise, neither ultimate simplicity nor ultimate plurality properly applies. By contrast, he believes that the thesis and antithesis of each of the last two antinomies are actually compatible rather than contradictory: there is freedom as applied to persons as rational subjects, while all objects in the realm of physical appearances act through natural necessity; likewise, there is an absolutely necessary Being (God) who is the Cause of the world of phenomenal appearances, although there is no absolutely necessary Being within the realm of such appearances.[130] But what is true of reality as a whole, of us as rational subjects, and of God remains a matter of metaphysical speculation, scientific knowledge being confined to the natural world of bodies.

Bodies

Although, as we shall see, Kant is an idealist in his theory of knowledge, he rejects any attempt to deny the reality of physical beings or to reduce their reality to mere ideas in the minds of its perceivers. "On the contrary," he asserts, "things as objects of our senses existing outside us are given" and never doubted. He continues,

> Consequently, I grant by all means that there are bodies without us, that is, things which, though quite unknown to us as to what they are in themselves, we yet know by the representations which their influence on our sensibility procures us, and which we call bodies.[131]

UNIVERSAL LAWS OF NATURE. Although experience never reveals the necessary nature of bodies as "things in themselves," we do experience their appearances and actions and can use that experience as a foundation for the principles of physical science:

> for instance, the propositions that "substance is permanent," and that "every event is determined by a cause according to constant laws," etc. These are actually universal laws of nature.

Antinomy (from the Greek *antinomia*, meaning conflict in law). The mutual contradiction of two principles, each of which appears to be true and can be supported, especially in Kant

Antithesis (from the Greek *antitithenai*, meaning to oppose). An idea or proposition set forth in opposition to another (as in Kant's discussion of the antinomies); in Hegelian thought, such opposition is the second phase of a dialectical process, leading to a synthesis of that antithesis and the thesis to which it is opposed

Thesis (from the Greek *tithenai*, to put or place). An idea formulated or a proposition put forward; in Hegelian thought, this represents the first phase of a dialectical process, in which that thesis is placed in opposition to another (its antithesis), leading to a higher unity of the two (their synthesis)

Through rational reflection on experience we can devise a scientific system of such "universal laws of nature," as Newton, for example, has done. Thus, through physical science, "we know nature as nothing but the totality of appearances" and derive their laws "from the conditions of their necessary unification" in our own consciousness. Against the traditional view, Kant maintains that

> we must not seek the universal laws of nature in nature by means of experience, but **conversely** must seek nature, as to its universal conformity to law, in the conditions of the possibility of experience, which lie in our sensibility and in our understanding.

Science requires that bodies follow certain universal and necessary laws because, otherwise, they could not be physical objects of human experience and subjects of knowledge at all. The entire natural realm of bodies or

> the sensible world is nothing but a chain of appearances connected according to universal laws.[132] This is the world of physical experience.

MATTER AND MOTION. As a Newtonian, Kant conceives of the phenomenal world of bodies in terms of the correlated concepts of matter and motion.

> Matter is the movable insofar as it fills a space. To fill a space means to resist everything movable that strives by its motion to press into a certain space.

As an object extended in space, a body resists other bodies by forces of repulsion, so that no two bodies can fill the same space at the same time. Thus, he says, "The concept of matter is reduced to nothing but moving forces." By definition, says Kant, "A body" is "matter between determinate boundaries (and such matter therefore has a figure)." All matter being subject to moving forces, any "mass of determinate shape is called a body." Matter is essentially movable, and motion can be experienced and known only in terms of phenomenal appearances. Kant concludes his *Metaphysical Foundations of Natural Science* with the acknowledgment that we naturally want to pass beyond this "to grasp the absolute totality of all conditions" regarding bodies, but we must beware of supposing that such knowledge—passing from physics into metaphysics—is possible.[133]

Kant holds that underlying all qualities and representations in "our empirical concept of a body" are the ideas of space and substance, which will require

critical analysis. Later, he writes that it is the mind itself that imposes "order and regularity" on the welter of physical appearances we experience, making physical science possible as "objectively valid." The mind imposes on physical reality a "Principle of Permanence of Substance," similar to the Newtonian law of the conservation of matter, that allows us to make sense of physical change; it also imposes a "Principle of Succession in Time, in accordance with the Law of Causality," similar to the Newtonian idea of force as the cause of physical change; and, third, it imposes a "Principle of Coexistence, in accordance with the Law of Reciprocity or Community," similar to the Newtonian idea of all masses exerting some force on all others in a system of gravitational interaction. Kant calls these principles of physical science "the three analogies of experience"; they allow us to think about bodies as enduring through time, as effecting change in succeeding times, and as coexisting simultaneously. On this view, bodies are dynamic centers of moving forces. Thus, we conceive of the natural order of bodies.

> By nature, in the empirical sense, we understand the connection of appearances as regards their existence according to necessary rules, that is, according to laws.

None of this says anything about what bodies must be like in themselves and apart from our human experiences of them. And neither does any of this cast doubt on the reality of bodies as "*material* idealism" might try to do. Kant rejects even "the *problematic* idealism of Descartes," as he calls it, for doubting the reality of the material world until he can derive it from his own existence. By contrast, he holds that "the consciousness of my existence is at the same time an immediate consciousness of the existence of other things outside me"; there is no knowledge of self in a vacuum. So we do know bodies, as is evidenced by physical science. "We ought, however, to bear in mind that bodies are not objects in themselves which are present to us, but a mere appearance of we know not what unknown object" in our experience, known only as phenomena. Reason leads us to think of an underlying ground of unity of such phenomena, without which we would have no ultimately coherent understanding of empirical truth;[134] nevertheless, this idea of the ground of phenomenal appearances is metaphysical, rather than physical, and not knowable. As we are about to see, this limitation of knowledge to phenomenal appearances, rather than to things in themselves, applies to the human personality as well as to bodies.

Personality

THE UNKNOWABLE SELF. Like our idea of the cosmos, or world as an ordered whole, our psychological idea of the self is metaphysical. As we ascribe all qualities of external sensation to objects called bodies, which are not knowable in themselves, "all the predicates of an internal sense refer to the *ego,* as a subject" which is likewise intrinsically unknowable. We experience our own states of consciousness—our thoughts, feelings, desires, and so forth; and we attribute them to an *"absolute subject"* which we cannot experience and cannot know but should regard as merely an idea of reason. Although this idea never functions in such a way as to constitute knowledge, it nevertheless "serves very well as a **regulative** principle totally to destroy all **materialistic** explanations of the internal phenomena of the soul," such as those of Hobbes. But we must beware of any "supposed **cognition** of the substance of our thinking being," since it transcends the limits of "the complex of experience" that is possible for us. Even thinking of the self or soul in terms of the concept of substance is potentially misleading, since that concept implies a degree of permanence which, in this case, "cannot be proved of it" because we cannot theoretically prove the soul's permanence "after death," as we would like to do.[135]

THE SELF AS MORAL AGENT. Although we cannot theoretically know the human personality in itself (apart from its states of consciousness, traits, and dispositions), we experience the self as a moral agent and, for practical purposes, should regard the human person as "an end in himself" having "an absolute worth." As such, he should never be treated as a mere thing or object. As Kant writes in his *Grounding,*

> rational beings are called persons inasmuch as their nature already marks them out as ends in themselves, i.e., as something which is not to be used merely as means and hence there is imposed thereby a limit on all

arbitrary use of such beings, which are thus objects of respect.

This is the basis of Kant's claim that all persons, as such, "have dignity, i.e., unconditional and incomparable worth"; it is our "rational nature" and capacity for **autonomy** that render persons worthy of respect. "Autonomy of the will is the property that the will has of being a law to itself," the capacity to think for oneself, to make one's own choices, and to be responsible for one's own actions. Such autonomy presupposes human freedom (which we shall discuss more carefully in a later section), the capacity of self-determination, as opposed to bodies, whose actions are naturally determined "through the influence of alien causes." It is as rational beings, rather than specifically as human beings, that we are free, so that freedom would naturally pertain to all persons, or rational beings.[136]

Kant admits that he cannot theoretically prove "freedom to be something actual in ourselves and in human nature," but he "must presuppose it" as a **postulate** of practical reason, required for the sake of moral experience. On this view there are two legitimate perspectives on human nature: we adopt "one point of view when by means of freedom we think of ourselves as a priori efficient causes" of our own actions "and another point of view when we represent ourselves with reference to our actions as effects" of our bodies on other bodies in our environment. The human person, on this view, belongs to two realms, "a world of sense and a world of understanding"; we know the body and empirical ego in terms of appearances in the world of sense, whereas we have rational beliefs, never constituting knowledge, regarding the self as freely functioning in the realm of moral action. Through inner sense a person can know himself in terms of psychological phenomena "as belonging to the world of sense"; but as a self-determining agent, "he must count himself as belonging to the intellectual world, of which he has, however, no further knowledge." Reason is that faculty in human nature which transcends sensibility and even understanding and which "shows such a pure spontaneity in the case of what are called ideas that it goes far beyond" the limits of the world of sense. "Therefore a rational

---

Regulative (from the Latin *regula*, meaning a rule). Serving the heuristic function of guiding further thought and action, as opposed (in Kant) to the constitutive function of ideas that can lead to knowledge

being," Kant concludes, "has two standpoints from which he can regard himself" legitimately: "first, insofar as he belongs to the world of sense subject to laws of nature (**heteronomy**); secondly, insofar as he belongs to the intelligible world subject to laws" of morality, "which, independent of nature, are not empirical but are founded only on reason" (human autonomy). It is as a rational being "belonging to the intelligible world" that man has a self-determining will of his own; as an animal "belonging to the world of sense," man is subjected to various "desires and inclinations" impinging on that will. Kant speaks of man's autonomous rational will as "his proper self," which acknowledges its duty, can take an interest in and be satisfied by doing it, and can causally determine the body to act "in accordance with rational principles." Thus, the body, its inclinations, and its actions, all of which are phenomena in the world of sense, are "subordinated" to the autonomous rational will which is "our proper self."[137]

SENSE, IMAGINATION, AND APPERCEPTION. In the first *Critique* Kant speaks of "three original sources (capacities or faculties of the soul)" of the mind's experiences, "namely *sense, imagination,* and ***apperception*.*"* Through sensation the mind intuits, or directly experiences, a manifold of representations of objects; through imagination the mind synthesizes this manifold into coherent patterns of experience; and through apperception the mind relates all its experiences to itself as the foundation of their unity. All knowledge and all coherence of experience presuppose a "pure" (or nonempirical, nonphenomenal) conscious source of its unity. "This pure original unchangeable consciousness," says Kant, "I shall name transcendental apperception" (the word "transcendental" referring to its being a **necessary condition** of experience). "*Sense* represents appearances empirically in *perception, imagination* in *association*" with one another, and *apperception* refers them to the self experiencing them all as objects of its experience. Kant explains, "For it is only because I ascribe all perceptions to one consciousness (original apperception) that I can say of all perceptions that I am conscious of them." Thus, the unity of perceptions in any person's

experience requires that they all be related to the "apperception" of his conscious self.

> The abiding and unchanging "I" (pure apperception) forms the correlate of all our representations in so far as it is to be at all possible that we should become conscious of them.

Kant sounds somewhat like Descartes when he writes, "It must be possible for the 'I think' to accompany all my representations"; for there cannot be thoughts without a thinker experiencing those thoughts. Yet, unlike Descartes, Kant denies that the thinking thing can be adequately represented or known in itself. He calls it "*pure apperception,*" he says,

> because it is that self-consciousness which, while generating the representation "*I think*" (a representation which must be capable of accompanying all other representations, and which in all consciousness is one and the same), cannot itself be accompanied by any further representation.

It is my experience of my perceptions as all being mine that leads me to the idea of an enduring, identical self; this "apperception," then, is "transcendental," in the sense that we discover it as a necessary condition of any coherent cognitive experience at all.

> The **synthetic** unity of consciousness is, therefore, an objective condition of all knowledge. It is not merely a condition that I myself require in knowing an object, but it is a condition under which every intuition must stand in order *to become an object for me.*[138]

Like Descartes, then, Kant maintains that we are conscious of our own existence as thinking things. But, unlike Descartes, he says, "This *representation* is a *thought,* not an *intuition*" providing any knowledge of the nature of the mind in itself, which we cannot intuit, or directly experience, at all, since all our intuition is sensible.

> Accordingly I have no *knowledge* of myself as I am but merely as I appear to myself. The consciousness of self is thus very far from being a knowledge of the self.

We have a functional consciousness of the mind, as it exercises, for example, its "higher faculties of knowledge," namely "*understanding, judgment,* and *reason*" (which we shall discuss in the following section). So, we are aware of the existence of a thinking subject

---

Heteronomy (from the Greek *heteronomos*, meaning other law).   The condition of being under the control of desires, inclinations, other people, or anything beyond one's own rational will (in Kant, contrasted with *autonomy*)

through experience of its operations but can achieve no knowledge of its essential nature since all our intuition is derived from sensibility and oriented to phenomenal appearances as its objects.[139]

THE IDEA OF THE SOUL.   Kant's first *Critique* contains a long and extremely difficult chapter (entitled "The **Paralogisms** of Pure Reason") in which he critically analyzes the metaphysical idea of the soul. Without attempting to plumb the depths of this chapter, which can be seen as reflections on the rational psychology of metaphysicians like Descartes, we can briefly consider a few key points. Personal, subjective experience—the "I think" or *cogito* of Descartes—is the starting point of self-consciousness. It naturally leads us to speculate about the nature of the self or soul doing the thinking. Thus, we might be metaphysically drawn to suppose that the soul is a simple reality, a unitary substance existing as a subject in relation to possible objects of experience. (As we shall see in the following section, all of these representations of the soul involve the illegitimate application of categories of understanding to what is not, and cannot be, an object of experience.) We are led to suppose, through the logic of rational psychology, that such a simple substance must be immaterial and thus incorruptible and that, as an intelligent subject, it has *personality*; combining all this we are led to view it as spiritual yet in some working community with the animal body, of which it must be the principle of life. But, being spiritual and incorruptible and having intellectual functions independent of body, it would also seem to be immortal. (We see reasoning of this sort, for example, in the rational psychology of Plato and Aquinas.) The problem, however, is that all this metaphysical speculation is based on the mistaken assumption that the starting point of the "I think" provides us with insight into the nature of the self and "may contain perception of an existent (the Cartesian *cogito, ergo sum*)."[140] But, in fact, Kant maintains, the "I think" only leads us to an awareness of an unknowable self, which functions as the transcendental unity of apperception, a pure subject, rather than an object of introspective perception.

THE EXERCISE OF RATIONAL WILL.   In the second *Critique* Kant analyzes "personality" in terms of "the freedom and independence from the mechanism of nature" arising from the exercising of rational will. It is as persons that rational beings are to be regarded as intrinsically valuable ends in themselves and never merely as means to the extrinsic ends of others. "This idea of personality awakens respect" for the dignity of all rational beings.[141]

CULTURE AS OUR ULTIMATE PURPOSE.   In his third *Critique* Kant observes that persons are attracted to objects regarded as "*pleasant*, or *beautiful*, or *sublime*, or *good*"; pleasure motivates our desires for enjoyment, beauty is satisfying to our disinterested judgment, the sublime leads us to contemplate what inspires awe, and the good is the object of moral experience. It is the subjects who experience objects in such varied ways that Kant regards as "the *ultimate purpose* of nature here on earth, in reference to whom all other natural things constitute a system of purposes" as means to the ends of persons. If we ask what is nature's ultimate purpose for man, Kant answers that it is "his *culture*" rather than happiness. "For it is not his nature to rest and be contented with the possession and enjoyment of anything whatever." Happiness, in order to be good, must be deserved. In this life as we know it, human nature seems forever to want more than whatever is available. Although man is "entitled to be the lord of nature," this is in virtue of "his having an understanding and the will" to act for higher purposes; but these faculties must be carefully developed in order to flourish.

> Therefore, culture alone can be the ultimate purpose which we have cause for ascribing to nature in respect to the human race (not man's earthly happiness or the fact that he is the chief instrument of instituting order and harmony in irrational nature external to himself).

But this development of the human person that Kant calls our "culture" can only be achieved in the context of "a *civil community*" that crosses national borders and involves international cooperation—"a *cosmopolitan* whole, i.e. a system of all states that are in danger of acting injuriously upon one another."

Paralogism (from the Greek *paralogos*, meaning contrary to reason).   In Kant, any of four fallacious arguments meant to prove something about the nature of the soul or pure ego

Otherwise, the threat of war is certain to disrupt and undermine the process of human culture. It is as a moral subject that "man is the final purpose of creation," according to Kant, "to which the whole of nature is teleologically subordinated"[142] as means to a more ultimate end.

DEVELOPING HUMAN CAPACITIES. He discusses this topic of human culture in a different form in the first four theses of his "Idea for a Universal History." His first thesis is teleological, maintaining,

> All natural capacities of a creature are destined to evolve completely to their natural end,

since otherwise, life might be reduced to a chaotic, "aimless course" determined by "blind chance." His second thesis says,

> In man (as the only rational creature on earth) *those natural capacities which are directed to the use of his reason are to be fully developed only in the race, not in the individual,*

since an individual's lifespan is too brief to allow for the necessary cultivation. His third thesis maintains,

> Nature has willed that man should, by himself, produce everything that goes beyond the mechanical ordering of his animal existence, and that he should partake of no other happiness or perfection than that which he himself, independently of instinct, has created by his own reason;

here again, we see the subordination of happiness to culture, which is deemed a necessary condition of our worthiness of happiness. And his fourth thesis says,

> The means employed by Nature to bring about the development of all the capacities of men is their antagonism in society, so far as this is, in the end, the cause of a lawful order among men;

for without such a stimulus prodding us, we might lack sufficient motivation to develop our capacities. He explains this "antagonism" among humans in terms of an "unsocial sociability of men, i.e., their propensity to enter into society, bound together with a mutual opposition which constantly threatens to break up the society." Unlike Hobbes, he holds that human nature comprises "an inclination to associate with others"; but, like Hobbes, he is struck by a contrary tendency to isolation and natural hostility.[143]

WILL SUBJECT TO REASON. Like Hobbes, Kant thinks that the will must be subject to reason if a just society is ever to be achieved. In the introduction to the *Metaphysics of Morals* he distinguishes between "free will," determined by reason, and "animal will," which is "determined only by inclination." Our human will is not "pure" because it is "affected but not determined by impulses" of desire. It is free insofar as it is subject to rationally determined universal moral laws. As he says in *The Metaphysical Elements of Justice*, the freedom of our will is not theoretically provable, as we have seen, because it is "completely supersensible"; and it coexists with the natural necessity of our bodily actions. On this dualistic view, man can be both free as a **noumenal** being in himself and extrinsically determined as a phenomenal physical being. His dignity is seen as a function "of his humanity considered as a personality, independently of physical determinations (*homo noumenon*). In contradistinction to this, man can be regarded as a subject affected by these determinations (*homo phaenomenon*),"[144] this latter perspective representing our animality.

HUMAN UNIQUENESS. At the beginning of his *Anthropology* Kant writes,

> The fact that man is aware of an ego-concept raises him infinitely above all other creatures living on earth. Because of this, he is a person; and by virtue of this oneness of consciousness, he remains one and the same person despite all the vicissitudes which may befall him.

Human dignity is rooted in personality, which is a function of self-awareness, as Socrates recognized so many centuries earlier. We still need to consider, however, human emotions, a dimension of human nature which students often mistakenly assume Kant ignores. Indeed, his *Anthropology* deals with our emotions and passions. Passions are inclinations "which can hardly, or not at all, be controlled by reason"; and, as such, they are dangerous. "On the other hand, emotion is the feeling of a pleasure or displeasure at a particular moment," which need not affect reason at all. We think

---

Noumenon (plural, **noumena**). In Kant, a rational idea, transcending all possible experience, of a thing-in-itself, as the unknowable ground of phenomenal appearances

there is something unfortunately wrong with a person who is devoid of emotion. "Passion, on the other hand, no man wishes for himself. Who wants to have himself put in chains when he can be free?" There are two sorts of passions—"those of natural inclination (innate) and those arising from the culture of mankind (acquired)"; sexual passion is an example of the first sort, while "ambition, lust of power, and avarice" are examples of the second. Kant also describes four general types of psychological temperaments: first, the sanguine person, whom Kant calls "Light-Blooded," tends to be "carefree and full of expectation," but frivolous, "a good companion, jocular, and high-spirited"; second, the melancholic temperament, which he labels "Heavy-Blooded" in nature, "thinks deeply" and takes things, including commitments, very seriously; third, the choleric temperament, which Kant calls "Hot-Blooded," is "hot-tempered," quick to take offense, "fond of appearance and the pomp of formalities," and driven by pride; and, fourth, the phlegmatic temperament, which he labels "Cold-Blooded," has a "tendency to inactivity" but is persistent and even-tempered. Temperament, "what nature makes of man," should not be confused with character, "what man makes of himself"; the former may have a utilitarian value, but the latter "has an inner value" or moral worth. The human capacity for self-development renders us unique in the animal kingdom; for "man as an animal endowed with capability of reason (*animal rationabile*) can make himself a rational animal (*animal rationale*)." Man's uniqueness among all earthly creatures consists of a combination of "his technical gift for manipulating things" ably, "his pragmatic gift (being clever in the use of others for his own purposes), and his moral gift of character (so that he can act toward himself and others according to the principle of freedom under the law)." Technically, we create fine and powerful tools to serve our needs and interests; pragmatically, we relate to others socially and become civilized through culture; and, morally, we view ourselves and others as free subjects and agents.[145]

THE CONFLICT BETWEEN GOOD AND EVIL. In *Religion within the Limits of Reason Alone* Kant considers the question of whether "*Man is* (by nature) *either morally good or morally evil*," indicating that it is possible that man is neither or both. He writes of three dimensions of human nature: first, a "predisposition to *animality* in man, taken as a *living* being" in the physical world; second, a "predisposition to *humanity* in man, taken as a living and at the same time a *rational* being"; and, third, a "predisposition to *personality* in man, taken as a rational and at the same time an *accountable* being," or moral agent. As animals, we are subject to "the *beastly* vices of *gluttony* and *drunkenness, lasciviousness*, and *wild lawlessness* [in relation to other men]"; as humans, we are subject to excessive pride, "*jealousy* and *rivalry*," as well as "the *diabolical vices*" of "*envy, ingratitude, spitefulness*, etc." But it is as persons that we bear a moral responsibility to resist such inclinations. At any rate, all three of our natural predispositions are good in themselves. Nevertheless, there is a natural human propensity towards evil, which can be analyzed in terms of the three aspects of "the *frailty* of human nature," its "*impurity*," and its "*wickedness*." Our frailty has to do with weakness of will, our impurity with the selfish motives that can clash with moral ones, and our wickedness with the tendency to subordinate moral duty to selfish desires. So man is naturally evil in the sense that he has propensities to defy moral obligations. Kant makes it clear that neither our sensuous nature nor reason in general is to blame for such evil tendencies, that it is to be located in our free will, which can choose either badly or well. (In Christian theology, this is related to the doctrine of **original sin**.) And we have a moral duty to try our best to resist these evil tendencies and continually to choose the good as revealed by reason.

> Natural inclinations, *considered in themselves*, are *good*, that is, not a matter of reproach, and it is not only futile to want to extirpate them but to do so would also be harmful and blameworthy. Rather, let them be tamed and instead of clashing with one another they can be brought into harmony in a wholeness which is called happiness.

Consequently, human nature is also naturally good, in that we have a propensity to moral behavior and to the sort of integrity that results from harmoniously ordering our personality and behavior. Thus, human nature comprises a conflict between good and evil tendencies, and we must use free will responsibly to pursue the former and shun the latter. Kant regards Jesus as the personification of the "ideal of moral perfection," a model we should strive to emulate.[146] Human personality, then, can be made good by the conscientious use of our own freedom. But this requires that we follow reason, which is oriented towards, but often falls short of, knowledge.

Knowledge

In his precritical writings, such as *New Exposition* of 1755, Kant maintains a fairly traditional rationalistic epistemology, arguing, for example, that there cannot be "one *sole*, absolutely first, universal principle of all truths," such as Aristotle's logical principle of **noncontradiction**, and arguing for the principle of identity in an affirmative ("*Whatever is is*") and a negative ("*Whatever is not is not*") form.[147] In the Inaugural Dissertation, of 1770, he distinguishes between "*sensitive*" and "*intellectual*" cognition, holding that the objects of sensitive knowledge are "representations of things *as they appear*," whereas those of intellectual thought are "representations of things *as they are*." Against traditional rationalists, he now denies that we can have "an *intuition* of things intellectual," saying we have "only a *symbolic cognition*" of them, our human intuition being "always *passive*" and derived from sense, unlike God's "perfectly intellectual" intuition, for example. And he warns against the dangers of confusing these two sorts of intuition, saying that "great care must be taken *lest the domestic principles of sensitive cognition transgress their boundaries and affect things intellectual*."[148] Here we see some of the seeds of his critical epistemology (no doubt germinated by the thought of Hume), which would root all knowledge in sensibility and restrict the legitimate use of concepts of knowledge to the realm of phenomena, while nevertheless speculating about intellectual ideas of pure reason, for which we have no corresponding intuitions. Let us now turn to the more famous works of his critical philosophy, starting with the relatively more accessible *Prolegomena*.

ANALYTIC VS. SYNTHETIC JUDGMENTS.   Since knowledge requires judgments, it will be helpful to distinguish types of possible judgments.

> Analytic judgments express nothing in the predicate but what has been already actually thought in the concept of the subject, though not so clearly and with the same consciousness.

For example, the judgment, "All bachelors are unmarried" is analytic, or "merely *explicative*," in that an analysis or explication of the subject concept ("bachelors") reveals that it already contains the predicate ("unmarried") as part of its meaning. The principle of noncontradiction governs all analytic judgments; thus a denial of that judgment about bachelors yields a self-contradictory statement, which must be false, rendering the original judgment universally and necessarily true. By contrast, synthetic judgments are genuinely informative "or *ampliative*" in the sense that their predicate terms provide new information not already contained in their subjects, thus amplifying or adding to the content of their subject terms. For example, in the judgment, "Some students are left-handed," there is nothing in the subject concept that implies anything about left-handedness. Obviously, the principle of noncontradiction cannot suffice to determine the truth of such judgments, since they are not a matter of definition (although, of course, they must not violate the principle of noncontradiction). Judgments of common sense and ordinary experience are synthetic, or what Hume called "matters of fact"; Kant holds that mathematical judgments are also synthetic, whereas Hume considered them analytic, or what he called "relations of ideas." However, mathematical judgments, as Hume and Kant would agree, unlike those of ordinary experience, are *a priori*, in the sense that their truth is universal, necessary, and not contingent on any concrete experience; in contrast, the judgment about left-handed students need not always be true, and its truth or falsehood can only be ascertained by concrete experience.[149]

Kant is particularly interested in judgments that are both synthetic (factually informative) and *a priori* (universally and necessarily true), as he thinks fundamental laws of science and principles of metaphysics should be. But before Kant himself, "no one, not even Hume, was led to make investigations concerning judgments of this kind," so that Kant is blazing a new trail, never traveled before by either dogmatic rationalists like Descartes and Leibniz or sceptical empiricists like Hobbes and Hume. "Weary therefore of dogmatism, which teaches us nothing, and of scepticism, which does not even promise us anything" in the way of factual certainty, Kant is the first to ask the question, "How are synthetic propositions *a priori* possible?" It is easy to understand that analytic statements are *a priori* since they are matters of definition "entirely founded on the principle of contradiction." Likewise, "synthetic ***a posteriori*** judgments" (those that are both informative and contingent on concrete experience) are simply verified or falsified by experience. But synthetic *a priori* propositions are neither matters of definition nor contingent on experience. Yet Kant is certain (of what Hume would deny) that there are such judgments, since basic laws of science (and, Kant would add, mathematical judgments) are of this sort. So he asks his novel question and points out that metaphysics, if it is ever to qualify as a science, "stands or falls with the solution of this problem; its very existence depends upon it." If all truths are either analytic or synthetic *a posteriori*, as Hume thought, then there is no place for metaphysics, which purports to deliver informative truths that are universally and necessarily so—in which case, Hume's inflammatory verdict that all works of metaphysics should be cast into the flames as worthless might seem appropriate. Until this problem is solved, future work in metaphysics is presumptuous, or "dogmatic," in Kant's sense. As he puts it rather grandly,

> All metaphysicians are therefore solemnly and legally suspended from their occupations till they shall have satisfactorily answered the question: *How are synthetic cognitions a priori possible?*[150]

Kant's own complicated answer to the question constitutes his critical epistemology, the core of his entire transcendental philosophy.

Forms of Sensibility.   As he did in his precritical Inaugural Dissertation, Kant repeats here that we humans, unlike God, are not capable of any original, *a priori* intellectual intuitions, all of our intuitions of objects being derived from sensibility. Nevertheless, we do have *a priori* concepts, such as those "of quantity, of cause, etc." that are not derived from experience itself, although their legitimate application must be empirical. Likewise, there are two *a priori*

forms of sensibility, space and time, which in themselves have no content but serve as structures within which objects can be intuited. Thus, space and time are not things like tables and chairs; but they are forms in the mind used to organize our experiences of such things as tables and chairs. However, these forms of sensibility legitimately apply to "objects only as they *appear* to us (to our senses), not as they are in themselves"—that is, to our human representations of tables and chairs rather than to whatever those realities we call tables and chairs may be independently of our experiences of them. Kant tries to show that the alleged synthetic *a priori* truths of mathematics are possible because they relate to these *a priori* forms: "Now, the intuitions which pure mathematics lays at the foundation of all its cognitions and judgments which appear at once apodeictic and necessary are space and time" (the word "apodeictic" here means universally true). Thus, he says, "Geometry is based upon the pure intuition of space. Arithmetic attains its concepts of numbers by the successive addition of units in time." So, mathematical knowledge is possible because it is grounded in these *a priori* "forms of our sensibility, which must precede all empirical intuition, i.e. perception of actual objects," but which are not themselves objects of empirical intuition.[151]

Thus, space and time are organizational structures of the mind, rather than empirical concepts. This does not, of course, condemn space and time or the sensible world they structure to the status of "mere illusion." We can distinguish genuine from illusory representations by their degree of coherence, and we shall be secure as long as we do not assume that what our senses reveal as appearances necessarily corresponds to the things themselves whose appearances we experience. Kant writes,

> if I consider all the representations of the senses, together with their form, space and time, to be nothing but appearances, and space and time to be a mere form of the sensibility, which is not to be met with in objects out of it, and if I make use of these representations in reference to possible experience only, there is nothing in my regarding them as appearances that can lead astray or

---

A posteriori (literally, in Latin, from the subsequent).   Following and dependent on some particular sense-experience, empirical, as opposed to *a priori*

cause illusion. For all that, they can correctly cohere according to rules of truth in experience

and qualify as genuine. Although Kant is an idealist, viewing time and space as forms of sensibility in the mind rather than objects outside the mind, his philosophy is merely a "transcendental, or better, *critical* idealism," in the sense that it critically analyzes our *a priori* forms, concepts, and ideas as necessary conditions of experience that are to be found in the mind alone. He never denies the reality of external things independent of the mind; indeed, unlike Descartes, he does not even call that into question, "since," as he puts it, "it never came into my head to doubt it."[152]

OBJECTIVE, SCIENTIFIC KNOWLEDGE. So much for our ordered perceptual judgments. Now let us consider the possibility of objective knowledge, such as science purports to deliver, "the cognition of nature, the actuality of which can be confirmed by experience." We can distinguish between "mere *judgments of perception*," which are "only subjectively valid" for the perceiver under certain circumstances, and "*judgments of experience*," which "have objective validity" for people in general. What must be added to the former to yield the latter are universally necessary (therefore *a priori*) concepts of the understanding. Kant says that

> if we have reason to hold a judgment to be necessarily universally valid (which never rests on perception, but on the pure concept of the understanding under which the perception is subsumed), we must consider it to be objective also, that is, that it expresses not merely a reference of our perception to a subject, but a quality of the object.

The basis of any objectively valid judgment of experience must be the perceptions of sensible intuition; but, in addition, the understanding must form judgments about those perceptions, using one or more of its *a priori* concepts or categories. Kant offers a good example in a footnote. We subjectively perceive that a stone becomes warm when the Sun shines on it, without understanding any necessary link between those two events, which, for all we know thus far, may just spatio-temporally happen to be related.

> But if I say: the sun warms the stone, I add to the perception a concept of the understanding, viz., that of cause, which necessarily connects with the concept of sunshine that of heat, and the synthetic judgment

becomes of necessity universally valid, viz., objective, and is converted from a perception into experience.[153]

Kant next provides a "Table of the Concepts of the Understanding," organized into four sets, each containing three concepts: the categories of quantity (unity, plurality, and totality), those of quality (reality, negation, and limitation), those of relation (substance, cause, and community), and those of modality (possibility, existence, and necessity). Objects can only be known or understood in terms of one or more of these categories, which only legitimately apply to phenomena of experience (and not necessarily to any things in themselves). Hume was correct that these concepts, such as substance and causality, are neither innate ideas nor mere inductive generalizations from experience; but he was mistaken in supposing that they are the contingent products of imagination. When we know that the sunlight causes the stone to become warm, the necessary connection Hume was seeking is the "necessary and universally valid" concept of the understanding (or category) of causality. Hume mistakenly tried to derive necessary connection from experience; but, in a way, he had things upside down when he asserted that the categories "are not derived from experience, but experience is derived from them." The categories are *a priori* concepts (not innate ideas, since they are formal structures of the mind with no content of their own) which the mind brings to its perceptions to constitute objectively valid, knowable experience. They "can never be referred to things in themselves, but only to appearances," as far as their legitimate application goes. Yet we cannot help referring phenomenal appearances to "*noumena*," that is, ideas of things in themselves, which we can only think about and talk about in terms of categories, which are the tools of our cognitive discourse:

> The understanding therefore, by assuming appearances, grants also the existence of things in themselves, and thus far we may say that the representation of such things as are the basis of appearances, consequently of mere beings of the understanding, is not only admissible but unavoidable.

Thus, the speculations of metaphysics are generated. "There is indeed something seductive in our pure concepts of the understanding which tempts us to a transcendent use—a use which transcends all possible experience." We succumb to this temptation when engaged in metaphysical speculation, as human reason naturally inclines us to do. The noumenal ideas of reason are merely problematic, with no empirical content and thus beyond the limits of possible knowledge.[154]

The synthetic judgments of science can be *a priori* because they involve the empirically verified application of universally necessary concepts of the understanding to data derived from perceptual observations.

> For we know nature as nothing but the totality of appearances, i.e., of representations in us; and hence we can only derive the law of their common connection from the principles of their connection in us.

Known as Kant's "**Copernican revolution**," this inverts the traditional view; instead of maintaining that our minds must conform to laws that are already in the natural world, he holds that phenomena of the natural world must meet the requirements of the mind in order to be possible objects of human experience and knowledge. As he puts it, "we must not seek the universal laws of nature in nature by means of experience, but conversely must seek nature, as to its universal conformity to law, in the conditions of the possibility of experience, which lie in our sensibility and in our understanding." Because it is contrary to our usual way of thinking of the relationship between the mind and objects of scientific knowledge (as was the revolutionary **heliocentric** theory of Copernicus), Kant's theory "seems at first strange"; yet he is confident that "*the understanding does not derive its laws (a priori) from, but prescribes them to, nature.*" Again, the limitation embedded in this position is that science can only legitimately apply the concepts of the understanding, which are essential to knowledge, to "nature as an object of possible experience" and not to "the nature of things in themselves." Kant credits Aristotle with having collected certain "elementary concepts under the name of categories." But not until Kant himself were they systematically ordered, presented as the universally necessary conditions of all knowledge, distinguished from the forms of sensibility, and restricted "to use merely in experience." Without such a careful development of the categories, he says, "they are quite useless and only a miserable list of names, without explanation or rule for their

use."[155] At this point Kant has allegedly accounted for the possibility of our mathematical and scientific knowledge.

THE PROJECT OF METAPHYSICS.   The next issues are how metaphysics is generally possible and whether metaphysical knowledge is possible. (If so, how? and, if not, why not?) As mathematics was related to the forms of sensibility (space and time) and scientific knowledge to the concepts of the understanding (the twelve categories), metaphysics involves certain ideas of pure reason, which "aim at the completeness, i.e., the collective unity, of all possible experience, and thereby go beyond every given experience. Thus they become *transcendent*." We have already considered two of these three ideas of pure reason—those of the cosmos, or world as a whole, on the one hand, and the self or soul, on the other—in previous sections; and we shall discuss the third one—God—in a later section. However, we should understand that reason naturally strives to view all conditioned appearances in the light of unconditioned reality, speculating about things in themselves as the ultimate grounds of psychological, cosmological, and religious experience, conceived of, respectively, as the soul, the cosmos, and God. These three ideas of reason are different from the twelve categories of the understanding in that they can never be used to constitute human knowledge since they have no empirical, sensible basis whatsoever. Indeed, they tend to lead to an "unavoidable illusion," which can never be dispelled "by any objective and dogmatic inquiries into things, but only by a subjective investigation of reason itself" of the sort represented by Kant's own epistemology. We might even be tempted hastily to assume (as a follower of Hume could do) that these ideas have no value at all. Certainly, their use is different from that of the categories, because they can never constitute knowledge. But the human mind does not function for knowledge alone. Instead, these ideas are sources of rational faith that can serve the heuristic purpose of regulating human thought and action. As such, they are valuable to us, so long as we avoid the mistake of considering "that which is merely *regulative* to be

---

Copernican revolution.   Kant's attempt to view objects of experience as needing to meet the requirements of the mind, rather than the traditional view that the ideas of the mind must meet the requirements of objects of experience (analogous to Copernicus's adopting a new model of the solar system, as having all planets moving around the Sun, to replace the old model of the Earth as stationary in the middle of the universe, with all other heavenly bodies revolving around it)

constitutive." For example, Kant says, "Natural science will never reveal to us the internal constitution of things, which, though not appearance, yet can serve as the ultimate ground for explaining appearances." Yet it is useful to the enterprise of natural science that we should continually strive to understand more and thus keep pushing back the frontiers of knowledge. "The sensible world is nothing but a chain of appearances connected according to universal laws." Although "it is not the thing in itself," it does "point to that which contains the basis of this appearance, to beings which cannot be cognized merely as appearances."[156]

It is only in the noumenal idea of such a thing in itself that "reason finds that completion and satisfaction, which it can never hope for" in the realm of mere phenomenal appearances. The function of this sort of idea is "to guide the use of reason within the world of sense according to principles of the greatest possible (theoretical as well as practical) unity." In the process, the ideas of reason elevate the mind above the limited prejudices of materialism, naturalism, and fatalism (all three of which appear to some degree in Hobbes) that threaten to restrict our thought. Thus, the possibility of metaphysical inquiry is rooted in the speculative ideas of reason, which aim to comprehend the underlying unity of conditions of all appearances. But because these ideas can never constitute knowledge, "we can never produce science, but only a vain dialectical art" in the area of metaphysics. Unlike Hume, however, Kant does not call for the abandonment of metaphysics, but merely for its reform through critical epistemology. Meanwhile, the old traditional metaphysics of thinkers from Plato through Descartes and Leibniz, he believes, has been exposed as illusory: "Critique stands in the same relation to the common metaphysics of the schools as chemistry does to alchemy, or as astronomy to the astrology of the fortune teller." He continues, "I pledge myself that nobody who has thought through and grasped the principles of critique, even only in these *Prolegomena*, will ever return to that old and sophistical pseudo-science." Yet it is unthinkable and undesirable that "the human spirit will ever give up metaphysical researches," which fill a natural speculative need of reason.[157]

We need a new approach to metaphysics, which, "after all this bustle and noise" of two millennia of philosophizing, "still remains as it was in the days of Aristotle," with no clear progress made before the advent of the Kantian critique itself. Although he does not spell out his alternative clearly here, Kant indicates that the new, reformed approach to metaphysics will not be that of an alleged science of "theoretic knowledge," but rather a system of "rational faith which alone may be possible for us, sufficient to our wants, and perhaps even more salutary than knowledge itself."[158] This would be rational faith in a free, morally responsible, immortal personal soul operating in the context of the cosmos or world ordered by laws and subject to the governance of God. The elements of this system, because they are not accessible to sensible experience, cannot be objects of knowledge but are postulates of practical reason (as we shall see in later sections).

KNOWLEDGE AND FAITH.   Kant's best and fullest articulation of his theory of knowledge is not in the *Prolegomena* at all, but in his first *Critique*, where it receives a sophisticated, high-powered, carefully argued presentation. Unfortunately, that is far too detailed and difficult a treatment for us to do anything more with it than surface skimming; but we can, at least, extract some of its best known aspects. The finest statement of Kant's Copernican revolution appears in the preface to the second edition: "Hitherto it has been assumed that all our knowledge must conform to objects. But all attempts to extend our knowledge" on this model have "ended in failure. We must therefore make trial whether we may not have more success . . . if we suppose that objects must conform to our knowledge." This inversion of the traditional **correspondence theory** leads him, as we have seen, to the dramatic conclusion that knowledge must be limited within the bounds of possible experience and is not available in the area of metaphysical ideas. Nevertheless, he maintains,

> even the *assumption*—as made on behalf of the necessary practical employment of my reason—of *God, freedom,* and *immortality* is not permissible unless at the same time speculative reason be deprived of its pretensions to transcendent insight.

As we shall see, such metaphysical ideas are matters of belief which are rationally justified in relation to our moral experience. But this would be a sad and sorry substitute if it were possible for us to know them. This is what he means by his famous sentence,

I have therefore found it necessary to deny *knowledge*, in order to make room for *faith*

(*Ich musste also das Wissen aufheben, um zum Glauben Platz zu bekommen*). These three ideas—of "the freedom of the will, the immortality of the soul, and the existence of God"—are ultimate objects of speculative reason[159] and function quite well at the level of rational faith.

BETWEEN RATIONALISM AND EMPIRICISM. In analyzing the elements of human knowing, Kant steers a middle path between modern rationalists like Descartes and Leibniz, on the one hand, and modern empiricists like Hobbes and Hume, on the other. With the latter he says, "There can be no doubt that all our knowledge begins with experience," for we have no innate ideas with any content. "But though all our knowledge begins with experience, it does not follow that it all arises out of experience," he adds. For the data derived from experience do not suffice to constitute knowledge, since our only source of intuition of data is sensibility. Kant holds that "there are two stems of human knowledge, namely, *sensibility* and *understanding*," either without the other being inadequate. "Through the former, objects are given to us; through the latter, they are thought." Thanks to sensibility, intuitions are available to us; but it is the understanding that provides the concepts without which those intuitions cannot be thought. Here is where the rationalists were correct, in realizing that the mind must contain certain *a priori* tools as necessary conditions of human knowing, though they misinterpreted those as innate ideas. "Intuition and concepts constitute, therefore, the elements of all our knowledge, so that neither concepts without an intuition in some way corresponding to them, nor intuition without concepts, can yield knowledge." Both are essential, and neither can perform the function of the other. "Thoughts without content are empty, intuitions without concepts are blind." Truth, or "the agreement of knowledge with its object," can only be established through the coordination of sensible intuitions and concepts of the understanding. In our quest for truth, we use a hierarchy of the three mental faculties we have discussed:

All our knowledge starts with the senses, proceeds from thence to understanding, and ends with reason, beyond which there is no higher faculty to be found in us.[160]

The three ideas of reason (those of the soul, the cosmos, and God), which transcend all possible natural experience, aim at unconditional completeness underlying all representations—"the *first* containing the absolute (unconditioned) *unity* of the *thinking subject*, the *second* the absolute *unity of the series of conditions of appearance*, the *third* the absolute *unity of the condition of all objects of thought in general*." Corresponding to these three ideas are the three areas of metaphysics, rational psychology, rational cosmology, and rational theology. These metaphysical "ideas never allow of any constitutive employment," in the sense that they can never constitute knowledge. "On the other hand, they have an excellent, and indeed indispensably necessary, regulative employment, namely, that of directing the understanding towards a certain goal" that can guide or regulate further thought and action. We reasonably act "*as if*" we have a soul, live in a cosmos, and are related to a God, each idea having "only a heuristic" practical value for us and being "postulated only problematically" rather than known with certainty. We can only understand this, however, by rising above the "*dogmatic*" assumptions of traditional rationalists like Descartes and passing through the crucible of the "*sceptical*" reductions of rigorous empiricists like Hobbes and Hume to reach the stage of "the *criticism* of reason" itself, represented by Kant's own philosophy. It is only after this third stage of philosophical development has been reached that we can have the necessary perspective for adequately answering Kant's three celebrated questions:

1. What can I know? *Was kann ich wissen?*
2. What ought I to do? *Was soll ich tun?*
3. What may I hope? *Was darf ich hoffen?*

Where dogmatism threatens to inflate matters of belief into knowledge-claims and scepticism tends to reduce all knowledge to belief and all faith to mere opinion, the critical philosophy maintains the proper distinctions among opinion, belief, and knowledge (*Meinen, Glauben, und Wissen*). Mere opinion, far from resting on objectively sufficient evidence, is not even subjectively sufficient; rational belief is "only subjectively sufficient," not resting on objectively sufficient evidence; and genuine knowledge rests on evidence that "is sufficient both subjectively and objectively."[161] This epistemology requires a new interpretation of human freedom, religious faith, and immortality, as we are about to see.

Freedom

We think of the human will as acting freely, at least sometimes independent of extrinsic necessity. Kant believes that man is both a phenomenal being and a noumenal reality. As a phenomenal being, the human person has a body which behaves in accordance with causal determinism. "In its intelligible character," however, "this same subject must be considered free from all influence of sensibility and from all determination through appearances." As a noumenal reality, the human person transcends the realm of phenomenal sensibility. "And consequently, since natural necessity is to be met with only in the sensible world, this active being must in its actions be independent of, and free from all such necessity." It is as a rational being, as we have seen, that man transcends the realm of sensibility.

> Reason therefore acts freely; it is not dynamically determined in the chain of natural causes through either outer or inner grounds.

Here in the first *Critique* Kant distinguishes between a "purely *animal*" will (*arbitrium brutum*), which is determined only "*pathologically*," that is by feelings, inclinations, and "sensuous impulses," and "freewill" (*arbitrium liberum*), which can act on rational motives. Both act upon laws, the animal will on extrinsic physical laws of stimulus-response and instinct and free will on practical laws of morality. Human freedom is an exception to the natural laws of extrinsic causal determination and is a transcendental necessary condition of moral responsibility; and it is problematic in the sense that it can never be proved or rendered an object of theoretical knowledge:

> Transcendental freedom is thus, as it would seem, contrary to the law of nature, and therefore to all possible experience; and so remains a problem.[162]

It does not neatly connect with the rest of our experience but reflects the duality of human nature.

FREEDOM AND NECESSITY. As we have seen, freedom and necessity constitute the third of four metaphysical antinomies of pure reason, both the thesis of freedom and its antithesis of natural necessity being supportable by plausible argumentation. In the *Prolegomena* Kant observes that the confusion arises from our thinking of phenomenal objects of sensibility as

things in themselves (which leads us to imagine that their principles of natural necessity must be "laws of things in themselves") or from our conceiving of "the subject of freedom," the self or human will, "as mere appearance" (and therefore subject to the causal laws that govern all phenomena). But if we recognize that the duality of human nature is such that we are both phenomenal beings, subject to laws of natural necessity, and noumenal persons, having the capacity of free choice, and that these are two different levels of humanity, the apparent conflict is resolved:

> Nature and freedom therefore can without contradiction be attributed to the very same thing, but in different relations—on one side as an appearance, on the other as a thing in itself.

It is only as rational and free that the human person can respond to "the *ought*" of moral obligation. Because of our dual nature freedom and necessity coexist in us with no genuine conflict.

> Thus practical freedom, viz., the freedom in which reason possesses causality according to objectively determining grounds, is rescued; and yet natural necessity is not in the least curtailed with regard to the very same effects, as appearances.[163]

As personal agents, we freely determine our own wills (sometimes in accordance with rational moral motives); but, as physical bodies, we act according to natural laws.

BEYOND THE LIMITS OF KNOWLEDGE. Remember that all of this is presented as a matter of belief rather than of knowledge. Why can we not theoretically know that the human person is free? The brief answer, already indicated, is that this concerns the noumenal reality of human nature and that only phenomenal appearances are knowable. A more careful answer is that two conditions must always be met in order for anything to be known: first, it must be accessible as a possible object of experience in the phenomenal world; and, second, we must be able to think of it, as spatio-temporally intuited, in terms of one or more of the twelve categories of the understanding. But here both conditions must go unmet: the idea of free personality defies the legitimate application of categories of the understanding because it is not among the appearances of phenomenal intuition.

FREEDOM AND MORALITY. The final section of Kant's *Grounding* deals at length with human freedom. There he argues that freedom must be presupposed as a "property of the will of all rational beings." For, among other things, a rational being is one "that is practical, i.e., that has a causality in reference to its objects"; it is a subject and an agent. But it can only function as a practical agent if it has "a will of its own"; hence, it must be free. But this argument hinges on certain assumptions about the essential nature of a rational being, assumptions which a strict materialist and hard determinist need not accept. This is why Kant admits that "we could not prove freedom to be something actual in ourselves and in human nature. We saw merely that we must presuppose it if we want to think of a being as rational," in the sense of a responsible moral agent. Kant admits that there is "a sort of circle" in our thinking about the relationship between freedom and morality: "we assume that we are free so that we may think of ourselves as subject to moral laws," and we "think of ourselves as subject to moral laws because we have attributed to ourselves freedom of the will." But it is not a **vicious circularity**; rather, these two ways of thinking are correlative and complementary. As we have seen, none of this compromises our being subject to laws of natural necessity as phenomenal beings; for the duality of humanity is such that we belong to two worlds, "a world of sense and a world of understanding." We experience and know ourselves as phenomena in the natural world of sense; yet we believe ourselves to be free agents on the basis of our moral experience, which is the object of reason rather than of the scientific understanding. "Freedom is, therefore, only an idea of reason whose objective reality is in itself questionable"—for example, by determinists—because it is unprovable and different from the natural operations of sensible experience. In this sense, "freedom is a mere idea, whose objective reality can in no way be shown in accordance with the laws of nature and consequently not in any possible experience" drawn from the phenomenal world. "It holds only as a necessary presupposition of reason"[164] needed to account for the possibility of moral experience (which we shall discuss in the next section).

In the second *Critique* Kant distinguishes "freedom in the negative sense," or independence of all extrinsic causal determination, from "freedom in the positive sense," which is the autonomous, self-determining legislation of practical reason. Hobbes, for example, conceived of human liberty simply in terms of negative freedom. "The moral law adds to the negative concept a positive definition, that of a reason which determines the will directly" to act according to duty. Ultimately, as Hume seemed to recognize, even negative freedom is not empirically verifiable, since even if the will is only directly determined from within, by its own character, values, motives, and propensities, what external events causally determined them remains an open question. Both negative and positive freedom remain unknowable. "Thus the concept of freedom is made the regulative principle of reason."[165] We believe we are free, act "as if" we are, and the belief regulates our conduct and pragmatically works in ordering our lives. Freedom is a necessary presupposition of moral responsibility.

Morality

In the 1760s, when he was most under the influence of Hume, Kant tended to identify human emotions as the source of moral perception. In his *Enquiry*, of 1763, for example, he maintains that "the faculty of representing what is *true* is *knowledge*; whereas the faculty of perceiving what is *good* is *feeling*"; on this view, moral judgment "is completely unprovable" by reason, being immediately derived from "an unanalyzable feeling of the good."[166] In the *Observations*, of 1764, while rejecting Hume's "good-natured passion" of sympathy as the basis of morality, he does see the source of moral virtue as "the *feeling of the beauty and dignity of human nature*."[167] But this is a mere transitional position in Kant's thinking on morality, which would be repudiated by his mature critical philosophy.

THE FOUNDATION OF KANT'S ETHICAL SYSTEM. Kant's best known and most accessible work on ethics is his *Grounding*, of 1785; unfortunately, too many people know Kant's moral philosophy only in relation to this one work, which, as the title (*Grundlegung* literally means "laying the foundation") indicates, provides merely the foundation of his ethical system, making it a good starting point for a discussion of that system so long as we see how the

---

Vicious circularity. A property of argumentation whose circular reasoning is sufficiently pernicious to render the entire argument worthless (e.g., "God must exist because the Bible says God exists, the Bible is the word of God, and God cannot lie")

superstructure is erected on that foundation. The little preface of the work declares the author's independence of all empirical approaches to ethics, such as those of Aristotle, Hobbes, and Hume. His reason is the conviction that, if any ethical principle "is to be morally valid, i.e., is to be valid as a ground of obligation, then it must carry with it absolute necessity." But every empirical approach to ethics, by its very nature, "is only very contingent and uncertain," leaving us adrift in the shoals of probability judgments. It is as if Kant is saying that all genuinely moral principles must be certain and necessary; and, since all empirically derived principles are "contingent and uncertain," no empirically derived principles can be genuinely moral ones. Kant promises that "some day" he will complete the moral system of which "this *Grounding*" is to provide the "foundation" (a promise he kept by the end of the century) and protests that this little work is "intended for nothing more than seeking out and establishing the supreme principle of morality."[168] This last point is particularly important for those who attack his ethical system as too formal, abstract, and so forth, on the basis of this work alone, with little or no attention to the other works (also discussed below) that constitute its larger part.

A GOOD WILL. In a well-known sentence from the *Grounding*, Kant writes,

> There is no possibility of thinking of anything at all in the world, or even out of it, which can be regarded as good without qualification, except a *good will.*

He argues his point by dividing other values (notice that he does not deny they are good) into those of the mind (such as "intelligence, wit, judgment," and so forth), those of character (such as "courage, resolution, perseverance"), and those of fortune (such as "power, riches, honor, even health," as well as happiness) and showing how these can "become extremely bad and harmful" if combined with ill will; no combination of them is sufficiently good without being joined to good will. A good will, unlike most of them, is intrinsically good rather than merely consequentially good (to use a distinction from Plato and Aristotle). In a rare exercise of poetic simile, Kant writes that even should a good will lead to no desirable consequences, "yet would it, like a jewel, still shine by its own light as something which has its full value in itself." What is distinctive about us, among

all the animals, is our reason. What function can reason uniquely serve in us? It does not guarantee happiness here and now; indeed, sometimes it seems an obstacle to short-term, selfish satisfaction of desire. What it can do is lead us to become persons of good will, which must be "the highest good" (though, divorced from happiness, not the "complete good") for humans, as well as "the condition of all the rest, even of the desire for happiness," which is undeserved without the presence of good will.[169]

What, then, is a good will? It is one that strives to do its moral duty out of a respect for the moral law. First, it must avoid actions which it believes "contrary to duty"; second, it is not manifest in cases where we have no immediate inclination to do the action (such as paying our taxes) and only choose it as a means to some extrinsic end (such as blindly supporting one's government or staying out of trouble with the Internal Revenue Service); third, the good will is also not obvious in cases where we have an immediate inclination to do our duty (such as to preserve one's own life under ordinary circumstances); fourth, it is most readily apparent in cases where we deliberately do our duty in opposition to our immediate inclinations (as when "an unfortunate man, strong in soul and more indignant at his fate than despondent or dejected, wishes for death and yet preserves his life without loving it.") So, it is not enough to do one's duty deliberately; a good will does this for a moral motive. Kant provides a fine example of this point. Beneficence, or trying to help other persons who need our help, is a moral duty; yet for some people, who are temperamentally sympathetic, compassionate, and benevolent, this duty can be performed with no sense of obligation at all; Kant holds that "in such a case an action of this kind, however dutiful and amiable it may be, has nevertheless no true moral worth," because it is not motivated by a sense of duty. But now Kant twists the example a bit to make it one of a former philanthropist, who, falling on hard times, loses his benevolence:

> Suppose then the mind of this friend of mankind to be clouded over with his own sorrow so that all sympathy with the lot of others is extinguished, and suppose him still to have the power to benefit others in distress, even though he is not touched by their trouble because he is sufficiently absorbed with his own.

Bereft as he is of any immediate inclination to help, suppose he nevertheless tears himself from this deadly insensibility and performs the action . . . solely from duty—then for the first time his action has genuine moral worth

that is obvious, because it is clear that it is motivated by a sense of obligation.[170]

Thus far, Kant has been arguing that an action must be motivated by a sense of duty to have moral worth. Second, he maintains, the moral worth of an action is derived from its motive rather than from any goal to which performing it may be a means. The motive in this case is what Kant calls "the maxim," that is, the agent's subjective principle of will, which explains why he chose to perform the act. Third, Kant defines duty (in terms of which he has already defined a good will) as "the necessity of an action done out of respect for the law."[171] This is a moral (not a physical or metaphysical) necessity, which does not compromise the will's freedom.

THE CATEGORICAL IMPERATIVE.   What Kant has done, in the scope of a few pages, is undermine any attempt to ground morality in empirical considerations, such as inclinations and consequences. This leads to his first statement of an ethical principle:

> Since I have deprived the will of every impulse that might arise for it from obeying any particular law, there is nothing left to serve the will as principle except the universal conformity of its actions to law as such, i.e., I should never act except in such a way that I can also will that my maxim should become a universal law.

This is the first statement of what Kant goes on to call the "**categorical** imperative"; this version of it is sometimes called the principle of **universalizability**. It challenges us to consider, whenever we have doubts about the moral legitimacy of something we are tempted to do, whether we could rationally will that such behavior be universalized, that is, performed by all people in morally similar circumstances (rather like the parent who admonishes her miscreant child with the query, "What if everyone acted like that?") Perhaps realizing that the point needs illustration, Kant provides his favorite example, that of the false promise: "When I am in distress, may I make a promise with the intention of not keeping it?" He points out that there are two legitimate interpretations

of that "may I," one pragmatic, the other moral. Pragmatically speaking, it *might* pay off for me selfishly (in terms of satisfying my own desires) to do this. But it could not be morally right, as we see when we apply the principle of universalizability as a test.[172]

Could we reasonably will that everyone who is in distress should deliberately make a false promise to escape his difficulties?

Once we consider the logical implications of thus universalizing false promises, we see that this would be irrational. As Kant says,

> Then I immediately become aware that I can indeed will the lie but can not at all will a universal law to lie. For by such a law there would really be no promises at all, since in vain would my willing future actions be professed to other people who would not believe what I professed.

In other words, if the act of making false promises were universalized, the entire practice of making and trusting promises would collapse, in which case my promise would not be believed and therefore would not succeed in achieving what it is designed to achieve. Universalizing false promises would be counterproductive to the purposes for which one is tempted to make a false promise in the first place. Notice that this is not utilitarian reasoning. The bad consequences of universalizing false promises are *not* what make them wrong (Kant would hold that John Stuart Mill is mistaken on this point); they only serve to help us realize that false promises are **intrinsically** wrong. As Kant puts the point,

> I only ask myself whether I can also will that my maxim should become a universal law. If not, then the maxim must be rejected, not because of any disadvantage accruing to me or even to others, but because it cannot be fitting as a principle in a possible legislation of universal law, and reason exacts from me immediate respect for such legislation.[173]

since morality requires this universal dimension.

MORALITY THROUGH REASON.   Kant admits that doubt can always be raised as to the possibility of our ever acting from a disinterested sense of duty, that "there have always been philosophers who have absolutely denied the reality of this disposition in human actions and have ascribed everything to a more or less refined self-love." These would be egoists like

---

Universalizable.   Able to be reasonably applied to all actions of a particular sort in morally similar circumstances; Kant uses universalizability as a criterion for testing whether the maxim of an action is morally justifiable

Hobbes. Anticipating Freud's idea of subconscious motives by more than a century, Kant acknowledges,

> We like to flatter ourselves with the false claim to a more noble motive; but in fact we can never, even by the strictest examination, completely plumb the depths of the secret incentives of our actions.

There is always the danger of self-deception regarding our actual motives, at the base of which may lie "the dear self" of egoism. Believing the egoists are mistaken, however, Kant points out that the "ought" of moral obligation remains independent of the "is" of factual description, that

> even if there never have been actions springing from such pure sources, the question at issue here is not whether this or that has happened but that reason of itself and independently of all experience commands what ought to happen. Consequently, reason unrelentingly commands actions of which the world has perhaps hitherto never provided an example and whose feasibility might well be doubted by one who bases everything upon experience.

As an illustration, he says that we have a duty to be sincere in our friendship relations and that that duty would not be diminished one iota by the fact (if it were one) that in the history of humanity "there might never have been a sincere friend." Moral principles are independent of empirical examples; even Christ, "the Holy One of the gospel," can only be "recognized as such" with reference to an independent "ideal of moral perfection" to which he measured up. The value of moral examples is that they provide encouraging models that we should strive to follow. But moral principles themselves should be "pure" in springing from reason alone, rather than derived from examples or from "the particular constitution of human nature" or from authority; nor should they be based on a hodge-podge mixture of rational and empirical considerations, since this would "make the mind waver between motives" at variance with one another, only accidentally leading to the good, if at all. He holds that "moral principles are not grounded on the peculiarities of human nature" but arise from reason, so that they "must be derivable for every rational nature, and accordingly for human nature." Morality, as Hume recognized, must somehow motivate behavior. It is the will that must choose, but (contrary to Hume) Kant says that "the will is nothing but practical reason." Far from being distinct from reason, it is reason in its practical dimension; "the will is

a faculty of choosing only that which reason, independently of inclination, recognizes as being practically necessary, i.e., as good."[174]

HYPOTHETICAL VS. CATEGORICAL IMPERATIVES. The human will, as practical reason, can respond to "an imperative," that is, "a command (of reason)," which is typically expressed in prescriptive language about what *should* or *ought not* to be done. Kant distinguishes two main types of imperatives: "hypothetical" (or conditioned) ones versus "categorical" (or unconditioned) ones. He breaks down the hypothetical ones into the "problematic" kind (where there is no sufficient reason to suppose that the condition applies) and the "assertoric" kind (where it is reasonable to assume that the condition does apply). The statement, "If you want to learn French, you should take Bonhomme's review course," is an imperative, because it tells you what you ought to do; but that is conditioned by an "if" hypothesis, which is "problematic" in the sense that it is unclear whether the condition does or does not apply. By contrast, the statement, "If you want to be happy, then you should treat others decently," is "assertoric" in the sense that it is reasonable to suppose that the "if" condition does apply. But, against all "hypothetical" imperatives, categorical ones, such as "You ought to tell the truth" and "You should never commit adultery," have no "if" conditions attached to them at all. (Kant calls the "problematic" ones technical imperatives of skill and the "assertoric" ones pragmatic imperatives of prudence.) Moral principles must be categorical rather than contingent or hypothetical. "The categorical imperative is an a priori synthetic practical proposition"—"practical" because it says how we should act, "synthetic" because it is not true by definition but is genuinely informative, and "a priori" because it is universally and necessarily binding on all rational agents. Kant maintains that "there is only one categorical imperative," although it can be expressed in terms of various formulas. We have already seen a preview of the formula of universalizability, which is restated now in two slightly different ways:

> Act only according to that maxim whereby you can at the same time will that it should become a universal law.

Its second version

> may be expressed thus: Act as if the maxim of your action were to become through your will a universal law of nature.[175]

TYPES OF MORAL DUTIES. Kant classifies moral duties into four types. First, we can distinguish between "duties to ourselves and to others"; and, second, we can distinguish between "**perfect** and imperfect **duties**," where a perfect one "permits no exception in the interest of inclination" and an imperfect duty is less strict, allowing the agent some discretion (for example, in choosing when to exercise it or towards whom). He provides an example of a violation of each type of duty to illustrate the reasoning of the principle of universalizability. First, suicide violates our "perfect" duty to self-preservation; if all people killed themselves when their lives became frustrating or painful, our earth would become a planetary graveyard. Second, a false promise is a violation of our "perfect" duty to be truthful towards all others all the time; and, as we have seen, if the act of falsely promising were universalized, the entire institution of giving our word would collapse, since no one could reasonably trust it. Third, a life of neglecting to develop one's talents violates the "imperfect" duty (to oneself) of self-improvement; if we universalized such a violation, culture and civilization would disintegrate. And, fourth, social apathy—not caring about or ever trying to help others—violates the "imperfect" duty (to others) of beneficence; if we universalized social apathy, we would deprive ourselves (as well as everyone else) of "the love and sympathy" we might need at some point. As if in response to Hume's "sensible knave" problem, Kant points out the irrational character of wishing to make oneself the sole exception to rules: on the one hand, we want the rules to apply universally, and, on the other, we want to make an exception "for ourselves (or just for this one time) to the advantage of an inclination." But this is "a contradiction in our own will, viz., that a certain principle be objectively necessary as a universal law and yet subjectively not hold universally but should admit of exceptions."[176] Once exceptions to rules start being considered, it is reasonable to ask why this one exception and not those others, which seem morally similar?

THE CATEGORICAL IMPERATIVE REFORMULATED. A second major formulation of the categorical imperative is based on Kant's distinction between things (even living things), which are objects having value and appropriately used merely as means to extrinsic ends, and persons (including humans), who are subjects having dignity and worthy of respect as "ends in themselves," so that they are "not to be used merely as means." He articulates the principle thus:

> Act in such a way that you treat humanity, whether in your own person or in the person of another, always at the same time as an end and never simply as a means.

The adverbial qualifier "simply" is important here. It is morally permissible to use your barber as a means to getting your hair cut, so long as you respect him as a person, with his own thoughts, feelings, and values, and do not treat him (or relate to him) as you would (to) his combs, scissors, clippers, and other instruments. Kant reviews his four examples of immoral actions, showing how this formulation of the categorical imperative allegedly applies. First, the suicide, in killing himself, uses his own person "merely as a means" to escaping his misery. Second, the person making a false promise uses the other (to whom it is made) as a gullible means to his own selfish purposes. Third, the one who neglects to develop any of his talents uses his own life merely as a means (to self-gratification, to peace and quiet, or to whatever). Fourth, the socially apathetic person fails to respect the rest of humanity as intrinsically valuable ends in themselves, viewing it merely as a possible obstruction or threat to his own selfish desires. Kant calls this second major formulation the "principle of humanity," although it might have been better called the principle of personality, since it applies to all rational beings, whether they be human or not. In a footnote Kant maintains that his categorical imperative, despite superficial similarities, is not merely the Golden Rule in philosophical attire, since the latter is ill-equipped to handle any duties to oneself; clearly, some people would be willing that others should not care about them so long as they did not have to bother about others, and, for example, hardly anyone would wish to be punished when guilty, even though the punishment is just and should be imposed.[177]

The third major formulation of the categorical imperative is the principle of autonomy, which builds on Kant's idea of the human person as free, in some sense, of the external determinations of natural

---

Perfect duty. From Kant on, a moral obligation allegedly permitting no exceptions in the interest of inclinations, as opposed to an imperfect duty, which allows some discretionary choosing, for example, as to when or towards whom the duty will be fulfilled

necessity and able to think for herself, make her own choices, and be responsible for her own actions. As an autonomous agent, she can do what she thinks right, thus contributing to the determination of the moral law as an active participant in the legislating process. Kant boasts that no other ethical theory prior to his own adequately respects this dimension of human autonomy. Other systems say we should act in certain ways because it will make us happy or because God commands it or because it will increase our ability to get along with others in society. But Kant maintains that we should determine for ourselves what is right, using our own disinterested reason, and do it because we think it right. He says, "I want, therefore, to call my principle the principle of the autonomy of the will, in contrast with every other principle, which I accordingly count under heteronomy." He asks us to view ourselves as legislating members of "a kingdom of ends," a free and equal association of rational agents, a sort of ideal ethical republic, of which God is the "sovereign." All other persons are members of this "kingdom of ends," above all price (or extrinsic value), having what Kant calls "unconditional and incomparable worth." As members, we must strive to be persons of good will. The principle of autonomy is stated thus:

> Act in accordance with the maxims of a member legislating universal laws for a merely possible kingdom of ends.

It challenges us to think of the maxims for our actions as establishing precedents that will serve as universal law.[178]

By contrast, any attempt to determine what is right in terms of external authorities or extrinsic consequences is considered heteronomous, focusing outside our own moral reason rather than within. All heteronomous moral systems, dismissed as spurious, "are either empirical or rational." Empirical ones can be "drawn from the principle of happiness," as are those of Aristotle, Hobbes, Hume, and utilitarians.

> Empirical principles are wholly unsuited to serve as the foundation for moral laws. For the universality with which such laws ought to hold for all rational beings without exception . . . is lost if the basis of these laws is taken from the particular constitution of human nature or from the accidental circumstances in which such nature is placed.

Among all heteronomous principles, that of egoism "is the most objectionable" of all, being purely self-serving. Among rational systems, there is theological ethics, such as the views of Augustine and Aquinas, "whereby morality is derived from a divine and most perfect will." This is preferable to empirical approaches, in that it will yield universal law; but it still leaves us passive recipients of rather than active participants in the legislating process, since "the will does not give itself the law, but a foreign impulse gives the law to the will."[179] Whereas a good child behaves himself by doing as he is told, we expect a morally good adult to be involved in helping to determine what is right and to establish morality.

VIRTUE AND HAPPINESS. In his second *Critique*, referring to his claim that a respect for moral law is the only motive that confers moral worth on an action, Kant says,

> It is a very beautiful thing to do good to men because of love and a sympathetic good will, or to do justice because of a love of order. But this is not the genuine moral maxim of our conduct, the maxim which is suitable to our position among rational beings.

Whereas virtue is the highest good we can achieve by our own efforts in this life, "the perfect good," towards which we should work as an ideal, is a proportionate "connection of virtue with happiness." Against the utilitarians Kant writes that "morals is not really the doctrine of how to make ourselves happy but of how we are to be *worthy* of happiness"; and this is by becoming virtuous persons of good will. In the famous words of its conclusion, which were also his epitaph, Kant expresses his reverence for both the cosmic world order and the moral order:

> Two things fill the mind with ever new and increasing admiration and awe, the oftener and more steadily we reflect on them: the starry heavens above me and the moral law within me[180]

(*der bestirnte Himmel über mir, und das moralische Gesetz in mir*).

Kant is sometimes accused of utterly divorcing feelings from his theory of morality. But in *Religion* he writes that "a heart which is happy in the *performance* of its duty (not merely complacent in the *recognition* thereof) is a mark of genuineness in the virtuous disposition." He makes it clear that a virtuous character "must need beget a joyous frame of mind, without which man is never certain of having really *attained a love* for the good." Kant also holds that "ought" implies "can," in that we cannot be obliged to do something that is impossible. For example, "when the moral law commands that we *ought* now to be better men, it follows inevitably that we must be *able* to be better men."[181] We shall see the significance of this principle in later sections.

JURIDICAL VS. ETHICAL LAWS. Important material can also be found in *Metaphysics of Morals*. In its general introduction, he points out that moral laws can be either "*juridical*" or "*ethical*," an action being considered legal when it agrees with juridical laws (such as those of the state) or moral when it follows ethical ones. He again repudiates all empirical approaches to morality, including the "eudaemonism" of thinkers like Aristotle, which are too contingent on our inclinations and circumstances and thus too prone to relativism and impotent to deliver a universally necessary categorical imperative. Juridical duties can have empirical inclinations as their incentives, whereas ethical duties require "the Idea of duty arising from the law" as "the incentive of the action," if it is to have moral worth. Ethical duties can apply even where civil law is not coercive, as in the case of a legally nonbinding promise. "Ethical legislation is that which cannot be external (though the duties may be external); juridical legislation is that which can also be external." The duty to keep one's promise is external, in that it concerns interpersonal commitments; "but the command to do so merely because it is a duty, without regard to any other incentive, belongs only to internal legislation" and is therefore ethical. Kant defines moral obligation as "the necessity of a free action under a categorical imperative of reason"; this is a moral (rather than a physical or metaphysical) necessity, which does not compromise, but rather requires, freedom. "An action is *allowed* (*licitum*) if it is not opposed to obligation." In addition to such morally permissible action, there is also morally impermissible or prohibited action, as well as morally obligatory "action to which a person is bound." Any action (and this includes most of those we ordinarily commit) is permissible or "merely allowed" if it "is neither commanded nor prohibited." Thus, we can speak of three types of laws—those "of permission," those "of command," and those "of prohibition." Only persons are directly related to morality; "moral personality is nothing but the freedom of a rational being under moral laws (whereas

psychological personality is merely the capacity to be conscious of the identity of one's self in the various conditions of one's existence)." By contrast, a thing has no direct relationship to moral law. The concept of "right or wrong in general" is likewise defined in relation to what accords with or is opposed to moral duty, a deed that is wrong being "a *transgression*," an "unintentional transgression" being "mere neglect" and an "intentional transgression" being considered "a crime." Kant also distinguishes between "*natural laws*," which can be rationally recognized without any external legislation, and *positive laws,* such as some civil laws of the state, "that would neither obligate nor be laws without actual external legislation." The ultimate principle of all moral law is the categorical imperative, presented here in the formula of universalizability. Any morally binding law can be expressed as "a proposition that contains a categorical imperative (a command)." Any law implies a "*lawgiver* (*legislator*)." For positive law, the lawgiver is human; whereas natural law comes "from the Will of a supreme lawgiver," God. Punishment is appropriate for those who violate laws we can be rightly compelled to obey; and reward is appropriate for "meritorious" action that is "in accordance with duty" but that goes beyond what we "can be compelled to do by the law."[182]

DUTIES TO OURSELVES AND TO OTHERS. In *The Metaphysical Principles of Virtue*, Kant observes that our duties to ourselves can be "duties of omission," having to do with our "moral *health*" or "duties of commission," pertaining to "man's moral affluence." If we omit to take care of our own virtuous characters or fail to improve ourselves, we are violating duties to ourselves. We have perfect duties to ourselves as moral agents, needing to preserve our own dignity, and as animals, naturally aiming at self-preservation, the preservation of our species, and the preservation of the capacity to use our own powers effectively. Vices that violate our perfect duties to ourselves as moral agents are "*lying, avarice*, and *false humility* (servility)"; actions that violate our perfect duties to ourselves as animals are suicide, illicit sexual behavior, and immoderate use of food and drink (gluttony and drunkenness). We also have imperfect duties to ourselves, having to do with the cultivation of our "natural powers (of the spirit, of the mind, and of the body) as means to all kinds of possible ends," as well as with our need for moral improvement, involving the purity of our dispositions towards duty and the performance of our duty more fully.[183]

Our duties to others include our obligations to love and respect all persons, whatever their relationships to us may be. "Now love is not understood here as feeling" of any sentimental sort. "Instead, love must be thought of practically, as the maxim of benevolence; and this maxim results in beneficence." So, it translates into wishing others well and being disposed to act for their well-being. Likewise, respect for others is no sentimental feeling but a limitation on our own self-image by a regard for the dignity of other persons. The duty to love others requires that we make their ends "(as long as they are not immoral)" our own; the duty to respect others forbids our treating them merely as means to our own selfish ends. Love of others involves "duties (a) of beneficence, (b) of gratitude, (c) of sympathy"; three vices corresponding to these are "envy, ingratitude, and malice." Respect for others requires a certain amount of modesty in comparing oneself to them; to refuse others the respect due them is to show contempt. Three vices involving a lack of respect for others are "(a) pride, (b) calumny, and (c) mockery." Finally, Kant observes that "virtue must be acquired (and is not innate)"; it must be taught and learned by practice.[184]

LYING. In his paper "On a Supposed Right to Lie from Altruistic Motives," Kant responds to a utilitarian challenge against his alleged categorical injunction against deliberate deception. A French utilitarian (named Benjamin Constant) asks that Kant consider whether it would not be right to lie to a murderer who asks whether our friend, whom he means to kill, is hiding in our house. Kant defines "a lie" as any "intentional untruthful declaration to another person" and claims that it is always harmful in barring other persons from access to the truth. Kant sticks to his guns, even in the face of this difficult case, saying, "To be truthful (honest) in all declarations, therefore, is a sacred and absolutely commanding decree of reason, limited by no expediency," including even the wish to protect a (relatively) innocent human life.[185] Thus, such a "perfect" categorical duty can never be made contingent on circumstances and likely consequences.

SEXUAL MORALITY. In *Lectures on Ethics* Kant writes that moral goodness requires "the submission of our will to rules whereby all our voluntary actions are brought into a harmony which is universally valid." We have already seen, however, that these moral rules are legislated from within, rather than imposed on our wills from without. Kant defends the traditional, conservative Christian view, saying that the right to use another's sex organs "for the satisfaction of sexual desire" can only be defensible in the context of more holistic rights to the entire person. "But how am I to obtain these rights over the whole person? Only by giving that person the same rights over the whole of myself. This happens only in marriage." When two people mutually contract to give themselves entirely to one another in marriage, that confers on each a right to the other which is not legitimately derivable otherwise.

> Matrimony is the only condition in which use can be made of one's sexuality. If one devotes one's person to another, one devotes not only sex but the whole person; the two cannot be separated.

Sexual activity divorced from this complete, monogamous, mutual giving of self violates the principle of humanity involving the use of oneself and/or the other person merely as a means; it degrades, rather than respects, human dignity.

> Every form of sexual indulgence, except in marriage, is a misuse of sexuality.[186]

MORAL TRAINING. In *Education* Kant writes,

> Man must develop his tendency towards *the good*. Providence has not placed goodness ready formed in him, but merely as a tendency.

As we have seen, human nature also comprises a rival propensity to evil which must be overcome. It is important that education include, as a primary component, "*moral training*." After all, morality is not a blind, mechanical adherence to rules but "a matter of character." We must learn to practice the motto of the Stoics, *Sustine et abstine*, "bear and forbear," to develop strong, stable, virtuous characters. Children must be taught to avoid the vices of malice ("envy, ingratitude, and joy at the misfortune of others"), of baseness ("injustice, unfaithfulness [deceitfulness]), dissoluteness"), and of narrow-mindedness ("unkindness, niggardliness, and idleness"), as well as to cultivate "virtues of merit" (including "magnanimity . . . , benevolence, and self-command"), virtues of obligation (including "honesty, propriety, peaceableness"), and virtues of innocence (including "honourableness, modesty, and content").[187]

Society

KANT'S SOCIAL CONTRACT THEORY. In his work "On the Common Saying: 'This May be True in Theory, but it does not Apply in Practice,'" Kant presents a non-Hobbesian version of the social contract theory. Against Hobbes, Kant believes man's rational nature is such that social union is not merely instrumentally valuable as a means to other ends (like security), but it is "an end in itself" and even "an absolute and primary duty," which can only be satisfactorily fulfilled in the context of "a civil state, i.e. a commonwealth." Not only is socialization intrinsically valuable; but we need a social order to guarantee "the *right* of men *under coercive public laws* by which each can be given what is due to him." Human beings have a right (even apart from the pursuit of happiness) to engage in free activity in a social context. Indeed, for Kant, the very concept of "right" is related to freedom:

> *Right* is the restriction of each individual's freedom so that it harmonizes with the freedom of everyone else (in so far as this is possible within the terms of a general law). And *public right* is the distinctive quality of the *external laws* which make this constant harmony possible.

In a civil constitution free persons are interrelated under coercive external laws, to which they are mutually subject while retaining their freedom. By agreeing to and participating in the social contract, citizens exercise their freedom to help constitute such law. A legitimate civil state should be built on three social principles:

1. The *freedom* of every member of society as a *human being*.
2. The *equality* of each with all others as a *subject*.
3. The *independence* of each member of a commonwealth as a *citizen*.[188]

Of the first of these principles, Kant says,

> No-one can compel me to be happy in accordance with his conception of the welfare of others, for each may seek his happiness in whatever way he sees fit, so long as he does not infringe upon the freedom of others to pursue a similar end which can be reconciled with the freedom of everyone else within a workable general

law—i.e. he must accord to others the same right as he enjoys himself.

This account incorporates a liberal conception of tolerance of others' choices of their own lifestyles. Regarding the second principle, Kant writes that members of society, except the ruler or head of state, who has special authority and responsibilities, "are all equal as subjects *before the law*"; this includes an equality of opportunity in the sense that "every member of the commonwealth must be entitled to reach any degree of rank which a subject can earn through his talent, his industry and his good fortune." It does not require a socialistic equality of possessions, but it rules out recalcitrant hereditary inequality (as, for example, in a caste system). No member of society can legitimately forfeit this social equality except through the commission of "some crime of his own." On the third principle, Kant maintains that, among the members of society, full-fledged citizens are co-legislators, involved in making the laws or choosing those who are to do so. "The basic law, which can come only from the general, united will of the people, is called the *original contract*." As members of society, we are all subject to it; those who also have the right to vote on legislation are citizens of the commonwealth. Kant thinks that any adult male who is "his *own master*" and has "some *property* (which can include any skill, trade, fine art or science) to support himself" should qualify as a citizen. In the legislating process, unanimity is unlikely, and majority rule should prevail.[189]

Kant makes it clear that the social contract need not be historical fact: "It is in fact merely an *idea* of reason, which nonetheless has undoubted practical reality." In subscribing to society and deriving benefits from our membership in it, we implicitly and tacitly oblige ourselves to obey its laws and respect its established authorities. We are bound to contribute to "the public welfare," which requires that everyone's freedom be guaranteed "within the law, so that each remains free to seek his happiness in whatever way he thinks best, so long as he does not violate the lawful freedom and rights of his fellow subjects." Therefore, rebellion against the social order is absolutely forbidden.

> And even if the power of the state or its agent, the head of state, has violated the original contract by authorizing the government to act tyrannically, and has thereby, in

the eyes of the subject, forfeited the right to legislate, the subject is still not entitled to offer counter-resistance.

For if a subject disputes the authority of his sovereign, who is to decide between them? "Neither can act as judge of his own cause. Thus there would have to be another head above the head of state to mediate between the latter and the people, which is self-contradictory." Nevertheless, Kant maintains, "the people too have inalienable rights against the head of state, even if these cannot be rights of coercion." He explicitly disagrees with the Hobbesian view that the sovereign "can do no injustice to a citizen, but may act towards him as he pleases." Kant calls this idea "quite terrifying"; against it he says that every person "has his inalienable rights, which he cannot give up even if he wishes to." For example, citizens should have the right to express their own opinions in public, even regarding what seems unjust in the ruler.

> Thus *freedom of the pen* is the only safeguard of the rights of the people, although it must not transcend the bounds of respect and devotion towards the existing constitution.

The denial of this right can bar the ruler from knowing what should be known in order to rectify wrongs. But the concept of *"political right"* has *a priori* "binding force for human beings" regardless of utilitarian consequences.[190]

THE PROBLEM OF A GOOD SOCIETY. In "Idea for a Universal History" Kant writes,

> *The greatest problem for the human race, to the solution of which Nature drives man, is the achievement of a universal civic society which administers law among men.*

The reason this is so difficult in practice is that lawful order must be established among people who have some antagonism towards one another without destroying their freedom. The solution lies in the idea of "a perfectly just civic constitution" to which they can freely subject their wills. Kant writes, *"This problem is the most difficult and the last to be solved by mankind."* On the one hand, man needs a political master; but, on the other, he must retain his freedom. Indeed, this is a task we are still striving to accomplish, whose "complete solution is impossible," but it is an ideal we must asymptotically approach.

> *The problem of establishing a perfect civic constitution is dependent upon the problem of a lawful external relation among states and cannot be solved without a solution of the latter problem.*

The ills of international conflict, including war and the preparation for it, are so grave that international cooperation must be pursued.

> In a league of nations, even the smallest state could expect security and justice, not from its own power and by its own decrees, but only from this . . . united power acting according to decisions reached under the laws of their united will.

The evils of savagery so threaten progress that we find ourselves forced to seek peace. We have become cultured and civilized in our enlightened age but must work to become more fully moral. Kant pulls this together thus:

> *The history of mankind can be seen, in the large, as the realization of Nature's secret plan to bring forth a perfectly constituted state as the only condition in which the capacities of mankind can be fully developed, and also bring forth that external relation among states which is perfectly adequate to this end.*

Political progress must involve improved international relations. Effort towards these goals is not only what is right but, in a sense, what we owe future generations, since "human nature is so constituted that we cannot be indifferent to the most remote epoch our race may come to." We must work to spread enlightenment, though this is a gradual and often difficult process.[191]

In "Conjectural Beginning of Human History" Kant demythologizes the Genesis story, arguing that it is reasonable to suppose that there was a single first adult pair of humans living in a relatively secure and comfortable environment, able to walk, converse, and think, originally guided by instinct alone until reason stirred in them, after which artificial desires began to emerge in them. They discovered in themselves the power of free choice, after which it was impossible for them to return to mere subjection to instinct. After the move from instinct to rational freedom, the "third step" of their evolution consisted in their achieving a "conscious *expectation of the future*," which also was a "source of care" and anxiety for them. Then "a fourth and final step" was towards self-awareness, the realization that they represent "the true end of nature," other creatures being "mere means" to the realization of their ends. This constitutes at least a basic grasp of the principle of humanity, that all rational beings, like them, are ends in themselves and morally equal. Thus, the Genesis story provides a symbolic representation of man's gradual "progress toward perfection," his evolving "transition from an uncultured, merely animal condition to the state of humanity, from bondage to instinct to rational control—in a word, from the tutelage of nature to the state of freedom." The fall represents a misuse of the freedom discovered, violating the moral law; and the expulsion from paradise symbolizes the punishment appropriate to such wrongdoing. "The following period began with man's passage from an age of comfort and peace to one of labor and strife." Humans were always social; but now they "had to band together and build villages" for mutual support in a more hostile environment. This was the beginning of culture and public order. Despotism and slavery ensued as some arrogated to themselves unequal, superior power. War and the endless preparation for war became part of the human condition; thus, fear, anxiety, and insecurity impelled man to "cultural progress," a process of social evolution which continues today; "and nature itself has given the vocation to everyone to contribute as much to this progress as may be within his power."[192]

POLITICAL MAXIMS.   One of Kant's greatest social essays is "Perpetual Peace," in which he explains the means necessary to minimize human conflict. Peace treaties should be more than truces, barring future warfare. Second, states, which are human societies and not merely plots of territory, should not be appropriated by other states. Third, we should work to abolish standing armies, which threaten war. Fourth, states should not go into debt to amass war machinery. Fifth, no state should interfere with the government of any other sovereign state. And, sixth, there should be no use of international disreputable acts, such as political assassinations, genocidal campaigns of extermination, and spies. Kant holds that governments should be "republican," meaning they should be constitutional, based on principles of freedom, submission to authority, and equality, characterized by a separation of political powers, and representative of the will of their people. He again calls for an international "league of nations" to protect the peace and preserve freedom. Our cosmopolitan status as citizens of the world should promote the ideal of "Universal Hospitality," meaning the right of a person not to be treated like an enemy when in a foreign country (not, however, the right to remain there permanently). We should go beyond nationally protected civil rights to

an awareness of "human rights" for all, since the "community of the peoples of the earth has developed so far that a violation of rights in one place is felt throughout the world." Kant believes that nature has contrived to push us towards international harmony, even when we fail to realize the significance of our efforts and are motivated by selfish considerations alone. Republican government (as explained) "is the only one entirely fitting to the rights of man. But it is the most difficult to establish and even harder to preserve," because it is not extremely efficient and requires patient cooperation. But it is "our duty to work toward this end" as best we can. Philosophers' views should be consulted by political leaders for the good of society, though Kant rejects the Platonic dream of philosopher-rulers as unrealistic and undesirable. We have a duty to try to improve defective government, but we should be cautious in doing so, realizing that even defective government is preferable to anarchy. Kant condemns three immoral political maxims:

1. Do what you want and then make excuses.
2. If you have done something wrong, deny it.
3. Divide and conquer.

These are principles of political moralism, which tends to be merely pragmatic and utilitarian; against this, Kant advocates "moral politics," saying that "true politics can never take a step without rendering homage to morality." There should never be any pragmatic compromise between morality and expedience. "The rights of men must be held sacred, however much sacrifice it may cost the ruling power." Kant also advocates a principle of publicity: "All actions relating to the right of other men are unjust if their maxim is not consistent with publicity," in other words, if they have to be done secretly in order to succeed. For this reason, he thinks that revolution tends to be wrong. He concludes the essay by assuring us that perpetual peace is not an empty idea but a goal that we are steadily approaching.[193]

HUMAN PROGRESS.   In his essay "An Old Question Raised Again: Is the Human Race Constantly Progressing?" Kant refuses to interpret the question in terms of the perpetual increase in happiness, dismissing eudaemonism as ultimately "untenable" and viewing it rather in terms of moral improvement. He maintains that we are making gradual progress, but he warns that it is not inevitably constant and that since it depends on our free will, the tide can always (at least temporarily) turn. We cannot infallibly predict free choices; although "man can *see*" the actions resulting from them, we can "not *foresee* with certainty" what they will be. He expresses enthusiasm for the French Revolution, which indicates a concern for the rights and liberties of strangers. He applauds "the evolution of a constitution in accordance with natural law" and establishing of republican government. "This evolution leads to striving after a constitution that cannot be bellicose, that is to say, a republican constitution." These are moral goals towards which civilization is advancing. Although progress depends on our will and is therefore not inevitable, Kant predicts, in answer to his own question, "The human race has always been in progress toward the better and will continue to be so henceforth." This confidence is linked, of course, with his commitment to the gradual unfolding of Enlightenment in our species. He compares the idea of a peaceful republican government to "a Platonic Ideal," which should be viewed as "not an empty chimera, but rather the eternal norm for all civil organization." And he avers that we have a duty to contribute to the establishment and maintenance of such government. Kant's rosy prediction is that violence will continue to diminish, charity will increase, people will become more trustworthy, and we shall move forward towards "the realization of the cosmopolitan society," bursting the limits of nationalism. He thinks that these future trends are unlikely to occur at the "grass-roots" level, "*from bottom to top*," but must occur "*from top to bottom*,"[194] under the direction of enlightened leadership.

JUSTICE. In *The Metaphysical Elements of Justice* Kant writes that a proper understanding of that social virtue must meet three conditions: first, the concept pertains only to external, practical interpersonal relationships; second, it pertains only to the relations between one person's will and another's (not to wishes, desires, or needs); and, third, "the matter [content] of the will, that is, the end that a person intends to accomplish," is irrelevant. Given these three restrictions, he writes,

> Justice is therefore the aggregate of those conditions under which the will of one person can be conjoined with the will of another in accordance with a universal law of freedom.

Here we see an intrinsic link between justice and a will subject to universal law (so that it is a moral matter), as well as an essential connection to human freedom. "Hence the universal law of justice is: act externally in such a way that the free use of your will is compatible with the freedom of everyone according to a universal law." The idea of universalizability is embedded here; justice requires that a person be free to do whatever is compatible with the freedom of all other persons in morally similar circumstances. To use an all-too-familiar example, justice requires that we should ordinarily have sufficient freedom of movement to wave our arms and hands around, but "my freedom to swing my fists ends where your nose begins," because one person cannot ordinarily strike another forcibly without violating his freedom to move about and function without pain. Justice is compatible with coercion to prevent violations of others' freedom; for example, the ordinary rule against punching someone else in the nose is legitimately suspended for purposes of self-defense, if a fist in the face is what is needed to repel a vicious assault. The social virtue of justice relates to both "natural Law" and "positive (statutory) Law," so that we can speak of both "innate rights and acquired rights." Kant maintains that "the one sole and original right that belongs to every human being by virtue of his humanity"—that is, the only innate human right—is the right to freedom or "independence from the constraint of another's will." We should realize that his ethical theory is **deontological** or duty-based, not fundamentally rights-based. Rights are derivative from duties; and the reason we have an innate human right to freedom is that otherwise we are incapable of choosing to act on duty. All other rights are either consequent to this one or defined by the laws of society. Kant analyzes this innate right to freedom in three dimensions:

1. It includes an element of innate equality, such that no one should be "bound by others to do more than one can also reciprocally bind them to do."

2. It includes an element of autonomy, such that each person is "his own master," so long as "he has done no injustice" rendering him liable to punishment.

3. It includes an element of political liberty "to do anything to others that does not by itself detract from what is theirs."[195]

Kant, thus, fundamentally defines justice in terms of a person's right to freedom rather than, as Hume did, in terms of property rights.

Nevertheless, Kant also includes property rights in his discussion of justice.

> An object is mine *de jure* (*meum juris*) if I am so bound to it that anyone else who uses it without my consent thereby injures me.

It is a violation of justice for one person to take and use another's wristwatch without permission, depriving the rightful owner of its use. Kant postulates that the relationship between persons (subjects) and things (objects) is such that, in principle, "it is possible to have any and every external object of my will as my property." If an external object belongs to no one else, you could theoretically appropriate it; if it does already belong to another, just transactions are possible that could make it yours. The civil law should never abrogate natural law, as it would by arbitrarily and unnecessarily depriving a person of his property. In the state of nature, "prior to the civil constitution," people already have property holdings. "A nonjuridical state of affairs, that is, one in which there is no distributive legal justice, is called the state of nature"; it should be distinguished from the state of "civil society," which "stands under distributive justice" rules. Against Hobbes, Kant asserts, "Even in a state of nature, there can be legitimate societies (for example, conjugal, paternal, domestic groups in general)"; he maintains that we have a moral duty—apart from considerations of pragmatic self-interest—to enter juridical society. Also, against Hobbes, Kant distinguishes between any sort of "civil union," which can be between master and servant, and a true "society," which requires "coequal partnership" and which is the appropriate product of civil union. The social virtue of justice, as the viable alternative to violence, grounds a "postulate of public Law," which demands, "If you are so situated as to be unavoidably side by side with others, you ought to abandon the state of nature and enter, with all others, a juridical state of affairs, that is, a state of distributive legal justice." Presumably, the opening qualifier excuses us from seeking out others if they are geographically far removed from us. Our conduct towards others in society is to be governed by reciprocally binding rules, and coercion against others is legitimate for self-defense and in protecting society against those who would flaunt the rules in violation of rights. A civil society, "viewed as a whole in relation to its own members," is what is called "*the state*"; insofar as it springs from "the common interest of all in having a juridical condition," it is "a *commonwealth.*" A civil society supplies the guarantee of publicly enforced laws of justice missing in the state of nature, where there is "no competent judge."[196]

LEGISLATIVE, EXECUTIVE, AND JUDICIAL AUTHORITIES. A state comprises three main sorts of authority, whether or not these be wielded by three different sets of people.

> The sovereign authority resides in the person of the legislator; the executive authority resides in the person of the ruler (in conformity to law), and the judicial authority (which assigns to everyone what is his own by law) resides in the person of the judge.

In our own society, the houses of Congress, the President, and the judiciary system, respectively, wield these three authorities. Legislative authority should reflect the united will of the citizens. A citizen can be identified by three attributes: "first, the lawful freedom to obey no law other than one to which he has given his consent," at least indirectly by committing himself to complying with majority rule; "second, the civil equality of having among the people no superior over him except another person whom he has just as much of a moral capacity to bind juridically as the other has to bind him"—any citizen can have authority (elected or appointed) over any other; and, "third, the attribute of civil independence" based on "his own rights and powers as a member of the commonwealth" rather than on "the arbitrary will of another person in the society." All citizens, as such, must have voting rights, a prerequisite of which is physical and economic independence; women are said to "lack civil personality" and voting rights to the extent that they depend on others (their fathers, husbands, sons, and so forth) for their "support (subsistence and protection)."[197]

The social contract that constitutes the moral foundation of civil society need not be an historical fact; indeed, Kant thinks it pointless and potentially dangerous to ask whether such an historical agreement can be discovered as its basis. He repeats here that there is never a moral right to violent rebellion against the state, calling it "high treason" worthy of "no lesser punishment than death." It might be possible to dethrone a ruler nonviolently, but "the formal execution of a monarch" is an abomination; and Kant says it "fills the soul . . . with horror" to contemplate "the fate of Charles I or Louis XVI." He does believe that the "negative resistance" of the people's representatives (in Parliament) to a ruler's demands can be morally legitimate; for example, a congress might refuse to support (and fund) the chief executive's call for war. Also, if a revolution has succeeded (as in the American Colonies) and has generated a new constitution, "the illegitimacy of its beginning and of its success cannot free the subjects from being bound to accept the new order of things as good citizens." Although a political sovereign does not own his subjects, since they are always rightly free citizens, they belong to him as "his people," subject to his command. The sovereign has the right to levy taxes on his subjects "for their own conservation, in particular, for the relief of the poor, foundling hospitals, and churches"; and the rich can be properly required to help support the poor.[198]

Magistrates have the right—and even the duty—to punish those convicted of having committed crimes. A convicted criminal can forfeit his rights of citizenship. Private crimes, as when one citizen cheats another, are "brought before a criminal court." Some crimes are violent, whereas others are merely "of a base character." Punishment should never be justified on utilitarian grounds, merely in terms of allegedly beneficial consequences. Indeed, a conviction is necessary before the utilitarian benefits of punishing should even be considered:

> The law concerning punishment is a categorical imperative, and woe to him who rummages around in the winding paths of a theory of happiness looking for some advantage to be gained.

The "principle of equality" must prevail in meting out punishments; it is unjust for one person to receive an extremely severe punishment, while another gets a proverbial "slap on the wrist" for the same crime. Kant thinks that mandatory labor is appropriate for prisoners, lest they be merely supported by the society they have violated. The death penalty is the only appropriate punishment for convicted, premeditated murderers.

> In this case, there is no substitute that will satisfy the requirements of legal justice. There is no sameness of kind between death and remaining alive even under the most

miserable conditions, and consequently there is no equality between the crime and the retribution unless the criminal is judicially condemned and put to death.

Kant does not approve of maltreatment (for example, torture) of even the worst prisoners. But he says that even if a society were to disband, before it does so it has an obligation under justice to execute "the last murderer remaining in prison." The only appropriate justification for any sort of punishment is retribution—not utilitarian restraint, as in Hobbes, or spiritual rehabilitation, as in Plato. Kant is anxious about abuses possible in a sovereign's pardoning a criminal, "either by mitigating or by entirely remitting the punishment," because it might undermine the norms of justice. He thinks such executive pardons are legitimate only in the case of crimes committed against the sovereign himself. "But, even in these cases, he cannot allow a crime to go unpunished if the safety of the people might be endangered thereby,"[199] as when the perpetrator obviously intends to continue inciting violent rebellion.

TYPES OF GOVERNMENT. Like so many political philosophers before him, Kant distinguishes three main types of government, depending on the relationship between state authority and the people: "a single person in the state has command over all, or several persons who are equal and united have command over all the rest, or all the people together have command over each person, including themselves." These are, respectively, "autocratic, aristocratic, or democratic" forms of government. Democracy is the "most complex" and least efficient of the three; autocracy is the simplest and most efficient, though also "the most dangerous" in being liable to oppressive despotism. Whichever form of government is adopted, a republican constitution is needed, "in which the law is autonomous and is not annexed to any particular person." Any of the three forms of government is compatible with such a republican constitution.

> Every true republic is and can be nothing else than a representative system of the people if it is to protect the rights of its citizens in the name of the people.

Such a republican constitution provides safeguards, whether the sovereign executive power be vested in one, some, or all of the citizens.[200]

WAR AND PEACE. Despite his advocacy of peace, Kant holds that a society has the right to go to war to protect itself from injury by another state, where there is no international judicial process with authority to resolve disputes. For example, threats against "a balance of power among all states" can be destabilizing enough to provoke legitimate fears of attack that call for retaliatory action. But even in a just war there are rights to be respected and reasonable limits on proper conduct; it is not the case that "all's fair in war." It is wrong to wage a punitive war, a war of extermination, or a war of subjugation, for example, no matter how threatened or violated we may have been. Spies, assassins, guerrillas, and rumor-mongers are morally wrong as are treachery and the plundering of vanquished peoples. A treaty concluding a war must not deprive the conquered citizens of their civil freedom, ought not to establish any form of "hereditary slavery," and should include "a general amnesty." The rights of neutrality, of security, and of reciprocal alliances are to be respected, though this "does not include the right to form a league for aggression and internal aggrandizement."[201]

In order to promote perpetual peace we should work to establish "a universal union of states," which would function as "a free and essentially arbitrary combination of various states that can be dissolved at any time. As such, it should not be confused with a union (such as that of the American states) that is founded on a political constitution and which therefore cannot be dissolved." This "rational Idea of a peaceful, even if not friendly, universal community of all nations on earth that can come into mutual active relations with one another" should serve as a regulative guide. Nor does Kant believe that oceans so separate nations that they can ignore one another safely, since, "thanks to navigation," they can be crossed and typically allow for international commerce. Appropriating newly discovered land can be legitimate, so long as it does not involve encroaching on others' property. For example, the land of "the American Indians" should only be appropriated by contractual agreements with them, not by violent force; and, even then, no unfair advantage should be taken of their ignorance or lack of sophistication. We should constantly strive to be just towards others and to promote world peace, which is admittedly an ideal that has never been achieved.

We must, however, act *as though* perpetual peace were a reality, which perhaps it is not, by working for its establishment and for the kind of constitution that seems best adapted for bringing it about (perhaps republicanism in every state).

The whole ultimate purpose of international law should be to promote justice and establish "a universal and enduring peace."[202]

FRIENDSHIP. In *Lectures on Ethics* Kant emphasizes the importance of our "respect for the rights of others" in powerful words:

> There is nothing more sacred in the wide world than the rights of others. They are inviolable. Woe unto him who trespasses upon the right of another and tramples it underfoot!

He discusses the social relationship of friendship, in which our natural motive of self-love can be "superseded by a generous reciprocity of love" for others. Friendship is a moral ideal at which we should aim, even if there is never any empirical proof of mutual sincerity in a friendship relation. "There are three types" of social relationships that might be considered friendly, "based respectively on need, taste, and disposition." Two people can be pragmatically drawn to each other merely because they are in a position to be of mutual assistance to one another. "The friendship of taste is a pseudo-friendship," based on the contingent and possibly temporary pleasure we enjoy from associating with certain people. The third type of social relationship "is one of pure, genuine disposition, and is friendship in the absolute sense." It is always a particular association of particular people to one another, in which each person "can reveal his disposition to another and enter into communion with him." Thus, it essentially requires mutual trust. It is not necessary that friends think alike; "on the contrary, difference in thought is a stronger foundation for friendship, for then the one makes up the deficiencies of the other." But what is required is basic agreement regarding their "intellectual and moral principles," if they are going to be able to trust one another and confide in one another successfully. Even true friendships of the third type can come to an end. But when they do, our respect for friendship should prevent us from betraying confidences or speaking ill of former friends. Not everyone is a potential friend of all, since friendship is particular and requires intellectual and moral compatibility. Yet some people are so congenial and amiable that they seem to be "everybody's friends."[203]

Religion

KANT'S PRECRITICAL IDEAS. In the preface of his early scientific work, *Universal Natural History and Theory of the Heavens* Kant points to the harmonious order of the universe as indicative of a divine Designer; near the end of the work, he writes, "The whole creation is penetrated by His energy."[204] In his *New Exposition* he uses similar causal reasoning, subscribing to the rationalist notion that there must be a sufficient "determining reason" for everything; he briefly considers "the Cartesian argument" that existence is necessarily included in the very essence of God. Kant himself holds that God is that "being whose existence is prior to the very possibility" of anything at all. On this view, the possibility of any reality must presuppose a necessarily existing Being.[205]

In a third precritical work, *The One Possible Basis for a Demonstration of the Existence of God*, Kant warns that an attempt to prove God's existence "requires that one venture into the fathomless abyss of metaphysics. This is a dark ocean without coasts and without lighthouses." By now he is denying the Cartesian thesis that existence is a "predicate or determination of any thing," in effect disputing a premise of the modern version of the ontological argument. He claims that one could deny all existence without any logical "internal contradiction," but then one would also have to deny all possibility. But we cannot deny all possibility whatsoever. "Consequently it is absolutely impossible that nothing at all exist." So, something must exist as necessary ground of possibility. "Accordingly something exists in an absolutely necessary fashion." He proceeds to argue that it must be one, simple, immutable, eternal, the highest reality, and a spirit. After providing such argumentation, however, Kant concludes this book with a caution, "It is thoroughly necessary that one be convinced of God's existence; but it is not nearly so necessary that it be demonstrated."[206]

THE THEOLOGICAL IDEA. Let us now move from that background on Kant's precritical ideas to the far more famous and important views of his critical philosophy, starting with a quick look at what he says near the end of the *Prolegomena* before moving on to each

Critique. In discussing the fourth antinomy (regarding whether all reality is contingent or whether there is an absolutely necessary Being), he argues that God can necessarily exist as "the cause *of* the appearances" of the world, even though all existence *in* the world of phenomenal appearances be contingent. Then, in discussing the theological "idea of a most perfect primal being," he maintains that we reasonably presuppose a source of the "connection, order, and unity" of the phenomenal order we experience, but without dogmatically "making the subjective conditions of our thinking objective conditions of objects themselves."[207]

DEISM, THEISM, AND ANTHROPOMORPHISM. Later, Kant presents an interesting discussion of deism versus **theism** and the use of analogous language in speaking of God. For example, we can only intelligibly think and talk about divine understanding in terms that relate it to our own, which "must receive its intuitions by the senses and which is occupied in bringing them under rules of the unity of consciousness," despite the fact that we do not imagine that this is the way God's understanding functions at all. Likewise for our attempts to understand the divine will, which we must conceive in relation to our own, which is distracted by selfish needs and tempted by desires, all of "which is wholly incompatible with the pure concept of the Supreme Being." But if we are going to think and talk of God at all, we are forced to do so in terms derived from our own limited experience, even while recognizing their inadequacies. Kant writes,

> Hume's objections to deism are weak, and affect only the proofs, and not the deistic assertion itself. But as regards theism, which depends on a stricter determination of the concept of the Supreme Being, which in deism is merely transcendent, they are very strong.

Where Hume's arguments are effective is in exposing the inadequacies of theological anthropomorphism, as theism's determinations of the divine nature in crude human terms. Kant distinguishes between "*dogmatic* anthropomorphism," which he opposes because it presumes to have knowledge where none is possible, and "a *symbolic* anthropomorphism," whereby we recognize that we are merely conceiving of God as appearing "in relation to the world of which I am a part" and

---

Theism (from the Greek *theos*, meaning god). Belief in the existence of God or gods

not as God intrinsically is. Thus, the idea of God is "sufficiently determined *for us*," though it cannot be determined "absolutely and *in itself*." For example, "reason is attributed to the Supreme Being," but only symbolically, "according to analogy." Kant maintains that this approach allows us to achieve a "**mean** between dogmatism, which Hume combats, and skepticism, which he would substitute for it." This also establishes natural theology as functioning regulatively "in order to guide the use of reason within the world of sense according to principles of the greatest possible (theoretical as well as practical) unity," and not constitutively for the achievement of scientific knowledge.[208]

GOD'S EXISTENCE.   One of the most famous parts of Kant's philosophical theology is his critique of the traditional theoretical arguments for God's existence in his first *Critique*. He maintains that there are three such approaches:

1. That which begins with "determinate experience and the specific constitution of the world of sense as thereby known" is the "*physico-theological*" argument from design.
2. That based on "experience which is purely indeterminate, that is, from experience of existence in general" is "*cosmological*" reasoning.
3. Those which "abstract from all experience, and argue completely *a priori* from mere concepts, to the existence" of God are "*ontological*."

No other arguments for God's existence are possible, from a theoretical perspective. He proceeds to criticize these three approaches in reverse order because he is confident that the first tends to presuppose the second and that the second tends to assume the first (in the way they get used).[209]

The ontological argument tries to demonstrate that God exists necessarily from an analysis of the very concept of God. If this is an analytic or "identical proposition," its predicate can only be denied if we also deny its subject. Consider, as an example, the statement that all triangles are figures with three internal angles. "To posit a triangle, and yet to reject its three angles, is self-contradictory; but there is no contradiction in rejecting the triangle together with its three angles." The same holds true for the proposition, "God is omnipotent," which is also "a necessary judgment." At least Kant believes that omnipotence belongs to the very concept of God, so that we cannot logically deny the former without also denying the latter. But there is no logical problem with an atheist denying both omnipotence and God together. "The only way of evading this conclusion is to argue that there are subjects which cannot be removed" or denied at all. But this would involve begging the question by assuming what we are trying to prove, namely "that there are absolutely necessary subjects," including God. The assertion, "God exists," if it is a genuine proposition, must be either analytic or synthetic. If the former, then existence adds no new idea to the subject concept, God, and the assertion is true by definition, making it "nothing but a miserable **tautology**." On the other hand, if considered a synthetic proposition, then its predicate can be denied of its subject without any logical contradiction. But, in fact, Kant maintains, "'*Being*' is obviously not a real predicate" at all. "It is merely the positing of a thing" and constitutes "merely the copula of a judgment," linking subject and predicate. The concepts of "God" and "God existing" are identical in content. "Otherwise stated, the real contains no more than the merely possible. A hundred real thalers do not contain the least coin more than a hundred possible thalers" in their concepts. So the assertion, "God exists," explicitly contains no predicate. "Whatever, therefore, and however much, our concept of an object may contain, we must go outside it, if we are to ascribe existence to the object." But this resorting to experience is precisely what the ontological argument would avoid, so that it does not even seek, let alone find, grounds for maintaining God's existence.

The attempt to establish the existence of a supreme being by means of the famous ontological argument of Descartes is therefore merely so much labour and effort

---

Physicotheology.   Kant's name for that branch of philosophical theology that argues from design to prove God's existence

Tautology (from the Greek *tautologos*, meaning repeating what has been said).   Loosely, a repetition of the same ideas, though, perhaps, in different words (e.g., "visible to the eye")

lost; we can no more extend our stock of [theoretical] insight by mere ideas, than a merchant can better his position by adding a few noughts to his cash account.[210]

By contrast with the ontological argument, the "*cosmological proof*" seems more "natural," in that it contains at least an empirical premise, namely, that some object of experience exists, trying to account for that in terms of some "absolutely necessary being," which is God. This is the sort of argument Aquinas used and Descartes developed in the third of his *Meditations*. The argument is only empirical "for a single step," in concluding that some necessary being exists. To the extent that it goes on to identify that with a perfect, most real being, however, it "abandons experience altogether" and smuggles in reasoning of "the ontological proof," which has already been criticized. But even in the empirical phase of the cosmological argument "there lies hidden a whole nest of dialectical assumptions" detected and undermined by Kant's critical epistemology. Most fundamentally, it uses the category of causality, which "is applicable only in the sensible world" of phenomenal appearances, to apply to an alleged necessary cause of the world as a whole (the cosmos). As we have seen, on Kantian grounds, this is illegitimate and can never constitute knowledge. The argument also assumes "the impossibility of an infinite series of causes," an assumption that has never been justified "even within the world of experience, still less beyond this world in a realm into which this series can never be extended." Further, the argument involves a confusion of "the logical possibility of a concept of all reality united into one" cosmos with "the transcendental possibility of such a reality," that would require a supporting intuition (of which we are incapable in this life) for its justification. It would be acceptable if those employing this argument recognized that it only leads us to "a *regulative principle* of reason, which directs us to look upon all connection in the world *as if* it originated from an all-sufficient necessary cause." But proponents of the argument are not satisfied with viewing it as anything less than a logical demonstration yielding knowledge, "thus changing a *regulative* into a *constitutive* principle."[211]

Third, there is the argument from design, which Kant calls "the physico-theological proof," leading from our experience of particular features of the world of appearances as richly varied but harmoniously ordered to the conclusion that God must exist as the intelligent, powerful source of this order. Kant says, "This proof always deserves to be mentioned with respect. It is the oldest, the clearest, and the most accordant with the common reason of mankind. It enlivens the study of nature" by encouraging us to view the natural order as intelligible. It has the psychological (not necessarily logical) effect of rendering belief in God as "an irresistible conviction." But, like Hume, who also criticized the proof while regarding it as the best of the traditional theoretical arguments for God, Kant warns that it does not work as a logical demonstration leading "to apodeictic certainty" and by itself "can never establish the existence of a supreme being, but must always fall back upon the ontological argument," which has already been criticized, to show that the designer of the natural order is a perfect, most real Being. By itself, the argument from design is an extremely limited probability argument. "The utmost, therefore, that the argument can prove is an *architect* of the world," limited by the materials available for design, and "not a *creator* of the world to whose idea everything is subject." But, of course, this falls far short of the goal of natural theology, to demonstrate "an all-sufficient primordial being." The argument is valuable in leading us to "admiring the greatness, wisdom, power, etc., of the Author of the world, but can take us no further." In order to show that the Designer is also "an absolutely necessary being," the unreliable cosmological argument must be smuggled into play; and to show that it is a perfect "*ens realissimum*," the discredited ontological argument must be employed. "Thus the physico-theological proof of the existence of an original or supreme being rests upon the cosmological proof, and the cosmological upon the ontological." All of them fail to be logically cogent. But, Kant adds, "besides these three, there is no other path open to speculative reason"[212] for proving God's existence.

MORAL THEOLOGY. This negative conclusion, however, is not the end of Kant's discussion even here in the first *Critique*. Natural theology, which reasons to "the properties and the existence of an Author of the world from the constitution, the order and unity,

---

Ens realissimum (from the Latin, literally meaning the most real Being).   A term Kant uses for God

exhibited in the world," includes "*moral theology*," as well as the "physico-theology" we have been discussing, to the extent that the world can be viewed as comprising free causality, as well as natural causality. The moral theologian (Kant, in contrast to Hume, for example) subscribes to theism and the belief in "a *living God*" in relation to our world, rather than merely to deism and the belief in an abstract, original metaphysical principle not necessarily bound up with our world now at all. Anticipating somewhat the **moral argument** of his next *Critique*, Kant writes here,

> Now since there are practical laws which are absolutely necessary, that is, the moral laws, it must follow that if these necessarily presuppose the existence of any being as the condition of their *obligatory* power, this existence must be *postulated*.

In the ethical works he would write during the next several years, Kant does not make the "*obligatory* power" of moral laws contingent on God after all. But he does keep the promise made here:

> At some future time we shall show that the moral laws do not merely presuppose the existence of a supreme being, but also, as themselves in a different connection absolutely necessary, justify us in postulating it, though, indeed, only from a practical point of view.[213]

Kant writes "that the doctrine of the existence of God belongs to doctrinal belief," standing in an intermediate position between mere opinion and certain knowledge. Such "belief is, from the *objective* point of view, an expression of modesty," falling short of knowledge-claims, "yet at the same time, from the *subjective* point of view, an expression of the firmness of our confidence." Yet this belief, like the one in immortality we shall discuss in the next section, is more than theoretical and speculative; it is also a "moral belief," having practical implications for our conduct as moral agents. Kant says,

> I inevitably believe in the existence of God and in a future life, and I am certain that nothing can shake this belief, since my moral principles would thereby be themselves overthrown, and I cannot disclaim them without becoming abhorrent in my own eyes.

This moral belief provides us with a conviction tantamount to subjective, but not objective, certainty. As Kant puts the point,

I must not even say, "*It is* morally certain that there is a God, etc.," but "*I am* morally certain, etc."[214]

A celebrated aspect of Kant's philosophical theology, after his criticism of the traditional theoretical proofs, is his own moral argument for God, contained in his second *Critique*. We recall that in his ethical theory Kant distinguishes between the supreme good we can achieve by our own efforts in this life, which is moral virtue, and the perfect or complete good of "happiness proportional to that morality," which we cannot fully achieve in this life. Yet since that perfect good is an ideal towards which we should aim, and since "ought" implies "can," it must be possible; and we are rationally justified in believing in the necessary condition of that possibility. Therefore, he concludes, reason "must postulate the existence of God as necessarily belonging to the possibility of the highest good" (*die Existenz Gottes, als zur Möglichkeit des höchsten Guts*), this being an object of practical faith. Since neither we nor anything in our finite world can suffice to guarantee the perfect good, it is "possible only on the supposition of a supreme cause of nature which has a causality corresponding to the moral intention," as well as attributes of "understanding and will." It would be irrational to conceive of ourselves as obligated to pursue an impossible ideal. "Therefore it is morally necessary to assume the existence of God" (*es ist moralisch nothwendig das Daseyn Gottes anzunehmen*). He proceeds to observe that "this moral necessity is subjective, i.e., a need, and not objective," that it is "a hypothesis" of "pure *rational faith*." On this view, religion is founded on morality, rather than the other way around. "Religion is the recognition of all duties as divine commands, not as sanctions, i.e., arbitrary and contingent ordinances of a foreign will, but as essential laws of any free will as such" (*zur Religion, d.i. zur Erkenntniss aller Pflichten als göttlicher Gebote*). Here "morals is not really the doctrine of how to make ourselves happy but of how we are to be *worthy* of happiness."[215]

In his third *Critique* Kant develops a theory of "*moral teleology*," which, he maintains, "supplies the deficiency in *physical teleology* and first establishes a *theology*." Whereas "*physical teleology*" only leads us "to assume the being of an intelligent world

Moral argument. In Kant, the postulation of God as practically necessitated by our moral consciousness

cause," it is "*moral teleology*" which relates to our own practical goals and final purpose. Because we morally aim at happiness in conformity with virtue, seeing "*morality* as worthiness to be happy," and cannot see these two goods as necessarily "*connected* by merely natural causes," it becomes practically necessary that we "assume a moral world cause (an author of the world)" as a warrant of such possibility, as "governor of the world" (not merely its designer), as well as "its moral lawgiver." The perfect, complete, "*highest good* in the world," God, and "the immortality of the soul" are all "mere things of faith," which cannot be objectively established and hence are strictly unknowable, but which are reasonably believed from a "practical point of view." Faith in such matters is a habit, a "moral attitude of reason as to belief in that which is unattainable by theoretical cognition." By means of faith the mind is able "to assume as true, on account of the obligation in reference to it, that which is necessary to presuppose as condition of the possibility of the highest moral final purpose." As such, it is "trust in the attainment of a design" that is moral in character. The God to which such moral faith leads us should only be conceived "according to analogy,"[216] with no pretence that we can have knowledge of God's intrinsic nature apart from the way it appears in our rational experience.

In his *Lectures on Philosophical Theology* Kant says that

> religion is nothing but the application of theology to morality, that is, to a good disposition and a course of conduct well-pleasing to the highest being.

Theology can be based on "reason" or on "revelation"; rational theology, in turn, can be "either *speculative*" in nature "or *moral*." Speculative theology is either "*transcendental*" (as in the use of ontological reasoning) or "*natural*," the latter including both "*cosmotheology*" and "*physicotheology*." Transcendental theology leads us to "represent God as the *cause* of the world"; natural theology (both cosmological and teleological) leads to the idea of "the *author* of the world, as a living God"; and moral theology leads us to "represent God as the *ruler* of the world." Whereas deism believes in an abstract metaphysical principle that is "wholly idle and useless" to us and our practical pursuits, theism believes "in a *living* God who has produced the world through knowledge and by means of his free will." Kant subscribes to moral theism, the

belief that God is not only living and related to us but is "the author of our moral laws." The God of moral theism must be omniscient to know our intentions, omnipotent to be able to order the natural realm, and holy and just to ensure the perfect good.[217]

Kant appreciates the objections Hume raised in his *Dialogues* against physicotheology. But they altogether miss the point of moral teleology, where God is conceived as "a necessary postulate" of practical reason, in terms of "the moral perfections of *holiness, benevolence*, and *justice*." These are three dimensions of the moral nature of God "as a *holy lawgiver*, a *benevolent sustainer of the world*, and a *just judge*." The problem of evil is a threat in philosophical theology insofar as it tends to call into question all three of these moral attributes. But it is man's (and, perhaps, also other rational creatures') freedom, autonomy, and responsibility for his own development that render "the incompleteness" of evil possible. The physical evils of the world constitute an incentive for progress, "a special arrangement for leading man toward happiness." As for the disproportion "between good conduct and well-being," Kant is convinced that it is temporary and will be rectified in the hereafter. On account of the limitations on our experience, we cannot even calculate a probability of God's being but must leave it a practical conviction, "a necessary *postulate*" of moral faith. Denying God does not lead to any logical contradiction but rather to the practical absurdity of our being obligated to strive for a goal for which no ground of possibility is granted.[218]

TRUE MORAL RELIGION. Kant's *Religion within the Limits of Reason Alone* considers the postulate of God that "arises out of morality" without being the basis of moral obligation.

> Morality thus leads ineluctably to religion, through which it extends itself to the idea of a powerful moral Lawgiver, outside of mankind, for Whose will that is the final end (of creation) which at the same time can and ought to be man's final end.

Here he distinguishes between a religion of "mere worship," which "*endeavors to win favor*" with God in a selfish manner, which he criticizes, and true "*moral* religions, i.e., religions of *good life-conduct*," which he endorses. True moral religion, he says, "must consist not in dogmas and rites but in the heart's disposition to fulfill all human duties as divine commands." Miracles are possible, but belief in them should not be regarded as essential. They would be "events in the world the *operating laws* of whose causes are, and must remain, absolutely unknown to us" and could be either "*theistic*," directly caused by God, or "*demonic*," caused by good or bad spirits. God should be regarded as the "highest lawgiver of an ethical commonwealth with respect to whom all *true duties*, hence also the ethical, must be represented as *at the same time* his commands." God should also be conceived "as moral ruler of the world" even now. The "*church invisible*" is our idea of all persons of good will united under "moral divine world-government," as in the kingdom of ends, whereas the "*visible church* is the actual union of men into a whole which harmonizes with that ideal" in this life.

> The true (visible) church is that which exhibits the (moral) kingdom of God on earth so far as it can be brought to pass by men.

Religion which is "*merely statutory*" is based on laws historically revealed and to be obeyed. By contrast, moral legislation is naturally knowable and is the necessary "condition of all true religion." Likewise, cultic rules of worship are arbitrary and less essential than moral "life-conduct." We should have respect for revealed scriptures. Various churches are different denominational expressions of true religion.

> There is only *one* (true) *religion;* but there can be *faiths* of several kinds.

Thus, Judaism, Islam, and Christianity (and, within the latter, Protestantism and Catholicism) are different denominational faiths within the same true religion of ethical monotheism.[219]

Kant does not think that religious feelings are essential, since feeling is a private, personal matter. Moral religion believes in God

1. as the omnipotent Creator of heaven and earth, i.e., morally as *holy* Legislator,
2. as Preserver of the human race, its *benevolent* Ruler and moral Guardian,
3. as Administrator of His own holy laws, i.e., as *righteous* Judge.

Kant defines moral religion as "the recognition of all duties as divine commands" (*das Erkenntniss aller unserer Pflicten as göttlicher Gebote*). He discusses Christianity in terms of natural (rather than supernatural) religion. He considers Jesus as "the wise Teacher" of the Gospels, "of whom an historical

record" is available to us, who, though not "the *founder* of the *religion*" of moral theism, should be revered "as the founder of the first true *church*." Kant analyzes the moral teachings of Jesus, as recorded in the Gospel of Matthew, in such a way as to make them sound like forerunners of the Kantian ethic. Kant dismisses mere statutory religion, with no regard to the cultivation of moral good will, as mere "*pseudo-service*," pretending to honor God with no genuine spiritual conversion, but merely through the outward displays of sacrifices, cultic rituals, penances, and so forth. By contrast, enlightened religion identifies true "service of God" as autonomously chosen "moral service," with no place for the "fetish-worship" of "Clericalism." In genuine moral religion mere "*piety* (a passive respect for the law of God)" should never substitute for "*virtue* (the application of one's own powers in discharging the duty which one respects)."[220]

Immortality

SOME PRECRITICAL IDEAS. In his pre-critical *Dreams of a Spirit Seer* Kant approaches the scepticism of Hume (some of whose works had recently been translated into German and studied by Kant) when he sarcastically writes of "the Wonderland of Metaphysics." There, Kant says,

> Folly and wisdom are separated by such indistinct borderlines that one can hardly walk for any length of time on the path of one without straying a little into the path of the other.

Yet it is precisely metaphysics, he sardonically adds, "with whom destiny made me fall in love hopelessly though I can but rarely pride myself on any reciprocated favours on her part." A part of metaphysical speculation that attracted Kant's attention is that which concerns the immortality of the soul. Even as early as 1766, perhaps under the influence of Hume, Kant seems resigned to the impossibility of metaphysical knowledge and writes here,

> If we begin to realize in the course of investigations that a convincing philosophical insight in the case examined is an impossibility, we shall have no more difficulty in admitting that such kind of knowledge is quite useless and unnecessary in any case.

He sees no reason to assume that certainty about life after death will ensure "honest or virtuous" behavior and worries about the person who "shuns the exercise of wicked acts but nourishes a vicious character because he loves the rewards of virtuous acts but hates virtue itself." Base characters might use knowledge of immortality not as grounds for becoming persons of good will but "to devise means of staving off the threatened consequences which await them in a future life." On the other hand, he says, it does seem appropriate that persons of good will should reasonably believe in immortality. As he writes,

> there has never been a righteous soul who could have endured the thought that death is the end of all, and whose noble disposition did not raise in him the hope of a future life. Thus it appears in conformity with human nature and the purity of morals to base the expectation of a future life upon the feeling of a noble soul rather than found morality on the hope of another life, i.e., the other way round.

Here Kant is clearly viewing the issue as one of rational belief and says that "moral faith leads man without deviation to his true purpose," so that knowledge of immortality, whether or not it is possible, is superfluous. He suggests that it may even be presumptuous of us to try to achieve it here:

> Human reason was not meant to try and part the highest clouds in heaven or lift from our eyes the curtains in order to reveal to us the secrets of the other world.

We should lead the sorts of virtuous lives now that will render us practically worthy of eternal reward rather than straining for some theoretical knowledge that may be unavailable anyhow. He ends the work thus:

> As our destiny in the future world most likely depends on the way in which we manage our jobs in this world, I shall conclude in the words of *Candide* whom Voltaire after so many school disputes allows to conclude: let's seek our happiness and cultivate our garden.[221]

It is this focus on practical action over theoretical speculation that characterizes Kant's more famous critical discussion of the topic as well.

THE PROSPECT OF A FUTURE LIFE.   In his first *Critique* Kant maintains that our "hope of a *future* life" is grounded in that characteristic of human nature that renders us never "capable of being satisfied by what is temporal." We have already discussed freedom and God, two of Kant's three postulates of practical reason, and are now dealing with the third. In a footnote later in this book he writes, "Metaphysics has as the proper object of its enquiries three ideas only: *God, freedom,* and *immortality*—so related that the second

concept, when combined with the first, should lead to the third as a necessary conclusion," although its necessity is practical rather than logical. If we use our freedom in choosing between good and evil and there is a just God ruling the moral order, then it seems there ought to be a future life in which good is rewarded and evil punished, as cannot be counted on in this life. Like Hume, Kant rejects all theoretical attempts to demonstrate the immortality of the soul.

> Yet nothing is thereby lost as regards the right, nay, the necessity, of postulating a future life in accordance with the principles of the practical employment of reason.[222]

In his second *Critique* Kant unfolds the reasoning underlying this postulating of immortality. Remember Kant's claim that we are morally obliged to strive for the perfect good of happiness proportional to virtue, which we cannot achieve in this life by our own efforts. This requires a "complete fitness of the will to the moral law . . . of which no rational being in the world of sense is at any time capable." The best we can do is make continual progress towards the goal of this "complete fitness," which would not extend far if biological death were the end of us. "This infinite progress is possible, however, only under the presupposition of an infinitely enduring existence and personality of the same rational being; this is called the immortality of the soul."[223] As a matter of rational faith, Kant holds that justice will ultimately prevail; to the extent that we have led virtuous lives as persons of good will, we shall achieve fulfillment as moral agents.

Fulfillment

HAPPINESS.   In the *Grounding* Kant defines human "happiness" in terms of a "complete well-being and contentment with one's condition." He admits that

> the concept of happiness is such an indeterminate one that even though everyone wishes to attain happiness, yet he can never say definitely and consistently what it is that he really wishes and wills.

The reason that it remains such a nebulous, problematic concept is that our understanding of it is so inescapably contingent on fragmentary, impressionistic, limited experience that we have only a vague notion of "a maximum of well-being" that endures permanently. Happiness, in this life, remains merely an empirical ideal—"not an ideal of reason but of imagination."[224]

Near the end of his first *Critique* Kant writes,

Happiness is the satisfaction of all our desires, *extensively*, in respect of their manifoldness, *intensively*, in respect of their degree, and *protensively*, in respect of their duration.

He distinguishes between "*happiness,*" which is a purely empirical concept, since "only by means of experience can I know what desires there are which call for satisfaction," and the "*worthiness of being happy,*" which is a moral concept. We should not pursue virtue for the selfish purpose of achieving happiness. But we should use our freedom to act in such a way that we shall become *worthy* of happiness; and *then* we shall have reason to "hope for happiness." As we have seen, the realization of this hope is contingent on the existence of God and human immortality as conditions of its coming to pass. Neither happiness, which is a good, nor moral virtue, which is the highest good we can achieve by our own efforts in this life, is the ultimate. "To make the good complete, he who behaves in such a manner as not to be unworthy of happiness must be able to hope that he will participate in happiness." The "supreme good" of happiness allocated "in exact proportion with the morality of the rational beings who are thereby rendered worthy of it" is an ideal of the "intelligible world only" and not to be expected in this "sensible world" of physical bodies.[225]

In the *Lectures on Philosophical Theology* Kant distinguishes between two different conceptions of happiness: "One consists in the *satisfaction of desires*. But desires always presuppose needs," which in this life always recur or go partially unsatisfied. "But there is also the possibility of a kind of happiness which is *mere enjoyment*, without any needs." This is more easily attained but is inferior in that its achievement is a matter of luck and fails to motivate us to strive to be better. It is so static and passive an experience that Kant comments, "Any man who wanted to be happy in this way would be the most useless man in the world. For he would completely lack any incentives to action." We should favor the more dynamic concept of happiness "as a *progress toward contentment*," recognizing that this requires "labor, difficulty, effort," and an ongoing "striving" for an ideal that we can never reach in this life. "Well-being is inseparably combined with good conduct," and our ultimate fulfillment must be a continuation and consequence of the character developed now.

Moral perfection in this life will be followed by moral growth in the next, just as moral deterioration in this life will bring a still greater decline. After death man will continue with his development and the predisposition of his abilities.[226]

Thus, Kant views the physical death of the body as an event through which we pass in our continuous, ongoing process of self-fulfillment.

MORAL PERFECTION. As for true contentment in this life, he says in his *Anthropology*, "It is not attainable for mankind, neither in the moral aspect (to be content with oneself and one's good conduct), nor in the pragmatic aspect (as to one's well-being which he intends to acquire through skill and cleverness)." But our lack of contentment should be viewed as a stimulus to further effort and progress, rather than as a curse. "To be (absolutely) contented with life would mean inactive rest, the cessation of all motivation," which would constitute a kind of living death.[227]

The last little section of Kant's *Lectures on Ethics* discusses "The Ultimate Destiny of the Human Race." There our fulfillment is defined in terms of developing "moral perfection, provided that it is achieved through human freedom, whereby alone man is capable of the greatest happiness." We cannot have it thrust upon us but must achieve it through the deliberate use of our rational faculties. He says,

> God's will is not merely that we should be happy, but that we should make ourselves happy, and this is the true morality. The universal end of mankind is the highest moral perfection.

To the extent that we can achieve this in the present life, we can help to establish "the kingdom of God on earth" as a precursor of what awaits us in the afterlife. But, Kant soberly warns us, "the hope of it is still distant; it will be many centuries before it can be realized."[228] The glory of moral enlightenment is that it illuminates this goal and gives us practical encouragement for pursuing it.

REFLECTIONS

Hume and Kant are the two greatest philosophers of the eighteenth-century Enlightenment. Despite important differences between them, they utilize a similar critical methodology and represent the Enlightenment ideals of reason, experience, science, and progress. In different ways, they challenge the traditions of their times, advocating individual autonomy over any unquestioning conformity to authority. Although we should not exaggerate their similarities, there is some legitimacy to Herder's calling Kant (in a letter of 1781) "a Prussian Hume." It appears that Kant passed through a brief sceptical period of his own, during his years as a *Privatdozent*, which was probably inspired by his study of Hume. But, significantly, this was merely a transit stop on Kant's intellectual journey from the rationalism in which he was educated to his own unique system of transcendental criticism, in which he typically performs a critical analysis of various forms of human experience and knowledge to determine what universal and necessary conditions must be granted as grounds of their possibility.

REALITY.   In his theory of reality Kant does make an advance beyond the phenomenalism of Hume, without, however, lapsing back into the naive realism of rationalists. While conceding Hume's point that we can know nothing metaphysical of reality in itself, apart from its appearances in our phenomenal experience, he leaves open the path of our rational speculation, regarding it as having heuristic or regulative value in guiding further thought and action. One might question the legitimacy of postulating noumenal ideas of things regarded as essentially unknowable. Hegel, for example, tends to wonder how the concept of an unknowable thing-in-itself can be anything but worthless. But, in defense of Kant, we might retort that, though knowledge may be the ideal goal of all cognitive thought, rational faith, falling short of that ideal, can still be quite valuable.

BODIES.   Second, in his analysis of bodies and the physical world of experience, Kant saves scientific knowledge from the scepticism of Hume, which threatens to reduce all laws to mere inductive generalizations. On Kant's view, the concepts of the understanding provide universal and necessary structures that make possible scientific knowledge. The catch, of course, as we have seen, is that this is physical rather than metaphysical knowledge, extending only within the parameters of possible natural experience.

PERSONALITY.   His treatment of the human personality, our third topic, is far richer and more complex than Hume's notion of a "bundle of perceptions." He agrees with Hume that the rationalist claim to

introspective knowledge of the self as a metaphysical subject is unfounded. But, unlike Hume, Kant realizes that we can experience the self in action, for example, in exercising moral choices; even though this experience does not provide any intuition into the content of the self, it does justify our postulating a self as a formal agent. It also seems correct that the mind passively has sense experiences, actively produces imaginative experiences, and reflectively encounters the experience (of "apperception") of itself as being the locus of those other experiences. As we have seen, Kant also takes human emotions seriously in his philosophical psychology. And his tridimensional view of human nature as animal, rational, and personal is valuable, even if it is not quite clear how these three dimensions coherently interrelate.

KNOWLEDGE.   Fourth, Kant's theory of knowledge is perhaps that facet of his philosophy for which he is most famous. Thanks to Kant, the history of philosophy made the "transcendental turn" away from the naive assumption that, when we know, ideas in our minds (somehow) conform to objects outside our minds and towards the critical consideration of universal and necessary conditions of any human experience and knowledge at all. His boast that no one ("not even Hume") before him investigated the grounds of synthetic *a priori* judgments is justified. He was probably mistaken (and Hume correct) about mathematical statements being synthetic since their truth does seem to hinge entirely on conceptual interrelations. But Kant's conception of synthetic *a priori* concepts is crucial to the understanding of the science and metaphysics of that era. His analysis of space and time as forms of sensibility whereby the mind structures its experiences, rather than objects of experience, is brilliantly original, as is his notion of the concepts of the understanding as the innate categories applied by the mind to its data in order to constitute knowledge. One might wonder whether the categories are limited to the twelve he names; why, for example, isn't his own concept of personality a separate category, rather than a particular sort of substance? But the Copernican revolution, whereby the mind is seen as imposing its conditions on all objects of possible knowledge, is an extremely important development in intellectual history. His analysis of the relationships among sensibility, the understanding, and reason—

each with its own *a priori* structures—is impressive as well. And, finally, his development of the metaphysical ideas of speculative reason as having "regulative" (rather than "constitutive") value is at least provocative, as a way of taking them more seriously than Hume does without rashly regarding them as knowable.

FREEDOM.   Regarding our fifth topic, Kant's theory of human freedom avoids slipping into determinism, as Hume's analysis does, extending greater respect for our experiences of autonomous choice. Kant's theory does deepen the dualism of his conception of human nature, since all actions of the body and animal will are still seen as extrinsically necessitated. People who are troubled by this dualism will wonder whether, to what extent, and how the phenomenal and noumenal sides of our nature can ever be integrated. But, apart from this worry, Kant's view of human freedom as a postulate of practical reason steers a healthy middle path between the dogmatic assumption that it is theoretically knowable and Hume's sceptical collapsing of it into determinism.

MORALITY.   Sixth, his theory of morality is also revolutionary, since never before had any philosopher developed so purely deontological an ethics, which places so much fundamental emphasis on human autonomy. And here again, Hume's influence was crucial, the inadequacies of his ethical emotivism driving Kant to a radical moral rationalism that never flirts with the temptation to base an "ought" on any "is." There is a radical parting of the ways between Kant and Hume on the subject of moral psychology, Kant being strenuously opposed to Hume's conception of reason as a "slave of the passions." Kant's categorical imperative, in all three of the formulations we have considered, provides a valuable rational test of moral permissibility and is an inspired tool for helping us to adopt a more objective judgment. At the same time, it is not obvious that consequences and emotions must be irrelevant to the calculation of right and wrong, particularly if those are consequences vitally affecting the well-being of persons and if emotions are essential to the nature of human persons. Nor need we, in subscribing to his categorical imperative, feel compelled to accept his way of applying it. One might reasonably

view the imperative as a categorical formal principle, for example, pointing to duties that are ***prima facie*** binding, unless and until they come into conflict with other such duties, at which point consequences do legitimately enter into the moral equation. Finally, we should note that Kant does place a great deal of emphasis on the development of virtuous character, as Hume did (and as Aristotle did long before that).

SOCIETY.   As for our seventh topic, in discussing the foundations of society, Kant improves on the Hobbesian version of the social-contract theory, meeting criticisms Hume raised against it. He agrees with Hume that human nature is intrinsically social and altruistic, and not isolationist and egoistic. He never suggests that the contract need be a historical fact but views it as an implicit free commitment we make to cooperate with others, by which we are morally bound. Kant's ideal of a republican government, with a separation of powers, is compatible with Hume's (and opposed to Hobbes's preferences), though he is too dogmatically extreme in his categorical denunciation of all political revolutions, even as a last resort for defending one's liberty. Kant's notion of nature's "secret plan" for civilizing mankind anticipates a peculiar plank in the platform of Hegel's philosophy of history, but Hegel is in tension with Kant's idea of freedom and autonomy. Kant's proposals for peace, in general, and his call for a League of Nations, the abolition of international subterfuge, the cultivation of universal hospitality, and a respect for human rights everywhere, in particular, are admirable. At the same time, Kant's vision is occasionally limited by the blinders of his own culture, as, for example, in his failure to realize that women should be extended the opportunities that will render them worthy of full-fledged citizenship. Finally, he presents what is probably the most sophisticated analysis of justice developed prior to our own century (the contemporary American philosopher John Rawls has recently gone further; see Chapter VI, Alternatives), one that is far superior to Hume's conventional, relativistic reduction of justice to property rights.

RELIGION.   Eighth, Kant's analysis of religion is a mixed achievement. His assessment of the traditional arguments for God's existence goes even further than

---

Prima facie (literally, in Latin, at first appearance).   What initially or ordinarily appears to be the case

Hume's did and seems impressively on-target; historically, the old arguments seem never to have recovered from his critique, though Hegel valiantly tries to help them do so. (By the time we get to James, for example, it is pretty well taken for granted that they are dead as logical demonstrations.) On the other hand, Kant's own moral argument for God is quite unconvincing because it is based on an unsupported, dubious premise that we have a moral obligation to try to bring about the complete good of a perfect conformity of happiness and moral virtue. The best one can reasonably support here is the claim that we have a duty to promote, to the best of our limited abilities, a just proportion between good action and happiness. But this does not necessitate anything like Kant's moral Legislator and holy Judge. The argument from design, as including Kant's moral teleology, remains the best psychological basis (never tantamount to a cogent logical demonstration) for rational faith in God. Kant's treatment of religion is valuable as far as it goes, but it may play down too much the elements of community (which Hegel will emphasize) and of feeling (which James will stress). Also, it is frustrating to realize how careful Kant is, as a Christian philosopher, not to reveal his views on whether Jesus was literally and uniquely God incarnate.

IMMORTALITY. Kant's treatment of immortality (our ninth topic) as a postulate of practical reason based on the moral argument is subject to the same criticism as offered in the preceding paragraph. If, indeed, Kant has mistaken what our moral obligation is regarding the highest good, the argument unravels. He would do better to strip away this shaky support, leaving the matter at the level of a hope of the moral imagination or of a matter of faith for which no rational argumentation is conclusive—putting his view close to Hume's.

FULFILLMENT. Finally, Kant's discussions of human fulfillment seem on the right track, in viewing it as a dynamic, ongoing "progress towards contentment" that must be conditioned by a moral worthiness to be happy. But again, as in his ideas on religion, there may be insufficient attention paid to the role of interpersonal community in human fulfillment and too much focus on individualistic considerations.

* * *

Kant, like Hume, offers an intricate, coherent philosophy of human nature, animated by the ideals of the Enlightenment. Both thinkers follow the clash between early modern rationalism (Descartes, Spinoza, and Leibniz) and early modern empiricism (Hobbes and Locke). Where Hume's system is valuable as both a critique of traditional views and an exploration of the logical conclusions of radical empiricism, Kant's is a proposal for a radically new approach that synthesizes the best of traditional rationalism (as in Descartes) and empiricism (as in Hume). Kant locates knowledge in the understanding (rather than in reason like the rationalists or in sensibility like the empiricists), which presupposes sensibility and restricts the cognitive range of reason. While rejecting the rationalists' doctrine of innate ideas, he avoids the empiricists' ***tabula rasa*** theory with his intermediate view of *a priori* structures of the mind. He agrees with the rationalists (against Hume) that some of our factual reasoning is universally and necessarily true, but he disagrees with them (siding with Hume) on the possibility of metaphysical knowledge. While believing in things-in-themselves (like the rationalists), Kant restricts knowledge to phenomenal appearances (like Hume). Although sceptical of metaphysical knowledge (like Hume), however, Kant (like the rationalists) staunchly affirms the value of metaphysical inquiry. He rejects both the theoretical proofs of God of the rationalists and the minimalistic deism of Hume, preferring the approach of moral experience. His approach to morality is a fresh alternative to both the traditionalism of the rationalists and the relativism of Hume. On so many of these dimensions of a philosophy of human nature Kant offers us the insights of a new perspective, informed by his own earlier allegiance to rationalism and challenged by the acute critique of Hume. In the relationship between Hume's ideas and Kant's we see the intellectual dialogue of eighteenth-century Enlightenment thought at its best.

QUESTIONS

1. What can Hume claim to know about reality? What are the advantages and disadvantages of this view?

2. What do we experience of bodies? What difference (if any) does it make that we do not actually experience their continuous, uninterrupted existence?

3. How does Hume explain the relation between impressions and ideas? Why does this explanation seem adequate or inadequate?

4. How is Kant's theory of reality dualistic? What do you consider the strengths and weaknesses of such dualism?

5. Why is moral agency essential to Kant's view of personality? Why is he correct or incorrect to insist on this?

6. What are three different formulations of Kant's categorical imperative? Why would you agree or disagree that these are forms of the same fundamental moral principle?

7. What are the problems with Hume's phenomenalistic "bundle" theory of human personality? How does Kant's dualistic view try to solve those problems, and what difficulties does it exhibit?

8. How does Hume's epistemology drastically reduce what seems knowable, and why is this worrisome? How does Kant's epistemology attempt to improve matters, and what problems does it represent?

9. In what sense does Hume really believe in human freedom? Why is this inadequate from Kant's point of view? Can Kant have it both ways with his dualistic theory of freedom and determinism? Explain.

10. How does Hume's emphasis on feelings affect his ethics? From Kant's perspective, what is to be said about that approach? Which thinker seems more correct here, and why?

11. Is Hume really an atheist, as he has been accused of being? If so, why does he pretend otherwise? If not, what sort of Deity does he believe in? Ultimately, is Kant's view of God and religion any better than Hume's—why or why not?

12. How does Hume tear down the arguments for immortality? What sort of new argument does Kant propose? What do you think of the reasoning of each thinker on this issue?

ALTERNATIVES

ROUSSEAU

Perhaps the most important philosophical figure between Hume and Kant was Jean-Jacques Rousseau, who was born in the Republic of Geneva, an independent city-state, in 1712 (a year after Hume's birth), of Calvinist parents. His mother died a few days after giving birth to him. When Rousseau was ten, his father had to leave Geneva after wounding a man with whom he had quarreled. The boy was later apprenticed to a brutal engraver from whom he ran away. He came under the protection of the Baroness de Warens, through whose influence he converted to Catholicism. After moving to France, he met distinguished members of the Enlightenment, including Diderot and Voltaire. He took Thérèse Levasseur, a semiliterate, lower-class hotel maid, as his mistress. He writes that she bore him five children, all of whom were turned over to a foundling hospital,

long before he married her. He invented a system of musical notation, and Diderot invited him to write articles on music for the great *Encyclopedia* he was editing. In 1750, Rousseau submitted an essay in which he argues eloquently that modern culture corrupts man's natural goodness, that social progress is illusory, and that civilization has not made us happier or better; the essay, which went against the grain of mainstream Enlightenment thought, nevertheless won a prize from the Academy of Dijon. In a second essay, Rousseau argues, against Hobbes, that our natural state was happy and wholesome, as well as free and solitary, that people were originally free of the artificial inequalities of society, but that society evolved as a mechanism for collectively coping with economic shortage, bringing with it a loss of freedom, equality, and natural virtue. Rousseau renounced Catholicism, reverting to Protestantism in order to regain his Genevan citizenship. A wealthy patroness had a beautiful home, called the Hermitage, built for him on her estates, where he wrote a novel, *The New Heloise*, as well as the two books to be discussed here, his *Social Contract* and *Émile*. These last two books were condemned in Geneva and in France, with orders for Rousseau's arrest issued in both places. He fled to the protection of Frederick II of Prussia, but his house was stoned there, leading him to run to the Swiss canton of Bern; when he was expelled from Bern, he accepted Hume's invitation to go to England, where his paranoid suspicions and slanderous remarks soon angered the genial, normally imperturbable Hume. Rousseau returned to France as a guest of the Prince de Conti. He spent the last twelve years of his life as a mentally disturbed drifter, copying music for a living, before dying in 1778; in 1794, his remains were laid to rest near those of Voltaire in the Panthéon in Paris.

Rousseau's masterpiece, *The Social Contract* (1762), opens with the powerful claim that man is born free yet everywhere is in chains. This expresses his belief in natural human liberty, stripped away by the artificial conventions of society. He agrees with Aristotle that those born into slavery are slavish by nature but insists that this is so, contrary to human nature, which should be free and equal. People can be forced to alienate their liberty; yet might does not create right. All socio-political rights and responsibilities must be derived from the agreement of some original compact, as Hobbes and Locke taught, which moves us out of a state of nature into one of civil society. In making this transition, we trade our natural liberty for civil liberty; we give up our right to grab what we can get but gain the moral freedom of self-mastery and equality as citizens under the law. Political sovereignty requires the subordination of private interests to the general will (*volonté générale*), which always tends to the preservation and well-being of the whole of society. Because the general will is infallible, it cannot be identified with the will of a majority of individuals or even with the unanimous will of all, both of which can be selfish and mistaken. The participants in the social contract jointly retain political sovereignty, rather than (as in Hobbes) handing it over inalienably to others; also, the state's control over the individual is limited to what concerns the welfare of the community, and violations of liberty or property

rights beyond this limit can nullify the contract and absolve the citizen of further political obligation. But within these legitimate parameters, a citizen can be "forced to be free" and to conform to the requirements of law. All legitimate government must be republican, with legislation democratically passed by the citizens, although the administration of those laws can be democratic, if a state is small, aristocratic, if it is mid-sized, or monarchical, if it is quite large.

The themes of republican government, the moral equality of all, and autonomous self-legislation would exert great influence on Kant. Also, though Rousseau did not advocate revolution, his political writings would serve as a catalytic agent for the French Revolution, inspiring its ideals of liberty, equality, and fraternity; indeed, Napoleon is reputed to have said that the Revolution would not have occurred without Rousseau.

If people are to be capable of self-government and to take advantage of political liberty, they must be educated for it. Rousseau's *Émile* (1762) tries to provide a model for the education of healthy citizens. It too begins with a powerful opening sentence, to the effect that everything is good as it comes from the hand of the Author of nature but degenerates in the hands of man. The natural goodness of children must be nurtured rather than corrupted, encouraged to thrive rather than stifled. Rousseau advocates a "negative education," designed to foster the free development of a child's own nature, to protect his heart from vice, and to guard his mind from error. His educational program comprises four steps, geared to the age of a child. In the first five years of life, a child should be free to explore the environment of sense perception, without binding swaddling clothes, without his natural desires and inclinations being checked, without disciplinary punishment; the emphasis should be on physical development (rather than on intellectual or moral education) and the gaining of experience. Between the ages of five and twelve, the child should enjoy sports and physical contact with his environment, rather than yet learning to read; his moral training should arise from experiencing the natural consequences of his actions, rather than from external restrictions. During early adolescence, from twelve to fifteen, a child should learn to read, with Rousseau particularly recommending Defoe's *Robinson Crusoe*, as teaching self-reliance; the child's formal intellectual education in the arts and science begins at this stage, building upon his natural curiosity, and he should learn a trade. The period of late adolescence, from fifteen to twenty-one, involves a study of history, religion, and socio-political-economic matters, to prepare the young man for healthy relationships with others. At the age of twenty-one, when the student's course of education is complete, he can marry. It is interesting that this educational program, designed to develop a good citizen for political society, is for boys only, Émile being the model student. In the final book of the work, Rousseau focuses on Sophy, a girl, who is to be trained to serve and to be a charming helpmate for Émile, when he has become a man. So, there is no commitment to equality of the sexes here, and only males should be trained for the political involvement of active citizenship. Rousseau's radical theory influenced the development of naturalistic educational psychology and served as a seminal source of Romanticism.

*　　*　　*

Let us next consider a couple of important younger thinkers near the end of the Age of Enlightenment: Jeremy Bentham (1748–1832), an Englishman, and Johann Gottlieb Fichte (1762–1814), a German. Bentham, in the empirical tradition, is one of the most important intellectual links between Hume and Mill; Fichte, in the idealist tradition, is a key link between Kant and Hegel. (Both Mill and Hegel are considered in our next chapter.) As Bentham actively promoted liberal reform in Great Britain, Fichte aroused nationalistic feelings in Germany.

BENTHAM

Jeremy Bentham was born in 1748 (the year Hume published his *Enquiry Concerning Human Understanding*). He was a child prodigy, reading history at the age of three, learning Latin at the age of five, and speaking French at the age of eight. He attended Oxford University, where he studied law, and was called to the bar in 1767, in accordance with his father's wishes; but his concerns were for legal and penal reform rather than for actual legal practice. He extended Adam Smith's *laissez-faire* principle to oppose government interference in all economic areas

as harmful and counterproductive. Bentham spent almost all his life in England, except for an extended visit, in the 1780s, to his brother, who held an industrial appointment in Russia. Bentham enjoyed robust health throughout his long life.

Bentham wrote *A Fragment on Government*, *The Book of Fallacies*, and *Rationale of Judicial Evidence* (edited by his young disciple, John Stuart Mill), as well as his *Introduction to the Principles of Morals and Legislation* (1789), considered here. He was the head of a movement of "philosophical radicals" and founded University College, London, where his embalmed body still remains. Bentham established a liberal journal, the *Westminster Review*, in 1824; many practical utilitarian changes he promoted were contained in the Reform Bill of 1832, which passed in the year of his death.

As a psychological hedonist, Bentham focuses Hume's attention to feelings on those of pleasure and pain, which he regards as the ultimate motivating forces of all human action. Whereas for Hume, utility is one of the two legs (along with natural sympathy) on which morality stands, Bentham makes it the sole foundation of morals. His ultimate principle, the principle of utility, maintains that actions are worthy of approval to the extent that they tend to increase the happiness (measured in terms of pleasure and the absence of pain) of the people involved and worthy of disapproval to the extent that they tend to decrease that happiness. Moral language is meaningful only when interpreted thus. On this view, no action can be absolutely right or wrong; rather, the morality of every action is relative to the greatest happiness of the greatest number. We can easily detect how radically different this is from Kant's ethics, which is more absolutist, duty-based (or deontological) rather than consequentialist, and rationalistic rather than hedonistic.

Bentham holds that there are four sorts of sanctions which motivate us to follow the principle of utility and that all of them concern different sources of pleasure and pain. Physical sanctions have to do with natural pleasurable and painful consequences; political sanctions concern the law and its punishments; social sanctions stem from popular opinion; and

---

Laissez-faire (literally, in French, allow to do).　An economic theory, associated with Adam Smith, that government should generally not interfere in the competitive activities of its citizens but should allow free enterprise; loosely, noninterference

religious sanctions relate to beliefs about how the Deity might deal with us. Thus, in Bentham's day, all four of these sanctions might have motivated us to avoid committing adultery: for fear of contracting venereal disease (physical), for fear of being imprisoned for breaking the law of the state (political), for fear of the social disapproval of others (social), and for fear of God's condemning us to hell (religious). These are all what Mill will call external sanctions. Finally, Bentham offers us seven criteria for measuring pleasures and pains:

1. Their intensity (how acutely felt they are),
2. Their duration (how long they are experienced),
3. Their certainty (how reliably predictable they are as consequences),
4. Their propinquity (how closely in time they follow the action as its consequences),
5. Their fecundity (the likelihood of pleasures generating further pleasures or pains causing more pains),
6. Their purity (how uncontaminated pleasures are by pains or pains by pleasures), and
7. Their extent (the number of people affected by them).

Mill will regard all these as quantitative criteria and suggest (against Bentham) that we should also consider qualitative distinctions. But Bentham's ideal is to use such strictly quantitative standards to establish (at least in theory) a hedonic calculus, a method for precisely calculating the pleasurable and painful consequences of actions.

FICHTE

Johann Gottlieb Fichte was born in 1762 (during the period when Kant was a *Privatdozent at* the University of Königsberg). He studied theology at the University of Jena, before transferring to the Universities of Wittenberg and Leipzig. After enthusiastically studying Kant, he traveled to Königsberg in 1791 to visit the aging philosopher. As opposed to empiricists like Hume, Bentham, and Mill, Fichte is an idealist like Kant and Hegel. Indeed, he became famous by being mistaken for Kant. Fichte wrote a *Critique of Revelation*, which was published anonymously in Königsberg in 1792; it was so Kantian in character (as well as in its title) that people assumed it was by Kant. When

Kant set the record straight, Fichte was offered a professorship at the University of Jena. However, Fichte was by no means a Kant-clone and developed his own philosophy in his *Science of Knowledge* (1794) and *System of Ethics* (1798). In 1799, under accusations of atheism, Fichte had to leave Jena. Later, he was appointed dean of the philosophical faculty at the newly founded University of Berlin, where he later served as rector for a year. He and his wife were involved in the Prussian opposition to Napoleon; in 1814, he caught typhus from his wife, who had contracted it while working as a war nurse, and soon died of it.

The Vocation of Man, published in 1800, comprises three sections: Book One, "Doubt," may be somewhat identified with Hume's view; Book Two, "Knowledge," with Kant's; and Book Three, "Faith," with Fichte's own unique position. Book One shows how we move from experience to doubt. From an empirical standpoint we have many ideas about the world. Objects appear substantial and perceivable in terms of determinate properties. Reality, as we experience it, seems determined by an endless series of cause-effect relations. But then we too are part of this natural order, products of external forces. Yet we sometimes think of ourselves as somehow independent and free, with adequate grounds for virtue and vice, remorse and conscience, punishments and rewards. The source of autonomy cannot be located in the body or in sensuous inclinations, but in thought and will. But is this notion legitimate, or is freedom an illusion? Either we must follow our hearts, believing in moral freedom, or adopt the implications of empiricism, viewing ourselves as subject to the determinations of the natural order. We must choose between these alternatives and suffer a dreadful doubt as long as we remain undecided. (As we shall see, Hegel also views empiricism as generating a sceptical doubt to be overcome at a higher level.)

Book Two develops a Kantian idealism. Our perception implies the capacity for self-awareness. We directly experience only our own states of consciousness, not external objects, and can only perceive things (including our own bodies) as they appear to us, inferring connections through a principle of causality. But how do we know (Hume's doubt) that the principle objectively applies? To justify this belief by an appeal to independent sense objects would be circular because our only basis for believing them independent is that they seem governed by this principle of causality. Our knowledge of causality must be prior to and independent of our knowledge of sense objects. We intuit that the principle of causality comes from us and is *a priori* (as Kant taught). Consequently cognitive consciousness implies self-consciousness (as Hegel will teach). We can only know ourselves and our own conscious states and never external reality in itself, including that of other persons. But then knowable reality becomes a dreamlike system of images, and knowledge turns out to be empty.

Book Three asserts that our vocation is not mere knowledge, but action, which should be the final purpose of knowledge. What we must recognize is that all knowledge presupposes faith. This may sound like Kant's postulates of practical reason; yet Fichte (anticipating James) grounds faith in the will, rather than

in the intellect. Faith is a commitment of the will that tends to action; and it is moral action that fulfills the "vocation" of human nature. We must respect others as fellow persons. We must believe we are free, follow conscience, and do our duty as persons of good will (Kantian), regardless of consequences (antiutilitarian). We thus see ourselves as belonging to a supersensible world, governed by moral laws, as well as the sensible one, governed by physical laws. The infinite divine will is our original source and mediates between each of us and the spiritual world. Towards the end of the book, Fichte seems to be headed towards a religious **panentheism**, such as we shall see adopted by Hegel. Thus, at the end of the eighteenth century, Fichte leads us to the greatest philosopher of the nineteenth, as Bentham, the father of utilitarianism, paves the way for Mill, the most famous utilitarian.

Notes

1. David Hume, *Essential Works of David Hume*, ed. Ralph Cohen (New York: Bantam Books, 1965), p. 2. This book is henceforth called "*Essential.*"

2. David Hume, *The Letters of David Hume*, 2 vols., ed. J. Y. T. Grieg (London: Oxford Univ. Press, 1969), Vol. I, p. 13. This work is henceforth called "Grieg."

3. *Essential*, p. 2.

4. Grieg, Vol. I, pp. 13, 9–10.

5. Ibid., pp. 13–14, 16–18.

6. *Essential*, pp. 2–3.

7. David Hume, *New Letters of David Hume*, ed. Raymond Klibansky and Ernest C. Mossner (London: Oxford Univ. Press, 1954), pp. 1–3. This book is henceforth called "*New.*"

8. *Essential*, p. 3.

9. *New*, p. 10.

10. Grieg, Vol. I, pp. 57, 59–60.

11. *New*, p. 17.

12. Grieg, Vol. I, pp. 90, 94–95, 101; for more on the unsuccessful invasion of Brittany, see David Hume, *Essays Moral, Political, and Literary*, ed. T. H. Green and T. H. Grose (London: Longmans, Green, and Co., 1912), Vol. II, pp. 443–60. This work is henceforth called "*Essays.*"

13. *Essential*, pp. 3–4.

14. David Hume, *Letters of David Hume to William Strahan*, ed. G. Birkbeck Hill (London: Oxford Univ. Press, 1888), p. xxii. This book is henceforth called "Hill."

15. *Essential*, pp. 4–5.

16. Ibid., pp. 5–6.

17. Grieg, Vol. I, p. 111.

18. Ibid., Vol. I, p. 393.

19. *Essential*, p. 7.

20. Grieg, Vol. I, pp. 457, 469, xxv; Vol. II, p. 335.

21. Ibid., Vol. II, p. 114.

22. *New*, p. 155.

23. Grieg, Vol. II, pp. 303, 306.

24. *Essential*, pp. 7–8.

25. Hill, pp. 330, 345, 364.

26. *Essential*, p. 8.

27. Grieg, Vol. II, p. 452.

28. *Essential*, p. 150.

29. David Hume, *A Treatise of Human Nature*, ed. L. A. Selby-Bigge (London: Oxford Univ. Press, 1967), pp. 16, 19, 66. This book is henceforth called "*Treatise.*"

30. Ibid., pp. 66–67, 103, 108, 232–34.

31. Ibid., pp. 33–35, 38–40, 187–93, 198–99, 204–6, 209, 212, 215–16.

32. *Essential*, pp. 103–4, 108, 159.

33. Ibid., pp. 44, 46–47, 52, 58, 91.

34. Ibid., pp. 535, 543–44.

35. *Treatise*, pp. xix–xxi.

36. Ibid., pp. 118n., 176–79.

37. *Essential*, pp. 121–23.

Panentheism (from the Greek *pan*, meaning all, *en*, meaning in, and *theos*, meaning God). The view that God is immanent in the world without being simply identical with the world (as in pantheism)

38. *Treatise*, pp. 207, 232–34, 251–52.

39. Ibid., pp. 253–54, 259–62, 265, 633–36.

40. Ibid., pp. 275–77, 286, 298–99.

41. Ibid., pp. 316–18, 329–31, 367, 369, 382, 387.

42. Ibid., pp. 399, 417, 419, 437–39.

43. Ibid., pp. 487, 575–76. See "Of the Dignity or Meanness of Human Nature," in David Hume, *Of the Standard of Taste and Other Essays*, ed. John W. Lenz (Indianapolis: Bobbs-Merrill, 1965), pp. 143–45, for a further critique of psychological egoism. This book is henceforth called *"Taste."*

44. *Essential*, pp. 49–50, 52–54.

45. *Treatise*, pp. 2–8.

46. *Essential*, p. 56.

47. Ibid., pp. 57, 62.

48. Ibid., pp. 63–65.

49. Ibid., pp. 67–69, 71–72.

50. Ibid., pp. 74–75, 77.

51. Ibid., pp. 79–81.

52. Ibid., p. 85.

53. Ibid., pp. 89–98.

54. Ibid., pp. 98–101, 120.

55. Ibid., pp. 155–56, 162–64, 167.

56. *Treatise*, pp. 180–81, 269–71.

57. *Essential*, pp. 85, 103–6.

58. Ibid., pp. 106–8.

59. Ibid., pp. 109–11.

60. Ibid., pp. 111–14.

61. Ibid., pp. 115–17.

62. *Treatise*, pp. 312, 404–5, 408–9, 413–15. In his essay "Of National Characters," Hume distinguishes between *"moral* causes . . . which are fitted to work on the mind as motives or reasons" and *"physical* causes"—*see* David Hume, *Essays Moral, Political, and Literary*, rev. ed., ed. Eugene F. Miller (Indianapolis: LibertyClassics, 1987), p. 198.

63. *Treatise*, pp. 415–16.

64. *Essential*, pp. 180–84.

65. Ibid., pp. 185–94.

66. Ibid., pp. 198–201.

67. Ibid., pp. 212–14, 216.

68. Ibid., pp. 221–22, 224.

69. Ibid., pp. 225, 233–34, 239–44, 247–48, 251–52.

70. Ibid., pp. 253–54, 259–60, 263.

71. Ibid., pp. 264–67.

72. Ibid., pp. 268–71.

73. Ibid., pp. 272–74, 276.

74. Ibid., pp. 278–81, 292.

75. *Essays*, p. 139.

76. David Hume, *David Hume's Political Essays*, ed. Charles W. Hendel (New York: Liberal Arts Press, 1953), p. 101. This book is henceforth called *"Political."*

77. *Treatise*, pp. 457, 467–69, 475.

78. *Taste*, pp. 152–60.

79. *Essential*, pp. 148, 166–67.

80. *Political*, pp. 44–51; see also the brief selections from Hume's *History of England* included in that book, on pp. 61–63.

81. Ibid., pp. 54–56, 60–61.

82. Ibid., pp. 64–66.

83. David Hume, *David Hume: Philosophical Historian*, ed. David Fate Norton and Richard H. Popkin (Indianapolis: Bobbs-Merrill, 1965), pp. 373–75.

84. *Essential*, pp. 194–95, 206–7.

85. *Treatise*, pp. xix–xx, 485–86, 493, 496, 539–41, 546–47, 549–54, 556–59, 561, 567–69.

86. *Essential*, pp. 466–67, 469, 477–78, 480–82.

87. Ibid., pp. 485–92.

88. Ibid., p. 54.

89. Ibid., pp. 124–27.

90. Ibid., pp. 128–33, 139, 141–42.

91. Ibid., pp. 142, 145–46, 150.

92. Ibid., pp. 150–54, 166.

93. Ibid., pp. 304, 307, 315–16.

94. Ibid., pp. 316–24.

95. Ibid., pp. 335–39.

96. Ibid., pp. 353–55.

97. Ibid., pp. 358–65.

98. Ibid., pp. 366–67, 374.

99. Ibid., pp. 379, 381–82, 385, 388.

100. *Taste*, pp. 114, 117, 146–49.

101. David Hume, *The Natural History of Religion*, ed. H. E. Root (Stanford, CA: Stanford Univ. Press, 1957), pp. 21, 26, 30, 32, 38, 41–43, 72, 74, 76.

102. *Treatise*, p. 114.

103. *Taste*, pp. 161–62.

104. Ibid., pp. 162–65.

105. Ibid., pp. 165–67.

106. *Essential*, pp. 218, 261, 263.

107. *Taste*, pp. 25–26, 51.

108. Ibid., pp. 103, 106, 110–11, 115, 117, 137–38.

109. Immanuel Kant, *Anthropology from a Pragmatic Point of View*, trans. Victor Lyle Dowdell (Carbondale: Southern Illinois Univ. Press, 1978), pp. 4–5n. This book is henceforth called *"Anthropology."*

110. Immanuel Kant, *Education*, trans. Annette Churton (Ann Arbor: Univ. of Michigan Press, 1960), p. 93. The book is henceforth called *"Education."*

111. Immanuel Kant, *On History*, ed. Lewis White Beck, essays trans. Lewis White Beck, Robert E. Anchor, and Emil L. Fackenheim (Indianapolis: Bobbs-Merrill, 1963), pp. 9–10. This work is henceforth called *"On History."*

112. *Anthropology*, p. 6n.

113. Immanuel Kant, *Kant: Philosophical Correspondence, 1759–99*, ed. and trans. Arnulf Zweig (Chicago: Univ. of

Chicago Press, 1967), pp. 89, 91. This book is henceforth called "*Correspondence*."

114. *On History*, p. xxviii.

115. *Correspondence*, p. 54.

116. Ibid., pp. 77, 88. He writes about hypochondria in *Anthropology*, pp. 108–9, and in Immanuel Kant, *The Conflict of the Faculties*, trans. Mary J. Gregor and Robert E. Anchor (New York: Abaris Books, 1979), pp. 187, 189. This book is henceforth called "*Conflict*."

117. *Correspondence*, p. 185.

118. Ibid., pp. 48, 56, 58, 71–73, 89, 100; cf. pp. 105–6.

119. Immanuel Kant, *Philosophy of Material Nature*, trans. James W. Ellington (Indianapolis: Hackett Publishing Co., 1985), p. 6. This book (combining the *Prolegomena* and *Metaphysical Foundations of Natural Science*) is henceforth called "*Nature*."

120. *Correspondence*, p. 150.

121. Ibid., pp. 122n, 163–64n, 173.

122. *On History*, pp. 3–5.

123. *Correspondence*, p. 205. Compare Immanuel Kant, *Logic*, trans. Robert S. Hartman and Wolfgang Schwarz (Indianapolis: Bobbs-Merrill, 1974), p. 29. This work is henceforth called "*Logic*." *See also* Immanuel Kant, *Immanuel Kant's Critique of Pure Reason*, trans. Norman Kemp Smith (New York: St. Martin's Press, 1965), pp. 635–36. This book is henceforth called "First *Critique*."

124. *Correspondence*, pp. 217–20; Wollner's note and Kant's letter can also be found in *Conflict*, pp. 11–19.

125. *Correspondence*, pp. 223–25, 251.

126. Immanuel Kant, *Critique of Judgment*, trans. J. H. Bernard (New York: Hafner Publishing Co., 1968), pp. 261–63. This book is henceforth called "Third *Critique*."

127. *Nature*, pp. 1–7, 11.

128. First *Critique*, pp. 7, 392–93; cf. *Nature*, Book II, p. 3, for Kant's analysis of "nature."

129. First *Critique*, pp. 393–94, 396, 402, 409, 415.

130. *Nature*, pp. 80–83, 85–87.

131. Ibid., pp. 32–33.

132. Ibid., pp. 38–39, 49, 61, 94.

133. *Nature*, Book II, pp. 40, 43, 78, 80, 95–96, 118, 134.

134. First *Critique*, pp. 45, 147, 212, 216–18, 228, 233, 236–37, 244–45, 356, 392n, 538.

135. *Nature*, pp. 75–76.

136. Immanuel Kant, *Ethical Philosophy*, trans. James W. Ellington (Indianapolis: Hackett Publishing Co., 1983), pp. 35–36, 41, 44, 49–50. This book (which combines Kant's "Grounding for the Metaphysics of Morals" as Book I and his "Metaphysical Principles of Virtue" as Book II) is henceforth called "*Ethical*."

137. Ibid., pp. 51–54, 57–60.

138. First *Critique*, pp. 127n, 136, 141, 145–46, 152–53, 155–56.

139. Ibid., pp. 168–69, 176, 246.

140. Ibid., pp. 330–32.

141. Immanuel Kant, *Critique of Practical Reason*, trans. Lewis White Beck (Indianapolis: Bobbs-Merrill, 1956), pp. 89–90. This book is henceforth called "Second *Critique*."

142. Third *Critique*, pp. 106–8, 279–83, 286.

143. *On History*, pp. 12–15.

144. Immanuel Kant, *The Metaphysical Elements of Justice*, trans. John Ladd (Indianapolis: Bobbs-Merrill, 1965), pp. 13, 46. This book is henceforth called "*Justice*." Compare *Ethical*, Book II, p. 78. *See also* Immanuel Kant, *What Real Progress Has Metaphysics Made in Germany since the Time of Leibniz and Wolff?* trans. Ted Humphrey (New York: Abaris Books, 1983), p. 73. This book is henceforth called "*Metaphysics*."

145. *Anthropology*, pp. 9, 155–57, 175, 198–200, 203, 238–41.

146. Immanuel Kant, *Religion within the Limits of Reason Alone*, trans. Theodore M. Greene and Hoyt H. Hudson (New York: Harper & Row, 1960), pp. 17–18, 21–25, 27, 30, 32, 35–36, 51, 54–57. This book is henceforth called "*Religion*."

147. Immanuel Kant, "A New Exposition of the First Principles of Metaphysical Knowledge," trans. F. E. England, included as an appendix to F. E. England, *Kant's Conception of God* (New York: Humanities Press, 1968), pp. 215–16. Kant's work is henceforth called "Exposition."

148. Immanuel Kant, *Kant: Selected Pre-Critical Writings and Correspondence with Beck*, trans. G. B. Kerford and D. E. Walford (Manchester, England: Manchester Univ. Press, 1968), pp. 54–55, 60–61, 81. This book is henceforth called "*Pre-Critical*."

149. *Nature*, pp. 12–13.

150. Ibid., pp. 18–21, 23.

151. Ibid., pp. 26–28.

152. Ibid., pp. 34–37; cf. *Metaphysics*, p. 69.

153. *Nature*, pp. 40–44.

154. Ibid., pp. 46, 51, 53, 55–59.

155. Ibid., pp. 61–62, 64–66. For a different (and much less famous) account of sensation, imagination, memory, and understanding, see *Anthropology*, pp. 29–31, 40–41, 49, 56–57, 73–74, 90–92, 94.

156. *Nature*, pp. 70–74, 90, 93–94.

157. Ibid., pp. 95, 101, 103, 105–7.

158. Ibid., pp. 108, 110.

159. First *Critique*, pp. 22, 29, 631.

160. Ibid., pp. 41, 61–62, 92–93, 97–98, 300.

161. Ibid., pp. 323, 533, 535, 550–51, 556, 558–59, 564, 607, 635, 646; cf. *Logic*, pp. 29, 72–81; *see also* Third *Critique*, pp. 319, 325–27, and *Metaphysics*, pp. 61, 125, 131, 133.

162. First *Critique*, pp. 469, 476, 633–34.

163. *Nature*, pp. 84–87; cf. Third *Critique*, p. 32.

164. *Ethical*, pp. 50–52, 56, 58–59.

165. Second *Critique*, pp. 33, 49–50.

166. *Pre-Critical*, p. 33.

167. Immanuel Kant, *Observations on the Feeling of the Beautiful and Sublime*, trans. John T. Goldthwait (Berkeley: Univ. of California Press, 1965), pp. 58, 60, 62–64. (Section Three of this book may be cited by radical feminists as indicative of Kant's alleged sexism; but that issue is not being considered here, since this is an early, pre-critical work and his remarks on this topic do not appear in the writings of his maturity.)

168. *Ethical*, pp. 1–5.

169. Ibid., pp. 7–9.

170. Ibid., pp. 9–11.

171. Ibid., pp. 12–13.

172. Ibid., pp. 14–15.

173. Ibid., p. 15.

174. Ibid., pp. 19–23; in his First *Critique* Kant writes, "Nothing is more reprehensible than to derive the laws prescribing what *ought to be done* from what *is done*" (p. 313).

175. *Ethical*, pp. 24–26, 29–30.

176. Ibid., pp. 30–33.

177. Ibid., pp. 35–37.

178. Ibid., pp. 38–44.

179. Ibid., pp. 45–48.

180. Second *Critique*, pp. 85, 115, 117, 134, 166.

181. *Religion*, pp. 19n, 43, 46. Elsewhere Kant writes, "For it would not be a duty to strive after a certain effect of our will if this effect were impossible in experience"—*see* Immanuel Kant, *Kant's Political Writings*, ed. Hans Reiss, trans. H. B. Nisbet (Cambridge, England: Cambridge Univ. Press, 1977), p. 62. This book is henceforth called "Kant *Political*."

182. *Justice*, pp. 13, 15–16, 19–21, 23–29.

183. *Ethical*, Book II, pp. 79–81, 108–10.

184. Ibid., pp. 113–14, 116, 123, 127–28, 130, 145.

185. Immanuel Kant, *Critique of Practical Reason and Other Writings in Moral Philosophy*, ed. and trans. Lewis White Beck (Chicago: Univ. of Chicago Press, 1949), pp. 298–301, 347–48.

186. Immanuel Kant, *Lectures on Ethics*, trans. Louis Infield (Indianapolis: Hackett Publishing Co., 1980), pp. 17, 167–69. This book is henceforth called "*Ethics*."

187. *Education*, pp. 11, 20, 96, 98–99, 107–8; *see Anthropology*, pp. 205–6, for Kant's list of five negative principles of character formation.

188. Kant *Political*, pp. 73–74.

189. Ibid., pp. 74–79.

190. Ibid., pp. 79–81, 84–86; cf. *Anthropology*, pp. 247–49.

191. *On History*, pp. 16–22.

192. Ibid., pp. 54–60, 63–68.

193. Ibid., pp. 85–90, 93–94, 96–98, 100, 102–3, 105–6, 108, 111–12, 114–16, 119–20, 122, 126–30, 135.

194. Ibid., pp. 140–42, 144, 146–48, 150–52. For further discussion of Kant's views on social evolution, see Wayne Paul Pomerleau, "Kant's Theory of Human Culture as the Meaning of History," *Logos*, 4 (1983), 25–38.

195. *Justice*, pp. 34–36, 43–44.

196. Ibid., pp. 51–52, 65, 70–72, 75–76.

197. Ibid., pp. 78–79.

198. Ibid., pp. 84, 86–87, 89–90, 92–93.

199. Ibid., pp. 99–102, 107–8.

200. Ibid., pp. 109–10, 112–13.

201. Ibid., pp. 118–22.

202. Ibid., pp. 123–26, 128.

203. *Ethics*, pp. 193–94, 200–209; *see also Ethical*, Book II,

pp. 135–39, where Kant analyzes the idea of friendship as "the union of two persons through equal mutual love and respect."

204. Immanuel Kant, *Kant's Cosmogony*, ed. Willy Ley, trans. W. Hastie (New York: Greenwood Publishing Co., 1968), pp. 14, 153.

205. Exposition, pp. 222–25.

206. Immanuel Kant, *The One Possible Basis for a Demonstration of the Existence of God*, trans. Gordon Treash (New York: Abaris Books, 1979), pp. 43, 45, 57, 59, 63, 69, 71, 79, 81, 83, 87, 239.

207. *Nature*, pp. 87–89.

208. Ibid., pp. 95–101.

209. First *Critique*, pp. 499–500.

210. Ibid., pp. 502–7.

211. Ibid., pp. 508–12, 517.

212. Ibid., pp. 519–24.

213. Ibid., pp. 525–27.

214. Ibid., pp. 648–50.

215. Second *Critique*, pp. 129–30, 134; cf. *Logic*, p. 98. For more on Kant's critical and constructive treatment of argumentation for God, see Wayne P. Pomerleau, "Does Reason Demand That God Be Infinite?" *Sophia*, 4, No. 2 (July 1985), especially pp. 19–20, 22.

216. Third *Critique*, pp. 295, 298, 301, 306–7, 321–22, 324, 338. In his *Metaphysics*, p. 131, Kant presents the three basic articles of his moral faith: "I believe in one God, original source of all good in the world, as its ultimate end"; second, "I believe in the possibility of harmonizing this ultimate end with the highest good in the world, as far as it pertains to men"; and, third, "I believe in a future life as the condition of the perpetual approach of the world to the highest good possible in it." *See also Correspondence*, pp. 80–83.

217. Immanuel Kant, *Lectures on Philosophical Theology*, trans. Allen W. Wood and Gertrude M. Clark (Ithaca, NY: Cornell Univ. Press, 1978), pp. 26, 28–30, 41. This book is henceforth called "*Theology*." Although we cannot discuss it here, Kant's advice regarding what children should be taught about religion is interesting—*see Education*, pp. 111–14.

218. *Theology*, pp. 99–101, 109–12, 115–22. For another perspective on Kant's treatment of the problem of evil, see his 1791 essay "On the Failure of All Attempted Philosophical Theodicies," translated by Michel Despland in his book, *Kant on History and Religion* (Montreal: McGill-Queen's Univ. Press, 1973), pp. 283–97.

219. *Religion*, pp. 4–6, 7n, 47, 79–81, 90–92, 95, 97–98; cf. *Ethics*, pp. 95–99, 112. See also "The End of Things," where Kant discusses Christianity, as a religion "worthy of love" as well as of respect, and Christ as a humanitarian teacher—*On History*, pp. 81–84. Although it is too fragmentary and problematic to be discussed here, an interesting set of remarks on "the idea of God" can be found in Immanuel Kant, *Opus Postumum*, ed. Eckhart Forster, trans. Eckhart Forster and Michael Rosen (New York: Cambridge Univ. Press, 1993), pp. 200–17.

220. *Religion*, pp. 105, 131, 142, 146–50, 156–57, 167, 189.

221. Immanuel Kant, *Dreams of a Spirit Seer and Other Related Writings*, trans. John Manolesco (New York: Vantage Press, 1969), pp. 76–77, 90, 96–98.

222. First *Critique*, pp. 31, 325n, 379; *see also Religion*, p. 149n.

223. Second *Critique*, pp. 126–27. "The End of All Things" contains a very interesting discussion of "the Final Judgment" (*On History*, pp. 70–78), though it is not essential for our purposes.

224. *Ethical*, pp. 7, 27–28; cf. Second *Critique*, p. 129.

225. First *Critique*, pp. 636, 638–41.

226. *Theology*, pp. 119, 124.

227. *Anthropology*, pp. 135–36.

228. *Ethics*, pp. 252–53.

Bibliography

GENERAL

Berlin, Sir Isaiah. *The Age of Enlightenment.* New York: Mentor Books, 1956.

Copleston, Frederick, S.J. *A History of Philosophy,* Vol. V, Part II, VI. Garden City, NY: Image Books, 1964.

Jones, W. T. *Hobbes to Hume,* 2d ed. New York: Harcourt, Brace & World, 1969.

Jones, W. T. *Kant and the Nineteenth Century,* 2d ed., rev. San Diego: Harcourt Brace Jovanovich, 1975.

HUME   *Primary Sources*

David Hume: Philosophical Historian. Ed. David Fate Norton and Richard H. Popkin. Indianapolis: Bobbs-Merrill, 1965.

David Hume's Political Essays. Ed. Charles W. Hendel, Jr. New York: The Liberal Arts Press, 1953.

Dialogues concerning Natural Religion. Ed. Richard H. Popkin. Indianapolis: Hackett Publishing Co., 1980.

An Enquiry concerning Human Understanding. Ed. Antony Flew. La Salle, IL: Open Court, 1988.

An Enquiry concerning Human Understanding, 2nd ed. Ed. Eric Steinberg. Indianapolis: Hackett Publishing Co., 1993.

An Enquiry concerning the Principles of Morals. Ed. J. B. Schneewind. Indianapolis: Hackett Publishing Co., 1983.

Essays Moral, Political, and Literary, rev. ed. Ed. Eugene F. Miller. Indianapolis: LibertyClassics, 1987.

The Essential David Hume. Ed. Robert Paul Wolff. New York: New American Library, 1969.

Essential Works of David Hume. Ed. Ralph Cohen. New York: Bantam Books, 1965.

Hume Selections. Ed. Charles W. Hendel, Jr. New York: Charles Scribner's Sons, 1955.

The Letters of David Hume, 2 vols. Ed. J. Y. T. Grieg. London: Oxford Univ. Press, 1969.

Letters of David Hume to William Strahan. Ed. G. Birkbeck Hill. London: Oxford Univ. Press, 1888.

The Natural History of Religion. Ed. H. E. Root. Stanford, CA: Stanford Univ. Press, 1957.

New Letters of David Hume. Ed. Raymond Klibansky and Ernest C. Mossner. London: Oxford Univ. Press, 1954.

Of the Standard of Taste and Other Essays. Ed. John W. Lenz. Indianapolis: Bobbs-Merrill, 1965.

Political Writings. Ed. Stuart D. Warner and Donald W. Livingston. Indianapolis: Hackett Publishing Co., 1994.

A Treatise of Human Nature. Ed. L. A. Selby-Bigge. Oxford, England: Oxford Univ. Press, 1967.

Writings on Religion. Ed. Antony Flew. La Salle, IL: Open Court, 1992.

Secondary Sources

Ayer, A. J. *Hume.* Oxford, England: Oxford Univ. Press, 1980.

Basson, A. H. *David Hume.* London: Penguin Books, 1958.

Chappell, V. C., ed. *Hume: A Collection of Critical Essays.* Garden City, NY: Doubleday & Co., 1966.

Knight, William. *Hume.* Port Washington, NY: Kennikat Press, 1970.

Merrill, Kenneth R., and Robert W. Shahan, eds. *David Hume: Many-sided Genius.* Norman: Univ. of Oklahoma Press, 1976.

Norton, David Fate, ed. *The Cambridge Companion to Hume.* New York: Cambridge Univ. Press, 1993.

Pears, David. *Hume's System.* New York: Oxford Univ. Press, 1990.

Stroud, Barry. *Hume.* London: Routledge & Kegan Paul, 1977.

Wright, John P. *The Sceptical Realism of David Hume.* Minneapolis: Univ. of Minnesota Press, 1983.

KANT   *Primary Sources*

Anthropology from a Pragmatic Point of View. Trans. Victor Lyle Dowdell. Carbondale: Southern Illinois Univ. Press, 1978.

The Conflict of the Faculties. Trans. Mary J. Gregor and Robert E. Anchor. New York: Abaris Books, 1979.

Critique of Judgment. Trans. J. H. Bernard. New York: Hafner Publishing Co., 1968.

Critique of Practical Reason. Trans. Lewis White Beck. Indianapolis: Bobbs-Merrill, 1956.

Critique of Practical Reason and Other Writings in Moral Philosophy. Ed. and trans. Lewis White Beck. Chicago: Univ. of Chicago Press, 1949.

Dreams of a Spirit Seer and Other Related Writings. Trans. John Manolesco. New York: Vantage Press, 1969.

Education. Trans. Annette Churton. Ann Arbor: Univ. of Michigan Press, 1960.

The Essential Kant. Ed. Arnulf Zweig. New York: New American Library, 1970.

Ethical Philosophy. Trans. James W. Ellington. Indianapolis: Hackett Publishing Co., 1983.

Grounding for the Metaphysics of Morals. Trans. James W. Ellington. Indianapolis: Hackett Publishing Co., 1981.

Immanuel Kant's Critique of Pure Reason. Trans. Norman Kemp Smith. New York: St. Martin's Press, 1965.

Kant: Philosophical Correspondence, 1759–99. Ed. and trans. Arnulf Zweig. Chicago: Univ. of Chicago Press, 1967.

Kant: Selected Pre-Critical Writings and Correspondence with Beck. Trans. G. B. Kerford and D. E. Walford. Manchester, England: Manchester Univ. Press, 1968.

Kant Selections. Ed. Lewis White Beck. New York: Macmillan Publishing Co., 1988.

Kant Selections. Ed. Theodore M. Greene. New York: Charles Scribner's Sons, 1957.

Kant's Cosmogony. Ed. Willy Ley. Trans. W. Hastie. New York: Greenwood Publishing Co., 1968.

Kant's Political Writings. Ed. Hans Reiss. Trans. H. B. Nisbet. Cambridge, England: Cambridge Univ. Press, 1977.

Lectures on Ethics. Trans. Louis Infield. Indianapolis: Hackett Publishing Co., 1980.

Lectures on Philosophical Theology. Trans. Allen W. Wood and Gertrude M. Clark. Ithaca, NY: Cornell Univ. Press, 1978.

Logic. Trans. Robert S. Hartman and Wolfgang Schwarz. Indianapolis: Bobbs-Merrill, 1974.

The Metaphysical Elements of Justice. Trans. John Ladd. Indianapolis: Bobbs-Merrill, 1965.

"A New Exposition of the First Principles of Metaphysical Knowledge." Trans. F. E. England. Included as an appendix to F. E. England. *Kant's Conception of God*. New York: Humanities Press, 1968.

Observations on the Feeling of the Beautiful and Sublime. Trans. John T. Goldthwait. Berkeley: Univ. of California Press, 1965.

"On the Failure of All Attempted Philosophical Theodicies." Trans. Michel Despland. In Michel Despland. *Kant on History and Religion*. Montreal: McGill-Queen's Univ. Press, 1973.

On History. Ed. Lewis White Beck. Essays trans. Lewis White Beck, Robert E. Anchor, and Emil L. Fackenheim. Indianapolis: Bobbs-Merrill, 1963.

The One Possible Basis for a Demonstration of the Existence of God. Trans. Gordon Treash. New York: Abaris Books, 1979.

Opus Postumum. Ed. Eckhart Forster. Trans. Eckhart Forster and Michael Rosen. New York: Cambridge Univ. Press, 1993.

Perpetual Peace and Other Essays. Trans. Ted Humphrey. Indianapolis: Hackett Publishing Co., 1983.

Philosophical Writings. Ed. Ernst Behler. New York: Continuum Publishing Co., 1986.

The Philosophy of Kant. Ed. Carl J. Friedrich. New York: Modern Library, 1949.

Philosophy of Material Nature. Trans. James W. Ellington. Indianapolis: Hackett Publishing Co., 1985.

Prolegomena to Any Future Metaphysics. Trans. by Paul Carus. Rev. James W. Ellington. Indianapolis: Hackett Publishing Co., 1977.

Religion within the Limits of Reason Alone. Trans. Theodore M. Greene and Hoyt H. Hudson. New York: Harper & Row, 1960.

What Real Progress Has Metaphysics Made in Germany since the Time of Leibniz and Wolff? Trans. Ted Humphrey. New York: Abaris Books, 1983.

Secondary Sources

Broad, C. D. *Kant: An Introduction*. Ed. C. Levy. Cambridge, England: Cambridge Univ. Press, 1978.

Guyer, Paul, ed. *The Cambridge Companion to Kant*. New York: Cambridge Univ. Press, 1992.

Jaspers, Karl. *Kant*. Ed. Hannah Arendt. Trans. Ralph Manheim. New York: Harcourt, Brace & World, 1962.

Kemp, John. *The Philosophy of Kant*. New York: Oxford Univ. Press, 1968.

Körner, S. *Kant*. London: Penguin Books, 1955.

Scruton, Roger. *Kant*. Oxford, England: Oxford Univ. Press, 1983.

Walker, Ralph C. S. *Kant*. London: Routledge & Kegan Paul, 1978.

Werkmeister, W. H. *Kant: The Architectonic and Development of His Philosophy*. La Salle, IL: Open Court, 1980.

Werkmeister, W. H., ed. *Reflections on Kant's Philosophy*. Gainesville: University Presses of Florida, 1975.

Wolff, Robert Paul, ed. *Kant: A Collection of Critical Essays*. Garden City, NY: Doubleday & Co., 1967.

Historical Background

«« «« «« «« «« «« «« «« «« «« «« «« «« «« «« «« «« «« «« «»»» »» »» »» »» »» »» »» »» »» »» »» »» »» »» »» »

o speak of the first eight decades of the nineteenth century as the Age of Ideology is not necessarily disparaging. The concept of ideology originated at the end of the eighteenth century in France and refers to a system of ideas oriented to practical action. In this respect, for example, Bentham was generating a **utilitarian** ideology a few years before the word was coined. Early in the nineteenth century, Napoleon gave the word a derogatory connotation; ironically, Karl Marx, the most famous ideologist of the century, used it as a term of contempt. Whether or not we maintain the negative connotation, however, the great theories of this century tend to carry with them some practical agenda or other, which can be **conservative** (as in Hegel) or **liberal** (as in Mill). Mirroring the intellectual clash of ideas during the period were conflicts of battling armies from the Napoleonic wars at the beginning of the century to the Franco-Prussian War near the end of the period.

In 1799, Russia and Austria, reacting against French foreign policy, united forces, successfully attacked, and drove the French troops out of Italy. This defeat, combined with rampant inflation in France, provided Napoleon with an opportunity to overthrow the government in October, institute a new constitution, and set himself up as First Consul. He defeated Austria as he had a few years earlier and once more engaged the English as he had in Egypt; in 1802, the British signed a peace treaty with France at Amiens. Napoleon then could turn his attention to domestic reforms, extending religious tolerance, establishing a central bank, expanding education, constructing roads, bridges, and canals, and setting up the Napoleonic Code of law, enacted in 1804. That year, Napoleon had himself named emperor. But war erupted again the next year, when he beat the Austrians and Russians at Austerlitz but was defeated by the British navy under Nelson in the Battle of Trafalgar. In 1806, the old Holy Roman Empire was dissolved, Napoleon routed the Prussian army of Frederick William III at Jena, and his troops occupied almost all of Prussia. The following year, Russia's young czar, Alexander I, had to submit to the French at Tilsit. By annexing the papal states in 1808 and imprisoning Pope Pius VII the following year, Napoleon antagonized Catholics.

Conservatism (from the Latin *conservare*, meaning to preserve, maintain). A political ideology committed to conserving traditional values and therefore tending to maintain the existing order and to resist change (often opposed to liberalism)

Liberalism (from the Latin *liber*, meaning free). A political ideology committed to personal freedom and tending to promote (nonrevolutionary) progress and reform of the existing order (often opposed to conservatism)

In 1812, Napoleon invaded Russia in June, fought the costly Battle of Borodino in September, lost half his army taking Moscow, and encountered serious difficulties securing provisions for his forces. Napoleon's appeals for peace were ignored by Czar Alexander, whom Napoleon had previously insulted; and the Russian army, led by Kutuzov, blocked the French escape towards the warmer climate to the south. The French retreat was a terrible fiasco. By the time the French forces reached Prussia, they were very vulnerable; in October of 1813, they were decisively beaten by a coalition of Prussians, Russians, Austrians, and Swedes in the Battle of Leipzig. Meanwhile, England, Holland, and Spain coordinated their attacks, leading to the occupation of Paris in March of 1814 and Napoleon's abdication. A brother of King Louis XVI was recalled from English exile, installed as constitutional monarch, and called Louis XVIII. After a ten-month exile at Elba, Napoleon escaped and resumed military command but was crushed by the English (under the Duke of Wellington) and the Prussians (under Gebhard Leberecht von Blücher) at Waterloo in 1815. Napoleon was banished to the remote island of St. Helena, where he died five-and-a-half years later, and Louis XVIII was restored as monarch. In June of 1815, the Congress of Vienna, with Prince Clemens Metternich, the Austrian chief minister, presiding, established a peaceful balance of power, granting the French authority over all the territories they had controlled in 1790.

Meanwhile, during this Napoleonic era, the United States was attempting to follow the isolationist injunctions of its first president, George Washington. In 1803, the government of Thomas Jefferson purchased the French Louisiana territory from Napoleon, doubling the size of the country. The Lewis and Clark Expedition surveyed the purchased territory and explored the continent to the Pacific coast. In 1807, Robert Fulton's steamship operated successfully on the Hudson River; this invention also facilitated westward expansion. The United States renewed warfare with England in 1812, during the British Regency period, in which the insane King George III could not rule and the Prince of Wales governed. Andrew Jackson defeated the British in the Battle of New Orleans two

weeks after the war had been concluded by the Treaty of Ghent in 1814.

A climate of political liberalism, advocating individual freedom and the right to private property, began to spread in Europe, inspired by the *Declaration of the Rights of Man and Citizen* proclaimed during the French Revolution. In Germany university students were calling for constitutional government and national unity; Metternich convened the Congress of Carlsbad in 1819 in order to quash such reforms, and censorship measures were imposed in Germany. In England the conservative Tory party ruled from 1815 to 1830, blocking the passage of much progressive legislation. Agitation for liberal policies in Russia was crushed under czars Alexander I and Nicholas I during this period. The United States sought to exclude European colonial influence by issuing the Monroe Doctrine in 1823, designed to stop further foreign power-grabbing in the Western Hemisphere. Especially after Andrew Jackson became president (in 1829), American democracy gradually expanded. Soon thereafter, the French statesman Alexis de Tocqueville visited the United States and published his *Democracy in America*, warning of the dangers of the "tyranny of the majority."

In the arts, Romanticism, emphasizing human passions, an appreciation of beauty and imagination, and a sense of oneness with nature, influenced literature in Germany (Johann Wolfgang von Goethe, Johann Christoph Friedrich von Schiller, August Wilhelm von Schlegel, and Heinrich Heine), France (Victor Hugo and Alexander Dumas, *père et fils*), England (William Wordsworth, Samuel Taylor Coleridge, Percy Bysshe Shelley and his second wife, Mary Wollstonecraft Shelley, daughter of the equal-rights advocate, Mary Wollstonecraft, John Keats, and Lord George Gordon Byron), Russia (Alexander Pushkin), and the United States (Edgar Allan Poe, James Fenimore Cooper, and Walt Whitman). Romantic music flourished with Franz Schubert, Robert Schumann, Hector Berlioz, Felix Mendelssohn, Frédéric Chopin, Franz Liszt, Gioacchino Rossini, and Johannes Brahms.

In 1830, the July Revolution erupted in France following an antiliberal crackdown; the king abdicated and fled to England for safety. The relatively liberal Duke of Orléans, Louis Philippe (the "umbrella king"), assumed the throne, abolishing censorship and extending voting rights. These reforms helped restore peace and inspired liberalization elsewhere. Some German princes accepted constitutions. In England the liberal Whig party came to power that same year; in 1832, a Reform Bill was passed (to be followed by a Second Reform Bill in 1867), and the enslaving of black people was abolished throughout the British Empire in 1833. The Industrial Revolution was underway (with railway locomotives operating by this time), and bourgeois middle-class interests were gaining currency. *Laissez-faire* policies, based on the theory of Adam Smith, the eighteenth-century Scottish economist, promoted **capitalistic** development and the protection of private property. Labor laws protecting women and children from being exploited in factories were passed in England, and, by 1847, they could not be worked more than ten hours a day in certain trades. Utilitarian **ethical** ideas, promoting maximum human happiness, were promulgated by Jeremy Bentham and encouraged moves towards further liberal reforms.

With the growing liberalism in Europe, **socialistic** ideas were spreading, generating a series of revolutions in 1848, the year in which *The Communist Manifesto* of Karl Marx and Friedrich Engels was published. Such a revolution in France toppled the middle-class-oriented government of King Louis Philippe, who abdicated and fled to England. A republic was proclaimed, but socialists were excluded from the government, and further rebellion erupted. In December, Louis Napoleon (Napoleon Bonaparte's nephew) was elected head of the Second Republic. He proceeded to sponsor legislation restricting labor exploitation and relieving poverty and opposed a move by the legislature to disenfranchise some voters. The February Revolution in France inspired rebellions in Germany. Frederick William IV accepted a liberal constitution and managed to retain power; the Frankfurt Assembly drew up a document on the "Fundamental Rights of the German Nation" before the end of that year. Revolts in Italy proved to be only temporarily successful. Although none of these revolutions fully achieved its goals, they all

helped spread constitutional government and gave more influence to the working classes. In 1852, Louis Napoleon had himself made Emperor Napoleon III of France. During the Crimean War (1854–56), in which Russia was defeated (by Turkey, England, and France), Czar Nicholas I died, succeeded by his son Alexander II, who instituted reforms, leading to the abolition of serfdom in 1861.

In education national elementary school systems developed in nineteenth-century Europe. In France public primary schools and some secondary schools had been established by the end of the eighteenth century. In England grammar schools were set up for children of the upper classes by the beginning of the nineteenth century. In 1817, Prussia established a national Department of Education. In America higher education started being available to women with the opening of Mount Holyoke in 1837; coeducational higher education began at Oberlin College, in Ohio, in 1834. Throughout most of the nineteenth century, American colleges provided undergraduate liberal arts education but little graduate work, until Yale organized graduate studies in 1858, with a Ph.D. being conferred three years later.

The push for political equality for women became more pronounced. In 1848 at Seneca Falls, New York, Elizabeth Cady Stanton and other feminists proposed the right of women to vote. In 1869, Mrs. Stanton and Susan B. Anthony formed the National Woman Suffrage Association to campaign for a woman's suffrage amendment to the federal constitution. Beginning with Wyoming in 1869, some states granted the vote to female citizens. In England in 1851, a resolution favoring women's suffrage was presented in the House of Lords. A bill was presented in the House of Commons in 1870 for the same cause. These initiatives to grant women the right to vote on a national level in America and Europe would not prove successful until the next century, however.

Western expansion was an important theme in nineteenth-century America. The Louisiana Purchase had given the United States a common border with Texas, and Americans were eager to "liberate" that

---

Capitalism. A socio-economic system in which private capital or wealth is used in the production and distribution of goods

Socialism. A socio-economic system in which the society as a whole owns the means of producing and distributing goods; in Marxist theory socialism is a transitional state between the overthrow of capitalism and the achievement of the classless society of communism

territory from the Spanish and appropriate it for themselves. It was thought that America's "Manifest Destiny" involved continental expansion. Texans revolted against the Mexicans and were massacred at the Alamo. But then the drive for independence proved successful; and in 1845, the Republic of Texas was annexed by the United States and became a slaveholding state. Three years later, Mexico formally ceded California to the United States; gold was discovered there, triggering a rush of miners and settlers into the territory, which became a free state in 1850.

The slavery problem was heating up in America, dividing the predominantly industrial North from the agricultural South, with the extension of slavery to the Western territories a prickly bone of contention. The Republican Party was formed in 1854 with a definite antislavery agenda and Abraham Lincoln became its presidential candidate in 1860. When he was elected, southern states seceded, and civil war erupted between the northern forces fighting to maintain the Union and the southern forces of the secessionist Confederacy. On New Year's Day of 1863, Lincoln formally issued his Emancipation Proclamation, declaring free all slaves residing in territories in rebellion against the federal government. In 1865, the Civil War ended, with the North victorious, after General Robert E. Lee surrendered to General Ulysses S. Grant at the Appomattox Courthouse in Virginia; that same year, the Thirteenth Amendment to the Constitution forbade slavery anywhere in the United States. The Reconstruction Act divided the defeated South into military districts, each of whose army commanders had supreme authority. Southern states were readmitted to the Union, but with newly written constitutions. Northern "carpetbaggers" and southern "scalawags" gained control of state governments there. Racial animosity boiled, giving rise to the Ku Klux Klan, which violently intimidated blacks. In 1870, the Fifteenth Amendment to the Constitution assured the right to vote to all citizens, regardless of race. Yet "Jim Crow" legislation in southern states was quickly passed to maintain and sanction racial segregation. Meanwhile, the United States had purchased Alaska from Russia in 1867 and was completing its first transcontinental railway, facilitating the settling of the West.

In Europe Italy was becoming unified, with Victor Emmanuel II becoming the king of the constitutional monarchy in 1861 and Florence its capital city; Venice was not included in the new nation until 1866 and Rome not until 1870. In 1862, King William I appointed Otto von Bismarck as Prime Minister of Prussia, which went to war with Austria in 1866 and then with France in 1870. During the Franco-Prussian War, Emperor Napoleon III was captured, held prisoner in Germany, and deposed. In 1871, Bismarck became Germany's first chancellor, forming an empire; he established an alliance with Austria in 1873, which was joined by Russia.

During this time music, literature, and painting produced dazzling riches beyond what has been mentioned earlier in connection with Romanticism. The German Ludwig van Beethoven composed concertos, sonatas, and his nine symphonies; fellow German Richard Wagner composed great dramatic operas. The Norwegian composer Edvard Grieg wrote *Peer Gynt*, and in Russia Peter Ilyich Tchaikovsky composed such mellifluous works as *Romeo and Juliet* and *Swan Lake* in addition to his six symphonies. In fictional literature, the achievements of this period are astonishing. In England Charles Dickens published one great novel after another, including *David Copperfield* and *Hard Times*; Alfred Lord Tennyson wrote poetry, as did Robert Browning and his wife, Elizabeth Barrett Browning. The great English novelists Jane Austen (*Pride and Prejudice* and *Emma*), Charlotte Brontë (*Jane Eyre*), her sister Emily Brontë (*Wuthering Heights*), and Mary Ann Evans (who wrote *Middlemarch* under the pen name of George Eliot) flourished at this time. American literature had clearly found its voice, thanks to the remarkable achievements of Washington Irving (*The Legend of Sleepy Hollow*), James Fenimore Cooper (the five novels of the *Leatherstocking Tales*), Nathaniel Hawthorne (*The Scarlet Letter*), Emily Dickinson's poetry, Herman Melville (*Moby Dick*), and Mark Twain (*The Adventures of Huckleberry Finn* and *Life on the Mississippi*). Acclaimed French authors of this time included Honoré de Balzac (*Le Père Goriot*), Gustave Flaubert (*Madame Bovary*), and Henri Stendhal (*The Red and the Black*). It was also a fertile period for Russian literature, including the work of Nikolai Gogol (*Dead Souls*), Ivan Turgenev (*Fathers and Sons*), Fyodor Dostoevsky (*Crime and*

Punishment), and Leo Tolstoy (*War and Peace*). The great English landscape painters, Joseph Mallord William Turner and John Constable, were working at this time, as were French painters Eugène Delacroix, Jean Auguste Dominique Ingres, and Jean François Millet, the Spaniard Francisco de Goya, and Americans James Abbott McNeill Whistler and Winslow Homer. Photography, which developed in the 1830s, was epitomized by the Englishman William Henry Fox Talbot, Frenchmen Louis Jacques Mandé Daguerre and Gaspard Félix Tournachon (better known as Nadar), and the American Mathew Brady. In science Charles Darwin's *Origin of Species* was published in 1859, supporting the ancient theory of evolution with the doctrine of **natural selection**; Michael Faraday discovered electromagnetic induction, and the Austrian monk Gregor Johann Mendel discovered the laws governing genetics. George Boole developed the field of symbolic logic, and Carl Friedrich Gauss made important discoveries in various areas of mathematics and astronomy. The archaeological discoveries of dinosaurs (1811), Neanderthal man (1856) as well as those of Mayan civilization (1839) and ancient Troy (1871) amazed mankind and changed our worldview. This was also a period of creative inventors, including Americans Samuel F. B. Morse, who perfected, patented, and promoted the telegraph to facilitate communication, and Thomas Edison, famous for his work on electric lighting and the phonograph.

The intellectual history of the nineteenth century has Hegel following in the idealistic path of Johann Gottlieb Fichte and Friedrich Wilhelm Joseph von Schelling. German thinkers opposed to Hegel include Friedrich Schliermacher, Arthur Schopenhauer, and Ludwig Feuerbach, as well as Karl Marx. John Stuart Mill follows the lead of Jeremy Bentham and his own father, James Mill, as well as being influenced by William Whewell and Auguste Comte and being opposed to the rationalism of William Hamilton. Other significant philosophers of this period are Charles Bernard Renouvier, Herbert Spencer, Henry Sidgwick, and the early existentialists, Søren A. Kierkegaard and Friedrich Wilhelm Nietzsche.

But it is chiefly the political ferment of this period that gives rise to its being labeled the Age of Ideology, since its theoretical systems are oriented to meeting social needs and advancing political agendas. In general, European history through the first eight decades of the nineteenth century reflects a move from conservatism and absolutism to liberalism and individualism. This shift is also indicated in the two nineteenth-century **philosophers** upon which this chapter concentrates, Hegel and Mill.

Natural selection.   The Darwinian principle that organisms with heritable variations that are better adapted to their environment are more likely to survive and successfully propagate

Hegel

Reason rules the world.

PHILOSOPHY OF HISTORY

BIOGRAPHY

Georg Wilhelm Friedrich Hegel was born on August 27, 1770 (the year in which Kant began his professorship at Königsberg), in Stuttgart (in southwest Germany). His father, Georg Ludwig Hegel, was a civil servant in the department of finance of the duchy of Württemberg in Swabia; his mother, Maria Magdalena Louisa Hegel, his sister, Christiane Luise Hegel (born in 1773), and his brother, Georg Ludwig Hegel (born in 1776), completed the family. Hegel (the future philosopher) nearly died of smallpox at the age of six. In 1780, he began attending Gymnasium Illustre. The next year, his mother died; near the end of his own life Hegel observed the anniversary of her death, writing his sister that he held it "forever in my memory."[1] Hegel was a conscientious, hardworking student, though he was not considered exceptionally gifted. He loved Greek poetry and kept a bilingual journal in German and Latin.

In 1788, he graduated from the *gymnasium* and enrolled in the Protestant **theological** seminary at Tübingen, as his father wished, presumably with the intention of training to become a Lutheran pastor. He was nicknamed "The Old Man" (*der Alte*)[2] for his serious, disciplined, studious manner. A year later, the year of the French Revolution, he shared quarters at the seminary with Schelling, the future philosopher, and the future Romantic poet Johann Friederick Christian Hölderlin. They supposedly planted a "liberty tree" as an expression of their enthusiastic support of the Revolution; Hegel is said to have quarreled with his father about it.

Hegel received his Master of Philosophy degree in 1790 and proceeded to prepare for his theology examinations, which he passed in September of 1793, the year in which he wrote his "Tübingen Essay." His graduation certificate said he was of good character and knowledgeable in theology and philology, though of modest philosophical ability. When he left the seminary he was poor and disinclined to take up parish work. So, the next month he became a family tutor in the home of C. F. Tschügg, in Bern, Switzerland. He was unhappy there but had access to a good library, which facilitated his studies; and there he wrote his "Berne Fragments" on religion. In a letter to Schelling he complains of his "remoteness from the centers of literary activity" and expresses his longing for another situation; he also expresses his ongoing interest in the French Revolution, condemning "the complete ignominy of Robespierre's party." A month later, he writes Schelling again, complaining of his "remoteness" and lack of time, commenting on the dangerous attempts of theologians at Tübingen to appropriate Kant's philosophy for orthodox purposes, and closing with the **Enlightenment** slogan, **"Reason and Freedom remain our password."** He writes Schelling, "From the Kantian system and its highest completion I expect a revolution in Germany." He expresses his confidence that it will inspire something comparable to what has happened in France:

> The philosophers are proving the **dignity** of man. The peoples will learn to feel it. Not only will they demand their rights, which have been trampled in the dust, they will take them back themselves.

In still another letter, he embraces the Kantian "**postulate** according to which practical reason governs the world of appearances," as "illuminated" by Schelling's own "splendid" writing.[3] Hegel wrote a "Life of Jesus" and *The Positivity of the Christian Religion* in 1795. In January of 1797, he obtained a tutor's post with a family in Frankfurt, Germany, thanks to the assistance of his friend Hölderlin there. The following year, he wrote *The Spirit of Christianity and Its Fate.*

Early in 1799, he received a note from his sister, Christiane, informing him that their father had just "died most quietly and peacefully." Hegel inherited a legacy sufficient to free him from tutoring, as he wrote in 1800 to Schelling, who had succeeded to Fichte's professorship at the University of Jena (in East Germany). Now that he could afford to leave Frankfurt, Hegel wrote, "I am looking for inexpensive provisions, a good beer for the sake of my physical condition, [and] a few acquaintances." The next year, Schelling helped Hegel to become a *Privatdozent*, an unsalaried lecturer, at Jena, on the strength of his *Philosophical Dissertation on the Orbits of the Planets* of that same year. There Hegel earned money by charging attendance fees for his lectures on logic and **metaphysics**. His first published book, *The Difference between Fichte's and Schelling's Systems of Philosophy*, appeared that year, defending the latter against the former. At the end of 1801, Hegel wrote, "Presently something new is being launched, namely the first issue of a *Critical Journal of Philosophy*, which I am editing with Schelling—with whom I am lodging." He expresses his hope that the *Journal* will provide an antidote "to unphilosophical rubbish" that abounds.[4] His essay *Natural Law* and his *Faith and Knowledge* were published in the *Journal* in 1803, the year Schelling left Jena to accept a chair at Würtzburg. By 1804, Hegel had thirty students (whereas he had had only eleven in 1801). The following year, he was promoted to extraordinary professor and began lecturing on the history of philosophy.

Meanwhile, Hegel was working on his philosophical masterpiece, the *Phenomenology of Spirit*. He had used up the inheritance from his father; though he now had a salary at the university, his need for money drove him to sign a publishing contract for the *Phenomenology*, for which he received an advance payment in return for his agreement to severe penalties if he failed to get the completed manuscript to the publisher by October 18, 1806 (he would need to have it in the mail by the 13th). In 1806, he writes, "Luther made the Bible speak German. . . . I may say of my endeavor that I wish to try to teach philosophy to speak German." In another letter, he reports, "The printing was begun in February" of 1806. The problem was that Napoleon's French troops had invaded Prussia. On October 8th, Hegel mailed "half the manuscript," promising to send the rest a few days later. But four days later, Napoleon bombarded the city of Jena. Hegel describes the next day, which should have been the deadline for mailing the manuscript, as

> the day the French occupied Jena and the Emperor Napoleon penetrated its walls. . . . I saw the Emperor—this world-soul—riding. . . . It is indeed a wonderful sensation to see such an individual, who, . . . astride a horse, reaches out over the world and masters it.

Hegel missed his deadline, although his legal advisor assured him that he would not be liable for the results of an act of war.[5]

The book was published in March of 1807, and Hegel was less than satisfied with the results. He writes to Schelling that May, complaining of the "unfortunate confusion" surrounding "the entire process" of its production:

> Make allowances for the greater want of form in the last sections by recalling that I actually completed the draft in its entirety in the middle of the night before the Battle of Jena.

He also warns that the preface of the book attacks "the shallowness" of some of Schelling's followers. Though Schelling was five years younger than Hegel, he was also the quicker prodigy; and the latter had appeared the disciple of the former until the publication of the *Phenomenology*, which was Hegel's philosophical declaration of independence. Schelling did react to what he called "the polemical part of the Preface,"[6] and their friendship ended.

Academic operations in Jena were so disrupted by Napoleon's occupation that the university closed, preventing Hegel from completing his courses. Hegel's lodgings were "plundered" and left in disarray. But Hegel also had to leave as a result of impregnating his landlord's wife, Christiana Burkhardt. In February of 1807, Mrs. Burkhardt gave birth to Hegel's son, Ludwig, in Jena. The following month, Hegel began editing a French-controlled newspaper in Bamberg (in Bavaria, a German province that had appeased Napoleon). Hegel, who admired the style of French newspapers, saw the job as "only temporary," lasting perhaps "two to three years," which would allow him time to pursue his literary ambitions. More specifically, he was beginning work on his *Logic*. Mainly he wanted the steady income and jokingly modified the wording of *Matthew* 6:33:

> I have convinced myself by experience of the truth of the biblical text which I have made my guiding light: "Strive ye first after food and clothing, and the Kingdom of God will fall to you as well."

But by 1808, he found his work at the *Bamberg Newspaper* annoying (because of struggles with censors) and undignified, appealing to a friend to help him return to academia. He also expressed some feelings of guilty conscience over impregnating Mrs. Burkhardt.[7]

That friend to whom he had appealed, Friedrich Immanuel Niethammer, who was reorganizing schools in Bavaria, appointed Hegel rector and philosophy professor at the *gymnasium* in Nuremberg towards the end of 1808. The school was dedicated to "classical studies." Hegel thanks and praises Niethammer for tightening and strengthening the curriculum. In 1810, Hegel writes Niethammer, urging the continued secularization of the school system and reporting that members of his faculty "are extremely displeased at having to go to church for religious instruction. What is **essentially** at stake is the former subordination of the teaching profession to the clergy. . . . Yet I know that you do all you can in favor of liberality." Hegel had suffered the anxieties of "hypochondria to the point of exhaustion" awhile, and Niethammer expressed the hope that he might marry.[8]

In early 1811, Hegel was courting Marie von Tucher, from an **aristocratic** family in Nuremberg, with poetry he had written. Just before mid-April, he sent her a poem, part of which reads:

Narrow bands dividing us, fall away!
Sacrifice alone is the heart's true way!
I expand myself to you, as you to me.
May what isolates us go up in fire, cease to be.
For life is life only as reciprocated,
By love in love is it alone created.

Then, shortly after mid-April, confident of having won her love, he wrote another poem, the first stanza of which exults,

You are mine! A heart as yours I may call mine.
In your look may I divine
Love's look returned, oh bliss,
Oh highest happiness!

That summer, he wrote his fiancée, trying to assure her that they will be "entirely happy" together, despite his "melancholy" and "hypochondriacal pedantry." When they married, Hegel was forty-one years old, while she was just less than half his age. In early October, Hegel writes Niethammer that

—apart from a few modifications still to be desired—I have now reached my earthly goal. For what more does one want in this world than a post and a dear wife?

He even expresses the hope that his recent marriage might have the beneficial effect of rendering him "more popular and easily accessible" with his students. At the same time he had begun to fear "that there might be almost too much philosophical instruction in the gymnasium"[9] for boys so young.

In the summer of 1812, Hegel's wife gave birth to a daughter, who died just a few weeks later. A few days after the infant's death, Hegel wrote Niethammer of his wife's grief, adding, "I suffer doubly, from the loss I have suffered and from the pain she feels." Over nineteen years later, several weeks before his own death, Hegel wrote a letter of condolence to a friend who had lost a child, telling of his own daughter's death. Towards the end of that year, Hegel's doubts about the appropriateness of much philosophical instruction in the *gymnasium* were deepening. He felt ambivalent because of his dual roles. As rector, he thought he had an "official duty" to express such doubts to Niethammer. "Yet," he asks rhetorically, "how am I, professor of philosophical preparatory sciences, to fight against my own discipline and post, undermining the basis of my own livelihood?" In June of 1813, Hegel's son Karl was born; in September of the following year, his son Immanuel was born.[10] Hegel apparently had a happy marriage and enjoyed a loving family life. During these years (1812–16) he was also completing his *Science of Logic*, published in installments.

Consequently, he was offered professorships by the universities of Erlangen, Heidelberg, and Berlin. In his correspondence negotiating for these positions, he writes that he strives to "unite clarity with both depth and appropriate elaboration" in his teaching but insists that effective "philosophy instruction" requires "a *definite methodological procedure*, encompassing and *ordering detail*" and that "philosophy must never be *edifying*." Heidelberg's offer was particularly flattering, and Hegel accepted it in August of 1816 (prior to his receiving the one from Berlin). The following year, after Hegel and his wife had moved to Heidelberg, Ludwig, Hegel's illegitimate son, moved in with them, following the death of his mother, and they adopted him.[11] At the university Hegel began lecturing on **aesthetics**, and he published his *Encyclopedia of the Philosophical Sciences* in three parts (a logic, a philosophy of nature, and a philosophy of **mind**).

In 1818, Hegel accepted a second offer from the

University of Berlin, filling the philosophy chair that had been left vacant since Fichte's death in 1814. There he found his students "receptive to and interested in philosophy," though by 1819 he had "not yet found a circle of friends" such as he had enjoyed in Heidelberg. He liked being in the "center of things" in Berlin, and after a while he was given a salaried teaching assistant. Late the following year, his *Philosophy of Right* was published. It reflects the fifty-year-old Hegel gone conservative and having become an intellectual spokesman for the Prussian state. He sent a copy to one of its officials, with a letter saying that his writings aim

> to demonstrate the harmony of philosophy with those principles generally required by the nature of the state. But most immediately they aim at showing agreement with the principles which the Prussian state—belonging to which necessarily gives me great satisfaction—has had the good fortune of having upheld and of still upholding under the enlightened Government of His Majesty the King and Your Highness's wise leadership.[12]

In 1821, Hegel began lecturing on the philosophy of religion at Berlin and the year after on the philosophy of history.

Hegel traveled widely the next few years; he met with Goethe at Weimar in the fall of 1827. That year, he also revised and published a second edition of his *Encyclopedia*. In 1829, he was elected rector of the University of Berlin; by this time, he had become quite famous. A bust of him was sculpted by a Professor Wichmann, and the Hegelian philosophy was spreading in various German universities. However, he was also pressed to defend himself against charges of **pantheism**. In 1826, he had proclaimed, "I am a Lutheran, and through philosophy have been at once completely confirmed in Lutheranism"; in another letter that same year he described himself as "a professor who prides himself on having been baptized and raised a Lutheran, which he still is and shall remain." He realized that "all speculative philosophizing on religion permits of being led to **atheism**." He describes himself as "an anxious man" who does "like tranquility," adding that he hates "to see a storm rise up every year, even if I can be persuaded that at most only a few drops of a light rain will touch me." When his religious orthodoxy was challenged, it

became "necessary to attack this rubbish head-on," to confront all "the twaddle about pantheism."[13]

But, in general, Hegel's thirteen years at Berlin were quite fulfilling for him. In 1827, he proudly writes, "my philosophy has now gained more widespread currency, and . . . more and more universities are offering lectures according to my ideas." Three years later, he published a third edition of his *Encyclopedia*. In early 1831, he wrote his sister about a "copper engraving" of him that had been done, as well as about his image being "imprinted on a medal."[14] When the cholera epidemic hit Berlin that year, Hegel, who had begun revising his *Phenomenology*, was among its first victims, dying in his sleep on November 14, the day after he fell ill. He was buried next to Fichte in Berlin. His four great lecture series were published posthumously: *Philosophy of History*, *Philosophy of Fine Art*, *History of Philosophy*, and *Philosophy of Religion*.

Reality

THE WORLD SPIRIT. Like other great thinkers we have studied, Hegel locates his philosophy of human nature in the context of a broader theory of reality. This theory can be considered one of **monistic idealism**, in that it maintains that all reality is ultimately spiritual in nature and that all things real are ultimately one. In his introduction to *The Philosophy of History* he writes that the only **presupposition** that philosophy "brings with it" to the study of history is "the thought that Reason rules the world" and that this presupposition is justified "in philosophy itself." This Reason is "*substance* as well as the *infinite* power"; it is "the *infinite material* of all natural and spiritual life." Metaphysically, Reason is the **Absolute Idea**, the ultimate reality.

> That this Idea is the True, the Eternal, simply the Power—that it reveals itself in the world, and that nothing else is revealed in the world but that Idea itself, its glory and majesty

—is supposedly the **conclusion** established by Hegelian philosophy. On this view, world history is "the rational, necessary course of the World Spirit, the Spirit whose nature is indeed always one and the same, but which reveals this one nature in the world's reality." Hegel observes that this is an old idea in

---

Absolute Spirit/Mind/Idea. The ultimate, unconditioned, uncaused, complete Reality, especially in Hegelian thought

philosophy, going back to the pre-Socratic Anaxagoras, whose view was such a welcome contrast to **materialistic** theories of reality that Aristotle considered him "like a sober man" among the drunks. Theologically, the view "that Reason rules the world" is related to God's governing reality through "divine providence." But if this is, indeed, an accurate picture, then "the doctrine (which has now become a prejudice) that it is impossible to know God" becomes an obstacle to our access to truth.[15]

On the Kantian principle that "ought" implies "can," that we cannot be required to attempt the impossible, such a view, which is advocated by Kant, purportedly flies in the face of our obligation to know. However, Hegel adds, "God wants no narrow-minded **souls** and empty heads for His children," but wants us to pursue, achieve, and value the very sort of "knowledge of Him" that should arise from divine revelation and that the Kantians deem unavailable to us. All of "*world history*," which "includes both physical and mental nature," according to Hegel, "takes place in the realm of Spirit." But if the nature of reality is spiritual, we must try to understand the nature of Spirit.

> Just as the essence of matter is gravity [that is, in being determined by a force outside it], so the essence of Spirit is its freedom [that is, in its self-determination].

We shall consider this notion of freedom in more detail in a later section. But we may now consider further the "complete antithesis" between matter and Spirit.

> Matter has weight insofar as it strives toward a central point outside itself. It is essentially composed of parts which are separable.

All matter, as Descartes observed, is **extended** and divisible; and, as Newtonian physics shows, is subject to gravitational forces that may determine its behavior.

> Spirit, on the other hand, is that which has its center in itself. Its unity is not outside itself; rather it has found it within its own self. . . . Spirit is **autonomous** and self-sufficient.[16]

That is, Spirit, which comprises all of nature, is opposed to matter in being conscious, self-conscious, and capable of self-determination.

SALIENT CHARACTERISTICS OF HEGEL'S METAPHYSICS. Hegel's renowned metaphysical theory is arguably the most demanding topic to be covered in this book. The twists and turns of its details are both subtle and complex. So, before plunging further into it, let us consider some of its most salient characteristics, which might provide us with a framework on which to hang those details. First, his system is an idealism, in the sense that it regards reality as fundamentally spiritual, as we have just seen. Second, Hegel is a monist, in that he conceives of all reality as ultimately one, despite the apparent multiplicity of this world. Third, Hegel is a **panentheist**, for whom that one all-encompassing reality, the World Spirit or Absolute, is God, with the things of this world being spatio-temporal "moments" or aspects of the whole. Fourth, Hegel invents a **dialectical logic** to help us achieve knowledge of the **synthetic** unity in which all antithetical conflict is allegedly resolved. Hegel's idealism, monism, panentheism, and dialectical logic, taken together, can invite us to conceive of all objects of experience as interlocking pieces of a jigsaw puzzle whose complete assembly would present us with a picture of all reality. Though he is a rationalist, rather than a Romantic thinker, Hegel was influenced by the Romantic movement. His emphasis on the underlying unity of all reality and his identification of that with the divine is reminiscent of Romantic literary writers and artists. We should also recognize, as we proceed, that he sometimes adopts an eccentric use of familiar concepts, such as "substance" and "truth" (as when "the substance of" something is used to mean its essence or when "the truth of" something refers to its fulfillment).

IDEALISM AND MONISM. A more rigorous presentation of this theory of reality can be found in Hegel's masterpiece, his *Phenomenology of Spirit*. In its preface he writes "that Substance is essentially Subject"; that is, reality as it ultimately is can best be described in spiritual terms. It can be considered apart from its relationships ("**in itself**" or *an sich*), as determined by its relationships ("**for itself**" or *für sich*), or both at once ("**in and for itself**" or *an und für sich*), for it is

---

In-itself.   Sartre's term (*en-soi*) for all reality that is not conscious, free, and responsible for its own actions, as opposed to "for-itself" (*pour-soi*); for Hegel, "in itself" refers to reality in its immediacy, apart from any relationships

For-itself.   Sartre's term (*pour-soi*) for personal consciousness, that reality which exists as free and is radically individual and responsible, as opposed to all other reality, which he calls "in-itself" (*en-soi*); for Hegel, "for itself" refers to reality as it is determined by its relationships

both genuinely self-contained and genuinely relational. As he puts it, "The spiritual alone is the *actual*; it is essence, or that which has *being in itself*." So reality, viewed initially as unrelated and undetermined, is essentially spiritual. But, second, "it is that which *relates itself to itself* and is *determinate*, it is . . . *being-for-self*" or actually determined as spiritual. And, third, these two dimensions, though different, are synthesized so that "*in and for itself*" reality "is spiritual Substance." The truth of idealism, established by the *cogito* "found in Descartes's metaphysics," as well as by his use of the **ontological argument**, is "that being and thought are, *in themselves*, the same,"[17] even if we do not treat them as conceptually identical.

Thus far, we have emphasized Hegel's idealism. But we must also establish his monism, the idea that reality, besides being spiritual, is ultimately one, all of its aspects being abstractions except in relation to it. He tells us that "only the whole has true actuality." The term he uses for dimensions of reality considered in abstraction from the whole is "moments," and he analyzes the **ontological** status of four of the most important ones we shall be considering: "but the moments of the whole, consciousness, self-consciousness, Reason, and Spirit, just because they are moments, have no existence in separation from one another." Hegel's Absolute Spirit is never static but dynamically expresses itself. As he writes near the very end of the *Phenomenology*, it expresses itself spatially as Nature and temporally as History.[18]

TOWARDS A NEW LOGIC. In the *Encyclopedia Logic* Hegel observes that the objects of philosophy and religion are "the same," namely "the Truth" (in the sense of its fulfillment) about reality, which is God. This claim may strike us as odd, but it makes sense in the context of Hegel's monistic system. His idea of logic is not some Aristotelian sets of forms of reasoning but is rather a systematic knowledge of reality. As he writes,

> Logic therefore coincides with Metaphysics, the science of things set and held in thoughts—thoughts accredited able to express the essential reality of things.

Thought can comprehend reality because it is its "heart and soul," because Spirit "governs the world" as "its **immanent** principle." This repudiation of the Aristotelian theory of logic as "concerned with forms only" will call for a new logic whose built-in content is the truth about reality.

> The study of truth, or . . . **consistency**, constitutes the proper problem of logic.[19]

We shall examine this new logic in our section on "Knowledge."

For now, we can observe that a metaphysical logic must be theological if Hegel is correct that reality is ultimately divine: "God is more than life: he is Spirit. And therefore if the thought of the Absolute takes a starting-point," as it must, the most adequate one "will be found in the nature of spirit alone." The object of thought is the totality of reality "as a whole, God, the Absolute Object." But, as we have seen, being is not merely the object of thought; Hegel's idealism argues for "the indissoluble connection between the notion or thought and being." To the extent that it is adequate and actualized, reality is "the Idea"—both "the one **universal** *substance*" and "a *subject*" or Spirit. The Idea is a dialectical **process** in which "thought and being," the "finite and infinite," the "subjective" and "the objective" are neither merely opposed nor simply united, but in which "the infinite overlaps and includes the finite, thought overlaps being, subjectivity overlaps objectivity." Reality, as adequate and actualized, incorporates a "harmony between the 'is' and the 'ought to be,'" which "is not torpid and rigidly stationary"[20] but an ongoing dynamic process.

THE ABSOLUTE IDEA. The final chapter of Hegel's *Science of Logic* deals with "The Absolute Idea" or "Notion." The Notion (*der Begriff*) is a concrete (not abstract), all-inclusive (or comprehensive) universal, which contains (and is the sum-total of) all the categories of thought and reality (both of which, as we have seen, are ultimately spiritual). Theologically, this is God, and Hegel tells us that it "has personality" within it. Apart from it, or taken in abstraction from it, everything "is error and gloom, opinion, striving, caprice, and transitoriness; the Absolute Idea alone is Being, imperishable Life, self-knowing truth, and the whole of truth." This, he says, is "the only object and content of philosophy" (as well as of "art and

---

Immanence.   Presence in something else, inherence, as opposed to transcendence; for example, the God of panentheism is immanent in the things of this world

religion"). But the Notion or Absolute Idea is all of reality. Its "activity" is the dynamic process, "the self-determining and self-realizing movement" of Spirit. Apart from it there is nothing. "Consequently it may well be said that every beginning must be made from the Absolute, while every progress is merely the exhibition of the Absolute in so far as that which is in itself is the Notion."[21] The Absolute Idea is allegedly known through reason's use of dialectical logic.

DIALECTICAL REASONING. Dialectic is a science that was founded by Plato and revivified by Kant and is more fully developed and utilized by Hegel himself to reveal the truth of reality. It sees thought and reality (which, we recall, are ultimately one) as encompassing "opposites" that not only **contradict** each other but "are transitions" to higher "syntheses." In dialectical logic, any immediate object of thought must be "mediated and related to an Other," with which it is in tension. Yet these opposites must be accepted as indicative of reality itself. We must not be intimidated (as Kant allegedly was) by the laws of Aristotelian logic (the principles of **identity**, **noncontradiction**, and **excluded middle**) into backing off from contradictions. Rather, they must be overcome through "the **negative** of the negative," rising above opposition to a higher synthesis, which will constitute a "**transcendence** of the contradiction." Thus, as the old Aristotelian **syllogism** is **triadic** (containing three logical terms related in three **propositions**), so dialectical reason will be triadic in its knowledge of reality, determining an object of thought (sometimes called a "**thesis**"), its opposite (sometimes called the "**antithesis**"), and the dynamic transcendence of their contradiction (sometimes called the "synthesis"). For example, if we try to understand the concept of mind (an original "thesis"), we do so, in part, by contrasting it with its opposite, matter (an "antithesis"). Like Descartes, we can elaborate their radical differences, negating any identity between them. From the perspective of Aristotelian logic, they cannot be

identical. But Hegel's dialectical reasoning allegedly overcomes this opposition to arrive at a higher truth (or "synthesis"), that matter and mind are essentially interrelated as aspects of the same underlying reality, the Absolute. The result of dialectical reasoning is allegedly progressively adequate knowledge of the truth of reality. "The first two moments of the triplicity are the abstract and false moments, which for this very reason are dialectical" in pointing to increasingly higher syntheses. But in this dialectical process nothing is ever completely lost, in that every higher synthesis "carries with it all that it has acquired" from previous oppositions. Thus, Kantian objections based on the alleged "limits of human **cognition**" that prevent us from rising above contradictions of logical understanding are counterproductive in that they threaten to make us give up the quest prematurely. Every beginning must be recognized as incomplete, yet necessary. It is dialectical logic which will rise above the limits of the understanding, overcome opposition, and constitute knowledge of the Absolute Idea, "the whole of its reality, into the system of philosophic science."[22]

RATIONALITY AND ACTUALITY. One of the most famous sentences in all of Hegel's writings, from the preface to his *Philosophy of Right*, says,

What is rational is actual and what is actual is rational.

This does not mean that anything real, as it presently exists, must be rational, but only that reality is rational to the extent that it achieves its ideal or actualizes its essence. To the extent that something is "actual," it must meet the requirements of Hegelian logic, be in principle intelligible, and measure up to rational standards. In the introduction to his *Encyclopedia Logic* Hegel admits that this claim has met with "expressions of surprise and hostility." Yet, he observes, religion's concept of God's divine providence confirms it all "too decidedly."[23] Reality as fully actualized, on this theory, is one, spiritual in nature, and rationally knowable.

Identity. The quality of remaining the same or the condition of two things being the same; in Aristotelian logic, the law of identity maintains that everything is what it is and cannot simultaneously be something other than what it is

Excluded middle, law or principle of. A basic law of Aristotelian logic asserting the truth of the disjunction of any (significant) proposition together with its negation (e.g., there either is or is not a one-hundred-year-old philosopher now teaching somewhere in the United States)

Triadic. Threefold or pertaining to a triad, or group of three (things, properties, ideas, etc.)

Bodies

ORGANIC PURPOSE.   In a passage in the *Phenomenology* on organic nature Hegel writes that an "*organism*" exhibits a self-contained unity to which external relationships are subordinate, such that "every determinateness through which it is open to an other is controlled by the organic simple unity." Human reason tries to discover scientific laws, such as principles of environmental adaptation, in order to explain the behavior of organisms—for example, "animals belonging to the air have the nature of birds, those belonging to water have the nature of fish, animals in northern latitudes have thick, hairy pelts, and so on." But such laws of observational reason "cannot be other than superficial" and merely emphasize "the *great influence* of environment," rather than explaining any real **necessity**; "such laws are seen at a glance to display a poverty which does not do justice to the manifold variety of organic Nature." Observational reason discovers only external **teleological** purposes and fails to disclose the true teleology of nature, the Notion or Idea as "the organism's own *essence*." This concept of organic purposes, "to which Reason in its role of observer rises," must be dialectically developed further before we reach the truth of idealism. Aristotle's concepts of genus and species are valuable as tools reason can use to understand the relationship between universals and particulars in biological nature; for "between the actual existence or shape, i.e. the self-developing individual, and the organic universal or the genus, there comes the *determinate* universal, the *species*."[24] Thus, the category of iris helps us to relate this particular flower to plant life in general.

NATURE AND SPIRIT.   Hegel's most important treatment of material reality is in his *Philosophy of Nature*. In its introduction he confronts the ambivalence with which an idealist might consider physical nature, saying that it "both attracts and repels us: attracts us, because Spirit is presaged in Nature; repels us, because Nature seems an alien existence, in which Spirit does not find itself" initially and obviously represented. There is a superficial antithesis between the natural and spiritual realms which must be transcended in the recognition that "Nature is Spirit estranged from itself"—that is, as expressed in time and space. The Absolute Idea (or God) dynamically generates what appears to be its opposite, through which its self-development and self-expression will be possible: "Nature is the Idea in the form of otherness." It appears as opposed to divinity; yet as an expression of the Absolute Idea, "Nature is divine." Unlike Spirit, which is essentially free, "Nature exhibits no freedom. . . , but only *necessity* and **contingency**." Hegel credits Kant with reviving the philosophy of nature but faults him for not transcending the view of "the reflective Understanding" and thus for seeing physical "forces of attraction and repulsion" merely "as fixed mutual opposites" rather than in dialectical tension with each other in the world of bodies.[25]

BODIES IN TIME AND SPACE.   At its simplest level material reality seems inert, quantitatively measurable, and analyzable in terms of "*bodies*" related to one another. "The body," he writes, "is *essentially* spatial and temporal, but as being *in* space and *in* time." There is even a dialectical tension between a body viewed spatially (from which perspective "the body *endures*") and seen temporally (from which perspective "it is *transitory*"). In fact, both of these apparently opposed perspectives are true, and their relationship points to "the unity which holds together the two moments *in their opposition*, i.e. *motion*." Thus far, we are considering bodies at a simple level and are encountering the analysis of Newtonian physics given Hegel's own dialectical twist. At a higher level "the individual body" must be viewed as a "*physical* totality" of characteristics which determine the specific sort of body it is—e.g., mineral, vegetable, animal, human. "The body, as *subject* of these determinations, contains them as *properties* or *predicates*, but in such manner that they are at the same time a relationship" constituting a unity of physical form. "Body, as mechanical totality, is form developed through and through within itself."[26]

INORGANIC AND ORGANIC MATTER.   Physical reality encompasses both inorganic matter, such as a rock, and organic matter, such as the human body, which is of greater interest to us here. "We have now to make the *transition* from inorganic to organic Nature, from the prose to the poetry of Nature." It is especially in "the *animal* organism" that we experience ecologically interconnected vitality. Organic nature comprises a "plurality of living things" that are so interdependent as to indicate "*one* Life, one organic system of Life." Again, we can consider dialectical relationships in an animal organism: from the perspective of "*sensibility*" it can appear self-contained, "an undivided identity of the subject with itself"; but, as opposed to this, from the perspective of its "*irritability*," it exhibits "a capacity for being stimulated from outside," as well as a "reaction outwards to the stimulation," so that it is obviously in community with other bodies; and, third, there is "the unity of these moments," represented by its "return to itself from its relation with the outside world," for example in "*reproduction.*" The Aristotelian concept of teleology is still useful for understanding the workings of animal organisms, and Kant (again) gets credit for resurrecting it, although we should remember that there are both the ends of conscious life and "purposive activity acting unconsciously," as in animal instinct. Finally, it is in the human body, as the greatest physical "instrument of spirit," that all aspects of organic life "attain their most perfect development."[27] So nature is dialectically related to Spirit, bodies move and interact in time and space, physical reality comprises both inorganic and organic matter, and the human body is that organism which is the physical matrix of the human personality.

Personality

THE IDEA AND HUMAN PASSION. Perhaps the gentlest way to begin piecing together Hegel's theory of human personality is to examine what he says in the introduction to his popular work *The Philosophy of History* before turning to his more demanding but philosophically more impressive *Phenomenology.* Remembering that he views human history as the expression of Spirit in time, we find him claiming that "the actions of human beings stem from their needs, their passions, their interests, their characters and talents," rather than merely (as we might mistakenly guess) from their cognitive reason. Thus, the forces driving the flywheels of history are human "passions, the aims of particular interests, the satisfaction of selfish desire." Considered from a certain perspective, history can seem "a drama" of tragic loss, and we can "be filled with grief" over its waste. Yet there is a fateful necessity to the historical process, as the self-expression of Absolute Spirit. Obviously, it

comprises a great deal of human suffering. "But as we contemplate history as this slaughter-bench, upon which the happiness of nations, the wisdom of states, and the **virtues** of individuals were sacrificed," we must place all that in the larger context of history's "ultimate goal" and the necessary means to its achievement. The movers and shakers of history, driven by their own needs and inclinations, seek personal satisfaction of desire, little suspecting the rational pattern into which their selfish passions are interwoven.[28]

Hegel holds that the historical process interrelates two great elements:

> the first is the Idea, the other is human passion; the first is the warp, the other the woof in the great tapestry of world history that is spread out before us.

These two elements might seem to run at cross-purposes with each other but are actually dialectically interwoven. Individual humans strive for personal and social welfare, but they only tend to achieve it to the extent that their behaviors are appropriate to their circumstances. "But world history is not the place for happiness," Hegel comments. "Periods of happiness are empty pages in history, for they are the periods of harmony, times when the antithesis is missing," as it rarely is absent, given that forces of opposition and tension drive history. The outcome of action is usually "something other than what the agents aim at" and desire. What makes leaders great is a fortunate coincidence between their selfish desires and the requirements of universal Reason:

> The historical men—the *world-historical individuals*— are those whose aims embody a universal concept.

Hegel uses Julius Caesar as his example. When Caesar led his troops across the Rubicon River into Rome in 49 B.C. against the orders of the Roman Senate, he was driven by personal ambition. Yet this act changed history, since

> Caesar became the sole ruler of the state. The accomplishment of his originally negative aim—i.e., the autocratic control of Rome—was at the same time an essential determination in the history of Rome and of the world.

With a consolidation of power, Rome was more easily able to spread its law, ideals, and culture through the Empire, advancing the rational cause of developing civilization.

The great men in history are those whose own particular aims contain the substantial will that is the will of the World Spirit.

Yet they do not realize such broader implications of their actions.

These heroic individuals, in fulfilling these aims of theirs, had no consciousness of the Idea at all.

This may help explain the fact that they tend not to lead happy lives.

They die young, like Alexander; they are murdered, like Caesar; they are exiled, like Napoleon.

Yet unwittingly and, perhaps, even unwillingly, they are serving higher purposes. "This may be called the *Cunning of Reason*" (*die List der Vernunft*), Hegel writes, "that it allows the passions to work for it, while what it brings into existence suffers loss and injury."[29]

The personal desires of even these heroes pale in significance in relation to the purposes of the Absolute:

Compared to the universal, the particular is for the most part too slight in importance: individuals are surrendered and sacrificed. The Idea pays the ransom of existence and transience—not out of its own pocket, but with the passions of individuals.

It is only in the area of personal values—of "*morality, ethics, religious commitment*"—that individuals "are to be regarded as ends in themselves," as Kant says; and these, of course, are areas of rational freedom. Here human personality does seem to have **intrinsic** dignity. Otherwise, however, "whatever can claim to be noble and grand in the world still has something higher above it. The claim of the World Spirit supersedes all particular claims" made by great historical figures, let alone by ordinary people. Still, what sets humans apart from other animals is the capacity for rational thought, self-awareness, and free action.[30]

THE MASTER-BONDSMAN DIALECTIC. Hegel's most famous and most important treatment of human personality is in his *Phenomenology*, which traces its development dialectically from the most rudimentary awareness to the highest reaches of absolute knowledge (*das absolute Wissen*). In the preface he again minimizes the significance of any particular individual. But there is a general pattern of development whereby we can understand "Life as a *process*." In order for consciousness to become self-consciousness

it must encounter another consciousness, from which it seeks recognition; for "self-consciousness is Desire."[31] Consciousness finds that it cannot merely and simply appropriate or destroy another consciousness, as it might a physical object, and still achieve satisfaction of desire.

This throws us into the famous passage on "Lordship and Bondage," which may be Hegel's most brilliant illustration of the dialectic at work. Encountering another consciousness, a human personality can pursue "the process of Recognition" in a **potentially** fruitful way. Mere physical objects, such as sticks and stones, cannot confer personal recognition; for that another person is needed. But the tendency is to relate to another person as one would to any object—to try to "supersede this otherness of itself." This tendency is bilateral, each subject trying to relate to the other as mere object. "Thus the movement is simply the double movement of the two self-consciousnesses." Each can become aware that the other is objectifying it as it would the other and is therefore, like itself, a person: "They *recognize* themselves as *mutually recognizing* one another." There is simultaneously an antithesis and mutual need between them. In some respects the easiest solution to this conflict is to destroy the other as another person, so that "each seeks the death of the other" and attempts "the staking of its own life." To some extent such "a life-and-death struggle" is necessary for the realization of self-conscious autonomy. For example, if a child is to mature into a healthy adult, she must experience a development of views and values in conflict with those of other persons; one's self-image is inevitably molded by the acceptance/rejection ratio struck in interpersonal relationships. But, as Hegel proceeds to show, if the struggle issued in the literal destruction of the other as a person, the outcome would be counterproductive.[32]

What we desire from other people that we can never get from physical objects, machines, and non-human animals is personal recognition. The destruction of another person leaves only a corpse, incapable of granting that to another or enjoying it from another. Thus, it can happen that one person "learns that life is as essential to it" as is the satisfaction of desire, backs down from the struggle, preferring life to independence, and becoming subject to the other's will. This gives rise to a primitive interpersonal relationship that falls far short of any true community. We see a resolution of the conflict between two individuals—

> one is the independent consciousness whose essential nature is to be for itself, the other is the dependent consciousness whose essential nature is simply to live or to be for another. The former is lord, the other is bondsman.

The master has preferred independence to life itself and now controls the actions of the subjected other, whose will is no longer his own; the other must work at the beck and call of the master, who enjoys the fruits of the other's labor. The other's slavish and fearful preference for life itself "holds the bondsman in bondage; it is his chain from which he could not break free in the struggle, thus proving himself to be dependent." The master gets the recognition originally desired from the bondsman, who must treat him as lord, and apparently need offer no recognition to the other in return.[33]

It looks as if the synthesis of lordship and bondage has generated one-sided independence and one-sided dependence. But the Hegelian dialectic is more subtle than that and proceeds to show that such a one-sided inequality is unstable and that the relationship "has in reality turned out to be something quite different" from what appeared at first blush. The master ironically becomes dependent on the expertise, industry, and labor of the bondsman; even the master's recognition rings hollow, since its source is a slavish bondsman. Meanwhile, the bondsman too becomes other than was suspected; in subservience, motivated by fear, the bondsman learns to master the environment by labor. "Through his service he rids himself of his attachment to natural existence in every single detail; and gets rid of it by working on it." The bondsman must become creative and productive; in mastering his environment, he achieves a kind of recognition and satisfaction. Hegel alludes to *Psalms* 111:10 to the effect that "the fear of the lord is indeed the beginning of wisdom"; yet he shows how the bondsman, through work, can master existence itself, which originally motivated the fear, and realize "that it is precisely in his work wherein he seemed to have only an **alienated** existence that he acquires a mind of his own."[34] Yet he is still a bondsman, subject to an alien will.

Here is a dramatic reversal or "counter-thrust" (*Gegenstoss*) found in Hegel's dialectic. The human personality cannot be fulfilled either by merely dominating another as superior or by being subservient to another as inferior, although both of these extremes are sufficiently frustrating and miserable to propel us to further development.

THE STAGE OF STOICISM. Interpersonal conflict between master and bondsman is a phase through which the human personality must pass, although it turns out to be a lower rung on a ladder to be climbed. Next, the dialectical process of evolving self-consciousness (for both the lord and the bondsman) rises through the stages of **stoicism**, **scepticism**, and the "unhappy consciousness," which turn out to be increasingly profound depths of alienation. (The mixed metaphors here are deliberate: as self-consciousness mounts higher in its evolution, it inevitably encounters more terrible depths of alienation, until a major reversal or "counter-thrust" occurs which will spin it out of the cycle of individualistic self-consciousness altogether into the levels of free, concrete mind—reason and spirit—in which community becomes crucial.) The frustrations, limitations, and misery of both poles of lordship and bondage suffice to drive self-consciousness to deny external reality as essential and to seek refuge in the infinitude of its own thought.

> In thinking, I *am free*, because I am not in an *other*, but remain simply and solely in communion with myself.

Despairing of its capacity to achieve true independence in interpersonal relationships, consciousness turns in upon itself. This stage of development is historically "called Stoicism. Its principle is that consciousness is a being that *thinks*" (*denkendes Wesen*). We might compare this view with that of Descartes's "thinking thing" (*res cogitans*). At any rate, it evolves as a rejection of or

> negative attitude towards the lord-and-bondsman relationship. As lord, consciousness does not have its truth in the bondsman, nor as bondsman is its truth in the lord's will and in his service; on the contrary, whether on the throne or in chains, in the utter dependence of its individual existence, its aim is to be free, and to maintain that lifeless indifference which steadfastly withdraws from the bustle of existence, alike from being active as passive, into the simple essentiality of thought.

In using the phrase "on the throne or in chains," Hegel must be thinking of Marcus Aurelius, the Roman emperor, and Epictetus, a slave of the Romans, who were two of the most famous historical Stoics. In Stoicism self-consciousness becomes "*indifferent* to natural existence," preferring the freedom of its own thought. Yet Hegel points out that this is merely an empty, abstract freedom, devoid of any solid content, precisely because of being cut off from external reality. "Stoicism, therefore, was perplexed when it was asked for what was called a 'criterion of truth as such,' i.e. strictly speaking, for a *content* of thought itself." What are valued are truth and goodness, whose essence allegedly "shall consist in reasonableness." But, absent connections with the world, this remains an idle abstraction:

> The True and the Good, wisdom and virtue, the general terms beyond which Stoicism cannot get, are therefore in a general way no doubt uplifting, but since they cannot in fact produce any expansion of the content, they soon become tedious.

The irony is deliberately dramatic, in that Stoicism becomes alienated from its own ideas and ideals.[35]

THE STAGE OF SCEPTICISM.   With this alienation from its own essential values, self-consciousness has entered the realm of "Scepticism," in which it "annihilates the being of the world in all its manifold determinateness" and encounters itself "as a real negativity." Nothing seems immune to the corrosive acid of sceptical self-consciousness. "Dialectic as a negative movement" here blasts into oblivion all purported truth and value. It experiences itself as *"absolute dialectical unrest,"* oscillating in a "thoughtless rambling which passes back and forth" from one idea to its opposite, "both bewildered and bewildering." In a marvelous metaphor, Hegel compares its mental chatter to "the squabbling of self-willed children" who relentlessly go back and forth in vocal opposition to one another, frequently changing sides, and "by contradicting *themselves* buy for themselves the pleasure of continually contradicting *one another.*" There is a kind of freedom of thought here, but it is one of sheer negativity, in which self-consciousness is torn apart and alienated from itself, because it is stripped of any stable ideas and values.[36]

THE STAGE OF UNHAPPY CONSCIOUSNESS.   Hegel calls the result of this most profound stage of alienation "the *Unhappy Consciousness*" (*das unglückliche Bewusstsein*). We might think of the troubled young Augustine as an example of this alienation. "The *Unhappy Consciousness*" also relates to Sartre's notion of being what we are not and not being what

we are. "This *unhappy, inwardly disrupted* consciousness" has internalized the struggle for supremacy of lordship and bondage. "Here, then, we have a struggle against an enemy, to vanquish whom is really to suffer defeat." Since consciousness is at war with itself, agony is inescapable.[37]

Personality must mount this spiral ladder of increasingly profound alienation (from others, in the lord-and-bondsman relationship, then from external reality, in the stage of stoicism, then from its own ideas and ideals, in the stage of scepticism, and finally from itself, in the stage of the unhappy consciousness) in its quest for independence, so long as it mistakenly assumes a subject-object dichotomy between itself and external reality. In order to overcome this assumption, it must evolve from self-consciousness, which is merely individualistic, to reason, which is universal.

THE STAGE OF REASON.   Through the stages just examined self-consciousness "has been concerned only with its independence and freedom" in an **atomistic**, selfish manner reminiscent of the Hobbesian **state of nature**. Because it has not yet learned idealism's truth of the identity of the actual and the rational, self-consciousness never could "understand the world; it desired it and worked on it, withdrew from it into itself and abolished it as an existence on its own account, and its own self *qua* consciousness" in the stages we have just considered. But now, as we enter the level of reason, there is a massive reversal of outlook. "Reason is the certainty of consciousness that it is all reality; thus does idealism express its Notion," though it is initially only the subjective idealism (represented by Kant and Fichte) that is a preparation for the objective idealism of Spirit and Hegel's own absolute idealism. Reason "merely asserts that it is all reality, but does not itself comprehend this" truth as yet. This constitutes an immature, "one-sided, spurious idealism" that cannot dialectically grasp the truth of its own proclamation.[38] Reason remains individualistic, and its identification with reality remains abstract.

THE STAGE OF SPIRIT.   By contrast, Spirit sees itself as essentially social and in community with reality as a concrete universal.

> Reason is Spirit when its certainty of being all reality has been raised to truth, and it is conscious of itself as its own world, and of the world as itself.

As a result of socialization, the sense of otherness is fading, the self embracing "a world which has completely lost the meaning for the self of something alien to it, just as the self has completely lost the meaning of a being-for-self separated from the world." Spirit is the ultimate reality, "*actual* and *alive*," the dynamically developing matrix of all phenomenology: "Spirit is thus self-supporting, absolute, real being" (*Wesen*), or God. "All previous shapes of consciousness are abstract forms of it." It absorbs empirical consciousness, self-consciousness, and reason into itself. It is essentially social. "The *living ethical* world is Spirit in its *truth*," no longer isolated and alienated from its environment. Objectively, it comprises "the *realm of culture*," subjectively, "the *world of belief or faith*." The very idea of personality connotes legal status of members of society, related, as citizens, in "an equality, in which all count the same, i.e. as *persons*."[39]

THE CAPACITY FOR RIGHTS. This takes us to the discussion of his *Philosophy of Right*, where, from the perspective of abstract right (even prior to Morality and the socio-political Ethical Life), "the subject is a person," on the one hand, determined internally by "caprice, impulse, and desire, as well as by immediate external facts" and, on the other, self-known "as something infinite, universal, and free." This capacity for self-knowledge is crucial here as what realizes a subject's potentiality to be a person. "Personality essentially involves the capacity for rights," from this perspective, requiring mutual interpersonal respect. "Hence the imperative of right is: 'Be a person and respect others as persons.'" Persons, as such, have the right to own and transfer property through contractual agreement. As Kant did, Hegel draws a contrast between persons, free and holders of rights, and things, "not free, not personal, without rights." Persons can own and contract for things, which most obviously comprise physical objects, such as this watch and that house. Yet things are not limited to bodies.

> Mental aptitudes, erudition, artistic skill, even things ecclesiastical (like sermons, masses, prayers, consecration of votive objects), inventions, and so forth, become subjects of a contract, brought on to a parity, through being bought and sold, with things recognized as things.

A person's "right of appropriation" allows him properly to make things (in this broad sense) objects of his will. Hegel criticizes Plato for denying this natural right to private property—presumably to the Guardians in his *Republic* (or, less famously, in *Laws*, Book V, 739). The legal status of a person is so linked to ownership rights for Hegel that he writes that "property is the *embodiment* of personality." What is wrong with slavery, such as was defended by Aristotle, is that it treats a person as a thing, refusing to respect his right to self-determination. Human nature is essentially "distinguished from beast in virtue of thinking" and willing, though these are the theoretical and practical dimensions of mind and "surely not two faculties" separate from each other. "Will without freedom is an empty word," so that every person's right to self-determination as a practical agent must be respected. "An animal acts on instinct, is driven by an inner impulse and so it too is practical, but it has no will." To deny a person freedom of action is to treat him like a beast, which must be driven by "impulses, desires, inclinations." We share these with the beast, "but it has no will and must obey its impulse if nothing external deters it. Man, however, the wholly undetermined, stands above his impulses" with free will. Thus, freedom (of thought and of action) is inseparable from personality[40] (and will be discussed further in the section devoted to that topic).

MIND. Self-consciousness and mental activity are fundamental to Hegel's conception of personality. In *Philosophy of Mind* he invokes the Socratic **maxim** of the Delphic oracle, "*Know thyself*," as an "'absolute' commandment" by which we are bound to try to understand human nature. "The knowledge it commands means that of man's genuine reality—of what is essentially and ultimately true and real—of mind as the true and essential thing." We must understand that mind is essentially a dynamic, "absolutely restless being, pure activity, the negating or ideality of every fixed category of the abstractive intellect." Unlike material nature, all of whose processes are necessarily determined, mind is essentially free:

> The substance of mind is freedom, i.e. the absence of dependence on an Other, the relating of self to self.

Mind or Spirit (*Geist*) develops "in three stages"— first as "*Mind Subjective*," then as "*Mind Objective*," and finally as "*Mind Absolute*." Subjective mind is represented as soul, as consciousness, and as independent subject. Objective mind involves law, morality, and social relationships. Absolute mind (*der absolute Geist*) comprises art, religion, and philosophy and grasps the Absolute Spirit as "the one and universal *substance*" underlying all reality.[41] Mind is that aspect of personality, through which human knowledge is possible.

Knowledge

PHILOSOPHY AS A TRUE SCIENCE.   We have already adumbrated Hegel's **epistemology** in previous sections but now will directly tackle its presentation, especially in the *Phenomenology* and his works on logic. The preface to the former specifically deals with scientific cognition. Its second paragraph attacks the "conventional" black-and-white thinking that "gets fixated on the antithesis of truth and falsity" and bifurcates between its own simplistic **dogmatic** truths and all other views as erroneous. "It does not comprehend the diversity of philosophical systems as the progressive unfolding of truth, but rather sees in it simple disagreements." Hegel states his own goal of making philosophy a true science, advancing it from the mere "*love* of knowing" to "*actual* knowing." Knowledge must be of reality, which, as we have seen, is Absolute Spirit. Yet this must not be represented by the sort of "monotony and abstract universality" that Hegel derides as "the abyss of vacuity," in which the Absolute appears "as the night in which, as the saying goes, all cows are black." Like any true science, philosophy must become a "full body of articulated cognition" of reality as concretely (not abstractly) universal. Kant's philosophy had to settle for **phenomenal** knowledge of mere appearances, stopping short of knowledge of reality in itself, consigning the comprehensive grasping of metaphysical truth to the domain of belief. But, for Hegel, a mere series of slices of reality will never suffice to constitute genuine knowledge. "The True is the whole" (*Das Wahre ist das Ganze*). This is important, in that nothing short of the totality of reality can ever be any more than an abstraction or can ever be adequately known; completeness thus becomes the criterion of adequacy. "But the whole is nothing other than the essence consummating itself through its development."[42] The Absolute is not real and cannot be known apart from this dynamic self-realization.

But this philosophical science will require a new logic that transcends the rigid dichotomies of the Aristotelian logic of reflective understanding and recognizes that any "basic proposition" we may imagine, "if true, is also false" and can be refuted by "pointing out its defect" or inadequacy, insofar as it omits aspects of the True. The dialectical logic of reason will establish **coherent** and comprehensive knowledge by employing **negation** as a means of exposing the limitations of any "initially one-sided form" and then moving beyond them to a more inclusive, and hence more adequate, grasp of reality. It must overcome the static categories of the old logic. For example, although we conceptually distinguish between matter and mind, we should not be misled into the sort of dualism (as in Plato, Descartes, or Kant) that cannot recognize that they interpenetrate each other: all matter is the expression of Mind in space, and all human minds, as we encounter them, are incarnated in matter, so that we experience a dynamic unity of the two. Reality must be known (illogically, an Aristotelian might object) as both wildly restless and in peaceful tranquillity:

> The True is thus the Bacchanalian revel in which no member is not drunk; yet because each member collapses as soon as he drops out, the revel is just as much transparent and simple repose.

Elements or moments of reality cannot adequately stand alone, independent of their supporting context. To analyze reality into disjointed, **categorically** labeled bits and pieces, as does Kant, with his static categorical understanding, is to reduce it to "a skeleton with scraps of paper stuck all over it," devitalized and "stripped" of "all the flesh and blood" that are natural to it. "The excellent, however, . . . cannot escape the fate of being thus deprived of life and Spirit, of being flayed and then seeing its skin wrapped around a lifeless knowledge" so long as the "pigeon-holing process" of the understanding prevails. "A table of contents is all that it offers, the content itself it does not offer at all." Only dialectical reason can adequately reveal the truth of idealism, "that Being is Thought," and ultimately illuminate and comprehend "the identity of Thought and Being." Whereas the understanding's logic is merely negative and destructive, the dialectical logic of reason is positive and constructive. Because reality is dynamic, so logic must be; "the dialectical movement" of reason will replace the static, abstract syllogistic proofs of Aristotelian understanding.[43]

LIMITED CONCEPTIONS OF KNOWLEDGE. A second seminal passage for Hegel's epistemology is his introduction to the *Phenomenology*, which begins with a critique of the view of knowledge "either as the instrument to get hold of the Absolute, or as the medium through which one discovers it." An instrument for apprehending objects, such as a pair of tongs or forceps, must distort those objects to some extent in grabbing them; likewise, seeing objects through a medium, such as a lens or pane of glass, inevitably distorts their appearances. "Either way we employ a means which immediately brings about the opposite of its own end," assuming that is to apprehend objects as they independently are in themselves. Further, a model of "cognition as an *instrument* and as a *medium*" presupposes not only "a *difference between ourselves and this cognition*," but also a subject-object distinction between knower and known. Indeed, these "useless ideas and locutions about cognition" only generate "excuses" for not pursuing knowledge of the Absolute at all (as in Hume and Kant) and should be rejected. A system of merely "phenomenal knowledge" divorced from any cognition of reality in itself "seems not to be Science" at all, so much as a sceptical "pathway of *doubt*, or more precisely as the way of despair," epistemologically speaking. It seems preferable to encourage confidence in Spirit's competence to know the truth about reality and in the mind's capacity for dialectical progress through "*determinate* negation." This would be a fully adequate idealistic epistemology, whose goal is the realization that

> Notion corresponds to object and object to Notion. Hence, the progress towards this goal is also unhalting, and short of it no satisfaction is to be found at any of the stations on the way."[44]

Human consciousness obviously has limits. But through the use of dialectical reasoning it can allegedly transcend its own limits to achieve knowledge of reality. However, we need an "underlying *criterion*" to determine when and to what extent knowledge has been achieved. But this must come from consciousness itself, rather than from outside. The traditional **correspondence theory** and Kant's inverted model of it both purport to give us our epistemological criterion.

> If we designate *knowledge* as the Notion, but the essence or the True as what exists, or the *object*, then the examination consists in seeing whether the Notion corresponds to the object.

This is the traditional model, used, for instance, by Aquinas, viewing the object to be known as the independent variable and the ideas of the would-be knower as the dependent.

> But if we call the *essence* or in-itself of the *object* the *Notion*, and on the other hand understand by the *object* the Notion itself as *object*, viz. as it exists *for an other*, then the examination consists in seeing whether the object corresponds to its Notion.

Hegel's language in this sentence is awfully thick and obscure; but, for our purposes, we can illustrate his point by the model of Kant's "**Copernican revolution**," seeing the formal structures of the knowing mind as the independent variable to which the appearances of objects must correspond, if they are to become objects of knowledge. When Hegel dismisses these two correspondence models as essentially "the same," he is sensitive to their dichotomizing subject and object in such a way that we can never know that the criterion has been met, yielding knowledge of reality as it is in itself. So both versions of the correspondence theory seem bankrupt. What is needed is the new logic of reason, which alone can grasp the "*dialectical* movement" of reality, the path of which is "the Science of the *experience of consciousness*." This bridges the gap between the knowing mind and knowable reality, seeing them as dialectically interrelated aspects of "the entire realm of the truth of Spirit." In knowing reality, consciousness no longer encounters "something alien," but comes to know itself. "And finally, when consciousness itself grasps this its own essence, it will signify the nature of absolute knowledge itself."[45] This is the all-encompassing whole that is Spirit, and any partial knowledge that falls short of this totality is, to that extent, inadequate.

EMPIRICAL CONSCIOUSNESS. Hegel offers us yet another ingenious illustration of the dialectic at work in the three sections on empirical consciousness in the *Phenomenology*, dealing with sensation, perception, and understanding. The most primitive sort of awareness is "of the immediate or of what simply *is*" through sensing an object. "In *ap*prehending it, we must refrain from trying to *com*prehend it," however, if this is to remain so immediate. Nevertheless, such sense-certainty "proves itself to be the most abstract and poorest *truth*. All that it says about what it knows is just that it *is*; and its truth contains nothing but the sheer *being* of the thing." What can be "known" at such a primitive level is merely "a pure *this*" as individual but indeterminate being. Spatio-temporally, we can speak of it as "Here" and "Now." Yet what do we mean by "This," "Here," and "Now"? "This" is whatever is the object of sensation at any given moment; "here" is relative to the shifting location of the person sensing; and "now" is the ever vanishing moment of time between what has been (but is no more) and what will be (but is not yet). Sense-certainty was to be purely objective and particular; yet any attempt to characterize it is universal and focused around an unknown subject. The immediacy of sense-certainty turns out to be illusory, in that a subject-object complex proves to be essential to it, the subject is "a pure [act of] intuiting" with no determinate character, and the object is known only most abstractly as being.[46]

Second, in perception the object is no longer bare being but is revealed "to be *the thing with many properties*." The simple, indeterminate This of sense-certainty has now been "superseded" (*aufgehoben*). This verb "to supersede," also sometimes translated as "to **sublate**" (*aufheben*), is one for which we have no common English equivalent. It has various meanings which seem **inconsistent**, but all of which Hegel sometimes intends: it means to abolish or negate; it also means to preserve or maintain; and again, it means to lift up or elevate. These various meanings render it an ideal concept (in both verb form and noun form) to represent the Hegelian dialectic. At any rate, perception cancels the indeterminacy of the This, while maintaining the This as object of experience and raising it to a higher level. Hegel illustrates perception's grasping of a determinate thing in terms of particular properties:

> This salt is a simple Here, and at the same time manifold; it is white and *also* tart, *also* cubical in shape, of a specific gravity, etc. All these many properties are in a single simple "Here," in which, therefore, they interpenetrate.

Lest we miss the dialectical analysis, he observes that there are three "moments":

(a) an indifferent, passive universality, the *Also* of the many properties . . . ;

(b) negation, . . . or the *One*, which excludes opposite properties; and

(c) the many *properties* themselves, the relation of the first two moments,

whose antithesis is thus synthesized. The object of perception is one thing with many properties, "a *community*" (*Gemeinschaft*). There seems a contradiction in the reflection that the one grain of salt could have so many different characteristics, unless its multiplicity is introduced by the perceiver. "So in point of fact, the Thing is white only to *our eyes, also* tart to *our* tongue, *also* cubical to *our* touch, and so on. We get the entire diversity of these aspects, not from the Thing, but from ourselves." But this reintroduces the subject as an essential player in what was to have been objective experience. Yet if this is true perception, the many properties must really characterize the one Thing. The grain of salt

> itself is the *subsistence of the many diverse and independent properties*. Thus, we say of the Thing: *it is* white, *also* cubical, and *also* tart, and so on. But *in so far* as it is white, it is not cubical, and *in so far* as it is cubical and also white, it is not tart, and so on.

We thus become aware that reality itself contains opposing elements of truth coexisting as antithetical, that the apparently simple grain of salt is far from simple after all.[47]

In attempting to come to terms with such complexity, consciousness "enters the realm of the Understanding." This is the third level of empirical consciousness. Thus far, in its attempts at objectivity, it has failed to appreciate itself as bound up with its object. It can try to understand the relationship of its object's unity and diversity in terms of a scientific concept such as that of "*Force*." Here consciousness is making its own distinct contribution to the process, "the two sides" of which, "the percipient and what is perceived," are both united and distinct. But empirical consciousness operating at the level of scientific understanding leads to the dichotomy we have seen represented in Kant's philosophy between "a surface show" of "*appearance*" and its "*inner truth*" of "a *supersensible* world" allegedly transcending "the world of *appearance*." But that "inner world" remains bare

---

Sublation.   In dialectical (e.g., Hegelian) philosophy, the resolution of opposites, or antitheses, into a higher unity, or synthesis; Hegel's word for it, *Aufhebung*, simultaneously means cancellation, preservation, and elevation

and devoid of content, "a *pure beyond*, because consciousness does not yet find itself in it." If the supersensible realm is conceived as a cognitive "*void*" beyond the possible grasp of consciousness, it will be written off as "unknowable," though this is not necessarily, as the Kantians suppose, "because Reason is too short-sighted or is limited." The result is an unfortunate **phenomenalism** which posts "No Entry" signs at the periphery of "the world of appearance." Yet we now have the elusive phantom of an "inner world, or supersensible beyond," which, though unknowable, is allegedly the reality underlying the phenomenal realm. What good is it, and what serious explanatory work can it do for us? One Kantian response is that "the *supersensible* world is an inert *realm of laws* which, though beyond the perceived world," governs its actions. But it seems mysterious how we can provide a scientifically adequate explanation of anything based on that which is, in principle, beyond all possible experience and thus unknowable. An explanation of the world of appearances in terms of a "play of Forces" remains inadequate unless and until we transcend mere empirical consciousness and move through self-consciousness and reason to Spirit.[48]

ABSOLUTE KNOWLEDGE. The final section of the *Phenomenology*, on Absolute Knowing, represents the journey's end. Ultimately, all antitheses must be synthesized, all dichotomies must be overcome, and "consciousness must know the object as itself." Yet this knowledge must be dialectically achieved, the result of a phenomenological "process of coming-to-be," rather than merely some summary conclusion. In order to achieve complete knowledge,

> Spirit attains to a knowledge of itself not only as it is *in itself* or as possessing an absolute *content*, nor only as it is *for itself* as a form devoid of content, or as the aspect of self-consciousness, but as it is both *in essence and in actuality*, or *in and for itself*.

The synthesis of what Spirit is "in itself" (its essential spiritual content) and what it is "for itself" (pure form of intentional activity) will be what it is "in and for itself" (its completeness as self-knowing reality). The satisfaction of this achievement discloses the counterpart of the "unhappy consciousness" discussed above: "the 'beautiful soul' is its own knowledge of itself in its . . . *pure inwardness* as Spirit. It is not only

the intuition of the Divine but the Divine's intuition of itself."[49]

This divine reality, which Spirit recognizes itself to be, is a dynamic, cyclical process of becoming, which "presupposes its beginning and reaches it only at the end." Religion reveals the Absolute Spirit to which human spirit is essentially related "earlier in time" than philosophy does, but only the latter can express that truth adequately. In absolute knowledge "Spirit has concluded the movement" of its self-expression and development, "its own restless process of superseding itself, or *negativity*." Unlike phenomenology, in which each moment must be negated and transcended, absolute knowledge is transphenomenological and "unites the objective form of Truth and of the knowing Self" completely. What is known in absolute knowledge "is *the absolute Notion*," the True as a whole, Spirit as self-revealed. But the "path" to that knowledge is the one we are tracing, through the various forms or manifestations Spirit assumes in its self-expression and development in nature and history. Lest it remain "lifeless and alone," there must be a "Calvary of absolute Spirit," in which its radical otherness dies so that it may rise again, having fully actualized and achieved full realization of its "throne."[50]

THE NEW DIALECTICAL LOGIC. To get a better understanding of Hegel's dialectical logic, we should consider his *Science of Logic*; in its introduction, he criticizes traditional Aristotelian logic, which focuses on "the *bare form* of cognition" and "abstracts from all *Content*." First, this abstraction to "only the rules of thinking" with no regard for content is "most inept." Second, it presupposes a false dichotomy between "the *Content* of knowledge and the Form of knowledge (or *Truth* and *Certainty*)." Third, this assumes a separation "of Object and Thought," such that one might suppose that "the Object, as a thing-in-itself, simply remains a something beyond Thought," as in the Kantian epistemology. But these are interconnected prejudicial errors. Although we can conceptually distinguish between "*Things* and the *Thinking* of them," we should realize that they "are in harmony" with one another, "that thought in its immanent determinations, and the true nature of things, are one and the same content." As we have seen, this is the fundamental thesis of monistic idealism. "But *reflective* Understanding," using the old Aristotelian logic and insisting "that Truth rests upon sense-reality," thinks reason impotent to generate any factual knowledge at all. We might consider Hobbes, Hume, and Kant as examples of this, from Hegel's perspective.

> In this renunciation of Reason by itself, the concept of Truth is lost; it is restricted to the cognition of merely subjective Truth, of mere appearance, of something to which the nature of the thing itself does not correspond; *knowing* falls back into *opinion*.

Reflective understanding, on seeing contradictions in appearances, backs off in deference to the basic laws of Aristotelian logic. But what is needed is a higher logic that will recognize "that the contradiction is just the lifting of Reason above the limitations of Understanding, and the dissolution of these."[51]

The Kantian *"criticism of the Forms of Common Understanding"* denies these Forms any *"applicability to things in themselves."* But then they are worthless and may as well be forsaken. Hegel is attempting to move beyond the polarized dichotomies of the Kantian critique and to see logic as metaphysical, rather than as merely formal, so that the logical is really ontological. But without the "living concrete unity" of Spirit that is reality, logic remains abstract and "destitute of solid content and substantial filling." Hegel points out that he has already utilized the new dialectical logic in his *Phenomenology*, demonstrating that "pure Science" is a synthesis of thought and reality.

> Logic is consequently to be understood as the System of Pure Reason, as the Realm of Pure Thought. *This realm is the Truth as it is, without husk in and for itself. . . . God as he is in his eternal essence before the creation of Nature and of a Finite Spirit.*

He briefly traces some of the history of idealism from Anaxagoras through Plato to the "Critical Philosophy" of Kant and Fichte. He criticizes Kant's complacent acceptance of the old, traditional logic; granted that

> Logic has not taken any step backwards since Aristotle,—but also it has taken no step forwards.

The lack of progress or compelling results in more than two millennia is indicative of its bankruptcy and the fact "that Logic is all the more in need of a thorough overhaul." He claims that "the need of a transformation of Logic has long been felt" by thinkers and even that the old, traditional "Logic has become contemptible" because it is "so empty and lifeless,"

so "immovably rigid." It is not even surprising that logical thought has **reductionistically** "been identified with Reckoning, and Reckoning with this Thinking,"[52] as we have seen done by Hobbes.

So what is to be done?

> In order that these dead bones of Logic may be revivified by Mind, and endowed with content and coherence, its Method must be that by means of which alone Logic is capable of becoming a Pure Science.

Prior to Hegel, philosophy had yet to discover the power of dialectical logic to show

> that Negation is just as much Affirmation as Negation, or that what is self-contradictory resolves itself not into a nullity, into abstract Nothingness, but essentially only into the negation of its *particular* content,

which can and must be transcended by a more inclusive synthesis. This, then,

> is a new concept, but a higher, richer concept than that which preceded; for it has been enriched by the negation or opposite of that preceding concept, and thus contains it, but contains also more than it, and is the unity of it and its opposite.

This is a fine description of *"the Dialectic,"* which Hegel has discovered and utilized, although he concedes that it is still "capable of much improvement." The ancient use of dialectic, even in Plato's great dialogue the *Parmenides*, was merely for the negative purposes of refutation.

> Kant set Dialectic higher, and this part of his work is among the greatest of his merits,—for he freed Dialectic from the semblance of arbitrariness attributed to it in ordinary thought, and set it forth as *a necessary procedure of Reason*

itself. Nevertheless, it was still seen as playing the negative role of helping us to detect **transcendental** illusion. This leads to the unfortunate conclusion

> that Reason is incapable of cognition of the Infinite;—a strange result, for—since the Infinite is the Reasonable—it amounts to saying that Reason is incapable of cognizing that which is Reasonable.[53]

The true dialectic will find "the Positive in the Negative" and lead reason to "*Speculative knowledge*." This will take us beyond a merely abstract and formal conception of logic to one which will disclose "Universal Truth." It must be nonsensory, nonemotional, and nonconjectural, establishing reason's cognitive independence in its pursuit of "the Absolute Truth." In the process, the supposed dichotomy between knowing subject (mind) and object known (reality or truth) must "be overcome" or mediated.

This will take us beyond Kant, who nevertheless remains historically important for three reasons: first, his work "remains the basis and beginning of modern German philosophy"; second, his conclusions, "that reason can cognize no **valid** content, and with regard to absolute truth must be referred to faith," are still commonly accepted; and, third, they then provide "a pillow for intellectual sloth," which has an excuse not to try to know the allegedly unknowable. The new dialectical logic will also allegedly replace the older metaphysics (e.g., of Aquinas and Descartes), which has "earned the just reproach" (e.g., by Hume and Kant) of "uncritically" employing its basic concepts "such as Soul, World, God."[54] The dialectic will allegedly involve a more dynamic and coherent theory of reality.

THE DIALECTIC AS AN ACTIVITY OF REASON.   Let us also consider some of the treatment of knowledge in the *Logic* of Hegel's *Encyclopedia*. In its introduction he counters the allegedly Aristotelian slogan that nothing can be in the intellect that was not first in sense experience with a maxim of "speculative philosophy" to the effect that nothing could be in the senses that had not been in the intellect. This establishes his idealistic point of view in opposition to that of **empiricism**. He again criticizes the purportedly Kantian notion that knowledge is an "instrument" that should be critically examined before being used.

> But the examination of knowledge can only be carried out by an act of knowledge. To examine this so-called instrument is the same thing as to know it. But to seek to know before we know is as **absurd** as the wise resolution of Scholasticus, not to venture into the water until he had learned to swim.

Hegel is determined to avoid Kant's queasy anxieties about the oppositions of speculative reason: "To see that thought in its very nature is dialectical, and that, as understanding, it must fall into contradiction—the negative of itself—will form one of the main lessons of logic," which must be a systematic and comprehensive science of the Absolute. "Truth, then, is only possible as a universe or totality of thought." Later, Hegel points out that this view requires us to go beyond the "divorce between thought and thing" perpetrated by "the Critical Philosophy" of Kant at the expense of any possible metaphysical knowledge. "*Logic therefore coincides with Metaphysics, the science of things set and held in thoughts*—thoughts accredited able to express the essential reality of things." If truth is an all-encompassing whole, then its logical study will require "consistency" or coherence, rather than correspondence, as an ultimate criterion.[55]

Phenomenal experience, called for by the "Empiricism" of Hume and the "Critical Philosophy" of Kant, cannot be adequate as "the one sole foundation for cognitions." Nor should we assume, as Kant's "subjective idealism" does, that "the categories, such as unity, or **cause** and effect, are strictly the property of thought" in us "and not also characteristics of the objects" of thought. This rash assumption leads to the dangerous denial of reason's capacity to know reality in itself. It seems inconsistent that we can only know phenomenal appearances and yet make claims about how reality itself lies beyond the limits of that knowledge: "No one knows, or even feels, that anything is a limit or defect, until he is at the same time above and beyond it." Like Descartes (in the third of his *Meditations*), Hegel argues that grasping the finite presupposes an awareness of the infinite. When merely used negatively by the logic of the understanding, he comments, "Dialectic becomes Scepticism" in its denial of reality as intrinsically knowable. "But in its true and proper character, Dialectic is the very nature and essence of everything," seen as dynamically and necessarily interconnected with everything else. "Everything that surrounds us may be viewed as an instance of Dialectic," the overarching pattern encompassing all of reality. The sceptical understanding (*Verstand*) is only **analytically** aware of the negative dimension of Dialectic, while speculative reason (*Vernunft*) synthetically recognizes the positive unity of opposites.[56]

BEING AND BECOMING AS AN ILLUSTRATION.   Hegel provides a now-famous illustration. Let us consider the most abstract idea of all—"Pure Being" is "simple and indeterminate." But then it can be neither experienced nor imagined.

> Being, as Being, is nothing fixed or ultimate: it yields to dialectic and sinks into its opposite, which, also taken immediately, is Nothing.

Since everything that can be experienced must be determined in some way(s) or other, purely indeterminate Being is Nothing at all, or its very contradiction. The understanding, using Aristotelian logic, might panic at this point. How can Being be its opposite,

Nothing or non-Being, "the absolutely negative"? But they are not merely opposites. Rather, they are united in the process of "Becoming." In becoming an oak tree an acorn both is and ceases to be an acorn. Nor is this merely a philosophical joke or semantic trick. "Becoming is the unity of Being and Nothing" in things as well as in thought. It is a richer, more concrete idea than either of the antitheses it synthesizes. Yet a richer, more concrete idea than it is that of Life, as Mind is a higher idea than that of Life. Thus, dialectical reason helps us progress from indeterminate abstractions to increasingly determinate conceptions of reality. Hegel asks us to notice how, in thus rising dialectically, we exploit "the double meaning of the German word *aufheben* (to put by, or set aside). We mean by it (1) to clear away, or annul. . . ; (2) to keep, or preserve." In the first, negative sense, Becoming denies the abstractions of Being and Nothing; but in the second, positive sense, it maintains aspects of what they involved. This clearly takes us beyond the limitations of the Aristotelian "Laws of Thought." On this dialectical view, nothing is simply self-identical, and there is always a middle ground between opposites. "Contradiction is the very moving principle of the world,"[57] rather than a sign of erroneous thinking. We must beware of abdicating the quest for rational knowledge of reality. The mind is naturally oriented to knowledge as the will is to free action.

Freedom

HISTORICAL STAGES OF FREEDOM. Hegel's most renowned discussion of freedom is in the Introduction to his *Philosophy of History*. Indeed, one of the most memorable passages in all his writings traces the evolution of freedom in three great stages of world history.

> In the world of the ancient Orient, people do not yet know that the Spirit—the human as such—is free. Because they do not know this, they are not free. They know only that *one* person is free; but for this very reason such freedom is mere arbitrariness, savagery, stupefied passion.

We should notice Hegel's remarkable causal connection in this passage between freedom and knowledge. He continues,

> This *one* person is therefore only a despot, not a free man.

We might think of the emperors of ancient China, who held unmitigated sway but were rigidly bound by the responsibilities of ruling.

> It was among the Greeks that the consciousness of freedom first arose, and thanks to that consciousness they were free. But they, and the Romans as well, knew only that *some* persons are free, not the human as such.

The ones who were free were the citizens. "Even Plato and Aristotle," enlightened as they were, failed to achieve a sufficiently universal perspective to recognize that persons as such should be free; hence they accepted (and, in Aristotle's case, defended) the institution of slavery.

> It was first the Germanic peoples, through Christianity, who came to the awareness that *every* human is free by virtue of being human, and that the freedom of spirit comprises our most human nature.

For instance, we have seen this view strongly advocated in Kant's moral and social philosophy. The tracking of this evolution through three great stages leads Hegel to the thesis of this course of lectures:

> World history is the progress in the consciousness of freedom—a progress that we must come to know in its necessity.

To put this in the teleological language of Aristotle, "Spirit's consciousness of its freedom, and hence also the actualization of that very freedom," constitutes the *"final goal of the world,"* towards which we are heading willy-nilly. "It is this goal to which all the sacrifices have been brought upon the broad altar of the earth in the long flow of time." And, putting it in religious terms, it is also "God's will for the world." This progressively evolving human freedom must involve knowing, willing, and producing in accord with universal ideals "such as Right and Law"; and ultimately this must be achieved through the state. This gradual historical development is not as simple as it may sound, but it occurs dialectically. Each new determination of freedom is likely to encounter opposition; however, it "thereby gains in this negation (*Aufheben*) an affirmative, richer, and more concrete determination."[58]

FREE WILL. In his *Philosophy of Right* Hegel locates the origin of right in the will.

> The will is free, so that freedom is both the substance of right and its goal, while the system of right is the realm of freedom made actual.

The realization of mutual freedom establishes a context of right but is also promoted by that social matrix. As mind evolves from the level of mere feeling to that of pictorial thinking to that of conceptual thought, "will, as practical mind in general," also develops. It is a mistake to compartmentalize mind in such a way that its intellect and will are seen as two radically distinct faculties. It is also unfortunate to reduce freedom of the will to mere "negative freedom, or freedom as the Understanding conceives it," namely as just a Hobbesian absence of external restraints. Positively, freedom should be viewed as self-determination in realizing one's own potential. True "freedom of the will," in a positive sense, "is the *self-determination of the ego.*" Mere negative "freedom of the will is arbitrariness (*Willkür*)," a contingent freedom *from* rather than a self-sufficient freedom *for*.

> If we hear it said that the definition of freedom is ability to do what we please, such an idea can only be taken to reveal an utter immaturity of thought, for it contains not even an inkling of the absolutely free will, of right, of ethical life, and so forth.

Yet this is the lamentable common conception of human freedom. What is needed here is an ideal object freely willed rather than the merely abstract capacity to do as one pleases. "The definition of the concept of the will in abstraction from the Idea of the will is 'the free will which wills the free will'" without any concrete purpose. Yet the conceptual opposition between subjective freedom and its objective purposes must be dialectically superseded:

> The will's activity consists in annulling the contradiction between subjectivity and objectivity and giving its aims an objective instead of a subjective character, while at the same time remaining by itself in objectivity.

What commonly passes for freedom is too subjective and contingent to be worthwhile.

> The man in the street thinks he is free if it is open to him to act as he pleases but his very arbitrariness implies that he is not free. When I will what is rational, then I am acting not as a particular individual but in accordance with the concepts of ethics in general.[59]

Positive freedom must be social and in accordance with moral ideals.

In *Philosophy of Mind* Hegel develops this theory further: "True liberty, in the shape of moral life, consists in the will finding its purpose in a universal content, not in subjective or selfish interests." Happiness (*Die Glückseligkeit*) is abstract and individualistic,

whereas true freedom is concrete and universal. Whether happy or not, as autonomous, "the will is an *actually free will.*" The Free Mind (*Der freie Geist*) is a self-realizing, coherent "unity of theoretical and practical mind." Hegel writes, "Whole continents, Africa and the East, have never had this Idea, and are without it still. The Greeks and Romans, Plato and Aristotle, even the Stoics, did not have it." They rather viewed human freedom as contingent on circumstances of birth, such as citizenship, or "strength of character, education, or philosophy" (wisdom conferring it on even the stoical slave like Epictetus). "It was through Christianity that this Idea came into the world." Then for the first time, each person "*as such*" was recognized as of "infinite value as the object and aim of divine love, destined as mind to live in absolute relationship with God himself, and have God's mind dwelling in him: i.e. man is implicitly destined to supreme freedom." Hegel's triadic analysis of "free will" is in terms of, first, law or "*formal, abstract right*," second, "*morality* of the individual conscience," and, third, "the ethics of actual life in family, civil society, and State," each of these being a higher, richer, more adequate phase than its predecessor. At the level of law (*das Recht*), freedom involves the right to own, use, and contract for private property. At the level of moral conscience (*Moralität*), it involves the capacity to see, will, and do its duty. And at the level of social ethics (*die Sittlichkeit*), interpersonal relationships particularize "*ethical duties*" and "*virtue*"; these are the relationships of "the *Family*," of "*Civil Society*," and of "the *Political Constitution*" or the state,[60] which we shall consider in more depth in our section on "Society."

Morality

THE HEDONIST AND THE MORAL REFORMER. For Hegel morality tends to be so individualistic as to represent a lower level than social ethics, and he discusses the evolution from the former to the latter in his *Phenomenology*. (His discussion of "morality" represents another odd use of a familiar concept since he identifies it with abstract individualism, as opposed to social ethics.) At the level of morality, practical reason moves from a self-indulgent desire for **hedonistic** pleasure through a self-righteous desire for moral reform to a self-sacrificing desire for heroic virtue. The hedonist interprets morality in terms of the gratification of his own desires and "takes hold of life much as a ripe fruit is plucked, which readily offers itself to the hand that takes it." But the hedonist destroys the object of his desire in enjoying it. The failure of hedonism is that satisfaction is perpetually fleeting and transitory in abstraction from society; "an individual," detached from other persons in the pursuit of selfish pleasure, "is only a moment" to be superseded by higher value. This can be corrected by "*the frenzy of self-conceit*" of the moral crusader, who, unlike the selfish hedonist, exhibits "the earnestness of a high purpose which seeks its pleasure in displaying the *excellence* of its own nature, and in promoting the welfare of mankind." Yet the reformer ends up alienating himself morally from his own individuality by serving an abstract ideal. Like the "unhappy consciousness" of an earlier phase of development, the moral reformer finds himself in danger of being torn apart.

> The heart-throb for the welfare of humanity therefore passes into the ravings of an insane self-conceit, into the fury of consciousness to preserve itself from destruction.

It strangely cleaves to individuality by denouncing it altogether as "the principle of the perversion" underlying its own alienation and driving moral reason to embrace virtue in a spirit of self-sacrificing heroic commitment. But initially this will to virtue is mere potentiality. "The good or the universal, then, as it comes to view there, is what are called gifts, capacities, powers" (*Gaben, Fähigkeiten, Kräfte*), which can be used well or misused badly. It is "the knight of virtue's" fate that he must engage in "a sham-fight which he *cannot* take seriously—because he knows that his true strength lies in the fact that the good exists absolutely in its own right," independent of his trivial efforts.[61]

MORAL REASON AND INDIVIDUALITY. Moral virtue thus "is conquered by the 'way of the world'" because it is still too abstract and individualistic, despite the effort to effect "the sacrifice of individuality." To deny the individuality of consciousness is to wander through a never-never land of abstractions. The ideals of moral virtue "are empty, ineffectual words which lift up the heart but leave reason unsatisfied, which edify, but raise no edifice." Like Don Quixote, the heroic knight of virtue is shown to have been tilting

with windmills. Yet in the process of this revelation consciousness learns "that the 'way of the world' is not as bad as it looked" to the extent that it participates in "the reality of the universal. With this lesson in mind, the idea of bringing the good into existence by means of the sacrifice of individuality is abandoned." The "cunning" of Reason is such that individuality "is better than it thinks, for its action is at the same time an implicitly universal action." Like Julius Caesar, we act as individuals but unwittingly (and perhaps unwillingly) serve higher interests than our own. As a moral law-giver, Reason transcends that third level of heroic virtue to specify moral duties:

> "Everyone ought to speak the truth." In this duty as expressed unconditionally, the condition will at once be admitted: *if* he knows the truth. The commandment, then, will now run: everyone ought to speak the truth at all times, according to his knowledge and conviction.

An irony of moral reason that applies to Kantian ethics is that it strives to be categorical, yet it must regard circumstantial conditions to be practical. The rule prescribing truth-telling must presuppose knowledge of the truth (which is contingent) or remain purely formal. "Another celebrated commandment is: 'Love thy neighbour as thyself.'" This moral requirement of beneficence "aims at removing an evil from someone and being good to him." But again, this presupposes contingent knowledge of "what is bad for him" but removable "and what in general is good for him; i.e. I must love him *intelligently*. Unintelligent love will perhaps do him more harm than hatred" and be counterproductive. The problem is that such attempts at categorical imperatives either "stop short" at abstract formalities or must be qualified by contingent conditions rendering them less than truly categorical.[62] Thus far, in this section, we have been focusing on moral Reason.

ETHICAL SPIRIT AND THE COMMUNITY. Now let us move to the higher level of ethical Spirit, as discussed by the *Phenomenology*. The major difference here is the emerging significance of "the community" (*Gemeinwesen*) as a matrix of value. "As *actual substance*, it is a nation, as *actual consciousness*, it is the citizens of that nation" (*Volk*). The spirit of this community "can be called the human law," arising out of "the prevailing custom" (*Sitte*) of society and binding on its members. "Confronting this clearly manifest ethical power there is, however, another power, the Divine Law," with which conflict is possible. As Aristotle observed, the most basic "*natural* ethical community" is "the Family," whose members are bound together by ethical responsibility and not merely by sentimental feelings or love. Any of its members, "so far as he is not a citizen but belongs to the Family" as his only social unit, has a merely shadowy public reality. Hegel writes that "the essence of ethical life" is "duty," which ideally should be "without contradiction. Consequently, we are not faced with the sorry spectacle of a collision between passion and duty, nor with the comic spectacle of a collision between duty and duty." Ethical "character" is committed to its duty. But what if the duty enjoined by "the divine law" conflicts with that of "human law," as in the tragic case of Sophocles' Antigone? It may not be clear how the dilemma can be resolved. Although trying to do its duty, in every such dilemma "the moral consciousness sees only an *occasion* for acting, but does not see itself obtaining, through its action, the happiness of performance and the enjoyment of achievement." Yet it cannot entirely "forego happiness" either. Thus, it postulates a "harmony of morality and Nature" as "a demand of Reason"; second, it postulates **immortality**, its own existence "projected into a future infinitely remote"; and, third, it postulates God as "*another* consciousness," which renders the moral laws "sacred, or which knows and wills them as duties."[63]

Here we have Kantian postulates of practical reason, made necessary by the unfortunate disjunction of morality and happiness. Kantian morality is incomplete or "imperfect" in that—despite all the talk of autonomous self-legislation—its moral duties "have their truth only in another being and are made sacred—which they are *not* for the moral consciousness—by a holy lawgiver." But, worse yet, moral consciousness uses the postulated God merely as a supporting prop, allegedly without ever being "in earnest about the holiness of this other being." This is a sort of "dissemblance" (*Verstellung*) or "hypocrisy" on its part (which Hegel describes in a way that anticipates Sartre's analysis of **bad faith** more than a century later). Yet moral consciousness cannot abide its own duplicity; "and, in order to preserve the purity of its heart, it flees from contact with the actual world" into an idle "yearning" of good intentions, becoming "an unhappy, so-called 'beautiful soul'" (*schöne Seele*), as Goethe said, "and it vanishes like a shapeless vapour that dissolves into thin air." The problem is that the ideal of Kantian morality, "duty for duty's sake," is a mere phantom, and the moral consciousness must realize this at some level and thus judge itself harshly.

> No man is a hero to his valet; not, however, because the man is not a hero, but because the valet—is a valet.

Likewise, the well-intentioned "beautiful soul" may be morally heroic but cannot escape harsh judgment from "the *moral* valet" (*Kammerdiener der Moralität*) within itself. Such alienation can lead to dire results, Hegel thinks—"this 'beautiful soul', then, being conscious of this contradiction" between its ideals and its actual capacities, "is disordered to the point of madness, wastes itself in yearning and pines away in consumption,"[64] like the romantic poet Novalis. In order to overcome this alienation, Spirit must rise beyond abstract morality to the level of social ethics.

SOCIAL ETHICS. In his *Philosophy of Right* Hegel writes that "the truth about Right, Ethics," and so forth lies in the customary "morality of everyday life." He repudiates both Kantian and utilitarian moral formulas, saying,

> The maxim: "Ignore the consequences of actions" and the other: "Judge actions by their consequences and make these the criterion of right and good" are both alike maxims of the abstract Understanding.

Kantian ethics, in particular, comes under fire as "an empty formalism" reducible "to the preaching of duty for duty's sake," as we have seen. He attacks "the notorious maxim: 'The end justifies the means'" as either a "trivial and pointless" formula (if interpreted to mean that the means, as means, must be justified relative to their end) or reprehensible (if interpreted to mean that criminal means may be employed for the achieving of desirable ends). "Subjective opinion" (**subjectivism**), which is what morality in the abstract turns out to be, is denounced as an inadequate "measuring-rod of right and duty." A morality based

---

Bad faith. Self-deception, the attempts of consciousness to deny its own freedom and shirk responsibility (in Sartre)

on good intentions is dangerous; for "thereby ethics is reduced to the special theory of life held by the individual and to his private conviction." Subjective conviction without objective knowledge is too unreliable. What is needed is a transition from abstract morality (*Moralität*), which is individualistic, to concrete ethical life (*Sittlichkeit*), which is social and synthesizes freedom and actuality. "Thus ethical life is the concept of freedom developed into the existing world and the nature of self-consciousness." Hegel considers a Kantian conformity of a person's actions "with the duties of the station to which he belongs" to be mere "rectitude" (*Rechtschaffenheit*) or respectability and interprets virtue, as the ancient Greeks did, in a social context: "Virtue is the ethical order reflected in the individual character so far as that character is determined by its natural endowment." Like Aristotle, he identifies virtue with socially valuable habits:

> But when individuals are simply identified with the actual order, ethical life (*das Sittliche*) appears as their general mode of conduct, i.e. as custom (*Sitte*), while the habitual practice of ethical living appears as a second nature which, put in the place of the initial, purely natural will, is the soul of custom.

As a member of society, a person finds that his rights and his duties are correlative. As we have seen, the three most important social organizations of ethical life are "the *Family*," the association of persons, driven together by mutual need, called "*Civil Society*," and "*the State*" or a constitutional, unified political order.[65]

Society

A COLLECTIVIST VIEW OF SOCIETY. In the *Phenomenology* Hegel advocates a collectivistic theory of society that might nowadays be called communitarianism. He says it is only in the social context of "a free nation" that an individual "finds his essential character" (*Bestimmung*) and never in isolation. "The wisest men of **antiquity** have therefore declared that wisdom and virtue consist in living in accordance with the customs of one's nation." Even in this first great book of Hegel's there is an apparent deference to the *status quo*. He writes that society's "ethical order exists merely as something *given*" in "the customs and laws in their entirety" and laments the rebellion of individuals who presumptuously and self-righteously oppose

them. "The *community*, the superior law whose validity is openly apparent, has its real vitality in the government" (*Regierung*), as the matrix of human law. A more profound and eternal authority, however, underlies that: "The community therefore possesses the truth and the confirmation of its power in the essence of the Divine Law and in the realm of the nether world." This, in turn, governs "the three relationships" of the family, those "of husband and wife, parents and children, brothers and sisters." Of these, the first is fundamental, naturally leading to the second; but it is difficult to think of any other philosopher who has taken the third of these relationships as seriously as Hegel does (this might reflect his affection for his own sister, Christiane).[66]

In a section referring to the French Revolution and its aftermath Hegel blames the utilitarian cult of individualism and "the Useful" for the pursuit of "*absolute freedom*" (*absolute Freiheit*) and the subsequent reign of terror it spawned. The stable bonds of society are imperiled by "this absolute freedom" to the extent that "all social groups or classes which are the spiritual spheres into which the whole is articulated are abolished" in the name of abstract ideals of equality and public utility. Hegel is eloquent in characterizing the worthlessness of such ideals and the appalling bankruptcy to which they lead: "Universal freedom, therefore, can produce neither a positive work nor a deed; there is left for it only *negative* action; it is merely the *fury* of destruction." His historical reference here, no doubt, is to the French Terror of 1793. As Paul says that "the wages of sin is death" (*Romans* 6:23), Hegel contends that the natural consequence of absolute freedom is death of the sorriest sort: "It is thus the coldest and meanest of all deaths, with no more significance than cutting off a head of cabbage" (surely a reference to the guillotine, the French execution instrument of choice). The terror associated with the anarchy of absolute freedom, and especially "the fear of death," cows people into submission to social oppression that is like lordship and bondage at a more advanced level. Thus, according to Hegel, "the Utility of the Enlightenment" leads to the foolish pursuit of radical equality and absolute freedom, culminating in the disastrous "death that is without meaning, the sheer terror of the negative that contains nothing positive."[67]

A more accessible discussion of society is in the introduction to Hegel's *Philosophy of History*. Spirit, expressing itself in time and history, assumes the form of political organization.

> This essential being is itself the union of two wills: the subjective will and the rational will. This is an ethical totality, the *state*. It is the reality wherein the individual has and enjoys his freedom—but only insofar as he knows, believes, and wills the universal.

He is speaking here of the state insofar as it measures up to the rational ideal of political society, and not necessarily of the state as we empirically find it existing around us. Unlike Hobbes, he is not talking of negative freedom from the encroachments of others. "As against this negative concept of freedom, it is rather law, ethical life, the state (and they alone) that comprise the positive reality and satisfaction of freedom. The freedom which is limited in the state is that of caprice," merely selfish, negative freedom to do as one arbitrarily pleases. "The State is the externally existing, genuinely ethical life," rather than any set of merely individualistic groupings and pursuits. "We must understand, further, that all the value that human beings possess, all of their spiritual reality, they have through the State alone." Later, we shall see how diametrically opposed to this collectivistic view is the individualism of Mill. But Hegel carries this glorification even further, saying, "The State is the divine Idea, as it exists on earth." Since this is allegedly the matrix of true freedom, he adds,

> Only the will that is obedient to the law is free, for it obeys itself and, being self-sufficient, it is free. Insofar as . . . the subjective will of human beings submits to laws, the antithesis between freedom and necessity disappears. The rational is the necessary.

If this theory strikes us as peculiar, we should try to remember that Hegel is speaking of positive freedom to be all we should be and that his context is the state as rationally realized.[68]

He explicitly repudiates the "state of nature" and **social contract** theory of Hobbes, which maintains "that the human being is free by nature, but that in society and in the state . . . he must limit this natural freedom of his." He also attacks as "false and dangerous" the democratic "assumption that *only* the people possess reason and insight" into what is politically best. He presents the traditional trichotomy of "forms of government," classified as "**monarchy**, aristocracy, and **democracy**," asking which is best, but meaning by that the one "most effectively" equipped to fulfill "the intrinsic purpose of the state"—that is, to measure up to some preconceived ideal. He maintains that states are initially authoritarian, but evolve towards constitutional monarchy in which power is consolidated, on the one hand, but freedom is fostered, on the other. He critically considers the popular "prejudice" in favor of representative government, denouncing it as "malicious," as "a trick of bad will, suggesting that the people are the totality of the state after all. Underlying this idea, moreover, is the principle of individuality," of which he is a declared enemy. (We shall see Mill on the other side of this ideological line.) Hegel sees the state as "the basis and the center of the other concrete aspects of the life of a people—its art, its laws, its ethics, its religion, its science," to such an extent that he might be accused of sowing seeds of political totalitarianism. Far from accepting a Jeffersonian "separation of church and state," he holds that "the state rests upon religion." By this he does not mean anything as innocuous as that religions encourage citizens to be politically obedient; he rather means "that the state has its roots in religion, . . . that religion is prior, and that the state has arisen from it and continues to do so." He labels it "foolishness" to imagine that we can "invent and institute types of government without taking account of religion." No individual can transcend his own culture, including its religious dimensions. Indeed, he seems to advocate a sort of cultural **determinism** when he says,

> The form of the state as we know it can exist only in the context of a definite religion—just as only *this* philosophy and only *this* art can exist in *this* state.

This is what Enlightenment thought allegedly fails to recognize with its misguided emphasis on

> the isolation of individuals from one another, and from the community as a whole; the individual's destructive selfishness and vanity break in with the search for personal advantage and satisfaction at the expense of the whole.

(Because of its geographical separation from war-torn Europe, he says, "America is therefore the land of the future. In the time to come, the center of world-historical importance will be revealed there. . . . It is the land of longing for all those who are weary of the historic arsenal that is old Europe.") Hegel compares the progress of world history to the Sun, in that it "rises in the East," then "goes from East to West," and will finally "sink in the West." In the ancient Orient, the despotism of a single person recognized as free prevailed; then in "the Greek and Roman world" some were acknowledged as free, and democracy and aristocracy prevailed; most recently, in the cultures of Germanic Christianity, "*All* are free [as persons]," and constitutional monarchy prevails. In yet another metaphor, he compares Oriental society to "the childhood stage of history," Greek society "to the period of adolescence," Roman society to "history's manhood," and Germanic society to its mature "old age."[69] Still, through all these stages, it is society, rather than individuality, that maintains a primacy.

FAMILY, CIVIL SOCIETY, AND THE STATE.   But Hegel's definitive work on this topic is his *Philosophy of Right*. He warns us that philosophy, as practiced in his German culture, is not a private pursuit as it was among the ancient Greeks, but is done "in the service of the state." However alarming this may sound to us, it is not as subservient as we may imagine, referring mainly to the fact that German philosophers of his day were professors in state universities and, thus, civil servants. The role of philosophy is more that of speculative analysis based on past experience than that of prophecy of the future. This seems to be the meaning of his famous but cryptic remark,

> When philosophy paints its grey in grey, then has a shape of life grown old. By philosophy's grey in grey it cannot be rejuvenated but only understood. The owl of Minerva spreads its wings only with the falling of the dusk.

We can best understand a culture or social phenomenon philosophically after it has occurred and stood the test of time. Any state must maintain order and administer justice. It has a duty as well as a right to punish criminals; but, further, the criminal himself allegedly has a right, as "a rational being," to be dealt with justly through proper punishment. As a member of society, he owes his punishment to it. Nor is this the result of a social contract and the state's categorical need to protect individuals' life and property, as Hobbes might suppose. "On the contrary," the state "is that higher entity which even lays claim to this very life and property and demands its sacrifice" for the public good. As we have seen, the three great organizations of ethical life for Hegel are the family, civil society, and the state. Let us now consider aspects of his analysis of each.[70]

Members of a family should be united by love. The family's relationships comprise the marriage of husband and wife, their physical property and capital, the education of their children, and the eventual dissolution of the family unit. The marriage should be characterized by "love, trust, and common sharing"; it should be freely consented to, solemnly declared, and acknowledged by the community. Hegel sees the husband as the "powerful and active" partner, whose role is to maintain a good home. He admits that women "are capable of education," but not in areas that require universal reason, such as philosophy; and he maintains that the state is "in jeopardy" when women are in charge of the government. A prosperous family needs "possessions specifically determined as permanent and secure, i.e. it requires capital," jointly owned by the family as a whole but properly administered by the head of the family. The children of a family are "the embodiment" of the love of the parents; they "have the right to maintenance and education at the expense of the family's common capital." They must be disciplined in such a way that their "potential freedom" can be realized. Once they "have been educated to freedom of personality, and have come of age," they typically strike off on their own and establish their own family units. Finally, with "the death of the parents" a family is dissolved and its capital passed on through inheritance.[71]

Moving on to his analysis of civil society, Hegel discusses it as "a system of complete interdependence, wherein the livelihood, happiness, and legal status of one man is interwoven with the livelihood, happiness, and rights of all." The members of civil society are interdependently involved in a system of economic needs arising out of human nature itself. Man's physical needs must be met in order that his spiritual nature might be fulfilled; the abysmal alternative "would simply be the condition in which the mental is plunged in the natural and so would be one of savagery and unfreedom." Cooperative work and "the division of labour" allow members of civil society to meet their economic needs. The system of capital is such that, "by a dialectical advance," an individual's labor is beneficial for the community, so "that each man in earning, producing, and enjoying on his own account is *eo ipso* producing and earning for the enjoyment of everyone else." (This idea can be compared to Adam Smith's "invisible hand" theory.) Humans "are made unequal by nature," in their talents, abilities, industry, etc. In civil society, rather than being abolished, this extends "to an inequality of skill and resources, and even to one of moral and intellectual attainment." Hegel condemns the "demand for equality" in civil society as "a folly of the Understanding," blindly committed to realizing its abstract ideals. The economic system, rather, seems to need "class-divisions." The "business class," in particular, represents essential skills of "craftsmanship," of "manufacture," and of "trade" in industrial society. In addition to meeting economic needs, civil society must also administer justice. "It takes over the pursuit and the avenging of crime"; through "the annulment of the crime" by retributive punishment, "the law is restored and its authority is thereby actualized," while the criminal himself is reconciled to justice. Third, civil society must exercise public authority in caring for the poor, providing opportunities for work, and maintaining a decent "standard of living" for all.[72]

The third organization of ethical life (after the family and civil society) is the state, which Hegel grandly describes as "the actuality of the ethical Idea." Again, we should remember that he is speaking of the state insofar as it is rational. As such, he says, "this final end has supreme right against the individual, whose supreme duty is to be a member of the state." The rationality of a state involves its "unity of objective freedom (i.e. freedom of the universal or substantial will) and subjective freedom (i.e. freedom of everyone in his knowing and in his volition of particular ends)." The state, "as a self-dependent organism," involves "*Constitutional Law*"; in its relations with other states, it is subject to "*International Law*"; and, as an expression of absolute Spirit in time, it is part of "the process of *World-History*." We shall consider each of these three dimensions to some extent. "The constitution is rational in so far as the state inwardly differentiates and determines its activity in accordance with the nature of the concept." This is fairly obscure, but Hegel seems to be calling for "a division of powers within the state" into the crown, the executive, and the legislature, which are nevertheless

collaborating in ruling the state. The best form this unity can take is that of "constitutional monarchy." The ancient trichotomy of government by one (monarchy), by some (aristocracy), and by the many (democracy) can be realized in different state powers in a constitutional monarchy: "The monarch is a *single* person; the *few* come on the scene with the executive, and the *many* en masse with the legislative." The state should be considered "an organism" rather than merely "an aggregate" (as it is by individualists like Mill). "The right to pardon criminals" is found only in "the sovereignty of the monarch." The executive requires an organized division of labor in which people "forgo the selfish and capricious satisfaction of their subjective ends" for the public good. It will comprise civil servants who should be from "the middle class, the class in which the consciousness of right and the developed intelligence of the mass of the people is found," and who will be institutionally checked from assuming aristocratic control. "The legislature is concerned (a) with the laws as such in so far as they require fresh and extended determination; and (b) with the content of home affairs affecting the entire state." Whereas the legislature passes the laws, the monarch has ultimate decision-making authority, and the executive is its principal advisory body. Hegel is ambivalent regarding the expression of the people's wishes: "Public opinion therefore deserves to be as much respected as despised"—respected as an expression of "genuine needs" but despised as merely opinion rather than informed knowledge. "Thus to be independent of public opinion is the first formal condition of achieving anything great or rational" in government. "Freedom of public communication," which includes freedom of both "the press and the spoken word," should be protected by law, but its excesses should be punished; it should never be interpreted as a license "to say and write whatever we please." Such license is dangerous and should be regulated by law; for example, Hegel writes that "traducing the honour of anyone, slander, abuse, the contemptuous caricature of government, its ministers, officials, and in particular the person of the monarch, defiance of the laws, incitement to rebellion, &c., &c., are all crimes" in a well-ordered state. Hegel is far more accepting of warfare than Kant was. He writes, "War is not to be regarded as an absolute evil"; as a becalmed sea becomes foul unless occasionally stirred by blowing winds, "so also corruption in nations would be the product of prolonged, let alone 'perpetual', peace," such as Kant advocated. War can promote the virtue of courage (as even the pacifist William James will have to acknowledge in his call for alternatives).[73]

INTERNATIONAL RELATIONS.   Moving from constitutional law to a discussion of international law, Hegel avers "that every state is sovereign and autonomous against its neighbours" and should be related to them in mutual recognition. States will have their disagreements and try to resolve them peacefully; but sometimes, when such efforts fail, issues "can only be settled by war." The development of states and their relationships with other states occurs as part of the process of world history, which Hegel regards as the final "court of judgement." Its outcome, he assures us, will accord with reason and not be "the verdict of mere might." World history operates at a higher level than our moral ideals, "talents and their achievements, passions strong and weak," and impressions of the "fortune and misfortune of states and individuals." In any given era a particular nation which best represents that phase of the self-expression of the absolute Idea tends to be "dominant in world history" at that particular time and legitimately to hold sway internationally.

> In contrast with this its absolute right of being the vehicle of this present stage in the world mind's development, the minds of the other nations are without rights, and they, along with those whose hour has struck already, count no longer in world history.

Every such "world-historical nation" will undergo a process of rising influence followed by gradual decline, after which it will be eclipsed. Meanwhile, ordinary individuals function merely as "the living instruments" for effecting its actions. "For the deeds of the world mind, therefore, they receive no honour or thanks either from their contemporaries or from public opinion in later ages." More "civilized nations" consider less developed peoples "barbarians" and treat them accordingly. "The civilized nation is conscious that the rights of barbarians are unequal to its own and treats their autonomy as only a formality." We have already discussed "(1) the Oriental, (2) the Greek, (3) the Roman, (4) the Germanic" civilizations as progressively developing "world-historical realms," and they are analyzed again here.[74]

* * *

In the "Additions" (*Zuzätze*) drawn from his lecture notes Hegel makes a couple of astonishing statements. First, he says, "The march of God in the world, that is what the state is" (*Es ist der Gang Gottes in der Welt, dass der Staat ist*). Again, we must bear in mind that he is talking about the state insofar as it measures up to a rational ideal, rather than any particular existing state. Second, he says, "Man must therefore venerate the state as a secular deity."[75] This claim too is dangerously open to misinterpretations fostering a fascist deification of some actually existing political order.

Religion

KANTIAN CRITIQUES OF POSITIVE RELIGION.   Much of Hegel's early (i.e., pre-*Phenomenology*) work deals with religion and is intrinsically rather interesting, as well as revealing of the development of his thought. His "Tübingen Essay" of 1793 distinguishes between "objective religion," which emphasizes understanding, **argumentation**, and thought, and "subjective religion," which "expresses itself only in feelings and action," considering the latter the essential dimension. Hegel maintains that religious rituals and other "forms of worship do no real honor to God—that right conduct is the form of service most pleasing to him" (which sounds rather Kantian), ridiculing the idea that we "can curry God's favor by some means other than a will that is in itself good." He defends folk religion as natural and compatible with human freedom; by contrast, Christianity is depicted as alienating us from the natural to orient us towards the supernatural.[76]

Then in his "Berne Fragments" of 1793–94 Hegel writes, "Supposedly the chief design and accomplishment of the Christian religion is to better man morally and make him more pleasing to God." But onto this core has grown a horrible complex of counterproductive phenomena, which has "burgeoned into the most shocking profusion of repressive institutions and ways of deluding mankind: oral confession, excommunication, penances, and a whole array of disgraceful monuments to human self-abasement." What reason finds valuable in religion is "the great principle that duty and virtue are self-sufficient"; but this becomes sullied when anything more "than the merest association with the idea of God" is invoked. Consider how Kantian the following sentence sounds:

> Religion's proper task is to strengthen, by means of the idea of God as moral lawgiver, what impels us to act ethically and to enhance the satisfaction we derive from performing what our practical reason demands, specifically with regard to the ultimate end that reason posits: the highest good.

By this notion of "the highest good," he means precisely what Kant did, "namely morality and a form of happiness commensurate with it." Meanwhile, belief in "the historical person of Christ" is a matter of empirical testimony rather than "any requirement of practical reason." He comments sarcastically that taking such matters on faith "is far easier than cultivating the habit of thinking for ourselves" and describes belief in Jesus as "faith in a personified ideal."[77] This is typical of Enlightenment thought, against which Hegel had yet to rebel.

"The Life of Jesus" of 1795 portrays Jesus as advocating a Kantian morality, preaching, "if you cannot love your enemies, at least respect the humanity in them." He urges us to devote our entire lives to moral duty and virtue and not to try to "curry favor with God" through prayers, rituals, and "a lot of words." The kingdom of God is characterized as a Kantian realm of ends, "a kingdom in which all rational beings will make nothing but the law their rule of conduct." Instead of espousing the Golden Rule, Hegel's Jesus employs a version of the categorical imperative:

> "To act on principles that you can will to become universal laws among men, laws no less binding on you than on them"—this is the fundamental law of morality.

Far from being a miracle-worker himself, he repudiates "miracle-makers," rather performing an occasional "act of kindness" toward others. He advocates autonomous self-governance as required by human dignity, rather than the authority of "ecclesiastical statutes," which violates it. He only asks his disciples to heed the rational voice of conscience: "This inner law is a law of freedom to which a person submits **voluntarily**, as though he had imposed it on himself." Only those who sacrifice everything for the sake of moral duty are held to be worthy of the kingdom of God. He says to his disciples, "'What I leave you is the commandment to love one another and the

example of my love for you. Only through this mutual love are you to distinguish yourselves as my friends.'" The strikingly **humanistic** story tellingly ends with the burial of Jesus in the tomb and contains no reference to any **resurrection**.[78]

The Positivity of the Christian Religion, also written in 1795, has a rather negative tone to it. In its very first section Hegel writes

> that the aim and essence of all true religion, our religion included, is human morality, and that all the more detailed doctrines of Christianity . . . have their worth and their sanctity appraised according to their close or distant connection with that aim.

He praises Jesus for advocating a religion of morality that would fulfill, rather than frustrate, human freedom. By contrast with such "a purely moral religion," Hegel launches a withering assault on "positive religion, i.e., a religion which is grounded in authority and puts man's worth not at all, or at least not wholly, in morals." Christianity has unfortunately become a positive religion in this sense of emphasizing ritualistic practices and submission to authority rather than autonomy and rational duty. Positivity inevitably strays from "the essence of any true religion, the Christian religion included," which is "the establishment of human duties and their underlying motives in their purity and the use of the idea of God to show the possibility of the *summum bonum*." Whereas true religion considers adherents of all other sects fraternally as fellow friends of virtue, positive religion is jealous of its own authority and arrogantly pities or loathes followers of other sects. Anticipating the developments of his mature philosophy, Hegel claims that religion

> becomes glaringly positive if human nature is absolutely severed from the divine, if no mediation between the two is conceded except in one isolated individual, if all man's consciousness of the good and the divine is degraded to the dull and killing belief in a superior Being altogether alien to man.

He warns that a careful discussion of this issue is impossible without "a metaphysical treatment of the relation between the finite and the infinite."[79]

HEGEL VS. KANT. In *The Spirit of Christianity and Its Fate*, written in 1798, Hegel is withdrawing his allegiance to Kantianism and becoming more sympathetic to his own religious tradition. He defends the moral mission of Jesus against both the alternative of the

Mosaic Law and that of Kantian ethics, especially in the expression of that mission "in the Sermon on the Mount." He criticizes Kant for allegedly misinterpreting Christ's injunction, "Love God above everything and thy neighbor as thyself," as a duty to love, saying that "in love all thought of duty vanishes." He attacks the Kantian dichotomy between inclination and law, maintaining that "love" unites them "as the relation of differents to one another." Hegel holds that the moral message of Jesus signals an "extinction of law and duty in love," such as Kantian ethics forbids. "The son of God is also son of man; the divine in a particular shape appears as a man. The connection of infinite and finite is of course a 'holy mystery,'" from the perspective of the sort of "reflective thinking" Kant uses, with its traditional categories of Aristotelian logic. We can only rise above the limitations of "reflective thinking" if we are infinite too. "Faith in the divine is only possible if in the believer himself there is a divine element which rediscovers itself, its own nature, in that on which it believes, even if it be unconscious that what it has found *is* its own nature." True faith in the infinite requires that man be infinite. "Hence faith in the divine grows out of the divinity of the believer's own nature; only a modification of the Godhead can know the Godhead." As if fearing that this sounds too heterodox to be taken seriously, Hegel adds, "All thought of difference in essence between Jesus and those in whom faith in him has become life, in whom the divine is present, must be eliminated."[80] This will be a goal of his more mature philosophy of religion.

But let us first briefly consider one last early work, his *Faith and Knowledge* of 1802. In its introduction, Hegel attacks the Kantian denial of God as a possible object of knowledge and relegation of God to an idea of rational faith:

> Reason, having in this way become mere intellect, acknowledges its own nothingness by placing that which is better than it in a *faith outside and above* itself, as a *beyond* [to be believed in].

On this view, the height of philosophical truth is purportedly that nothing can be known of God.

> Thus what used to be regarded as the death of philosophy, that Reason should renounce its existence in the Absolute, excluding itself totally from it and relating itself to it only negatively, became now the zenith of philosophy. By coming to consciousness of its own nothingness, the Enlightenment turns this nothingness into a system.

Hegel labels this inadequate system "an idealism of the finite" because it artificially and arbitrarily restricts the role of reason within the bounds of sensible intuition. "In this situation philosophy cannot aim at the cognition of God, but only at what is called the cognition of man." However, as we have seen, Hegel's philosophy is designed to show that the latter dialectically leads to the former. On the faulty assumption that the idea of God is devoid of any cognitive content, Hegel says, "Kant is quite correct in making this empty unity a merely **regulative** and not a **constitutive** principle," since it could only constitute knowledge if it contained a content to be known. But this regulative idea of "the practical faith of the Kantian philosophy," properly understood, shows "that infinite thought is at the same time absolute reality" or establishes, as Hegel likes to say, "the absolute identity of thought and being," which was the point of "the ontological proof" which Kant is famous for supposedly dismantling. At the end of his conclusion Hegel describes this tragic abdication as philosophy's "speculative Good Friday" in which reason dies "in the . . . harshness of its Godforsakenness." Yet his final sentence anticipates "its resurrection" in the all-encompassing absoluteness.[81]

ENLIGHTENMENT THOUGHT ON RELIGION. In his *Phenomenology*, Hegel attacks the Enlightenment's view of religion as merely "a creation of consciousness itself." Enlightenment thought fails to do justice to the reality of the Absolute Spirit, by attacking the *object* of belief as **anthropomorphic** (as Hume did). Second, it challenges the *basis* of religious faith as without adequate evidence (again Hume comes to mind). Third, Enlightenment thought criticizes the *manner* of religious belief, its sacrifices and ritualistic practices, which it considers "foolish." But, in so doing, it implicitly reduces the goals of human action to finite purposes and relegates ideals to the arena of "pure intention." Beyond these problems with this critique of the object, basis, and manner of religion, however, the negative "truth" of the Enlightenment is that "absolute Being" has no cognitive content. Beyond this alleged "truth," Enlightenment thought offers mere utility, the perspective that "everything is *useful*" to the extent that it is at all worthwhile. It optimistically regards man as good, holding that "*everything* exists for his pleasure and delight." As things are judged with reference to their utility to man, so is man judged in terms of his utility to others. "The extent to which he looks after his own interests must also be matched by the extent to which he serves others, and so far as he serves others, so far is he taking care of himself: one hand washes the other." From Hegel's perspective this characterization would apply to the thought of Adam Smith before him as well as to that of John Stuart Mill after him. And what of religion in connection with this alleged Enlightenment view? It gets ground through the same mill. "The *relation* to absolute Being, or religion, is therefore of all useful things the supremely useful; for it is pure utility itself" to be allied with God. Religious faith rightly regards this self-serving attitude as "an abomination" and "utterly detestable." Enlightenment thought wrongs religious faith by setting up a straw man caricature of it in order easily and ceremoniously to tear it apart.[82]

NATURAL, AESTHETIC, AND REVEALED RELIGION. Subsequently, having covered "*consciousness, self-consciousness, Reason*, and *Spirit*" as the four main "moments" in the evolution of mind, Hegel writes that religion "presupposes that these have run their full course" and is their sum-total and truth, as dialectically advanced. Religion preserves and elevates what was of ultimate value in those earlier stages, canceling out what was flawed and inadequate. Hegel's triadic analysis will focus on natural religion, then on aesthetic religion, and finally on revealed religion. Natural religion, which Hegel conceives as primarily Oriental (meaning Asian and Egyptian), pursues an objective view of God as Substance. He will consider various forms of it which are "different aspects of a *single* religion." The first form is the Persian religion of Zoroastrianism, which views "*God as Light*," related to human consciousness as "*lord and master*" and having eternal "*darkness*" as its supernatural counterpart. The second form is that of animistic religions, primarily of India, that regard plants and animals as embodiments of spirits to be worshipped. The third form of natural religion is the Egyptian veneration of the "*artificer*" (*der Werkmeister*), which produces "pyramids and obelisks," the sphinx, the "ambiguous being which is a riddle to itself," and cryptic, puzzling language. The end result of this evolution of forms of natural religion is the insight that "Spirit is *Artist*" (*Der Geist ist Künstler*).[83]

This insight takes us into the second stage of aesthetic religion, which, for Hegel, is paradigmatically Greek. Like natural religion, it assumes three progressively advanced forms; but they regard the object as Subject rather than merely as "universal substance." The first of its forms is the "*abstract work of art*," such as appears in religious sculpture, hymns, oracles, cults, sacrifices, and temple architecture. The second form of aesthetic religion is the "*living work of art*," such as appears in "the enthusiasm" of ecstatic dances and "the festival." Its third form is the "*spiritual work of art*," in which the deities of folk religion "unite in a single pantheon"; here we see the development of religious literature, such as "the Epic" (e.g., Homer), "Tragedy" (e.g., Sophocles), and "Comedy" (e.g., Aristophanes), in Greece.[84] (It is indicative of Hegel's infatuation with Greek culture that he views its religion as superior to all the Oriental ones and inferior only to ethical monotheism, as well as that he devotes more than three times as much space to it as to the Oriental ones.)

But higher than either natural or aesthetic religion is the revealed religion of monotheism, particularly Christianity. Here the object of reverence is neither merely "*Substance*" nor merely "*Subject*" but is the synthesis of the two, infinite "Spirit." Comedy could ridicule the gods, while tragedy lamented the idea that (in the words of a Lutheran hymn) "God is dead." But with the evolution of human nature, the old symbols lose their currency: "Trust in the eternal laws of the gods has vanished, and the Oracles . . . are dumb. The statues are now only stones," and the hymns idle sing-song shouts (in much of this Hegel anticipates the atheistic Nietzsche). "The tables of the gods provide no spiritual food and drink, and in his games and festivals man no longer recovers the joyful consciousness of his unity with the divine." With Christianity the idea of divine incarnation offers a higher perspective on the relation of the finite and the infinite; the God-man is Spirit made flesh in "that it has an *actual* mother but an *implicit* father" (*dass er eine wirklich Mutter, aber einen ansichseienden Vater hat*), its mother representative of human self-consciousness and its father of divine Substance. Here emerges the idea "that Spirit is *immediately present* . . . as an *actual man*, that the believer . . . *sees, feels*, and *hears* this divinity" in the person of Jesus. "This incarnation of the divine Being . . . is the simple content of the absolute religion" of Christianity. "In this religion the divine Being is known as Spirit," because it is "*revealed*" as such. Absolute Spirit, a synthesis of Substance and Subject, turns out not to be alien to us, after all. "The divine nature is the same as the human, and it is this unity that is beheld" (*angeschaut*). It is in the "absolute religion" of Christianity, then, that "God is *revealed as He is*; He is immediately present as He is *in Himself*, i.e. He is immediately *present* as Spirit." The universal "joy" of this revelation, communicated through the good news of the gospels, "enters self-consciousness and seizes the whole world." Religious communities are informed with its Spirit and communicate their beliefs in the "*form of picture-thinking*" or symbolic expression, as, for instance, in the myths of creation, a fall from grace, and an act of atonement. But what still must be achieved, even in the "absolute religion," is the transcendence of such **dualistic** symbolic picture-thinking by the more adequate monistic conceptual thought of philosophy.[85]

OUR KNOWLEDGE OF GOD. Let us next consider portions of each of the three volumes of Hegel's *Encyclopedia*. In its *Logic* he writes that "a reason-derived knowledge of God is the highest problem of philosophy." As we have seen, he is critical of the Kantian philosophy for confining all knowledge to the sense-based understanding; it is guilty of giving up on cognition of the highest reality, unlike the great **medieval** thinkers, such as Augustine and Aquinas, for whom true theology was "at the same time a real philosophy of religion" and not merely systematic doctrinal beliefs derived from authority. The sort of demonstration of God's existence that reflective understanding uses (as in Aquinas and Descartes) must rest on presuppositions, "which will then constitute the ground of his being." But if God is the source of all other reality, this lands us in the thickets of **circular reasoning**. This "has in modern times led some to say that God's existence is not capable of proof," strictly speaking—e.g., Hume and Kant. But the demonstrations of reason proceed to show how their epistemological starting points are ontologically derived from God. Thus, "what men call the proofs of God's existence are, rightly understood, ways of describing and analysing the native course of the mind, the course of *thought*" as it rises "beyond the world of sense, its passage from the finite to the infinite, the

leap into the supersensible which it takes when it snaps asunder the chain of sense" that would restrict the movements of reason. As acts of the understanding, anchored in the phenomenal world, theological proofs do fail; but as works of reason, effecting an "upward spring of the mind" towards ultimate reality, they bring about a "process of exaltation" transcending mere appearances.[86]

It is a mistake to conceive of God, as the reflective understanding does, as "*a* Being, even the highest," separate from other beings; God is rather "*the* Being," apart from which nothing has any reality at all—and only reason can grasp this truth. Hegel's God is not only the absolute Substance, but an "absolute Person." He rejects the impersonal, uninvolved God of **deism** (e.g., of Hume) as "merely the mode in which the understanding thinks God: whereas Christianity . . . contains the rational notion of God" as personal and involved. The God of Christianity cares for the ultimate welfare of all personal creatures, which hinges on their feeling of oneness with the Infinite. The key to "salvation and the blessedness of men" is "laying aside our immediate subjectivity . . . and learning to know God as our true and essential self."[87] But this is beyond the capacity of the dualistic understanding, and it can only be accomplished by reason.

In the second part of the *Encyclopedia*, his *Philosophy of Nature*, Hegel writes that God is "that Being in whom Spirit and Nature are united." This seems an unorthodox statement of the relationship between God and the natural world that appears to compromise divine transcendence; but it is of a piece with Hegelian monism, as we have discussed it.

> God reveals Himself in two different ways: as Nature and as Spirit. Both manifestations are temples of God which He fills, and in which He is present.

The purely transcendent deity of orthodox monotheism is merely a detached abstraction. In a veiled reference to the doctrine of the Trinity, Hegel indicates that that is one perspective on God, which is inadequate apart from others:

> God, as an abstraction, is not the true God, but only as the living process of positing His Other, the world, which, comprehended in its divine form is His Son; and it is only in unity with His Other, in Spirit, that God is Subject.[88]

It is the idea that the world has a "divine form" and is "in unity" with God that pushes Hegel into the controversial position of panentheism—the monistic view that all things, insofar as they are real, are in God and, to that extent, divine. A panentheist would adopt a more literal interpretation of the scriptural passage that says in God "we live, and move, and have our being" (*Acts* 17:28) than would an orthodox Christian. Hegel rhetorically asks, "If God is all-sufficient and lacks nothing, why does He disclose Himself in a sheer Other of Himself?" The implication is that God is not self-sufficient apart from the world, that the nature of the "divine Idea" requires it "to disclose itself, to posit this Other outside itself and to take it back again into itself, in order to be subjectivity and Spirit."[89]

In his *Philosophy of Mind*, the third part of the *Encyclopedia*, Hegel writes that "*religious* consciousness . . . pierces through the seemingly absolute independence of things to the one, infinite power of God operative in them and holding all together." He holds that "Christian theology," employing the "picture-thinking" language of the Trinity, conceives of God as involved in "the process . . . of positing its Other" and then "positively overcoming" the otherness in love. He avers that "the spirituality of God is the lesson of Christianity," expressed in the "picture-thinking" language of religion. The "ultimate purpose" of philosophy is to grasp this truth conceptually: "*The Absolute is Mind* (Spirit)—this is the supreme definition of the Absolute." From the perspective of monistic idealism, it is the dynamic nature of Absolute Spirit that it expresses itself as "Nature and finite mind, so that this Other loses all semblance of independence." Oriental and Jewish religions (as well as that of the Enlightenment) view God as "abstract" and merely transcendent; the Greeks represent the gods as determinate individuals dynamically involved with our world; and in Christianity "the immanently differentiated *one* nature of God, the totality of the divine mind in the form of unity, has first been manifested."[90] This is the proper subject matter of philosophy in its quest for absolute knowledge.

The final section of the *Encyclopedia*, on "Absolute Mind," deals with this in some detail. It maintains that "belief or faith is not opposite to . . . knowledge" but is rather "only a particular form of the latter." The goal of "Philosophy of Religion," he writes, is "to discover the logical necessity" in the Absolute's process of self-determination and self-expression. Even beautiful art, in its own limited way, strives to grasp this truth. The

"revealed religion" (*die geoffenbarte Religion*) of Christianity implies a duty to pursue "speculative comprehension" of the very sort that Enlightenment thinkers such as Hume and Kant considered impossible. What we must come to understand is the mutual interdependence of the finite and the infinite:

> God is God only so far as he knows himself: his self-knowledge is, further, a self-consciousness in man and man's knowledge *of* God, which proceeds to man's self-knowledge *in* God.

Philosophy must know Absolute Spirit dialectically. Its abstract thesis is God "as eternal content, abiding self-centred" Being; its opposed antithesis is in terms of a "distinction of the eternal essence from its manifestation, which by this difference becomes the phenomenal world"; and its synthesis apprehends an "infinite return, and reconciliation with the eternal being, of the world it gave away." Hegel analyzes each of these three—"the 'moment' of *Universality*," then "the 'moment' of *particularity*," and finally "the 'moment' of *individuality*"—in a single paragraph. Although religion's form of "picture-thinking" differs from philosophy's form of dialectical rational thought, Hegel writes, "the content of religion and philosophy is the same," namely, God or Absolute Spirit. It has been so common to pit them against each other and to accuse philosophy of either atheism ("that it has *too little* of God") or pantheism ("that it has *too much* of him"). But Hegel voices some doubt that any serious philosopher has actually subscribed to a crude pantheistic belief that everything, as it is in itself, is equivalent to God. (This should be distinguished from panentheism, previously discussed, the view that everything actually exists *in* God, without, by itself, being identical to God.) Even Hinduism, which he labels "the maddest of polytheisms," is not really a pantheism, for "which everything is God, and God everything" taken by itself. As we have seen, Hegel was himself accused of pantheism, but he regards this as a "shallow" misunderstanding of his philosophical system.[91]

ART, RELIGION, AND PHILOSOPHY. The introductions to Hegel's lecture series on art, religion, and the history of philosophy all contain more interesting ideas that are pertinent here. "Fine art is not real art," he says, until "it has taken its place in the same sphere with religion and philosophy and has become simply a mode of revealing to consciousness and bringing to utterance the divine nature." Thus, its content is identical to that of religion and philosophy, namely Absolute Spirit or God. True art recognizes that this is revealed in human nature itself. "For not only is there a divinity in man, but in him it is operative under a form that is appropriate to the essence of God, in a mode quite other and higher than in nature." In Christianity God is revealed "as a person, as a subject," and Christian art reflects the essential, personal relationship between the divine and the human. There is an evolution from "the *symbolic* form of art" (e.g., architecture) to the "classical form of art" (e.g., sculpture) to the "romantic form of art" (e.g., painting, music, and poetry); but all serve to reveal the infinite Spirit as "the self-unfolding Idea of beauty."[92]

Hegel's entire philosophical system is remarkably **theocentric**:

> God is the beginning of all things and the end of all things. . . . He is the centre which gives life and quickening to all things and which animates and preserves in existence all the various forms of being.

If philosophy is understood to be the pursuit of knowledge of reality, it must be religious.

> The object of religion as well as of philosophy is eternal truth in its objectivity, God and nothing but God, and the explication of God. Philosophy is not a wisdom of the world, but is knowledge of what is not of the world.

In addition to the anti-Kantian tenor of this statement, we might also observe how removed its stance is from that of empiricists such as Hume and Mill. Hegel continues, "Philosophy, therefore, only unfolds itself when it unfolds religion, and in unfolding itself it unfolds religion." Few other modern thinkers so heavily accentuate this commonality.

> Thus religion and philosophy come to be one. . . . Philosophy is thus identical with religion. . . . It is in the peculiar way in which they both occupy themselves with God that the distinction comes out.

In other words, they are similar in content but differ in form. Both study the Absolute as it is revealed. "Nature, finite spirit, the world of consciousness, of intelligence, and of will are embodiments of the divine Idea." Thus, in coming to understand these phenomena of experience, we learn more adequately to grasp the Absolute. More specifically, we come to see that there is no ultimate dichotomy between the infinite

and the finite, that "there cannot be a Divine Spirit and a human, which are *absolutely different*." Hegel scorns the Kantian prejudice of his own era, that everything but God is knowable: "Formerly the mind found its supreme interest in knowing God, and searching into his nature. It had and it found no rest unless in thus occupying itself with God," he says in what could be a paraphrase of Augustine. Through religious philosophy we achieve a spiritual elevation:

> In thinking I lift myself up to the absolute above all that is finite, and am infinite consciousness, while I am at the same time finite consciousness.

So Hegelian philosophy not merely considers the relationship between God and humans but helps to establish it as actually realized. Religious faiths other than our own should be respected as grasping part of the truth, even if a different part from that to which we have access. "Therefore in them we have not to do with what is foreign to us, but with what is our own." The ultimate truth must be all-encompassing, and all perspectives on it are valuable.[93]

Unlike religion, philosophy must rationally "justify its beginning and its manner of knowledge" rather than resting it on faith, authority, and tradition. But the empirical and Kantian ways of doing this, emphasizing "the limitations of human thought," undermine the prospects of religious knowledge. Hegel may have Kant in mind when he says,

> The man who speaks of the *merely* finite, of *merely* human reason, and of the limits to mere reason, lies against the spirit, for the spirit as infinite and universal, as self-comprehension, comprehends itself not in a "merely" nor in limits, nor in the finite as such.[94]

Dialectical reason supplies philosophy with a cognitive method that gives it a form for grasping the Absolute that is more adequate than the picture-thinking of religion, as religion's form is superior to that of art.

GOD AND THE WORLD. Let us conclude our study of Hegel's discussion of religion by briefly considering passages from the body of his lectures on that topic. As we have seen, he wants to rethink the proper role of arguments for divine reality:

> What has to be done, therefore, is to restore the proofs of the existence of God to their place of honour, by divesting them of what is inadequate in them.

This is particularly timely in the wake of the blistering assault on them by Hume and Kant. More specifically, we must beware of suggesting that God's existence is "dependent on the Being of the finite." Human reason rises from finite contingency to infinite necessity. We must concede that the Infinite cannot be **deduced** from the finite and that any "proof of the existence of God is nothing but the description of that act of rising up to the infinite." Reason contemplates "the Absolute Notion" and dialectically realizes that

> the Idea of Spirit means the unity of divine and human nature. . . . Spirit is accordingly the living Process by which the implicit unity of the divine and human natures becomes actual.[95]

In the philosophy of religion we can come to synthesize the old antitheses between finite and infinite, natural and supernatural, temporal and eternal, human and divine. The concrete picture-thinking illustration of this synthesis that the Christian religion offers us is the person of Jesus Christ, the God-man. Not only was Jesus divine, but so (allegedly) are we and all natural things one with Absolute Spirit; "they have no independent Being as against it, and neither has it, consequently, as against them. There is only one Being, . . . and things by their very nature form part of it." This is monistic panentheism, the view that there is a single all-encompassing divine Reality, in which all objects of experience are contained. "Everything is thus included in it, and it is immediately present in everything." It is not the same as the more simplistic pantheism, which deifies "every existing thing in its finitude and particularity" as, in itself, being God. Hegel denies that any serious philosopher has ever embraced so crude a doctrine: "Such an absurd idea has never come into anybody's head outside of the ranks of these opponents of Pantheism." What Hegel does contend—and what makes his thought different from that of every other philosopher we are considering—is that "there is no gulf between the Infinite and the finite."[96] The truth of religion—adequately expressed only by philosophy—is that God and the world, including human nature, are one.

Immortality

Hegel is difficult to pin down on the topic of immortality. (After his death, his followers disagreed as to whether he even believed in personal immortality.) As we are about to see, this difficulty is not for lack of passages in which he discusses it, but rather because

of the ambiguous, noncommittal nature of his treatment. In *The Spirit of Christianity and Its Fate* he criticizes the Jews for their lack of positive freedom, or autonomous self-determination, and rhetorically asks,

> How could they have hoped even for the poor immortality in which the consciousness of the individual is preserved, how could they have wished to persist in self-subsistence who had in fact renounced the capacity to will and even the very fact of their existence

because of their attachment to externals? Immortality in the sense of a permanent preservation of personal consciousness seems orthodox in Christianity, and it is unclear here why he considers this a "poor" conception. Towards the end of that early essay he criticizes early Christians' view of "the immortality of the soul" in terms of "a resurrection of the body." He prefers what he calls "the Greek view that body and soul persist together in one living shape" rather than as separate Cartesian substances mysteriously united. In his *Philosophy of Nature* Hegel writes, "Thought, as this universal which exists for itself, is *immortal being*; mortal being is that in which the Idea, the universal, exists in an inadequate form."[97] But this is no ringing endorsement of personal human immortality as long as our finite spirit is seen as an "inadequate" expression of the Absolute.

In the *Lectures on the Philosophy of Religion* Hegel says of the religious believer,

> Knowing himself in God, he at the same time knows his imperishable life in God; he knows of the truth of his Being, and therefore the idea of the *immortality of the soul* here enters as an essential moment into the history of religion. The ideas of God and of immortality have a necessary relation to each other.

This statement (with whose last sentence James will agree) is ambiguous enough not to commit Hegel himself to personal immortality. He seems to be denying immortality as any unique future state when he says that "the immortality of the soul must not be represented as first entering the sphere of reality only at a later stage; it is the actual present quality of Spirit." It may be that we participate in this only to the extent that we are part of the Absolute. He links belief in immortality to an important Christian doctrine: "The soul, the individual soul, has an infinite, an eternal quality, namely, that of being a citizen in the Kingdom of God." But he is not explicitly embracing this as his own view. Finally, in his *Lectures on the Proofs of the Existence of God* he says, "Spirit is immortal; it is eternal; and it is immortal and eternal in virtue of the fact that it is infinite, that it has no such spatial finitude as we associate with body."[98] Is this describing us or the Absolute or both, and what is the nature of our own immortality, if any? The answers to these questions are not clear, although they are quite relevant to a theory of human nature.

Fulfillment

We have already considered something of Hegel's critique of the Enlightenment's utilitarian conception of happiness. In his *Philosophy of Right* he analyzes such an empirical understanding of human "welfare or happiness" as the "satisfaction" of our "needs, inclinations, passions, opinions, fancies, &c." Unfortunately, his presentation of his own view of the fulfillment of human nature is rather thin. In his early *Faith and Knowledge* he writes, "Every philosophy sets forth nothing else but the construction of highest bliss as Idea." This "highest bliss" for mankind inevitably involves some relationship between rational activity and satisfaction, which tend to blend into each other. He condemns the empirical, merely **naturalistic** idea of happiness, but he admits, "Polemics against happiness will be dismissed as empty chatter when this happiness is recognized to be the blissful enjoyment of eternal intuition." This sounds rather like Aquinas, but Hegel fails to characterize "the bliss of eternal vision"[99] in any definite manner and to commit himself clearly to believing that we, as human individuals, will experience it hereafter.

In *Philosophy of Mind* Hegel writes that a higher conception of "*happiness*" than the empirical one requires "the subordination of *particular* impulses to a

universal"; both the particular impulses and the universal "are, in their mutual externality, untrue, and that is why they come together in the will that wills the *concrete* universal." Without the subordination of our impulses to the universal, they remain "a mere negative" antithesis, and happiness (*die Glückseligkeit*) remains "abstract and merely imagined." The higher conception towards which we reasonably aim might better be called "well-being" (*das Wohl*).

> Happiness (good fortune) is distinguished from well-being only in this, that happiness implies no more than some sort of immediate existence, whereas well-being is regarded as having a moral justification.[100]

Given Hegel's ambiguity about personal immortality, we should not be surprised that he does not specify whether, and to what extent, such welfare extends beyond this life. Yet, here again, the issue is germane to an understanding of his theory of human nature.

REFLECTIONS

Hegel is chronologically the last of the monumental speculative system builders in the history of philosophy. If greatness is measured in terms of towering influence on subsequent thought, he is one of its greatest thinkers. As Kant effected a "transcendental turn" in Western philosophy that was revolutionary, Hegel brought about a "dialectical turn" that has been comparable. Indeed, it is difficult to exaggerate his importance. Virtually every new philosophy we study that developed in the last century and a half—**voluntarism**, **Marxism**, **logical positivism**, **existentialism**, neo-idealism, **pragmatism**, process thought, phenomenology, and analytic philosophy—can be seen as either an extension of or a reaction against Hegelian thought. It has had its ups and downs in

---

Voluntarism (from the Latin *voluntas*, meaning will).   The doctrine that will is the fundamental principle in human experience and/or in all of reality

Marxism.   A political and economic ideology, stemming from the ideas of Marx and Engels, calling for a revolutionary class struggle designed to overthrow the system of capitalism, move us through socialism, and achieve a communist society

Logical positivism.   A twentieth-century philosophical movement that began in the 1920s and flourished until the 1950s, which holds that any empirical statement must be verifiable (or, sometimes, falsifiable), at least in principle, in order to be cognitively meaningful; this renders metaphysical (and theological) utterances literally nonsensical and reduces value (including ethical) statements to expressions of emotional preferences

Existentialism.   A philosophical movement that began in the middle of the nineteenth century and became popular in the twentieth, teaching that human consciousness is individual, is free rather than being determined by some alleged common essence, and is a source of values

Pragmatism (from the Greek *pragma*, meaning deed or action).   A philosophical movement of the late nineteenth and twentieth centuries (beginning with Peirce and popularized by James), emphasizing the practical usefulness of ideas and beliefs as the criterion of their meaning and truth

popularity during that century and a half, but lately it seems to be coming back into vogue. Hegel is significant as the best critic of Kant ever, as the most radical proponent of monistic idealism, and as the first Western thinker since Aristotle to invent (he might prefer to say discover or refine) a dramatically different logic. The roots of his system, which are most vulnerable to criticism, are his monistic theory of reality and his dialectical theory of knowledge.

REALITY. His theory of reality is every bit as fundamental to his view of human nature as Hobbes's was to his. If Hegel is correct, all of reality is ultimately one and is spiritual (monistic idealism). Two opposite reactions to this theory are possible: we can either regard it as exhilarating in that it elevates everything to a grand and glorious status by viewing it as part of an infinite, all-embracing whole or consider it (as existentialists and James do) an obliteration of individuality and personal integrity. But whichever way we tend to cut on the implications of the theory, we would do well, as critical thinkers, to demand what evidence Hegel has given us for the alleged unity of reality and thought. Even if we carefully interpret his theory as he would have us do, the claim that rationality and actuality are identical flies in the face of common sense and ordinary experience. So, it is appropriate to ask for proof. Supposedly his entire logical (i.e., ontological) system constitutes that evidence, though each of us must judge how convincing or unconvincing it is.

BODIES. Second, Hegel's discussion of bodies is most remarkable for the amount of serious attention paid to the world of organic nature, given the context of an idealistic theory of reality. The fact that he dedicates an entire, substantial book of his *Encyclopedia* to it is as striking as it would have been if the materialistic Hobbes had written a whole book on spiritual reality. Even though Hegel does not seem to have anything dramatically new to offer in physical science, what is striking is his analysis of bodies as physical expressions of Absolute Spirit in time and space.

PERSONALITY. Hegel's view of personality, our third topic, seems marred by his lack of respect for the human individual as intrinsically valuable. One can easily be offended by his cavalier attitude towards the sufferings of human individuals on the sacrificial "slaughter bench" of history and his overreaction

against happiness as a legitimate goal of the historical process. Furthermore, his famous idea of humans being historically used as pawns by "the Cunning of Reason" seems difficult to square with our ordinary conception of freedom. Nor does it suffice that he tries to make an exception of the values-oriented dimension of our lives, since it is artificial to dichotomize our values from our natures as persons. The analysis of the dialectical development of personality through the stages of lordship and bondage, stoicism, scepticism, and the unhappy consciousness is brilliantly imaginative, ranking these passages from the *Phenomenology* (along with Plato's allegory of the cave, the first two of Descartes' *Meditations*, and Sartre's section on "bad faith") among the magical moments in the history of philosophy. The problem is that, for all its brilliance, it is so contrived that few people believe it represents any necessary development outside Hegel's own fertile imagination. Hegel does have a more dynamic analysis of human personality than any other thinker we have considered thus far (even Kant, with his fixed structures of the mind). But this may well raise the question of whether anything stable is left to constitute a human nature or whether everything about us is in process; thus, he may be unwittingly (and even unwillingly) leading us down the road to Sartre's denial of human nature altogether.

KNOWLEDGE. Fourth, Hegel offers us what is arguably the most underappreciated theory of knowledge in the history of philosophy. His critique of Kant's epistemology may be the most acute ever developed, and his presentation of a new logic in support of his claims of rational knowledge of reality in itself is most significant. The postulate that truth must be all-encompassing tends to bias Hegelian epistemology in line with his monistic ontology. It is a pernicious doctrine in the sense that it condemns us to untruth, since our human perspective—even at the level of "absolute knowing"—would seem always to remain exactly that, a *human perspective*; nor does the dogmatic assertion that we are also infinite help here, since we remain finite and limited even in the use of reason. Hegel's critique of the models of cognition as an instrument or a medium is doubly flawed. First, he does not spell out the identity of the perpetrators, let alone where they use such language. (One supposes he means to include Kant as well as the empiricists, but is this fair to Kant?) Next, the **analogies** between the nonphysical process of knowing and material objects inevitably limp. (Surely a *physical* instrument or medium will distort to some extent; but why should we assume the same of an immaterial one?) Also, Hegel is too quick to dismiss the traditional subject-object dichotomy in epistemology, again because of his monistic presuppositions. His application of the dialectic to the stages of sense-certainty, perception, and scientific understanding is another *tour de force*; but, again, it illustrates what a Procrustean bed the dialectic can become—on which phenomena to be examined are stretched or hacked up to fit preconceived patterns. He may be correct in criticizing reflective understanding for stopping short at the sight of negative antitheses and in recommending dialectical reason as providing knowledge of higher, positive syntheses; but he has not proved his point, and his illustrations, however ingenious, seem too contrived to be convincing. He is right to admonish Kant for complacently and uncritically accepting the old Aristotelian logic, and he deserves our admiration for inventing an alternative approach; but that is not to say that this new logic works in providing the higher knowledge he advocates. Finally, his collapsing of the distinction between true logic and metaphysics is a bold but suspect move, dependent on unjustified assumptions of monistic idealism.

FREEDOM. Regarding our fifth topic, Hegel's analysis of human freedom is more sophisticated than that of almost any of his predecessors (Kant being the noteworthy exception) because of his acknowledgment of the dialectical dynamic between a negative freedom from external restraints and a positive freedom for self-determination. But, ironically, he leaves these as antitheses in mutual opposition, rather than working out the sort of dialectical synthesis that does anything more than subordinate the former to the latter. (Mill, who is an empiricist of the sort Hegel despises and not a dialectical thinker at all, does a strangely better job of truly reconciling the two.) "True liberty" is needlessly opposed to the individualistic pursuit of happiness (as it might be by a Platonist or an Aristotelian), rather than constructively synthesized with it. Hegel's analysis of history as the progressively expanding development of the

consciousness of freedom is an illuminating interpretive idea (essentially Kantian in origin), but it is a dangerous illusion to suppose that the process is necessary and inevitable, regardless of our conscious human choices. Hegel's division of history into three great periods, however provocative and memorable, is an arbitrary and chauvinistic **generalization**: it is not clear that all of the most ancient civilizations were autocratic, nor were they all (or even typically) Oriental; the citizen governments of ancient Greece and Rome were not necessarily representative of their times; and the Germanic peoples of modern times were not unique in their respect for human freedom as such, to the extent that they exhibited it at all.

MORALITY. Sixth, Hegel's theory of morality, like his epistemology, is explicitly pitted against the Kantian alternative. He is so prejudiced against individualism that he continually condemns "morality" as abstract in favor of social ethics, which is allegedly more concrete because rooted in cultural customs. But there are bad societies, and cultural customs can be irrational and perversely immoral; in his own peculiar way Hegel runs the risk of deriving a **prescriptive** "ought" from a descriptive "is" (remember Hume's great distinction and challenge here). Hegel may be correct that Kant's postulates of practical reason are necessitated by his mistaken dichotomy of morality and happiness; but Hegel himself has the same problem, even if he does not resort to the same solution. (As we shall see, Mill tries to solve the problem by denying the distinction altogether.) Hegel is unfair in repudiating Kantian ethics as "an empty formalism"; there is serious, engaging content to its principles, as Hegel should have recognized.

SOCIETY. As for our seventh topic, Hegel's theory of society reflects the same distrust of and disrespect for the individual as does his theory of morality. Even while preserving a language of liberty and representative government, he advocates a dangerous collectivism that tends to deify the state. Though it is a great book, his *Philosophy of Right* can be reasonably read as a manifesto of authoritarianism and a reactionary apology for the *status quo*. Although he favors a separation of powers, his monarch (like Hobbes's) is to have sovereign authority. Nor is it surprising that he is ambivalent towards freedom of expression (as Mill will not be). In comparison with Kant before him or

James afterwards, Hegel is too quick to justify war as a necessary resolution of international conflicts, too antiegalitarian, and too willing to excuse the actions of dominant cultures towards their neighbors.

RELIGION. Eighth, Hegel's analysis of religion is carefully worked out, and we can trace its development from his early works, which present an extreme form of Kantianism, through those that reject Kantianism, to his mature position, which has been described here as panentheism. Hegel's evolution from a critic of Christianity as a "positive religion" to his defense of it as the "absolute religion" is quite striking. Although his treatment is oversimplified and often exhibits the Procrustean use of dialectic mentioned above, his mature (i.e., from the *Phenomenology* on) discussion of specific religious traditions and their doctrines is a fascinating phenomenology of religions. His attempt to reinterpret the proofs of God's existence as legitimate presupposes his controversial denial of knowledge of reality through the understanding and his assertion of it through speculative reason. His eccentric notion that the content of philosophy (and, for that matter, that of art) is identical to that of religion may have little to recommend it, apart from its compatibility with his underlying monistic world-view. Finally, the thesis that the point of religion and metaphysics is to help us realize that we are infinite and one with God is flatteringly attractive, but it also seems arrogant and in need of far more careful justification than he is prepared to provide.

IMMORTALITY. Hegel's brief and scattered discussions of immortality, our ninth topic, are annoyingly ambiguous (as Aristotle's were). Does Hegel believe in human immortality or merely wish to consider others' views on it without committing himself one way or the other? If he does believe in it, is it a personal survival of individual consciousness after death or some impersonal reabsorption into Absolute Spirit? One cannot answer these questions with any confidence. It is as if he regarded the issue as largely extraneous to his system.

FULFILLMENT. Finally, Hegel's treatment of the ultimate fulfillment of human nature is equally fuzzy, although it seems less likely that he would think this a tangential issue. It is difficult to say why he does not present his views on this topic more carefully. Perhaps the answer is a combination of two factors—that his overreaction against the Enlightenment idea of happiness affords him no definite place to go with the matter in this life and that his fuzziness about personal immortality leaves him without any adequate foundations for speculation about the matter hereafter.

* * *

Hegel is one of those great thinkers (perhaps Plato and Hobbes are others) who are more important for challenging established ideas and provoking reactions in others than for the correctness of their own views. As the preceding ten paragraphs would suggest, Hegel's theory seems problematic on every topic we have examined. Yet he offers us a unique and inspiring world-view, featuring a conception of human nature unlike that of any other thinker we are considering. For Hegel we are expressions of and included in an all-encompassing Absolute Spirit. Our mandate is to soar beyond sense experience and empirical understanding to speculative reason by means of the dialectic, in the theoretical areas of our lives, and to transcend individuality to conform ourselves to the requirements of a much broader community, in the practical areas. On almost all counts a strikingly contrasting voice in nineteenth-century philosophy is that of John Stuart Mill.

Mill

Human nature is not a machine to be built after a model, and set to do exactly the work prescribed for it, but a tree, which requires to grow and develop itself on all sides, according to the tendency of the inward forces which make it a living thing. ON LIBERTY

BIOGRAPHY

John Stuart Mill was born on May 20, 1806 (the year before Hegel's *Phenomenology* was published), in London, the oldest child of James and Harriet Burrow Mill. For details of much of John Stuart Mill's life we have access to his *Autobiography* as well as to some of his voluminous correspondence. His father was an intellectual, a progressive liberal, and a devoted disciple of Jeremy Bentham, the founder of the utilitarian movement. In 1809, James Mill took his son to visit Bentham and began an educational experiment in which the father undertook the instruction of the three-year-old on his own, teaching him Greek language and literature from that early age. By the age of seven, the boy was reading Platonic dialogues (though he admits that he could not understand one of them, the *Theaetetus*, at that time). Within a year, he began studying Latin, Euclidean geometry, and algebra. He was also assigned to instruct his younger siblings in some of what he had been taught. He read history and composed verses. He enjoyed learning theoretical science and, at about the age of twelve, began studying the logic of Aristotle, followed by that of Hobbes. Meanwhile, the elder Mill was writing a history of British India, published in 1818, which the boy had helped

proofread and which led to James Mill's salaried appointment as an Assistant to the Examiner of India Correspondence in 1819. At that later time, the father also led the boy "through a complete course of political economy." Two important features of the boy's education were that his father would explain why things needed to be learned while he instructed and would encourage his son to think for himself, even to disagree with his father, rather than leaving him "crammed with mere facts, and with the opinions or phrases of other people," passively absorbed and uncritically accepted. During his childhood, John was not given opportunities to play with others; he writes that his father "was earnestly bent upon my escaping not only the ordinary corrupting influence which boys exercise over boys, but the contagion of vulgar modes of thought and feeling." In 1820, John visited France for about a year as a guest of Sir Samuel Bentham (the philosopher's brother). After his return to England in 1821, he resumed his studies, but he no longer regarded his father as his "schoolmaster."[101]

The published version of Mill's *Autobiography* makes no mention of his mother, despite his father's being one of its most prominent figures. An unpublished early draft says, "My father's older children neither loved him nor with any warmth of affection anyone else." He writes there that "a really warm-hearted mother" would not only have rendered his father more lovable but also would have imparted loving inclinations to the children. Yet his own mother, he says,

> with the very best of intentions only knew how to pass her life drudging for them. . . . I thus grew up in the absence of love and in the presence of fear; and many and indelible are the effects of this bringing-up in the stunting of my moral growth.

He adds,

> I acquired the habit of leaving my responsibility as a moral agent to rest on my father and my conscience never speaking to me except by his voice.

Another curious feature of Mill's upbringing was that he was raised "from the first without any religious belief, in the ordinary acceptation of the term"; his father, who had been disciplined in Scottish Presbyterianism and licensed as a preacher, had broken with orthodox religion and become an **agnostic**, taking particularly strong exception to the doctrine that a good God would condemn personal creatures to eternal damnation. James Mill thought that we can know nothing of the answers to our ultimate metaphysical and theological questions for lack of experience, but made sure his son became "acquainted with what had been thought by mankind on these impenetrable problems." As John Stuart Mill writes,

> I am thus one of the very few examples, in this country, of one who has, not thrown off religious belief, but never had it. . . . I looked upon the modern exactly as I did upon the ancient religion, as something which in no way concerned me.

He does criticize his father for a lack of tenderness towards his children, saying that he "resembled most Englishmen in being ashamed of the signs of feeling, and by the absence of demonstration, starving the feelings themselves." He writes that his father's "temper was constitutionally irritable" but that at least John's younger siblings "loved him tenderly: and if I cannot say so much of myself, I was always loyally devoted to him." While growing up, he saw a great deal of Jeremy Bentham, "owing to the close intimacy which existed between him and my father." Every summer he and his father visited Bentham's house, and the Mills eventually rented a house near Bentham's.[102]

"During the winter of 1821–2," after returning to England from France, the teenager studied law with John Austin, a follower of Bentham, who later taught jurisprudence at the University of London. Mill was also given a treatise on Bentham's thought. "The reading of this book was an epoch in my life; one of the turning points in my mental history." He had already been trained in Benthamism. As he says, "The Benthamic standard of 'the greatest happiness' was that which I had always been taught to apply." But now he saw all references "in morals and legislation" to **natural law** and moral intuition repudiated "as dogmatism in disguise" and became convinced "that all previous moralists were superseded." He now understood the "principle of utility" to be the ultimate moral "keystone":

> It gave unity to my conceptions of things. I now had opinions; a creed, a doctrine, a philosophy; in one among the best senses of the word, a religion; the inculcation and diffusion of which could be made the principal outward purpose of a life.

In the winter of 1822, he formed a small "Utilitarian Society," which read together and met every other

week for discussions; its numbers remained in the single digits until it disbanded in 1826. In May of 1823, Mill's father helped him secure "an appointment from the East India Company, in the office of the Examiner of India Correspondence, immediately under himself." Here at India House, the younger Mill would continue to work "for the next thirty-five years,"[103] though usually for only a few hours each day on official business, leaving him the leisure and energy to pursue his writings. Also in 1823, he was arrested for disseminating birth-control pamphlets (then considered obscene) in a working-class district of London; although sentenced to fourteen days imprisonment, he was actually jailed only overnight.

During that same year, Bentham established the *Westminster Review*, offering the editorship to James Mill, "who declined it as incompatible with his India House appointment." John Stuart Mill began publishing articles in it in 1824 and was its most frequent contributor for a while. Liberalism was on the rise in England, with an ever increasing commitment to "representative government, and complete freedom of discussion." The young Mill was zealous on its behalf, but only intellectually, in the manner of "a mere reasoning machine," his father having discouraged any attention to feelings, including that of "genuine benevolence, or sympathy with mankind." In 1825, the younger Mill worked at editing Bentham's *Rationale of Judicial Evidence* for publication (in five volumes). At this time, he also learned German, studied Hobbes's logic again, and helped found a London debating society. The combination of overwork and suppression of feelings precipitated what he calls "a crisis in my mental history," a prolonged period of depression, in the autumn of 1826. His description is gripping:

> In this frame of mind it occurred to me to put the question directly to myself: "Suppose that all your objects in life were realized; that all the changes in institutions and opinions which you are looking forward to, could be completely effected at this very instant: would this be a great joy and happiness to you?" And an irrepressible self-consciousness distinctly answered, "No!" At this my heart sank within me.

His profound disillusionment at this realization could not be reasoned away. Nor was there anyone to whom he could explain it, especially not to his father. As he writes, "I sought no comfort by speaking to others of what I felt. If I had loved any one sufficiently to make confiding my griefs a necessity, I should not have been in the condition I was." All his life had been a training period for the work of progressive reform; but now, he felt "left stranded at the commencement of my voyage, with a well-equipped ship and a rudder, but no sail." He continued his work at India House "mechanically, by the mere force of habit," but did not believe he could endure for more than a year. However, in less than that time, he "was moved to tears" on reading a passage about the death of an author's father, and this proved to be something of a breakthrough. He suffered relapses, but "the cloud" of his misery gradually withdrew. He drew two conclusions from this traumatic experience: first, that only those people are truly happy "who have their minds fixed on some object other than their own happiness; on the happiness of others, on the improvement of mankind, even on some art or pursuit, followed not as a means, but as itself an ideal end"—in other words, that one's own personal happiness can only be a by-product of other worthwhile endeavors; and second, that "human well-being" requires a "cultivation of the feelings," such as had been neglected in his own upbringing. He was particularly comforted by reading the poetry of Wordsworth. "The result was that I gradually, but completely, emerged from my habitual depression, and was never again subject to it." He developed an intimate friendship with novelist and critic John Sterling, who confided that he and others had regarded Mill "as a 'made' or manufactured man" up to that time. In 1828, Mill was promoted to Assistant Examiner in India House; the following year (in which his father's *Analysis of the Phenomena of the Human Mind* was first published) he withdrew from attending the debating society. He began studying writings by authors of the socialistic "St. Simonian school in France," including Auguste Comte, who was then calling himself "a pupil of Saint-Simon." In early 1830, Mill started writing down some of his ideas on logic, including on "the problem of **induction**." He came to grips with the problem of "Philosophical Necessity," which had haunted him during his period of dejection (as it later bedeviled William James in his). "I saw that though our character is formed by circumstances, our own desires can do much to shape those circumstances." After the French Revolution of 1830 erupted, Mill "went at once to Paris," where he met the Marquis de Lafayette. In that year and the following one, he wrote "Essays on Some Unsettled Questions of Political Economy"; and in 1831, he published seven articles, entitled "The Spirit of the Age,"[104] in the *Examiner*.

In 1835, Mill edited the *London Review*, which became the *London and Westminster Review* in 1836 and which he continued to edit (and eventually own) until 1840; he introduced the practice of having every article "bear an initial, or some other signature, and be held to express the opinions solely of the individual writer," rather than necessarily reflecting the editorial perspective of the *Review* itself. Meanwhile, his father's health had declined; "his symptoms became unequivocally those of pulmonary consumption, and after lingering to the last stage of debility, he died on the 23rd of June, 1836." In a way the father's death had a liberating effect on his son, who did not feel "bound to defer" to "any other radical writer or politician." In the year of his father's death, he was promoted at India House. In 1838, his article "Bentham" was published in the *Review*; and in 1840, his paper "Coleridge" was published in its last issue under his proprietorship. Mill then proceeded to finish his *System of Logic*, which he had been working on intermittently and which was published in two volumes in 1843; he was surprised and puzzled by its considerable success as an empirical alternative to the **rationalistic** perspective of "the intuitive philosophers."[105]

In 1830, Mill had met Mrs. John Taylor, who was a couple of years younger than he and was married to a considerably older merchant. He describes Harriet Taylor as "the most admirable person" he ever knew:

> To her outer circle she was a beauty and a wit, with an air of natural distinction, felt by all who approached her: to the inner, a woman of deep and strong feeling, of penetrating and intuitive intelligence.

He maintains (perhaps extravagantly) that

> her profound knowledge of human nature and discernment and sagacity in practical life, would, in the times when such a carrière was open to women, have made her eminent among the rulers of mankind.

He attributes to her "the noblest and best balanced" sort of "moral character," as well as a "passion" for social justice. He describes his debt, "even intellectually, to her" as "almost infinite," attributing to her influence whatever practical dimension is of value in his writings.

Mill's "incomparable friend," Mrs. Taylor, lived much of the time with her daughter, Helen, separate from her husband, despite the scandalous rumors this aroused in Victorian England. Mill writes that their relationship "was one of strong affection and confidential intimacy only" and that they tried to be careful not "to bring discredit on her husband." Partly under her influence Mill seemed to be moving in the direction of democratic socialism, while repudiating "that tyranny of society over the individual which most Socialistic systems are supposed to involve." He came to see the pivotal "social problem of the future" as one of "how to unite the greatest individual liberty of action, with a common ownership in the raw material of the globe, and an equal participation of all in the benefits of combined labour."[106]

In 1844, he published *Some Unsettled Questions of Political Economy*; and his *Principles of Political Economy* was published in two volumes just prior to the outbreak of "the French Revolution of 1848"; like the book on logic, *Principles* was quite successful[107] and went through several editions during his lifetime.

Before proceeding with this chronology, it might be interesting to consider briefly some of what Mill writes in his *Letters* between the end of his depression and his marriage in 1851. In 1831, he wrote his dear friend John Sterling that "the only thing that I believe I am really fit for is the investigation of abstract truth, and the more abstract the better"; his work was far more theoretical than practical, focusing on "principles of morals, government, law, education, above all self-education." The following year, he wrote Thomas Carlyle, "I am rather fitted to be a logical expounder than an artist." In 1833, he wrote Carlyle again, conceding that "most of the highest truths are, to persons endowed by nature in certain ways . . . , intuitive," needing "neither explanation nor proof," though these latter constitute his own logical methods. Later that year, he described in another letter to Carlyle his "peculiar" view that the finest of people of both genders combine "the highest measure of what are considered feminine qualities" with "the highest masculine qualities," rather than being stereotypically male or female. The next year, he wrote Carlyle that his fellow utilitarians were so much more experienced and practical than he and that, by comparison, he,

a schoolboy fresh from the logic school, had never conversed with a reality, never seen one, knew not what manner of thing it was, had only spun . . . deductions from assumed **premises**[11]

—a striking remark, coming from a man who would become one of the greatest of philosophical empiricists. In 1836, he wrote E. Lytton Bulwer that the *Review* needed to foster "a utilitarianism which takes into account the whole of human nature; not the ratiocinative faculty only"—one "which holds feeling at least as valuable as thought." On hearing that John Sterling was dying, in 1844, he wrote him,

I have never so much wished for another life as I do for the sake of meeting you in it. The chief reason for desiring it has always seemed to me to be that the curtain may not drop altogether on those one loves and honours.[108]

In these snatches from his correspondence after his depression we see both Mill's self-critical attitude and his appreciation of the role of feelings in human nature.

In July of 1849, John Taylor died of cancer, and Mill and Harriet married in April of 1851. Some might think this legitimized what had been a scandalous relationship; but their friendship up to that point was probably platonic. In 1854, when Mill was working on his *Autobiography*, his wife urged him to reveal the nature of their relationship candidly—as one of "strong affection, intimacy of friendship, and no impropriety"; she added that doing so could provide "an edifying picture for those poor wretches who cannot conceive friendship but in sex—nor believe that expedience and the consideration for feelings of others can conquer sensuality." By 1853, Mill had begun showing signs of consumption, and the following year (the year of his mother's death), he thought he was dying of tuberculosis, "the family disease." Between December of 1854 and June of 1855, he took an extended recuperative holiday "in Italy, Sicily, and Greece." In 1856, he was appointed Chief of the Office of the Examiner of India Correspondence, holding that position for "a little more than two years" until retiring from the East India Company with a "liberal compensation granted" him. He and his wife had been working on his essay *On Liberty*, but she died of tuberculosis at Avignon, France, on November 3, 1858. He "bought a cottage as close as possible to the place where she is buried" in Avignon, where he and his stepdaughter, Helen, could spend "a great portion" of every year. The first two volumes of his *Dissertations and Discussions* were published in 1859. In February of that same year, he also published *On Liberty*, which he predicted "is likely to survive longer than anything else that I have written (with the possible exception of the 'Logic')." He dedicated it to Harriet's memory and refused ever to make any "alteration or addition to it," beyond where her death left it. In 1860 and 1861, he wrote *Considerations on Representative Government* (published in 1861), *The Subjection of Women* (published in 1869), and *Utilitarianism*, "first published, in three parts, in successive numbers of Fraser's Magazine" in 1861 "and afterwards reprinted in a volume" in 1863. In early 1862, he published "The Contest in America" in *Fraser's Magazine*, taking the side of the North in the Civil War, because of his strong anti-slavery sentiments. In 1865, he was elected Lord Rector of Saint Andrew's University and published both *An Examination of Sir William Hamilton's Philosophy* and *Auguste Comte and Positivism*. He also was a pioneer in resigning his author's royalties in order to have printed "cheap People's Editions of those of my writings which seemed the most likely to find readers among the working classes."[109]

Also in 1865, he was approached "by some electors of Westminster" to run for a Parliamentary seat in the House of Commons. He agreed on condition that he not have to canvass for votes or incur any personal expenses in the campaign. And he said that, if elected, he would not give any of his "time and labour to their local interests." He told the electors that he favored extending the suffrage to women and refused to discuss only his "religious opinions." To his amazement, Mill was elected over his Conservative opponent and served a three-year term. In Parliament he spoke in favor of capital punishment, women's suffrage, personal political representation, the granting of more autonomy to Ireland, and a Reform Bill. His Tory opponents quoted against him his earlier published reference to "the Conservative party" as "the stupidest party"; but this backfired on them when they came popularly to be called "'the stupid party' . . . for a considerable time afterwards."[110]

In 1867, Mill published the third volume of his *Dissertations and Discussions* and delivered his inaugural address at St. Andrews. He also began a revised edition of his father's *Analysis of the Phenomena of the Human Mind*, which was published in two volumes in 1869. Meanwhile, his advocacy of liberal causes in Parliament had not endeared him to most of his constituents, and in the new election of 1868 he

was "thrown out" of office. From then on he alternated between living in London and staying in Avignon.[111] On Saturday, May 3, 1873, he walked fifteen miles on a botanical expedition; two days later, he suffered a fever. On Wednesday, May 7th, he died in Avignon, murmuring to his adopted daughter, Helen, "You know that I have done my work." His autobiography, edited by her, was published that year; there followed the publication in 1874 of his *Three Essays on Religion* (*Nature*, *Utility of Religion*, and *Theism*), in 1875 of the fourth volume of his *Dissertations and Discussions,* and in 1879 of his uncompleted "Chapters on Socialism," edited by Helen Taylor. In 1910, the *Letters* of Mill (whom Prime Minister Gladstone called "the saint of rationalism"), edited by Hugh Elliott, was published.

Reality

Mill's essay *Nature* sets up his discussion of whether we should follow nature in our behavior (to be considered below in our "Morality" section) with a preliminary analysis: "Nature means the sum of all phenomena together with the causes which produce them." For a rigorous empiricist like Mill (or Hobbes or Hume), reality reduces to such an aggregate. Scientific progress consists in the gradual learning, "either by direct observation or by reasoning processes grounded on it," of the regular causal conditions of natural phenomena—the "laws of nature." All reality falls, at least in principle, within this sphere.

> Nature, then, in this its simplest acceptation, is a collective name for all facts, actual and possible, or (to speak more accurately) a name for the mode, partly known to us and partly unknown, in which all things take place.

The apprehension of reality as a whole is an ideal towards which science works. In this inclusive sense of the word (as opposed to a narrower one that refers to all reality apart from any human agency) nature "means all the powers existing in either the outer or the inner world and everything which takes place by means of those powers."[112] This idea should encompass any talk of the human mind and even of God.

Mill follows not only Hobbes's and Hume's empiricism, but also their phenomenalism, restricting knowable reality to phenomena, or things as they appear experientially. "What the mind is, as well as what matter is, or any other question respecting Things in themselves, as distinguished from their sensible manifestations, it would be foreign" to us to try to specify. He will not speculate, for example, about "the mind's own nature," as opposed to the mental phenomena of "Thoughts, Emotions, Volitions, and Sensations" (as we shall see below in our section on "Personality"). We must deal with the facts of natural reality; and "the distinction between mental and physical facts, between the internal and the external world," is merely useful for purposes of classification.[113]

Bodies

In his *System of Logic* Mill empirically defines a body as "the external cause to which we ascribe our sensations." When experiencing gold, we see a yellow color and feel a certain solidity, being directly aware of only our sensations, but regarding them "as produced by something" external to us, which we call "a body." Our sensations do not seem to coalesce randomly, but according to orderly regularities. It is an open metaphysical question whether there might be a material substance underlying the phenomenal qualities of a physical object. At any rate Mill agrees with other modern thinkers, including Hume, "that *all we know* of objects is the sensations which they give us, and the order of the occurrence of those sensations." Again, the intrinsic nature of body, like that of mind, must remain unknowable: "As body is the mysterious something which excites the mind to feel, so mind is the mysterious something which feels and thinks." Any knowledge of the qualities, relations, and quantities of bodies must be grounded "in our sensations or states of feeling"[114] drawn from experience.

In *An Examination of Sir William Hamilton's Philosophy* Mill rests his argument "that the belief in an external world is not intuitive, but an acquired product" on several postulates, all of which are allegedly justified by experience. The first of these (observed earlier by Hume) is that the human mind expects possible future sensations on the basis of actual past sensations. The second is that the mind associates its ideas in accordance with regular laws, including:

1st. Similar phenomena tend to be thought of together.

2nd. Phenomena which have either been experienced or conceived in close contiguity to one another, tend to be thought of together. . . .

3rd. Associations produced by contiguity become more certain and rapid by repetition, . . .

4th. When an association has acquired this character of inseparability, . . . the belief we have in their [appearances'] coexistence, though really a product of experience, seems intuitive.

Mill holds that this explains our acquired belief that there is an external world of bodies outside our minds.[115]

He uses the example of "a piece of white paper on a table," which we can see when we are in a room with it and which we are convinced continues to be there when we have left the room. What our belief really amounts to is the conviction that we could easily repeat those visual sensations upon entering that room again.

> The conception I form of the world existing at any moment, comprises, along with the sensations I am feeling, a countless variety of possibilities of sensation,

expected on the basis of past experience. Bodies existing in an external world, on this theory, are merely such "possibilities of sensation," which we are more or less confident we could experience under certain circumstances.

> These various possibilities are the important thing to me in the world. My present sensations are generally of little importance, and are moreover fugitive: the possibilities, on the contrary, are permanent,

or relatively enduring in time. The importance of that piece of paper on the table can extend far beyond the sense data we experience in relation to it at any moment. Although actual sensations come and go, "the possibilities remain" and "are independent of our will," belonging to others as well as to us. We believe in the external reality of that body in the sense that it could, under certain circumstances, be experienced by anyone, though we can experience only our own sensations: "The permanent possibilities are common to us and to our fellow-creatures; the actual sensations are not." This leads to Mill's phenomenalistic analysis of bodies: "Matter, then, may be defined, a Permanent Possibility of Sensation." In this sense, even the sceptical Hume believed in bodies. Mill criticizes "the strangely **sophistical** reasoning" of Kant that the properties of bodies are all relative to our experience, though the bodies themselves are independent external realities[116]

Personality

A PHENOMENALISTIC ANALYSIS OF MIND.   Later in the *Examination* Mill applies the same phenomenalistic approach to the analysis of the mind, again asserting that we have "no conception" of it in itself, "as distinguished from its conscious manifestations." Nevertheless, we think of it, as we do of a body, as "a permanent something, contrasted with the perpetual flux of the sensations and other feelings or mental states which we refer to it." Just as we believe in a body not presently perceived because we think of it in terms of permanent possibilities of sensation, so we believe in the continued reality of mind, even "when it is not feeling, nor thinking, nor conscious of its own existence," as an enduring possible source of such states. Of course, we think of ourselves as mental personalities in an environment with others. This view is based on an inductive argument from analogy. In ourselves, we experience causal connections between our own bodies and our mental states and then between our mental states and our behavioral responses; for example, we see an immediate physical threat, which causes us to feel fear, prompting our running away. In the case of others, we have sensory evidence "for the first and the last links of the series, but not for the intermediate link" of their mental states. We infer that there must be some connecting link in others comparable to that we experience in ourselves and that, instead of being mere "automatons," they are mental personalities like us. What is mysterious is how this series of mental states, whether our own or someone else's, can be self-aware, can remember the past, and can anticipate the future; this problem (which also pertained to Hume's phenomenalistic "bundle" theory of personality) seems "inexplicable" to Mill.[117]

It is in the *System of Logic* that Mill most carefully develops his theory of mental personality. We have no experience, and hence no knowledge, of the essential nature of the mind and are directly aware of only "a certain 'thread of consciousness' " (as Mill's father had expressed it)—"a series of feelings, that is, of sensations, thoughts, emotions, and volitions, more or less numerous and complicated." It is true that we think of ourselves or our minds as mental entities distinct from such states of consciousness, but this is transcendent metaphysical speculation on our part.

Minds not only are affected by sensory experiences but also can affect other minds. "A mind does not, indeed, like a body, excite sensations, but it may excite thoughts or emotions," including, especially, those "of approbation or blame,"[118] which will prove relevant to morality and social relationships.

EXACT AND INEXACT SCIENCES.   Mill's *System of Logic* is a particularly valuable source for his development of a "science of human nature." There he defends the views that there are inexact, as well as exact, sciences and that "the thoughts, feelings, and actions of sentient beings" can be the subject-matter of an inexact science. "Any facts are fitted, in themselves, to be a subject of science, which follow one another according to constant laws," he avers. Meteorology, for example, is an inexact science, because of the difficulty of collecting and processing all the data relevant to explaining and predicting specific weather patterns; yet there is no doubt that the latter do depend upon uniform natural laws. Sometimes, as in the case of astronomy, inexact sciences become exact.[119]

PSYCHOLOGY, THE SCIENCE OF HUMAN NATURE.   "The science of human nature," Mill claims, is an inexact science.

> The phenomena with which this science is conversant being the thoughts, feelings, and actions of human beings, it would have attained the ideal perfection of a science if it enabled us to foretell how an individual would think, feel, or act throughout life, with the same certainty with which astronomy enables us to predict the places and the occultations of the heavenly bodies.

The fact that this is not possible is due merely to the inevitable lack of complete and precise data regarding character, circumstances, and their intersection. Even so, we can make reliable statistical predictions, as we do regarding upcoming political elections. A "science of human nature" requires observable phenomena and laws explaining them. The "mental phenomena" we experience "consist of Thoughts, Emotions, Volitions, and Sensations," which comprise "the various feelings" of human nature. All such mental states are "immediately caused either by other states of mind or by states of body"; the first case falls within the domain of "Psychology, or Mental Philosophy," whereas the second will "belong to the province of Physiology." Mill sees these as irreducibly different sciences and denies that all mental phenomena can ultimately be "deduced from the physiological laws of our nervous organisation."[120]

Psychology, or the "science of human nature," is essentially built on "the uniformities of succession, the laws, whether ultimate or derivative, according to which one mental state succeeds another—is caused by, or at least is caused to follow, another." So, it is important that we be able to set forth these laws. The first "is expressed by saying, in the language of Hume, that every mental *impression* has its *idea*" as a possible correlate. "Secondly, these ideas, or secondary mental states, are excited by our impressions, or by other ideas, according to certain laws which are called Laws of Association." Three of these may be specified: first, "that similar ideas tend to excite one another"; second, when any two impressions have been experienced together, "then whenever one of these impressions, or the idea of it, recurs, it tends to excite the idea of the other"; and third, "that greater intensity in either or both" of two associated impressions produces the same effect as "a greater frequency of conjunction." (Mill refers to his father's *Analysis of the Phenomena of the Human Mind* as a "masterly" treatment of such laws of association.) These psychological laws are empirical rather than *a priori*. "An Empirical Law," Mill writes, "is an uniformity, whether of succession or of co-existence, which holds true in all instances within our limits of observation, but is not of a nature to afford any assurance that it would hold beyond those limits." Mill is very sensitive to the widely varying circumstances in which these laws of human nature are operative. Individuals within the same culture have different experiences, and diverse cultures diverge significantly in theirs.[121] Thus, despite the stable universality of human nature, it is difficult to be very precise in analyzing particular individuals or very accurate in predicting their behavior.

ETHOLOGY, THE SCIENCE OF CHARACTER. Our characters are variously developed in different sets of circumstances. Still, Mill is confident that "there exist universal laws of the Formation of Character," which are deducible "from the general laws of mind," and calls the science based on these laws "Ethology, or the Science of Character," comprising "the formation of national or collective character as well as individual,"

So, whereas psychology is an "experimental science" of mental personality, ethology, the science of character formation, is a "deductive science" derived from psychology. Mill admits that ethology has not yet been developed either extensively or systematically as a science in his day. If we are to be able to control our social environment for good utilitarian purposes, it is important that this be done. Learning to form desirable character through proper education is a valuable step to social progress. Any conclusions to which we are led by this science of ethology "must undergo a perpetual verification and correction from the general remarks afforded by common experience respecting human nature in our own age, and by history respecting times gone by." We cannot afford to trust *a priori* principles, dogmatically maintained in the absence of empirical confirmation.[122] For in our understanding of the human personality too much is at stake regarding our social well-being.

Knowledge

AN EMPIRICAL THEORY OF KNOWLEDGE. In his *Examination* Mill maintains that the "most fundamental questions in philosophy" concern what we can know of external reality and the evidence that renders such knowledge possible. In this respect of viewing epistemology as the basic area of philosophy, Mill is a typically modern thinker. Our knowledge of physical objects is strictly derived from sense experience, claims the empirical Mill.

> By those channels and no otherwise we learn whatever we do learn concerning them. Without the senses we should not know nor suspect that such things existed. We know no more of what they are, than the senses tell us, nor does nature afford us any means of knowing more.

The properties of such objects are identified with their powers to produce sensations in us. He subscribes to "the doctrine of the **Relativity** of Knowledge to the knowing mind," which could assume either "the most extreme form" (represented by Hume), which holds that the possibilities of phenomenal sensations are all we have any reason to believe external objects are, or a more moderate form (represented by Kant), which maintains that they are all we can know of external objects in our present state but that they are the appearances of some underlying **noumenal** reality.[123]

INDUCTIVE LOGIC.   To see Mill's more original contributions to epistemology, we must turn to his *System of Logic*. He sees logic as including both "the science of reasoning" and an art which is "founded on that science," meaning by "reasoning" both deductive "syllogizing" and "induction." The function of logic is to guide our thoughts "in the pursuit of truth." Some truths are known to us directly in "Intuition," whereas others are known "through the medium of other truths," by "**Inference**"; the former provide "the original premises" for the latter (as Descartes had observed a couple of centuries earlier). The mind entertains two sorts of propositions, "essential" ones, which are "purely verbal," and **accidental** ones, which purport to characterize reality, a distinction Mill identifies with Kant's *"analytic"* vs. *"synthetic"* judgments. Reasoning or inference is commonly held "to be of two kinds: reasoning from particulars to generals, and reasoning from generals to particulars; the former being called Induction, the latter Ratiocination or Syllogism." Induction infers a proposition from "*less general*" propositions, while deduction infers one "from propositions *equally* or *more* general." But Mill points out that even the most "general proposition," if synthetic, is a conclusion of prior inferences "collected by induction." Thus, induction is fundamental to all reasoning regarding truths that are "not self-evident" and is defined as "the operation of discovering and proving general propositions," which are merely "collections of particulars." Through inductive reasoning the mind infers "that what is true of certain individuals of a class is true of the whole class, or that what is true at certain times will be true in similar circumstances at all times." No mere descriptive summary of observed facts, such as Kepler's characterization of planetary orbits as elliptical, is a genuine inference or can be true induction, which must involve "Generalization from Experience." True induction "consists in inferring from some individual instances in which a phenomenon is observed to occur, that it occurs in all instances of a certain class; namely, in all which *resemble* the former, in what are regarded as the material circumstances." Thus, induction presupposes "that the course of nature is uniform,"[124] an assumption which our pragmatic experience supports.

We believe that "the future will resemble the past," insofar as empirical phenomena are properly described and subsumed under properly formulated laws. This belief "that the course of nature is uniform, is the fundamental principle, or general axiom, of Induction"; yet it is "itself founded on prior generalizations." This would seem to generate a kind of circularity. The principle of the uniformity of nature is a postulate; as such, it is never strictly provable but is supported by experience and is the **necessary condition** that must be assumed in order that any informative proposition whatsoever may be proved.[125]

CAUSAL REASONING.   A most important empirical generalization is "the Law of Causation," which holds "that every fact which has a beginning has a cause," which "invariably and *unconditionally*" precedes it. Mill's experimental methods for determining causes are quite famous, the simplest being his "Method of Agreement" and his "Method of Difference." He states the first as follows:

> *If two or more instances of the phenomenon under investigation have only one circumstance in common, the circumstance in which alone all the instances agree, is the cause (or effect) of the given phenomenon.*

For example, if twenty people in the world have gotten a rare, mysterious disease and are found to share in common only the fact that, prior to contracting it, they were all bitten by a mosquito carrying a certain microorganism, then being bitten by that sort of insect is the cause of that disease. Here is Mill's statement of the Method of Difference:

> *If an instance in which the phenomena under investigation occurs, and an instance in which it does not occur, have every circumstance in common save one, that one occurring only in the former; the circumstance in which alone the two differ, is the effect, or the cause, or an indispensable part of the cause, of the phenomenon.*

To continue our example, if the only two people bitten by such an infected mosquito and not contracting the disease significantly differed from all the victims of the disease only in having had an experimental inoculation, then the vaccine was causally related to their remaining free of the disease. Mill points out that both of these methods involve "*elimination*": the Method of Agreement eliminates all differences to determine what is causally related, while the Method of Difference eliminates points of agreement to determine what is causally related. The Method of Difference tends to be most useful in cases where "artificial experimentation" (as with inoculation) is possible, while the Method of Agreement is more useful in cases where we can only observe the facts, rather than manipulate circumstances.[126]

These two methods of inductive reasoning can be combined to form "the Joint Method of Agreement and Difference," which Mill expresses thus:

> If two or more instances in which the phenomenon occurs have only one circumstance in common, while two or more instances in which it does not occur have nothing in common save the absence of that circumstance; the circumstance in which alone the two sets of instances differ, is the effect, or the cause, or an indispensable part of the cause, of the phenomenon.[127]

If the twenty people bitten by infected insects and contracting the disease are alike only in not having been vaccinated and the two people bitten by infected insects but remaining free of the disease are alike only in having been inoculated, the vaccination is the causal difference between getting and not getting the disease, once bitten.

A fourth method of causal reasoning, "the Method of Residues," can be seen as a variant of the Method of Difference:

> Subduct from any phenomenon such part as is known by previous inductions to be the effect of certain antecedents, and the residue of the phenomenon is the effect of the remaining antecedents.

Suppose that we have already determined that the students who get a grade of at least C on a certain history examination are of at least average intelligence, have attended class regularly, and have also slept within twenty-four hours of taking the exam, while those who get at least a grade of B have also studied the material within a week of taking the exam, and that we want to find the causal antecedents for the "residue" of students getting grades above a B; if the only remaining difference is that they have read a certain primary source in preparing for the exam, that is probably the causal difference between their performance and that of students who scored lower. We might notice that these last two methods of causal reasoning, like the first two, employ some sort of elimination of phenomenal circumstances. But sometimes we cannot manipulate circumstances that are always present and can only observe their modifications. For example, the Moon is always present in our celestial environment but naturally varies in its observable spatial location relative to us; and we can observe a corresponding variation in the rise and fall of the

tides. By a fifth method of causal reasoning, "the Method of Concomitant Variations," we conclude that the gravitational attraction of the Moon, varying with its position relative to certain parts of the Earth, "wholly or partially" determines the rise and fall of the tides. Mill states this method thus:

> Whatever phenomenon varies in any manner whenever another phenomenon varies in some particular manner, is either a cause or an effect of that phenomenon, or is connected with it through some fact of causation.[128]

Sometimes, of course, we can ourselves produce the variations, as when we determine how much time to spend preparing for that history exam, which could be correlated with corresponding grades of test results.

These empirical methods of causal reasoning are crucial for our discovery of patterns of succession among phenomena of experience and, thus, are essential to human knowledge. Mill was the first to map them out so clearly.

Freedom

MILL'S DOCTRINE OF NECESSITY.   Thus far, we have seen that Mill adopts a phenomenalistic view of reality, conceives of bodies as relative to our sensations of them, defends psychology as a "science of human nature," and presents an empirical theory of knowledge that emphasizes inductive logic and causal reasoning. We can reasonably expect that his treatment of human freedom, consonant with this perspective, tilts towards determinism. His most famous discussion of this topic is "Of Liberty and Necessity," in *A System of Logic*, where he addresses "the celebrated controversy concerning the freedom of the will" by holding all "human volitions and actions to be necessary and inevitable," subject to the law of causality, like all other events. He says that this position "is commonly called the doctrine of Necessity," although there are problems with that term, which strikes many of us as "humiliating to the pride, and even degrading to the moral nature, of man." Yet Mill maintains that "the doctrine called Philosophical Necessity" is supported by universal experience and correctly claims

> that, given the motives which are present to an individual's mind, and given likewise the character and disposition of the individual, the manner in which he will act might be unerringly inferred; that if we knew the person thoroughly, and knew all the inducements which are

acting upon him, we could foretell his conduct with so much certainty as we can predict any physical event.[129] Two key words here are "motives" and "character," since they are internal causes of actions we tend to regard as free.

To say that some of our actions are "caused" (at least in part) by a **conjunction** of motives and character is merely to point to an "invariable, certain, and unconditional sequence," and not to any "mysterious compulsion." Here Mill is clearly embracing Hume's view of causal necessity. Unfortunately, it seems, this concept of causal necessity too often "involves much more than mere uniformity of sequence: it implies irresistibleness." We do not wish to think that we could never conceivably act otherwise than we do act, for such an idea is humiliating to human dignity and destructive of moral responsibility. But that is not what Mill's doctrine of necessity asserts. "When we say that all human actions take place of necessity, we only mean that they will certainly happen if nothing prevents." Those last three words are crucial, since often the will, driven by other motives or different dimensions of character, *could* move us to act differently from the way we do act. Another way of putting the point is to say that Mill is not a fatalist. He denies that "there is no use in struggling against" whatever is happening, "that it will happen however we may strive to prevent it." The reason he denies such fatalism is his conviction that, under ordinary circumstances, a human being "has, to a certain extent, a power to alter his character," however difficult this may be in fact. It is true that a person's "character is formed by his circumstances"; nevertheless, Mill avers, "his own desire to mould it in a particular way is one of those circumstances, and by no means one of the least influential." Other people, like our parents, helped to form our characters as we were developing. "We are exactly as capable of making our own character, *if we will*, as others are of making it for us." Indeed, on this view, our precious "feeling of moral freedom" is nothing more than this conviction that we are "able to modify our own character *if we wish*" to do so. "A person feels morally free who feels that his habits or his temptations are not his masters, but he theirs: who even in yielding to them knows that he could resist" if he so chose. To the extent that the concept of "Necessity" is identified with the denial of the mind's capacity "to co-operate in the

formation of its own character," it is an "objectionable term."[130]

THE ROLE OF MOTIVES.   Having discussed the causal determination of character, let us briefly consider the role of motives. "When the will is said to be determined by motives, a motive does not mean always, or solely, the anticipation of a pleasure or of a pain," as a narrower psychological hedonist (such as Callicles, in Plato's *Gorgias*) would claim. We can come to desire actions and character traits, once associated with pleasure and the avoidance of pain, without any present reference to them. For example, "the moral hero" may have once viewed self-sacrifice as a means to pleasure and continue to pursue it, even though it no longer seems conducive to pleasure; this is because of a "habit of willing," which is "commonly called a purpose" and helps to establish "a confirmed character."[131] In summary, all of our actions are causally determined; but some of them are determined, at least in part, by our characters and motives, over which we allegedly have some control.

MILL'S DETERMINISTIC POSITION.   The other important source for Mill's discussion of this issue is the chapter of his *Examination*, "On the Freedom of the Will"; indeed, though less famous than the treatment in the *Logic*, in some ways (apart from its critique of the opposing theory of Hamilton and Mansel) it is the more valuable analysis. First, Mill admits that we never experience a causal "*nexus*" between determining antecedent conditions and a voluntary action, but only "an invariable sequence." But, on Mill's Humean view of causality, that is true of even physical causes and effects. As he writes, our "volitions do, in point of fact, follow determinate moral antecedents with the same uniformity, and (when we have sufficient knowledge of the circumstances) with the same certainty, as physical effects follow their physical causes." What are these "moral antecedents" that causally determine voluntary actions? Mill explains that they are "desires, aversions, habits, and dispositions, combined with outward circumstances suited to call those internal incentives into action." (These are what the *Logic* identified as our motives and characters.) These "moral antecedents," in turn, have causes, some of which are "mental," such as the influences of education. But this only accentuates, rather than dispels, the essential role of causal determination in even voluntary actions:

> A volition is a moral effect, which follows the corresponding moral causes as certainly and invariably as physical effects follow their physical causes.[132]

Second, Mill attacks our alleged consciousness of the ability to act differently from the way we do act by denying that we can ever be conscious of what we are "*able* to do," apart from what we actually do:

> Consciousness is not prophetic; we are conscious of what is, not of what will or can be. We never know that we are able to do a thing, except from having done it, or something equal or similar to it.

But, if Mill is correct here, our alleged consciousness of the ability to act otherwise, far from being the object of experience, is merely a misleading "interpretation of experience."[133]

Third, the more accurate interpretation is that we sometimes *feel* that we "could have chosen the other course" of action *if* circumstances had been such that we "*preferred it.*" Mill invokes the example of murder—given his character, a person will "elect to murder" or "elect to abstain" from murder depending on "external motives," such as his knowledge (e.g., that there are no witnesses about or that his society punishes this sort of crime by execution), and/or "internal motives," such as his desires (e.g., to have revenge on his enemy or to avoid punishment). Our desires, Mill maintains, determine our actions, regardless of moral character:

> The difference between a bad and a good man is not that the latter acts in opposition to his strongest desires; it is that his desire to do right, and his aversion to doing wrong, are strong enough to overcome, and in the case of perfect virtue, to silence, any other desire or aversion which may conflict with them.

Moral education is so important because it disciplines will and habituates it in preferring right to wrong; "but the will can only be educated through the desires and aversions," to which our human nature is so susceptible.[134]

Fourth, Mill defends the viability of "moral responsibility" in relation to his deterministic theory by identifying it with punishment: "When we are said to have the feeling of being morally responsible for our actions," what we experience is "the feeling of liability to punishment"—either that it is likely or that it is

deserved. Far from destroying the justification of punishment, the deterministic theory, Mill believes, is its necessary condition. If character and motives do not help determine the will, if the will is free of all external determination, then punishment—which should be designed to reform character and improve motives—has "no power of acting on the will" and is undeserved. Thus, of the two utilitarian purposes of punishment—"the benefit of the offender himself and the protection of others"—the first would evaporate on the free-will theory.[135]

Fifth, Mill's deterministic position is not fatalistic. "Real fatalism is of two kinds," he writes. "Pure" fatalism "holds that our actions do not depend on our desires" but merely on forces external to us; as we have seen, Mill staunchly holds the opposite. "Modified Fatalism," like Mill himself, "holds that our actions are determined by our will, our will by our desires, and our desires by the joint influence of the motives presented to us and of our individual character"; but, unlike Mill, it also allegedly maintains "that, our character having been made for us and not by us, we are not responsible for it, nor for the actions it leads to, and should in vain attempt to alter them." Mill defends our moral responsibility and our capacity to reform.[136]

Finally, he attacks Kant's distinction between our phenomenal actions, which are causally necessitated, and free acts of will changing our character for better or worse. By means of this dualistic distinction, "the philosopher of Königsberg" allegedly compromises "the consistency of his theory." Mill objects that our will to change our character is itself determined by antecedent causal circumstances.[137] His own theory of **compatibilism** (that human freedom is compatible with causal necessity) here, as in his *Logic*, is thoroughly empiricist.

Morality

In the *Logic* Mill maintains that morality or "practical ethics" is not a science because it employs "the imperative mood," expressing what should be, rather than "the indicative," expressing what is. "Now, the imperative mood is the characteristic of art," or skilled activity, rather than of science, he says. "Whatever speaks in rules or precepts, not in assertions respecting matters of fact, is art; and ethics or morality is properly a portion of the art corresponding to the sciences of human nature and society."[138]

THE PRINCIPLE OF UTILITY.   But if ethics is not a science, we should beware of attempts to deduce as certain correct forms of behavior "from supposed universal practical maxims" (as rationalists like Kant do) or even to establish universal rules of conduct that are impervious to circumstances. Although science is valuable for connecting ends with means, only art can define our ultimate ends.

> Every art has one first principle, or general major premise, not borrowed from science; that which enunciates the object aimed at, and affirms it to be a desirable object.

Whereas medical art affirms that curing disease is a good end, medical science establishes effective means to doing so. As if referring to Hume's is-ought distinction, Mill discriminates between scientific propositions establishing matters of fact (e.g., "an existence, a co-existence, a succession, or a resemblance") and prescriptive propositions ("of which the predicate is expressed by the words *ought* or *should*"). These prescriptive propositions may imply, "as a matter of fact," that what is upheld as desirable "excites in the speaker's mind the feeling of approbation." Yet that is a secondary matter that cannot justify the approval of anyone, including the speaker himself. That would require a practical first principle: "There must be some standard by which to determine the goodness or badness, absolute and comparative, of ends or objects of desire." There must be a single such ultimate criterion to avoid the sort of conflicts that would regard an act as "approved by one" principle "and condemned by another." Though he does not justify his view here, Mill declares that "the general principle to which all rules of practice ought to conform, and the test by which they should be tried, is that of conduciveness to the happiness of mankind."[139] This is the famous principle of utility.

TWO APPROACHES TO ETHICS.   Mill's *Utilitarianism*, one of the most influential works of ethical theory ever written, begins by focusing on "the controversy respecting the criterion of right and wrong" that has raged since "the dawn of philosophy." In approaching the problem of "the foundation of morality," disputed since the debate between "the youth Socrates" and "the old Protagoras," Mill distinguishes two possible approaches, both of which seek "general laws" that can be applied to particular cases. What he calls "the intuitive school" maintains that "the principles of morals are evident *a priori*" through reason independent of concrete experience; this approach is best represented by Kant. Mill criticizes it for rarely listing its alleged "*a priori* principles" or reducing them to some ultimate "ground of obligation" (although he does not specifically accuse Kant of failing in these respects). "According to the other doctrine" of ethics, which Mill names "the inductive" approach, "right and wrong, as well as truth and falsehood, are questions of observation and experience." As an empiricist, Mill clearly favors the latter approach, which will lead him to "the principle of utility, or, as Bentham latterly called it, the greatest happiness principle." He refers to Kant as "the most illustrious" proponent of the "intuitive" approach and quotes one formulation of his categorical imperative. Yet he criticizes Kant as a crypto-utilitarian in the sense that that principle allegedly "fails, almost grotesquely, to show that" there would be anything wrong with even "the most outrageously immoral rules of conduct," apart from "the *consequences* of their universal adoption."[140]

THE ISSUE OF PROOF.   We should never expect a strict demonstration, or "direct proof," of any ultimate principle, although later Mill will try to provide "such proof as it is susceptible of." This is the same point he made earlier in the *Logic*, that science can only demonstrate links between means and ends and not conclusively establish the ends themselves. However, he warns, this does not imply that our "ultimate ends" are or should be matters of "blind impulse or arbitrary choice," for they are capable of argument or "proof" in a broader sense of the word: "The subject is within the cognizance of the rational faculty; and neither does that faculty deal with it solely in the way of intuition." Mill will present an argument for utilitarianism, in this larger sense of rational considerations, "capable of determining the intellect either to give or withhold its assent to the doctrine; and this is equivalent to proof."[141] But other matters must be discussed before such an attempt at argumentation is made.

THE PRINCIPLE OF UTILITY AND ITS DEFENSE.   Foremost among these is the most famous statement of the principle of utility:

The creed which accepts as the foundation of morals, Utility or the Greatest Happiness Principle, holds that actions are right in proportion as they tend to promote happiness, wrong as they tend to produce the reverse of happiness.

Here right and wrong are measured with reference to the ultimate good of happiness. But happiness itself must be measured in terms of some criteria:

By happiness is intended pleasure and the absence of pain; by unhappiness, pain and the privation of pleasure.

This will provide Mill with a strictly empirical moral criterion, based on the hedonistic assumptions

that pleasure and freedom from pain are the only things desirable as ends; and that all desirable things (which are as numerous in the utilitarian as in any other scheme) are desirable either for the pleasure inherent in themselves, or as means to the promotion of pleasure and the prevention of pain.

This view makes right and wrong relative to experience (though not purely subjective) and is a far cry from Kantian **deontology.**[142]

Next, Mill attempts to defend his theory against various standard criticisms, of which we shall consider eight. First, critics have traditionally accused hedonists, from Epicurus on, of adopting too demeaning a theory, "a doctrine worthy only of swine," who live for bestial pleasures and avoid pain at all costs. Mill's response is that it is not hedonists, "but their accusers, who represent human nature in a degrading light" by failing to recognize that, given our higher faculties, we are not content with physical pleasures. "But there is no known **Epicurean** theory of life which does not assign to the pleasures of the intellect, of the feelings and imagination, and of the moral sentiments, a much higher value as pleasures than to those of mere sensation." Indeed, here is one of Mill's few disagreements with Bentham's purely quantitative interpretation of utilitarianism:

It is quite compatible with the principle of utility to recognize the fact that some *kinds* of pleasure are more desirable and more valuable than others. It would be absurd that while, in estimating all other things, quality is considered as well as quantity, the estimation of pleasures should be supposed to depend on quantity alone.

But this introduces a new problem (which Bentham did not face) of how qualitatively to decide among pleasures. Mill's answer is that if people who have experienced any two types of pleasure tend to prefer one over the other, that one is "the more desirable

pleasure"; and he thinks that experience reveals that such people tend to prefer the sort of pleasure "which employs their higher faculties" over the mere gratification of animal appetites. In this alleged fact of human nature consists the "sense of dignity, which all human beings possess in one form or another." As Mill expresses the point in one of the most well-known of all his sayings,

It is better to be a human being dissatisfied than a pig satisfied; better to be Socrates dissatisfied than a fool satisfied. And if the fool, or the pig, are of a different opinion, it is because they only know their own side of the question.

Mill also emphasizes that "the utilitarian standard" is nonegoistic, that it "is not the agent's own greatest happiness, but the greatest amount of happiness altogether," thus distinguishing his ethical theory from the **egoistic** one of Hobbes. So, utilitarianism requires that we act for the greatest possible happiness of ourselves and others, measured in terms of "an existence exempt as far as possible from pain, and as rich as possible in enjoyments, both in point of quantity and quality."[143]

The second objection is a two-edged one, to the effect that the object of utilitarianism, happiness, "is unattainable" and/or unnecessary. Mill maintains that it is "unattainable" only to the extent that we adopt an unrealistic conception of happiness. A more **realistic** view of happiness is

not a life of rapture, but moments of such, in an existence made up of few and transitory pains, many and various pleasures, with a decided predominance of the active over the passive, and having as the foundation of the whole not to expect more from life than it is capable of bestowing;

on this interpretation, human happiness is possible and normally requires some balance of "tranquillity" and "excitement." Indeed, Mill expresses his optimistic assurance that our prospects for happiness are improving. On the other hand, he admits that people can live without happiness, as all too many (he estimates "nineteen-twentieths of mankind") do and that people can even choose to lead lives of self-sacrifice. Yet he insists that this is only good to the extent that it is conducive to the greatest happiness overall. When it is so conducive, self-sacrifice is admirable and reinforces the **altruistic** view "that the happiness which forms the utilitarian standard of what is right in conduct is not the agent's own happiness but that of all concerned." The moral ideal—far from Hobbesian egoism—is that we should try to be as impartial as possible in choosing between our own welfare and that of others.[144]

A third objection is that utilitarianism is too demanding in requiring that we be motivated by a concern for "the general interest of society." In response, Mill distinguishes between action-morality and agent-morality and insists that "utilitarian moralists have gone beyond almost all others in affirming that the motive has nothing to do with the morality of the action, though much with the worth of the agent." He offers a vivid example, claiming that the person who deliberately saves another "from drowning does what is morally right," regardless of his motive; on the other hand, the vileness of his motive may be relevant to our moral estimation of his character.[145]

Fourth, the utilitarian view can be accused of being too cold and calculating, in focusing on the reckoning of consequences. In response, Mill points out that we can and should consider more than "the rightness and wrongness of their actions," in judging the virtuous character of persons.[146]

Fifth, utilitarianism is sometimes attacked "as a *godless* doctrine." But there is no reason that it should be, especially if we believe in a Deity that cares for our welfare: "If it be a true belief that God desires, above all things, the happiness of His creatures, and that this was His purpose in their creation, utility is not only not a godless doctrine, but more profoundly religious than any other."[147]

Sixth, utilitarianism "is often summarily stigmatized as an immoral doctrine by giving it the name of Expediency," as "opposed to the Right." But if that connotes selfishness or serving short-term interests, Mill's sort of utilitarianism is not guilty. He uses the example of the rule against lying, which has significant utilitarian value and should normally be followed. "Yet that even this rule, sacred as it is, admits of possible exceptions is acknowledged by all moralists," says Mill (forgetting about Kant), indicating that all such rules are relative rather than absolute.[148]

Seventh, the principle of utility may be attacked as impractical in the sense that we often lack the time to calculate likely consequences in the urgent circumstances of practical decision making. Mill responds that we need not start from scratch and can always base our judgments on the past experiences of

ourselves, others we have known, and people throughout recorded history. He sarcastically comments,

> There is no difficulty in proving any ethical standard whatever to work ill, if we suppose universal idiocy to be conjoined with it; but on any hypothesis short of that mankind must by this time have acquired positive beliefs as to the effects of some actions on their happiness.

Indeed, the rules of morality, including that against lying, reflect those beliefs that are derived from past experience.[149]

Finally, utilitarianism is suspected of providing us with an all-too-convenient excuse for making "an exception to moral rules" in favor of ourselves. But, Mill answers, every ethical theory is susceptible to abusive misapplications. The "knotty points" of moral dilemmas are such that there can always be conflicting rules and obligations. We need an ultimate principle, such as that of utility, to serve as "umpire" in such cases.[150]

MORAL SANCTIONS.   Mill considers the sanctions supporting the principle of utility—"what are the motives to obey? or, more specifically, what is the source of its obligation?" He observes that "sanctions are either external or internal" and that utilitarianism incorporates both types. The external sanctions derive from our hope for rewards and fear of punishment, whether those be natural, social, or religious. "The internal sanction of duty," by contrast, is "a feeling in our own mind," providing a sense of moral satisfaction or of remorse, and constituting "the essence of Conscience." He regards this "subjective feeling" as the "ultimate sanction" of morality, in the sense that it is inescapable for those in whom it has been inculcated.[151]

MORAL FEELINGS.   Another major issue is whether our "feeling of duty is **innate** or implanted" in us by our social environment. Mill's view is that "moral feelings are not innate" in human nature but are "acquired." Nevertheless, they are "natural" to us in the sense that we are born with the capacity to develop "the moral faculty," given conducive circumstances. Likewise, he avers, "It is natural to man to speak, to reason, to build cities, to cultivate the ground, though these are acquired faculties," rather than activities pursued from the beginning of our lives. This capacity is rooted in "the social feelings of mankind—the desire to be in unity with our fellow creatures, which is already a powerful principle in human nature." Mill believes (against Hobbes and with Hume) that these natural sentiments render us altruistic, normally concerned about the well-being of others, as well as for our own, providing a psychological foundation for morality. He even anticipates a social climate in which it might "be taught as a religion." Thus, the "whole force of education" might be brought to bear to facilitate the acquisition of a sense of duty. Mill admits that this concern for others is "inferior in strength to their selfish feelings" for some people and that in others it can be "wanting altogether." But it is a powerful sanction for those who possess it and can be socially reinforced as "the ultimate sanction of the greatest happiness morality."[152]

THE DESIRABILITY OF THE GENERAL HAPPINESS. Mill argues that "the general happiness" is the only complete, ultimate, intrinsic end of human nature. He reminds us that no direct demonstration of "first principles," including the principle of utility, is possible. The argument proceeds in two steps. First, Mill uses analogies to show "that happiness is desirable": just as we know something is visible from the empirical fact that it is actually seen or that something is audible because it is heard, so we know that something is desirable if it is actually desired. But experience reveals (as Aristotle knew full well) that people do desire happiness; therefore, happiness must be desirable. But whose happiness is desirable? Is it merely the agent's own, as Hobbes indicated? No, reality is not so atomistically compartmentalized as that, which the second step of Mill's argument is designed to show. Since each individual desires his or her own personal happiness, we must collectively desire "the general happiness." After all, your happiness is causally bound up with the well-being of the groups of which you are a member, to the extent that that membership matters to you; we are not isolated individuals, and our interests cannot be utterly divorced from their social contexts. Thus, "the general happiness" is desirable as at least "*one* of the ends of conduct." If we want to say that this is *the* ultimate end, as Mill does, we must consider the Kantian claim that virtue fits that description. Mill admits that some people, like Kant, desire virtue "and the absence of **vice** no less really than pleasure and the absence of pain." Far from denying that virtue is an intrinsic good for

such people, Mill admits it but explains that it has evolved, in their minds, from being a mere means to the end of happiness to becoming an essential component part of their happiness:

> What was once desired as an instrument for the attainment of happiness, has come to be desired for its own sake. In being desired for its own sake it is, however, desired as *part* of happiness.

So it is with everything other than happiness itself—it is desirable either as a means to happiness or because it is conceived of as a component part of happiness. The reason for this alleged fact is that "human nature is so constituted" as to render it so.[153]

JUSTICE. Mill confronts and tries to solve the problem of justice. He begins with the concession, "In all ages of speculation one of the strongest obstacles to the reception of the doctrine that Utility or Happiness is the criterion of right and wrong has been drawn from the idea of Justice."[154] Suppose, for example, that sometime in the next fifty years technology will have developed to the point that we can render ninety-five percent of the members of society deliriously happy and free to do whatever they like throughout their lives, if we enslave the remaining five percent (say, those who are born both left-handed and green-eyed) as lifelong workers running and maintaining our machinery. We need not envision whips and chains; the minority will simply work as most of us do today, in relatively sanitary, safe conditions, with vacation time, and so forth. But the catch is that they have no choice about being society's designated workers, due to circumstances beyond their control (such as being born both left-handed and green-eyed). They might (and many of us would) say that it was unjust (or unfair) to deprive them of the liberty granted most other members of society because of the results of some biological lottery. Yet if we assume that the situation could be manipulated for the greatest happiness of the greatest number of people, it appears we have a conflict between justice and utility. Or do we?

In responding to this objection, Mill carefully analyzes the concept of justice, as he has already analyzed the concept of utility. He focuses on five standard meanings of justice and injustice. First, we think that justice requires a respect for people's "*legal rights*" and that it is unjust to violate them; for example, you could legitimately complain that the thief who "ripped off" your hard-earned money did you an injustice. Second, justice requires that we respect "a *moral right*" of another, even if it is not legally protected; for example, if the libel laws do not cover a certain form of slander, you could nevertheless be warranted in complaining that someone smearing your reputation has done you an injustice. Third, justice requires that we try to give each person what "he *deserves*," whether we feel like it or not; for example, if you meet all the requirements for a course with good-to-excellent achievement, your teacher does you an injustice in flunking you. Fourth, "it is confessedly unjust to *break faith* with any one"; if you give your word to meet an associate for lunch tomorrow, justice requires that you keep faith with her. Fifth, in certain circumstances, defined in terms of social roles, justice requires impartiality so that it is "inconsistent with justice to be *partial*"; for example, it would be unjust for the judge, in a court of law, to acquit a defendant on the basis of good looks or to condemn one because of offensive body odor, since justice requires impartial rulings based on the evidence presented. Mill briefly considers "*equality*" as a perspective on justice but backs away from endorsing it with the flip comment, "Each person maintains that equality is the dictate of justice, except where he thinks that expediency requires inequality."[155]

Now Mill sets about to find the common denominator in all these conceptions of justice, "the mental link which holds them together." He observes that, etymologically, the word relates to "the ordinances of law" and concludes "that the *idée mère*, the primitive element, in the formation of the notion of justice, was conformity to law." We psychologically tend to think that people "ought to be compelled" to meet obligations of justice by the punishments of law or public opinion or pangs of conscience. Mill connects this with the Kantian distinction between "duties of perfect and of imperfect obligation," the former engendering correlative rights in someone, while the latter do not. If one person has a "**perfect**" **duty** to be honest in dealing with another, that second person has a right to honest treatment; by contrast, the beggar you meet on the street corner has no right to your money, despite the fact that you have an "imperfect obligation" to be charitable to the unfortunate. In this sense,

justice involves "duties of perfect obligation" which others have a right to have met.

> Justice implies something which it is not only right to do, and wrong not to do, but which some individual person can claim from us as his moral right.

Summarizing the discussion thus far, Mill claims that "the two essential ingredients in the sentiment of justice are the desire to punish a person who has done harm, and the knowledge or belief that there is some definite individual to whom harm has been done."[156]

We are ready for Mill's response to the alleged conflict between justice and utility. It turns out "that justice is a name for certain moral requirements, which, regarded collectively, stand higher in the scale of social utility, and are therefore of more paramount obligation, than any others." For example, the requirement to preserve innocent human life is such that under certain circumstances, "it may not only be allowable, but a duty, to steal, or take by force, the necessary food or medicine" that will save people from death; justice may permit or even require such theft. But now notice the interpretive spin Mill is giving to the term:

> Justice remains the appropriate name for certain social utilities which are vastly more important, and therefore more absolute and imperative, than any others are as a class.[157]

In other words, **contrary** to specious appearances, justice allegedly cannot really conflict with utility because it *is* the most obligatory of all "social utilities" and, of course, cannot conflict with itself.

Dissociating Morality from Nature.   In his essay *Nature* Mill considers whether we can safely correlate the "goodness" of "any mode of thinking, feeling, or acting" with the extent to which it is "according to nature," as the Stoics and Aquinas once taught. Like Hume, Mill wants to distinguish between "what is," as studied by "science and history," and "what ought to be," as considered by "art, morals, and politics." But the concept of "nature," whether used to refer to all of reality or to reality in the absence of any "voluntary human intervention," has to do with fact rather than with value. Yet it must become a value-laden word in order to provide us with "a test of right and wrong, good and evil." Thinkers who wish to make this move (like Aquinas) want to associate the idea of nature with that of law. Indeed, we do speak of both scientific laws (of fact) and moral and political laws (of value). We have to conform to physical laws of nature, whether wittingly or unwittingly, except to the extent that we are able to extricate ourselves from the circumstances in which they apply. But should we take seriously the idea of following nature, "as an ethical maxim," where "nature" is interpreted to refer to reality as it is independent of all human agency? Mill's answer is that to do so would be "palpably absurd" and contrary to all human initiative:

> If the natural course of things were perfectly right and satisfactory, to act at all would be a gratuitous meddling, which, as it could not make things better, must make them worse.

Plowing fields, growing crops, building houses, designing and wearing clothes are all, he points out, "direct infringements of the injunction to follow nature." The developments of civilization presuppose natural imperfections to be improved. But why should we regard nature as morally admirable, anyhow?

> In sober truth, nearly all the things which men are hanged or imprisoned for doing to one another are nature's everyday performances. Killing, the most criminal act recognized by human laws, nature does once to every being that lives, and in a large proportion of cases after protracted tortures

such as we would attribute to moral monsters. Nature routinely deprives creatures of their means of livelihood as well.

> Either it is right that we should kill because nature kills, torture because nature tortures, ruin and devastate because nature does the like, or we ought not to consider at all what nature does, but what it is good to do.

Mill pushes the logic of his critique to its conclusion:

> If it is a sufficient reason for doing one thing that nature does it, why not another thing? If not all things, why any thing?

Should we follow our natural instincts and behave like other animals? Mill answers, very much to the contrary,

> that nearly every respectable attribute of humanity is the result, not of instinct, but of a victory over instinct; and that there is hardly anything valuable in the natural man except capacities—a whole world of possibilities, all of them dependent upon eminently artificial discipline for being realized.

The very development of moral character requires that we rise above natural instinct. "The truth is that there is hardly a single point of excellence belonging to human character which is not decidedly repugnant to the untutored feelings of human nature." Thus, our

moral duty—regarding both nature in general and human nature in particular—is "not to follow but to amend it."[158]

Like Hume, Mill would divorce the realm of descriptive fact from the prescriptive sphere of value:

> Conformity to nature has no connection whatever with right and wrong. . . . That a thing is unnatural, in any precise meaning which can be attached to the word, is no argument for its being blamable.

The maxim that we ought to "follow Nature" is either meaningless and superfluous (if we are referring to the physical and mental laws to which we are inevitably bound) or "irrational and immoral" (if we are referring to the adoption of the nonhuman natural order as a model for our voluntary actions).[159] It is far better to use the capacities of human nature to change our environment and rationally control our animal instincts in pursuit of the utilitarian goal of the greatest happiness for the greatest number of persons.

Society

JUSTICE AND SOCIAL CONDUCT.   Let us continue examining Mill's analysis of justice in *Utilitarianism*, but now with reference to his social theory. He holds that "the idea of justice" comprises "a rule of conduct," generally applicable to all and oriented toward their well-being, on the one hand, and "a sentiment which sanctions the rule," by a willingness that violators should be punished, on the other. Rules of social justice, as we have seen, are correlated with people's rights to expect them to be enforced.

> When we call anything a person's right, we mean that he has a valid claim on society to protect him in the possession of it, either by the force of law, or by that of education and opinion.

The justificatory grounds of all social rights are those of "general utility," rather than any alleged *a priori* foundations, and our need for security is so basic as to require constant social protection.[160]

Mill acknowledges the broad-based relativity of our views of justice from one society to another or among individuals within the same society. He illustrates the point with three examples:

1. Different views on the proper justification of punishment,
2. Varying opinions on how much people with different talents and skills should be paid for their contributions to society, and

3. The problem of what constitutes a fair method of taxation.

(In the course of discussing the first of these, Mill repudiates the social contract theory, calling it "a mere fiction," which is useless for justifying our obligations to society.) Justice turns out to be a collective "name for certain classes of moral rules, which concern the essentials of human well-being more nearly, and are therefore of more absolute obligation, than any other rules for the guidance of life." Most important among the rules of justice (to which, we recall, rights attach) are those of nonmaleficence, forbidding us "to hurt one another" and proscribing "wrongful interference with each other's freedom"; for these affect needs and interests which are "vital to human well-being" rather than being tangential or secondary. "The most marked cases of injustice" are actions "of wrongful aggression, or wrongful exercise of power over some one; the next are those which consist in wrongfully withholding from him something which is his due." Justice requires that people be given what they deserve and, in certain circumstances, that impartiality be observed. It follows from this "that society should treat all equally well who have deserved equally well of *it*." Mill maintains that the principle of utility itself should be interpreted in terms of a presumption of a basic equality of persons involved, in accordance with "Bentham's dictum, 'everybody to count for one, nobody for more than one.' " All people, as such, have an equal ***prima facie*** claim to happiness, on this view. Furthermore, they all "have a *right* to equality of treatment, except when some recognized social expediency requires the reverse." That last qualifying phrase is important for showing that equality is not an intrinsic value, but is relative to social utility. When social inequalities cease to be considered expedient, we come to regard them as unjust. Indeed, social progress can be viewed in terms of the evolution from inequality to greater equality and the corresponding erosion of "the aristocracies of colour, race, and sex."[161] Here we can already discern hints of the social liberalism that will radically distinguish Mill from Hegel's conservatism.

SOCIAL LIBERTY. Let us now turn to an analysis of Mill's greatest work of social philosophy, *On Liberty*, which is arguably the most impressive philosophical statement of political liberalism of all time. Mill defines his topic as civil "or Social Liberty: the nature and limits of the power which can be legitimately exercised by society over the individual." He points out that the "struggle between Liberty and Authority" is different in recent times from what it was in earlier ages. Formerly, the interests of subjects were pitted against those of the sovereign authority, and liberty was measured in terms of "protection against the tyranny of the political rulers." A ruler's power was historically limited by securing his "recognition of certain immunities, called political liberties or rights," and/or through "the establishment of constitutional checks." But with the rise of recent democratic government, the split between sovereign and subjects has been fused, and people are increasingly governing themselves, if not directly, then at least through their elected representatives.[162]

With the emergence of the American "democratic republic," we realize that the problem of liberty has shifted. Because of the political procedures of majority rule, "the tyranny of the majority" (as Alexis de Tocqueville calls it) is a new problem "against which society requires to be on its guard." Society itself, in the form of a majority of its members, can become a tyrant, imposing its own views and values on minority groups, by means of the sanctions of law and public opinion. We ought to be able to determine a reasonable limit to such imposition as a check against our natural tendency to want others to conform to our own standards. Personal "likings and dislikings" get communicated and shared, threatening to become social expectations. What is needed is a criterion for testing "the propriety or impropriety" of social interference in personal preferences. Mill proposes his "very simple principle" as such a criterion:

> That principle is, that the sole end for which mankind are warranted, individually or collectively, in interfering with the liberty of action of any of their number, is self-protection.

We might call this formulation his "self-protection" principle. It is followed immediately by a different formulation of the same idea:

> That the only purpose for which power can be rightfully exercised over any member of a civilized community, against his will, is to prevent harm to others.

This might be labeled Mill's "harm" principle. He proceeds to say that a person's "own good, either physical or moral, is not a sufficient warrant" for interfering with his liberty. "He cannot rightfully be compelled to do or forbear because it will be better for him to do so, because it will make him happier, because, in the opinions of others, to do so would be wise, or even right," though these may be adequate grounds for reasoning with or trying to persuade him. Mill is distinguishing here between purely self-regarding and other-regarding behavior:

> The only part of the conduct of any one, for which he is amenable to society, is that which concerns others. In the part which merely concerns himself, his independence is, of right, absolute.

He proceeds to specify that the criterion only applies to mature adults, not to children or the irresponsible or members of primitive societies.[163]

As a citizen of the British Empire, he defends progressive, enlightened, benevolent despotism as "a legitimate mode of government in dealing with barbarians, provided the end be their improvement, and the means justified by actually effecting that end." He might observe that that has turned out to be the case with Great Britain's colonial rule of India, for instance. In arguing his point, Mill deliberately avoids making any appeal to "the idea of abstract right," preferring to rest his case on "utility as the ultimate appeal on all ethical questions," so long as this is broadly interpreted in terms of "the permanent interests of man as a progressive being" rather than narrowly as short-term expediency. He carves out three spheres of human action that should be protected by his "very simple principle" of liberty: "first, the inward domain of consciousness; demanding liberty of conscience, in the most comprehensive sense; liberty of thought and feeling; absolute freedom of opinion and sentiment on all subjects, practical or speculative"; second, there is freedom of personal lifestyles, "liberty of tastes and pursuits," so long as we refrain from harming others; and, third, there is freedom of association, the liberty to unite with those of our choice, "for any purpose not involving harm to others," so long as that association is not brought about by force or deceit. The freedom of any society, according to Mill, is contingent on the extent to which these liberties are granted and protected.

> The only freedom which deserves the name, is that of pursuing our own good in our own way, so long as we do

not attempt to deprive others of theirs, or impede their efforts to obtain it.[164]

The remainder of *On Liberty* explores some of this liberty principle's implications and applications.

FREEDOM OF EXPRESSION. Mill presents what may be the best argued defense of freedom of expression in the history of philosophy. Even if government restrictions here reflect majority opinion in constitutional countries, Mill decries them as "illegitimate," regardless how numerically overwhelming that majority may be.

> If all mankind minus one, were of one opinion, and only one person were of the contrary opinion, mankind would be no more justified in silencing that one person, than he, if he had the power, would be justified in silencing mankind.

This is fine rhetoric, but its underlying reasoning must also be examined. Let us begin with the modest acknowledgment that none of us is ever infallible; thus, for all we know, any unpopular opinion may be true or false or some mixture of the two.[165]

First, then, if it is true, by suppressing it we deprive people of access to its truth, and truth is a good of the mind, the deprivation of which tends to be detrimental. Public policy requires that we adopt certain views and act upon them; nor should we be "wishy-washy," vacillating indecisively between an opinion and its contrary. However, Mill says,

> There is the greatest difference between presuming an opinion to be true because, with every opportunity for contesting it, it has not been refuted, and assuming its truth for the purpose of not permitting its refutation.

We are only justified in assuming a truth and acting on it to the extent that we have allowed it to be critically challenged. The cultivation of truth requires an openness to alternative points of view. Nor should we swallow that "piece of idle sentimentality" that assumes that truth, by its very nature, will always prevail against any and all persecution. "The real advantage which truth has, consists in this: that when any opinion is true, it may be extinguished once, twice or many times, but in the course of ages there will generally be found persons to rediscover it," until one of its reappearances occurs in circumstances favorable to its continuation. In an intellectually oppressive climate, not only truths but capable minds can be stifled. In the spirit of Socrates, Mill avers,

No one can be a great thinker who does not recognize, that as a thinker it is his first duty to follow his intellect to whatever conclusion it may lead. Truth gains more even by the errors of one who, with due study and preparation, thinks for himself, than by the true opinions of those who only hold them because they do not suffer themselves to think.[166]

Second, the unpopular opinion to be suppressed may, in fact, be false, and the majority opinion may be correct; even so, the latter, if not exposed to any possible criticism, is liable to "be held as a dead dogma, not a living truth," and this sort of "truth" is hardly distinguishable from superstition. We cannot genuinely understand the significance of a truth without a critical awareness of opposing views, as they are expressed by advocates who earnestly believe them. Where we cannot find such advocates, we need to devise such an effective substitute as the "Socratic dialectics, so magnificently exemplified in the dialogues of Plato," to challenge our own views. Meanwhile, to the extent that we can find articulate critics of the *status quo*, Mill proclaims, "let us thank them for it, open our minds to listen to them, and rejoice" that they will do for us what we might find difficult to do for ourselves.[167]

Third, the most common situation is that a generally accepted opinion is partly true, while an unpopular rival view represents another portion of the truth. Since the conflict of rival views can elicit the greater whole of truth of which each represents a part, the suppression of such collisions is a "formidable evil" obstructing such an intellectual good. When people can hear both sides of a dispute, "there is always hope" for progress; "it is when they attend only to one that errors harden into prejudices." Mill thus defends the freedom to express unpopular opinions, whether they be true, false or mixed.[168]

INDIVIDUALITY. Mill next presents one of the most powerful defenses of human individuality ever mounted, the idea being that people should be free to adopt their own lifestyles "without hindrance, either physical or moral, from their fellow-men, so long as it is at their own risk and peril" and puts nobody else in any danger. An individual "must not make himself a nuisance to other people. But if he refrains from molesting others in what concerns them, and merely acts according to his own inclination and judgment in things which concern himself" alone, they should respect his liberty. Given that none of us is perfect or

infallible, "it is useful" to society "that there should be different experiments of living," so that we can test which seem to work best. Living in accordance with one's own personality and character is conducive to both "human happiness" and "individual and social progress." But, unfortunately, Mill observes, "individual spontaneity" is rather unappreciated, and the majority tends to want everyone to conform to its ways. It is unhealthy for us merely to conform to external expectations rather than living in ways that are best for us.

> Human nature is not a machine to be built after a model, and set to do exactly the work prescribed for it, but a tree, which requires to grow and develop itself on all sides, according to the tendency of the inward forces which make it a living thing.

Unlike machines, we should not perfectly replicate one another; like other organic beings, we require a certain measure of individuality for a healthy life. When we attribute "character" to a person, it is a tribute to his individuality, to the fact that his "desires and impulses are his own" and his actions unlike those of an automaton. Unfortunately, the common tendency, encouraged by the social pressures of conformity, is "to degenerate into the mechanical." This is detrimental to the development of human genius, which, though important for progress, tends not to be appreciated by the mass of "unoriginal minds." Thus, collective mediocrity tends to flourish in society. We ought to encourage "exceptional individuals" in their difference and to regard nonconformity as a social service, being grateful even for eccentricity, which is often a matrix for "genius, mental vigour, and moral courage," all of which are beneficial.[169]

By contrast, the "despotism of custom," which would crush expressions of individuality, is a great obstacle to human progress. Mill thinks that Eastern cultures tend to be static because they have historically languished under the yoke of custom; China, for example, despite prodigious talent and even wisdom, has remained stagnant "for thousands of years; and if they are ever to be farther improved, it must be by foreigners," he claims. What has rendered Europe so much more progressive is its relative cultivation of variety. Mill agrees with von Humboldt that the two "necessary conditions of human development" are freedom and variety and thinks the second to be diminishing daily in his own society.[170]

SOCIETAL AUTHORITY IN RELATION TO INDIVIDUAL ACCOUNTABILITY. Mill tries to set limits to society's legitimate authority over the individual, beyond the areas of freedom of expression and personal lifestyle. His general judgment is, "To individuality should belong the part of life in which it is chiefly the individual that is interested; to society, the part which chiefly interests society." Negatively put, we can be legally prevented from injuring the legitimate interests of others and violating their rights; positively expressed, we can be legally forced to bear our fair share of responsibility for the protection of society. In other areas affecting the well-being of others, society may legitimately punish us "by opinion, though not by law." But wherever a person's action affects only his own interests or need not affect others unless they so choose, he should enjoy "perfect freedom, legal and social, to do the action and stand the consequences." Mill's argument here is that when society interferes in self-regarding behavior, it does so on general assumptions that are either mistaken or, "even if right," likely to be "misapplied to individual cases." We can legitimately avoid people we do not like and even warn others of what we consider their potential danger. Mill is sensitive to the difficulty in drawing a hard-and-fast distinction between other-regarding and purely self-regarding conduct, since we are members of society as well as individuals and there is, at least, the permanent danger of bad example to others. He admits that damage to oneself can adversely impact on others and thus pass out of the purely "self-regarding class" of actions. Still, though it may not always be clear-cut, he believes the distinction to be legitimate. For example, he says, "No person ought to be punished simply for being drunk; but a soldier or a policeman should be punished for being drunk on duty," because he thus endangers the public he is charged to protect. "But the strongest of all the arguments against the interference of the public with purely personal conduct, is that when it does interfere, the odds are that it interferes wrongly."[171] Since this interference is wrong because of the harm it is likely to do, this is a distinctly utilitarian argument.

Mill exhibits "specimens of application" of his "two maxims," that individuals are not accountable to society for their purely self-regarding actions and that they are accountable for other-regarding actions that threaten the interests of other people. Sometimes,

indeed, utility requires that society not interfere even with actions that do or might harm others, as in the case of competitive activity that leads to one person being preferred over another for a desirable prize or position. Although drunkenness *per se* is normally "not a fit subject for legislative interference," the person who has proved himself a violent drunk, given to physical abuse of others, can be legitimately restricted from becoming drunk. Likewise, idleness is often purely self-regarding but can be properly punished, even by compulsory labor, if it leads to neglecting to support one's children. Third, some actions can be rightly punished if done publicly (though not if done privately), because they then constitute "offenses against decency." Mill thinks that fornication and gambling should be legally tolerated, but has difficulty deciding whether a person should be allowed "to be a pimp, or to keep a gambling-house."[172]

Even when government interference does *not* violate personal liberty, it may be objectionable on any combination of three grounds. "The first is, when the thing to be done is likely to be better done by individuals than by the government. Speaking generally, there is no one so fit to conduct any business, or to determine how or by whom it shall be conducted, as those who are personally interested in it." Second, even when government can act more effectively than individuals, their "own mental education" may require their acting for themselves. Third, even when that is not an issue, there is always "the great evil of adding unnecessarily" to the power of government in relation to that of individual citizens. Mill contrasts the Russian Empire, with its bureaucratic paralysis, unfavorably with the American people, who are used to transacting public business for themselves. His formula for good government is—"the greatest dissemination of power consistent with efficiency; but the greatest possible centralization of information, and diffusion of it from the centre." He ends with the non-Hegelian warning that individuality should never be sacrificed on the altar of the State.[173]

REPRESENTATIVE GOVERNMENT. In his *Considerations on Representative Government* Mill argues that that is "the ideally best form of government." No matter how good (e.g., enlightened and benevolent) an autocrat might be, "despotic monarchy" renders citizens "mentally passive" and dependent on others. "They exercise no will in respect to their collective interests." Mill advocates representative government, in which political authority "is vested in the entire aggregate of the community, every citizen not only having a voice in the exercise of that ultimate authority, but being, at least occasionally, called on to take an actual part in the government by the personal discharge of some public function, local or general"; for example, we elect our legislators and are sometimes called upon to perform jury duty. Mill rests his advocacy of representative government on two principles: "The first is that the rights and interests of every or any person are only secure from being disregarded when the person interested" can, and is inclined to, demand them. "The second is that the general prosperity" of society is directly proportional "to the amount and variety of the personal energies enlisted in promoting it." Combining these two principles, Mill infers that good government requires that citizens be "self-*protecting*" and "self-*dependent*." Nevertheless, it remains "an open question" as to precisely what functions of good government citizens should discharge. "Great varieties in this respect are compatible with the essence of representative government, provided the functions are such as secure to the representative body the control of everything in the last resort." Also, the people can "control" the business of government without actually having to do it themselves, as we elect legislators to vote on budget matters.[174]

Mill distinguishes between a pure democracy, in which all the people, equally represented, govern themselves, and the more commonly practiced democracy, in which the people as a whole are governed by "a mere majority," which is "exclusively represented." The latter is "a government of privilege," which tends "to the complete disfranchisement of minorities." Mill thinks that minorities should themselves have proportional representatives, even if those will inevitably be outvoted by the representatives of the majority. The disfranchisement of any citizens is not only harmful to them but corrosive of democratic society itself. "There ought to be no pariahs in a full-grown and civilized nation, no persons disqualified, except through their own default." There will always be insufficient incentive to consider the needs and interests of those excluded from voting rights.

> No arrangement of the suffrage, therefore, can be permanently satisfactory in which any person or class is peremptorily excluded, in which the electoral privilege is not open to all persons of full age who desire to obtain it.

However, Mill does think a literacy requirement is appropriate.[175]

EQUAL OPPORTUNITIES FOR WOMEN. In reaction to the fact that women were still denied the vote in Mill's day, in *The Subjection of Women* he states his thesis—

> That the principle which regulates the existing social relations between the two sexes—the legal subordination of one sex to the other—is wrong in itself, and now one of the chief hindrances to human improvement; and that it ought to be replaced by a principle of perfect equality, admitting no power or privilege on one side, nor disability on the other.

Of course, this would require equal educational, vocational, and political opportunities for both genders. Mill recognizes that some people (like Aristotle) will object that the government of women by men is "natural." But every domination of some people by others can be rationalized in the same specious manner, including slavery (again Aristotle comes to mind for us as for Mill). Unfortunately, even great rationalizers tend to confuse what is customary with what is "natural," when it seems to their advantage to do so. A second frail objection to equality of the sexes is the claim that women voluntarily accept their social status relative to men, and generally do so without complaints. But, in fact, by the time Mill was publishing this, women were protesting their exclusion from the political process (and Mill himself had presented to Parliament their petition for voting rights). Since time immemorial, women have complained "of ill usage by their husbands" to the extent that they could do so safely; but, while subject to their husbands' physical and fiscal power, women are limited in their freedom to rebel. Men mentally enslave women through propaganda and fear.[176]

Given the tyranny of custom, it is hardly surprising that almost every thinker until recently has assumed the social inequality of the sexes "to be a fundamental and unalterable fact in human nature." But the progressive course of history militates against this old assumption. For the special characteristic of **modernism** is the conviction

> that human beings are no longer born to their place in life, and chained down by an inexorable bond to the

place they are born to, but are free to employ their faculties, and such favourable chances as offer, to achieve the lot which may appear to them most desirable.

(We recall that Hegel, while not drawing the liberal conclusions of Mill, saw the direction of history in terms of the gradual progression of human freedom.) This modern spirit does not entail the annihilation of value preferences.

> It is not that all processes are supposed to be equally good, or all persons to be equally qualified for everything; but that freedom of individual choice is now known to be the only thing which procures the adoption of the best processes, and throws each operation into the hands of those who are best qualified for it.

A person's gender should no more determine her social position than should her race or family background. There are rarely enough talented people to accomplish well the most difficult and important social tasks; and it is damaging to society to deprive it of the contributions of gifted people because of artificial prejudices. In all advanced countries of modern times (especially after the end of the American Civil War) Mill considers the legal discrimination against women to be the "single relic of an old world of thought and practice," an affront to both "justice and expediency." For the utilitarian advantage of "humanity in general," we should put the matter to the test of experience.[177]

Unless and until we grant women equal opportunities, we cannot know what the practical consequences would be. Indeed, as matters stand, what appears as "the nature of women is an eminently artificial thing," the product of "forced repression in some directions, unnatural stimulation in others." Mill thinks that very few men can really understand the thoughts and feelings of even the most important women in their lives because of the artificial strictures of society. He realizes that progress here will only come gradually because of a conservative attachment to the *status quo* and of a reluctance to risk change; he further recognizes that effort will be needed to effect even gradual progress. We should also note that he *refuses* to advocate what today we would call "affirmative action" but only calls for equal opportunity.[178] His argument for that objective is clearly utilitarian in nature.

MILL'S ECONOMIC THEORY.   Let us briefly consider Mill's *Principles of Political Economy*, in which he holds that there will always be limits to the goods available to us, regardless of how our modes of production might change; but what is quite variable is "the Distribution of Wealth" (a point Marx makes even more forcefully at about the same time). The way wealth is distributed varies with the customs of society and with the views of its rulers. Private property, though defensible on utilitarian grounds, could be replaced by a system in which the people generally hold land and the modes of production in common. Critics of private property either advocate "absolute equality in the distribution" of physical goods (these are **communists**) or allow inequality so long as it is not based on accidental circumstances, such as parentage. Mill thinks some such social scheme might be practicable and would like to see a system that fosters a "greater amount of public spirit" than does his own social order. Indeed, he would rather have a communistic system than continue the current social order in which wealth is so unjustly distributed in relation to labor. Still, he is hopeful (unlike Marx) that the system of private property might undergo a gradual progressive evolution that would render it more just.[179]

Mill considers the extent to which government should control the affairs of society. There is "the *authoritative* interference of government" in the actions of individuals; but there is also a nonauthoritative form of intervention, whereby government advises and informs citizens (consider how our government educates about the dangers of smoking without outlawing smoking). The legitimacy of authoritative government intervention is far more limited than that of the second type; Mill tends to be suspicious of the first type and supportive of the second. The burden of proof, Mill avers, "always lies on the defenders of legal prohibitions." By contrast, government's informing and advising its citizens represents "no infringement of liberty, no irksome or degrading restraint." Nevertheless, even here people should not become too dependent on their governments even for information and advice. "*Laissez-faire*, in short, should be the general practice: every departure from

---

Communism.   A socio-economic system characterized by an absence of classes and common ownership of property; in Marxist thought, this is the ideal end towards which the revolutionary struggle to overthrow capitalism is a necessary means

it, unless required by some great good, is a certain evil." However, this presupposes that the people should be educated to inform and think for themselves. Public education is valuable, although "government must claim no monopoly" on educating its citizens. Sometimes, government must intervene by law, as in the case of labor legislation to curtail the exploitation of workers by owners.[180]

In his *Chapters on Socialism* Mill celebrates the Reform Act of 1867 for increasing the electoral power of the working classes. He is confident that labor will soon find effective but peaceful means of utilizing that power to protect their interests against established institutions and the ruling class and that this will provide a healthy alternative to the dangers of violent revolution (called for by Marx). He believes it quite proper for the working classes to demand a fair, impartial reexamination of the present capitalist system, which could move society in the direction of socialism. It is easy to identify and lament the evils of the current system—poverty, crime and vice, selfish competition, and so forth. Yet socialists tend to exaggerate these ills and the role of the capitalist system in fostering them, as well as to present a very one-sided analysis of competition. In defense of the *status quo* Mill writes, "The present system is not, as many Socialists believe, hurrying us into a state of general indigence and slavery from which only Socialism can save us." Indeed, Mill thinks the current system is gradually reforming itself so as to decrease its "evils and injustices." And he believes that "the principal defects of the present system" can be corrected, while realizing the primary advantages of socialism, "by arrangements compatible with private property and individual competition,"[181] with no need for a communist revolution and an overthrow of the capitalist system.

CAPITAL PUNISHMENT. Finally, Mill's parliamentary speech, "Capital Punishment," represents a somewhat surprising position for a progressive thinker and one of the great champions of liberal reform. Indeed, at its beginning Mill indicates his wish that he could support the 1868 motion to abolish the death penalty. But he takes his stand on utilitarian grounds:

> I defend this penalty, when confined to atrocious cases, on the very ground on which it is commonly attacked— on that of humanity to the criminal; as beyond comparison the least cruel mode in which it is possible adequately to deter from the crime.

He is convinced that it is more humane "than imprisonment with hard labour for life," an alternative "attempt to repress murder." The death penalty not only prevents convicted felons from repeating their crimes against society but also restrains others from following their bad example. We should be careful, however, to restrict it to the punishment of only those convicted of "the most atrocious crimes," like first-degree murder, since otherwise people will hesitate to impose it and it will lose its effectiveness as a deterrence. Mill admits that the strongest argument against capital punishment is rooted in the possibility of an incorrigible error. Yet he is confident that with our legal procedures (the adversarial system, the presumption of innocence, rules of evidence, and an appeals system) such gross mistakes will remain "extremely rare." Indeed, the shocking gravity of this ultimate sanction, he thinks, makes us all the more careful. In conclusion, although he supports "the limitation of death punishment" (in accordance with a bill of 1867), Mill opposes its "total abolition" on utilitarian grounds.[182]

Religion

AN EMPIRICAL AND UTILITARIAN APPROACH TO GOD. Mill approaches the topics of God and religion from the empirical and utilitarian perspective as well. In his *Examination* he attacks Hegel's all-encompassing conception of God as illogical, saying we must "admit, either that there is no Absolute Being, or that the law, that contradictory propositions cannot both be true, does not apply to the Absolute." Hegel chose the latter side of the alternative," viewing God as beyond the law of noncontradiction, while Mill clearly favors the former alternative, denying the Deity of panentheism. Against rationalists and idealists like Hegel, Mill holds that our ideas of God must be firmly rooted in our knowledge of physical nature and human nature. Thus, our sense of divine attributes must be "relative" to our phenomenal experience. He insists that we should be honest in our use of religious language, using it to mean what it signifies when applied to earthly things, apart from the limits necessitated by the physical world. He does not "pretend to know" what infinity really entails; but, he maintains, "I know that infinite goodness must be goodness, and what is not consistent with goodness, is not consistent with infinite goodness." In a particularly powerful sentence

Mill refuses to use religious language in a hypocritical, sycophantic manner:

> I will call no being good, who is not what I mean when I apply that epithet to my fellow-creatures; and if such a being can sentence me to hell for not so calling him, to hell I will go.

Against the Hegelians, Mill protests that "the law of contradiction is a law of human thought." It is merely insincere flattery to say that God is good but not in the sense in which anything we experience is good (e.g., that God's goodness is not like ours). Either we have experiential grounds for predicating a quality of God or "it is simply the unknown attribute of a thing unknown" and no fit object of religious worship. Either "the moral attributes of God" signify what they do when used to describe humans or Hume was correct in holding "that we ought not to ascribe any moral attributes to God at all." We shall soon consider argumentation for God; but for now we can observe that Mill, like Hume, regards "the **Design argument**" as "the best," and "by far the most persuasive," available.[183]

EVIL AS INDICATIVE OF A FINITE GOD.   Turning to Mill's *Three Essays on Religion*, we see *Nature* attacking natural theology's sophistry in explaining away the horrible evils of the world. If we want to be honest and call the misery of sentient creatures evil, then logic should point us to a limited creator:

> If the maker of the world *can* all that he will, he wills misery, and there is no escape from the conclusion.

Nor is it credible to say that this misery is a necessary means to the dominion of virtue and the prevailing of justice, for misery does not seem to promote virtue widely, and happiness and misery seem unjustly rationed in proportion to virtue. Mill's conclusion points to some likelihood of a finite designer or creator—

> that the Principle of Good *cannot* at once and altogether subdue the powers of evil, either physical or moral; could not place mankind in a world free from the necessity of an incessant struggle with the maleficent powers, or make them always victorious in that struggle, but could and did make them capable of carrying on the fight with vigor and with progressively increasing success.

(As we shall see, James will adopt both the content and the tone of this claim.) A finite God might have moral attributes, in our sense of the words, but be limited in power, doing the best it can, given "the fetters which impede its free action."[184]

RELIGIOUS BELIEF.   In *Utility of Religion* Mill reflects on an age that wants to believe but finds the old arguments supporting religious faith no longer compelling. The evidence seems to pull us away from the doctrines of the past; yet it is thought that they still have a stabilizing, edifying utilitarian value.

> It is a most painful position to a conscientious and cultivated mind to be drawn in contrary directions by the two noblest of all objects of pursuit—truth and the general good.

But the time has come to question the utility of traditional doctrines. Mill asks what are their social and their personal advantages: "What amount of benefit to social interests . . . arises from religious belief? And what influence has it in improving and ennobling individual human nature?" Even if religious teachings have helped to civilize and morally improve us, he thinks, it is because they were inculcated in early childhood rather than because they were religious. The power of public opinion and moral education is significant whether or not it is religious. Nor does Mill believe the association with hopes of eternal reward and fears of eternal damnation very compelling for most people, given their remoteness and uncertainty, as well as people's self-excusing rationalizations. And the evil imbedded in ascribing supernatural origins to morality is that it becomes so dogmatically consecrated as to be beyond any permissible critical reflection. Overall, the social benefit does not seem to outweigh the detriment.[185]

What, then, of religion's utility for individual development? It seems to satisfy certain aspirations for transcendence and to provide consolation for people who are suffering. But could not the altruistic concern for our fellows and the future of our species do this as well? On a smaller scale, patriotism serves this purpose. Why can this "love of country" not be expanded? "The essence of religion is the strong and earnest direction of the emotions and desires toward an ideal object, recognized as of the highest excellence, and as rightfully paramount over all selfish objects of desire," says Mill. But, he adds, "This condition is fulfilled by the Religion of Humanity in as eminent a degree and in as high a sense as by the supernatural religions." It has the advantage of being more "disinterested." Second, it would encourage the active use of our capacities, rather than a passive acceptance. However, it does not offer us the prospect of personal immortality (which we shall discuss further in the following section); but Mill deems this a superfluous—and even tedious—idea, especially for those achieving happiness here and now.[186] So, on balance, the individual benefits of religious belief seem no more impressive than its social utility.

GOD'S EXISTENCE. Mill's most important work on religion is *Theism*, where he asserts that polytheism's belief in many gods "is immeasurably more natural to the human mind than monotheism's belief in one author and ruler of nature" and that the former does not naturally tend to transform itself into the latter. Monotheism's view of the world as following a single orderly plan is a consequence of scientific thought. It is because monotheism can thus claim scientific grounding that it lends itself to philosophical inquiry. Mill raises two questions. "First, is the theory which refers the origin of all the phenomena of nature to the will of a creator consistent or not with the ascertained results of science?" Mill thinks it is consistent as long as that theory views God as "governing the world by invariable laws" rather than "by acts of variable will." His second question asks, what is the scientific value of the evidence allegedly supporting theism? In order to be scientifically respectable, an argument must be empirical, using "the *a posteriori* method."[187]

Mill evaluates four such arguments: The argument for God as "a First Cause" presupposes that everything we know about owes its existence to some causal source, and thus so must the world. But Mill corrects the presupposition to say, "not that everything which we know derives its existence from a cause, but only every event or change." The world as a whole need not be an event and, for all we know, may be permanent, despite ongoing changes within its framework. Nor does it help to say that our minds could only have been causally produced by a "creating mind," because it leaves open the issue of how any mind can be eternal and ungenerated—a hypothesis ungrounded in any human experience of reality. Second, Mill quickly and easily dismisses the argument from general consent as having "little weight" in determining the truth; from the fact that many people have believed, nothing follows regarding what we

should (let alone, must) believe. Mill criticizes the third argument, which he calls "the argument from consciousness," used by Descartes and his followers, inferring God's necessary existence from the alleged claim that we "clearly and distinctly apprehend" that existence is conceptually inseparable from the very idea of God. But since the critique of ontological reasoning by Kant, Mill says, this approach "is not likely to satisfy anyone in the present day." Fourth, the design argument is the most scientifically respectable, offering itself for judgment "by the established canons of induction" and being "wholly grounded on experience." Mill's verdict is that, "though it has some force, its force is very generally overrated" by those advocating it. He agrees with Hume that the evidence of cosmic design reduces "only to the inferior kind of inductive evidence called analogy." The argument itself, based on that shaky evidence, employs the inductive method of agreement. But intelligent design is not the only plausible explanatory principle of the adaptations we find in nature; thanks to the influence of Charles Darwin's work in evolutionary theory, Mill can propose the alternative "principle of 'the survival of the fittest' " or natural selection. His final judgment here is that we have "no more than a probability" favoring "creation by intelligence" and that "the various other arguments of natural theology" cannot contribute anything to the increasing of that probability.[188]

GOD'S NATURE. Given this evaluation of the arguments for God's existence, what is the nature of the Deity indicated? It would seem that "the power, if not the intelligence," of God "must be so far superior to that of man as to surpass all human estimate," if God did design the universe; but, surely, neither omnipotence nor omniscience follows from this. Indeed, the very idea of design suggests contrivance, "the adaptation of means to an end," the need for which indicates "the limitation of power." There is no reason to believe that "matter and force" were created by the Deity, rather than being coeternal materials to be employed in accordance with a designing plan; but then God's power was limited by the materials to be used. Thus, omnipotence is not called for as a divine attribute. If God's power is limited, omniscience could be defended; yet there is no evidence to require it. Indeed, the defects of creation seem too striking to support divine omniscience, even allowing limits on God's power. It is particularly problematic how we can argue that "the Creator foresees all the future, that he foreknows all the effects that will issue from his own contrivances." The indications of natural design, as Hume recognized, offer even less evidence of God's moral attributes. Things seem adapted for the limited endurance of sentient creatures, but not so obviously for their good. Their pleasures and pains seem mainly adaptation mechanisms for temporary survival and perpetuation of their species. There may be slight indications of benevolence in the Creator/Designer; but to the extent that natural happiness is viewed as a primary objective, "in our corner of the universe at least," the plan seems to have been "an ignominious failure." We humans, at least, have the capacity to modify nature and improve ourselves and our environment. This could be viewed as itself a divine blessing; yet it comes at a "frightful cost" in terms of painful struggle and ongoing suffering, straining credulity for those wanting to subscribe to absolute loving benevolence on God's part. Other moral attributes, such as divine justice, are lacking in any evidential basis whatsoever. So, natural theology points to a Deity of great but limited power, of great but possibly limited intelligence, who may be somewhat benevolent towards some creatures but, for all we can tell, is lacking in other moral attributes.[189]

Mill does (anticipating James) defend "the indulgence of hope" in religious matters, deeming its beneficial consequences significant:

> It makes life and human nature a far greater thing to the feelings and gives greater strength as well as solemnity to all the sentiments which are awakened in us by our fellow creatures and by mankind at large.

He especially appreciates the hopeful model of human behavior personified by Christ. Finally, he points to a psychological advantage of his idea of a limited Deity—it can encourage "the feeling of helping God . . . by a voluntary co-operation which he, not being omnipotent, really needs."[190] Thus, our efforts to do good—interpreted in a utilitarian manner, of course—can be thought to have cosmic significance.

Immortality

The section "Immortality" in *Theism* is a most valuable source for Mill's views on that topic. He divides his analysis into two parts: first he considers reasons to believe in it apart from antecedent religious prejudices, and then he turns to reasons that are religiously supported. The speculative arguments of philosophers (his examples are those of Plato's *Phaedo*) hinge on a view of the soul as a single, indivisible substance, not subject to dissolution, whatever happens to its associated body. But there is no evidence for such a substantial soul. Indeed, Mill thinks it more respectable in his day for thinkers to follow Hume's lead in regarding it "as the name of a bundle of attributes . . . of feeling, thinking, reasoning, believing, willing, etc.," all of which are the products of "bodily organization" and which cannot reasonably be supposed to survive when that bodily organization breaks down. Scientific study gives us every reason to believe that "cerebral action is, if not the cause, at least, in our present state of existence, a condition *sine qua non* of mental operations." (We shall see later that William James tackles this point from an interesting perspective.) Still, Mill admits, this does not disprove immortality but only highlights the lack of evidence on its behalf; and, of course, we may suppose that our clusters of "states of consciousness" somehow survive the deaths of our bodies. As we have seen, Mill thinks our states of consciousness are the most obviously real objects of our experience; but we have no experiential basis for thinking that mind can function independently of body. Other nonreligious sources of the belief in immortality are our reluctance to accept our own ends and our conditioning by teachings traditional in human culture. "As causes of belief," Mill says, these "are most powerful. As rational grounds of it they carry no weight at all." He next turns to the religiously supported reasons for such belief. These include "the goodness of God," the unlikelihood that God would annihilate the noblest of earthly creatures, and the improbability that God "would have implanted in us an instinctive desire of eternal life," which was fated for "complete disappointment." Mill grants that these reasons would have some weight if we had independent grounds for thinking God infinitely perfect. But, as we have seen, the evidence points to a finite Deity, whose goodness and/or power may be so limited as not to be able to deliver the immortality we may or may not be programmed to desire. Nevertheless, Mill defends our right "to hope for a future state as a possibility," despite the absence of any compelling evidence supporting that hope.[191]

On a more personal note, some of his diary entries of 1854 (the year he thought he was dying of tuberculosis) are striking. On March 19, he writes that "belief in a life after death" should only be consoling to those who fancy themselves God's favorites and that the rest of us might do better to accept "the cessation of our consciousness when our earthly mechanism ceases to work." On March 24, he indicates that all philosophical arguments for immortality presuppose a correlation between the nature of reality and our own wishful thinking. On April 4, he deems the privilege of not dying until we like to be preferable to the tedious burden of "being immortal."[192] It does not seem likely that Mill himself entertains the hope of personal immortality.

Fulfillment

THE DEVELOPMENT OF CHARACTER. Thus, it should be no surprise that his conception of the fulfillment of human nature is this-worldly. It consists in the progressive realization of what *On Liberty* calls "the distinctive endowment of a human being." This comprises the "human faculties of perception, judgment, discriminative feeling, mental activity, and even moral preference," all of which, to some extent, should be connected with personal choice and actively exercised. People readily admit that our thoughts should be our own but tend to be wary of the notion, which Mill defends, that "our desires and impulses should be our own likewise," rather than ingrained in us or imposed on us by external sources. "A person whose desires and impulses are his own—are the expression of his own nature, as it has been developed and modified by his own culture—is said to have a character." When those desires and impulses are vigorous as well as original, "he has an energetic character."[193] The fulfillment of our human nature requires the development of character.

A MODEST SENSE OF FULFILLMENT. Happiness is the name Mill tends to give to the state in which human nature is best fulfilled. In *Utilitarianism* he dismisses as impossible the naive view of happiness as never-ending, deliriously "pleasurable excitement." The happy life is rather one encompassing "many and various pleasures," active as well as passive, relatively "few and transitory pains," and a realistic expectation of what life has to offer. He insists that many people

actually achieve happiness in this sense, and that their lives strike a personally satisfying balance between tranquillity and excitement. "With much tranquillity, many find that they can be content with very little pleasure: with much excitement, many can reconcile themselves to a considerable quantity of pain." There is no reason to think that people cannot achieve fulfillment in this modest sense. Only lazy people fail to find any of life's excitements satisfying; and only those in whom the lust for excitement has become obsessive dismiss all tranquillity as "dull and insipid." Another reason people fail to appreciate the happiness available to them is their own selfishness, which bars them from being satisfied with what they have and from appreciating the well-being of others. Still another "principal cause which makes life unsatisfactory is want of mental cultivation." Mill is confident that a mind that has been taught "to exercise its faculties" will normally encounter "sources of inexhaustible interest in all that surrounds it: in the objects of nature, the achievements of art, the imaginations of poetry, the incidents of history, the ways of mankind, past and present, and their prospects in the future." Everyone raised in civilized countries should have access to the sort of "mental cultivation" that makes available all these sources of fulfillment. "In a world in which there is so much to interest, so much to enjoy, and so much also to correct and improve," people who have developed their abilities should be capable of happiness, to the extent that their lives are free of "the great sources of physical and mental suffering," poverty, disease, and social cruelty. Mill is optimistic in holding that these "great positive evils" are quite "removable, and will, if human affairs continue to improve, be in the end reduced within narrow limits." What is needed is collaborative effort to conquer them.[194] This, in turn, requires socio-political coordination.

GOOD GOVERNMENT AND THE GOOD OF HUMANITY. Mill's *Considerations on Representative Government* contains an underappreciated passage on the correlation between good government and "the general good of humanity." He is arguing that we need a socio-political system that will promote active effort in people rather than passive acquiescence. There are "three varieties of mental excellence, intellectual, practical, and moral." The intellectual flourishing of human beings requires that they actively use their minds.

Second, practical excellence requires "active and energetic character." Third, even moral superiority requires a striving for virtue. A good social order encourages its people to exercise their powers. Even contentment, which might be partially identified with human fulfillment, can become a contemptible smugness, if divorced from both the quest for spiritual development and the wish to help other people:

> The contented man, or the contented family, who have no ambition to make anyone else happier, to promote the good of their country or their neighborhood, or to improve themselves in moral excellence, excite in us neither admiration nor approval.[195]

MILL RELATED TO ARISTOTLE.   Even though neither Mill nor the followers of Aristotle might appreciate the comparison, Mill's conception of human fulfillment or happiness is rather Aristotelian: flourishing individuals require active self-realization of their capacities in the context of a good society. Like Aristotle, Mill tends to naturalism and empiricism, has a limited theology without the advocacy of religious practices, and is agnostic about personal immortality. Unlike Aristotle, Mill is a phenomenalist, a hedonist, a determinist, and an individualist. Both made great contributions to logical theory, and both have profoundly influenced the ways in which we think about ourselves, our fellow humans, and our world.

REFLECTIONS

It is unfortunate that Mill rarely discusses Hegel's ideas explicitly and seems to have had little direct knowledge of the details of Hegel's writings, so that his own theory does not play off his predecessor's as neatly as Aristotle's does off Plato's, Kant's off Hume's, and so forth. Nevertheless, one reason for selecting Mill from all the important post-Hegelian thinkers of the nineteenth century is the striking contrast between his ideas and those of Hegel, constituting a mock debate between them on virtually all ten of our topics. (Another reason, as we have seen, is that Hegel and Mill together represent a move, during that century, from conservative communitarianism to liberal individualism; and, of course, an obvious third reason is the powerful influence of Mill's views on inductive logic, utilitarian ethics, and progressive political theory.) Mill advocates as refined and radical a

form of empiricism as the refined and radical form of rationalism Hegel presents. In many ways their theories feature opposing strengths and weaknesses, in the sense that Mill's advantages tend to correspond to Hegel's disadvantages and Mill's shortcomings tend to correlate with Hegel's best achievements. It may be that a better theory than either might lie between their opposing viewpoints.

REALITY.   Like Hegel (and others we have studied before this chapter), Mill grounds his entire philosophical system in his theory of reality. His analysis of Nature, as the aggregate of all possible phenomena, is plausible enough. But why should we grant his implicit reduction of all reality to Nature in this sense? Although it seems correct to say that we humans here and now can only know reality as it appears to us phenomenally, we should be hesitant to conclude that that is all there is.

BODIES.   Second, regarding bodies, Mill likewise confuses legitimate epistemological claims with dubious ontological ones (or implicitly infers the latter from the former). He is probably right that we only *know* bodies in terms of their phenomenal appearances. But it does not follow that bodies *are* no more than the clusters of their phenomena or the "permanent possibilities" of our sensations. On the other hand, this view is no stranger than Hegel's notion that bodies are the physical expression of Absolute Spirit in space. Might not a healthier middle-ground position be the Kantian dualism Mill repudiates, the view that bodies are independent physical realities, though their properties are only given in experience as relative to perceivers like us?

PERSONALITY.   Mill's theory of personality, our third topic, does not undermine human individuality to the extent that Hegel's does; but it is also less dynamic and is presented in a far less dialectically brilliant manner. Mill's reliance on Hume is a mixed blessing (or mixed curse, depending on one's point of view): on the one hand, it is reductionistic in limiting the personality to its phenomena and its states of consciousness and in imagining that empirical laws of association provide sufficient explanation for all its work; on the other hand, Mill thus advances Hume's dream of establishing psychology as what we today would call a social science. But, unlike psychology, philosophy should view the human personality as the metaphysical ground of empirical consciousness rather than as merely equated with its phenomenal states.

KNOWLEDGE. Fourth, a portion of Mill's theory of knowledge is of tremendous lasting value. Earlier, we observed how underappreciated Hegel's epistemology has been. This is also somewhat true of Mill's, whose theory of knowledge is less ingenious but more plausible than Hegel's. Is it a deficiency that this strictly empirical theory lacks any sense of universal, necessary *a priori* structures, such as Kant emphasizes? Even if it is, though, Mill's canons of causal reasoning constitute a magnificent analysis of principles that are crucial to scientific thinking, and he deserves great credit for being the first to articulate them so clearly.

FREEDOM. As for our fifth topic, Mill's conception of human freedom seems a more plausible form of determinism than we have seen earlier (in Hobbes or Hume) because of its recognition that we can contribute to the causal determination of our own motives and character, if we so choose. But, by eliminating free will altogether, he ultimately reduces this "choice" to external factors (of heredity and/or environment) which are beyond our personal control, collapsing the distinction he wants to preserve between his own position and fatalism and undermining (as all determinism inevitably does) the very sort of moral responsibility his ethical theory requires (and which he implausibly identifies with punishment). We might do better to adopt Kant's dualistic theory, which Mill attacks, as showing that all actions are determined phenomenally, as events in the physical world, while some of them, which we rightly regard as free, are autonomously chosen by a self-determining noumenal will.

MORALITY. Sixth, Mill's analysis of morality is like Hegel's in presenting itself as an alternative to Kant's deontological absolutism and in collapsing the distinction between what is and what should be. The facts that people desire happiness and approve of some sorts of conduct on consequential grounds are not conclusive in showing how they ought to behave. Only a theory that is fundamentally *a priori* and deontological (like Kant's) can avoid this problem. Mill is wonderfully self-critical (a mark of a first-rate philosopher) and honestly confronts the serious objections to his own theory, most of which he handles well. However, the accusation that hedonists demean human nature by thinking it ultimately motivated by pleasure and an aversion to pain should not be lightly dismissed. A sense of duty may well be a basic motivating force independent of pleasure and pain and contributing to our dignity as rational agents. Mill's qualitative distinctions among pleasures and pains render his theory more sophisticated than Bentham's purely quantitative model; however, it is doubtful that the issue of how we should qualitatively rank pleasures can be as neatly settled as Mill suggests (again the is-ought distinction is a problem). He does effectively show how unfair it is to tar his brand of utilitarianism (or Bentham's, for that matter) with the brush of egoism. His ethics is a form of **consequentialism**, regarding the morality of all actions as relative to their likely consequences. But there is a problem with our capacity to predict consequences of actions before they occur, which is normally a mere matter of probable guesswork; our vision of the future is usually too cloudy to see very far down the line. Even worse, we should ask whether some actions are not inherently wrong, regardless of consequences. For example, what possible set of circumstances or likely consequences could justify torturing human babies to death merely for the sadistic amusement of the torturer? If none, then it seems Kantian absolutism is closer to being correct. Mill does well to point out that ultimate principles, including those in ethics, are not strictly demonstrable and nevertheless to try to offer what rational considerations he can on behalf of his principle of utility. Yet it is not a convincing argument, because it trades on an ambiguity in the word "desirable." We must interpret this word as meaning "able to be desired" in order for the analogy (with "visible" and "audible") to work, yet that is not what we mean, in a moral context, when we declare anything desirable; we mean that it "ought to be desired," which breaks the analogy and leads to Mill's inferring an "ought" from an "is" in precisely the manner against which Hume warned. The worst objection against utilitarianism remains the justice obstacle; unfortunately, Mill verbally dissolves, rather than solves, the problem, with his slick definition of justice in terms of "social utilities." On the other hand, his critique of the natural-law equation of morality and the following of nature is masterful.

SOCIETY. Mill offers a very welcome alternative to the conservative, authoritarian model of society (our seventh topic) that we saw Hegel advocating. Indeed, of all the views on society represented in this book, Mill's is probably the most acceptable to most of us who live in liberal democracies today. *On Liberty*, in particular, is a strikingly fine defense of limits on government, freedom of expression, and political autonomy in choosing one's own lifestyle. In theory, Mill's position seems admirable. However, a major bone of contention concerns the practical legitimacy of his pivotal distinction between other-regarding and purely self-regarding conduct, as he himself seems to acknowledge. In a way the problem is similar to one brought out in relation to utilitarian ethics: can we discern future consequences well enough to say whether they will affect the interests of others, as well as those of the agent? In defense of Mill here, we might observe that it is unfair to require certainty in such matters, which always necessarily involve fallible judgment, but that such judgment is relatively reliable in proportion to careful thought and association with the findings of past experience. Mill's defense of equal opportunity for women seems remarkably ahead of his time, and his urging us at least to experiment with socio-economic evolutionary reforms (that can help defuse calls for violent revolution) has also proved prophetic; not only have women attained greater equality in our own century, but moves towards social legislation and welfare programs have become a vital part of our own political economy. It is admirable that Mill not only advocated liberal reforms in his writings but fought for them politically in his own life.

RELIGION. Eighth, there is something refreshingly bracing about the clarity of Mill's approach to religion, as compared with the speculative fuzziness of Hegel's, particularly in its insistence that we preserve the integrity of ordinary human logic and language in talking (and thinking) about God and in how seriously it takes the problem of evil. Mill does well to question the usefulness of religious belief since its uncritical assumption can deter us from seriously considering its evidential grounds; however, he is excessively negative in assessing that utility, and it seems that religion historically and currently does provide a useful service of civilizing human nature, nurturing the regard for transcendent ideals and inspiring lofty aspirations. His critique of arguments for the existence of God is generally quite reasonable and continues the trend from Hume through Kant to James (the exception being Hegel) we are studying here; however, he may be too hard on the design argument, in failing to point out that it is compatible with (and not merely an alternative to) evolutionary theory and that it is particularly valuable in accounting for the origin of mind (rather than merely of matter) in the universe.

IMMORTALITY. Regarding our ninth topic, Mill's treatment of immortality is as superficial as that of other radical empiricists (including Hobbes and Hume before him and James after him) and (except for Hobbes, who had religious reasons for concern) indicative of their general lack of much personal commitment to the topic. Mill's criticisms of traditional reasons for belief in immortality are appropriate, but his lack of sympathy for it minimizes his chances of pursuing the issue of whether, for example, it might function as what Kant calls a postulate of practical reason or what James will identify as a valuable postulate of human rationality.

FULFILLMENT. Finally, Mill's analysis of the fulfillment of human nature is arguably the richest naturalistic one (i.e., one divorced from any consideration of life after death) we are studying. Aristotle probably offers the most famous and most influential of all naturalistic philosophical conceptions of human fulfillment. But Mill's respect for individuality and the personal dignity of all humans as persons renders his analysis here even more impressive. Of course, the question remains whether a view of human fulfillment confined within the parameters of this life (from womb to tomb) can be adequate and satisfying.

*　*　*

Like all the other thinkers on whom this book is focusing, Mill offers us a complex and comprehensive philosophical system. It presents a stark contrast to that of Hegel, in being empirical, realistic, phenomenalistic, **pluralistic**, deterministic, hedonistic, and individualistic (with Hegel's system being rationalistic, idealistic, metaphysical, monistic, dialectical, abstract, and communitarian); Mill repudiates Hegel's new logic and returns us to traditional Aristotelian logic, with which common sense and science are more comfortable; yet Mill makes new contributions even here with his canons of causal reasoning. The intellectual integrity of his analyses is admirable. The unfortunate thing about the reception of Mill's philosophy is that few people are familiar with it beyond its utilitarian ethics and liberal socio-political theory. Both of these aspects have proved enormously important to the development of Western civilization. But, as we have seen, they are two crucial pieces of a much larger whole and are supported by other, more fundamental portions of this impressive theory. Although Hegel remains the greatest philosophical genius of the nineteenth century, Mill presents a valuable perspective on human nature in all its various dimensions.

QUESTIONS

1. *What is Hegel's conception of reality? How could it be productively supported or challenged?*

2. *How does Hegel view human history? What seems to you particularly insightful or disturbing about this perspective?*

3. *What can we say about Hegel's God, the Absolute Spirit of his system? How adequate is it as an object of religious worship?*

4. *In what sense is Mill's analysis of reality, in general, and of bodies, in particular, phenomenalistic? What do you think about such an analysis, and why?*

5. *What is the "science of human nature" for Mill? Do you agree that it can be truly scientific, and why or why not?*

6. *What is Mill's principle of utility, and how does he argue for it? Why would you accept or reject this principle and argument?*

7. *What does Hegel really mean by identifying the* "rational" *and the* "actual"? *Why is that so important to his theory? And what might Mill say in response?*

8. *How does Hegel's dialectic supposedly work in showing that every person is ultimately related to society, to God, and to all of reality? Why would Mill disagree?*

9. *How does knowledge differ for Hegel and for Mill? What are the advantages and disadvantages of each view?*

10. *Are individual human beings genuinely free for Hegel and/or for Mill? If so, in what sense? If not, why not?*

11. *What might be a relatively acceptable middle ground between Hegel's communitarian view of society and Mill's individualistic analysis?*

12. *How could Hegel's and Mill's theories point us towards an adequate view of the relationship between God and human nature?*

ALTERNATIVES

Three extremely important nineteenth century thinkers after Hegel and Mill are the Danish Søren A. Kierkegaard and the Germans Karl Marx and Friedrich Nietzsche. Kierkegaard studied theology at the University of Copenhagen and was a devout Christian; both German thinkers attended the University of Bonn for a while and were atheists. All three of them reject both Hegel's reactionary idealism and the liberal utilitarianism of Mill as inadequate for providing a lastingly beneficial solution to the human predicament. Marx is the father of communism; the other two are the first philosophical existentialists.

KIERKEGAARD

Søren A. Kierkegaard was born in 1813 (during the period Hegel was completing his *Science of Logic*). He spent almost all his life in Copenhagen, the intellectual center of Scandinavia. Although he enrolled in the University of Copenhagen as a theology student in accordance with his father's wishes, his chief interests were philosophical and literary. His tutor, Hans Martensen, was a Hegelian, and the university was becoming a bastion of Hegelian thought, which Kierkegaard rejected as too abstract to be personally relevant. He frittered away his time as a dabbling dilettante until after his father died, at which time he successfully completed the study of theology. Soon after receiving his master's degree in philosophy, he broke off his engagement to a teenage girl, pretending to be an insensitive cad, though apparently he did so because he was reluctant to subject her to his profound melancholy and because he could not see how a genuine commitment to her could be compatible with a total love of God. The grief-stricken Kierkegaard went to Berlin, where he attended classes of the elderly Schelling, sarcastically writing his brother that Schelling was too old to give lectures and he too old to attend them. After Kierkegaard returned to Copenhagen in 1842, he began work on the prolific outpouring of writings to be published during the next seven years. After the publication of his philosophical masterpiece, the *Concluding Unscientific Postscript*, in 1846, Kierkegaard picked a quarrel with the satirical newspaper, *The Corsair*, which proceeded savagely and relentlessly to ridicule him. The last couple of years of his life were marked by an even more painful controversy with the Danish Lutheran Church, which he attacked in print for what he called its smug, self-righteous, hypocritical "Christendom" and whose religious services he ceased attending. In 1855, he collapsed in the street and was taken to the hospital, where he refused most visitors, including his brother, would not receive the sacrament from any pastor, and died.

Kierkegaard's philosophically most important works were written under pseudonyms. This eccentric literary device is mischievously designed to protect the author from being too readily identified with the views expressed, to allow dialectical contradictions to emerge between different lines of thought, and to make it difficult for scholars to cast them into any tidy system. His great works of the 1840s—from *Either/Or* (1843) through *Sickness unto Death* (1849)—emphasize such **existential** themes as individual human existence, freedom and responsibility, and existential emotions and will as more fundamental than reason in defining our lives. In man, soul and body are united in a spiritual self, which synthesizes the finite and the infinite, the temporal and the eternal, necessity and freedom. As opposed to the static being of all other finite things, human existence is an ongoing, dynamic process of becoming. It is also intrinsically individual, more radically so than has been

suggested by any thinker we have previously considered; against the communitarian spirit of Hegelian thought, Kierkegaard wanted to be identified on his tombstone as "the individual." For him freedom is not an abstract philosophical topic but a practical matter of commitment, for which we humans are irrevocably responsible.

Kierkegaard, the father of existentialism, maps out three spheres of human existence. The aesthetic life is one predominantly spent in pursuit of pleasure and excitement, avoiding pain and boredom, one of romantic hedonism, unmarked by any lasting commitments. The ethical life is fundamentally concerned with a choice between good and evil and recognizes universally binding imperatives. Whereas Don Juan, the self-indulgent, adventurous seducer, is an apt model of the aesthetic life, the Greek leader and tragic hero Agamemnon, the "knight of infinite resignation," who sacrifices his daughter Iphigenia on the altar of universal duty, is an exemplar of the ethical life. The religious sphere of existence requires a different sort of commitment, to God rather than to universal principles. The Old Testament Abraham is Kierkegaard's favorite example of the religious man of faith, a "knight of hidden inwardness," for whom there can be a "teleological suspension of the ethical" in deference to God's will. Kierkegaard goes on to distinguish between the religion of immanence, represented by Hegelians, which tries rationally to relate the human and the divine, and the **paradoxical** Christian religion, which emphasizes the radical transcendence of God and the mystery of the Incarnation, which resists all attempts at dialectical sublation.

In his philosophical, pseudonymous works, Kierkegaard refuses to call himself a philosopher and is severely critical of modern philosophical rationalists from Descartes through Hegel.[196] In his *Philosophical Fragments* of 1844, Kierkegaard assails rationalistic proofs of God's existence as requiring a nonlogical "leap" either from ideal concepts to actual being (in ontological argumentation) or from the facts of reality as we experience them to their interpretation as divine effects (in empirical argumentation). The very presumption of demonstrating divine existence fails to recognize that God is essentially "the Unknown," an object of religious faith, rather than of philosophical knowledge. In the *Postscript* this distinction between faith and reason is brilliantly explored, with the weapon of the dialectic adroitly wielded against the Hegelians. Is a system of thought possible? Yes, a logical system certainly is possible because it abstracts from existence. Is an existential system possible? Reality is a knowable system for God, who is eternal and radically transcendent. But, no, an existential system is not possible for humans, precisely because we cannot abstract ourselves from and transcend the existential process of temporal becoming. Where Hegel posits the identity of subject and object, the unity of thought and being, Kierkegaard insists that existence separates these antitheses so that a dialectical synthesis is never possible for us. Unlike the Hegelian, who seeks rational, objective knowledge, Kierkegaard maintains that we must strive for subjective, passionate commitment.

MARX

Karl Marx, who was born in 1818 (five years after Kierkegaard's birth), was the son of a Jewish lawyer, who later converted to Lutheranism. After transferring from the University of Bonn, where he had studied law, to the University of Berlin, where he shifted to philosophy and began associating with left-wing "Young Hegelians," who, following Hegel's death, adopted radical political and theological positions, he received a Doctor of Philosophy degree from the University of Jena. The following year, 1841, he began editing the recently launched *Rheinische Zeitung* in Cologne (which was suppressed by Prussian authorities the next year) and rejecting Hegelianism. He went to Paris for a couple of years, where he encountered prominent socialists, like Pierre Proudhon, studied important economists, including Adam Smith, and befriended Friedrich Engels (1820–1895), the son of a wealthy industrialist in England, who would become his collaborator. In 1845, Marx was expelled from France and went to Brussels; two years later, he joined the Communist League and was charged to write up, with Engels, the synopsis of its goals and principles that would become the *Communist Manifesto*. After the collapse of the revolutions of 1848, Marx, then in Germany, was tried for treason and acquitted; he returned to Paris. But when he was again expelled from France the following year, he and his family moved to London, where he spent the rest of his life in poverty and dependent on Engels for financial assistance, until his death in 1883.

In the last of his "Theses on Feuerbach" Marx takes philosophers to task for merely offering various interpretations of the world rather than mobilizing to change it. He was greatly influenced by Hegel's concept of alienation, as presented most memorably in the section on "Lordship and Bondage," and adapted it (for example in his *Economic and Philosophical Manuscripts of 1844*) to the class struggle between laborers and the owners of the modes of production. He is like Mill in being passionately concerned about the welfare of the workers. But, unlike Mill, he denies the feasibility of progressive reform and calls for the abolition of private property and the replacement of capitalism with communism.

Marx admires the Hegelian dialectic for its insight into the dynamic movement inherent in reality and the idea that the conflicts of negative opposition can generate creative results. But, as he observes in his "Critique of the Hegelian Dialectic and Philosophy," this must be attached to a naturalistic humanism rather than to Hegel's abstract idealism. *The German Ideology* (1846) calls for ideas grounded in natural experience rather than the notion that ideas determine material conditions. In their famous *Communist Manifesto* (1848) Marx and Engels analyze social reality as the struggle between the bourgeoisie (who own the means of production in industrial society) and the proletariat (or laboring class). The former exploit the latter, demanding as much labor as possible in return for the lowest possible wages (while workers may wish to offer the least amount of labor for as much compensation as they can get). The conflict between these antithetical forces can only be ultimately resolved through revolution, which will destroy class structures altogether and lead to the classless society (after an indefinite interim period of the **dictatorship** of the proletariat). In this visionary communist society, according to *The German Ideology*, people will supposedly be free to be generalists and to pursue their own interests.

Marx does not trust Mill's liberal ideals of justice, progress, and liberty. Such abstractions are merely bourgeois band-aids over the mortal wounds of capitalist society, all the more dangerous for encouraging

---

Dictatorship. Autocratic government by an absolute ruler with unrestrained power

the illusion that we are curing our ills. Religion is another lethal illusion, distracting us from the real problems of the real world, offering us the false comfort of opium, to which we become addicted. Hegel's idealistic view of religion is particularly alienating; but even Mill's more modest sense of the hope religion represents would appear unhealthy from this perspective. Marx published the first volume of *Capital*, his great work of political economy, in 1867, the second and third volumes being published after his death by Engels, in 1885 and 1894, respectively. His influence on the twentieth century has been profound due to the appeal of his communistic theory to the disadvantaged, to the Communist Revolution in Russia, and to the prolonged exercise of power by Communist parties in the former Soviet Union, its satellites in Eastern Europe, and the People's Republic of China.

NIETZSCHE

Friedrich Wilhelm Nietzsche was born in 1844 (the year Marx published his *Economic and Philosophical Manuscripts*). The son of a Lutheran pastor, he studied classical philology and was appointed to a professorial chair at the University of Basel before his twenty-fifth birthday. But frail health and discontent with academia led to his resigning about a decade later. He served in the ambulance corps of the German army during the Franco-Prussian War, but illness led to a physical collapse. He spent the next decade as a productive, but lonely, writer. Perhaps as a result of syphilis contracted during his student days, he became insane in 1889, never completely recovering in the last eleven-and-a-half years of his life, and dying in 1900.

Nietzsche is among the most controversial of all philosophers, provocative in the challenges he raises against smug assumptions of such other thinkers as Hegel and Mill. In *The Gay Science* (1882) he has a madman proclaim the death of God. He does not mean this in Hegel's sense of a symbolic death representing the overcoming of the gulf between the natural and the supernatural or even as suggesting Mill's idea that we should give up on the infinitely perfect God of Judeo-Christian mythology in favor of a finite God. As the first atheistic existentialist (we shall study another, Sartre, in the next chapter), Nietzsche means that that archaic concept has outlived its usefulness and that we must learn to live, strive,

and thrive as best we can without it. Indeed, from his perspective, modern philosophers, from Descartes through Hegel, might be said to have killed God by reductive analysis.

If anything, Nietzsche is even more contemptuous than Marx of mainstream philosophers such as those on whom this book is focusing. In *Beyond Good and Evil* (1886) he attacks what he calls "the Prejudices of Philosophers," including their basic quest (evident in all twelve of the thinkers emphasized here) for truth and certainty. He asks why we should not prefer *un*truth and *un*certainty, if they might prove valuable? Whereas others pursue the will-o'-the-wisp of Truth, he claims that all life (including ours) is essentially the Will to Power. He obviously despises the philosophical theories of his own German culture, including those of Kant and Hegel. But Nietzsche's *Genealogy of Morals* (1887) exhibits equal contempt for English thinkers, including utilitarians like Mill, whose values indicate a herd mentality. Unlike Mill, who wants us to adopt and practice a single ethics for the welfare of all, Nietzsche distinguishes between a master morality, which identifies the good with what is naturally noble and the bad with what is base, and a slave morality, which distinguishes between the good (which serves the interests of inferior weaklings) and the evil (identified with the values of strong aristocrats). We might notice a parallel between this view that naturally superior and naturally inferior people have distinct sets of values and Hegel's dialectical relationship between lord and bondsman. In *Thus Spoke Zarathustra* (1883–85) Nietzsche eagerly anticipates the coming of the overman (*das Übermensch*), who will be the fulfillment of human nature; man, as we know him, is allegedly a mere link between beast and overman.

In his *Twilight of the Idols* (1889) Nietzsche assails as vain the traditional ideals of reason, free will, and moral objectivity. The philosophical abstraction of reason pushes us to distinguish between appearances and reality, introducing a false dichotomy in our thinking (as in Kant), and to distrust our senses (as in Plato). The idol of free will seems merely a smokescreen for encouraging guilty pangs of conscience and for justifying punishment. For Nietzsche, the very notion of moral facts is illusory; all we have are the subjective interpretations of moral judgments. Not only is Nietzsche significant as the first atheistic existentialist, but his critique of the assumptions of mainstream modern philosophy is now acclaimed as the origin of "postmodern" thought, which challenges the notion of any universal and necessary epistemological foundations

accessible through any methodology. At any rate, like Kierkegaard and Marx, Nietzsche presents a radical theory which can shock us into questioning some of the most basic ideas, assumptions, and principles of such thinkers as Hegel and Mill.

Notes

1. G. W. F. Hegel, *Hegel: The Letters*, trans. Clark Butler and Christiane Seiler (Bloomington: Indiana Univ. Press, 1984), p. 420. This book is henceforth called *"Letters."*

2. Ibid., p. 18.

3. Ibid., pp. 28–29, 31–32, 35, 41.

4. Ibid., pp. 420, 63–64, 89.

5. Ibid., pp. 107, 110, 114–15.

6. Ibid., pp. 79–80.

7. Ibid., pp. 116, 126, 130, 134, 142, 167–69, 425.

8. Ibid., pp. 188, 210, 561, 181.

9. Ibid., pp. 237–38, 243–44, 255, 258.

10. Ibid., pp. 269–71, 283, 296, 313, 429.

11. Ibid., pp. 338, 340–42, 351, 433–34.

12. Ibid., pp. 381, 450–51, 470, 459–60.

13. Ibid., pp. 709–10, 421, 644, 556, 520, 532, 467, 470, 535.

14. Ibid., pp. 556, 422.

15. G. W. F. Hegel, *Introduction to the Philosophy of History*, trans. Leo Rauch (Indianapolis: Hackett Publishing Co., 1988), pp. 12–15, 17. This book is henceforth called *"History."*

16. Ibid., pp. 17, 19–20. For more on the relationship between Nature and Spirit, *see* G. W. F. Hegel, *Hegel's Philosophy of Nature*, trans. A. V. Miller (London: Oxford Univ. Press, 1970), p. 3. This book is henceforth called *"Nature."*

17. G. W. F. Hegel, *Phenomenology of Spirit*, trans. A. V. Miller (New York: Oxford Univ. Press, 1979), pp. 14, 352. This book is henceforth called *"Phenomenology."*

18. Ibid., pp. 413, 492.

19. G. W. F. Hegel, *Hegel's Logic*, trans. William Wallace (London: Oxford Univ. Press, 1975), pp. 3, 36–37, 40–41. This book is henceforth called *"Logic."*

20. Ibid., pp. 84, 256–57, 275, 279, 291.

21. G. W. F. Hegel, *Hegel's Science of Logic*, trans. W. H. Johnston and L. G. Struthers (London: George Allen & Unwin, 1951), Vol. II, pp. 466, 468, 471. This book is henceforth called *"Science."*

22. Ibid., pp. 473, 475–80, 482–85.

23. G. W. F. Hegel, *Hegel's Philosophy of Right*, trans. T. M. Knox (New York: Oxford Univ. Press, 1967), p. 10. This book is henceforth called *"Right."* *See also Logic*, p. 9.

24. *Phenomenology*, pp. 154–56, 176.

25. *Nature*, pp. 3, 14–15, 17, 45.

26. Ibid., pp. 47, 178, 214.

27. Ibid., pp. 270, 273, 357, 388–89, 421–22.

28. *History*, pp. 23–26.

29. Ibid., pp. 26, 29–30, 32–33, 35.

30. Ibid., pp. 35–36, 40, 74.

31. *Phenomenology*, pp. 45, 107, 109.

32. Ibid., pp. 111–14.

33. Ibid., pp. 115–16.

34. Ibid., pp. 116–19.

35. Ibid., pp. 120–22.

36. Ibid., pp. 123–26.

37. Ibid., pp. 126–27.

38. Ibid., pp. 139–42.

39. Ibid., pp. 263–65, 290.

40. *Right*, pp. 37–38, 40–42, 45, 48, 226–27, 229, 235. *See also Logic*, pp. 44–45, and G. W. F. Hegel, *On Art, Religion, Philosophy: Introductory Lectures to the Realm of Absolute Spirit*, ed. J. Glenn Gray (New York: Harper & Row, 1970), p. 115. This last collection is henceforth called "Gray."

41. G. W. F. Hegel, *Hegel's Philosophy of Mind*, trans. William Wallace and A. V. Miller (London: Oxford Univ. Press, 1971), pp. 1, 3, 15, 20–29, 153, 155–56, 171–76, 179, 185, 187, 192, 225–26, 228–29, 238, 243, 292. This book is henceforth called *"Mind."* For more on the soul, *see* Georg Wilhelm Friedrich Hegel, *Lectures on the Philosophy of Religion*, trans. E. B. Speirs and J. Burdon Sanderson (London: Routledge & Kegan Paul, 1968), Vol. III, p. 343. This book is henceforth called *"Religion."*

42. *Phenomenology*, pp. 2–3, 9–11.

43. Ibid., pp. 13, 27, 31–33, 36, 40.

44. Ibid., pp. 46–51.

45. Ibid., pp. 52–53, 56–57.

46. Ibid., pp. 58–64, 66.

47. Ibid., pp. 67–74.

48. Ibid., pp. 77, 81–82, 87–91, 101.

49. Ibid., pp. 480, 483.

50. Ibid., pp. 487–88, 490–93.

51. *Science*, Vol. I, pp. 53–56.

52. Ibid., pp. 57–63.

53. Ibid., pp. 64–67.

54. Ibid., pp. 67–75. *See* the section on Kant in G. W. F. Hegel, *Lectures on the History of Philosophy*, trans. E. S. Haldane and

Frances H. Simson (London: Routledge & Kegan Paul, 1955), Vol. Three, especially pp. 476–78, as well as the "Final Result" of that lecture series, Vol. Three, pp. 545–53. For earlier Hegelian treatments, *see* G. W. F. Hegel, *The Difference Between Fichte's and Schelling's Systems of Philosophy*, trans. H. S. Harris and Walter Cerf (Albany: State Univ. of New York Press, 1977), pp. 79–80, 89–91, 94, 96, and G. W. F. Hegel, *Faith and Knowledge*, trans. Walter Cerf and H. S. Harris (Albany: State Univ. of New York Press, 1977), pp. 55–56, 59, 64, 67–69, 77, 84–85. This last book is henceforth called *"Faith."*

55. *Logic*, pp. 12, 14–15, 19–20, 35–36, 41. *See also Nature*, p. 10, and Gray, pp. 88, 176, 216, 227–28, 234, 278–79.

56. *Logic*, pp. 65, 70, 72–73, 91–96, 116–19.

57. Ibid., pp. 124–30, 132–33, 142, 167, 172–74.

58. *History*, pp. 21–23, 63, 67. *See also Logic*, p. 220, and Gray, pp. 223, 303.

59. *Right*, pp. 20–23, 27, 32–33, 230. *See also* G. W. F. Hegel, *Natural Law*, trans. T. M. Knox (Philadelphia: Univ. of Pennsylvania Press, 1975), pp. 89–91, 121. This book is henceforth called *"Law."*

60. *Mind*, pp. 228, 238–40, 243–46, 251, 254–55.

61. *Phenomenology*, pp. 218, 221–23, 226, 230–31.

62. Ibid., pp. 233–35, 254–56.

63. Ibid., pp. 267–70, 279–80, 366–70.

64. Ibid., pp. 380, 383, 400, 404, 407; cf. *Law*, p. 113.

65. *Right*, pp. 3, 80, 90, 97–101, 103, 105, 107–10.

66. *Phenomenology*, pp. 214–15, 272–74.

67. Ibid., pp. 355–57, 359–62.

68. *History*, pp. 41–42.

69. Ibid., pp. 43, 46–47, 49–56, 80, 90, 92–97. Although they are not particularly important for our purposes, some interesting ideas can be found in G. W. F. Hegel, *Hegel's Political Writings*, trans. T. M. Knox (London: Oxford Univ. Press, 1964); *see*, for example, "The German Constitution," especially pp. 143–64, 234–37, "On the Recent Domestic Affairs of Wurtemberg," pp. 243–45, and "The English Reform Bill," especially pp. 295–97, 321–24, 329–30.

70. *Right*, pp. 7, 13, 70–71, 110.

71. Ibid., pp. 110–14, 263–64, 116–19.

72. Ibid., pp. 123, 127–32, 141, 148–50.

73. Ibid., pp. 155–56, 160, 174–76, 180–81, 282, 186, 290, 190–91, 193, 195, 204–7, 209–10, 295–96. In connection with Hegel's critique of Kant's political philosophy, *see Law*, p. 132, where he warns that we should not try "escaping into the shapelessness of cosmopolitanism, still less into the void of the Rights of Man, or the like void of a league of nations or a world republic. These are abstractions and formalisms."

74. *Right*, pp. 212–14, 216–22.

75. Ibid., pp. 279, 285.

76. G. W. F. Hegel, *Three Essays, 1793–1795*, ed. and trans. Peter Fuss and John Dobbins (Notre Dame, IN: Univ. of Notre Dame Press, 1984), pp. 32–36, 42, 45, 56.

77. Ibid., pp. 70, 72, 81, 93–94, 96, 98–99.

78. Ibid., pp. 112–18, 127, 141–42, 154, 165.

79. G. W. F. Hegel, *Early Theological Writings*, trans. T. M. Knox (Philadelphia: Univ. of Pennsylvania Press, 1971), pp. 68–69, 71, 86, 91–92, 176. This book is henceforth called *"Early."*

80. Ibid., pp. 205–6, 212–15, 223, 262, 266, 268.

81. *Faith*, pp. 56, 60, 64–65, 80, 94, 191.

82. *Phenomenology*, pp. 334, 337–40, 342–43.

83. Ibid., pp. 412–13, 417–21, 424.

84. Ibid., pp. 424, 427, 430–35, 438–40, 443, 450–51.

85. Ibid., pp. 453, 455, 457–63, 467–68, 473–74, 476–77.

86. *Logic*, pp. 57–58, 81–82, 104.

87. Ibid., pp. 164, 214, 246, 260–61.

88. *Nature*, pp. 8, 13.

89. Ibid., pp. 13–14.

90. *Mind*, pp. 12, 17–20.

91. Ibid., pp. 292, 296–300, 303–5, 307, 312–13.

92. Gray, pp. 29, 56, 104, 110–15, 119–27.

93. Ibid., pp. 129, 145, 151, 157, 160, 186, 198, 200.

94. Ibid., pp. 269, 277–79, 283.

95. *Religion*, Vol. I, pp. 168, 170–71; Vol. II, p. 349. For more on the proofs of God's existence, *see Religion*, Vol. III, pp. 156, 164, 216, 229. Hegel's view on the relationship between philosophy and religion is discussed further in Wayne P. Pomerleau, "The Accession and Dismissal of an Upstart Handmaid," *The Monist*, 60 (April 1977), 213–20.

96. *Religion*, Vol. III, pp. 129, 315–16, 319, 348.

97. *Early*, pp. 196, 297–98; *Nature*, p. 444.

98. *Religion*, Vol. I, pp. 79, 314; Vol. III, pp. 57, 105, 302.

99. *Right*, p. 83; *Faith*, pp. 59–60.

100. *Mind*, pp. 229, 238, 250.

101. John Stuart Mill, *Essential Works of John Stuart Mill*, ed. Max Lerner (New York: Bantam Books, 1961), pp. 12–20, 24–28, 30, 41, 44. This book is henceforth called *"Essential."*

102. Ibid., pp. 3–4, 31–34, 39–41.

103. Ibid., pp. 45–47, 54–55.

104. Ibid., pp. 60, 63, 68, 70, 73, 76–77, 83–84, 86–92, 95–97, 100–103, 105, 109.

105. Ibid., pp. 119–21, 123, 130–34.

106. Ibid., pp. 111–14, 135–37.

107. Ibid., pp. 138–39.

108. John Stuart Mill, *The Letters of John Stuart Mill*, 2 vols., ed. Hugh S. R. Elliott (London: Longmans, Green, and Co., 1910), Vol. I, pp. 8, 35, 54, 70–71, 88, 103–4, 127. This book is henceforth called *"Letters."*

109. *Essential*, pp. 141–42, 2, 142–43, 148–51, 153, 155–56, 158, 161–62.

110. Ibid., pp. 163–68.

111. Ibid., pp. 179–80, 182.

112. Ibid., pp. 368–70.

113. John Stuart Mill, *A System of Logic*, 5th ed. 2 vols. (London: Parker, Son, and Bourn, 1862), Vol. II, p. 428. This book is henceforth called *"Logic."*

114. Ibid., I, pp. 61–64, 68, 82–83.

115. John Stuart Mill, *An Examination of Sir William Hamilton's Philosophy* (London: Longman, Green, Longman, Roberts & Green,1865), pp. 190–92. This book is henceforth called "*Examination.*"

116. Ibid., pp. 192–93, 196, 198, 161.

117. Ibid., pp. 205, 208, 212–13. In John Stuart Mill, *Theism*, ed. Richard Taylor (Indianapolis: Bobbs-Merrill, 1957), p. 50, Mill maintains that our own mental states "are the only things which we directly know to be real, all things else being merely" their "unknown conditions."

118. *Logic*, I, pp. 68, 80–81.

119. John Stuart Mill, *The Logic of the Moral Sciences* (La Salle: Open Court, 1988), pp. 30–32. This book (which is Book VI of Mill's *A System of Logic*) is henceforth called "*Moral.*"

120. Ibid., pp. 32–38.

121. Ibid., pp. 38–39, 46, 49.

122. Ibid., pp. 50, 54, 58–60.

123. *Examination*, pp. 6–12.

124. *Logic*, Vol. I, pp. 3–5, 127–28 (including note), 185–86, 218, 313–14, 319, 324, 337–38, 341.

125. Ibid., pp. 342–43.

126. Ibid., pp. 363, 377, 425, 428–30, 433.

127. Ibid., pp. 435–36.

128. Ibid., pp. 436–37, 440–41.

129. *Moral*, pp. 22–23; cf. Mill's diary entry for Feb. 27, 1854, in *Letters*, Vol. II, p. 375.

130. *Moral*, pp. 23–28.

131. Ibid., pp. 28–29.

132. *Examination*, pp. 500–501.

133. Ibid., pp. 503–4.

134. Ibid., pp. 504–5.

135. Ibid., pp. 506–7, 510.

136. Ibid., p. 516.

137. Ibid., p. 517.

138. *Moral*, p. 134.

139. Ibid., pp. 137, 140, 142–43; cf. Mill's brief diary entry of March 23, 1854, in *Letters*, Vol. II, p. 381.

140. *Essential*, pp. 189–92.

141. Ibid., p. 192.

142. Ibid., p. 194.

143. Ibid., pp. 195–99.

144. Ibid., pp. 199–204.

145. Ibid., pp. 205–6.

146. Ibid., pp. 206–7.

147. Ibid., p. 208.

148. Ibid., p. 209.

149. Ibid., p. 210.

150. Ibid., pp. 211–12.

151. Ibid., pp. 212–15.

152. Ibid., pp. 216–20.

153. Ibid., pp. 220–24.

154. Ibid., pp. 226–27.

155. Ibid., pp. 228–31.

156. Ibid., pp. 231–36.

157. Ibid., p. 248.

158. Ibid., pp. 371–77, 381–82, 390–91, 395.

159. Ibid., pp. 399–401.

160. Ibid., pp. 237–39.

161. Ibid., pp. 240–48; cf. *Moral*, pp. 61, 63, 100–103, 115–16, for Mill's views on social science and social progress.

162. *Essential*, pp. 255–57.

163. Ibid., pp. 257–63.

164. Ibid., pp. 263–66.

165. Ibid., pp. 268–69.

166. Ibid., pp. 269–72, 280, 284.

167. Ibid., pp. 285–87, 294–95.

168. Ibid., pp. 295, 301–2.

169. Ibid., pp. 304–5, 308, 313–15.

170. Ibid., pp. 318–20.

171. Ibid., pp. 322–25, 327–30.

172. Ibid., pp. 340, 343–45.

173. Ibid., pp. 354–60.

174. John Stuart Mill, *Considerations on Representative Government*, ed. Currin V. Shields (New York: The Liberal Arts Press, 1958), pp. 36–37, 42–43, 68, 70–71. This book is henceforth called "*Government.*"

175. Ibid., pp. 102–4, 131–32.

176. John Stuart Mill, *The Subjection of Women*, ed. Susan Moller Okin (Indianapolis: Hackett Publishing Co., 1988), pp. 1, 12–16.

177. Ibid., pp. 17–21.

178. Ibid., pp. 21–28.

179. John Stuart Mill, *Principles of Political Economy and Chapters on Socialism*, ed. Jonathan Riley (Oxford, England: Oxford Univ. Press, 1994), pp. 5–12, 14–15.

180. Ibid., pp. 324–27, 332–35, 341, 349–51.

181. Ibid., pp. 373–75, 378–81, 384–85, 403–4, 412–13, 421.

182. John Stuart Mill, "Capital Punishment," in *Collected Works of John Stuart Mill*, ed. John M. Robson and Bruce L. Kinzer (Toronto: Univ. of Toronto Press, 1988), Vol. XXVIII, pp. 266–72.

183. *Examination*, pp. 44, 98–105, 491; *see Letters*, Vol. II, p. 93, where Mill writes that the study of Hegel "tends to deprave one's intellect" and has given him "a sort of sickening feeling," which he has "not yet entirely got rid of."

184. *Essential*, pp. 385–86, 396.

185. Ibid., pp. 402–6, 410–14, 418–19.

186. Ibid., pp. 419, 421–25, 429–31.

187. *Theism*, pp. 6–11.

188. Ibid., pp. 12–14, 18, 20–21, 24–25, 27–32; for Mill's appreciation of Darwin's work, *see Letters*, Vol. I, p. 236, and Vol. II, p. 181.

189. *Theism*, pp. 33–34, 36–37, 42–45.

190. Ibid., pp. 81, 84–86.

191. Ibid., pp. 46–55. In his *Examination*, p. 211, Mill anticipates James in maintaining that it is as plausible to suppose that "a thread of consciousness" might be "prolonged to eternity" as that some purely conjectural "spiritual substance for ever continues to exist."

192. *Letters*, Vol. II, pp. 380–81, 384.

193. *Essential*, pp. 307–9.

194. Ibid., pp. 200–202.

195. *Government*, pp. 47–50.

196. For more on his negative relationship to other modern philosophers, *see* Wayne P. Pomerleau, "Kierkegaard's Existential Critique of Modern Rationalists," *Explorations*, 8, No. 2 (Winter 1989), 27–38.

Bibliography

GENERAL

Aiken, Henry D. *The Age of Ideology*. New York: Mentor Books, 1956.

Copleston, Frederick, S.J. *A History of Philosophy*, Vol. VII, VIII, Part I. Garden City, NY: Image Books, 1965, 1967.

Jones, W. T. *Kant and the Nineteenth Century*, 2d ed., rev. San Diego: Harcourt Brace Jovanovich, 1975.

HEGEL   ***Primary Sources***

The Difference Between Fichte's and Schelling's Systems of Philosophy. Trans. H. S. Harris and Walter Cerf. Albany: State Univ. of New York Press, 1977.

Early Theological Writings. Trans. T. M. Knox. Philadelphia: Univ. of Pennsylvania Press, 1971.

Encyclopedia of the Philosophical Sciences in Outline and Critical Writings. Ed. Ernst Behler. New York: Continuum Publishing Co., 1990.

Faith and Knowledge. Trans. Walter Cerf and H. S. Harris. Albany: State Univ. of New York Press, 1977.

Hegel: The Letters. Trans. Clark Butler and Christiane Seiler. Bloomington: Indiana Univ. Press, 1984.

Hegel Selections. Ed. M. J. Inwood. New York: Macmillan, 1989.

Hegel's Lectures on the History of Philosophy, 3 vols. Trans. E. S. Haldane and Frances H. Simson. London: Routledge & Kegan Paul, 1955.

Hegel's Logic. Trans. William Wallace. London: Oxford Univ. Press, 1975.

Hegel's Philosophy of Mind. Trans. William Wallace and A. V. Miller. London: Oxford Univ. Press, 1971.

Hegel's Philosophy of Nature. Trans. A. V. Miller. London: Oxford Univ. Press, 1970.

Hegel's Philosophy of Right. Trans. T. M. Knox. New York: Oxford Univ. Press, 1967.

Hegel's Political Writings. Trans. T. M. Knox . London: Oxford Univ. Press, 1964.

Hegel's Science of Logic, 2 vols. Trans. W. H. Johnston and L. G. Struthers. London: George Allen & Unwin, 1961.

Introduction to the Philosophy of History. Trans. Leo Rauch. Indianapolis: Hackett Publishing Co., 1988.

Lectures on the Philosophy of Religion, 3 vols. Trans. E. B. Speirs and J. Burdon Sanderson. London: Routledge & Kegan Paul, 1968.

Natural Law. Trans. T. M. Knox. Philadelphia: Univ. of Pennsylvania Press, 1975.

On Art, Religion, Philosophy: Introductory Lectures to the Realm of Absolute Spirit. Ed. J. Glenn Gray. New York: Harper & Row, 1970.

Phenomenology of Spirit. Trans. A. V. Miller. New York: Oxford Univ. Press, 1979.

The Philosophy of Hegel. Ed. Carl J. Friedrich. New York: Modern Library, 1954.

Three Essays, 1793–1795. Ed. and trans. Peter Fuss and John Dobbins. Notre Dame, IN: Univ. of Notre Dame Press, 1984.

Secondary Sources

Beiser, Frederick C., ed. *The Cambridge Companion to Hegel*. New York: Cambridge Univ. Press, 1993.

Findlay, J. N. *The Philosophy of Hegel*. New York: Collier Books, 1962.

Harris, Errol E. *The Spirit of Hegel*. Atlantic Highlands, NJ: Humanities Press, 1993.

Inwood, Michael, ed. *Hegel*. New York: Oxford Univ. Press, 1985.

Kaufmann, Walter. *Hegel. A Reinterpretation*. Garden City, NY: Doubleday & Co., 1966.

MacIntyre, Alasdair, ed. *Hegel: A Collection of Critical Essays*. Garden City, NY: Doubleday & Co., 1972.

Mure, G. R. G. *The Philosophy of Hegel*. London: Oxford Univ. Press, 1965.

Singer, Peter. *Hegel*. Oxford, England: Oxford Univ. Press, 1983.

Soll, Ivan. *An Introduction to Hegel's Metaphysics*. Chicago: The Univ. of Chicago Press, 1969.

Solomon, Robert C. *In the Spirit of Hegel*. New York: Oxford Univ. Press, 1983.

Stace, W. T. *The Philosophy of Hegel*. New York: Dover Publications, 1955.

MILL   *Primary Sources*

Collected Works of John Stuart Mill, Vol. XXVIII. Ed. John M. Robson and Bruce L. Kinzer. Toronto: Univ. of Toronto Press, 1988.

Considerations on Representative Government. Ed. Currin V. Shields. New York: The Liberal Arts Press, 1958.

Essential Works of John Stuart Mill. Ed. Max Lerner. New York: Bantam Books, 1961.

An Examination of Sir William Hamilton's Philosophy. London: Longman, Green, Longman, Roberts & Green, 1865.

The Letters of John Stuart Mill, 2 vols. Ed. Hugh S. R. Elliott. London: Longmans, Green, and Co., 1910.

The Logic of the Moral Sciences. La Salle, IL: Open Court, 1988.

On Liberty. Ed. Elizabeth Rapaport. Indianapolis: Hackett Publishing Co., 1978.

Principles of Political Economy and Chapters on Socialism. Ed. Jonathan Riley. Oxford, England: Oxford Univ. Press, 1994.

Selected Writings of John Stuart Mill. Ed. Maurice Cowling. New York: New American Library, 1968.

The Subjection of Women. Ed. Susan Moller Okin. Indianapolis: Hackett Publishing Co., 1988.

A System of Logic, 5th ed., 2 vols. London: Parker, Son, and Bourn, 1862.

Theism. Ed. Richard Taylor. Indianapolis: Bobbs-Merrill, 1957.

Utilitarianism. Ed. George Sher. Indianapolis: Hackett Publishing Co., 1979.

Secondary Sources

Britton, Karl. *John Stuart Mill*, 2nd ed. New York: Dover Publications, 1969.

Robson, John M., and Michael Laine, eds. *James and John Stuart Mill/Papers of the Centenary Conference*. Toronto: Univ. of Toronto Press, 1976.

Ryan, Alan. *J. S. Mill*. London: Routledge & Kegan Paul, 1974.

Schneewind, J. B., ed. *Mill: A Collection of Critical Essays*. Garden City, NY: Doubleday & Co., 1968.

Thomas, William. *Mill*. Oxford, England: Oxford Univ. Press, 1985.

Thompson, Dennis F. *John Stuart Mill and Representative Government*. Princeton: Princeton Univ. Press, 1976.

Historical Background

《《《《《《《《《《《《《《《《《《《《《《《《《《《《《》》》》》》》》》》》》》》》》》》》》》》》》》》

owards the end of the nineteenth century, in Vienna Sigmund Freud developed psychoanalytic techniques that would revolutionize the fields of psychiatry and psychology and that would have a major impact on twentieth-century thought. Also, in the wake of Hegelian **idealism** and various ideological reactions against it, such as Mill's **utilitarian, liberal empiricism**, a variety of forms of **philosophical** analysis began to emerge, each with its own distinctive focus. In America there was the **pragmatic** analysis of Charles Sanders Peirce and William James; Henri Bergson and Alfred North Whitehead developed **process** analysis; Bertrand Russell and A. J. Ayer did **logical** analysis; Edmund Husserl pursued **phenomenological** analysis; Jean-Paul Sartre blended the **existential** analysis of Kierkegaard and Nietzsche with phenomenology; Ludwig Wittgenstein and his followers did linguistic or conceptual analysis. Philosophers are typically trained in and aligned with one of these "camps," tending to dismiss others as irrelevant or narrow-minded or fuzzy-headed, rather than carefully and critically assessing their contributions, leaving us with an array of philosophical factions. Other important philosophers up to the middle of the twentieth century include Gottlob Frege, a German; William K. Clifford, George Edward Moore, and Robin George Collingwood in Great Britain; and Josiah Royce, John Dewey, and George Santayana in America.

Queen Victoria's sixty-four-year reign over the British Empire lasted until the beginning of the twentieth century. In 1899 (two years before she died), Britain became involved in the Boer War in South Africa, as a result of which British sovereignty was accepted by the Boers (South Africans of Dutch extraction), but representative government was eventually set up. In Prussia in the 1880s Otto von Bismarck instituted health, accident, and old-age insurance for German workers. But his fortunes declined, and he was dismissed from office in 1890 by William II (the grandson of Queen Victoria), who had been Emperor of Germany since 1888. In 1881, the reform-minded Czar Alexander II of Russia was assassinated, being succeeded by the reactionary Alexander III. The **communist** teachings of Marx and Engels were spreading among Russia's industrial workers. In 1891, Pope Leo XIII issued *Rerum Novarum*, an encyclical condemning **socialism**, communism, and liberalism but calling for improved conditions for the working classes. In France, the trial for treason of Captain Alfred Dreyfus, a Jewish army officer, caused an international furor and led to drastic anticlerical measures in French government. After Japan won a war with Russia in 1905, there was an insurrection of munitions workers in St. Petersburg, with thousands of casualties, followed by a general strike, leading to the czar's acceptance of a constitution, the Duma (a representative legislature), and multiple legal political parties, including the Bolsheviks.

In America the last major violent confrontation with Indians occurred at Wounded Knee, in 1890 (fourteen years after General Custer's defeat in the Battle at the Little Bighorn). In 1898, after the conclusion of the Spanish-American War (in which Theodore Roosevelt won distinction for leading his "Rough Riders"), the United States annexed Puerto Rico and the Philippines. In 1901, Roosevelt began serving his eight years as president, becoming even more famous as a "trust buster" and an early conservationist. In 1903, in North Carolina, Wilbur and Orville Wright made the first brief airplane flights. That same year, the United States concluded a treaty with the newly declared republic of Panama, allowing the perpetual lease of a ten-mile strip of land through the isthmus on which the Panama Canal would be dug (it was finally opened in 1914). Many western states entered the Union near the turn of the century, with Arizona becoming the forty-eighth state in 1912.

On June 28, 1914, Austrian Archduke Francis Ferdinand (with his wife) was assassinated by Serbian nationalists in the Bosnian city of Sarajevo, provoking an indignant firestorm in Austria-Hungary against Serbia. A month later, Austria declared war on Serbia. Other European countries took sides. Germany declared war against Russia, France, and Belgium, and the British government declared war on Germany, as Japan did later. Germany was allied with the Ottoman Empire, Bulgaria, and Austria-Hungary. The Germans conquered Belgium and moved into France. Russian armies invaded German East Prussia and Austrian Galicia but were defeated and expelled from German territory; by 1916, German forces had pushed into Russia itself. In February of 1917, Czar Nicholas II was overthrown and abdicated; a liberal provisional government was set up by the Duma, but by October, it was toppled by the Bolsheviks, led by V. I. Lenin, who established an armistice with Germany and included Leon Trotsky and Joseph Stalin in his government. By 1918, a constitution had established a dictatorship of the proletariat and one-party rule for Communism.

American President Woodrow Wilson had tried to keep the United States neutral in the war, but this became increasingly difficult. When the British liner "Lusitania" was sunk by the Germans in 1915, with about one hundred American lives being lost, Wilson protested and pushed Germany to cease its unrestricted submarine warfare against transport ships. When Germany resumed submarine attacks in 1917, the United States declared war. By the following year, German armies were in full retreat; Germany and her allies were calling for peace. An armistice was concluded in November of 1918, the German Emperor abdicated, and a republic was set up. The Peace of Versailles was signed in June of 1919 (though not by either the United States or Russia). President Georges Clemenceau of France and Prime Minister Lloyd George of England pushed for harsh terms against the conquered Germany, which had to give up all of its colonies, cede Alsace-Lorraine to France, disband its fleet, surrender territory to the reincarnated Poland, reduce its army, cease military conscription, stop producing certain types of armaments, pay monetary war reparations, and admit blame for the devastations of the war. A **democratic** constitution was written for the Weimar Republic in Germany, calling for universal suffrage for all citizens (female as well as male), providing for parliamentary government, and guaranteeing civil rights. That same year, a League of Nations—promoted by Woodrow Wilson, although never joined by the United States—was established with an International Court of Justice. Also in 1919, Benito Mussolini formed a Fascist political party in Italy, establishing a Fascist government three years later and abolishing all political parties but his own.

Russia had granted women's suffrage in 1917. Two years later, Lenin sponsored the Third Comintern (Communist International), hoping to expand Communist influence abroad. By 1922, Bolsheviks had full control of most of Russia; about that time, Siberia and parts of the Ukraine were being consolidated into a Soviet Union, which was constitutionally established by 1923. But the next year Lenin died, leaving Leon Trotsky and Joseph Stalin to struggle for the leadership of the Communist Party, with Stalin establishing dictatorial power in 1929 and Trotsky being banished and later assassinated in Mexico.

In 1918, Great Britain granted women the vote, and the following year Pope Benedict XV came out in favor of women's suffrage. In 1920, the United States passed the Nineteenth Amendment to the Constitution giving women the vote. Progress was in the air; even the Republican administration that replaced the Democrats in 1921 adopted some programs of political and economic liberalism though becoming isolationist in its foreign-affairs policies. Business productivity boomed, and national spirits soared. Then came the "crash" of the New York Stock Exchange in October of 1929, precipitating the international crisis of the Great Depression. By 1930, a campaign of passive resistance against the British colonial rule in India had begun, under the leadership of Mohandas Gandhi.

Germany had joined the League of Nations in 1926, and military supervision of Germany by foreign powers had ceased. By 1932, the National Socialists ("Nazis") constituted the largest political party in Germany, which was frustrated by its social conditions and its treatment by the international community. The next year, Adolf Hitler became Chancellor of Germany, establishing totalitarian control, suppressing other political parties, and focusing national resentment against Jewish scapegoats. Germany withdrew from the League of Nations. Also in 1933, Franklin Delano Roosevelt became President of the United States, passing social security laws and launching large government work projects to counteract the ill effects of the Depression. Germany was rearming and making expansionistic claims on neighboring territories; compulsory military service was restored, and German troops were deployed to the previously demilitarized Rhineland. In 1935, Fascist Italy invaded Ethiopia; the League of Nations imposed economic sanctions against Italy, but they were not rigorously pressed. The following year, an alliance between Italy and Germany established the "Rome-Berlin Axis." That same year, the Soviet Union comprised thirteen republics, with the Politbureau, the executive committee headed by Stalin, wielding power. Also in 1936, civil war broke out in Spain; by 1939, General Francisco Franco, aided by Germany and Italy, had triumphed over the Popular Front, backed by Russia, and set up a Fascist government there.

In 1938, Hitler established an alliance between Germany and Austria, and he laid claim to the Sudetenland, which was the Germanic portion of Czechoslovakia. At a conference in Munich, Western democratic powers acceded to an "appeasement" of the Nazis. The following year, Hitler annexed the remainder of Czechoslovakia, and Western nations increased preparations for war. The Germans set up concentration camps throughout territories they occupied. There Jewish, Gypsy, and Communist inmates were forced to perform hard labor under the command of brutal guards. Several of these camps, such as Auschwitz, were designed for genocidal extermination. About six million Jews were eventually murdered in what has come to be called the Holocaust. In 1939, Germany attacked Poland, Norway, Denmark, Holland, and Belgium. It invaded France, in contempt of her much vaunted Maginot Line of defense; France surrendered, and a pro-German puppet government was organized at Vichy under Marshal Henri Pétain. Mussolini seized territories in southern France for Italy. Heavily besieged by German air power in the Battle of Britain, the British bravely dug in to defend themselves under their Prime Minister Winston Churchill. Despite a nonagression pact that had been signed for purposes of expediency between proponents of two opposing ideologies, German Fascism and Russian Communism, Hitler, mistrusting Russian intentions, invaded the Soviet Union in June 1941 along a 2000-mile front, reaching the outskirts of Moscow within a month. But this proved to be a fatal mistake on Hitler's part, just as it had been Napoleon's downfall; for Russia, with greater resources than Hitler had imagined, repelled the invasion, and Britain, under decreased pressure, was able to regroup and repel the Nazi threat.

On December 7, 1941, Japan (an ally of Germany and Italy) bombed the American fleet at Pearl Harbor, Hawaii, bringing the United States into the war on the side of England, France, and the Allies, against the Axis powers. In 1943, the Nazis were defeated at Stalingrad, and the German and Italian troops were retreating before Allied forces in North Africa; the Allies successfully invaded Italy, and Mussolini's government was toppled. In June of 1944, the Allied forces launched a major assault in Normandy, repelling the Germans. Soon, Allied incursions into the German homeland had begun. With Berlin burning, Hitler committed suicide, and Germany surrendered in May 1945. With Italy and Germany defeated, Japan remained at war until August of 1945, when American warplanes dropped atomic bombs on the Japanese cities of Hiroshima and Nagasaki, under orders from President Harry S. Truman. Japan surrendered and was occupied by American forces. Meanwhile, Germany was divided into four zones of occupation, the Soviets converting their East German zone into a Communist regime (as they had already done in Poland, Hungary, and Rumania). In 1945, the United Nations was formed, replacing the League of Nations, with five major powers (the United States, the Soviet Union, Great Britain, France, and China) being granted veto power in the Security Council. The next year, Nazi leaders were tried at Nuremberg for war crimes connected with the extermination of millions of Jews, Gypsies, and political activists; and a war in Indochina (which would last until 1954) erupted between the French and the Vietnamese nationalists, led by Ho Chi Minh.

In 1947, India gained independence, and the following year its famous advocate of civil disobedience, Mohandas Gandhi, was assassinated. The next year, the State of Israel was proclaimed, war broke out between Israel and the Arab League, the Soviet Union blockaded West Berlin, Communists and Nationalists fought for power in China, and Korea was divided into northern and southern portions. In 1949, the North Atlantic Treaty Organization was formed by Western allies; Mao Zedong set up a Communist government in China, and the Chinese Nationalist government fled to Taiwan; Germany was split into eastern and western parts; Russia ended its blockade of West Berlin and diplomatically recognized the People's Republic of China. In 1950, the Korean War broke out between Communist North Korea, supported by the People's Republic of China, and South Korea, backed by military forces of the United Nations; it lasted for three years, ending in a stalemate after exacting a toll of millions of casualties. Also in 1954, Senator Joseph McCarthy's charges of large-scale Communist infiltration into the U.S. State Department were found to be false, and he was condemned by the Senate.

Most of the second half of the twentieth century has been marked by a "cold war" between the democratic West, under American leadership, and Soviet Communism, under Russian leadership. After Soviet Premier Stalin died in 1953, East-West relations periodically thawed and chilled, being strained, three years later, by the Russian invasion of Hungary to crush an anti-Soviet revolt. In 1962, the Soviets started constructing nuclear missile bases in Cuba, as part of a massive arms race with the West; after President John F. Kennedy ordered a naval blockade of Cuba to prevent nuclear weapons from reaching the island, Soviet Premier Nikita Khrushchev had the missile sites dismantled, ending this Cuban missile crisis, which some feared might precipitate a third World War. In 1968, Soviet troops invaded Czechoslovakia to crush a liberal reform movement there. Meanwhile, the space race had begun, with the Soviets taking an early lead in the late 50s with the launching of Sputnik I in 1957, and the Americans catching up in the late 60s, landing men on the Moon in 1969.

In 1959, Alaska and Hawaii became the forty-ninth and fiftieth states in the American Union. The 60s was a particularly turbulent decade in America and around the world. Riots and large-scale demonstrations were rampant. African nations continued gaining independence from European colonialization in the 60s and 70s. Hostilities continued in the Middle East between Israel and surrounding Arab countries, with Israelis winning the "Six Day War" in 1967, only to be attacked by Egyptians and Syrians six years later in the Yom Kippur War of 1973, also won by the Israelis. Important American political figures were assassinated in the 60s, including President Kennedy, black nationalist leader Malcolm X, civil rights leader Martin Luther King, and Senator Robert F. Kennedy, brother of the slain president. By the second half of this decade, American involvement in a civil war in Vietnam escalated dramatically, with more than half a million Americans assigned to military service there at one time and heavy bombing from the air. The war spread to Laos and Cambodia. Long after American public opinion had turned against the "quagmire," President Richard M. Nixon began deescalating the American presence and participation, with all American troops being withdrawn by 1973 and

South Vietnam falling to the Communists in 1975. The Watergate scandal erupted in 1972, during a presidential election campaign, when men were caught burgling the Democratic Party headquarters at the Watergate complex in Washington. President Nixon denied any involvement on the part of the White House; but when tapes he had secretly recorded concerning Watergate were discovered and some of his aides were convicted of conspiring to cover up and obstruct justice, Nixon was forced to resign in 1974, rather than risk possible impeachment from office.

In the midst of all this turmoil and conflict, there were great cultural achievements over the decades. In France, at the turn of the century, Auguste Rodin was creating some of the finest sculptures of **modern** times, such as *The Thinker*; some years later Constantin Brancusi was concerned with formal simplicity and coherence in sculptures such as *The Kiss*. In painting, an unprecedented period of experimentation began, centered in France. Impressionists, such as Édouard Manet, Edgar Degas, Claude Monet, Pierre Auguste Renoir, Camille Pissarro, and Mary Cassatt, used short brush strokes of bright colors in immediate juxtaposition to represent the effect of light on objects. Dissatisfied with the limitations of impressionism, post-impressionists Paul Cézanne, Georges Seurat, Henri de Toulouse-Lautrec, Vincent van Gogh, Paul Gauguin, and Edvard Munch pursued other directions. The most important Fauvists (wild beasts) were Henri Matisse and Georges Roualt. Pablo Picasso worked in a large variety of styles and media. Expressionists included Vassili Kandinsky, Piet Mondrian, and Kazimir Malevich. Freudian psychoanalytic thought inspired the fantasy art of Marcel Duchamp and surrealist Salvador Dali. Other prominent twentieth-century artists included realists Edward Hopper and Georgia O'Keeffe; abstract expressionists Jackson Pollock and Willem de Kooning; pop artists Andy Warhol and Jasper Johns and color fielder Mark Rothko; photographers Alfred Stieglitz and Edward Steichen; and architects Antoní Gaudi and Frank Lloyd Wright.

With regard to musical developments during this period, the Austrian Gustav Mahler wrote nine magnificent symphonies (and an incomplete tenth); the German Richard Strauss broke new ground in orchestration and brought the tone poem to a new level of refinement; Frenchmen Claude Debussy and Maurice Ravel incorporated conceptual elements of visual impressions into their music, thereby ushering in a musical movement of the same name; the Russian Igor Stravinsky shocked the musical world with the premiere, in 1913, of his composition *The Rite of Spring*; the Austrian Arnold Schoenberg introduced the twelve-tone system of tonal organization; the Hungarian Béla Bartók synthesized elements of authentic folk music (drawn from his own ethnomusicological research) and contemporary ideas concerning form, harmony, and orchestration. American popular song flourished during this period, due in large part to the immense popularity of Broadway musicals, such as those written by Jerome Kern, George Gershwin, Cole Porter, Richard Rodgers, and Irving Berlin. This period also witnessed the birth of jazz, one of the United States' only truly indigenous art forms. Some key figures in jazz included trumpeter Louis Armstrong, composer/pianist Edward Kennedy ("Duke") Ellington, and saxophonists Charlie Parker and John Coltrane. Finally, there was the advent of rock-'n'-roll; some notable figures within this style included Chuck Berry, Elvis Presley, and the Beatles.

Literature continued to flourish. American novelists of the period included: Henry James (*The Portrait of a Lady*), Edith Wharton (*The Age of Innocence*), William Faulkner (*The Sound and the Fury*), Ernest Hemingway (*The Sun Also Rises*), J. D. Salinger (*The Catcher in the Rye*), and John Updike (the *Rabbit* series); among English and Irish novelists were Thomas Hardy (*Jude the Obscure*), Joseph Conrad (*Heart of Darkness*), George Orwell (*Nineteen Eighty-Four*), D. H. Lawrence (*Sons and Lovers*), and James Joyce (*Ulysses*); Continental novelists were exemplified by Thomas Mann (*The Magic Mountain*), Franz Kafka (*The Trial*), Jean-Paul Sartre (*Nausea*), and Albert Camus (*The Stranger*). Playwrights included Henrik Ibsen, Oscar Wilde, George Bernard Shaw, Eugene O'Neill, and Arthur Miller. Among prominent poets were T. S. Eliot, Robert Frost, and Carl Sandburg.

In science French chemist Louis Pasteur experimented with bacteria, developed the process of pasteurization, and produced a vaccine against anthrax, which was also used effectively against rabies. Later, in France, Pierre and Marie Curie did pioneer work on radioactivity. German-born Albert Einstein produced his theory of relativity, before being denied his German citizenship, for being Jewish, and coming to America. American Jonas Salk developed an effective vaccine against the polio virus. Technological inventions that have changed our lives during this period included the automobile, motion pictures, radio, television, jet aircraft engines, and computers.

During the twentieth century, many philosophers have been influential, in addition to James and Sartre, on whom this chapter will focus. Martin Buber was a significant Jewish philosopher, as Paul Tillich was a noteworthy Protestant one. Among Catholic philosophers, Jacques Maritain, Gabriel Marcel, and Frederick Copleston, S.J., have made their marks. Existentialists Martin Heidegger and Simone de Beauvoir have followers. Gilbert Ryle, John Hick, and Antony G. N. Flew have all worked in England. In America, Philippa Foot and Robert Nozick are making valuable contributions. The thought of Jürgen Habermas, a German, is also proving influential.

Let us conclude this historical background by briefly treating events occurring thus far in the last quarter of our century. In 1976, Mao Zedong, Chairman of the Communist Party in the People's Republic of China, died, after which China began to open up somewhat to the outside world. American President Jimmy Carter worked for nuclear arms control and international human rights in the late 1970s and helped bring about a peace treaty between Israel and Egypt. In 1980, after a protracted guerrilla war, a general election was held in Rhodesia, leading to a black government taking office and the beginning of the genuinely independent country of Zimbabwe. In 1990, the European Economic Community (the "Common Market") moved towards the more unified political ties of a European Union; and the following year, apartheid was abolished in South Africa. Perhaps most surprising of all, however, was the collapse of the Soviet Union and the relinquishing of its control over Eastern Europe, with the demolition of the Berlin Wall and the fall of Communist regimes in Hungary, Czechoslovakia, and Poland in 1989–90. The Soviet Union allowed the Baltic republics of Estonia, Latvia, and Lithuania to regain their independence and then itself broke up, with most of its member republics becoming loosely federated in a commonwealth of independent states. Finally, what had been Communist Yugoslavia disintegrated, with Serbs, Croats, and Muslim Bosnians warring among themselves.

The last century or so has rightly been called the Age of Analysis. In the mass movements of social change, in the struggles for power, self-determination, and political rights, it was important to analyze the human condition as it is and as it could become. Two psychologically perceptive philosophical **humanists** who did so were the American William James and the Frenchman Jean-Paul Sartre. The pragmatism of the former and the individualism of the latter are both quite symptomatic of our contemporary culture. The alternatives we consider are Ludwig Wittgenstein, the coauthors, Robert S. Downie and Elizabeth Telfer, and John Rawls.

BIOGRAPHY

William James was born on January 11, 1842 (one year before Mill published his *System of Logic*), in New York City, the oldest of five children of Henry James, Sr., and his wife Mary Walsh James. He was named after his paternal grandfather, William James of Albany, from whom Henry Sr. had received a legacy sufficient to allow him to devote the remainder of his life to studying and writing **theology**. In 1843, Henry James, Jr., was born (he would become one of America's most distinguished writers of fiction), followed by Garth Wilkinson (called "Wilky") in 1845, Robertson (called "Bob") in 1846, and Alice in 1848. The life of the James family appears to have been vibrant, if unsettled. They moved back and forth between Europe and America, giving the five children a fluency in languages as well as a cosmopolitan upbringing, though they never remained in any school for very long. Once, while in England, they met John Stuart Mill.

As a child, William James loved to draw. His brother Henry later wrote, "As I catch W. J.'s image, from far back, at its most characteristic, he sits drawing and drawing, always drawing." Since William wanted to try becoming a painter, the family (returning from Germany and Switzerland) settled in Newport, Rhode Island, where William could study painting with William Morris Hunt, the leading portraitist in America at that time. But within a year, William abandoned the goal of becoming a painter, apparently believing that he would never be better than mediocre at it. In 1861, he entered the Lawrence Scientific School at Harvard University (ill health apparently kept both him and brother Henry out of the Civil War, in which their younger brothers Wilky and Bob served in black regiments). William studied chemistry and then physiology before entering Harvard Medical School in 1864, when the family moved to Boston. But then he took a year (1865–66) off to join the Thayer expedition to Brazil, led by the famous Swiss-born naturalist, Louis Agassiz, the trip being marred by James's ill health. So in 1866, he returned from South America, resuming work in medical school, and the James family moved from Boston to Cambridge. But from 1867 to 1868, William left Massachusetts again to study physiology and medicine at the University of Berlin (Hegel's school) and to try to recover his health. He wrote to his father of his excitement in reading Kant: "I began the other day Kant's 'Kritik,' which is written crabbedly enough, but which strikes me so far as almost the sturdiest and honestest piece of work I ever saw" (this was one of the few times he would ever praise Kant's work in writing). He also discovered the writings of a French neo-Kantian, as he proceeds to tell his father, "one Charles Renouvier, of whom I never heard before but who, for vigor of style and compression . . . is unequalled by anyone. He takes his stand on Kant." Although unsuccessful at curing his mysterious back pains, James returned to Harvard, passed his medical exams, and received the M.D. in June of 1869, though with no intention of practicing medicine.[1] Indeed, he did not seem to have a clue as to what to do with the remainder of his life.

In 1869, shortly after receiving his medical degree, James's symptoms became increasingly severe. Now his scientific training was threatening his capacity to believe in freedom of the will and the legitimacy of struggling for moral ideals; he was lurching towards a hopeless **determinism**, experiencing a brooding, self-absorbed depression. A thinly veiled case history in his *Varieties of Religious Experience* vividly recalls his pathetic sight of an epileptic patient in an asylum he visited as a medical student, a young man, "entirely idiotic, who used to sit all day . . . with his knees drawn up against his chin." James, the young M.D., could not dispel the awful sense that, if determinism prevailed, there was nothing he could possibly do to prevent himself from assuming a similar vegetative state: "*That shape am I*, I felt, **potentially**. Nothing that I possess can defend me against that fate, if the hour for it should strike for me as it struck for him." He reports that he found himself reduced to "a mass of quivering fear" at this terrible thought, after which "the universe was changed for me altogether. I awoke morning after morning with a horrible dread at the pit of my stomach, and with a sense of the insecurity of life that I never knew before."[2] He became a virtual invalid in his parents' Cambridge home.

By February 1870, James faced a moral decision of grave personal significance; he must either renounce the life of moral activity as a groundless fantasy or find a way to commit himself to it intensely and intently. In an entry in his diary, dated April 30, 1870, James explains that studying the **voluntarism** of Renouvier provided him with the psychic ammunition needed to resolve the issue:

> I think that yesterday was a crisis in my life. I finished the first part of Renouvier's second "Essais" and see no reason why his definition of Free Will—"the sustaining of a thought *because I choose to* when I might have other thoughts"—need be the definition of an illusion. At any rate, I will assume for the present—until next year—that it is no illusion. My first act of free will shall be to believe in free will.

There were times in his depressed state when "suicide seemed the most manly form to put my daring into." But from then on, James began gradually recovering and was increasingly capable of affirming a life of "doing and suffering and creating."[3] Nevertheless, throughout his adult life life James experienced various physical symptoms—eye strain, back pains, digestive problems, and periods of exhaustion—which appeared to be of a psychosomatic nature, as well as periods of moodiness and depression.

In August 1872, James's former chemistry professor, Charles William Eliot, now President of Harvard, offered him a position as Instructor of Physiology, and he was well enough to accept, beginning a career of more than a third of a century on the Harvard faculty. In 1873, he became Instructor of Anatomy and Physiology. But ill health forced him to travel to Italy, where he recuperated from 1873 to 1874. The following year, he taught his first psychology course at Harvard, using the physiological approach he had learned from the Germans. The next year, he set up the first psychology laboratory in America and was promoted to Assistant Professor of Physiology. In 1877, his course on physiological psychology was sponsored by the Philosophy Department. About that time, his father returned home after a meeting of the Radical Club to announce that he had met there William's future wife, a schoolteacher named Alice Howe Gibbens (the daughter of a medical doctor). Though William was not eager to meet her, the thirty-four-year-old man and the twenty-seven-year-old woman were eventually married in Boston on July 10, 1878, and seem to have had a stable marriage. She was intelligent, sensitive, witty, and understanding of and sympathetic to his intellectual obsessions and emotional moodiness. They lived comfortably but modestly in Cambridge (later adding a summer house in Chocorua, New Hampshire). Like his parents, they had five children, naming the first two (born in 1880 and 1882) Henry and William; Herman (1884), Margaret Mary (1887), and Alexander Robertson (1890) followed.

In 1878, James also agreed to write a psychology textbook. He was asked to produce a complete manuscript in a year, protested, and was given two years to complete it, not anticipating that it would take twelve years. But even when he contracted to write the book, he was getting restless to move from psychology to philosophy. Throughout much of the 1870s, he was an active member of a "**Metaphysical** Club," in which he discussed philosophy with friends and fellow intellectuals, including Oliver Wendell Holmes and Charles Sanders Peirce, the founder of American pragmatism. In 1879, James began teaching philosophy at Harvard, becoming Assistant Professor of Philosophy the following year. The preceding year, he had published "Remarks on Spencer's Definition of **Mind** as Correspondence" in the *Journal of Speculative Philosophy* and "Quelques Considérations sur la Méthode Subjective" (in his own fluent French) in Renouvier's *Critique Philosophique*. In July of 1879, part of his important essay on "The Sentiment of Rationality," which he then called the "only decent thing I have ever written," was published in *Mind*, the latter part being an address he had delivered to the Harvard Philosophical Club in 1880. He became increasingly impatient with psychology, referring to it as "a nasty little subject" and becoming irritated when he was identified as a "psychologist."[4] He was promoted to Professor of Philosophy in 1885 (and, in 1889, to Professor of Psychology).

In 1890, James's masterful *Principles of Psychology* was finally published in two volumes in Henry Holt's "American Science Series." James wrote to Holt complaining about its excessive length (about 1400 pages):

> No one could be more disgusted than I at the sight of the book. *No* subject is worth being treated of in 1000 pages! Had I ten years more, I could rewrite it in 500; but as it stands it is this or nothing—a loathsome, distended, tumefied, bloated, dropsical mass.

Almost a month later, he wrote his brother Henry, concerning his "tedious book," as follows:

> As "Psychologies" go, it is a good one, but psychology is in such an ante-scientific condition that the whole present generation of them is predestined to become unreadable old **medieval** lumber, as soon as the first genuine tracks of insight are made. The sooner, the better, for me!

The book was quite successful, but its most obvious liability was its massive size. So, the next summer, James prepared an abridged version, published in 1892 as *Psychology: Briefer Course*. Between them, the two books became standard psychology texts, the larger one being called the "James," the shorter one, "Jimmy." After 1892, James diverted his attention from psychology, except for a residual interest in "the borderland between normal and pathological mental states" and the psychology of "religious experience." In 1892–93, James took a sabbatical in Europe with his family. About a month before they sailed, he wrote, "Both Alice and I need a 'year off.'"[5] They went to Germany, Switzerland, Florence, and London; and the break from his university activities allowed James to be replaced as director of Harvard's psychology laboratory.

After completing his sabbatical, James returned to teaching philosophy and writing lectures with renewed vigor. In 1896, he offered his first course on Kant's philosophy. A valuable collection of his lectures was published in 1897, entitled *The Will to Believe and Other Essays in Popular Philosophy*, dedicated to his friend Charles Sanders Peirce. James

taught courses at Radcliffe College and in Harvard's summer school to supplement his regular university salary. He visited the University of California at Berkeley in 1898, where he presented a lecture, "Philosophical Conceptions and Practical Results," which helped launch pragmatism as a native American school of philosophy. In 1899, his *Talks to Teachers on Psychology: and to Students on Some of Life's Ideals* developed "a definite view of the world and of our moral relations to the same."[6] He was partly driven to work so hard by a concern about money, his Harvard salary being quite modest and his books not yet earning much in royalties.

He found himself overwhelmed with faculty responsibilities that detracted from his research and writing time. As he wrote to Renouvier,

> Our University moreover inflicts a monstrous amount of routine business on one, faculty meetings and committees of every sort, so that during term-time one can do no continuous reading at all—reading of books, I mean. When vacation comes, my brain is so tired that I can read nothing serious for a month.

In a letter to another friend, James complained,

> Last year was a year of hard work, and before the end of the term came, I was in a state of bad neurasthenic fatigue, but I got through it outwardly all right.

This led to a physical breakdown in 1899, for which James traveled to Nauheim, Germany, for recuperative treatment. He and his wife also visited England, southern France, Switzerland, and Rome; he took medicinal baths and consulted with specialists. He was also busy with studies on religious experience, in preparation for his upcoming Gifford Lectures at the University of Edinburgh in 1901–2. But he was homesick. In a letter he wrote from England he expressed appreciation for his surroundings but wrote, "Still, one loves America above all things, for her youth, her greenness, her plasticity, innocence, good intentions, friends, everything." After arriving in Edinburgh, he wrote, "Edinburgh is surely the noblest city ever built by man." Yet later that month, he wrote to a correspondent, "Beautiful as the spring is here, the words you so often let drop about American weather make me homesick." Nevertheless, the Gifford Lectures did generate a temporary renewal of energy for James. The lectures were published in June of 1902, after he returned to America, as *Varieties of Religious Experience*. They sold well and eased

James's concerns about having sufficient money to support his family. Yet he was less than satisfied with their contents. His goal had been to blend the findings of religious psychology with insights of metaphysical speculation, whereas the actual balance tilted heavily in favor of the former. He expressed his pique to F. C. S. Schiller, a friend and fellow pragmatist at Oxford, exaggerating, "The Gifford lectures are all facts and no philosophy." (In that same letter he urges Schiller to "drop the thought" of his being awarded an honorary degree by Oxford.)[7]

After he returned to Harvard from Scotland, he attempted to restrict his teaching in order to devote his time and energy to developing his own philosophy. He gave lectures, away from the Harvard campus, in which he tried out his ideas on various audiences. Having gotten the Gifford Lectures published, he writes, "I decided that everything was cleared and that my duty was immediately to begin writing my metaphysical system."[8] In fact, most of his purely philosophical work was written in these last eight years of his life. In the spring of 1905, he traveled to Greece, longing to visit Athens; on his return, he delivered his lecture "The Notion of Consciousness" (in French) at the Fifth International Congress of Psychology in Rome. When he returned home in early June, a letter was awaiting him, informing him that he had been elected to the newly established and prestigious American Academy of Arts and Letters, to which his younger brother Henry had already been elected. There seems to have been a loving rivalry between the brothers, each of whom had a prodigious mastery of words and ideas; indeed, it has been said (by the novelist Rebecca West) that Henry wrote fiction as thought-provoking as if it were philosophy, and William wrote philosophy with such literary flair as if it were fiction. At any rate, James declined membership in the Academy, perhaps partly resenting his brother's beating him to the honor and partly because of his own reluctance to accept awards from elitist groups that do not seem to perform any useful practical service.

In 1906, James obtained a leave of absence from Harvard to accept a visiting professorship at Stanford for the spring term. But in April, his California lecture series was interrupted by the great San Francisco earthquake. He went to San Francisco on the day of the disaster and reported his observations in a paper, "On Some Mental Effects of the Earthquake."[9] That November, he delivered his lectures comprising *Pragmatism* at the Lowell Institute in Boston and then, two months later, at Columbia University; they were published in the spring of 1907. James was worried about running out of time before he could finish his philosophical system. As he wrote to his brother Henry in late 1906, "I live in apprehension lest the Avenger should cut me off before I get my message out. . . . It is an esthetic tragedy to have a bridge begun, and stopped in the middle of an arch." In February 1907, he resigned all his official duties at Harvard to dedicate his remaining energy to the completion of his philosophical system. (In a touching last class meeting, his undergraduates gave him a silver cup; his graduate students presented him with an inkwell.) Hoping to achieve prolific productivity, he wrote, "I expect to shed truths in dazzling profusion on the world for many years." Apparently, James did not consider himself a particularly good teacher; towards the end of his life, at least, he grew to dislike teaching and regularly considered resigning (in January of 1905, President Eliot pleaded with him not to do so). In another letter, written the following month, he wrote that a professor has two "functions: (1) to be learned and distribute bibliographical information; (2) to communicate truth." He saw himself as inadequate in balancing those two tasks: "Hitherto I have always felt like a humbug as a professor, for I am weak in the first requirement. Now I can live for the second with a free conscience." A couple of months after his resignation, he wrote his son Bill, "I have got my 'Pragmatism' proofs all corrected. The most important thing I've written yet, and bound, I am sure, to stir up a lot of attention. But I'm dog-tired." A few days later, he wrote his brother Henry,

> I have just finished the proofs of a little book called "Pragmatism" which even you may enjoy reading. . . . I should n't be surprised if ten years hence it should be treated as "epoch-making," for of the definitive triumph of that general way of thinking I can entertain no doubt whatever—I believe it to be something quite like the protestant reformation.

In that same letter he wrote,

> You can't tell how happy I am at having thrown off the nightmare of my "professorship." As a "professor" I always felt myself a sham, with its chief duties of being a walking encyclopedia of erudition. . . . I can now live for truth pure and simple, instead of for truth

accommodated to the most unheard-of requirements set by others.[10]

James, now sixty-five years old, suffered from angina pains and chronic shortness of breath. He was invited to deliver the Hibbert Lectures at Manchester College, Oxford, and reluctantly agreed to do so. In these lectures of 1908 (published in 1909 as *A Pluralistic Universe*) he deliberately attacked the Hegelian absolute idealism that was rampant in England at that time. As he wrote his brother Henry from the boat sailing over, "I have been sleeping like a top, and feel in good fighting trim again, eager for the scalp of the **Absolute**. My lectures will put his wretched clerical defenders fairly on the defensive." At the same time, since the publication of his *Pragmatism*, James himself was under attack. In a letter written shortly after attending what he called "a really delightful meeting" of the American Philosophical Association (James had been elected as president of both that society and the American Psychological Association), James reported that "everyone cursed my doctrine and Schiller's about 'truth.'" He admitted that his breezy, reckless, racy use of language created a bias against his ideas in the minds of fellow intellectuals: "I find that my free and easy and personal way of writing, especially in 'Pragmatism,' had made me an object of loathing to many respectable academic minds."[11] In 1909, he published *The Meaning of Truth*, a collection of essays defending his views.

In early 1910, James was having more heart trouble and traveled to Europe to consult a specialist in Paris and take the medicinal baths at Nauheim, in Germany. But his fatigue got the better of him, and he sailed home a few months later. Walking, talking, and writing had all become excruciating for him. He was trying to finish his textbook *Some Problems of Philosophy* (which was edited by his son Henry after his death and published in 1911). After arriving in America in mid-August, he went directly to the family's summer house in Chocorua, New Hampshire. He died there on August 26, 1910. His body was carried back to Cambridge, a funeral service was conducted in the college chapel, and, after cremation, his ashes were placed near the graves of his parents. In 1911, his *Memories and Studies*, with a preface by his son Henry, was published; his *Essays in Radical Empiricism*, edited after his death by Ralph Barton Perry,

was published in 1912; in 1920, some of his *Collected Essays and Reviews*, with a preface by Perry, and *The Letters of William James*, in two volumes, edited by his son Henry, were published.

Reality

As a radical empiricist, James (like Hobbes and Hume) tries to anchor his reflections on the nature of reality in the findings of concrete perceptual experience, but with two differences. First, he is not as **atomistic** in his interpretation of those findings, maintaining (as we shall see) that we perceive connections as well as independent data of impressions. And, second, he places much more emphasis, as a pragmatist, on the extent to which our thoughts are guided by our practical needs and interests. In one of his first published reviews (1875), he adumbrates this lifelong theme when he writes that "our opinions about the nature of things belong to our moral life,"[12] using the word "moral" in a broad sense equivalent to what we would call "practical."

JAMES VS. HEGEL. During the last thirty years of James's life the dominant theory of reality in America and Great Britain was that of Hegelian idealism. So, it is appropriate that James uses that perspective as a foil for his own. In 1882, his article "On Some Hegelisms" was published, in which he attacks that **monistic** view of reality as an "absolute block whose parts have no loose play" (in the sense that the actions of every piece are utterly determined by the whole), as one in which all individuality gets absorbed in the Absolute, and as one in which discontinuities, radical otherness, and abrupt novelties are denied. Whereas Hobbes and Hume emphasize the atomic individuality of the real, as if interconnections are artificial, arbitrary, and imaginary, Hegel goes to the opposite extreme, merging everything into an "all-or-nothing" cosmic "principle of totality," whose "glue" is **dialectical** conflict and from which all escape (to freedom and individuality) becomes impossible. As James remarks, his "system resembles a mouse-trap, in which if you once pass the door you may be lost forever. Safety lies in not entering." James strives for a middle ground between the extremes, explaining that the "three great continua . . . of memory or personal consciousness, of time and of space" present the perceptual data of reality as interconnected without being entirely inextricable. "The things we meet are many, and yet are one; each is itself, and yet all belong together; continuity reigns, yet individuality is not lost." James ends the essay by offering eleven reasons for his repudiation of the Hegelian theory of reality.[13]

AN EMPIRICAL, PRAGMATIC STANCE. In a chapter of his *Principles of Psychology* entitled "The Perception of Reality," James writes of seven different realms of the real for us human subjects.

1. "The world of sense, or of physical 'things' as we instinctively apprehend them," tends to be the touchstone of what most of us count as "real" for us.

2. "The world of science, or of physical things as the learned conceive them," in terms of physical forces and scientific laws, is another layer of reality for the educated.

3. "The world of ideal relations, or abstract truths believed or believable by all," involves the truths of logic, mathematics, **ethics**, **aesthetics**, and metaphysics.

4. "The world of 'idols of the tribe,' illusions or prejudices common to the race" of all humans, includes, for example, the appearances that the heavens move around the Earth, that the Sun literally "rises" in the east and "sets" in the west, and that our planet is flat.

5. "The various supernatural worlds, the Christian heaven and hell, the world of the Hindu mythology," and the worlds of fiction are real to certain cultures.

6. "The various worlds of individual opinion" are as numerous as the human beings who are thinking.

7. "The worlds of sheer madness and vagary" are real for those who have lost touch with the reality common to most of us.

We inhabit many of these realms through most of our conscious lives and normally are quite capable of discriminating among them. "Each world *whilst it is attended to* is real after its own fashion; only the reality lapses with attention." James goes on to argue that an object must do more than appear in conscious experience to be considered real—"it must appear both *interesting* and *important*" to the person experiencing it. In this sense, what we believe to be real is viewed as in "*relation to our emotional and active life.*" As

James comments, "Hume's account of the matter was then **essentially** correct, when he said that belief in anything was simply the having the idea of it in a lively and active manner."[14]

On the one hand, reality is somehow objectively given; but, on the other, it is subjectively experienced. "*The fons et origo of all reality, whether from the absolute or the practical point of view, is thus subjective, is ourselves.*" It seems that for James, as for Hume and Kant, we can have no conception of reality as it is in itself, independent of us and our experience of it. But this also means that our own reality is the absolute foundation for us, "*the ultimate of ultimates for our belief.*" James compares it to "the **cogito**" of Descartes, in that it is the basis on which our entire systems of beliefs get built.

> *Whatever things have intimate and continuous connection with my life are things of whose reality I cannot doubt.* Whatever things fail to establish this connection are things which are practically no better for me than if they existed not at all.

What we experience as real commands our attention, in a lively manner, tends to stimulate our wills to act, and generally involves our emotional interests.

> As a whole, sensations are more lively and are judged more real than conceptions; things met with every hour more real than things seen once; attributes perceived when awake, more real than attributes perceived in a dream.

The regular objects of waking sensation normally remain our touchstone:

> *Sensible objects are thus either our realities or the tests of our realities. Conceived objects must show sensible effects or be disbelieved.*

There is a dovetailing of James's empiricism and his pragmatism. Different theories of reality—such as those of monism and pluralism—might vie for our allegiance as explanations of experience.

> Which theory is then to be believed? *That theory will be most generally believed which, besides offering us objects able to account satisfactorily for our sensible experience, also offers those which are most interesting, those which appeal most urgently to our aesthetic, emotional, and active needs.*[15]

This last quote illustrates James's emphasis on connections with the practical interests of "our moral life."

MONISM, PLURALISM, AND MELIORISM. In his "Philosophical Conceptions and Practical Results," which helped launch the pragmatic movement in 1898, James focuses on this oldest of metaphysical issues (which dates back to Thales, the first of pre-Socratic Greek philosophers), the problem of the One and the Many. Is reality ultimately one, as Hegel and the monists maintain, or is it ultimately many, as Hume and the atomists contend? Now James wants to explore the practical significance of viewing the world as one. It ought to follow "that we can pass from one part of it to another without letting go of the thing." James observes that in a physical sense this is true of the sensible universe of time and space, but not where mental reality enters the picture, "for there is no obvious transition from one mind to another, or from minds to physical things." A second pragmatic "meaning of oneness is susceptibility of collection." But we cannot "collect" the universe, as we can a pack of playing cards, either physically or mentally. A third meaning of oneness is "generic sameness," in which sense our world is too varied to be one. "Its elements have, however, an affinity or commensurability with each other, are not wholly irrelevant, but can be compared, and fit together after certain fashions."[16] James is moving in the direction of a relational pluralism that steers a middle path between Humean atomism and Hegelian monism.

At the beginning of *Pragmatism* James makes it clear that philosophy is essentially our way of defining a conception of reality that constitutes a livable world-view:

> For the philosophy which is so important in each of us is not a technical matter; it is our more or less dumb sense of what life honestly and deeply means. It is only partly got from books; it is our individual way of just seeing and feeling the total push and pressure of the cosmos.

Consider, for example, the metaphysical problem of **substance**. We experience, think of, and talk about the world in terms of things, like pieces of chalk and wood, known only through their qualities and relations. "A group of attributes is what each substance here is known-as, they form its sole cash-value for our actual experience. The substance is in every case revealed through *them*." But therefore all **knowledge**-claims about substances in themselves—whether

material or spiritual—become subject to the criticisms of thinkers like Hume. Again consider the alleged oneness of reality.

1. The "world is at least *one subject of discourse*" for us, as is indicated by words like "world," "reality," and "universe."

2. Space and time do constitute, for us, "vehicles of continuity by which the world's parts hang together."

3. We experience regular lines of influence among the world's parts, our input contributing to their interconnectedness.

4. **Phenomena** may be regarded as subject to a "*causal unity*," as, perhaps, that of divine providence.

5. The "most important sort of union that obtains among things, pragmatically speaking, is their *generic unity*. Things exist in kinds" and are therefore classifiable.

6. Reality may be regarded as having a "*unity of purpose*," with more local goals subordinate to more global ones.

7. "*Aesthetic union* among things also obtains" among things so that they appear to "tell a story" to us.

8. In some systems of thought, such as that of Hegelian idealism, all reality is identified with "*one Knower*," for whom it constitutes "an *all enveloping noetic unity*."

So, in all these respects, reality may be viewed as one, "by as many definite **conjunctions** as appear. But then also *not* One by just as many definite **disjunctions** as we find." It is all relative to our point of view, from which reality may be conceived as either "a universe" or "a multiverse," but with no ultimate, absolute perspective available to us. The world is both one and many for human experience, although it may be "growing more and more unified by those systems of connexion at least which human energy keeps framing as time goes on." The problem with monism is that it can tolerate no loose ends or ragged edges in reality, whereas pluralism "will allow you any amount, however great, of real union" on the sole condition that "you grant *some* separation among things, some tremor of independence, some free play of parts on one another, some real novelty or chance, however minute." James clearly adopts the

---

Noetic (from the Greek *noetikos*, meaning intellectual).   Cognitive, having to do with the rational activity of intellect

perspective of pluralism and repudiates the all-or-nothing view of monism.[17]

The last two lectures of *Pragmatism* continue the discussion. In "Pragmatism and Humanism," James analyzes our "reality" in three dimensions. The "*first* part of reality from this point of view is the flux of our sensations," which we receive as data of experience. "The *second* part of reality, as something that our beliefs must also obediently take account of is the *relations* that obtain between our sensations or between their copies in our minds." It is this second dimension that atomists tend to minimize. "The *third* part of reality" consists of "the *previous truths* of which every new inquiry takes account"; they may be modified or even abandoned, but we tend to try to conserve them. Yet we should realize that all three of these dimensions of reality are person-relative. "Superficially," James acknowledges, "this sounds like Kant's view" of mental structures; "but between categories fulminated before nature began, and categories gradually forming themselves in nature's presence, the whole chasm between **rationalism** and empiricism yawns," dividing Kant from James. Like the rationalists, Kant conceives of reality as "*ready-made and complete from all eternity, while for pragmatism it is still in the making*" and dependent on us. Rationalism views reality as one genuine complete edition, with all alternative editions being deviations; pragmatism sees it as "unfinished, growing in all sorts of places, especially in the places where thinking beings are at work." From the rationalist point of view, the pragmatic conception of reality seems unstable and disreputable. "Such a world would not be *respectable* philosophically. It is a trunk without a tag, a dog without a collar in the eyes" of philosophical rationalism.[18]

In "Pragmatism and Religion" James connects monistic rationalism with the view that reality rests in more powerful hands than our own, so that we need not exert ourselves on its behalf: "Look back, *lie back*, on your true principle of being! This is the famous way of **quietism**, of indifferentism. Its enemies compare it to a spiritual opium." By contrast, pluralistic pragmatism believes in possibilities whose realization may depend on our exertion of effort. This distinction may be expressed in the religious framework of salvation as either necessary or possible, from the perspectives of monistic rationalism and pluralistic pragmatism.

> One sees at this point that the great religious difference lies between the men who insist that the world *must and shall be*, and those who are contented that the world *may be*, saved.

James relates this view to his notion of **meliorism**, the doctrine of betterment, as a middle ground between the equally deterministic doctrines of "pessimism," which considers "the salvation of the world impossible" no matter what we do, and "optimism," which "thinks the world's salvation inevitable" no matter what we do. "Meliorism treats salvation as neither necessary nor impossible. It treats it as a possibility," to whose realization we can contribute, if we so choose. In this sense, James believes, we can help "*create* the world's salvation" by our initiative and effort. He asks us to imagine God challenging us to become cocreators, with no prior guarantee of success:

> Suppose that the world's author put the case to you before creation, saying: "I am going to make a world not **certain** to be saved, a world the perfection of which shall be conditional merely, the condition being that each several agent does its own 'level best.' I offer you the chance of taking part in such a world. Its safety, you see, is unwarranted. It is a real adventure, with real danger, yet it may win through."

James asks us to take the challenge personally: "Will you trust yourself and trust the other agents enough to face the risk?" This is a rather dramatic way of posing meliorism's view of our involvement in reality, and James makes it clear that his own "healthy-minded buoyancy" leads him to accept the challenge. Yet he acknowledges that "there are morbid minds" that cannot stand the insecurity. "Pluralistic moralism simply makes their teeth chatter, it refrigerates the very heart within their breast." And, of course, they must make their own faith-commitment, though they should not pretend that **proof** is possible here.

> In the end it is our faith and not our logic that decides such questions, and I deny the right of any pretended logic to veto my own faith. I find myself willing to take the universe to be really dangerous and adventurous, without therefore backing out and crying "no play."

Quietism.   In twentieth-century thought (e.g., both James and Sartre), a negative term for a passive lack of commitment

Meliorism (from the Latin *melior*, meaning better).   In James, the view that the world, however good or evil it may be, can become better if we freely act to help improve it

The melioristic view requires this sort of concession, and James exclaims, "I am willing that there should be real losses and real losers, and no total preservation of all that is." A commitment to such a world necessarily involves an "element of 'seriousness,'" since our efforts could prove futile, as well as a trust in the cooperation of others. Religiously, it might also involve a trust in God. James says,

> I firmly disbelieve, myself, that our human experience is the highest form of experience extant in the universe. I believe rather that we stand in much the same relation to the whole of the universe as our canine and feline pets do to the whole of human life. They inhabit our drawing-rooms and libraries. They take part in scenes of whose significance they have no inkling.

So, we may participate in and can contribute to processes we cannot comprehend. This is the "melioristic type of **theism**" that James thinks intermediate between a "crude **naturalism**" with no room for "higher powers" and a "**transcendental** absolutism" that absorbs everything into such higher powers.[19]

In *Some Problems of Philosophy* James defines metaphysics as "the science of the most **universal** principles of reality (whether experienced by us or not), in their connection with one another and with our powers of knowledge." **Contrary** to the claim that all persons are either Platonists or Aristotelians, James prefers to draw the line between rationalists, who try to deduce facts from abstract principles, and empiricists, who inductively generate principles from concrete facts. On this view, Plato and Aristotle, Augustine and Aquinas, Descartes and Hegel are all rationalists, while Hobbes, Hume, and Mill are empiricists. James admits, "Kant may fairly be called mixed"; and he warns that he himself "is weakly endowed on the rationalist side" and has "a strong leaning towards empiricism."[20]

In his chapter "The One and the Many," James redefines the pivotal issue between monism and pluralism. "Pluralism stands for the distributive, monism for the collective form of being." The former must allow the real to be distributed in such a way that there is some disconnection, no matter how little; the latter cannot allow any disconnection whatsoever. Although (as we have seen) acknowledging that "the world is 'one' in some respects," he sides with pluralism as "more 'scientific,'" as more conducive to "the moral and dramatic expressiveness of life," and as

having the logical advantage of not being "obliged to stand for any particular amount of plurality" but prevailing so long as "the smallest morsel of disconnectedness" can be discovered. "'Ever not quite' is all it says to monism." James later reviews the history of causal analysis, beginning with Aristotle's four causal principles, including Hume's critique of causal knowledge and Kant's treatment of causality as an *a priori* category of the understanding. But his reservation about this entire "conceptual view" of causation has to do with its threatened "**negation** of real novelty." To the extent that an event or reality is causally determined, spontaneity and free possibility get excluded. James wants a place left for "what John Mill calls unconditional causes" of desire and free will.[21] As a pluralist, meliorist, and pragmatist, James calls for free will as an exception to the necessary laws of extrinsic determination and as the ground of novelty in the realms of reality.

Bodies

Like Hume and Kant, James does not believe that we can know things as they are in themselves, including the physical realities we call bodies and the mental realities we call minds.

> In their purity the substance "consciousness" and the substance "matter" are impossible to analyze out,—we cannot penetrate far enough into the insides of things to gain an intuition of them.

Of course, bodies are given as phenomenal objects of perceptual experience, and a person's own body represents "an omnipresent material object" in his experience.[22] But, like Mill, James seems to analyze material reality in terms of the more or less permanent possibility of sense experience. As he writes in *Some Problems of Philosophy*,

> Certain *grouped sensations*, in short, are all that corporeal substances are *known-as*, therefore the only meaning which the word "matter" can claim is that it denotes such sensations and their groupings.[23]

It is the behavior of other human bodies that leads us to attribute minds to other persons. In his *Essays in Radical Empiricism* James writes,

> Why do I postulate your mind? Because I see your body acting in a certain way. Its gestures, facial movements, words, and conduct generally, are "expressive," so I deem it actuated as my own is, by an inner life like mine.

This **argument from analogy** for other minds is again similar to one used by Mill. James goes on to ask, "But what is 'your body' here but a percept in *my* field? It is only as animating *that* object, *my* object, that I have any occasion to think of you at all."[24] In other words, my very awareness of other persons is utterly dependent on my perceptual experience of their bodily behavior.

James is far less interested in the nature of bodies than he is in the question of whether physical reality could be the ultimate source of everything—that is, whether **materialistic** naturalism or religious theism is a more satisfactory theory. He raises this question in his essay "Philosophical Conceptions and Practical Results." He denies that objective scientific evidence can decide the issue either way, if that issue is framed as one about the past origin of our world. "Matter and God in that event mean exactly the same thing—the power, namely, neither more nor less, that can make just this mixed, imperfect, yet completed world." If it is merely a question of how to account for what has already come to be, it would seem to lack sufficient pragmatic significance to render it worth pursuing.

> As far as the past facts go, indeed there is no difference. These facts are in, are bagged, are captured; and the good that's in them is gained, be the atoms or be the God their cause.

But if we consider the issue from the perspective of possible future significance for our lives, it becomes a different story.

> Theism and materialism, so indifferent when taken retrospectively, point when we take them prospectively to wholly different practical consequences, to opposite outlooks of experience.

If materialism is correct, we have nothing to which we can ultimately look forward but a "dead universe" in which all our ideals and efforts have evaporated into nothingness.

> Dead and gone are they, gone utterly from the very sphere and room of being. Without an echo; without a memory; without an influence on aught that may come after, to make it care for similar ideals. This utter final wreck and tragedy is of the essence of scientific materialism.

By contrast, theism offers a causal explanation of our world which carries with it the hope that values will be ultimately realized.

> A world with a God in it to say the last word, may indeed burn up or freeze, but we then think of Him as still mindful of the old ideals and sure to bring them elsewhere to

fruition; so that, where He is, tragedy is only provisional and partial, and shipwreck and dissolution not the absolutely final things.[25]

So, for pragmatic reasons, associated with the values of "our moral life," James opts for theism over materialism, rejecting bodies as the ultimate source of our world. Yet, as we have seen, physical reality is important as the primary object of perceptual experience and the basis for our belief in other persons.

Personality

CONSCIOUSNESS.   As early as 1878, three years after teaching his first psychology course, James was writing about consciousness. He holds, "'Mind,' as we actually find it, contains all sorts of laws—those of logic, of fancy, of wit, of taste, decorum, beauty, morals, and so forth, as well as of perception of fact." This may sound like Kant's structures of the mind; however, for James these "laws" are not **innate** and *a priori* but have "grown up in the course of evolution." He also, like Kant, emphasizes the active role played by the mind in the process of **cognition**. In "A Plea for Psychology as a 'Natural Science,'" published a couple of years after his *Principles of Psychology*, James says the discipline has not yet been established, that it is in a condition comparable to that of physics prior to Galileo. He expresses his wish, "by treating Psychology *like* a natural science, to help her become one." But this will require a break from past approaches. Remembering that "psychology" means the study of the **soul** and that theoretical speculation about abstract spirit has proved inconclusive in the past, James proposes to abandon all talk of "the soul, the transcendental ego," and so forth.[26]

Let us turn to the *Principles* themselves, remembering that much of what is written there also appears in James's abbreviated *Psychology: Briefer Course* (references to both will often be provided for the reader's convenience). He initially defines Psychology as "the Science of the Mental Life, both of its phenomena and their conditions. The phenomena are such things as we call feelings, desires, cognitions, reasonings, decisions, and the like"—in other words, all states of consciousness. He observes that the "'associationist' schools" of Hume and Mill have "constructed a *psychology without a soul*," using the empirical method. Yet there must be some mental agent, whether it be called soul, mind, consciousness, or brain. Next, James proposes as a "general law that *no mental modification ever occurs which is not accompanied or followed by a bodily change*," since all our mental phenomena occur in a physical context. Third, he would have us recognize that consciousness is naturally **teleological** in its activities:

> The pursuance of future ends and the choice of means for their attainment are thus the mark and criterion of the presence of mentality in a phenomenon. We all use this test to discriminate between an intelligent and a mechanical performance.

From the perspective of science, it seems "that *the cortex is the sole organ of consciousness in man*," although this assumption should be regarded as a **postulate** rather than as a datum. The brain responds to stimuli which can, individually or collectively, "*excite a nerve-centre to effective discharge*"[27] in neural activity, experienced as states of consciousness.

To a great extent persons behave according to habit, "*due to the plasticity of the organic materials of which their bodies are composed*." Our acting on habit involves certain practical effects. First, it simplifies movements needed to achieve certain results and economizes energy expended; and, second, it decreases the amount of conscious attention needed to perform the actions. "Habit is thus the enormous flywheel of society, its most precious conservative agent." It is to our advantage to cultivate "*as many useful actions as we can*" as habits. Indeed, James exclaims about how "miserable" human life would be to the extent it was devoid of habit and in need of deciding about every petty activity.[28]

In his famous discussion of "the stream" of consciousness, he begins, rather as Descartes did (without the Cartesian metaphysical knowledge-claims), with the fundamental fact that "*thinking of some sort goes on*." In analyzing consciousness he articulates five basic characteristics:

1. "Every thought tends to be part of a personal consciousness" or mind or self, to be "*owned*" rather than abstract and freely floating.
2. "Within each personal consciousness thought is always changing" and never static or permanent.
3. "Within each personal consciousness thought is sensibly continuous" rather than chopped up into discrete atomic bits, as Hume thought. Here is where James's metaphor of "the stream of thought" is apt, emphasizing its continuity. (He also compares it to bamboo, whose joints

constitute a genuine part of, rather than a real break in, the wood.) We can think of the process of thinking as like the "alternation of flights and perchings" in the life of a bird, the stream of thought comprising "*substantive parts*" focused upon ("*the resting-places*") and "*transitive parts*" traversed to get from one focus to another ("*the places of flight*"). Every focal part of consciousness is also enveloped by a "*psychic overtone, suffusion, or fringe*" providing a context that can itself enter into the spotlight of attention for thought.

4. "It always appears to deal with objects independent of itself," so that two different minds can attend to a common object. James rejects the Kantian belief that all consciousness also distinguishes between itself and its objects as "a perfectly wanton assumption," holding that such discrimination can occur but does not always do so in thought.
5. "It is interested in some parts of these objects to the exclusion of others, and welcomes or rejects—*chooses* from among them, in a word—all the while."

Our capacity to ignore things not perceived as relevant to our interests is important. Like Hume he compares the human mind to "a theatre," but he emphasizes the deliberate selection of certain scenarios rather than other possible ones. And human nature is such that there is significant agreement (as well as some diversity) in those parts of experience we choose to notice and those we ignore.[29]

THE SELF. James's analysis of the self on which we can focus our consciousness is also important. First, he distinguishes between the self known as object, the "Empirical Self" or *me* and our idea of the self as subjective knower, the "pure Ego" or "I." What is the "Empirical Self," according to James? "*In its widest possible sense*," he writes, "*a man's Self is the sum total of all that he CAN call his*, not only his body and his psychic powers, but his clothes and his house, his wife and children, his ancestors and friends, his reputation and works, his lands and horses, and yacht and bank-account." Its constituents include

(a) The material Self;
(b) The social Self;
(c) The spiritual Self.

The core of a person's "material Self" is his body, certain parts of which (for example, the central nervous system) seem more intimately his than others (such as fingernails). It also includes his clothing, his immediate family, and his home. A person's "social Self" is his recognition by other members of society (what Hegel, in his section on the master-servant dialectic, describes us as fighting to achieve). A person has as many social selves as he has distinct reputations with others who recognize him socially. James observes that the "most peculiar social self" a person tends to have arises from the relationship of romantic love. "A man's *fame*, good or bad, and his *honor* or dishonor, are names for one of his social selves." A person's "spiritual Self" is his "inner or subjective being, his psychic faculties or dispositions," what we would call his personality. James suggests that we can arrange the various constituents of the "Empirical Self," as just analyzed, "in an *hierarchical scale, with the bodily Self at the bottom, the spiritual Self at top, and the extracorporeal material selves and the various social selves between*." All the elements of the "Empirical Self" have a tendency to excite attention in the stream of consciousness. We may also speak of a person's "selfishness" as his sense of and concern for self, with its "most palpable" form being bodily:

> My own body and what ministers to its needs are thus the primitive object, instinctively determined, of my *egoistic* interests. Other objects may become interesting derivatively through association with any of these things, either as means or as habitual concomitants.[30]

(This last point might sound like Hobbes.)

James next discusses the "pure Ego." We have a sense of personal identity (which Hume struggled to account for) grounded in either the sameness of our perceptions or their continuity in the mind. We are speculatively tempted to try to develop a systematic theory of personal identity. "The 'Soul' of Metaphysics and the 'Transcendental Ego' of the Kantian Philosophy are," he says, "but attempts to satisfy this urgent demand." The "spiritualist theory" of medieval **scholasticism**, for example, speaks of the soul as an individual, immaterial, simple, free substance, which could be **immortal**; Plato, Aristotle, Augustine, Aquinas, and Descartes all held it in some form or other, whereas Hume and Kant undermined the confidence that we could know anything of the sort. "The Soul-theory," says James, is "a complete superfluity, so far as accounting for the actually verified facts of conscious experience goes." Nor does it warrant the

sort of personal immortality that would seem of vital significance to most people (as Aristotle apparently realized). James writes, "My final **conclusion**, then, about the substantial Soul is that it explains nothing and guarantees nothing." Second, the "associationist theory" is identified with Hume's famous **phenomenalistic** view of the self as a bundle of perceptions. James praises Hume for his introspective analysis but blames him for going on "to pour out the child with the bath" by reducing the Self to "nothing but Diversity, diversity abstract and absolute" as the spiritualistic substantialists reduce it to "nothing but Unity, unity abstract and absolute." Despite his **epistemology**, which should lead to a phenomenalistic repudiation of all metaphysics, in generating the bundle theory of the Self, says James, "Hume is at bottom as much of a metaphysician as Thomas Aquinas." And later associationists tended to follow suit. Indeed, Mill "seems to fall back upon something perilously near to the Soul" in his refusal to admit that "there might after all *be* no 'real tie'" associating our states of consciousness. From this perspective, James avers, Mill's views "may be regarded as the *definitive bankruptcy of the associationist description* of the consciousness of self." A third attempt to define the "pure Ego" is represented by the "transcendentalist theory" of Kant. But his transcendental Ego, or the "*I think*" that represents a "unity of **Apperception**," is a useless Subject devoid of "any positive attributes"— pure form with no experienceable content, a **noumenal** idea that is, in principle, humanly unknowable. However, in asserting reality of an unexperienced and unknowable agent, according to James, "Transcendentalism is only Substantialism grown shame-faced, and the Ego only a 'cheap and nasty' edition of the soul." In Hegel this vacuous transcendental psychology becomes "a raging fever," heating up an entire system of absolute idealism with no traces of "any definite psychology." James himself conceives of the "I" not as a thing but as "a *Thought*, at each moment different from that of the last moment, but *appropriative* of the latter, together with all that the latter called its own." This is as far as psychological science allows James to go. He can "postulate" a personal "*knower*" appropriating the thought; but the issue of defining the nature of that "*knower*" will inevitably "become a metaphysical problem"[31] **transcending** the bounds of science.

ATTENTION, DISCRIMINATION, ASSOCIATION, AND MEMORY. We have seen that an important characteristic of consciousness is its capacity for attention. We fortunately ignore millions of data every day because they do not seem sufficiently relevant to our personal interests. Our experience is inevitably a function of selective attention.

> Every one knows what attention is. It is the taking possession by the mind, in clear and vivid form, of one out of what seems several simultaneously possible objects or trains of thought.

It is difficult for the human mind to attend to more than a single object or train of thought at a time, unless they be very habitual or attention is quickly shuttling back and forth. James thinks that multiple attentions to tasks that are nonautomatic, as is illustrated "in the story of Julius Caesar dictating four letters whilst he writes a fifth," would require "a rapid oscillation of the mind from one to the next." We can distinguish between **voluntary** attention, derived from some interest(s) to be served by the effort, and passive attention, stimulated by sense-impressions or instincts. As a result of attention, the mind perceives, conceives, distinguishes, and remembers more sharply, while requiring less "reaction-time" to function. Selective attention allows us to distinguish and relate useful mental experience requiring a combination of discrimination and comparison. "The truth is that Experience is trained by *both* association and dissociation, and that psychology must be writ *both* in **synthetic** and in **analytic** terms." Hume's "simple impression," as loose and separate from other impressions, is relegated to the realm of "abstractions, never realized in experience." We experience "concreted objects" as clusters of impressions and only subsequently analyze them into parts. Without the capacity to discriminate, we would remain like the baby who, "assailed by eyes, ears, nose, skin, and entrails at once, feels it all as one great blooming, buzzing confusion." And we do associate ideas with one another to constitute **coherent** mental processes, as Hobbes, Hume, and Mill's father, James Mill, demonstrate. The mind also requires memory to function usefully; and what is remembered must be "*expressly referred to the past*, thought as *in the past*," and it "must be dated in *my* past." The greater the number of associations the mind establishes with others of its ideas, the more retentive of it memory tends to be. "Each of its

associates becomes a hook to which it hangs, a means to fish it up by when sunk beneath the surface."[32] So, attention, discrimination, association, and memory all interconnect in the workings of the mind.

SENSATION, PERCEPTION, AND IMAGINATION. As an empiricist, like Hobbes and Hume, James must rest his theory largely on sensation, perception, and imagination. A sensation is simpler than a perception. "Its function is that of mere *acquaintance* with a fact. Perception's function, on the other hand, is knowledge *about* a fact," relative to its associations with other facts. "But in both sensation and perception we perceive the fact as an *immediately present outward reality*, and this makes them differ from 'thought' and 'conception,' whose objects do not appear present in this immediate physical way." Once we have accumulated experiences that are mentally processed, we no longer have pure sensations, since the mind relates all its experiences, through discrimination and association. When adults speak of sensations, then, they mean "either certain *objects*, namely simple *qualities* or *attributes* like *hard, hot, pain*; or else those of our thoughts in which acquaintance with these objects is least combined with knowledge about the relations of them to other things." Imagination retrieves copies of past sensations and perceptions even after their external stimuli are no longer being experienced (something like Hobbes's view of decaying sense). "No mental copy, however, can arise in the mind, of any kind of sensation which has never been directly excited from without," so that imagination is utterly dependent on this source, according to James (as for Hobbes). Normally perception is a "*consciousness of particular material things present to sense*" (rather than imagined) and "*associated*" with further facts. Sometimes, we doubt how to interpret perception and can only form probability judgments concerning the things perceived, since these judgments depend on associations with things that usually arouse similar perceptions.[33]

BELIEF. Belief is a feeling of assurance that an idea or **proposition** is true or real, "the mental state or function of cognizing reality," as opposed to imagining or supposing it.

> In its inner nature, belief, or the sense of reality, is a sort of feeling more allied to the emotions than to anything else.

Disbelief, rather than being opposed to belief, is a negative belief; the true opposite of belief is doubt. James agrees with Mill that the feeling associated with belief is unique and not quite like (or explicable in terms of) any other feeling. Every proposition can be analyzed in terms of four constituent elements—

> the subject, the predicate, and their relation (of whatever sort it be)—these form the *object* of belief—and finally the psychic attitude in which our mind stands towards the proposition taken as a whole—and this is the belief itself.

We tend to believe our experiences to be real unless and until they conflict with other experiences or beliefs, which clash raises doubts. If I imagine Pegasus, the winged horse of ancient mythology, and believe him only to belong to the realm of fiction, there is no conflict. On the other hand, if I imagine "my old mare Maggie, having grown a pair of wings where she stands in her stall," this image will clash with the sensible reality of the spatio-temporal physical world and will be refuted by my taking a good look at Maggie in the barn. Logic distinguishes between **existential** and attributive judgments. It is true that my imaginary conception of Maggie attributes wings to her; but it is false that a winged horse actually exists in the sensible, spatio-temporal world.[34]

"The mere fact of appearing as an object at all is not enough to constitute reality." In order for an idea to be considered real (in any of the seven senses analyzed in a previous section), it "must appear both *interesting* and *important*" to the person thinking it. In this sense, what we count as real must have some "*relation to our emotional and active life,*" in that our beliefs are influenced by emotions and involve some tendency to act (we see the seeds of pragmatism here). People's belief in immortality (which we shall discuss later), for example, is conditioned by the desire for personal survival. Different theoretical systems of reality might vie for our allegiance. They should all be capable of accommodating the reality of the sensible world in some satisfactory way. But, assuming they meet this minimal requirement, which should we favor?

> That theory will be most generally believed which, besides offering us objects able to account satisfactorily for our sensible experience, also offers those which are most interesting, those which appeal most urgently to our aesthetic, emotional, and active needs.

So, here again, we see the needs and interests of "our moral life" vitally affecting our ideas. We demand that certain requirements be met in order that our experience should make sense to us. "Certain postulates are given in our nature; and whatever satisfies those postulates is treated as if real"[35] and believed.

INSTINCTS AND EMOTIONS.   James maintains that "*the most elementary single difference between the human mind and that of brutes*" consists of the **reasoning** capacity of abstract thought. However, because we are animals, we are also subject to instinctive behavior. "*Instinct is usually defined as the faculty of acting in such a way as to produce certain ends, without foresight of the ends, and without previous education in the performance.*" James thinks that at least some forms of sympathy, "that of mother with child, for example, are surely primitive" instincts. Sympathy is also an emotion. So, instincts and emotions overlap.

> Emotions, however, fall short of instincts, in that the emotional reaction usually terminates in the subject's own body, whilst the instinctive reaction is apt to go farther and enter into practical relations with the exciting object.

On the other hand, emotions tend to cover a larger range than instincts, sometimes being "excited by objects with which we have no practical dealings" at all, such as beautiful sunsets. We naturally tend to think of emotions as the effects of mental perception and as causing certain bodily expressions. "Common-sense says, we lose our fortune, are sorry and weep; we meet a bear, are frightened and run; we are insulted by a rival, are angry and strike." In each case, the emotion purportedly appears as the middle link. But James's theory "is that *the bodily changes follow directly the perception of the exciting fact, and that our feeling of the same changes as they occur IS the emotion.*" On this alternative model, the bodily change is the middle link between the mental perception and the emotion, so that "we feel sorry because we cry, angry because we strike, afraid because we tremble." On this view, emotions are the effects of changes in our bodily states, all of which can be felt, either "*acutely or obscurely*"; there is no more to an emotion than a consciousness of the feelings caused by changes in bodily states. "A purely disembodied human emotion is a nonentity," regardless of whether other beings, such as "pure spirits," might experience them. Yet James denies that this is a materialistic theory, as "the platonizers in psychology" will charge. He is only saying that emotions are physically caused, not denying that they can be of a spiritual nature. The theory does, however, underscore the interrelationship of "our mental life" and our bodily makeup.[36]

THE WILL.   We experience all sorts of desires; when a desire is accompanied by a sense that we shall not attain its object, "we simply *wish.*" By contrast, if we believe that the object of desire is attainable, "we *will* that the desired feeling, having, or doing shall be real"; and we can act to try to realize it. "The only ends which follow *immediately* upon our willing seem to be movements of our own bodies." By willing to do so, I can move my own arm; that physical motion, in turn, can cause the chair to move to a desired location. So, will or volition is a mental function that is secondary to such primitive ones as instincts and emotions; and it **presupposes** ideas stored in memory of possible movements that can bring about desired results. But what is the act of willing? "There is indeed the *fiat,* the element of consent, or resolve that the act shall ensue. This," says James, "to the reader's mind, as to my own, constitutes the essence of the voluntariness of the act." Our anticipated image of the effects of movement, combined with this "*fiat,*" precedes voluntary action. When we are undecided about what course of action to take, our minds deliberate among the various imaginary options before them; this deliberation tends to be accompanied by a "peculiar feeling of inward unrest" until a decision is made leading to a voluntary act of will.[37]

James sketches five types of decision of which the human mind is capable. "The first may be called *the reasonable type*" because it is determined by a preponderance of reasons or rational **arguments** to select one of the available options; it nevertheless feels "*free,* in that we are devoid of any feeling of coercion" in making the decision. The next two types of decision are determined by "some **accidental** circumstance" occurring outside or within our own minds. "In the *second type*" of decision we move "in a direction accidentally determined *from without*" as when we overhear a comment that influences the choice. "In the *third type* the determination seems equally accidental, but it comes from within" ourselves, as when we throw ourselves back into an habitual

pattern of behavior. "There is a *fourth form* of decision" occurring as a result of a sudden change of mood, as from easygoing to ambitious, which might be provoked by the onset of emotions such as "grief and fear," for example. "In the *fifth and final type* of decision," it is "we ourselves by our own wilful act" who have "inclined the beam" one way or the other; this **intrinsically** self-determined action is accompanied by a distinct "*feeling of effort,* absent from the former decisions." Few human decisions are of this fifth type,[38] which we shall later identify with the "will to believe."

When we intentionally "*ATTEND to a difficult object and hold it fast before the mind,*" our decisions regarding it seem most purely voluntary; what seems to count is the mental resolution involved, "and it is a mere physiological incident that when the object is thus attended to, immediate motor consequences should ensue," involving bodily action. "*Effort of attention is thus the essential phenomenon of will*" in voluntary decisions. The object of will is always some idea which we may find more or less resistant to our efforts to attend to it. On this view volition fundamentally involves "a relation, not between our Self and extra-mental matter (as many philosophers still maintain) but between our Self and our own states of mind." The extent to which we have free will boils down to the question of "the amount of effort of attention or consent which we can at any time put forth." This is ultimately a metaphysical issue (to be considered at length in a later section), which James maintains "is insoluble on strictly psychologic grounds." As we shall see, James regards freedom of the will as "a *moral* postulate about the Universe, the postulate that *what ought to be can be, and that bad acts cannot be fated, but that good ones must be possible in their place.*"[39] Yet science is ill-equipped to handle moral postulates regarding reality.

In his later treatment, "The Will" in his *Talks to Teachers,* James discusses habits of will as functions of two variables—"the stock of ideas" we have and the patterns of connections we have established between various ideas, on the one hand, and "action or inaction," on the other. Some acts of the will are particularly difficult, whatever our "volitional habits" might be, such as situations of moral dilemmas. Moral action essentially "*consists in the effort of attention by which we hold fast to an idea* which but for that effort of attention would be driven out of the mind by the other psychological tendencies that are there." So our "acts of voluntary attention," resulting from influential effort, are crucial to the moral life. James realizes that he is suspected of thus adopting "a mechanical and even a materialistic view of the mind" in this account of will and protests, against this suspicion, "in no sense do I count myself a materialist." For he does not believe that consciousness, as we experience it, "can possibly be *produced* by a nervous machinery," although he admits that "the *order*" of our ideas might be determined by the machinery of the brain and central nervous system and that the range of ideas with which we can function might be restricted by "the native and acquired powers" of the brain. But none of this destroys the possibility of free will, since the "duration and amount" of voluntary attention in terms of which it is defined still "*seem* within certain limits indeterminate. We *feel* as if we could make it really more or less, and as if our free action in this regard were a genuine critical point in nature—a point on which our destiny and that of others might hinge." The difference between the believer in free will and the determinist is that the former "believes the appearance to be a reality," whereas the latter "believes that it is an illusion." James insists that his "psychological and psychophysical theories" need not push him "to become a fatalist or a materialist" and, in fact, declares himself a free-willist.[40]

Tolerance of Others and Self-Realization. In his essay "On a Certain Blindness in Human Beings," he talks of how our feelings affect our judgments:

> Our judgments concerning the worth of things, big or little, depend on the *feelings* the things arouse in us.... Now the blindness in human beings ... is the blindness with which we all are afflicted in regard to the feelings of creatures and people different from ourselves.

James tells a story about a time when he visited the mountains of North Carolina and found the newly cleared land ugly due to the charred stumps of cut down trees; then, his driver commented on how pleased and proud the inhabitants were of having cultivated the land. James exclaims about his sudden realization of how prejudiced was his point of view: "I had been as blind to the peculiar ideality of their conditions as they certainly would also have been to the ideality of mine, had they had a peep at my strange

indoor academic ways of life at Cambridge." The point is that the feelings that energize a way of life, give it significance, and motivate deliberate action can be quite foreign and mysterious to others. We are often so divorced from the values of others that it can be healthy to try to look at things from their points of view. A certain amount of tolerance of others seems appropriate:

> Hands off: neither the whole of truth nor the whole of good is revealed to any single observer, although each observer gains a partial superiority of insight from the peculiar position in which he stands.

As James says in "What Makes a Life Significant" (expressing Mill's principle of liberty), "The first thing to learn in intercourse with others is non-interference with their own peculiar ways of being happy, provided those ways do not assume to interfere by violence with ours." We must all determine which ideals will give meaning to our own lives; and "morally exceptional individuals" are those who strive and struggle to realize their ideals. Given "this wonderful human nature of ours," life can be significant if such qualities as "inner joy, courage, and endurance are joined with an ideal." Yet all our "ideals are relative to the lives that entertain them." A value of education is that it can expose us to new ideals that we can incorporate into our own personal value systems. It is due to the "marriage" of "ideal aspirations" and personal **virtues** that the human "character of *progress*" is sustained, giving life significance.[41]

The Individual. James's theory of personality, while subscribing to the idea of a common human nature, places a great deal of emphasis on "The Importance of Individuals." In the essay of that name he approvingly quotes an uneducated carpenter as saying, "There is very little difference between one man and another; but what little there is, *is very important.*" He condemns "the talk of the contemporary sociological school about averages and general laws and predetermined tendencies" to the extent that it tends to minimize "the importance of individual differences" among people. In *The Varieties of Religious Experience* he illustrates his point about how all sentient creatures are individuals and, as such, resist generic classification with the story of an outraged crab who protests about being categorized as a crustacean by protesting, "I am MYSELF, MYSELF alone."[42]

MENTAL STATES AND PERSONALITY TYPES. Likewise "medical materialism" is taken to task for its **reductionistic** characterizations of mental states as "'nothing but' expressions of our organic disposition." Despite such attempts to discredit them as the neurotic consequences of bodily afflictions, we all consider some mental states as superior to and more desirable than others. And we do so for some combination of two reasons: "It is either because we take an immediate delight in them; or else it is because we believe them to bring us good consequential fruits for life." (We might recall here Socrates' view of things as worthwhile to the extent that they are pleasant and/or useful.) James later distinguishes between the "healthy-minded" personality, which exhibits an optimistic attitude of joyous buoyancy towards life, and the "morbid-minded" personality, which exhibits a pessimistic attitude of morose melancholy. It is difficult for these two personality types to respect one another. To those who are morbid-minded, "healthy-mindedness pure and simple seems unspeakably blind and shallow. To the healthy-minded way, on the other hand, the way of the sick soul seems unmanly and diseased." Of course, these are merely types to which individuals can more or less conform. A third personality type is what James calls "the divided self," which fluctuates between highs of exhilaration and lows of despair. James sees Augustine as "a classic example" of the divided self, his "half-pagan, half-Christian" upbringing leading him to feel guilt over the lustful pleasures he enjoyed, his **Manicheanism** providing a temporary theoretical world-view reflecting his own psychic ambivalence, and his conversion to Christianity leading him to yearn to control his own desires, but not too quickly. James is fascinated and pleased by the explorations in such abnormal psychology being conducted by Freud and others and at least interested in their idea of "the subliminal consciousness." He approves of the idea of a "*subconscious self*,"[43] although, as a philosopher, he would surely have thought Freud's notion of unconscious mental states quite **inconsistent**.

A THEORY OF PURE EXPERIENCE. In the last decade of his life, James's views on consciousness became increasingly radical. In "Does 'Consciousness' Exist?" he begins by observing how Kant "undermined" the traditional concept of "the soul" by denying it any knowable content and replaced it with the purely formal "transcendental ego." James admits that he has "mistrusted 'consciousness' as an entity" for twenty years and that the time has finally arrived when it should "be openly and universally discarded," although thoughts exist and the process of thinking is real. His denial of consciousness as "an entity" means that there is "no aboriginal stuff or quality of being, contrasted with that of which material objects are made, out of which our thoughts of them are made; but there is a function in experience which thoughts perform"—namely, the function of *knowing*. Against Cartesian **dualism** and Hegelian monism, James proposes a theory of "pure experience," according to which consciousness is not a thing but "a kind of external relation" to other parts of experience. The relation of consciousness, as we experience it, is always associated with bodily processes. "The 'I think' which Kant said must be able to accompany all my objects, is the 'I breathe' which actually does accompany them." As James points out, the word "spirit" etymologically means "breath." So, the idea of consciousness as a substantial reality independent of its objects is repudiated: "*That entity is fictitious, while thoughts in the concrete are fully real. But thoughts in the concrete are made of the same stuff as things are.*"[44]

In his paper "The Idea of Consciousness," James defines psychology as "the science of the facts of consciousness, or of *phenomena*, or yet again of the *states* of consciousness." Traditional schools of philosophical psychology—"Scholastic, Cartesian, Kantian, neo-Kantian"—dualistically separate the conscious subject from its objects. James confesses that from the days when he first started seriously doing psychology, "this old dualism of matter and thought, this supposedly absolute heterogeneity of the two, has always presented difficulties." Although we may have practical reasons for making such distinctions, he sees no reason "to attribute an essential difference between images and objects. Thought and reality are made of one and the same stuff, which is the stuff of experience in general." He concludes the essay by summarizing six theses:

1. "*Consciousness, as it is ordinarily understood, does not exist, any more than Matter*," that is, substantially.

2. "*What does exist, and makes up the part of truth*

that the word 'Consciousness' covers, is the susceptibility of the parts of experience to be
related" to "or known" by other parts of it.

3. "*This susceptibility is explained by the fact that*"
some parts of experience assume "*the role of
things known and others the role of knowing
subjects*" in relation to them.

4. "*We can clearly define these roles without going
outside of the stuff of experience itself, and without invoking anything transcendent,*" like Kant's
transcendental ego or Hegel's Absolute Spirit.

5. "*The attributions subject and object, the thing
represented and that which represents, thing and
thought,*" although practically useful, do not signify a substantial distinction of "*an **ontological**
order, as classical dualism would have it*" to be.

6. "*Finally, things and thoughts are not at all fundamentally heterogeneous; they are made of one
and the same stuff,*" which is indefinable but can
be called "experience in general."[45]

Knowledge

TYPES OF KNOWLEDGE. James's theory of knowledge is rooted in this empirical psychology, and his
Principles of Psychology is a good source in which to
commence our study of it: "*There are two kinds of
knowledge* broadly and practically distinguishable:
we may call them respectively *knowledge of acquaintance* and *knowledge-about*." Through the first we
directly encounter an object through experience without necessarily having any descriptive understanding
of it; through the second we understand an object in
terms of its relationships to other things. Of course,
the two types of knowledge complement each other.
"The grammatical sentence expresses this. Its 'subject' stands for an object of acquaintance which, by
the addition of the predicate, is to get something
known about it." Our acquaintance with things is established through intuitive feeling, while our knowledge about them proceeds from analytical thought.[46]

A PRIORI TRUTHS. James believes in *a priori* truths,
though he has little patience with the Kantian discussion of whether they can be synthetic as well as analytic. He confidently asserts that "*the mind is filled
with necessary and eternal relations which it finds between certain of its ideal conceptions, and which form
a determinate system.*" These *a priori* systems include those of mathematics and formal logic. "None

of these eternal verities has anything to say about
facts, about what is or is not in the world." These
truths are hypothetical rather than existential—given
that Socrates is a man and assuming that all men are
mortal, it necessarily follows that Socrates must be
mortal. But what of alleged metaphysical and moral
principles? Do any of them count as *a priori* truths?
We have inherited quite a few such principles from
intellectual history, such as, "Whatever is in the effect
must be in the cause" and "Nothing is or happens
without a reason." Are these necessary statements of
fact (what Kant calls synthetic *a priori*)? James denies it: "Such principles as these, which might be
multiplied to satiety, are properly to be called *postulates of rationality*, not propositions of fact." They are
useful for guiding theoretical inquiry and practical action, but it would be rash to claim that we know them
in a strict sense, even the crucial "principle that 'nothing can happen without a cause.'" Likewise, ethical
principles, ultimately are "mere postulates of rationality, so far as they transcend experience" in functioning **prescriptively**. Philosophy itself is founded
on the "widest postulate of rationality" of all, asserting "that the world *is* rationally intelligible," so that
our theorizing about it might prove worthwhile. In
conclusion, the propositions of logic, mathematics,
ethics, and metaphysics can serve as useful tools for
us but provide no factual knowledge.[47]

THE VALUE OF A THEORY. In James's first great
philosophical essay, "The Sentiment of Rationality,"
he speaks of our natural wish to escape puzzlement
and perplexity about ourselves and our world and of
the value of theories in helping us feel that things
make sense.

> This feeling of the sufficiency of the present moment, of
> its absoluteness,—this absence of all need to explain it,
> account for it, or justify it,—is what I call the Sentiment
> of Rationality,

he says. On the one hand, we want our theories to be
simple enough that they can be understood and thus
do their explanatory work. But, on the other hand, we
also expect a good theory to be detailed enough to
help us to distinguish among the many, varied objects
of experience.

> A man's philosophic attitude is determined by the bal-
> ance in him of these two cravings. No system of philos-
> ophy can hope to be universally accepted among men

which grossly violates either need, or entirely subordinates the one to the other.

James would say that Hegel's theory of reality sacrifices the clear details of experience to the monistic Absolute; "that of Hume, with his equally barren 'looseness and separateness,'" errs at the other extreme, offering no simple way of unifying those details. It is so difficult to balance these demands well and not to fall overboard towards clear details and away from simple unity or vice versa. But even if we do manage to strike this delicate balance, more is required of a theory than this.

> The interest of theoretic rationality, the relief of identification, is but one of a thousand human purposes. When others rear their heads, it must pack up its little bundle and retire till its turn recurs. The exaggerated dignity and value that philosophers have claimed for their solutions is thus greatly reduced,

to the extent that logic and theoretical accuracy are insufficient. This is the revolutionary feature of James's essay, its realization that theoretical satisfaction is only a **necessary condition**, and not a **sufficient condition**, of a valuable theory. Such a theory must also provide for "the feeling of rationality in its *practical* aspect." It must somehow serve our needs and interests as human beings.[48]

Two theories could be equally satisfactory from a theoretical perspective, in which case it would be reasonable for us to choose "that one which awakens the active impulses" more effectively. The most important pragmatic use of a good theory is that it should help, "*in a general way at least, banish uncertainty from the future.*" Philosophical pessimism fails to provide a theory of reality that is congruous with our natural "desires and active tendencies," rendering the future less secure rather than more so. "But a second and worse defect in a philosophy than that of **contradicting** our active propensities is to give them no object whatever to press against." Hobbes's reductionistic philosophy threatens to undermine any ultimate ground of value and to hurl us into the meaningless void of matter in motion.

> This is why materialism will always fail of universal adoption, however well it may fuse things into an atomistic unity, however clearly it may prophecy the future eternity. For materialism denies reality to the objects of almost all the impulses which we most cherish.

Knowledge of comprehension and knowledge of acquaintance are both oriented towards possible practical action. James quotes one of his favorite passages from Scripture (*Ezekiel* 2:1), "Son of Man, *stand upon thy feet* and I will speak unto thee," to illustrate the human need actively to do something useful with our knowledge. A third philosophy—in addition to those of pessimism and materialism—also fails to meet our practical needs: "Fatalism, whose solving word in all crises of behavior is 'all striving is vain,' will never reign supreme, for the impulse to take life strivingly is indestructible in the race" of humans. Still, there are various philosophies that do seem to satisfy both our theoretical requirements and our practical interests (including most of the ones we have studied thus far), and "personal temperament" inevitably influences our attraction towards some one among them. We commit ourselves in faith—meaning a "belief in something concerning which doubt is still theoretically possible"—in one philosophy or another; "and as the test of belief is willingness to act, one may say that faith is the readiness to act in a cause the prosperous issue of which is not certified to us in advance." We do not know a philosophical theory to be true, but believe in it and act accordingly. Its value and legitimacy for us go far beyond the realm of logical proof and objective evidence. "Pretend what we may, the whole man within us is at work when we form our philosophical opinions. Intellect, will, taste, and passion co-operate just as they do in practical affairs."[49]

Our faith in a philosophical theory renders it a "working hypothesis" for us. Many of us require of any theory that will promote the sentiment of rationality that it should account for some combination of the four postulates of "God, immortality, absolute morality, and free-will." But is it responsible to believe in such matters in the absence of scientific evidence? In response, James uses a favorite analogy: imagine a mountain climber who has gotten on the wrong side of a wide crevasse and who can only save himself from starvation and exposure by risking "a terrible leap" such as he has never attempted before and cannot know he can successfully make. If he doubts his ability, he will stand his ground and freeze to death or tentatively and in despair fall into the yawning abyss; but if he believes he can make the leap and does his best, he may succeed. "*There are then cases where faith creates its own verification,*" where belief, coupled with commitment to act, becomes a self-fulfilling prophecy, as does the refusal or inability to believe. James associates this view of philosophical theories in terms of believed postulates of rationality with his doctrine of meliorism. If we believe that the future can be better than it otherwise would be through our efforts, and act on that belief, our faith might create its own verification. The **sceptic**, who has no theoretical basis for effort, and the moralist, whose theory supplies energy for her initiatives, equally must act on faith in the absence of certain knowledge. All of us must try what theories we find most workable. It is as if "nature has put into our hands two keys, by which we may test the lock" of reality. "If we try the moral key *and it fits*, it is a moral lock. If we try the unmoral key and *it* fits, it is an unmoral lock." But each of us must judge for himself in such matters, with no objective, universal knowledge available, the "keys" being various postulates of rationality, including those "of God, of duty, of freedom, of immortality,"[50] all of which we shall discuss in detail in subsequent sections. Meanwhile, it might be worth remembering that it was Kant who first conceived of freedom, God, and immortality as postulates of practical reason, although James does not give him credit for originating this fruitful idea.

JAMES VS. KANT.   From the time he begins writing and teaching philosophy James rarely gives Kant credit for anything good, identifying him with the barren abstractions of German Idealism. In his "Philosophical Conceptions and Practical Results," James explicitly identifies his pragmatic method with the British tradition that includes Hume and Mill and dissociates it from the approach of Kant, saying,

> I believe that Kant bequeathes to us not one single conception which is both indispensable to philosophy and which philosophy either did not possess before him, or was not destined inevitably to acquire after him. . . . The true line of philosophic progress lies, in short, it seems to me, not so much *through* Kant as *round* him.

In a later essay James calls for the replacement of the view of truth as absolute, held by Kant and most earlier Continental philosophers, by a more humanistic conception. James is convinced that these lines of influence have merged to render the absolute view obsolete. First, it has been subjected to the criticisms of thinkers like Mill who "have emphasized the incongruence of the forms of our thinking with the 'things' which the thinking nevertheless successfully handles." Second, the doctrine of evolution has made us realize that the world is less fixed and more "plastic" than was once supposed and that all human functions are "adaptations" to our practical needs and interests. Third, the most recent findings of science have pulled us away from the precise certainties of Kant's Newtonian age and "reconciled us to the idea that 'Not quite true' is as near as we can ever get."[51]

TENDER-MINDED VS. TOUGH-MINDED PHILOSOPHERS. James's most famous treatment of epistemology is found in his *Pragmatism* lectures. In the first lecture he generalizes the "human temperaments" that incline us in philosophical directions as of two types, the "tender-minded" and the "tough-minded," which he associates with rationalism (philosophy based on abstract "principles") and empiricism (philosophy based on concrete "facts"), respectively. He says that the "tender-minded" rationalists tend towards intellectualism, idealism, optimism, religion, free will, monism, and **dogmatism**; by contrast, the "tough-minded" empiricists tend towards sensationalism, materialism, pessimism, irreligion, fatalism, pluralism, and scepticism. The extremes have trouble respecting one another. "The tough think of the tender as sentimentalists and soft-heads. The tender feel the tough to be unrefined, callous, or brutal." For most of us, though, the problem is that we want the best of both worlds.

> Facts are good, of course—give us lots of facts. Principles are good—give us plenty of principles. The world is indubitably one if you look at it in one way, but as indubitably is it many, if you look at it in another.

So, we would like to cling to both sides of the turntable; yet, as philosophers, we demand consistency. We live in an era of scientific fact, yet want to maintain our religious and moral values. Empiricism seems insufficiently value-oriented, and religious philosophers appear insufficiently empirical. This is what James calls "the present dilemma in philosophy." If we follow Plato, Augustine, Descartes, and Hegel down the "tender-minded" path of rationalism, we seem to lose contact with the world of empirical fact; on the other hand, if we follow Hobbes, Hume, and Mill down the "tough-minded" path of empiricism, we find our beliefs in freedom and values imperiled. How can we break this dilemma? James answers,

I offer the oddly-named thing pragmatism as a philosophy that can satisfy both kinds of demand. It can remain religious like the rationalisms, but at the same time, like the empiricisms, it can preserve the richest intimacy with facts.[52]

The next seven lectures proceed to articulate the details of this middle path.

THE CAMPING-TRIP ANECDOTE.   The second lecture, "What Pragmatism Means," is one of James's best-known essays. It begins with a "trivial anecdote" about how he was once on a camping trip with some friends, went on a walk away from camp, and returned to find all the others disagreeing about whether a man goes around a squirrel if he circles the tree on which it stands but the squirrel also moves around the tree, constantly keeping the tree between the man and itself. James answered that it "depends on what you *practically mean* by 'going round' the squirrel." If you mean moving from the north of it "to the east, then to the south, then to the west, and then to the north" again, the man obviously does go around it. "But if on the contrary you mean being first in front of" the squirrel, then to its right side, then facing its back, then to its left side, and then facing its belly again, the man does not go around it, since he is constantly facing the squirrel's belly.[53]

THE PRAGMATIC METHOD OF SETTLING DISPUTES. The point of the story is to illustrate the pragmatic method of settling disputes by examining their practical meanings.

> What difference would it practically make to any one if this notion rather than that notion were true? If no practical difference whatever can be traced, then the alternatives mean practically the same thing, and all dispute is idle. Whenever a dispute is serious, we ought to be able to show some practical difference that must follow from one side or the other's being right.

James reports that the pragmatic method was first introduced by his friend Charles Sanders Peirce in 1878 and was popularized twenty years later by his own lecture at the University of California. James is confident that it can be used effectively to eliminate many insignificant philosophical disputes.

> There can *be* no difference anywhere that doesn't *make* a difference elsewhere—no difference in abstract truth that doesn't express itself in a difference in concrete fact and in conduct consequent upon that fact, imposed on somebody, somehow, somewhere, and somewhen.

We have seen this pragmatic emphasis gradually emerging in James's thought, but now it appears full-blown:

> The whole function of philosophy ought to be to find out what definite difference it will make to you and me, at definite instants of our life, if this world-formula or that world-formula be the true one.

He thinks the pragmatic method has been employed for many centuries before Peirce began the movement, that Socrates, Aristotle, and Hume, for example, used it effectively. In a way it is a more generalized application of the principle of utility of John Stuart Mill, to whose memory, by the way, James dedicates *Pragmatism*.[54]

James admits that, as a method, it leans away from rationalism and towards empiricism, while maintaining that it is open to a wider range of results than traditional empiricism. He prefers to view philosophical theories as "*instruments*" or tools for finding answers rather than as already given answers. The attitude of pragmatism is one "*of looking towards last things, fruits, consequences, facts,*" as empiricism does, and "*away from first things, principles, 'categories,' supposed necessities*" so prized by rationalism. In addition to being a method, pragmatism also involves a particular theory of truth, which will be considered in more detail later, that views ideas as true to the extent that they are useful in helping us relate well to experience. When a novel experience fails to fit into an established web of old beliefs, James maintains, most of us try to preserve as much as we can of the old stock, "for in this matter we are all extreme conservatives," modifying it as little as possible to accommodate the new data. "New truth is always a go-between, a smoother-over of transitions. It marries old opinion to new fact so as ever to show a minimum of jolt, a maximum of continuity." Facts of experience are not, themselves, true. "Truth is *what we say about* them." And, on this theory, truth is relative to the pragmatic function "of giving human satisfaction in marrying previous parts of experience with newer parts" rather than being purely objective or absolute.[55]

So, pragmatism is primarily a method of inquiry and secondarily a theory of truth. Unlike the rationalist, who "is comfortable only in the presence of abstractions," James says that the pragmatist will "talk about truths in the plural, about their utility and satisfactoriness, about the success with which they 'work,'" generalizing only on the basis of concrete facts, like empiricists. James adds (perhaps with tongue in cheek),

> Your typical ultra-abstractionist fairly shudders at concreteness: other things equal, he positively prefers the pale and the spectral. If the two universes were offered, he would always choose the skinny outline rather than the rich thicket of reality. It is so much purer, clearer, nobler.

He is committed to a realm of Truth, like Plato's eternal Ideas or Hegel's Absolute, which is independent of all our values. By contrast, James holds that "truth is *one species of good. . . . The true is the name of whatever proves itself to be good in the way of belief, and good, too, for definite, assignable reasons.*"[56] As has already been indicated and will be explored in more depth later, what is good is relative to the needs and interests of persons.

KNOWLEDGE AND COMMON SENSE. In the fifth lecture, "Pragmatism and Common Sense," James describes his view as one of "noetic pluralism" because it is committed to multiple truths that are only "strung along" additively without completely interlocking in one already finished system. He says that "our knowledge grows *in spots*. The spots may be large or small, but the knowledge never grows all over." We conservatively prevent the spots from spreading too far or too quickly, clinging to "as much of our old knowledge, as many of our old prejudices and beliefs, as we can. We patch and tinker more than we renew," because it is disconcerting to have to accommodate radically spreading spots of knowledge. The major thesis of this lecture is that

> our fundamental ways of thinking about things are discoveries of exceedingly remote ancestors, which have been able to preserve themselves throughout the experience of all subsequent time.

These are the concepts of common sense, which remain fundamental to our thinking, although other ways of thinking (including the scientific and the philosophical) "have grafted themselves" on to this one. The most important of these concepts of common sense are those of "Thing; The same or different; Kinds; Minds; Bodies; One Time; One Space; Subjects and attributes; Causal influences; The fancied;

The real." Superficially, this may sound like Kant's doctrine of mental structures; but, for James, they are "constructions as patently artificial as any that science can show," rather than innate, have been handed down from one generation to the next through instruction, and have evolved in the ways in which they are conceived.

> Common sense appears thus as a perfectly definite stage in our understanding of things, a stage that satisfies in an extraordinarily successful way the purposes for which we think.

Its concepts prove quite adequate for the "utilitarian practical purposes" of ordinary life.[57]

But for purposes of understanding how the stuff and forces of the natural world interact and why the entire phenomenal world appears to us as it does experientially, common sense falls short. "Science and critical philosophy thus burst the bounds of common sense. With science *naif* **realism** ceases," the table being microscopically different from its macroscopic appearances. "With critical philosophy, havoc is made of everything," because the categories of common sense come to be recognized as filters through which we perceive reality rather than as reality's independent "way of *being*." Yet we turn to science and philosophy for ways of understanding ourselves and our world which common sense cannot supply.

> There are thus at least three well-characterized levels, stages or types of thought about the world we live in, and the notions of one stage have one kind of merit, those of another stage another kind. It is impossible, however, to say that any stage as yet in sight is absolutely more *true* than any other. Common sense is the more *consolidated* stage, because it got its innings first, and made all language into its ally.

Each stage proves pragmatically "*better*" for dealing with experience from a particular point of view. James concludes the essay by making two points. First, we should be suspicious about attributing any absolute truth to the findings of common sense, treating them rather as "only a collection of extraordinarily successful hypotheses." Second, the inability of any stage of thinking to establish absolute factual truth should "awaken a presumption favorable to the pragmatic view that all our theories are *instrumental*, are mental modes of *adaptation* to reality,"[58] rather than insights of certain knowledge.

THE RELATIONSHIP BETWEEN TRUTH AND FACTS. James's sixth lecture, "Pragmatism's Conception of Truth," says that new theories typically must pass through three phases of reception: first they are "attacked as absurd," then they are accepted as true but dismissed as "obvious and insignificant," and finally they are recognized as so importantly true that even their former enemies want to claim credit for their discovery. He believes that the pragmatic theory of truth is still in the first phase but is showing signs of entering the second. "Pragmatists and intellectualists both accept" the dictionary definition of truth as the agreement of our ideas with reality, differing, however, on how properly to interpret the terms "agreement" and "reality." Whereas the intellectualist sees true ideas as somehow copying what is already extramentally fixed and determined, the pragmatist asks of any idea or belief considered true, "What experiences will be different from those which would obtain if the belief were false? What, in short, is the truth's cash-value in experiential terms?" The answer is an instrumental one, related to how beliefs function for us. *"True ideas are those that we can assimilate, validate, corroborate and verify. False ideas are those that we can not."* Unlike the intellectualist, the pragmatist refuses to conceive of truth as an entity or "a stagnant property" inhering in an idea.

> Truth *happens* to an idea. It *becomes* true, is *made* true by events. Its verity *is* in fact an event, a process: the process namely of its verifying itself, its veri-*fication*. Its **validity** is the process of its valid-*ation*.[59]

This process conception of truth is at the core of the pragmatic theory.

James upsets traditionalists when he goes on to write of an idea,

> You can say of it then either that "it is useful because it is true" or that "it is true because it is useful." Both these phrases mean exactly the same thing, namely that here is an idea that gets fulfilled and can be verified. True is the name for whatever idea starts the verification-process, useful is the name for its completed function in experience.

It is as if Mill's utilitarian conception of what is beneficial has expanded out of the area of ethics into that of epistemology. In order to count as "true," a mental state must perform the "function of a *leading that is worth while*" for us in our dealings with reality. We are liable to suffer bad consequences when our ideas deviate from this pragmatic ideal.

> Woe to him whose beliefs play fast and loose with the order which realities follow in his experience; they will lead him nowhere or else make false connections.

Matters of experienced fact, then, are among the most crucial "realities" with which our ideas must agree. But because all of us are limited in our experiences, to some extent we must accept one another's verifications, reserving the theoretical right to verify for ourselves at some point. Thus, James compares our system of truths to the bank notes of a credit system, which we pass from person to person with little fuss "so long as nothing challenges them"; but once suspicions are raised about their authenticity, we can test to see if they are forgeries. As Hume explicitly recognized, James maintains that

> matters of fact are not our only stock in trade. *Relations among purely mental ideas* form another sphere where true and false beliefs obtain, and here the beliefs are absolute, or unconditioned,

their truth being assured by definition or as a matter of principle.

> It is either a principle or a definition that 1 and 1 make 2 . . . ; that white differs less from gray than it does from black; that when the cause begins to act the effect also commences. Such propositions hold of all possible 'ones,' of all conceivable 'whites' and 'grays' and 'causes,'

and are analytic, dealing with abstract relations among ideas. "Moreover, once true, always true, of those same mental objects. Truth here has an 'eternal' character," given those definitions and principles, being hypothetical rather than existential. So, as Hume seemed to recognize, matters of fact and relations of ideas (what Kant calls synthetic and analytic truths, respectively) constitute the "realities" with which existential and hypothetical truths must agree. A third sort of "reality" is the entire system of other truths to which our minds are already committed.[60]

Now more needs to be said about the meaning of "agreement," which intellectualists traditionally think of in terms of **correspondence** or copying. The pragmatist finds this too static an interpretation and says,

> To 'agree' in the widest sense with a reality *can only mean to be guided either straight up to it or into its surroundings, or to be put into such working touch with it as to handle either it or something connected with it better than if we disagreed.* Better either intellectually or practically!

This conception of agreement in terms of a useful "leading" is pragmatic and oriented towards future consequences rather than abstract and oriented towards past determinations. As James observes, this is an explicitly pluralistic view: "Our account of truth is an account of truths in the plural, of processes of leading . . . having only this quality in common, that they *pay*" for us. On this view truth is identified with expedient thinking, as what is "right" is identified (by both Mill and James) with expedient behavior. "Expedient in almost any fashion; and expedient in the long run and on the whole of course." And we should beware of imagining that any of our factual truths, definitions, matters of principle, or old beliefs are incorrigible, since human experience has a notorious habit of "*boiling over*" and forcing us to adapt, or even repudiate, old formulas.

> The 'absolutely' true, meaning what no farther experience will ever alter, is that ideal vanishing-point towards which we imagine that all our temporary truths will some day converge.

And there seems to be no reason to suppose that that ideal is actually reachable in human life as we know it. "Meanwhile we have to live to-day by what truth we can get to-day, and be ready to-morrow to call it falsehood." James challenges us to consider examples of what once passed for absolute truth: the **geocentric** astronomy of Ptolemy, which has been replaced by the **heliocentric** system of Copernicus, the theory of spatial relations represented by Euclidean geometry, which has been countered with newer geometrical systems, the traditional logic of Aristotle, which was challenged by the dialectical logic of Hegel, the scholastic metaphysics of Aquinas, which was opposed by the critique of modern times. We now recognize these views as "only relatively true, or true within those borders of experience. 'Absolutely' they are false." Like traditional theorists, pragmatists insist that there must be a link between truth and fact. "Truths emerge from facts; but they dip forward into facts again and add to them; which facts again create or reveal new truth." The relationship between truths and facts is dialectical and dynamic.

> The 'facts' themselves meanwhile are not *true*. They simply *are*. Truth is the function of the beliefs that start and terminate among them.

Traditional rationalists might agree that experience and our awareness of truth "are in mutation" but will never agree with the pragmatist "that either reality itself or truth itself is mutable. Reality stands complete

and ready-made from all eternity, rationalism insists," and "truth has nothing to do with our experiences."[61] This would-be line of defense is set to protect the rationalists from the assaults of pragmatism.

A Defense of Pragmatism. James's second great work of epistemology, *The Meaning of Truth*, is largely a defense of the theory presented in *Pragmatism* against its critics. He begins by defining cognition as "a function of consciousness" that is "self-transcendent," in the sense of referring to whatever the subjective knower regards as reality. In order for a state of consciousness to qualify as "knowledge," it must refer to an objective content for that knowing individual. James points out that one person's reality may not qualify as such for another: "If your feeling bear no fruits in my world, I call it utterly detached from my world; I call it a **solipsism**, and call its world a dream-world." Thus, what counts as knowledge is person-relative. We do, of course, act as if we share a common reality; that is to say,

> we believe that we all know and think about and talk about the same world, because *we believe our PERCEPTS are possessed by us in common.* And we believe this because the percepts of each one of us seem to be changed in consequence of changes in the percepts of some one else.

We mutually affect each other's experiences of reality. We can know things either "immediately and intuitively," as we know this sheet of paper held in our hands, or "conceptually or representatively," as we know "the tigers now in India," for example, or the scholastic system of philosophy of Thomas Aquinas. But what does it mean to say that we in America know "the tigers now in India"? Our thoughts indicate, refer to, are "mentally *pointing* towards" certain objects outside our minds which we believe to be elsewhere. But we must maintain the subject-object dualism in the sense that our "ideas and the tigers are in themselves as loose and separate, to use Hume's language, as any two things can be; and pointing means here an operation as external and **adventitious** as any that nature yields." Representative knowledge of an object leads the knower to it through the medium of experience of reality.[62]

In immediate, intuitive knowledge, by contrast, there is no need for any pointing across an intermediate space and time, since the thought directly encompasses its object. Unlike the "case of tigers in India," where, "the things known being absent experiences, the knowing can only consist in passing smoothly towards them through the intermediary context that the world supplies," in our immediate knowledge of the paper held in our hands, there is contact between subject and object through the body, so that they form two dimensions of *the datum, the phenomenon, or the experience.* The paper is in the mind and the mind is around the paper." Such immediate knowledge involves an identity of the object and the mental content, which is impossible in representative knowledge.[63]

COHERENCE, A NECESSARY CONDITION OF TRUTH. James criticizes the old correspondence theory of truth for naively assuming that true propositions simply "copy extra-mental realities." Not only is there the ambiguity wrapped around the issue of how an idea can "copy" or correspond to something other than an idea, but James sees no good reason to assume "that the sole business of our mind with realities should be to copy them." When we encounter reality through experience, we need to be able to relate to it profitably, whether or not this involves a process of "copying." Also, knowledge, although a valuable achievement, is only one of the possible ways in which we can fruitfully relate to reality. It is important to emphasize the relational quality of truth, and the traditional correspondence theory does this; but, for James, it is fundamentally "a relation, not of our ideas to non-human realities, but of conceptual parts of our experience to sensational parts. Those thoughts are true which guide us to *beneficial interaction* with sensible particulars as they occur, whether they copy these in advance or not."[64]

He summarizes his humanistic or pragmatic theory of truth in six theses. First, conformity to reality is a necessary condition of truth. Second, "reality" here means the conceptual and perceptual aspects of our experience. Third, "conforming" here means so taking account of reality as to yield results which are (intellectually and/or practically) satisfactory. Fourth, "taking account of" and "satisfactory," as used here, are primitive terms that cannot be defined in terms of more basic ones but are subject to a wide array of possible functions. Fifth, roughly speaking, "taking account of" reality must include "*preserving* it in as unmodified a form as possible," and this will be

unsatisfactory if it contradicts other realities of which we have also taken account. Thus, sixth, taking account of reality in a satisfactory way may either establish new truth or be subscribing to a previously established one.[65]

In "The Essence of Humanism" James argues that all knowing must occur in the context of personal experience and that "the knower and the object known must both be portions of experience." Our reality is thus given in the field of experience; "and what knows it is defined as an experience *that 'represents' it, in the sense of being substitutable for it in our thinking*, because it leads to the same associates, *or in the sense of 'pointing to it' through a chain of other experiences that either intervene or may intervene.*" So, when a person knows her dog, her ideas about it either adequately represent the actual dog and its behavior or lead to possible experiences that could put her into contact with them. As correspondence, pragmatically conceived, is a necessary condition of truth, so is coherence: "If a novel experience, conceptual or sensible, contradict too emphatically our pre-existent system of beliefs, in ninety-nine cases out of a hundred it is treated as false." Only in the most extreme of circumstances can we afford to throw entire systems of beliefs overboard, and these precipitate revolutionary crises in our thought. Coherence with sensible realities always remains the normal touchstone of truth: "Our ideas and concepts and scientific theories pass for true only so far as they harmoniously lead back to the world of sense."[66] So, like correspondence, coherence is a necessary condition of truth, which should be interpreted pragmatically.

PRAGMATIC TRUTH VS. INTELLECTUAL TRUTH. "*Existential* truth is incidental to the actual competition of opinions. *Essential* truth, the truth of the intellectualists," like Hegel, by contrast, is merely truth as possible and not yet actually established in our personal knowledge. Against Hegel and other idealists, James says, "It is less real, not more real, than the verified article; and to attribute a superior degree of glory to it seems little more than a piece of perverse abstraction-worship." We do often accept possible confirmation in place of actual verification, and it is useful for us to be able to do so. But actual, existential truth has both logical and metaphysical priority over possible, essential truth as its ultimate warrant. In "The Meaning of the Word Truth," James calls his account "realistic," rather than idealistic, and avers that it "follows the epistemological dualism of common sense," between knowing subject and object known, though both appear as interrelated in the field of experience. True statements must refer to some determinate object(s) in such a way as to facilitate some profitable adaptation of the mind(s) accepting them. No account of what it means for them to be "true" can be complete "without referring to their functional possibilities," as emphasized by pragmatism—it is a shortcoming of the traditional correspondence and coherence theories of truth that they do not do so. Unlike the intellectualist, who sees "three distinct entities in the field" of experience, a pragmatist refuses to make truth something independent of the relationship between reality and the process of knowing, as James makes clear in "A Dialogue." On this view, knowledge and truth are essentially correlative, rather than the latter being prior to and independent of the former. James identifies this pragmatic theory with his doctrine of radical empiricism, which "consists first of a postulate, next of a statement of fact, and finally of a generalized conclusion." First, the postulate holds that only what in some way is "drawn from experience" should be subject-matter for philosophical discussion. Second, the "statement of fact" maintains that "the relations between things, conjunctive as well as disjunctive, are just as much matters of direct particular experience, neither more so nor less so, than the things themselves." It seems that Hegel violates the postulate and that Hume fails to do justice to the statement of fact. Third, the "generalized conclusion" of radical empiricism is that "the parts of experience hold together from next to next by relations that are themselves part of experience," rather than being "loose and separate," as Hume imagined, and needing some "extraneous trans-empirical connective support," such as Hegel's Absolute, to hold them together.[67]

COMMENTS ON PHILOSOPHICAL SYSTEMS. In *Some Problems of Philosophy* James subscribes to the idea of Plato and Aristotle that philosophy begins in a sense of wonder. "It sees the familiar as if it were strange, and the strange as if it were familiar." The sense of wonder seems to be provoked by the interactions "of four different human interests, science, poetry, religion, and logic." Many of the greatest philosophies (including the ones studied here) are global systems of thought that purport to encompass all thought and reality. James's example of such a sweeping system is "Thomas Aquinas's great 'Summa,' written in the thirteenth century," in which "we find opinions expressed about literally everything, from God down to matter, with angels, men, and demons taken in on the way," with the interrelationships of the various elements of the system being taken very seriously. "A theology, a psychology, a system of duties and morals, are given in fullest detail, while physics and logic are established in their universal principles." And all of this is done for the sake of articulating knowledge. This is philosophy done on the grand scale and designed to impart a world-view. But philosophy is essentially the work of "*man thinking*, thinking about generalities rather than about particulars." It must proceed by methods of thinking that are peculiarly human, for the philosopher "observes, discriminates, generalizes, classifies, looks for causes, traces analogies, and makes hypotheses." All of these mental processes have "evolved gradually out of primitive human thought"; and, limited though they be, they are the tools with which we must work.[68]

We become acquainted with things through sense experience ("percepts"), as a result of which we form ideas or "representations" of them in our minds ("concepts"), sensation and thought being "interlaced" in our experience. Whereas percepts are continuous in the stream of consciousness, concepts are "discrete from each other in their several *meanings*." The flux of perceptual experience, in itself, "*means nothing*," and it is our concepts that assign meaning to its parts, which themselves flow into one another. Our concepts allow us to make "cuts" in the flux of perceptual experience. "The cuts we make are purely ideal"; but without them the flux remains "a big blooming buzzing confusion" for us. Unlike Kant, who sees the sensible flux as an intrinsically disconnected manifold to be united by the "transcendental ego of apperception," James sees the flux as intrinsically continuous, discrimination being introduced by the knowing mind for pragmatic purposes. Our concepts perform three services for us—they provide "an immense map of relations" which can practically guide our thought and action, they generate values that can motivate the will, and they alert us to "'eternal' truths," such as those of mathematics and formal logic, which transcend the particular facts of the sense world. Like Plato, James subscribes to a "logical realism" that views concepts as singular realities of which physical things can be seen as constituted through some sort of participation, so that this physical table is constituted as a perceptual object of flatness, tallness, hardness, and other concepts of which it somehow does "partake." But for Plato and his rationalistic followers, concepts are eternally "primordial and perceptual things are secondary in nature," whereas James views "concrete percepts as primordial and concepts as of secondary origin." James admits that his theory of knowledge is "somewhat eccentric in its attempt to combine logical realism with an otherwise empiricist mode of thought."[69]

Freedom

FREEDOM AND RATIONALITY.   Unlike his treatments of personality and knowledge, which are broadly spread out over many works during a period of many years, James's discussions of three of the four postulates of rationality mentioned—freedom, morality, and immortality (the exception being that of God)—are mainly focused in single essays. The great work in which he discusses human freedom is "The Dilemma of Determinism," at the beginning of which he boasts that he has a new perspective to offer, despite the prejudice "that the juice has ages ago been pressed out of the free-will controversy." He will proceed to show why he follows Renouvier (and, we might add, Kant) in subscribing to human freedom as a postulate of rationality. But first, James makes it a point to "disclaim openly on the threshold all pretension to prove to you that the freedom of the will is true. The most I hope is to induce some of you to follow my own example in assuming it true, and acting as if it were true." (Although he gives Kant no credit for it, this is a very Kantian point of view—assume it as a **regulative** idea of practical reason and act as if it were the case. We recall that James's own mental crisis was over the inability to believe in freedom and that it was the approach of the neo-Kantian

Renouvier that helped James pull himself out of his crisis.) Our first voluntary act of freedom should be to affirm freedom itself. He warns us that his argument will hinge on "two suppositions," both of which he has tried to develop carefully in his theory of knowledge. The first is that our theories about reality are designed to provide us with a sentiment of rationality; the second is that whenever we consider two rival theories, it is legitimate to consider that one truer which "seems to us, on the whole, more rational than the other."[70]

HARD DETERMINISM VS. SOFT DETERMINISM.   Another preliminary tactic is that James will try, for a while, to avoid using two words that are weighted with heavy emotional connotations, although later he will perversely embrace the second. "One is the eulogistic word *freedom*, and the other is the opprobrious word *chance*." Even proponents of free will tend to be nervous about admitting that it introduces chance into the universe; opponents often try to appropriate the language of freedom for their own purposes. James distinguishes between "hard determinism," which is honest enough not to "shrink from such words as fatality, bondage of the will, necessitation, and the like," and "soft determinism which abhors harsh words, and, repudiating fatality, **necessity**, and even **predetermination**, says that its real name is freedom; for freedom is only necessity understood, and bondage to the highest is identical with true freedom." In this sense, Hume is a "soft" determinist, although he prefers to use the word "liberty" rather than "freedom." James condemns the less forthright "soft" determinism as "a quagmire of evasion under which the real issue of fact has been entirely smothered" (as we saw it was in Hume's thought, which failed to pursue the issue of what ultimately determines the will in its voluntary actions). So, for a while, at least, James will use the words "determinism" and "indeterminism," words around which "no ambiguities hang."[71]

DETERMINISM VS. INDETERMINISM.   We should recognize that determinism and indeterminism are exclusive and exhaustive theoretical alternatives, that they constitute an either-or which exhausts the possibilities; but determinism and indeterminism contradict

---

Predeterminism.   The theory that every event is necessitated according to fixed causal laws; fatalism adds to this the idea that nothing we can do will affect the outcome that is determined; the theological view of predestination identifies God's will as the original source of all predeterminism

each other, so that one of them must be correct and the other must be incorrect. Determinism

> professes that those parts of the universe already laid down absolutely appoint and decree what the other parts shall be. The future has no ambiguous possibilities.

Everything that is had to be, and whatever will be is fated, with no exceptions.

> Indeterminism, on the contrary, says that the parts have a certain amount of loose play on one another, so that the laying down of one of them does not necessarily determine what others shall be. It admits that possibilities may be in excess of actualities.

Determinism believes everything to be either necessary or impossible, allowing no middle ground for unrealized possibilities; by contrast, indeterminism accepts that middle ground of possibilities as real rather than dismissing them as "pure illusions." As a matter of logic, this is a hard-and-fast distinction:

> The issue, it will be seen, is a perfectly sharp one, which no eulogistic terminology can smear over or wipe out. The truth *must* lie with one side or the other, and its lying with one side makes the other false.

Strangely enough, facts do not tilt us to one theory or the other, since the determinist and the indeterminist can be presented with identical facts.

> What divides us into possibility men and anti-possibility men is faiths or postulates—postulates of rationality. To this man the world seems more rational with possibilities in it,—to that man more rational with possibilities excluded.

James uses the example of how he will walk from Harvard University's campus to his own house after delivering this lecture. He could walk home by way of either Divinity Avenue or Oxford Street. But no one, including himself, can predict with absolute infallibility which route shall be chosen (even if he has decided, he could change his mind); however, "*after the fact*" both determinists and indeterminists can explain the chosen route in their own terms, so that the data of experience cannot provide a theoretically knock-down, drag-out proof. James admits he has "taken the most trivial of examples" here;[72] if no more were ever at stake than the way we walk home, we might doubt that it matters pragmatically.

THE BROCKTON MURDER CASE. But now let us consider a richer example, in which much more is at stake. Perhaps whipping out a copy of the newspaper and waving its headlines before his audience, James reminds them of the horrible details of a recent murder at Brockton (a suburb of Boston), in which a ruthless husband lured his wife to a deserted, isolated area, "shot her four times, and then, as she lay on the ground and said to him, 'You didn't do it on purpose, did you, dear?' replied, 'No'" and cold-bloodedly "raised a rock and smashed her skull." James emphasizes the gruesome details because he wants to elicit from the members of his audience (and from us, his readers) the psychological reaction of regret. "We feel that, although a perfect mechanical fit to the rest of the universe," the murder at Brockton "is a bad moral fit, and something else would really have been better in its place." But how can a consistent determinist deal with this reaction of regret? One way is to adopt the view of pessimism, holding both the murder and the reaction as elements of a world in which things must go from bad to worse.

> The judgment of regret calls the murder bad. Calling a thing bad means, if it means anything at all, that the thing ought not to be, that something else ought to be in its stead. Determinism, in denying that anything else can be in its stead, virtually defines the universe as a place in which what ought to be is impossible.

Both the murder and our regret are symptoms of a diseased reality. The pessimist takes a larger view than the rest of us: "It is absurd to regret the murder alone. Other things being what they are, it could not be different. What we should regret is that whole frame of things of which the murder is one member," says the pessimist. A peculiar determistic twist on pessimism is its inverse, "a systematic and infatuated optimism like that ridiculed by Voltaire in his Candide," which would extinguish our regrets by assuring us that somehow everything is determined to work out for the best, even if we cannot see how in the world that is possible.[73] Two modern German philosophers, Leibniz and Schopenhauer, have developed theories of optimism and pessimism, respectively. There is nothing inconsistent or theoretically illogical about their views, the problem being a practical one of how we can bear to live with a view that would have us resign ourselves to atrocities.

Another deterministic alternative, which James calls "*subjectivism*," sees experience as potentially increasing our knowledge, heightening our sensitivities, and animating our desires. "Subjectivism has three great branches,—we may call them scientificism, sentimentalism, and sensualism, respectively.

They all agree essentially about the universe, in deeming that what happens there is subsidiary to what we think or feel about it." To the extent that the murder at Brockton helps us understand what happens to the human skull when it is crushed by a huge rock, to the extent that it elicits feelings of compassion from us, to the extent that we become awash with the burning desire to punish the murderer, it might be said to be a good thing rather than bad. So, this is "what may be called the dilemma of determinism, so far as determinism pretends to think things out at all." One "horn" of the dilemma is pessimism (with its inverted twin of optimism), and the other is subjectivism. The second "horn" is as logically **consistent** as the first. The matter devolves to one of practical acceptability. Can we stand to live in a world in which pain, misery, suffering, disease, cruelty, and so forth cease to be viewed as intrinsically evil but must be seen as potentially good, depending on the effects they have on us as perceivers? James thinks that subjectivism is practically more acceptable than pessimism, but he still rejects it pragmatically for encouraging a passive quietism and for disparaging the value of energetic effort.[74]

THE PROBLEM OF REGRET. James repudiates all the attempted solutions to the problem of regret offered by determinism and is now prepared to state his own position, with frequent deliberate use of first person singular pronouns:

> I cannot understand the willingness to act, no matter how we feel, without the belief that acts are really good and bad. I cannot understand the belief that an act is bad, without regret at its happening. I cannot understand regret without the admission of real, genuine possibilities in the world.

He adds, as a more general assertion,

> Only *then* is it other than a mockery to feel, after we have failed to do our best, that an irreparable opportunity is gone from the universe, the loss of which it must forever after mourn.

He reminds us that he has not pretended to prove anything one way or the other and admits that his indeterministic theory "gives us a pluralistic, restless universe," which a friend of his (perhaps his idealistic colleague at Harvard, Josiah Royce) compared to "the sight of the horrible motion of a mass of maggots in their carrion bed." But, to continue the graphic metaphor, given that such evil "carrion as the

Brockton murder" does exist, it would be even more morally repulsive to believe that there are "no possible maggots" of freely chosen initiatives "to eat the latter up" rather than to leave it to rot there for all eternity. At this point James embraces the word "chance," which he had bracketed earlier, maintaining that "a world with a *chance* in it of being altogether good, even if the chance never come to pass, is better than a world with no such chance at all." As we have seen, meliorism embraces "the chance that in moral respects the future may be other and better than the past has been." He realizes that the members of his audience are likely to feel uncomfortable with the idea of a "chance" universe: "It certainly *is* a bad word to make converts with; and you wish I had not thrust it so butt-foremost at you,—you wish to use a milder term" like "freedom" or "liberty." He explains the "dash of perversity" in his choice of this word:

> The spectacle of the mere word-grabbing game played by the soft determinists has perhaps driven me too violently the other way; and, rather than be found wrangling with them for the good words, I am willing to take the first bad one which comes along, provided it be unequivocal.

He wants to avoid the hypocrisy that would "make a pretence of restoring the caged bird to liberty with one hand, while with the other we anxiously tie a string to its leg to make sure it does not get beyond our sight."[75] There is no "string" to assure that our chances will not fly away; we must try our best to use them as well and as wisely as we can.

Morality

JAMES'S CATEGORICAL IMPERATIVE. In one of his earliest essays (1878) James adumbrates the **relativistic** theory of morality he would later develop: "The truth appears to be that every individual man may, if it please him, set up his private **categorical** imperative of what rightness or excellence in thought shall consist in." This is, of course, a distortion of Kant's notion of the "categorical imperative" as universal and absolute. James proceeds to say that all our ideals "are, at best, postulates, each of which must depend on the general consensus of experience as a whole to bear out its validity." Although people can "attempt to forestall the decision" as to which ideals are worth their commitments, they inevitably do so "at their risk," since they must continue making choices and engaging in actions, even if they be of the drifting sort, all of which will potentially bear practical consequences.[76]

THE GENETIC ORIGIN OF MORAL VALUES. The great essay in which James discusses morality is "The Moral Philosopher and the Moral Life," in which he first distinguishes his perspective from the **absolutism** of thinkers like Kant and makes it clear that he regards moral values as person-relative or as humanistic. For he claims that "there can be no final truth in ethics any more than in physics, until the last man has had his experience and said his say." He also forswears "ethical scepticism" as destructive of the aim, shared by all moral philosophers, "to find an account of the moral relations that obtain." It is a fact that we experience moral ideals, and that fact is the starting point of ethics. James then discusses "the *psychological* question" about how our moral values originate, "the *metaphysical* question" about "the very *meaning*" of basic ethical terms, such as "good," "ill," and "obligation," and "the *casuistic* question" about what standard should be used to measure and rank various competing goods. The first of these questions might better be called the "genetic" question, for it inquires into the genetic origin of moral values. The moral intuitionist (perhaps like Kant) holds that we have an innate ability to recognize values that are binding independently of us, while the moral evolutionist (like Mill) maintains that our values develop in the course of, and as a result of, our experience. James credits the evolutionists with having "done a lasting service in taking so many of our human ideals and showing how they must have arisen from the association with acts of simple bodily pleasures and reliefs from pain." But he doubts that "all our sentiments and preferences" can be so explained. "The more minutely psychology studies human nature, the more clearly it finds there traces of secondary affections" that transcend mere **hedonistic** associations. These include "a vast number of our moral perceptions," which "deal with directly felt fitnesses between things and often fly in the teeth of all prepossessions of habit and presumptions of utility." James tells a story of an imaginary society in which millions of inhabitants are "kept permanently happy on the one simple condition that a certain lost soul on the far-off edge of things should lead a life of lonely torture"; he rhetorically asks if we would not find it "hideous" to enjoy such bliss experienced "as the fruit of such a bargain."[77] The story is supposed to show that human nature includes some capacity of intuitive moral sense complementing and even helping to generate our socially evolved values.

A PERSON-RELATIVE MORALITY. Next, he considers "the *metaphysical* question" about the ground of meaning for our basic moral concepts, making it clear that they are person-dependent:

> Surely there is no *status* for good and evil to exist in, in a purely insentient world. How can one physical fact, considered simply as a physical fact, be 'better' than another?

Moral qualities, he insists, cannot exist in a vacuum but "must be *realized*" in some thinking mind(s). But let a single sentient mind enter the picture, and moral values have a foundation. "Moral relations now have their *status* in that being's consciousness. So far as he feels anything to be good, he *makes* it good," moral values being entirely relative to his needs, interests, and desires. At this point, we have moved to a realm of "moral solitude" from that of a moral nulliverse. "If now we introduce a second thinker with his likes and dislikes into the universe, the ethical situation becomes much more complex" because the preferences of the two can conflict, in which case they can try to ignore or convince or dominate each other. "Such a world, in short, is not a moral universe but a moral dualism," devoid of any single intrinsically privileged perspective. "Multiply the thinkers into a pluralism, and we find realized for us in the ethical sphere" a world like our own "in which no one 'objective' truth, but only a multitude of 'subjective' opinions, can be found." But such chaos of values is philosophically intolerable, and ethics must attempt to impose some order upon it.[78]

One way in which we can do this is by assuming a moral order that is independent of humans and that is the ultimate source of all values, whether this be Plato's realm of eternal, immutable Ideas or Aquinas's **infinitely** perfect moral Legislator or Kant's Reason. The history of ethics is rife with disagreements among such rival absolutist systems.

> But the moment we take a steady look at the question, *we see not only that without a claim actually made by some concrete person there can be no obligation, but*

that there is some obligation wherever there is a claim. Claim and obligation are, in fact, coextensive terms.

This statement sets James's theory apart from all non-humanistic ones and presents a view of morality as person-relative.

> The only possible reason there can be why any phenomenon ought to exist is that such a phenomenon actually is desired. Any desire is imperative to the extent of its amount; it *makes* itself valid by the fact that it exists at all.

So, value becomes a function of desire, and our basic moral terms, such as "good," "bad," and "obligation," for example, "mean no absolute natures, independent of personal support. They are objects of feeling and desire, which have no foothold or anchorage in Being, apart from the existence of actually living minds." In a theory of moral theism God plays a prominent role in the determination of values, but not an exclusive role, so long as there are personal creatures. James makes it clear that whether or not there be a God "in yon blue heaven above us bent, we form at any rate an ethical republic here below," that ethics has "as genuine and real a foothold in a universe where the highest consciousness is human, as in a universe where there is a God as well,"[79] which, as we shall see, is the one in which he believes.

THE CASUISTIC QUESTION. What James calls "the *casuistic* question" in ethics asks how we can best order conflicting values. We want to avoid moral scepticism and **anarchy**, on the one hand, and an arbitrary, self-serving moral dictatorship, on the other, which is a difficult dilemma requiring an objective, impartial test. "That test, however, must be incarnated in the demand of some actually existent person," and that standard must be selected in some manner that is free of favoritism and prejudice. James quickly reviews nine famous solutions to the casuistic question that have been proposed historically (including several we have studied here). Thus,

1. "to be a mean between extremes";
2. "to be recognized by a special intuitive faculty";
3. "to make the agent happy for the moment";
4. "to make others as well as him happy in the long run";
5. "to add to his perfection or **dignity**";
6. "to harm no one";
7. "to follow from reason or flow from universal law";

8. "to be in accordance with the will of God"; and
9. "to promote the survival of the human species on this planet,

—are so many tests, each of which has been maintained by somebody to constitute the essence of all good things or actions so far as they are good." Here we see represented the views of Aristotle (Solution 1), egoism, though of a narrower sort than Hobbes's (Solution 3), Mill's utilitarianism (Solution 4), Kant (Solution 7), and Augustine and Aquinas (Solution 8). "No one of the measures that have been actually proposed has, however, given general satisfaction."[80]

The one James most favors is the utilitarian:

> The best, on the whole, of these marks and measures of goodness seems to be the capacity to bring happiness. But in order not to break down fatally, this test must be taken to cover innumerable acts and impulses that never *aim* at happiness.

James himself maintains that "the *most* universal principle" holds that "*the essence of good is simply to satisfy demand.* The demand may be for anything under the sun." There is no intrinsically bad demand, "for all demands as such are *prima facie* respectable, and the best simply imaginary world would be one in which *every* demand was gratified as soon as made." But because of limited resources and conflicting desires, this is practically impossible, "and there is always a *pinch* between the ideal and the actual which can only be got through by leaving part of the ideal behind." The ethical philosopher must be sufficiently down-to-earth to face this fact. "Some part of the ideal must be butchered, and he needs to know which part. It is a tragic situation, and no mere speculative conundrum, with which he has to deal." He must engage reality without being prejudiced by his own selfish interests. James maintains that moralists should accept as "the guiding principle for ethical philosophy" the rule "to satisfy at all times *as many demands as we can*" while also "awakening the least sum of dissatisfactions" possible. Despite his reputation as a liberal and an individualist, he adds,

> The presumption in cases of conflict must always be in favor of the conventionally recognized good. The philosopher must be a conservative, and in the construction of his casuistic scale must put the things most in accordance with the customs of the community on top.

This is, presumably, for reasons of stability, which has a pragmatic value of its own.

And yet if he be a true philosopher he must see that there is nothing final in any actually given equilibrium of ideals,

and that all values are subject to revision or replacement with evolving circumstances.[81]

THE EASYGOING AND THE STRENUOUS MOODS. James then reviews the key findings of the essay.

On the whole, then, we must conclude that no philosophy of ethics is possible in the old-fashioned absolute sense of the term. Everywhere the ethical philosopher must wait on the facts.

This is certainly consistent with James's stance of radical empiricism. "In point of fact, there are no absolute evils, and there are no non-moral goods," in his broad sense of "moral," as having to do with any values.

There is but one unconditional commandment, which is that we should seek incessantly, with fear and trembling, so to vote and to act as to bring about the very largest total universe of good which we can see. Abstract rules indeed can help; but they help the less in proportion as our intuitions are more piercing, and our vocation is the stronger for the moral life.[82]

This leads to James's analysis of "the moral life of man" in terms of "the difference between the easygoing and the strenuous mood." In the former mood we tend to want to avoid confict, "shrinking from present ill" as much as possible. "The strenuous mood, on the contrary, makes us quite indifferent to present ill, if only the greater ideal be attained" through concerted effort. "The capacity for the strenuous mood probably lies slumbering in every man, but it has more difficulty in some than in others of waking up." Here is where religion comes into play. We have already seen that James denies that ethics is dependent on God. But now he tells us that religious faith can contribute to the activating of the strenuous mood, so that

even if there were no metaphysical or traditional grounds for believing in a God, men would postulate one simply as a pretext for living hard, and getting out of the game of existence its keenest possibilities of zest.

Like Kant, he thinks that the full realization of a "stable and systematic moral universe" requires "a divine thinker" as coordinator.

In the interests of our own ideal of systematically unified moral truth, therefore, we, as would-be philosophers, must postulate a divine thinker, and pray for the victory of the religious cause.[83]

Society

Though his remarks on social theory tend to be brief and scattered, they do figure into his system, and he is particularly interested in the relationship between social progress and individual leadership as well as in the topic of war. The first sentence of his last book illustrates the point nicely, saying,

The progress of society is due to the fact that individuals vary from the human average in all sorts of directions, and that the originality is often so attractive or useful that they are recognized by their tribe as leaders, and become objects of envy or admiration, and setters of new ideals.[84]

WOMEN AND MARRIAGE. In 1869, about the time he received his medical degree (and before the onset of his mental crisis), James reviewed Mill's recently published *Subjection of Women*, which he finds entirely "noteworthy" for introducing the new ideal of equal opportunity. James does not believe that the evils against which Mill targets his attacks are as flagrant in America as in Europe:

The legal abuses are in large measure obsolete; the element of brutality which he makes so prominent in the masculine feeling of superiority is foreign; American husbands are as a rule less sensitive about their wives occupying a position of independent publicity than those of whom Mr. Mill writes.

James suggests that Mill "confounds" love with friendship—"Independence is Mr. Mill's personal ideal." It is an ideal proper to friendship, and the question is whether it is also appropriate to the partners in a marriage relation. James writes,

We think that the ideal of the representative American is opposed to this. However he might shrink from expressing it in naked words, the wife his heart more or less subtly craves is at bottom a dependent being.

It is "security and repose," rather than mutual independence, that seem essential to the American ideal of marital love. James does not say this as an argument against Mill's perspective so much as to emphasize "its extremely revolutionary purport." He recommends that "it ought to be read by every one who cares in the least degree for social questions,—and who does not?" He confidently says, "No one can read it without feeling his thought stimulated and enlarged" and predicts that many readers "will be converted by it." He suggests that Mill may have a "far-seeing" vision regarding "the inexorable outcome of the path of progress on which we have entered" in our recent steps of social evolution.[85]

AFRICAN-AMERICANS. In 1909, the year before his death, James wrote a letter discussing another social issue, advocating extending the vote to African-Americans. He praises his friend and former student at Harvard, W. E. B. Du Bois, as one of the "champions of coordinate & equally essential interests" and expresses the hope he will continue fighting for that cause which will prevent our turning "our civilization into an irrevocable caste-system."[86]

SOCIETY AND INDIVIDUALS. In his essay "Great Men and Their Environment," James explores the relationship between society and individuals by considering what produces socially great individuals. He thinks that the social environment is related to the great individual as the natural environment is related to the emergence of spontaneous variations in Darwinian thought—that is to say, the environment plays a selective role: "It chiefly adopts or rejects, preserves or destroys, in short *selects* him. And whenever it adopts and preserves the great man, it becomes modified by his influence in an entirely original and peculiar way," as new biological mutations can affect the natural environment that nurtured them. To some extent the social environment determines whether an individual will be sufficiently noticed to make a difference. "Not every 'man' fits every 'hour'. . . . A given genius may come either too early or too late" to be effective. He gives some examples: "John Mill in the tenth century would have lived and died unknown. Cromwell and Napoleon need their revolutions, Grant his civil war." Gifted individuals must arise in responsive social environments in order for "social evolution" to occur. "Both factors are essential to change. The community stagnates without the impulse of the individual. The impulse dies away without the sympathy of the community." In a sequel to this essay, entitled "The Importance of Individuals," he holds that it is gifted persons taking advantage of their circumstances who are the agents of social change:

> The zone of the individual differences, and of the social 'twists' which by common confession they initiate, is the zone of formative processes, the dynamic belt of quivering uncertainty, the line where past and future meet.[87]

In "What Makes a Life Significant," as we have seen, James adopts Mill's principle of "non-interference"

with others except for purposes of self-protection and the liberal principle of tolerance in our social relationships. Later in that essay he expresses his confidence in social progress, that "the world does get more humane, and the religion of democracy tends toward permanent increase" over time. This will predictably involve some difficult modifications of the *status quo*: "Society has, with all this, undoubtedly got to pass toward some newer and better equilibrium, and the distribution of wealth has doubtless slowly got to change."[88]

AGAINST IMPERIALISM. Regarding international relations, James was a pacifist and a vice president of an Anti-Imperialist League. This put him at odds with Theodore Roosevelt, his former student. Near the turn of the century, James attacks his former student's apparently undiscriminating militarism as an "abstract war-worship." Earlier that same year (1899), James had already written in protest against what he calls "The Philippine Tangle":

> We see by the vividest of examples what an absolute savage and pirate the passion of military conquest always is, and how the only safeguard against the crimes to which it will infallibly drag the nation that gives way to it is to keep it chained for ever.

He expresses sarcastic contempt for the hypocritical rationalizations used to justify such imperialistic adventures:

> We are to be missionaries of civilization, and to bear the white man's burden, painful as it often is. We must sow our ideals, plant our order, impose our God. The individual lives are nothing. Our duty and our destiny call, and civilization must go on.

The reality beneath the veneer must be exposed. As James puts it, "We are cold-bloodedly, wantonly and abominably destroying the soul of a people who never did us an atom of harm in their lives. It is bald, brutal piracy, impossible to dish up any longer in the cold pot-grease of President McKinley's cant."[89]

WAR AND PEACE. In his "Remarks at the Peace Banquet" (1904), James warns,

> Our permanent enemy is the rooted bellicosity of human nature. Man, biologically considered, . . . is the most formidable of all beasts of prey, and, indeed, the only one that preys systematically on his own species.

He doubts that a thousand years of peace, even if it were achievable, could possibly "breed the fighting disposition out of our bone and marrow," for it seems natural that we should idealize war, which provides such "thrills and excitements" to punctuate the tediousness of our habitual routines. "This is the constitution of human nature which we have to work against. . . . War is human nature at its uttermost" propensities. He therefore doubts that perpetual "universal peace" (of which Kant, for example, dreamed) or a global "general disarmament" is feasible, and urges instead the "preventive medicine" of minimizing conflicts and resolving them as peacefully as we can.[90] His most famous essay on international relations, "The Moral Equivalent of War," published in August 1910, the month he died, continues this line of thought.

> The essay begins with a realistic prognosis:

> The war against war is going to be no holiday excursion or camping party. The military feelings are too deeply grounded to abdicate their place among our ideals until better substitutes are offered.

As the title indicates, this is his theme. Modern warfare is too costly and too horrible to continue recklessly pursuing; yet it breeds qualities and ideals that are worth preserving. Unless and until we find an appropriate substitute that will maintain those values without the bloodshed, we shall continue lurching into military conflicts, such as the Spanish-American War (which James calls "our squalid war with Spain") of 1898. He says, "In my remarks, pacifist though I am, I will refuse to speak of the bestial side of the war-*régime*"; instead he focuses on those values and how they may be otherwise realized. Patriotism is a virtuous attitude, to be promoted, as is manly valor. We cannot blame those who wish to make sure that "Roosevelt's weaklings and mollycoddles" do not extinguish such values. And so it is with other qualities: "Fidelity, cohesiveness, tenacity, heroism, conscience, education, inventiveness, economy, wealth, physical health and vigor"—all can be nurtured by warfare and a nation's preparation for it. "So long as anti-militarists propose no substitute for war's disciplinary function, no *moral equivalent* of war," they will fail to advance the cause of pacifism effectively. In stating his own view, James calls it "nonsense" to assume that perpetual warfare is somehow fated. We have it within our power to oppose it and reduce its occurrences, if we energetically work at it. The philosopher's service here is to exercise the sort of creative thinking that will discover that "moral equivalent," and this is the one James performs here. Suppose, he suggests, "there were, instead of military conscription a conscription of the whole youthful population to form for a certain number of years a part of the army enlisted against *Nature*." This would be a program of national service, as opposed to military service, designed to raise the standard of living for members of our own society. "To coal and iron mines, to freight trains, to fishing fleets in December, to dish-washing, clothes-washing, and window-washing, to road-building and tunnel-making, to foundries and stoke-holes, and to the frames of skyscrapers, would our gilded youths be drafted off" to work for social progress. Thus would values of patriotic service, which we now associate with the military, be fostered without the drawbacks of warfare. "We should get toughness without callousness, authority with as little animal cruelty as possible, and painful work done cheerily because the duty is temporary" and obviously beneficial. James concludes by exclaiming, "It would be simply preposterous if the only force that could work ideals of honor and standards of efficiency into English or American natures should be the fear of being killed by the Germans or the Japanese." There must be some other, more constructive means of "awakening the higher ranges of men's spiritual energy";[91] and he believes he has discovered it.

Religion

A JUSTIFICATION OF FAITH. "The Will to Believe," James tells us, is "an essay in justification *of* faith, a defence of our right to adopt a believing attitude in religious matters, in spite of the fact that our merely logical intellect may not have been coerced." He lays the groundwork for his argument by carefully defining "a *genuine* option." A "**hypothesis**" is "anything that may be proposed to our belief," and "an *option*" is any "decision between two hypotheses." To be "genuine," an option must be "of the forced, living, and momentous kind." To say that an option is "living" (rather than "dead") is to indicate that both of its hypotheses are significant or meaningful relative to

---

Hypothesis (from the Greek *hupothesis*, meaning suggestion or supposition). An assertion that something may be the case; a proposition assumed as a basis for reasoning, argument, or action

the person deciding at the time of the decision; to say that it is "forced" (rather than "avoidable") means that it involves an either-or logical disjunction, such that one of the two hypotheses must be chosen and choosing either requires rejecting the other; and to say that an option is "momentous" (rather than "trivial") signifies that it is an extremely important decision opportunity.[92]

PASCAL'S WAGER. James reminds us of "Pascal's Wager" (named after Blaise Pascal, the seventeenth-century French mathematician and philosopher), the notion that we have no evidence for or against God's existence but should consider the stakes of believing or not believing for ourselves. If we believe in the God of monotheism and our belief turns out to be correct, we may be eternally rewarded, whereas we will have lost little if our belief turns out to be mistaken; on the other hand, if we choose not to believe in the God of monotheism and turn out to be wrong, we might face eternal damnation, whereas we will have gained little if we are correct. Pascal's conclusion is that the prudent course of action, given how much is potentially at stake, is to believe in God and act accordingly. James acknowledges that this seems a revoltingly calculating, selfish, and insincere approach to religious faith. As James rhetorically asks, "Can we wonder if those bred in the rugged and manly school of science should feel like spewing such subjectivism out of their mouths?" He invokes the contemporary W. K. Clifford as a case in point, emphasizing the intellectual irresponsibility of unjustified faith, when he says, "It is wrong always, everywhere, and for every one, to believe anything upon insufficient evidence." But then James points out that all of us have to accept all sorts of things on faith with no immediately available confirming evidence. He uses examples that would have been applicable to his ivy-league audience shortly before the turn of the century:

> Here in this room, we all of us believe in molecules and necessary progress, in Protestant Christianity and the duty of fighting for 'the doctrine of the immortal Monroe,' all for no reasons worthy of the name.

It is not argumentation or evidence that generates our beliefs in most such matters—"not insight, but the *prestige* of the opinions, is what makes the spark shoot from them and light up our sleeping magazines

of faith." This does not strike most of us as particularly irresponsible.

> Our faith is faith in some one else's faith, and in the greatest matters this is most the case. Our belief in truth itself, for instance, that there is a truth, and that our minds and it are made for each other,—what is it but a passionate affirmation of desire, in which our social system backs us up?

This is what James elsewhere might call philosophy's fundamental postulate of rationality, and its only justification can be in terms of pragmatic consequences. As a matter of fact, "our non-intellectual nature"—that is, our needs, interests, and desires—"does influence our convictions" in many matters of everyday thinking. "Pascal's argument, instead of being powerless, then seems a regular clincher," by analogy. At this point, James is ready to state the main thesis of his essay:

> *Our passional nature not only lawfully may, but must, decide an option between propositions, whenever it is a genuine option that cannot by its nature be decided on intellectual grounds,*

since the decision not to decide is itself a commitment and, as such, inevitably involves risk.[93] The conditions that we must be dealing with a "genuine option" and that it must not be determinable by rational argument or objective evidence are crucial to eliminate the license to believe anything we may fancy.

EMPIRICISM VS. ABSOLUTISM. James distinguishes between "the *empiricist* way" of thinking, which is open to new evidence, and "the *absolutist* way of believing in truth," which is so certain that it knows as to be impervious to any. We are all subject to the absolutist's recalcitrant sense of certainty. As James says,

> You believe in objective evidence, and I do. Of some things we feel that we are certain: we know, and we know that we do know. There is something that gives a click inside of us, a bell that strikes twelve, when the hands of our mental clock have swept the dial and meet over the meridian hour.

James himself is fiercely anti-absolutist but admits, "The greatest empiricists among us are only empiricists on reflection: when left to their instincts, they dogmatize like infallible popes." Of course, it would be desirable if we could decide the question of religious faith on intellectual grounds. He says,

Objective evidence and certitude are doubtless very fine ideals to play with, but where on this moonlit and dream-visited planet are they found?

As an empiricist, James believes that the only incorrigible factual certainty available to us is "the truth that the present phenomenon of consciousness exists." Beyond that, we should try to be open-minded about our beliefs. The various tests that purportedly assure us of objective factual certainty—including Descartes's criterion of "clear and distinct ideas guaranteed by the veracity of God" and Kant's "forms of synthetic judgment *a priori*"—have all failed to win consensus support.[94] So, we must humbly and honestly accept the fallibility of our own factual beliefs.

KNOWING TRUTH AND AVOIDING ERROR.   James articulates the two great commandments of our cognitive life: "*We must know the truth*; and *we must avoid error*." Far from being identical, obeying either can put us at risk of violating the other. A parting of the ways emerges among intellectuals when circumstances require that we choose between them which commandment should have priority.

> We may regard the chase for truth as paramount, and the avoidance of error as secondary; or we may, on the other hand, treat the avoidance of error as more imperative, and let truth take its chance.

Descartes and Clifford cautiously prefer to avoid the risk of error at all costs, even if that requires forfeiting a chance at the truth. By contrast, James expresses his own preference:

> Our errors are surely not such awfully solemn things. In a world where we are so certain to incur them in spite of all our caution, a certain lightness of heart seems healthier than this excessive nervousness on their behalf. At any rate, it seems the fittest thing for the empiricist philosopher.

Of course, we can simply put off deciding in most factual matters to which the will-to-believe argument does not apply. It does not matter to most of us whether there is intelligent extra-terrestrial life in the universe; so, we can postpone judgment on the issue unless and until conclusive evidence is forthcoming.[95]

VALUE ISSUES.   But James points out that issues of value (what he calls "moral questions") are different.

> *Moral questions* immediately present themselves as questions whose solution cannot wait for sensible proof. A moral question is a question not of what sensibly exists, but of what is good, or would be good if it did exist.

Whereas issues of scientific fact must be determined by the findings of the head, value issues concern what Pascal calls reasons of the heart. "The question of having moral beliefs at all or not having them is decided by our will," rather than by logical intellect. "If your heart does not *want* a world of moral reality, your head will assuredly never make you believe in one." Consider the commonplace illustration of human friendship:

> *Do you like me or not?*—for example. Whether you do or not depends, in countless instances, on whether I meet you half-way, am willing to assume that you must like me, and show you trust and expectation. The previous faith on my part in your liking's existence is in such cases what makes your liking come.

On the other hand, if we put off making overtures of friendship until sufficient objective evidence is available to show that our efforts will succeed, we shall never establish such an interpersonal relationship at all. "There are then cases where a fact cannot come at all unless a preliminary faith exists in its coming. *And where faith in a fact can help create the fact*, that would be an insane logic which should say that faith running ahead of scientific evidence" is irresponsible and immoral.[96]

THE PRAGMATIC BASIS FOR RELIGIOUS FAITH.   James applies this argument to religion, which generically makes two essential claims: "First, she says that the best things are the more eternal things," rather than the findings of here and now. "The second affirmation of religion is that we are better off even now if we believe her first affirmation to be true," because such belief enriches this life. Religious faith cannot be decided on intellectual grounds because no conclusive objective evidence is naturally forthcoming. It is a "forced" option in the sense that we must either commit ourselves to believing in the God of monotheism now or not, with no middle ground. It is "living" for many of us, in that both hypotheses—that the God of monotheism does or does not exist—are meaningful to us at this stage of our lives. And it is "momentous" insofar as it offers us ultimate fulfillment which we may not live to reconsider tomorrow. So for some people, at some times of their lives, it is a "genuine option" susceptible to the will-to-believe argument. Of course, whichever way we choose, we do risk error. But, as James exclaims, "Dupery for dupery, what proof is there that dupery through hope is so much worse than dupery through fear? I, for one, can see no proof." Thus, James forswears the presumption of **agnosticism** in favor of making the commitment of religious faith for essentially pragmatic reasons. He emphasizes that he is not defending irrational wishful thinking, "the faith defined by the schoolboy when he said, 'Faith is when you believe something that you know ain't true.'" After all, if we know something to be false, believing in it cannot be a "living" option. At any rate, when the conditions laid out apply, we should "respect one another's mental freedom" to exercise the right to believe.[97]

JAMES'S BELIEF IN GOD. In his essay "Reflex Action and Theism," James affirms his own supernaturalist belief

> that *some* outward reality of a nature defined as God's nature must be defined, is the only ultimate object that is at the same time rational and possible for the human mind's contemplation. *Anything short of God is not rational, anything more than God is not possible.*

There is, of course, considerable leeway regarding the nature of this God, but two features seem crucial.

> First, it is essential that God be conceived as the deepest power in the universe; and, second, he must be conceived under the form of a mental personality.[98]

THE CHESS-GAME ANALOGY. The last few paragraphs of "The Dilemma of Determinism" confront the problem of how a God, governing our world with divine providence, can be compatible with the indeterministic theory of free chance James advocates. He offers an analogy by way of reply. Imagine that God is a grand-master chess player and we humans are amateurs playing chess with God. Our moves are not fatalistically determined, but we are free to move our pieces as seems fit to us. Yet God "knows in advance" all the possible moves we could make, which are more and which less likely, and "how to meet each of them by a move of his own which leads in the direction of victory. And the victory inevitably arrives, after no matter how devious a course," for the master over the amateurs. James admits that this analogy renders God "subject to the law of time" rather than eternal. But he repudiates the traditional notion of divine eternal omniscience as "only just another way of whacking upon us the block-universe, and of denying that possibilities exist." He prefers to think of God as knowing past and present as fact but the future, in part, merely as possibility, allowing for genuine

human freedom. God does not, on this view, know from all eternity every "move" we shall choose. "Of one thing, however, he might be certain; and that is that his world was safe, and that no matter how much it might zigzag he could surely bring it home at last"[99] in an ultimate victory.

MYSTICAL EXPERIENCES. In his extraordinary book of religious psychology, *The Varieties of Religious Experience*, James defines "religion" broadly as "a collective name" for many different sorts of personal commitments, encompassing "*the feelings, acts, and experiences of individual men in their solitude, so far as they apprehend themselves to stand in relation to whatever they may consider the divine*." We note the emphasis here on religion as personal rather than as institutional or communitarian, the deliberate ambiguity regarding its object, which need not be the personal God of ethical **monotheism**, and the key element of emotional response. Religion offers a different key from that of science "for unlocking the world's" **mysteries**. James regards mystical experiences as among our best evidences supporting religious belief and analyzes them in terms of the four features:

1. "*Ineffability*"—they cannot be described adequately through conventional concepts to those who have not experienced them.

2. "*Noetic quality*"—they provide cognitive insight to those who have had them which seems tantamount to states of knowledge.

3. "*Transiency*"—they tend not to be sustainable for very long.

4. "*Passivity*"—they are not simply brought about by the mystic's own efforts of will.

James considers the question of whether there is "any *warrant for the truth*" of the mystic's beliefs, arguing three points:

1. "Mystical states, when well developed, usually are, and have the right to be, absolutely authoritative over the individuals" who experience them.

2. "No authority emanates from them which should make it a duty for those who stand outside of them to accept their revelations uncritically," since they do not provide objective evidence which is verifiable by others.

3. "They break down the authority of the non-mystical or rationalistic consciousness, based upon the understanding and the senses alone.

They show it to be only one kind of consciousness" and expose at least the possibility of alternative forms."[100]

AGAINST INTELLECTUALISM IN RELIGION. James holds that "feeling is the deeper source of religion" and that "theological formulas" are merely "secondary products." As we try to consolidate religious intuitions into doctrines, we form "**over-beliefs**, buildings-out performed by the intellect into directions of which feeling originally supplied the hint." So reason does play a role, but it is secondary. James attacks the "intellectualism in religion" (of which Descartes would be an example) that tries "to construct religious objects out of the resources of logical reason alone, or of logical reason drawing rigorous **inference** from non-subjective facts." He rejects the old rational arguments of philosophical theologians like Aquinas and Descartes, which "have stood for hundreds of years with the waves of unbelieving criticism breaking against them, never totally discrediting them in the ears of the faithful, but on the whole slowly and surely washing out the mortar from between their joints." The "**cosmological" argument**, the "**argument from design**," the "**moral argument**," and that from popular consent have all been crumbling in the century since Kant's death. "Darwinian ideas have revolutionized" our thinking about cosmic design because of the theory of **natural selection**; and, like Hume, we realize that we experience disorder as well as order, which militates against an infinitely perfect God. To the extent that we are tempted to find such arguments credible, however, the metaphysical attributes of God, such as divine simplicity, eternity, immutability, and self-sufficiency, seem irrelevant to our pragmatic concerns anyhow. By contrast, as Kant recognized, it is God's moral attributes, such as holiness, justice, and love, which are pragmatically significant, to the extent that they "determine fear and hope and expectation, and are foundations for the saintly life." But since philosophy has proved so unsuccessful at supporting either the existence or the nature of God by rational argumentation, James hopes it might take on the new role of moving "from theology into science of religions" and analyzing the data of religious experiences and beliefs to study comparatively their essential features, treating them "as *hypotheses*, testing them in all the manners, whether negative or positive, by which hypotheses are ever tested." Of course, it is such "a critical Science of Religions"[101] that James himself is attempting to help establish here.

BELIEF AND SALVATION. James analyzes religion generically as encompassing certain fundamental beliefs:

"**1.** That the visible world is part of a more spiritual universe from which it draws its chief significance;

2. That union or harmonious relation with that higher universe is our true end;

3. That prayer or inner communion with the spirit thereof—be that spirit 'God' or 'law'—is a process wherein work is really done, and spiritual energy flows in and produces effects" that believers can and do experience.

In addition to these three basic beliefs, he says, "Religion includes also the following psychological characteristics:—

4. A new zest which adds itself like a gift to life" and

"**5.** An assurance of safety and a temper of peace, and, in relation to others, a preponderance of loving affections."

James attacks "the 'Survival theory,'" which treats religion as an outdated relic of a bygone era, calling it "shallow" for dismissing "*private and personal phenomena as such*" and only taking seriously the publicly objective dimensions of experience. He values four dimensions of human experience rather than only one: "A conscious field *plus* its object as felt or thought of *plus* an attitude towards the object *plus* the sense of self to whom the attitude belongs"—all four of these should be taken seriously. Whereas different religions vary widely in their doctrines, James holds that the feelings and conduct associated with them tend to be remarkably similar. "The theories which Religion generates, being thus variable, are secondary; and if you wish to grasp her essence, you must look to the feelings and the conduct as being the more constant elements." Despite doctrinal variations, there is a common structure to the thought of

---

Over-belief.   In James, those religious beliefs a person holds over and above the core beliefs common to religions generally; for example, a Christian might subscribe to the over-belief that Jesus Christ was literally and uniquely God, while an Orthodox Jew or Muslim would not

religion. "It consists of two parts:—1. An uneasiness; and 2. Its solution." The first part is a diagnosis of what is naturally wrong with us—for example, in Christianity, the doctrine of **original sin**. The second part is a prescription as to how salvation is possible—for example, in Christianity, the teaching that we should accept the redemptive act of Christ and follow the way of life of which he is a model. James thinks that "the most interesting and valuable things about a man are usually his over-beliefs," and he is prepared to say something about what he believes regarding God and religion over and above the generic features he has already analyzed. He thinks that "the unseen region" of reality "is not merely ideal, for it produces effects in this world. When we commune with it, work is actually done upon our finite personality, for we are turned into new men." This leads him to conclude, "We and God have business with each other," so that the natural and supernatural realms of reality intersect, with the practical consequences of hope for the otherwise impenetrable future.

> God's existence is the guarantee of an ideal order that shall be permanently preserved. This world may indeed, as science assures us, some day burn up or freeze; but if it is part of his order, the old ideals are sure to be brought elsewhere to fruition, so that where God is, tragedy is only provisional and partial, and shipwreck and dissolution are not the absolutely final things.[102]

James distinguishes between "naturalists," who view all reality as part of the natural universe, and "supernaturalists," who believe in an unseen region beyond the natural universe; and he proclaims himself a supernaturalist who believes in a "crasser" or "piecemeal" interrelationship between the two realms. As he writes,

> Notwithstanding my own inability to accept either popular Christianity or scholastic theism, I suppose that my belief that in communion with the Ideal new force comes into the world, and new departures are made here below, subjects me to be classed among the supernaturalists of the piecemeal or crasser type,

as opposed to "the refined supernaturalists" who view the two realms of reality as divorced from each other. He does not believe that religious experience points "unequivocally" to the unique and infinite God of monotheism. "The only thing that it unequivocally testifies to is that we can experience union with *something* larger than ourselves and in that union find our

greatest peace." Philosophers, with their "passion for unity," tend to consolidate that reality into a single Being. However, James writes, "Anything larger will do, if only it be large enough to trust for the next step. It need not be infinite, it need not be solitary. It might conceivably even be only a larger and more godlike self," whose phenomenal expression the present self might be, with the universe being simply "a collection of such selves, of different degrees of inclusiveness, with no absolute unity realized in it at all. Thus would a sort of polytheism return upon us," to which James himself is not necessarily subscribing. Religion offers us no cognitive certainty but only "the chance of salvation." But for many of us this will suffice to render it meaningful and worthwhile. "No fact in human nature is more characteristic than its willingness to live on a chance." (Interestingly enough, this book is subtitled, *A Study in Human Nature*.) James realizes that these statements of his own religious over-beliefs "are unsatisfactory from their brevity," and he promises to add to them "in another book,"[103] which turned out to be *A Pluralistic Universe*.

THE HEGELIAN ABSOLUTE SPIRIT. In *Pragmatism* he analyzes the Hegelian notion of an Absolute Spirit, conceding that it does assure us that all ills are rectified, thus conferring on its believers the "right ever and anon to take a moral holiday, to let the world wag in its own way, feeling that its issues are in better hands than ours." This, says James, is the Absolute's "cash-value when he is pragmatically interpreted." If that were the end of it, James could subscribe to the belief himself, but it is not. As he says, "My belief in the Absolute, based on the good it does me, must run the gauntlet of all my other beliefs. Grant that it may be true in giving me a moral holiday," which is indeed desirable enough. But it also "happens to be associated with a kind of logic of which I am the enemy," because it compromises individuality and **autonomy**. So, says James, "I personally just give up the Absolute. I just *take* my moral holidays; or else as a professional philosopher, I try to justify them by some other principle."[104]

JAMES'S RELIGIOUS BELIEFS. In *A Pluralistic Universe* James does indeed further define his own religious over-belief. He criticizes "orthodox theism" for divorcing God from the natural world, exaggerating divine transcendence (as Hegel's **panentheism** over-estimates divine **immanence**):

> There is a sense, then, in which philosophic theism makes us outsiders and keeps us foreigners in relation to God, in which, at any rate, his connection with us appears as unilateral and not reciprocal. His action can affect us, but he can never be affected by our reaction,

on this orthodox view which undermines any genuine "social relation" between God and us. By contrast, both absolute idealism and James's pragmatic pluralism identify humans with the divine substance.

> But whereas absolutism thinks that the said substance becomes fully divine only in the form of totality, and is not its real self in any form but the *all*-form, the pluralistic view which I prefer to adopt is willing to believe that there may ultimately never be an all-form at all, that the substance of reality may never get totally collected, that some of it may remain outside of the largest combination of it ever made, and that a distributive form of reality, the *each*-form, is logically as acceptable and empirically as probable as the all-form.

James maintains "that there is a God but that he is finite, either in power or in knowledge, or in both at once." (Remember that the master-chess-player analogy rendered God temporal, rather than eternal, and limited divine knowledge of the future to possibilities rather than to pure facts.) He embraces "a pluralistic panpsychic view of the universe," in which there is a community of social relationships among multiple personal life-forms, including God's and ours. "We are indeed internal parts of God and not external creations, on any possible reading of the panpsychic system." To that extent he agrees with Hegelian idealism against orthodox theism's view of God as radically other. "Yet because God is not the absolute, but is himself a part when the system is conceived pluralistically," monism's view of God as absorbing all finite individuality should be rejected.

> Having an environment, being in time, and working out a history just like ourselves, he escapes from the foreignness from all that is human, of the static timeless perfect absolute.[105]

(James can be viewed here as contributing to the development of what would become process theology.)

Thus everything, including God, can be seen as environmentally related to at least some other things in reality, though nothing encompasses everything else, as in monism. "Things are 'with' one another in many ways, but nothing includes everything, or dominates over everything. The word 'and' trails along after every sentence," so that there is never a definitive conclusion in our experience. " 'Ever not quite' has to be said of the best attempts made anywhere in the universe at attaining all-inclusiveness. The pluralistic world is thus more like a federal republic than like an empire." Reality is both one (a "universe") and many (a "multiverse") from different points of view, its unity never obliterating its multiplicity but remaining what James calls "the strung-along type" of continuity. The view of things as intrinsically related to at least some other things distinguishes his "radical" empiricism from "the bugaboo empiricism of the traditional rationalist critics" like Hobbes and Hume, which chops "up experience into atomistic sensations, incapable of union with one another" unless and until that is artificially achieved by some knowing mind. We should notice that James never claims to have disproved the theory of monism or to have proved that of pluralism. He says, "The world *may*, in the last resort, be a block-universe; but on the other hand it *may* be a universe only strung-along, not rounded in and closed." He does articulate what is at stake if we accept either theory and indicates his reasons for preferring the latter to the former. But ultimately, it is a matter of belief rather than of knowledge, and he offers us his "faith-ladder" to illustrate the genesis and evolution of practical belief. We start with an idea, regardless of how or why it arose, and wonder whether it is true. Since "it is not self-contradictory," we realize that it "*might* be true somewhere." Next, we see that it "*may* be true" for us "here and now." Then we think that "it would be *well if it were true*, it *ought* to be true." From there we become sufficiently persuaded to think that it "*must* be true." Finally, we decide that it "shall be *held for true*" for us and act accordingly. In some cases, our belief, culminating in action, can help to make it true. "Not one step in this process is logical. . . . It is life exceeding logic, it is the practical reason for which the theoretic reason finds arguments after the conclusion is once there." In this case it can be used to generate the belief in pluralistic theism.[106]

James's most personal statement of his religious beliefs is in a questionnaire he filled out in 1904. He says that religion involves a belief in "a *social* reality," that God combines ideals and causal efficacy, that his personal God "must be cognizant and responsive in some way." He says,

> Religion means primarily a universe of spiritual relations surrounding the earthly practical ones, not merely relations of "value," but agencies and their activities.

His belief is based on neither logical argumentation nor his own personal religious experience, but on psychological "need." He says that he thinks of God "as a more powerful ally of my own ideals." He accepts the testimony of others who claim to have experienced God, although he has never had such a personal experience himself. He cannot pray without feeling "foolish and artificial." He has never "keenly" believed in immortality, but he does so more strongly in his old age than earlier. Furthermore, he does not accept the Bible as authoritative in religious matters, finding it "so human a book" as not to allow for "divine authorship."[107]

Immortality

James thinks that most of us would identify "personal immortality" with the crucial pragmatic difference potentially made by the God of ethical theism, focusing on the rewards and punishments due a person, after the death of his body, for the way he lived this life:

> Religion, in fact, for the great majority of our own race *means* immortality, and nothing else. God is the producer of immortality; and whoever has doubts of immortality is written down as an **atheist** without farther trial.

James admits that he regards the issue as

> a secondary point. If our ideals are only cared for in 'eternity,' I do not see why we might not be willing to resign their care to other hands than ours. Yet I sympathize with the urgent impulse to be present ourselves.[108]

IMMORTALITY IN GENERAL. As he wrote a single famous essay on the issues of freedom and morality (unlike the many important works he produced on God), there is a single crucial treatment of this fourth "postulate of rationality," his Ingersoll Lecture, "Human Immortality," first published in 1898. In the preface to its second edition he limits his focus from "immortality in general" to the project of "showing it to be *not incompatible* with the brain-function theory of our present mundane consciousness. I hold that it is so compatible, and compatible moreover in fully individualized form." Near the beginning of his lecture James admits that his "own personal feeling about

immortality has never been of the keenest order" but says he realizes that other people are vitally concerned about it. The lecture itself is structured as responses to two possible objections against belief in immortality.[109]

A FIRST OBJECTION ANSWERED. The first objection rises from the findings of contemporary science, which has supposedly established "that our inner life is a function of that famous material, the so-called 'gray matter' of our cerebral convolutions" of the brain. If consciousness is a function of brain states, as physiologists claim, the problem can be easily crystallized: "How can the function possibly persist after its organ has undergone decay?" James, "as a physiological psychologist," does accept "the great psycho-physiological formula: *Thought is a function of the brain*"; and he asks his audience to do so as well. "The question is, then, Does this doctrine logically compel us to disbelieve in immortality?" He wants to argue that it does not. But, in order to do so, he must distinguish different types of functions. The most common sort is the "*productive* function," as when a poet's activity produces a sonnet or when a seed germinating in the soil and sunlight produces a plant. James admits that immortality must be abandoned as impossible if consciousness is a function of the brain in this productive sense. But, he points out, there are at least two other sorts of functions we experience: "We have also releasing or permissive function; and we have transmissive function." Let us briefly consider an example of each. "The trigger of a crossbow has a releasing function: it removes the obstacle that holds the string, and lets the bow fly back to its natural shape," which produces the flight of the arrow, as the trigger itself does not. "In the case of a colored glass, a prism, or a refracting lens, we have transmissive function," since they transmit light without producing it. James continues, "My thesis now is this: that, when we think of the law that thought is a function of the brain, we are not required to think of productive function only; *we are entitled also to consider permissive or transmissive function*," neither of which rules out immortality as productive functioning does. "Suppose, for example, that the whole universe of material things—the furniture of earth and choir of heaven—should turn out to be a mere surface-veil of phenomena, hiding and keeping back the world of genuine realities."

Imagine that our physiological experience involves transmitting "or refracting the one infinite Thought which is the sole reality into those millions of finite streams of consciousness known to us as our private selves." Thoughts and experiences that have come to be ours through this process need not evaporate when the brain dies and that particular sequence of transmission ceases. What has been transmitted through our brains might go on to be otherwise expressed. Perhaps "that special stream of consciousness" that we now call ours will lose its personal identity. "But the sphere of being that supplied the consciousness would still be intact; and in that more real world with which, even whilst here, it was continuous, the consciousness might, in ways unknown to us, continue still." Thought, as we know it now, would still be a function of the brain; but the latter would be transmitting rather than producing the former. And on this view the possibility of that thought surviving the death of the brain would be preserved. This transmission theory has other advantages as well. It helps us get around the thorny problem of how matter can possibly produce mind. Second, it helps make sense of the experiences of the "rising and lowering of a psycho-physical threshold" of consciousness, since sometimes the brain can be transmitting more effectively than at other times. And, third, it connects with extra-sensory psychic experience, as "the production-theory" fails to do. James says that Kant's ideas of the relation between the noumenal self and the phenomenal body "come singularly close to those of our own transmission theory." He considers but refuses to tackle the question of whether this transmission theory supports the hope that "anything like those sweet streams of feeling which we know" as our own personal consciousnesses might survive "when the finiting organ drops away, and our several spirits revert to their original source and resume their unrestricted condition."[110]

A Second Objection Answered. Instead, he moves on to the second objection, that immortality would preserve an "incredible and intolerable number of beings." If any living consciousness is to live on, why should not all such creatures do so? "So that a faith in immortality, if we are to indulge it, demands of us nowadays a scale of representation so stupendous that our imagination faints before it." We might

be quite content that those with whom we closely identify should survive, but what of people we condemn as brutal primitives, and what about nonhuman, inferior species? James thinks this conceit is the result of "an invincible blindness" that makes us fail to recognize "the inner significance of alien lives" and set ourselves up as standards of worthiness. But, as a pluralist, James values the unique contribution represented by each distinct consciousness and thinks that the concern about "an over-peopled Heaven is a purely subjective and illusory notion, a sign of human incapacity, a remnant of the old narrow-hearted **aristocratic**" prejudice. In the name of sympathetic tolerance we should be open to the possibility that all living things have as serious a claim on immortality as we would make for our own.[111]

Fulfillment

The Pursuit of Happiness. In the lecture "Healthy-Mindedness" in *The Varieties of Religious Experience*, James says,

> If we were to ask the question: 'What is human life's chief concern?' one of the answers we should receive would be: 'It is happiness.' How to gain, how to keep, how to recover happiness, is in fact for most men at all times the secret motive of all they do, and of all they are willing to endure.

On this view, then, we are all natural utilitarians, served by Mill as our spokesman. To the happy person evil and sorrow seem relatively foreign and abstract. The healthy-minded person believes in (and is committed to) their gradual replacement by happiness. "The idea of a universal evolution lends itself to a doctrine of general meliorism and progress,"[112] such as Mill subscribed to and James himself endorses, so long as we strive to help to realize it.

No Universal Formula. Perhaps the best source for James's treatment of human fulfillment is his essay, "Is Life Worth Living?" He begins by offering "the jocose answer that 'it depends on the *liver*,'" and the joke comes interestingly close to capturing his final response that whether or not life is worth living is relative to particular persons and circumstances. The people who commit suicide answer the question in the negative, at least for themselves. The natural environment can provide either happy fulfillment or frustrated wretchedness.

Visible nature is all plasticity and indifference—a moral multiverse, as one might call it, and not a moral universe. To such a harlot we owe no allegiance; with her as a whole we can establish no moral communion; and we are free in our dealings with her several parts to obey or destroy, and to follow no law but that of prudence in coming to terms with such of her particular features as will help us to our private ends.

There is no **natural law** imperative to accept life passively as it is dealt us. Each of us must judge whether life offers fulfillment and what we should do if it does not. This includes the right to "step out of life whenever you please." But the acceptance of adversity might be rational to the extent that we "could be *certain* that our bravery and patience with it were terminating and eventuating and bearing fruit somewhere." Where we have no such certainty, submission may seem "a fool's paradise and lubberland," but "we are free to trust at our own risks anything that is not impossible." There may be a wider "unseen spiritual world" giving meaning to the suffering and adversity of human life as we know it now. Of course, this is a possibility rather than a certainty. "So far as man stands for anything, and is productive or originative at all, his entire vital function may be said to have to deal with maybes." But possibilities can bear life-affirming value; and, as we have seen, sometimes believing in a possibility and acting accordingly can contribute to its realization. Believing in possibilities and refusing to believe in them can be equally self-fulfilling prophecies (like the mountain climber trapped at the edge of the precipice). "You make one or the other of two possible universes true by your trust or mistrust,—both universes having been only *maybes*, in this particular, before you contributed your act." There is no universal formula for human fulfillment, but every person must seek his or her own. To the person who has given up on the possibility of fulfillment, James say, "Your mistrust of life has removed whatever worth your own enduring existence might have given to it." James suggests that the reality of a spiritual world might "in part depend on the personal response" which we make to experience. "God himself, in short, may draw vital strength and increase of very being from our fidelity."[113]

REALIZING OUR IDEALS. Human fulfillment consists in striving to help realize our ideals, whatever they may be.

If this life be not a real fight, in which something is eternally gained for the universe by success, it is no better than a game of private theatricals from which one may withdraw at will. But it *feels* like a real fight,—as if there were something really wild in the universe which we, with all our idealities and faithfulnesses, are needed to redeem.

As long as evil, pain, misery, ignorance, and disease, on the one hand, coexist with free choice, personal commitment, initiative, effort, and moral values, on the other, melioristic progress offers us possibilities of fulfillment. As James says,

These, then, are my last words to you: Be not afraid of life. Believe that life *is* worth living, and your belief will help create the fact.[114]

We should not expect to be handed personal fulfillment as a finished product, but we are free to work at producing it for ourselves and for others.

REFLECTIONS

Perhaps the first thing one notices about James's philosophy, as opposed to that of almost all other thinkers, is the vivid, vibrant verve of its style. He has been criticized for writing in the language of the marketplace (or even in that of the streets) rather than in the manner of the academy; but this renders his work more literary than that of any other thinker considered here thus far after Plato. In terms of the content of his thought, it develops a more attractive version of empiricism than those of Hobbes and Hume, because it is less atomistic in recognizing that we experience objects as related rather than as "loose and separate." But it does not escape the theoretical and practical relativism of those earlier theories. James offers a superb critique of and alternative to traditional rationalism, especially in its absolutist Hegelian form, but fails to appreciate the similarity (we might even dare to suggest the indebtedness) of his own philosophy to Kant's, as, for example, in the crucial notion of "postulates of rationality." In many ways Jamesian pragmatism can be viewed as a more generalized version of Mill's utilitarianism, and James has the relative advantage (indeed over every other thinker we have covered thus far) of framing his philosophical system from the background of a professional psychologist.

REALITY. He presents a rich and complex theory of reality, which has the advantages of viewing it as (at least partially) connected rather than as atomistic, as operative in different realms of experience, and as influenced by the values of those of us who experience it. He does a sophisticated job of showing how the world can be both one and many, in different respects. His view of mental categories that we learn and continue to apply to reality, because doing so provides us with the sentiment of rationality, is attractive and compatible with the Kantian theory of structures of the mind, except for the important issue of whether they are innate or acquired through experience. His theory of meliorism seems far more conducive to our energetic transactions with reality than either deterministic optimism or fatalistic pessimism could be.

BODIES.   Second, James may be correct (with Hume and Kant) that bodies are not knowable (by us) in themselves. But his pragmatic theory allows him to emphasize (more effectively than Hume or Kant could) how little this matters for any reasonable purposes of our lives. His Millian argument for the reality of other minds based on the observed behaviors of bodies may be disappointing, but there does not seem to be any good reason to expect that we should have evidence that is independent of bodily actions. Finally, his choice of theism over materialism as ultimate metaphysical explanation is appropriately forward-looking (oriented to practical consequences for the future) rather than backward-looking (focused on theoretical evidence drawn from the past).

PERSONALITY.   His theory of personality, our third topic, has more depth of insight and experiential justification than that of any other thinker we are considering. As one of the founding fathers of the new empirical psychology that was splitting off from philosophical speculation to become a social science, James was arguably the most important living psychologist for that decade between the publication of his *Principles* and the turn of the century (when Freud started publishing his great works). His characterizations of the stream of consciousness and the empirical self are brilliant landmarks of psychological analysis, which still ring true today. By contrast, his discussion of the pure Ego is more interesting for its tracing of the disappearance of the soul from philosophical psychology since about the time of Hume (and largely due to Hume's influence) than for its substituting of "appropriative Thought" for a thinker, which merely

duplicates Hume's problem of explaining how Thought itself can be personal, can remember, can appropriate, and so forth. If Thought is transmitted rather than produced by the brain, as James later seems to hold, the mystery becomes even more perplexing. His treatment of belief is a fine extension of Humean theory by means of pragmatic interests and values. His view of emotions as our feelings of bodily changes, rather than as their causes, is provocative, but it remains counterintuitive more than a century after he presented it. His denial of consciousness as a substantive entity and reduction of consciousness to a process of awareness is a logical conclusion of the trend in philosophical psychology from Hume on; but this denial seems unsatisfying to the extent that it leaves open the issue concerning of what consciousness is a process and in that it fails to answer the question of how consciousness occurs. (For example, if it is a process of the brain, how can a physical organ either produce or transmit mental awareness?) James's theory of "pure experience" is a good example of his occasionally baffling conceptual imprecision.

KNOWLEDGE.   Fourth, his theory of knowledge as involving both acquaintance and analysis is valuable, as is his use of the Kantian notion of "postulates of rationality." But he is too quick to dismiss the question of whether the mind can incorrigibly have certain factual knowledge (what Kant calls synthetic *a priori*) because of his aversion to anything innate that might pave the road to rationalism or idealism. His pragmatic insight into the need for acceptable theories to provide a "sentiment of rationality," rather than merely to pass logical muster, seems correct, as does his notion that sometimes faith can contribute to its own verification, although, until that occurs, we are dealing with subjective belief rather than objective knowledge. His own theory of knowledge, as he recognizes, is not impartial but leans heavily towards the "tough-minded" approach of empiricism and away from the "tender-minded" approach of rationalism, rather than being more middle-of-the-road like Kant's. Thus, he cannot deliver the grounds for any universal and necessary knowledge, such as Kant's theory provides, any more than Hume or Mill could. If an epistemology is to forswear any absolute factual Truth and portray all truths as relative to knowing minds, as James's does, then we need something like the pragmatic principle to furnish some semblance of objectivity; on the other hand, it threatens to collapse the distinction between what is usefully believed and what is known to be true. To characterize knowledge in terms of "beneficial" or "satisfactory" relations with fact is to introduce intractably subjective judgments; and it is difficult to substantiate such judgments without some objective criteria of beneficial satisfactoriness.

FREEDOM.   As for our fifth topic, James's discussion of freedom may be the best in the entire history of philosophy up to his time. The pre-Humean attempts to prove human freedom theoretically do, indeed, seem doomed to frustration and failure. The more practical approach, initiated by Kant, is far more fruitful, but James explores and explains its ramifications more powerfully than Kant (or anyone else) ever did. Belief in meliorism pragmatically requires indeterminism; and the corollary fact that it introduces an element of chance into the universe does not seem so frightfully alarming.

MORALITY.   Sixth, his theory of morality is relativistic without being subjectivistic, since value is relative to the greatest possible satisfaction of personal desire overall. It is nonegoistic but does not allow for any particular absolute rules or any particular absolute virtues. This flexibility is both its strength and its weakness. It does seem that the particular rules of moral practice are person-relative (whether or not the persons involved be human). And it may be that the only absolute principles are general ones like Kant's categorical imperative or James's principle concerning the maximal fulfillment of personal demands; perhaps the only absolute virtues are such broad ones as caring, commitment, and fidelity to ideals. But it seems wrong to hold that any desire, as such, is respectable and worthy of being satisfied unless it is outweighed by other conflicting demands; a sadistic desire to inflict pain on other innocent creatures merely for our own enjoyment is intrinsically wrong and could not be justified by some cost-benefit analysis (as James's own arresting example of the society kept deliriously happy at the price of one lost soul's permanent misery would seem to indicate). Utility may indeed be a component of moral value; but, like Mill, James mistakenly reduces the latter to the former.

SOCIETY.   His treatment of society (our seventh topic) is thin; and, apart from the remarks on war and peace, it is fairly unimpressive. His pragmatic ethical theory, combined with his tendencies to democratic liberalism, provides him with the materials for a socio-political theory that might look rather like Mill's. But he never carefully develops any such dimension of his system, perhaps because he did not have anything dramatically new to say in this area beyond the great work Mill had already accomplished. But another reason was probably his own distaste for and distrust of big government, large organizations, and society on the grand scale (feelings he expressed strongly in a letter of June 7, 1899). James knows that pragmatism requires some subordination of individual interests to the common welfare, but his heart is always with the individual. His ideas on a program of national service as providing a "moral equivalent of war" are visionary and being considered seriously by the highest level of executive politics in the United States now.

RELIGION.   Eighth, although much ridicule has been leveled against his "Will to Believe" argument, it is a respectable option, so long as the specified conditions are observed. James's study of religious experience is masterful, its greatest flaw (consistent with his failure to deal adequately with society) being its remarkable neglect of the community aspect of religious institutions. His notion of God and humans as collaborators in a common struggle against evil is attractive, while his idea of God as finite will be unappealing (perhaps even shocking) to those of us raised to believe in the infinitely perfect God of Western monotheism; yet this finite God may be more consistent with the fact of **evil** in the world.

IMMORTALITY.   Regarding our ninth topic, James's discussion of immortality is successful as far as it goes—in responding to the two objections he addresses in defense of it—but unsatisfying in its unwillingness or inability to commit to immortality as anything more than a logical possibility. Also, as he seems to recognize, in skirting the issue of whether the transmission theory supports belief in personal immortality, James avoids the crucial point of interest in the topic for most people.

FULFILLMENT.   Finally, his remarks on human fulfillment are also rather thin and relativistic, again defending more its possibilities than its reality. Given the combination of his rich psychological theory and his potentially fruitful system of pragmatism, it is disappointing that he does not further analyze how human potential can best be fulfilled.

* * *

Despite its shortcomings, James's philosophical system is first-rate, arguably the greatest ever produced in the Western Hemisphere. Although not its founder, he did more than any other thinker to popularize pragmatism, the only native American school of philosophy; and, in doing so, he made effective critical use of many of the influences from the history of European thought. In some ways his philosophy seems akin to existentialism—in its emphasis on human individuality, free choice, and responsible commitment—as if anticipating the work of thinkers like Sartre.

Sartre

We have to deal with human reality as a being which is what it is not and which is not what it is.

Being and Nothingness

BIOGRAPHY

Jean-Paul-Charles-Aymard Sartre was born in Paris on June 21, 1905 (three years after James published *Varieties of Religious Experience*), the son of Jean-Baptiste Sartre, a naval officer, and Anne-Marie Schweitzer Sartre. In *The Words*, the autobiography of his childhood, Sartre says his father "was already wasting away with the fevers of Cochin-China," when he met Anne-Marie, "married her, begot a child in quick time, me, and sought refuge in death." At the time of his father's death, Jean-Paul, sick with enteritis, was less than fifteen months old. Jean-Paul recovered, and his mother took him to live with her parents, Charles and Louise Schweitzer, in Meudon in 1907 (the year James published his *Pragmatism*). She "kept house for her parents," who treated her like a child, financially and psychologically dependent on them. Sartre writes, "The death of Jean-Baptiste was the big event of my life: it sent my mother back to her chains and gave me freedom." The boy was pampered and indulged rather than subjected to paternal discipline. As he says, "Had my father lived, he would have lain on me at full length and would have crushed me. As luck had it, he died young." Consequently, he says, using Freudian terminology, "I have no Superego." He regarded Anne-Marie more as "an elder sister" than as his mother. His grandfather, Charles Schweitzer, the most important man in his life, was a modern-language professor, who esteemed intellectual and literary values and who ruled over the household as "the patriarch. He so resembled God the Father that he was often taken for Him." Though grandfather Charles was a Protestant who made fun of Catholicism, the boy was raised as a Catholic by his mother and grandmother, despite the fact that neither of them had a great deal of religious conviction. Sartre describes the disparity between his well-behaved external conduct and his outrageously wicked thoughts, which made him feel all the more virtuous for not acting them out. Around 1909, he suffered leucoma in his right eye, causing "a white speck" in it and partial loss of vision; this would lead to his being "half-blind and wall-eyed." In those early years he had blond curls. His sole object was to please his elders, and he was the center of devoted attention. He writes, "My grandfather believes in progress; so do I: Progress, that long, steep path which leads to me." In 1911, the Schweitzer-Sartre family "left Meudon and moved to Paris," his grandfather having "recently founded the Modern Language Institute." *The Words* is divided into two parts: "Reading" and "Writing," indicative of how the boy's childhood largely revolved around his literary development. He says,

> I began my life as I shall no doubt end it: amidst books. In my grandfather's study there were books everywhere. . . .

> Though I did not yet know how to read, I already revered those standing stones.

The boy memorized a story that was read to him and then taught himself to read by going through the book himself, "half reciting, half deciphering," to match the remembered words with the written characters. He "was wild with joy" at the possibilities thus opened up for him. "The library was the world caught in a mirror. It had the world's infinite thickness, its variety." With this reading access to books, he "launched out into incredible adventures." Books were his link to the outside world. As he says,

> In Platonic fashion, I went from knowledge to its subject. I found more reality in the idea than in the thing.

There developed a kind of "idealism," which it took him some "thirty years to shake off." His lifelong devotion to literature (both fictional and philosophical) thus began. He writes, "I had found my religion: nothing seemed to me more important than a book. I regarded the library as a temple."[115]

In 1913, his grandfather enrolled him in the Lycée Montaigne (a lycée is a public secondary school in France) but became angry over the boy's poor performance the first day and withdrew him from the school the "very next day," quarreling with its principal. Instead, a Paris schoolteacher was engaged to give the boy private lessons. In 1914, Jean-Paul attended a public school in Arcachon and then the Poupon Academy in Paris, followed by more private tutoring. These early attempts at schooling were brief, fitful, and fairly unsuccessful. Thus, he writes, "Until the age of ten, I remained alone between an old man and two women." Jean-Paul writes of himself as "an imposter" putting on pretenses for them and, even worse, he "suspected the adults of faking" as well. He was uncomfortable with his own "unjustifiable body," although his mother kept assuring him that he was "the happiest of little boys," and he was inclined to believe this, having no inkling of his own forlornness. Though raised as a Catholic, Catholicism had little meaning for him and seems to have been another element of his family's bourgeois hypocrisy. His grandfather "never missed an opportunity to ridicule Catholicism," and his grandmother merely "pretended to be indignant" about it; meanwhile Sartre's mother "was careful not to intervene." He writes,

> I was a Catholic and a Protestant; I united the critical spirit and the spirit of submission. At bottom, the whole

business bored me. I was led to disbelief not by the conflict of dogmas, but by my grandparents' indifference.

God ceased to be a meaningful object of faith for the child. As he says, "Failing to take root in my heart, He vegetated in me for a while, then He died." The boy turned to writing for his own pleasure, casting himself in the role of the hero of his stories. It was prophesied that he would grow up "to be a writer"; his mother encouraged the notion, and his grandfather started putting his hand on the boy's head and bragging to his German pupils, "He has the lump of literature." After almost a hundred pages of sarcastic, self-effacing recollections, Sartre writes that by now "the reader has realized that I loathe my childhood and whatever has survived of it." He "wanted to die" but lived for his writing. For a while he heard voices talking in his head, as if he had a second self seeking expression. In October of 1915 his grandfather enrolled him in the Lycée Henri IV. In 1917, while waiting for some schoolmates, he tried

> to think of the Almighty. Immediately He tumbled into the blue and disappeared without giving any explanation. He doesn't exist, I said to myself with polite surprise, and I thought the matter was settled. In a way, it was, since never have I had the slightest temptation to bring Him back to life.[116]

In 1917, Sartre's mother remarried (this time, to a marine engineer named Joseph Mancy); mother, stepfather, and Jean-Paul moved to La Rochelle, where the boy entered the local lycée. He was unhappy at school and did not like his new stepfather. He thought of the time between moving to La Rochelle and going back to Paris in 1920 as the worst years of his life. But in the autumn of 1920, he did return to the Lycée Henri IV. The following June, he passed the first part of the baccalaureate, passing the second part in June 1922. He wrote a short story in 1922, which was published in 1923. In 1924, he entered the prestigious École Normale Supérieure. He later writes,

> In a sense the French university *system* formed me more than its professors, because in my time the latter, with only one or two exceptions, were very mediocre. But the system, above all the École Normale, I accepted as absolutely natural.

He thought the lectures "idiotic," he writes, "but only because the teachers" giving them "had nothing to tell us."[117]

He wrote a thesis in 1927 but failed the *agrégation* exam. After accepting the need to present more traditional philosophical ideas, he not only passed the exam in 1929, but took first place on it. During this period, he had been briefly engaged, unofficially, to a grocer's daughter. Then, he met Simone de Beauvoir (born in 1908), who took second place on the 1929 *agrégation* exam. Their close relationship endured for more than half a century, until his death in 1980, though they had no use for the bourgeois formalities of marriage.

In a long interview of June 1975, he says that she has been the central person in his adult life, that what has always been unique "is the equality of our relationship," and that they have been helpfully critical of each other's writings. In November of 1929, Sartre began eighteen months of military service, being demobilized in February of 1931. He began teaching philosophy at a lycée in Le Havre and, that summer, started his first version of what would become the novel *Nausea*. Then in September of 1933, he began a year's fellowship to study at the French Institute in Berlin, where he did research under Edmund Husserl, the founder of the phenomenological method. In 1934, he wrote *The Transcendence of the Ego*, a work of phenomenological philosophy, and completed a second version of his novel. That summer, he and de Beauvoir toured Germany, Austria, and Prague (this was one of several touring vacations he spent with her in the 30s); in October, he resumed teaching at Le Havre. He later writes,

> I was a teacher, because I had to earn a living. But I did not hate teaching, not at all, even though I found it very unpleasant to become an adult with all the responsibilities of an adult.

In 1935, he experimented with mescalin injections, producing depression and hallucinations. The depression lasted for several months; he interpreted it later "more or less as an identity crisis connected with this passage into adult life"[118] (perhaps like James after completion of his medical degree). That year his grandfather, Charles Schweitzer, died.

The following year, his work *Imagination* was published; he also started teaching in Laon. In 1937, *The Transcendence of the Ego* was published and *Melancholia* was accepted by the publisher Librairie Gallimard and published the following year, retitled *Nausea*. He later writes that in some ways the novel came closer to the truth about himself than *The Words*, which was "a kind of novel also," though a

construction in which he did believe. In his long interview of 1975 he says he still considers *Nausea* "the best thing I have done." 1938 was the year of the Munich conference, when Hitler succeeded in grabbing the Sudetenland. Sartre writes, "At the time of Munich I was torn between my individual pacifism and my anti-Nazi feelings. Yet for me, at least, anti-Nazi feelings were already becoming predominant" because it was becoming clear that Nazism was an enemy that would threaten France itself. In 1939, his book *The Wall* and his work *The Emotions: Outline of a Theory* were published, and he was conscripted into military service. This precipitated his growing social consciousness, as he reports:

> I suddenly understood that I was a social being when I saw myself torn from where I was, taken away from the people who mattered to me, and put on a train going someplace I didn't want to go, with other fellows who didn't want to go any more than I did.

He had to come to terms with the loss of the personal freedom that was so precious to him. He writes,

> Through this mobilization I had to encounter the negation of my freedom in order to become aware of the weight of the world and my ties with all the others and their ties with me.

In 1940, his *Psychology of Imagination* was published, and he was awarded a prize for *The Wall*. On June 21, 1940, when the Germans invaded France, he was taken prisoner of war with other soldiers from his unit and "experienced the profound alienation of captivity." This period was a "turning point" in his life, giving him a sense of solidarity with others, as he reports:

> It was then, if you like, that I abandoned my prewar individualism and the idea of the pure individual and adopted the social individual and socialism.[119]

In March of 1941, he escaped from the prison camp, posing as a civilian. The next month, he resumed teaching in Neuilly and started the Socialism and Liberty resistance group. He experienced the challenge of courage and the romance of true heroism. He later comments that

> the militant in the Resistance who was caught and tortured became a myth for us. Such militants existed, of course, but they represented a sort of personal myth as well. Would we be able to hold out against torture too?

In October, he began teaching at the Lycée Condorcet and dissolved Socialism and Liberty. In 1943, *The Flies* and *Being and Nothingness* were published; the latter he later analyzes as "a rationalist philosophy of consciousness" and "a monument of rationality." In May of 1944, his play *No Exit* premiered; it was published the following year. He later says that it was not just a fictional attempt "to 'repeat' *Being and Nothingness* in different words,"[120] but certain themes of his existential philosophy did carry over into the literary works of that period.

In July 1944 (following the Allied landings at Normandy), he and de Beauvoir escaped from Paris, after which he formed the editorial board for a new publication called *Modern Times*. In 1945, *The Age of Reason* (written 1938–41) was published, his stepfather died, and he refused the individual attention of the Legion of Honor. He visited America for several months and then returned to France. After the end of the war in Europe he vacationed with his widowed mother in the country. Thanks to his wartime experiences, he had become political. He says, "Before the war I thought of myself simply as an individual. I was not aware of any ties between my individual existence and the society I was living in." He thought of himself then as "a 'man alone,' an individual who opposes society through the independence of his thinking but who owes nothing to society and whom society cannot affect, because he is free." Before the war he "had no political opinions" and "did not vote." He lived to write and "did not see writing as a social activity." This had changed by the end of the war.[121] The first issue of *Modern Times* appeared in 1945.

In October of that same year Sartre delivered his famous lecture, "Existentialism Is a Humanism," in Paris at the Club Maintenant; this was the lecture that popularized existentialism (as James's lecture at Berkeley in 1898 had launched pragmatism as a popular philosophical movement). The existential philosophy was becoming the intellectual rage; the lecture was published in 1946, and he lectured on existentialism in Switzerland (as he had in Belgium the year before). In October of 1946, he moved into an apartment with his mother. His play *The Respectful Prostitute* premiered that same year. The following year, his *What Is Literature?* was serialized in *Modern Times*, and he started writing his play *Dirty Hands*, which premiered and was published in 1948. He participated in the founding of the R.D.R., a political action group for leftist militants. By the end of that year, the Vatican had

placed Sartre's works on its Index of Forbidden Books. In 1949, he convened (and subsidized) a meeting of the R.D.R. but then resigned from it before the end of that year.

In 1950, Sartre denounced the Soviet labor camps, and during the spring he visited the Sahara and other parts of Africa. He was rereading works of Karl Marx. As he later says,

> When I discovered the class struggle, this was a *true* discovery, in which I now believe totally, in the very form of the descriptions which Marx gave of it. Only the epoch has changed; otherwise it is the same struggle with the same classes and the same road to victory.[122]

The next year, his play *The Devil and the Good Lord* premiered and was published. In 1952, the first two parts of *The Communists and Peace* were published in *Modern Times*. He later says,

> I remained close to the Communists for four years, but my ideas weren't the same as theirs, and they knew it. They made use of me without becoming too involved, and they suspected that if something like Budapest happened, I would quit—which I did

when the Soviets invaded Hungary in 1956. Early in 1954, the third part of *The Communists and Peace* was published in *Modern Times*; and in May he attended a meeting of the World Peace Conference in Berlin. Later that year, he visited the Soviet Union for the first time and became vice president of the Franco-Soviet Association. He later admits to lying after that "first visit to the U.S.S.R. in 1954," to "saying nice things about the U.S.S.R.," about which his ideas were confused. In early 1955, *Modern Times* came out in support of the Algerian rebels against French colonialism. In 1956, he participated in a Communist-organized cultural congress in Venice, but later he condemned the Soviet invasion of Hungary, breaking with the Communists[123] and quitting the Franco-Soviet Association. He was coming to realize that the Soviet Union's invasion was the act "of an imperialist power" and was "essentially inspired by its antagonistic relations with the United States, and not by a principle of respect, of equality, vis-a-vis other socialist states."[124] That year, he had met Arlette El Kaim, who would later become his adopted daughter.

In 1957, Sartre went to Poland for the Polish premiere of *The Flies* and "started writing his *Critique of*

Dialectical Reason," which came to consume all his time. As he later reports,

> I worked on it ten hours a day, taking corydrane—in the end I was taking twenty pills a day. I really felt that this book had to be finished. The amphetamines increased the speed of my thinking and writing so that it was at least three times my normal rhythm, and I wanted to go fast.

This book is "a Marxist work written against the Communists." The Soviet aggression against Hungary the year before had led him to believe "that true **Marxism** had been completely twisted and falsified by the Communists." The brutal work schedule and use of amphetamine pills damaged his health. But, in response to a question about that trade-off, he comments,

> What is health for? It is better to write the *Critique of Dialectical Reason*—I say this without pride—it is better to write something that is long, precise, and important in itself than to be in perfect health.[125]

He also protested against the Algerian war and, in 1958, participated in a press conference on human-rights violations in Algeria. He was still hard at work on his *Critique* that year; in October, he suffered some heart trouble. In 1960, that first part of the *Critique* was published by Gallimard. That year, Sartre and de Beauvoir visited Cuba, where they met with Fidel Castro; Sartre also visited Yugoslavia and met with Marshal Tito.

In June of 1961, he moved his mother into a hotel, he and de Beauvoir taking an apartment in Paris. The following month, their apartment was bombed. The next January, his Paris apartment was bombed again, and he moved out. In March of 1962, he was elected vice president of the Congress of the European Community of Writers. He visited the Soviet Union three more times, meeting with Nikita Khrushchev. In 1963, he was back in the Soviet Union again for a writers conference in Leningrad and was received by Khrushchev in the republic of Georgia. That autumn, his autobiographical work *The Words*, the first version of which he had written nine years earlier, was published in *Modern Times*; then he visited Czechoslovakia with de Beauvoir in November. In 1964, he was awarded the prestigious Nobel Prize for Literature and refused it on grounds of principle, partly for fear of being turned into an institution and partly as a protest against its being awarded only to

Western writers and Soviet dissidents. His refusal to accept the prize caused a scandal, and he was roundly condemned for it. The following year, he adopted Arlette Elkaim (she had changed the spelling of her surname), a gifted musician with whom he liked to play duets (de Beauvoir's novel, *She Came to Stay,* concerns Elkaim's relationship with Sartre and de Beauvoir). Sartre was scheduled to give a series of lectures in the U.S. at Cornell University in April of 1965, but in protest against U.S. military intervention in Vietnam, Sartre canceled his visit to America. The next year, he joined Bertrand Russell's tribunal to investigate American war crimes in Vietnam. In May 1967, Sartre presided over a meeting of the Russell tribunal in Stockholm, having been asked to do so.[126] Later that year, he wrote *Vietnam: Imperialism and Genocide*, explaining the tribunal's findings that the American government was guilty of genocide in Vietnam. Back in May, he supported the student uprising in Paris; later, he accused the Communist party of betraying the student revolution.[127] In August, he condemned the Soviet invasion of Czechoslovakia, which he visited later that year. In 1969, his mother died. He protested against the expulsion of thirty-four dissident students from the University of Paris. Then in December, he appeared on French television to denounce the Americans' My Lai massacre in Vietnam and chaired a press conference on it.

In 1970, Sartre accepted the nominal editorship of several leftist publications, viewing "some form of libertarian socialism" as the only hope for mankind and identifying himself personally "with the revolutionary battles being fought throughout the world." The next year, he had a mild heart attack; yet he remained politically active. In 1972, convinced that "every man is a political animal," he agreed to edit a new daily paper called *Libération*. The following year, he suffered a more serious heart attack and was left partially blind after a couple of hemorrhages in his good (left) eye, which left him unable to read or write by himself. He withdrew from some of the left-wing publications that he had allowed to use his name. In 1975, he submitted to the long interview (to which we have been referring) on his seventieth birthday, saying (among other things) that he prefers to be called an "existentialist" to a "Marxist," if "a label is absolutely necessary" (though he does believe "the essential aspects of Marxism are still valid"); that the three things of most interest to him in life are music, philosophy, and politics; and that he feels that he has had a fairly good life.[128]

In 1976, a film on Sartre was released in Paris, and he accepted a doctorate from the Hebrew University, in Jerusalem. In an interview the next year, he declared that he was no longer a Marxist; that same year he published an appeal to Israel to respond to the peace initiative of President Sadat of Egypt. In 1978, he visited Israel with his adopted daughter, Arlette, to try to advance the cause of peace in the Mideast. The following year, he spoke at an Israeli-Palestinian conference organized by *Modern Times*. In March of 1980, he was hospitalized for edema of the lungs; he was only allowed one visitor at a time—Arlette in the mornings and evenings and de Beauvoir during the afternoons. He died on April 15, a day after going into a coma. The French president, Giscard d'Estaing, came to pay his respects. De Beauvoir actively participated in running *Modern Times* for a while after that and worked to promote the feminist movement; but without Sartre her interest in living seemed diminished, and she passed away almost exactly six years after his death. Since 1980, some of Sartre's previously unpublished and sometimes uncompleted works have been published posthumously, including a second part of the *Critique of Dialectical Reason*, edited by his adopted daughter, his *Notebooks for an Ethics*, and *Truth and Existence*, also edited by Arlette, his heir and literary executor. In his 1975 interview he explained that he did not want such works published until after his death because they were incomplete; as long as he was alive, the possibility of his returning to work on them remained, but, if published posthumously, they would be recognized as unfinished works presenting "ideas which are not completely developed."[129]

Reality

With Sartre we can do what has been impossible with his predecessors—turn to his fictional novels, short stories, and plays for an expression of his thought supplementing that of his philosophical writings. *Nausea*, the most famous of his novels, provides graphic insight into his theory of reality. The novel is presented in the form of a diary of an Antoine Roquentin, who, near its beginning, is trying to assure himself that he is not insane. Later, he identifies his self with his thinking and writes of "the hatred, the disgust of existing." As a takeoff on Descartes, he exclaims,

> I am, I exist, I think, therefore I am; I am because I think, why do I think? I don't want to think any more, I am because I think that I don't want to be.

Again, he wonders if he is mad. In a well-known scene about two-thirds of the way through the novel, Roquentin is sitting on a park bench examining the roots of a chestnut tree, which he describes as "this black, knotty mass, entirely beastly, which frightened me," because it provided a revelation of the nature of reality: "It is there, around us, in us, it is *us*." In the course of this experience "existence had suddenly unveiled itself. It had lost the harmless look of an abstract category: it was the very paste of things, this root was kneaded into existence." Here reality is forcing itself on the observer as unavoidably and fully there, in "flaunting abundance." From this perspective, reality appears an insurmountable obstacle to Roquentin: "*In the way*: it was the only relationship I could establish between these trees, these gates, these stones." And he comes to realize that he too is inescapably part of it: "And I—soft, weak, obscene, digesting, juggling with dismal thoughts—I, too, was *In the way*." He considers committing suicide in order to eliminate one superfluous reality but realizes that that would cure nothing, since his death, his corpse, his blood spilled on the stones of the park would themselves be part of this superfluous, unjustifiable reality. He feels the "**absurdity**" that is necessarily attached to himself and everything else: "I was *In the way* for eternity." He feels nauseous at the realization that he and everything else are without any adequate reason for being: "Absurd, irreducible; nothing—not even a profound, secret upheaval of nature—could explain it." His own reality, like that of the chestnut root, is seen as radically **contingent**; everything is superfluous or up for grabs, and nothing that exists is guaranteed. From this perspective reality constitutes a relentlessly oppressive environment: "Existence everywhere, infinitely, in excess, for ever and everywhere." Roquentin is disgusted by the realization that he is helplessly implicated in the irrational miasma of reality and no better than or radically different from anything else: "Every existing thing is born without reason, prolongs itself out of weakness and dies by chance." By the end of the novel he wants to achieve a permanent, stable sort of being, devoid of existential becoming; he imagines this might be achieved by producing a novel, as a finished work that will be accepted and appreciated as a complete achievement.[130] Roquentin's vision of reality encompasses the fullness of being (the chestnut root) and the nothingness of existential becoming (his own consciousness), viewing all of it as rationally inexplicable, superfluous, absurd, and therefore nauseating.

In the introduction to his philosophical masterpiece, *Being and Nothingness*, entitled "The Pursuit of Being," Sartre rejects the old "dualism of being and appearance," which dates back before Plato, as a false dichotomy. "For the being of an existent is exactly what it *appears*." He likewise repudiates the Aristotelian "duality of potency and act," saying, "The act is everything." Being as revealed is phenomenon for consciousness. Reality comprises "the being-**in-itself** (*l'être-en-soi*) of the phenomenon" and consciousness, or "being-**for-itself** (*l'être-pour-soi*)." Nonconscious being simply and fully "is what it is." In itself, says Sartre, "It is full positivity. It knows no otherness; it never posits itself as *other-than-another-being*." In itself it "can neither be derived from the possible nor reduced to the necessary" but is radically contingent, as was disclosed by Roquentin's intuition. It is in this sense that "being is superfluous (*de trop*) . . . Uncreated, without reason for being, without any connection with another being, being-in-itself is *de trop* for eternity." The being-for-itself of consciousness, although also "superfluous," is nevertheless the source of all relations, including those of possibility and necessity. Sartre repudiates the Hegelian notion of "being and non-being as two complementary and antithetical components of the real" as too abstract. Since nonbeing or nothingness must be "logically subsequent" to being "in order to deny it," they cannot be "on the same plane"; nor can negation be dialectically introduced "into being from outside" in the Hegelian manner.[131] Rather, consciousness becomes aware of itself as the source of negation at the heart of being.

Bodies

A body devoid of consciousness, according to *Being and Nothingness*, is a being-in-itself. "It is *itself*. It is an immanence which can not realize itself, . . . because it is glued to itself" and is not free to get outside itself. Unlike consciousness, it is incapable of self-awareness but is fully "opaque to itself." A body entirely is what it is (e.g., a rock) and is not what it is not (e.g., a plant). A body (such as a rock) depends on forces outside itself (such as a human hand) to become anything other than what it is (like a weapon). Sartre is not very interested in discussing the nature and operations of most bodies but does discuss the human body. He observes that consciousness can only relate to its world and can only establish interpersonal relationships through the body. "My body," he writes, "and the Other's body are the necessary intermediaries between the Other's consciousness and mine." Since we never have direct, immediate experience of another consciousness (this is the problem of solipsism, with which Descartes wrestled), it "remains always possible that the Other is only a body." We must rely on significant bodily behaviors to pass beyond this possibility reasonably. In his chapter "The Body" Sartre distinguishes between my body as it appears scientifically (a living organism "composed of a nervous system, a brain, glands, digestive, respiratory, and circulatory organs whose very matter is capable of being analyzed chemically into atoms of hydrogen, carbon, nitrogen, phosphorus, etc.") and "*my* body such as it is *for me*" in everyday experience. My body as I ordinarily experience it is my "primary relation to the in-itself" and the necessary condition of my "being-in-the-world." Only by abstraction can consciousness be severed from its world. "The for-itself is a relation to the world" existentially because consciousness is embodied and the body can only live and function in an environment. Embodied consciousness (which apparently is the only sort there is) experiences its own contingency (as what we shall call "**facticity**") yet "forever surpasses this contingency towards its own possibilities." There is no ontological dualism of body and consciousness, as for Descartes. Consciousness is not something separate

---

Facticity.   In Sartre, the totality of facts about a person that transcend his or her freedom

from the body in the body "The body is nothing other than the for-itself; it is not an in-itself *in* the for-itself." It is rather "the *situation* of the for-itself" as having to exist "as an engaged, contingent being among other contingent beings." To the extent that consciousness must be embodied and engaged in the world, "the body is a necessary characteristic of the for-itself." Sartre agrees with Plato (and Aristotle) that it is the body which individualizes consciousness, but denies that consciousness is a substantial soul that "can detach itself" from the body and function independently.[132]

Am I then identical with my body? Yes and no. As Sartre says, "I *am* my body to the extent that I *am*; I am *not* my body to the extent that I am not what I am." (This will become clearer in the next section, when we analyze the impossibility of consciousness's being merely what it is and its possibilities of becoming what it is not.) My body is a source of facticity, providing parameters within which the freedom of consciousness must function. It involves me in a past (including the circumstances of my birth, my class, my nationality, my physiological structure, my temperament), it relates me to a present environment (the need to breathe and the presence of others), and it orients me to a future (e.g., that of aging and death). "It is therefore in no way a contingent addition to my soul; on the contrary, it is a permanent structure of my being." My body, far from being extrinsic to me, is "the permanent condition of possibility for my consciousness as consciousness *of* the world and as a transcendent project toward my future" (that is, as possibly becoming anything other than what it already is). Consciousness's experience of "its facticity and its contingency" is what can assume the form of a "dull and inescapable nausea," such as that described by Roquentin. Sartre describes three dimensions of the body: first, that in which I exist in everyday life; second, that through which it "is utilized and known" by another person; third, my way of existing in relation to others. So, consciousness is embodied, and bodies exist environmentally. Sartre neatly expresses the point, saying that "consciousness is engulfed in a body which is engulfed in the world."[133]

Sartre is not a traditional materialist like Hobbes. But in an interview in May 1975 (which we have not considered thus far) he points out that a materialist would view matter as encompassing "the for-itself" of consciousness as well as "the in-itself," since he will define all reality as material.[134] Sartre's best discussion of materialism may be found in his 1946 essay "Materialism and Revolution." He accepts the Marxist idea "that man has no salvation other than the liberation of the working class," but he rejects the "monster" of materialism on which it is based, claiming that it "offers the revolutionary more than he asks for. For the revolutionary does not insist upon being a thing, but upon mastering things." Traditional materialism, "in decomposing man into behavior patterns," strips him of his dignity and thus plays into the hands of his would-be oppressors.

> It is the master who sees the slave as a machine. By considering himself a mere natural product, . . . the slave sees himself through his master's eyes . . . The materialist revolutionary's conception harmonizes with that of his oppressors.

Traditional materialism also undermines belief in freedom, which, as we shall see, is the keystone of Sartre's conception of the human person, locking all behavior into the conditioned necessity of a universal determinism. "But materialism is also monistic," not tolerating any genuine diversity of ideas. Yet social progress requires a theory that will "account for the plurality of freedoms and show how each one can be an object for the other while being, at the same time, a freedom for itself."[135] For all these reasons materialism is inadequate, and we must seek a more productive perspective on human personality.

Personality

CONSCIOUSNESS.   It is in his theory of the human person that Sartre's method of philosophical analysis best merges with his early interest in psychology. As he reports in that May 1975 interview mentioned in the preceding paragraph, his interest in philosophy initially stemmed from his belief that it would provide "a methodical description of man's inner states, of his psychological life." In those early years, he admits, "in my mind, philosophy ultimately meant psychology. I got rid of that conception later." Indeed he ends up rejecting any psychology that is not grounded in philosophy. In the 1940s, he reports, "I consider myself a Cartesian philosopher," especially in *Being and Nothingness*. He proceeds to admit that nonhuman animals are conscious, though his philosophical method does not provide the means to analyze their consciousness:

> I know that animals have consciousness, because I can understand their attitude only if I admit a consciousness. What is their consciousness? What is a consciousness that has no language? I have no idea,

he replies. He holds that every "consciousness is a psychic reality" but refuses to define every psychic reality as consciousness. The objects of consciousness "are outside consciousness and transcendent. Thus, it is impossible to say that consciousness is the only reality" that is psychic. Even the ego, the object of reflexive consciousness, is outside consciousness rather than its content. Consciousness is always intentionally directed towards some object(s). Through acts of consciousness we intend (that is, we direct consciousness towards) objects of intuition, knowledge coming later through a process of clarification, amplification, and so forth. As we shall see, Sartre develops an existential psychoanalysis. But, when asked whether it is not a psychology, he responds,

> No. Quite frankly, I do not believe in the existence of psychology. . . . I consider that psychology does not exist except in the sense of the empirical psychology that one does in novels"[136]

—for example, in the character analysis of Roquentin in his own *Nausea*.

EXISTENTIALISM.   With that as background, let us examine Sartre's most accessible study of the human person, that presented in his popular lecture "Existentialism." It begins by acknowledging three standard criticisms commonly raised against this theory. First, the Communists especially accuse existentialists of "inviting people to remain in a kind of desperate quietism" and advocating "a philosophy of contemplation" that is passive and unproductive. Second, both conservative and radical critics charge existentialism "with dwelling on human degradation, with pointing up everywhere the sordid, shady, and slimy, and neglecting the gracious and beautiful, the bright side of human nature" (our brief discussion of *Nausea* above might seem to support this charge). And, third, Christians accuse existentialists of "denying the reality and seriousness of human undertakings, since, if we reject God's commandments and the eternal verities, there no longer remains anything but pure

caprice" in the area of moral values, "with everyone permitted to do as he pleases and incapable, from his own point of view, of condemning the points of view and acts of others." We shall soon see how Sartre answers these objections. But he immediately provides a context for his theory by making it clear that it (like the theory of James) is explicitly humanistic, saying that "by existentialism we mean a doctrine which makes human life possible and, in addition, declares that every truth and every action implies a human setting and a human subjectivity."[137] Indeed, we shall see that this is the most subjective view of the human person extensively considered in all these studies.

He points out that "there are two kinds of existentialist," identifying them as "Christian" and "atheistic" (although "religious" or "theistic" would be a more inclusive label than "Christian," since there are also existentialists of other faiths); of course, these disagree over the existence of a God that created human nature, and Sartre himself is avowedly in the atheistic branch. "What they have in common is that they think that existence precedes essence, or, if you prefer, that subjectivity must be the starting point" for all human beings (*l'existence précède l'essence*). Whereas an artifact—"for example, a book or a paper-cutter"—must first be conceived as an idea in the minds of its inventors and producers before being made to exist in the world of space and time (i.e., its "essence" precedes its "existence"), a human being has no predetermined essence as a person (although she may have as a physical organism belonging to a biological species). Rather, she must first exist, as a conscious, free agent, defining her own personality (or personal "essence") by means of conscious experiences—her thoughts, choices, and actions. By contrast, for the theistic thinker (such as Aquinas or Descartes),

> the concept of man in the mind of God is comparable to the concept of paper-cutter in the mind of the manufacturer, and, following certain techniques and a conception, God produces man, just as the artisan, following a definition and a technique, makes a paper-cutter.

All eleven thinkers we have considered in depth before Sartre have assumed that there is a common, given human nature, despite deep-seated disagreements regarding how it should best be analyzed. For every one of them, as Sartre says,

Man has a human nature; this human nature, which is the concept of the human, is found in all men, which means that each man is a particular example of a universal concept, man.

Here is where Sartre's view is radical, denying that there is any common human nature determining individual human subjectivity. "What is meant here by saying that existence precedes essence" in the human person? "It means that, first of all, man exists, turns up, appears on the scene, and, only afterwards defines himself." Initially, the human person "is nothing"; she can only become "something" as a person by defining (even by creating) her own character. "Thus, there is no human nature, since there is no God to conceive it," according to Sartre's atheistic existentialism (*il n'y a pas de nature humaine*).

> Man is nothing else but what he makes of himself. Such is the first principle of existentialism. It is also what is called subjectivity.

It is by consciously choosing and acting that man "hurls himself toward a future" and determines the sort of person he will be; and, therefore, "man is responsible for what he is," however tempting it might be to shirk this responsibility and blame others. This is "subjectivism" in two respects. It "means, on the one hand, that an individual chooses and makes himself; and, on the other, that it is impossible for man to transcend human subjectivity." These two dimensions of subjectivism coalesce to underline our responsibility for our own choices. Like the Platonists, Sartre claims that "we can never choose evil. We always choose the good, and nothing can be good for us without being good for all." He maintains that this leads to our necessarily implicating all of humanity in our deliberate actions, which heightens the level of our responsibility enormously:

> Therefore, I am responsible for myself and for everyone else. I am creating a certain image of man of my own choosing. In choosing myself, I choose man.[138]

His subjectivism rules out not only any common human nature but also any independent objective values; we must create both ourselves (as persons) and our values, individually bearing full responsibility for doing so.

ANGUISH, FORLORNNESS, AND DESPAIR.   At this point he analyzes the three existential emotions of "anguish, forlornness, despair" (*angoisse, délaissement, désespoir*), which, unlike fear or anger, seem unique

to the human person and can therefore expose what is central to individual subjectivity. "First, what is meant by anguish?" It is a profound and inescapable sense of uneasiness felt by the person "who involves himself and who realizes that he is not only the person he chooses to be, but also a lawmaker who is, at the same time, choosing all mankind as well as himself"; this "feeling of his total and deep responsibility" seems to be the result of a radical Kantian autonomy devoid of any common human nature or objective universal values. Sartre admits that many people are unaware of any such anguish but maintains "that they are hiding their anxiety, that they are fleeing from it" in an attitude of what we shall discuss as "**bad faith**." He provides a couple of helpful examples. The Old Testament story of Abraham believing that an angel of God has ordered him to sacrifice his beloved son, Isaac, can illustrate the anguish of trying to act rightly without ever being able to secure any conclusive evidence of what is the right course of action. Second, the military officer who must decide whether to attack, hold his ground, or retreat is responsible for the soldiers under his command; even if orders have come down to him from his superiors, his anguish stems from having to interpret and obey those orders in this concrete situation.[139]

The second emotion of forlornness arises from our awareness that, in the absence of God and devoid of any common human nature, we are ultimately on our own in our decision making and the responsibility we bear for it. From this perspective, Sartre says that it is

> very distressing that God does not exist, because all possibility of finding values in a heaven of ideas disappears along with Him; there can no longer be an *a priori* Good, since there is no infinite and perfect consciousness to think it.

He quotes the Russian novelist Dostoevsky's dictum, "If God didn't exist, everything would be possible" as "the very starting point of existentialism," insisting that it is also the revelation of our ultimate forlornness. "We are alone, with no excuses," having created our own essences and values. We bear sole responsibility for the way we use—or fail to use—our freedom; and "man is condemned to be free" in the sense that, as long as he exists and functions as a person, he cannot help being free. Again, he provides a couple of helpful examples. He tells of a young man who had to decide whether to go to England to join the Free

French forces in their resistance against the Nazis or to stay home in France to care for his mother. This student came to ask Sartre for advice; but, respecting the young man's autonomy, Sartre refused to say which option should be preferred and urged him to choose for himself, lonely though that shouldering of responsibility would be. Second, Sartre tells of a young Jesuit he met when he was a prisoner of war, whose life had been a series of failures and who interpreted that failure pattern as a sign that he should devote his life to God, therefore, joining the Society of Jesus. Sartre seems to admire him for bearing the responsibility of personal commitment.[140]

The third existential emotion of despair follows those of anguish and forlornness, referring to the realization that we cannot ultimately rely on anyone else for anything. "It means that we shall confine ourselves to reckoning only with what depends upon our will." It is (initially, at any rate) a rather disturbing realization.

> But, given that man is free and that there is no human nature for me to depend on, I can not count on men whom I do not know by relying on human goodness or man's concern for the good of society.

In this vein, he provides a personal example of his own despair that anyone else will carry on his own political struggle after he has gone:

> Tomorrow, after my death, some men may decide to set up Fascism, and the others may be cowardly and muddled enough to let them do it. Fascism will then be the human reality, so much the worse for us.[141]

All three of these existential emotions—anguish, forlornness, and despair—are functions of human freedom and responsibility.

On Objections to Existentialism. Sartre is now ready to answer the three objections raised against existentialism at the outset of the lecture. To the accusation that it fosters a spirit of passive quietism, he replies,

> The doctrine I am presenting is the very opposite of quietism, since it declares, "There is no reality except in action."

He insists that a human being is "nothing else than the ensemble of his acts, nothing else than his life," his unrealized "potential" counting for nothing at all. But in that case the emphasis must be on involvement in and commitment to action. Second, far from merely dwelling on the negative and being pessimistic,

existentialism is characterized by "an optimistic toughness." It is true that existential fiction often focuses on "people who are soft, weak, cowardly, and sometimes even downright bad." But the message is always that they make themselves that way and that they have the ability to make themselves different at any time, if they so choose. Thus, far from existentialism being fundamentally pessimistic, Sartre claims, "there is no doctrine more optimistic, since man's destiny is within himself." Third, it is not true that existentialism involves a fundamental denial of all value or renders us unable to cast moral judgments on others or renders all choice and action arbitrary. Although it sees values as relative to individual human subjects, "what is not possible is not to choose" some values over others. As Sartre says, "I ought to know that if I do not choose, I am still choosing." Even the attempt to sit on the fence, forever avoiding any commitments, is itself an expression of value, which implicitly "involves all mankind," and for which the agent must "take full responsibility." We cannot altogether avoid making choices which have value implications affecting the sort of persons we become.

> Man makes himself. He isn't ready made at the start. In choosing his ethics, he makes himself.

Because our values relate to others as well as to ourselves, "one can still pass judgment on others," even though they do not share those values. For example, because freedom is a fundamental value for Sartre, he condemns dishonesty as undermining any "complete freedom of involvement" among people. Given this fundamental value he has chosen to embrace, he does condemn those who deny their freedom and shirk their responsibility:

> Those who hide their complete freedom from themselves out of a spirit of seriousness or by means of deterministic excuses, I shall call cowards; those who try to show that their existence was necessary, when it is the very contingency of man's appearance on earth, I shall call stinkers

(*des salauds*). If there is no God constituting the source of values, then they must come from us.

> Moreover, to say that we invent values means nothing else but this: life has no meaning *a priori*.[142]

But our creation of values, far from being arbitrary, is a response to our own existential experience. So, from Sartre's point of view, all three of the objections confronted at the outset of the lecture turn out to be unfair to existentialism.

DESCARTES, HOBBES, AND HEGEL.　He acknowledges the Cartesian germ of his theory, presents it as a preferable alternative to materialism, and expounds its humanistic character. He regards Descartes's "*I think; therefore I exist*," the basic experience of subjective consciousness, as the legitimate foundation of all philosophizing, "for outside the Cartesian *cogito*, all views are only probable." Second, the Cartesian approach, emphasizing personal consciousness and freedom, "is the only one which gives man dignity, the only one which does not reduce him to an object," as materialism inevitably does. "The effect of all materialism is to treat all men, including the one philosophizing, as objects." (Hobbes would presumably fall under this criticism, though Sartre does not discuss him explicitly.) But, against Descartes, he maintains that we experience ourselves, through the *cogito*, as being "in the presence of others," who are evidently "just as real to us as our own self." In becoming self-aware, a person not only becomes aware of other people but even "perceives them as the condition of his own existence." This view is similar to Hegel's view that personal identity can be established only in an interpersonal context of mutual recognition. Sartre says, "The other is indispensable to my own existence, as well as to my knowledge about myself." Thus, "intersubjectivity" is a feature of the "universal human condition," which Sartre accepts while denying that it is tantamount to any "human nature." That universal condition is allegedly man-made,[143] each of us contributing to its ongoing evolution by our own choices.

EXISTENTIALISM AS A HUMANISM.　Finally, he analyzes existentialism's character as a humanism. He does not mean by this that man is given as an absolute "end and as a higher value," calling this interpretation "absurd," since the human person "is always in the making" and never a fixed end.

> But there is another meaning of humanism. Fundamentally it is this: man is constantly outside of himself; in projecting himself, in losing himself outside of himself, he makes for man's existing; and, on the other hand, it is by pursuing transcendent goals that he is able to exist.

The very word "exist" etymologically means "to stand outside of"; metaphorically speaking, a person "stands outside of" himself to reflect on what he is and contemplate what he could become. The word "project" literally means "to throw forward"; in positing and pursuing goals, we hurl ourselves forward towards a future that will somehow differ from our present. Our goals are "transcendent" in the etymological sense that we "climb across" our actions to reach them. Sartre's theory is humanistic in holding that man exists by projecting himself towards transcendent goals with no predetermined common nature restricting this activity. This takes us back to his atheism. His brand of existentialism is humanistic rather than **theocentric**. If there were a God that created us, we would presumably share a common nature. Yet, Sartre insists,

> Existentialism isn't so atheistic that it wears itself out showing that God doesn't exist. Rather, it declares that even if God did exist, that would change nothing.[144]

THE DESIRE TO BE GOD.　Let us now supplement this relatively gentle approach to Sartre's theory of the human personality with material from his more rigorous *Being and Nothingness*; this material will be more demanding—but, taken in small pieces, it should now prove quite manageable. Since we have just been discussing his atheistic humanism, perhaps we can begin with his controversial passage on man's "desire to be God." Aware of his limits, man strives for completeness; radically contingent, he yearns for necessity; dependent on his physical and social environment, he longs for self-sufficiency. In creating values and reaching to realize them, man projects himself towards a future which transcends his present. These ideas of completeness, necessary being, self-sufficiency, and creativity are symbolically crystallized in our concept of God. Thus, Sartre writes, "To be man means to reach toward being God. Or if you prefer, man fundamentally is the desire to be God." Although this may appear to define "a human 'nature' or an 'essence,'" he does not think it does so in any way that compromises human individuality, freedom, and responsibility, since the ways in which we can express this "desire to be God" are overwhelmingly diverse and open-ended. Desire motivates free action and indicates what could be but currently is not the case.

> But since desire . . . is identical with lack of being, freedom can arise only as being which makes itself a desire of being.

That is to say, we act in order to convert what is not now so to what will become so. One person works her way through medical school to change herself from not being a doctor to a state of being one; another campaigns for a political cause to change his social environment from what it has not yet become to what it can be (e.g., egalitarian). When such projects assume a totalizing quest for completeness, they take on the character of the "desire to be God," which involves a self-contradictory project of "being-in-itself-for-itself."[145] Thus, we want to achieve an impossible synthesis of free consciousness ("for-itself"), on the one hand, and self-sufficient completeness ("in-itself"), on the other.

THE SYMBOL OF THE HOLE. This takes us to another noteworthy passage, which explores the symbol of "the hole." The inevitable, inescapable incompleteness of consciousness—its "nothingness" or the fact that it is no thing and cannot ever be a thing without ceasing to be consciousness—is symbolized by the hole. After sympathetically considering William James's metaphor of "a river," which "evokes the image of the constant interpenetration of the parts by a whole and their perpetual dissociation and free movement," Sartre opts for that of the hole. He observes that we seem to be fascinated by the desire to plug up holes. The baby sucks his thumb, the older child sticks a lollipop in his mouth, and the adult smokes his cigarettes. Sartre analyzes both sexual intercourse and the eating of food in similar terms. But all such attempts to fill up the holes in our being can only be temporarily and partially successful at best. So it is with the "holes" of our conscious personality, whose "nothingness" cannot be filled with "being" without ceasing to be "for-itself." The attempt to become fully adequate is tantamount to the "desire to be God" and to annihilate our own humanity. "Thus the passion of man is the reverse of that of Christ, for man loses himself as man in order that God may be born," whereas Christ ceased to be merely divine in order to be born human. "But the idea of God is contradictory and we lose ourselves in vain," because the nothingness of consciousness and the fullness of being are mutually exclusive; and God, as the ideal of "an In-itself-For-itself," is an empty symbol. Sartre's memorable conclusion is, "Man is a useless passion" (*l'homme est une passion inutile*).[146] We cannot fill

the "holes" of consciousness without destroying it, as by death or the onset of a permanent vegetative state.

BAD FAITH. Another intriguing passage is that on "bad faith" (*mauvaise foi*), which is different from ordinary lying in that it is self-deception rather than the conscious deception of others. "The liar intends to deceive and he does not seek to hide this deception from himself," as does the person in bad faith. Like the three existential emotions discussed previously, bad faith seems to be unique to human beings and therefore should help to reveal what it is to be a person. Sartre poses the issue thus: "What must be the being of man if he is to be capable of bad faith?"[147] He offers four examples to illustrate its patterns.

The first is of a woman on a date with a man whose intentions are sexual. She wants him to find her attractive and is flattered by his attentions, yet she is uncomfortable with a commitment to a sexual relationship with him. He seductively holds her hand, which she neither offers nor withdraws, preferring to try mentally to dissociate herself from it. As Sartre writes, "the hand rests inert between the warm hands of her companion—neither consenting nor resisting—a thing." She wants to think of herself as transcending that part of her body being held and to think of it as mere facticity, refusing to admit that she is "at once a *facticity* and a *transcendence*" in self-deception. "We shall say that this woman is in bad faith." Notice that Sartre does not care whether she does or does not establish a sexual relationship with the man; nor is it a question here of whether or not she deceives him. Sartre rather criticizes her for her dishonest mind games. Her hand is part of her, though there is more to her than that. Although she has not yet become his mistress nor has she rejected him, she can do either at any moment. "We have to deal with human reality as a being which is what it is not" (in other words, potentially may become what it now is not) "and which is not what it is" (that is, is never merely limited to what it presently is). If a person were pure being (in-itself)—simply what he is and not what he is not, like a rock—then bad faith would be impossible.[148]

Sartre's second example is of a café waiter, who sinks his own personality by playing the role of a waiter too avidly. "He bends forward a little too eagerly; his voice, his eyes express an interest a little too solicitous." Again, there is nothing wrong with a man being a dedicated, accomplished waiter. But the one who is in bad faith is pretending that that is all he is while on the job. "All his behavior seems to us a game. He applies himself to chaining his movements as if they were mechanisms." He tries to lose himself as a person in order to be merely and fully a waiter, as an "inkwell is an inkwell," though he is fooling himself in pretending that this is even possible. He cannot fully be any thing, including a waiter; as a person, he is forever "separated by nothing" from this and every other way of being. In a sense, of course, he is a waiter; but he can never be merely that.[149]

Sartre's third example is of a sad person who puts on and removes his sad behaviors like a mask. This sadness unifies and explains certain appearances.

> It is the meaning of this dull look with which I view the world, of my bowed shoulders, of my lowered head, of the listlessness in my whole body,

following the death of someone close. But it is punctuated by times of denial of the sadness and its concomitant behaviors.

> Let a stranger suddenly appear and I will lift up my head, I will assume a lively cheerfulness. What will remain of my sadness except that I obligingly promise it an appointment for later after the departure of the visitor?

Now deceiving the visitor does not make it bad faith; it is rather a question of whether I am trying to trick myself into believing that I am (simply) sad when I am not or no longer (somewhat) sad when I am. But we can never be simply sad and are always at least potentially sad, so that "the ideal of sincerity" appears as merely "a task impossible to achieve." In order to be either sincerely sad or sincerely devoid of all possible sadness, we would have to be merely what we are (that is, in-itself rather than for-itself).[150]

Sartre's fourth example is of a homosexual and his friend, whom he sarcastically calls "the champion of sincerity." The homosexual is in bad faith because he refuses to admit to himself that he is a homosexual, despite his sexual orientation, history, and ongoing activities. But his critical friend is also in bad faith in thinking that freedom can be reduced to a thing, in demanding (in the name of an elusive, illusory sincerity) that the homosexual "constitute himself as a thing" by reducing himself to his homosexuality. Ironically, it is the homosexual's friend's sincerity that renders his attitude destructive of freedom. "Thus the essential

structure of sincerity does not differ from that of bad faith since the sincere man constitutes himself as what he is *in order not to be it*"; in this case the friend makes himself a critic in order to convince the homosexual to admit what he is so that no further criticism will be appropriate. "In the final analysis the goal of sincerity and the goal of bad faith are not so different." Both involve a person's attempt to deny the complexity of consciousness and its inability to be anything fully and simply.[151]

Why are only humans uniquely capable of bad faith, and what does this tell us about ourselves? "The condition of the possibility for bad faith is that human reality, in its most immediate being, . . . must be what it is not and not be what it is." At some level bad faith must be believed by the person in that condition, since "bad faith is *faith*." Yet, at another level of consciousness, "bad faith is conscious of its structure." So not only is the deceiving person identical to the one being deceived (which is not the case in ordinary lying), but he both does and does not believe something (e.g., that he is a homosexual). "In this sense consciousness is perpetually escaping itself, belief becomes non-belief." Sadly, it seems impossible for us ever fully to be in good faith:

> The ideal of good faith (to believe what one believes) is, like that of sincerity (to be what one is), an ideal of being-in-itself. Every belief is a belief that falls short; one never wholly believes what one believes.

We are condemned to varying degrees of bad faith, as (and because) we are condemned to freedom. Attempting to deny itself, its freedom, and its responsibility in bad faith, consciousness tries

> to flee what it can not flee, to flee what it is. The very project of flight reveals to bad faith an inner disintegration in the heart of being.

In a peculiar footnote at the end of this chapter Sartre writes, "If it is indifferent whether one is in good faith or in bad faith, . . . that does not mean that we can not radically escape bad faith." To do so would be to achieve "authenticity," which he refuses to discuss here.[152] Though good faith be an impossible ideal, he seems to advocate striving for authenticity and to condemn bad faith; and the suggestion that we can "radically escape" the latter is tantalizing.

PERSPECTIVES ON CONSCIOUSNESS. Sartre stresses the perpetual intentionality of human consciousness, the phenomenological idea that it is always directed towards some object(s) or other:

> All consciousness, as Husserl has shown, is consciousness *of* something. This means that there is no consciousness which is not a *positing* of a transcendent object.

In this sense, for Sartre, consciousness is "positional in that it transcends itself in order to reach an object," which may or may not have reality outside of its being posited by consciousness. Since consciousness is merely the act of intentionality, it is not substantial; and the "ontological error of Cartesian rationalism" was the assumption that it is. "Consciousness has nothing substantial, it is pure 'appearance' in the sense that it exists only to the degree to which it appears." In this sense of not being substantial, the for-itself is "nothingness" or "total emptiness (since the entire world is outside it)." It exists and functions only in relation to being outside (and other than) itself, so that it can only interrogate itself through reflection on its awareness of what is other (and so that the Cartesian problem of solipsism is ruled out from the start);

> consciousness is a being such that in its being, its being is in question in so far as this being implies a being other than itself.

In analyzing and reflecting on its experience, consciousness is always (at least implicitly) questioning not only its objects but itself; as Sartre writes, "this man that I *am* . . . stands before being in an attitude of interrogation." In making distinctions through "a process of **nihilation**," consciousness denies certain conceivable identities, including that between itself and the being of its objects, introducing nothingness into its world.

> The Being by which Nothingness arrives in the world is a being such that in its Being, the Nothingness of its Being is in question.

Unlike its objects, consciousness is pure subjectivity and no thing. But this activity of questioning, of distinguishing, of denying its identity with its objects, and of introducing nothingness into its world presupposes human freedom, as is recognized by the Cartesian project of "systematic doubt."[153] It is the freedom and nothingness of consciousness that produce bad faith, which is only possible if consciousness is what it is not and is not what it is.

> Negation has referred us to freedom, freedom to bad faith, and bad faith to the being of consciousness, which is the requisite condition for the possibility of bad faith.

Let us now further explore Sartre's analysis of the structures of consciousness. Unlike the in-itself, which is "a fullness" of being, the for-itself "is a decompression of being," a "nothingness at the heart of being." Consciousness is pure subjectivity and freedom, never ontologically identical with the being of its objects.

> Yet the for-itself *is*. It *is*, we may say, even if it is a being which is not what it is and which is what it is not.

It is real, without having the fixed, determined being of its objects. Consciousness experiences its own existence as contingent, and "this contingency is what we shall call the *facticity* of the for-itself." Its existence is dependent rather than self-sufficiently necessary; it could have not been, it must exist and function as free subject, and it is going to cease to exist with the onset of death. "It has the feeling of its complete gratuity; it apprehends itself as being there *for nothing*, as being *de trop*," the idea so graphically described in *Nausea*. Unlike the in-itself, consciousness, as pure transcendence, is inevitably a lack of being.

> A lack presupposes a trinity: that which is missing or "the lacking," that which misses what is lacking or "the existing," and a totality which has been broken by the lacking and which would be restored by the synthesis of "the lacking" and "the existing"—this is "the lacked."

It is consciousness's lack of being that, as we have seen, is symbolized by the hole; and the impossible ideal of that restored totality is what Sartre has analyzed as the "desire to be God," a perfect synthesis of for-itself-in-itself. Consciousness's lack of being gives rise to desire, through which it is "haunted in its inmost being by the being of which it is desire." Even the Ego "does not belong to the domain of the for-itself" but "appears to consciousness as a transcendent in-itself, as an existence in the human world, not as *of the nature of* consciousness"[154] (more on this after the following paragraph).

Temporality is characteristic of consciousness, its three dimensions being "structured moments of an original synthesis" rather than independent realities.

Nihilation (from the Latin *nihil*, meaning nothing). In Sartre, the denial by consciousness of what is other than itself or even of its own facticity

Otherwise we will immediately meet with this **paradox**: the past is no longer; the future is not yet; as for the instantaneous present, everyone knows that this does not exist at all but is the limit of an infinite division, like a point without dimension.

The past of consciousness "has melted away into nothingness"; but, as it is remembered, it modifies our present reality. Sartre points out that the sense of belonging that a memory has—"or its 'intimacy,' according to James"—does not mitigate this feature of its being "a *present* modification" of consciousness. Our sense of our own past is inextricably identified with the facticity of the human person. "The past, in fact, like Facticity, is the invulnerable contingency of the in-itself which I have to be, without any possibility of not being it." To move to a second temporal dimension, Sartre writes, "My present is to be present. Present to what?" And the answer is, to the intended objects of consciousness, "to the world, in short to being-in-itself," which exists "as a totality" only as presented to consciousness. He says, "The For-itself is defined as presence to being," in the sense (as we have seen) that it always intends objects. The third temporal dimension, of the future, is only as a function of human consciousness. "The future, like the past, does not exist as a phenomenon of that original temporality of being-in-itself." As memory of the past involves a synthesis with the present, so does our anticipation of the future. Sartre illustrates this quasi-Kantian analysis of time as a mental structure with the example of a tennis player preparing for a projected move: "This position which I quickly assume on the tennis court has meaning only through this movement which I shall make immediately afterward with my racket in order to return the ball over the net." Through its projects consciousness envisions a future for which it can act and by which it "radically escapes the present." Here lies the freedom to which the for-itself is "condemned."[155] The dimensions of time have no reality independent of consciousness but are among its inescapable structures.

Let us next briefly consider three of Sartre's earliest works, which, though less important than *Being and Nothingness*, will offer valuable perspectives on consciousness to supplement the contributions of that great book. His monograph *The Transcendence of the Ego* (subtitled *An Existential Theory of Consciousness*) presents its thesis in its very first paragraph:

> We should like to show here that the ego is neither formally nor materially *in* consciousness: it is outside, *in the world.*

Or, as the title indicates, the ego *transcends* consciousness rather than being among its contents. He agrees with "Kant that 'the I Think *must be able* to accompany all our representations' " but denies that any ego "*in fact* inhabits all our states of consciousness." Sartre's phenomenological analysis of consciousness shows it to be intentional (i.e., directed towards objects) and fundamentally "not *positional*"; that is to say, "except in the case of reflective consciousness" (thinking about itself), it does not take "itself as its own object. Its object is by nature outside of it." Even when consciousness is engaged in the Cartesian *cogito,* there is a distinction between consciousness as it is fundamentally thinking and consciousness reflecting on itself thinking. So, if the ego were "a part of consciousness," rather than transcendent, it would be dichotomized into "the *I* of the reflective consciousness and the *I* of the reflected consciousness," subject versus object. Of course, we do have an idea of self; but it "appears only with the reflective act" and as the object or **noematic** correlate of a reflective intention." Nor is there any ontological difference between the ego as transcendental subject and the ego as psychological object: "The *I* is the ego as the unity of actions. The *me* is the ego as the unity of states and of qualities." Against Descartes, Sartre denies that the ego as subject enjoys any privileged self-evident status:

> My *I*, in effect, is *no more certain for consciousness than the I of other men.* It is only more intimate,[156]

since my consciousness constitutes it as my object.

A PHENOMENOLOGY OF EMOTIONS.   In *The Emotions: Outline of a Theory* he relates psychology to the phenomenological method he espouses, saying that psychology "tries to draw its resources exclusively from experience," utilizing our "spatial-temporal perception of organized bodies" as well as "the intuitive knowledge of ourselves that is called reflexive experience" (we have seen James developing psychological

---

Noema (from the Greek *noema*, meaning a thought).   In phenomenology, the sense or object of an act of intentional consciousness

theory on these same two foundations). Thus, empirical psychology strives to be factual. By contrast,

> phenomenology is the study of phenomena — not facts. And by phenomenon must be understood "that which manifests itself," that whose reality is precisely appearance.

A phenomenological study of emotions will do more than collect facts; it "will interrogate emotion *about consciousness* or *about man*," asking what the facts of our emotions reveal to us about the human person. As a phenomenologist, Sartre seeks the significance revealed by the facts about our emotions. He sees his own work here "as an *experiment* in phenomenological psychology," pushing beyond the facts to their significance as phenomena. He discusses the theory of William James describing emotions as states of consciousness manifesting physiological reactions. But, with "all the critics of James," Sartre points out that emotions are "*more*" and "*something else*" than merely "the consciousness of physiological manifestations." For example, in the emotion of fear, he writes, "it is inconceivable that a bodily state perceived for and in itself should appear to consciousness with this frightful character." But also, an emotion is always "something else" than the manifestation of facts, establishing "a certain relationship of our psychic being with the world." As such, it is not a manifestation of fact. "It is an organized and describable structure" of consciousness. In order to understand our emotions, we must grasp their functional "*signification*." Emotions have a "magical" quality, through which "consciousness changes the body, or, if you like, the body—as a point of view of the universe immediately inherent in consciousness—puts itself on the level of behavior," as, for example, in a pattern of "fight or flight." The "physiological manifestations" emphasized by James are mere "trivial disturbances" of the body rather than essential to emotional reaction. Thus, for Sartre, "emotion appears as a structure of consciousness" and not merely as a fact (or set of facts) to be observed. "It has a meaning; it *signifies something for my psychic life*."[157]

FEELINGS, IMAGES, AND THOUGHT. In *The Psychology of Imagination* Sartre discusses human feelings, images, and thought to try to discern what they indicate about the nature of personal consciousness. He gives credit to James for helping to advance "the physiology of feeling" but maintains that "the nature of feeling itself is not known any better" as a result of his efforts. He repudiates the analysis of feelings as "affective *states*, that is, inert contents which are carried by the stream of consciousness." Rather, each emotion is a mode "of self-*transcendence*" whereby consciousness affectively intends an object (i.e., is directed towards it with some feeling or other). "Hatred is hatred *of* someone, love is love *of* someone." As our feelings are identified with consciousness as its structures, so our images cannot be separated from our thought: "The image serves neither as illustration nor support for thought. It is in no way different from thought," its knowledge, intentions, and judgments. Our images are not, for example, merely the building blocks out of which we construct judgments. "In a word: the function of the image is *symbolic*." Through images consciousness tries "to *see*," and thus "to *possess*," its objects, although this attempt is never perfectly successful, since its images inevitably have a "character of unreality" distinguishing them from objects of perception. "What are the characteristics that can be attributed to consciousness" on the basis of these findings? Like Hegel's dialectical act of **sublation** (*Aufhebung*), in imagining, consciousness must be "at once *constituting*, *isolating* and *annihilating*." Again, Sartre illustrates his point with a tennis example. When a player anticipates his opponent's shot and rushes to the net to return it, consciousness is "*constituting*" a pattern of voluntary action, "*isolating*" the projected course of the ball off the racket, and "*annihilating*" its nature as a winning shot.[158] Here consciousness is intentionally synthesizing its perceptions, anticipations, and actions through imaginative thought.

ORESTES, AN EXISTENTIAL HERO. Sartre's view of the human personality as self-creative, nonsubstantial, intentional activity is grippingly portrayed in his play *The Flies*. At the beginning Orestes, the existential hero, describes himself as a "stranger" in his own land; prior to making any commitments, he is merely a drifter without any identity. His tutor wrongly associates his freedom with a lack of commitment, praising him for his relativism and saying that it renders him fit to "hold a chair of philosophy . . . in a great university." But Orestes' hollow freedom gives him nothing to call his own, not even a personality. He meets his estranged sister, Electra, who urges him to take action to avenge the murder of their father, Agamemnon. Orestes first tries to shirk the responsibility for such a drastic course of action, preferring to escape Argos and offering to take Electra with him back to Corinth. But she is disappointed in his lack of courageous resolve and denies him as her brother, so that his identity (in her eyes as well as his own) is tied to his commitments. He wants to develop an identity as a person and to belong somewhere. At first he prays for divine guidance but comes to realize that the gods have abandoned him so that he is forlorn in his anguish and despair. Realizing that no one else (human or divine) can determine his actions and identity, he becomes defiant. He immediately achieves a sense of belonging and ownership when he assumes responsibility for having to act upon his father's assassination, saying, "I must take a burden on my shoulders, a load of guilt so heavy as to drag me down." Electra notices the change in him at once and acknowledges him as her brother. Zeus, the head of the gods, considers Orestes dangerous now that he is exercising genuine freedom by committing himself to a course of action, saying, "Once freedom lights its beacon in a man's heart, the gods are powerless against him." Orestes kills Aegistheus (the king of Argos) and his paramour Clytemnestra (the mother of Orestes and Electra), as revenge for his father's murder. Towards the end of Act II he is embracing his own course of action: "I am free, Electra. Freedom has crashed down on me like a thunderbolt." Meanwhile, Electra seems to be regretting the ineradicable facticity of the actions and worrying that "the flies" or Furies, "the goddesses of remorse," will hound and torment them for what they have done. Near the beginning of Act III she is disavowing her responsibility for what has occurred, blaming her brother, who, by contrast, does accept his own responsibility. Orestes is unrepentant even before Zeus, asserting his ongoing commitment to the course of action he has chosen, proclaiming,

> I am no criminal, and you have no power to make me atone for an act I don't regard as a crime.

He further declares, "I *am* my freedom," accepting even the forlornness that must accompany it. Zeus abhors people like Orestes who exercise their freedom but is helpless to undo their freedom. Orestes tells him,

> You are God and I am free; each of us is alone, and our anguish is akin.

In the most well-known line of the play, he asserts that

> human life begins on the far side of despair

(*la vie humaine commence de l'autre côté du dés-espoir*). Electra has now embraced remorse for the action and surrendered herself to the bad faith of blaming everything on her brother, abdicating her responsibility and her autonomy as a free agent. In despair and forlorn, Orestes cries out, "I am alone, alone." Yet he has achieved an identity and declares himself to his people as the rightful king of Argos. Acknowledging that he cannot stay, he takes upon himself their fears and remorse, saying, "I wish to be a king without a kingdom, without subjects." As the play ends, he calmly strides away, with the screaming Furies hurling themselves after him.[159] Orestes, the existential hero, achieves a unique, self-created personality by means of his intentional thought and action, by formulating his own values, committing himself to them, and accepting responsibility for this use of his own freedom.

Knowledge

EXISTENTIALISM VS. ABSOLUTE IDEALISM. An existentialist ought to forswear the epistemology of absolute idealism, as Sartre does Hegel's. The latter's view of knowledge as retrospectively comprehending "truth-that-has-come-into-being" presupposes a "philosophy at the end of History." But Sartre observes that, as long as humans consciously exist, "History is never finished," so that the idealistic attempt to present epistemology as a completed system "can lead, from the point of view of knowledge, only to scepticism." What an existential epistemology requires is "the singularity of the universal and the universalization of the singular"[160]—universal truth must be concretely and individually realized, and existential individuality must express **universalizable** truth, since all human experience is within the dynamic, constantly changing matrix of ongoing history.

IMAGINATIVE CONSCIOUSNESS. One way to avoid the dead end of abstract idealism is to approach knowledge in terms of concrete images. In *The Psychology of Imagination* Sartre agrees with Descartes "that a reflective consciousness gives us knowledge of absolute certainty; that he who becomes aware 'of having an image' by an act of reflection cannot deceive himself." For our mental images are not merely contents of consciousness; an image rather *is* a consciousness. Sartre criticizes *"the illusion of immanence"* which philosophers and psychologists since Hume have embraced, which "is also the point of view of common sense," and which maintains that mental images are little "likenesses" of objects in consciousness. He expresses surprise that Hume and his followers fail to sense "the radical incongruity between consciousness and this conception of the image." If consciousness is a unified, intentional structure (rather than an empty box), such replicas could not be inserted into it without its continuity being arrested and its unity broken. Against this theory, Sartre writes,

> When I perceive a chair it would be absurd to say that the chair is *in* my perception. According to the terminology we have adopted, my perception is a certain consciousness and the chair is the object of that consciousness.

Thus, there is no image as a third something intermediate between consciousness and the chair. After all, says Sartre, "An image of a chair is not, and cannot be a chair." What could it mean to say that a nonmaterial image in the mind is *like* (or corresponds to) a material thing outside the mind? An image of a chair "is not the chair: in general, the object of the image is not itself an image." It would be more accurate to speak of a person's "imaginative consciousness" of a chair than her consciousness of the image of a chair, since her image is her consciousness; unfortunately, this flies in the face of linguistic usage. "To perceive, conceive, imagine: these are the three types of consciousness by which the same object can be given to us," rather than three different functions of some conscious agents. We cannot be mistaken about our images, as we can (and often are) about objects of perception. "Our attitude towards the object of the image could be called 'quasi-observation'"—that is, a type of "observation which teaches nothing" new, unlike perceptual observation. Imaginative consciousness intends the object it observes through images and thus knows it. "All consciousness is consciousness *of* something" intended as its object, whether that be an image or a chair or a right triangle. Through "reflection" we can become conscious of consciousness; but this is a second-order

mental activity. In perceptual consciousness, an object (like a chair) is posited "as existing. The image also includes an act of belief, or a positional act." But the object of imaginative consciousness need not be posited as existing. Unlike perceptual consciousness, which appears as passive, imaginative consciousness is "a spontaneity which produces and holds on to the object as an image," appearing as "creative, but without positing that what it has created is an object" that exists. An image, rather, has a "vague and fugitive quality" of "nothingness" as contrasted with things of perceptual observation, such as that chair. Sartre credits James with helping to shatter "the illusion of immanence" on which the old correspondence theory of knowledge was founded. As he writes, "James' objection carries its full weight here: what is that resemblance which goes out in search of images in the unconscious, the resemblance that precedes the consciousness we have of it?"[161] Again, on this view, consciousness is pure activity rather than a container; it intends objects but contains nothing "within" itself—not an ego or images or anything else. It can assume three forms—perceptual, conceptual, and imaginative; but in every case it is nonsubstantial, "nothingness."

CONSCIOUSNESS AS QUESTIONING. *Being and Nothingness* is not really a work of epistemology; yet it contains insights that are importantly relevant to Sartre's theory of knowledge. First, there is the emphasis on consciousness as questioning. In a puzzling sentence, he writes that

> the question is a bridge set up between two non-beings: the non-being of knowing in man, the possibility of non-being of being in transcendent being.

Human knowledge is an achievement of consciousness, rather than a being, and the object of consciousness is experienced as being what it could possibly not be. These subject and object poles of experience are connected by a question. But "the truth" is "a third non-being" that can emerge from the process of questioning. For example, a person questions whether what he sees is a wooden chair. He knows it looks like a wooden chair; second, there is the possibility of his being mistaken about the nature of the perceptual object; and, third, he comes to establish the truth of its being a wooden chair rather than, say, a plastic facsimile. These three dimensions of "non-being" can arise in the process of consciousness questioning its objects. "The permanent possibility of non-being, outside us and within, conditions our questions about being,"[162] which are prerequisites of knowledge.

INTUITIVE KNOWLEDGE. Sartre discusses knowledge further, writing,

> There is only intuitive knowledge. **Deduction** and discursive argument, incorrectly called examples of knowing, are only instruments which lead to intuition.

When reason and argumentation fail to achieve knowledge, they are mere indicators "which point toward an intuition beyond reach." If all knowledge is intuitive, it must involve the presence of consciousness to the object known. Most philosophers traditionally conceive of knowledge as the presence of an object to consciousness. But, Sartre points out, "Being-present, in fact, is an ekstatic mode of being of the for-itself." Only consciousness can be "ekstatic," standing outside itself to intend (or be present to) something else. Sartre concludes, "We are then compelled to reverse the terms of our definition: intuition is the presence of consciousness to the thing" known. On this view, knowledge is "a mode of being" of consciousness rather than "a relation established after the event between two beings," or "an activity of one of these two beings," or "a quality of a property or a virtue" of consciousness. "It is the very being of the for-itself in so far as this is presence to" an object of intuition. "Knowledge is nothing other than the presence of being to the For-itself, and the For-itself is only the nothing which realizes that presence." Whereas an idealist like Hegel thinks that being is reabsorbed in knowledge, Sartre's "radical reversal of the idealist position" holds that "knowledge is reabsorbed in being" in the intuitive presence of consciousness to it. Sartre agrees with realists that, in knowledge, "the For-itself adds *nothing* to the In-itself except the very fact that *there is* In-itself," which can only be a fact for consciousness. The body is the immediate object of intuition—the intuition of both the consciousness intimately associated with it and of other consciousnesses.[163] Through its body, consciousness has access to an external world of possible intuitions.

CONSCIOUSNESS AND KNOWLEDGE. Sartre did write an essay in existential epistemology, entitled *Truth and Existence*, which was only published after his death. Unlike other posthumous writings of Sartre, this one appears to be complete. It develops the theme of human consciousness questioning and seeking knowledge. He writes that "questioning comes into the universe through man." The human person becomes concerned about questions of whose answers he is ignorant.

> Thus man defines himself in relationship to an original ignorance. He possesses a profound relationship to this ignorance. He defines what he is and what he seeks in terms of it.

Sartre is more explicit than any of his predecessors that we have studied here in linking human existence to human knowledge, writing, "Man is defined by what he *can* know." As an absolute subject, consciousness "is nonsubstantial," as we have seen; we have also discovered that, for Sartre, although consciousness typically takes the In-itself for its object, "consciousness *cannot be* that of which it is conscious." As earlier philosophers (e.g., James) recognized, truth is a relationship between consciousness and being: "Truth is the being-as-it-is of a being for an absolute subject." More specifically for Sartre (here he differs from other thinkers we have studied), truth is the "progressive disclosure of Being," a matter of degree, rather than all or nothing at all. The figure of speech here suggests that Being is somewhat hidden from consciousness and that the developing knowledge of the truth about Being involves its gradual revelation to consciousness. The ideal of knowledge, pushed to its limit, involves a permanent, comprehensive revelation of Being in its entirety: "The ideal of Truth is only that *all* of Being be illuminated and that it remain so." But Being can only reveal itself to consciousness from the latter's partial, subjective points of view. (Compare this to Kant's thesis that humans, unlike God, are only capable of sensible intuition, which is necessarily partial, and not of intellectual intuition, which would be comprehensive.) Sartre goes beyond James's pragmatic relativism in dealing with truth to a position of existential subjectivism. He writes, "Truth is subjective. The truth of an age is its meaning, its climate, etc., to the extent that they are lived as the discovery of Being." As long as individual human subjects experience such discovery, they are dealing with "living" truths; when a truth loses its revelatory quality for existing human subjects, it becomes "dead" for them (we might compare this to James's distinction between "living" and "dead" options). Sartre outlines three stages of an idea: first, it is a conscious "project of deciphering an in-itself in the light of an end," so that it is a means to a practical goal; second is the phase of "its living verification, the moment when behavior absorbs itself in the object" of the idea; and, third, it is communicated to some other consciousness(es), by whom the statement is received as an in-itself. At this last point "the idea is dead," unless and until the people involved with it somehow recover its vital function of disclosing Being.[164]

A couple of dangers are implicit here. First, to the extent that man has turned away from the existential towards "the eternal" (Hegel may be an example), "he has preferred dead truths to living truths and he has created a theory of Truth which is a theory of death." And, second, since freedom is the "foundation of Truth," consciousness "can choose non-truth. This non-truth is ignorance or lie." We can prefer that Being remain concealed, because unveiling it is too awkward or painful for us. We may note that knowledge is intrinsically as practical a project for Sartre as it was for James—"all knowledge, even intellectual knowledge, is action." Consciousness can only unveil Being because it acts freely. But, **conversely**, Sartre also holds "that all free behavior is revelatory—unveiling" Being in some way or other. "Thus the structure of truth is necessarily that what *is* is illuminated by what is not"—by consciousness in its every free project. Sartre brings out the subjectivity of this process quite deliberately when he writes that

> I am the being through whom the truth will come from within into the world. To say that I do not know is to say that I am aware that I can know.

He invokes the Socratic profession of ignorance as implicitly "the most radical affirmation of man" that truth is knowable. But the process of coming to know the truth—revealing Being—requires practical action. If man were complete and self-sufficient consciousness (an "In-itself-for-itself" like God), human error and ignorance "would be impossible" (this is a problem for Hegel's philosophy, which sees us as implicitly divine). We start every project of knowing in ignorance and constantly risk error. Sartre writes that "there are only two realities about which I cannot make a mistake: the modes of the For-itself that I am and the presence of the In-itself"—as we have seen,

the first point is Cartesian, while the second involves a criticism of Descartes. When we settle for error or choose to accept our ignorance, we choose not to utilize our freedom to reveal Being. In this sense, for Sartre,

> the fear of truth is fear of freedom. Knowledge commits me as accomplice of the surging up of Being in the world and places me before new responsibilities,[165]

which, of course, can be shirked.

Mere opinion is different from knowledge of the truth, in that we passively accept opinion rather than actively develop it. "Opinion is no longer free and verifiable anticipation of Being." It lacks the dynamic character of knowledge and is merely static. "We *have* an opinion, we do not know why" in the sense of understanding the grounds of that opinion. "Opinion comes from heredity, our environment, education" (as Plato illustrates in his *Republic*). Sartre says, "Opinion being what it is, I feel no obligation at all to verify it. *Since* I am not responsible for it, why should I be obligated to find out if it is true?" (Think, for example, of the prisoners in Plato's allegory of the cave.) Sartre writes that "the *original truth*, the most manifest truth" for us, "is the existence of the For-itself in the midst of Being." As we have seen, "the unveiling of Being" requires an active project on the part of the for-itself. "Therefore all knowledge of being implies a consciousness of ourselves as free." Through reflection we can make this explicit. Truth is essentially a relationship between personal consciousness and reality, even if it comes to gain general currency. As Sartre writes,

> I discover Being through my project, and truth, before becoming *the* universal truth—through gift and verification across the entire human adventure—is *my* truth.

Thus, a subjective perspective is quite apt:

> In this sense, "to each his own truth" is a correct turn of phrase because each person defines himself by the living truth that he unveils.

On this view, "the criterion of truth" must be a relationship between subjective consciousness and objective Being. More specifically, "it is *Being* as presence" to consciousness. In knowledge we "grasp" Being as it becomes revealed, "and we can no more doubt it than we can doubt the *I think*" of the Cartesian *cogito*. Sartre maintains that there are "three possible ways" in which a truth can appear: "it is *my* truth; it is truth that has become for the other; it is universal truth."

The process always starts with personal action and individual appropriation; but then it can be shared interpersonally.

> As far as *universal* truth is concerned, it is a pure abstract statement, that is, the pure index of a permanent possibility, valid for everyone, of freely realizing a certain unveiling.

But, as we have seen, a danger embedded in this third stage is that of truth becoming "dead-truth or *fact*." Truth as a final, complete system is as much an unrealizable ideal for Sartre as it was for James:

> What renders Truth impossible is that man makes History and that he is still making it while knowing it. Thus man, by the very fact that he is free, is haunted by an absolute truth

which Sartre compares to "the Platonic ideal."[166] So, *Truth and Existence* develops an epistemological theory according to which knowledge of truth results from the conscious activity of existing individual subjects through which Being is revealed.

MARXISM AND EPISTEMOLOGY. The most important epistemological work Sartre published is his *Search for a Method*, which originally accompanied his *Critique of Dialectical Reason*; like the latter, it is a difficult, jargon-ridden essay marking his movement from the pure existentialism of the 1940s towards Marxism. He calls Marxism "the one philosophy of our time" and holds that "the ideology of existence," on which we have thus far focused, is merely "an enclave inside Marxism." Marxism has allegedly become the living philosophy of our time.

> A so-called "going beyond" Marxism will be at worst only a return to pre-Marxism; at best, only the rediscovery of a thought already contained in the philosophy which one believes he has gone beyond.

In Sartre's opinion, thinkers who merely develop and apply the ideas of such great philosophers as Descartes, Kant, and Hegel "should not be called philosophers" at all but "ideologists"; existentialism is classified as such an ideology, constructed in reaction against Hegelianism. But the **alienation** and conflict of the midnineteenth century generated the need for a new philosophy focused on "*material* work and revolutionary *praxis*," according to Sartre, a need that was met in the writings of Marx which emphasize "the priority of action (work and social *praxis*) over

knowledge as well as their heterogeneity." Sartre sees the dialectical materialism of Marx as "the only valid interpretation of history," even while affirming the value of existentialism as "the only concrete approach to reality."[167] Sartre holds that every epistemological philosophy must meet the socio-economic needs of an age and that Marxism's dialectical materialism meets ours.

The chapter "The Progressive-Regressive Method" in *Search for a Method* contrasts his own epistemological method with the "synthetic progression" of traditional dialectics, which settles for "pure *exposition*" and which cannot discover anything new. By contrast, he writes, "Our method is heuristic; it teaches us something new because it is at once both regressive and progressive." Normal knowing is "originally progressive," synthesizing actions or events as they follow one another in time; but it also requires a "regressive" movement, analyzing the causes or reasons explaining those actions or events. Sartre provides an example of my watching a companion in a library suddenly get up from his chair and walk towards the window. To understand why he is doing this, "regressive" analysis is needed to realize that "the room is too warm" and that I myself feel some "discomfort." I then interpret the significance of his action: "He is going 'to let in some air.'" The unity of his conduct and the situation now seems clear. "The movement of comprehension is simultaneously progressive (toward the objective result) and regressive (I go back toward the original condition)."[168] Knowledge of human activity normally requires a dialectic of "progressive" synthesis and "regressive" analysis. Marxism provides the dialectical progressive-regressive method that will allow us to achieve knowledge of existing human individuals in action in a social context.

Freedom

SARTRE VS. DESCARTES. It is impossible to detach the Sartrean understanding of human personality from radical freedom; indeed, he probably places more emphasis on this topic than any other philosopher studied here. As a French philosopher, Sartre is interested in and influenced by the thought of Descartes. In Sartre's essay "Cartesian Freedom," he writes that

---

Praxis (from the Greek *prassein*, meaning to do or practice). Practical human conduct; in Marx, it means a synthesis of theory and practice

Descartes's legacy has been the over-intellectualizing of freedom, so that we conceive of it in terms "of independent *thinking* rather than the production of a creative act," identifying it with abstract judgment. He credits Descartes with recognizing a vital link between human freedom and the negative thinking of doubt, so that the latter necessarily implies the former. Sartre writes that "no one before Descartes had stressed the connection between free will and negativity." What Descartes failed to emphasize was the practical creative productivity of this freedom. As "a good Christian" of his era, Descartes highlights the misuses of freedom, rather than its positive achievements. "Cartesian man and Christian man are free for Evil, but not for Good, for Error, but not Truth," as Sartre interprets their twisted emphases, both allegedly attributing the creative, productive use of freedom to God. "It took two centuries of crisis—a crisis of Faith and a crisis of Science—for man to regain the creative freedom that Descartes placed in God."[169] We have traced that development of two centuries in our studies here from Hume through Sartre himself.

CHOICE AND CONSCIOUSNESS. As with most of our topics, we must turn to *Being and Nothingness* for Sartre's most influential discussions of freedom. Not every event is an action, and he finds it "strange" how philosophers "have been able to argue endlessly about determinism and free will" in the absence of a clear understanding of action, which, Sartre says, "is on principle *intentional*." The very fact that being can influence our actions is indicative of freedom:

> It is only because I escape the in-itself by nihilating myself toward my possibilities that this in-itself can take on value as cause or motive. Causes and motives have meaning only inside a projected ensemble

of personal transcendence. Our awareness of external motives and causes emphasizes this transcendence. As Sartre says,

> I am condemned to exist forever beyond . . . the causes and motives of my act. I am condemned to be free. This means that no limits to my freedom can be found except freedom itself or, if you prefer, that we are not free to cease being free.

Because of the constant temptation of bad faith, consciousness is "such that in its being its freedom is at stake." As James tried to set up determinism and indeterminism as **exhaustive** and **mutually exclusive alternatives** (or logical **contradictories** of each other), Sartre proposes an all-or-nothing option—

> either man is wholly determined (which is inadmissible, especially because a determined consciousness—i.e., a consciousness externally motivated—becomes pure exteriority and ceases to be consciousness) or else man is wholly free.

If these are the only alternatives, the latter seems obviously correct. Nor is human freedom "limited to voluntary acts." Rather, the entire life of consciousness, "in so far as this existence is the nihilation of facticity"—i.e., every distinguishing thought—is freedom. Indeed, consciousness and freedom turn out to be identical, rather than the latter being predicated of the former (in an Aristotelian or Thomistic or Cartesian manner):

> One must be conscious in order to choose, and one must choose in order to be conscious. Choice and consciousness are one and the same thing.

Of course, choice is not a "thing" in any substantial sense; but, as we have seen, for Sartre, neither is consciousness. Sartre admits that we must exist in a situation, whose "facticity" (givenness beyond our control) constitutes parameters within which we must be free. Our planet and its climate, our race and class, our language, our heredity, the particular circumstances of our childhoods, our acquired habits, and so forth all provide a "coefficient of adversity" in relation to which we must act. But how we act in relation to all this is ultimately our choice (otherwise it is not genuine action at all). All facticity is significant only in relation to freedom. In itself, apart from any relation to human freedom, "the coefficient of adversity in things" is meaningless. A person's deprived, disadvantaged upbringing, for example, is only significant in light of her values and projects. For Sartre, the ultimate "*facticity* of freedom" is "the fact of not being able not to be free." Although Sartre advocates a theory of radical freedom, in the sense that it gets to the very roots of human consciousness, he does not

---

Contradictories. Two propositions, one of which must be true and the other of which must be false (i.e., it is impossible that both are true, and it is impossible that both are false)

suppose that our freedom can ever be absolute. It is always *"restricted"* by its horizon of facticity.

> Every choice . . . supposes elimination and selection; every choice is a choice of finitude. Thus freedom can be truly free only by constituting facticity as its own restriction.[170]

OUR SENSE OF RESPONSIBILITY. In "Freedom and Responsibility," an influential section of *Being and Nothingness,* Sartre writes,

> The essential consequence of our earlier remarks is that man being condemned to be free carries the weight of the whole world on his shoulders; he is responsible for the world and for himself as a way of being,

since he is the "author" or creator of his own essence and the world as constituted by his thoughts, choices, and actions. This sense of responsibility generates the existential emotions (of anguish, forlornness, and despair) already discussed. As Sartre puts it, "In this sense the responsibility of the for-itself is overwhelming since he is the one by whom it happens that *there is* a world." He makes some remarkable claims to emphasize the humanism of his perspective. For example, he maintains that "there is no non-human situation." This does not mean that events can only happen to humans. For instance, Sartre would not deny that dinosaurs were fighting and feeding centuries before the evolution of the human species. But a set of events must be related to consciousness and freely chosen values and projects to constitute a "situation." Another example of a strange claim he makes is that "there are no *accidents* in a life." Again, this is not a denial that unforeseen and unchosen events happen in our lives; in driving an automobile down the highway, a person might run over a nail and suffer a flat tire. But such events occur only in the context of our own web of actions, and we have control over and are responsible for how we deal with them; in short, they are never *pure* accidents as lived by us because, even if they kill us immediately (so that we have no opportunity for a deliberate reaction), we put ourselves in the situation in which the events could affect us. Sartre offers the provocative example of a person getting drafted into military service during a war. He might not support the war and might want to reject all available options to being drafted. Yet he can, Sartre observes, "always get out of it by suicide or by desertion" if he so chooses, so that it is a deceptive "cop-out" to protest that he has no freedom (and thus

no responsibility) in the matter. "For lack of getting out of it," Sartre insists, he has "*chosen* it. This can be due to inertia, to cowardice," or to a preference of "other values to the value of the refusal to join the war." Thus, Sartre deliberately accentuates our freedom and responsibility in even extremely undesirable situations, stripping us of the excuses we seek in bad faith. Of course, we can whine that we "did not ask to be born" and cannot help being free. But these are trivial truths about "our facticity"; they are impotent for getting us off the hook of responsibility for how we react to them. Part of our "facticity" is that we inevitably encounter ourselves as "*abandoned* in the world," in the sense of being "alone and without help, engaged in a world for which" we cannot avoid being responsible, even if we wish to shirk it.

> For I am responsible for my very desire of fleeing responsibilities. To make myself passive in the world, to refuse to act upon things and upon Others is still to choose myself, and suicide is one mode among others of being-in-the-world

—the mode of reducing oneself to a corpse. There is a dialectic between freedom and facticity; they are in tension with each other, and we never experience either without the other. Both are elusive; we can grasp neither in a pure form.

> Thus facticity is everywhere but inapprehensible; I never encounter anything except my responsibility,

Sartre says, which can continuously reinforce the existential emotions.

> It is precisely thus that the for-itself apprehends itself in anguish; that is, as a being which is neither the foundation of its own being nor of the Other's being nor of the in-itselfs which form the world, but a being which is compelled to decide the meaning of being—within it and everywhere outside it.

We tend to flee this anguish in bad faith.[171]

EMPIRICAL VS. EXISTENTIAL PSYCHOANALYSIS. Sartre's section, "Existential Psychoanalysis" indicates how therapy can provide help for persons who suffer neurotic symptoms as a result of choices that are not working for them. "The *principle* of this psychoanalysis is that man is a totality and not a collection" of behaviors, so that all expressions and actions potentially reveal that totality. Sartre compares and contrasts his own existential psychoanalysis with the more famous "empirical psychoanalysis" of the Freudians. For both types, he observes, "The goal of psychoanalysis is to *decipher* the empirical behavior patterns of man," to explain their significance. "Its *point of departure* is *experience*" in each case. "Both kinds of psychoanalysis" take seriously the "symbolic relations" of psychic phenomena "to the fundamental, total structures which constitute the individual person. Both consider that there are no primary givens such as hereditary dispositions, character, *etc.*" Both view the human person as dynamic and changing in a particular (and relevant) situation. "Empirical psychoanalysis and existential psychoanalysis both search within an existing situation for a fundamental attitude" that will explain troubling maladjustments. But, whereas the Freudian approach emphasizes experiences (especially those of early childhood) that happened to the patient (and for which he is not responsible), Sartre says, "Existential psychoanalysis seeks to determine the *original choice*" made by him (and thus for which he is responsible), from which more ordinary choices routinely follow. Unlike existential psychoanalysis, empirical psychoanalysis explains neurosis in terms of

> the hypothesis of the existence of an unconscious psyche, which on principle escapes the intuition of the subject. Existential psychoanalysis rejects the hypothesis of the unconscious; it makes the psychic act coextensive with consciousness.

For example, if a college student regularly and angrily rebels against all authority and is miserable as a result of doing so, there is a maladjustment to be dealt with. Whereas the Freudian might track the problem back to the student's repressed hatred of her father because he yelled at her and broke her doll when she was five, the existentialist might determine that she has consciously chosen to hate her father and to express that hatred by her bitter resentment of all authority in her life. This hatred of her father, displaced on all authority figures, is her "original choice" or "**fundamental project**," from which her everyday actions (and reactions) now stem. "But if the fundamental project is fully experienced by the subject and hence wholly conscious, that certainly does not mean that it must by the same token be *known*." Indeed, this is where professional therapy can be helpful. Sometimes, bad faith can block our capacity to know

something of which at some level we are conscious. Sartre repudiates the Freudian "supposition that the environment acts mechanically on the subject under consideration"—that, for example, the student's hatred and rebellion were simply caused by the father's behavior years ago—pushing us to take responsibility for our own problems. "Furthermore the psychoanalyst will never lose sight of the fact that the choice is living and consequently can be *revoked* by the subject." This is an important point—we remain free to change our own fundamental projects, however traumatic a process that may be. Existential psychoanalysis must see each consciousness as "*individual*" rather than simply of a type.

> Precisely because the goal of the inquiry must be to discover a *choice* and not a *state*, the investigator must recall on every occasion that his object is not a datum buried in the darkness of the unconscious but a free, conscious determination—which is not even resident in consciousness, but which is one with this consciousness itself.

Whereas "traditional psychoanalytic interpretation" is geared to helping a patient gain knowledge of what has happened to him, "existential psychoanalysis" is designed "to bring to light, in a strictly objective form, the subjective choice by which each living person makes himself a person." Sartre (perhaps too modestly) holds that this new existential approach to "psychoanalysis has not yet found its Freud."[172]

AN ILLUSTRATION OF ABDICATED FREEDOM. Sartre's play *The Respectful Prostitute* provides a dramatic illustration of how we can abdicate our freedom and shirk responsibility. The title character, Lizzie, lives in a racist Southern town in the United States and does not want to get involved in helping "the Negro," a fugitive she knows to be innocent. As she says on the very first page of the play, "I'm not buying anybody else's troubles, I got enough of my own. Beat it." Fred, one of her customers, self-righteously condemns her sin; he is in bad faith in refusing to acknowledge that the sin is also his, that he has been exploiting her and using her as a means to his own selfish ends. He does not want to tell her his name, which bothers her. By contrast, she admits to her own

---

Fundamental project (or **original choice**).   In Sartre, a basic way of existing, freely chosen by consciousness, from which one's everyday actions and reactions stem

sin yet dismisses it, saying, "But then, I've got so many on my conscience." Fred insults her by trying to pay her too little, and she gets angry. He threatens her with legal action and reveals that he is a son of Senator Clarke, but without disclosing anything as personal as his own name. She exposes his bad faith by demanding, "If it disgusts you to make love, why did you come here to me?" Fred exhibits his own racist attitude and disrespect for some human life in the course of their discussion and mocks Lizzie for wanting to tell the truth about what she knows concerning the Negro, against whom Fred wants her to testify. He bribes her by offering her five hundred dollars to lie: "Lizzie! Be reasonable! Five hundred dollars!" Tempted, she sobs, "I'm not reasonable, and I don't want your five hundred dollars. I just don't want to bear false witness." John, a policeman, threatens her with jail if she does not sign the phony statement against the Negro; but she still protests, "I don't want to lie." Up to this point she seems fairly admirable in her honest convictions. But by the end of the first scene Senator Clarke has joined the discussion, wheedling and conning her into signing the document, actually guiding her hand as she does so. As soon as she has signed the false statement, they all leave her; she rushes to the door uselessly crying, "Senator! Senator! I don't want to sign! Tear up the paper!" She has relinquished her freedom and integrity, feebly blaming others for what she has done—"Something tells me I've been had." At this point she has slipped into bad faith. Later, in talking with the senator again, she is still shirking responsibility by blaming her confusion on him; as she tells him, "I don't know where I am any more; you've mixed me up; you're too quick for me." After the senator leaves, the Negro returns, pleading with her to hide him. She refuses on the grounds that she does not want any trouble and accuses him of harming her by getting her involved. He appeals to her knowledge of his innocence; but she underscores her own bad faith by replying, "I don't know what's right any more. Just the same, a whole city can't be completely wrong." And, indeed, the entire racist town seems to want him punished. By the end of the play the Negro has run away, with racists shooting at him, and Fred is back, offering to make life easier for Lizzie by setting her up as his mistress, if she will agree to cater to his every whim. She does wearily hand over her freedom

to him and accept his offer. The play concludes with his patronizing her by patting her cheek and saying, "Then everything is back to normal again. My name is Fred."[173]

A QUEST FOR ABSOLUTE FREEDOM. The theme of human freedom is prominent in other works of Sartre's fiction as well. Let us briefly illustrate the point by a quick look at his "The Roads to Freedom" trilogy. In the first novel, *The Age of Reason,* Marcelle correctly accuses the main character, Mathieu, of wanting to be absolutely free. An annoyed Mathieu replies, "If I didn't try to assume responsibility for my own existence, it would seem utterly absurd to go on existing." This seems to express Sartre's view that we can only give meaning to our lives by utilizing our freedom and accepting responsibility. Much later in the novel Mathieu feels that he has achieved his personal quest, thinking that

> he was free, free in every way, free to behave like a fool or a machine, free to accept, free to refuse, free to equivocate. . . . He was alone, enveloped in this monstrous silence, free and alone, without assistance and without excuse, condemned to decide without support from any quarter, condemned forever to be free.

In *The Reprieve* Mathieu is thinking that as embodied consciousness (in his head, so to speak) he is radically different from all the "solid objects" outside himself: "Inside, nothing, not even a puff of smoke, there is no *inside*, there is nothing. Myself: nothing. I am free, he said to himself." Yet as he thinks, "I am my own freedom," he is filled with "a sense of desolation, . . . an anguish so transparent as to be utterly unseeable." For he cannot avoid being and exercising this freedom, which alienates him from the whole world of in-itself reality: "Outside the world, outside the past, outside myself: freedom is exile, and I am condemned to be free." There is also the burden of responsibility assuming the form of the question, "What shall I do with all this freedom?" He realizes that ultimately—beyond the realm of his own personal projects—it does not matter and considers committing suicide by throwing himself into the Seine. "He had no special reason for letting himself drop, nor any reason for not doing so." His life and his potential suicide are equally absurd in the sense of lacking any ultimate sufficient reason. He decides not to throw himself into the river and walks away, thinking, "Next time, perhaps." He shall remain free to choose rather than choosing to terminate his freedom now. In *Troubled Sleep*, the concluding novel of Sartre's trilogy, Mathieu is defiantly asserting his freedom by firing on the enemy for fifteen minutes. He thinks of each shot as exacting revenge for something or other:

> One for Lola, whom I dared not rob, one for Marcelle, whom I ought to have ditched. . . . This for the books I never dared to write, this for the journeys I never made, this for everybody in general whom I wanted to hate and tried to understand.

He sees his own gunshots as shattering the rules and values that others would impose on him as limits on his freedom:

> Thou shalt love thy neighbor as thyself—bang! in that bastard's face—Thou shalt not kill—bang! at that scarecrow opposite. He was firing on his fellow man, on Virtue, on the whole world: Liberty is Terror.

Mathieu achieves his goal of continuously shooting at the enemy for a full fifteen minutes. What is interesting is his spontaneous association of this action with the autonomous exercise of freedom. His thoughts indicate his exuberant feelings—"he was cleansed, he was all-powerful, he was free."[174] Throughout the discussion of this topic, we might observe, Sartre, unlike James, never tries to argue for freedom; rather, like Descartes, he considers it self-evidently implied by our acts of consciousness.

Morality

EXISTENTIAL ETHICS AND MORAL FREEDOM. Human freedom is always oriented towards some goal that is at least implicitly practical.

> This absolute end, this imperative which is transcendent yet acquiesced in, which freedom itself adopts as its own, is what we call a value.

All pursuit of value should respect human freedom and thus respect humans as "absolute ends. . . . It can therefore be identified with Kantian **good will** which, in every circumstance, treats man as an end and not as a means."[175] What is not so clear, however, is what sort of existential ethics should be developed to foster such respect for all human freedom. Indeed, in the interview of May 1975, Sartre denies that any already established moral system, such as that of "Kantian ethics," can retain "validity" today "because the moral categories depend essentially on the structures of the society in which we live" and our social structures have changed too radically. He puts the point quite strongly:

We are in a period without ethics, or, if you like, there are ethical theories but they are obsolete.

He holds that now "too many contradictions exist and ideas are too confused" for us to be able to live morally. "It has not always been impossible, will not always be, but it is today."[176] Yet Sartre does try to assemble the elements of an ethics.

In the final section of *Being and Nothingness*, "Ethical Implications," Sartre analyzes all value as a function of "*a lack*" of being recognized by consciousness and experienced with passion. He hopes that existential psychoanalysis will help us to "repudiate the *spirit of seriousness*," which imagines that values are objective, absolute, and "independent of human subjectivity," and will reconcile us with our own passionate desires. People who get beyond "the spirit of seriousness," Sartre assures us, realize "that all human activities are equivalent," in the sense of not being measurable by any transcendent standards (such as Platonic Ideas or the eternal will of God), "and that all are on principle doomed to failure," in that we can never fill up the "hole" of being that human consciousness necessarily is. His illustration is shocking:

> Thus it amounts to the same thing whether one gets drunk alone or is a leader of nations.

Since there is no objective standard against which we may judge our projects, it boils down to whether, and to what extent, they allow us to express our freedom and to fulfill our subjective passions. Sartre's existential theory is designed to "reveal to the moral agent that he is *the being by whom values exist*." It is because consciousness is nothingness, is never simply what it is (like the in-itself), and will forever experience its own lack in the form of passionate desires that it must transcend itself and create its own values (even if it does so by subscribing to those of others). In a very strange sentence, Sartre writes,

> A freedom which wills itself freedom is in fact a being-which-is-not-what-it-is and which-is-what-it-is-not, and which chooses as the ideal of being, being-what-it-is-not and not-being-what-it-is.[177]

This is not mere gobbledygook but requires interpretation. First, consciousness (the for-itself) *is* freedom (rather than having it) and should choose to be freedom (rather than to shirk it). Second, it is that sort of reality (nothing or not a thing) which is never (and cannot ever be) *merely* what it currently is. Third, it is always *potentially* what it is not yet. Fourth, its ideal is to transcend itself to *become* something more.

In *Notebooks for an Ethics* Sartre expresses his distrust of any "immediate morality" that strives to be objective because "it involves too much bad faith," in refusing to recognize that all values are subjective and relative to our needs and interests. Ethical theories as diverse as those of Plato, Aristotle, Augustine, Aquinas, Kant, and Hegel would all be subject to this suspicion; and, on this point, Sartre seems to be closer to the relativism of Hume and James, though he is more radical than either of them. Even authenticity, or the absence of bad faith, is not a legitimate objective value in its own right, for Sartre, who says, "If you seek authenticity for authenticity's sake, you are no longer authentic." We need to admit that its value is relative to our own subjective projects and the flourishing of freedom. As James distinguishes between "tender-minded" and "tough-minded" philosophers, Sartre expresses his preference for "a *tough* ethics" over a "*tender*" one, that is, "an ethics filled with hope." He condemns all abstract, formalistic approaches to ethics that merely yield the universal in favor of "a *concrete* ethics (synthesis of the universal and the historical)." Moral values emerge from our historical situations.

> Man is the source of all good and all evil and judges himself in the name of the good and evil he creates. Therefore *a priori* neither good nor evil.

Moral problems are practical and involve a conflict of values.

> Ethics is the theory of action. But action is abstract if it is not work and struggle.

Like Kant and Hegel, Sartre wants to incorporate the right of humans to be treated as ends in themselves and to have their freedom respected by others. He says,

> My freedom is the pure power of doing whatever does not limit the freedom of the other.

This ideal (which we have seen before) is the centerpiece of Sartrean ethics. As he puts it,

> Once I have posited that I can do anything at all so long as I do not interfere with the freedom of others, I think I have done enough from the point of view of freedom.

In this sense, arbitrary, unprovoked violence against others would infringe their rights, as does a deliberate lie, which violates another's free access to the truth needed to form and act on opinions and which "transforms man into a thing" to be used as a means rather than respecting him as an end in himself.[178]

A SUBJECTIVE THEORY OF MORALITY. Sartre asserts that his slogan, "We are condemned to be free," though easily misunderstood (literally speaking, it looks like a paradox), "is the basis of my ethics." The human person must simultaneously be both "a facticity surrounded by the world" and a free "project that surpasses" that facticity. "As project, he assumes his situation in order to surpass it." The Hegelian notion of *aufheben*—"to preserve in surpassing"—is operative here. We usually think of freedom as including a lack of condemnation and of condemnation as opposing freedom. But, as human beings, we are condemned to live with our own facticity (including the fact that we must be free), which limits our freedom. "But since I am free, I am constrained by my freedom to make it mine, to make it *my* horizon, *my* perspective, my morality, etc." There are no ready-made solutions to moral problems. "The answers are not to be *found* but to be invented and chosen." If an ethics is to develop dialectically, "we have to start from the idea of totality" of human projects in a concrete situation. This will involve conflicts and the need to resolve them. "Hence thesis—antithesis—synthesis." One person's freedom, goals, and values will inevitably conflict with those of another at some point. Ethics requires that "answers" be "invented and chosen" which respect both. "There are *totalities*, not *one* totality" in personal relationships, so that the ethical dialectic actually "resolves itself into a plurality of dialectics," without any Hegelian absolute unity to be achieved. (Sartre's pluralism and relativism of all values to personal needs and interests is rather similar here to James's.) The Good is person-relative.

> The Good cannot be conceived apart from an acting subjectivity, and yet it is beyond this subjectivity. Subjective in that it must always emanate from a subjectivity and never impose itself on the subjectivity from the outside, it is objective in that it is, in its universal essence, strictly independent of this subjectivity.

Here we see the ethical dialectic at work: the Good is both subjective (in its derivation) and transcendently objective (in its applicability)—a synthesis of two superficially opposed concepts. "So man has to be considered as the being through which the Good comes into the world"; yet he projects the Good as universal. We might recall that Hume sought a justifiable link between what is and what should be. Sartre writes that "the person is the bridge between being and the ought-to-be. But as such, he is necessarily unjustifiable."[179] This is the logical end of his subjective theory of morality.

A fine literary depiction of the human struggle for moral action can be found in Sartre's play *Dirty Hands*; of its seven acts, the first and last ones are set at about the same time, with the middle five being a flashback to two years earlier. The action occurs during the Second World War. The main character, Hugo Barine, has just been released from prison, where he was serving time for killing a man; and now he seeks to reunite with his old political faction and is trying to convince Olga, his former collaborator, that he can still be useful to the party. He exclaims, "It's funny to be free; it makes me dizzy." Olga says that she will "do as the party tells me" regarding Hugo, and he mocks her for thus abdicating her free choice to external authorities. But he is suspected of being "an undisciplined anarchistic individualist," and she must try "to find out if he's salvageable or not." So, he tells her his story, which begins in March of 1943. We learn that the situation involves three irreconcilable political groups, "the fascist government of the Regent," allied with Nazi Germany, Hugo's own Communist party, which is struggling against it to bring about "a classless society," and—between these two—"the Pentagon, which serves as a clandestine rallying-point for the bourgeois liberals and nationalists." The dramatic action revolves around Hoederer, one of their own leaders, who is branded a traitor because of his attempts "to negotiate with the Regent's men." Hugo is assigned to work as Hoederer's secretary, to spy on him, and ultimately to let in some assassins who will kill him. Hugo and his wife, Jessica, are taunting each other about the phony role-playing each is doing. She shows him a revolver she has found and asks him what it is for. He responds, "It's to kill Hoederer." She mocks him, and he wonders aloud, "Am I playing? Or am I being serious?" He desperately wants assurance that she loves him but cannot get her to become serious. Hugo is an idealist who is anxious to maintain his own self-respect. He desperately demands the truth, but Jessica scornfully retorts, "There is no truth." As she perceives, he cannot convince anyone else that he will "become a murderer," if he cannot first convince himself. He does

not yet know the truth of his own intentions. Hoederer admits, "I always trust people on principle"; he does place his trust in Hugo, which complicates matters, since Hugo wants to be trusted and respects Hoederer. Hugo does not know whether he can go through with his part in Hoederer's assassination; he means to do so yet realizes that it is merely another role (along with those of husband, revolutionary, and secretary) he will have to assume. He says, "An assassin is never really an assassin. They play at it, you understand." Hugo complains of Olga's lack of trust in him, and she concedes that he too is suspected of treason. He threatens to leave the party if he is replaced on this assignment, but she issues a counterthreat that a person "only leaves the party feet first." Hugo hates the idea of living without the trust of others. It seems that only Hoederer, the one he is assigned to betray, truly trusts him. Jessica cross-examines him harshly, pointing out the relativism of his convictions, that, if he had only met Hoederer earlier, he would be firmly on his side. Hugo protests, "To hear you, one would think that all opinions have the same weight, that one catches them like a disease." He is sure he is right. But when she challenges how he can possibly know what is right, he utters idealistic mumbo jumbo: "Politics is a science. You can demonstrate that you are right and that others are wrong." Jessica calls his bluff by daring him to convince Hoederer he is pursuing a wrong policy before killing him. In his subsequent discussion with Hoederer Hugo accuses him of compromising the party's program and thus betraying it. Hoederer asserts that any "party is always only a tool" for pursuing the goal of power; but Hugo protests that its only legitimate goal is the realization of ideas and ideals. Hoederer maintains that the deliberate deception of one's comrades is sometimes a necessary means to a valuable end, and Hugo (who, of course, is trying to deceive him) is outraged, saying, "All means are not good," to which Hoederer retorts, "All means are good when they're effective." He scolds Hugo for naively clinging to the purity of his ideals and being unwilling to soil his hands. In a famous passage, he exclaims,

> Well, I have dirty hands. Right up to the elbows. I've plunged them in filth and blood.

He correctly accuses Hugo of preferring abstract principles to real persons, whereas he claims to love people, for all their faults. Jessica tips off Hoederer about

Hugo's intentions. She accurately says, "He doesn't want to kill you. Not in the least. He thinks too much of you for that. It's just that he has his assignment." Hoederer agrees not to harm Hugo and to try to win him over. He does try, apparently prevailing, when Hugo sentimentally exclaims, "I know now that I could never shoot you because—because I like you." But a bit later Hugo returns to find him in a sexually suggestive situation with Jessica and shoots him to death. Was this the right thing to do or was it evil? It is difficult to say without knowing Hugo's real motives. Was he out of his mind with romantic jealousy or merely availing himself of a convenient opportunity to do his duty for the party? Even he seems uncertain. In the last act Olga asks him why he did it. He replies, "I—I killed him because I opened the door. That's all I know. If I hadn't opened that door—." He admits that jealousy may have been a factor. "But not about Jessica." He may have been jealous of Hoederer's authenticity and integrity. He is obviously struggling to be honest with himself and to overcome bad faith. He tells her, "I loved Hoederer, Olga. I loved him more than I ever loved anyone in the world." She offers to accept him back into the party as "salvageable." But he laughs, "Salvageable! What an odd word! That's a word you use for scrap." And indeed, this is what he has become for the party—he will either be reused or eliminated. She wants him to deny his act, since party policy has changed in the intervening two years, Hoederer's collaboration with the Regent is now viewed as a positive measure, and his reputation has been rehabilitated. But again, Hugo must make a moral decision. Should he go along with this "farce" and deny his own responsibility for Hoederer's death? Should he play the phony game in order to render himself "salvageable"? As he observes, "The crime itself cannot be salvaged, isn't that so? It was an error of no significance. To be left in the ash-can." He refuses to abjure his own action, even though he is honestly confused about its motive(s). He will not violate his moral values and dishonor the memory of Hoederer, whom he still loves and respects, by allowing his death to be dismissed as an accident. He knows that two party members are waiting outside to kill him unless he agrees to Olga's terms and she declares him "salvageable." The play ends with Hugo kicking the door open and shouting, "Unsalvageable!"[180] Here Sartre portrays his existential morality as subjective, relative to values individually created, and calling for personal authenticity. It makes not a particle of difference to how Hugo should act that no one apparently agrees with or is sympathetic to his project.

Society

SHAME. Although *Being and Nothingness* contains little about organized society, its Part Three, "Being-for-Others" (*Le Pour-Autrui*), deals entirely with interpersonal relationships. A third dimension of the human person, in addition to the for-itself of consciousness and the in-itself of the body, is this interpersonal for-others. Sartre describes the encounter with another consciousness in terms of a phenomenon such as shame (*la honte*). Imagine, he suggests, that "I have just made an awkward or vulgar gesture." It may be an insignificant act until I realize that someone else witnessed it. "Somebody was there and has seen me. Suddenly I realize the vulgarity of my gesture, and I am ashamed." At times like this we realize that we are the object of others' experiences, and shame arises as "an immediate shudder" at the recognition that others have seen us as we are. Sartre appreciates Hegel's point that "the Other is indispensable" to self-consciousness. In a psychological sense Hegel is correct that we must risk our lives in confronting others. There is a sense in which interpersonal relations do tend to the dominance-subordination so grippingly represented in his Master-Slave dialectic. Hegel teaches us that "being-for-others appears as a necessary condition for my being-for-myself." On the other hand, Hegel is "guilty of an epistemological optimism" in assuming that some "objective agreement can be realized between consciousnesses," where Sartre insists on "their ontological separation." In a well-known section on "The Look" ("*Le Regard*"), which might be compared with Hegel's Master-Slave dialectic and its treatment of the emergence of personal recognition, Sartre analyzes the discovery by consciousness of the alien point of view of another consciousness. The other constitutes her own world, of which she is the subjective center and in which I am an object. I have been displaced by a perspective that cannot be mine; "I cannot put myself at the center" of her world. Thus her "appearance among the objects of *my* universe" inevitably introduces "an element of disintegration in that universe." Her perspective in principle eludes me. "Thus suddenly an object has appeared which has stolen the world from me." Although "*the Other* is still an object *for me*," I am also her object; the identity of my world as the only one slips away.

> The appearance of the Other in the world corresponds therefore to a congealed sliding of the whole universe, to a decentralization of the world which undermines the centralization which I am simultaneously effecting.

This can make us feel as if "the world has a kind of drain hole in the middle of its being," through which it is draining away from us. Unlike a chair, another person is not merely our object, but another subject, which constantly threatens to objectify us. To recognize any object as another person "refers to my permanent possibility of *being-seen-by-him*. . . .'Being-seen-by-the-Other' is the *truth* of seeing-the-Other" as another person.[181]

Sartre provides a vivid example of a person crouched down and looking through a keyhole, motivated "by jealousy, curiosity, or vice" to spy on someone else. I might be totally absorbed in this activity. "But all of a sudden I hear footsteps in the hall. Someone is looking at me!" I immediately become self-conscious; "I see *myself* because *somebody* sees me." I realize that I am that other person's object and experience this recognition as shame. This objectification reduces me to being in the mode of "in-itself" and compromises my transcendence. (On this view, by the way, God is "the concept of the Other pushed to the limit" as omnipresent.) Shame is the consciousness "of being *an* object; that is, of *recognizing myself*" in this degraded, fixed, and dependent being which I am for the Other. Shame is the feeling of an *original fall*" from transcendence into another's world. Analysis reveals "three dimensions" of shame, all of which are necessary to the phenomenon: "*I* am ashamed of *myself* before the *Other*." (My shame before God is special, because God is conceived of not only as forever present but also as "a subject which can never become an object.")[182]

SEXUAL DESIRE AND LOVE.   In the chapter "Concrete Relations with Others" Sartre discusses sexual desire, love, and sadism and masochism as examples of interpersonal relations. His claim, "Conflict is the original meaning of being-for-others," says a great deal about his theory of the roots of society. The other's look takes "*possession*" of my body as its object, and

I cannot help wanting to recover my being from this appropriation. But I can only accomplish this by asserting my freedom. "Thus my project of recovering myself is fundamentally a project of absorbing the Other." Sartre characterizes love in such terms, maintaining that "to love is in essence the project of making oneself be loved" and that each person in a love relationship "is entirely the captive of the Other." He describes love as "alienated freedom," saying that anyone "who wants to be loved . . . by the mere fact of wanting someone to love him alienates his freedom."[183]

One way in which we can appropriate another's "free subjectivity through his objectivity-for-me is *sexual desire*." Sartre sees sexual desire and sexual repulsion as "fundamental structures of being-for-others," which can extend from birth to death, rather than as accidents contingent on our physiological nature. In sexual desire I encounter "not only the revelation of the Other's body but the revelation of my own body" as well. In my desire for the other, I can experience myself as overwhelmed by my own body; "in desire I make myself flesh *in the presence of the Other in order to appropriate the Other's flesh*." This physical appropriation of another person can take the form of "the caress" (*la caresse*), which is an attempt to shape and "*incarnate* the Other," as well as being an expression of desire. In sexual desire, as through a caress, "I throw myself toward the Other's facticity," incarnating myself in the process, a "disturbing" self-objectification. "Nevertheless desire is itself doomed to failure," for we cannot completely subordinate our transcendence or appropriate another subject. And sexual pleasure "is the death of desire," insofar as it kills it, at least temporarily. Obscenity is another phenomenon of interpersonal relationships and is opposed to gracefulness, in that it violates or debases (rather than expressing) transcendence. "In grace the body is the instrument which manifests freedom," by precise, self-determined action. Even a naked body, as we know, can be graceful, its perfect, spontaneous movements disguising or covering up its facticity. By contrast, ungraceful or obscene movements have a "*mechanical*" quality or awkwardness that emphasizes the body's facticity.[184]

The sadist, Sartre maintains, demands that the other's movements be mechanically obscene rather than gracefully free. The sadist tries to manipulate and appropriate the freedom of the other, even "by means of violence and pain." Love allegedly requires "freedom's self-enslavement." The masochist subjects his will to another's, his commanded physical movements becoming "the very image of a broken and enslaved freedom." So, sexual desire can lead to either sadism or masochism, the aggressive appropriation of another's freedom or the passive abdication of one's own. Even so-called "'normal' sexuality," Sartre holds, is a "sadomasochistic" blend. But what of those situations in which we find ourselves "not in conflict with the Other but in community with him"? Does the sense of "we" not sometimes connote a community of subjects who respect each other enough not to make objects of one another? Perhaps so, but the "We-as-subject" also has as its complement "We-as-object"; every community can be (and probably is) objectified by others. So, though there is the reality of "the *Mitsein*" ("being-with"), it is a secondary social phenomenon: "The essence of the relations between consciousnesses is not the *Mitsein*; it is conflict." Nor, as we have seen, is love a **counterexample**, for Sartre, who writes, "Love is a fundamental relation of the for-itself to the world and to itself" through another person, who gets used as "only a conducting body" mediating between the lover and his world.[185]

CONFLICT. Sartre's greatest play, *No Exit*, offers a memorable depiction of this view of interpersonal relationships. It features three main characters, Joseph Garcin, Estelle Rigault, and Inez Serrano, who are dead and are sharing a room in what can only be seen as hell. Garcin expresses the preference for solitude that is a theme of the play near its beginning, when he says, "I'd rather be alone." The characters have trouble being honest with one another because of their bad faith. Yet Inez is correct in observing, "Yes, we are criminals—murderers—all three of us. We're in hell, my pets; they never make mistakes, and people aren't damned for nothing." She acutely predicts that "each of us will act as torturer of the two others." Garcin has been shot as a cowardly traitor; Inez is a cruel lesbian who drove her cousin and his wife to commit suicide; Estelle cheated on her husband and drowned her illegitimate baby, driving her lover to suicide. Garcin needs the understanding Inez could provide but is too selfish to offer; Inez needs the love

of Estelle, who wants nothing to do with her; and Estelle yearns for the romantic affections of Garcin, who finds her too fatuous to be worthwhile. As Garcin points out, none of them "can save himself or herself," and the three are "linked together inextricably," condemned to make each other miserable. Their attempts to help each other and to ignore each other are equally futile. They alienate one another with a gaze ("the look") as well as with their words. Each threatens to reduce the transcendence of the others (to objectivity), yet each desires and needs something of another (as a subject). Every conscious personality is potentially at the mercy of every other, conflict being a perpetual structure of being-for-others. Garcin exclaims, "I understand that I am in hell" (*je comprends que je suis en enfer*). Sartre, of course, does not believe in any afterlife, and it is clear that the three characters represent us and that the room in which they are trapped is our hell on earth. In the most famous line of the play, Garcin proclaims,

Hell is—other people!

(*l'enfer, c'est les Autres*). And, just before the end of the play, Inez also supposedly speaks for all of us in saying,

So here we are, forever

(*Et nous sommes ensemble pour toujours*).[186] From the point of view of the Sartre of the 1940s, this is our fate, to torment (and be tormented by) others with whom we live. Such a perspective on interpersonal relations as fundamentally conflict might seem to provide little or no basis for a theory of society. Yet, like Hobbes, who moves from a comparable perspective to a theory of society, Sartre, as we shall see, tries to provide one.

MARXIST AND HEGELIAN INFLUENCES. Sartre's long interview of May 1975 is illuminating for his self-analysis of an "evolution," as he calls it, from his existential emphasis on individuals in interpersonal conflict to one (influenced by Marxism) on class action for social change. He says he started deliberately using the dialectic in his writings only after *Being and Nothingness*. The period of World War II, including the Nazi occupation of France, the Resistance, and the liberation by the Allies, moved him to focus more on the dynamic link between philosophical theory and practical action. As he says, "There is an evolution, but I don't think there is a break." Among other things, he came to realize the deficiency of his early treatment of society. As he admits, "What is particularly bad in *L'Etre et le Néant* is the specifically social chapters on the 'we.'" He recognizes that in that work, *Being and Nothingness*, he presented an extremely negative analysis of love, yet he still maintains that sadism and masochism are quite normal dimensions of love. He does assert that his early work provides an ontology, or general theory of being, that can provide a solid foundation for a view of society: "That is really where I differ from a Marxist. What in my eyes represents my superiority over the Marxists is that I raise the class question, the social question, starting from being, which is wider than class." He considers his *Critique of Dialectical Reason* "a truly dialectical work," in the sense that it tries to deal with society as an historical totality encompassing "lots of contradictory relationships within the whole and an interconnection of the whole that comes from the shifting of all these particular contradictions." He is reluctant to describe the *Critique* as "a Marxist work" (it is anti-Communist) but says it "is close to Marxism." He sees it as genuine "reflected philosophy" rather than as mere ideology. He foresees the approaching "end of Marxism" but wants to retain its emphasis on the "notion of surplus value, the notion of class—all of that reworked, however." Like the Marxists, he wants "a philosophy in which theory serves practice"; but, unlike them, he wants to focus on human freedom "as its starting point." He accepts the term "libertarian socialism" as describing his own position. Although he is not fond of labels, he prefers that of "existentialist" to that of "Marxist" near the end of his life. Nevertheless, he is anxious that treatments of his work not be restricted to the period up to 1949, saying, "I think that a study of my philosophical thought should follow its evolution."[187] This has to include some consideration of his *Critique*, however daunting a task its obscure, cryptic writing style might render it.

The Marxist dialectic, which Sartre appropriates, stems from the works of Hegel. What Sartre repudiates of Hegel is his assumption that we are "at the beginning of the end of History, that is to say, at that moment of Truth which is death," and his idealistic thesis that "the movement of Being and the process of Knowledge are inseparable." These points need correction.

Marx's originality lies in the fact that, in opposition to Hegel, he demonstrated that History *is in development*, that *Being is irreducible to Knowledge*, and, also, that he preserved the dialectical movement *both in* Being *and in* Knowledge.

The problem with Marxism, however, is that its attitude of reductionistic positivism minimizes the role of freedom; its materialism tries to locate human nature "outside" the human person "in an *a priori* law, in an extra-human nature, in a history that begins with the nebulae." Marx, like every thinker we have studied before him, believed in a predetermined, common human nature. There is a deterministic rationalism implicit in Marx's thought; but it is inconsistent with his teaching that we make our own history. As Sartre comments, "If this statement is true, then both determinism and analytical reason must be categorically rejected as the method and law of human history." In this case nothing should be assumed as historically inevitable. Sartre presents his own view, that

> men make History to precisely the extent that it makes them.

This always occurs in the context of "given circumstances and social conditions," including those of class conflict. Like Marx, Sartre is influenced by Hegel's Master-Slave dialectic but diverges from its interpretation of abstract idealism. He writes,

> The origin of struggle always lies, in fact, in some concrete antagonism whose material condition is *scarcity* (*la rareté*).

Hence, it is never simply a product of the need for psychological recognition but always has materialistic causal roots. "Hegel, in other words, ignored matter as a mediation between individuals" in a way that Sartre (and Marx) cannot abide. We live in an environment of moderate scarcity (part of our facticity) which both influences and is affected by our practical actions:

> *Scarcity* is a fundamental relation of *our* History and a contingent determination of our univocal relation to materiality.

Human activity (whether of an individual or a group) in a concrete context done for the sake of some goal(s) is called "*praxis*" by Sartre; and it is never altogether separate from our needs and ways of trying to meet them. "Every *praxis* is primarily an instrumentalisation of material reality." But every action is also somehow identifiable with society; since man is a social being, "*all things* are, directly or indirectly, social facts." All *praxis* involves "both man as a practical agent and matter as a worked product in an indivisible symbiosis." Human freedom expresses itself in a social "world of exploitation and oppression, in opposition to this world and as a negation of the inhuman *through values.*" Alienated by social conditions, consciousness chooses to act to rework its material environment, the matter embodying past *praxis* that Sartre calls "practico-inert being." The antagonism of class conflict seems universal and conditions our practical choices.

> Every system of values rests on exploitation and oppression; every system of values effectively negates exploitation and oppression . . . every system of values, in so far as it is based on a social practice, contributes directly or indirectly to establishing devices and apparatuses which, when the time comes (for example, on the basis of a revolution in techniques and tools) will allow *this* particular oppression and exploitation to be negated.[188]

It will be replaced by another social form, and the dialectic continues.

Individual *praxis* is rarely, if ever, likely to change the practico-inert enough to affect social alienation significantly, especially for those who are the victims of our economic systems. "The worker will be saved from his destiny only if the human multiplicity as a whole is permanently changed into a group *praxis.*" Thus collective action is needed, and we must unite to effect serious changes. "These transformations are wholly *material*; or rather, everything really takes place in the physico-chemical universe and the organism's power of assimilation and of strictly biological selection exists at the level of consumption." This emphasis of the Marxists is valuable and missing in Hegel. On the other hand, this materialism should not be pressed so far as to minimize the role of human freedom. As Sartre puts it,

> But one will never understand anything of human history if one fails to recognize that these transformations take place in a practical field inhabited by a multiplicity of agents, in so far as they are produced by the free actions of individuals.

Here is where Sartre's existentialism serves as a corrective against the one-sided emphases of Marxism. Individuals form social groups in order to pursue a common *praxis*, which is both "free individual" action and that of "a totalised multiplicity" (that is, an historically developing social group). By working together human beings can freely constitute their "individual *praxis* into common *praxis*. At this level, there is group behavior and there are group thoughts." The individual retains his individuality, yet his condition is affected by the social ensemble which he needs and to which he belongs. The individual's goals can always erupt into conflict with those of the group, yet in society neither exists without the other.

> The individual integrates himself into the group and the group has its practical limit in the individual.

A more or less stable dialectical synthesis is achieved in social life and action. Each member conceives of and tries to constitute the group in his own fashion, so that there may be as many "totalisations" or conceptions of a group as it has members; and each member denies conceptions other than his own, to the extent that they differ, leading to a lack of perfect cohesion or "detotalisation." Groups can conflict or cooperate; but a society is not any sort of group or collection of groups. In the concrete "material context of needs, dangers, instruments and techniques," the formation of society requires that certain conditions be met: first, "human multiplicities," or collections of individuals, must be "united *by a container or by a soil*," sharing a common space; second, these "multiplicities" must be historically divided into both "groups" (collections of individuals engaged in reciprocal action) and series (collections of individuals engaged in actions separate from each other); and, third, its basic internal relation (whether that be one of production or consumption or common defence) must ultimately associate (mutually cooperating) groups and series of people (having separate, and possibly opposed, goals). In a capitalist society, for example, the workers and owners of the means of production (bourgeoisie) share a geographic territory (such as France) as their living space, making up both bonded groups and separate series of people, and different groups with separate goals must relate to each other for the production of goods. There is a struggle for dominance between the two social classes. Given the structures of the capitalist system, each class needs and must cooperate with the other; yet, to the extent that the owners exploit and oppress the workers, the freedom and dignity due all humans is not fully respected. The workers suffer the results of their alienating social conditions.[189] This compromises their transcendence, constituting a destabilizing element in society.

Religion

THE NONEXISTENCE OF GOD.   Since Sartre is a dogmatic atheist, his views on religion can be dealt with rather briefly, focusing on the nonexistence of God, the empty ideal that God represents, and the potential bad faith of religious belief. His popular lecture on "Existentialism" reveals a conflict about the importance of atheism to his philosophy. First he says that the existentialist

> thinks it very distressing that God does not exist, because all possibility of finding values in a heaven of ideas disappears along with Him; there can no longer be an *a priori* Good, since there is no infinite and perfect consciousness to think it.

So, from the point of view of the absence of absolute values (and, as we have seen, from that of a lack of any predetermined common human nature), God's nonexistence is vitally significant.

> Indeed, everything is permissible if God does not exist, and as a result man is forlorn, because neither within him nor without does he find anything to cling to.

Yet in the last paragraph of the lecture, he insists,

> Existentialism isn't so atheistic that it wears itself out showing that God doesn't exist. Rather, it declares that even if God did exist, that would change nothing.

This later protestation that God's "existence is not the issue"[190] for existentialism seems inconsistent with the core of Sartre's theory.

GOD AS A SYMBOL.   He discusses the ideal that God represents in *Being and Nothingness*. He denies that there could be a God who comprehends the totality of reality, setting up a dilemma to argue his point. Either God's nature would be that of conscious for-itself or that of an in-itself that is beyond consciousness (he has postulated that those are the only two types of reality possible). But "if God is consciousness, he is integrated in the totality"; and, being part of it, God could not step outside it to comprehend it. On the other hand, "if by his nature, he is a being *beyond consciousness* (that is, an in-itself which would be its own foundation)," then either the totality will "appear to him only as *object*" (leaving out its dimensions of subjectivity) "or as *subject*" (in which case, it is other

than God, who can therefore "only experience it without knowing it"). Either way, this argument would conclude, the ideal of divine omniscience is impossible. God functions symbolically in our lives as "the ideal of a consciousness which would be the foundation of its own being-in-itself by the pure consciousness which it would have of itself." If the nature of consciousness is to be finite and contingent, then the ideal of an "in-itself-for-itself" must be unrealizable, and God is merely a symbol of our own all-too-human aspirations:

> God, value and supreme end of transcendence, represents the permanent limit in terms of which man makes known to himself what he is

—namely a desire for completeness and self-sufficiency. We strive to realize "an ideal synthesis" of "the in-itself and the for-itself" in our lives, an "integration" which "is always indicated and always impossible."[191] God merely represents this necessarily empty ideal.

CRITICISMS OF CHRISTIANITY.   Sartre saves his harshest criticisms of religious faith (which, given his own background, culture, and likely audience, is depicted as Christian) for his *Notebooks for an Ethics*, where he writes, "The Christian faith is bad faith," since "the very nature of God forbids us to believe in him"; it is both allegedly contradictory (as we have seen) and "opposed to the psychological structure of belief." For human belief must be built on "experience, intuition," and other "operations that can be *carried out*," But no such natural human operation can "be carried out when it is a question of God," the object of no possible "experience, intuition, etc." This pulls the very foundations out from under any alleged faith:

> Therefore we cannot found ourselves on any concrete operation, and so our belief is a belief *in nothing*. To be legitimate, it has to borrow from the sensory world of intuitions (nice old man, Christ on the cross), which is only possible for children or those who have a shoemaker's faith.

Religious belief, Sartre thinks, typically conceives of God as fixing us with the eternal gaze (the look) of a sovereign, a gaze which "ought-to-be. This is a convenient enough sort of falsification since a gaze is by nature freedom. God as the sovereign is the setting of our necessity." This provides us with a welcome limitation on our freedom and excuse from our responsibility. There is something dishonest about a belief in a self-sufficient God who, nevertheless, "has need of a free consciousness to reflect his work." If God must somehow give creation to an Other, that Other would need to be thoroughly independent and free—in short, an equal or "another God"—to be worthy as witness. But this notion is condemned as blasphemous by religion, which sees it as threatening to compromise the divine perfection: "God's risk is man's freedom." So religion tries to have it both ways, to view man as radically dependent on and belonging to God, on the one hand, and as genuinely free and morally autonomous, on the other. "But here we rediscover an element of the dialectic of the Master and the Slave" made famous by Hegel; man's required service is tainted by being externally required and thus unworthy of the presumed glory of his sovereign God. "Here we grasp at its source the Christian's game of bad faith, which shifts from one point of view to the other." He must fool himself into thinking that he is, somehow, both an "inessential" creature and yet "essential to the world and consequently to God,"[192] This duplicity seems objectionable.

Immortality

Sartre does not believe in human immortality and sees no reason to discuss it much. Yet he does write about death in such a way as to indicate his views on the end of a person's life. In *Being and Nothingness* he says, "By death the for-itself is changed forever into an in-itself in that it has slipped entirely into the past." With death consciousness ceases to be, leaving only a corpse. The reason behind his unequivocal position here is his conviction that "the body is a necessary characteristic of the for-itself." As he goes on to write, "the very nature of the for-itself demands that it be body; that is, that its nihilating escape from being should be made in the form of an engagement in the world," which must be mediated by the body. He says he agrees with Plato (although this may sound more like Aristotle) that it is the body "*which individualizes* the soul," while repudiating any reified view of soul as an entity that can "detach itself . . . from the body at death" and go on functioning. (It is interesting to note how talk of the soul has diminished in the history of philosophy of human nature since Hume, with contemporary thinkers such as James and Sartre preferring to speak of "consciousness" as not a substantial thing at all but rather an activity of a living

person.) For Sartre "there is no longer any *other side* of life, and death is . . . the final phenomenon of life." Death is part of human facticity and is "absurd" in the sense of not being rationally justifiable. Sartre rejects the sentimental notion that death provides meaning for our lives, saying that

> it is, on the contrary, that which on principle removes all meaning from life. If we must die, then our life has no meaning because its problems receive no solution and because the very meaning of the problems remains undetermined.[193]

Since we create all meaning, whose validity is relative to our own projects, it dies with us.

Whereas "life decides its own meaning" and "possesses essentially a power of self-criticism and self-metamorphosis which causes it to define itself as a 'not-yet,'" death annihilates all possibility of self-initiated change in consciousness, signalling an "*all done*. This means that for it the chips are down and that it will henceforth undergo its changes without being in any way responsible for them." It is only the survivors who can adopt an attitude towards those who have died.

> To be dead is to be a prey for the living. This means therefore that one who tries to grasp the meaning of his future death must discover himself as the future prey of others.

As long as we are alive, we can freely act so as to elude the definitions of others; but, with death, this capacity for transcendence evaporates. In this sense, Sartre writes, death "gives the final victory to the point of view of the Other," since "to die is to exist only through the Other, and to owe to him one's meaning." Consciousness is oriented towards death (and can know as much); but this is a contingent fact about it rather than part of its "ontological structure," unlike, for example, our finitude, which "is an ontological structure of the for-itself which determines freedom." As Sartre says, "human reality would remain finite even if it were immortal, because it makes itself finite by choosing itself as human," by projecting one set of possibilities to pursue "to the exclusion of others." Death is an aspect of our facticity and contingency as finite beings, and it is as absurd (or rationally unjustifiable) as is our birth. "*Mortal* represents the present being which I am for the Other; *dead* represents the future meaning of my actual for-itself for the Other." Impending death looms ahead for consciousness. "Thus death haunts me at the very heart of each of my projects" as its ultimate destiny. Yet, as long as we are conscious, we can never directly encounter this limit of our own deaths. "Since death is always beyond my subjectivity, there is no place for it in my subjectivity."[194]

"The Wall" is a well-known short story in which Sartre focuses on death (and, implicitly, the lack of immortality). The narrator is Pablo Ibbieta, a prisoner along with Tom Steinbock and Juan Mirbal, all of whom have been sentenced to die before a firing squad the following morning. Pablo remembers, "How madly I ran after happiness, after women, after liberty. Why? I wanted to free Spain . . . I took everything as seriously as if I were immortal." But now he realizes, " 'It's a damned lie.' It was worth nothing because it was finished. . . . death had disenchanted everything." He cannot comprehend his own death, yet the immanent prospect affects everything for him. More than anything else, he is gripped with the sense that nothing ultimately matters any longer—"several hours or several years of waiting is all the same when you have lost the illusion of being eternal." Pablo supposedly knows the whereabouts of an important rebel leader named Ramon Gris, and his captors are willing to trade Pablo's life and freedom for information leading to the arrest of Gris. Pablo stubbornly refuses to tell them where he thinks Gris is hiding, though for no good reason. He thinks, "I would rather die than give up Gris. Why? I didn't like Ramon Gris any more. My friendship for him had died" with the loss of hope for a future.

> They were going to slap a man up against a wall and shoot at him till he died, whether it was I or Gris or somebody else made no difference. I knew he was more useful than I to the cause of Spain but I thought to hell with Spain and anarchy; nothing was important.

So, Pablo perversely sends the authorities out on what he thinks will be a wild-goose chase for the sheer fun of making fools of them before he dies. He thinks, "It was a farce. I wanted to see them stand up, buckle their belts and give orders busily" on the illusion they were about to get their way. He later is freed and is astonished to learn that he is being freed because the authorities did indeed find Gris in the cemetery, where Pablo had jokingly told them he was hiding. As Pablo says in the closing words of the story, "Everything began to spin and I found myself sitting on the ground: I laughed so hard I cried."[195] Just as there can be no human nature or ground of absolute value without God, according to Sartre, so the lack of immortality and the prospect that death ends all renders life devoid of any ultimate meaning and absurd.

Fulfillment

In *Truth and Existence* Sartre considers the "classic question: Why does man live?" It is human consciousness, the ground of all "action and freedom," that is the origin of the concept of purpose. And it is a mistake to imagine that there is some already given purpose that constitutes fulfillment for all of us. Such an idea seems particularly outlandish given Sartre's conviction that there is no common human nature that might be oriented to such an objective goal. Hegel's notion of the "cunning of reason," for example, "has no place in subjectivity as free choice: it is quite simply the passage to the objective."[196] We must freely choose our own values and try to progress towards our own finite goals as best we can.

In *Notebooks for an Ethics* Sartre writes, "There is no reason to prepare a kingdom of morality or of happiness for strangers or unknown people at the price of injustice and unhappiness today. We have rather *today* to reach some improvement that will prepare the way for tomorrow's improvement." This is quite in line with his repudiation of idealistic conceptions of absolute purpose. He is sarcastically critical of the utilitarian conception of happiness as the be-all and end-all of man's existence: "Happy during the mass, happy when he counts on eternal life and on justice, happy when he prays, etc." The objectionable assumption is "that this happiness has to be installed in each person as a *state of affairs* completely cut off from the process that brought it about and, in particular, from the real situation." This alienates us from our present existence and locates happiness in an elusive future, objectifying us as instrumental means for bringing it about. Sartre writes of man, "Contradiction: if one does take care to give him happiness, it is because he is a free creature—but in order to give it to him, one turns him into an object." Rather the human subject, as free, must constitute his own meaning and work to realize it. Our best bet seems to be to try to pursue our own goals as honestly as possible, authenticity being a "source of joy" to the extent that it is achievable. A life of bad faith cannot be fulfilling, on Sartre's view of the human person. "For the authentic man, on the contrary, man's greatness," Sartre says, derives from an acceptance of his own limitations and contingency. "Thus the authentic man perpetually surpasses the temptation . . . *to be* everything."[197] We should accept our own freedom and responsibility, choosing and acting upon our own values while being sensitive to the ways in which our choices affect others, avoiding, to the extent that we can, bad faith and the illusion that we can ever fill up all the "holes" of our existence.

REFLECTIONS

Of all the theories of the human person we have emphasized here, Sartre's is the most individualistic and places the most radical emphasis on freedom and responsibility. His theories of knowledge and of values are the most subjective, and he is the only avowed atheist. All the other major theorists considered, from Plato through James, despite their obvious differences as to how it should be defined, could agree that we do all share a common human nature. As we have seen, Sartre views this as a myth, maintaining that each human person, rather, exercises freedom and consciousness to create his or her own individual nature, which is subject to constant change or ratification. From this perspective, a benefit of ending our studies with Sartre's theory is that it helps us critically to challenge that basic assumption. Are we humans like all other things in our world in this respect? Do all human beings in all cultures at all times in history under all circumstances share a common nature that sets parameters within which their individual personalities can develop? We should note that this is not a biological question. Of course, we are all members of the same biological species, genetically similar, with comparable DNA structures, and so forth. But what of human consciousness, the human personality, what philosophers of previous centuries used to identify as the soul? Is this so unique in each individual as not to allow for any common nature? Or, to put it in Sartre's terms, are we different from most other things in that our "existence precedes essence," defining it individualistically? This is the great critical issue raised by Sartre's theory. But, before dealing with it further, let us consider some reflections on his treatment of each of our ten topics.

REALITY. Sartre's theory of reality exaggerates the oppressive superfluity of all things. Reality is only "superfluous" or absurd if Sartre is correct in assuming that there is no ultimate rational explanation (whether that be a God or a process of scientific evolution) for it. In fact, the history of philosophy (including some of the thinkers studied here) is replete with efforts to identify the metaphysical source of reality; Sartre has not so much refuted any of those attempts as he has dismissed them all. But even if he were right about this, why should we be so neurotically obsessed with the ultimate absurdity of reality as his character Roquentin is, rather than accepting it and making the best of our world and of our lives while we can? Next, Sartre's dualism between "being-in-itself" and "being-for-itself," despite its perhaps annoying terminology, does seem to capture a fundamental dichotomy, in that we do experience differently conscious and nonconscious reality. The problem, though, is one that applies to every dualism since Plato's, that of relating the two realms. How does (or even could) consciousness originate in nonconscious being? Sartre leaves us unsatisfied by treating this as a metaphysical mystery and not trying to deal with it.

BODIES. Second, his theory of a nonconscious body as "being-in-itself," which simply is what it is and is not what it is not, is not particularly illuminating. Apparently, he does not care to discuss the nature of nonconscious bodies, except for the sake of drawing contrasts with consciousness, perhaps leaving that task to scientists. Far more significant is his solution to the problem of ontological dualism in the human person, his view that in us body and consciousness are one rather than constituting two different things that must be somehow related. Like James, he is trying to develop a more cohesive and integrated view. His idea of consciousness as always (and necessarily) embodied and situated in a world is at least plausible and simpler than some earlier theories. (Remember Aristotle's ambivalence on this issue.) This steers a middle path between the ontological dualism of Plato and the materialism of Hobbes. But what Sartre fails to do is shed any light on how and why consciousness emerges as a "nothingness" at the heart of the being of the human body.

PERSONALITY. As for our third topic, Sartre offers one of the most intriguing (because the most extreme of) theories of personality we have emphasized. On the one hand, he admits that nonhuman animals are conscious, which ought to render them "for-itself" like us; but, on the other, he seems to attribute the hallmarks of the for-itself only to humans. This suggests some fuzziness in his analysis, which might be solved by identifying the "for-itself" with self-consciousness, as found in humans, and by simply observing that Sartre is only really interested in human beings. He does an effective job of defining at least his own brand of existentialism in terms of the "existence precedes essence" formula, though it is not necessary to interpret that as radically as he would have us do. Can we seriously distinguish, as he would have us do, between a "human nature" and a "universal human condition," of which freedom is a fundamental structure? Why should we not, departing from his view, hold that human beings are unique among living beings on Earth in that they *participate* in defining their own personalities within the parameters established by their common human nature (including their biological organisms, their consciousness, their capacity for free action, and their tendency to social feelings)? Sartre's treatment of the three existential emotions is brilliant but again quite extreme. He is importantly correct in holding that we (it seems uniquely among creatures) experience anguish, forlornness, and despair; and *to some extent* we should, as free and responsible, conscious agents, do so. But why need this be seen as such an onerous, traumatic realization? Why not view it, in Jamesian fashion, as at least as much an adventurous opportunity as an awful burden, serious but not crushing? We may grant that our decisions must be ultimately ours; but that does not render us as desperately alone as Sartre's excessively individualistic theory maintains because of the very engagement in positive, cooperative social relationships that he downplays. We do learn to trust others to work with us for the realization of common goals, and this trust is not merely a mirage on the highway of despair. Sartre effectively defends existentialism against some criticisms, convincingly showing that it need not and does not advocate a passive quietism and that there is an "optimistic toughness" to it. On the other hand, he cannot dismiss its negative, pessimistic side, given his emphases on the superfluity of all reality and the ultimate meaninglessness of our projects; and he does seem to undermine the legitimacy of values by rendering them so subjective, although he convincingly shows that he is not advocating a nihilistic destruction of all values. His views on our "desire to be God" and our wish to fill up the "hole" of our being make the legitimate point that we are inescapably finite; but again, he pushes it too far in characterizing our attempts to realize our projects as "a useless passion." (James's meliorism may seem a far healthier perspective.) Sartre's discussion of "bad faith" is excellent. There is something uniquely revealing about our capacity for self-deception, and his insight that it stems from our not being merely what we are and our being potentially what we are not is quite apt. On the other hand, the quest for authenticity need not be impossible; granted that it is a matter of degree and that (perhaps) no one is absolutely and irrevocably authentic, some people are nevertheless, for all practical purposes, honest with themselves, so that it is an achievable (as well as a laudable) goal for us to pursue. Sartre may be correct that consciousness is pure intentionality of objects with no content in itself; if nothing else, this offers a challenging alternative to the more traditional view of it as a substantial but nonmaterial entity. His theory of emotions is refreshingly nonreductionistic compared to that of James; emotions are not merely our ways of being conscious of physical states but ways of relating psychically to our environment and organized structures of consciousness itself.

KNOWLEDGE. Fourth, Sartre's theory of knowledge has not yet become one of the most studied dimensions of his philosophy, largely because *Being and Nothingness*, his masterpiece and most widely read work, contains too few bits and pieces of epistemological ideas to amount to a systematic theory. Yet his focus on the conscious questioning of experience as the basis for knowledge is valuable and continues the historical line of thought of Plato and Aristotle that philosophy begins with intellectual wonder. His notion that all knowledge is intuitive and that deductive demonstration is not knowledge at all but merely an instrumental means to intuition seems a needlessly restrictive analysis of knowledge, and it would be more accurate to say that all forms of knowledge (including the demonstrative) require a foundation in intuition, as Kant claims. Sartre's posthumously published *Truth and Existence* reemphasizes the central importance of our "questioning" of experience and explores (as James did, in his own way) the idea that truth essentially relates consciousness and being. The metaphorical treatment of truth revealing hidden being is more provocative than illuminating. Perhaps the greatest problem with Sartre's epistemology (as with James's) is its relativism (his being worse than James's in that it edges us into subjectivism and does not stress objective pragmatic verification). Finally, his "progressive-regressive method" is a valuable tool for synthesizing an awareness of events leading to other events with explanatory analysis of why such sequences occur, although there is nothing radically new in this idea, apart from the name Sartre gives it.

FREEDOM.   His discussion of freedom, our fifth topic, is probably the most exciting dimension of his theory. Like Descartes, he is correct in identifying freedom as a fundamental structure of human consciousness, although it does not follow, as Sartre believes, that they are identical. He is also right, against Descartes, to emphasize the practical creative productivity of this freedom. His radical view of freedom as unlimited except by the fact of our having to be free is an exaggeration. Both Descartes and Sartre should recognize that our freedom is always practically limited by our awareness, which, in turn, is a function of our conscious experience. Sartre correctly emphasizes the serious responsibility attached to human freedom but dramatically exaggerates in thinking it "overwhelming." Kant's view may be preferable, that, as free agents, we bear moral responsibility for our choices, but that the primary thrust of this responsibility is that we should function as persons of good will, not imagining that we can control all the consequences of our actions. Likewise, Sartre goes too far when he denies that there are any accidents in life and insists that a person chooses his situation, even if it is only the most preferable of a range of bad alternatives. Of course, we are normally responsible for how we react to accidents in our lives; but they remain accidents, for which we are not responsible, and they can severely limit our subsequent choices. It is at least misleading and insensitive to say that the draftee who fights in a war he hates when his only alternatives are being shot and committing suicide has "chosen" that war. Sartre's proposed existential psychoanalysis is valuable in getting people to confront (and either endorse or abandon) their fundamental projects; but it is typically myopic in dismissing the importance of environmental occurrences (that constitute elements of the facticity of their past). Again, James's view of freedom as a "postulate of rationality" asserted in a context of limiting forces for the sake of making sense of our lives and contributing to progress seems not only more moderate but also more productive than Sartre's.

MORALITY.   Sixth, Sartre's subjective theory of morality seems even more objectionable than the relativistic one of James. Not only does Sartre assume that ethics must be relative to contingent, changing circumstances, but he offers no objective standard, such as that of pragmatic consequences, against which to measure values. The idea that we individually create all values is even more destabilizing (potentially anarchistic) than the view that we develop them socially. In this respect James's pragmatic humanism, despite its faults, seems more trustworthy than Sartre's existential humanism. Perhaps the reason Sartre never completed his *Notebooks for an Ethics* is that his ontology (specifically his philosophy of the human person) provides no adequate basis for asserting freedom as a fundamental universal value. On the one hand, he gives us an ethical subjectivism that renders all values functions of the free choices of individuals; yet, on the other hand, freedom and responsibility for our choices assume the position of fundamental values, with the inauthenticity of bad faith being categorically condemned. But why should we embrace our own freedom and responsibility, if we prefer self-deception? In denying moral objectivity, Sartre may be reducing all value judgments to unimpeachable statements of preference. Even if we do value our own freedom, however, why should anyone experience any obligation to respect the freedom of others? Sartre's subjectivism provides no springboard for moving from egoism to reciprocity (in this respect, even Hobbes's view is more cogent). Sartre's emphasis on the "totalities" of interpersonal relationships falls short of cogency since all such "totalities" seem arbitrary on his grounds. Ironically, his *Dirty Hands* seems only to emphasize this weakness.

SOCIETY.   Regarding our seventh topic, Sartre's treatment of society is equally deficient, for the same reason—namely, his subjective ontology cannot bear the weight. The section of *Being and Nothingness* titled

"The Look" is a brilliant psychological adaptation of Hegel's Master-Slave dialectic and grippingly represents the potentially threatening dimension of interpersonal relationships. Sartre here characterizes the tension between the subjectivity and the objectivity of humans more powerfully than any other philosopher (including even Hegel himself) ever has. But his excessively negative treatment of love, sexual desire, and community spoils the power of this treatment as a basis for a theory of society (to his credit, he acknowledges this in the interview of May 1975). *No Exit* magnificently captures both the arresting brilliance and the one-sided negativity of this theory of interpersonal relationships. Unfortunately, his *Critique of Dialectical Reason*, the big book in which he tries to rectify this problem, is so problematic that it only reinforces the suspicion that no viable theory of society can be built on such an excessively subjective version of existential thought. Part of the problem is the poor writing of the book (remarkable in that it comes from a winner of the Nobel Prize for Literature, who has shown himself to be capable of superb writing), which is jargon-ridden and obscurely prolix to the point of distraction. But, beyond the execrable style of the work, it attempts an awkward synthesis of existential freedom and subjectivity with Marxist-inspired social criticism and collective practice. Sartre's ambivalence towards material reality is a special problem here: to the extent that he emphasizes its importance, his theory of radical freedom is compromised; to the extent that he deemphasizes it, he loses his basis for the rhetoric about class struggle and the alienation of workers. Nor is his theory of society, as a "multiplicity" relating "groups" and "series," any better—it seems such a muddled step backward from both the organic model of Hegel and the libertarian model of Mill. The value of the *Critique* is that it exposes the inextricable link between a social theory and its underlying views on the human person and values. Even if Sartre's subjectivism does allow for a tenable social philosophy, it appears to be a remarkably poor basis for a cogent theory of collective action.

RELIGION.   Eighth, his views on God and religion are too dogmatic to be more than interesting. He rules out God as a mere symbol of human aspirations because of his unsubstantiated assumption that being-in-itself and being-for-itself are the two exhaustive and mutually exclusive sorts of reality. But this is merely a stipulative dichotomy. Why must all consciousness be contingent, finite, and perpetually incomplete, even granted that every *human* consciousness is so? In a sense Sartre has simply defined God out of existence, in an *a priori* manner, for Sartre's own ideological purposes (i.e., to preserve his radical conception of human individuality, freedom, and responsibility). Nor is his condemnation of religious belief as bad faith any more plausible. It certainly can have some foundation in our moral experience (as Kant maintained) and/or our mystical intuitions (as James thought), neither of which should be cavalierly dismissed without critical analysis. Although it is inconsistent to speak of a self-sufficient, infinite God needing anything else, this problem is easily cracked by either (with Aquinas) denying that this is a matter of need on God's part or (with James) denying that God is infinite and self-sufficient.

IMMORTALITY.   Sartre's dismissal of human immortality (our ninth topic) is likewise too facile. Unlike Hume and James, who are similarly sceptical, he never seriously entertains its possibility. This is because of his unjustified assumption that all consciousness must be embodied. His analyses of death, both in *Being and Nothingness* and in "The Wall," are fascinating. Yet, despite his efforts to defend existentialism against the charge that it is overly negative, these analyses are relentlessly pessimistic. If all human projects are ultimately absurd and all efforts ultimately collapse into meaninglessness, we cannot help wondering why anyone should bother. An untimely death, of course, can prevent a person from achieving her goals; but death, as anticipated by people, provides a temporal structure to life within which they can work to accomplish their plans. Again James's confident conviction that there are objective (though person-relative) values to be realized by fighting for them seems to offer us a more constructive incentive for initiative, effort, and action.

FULFILLMENT.   Finally, Sartre's ideas on human fulfillment are quite consistent with his subjective theory. If there is no common human nature, it seems unlikely that we could identify any universal way of fulfilling ourselves. But why should this not apply to his ideal of authenticity as well as to any other? If there is no common human nature to be fulfilled and if each individual must find his or her own personal satisfaction, why could not some people find their joy in the pursuit of a life of bad faith, more or less successfully concealing the anguish, forlornness, and despair that attend their own freedom and responsibility?

*   *   *

Despite the above criticisms, Sartre is extremely valuable as a radical challenge to earlier perspectives and as a corrective against the rationalism and collectivism of many of his predecessors. Although he goes too far, he is correct in emphasizing the uniqueness of the human individual, the fundamental role of consciousness in our existence, the central importance of freedom and responsibility, and the moral value of authenticity. Let us spurn his dubious distinction between a "human

nature" (which he rejects) and a "universal human condition" (which he accepts) and embrace human nature as encompassing some of the very elements on which he focuses, such as embodied consciousness, free self-actualization, and a balance of facticity and transcendence. If man is a personal animal, Sartre's theory does a far more effective job of discussing his personality than his animality. Other thinkers (such as Aristotle and Hobbes) have done better in analyzing man as a physical organism living in and dependent on a material environment. If human personality comprises dimensions of rational thought (emphasized by such disparate thinkers as Plato, Aquinas, Descartes, Hume, Kant and Hegel), moral freedom (emphasized, for example, by Augustine and James), and social action (emphasized by Mill, among others), Sartre deals with all of them.

QUESTIONS

1. *Make up your own examples of James's seven realms of reality. Do you think all of these should be considered "real," and can you think of other sorts of "reality" that James overlooks? Explain.*

2. *Why does James prefer the attitude of "meliorism" to either "optimism" or "pessimism"? Why would you agree or disagree here?*

3. *Against what criticism does James defend belief in the possibility of immortality? Why do you consider his argument here convincing or unconvincing?*

4. *What does Sartre mean by "being-in-itself" versus "being-for-itself"? Why does this seem to you an adequate or inadequate way of classifying reality?*

5. *What does Sartre mean by "bad faith" and the three existential emotions? Why do you suppose he considers these so important?*

6. *Why does Sartre deny that there is any such thing as "human nature"? Does he sneak the idea in the back door when he admits there is a "universal human condition"? Explain your answer.*

7. *Compare and contrast James's theory of the self and "stream" of consciousness with Sartre's view of consciousness as "nothingness" and a "hole" in being. Which do you think more accurate, and why?*

8. *How is James's theory of knowledge somewhat "existential," and how is Sartre's somewhat "pragmatic"? Despite the overlap, how do they fundamentally differ? Which seems more valuable, and why?*

9. *Why is freedom so crucially important to both James and Sartre? How do their approaches to this common topic significantly diverge? What are the strengths and weaknesses in each approach?*

10. *What would it mean to call James a moral relativist and Sartre a moral subjectivist? How might each criticize the other? Why do (don't) you think their theories of morality significantly different?*

11. *How do James and Sartre exhibit different attitudes towards our relationships with other members of society? Is Sartre's individualistic existentialism or his Marxist socialism closer to James's pragmatic progressivism? Why might many serious people be reluctant to agree with either of these thinkers here?*

12. *Why do James and Sartre reject the traditional Judeo-Christian conception of God? How are their discussions of religious faith radically opposed to each other? How might a believer reasonably respond to both of them?*

ALTERNATIVES

There does not seem to be any great, creative philosophical system-building since Sartre; nor has any particularly exciting philosophy of human nature emerged in the last few decades. But let us briefly consider three twentieth-century alternatives. The first is Ludwig Wittgenstein, one of the most famous and influential philosophers from this Age of Analysis. Our second alternative is actually a pair of professors of moral philosophy at Glasgow University—Robert S. (R. S.) Downie and Elizabeth Telfer—whose book, *Respect for Persons*, published in 1969, is far less famous than it deserves to be. Our final alternative is John Rawls, recently retired from the philosophy department at Harvard University, whose book, *A Theory of Justice* (published in 1971), is already very influential. All of these thinkers represent the broad perspective of contemporary analytic philosophy, which emphasizes conceptual analysis and represents the dominant approach to philosophy in English-speaking countries of the world for most of this century.

*　*　*

WITTGENSTEIN

Ludwig Wittgenstein was born in Vienna in 1889 (the year before the publication of James's *Principles of Psychology*), the youngest of eight children in a prosperous, cultured family. His father was a successful engineer and industrialist, and his mother was a pianist (Brahms was a frequent guest in their home). After studying engineering in Austria and Berlin, he went to the University of Manchester to study aerodynamics in 1911. However, when his interests shifted to mathematics and logic, he entered Cambridge University the following year to study with Bertrand Russell. During World War I, Wittgenstein served in the Austrian army and became a prisoner of the Italians in 1918. While imprisoned, he worked on his *Tractatus Logico-Philosophicus*, which was published in 1921. This is an odd and puzzling philosophy book because of both its content, which focuses on logic and language rather than seeking out the truth about reality, and its form, which consists largely of numbered aphorisms, the meaning of which is often quite obscure. Wittgenstein tries to show that philosophical problems stem from misunderstanding the logic of our

language; to offset this, he attempts to limit the legitimate expression of thought and to characterize whatever lies beyond that limit as nonsense. He depicts the world as a totality of independent, irreducible facts, none of which necessarily implicates any others; this position is referred to as logical atomism. Thoughts are logical pictures of facts and are expressed by propositions, whose linguistic signs are sentences. Language not only expresses thought but disguises or conceals its essence, which can be revealed by logical analysis. Such analysis shows most philosophical problems to be unsolvable, because they are nonsense, and to stem from our failure to understand the logic of our language. Philosophy is not a natural science, and its legitimate function is to provide an analysis of language leading to logical clarification. According to this "picture theory" of language, propositions are mental models of reality, and the limits of our language signify the limits of our world. The self or human subject is not a *part* of the world—thus, not an object of natural science—but is a *limit* of the world. Ethics, aesthetics, and metaphysics are all nonscientific because they transcend the legitimate limits of language. They enter the realm of the mystical, about which we cannot intelligibly speak, but which we must confront in silence. Wittgenstein acknowledges that even the propositions of his own book are unscientific nonsense; he compares them to a ladder, which, after we have climbed, we must throw away.

Thinking he had nothing to add to the *Tractatus*, he became a schoolmaster in Upper Austria from 1920 to 1926; annoyed by dull, lazy, frivolous pupils (he left after striking a student and being ordered by a judge to undergo psychological examination), he became an architect in Vienna for a couple of years. During this time, he produced no philosophical work but did attend meetings of the Vienna Circle, a group of intellectuals who developed a philosophy, called "**logical positivism**," based on his work (and also rooted in ideas of Hume). Wittgenstein, in turn, was influenced by their discussions to reconsider his own views on language.

In 1929, he returned to Cambridge, having given away the inheritance left him by his father. After the *Tractatus* was accepted as his doctoral dissertation, he spent most of the rest of his life teaching there; though he never published anything more during his lifetime, his influence was considerable because of his lectures and privately circulated copies of his manuscripts. He became a professor at Cambridge in 1937, was awarded a philosophy chair in 1939, resigned in 1947, and died of cancer in 1951. By the early 1930s, he had abandoned the "picture theory" of language; by the middle of that decade, he had begun writing his *Philosophical Investigations*, which would be published posthumously in 1953 and which developed a more flexible theory of language.

Curiously, the book begins with a quote from Augustine's *Confessions* representing the picture theory of language which the earlier Wittgenstein had advocated but which he now criticizes as inadequate. Language does far more than simply name objects pictured in thought. To capture his understanding of the rich complexity of language, let us consider three metaphors he employs. Linguistic activity uses words as tools. Imagine the many tools contained in a well-equipped tool box: hammers, pliers, wrenches, saws, screwdrivers, and so forth, each with its own special function. The words we use in language, likewise, serve a wide variety of functions. As the function of a tool is defined by its legitimate use, so the meaning of a word can often be defined by its usage in the language. A second metaphor is that of language-games. As there are indefinitely many possible games we can play, each defined by a set of rules governing activity in that game, so there are many human concerns and forms of life to which various linguistic activities are relevant: describing, commanding, reporting, questioning, praying, speculating, joking, thanking, cursing, etc. Exclamations, for example, cannot be adequately understood in terms of the naming of objects pictured in thought. Again, in many, but not all, cases meaning must be understood in terms of usage. Wittgenstein anticipates a Platonic objection to his analogy between uses of language and a variety of games: just as card games, board games, ball games, and so forth must share some common essence whereby they are all "games," so there must be some common essence shared by all uses of language. In response he introduces a third metaphor of family resemblances. It will not do to say, in dogmatic fashion, that there must be such common essences; we must rather look and see whether there are or not. When we

adopt this empirical approach, what we find is a complex network of similarities, relationships, and partially shared characteristics, comparable to members of a typical human family, no two of whom are identically alike, but all of whom share physical features and/or personality traits with some of their relatives. Likewise, the many uses of language share overlapping characteristics, even if we find no essence common to all of them. The later Wittgenstein of the *Investigations*, like the earlier Wittgenstein of the *Tractatus*, views the task of philosophy as therapeutic, to analyze alleged problems in such a way as to reveal the nonsense resulting from their transcendence of the legitimate limits of language. He says that every philosophical problem assumes the form of someone having lost his way; Wittgenstein's goal is to help the fly find its way out of the fly bottle. This analytic view of philosophy is described as a struggle against the linguistic bewitchment of our intelligence and is compared to treating an illness. If Wittgenstein is correct, the only proper function of philosophy is that of descriptive analysis; it can never provide the sort of theoretical foundation for thought and experience sought by all twelve of the great thinkers on whom this book has focused but must simply leave reality as it is. Because philosophical problems are ultimately nonsensical, they are not to be solved so much as their underlying confusion is to be dissolved. As Wittgenstein's earlier work influenced the development of logical positivism, so his later work exerted an immense influence on linguistic analysis (including what is sometimes called ordinary language philosophy) that continues today and is evident in the other philosophers we are about to consider.

DOWNIE AND TELFER

Robert S. Downie, born 1933, and Elizabeth Telfer, born 1935, are both graduates of Oxford University; they were Lecturers in Moral Philosophy at Glasgow University when *Respect for Persons* was published in 1969. Downie also published *Roles and Values* (1971), and Telfer wrote a highly respected paper on "Friendship" (also published in 1971).

In analyzing the idea of *Respect for Persons*, Downie and Telfer must explain what is uniquely characteristic of persons that renders them particularly worthy of moral respect. Adopting Mill's phrase, they announce that they are trying to define the "distinctive endowment of a human being." This quest, then, is for the "generic" human self, what we all essentially share in common that sets us apart from other sorts of beings. They proceed to adopt a basically Kantian view that what is morally special about humans is that they are persons and that personhood is to be analyzed in terms of rational will. Having rational will involves being able to make one's own choices and pursue one's own goals, to carry out one's own plans in an independent manner. So self-determination and autonomy are at the core of the possession of rational will. But, they admit, there is a third essential dimension of personhood typically undervalued by Kantians (but emphasized by Hume). This is the emotional dimension of feelings and sentience, which need not be separated from reason and will but which, in human persons, necessarily involves rational will. So, the three dimensions of personhood are the cognitive one of thinking, the conative one of willing, and the affective one of feeling. It is the dynamic combination of these capabilities that makes us moral agents worthy of respect. What Downie and Telfer mean by respecting a person is regarding him or her as intrinsically valuable. This is to cherish a person for what he is (rather than for what he has or does) or, in Kantian language, to treat him as an end in himself and not merely as a means to our own selfish ends.

Perhaps the most ingenious aspect of their book is to be found in the way Downie and Telfer apply this conception of respect for persons to the areas of "public" and "private" morality. Like ancient Greeks (e.g., Plato and Aristotle), great medieval thinkers (e.g., Augustine and Aquinas), and important modern philosophers (e.g., Hume and Kant), they are convinced that morality must cover both interpersonal relationships ("public") and virtuous qualities pertaining to one's own character ("private"). They analyze utility, equality, and liberty as the three primary values of public morality. Mill is right that we should care about and work for the happiness of persons; but he fails to explain clearly enough that the reason we should strive for a (Jamesian) maximum satisfaction of desires is that persons, by their nature, are intrinsically valuable. Kant is right that there should be a presumption of moral equality among all persons, such that universalizing rules is desirable as well as possible. And Mill is right to hold up liberty as a core

value, though this should be understood to involve social cooperation, as well as noninterference, with other persons. By "private" morality is meant that aspect of it that is "self-referring." This involves traditional virtues, such as prudence, courage, and temperance (discussed by Plato, Aristotle, Augustine, Aquinas, Hume, and Kant). But it also involves self-realization (or what Mill called self-development) and authenticity (advocated by Sartre). If we are to realize our own potential as persons and flourish, self-respect is needed. Respecting ourselves as persons is as morally important as respecting others. Self-respect requires relative independence and self-control. Though none of the elements of *Respect for Persons* is particularly original, what is impressive is the synthesis of ideas constructed by Downie and Telfer.

RAWLS

John Rawls was born in Baltimore in 1921 and received a doctorate in philosophy from Princeton University in 1950. After teaching at Harvard for about three decades, he retired in 1991. Although he is most acclaimed for *A Theory of Justice*, which was published in 1971, he has published numerous articles and, in 1993, a second book, entitled *Political Liberalism*.

A Theory of Justice, by John Rawls, is arguably the most important philosophy book published after 1970. Although primarily a work of political philosophy, it is based on an underlying conception of human nature. It views justice as the primary virtue of social institutions and employs a **social contract** theory to account for this virtue. As an analogue to the concept of the **state of nature** in traditional social contract models (as in Hobbes), Rawls uses "the original position" as a hypothetical explanatory device. We can imagine free and equal persons, who are rational agents, mutually disinterested in the sense of pursuing their own goods with little or no concern for the interests of others (in other words, they are not motivated by envy). We can imagine that they are operating under a "veil of ignorance," regarding their own special talents and characteristics, and are able to make mutually binding agreements concerning principles on which their society will be founded. This is again a basically Kantian model of human nature. But Rawls adds to this account Hume's notion that such persons live in an environment of moderate scarcity, such that there are not enough primary goods (rights, liberties, powers, opportunities, income, and wealth) for everyone to enjoy in an unlimited way, but there is enough that we can live decently by social cooperation. We need to construct and agree upon principles of justice that will enable us to meet our primary interests as persons and to achieve such social cooperation.

In order to be fair and effective, such principles would need to meet certain formal requirements. First, they must be *general*, or able to be formulated without being connected to particular individuals; second, they must be *universal* in application, applying to all members of society alike as moral persons; third, they must be *public*, in the sense that all members of society should be able to know about them; fourth, they should allow us to settle conflicting claims by *ordering* them in terms of relative justice; and, fifth, they should be *final*, in the sense of providing the ultimate court of appeal for practical decision making. Rawls argues that there are two principles of justice that meet all five of these conditions and that would be rationally chosen by persons in his hypothetical original position. The first requires maximum equal liberty, in the sense that each person should have a right to the greatest amount of basic liberty (civil rights such as are protected by the American Constitution) compatible with the same liberty for all

others. The second principle allows for social and economic inequalities only when two conditions are met:

1. Those inequalities must be reasonably expected to be to the advantage of all, including even the least advantaged.
2. Such advantages must be connected to offices and positions to which all people have equal opportunity.

The first of these principles of justice is to have priority over the second in that basic liberties must never be limited or rendered unequal for the sake of socioeconomic advantage; the second has priority over all utilitarian efficiency. These principles will allegedly provide a basis for social justice and promote self-respect (corresponding to the dimensions of public and private morality found in Downie and Telfer).

* * *

What we see in both *Respect for Persons* and *A Theory of Justice* is a basically Kantian model of human nature, onto which other elements may be grafted, used as a basis for further theorizing in the areas, respectively, of ethics and political philosophy. However sympathetic or unsympathetic we may be to these two books, they testify to the fundamental importance of having a clear conception of human nature, which one can articulate and for which one can argue.

Notes

1. William James, *The Letters of William James*, ed. Henry James (Boston: Little, Brown, and Co., 1926), Vol. One, pp. 22–23, 31–32, 47, 53, 56, 60–61, 84–85, 138, 140. This book is henceforth called "*Letters*."

2. William James, *The Varieties of Religious Experience* (New York: New American Library, 1958), pp. 135–36. This book is henceforth called "*Varieties*." *See also Letters*, Vol. One, pp. 145–46.

3. *Letters*, Vol. One, pp. 147–48; cf. p. 129.

4. Ibid., Vol. Two, p. 233; Vol. One, p. 203; Vol. Two, pp. 2–3.

5. Ibid., Vol. One, pp. 294, 296, 300–1; Vol. Two, p. 3; Vol. One, p. 319.

6. William James, *Talks to Teachers on Psychology: and to Students on Some of Life's Ideals* (New York: W. W. Norton & Co., 1958), p. 19. This book is henceforth called "*Talks*."

7. *Letters*, Vol. Two, pp. 45, 47, 105, 146, 165. On p. 58 he writes, "although religion is the great interest of my life, I am rather hopelessly non-evangelical, and take the whole thing too impersonally."

8. Ibid., p. 172.

9. William James, *Memories and Studies* (Westport, CT: Greenwood Press, 1968), pp. 209–26. This book is henceforth called "*Studies*."

10. *Letters*, Vol. Two, pp. 259, 266, 268, 276, 279–80.

11. Ibid., pp. 303, 300–301.

12. William James, *Collected Essays and Reviews* (London: Longmans, Green & Co., 1920), p. 11. This book is henceforth called "*Collected*."

13. William James, *The Will to Believe and Other Essays in Popular Philosophy* and *Human Immortality* (New York: Dover Publications, 1956), pp. 263–80, 290–94. This book is henceforth called "*Will*." *See also* "Monistic Idealism" and "Hegel and His Method," in William James, *Essays in Radical Empiricism and A Pluralistic Universe*, ed. Ralph Barton Perry (New York: E. P. Dutton & Co., 1971), pp. 158–60, 162–78, 181–84. This book is henceforth called "*Essays*." *See also* "A Pluralistic Mystic," in *Studies*, pp. 376, 409–10.

14. William James, *The Principles of Psychology* (New York: Dover Publications, 1950), Vol. Two, pp. 292–93, 295. This book is henceforth called "*Principles*."

15. Ibid., pp. 296–98, 300–301, 312.

16. *Collected*, pp. 430–33.

17. William James, *Pragmatism*, ed. Bruce Kuklick (Indianapolis: Hackett Publishing Co., 1981), pp. 7, 43–45, 63–69, 71, 73–74. This work is henceforth called "*Pragmatism*."

18. Ibid., pp. 110–12, 115–17.

19. Ibid., pp. 125, 127–34.

20. William James, *Some Problems of Philosophy* (New York: Longmans, Green and Co., 1931), pp. 31, 34–37. This book is henceforth called "*Problems*."

21. Ibid., pp. 114–15, 133, 142–43, 190–93, 196–201, 205, 214.

22. William James, *Manuscript Essays and Notes*, ed. Frederick H. Burkhardt, Fredson Bowers, and Ignas K. Skrupskelis (Cambridge, MA: Harvard Univ. Press, 1988), pp. 18, 54. This book is henceforth called "*Manuscript*."

23. *Problems*, pp. 122–23.

24. *Essays*, p. 42; cf. *Manuscript*, pp. 45–46.

25. *Collected*, pp. 414, 416–23.

26. Ibid., pp. 46–47, 316–17, 321–22.

27. *Principles*, Vol. One, pp. 1, 5, 8, 66, 82. *See also* William James, *Psychology: Briefer Course* (New York: Henry Holt and Co., 1910), pp. 1, 3–4, 119. This book is henceforth called "*Psychology*."

28. *Principles*, Vol. One, pp. 105, 112, 114, 121–22; *Psychology*, pp. 135, 138–39, 143–45.

29. *Principles*, Vol. One, pp. 224–26, 236–37, 239–40, 243, 258–59, 271–72, 274–75, 284, 288–89; *Psychology*, pp. 152–54, 157–60, 166–67, 170.

30. *Principles*, Vol. One, pp. 291–94, 296, 313, 319, 324, 334; *Psychology*, pp. 176–81, 190, 194.

31. *Principles*, Vol. One, pp. 339, 342–44, 347–48, 350–53, 357–66, 400–401; *Psychology*, pp. 196, 198, 200, 202–3, 215–16.

32. *Principles*, Vol. One, pp. 402–4, 409, 416–17, 424–25, 487–88, 594–97, 650, 662; *Psychology*, pp. 220–21, 16, 288, 294.

33. *Principles*, Vol. Two, pp. 1–3, 44, 76–77, 82–83; *Psychology*, pp. 12–14, 302, 312, 316–17.

34. *Principles*, Vol. Two, pp. 283–90; cf. William James, "The Psychology of Belief," *Mind*, XIV (July 1889), 321–28. This latter work is henceforth called "The Psychology of Belief."

35. *Principles*, Vol. Two, pp. 295, 308, 312, 317; cf. "The Psychology of Belief," pp. 328–52.

36. *Principles*, Vol. Two, pp. 360, 383, 410, 442, 449–53, 467; *Psychology*, pp. 391, 375–76, 378–81.

37. *Principles*, Vol. Two, pp. 486–88, 501, 527–28; *Psychology*, pp. 415–16, 419–20, 427–28.

38. *Principles*, Vol. Two, pp. 531–34; *Psychology*, pp. 429–34.

39. *Principles*, Vol. Two, pp. 561–62, 567–68, 571–73; *Psychology*, pp. 450, 455–57.

40. *Talks*, pp. 125–29.

41. Ibid., pp. 149–52, 165–66, 169–70, 183, 185–89; see the comparable discussion in "The Energies of Men," pp. 229–64 of *Studies*.

42. *Will*, pp. 256–57, 261–62; *Varieties*, p. 26.

43. *Varieties*, pp. 29–30, 83, 121, 137, 142–45, 189, 385–86. For more direct references to Freud, see William James, *Essays, Comments, and Reviews*, ed. Frederick H. Burkhardt, Fredson Bowers, and Ignas K. Skrupskelis (Cambridge, MA: Harvard Univ. Press, 1987), pp. 474–75, 532. This book is henceforth called "*Comments*." See also *Letters*, Vol. Two, p. 327, where James reports on going to hear Freud speak at Clark University in 1909.

44. *Essays*, pp. 3–9, 16, 22.

45. Ibid., pp. 108–10, 113, 120.

46. *Principles*, Vol. One, pp. 221–22; *Psychology*, p. 14.

47. *Principles*, Vol. Two, pp. 661, 663, 669–71, 675, 677, 688. For a further discussion of existential judgments versus value judgments, *see Varieties*, p. 23.

48. *Will*, pp. 63–67, 70, 75.

49. Ibid., pp. 75–77, 82–86, 88–92; for other passages invoking the quote from *Ezekiel*, *see Principles*, Vol. Two, p. 315, and "The Psychology of Belief," p. 349.

50. *Will*, pp. 95–97, 102–3, 107–9.

51. *Collected*, pp. 434–37, 448–49.

52. *Pragmatism*, pp. 8–13, 18.

53. Ibid., p. 25.

54. Ibid., pp. 25–27.

55. Ibid., pp. 28–33.

56. Ibid., pp. 33–34, 37.

57. Ibid., pp. 77–80, 82–83.

58. Ibid., pp. 84–87.

59. Ibid., pp. 91–92.

60. Ibid., pp. 93–96.

61. Ibid., pp. 96–98, 100–101.

62. William James, *The Meaning of Truth* (Ann Arbor: Univ. of Michigan Press, 1970), pp. 1, 6–8, 23, 36–37, 43–46. This book is henceforth called "*Truth*."

63. Ibid., pp. 46–50.

64. Ibid., pp. 78–82.

65. Ibid., pp. 100–101.

66. Ibid., pp. 126, 132, 134–35; "The Essence of Humanism" is also in *Essays*, pp. 100–107.

67. *Truth*, pp. 205–6, 217–20, 295–96, xxxvi–xxxvii; see also *Essays*, pp. 24–26, where James calls radical empiricism "essentially a mosaic philosophy, a philosophy of plural facts," and contrasts it with the "ordinary empiricism" of Hume and Mill.

68. *Problems*, pp. 7, 11, 15.

69. Ibid., pp. 47–51 (including footnote), 73–74, 106.

70. *Will*, pp. 145–46.

71. Ibid., pp. 149–50.

72. Ibid., pp. 150–52, 155–56.

73. Ibid., pp. 160–63.

74. Ibid., pp. 165–66, 170–71.

75. Ibid., pp. 175–80; *see Pragmatism*, pp. 54–56, and *Problems*, p. 145, for James's connection between a belief in free will and the possibility of genuine novelties in the world.

76. *Collected*, pp. 60–61.

77. *Will*, pp. 184–88.

78. Ibid., pp. 190–92.

79. Ibid., pp. 194–95, 197–98.

80. Ibid., pp. 198–200.

81. Ibid., pp. 201–6.

82. Ibid., pp. 208–9.

83. Ibid., pp. 211–14.

84. *Problems*, p. 3.

85. *Comments*, pp. 251, 253, 255–56.

86. Ibid., pp. 192–93.

87. *Will*, pp. 225–26, 229–30, 232, 259.

88. *Talks*, pp. 170, 178, 189.

89. *Comments*, pp. 162–66, 154–58.

90. *Studies*, pp. 300–301, 303–6.

91. Ibid., pp. 267, 269, 272, 275–77, 280, 283, 286–92, 295.

92. *Will*, pp. 1–4.

93. Ibid., pp. 5–9, 11.

94. Ibid., pp. 12–15.

95. Ibid., pp. 17–22.

96. Ibid., pp. 22–25; cf. William James, *Essays in Philosophy*, ed. Frederick H. Burkhardt, Fredson Bowers, and Ignas K. Skrupskelis (Cambridge, MA: Harvard Univ. Press, 1978), pp. 331–32, for a comparable statement of this sort of voluntarism, which James made about two decades earlier.

97. *Will*, pp. 25–30. *See Pragmatism*, p. 116, and *Letters*, Vol. Two, p. 207, for James's regrets over his "Will to Believe" title.

98. *Will*, pp. 115–16, 122.

99. Ibid., pp. 180–82.

100. *Varieties*, pp. 39–45, 47, 54, 107, 292–94, 323–28.

101. Ibid., pp. 329–31, 333–35, 338–41, 346–47.

102. Ibid., pp. 367, 371, 376–78, 380–81, 383, 388–90.

103. Ibid., pp. 392–97.

104. *Pragmatism*, pp. 35–36, 38.

105. *Essays*, pp. 134, 138, 269–70, 272.

106. Ibid., pp. 274–77; cf. James's "Faith and the Right to Believe," the Appendix to *Problems*, pp. 221–31, where he discusses the "faith-ladder," probabilities, and pluralistic meliorism, and William James, "Reason and Faith," *The Journal of Philosophy*, XXIV, No. 8 (April 14, 1927), 197–201, which also includes a treatment of the "faith-ladder." For more on James's view of God, see Wayne P. Pomerleau, "Does Reason Demand That God Be Infinite?" *Sophia*, 24, No. 2 (July 1985), especially pp. 22, 25.

107. *Letters*, Vol. Two, pp. 213–15.

108. *Varieties*, p. 395; cf. *Will*, p. 80.

109. "Human Immortality," at the end of *Will*, pp. viii, 3, 6.

110. Ibid., pp. 7, 10–18, 23–24, 28–30.

111. Ibid., pp. 31, 35–37, 39–41, 43–45.

112. *Varieties*, pp. 76, 83, 85.

113. *Will*, pp. 32, 37, 43–44, 46, 57–61.

114. Ibid., pp. 61–62.

115. Jean-Paul Sartre, *The Words*, trans. Bernard Frechtman (New York: Fawcett World Library, 1966), pp. 9–11, 13, 16–17, 20–21, 23, 25, 30–32, 37. This book is henceforth called "*Words*."

116. Ibid., pp. 48–49, 51–53, 59, 61–65, 90–91, 95–96, 102, 120, 136–38, 157.

117. Jean-Paul Sartre, *Between Existentialism and Marxism*, trans. John Mathews (New York: Morrow Quill Paperbacks, 1979), p. 61. This book is henceforth called "*Between*."

118. Jean-Paul Sartre, *Life/Situations: Essays Written and Spoken*, trans. Paul Auster and Lydia Davis (New York: Pantheon Books, 1977), pp. 32–33, 58–59, 46. This book is henceforth called "*Life*."

119. Ibid., pp. 15, 24, 46–48.

120. *Between*, pp. 34, 41, 10.

121. *Life*, pp. 44–45.

122. *Between*, p. 39.

123. *Life*, pp. 49, 86, 18.

124. *Between*, p. 119.

125. *Life*, pp. 18, 22.

126. Ibid., pp. 15, 26.

127. *Between*, pp. 67–83, 125–27.

128. *Life*, pp. 83–85, 54, 3–5, 36–38, 60, 91–92.

129. Ibid., pp. 74–75.

130. Jean-Paul Sartre, *Nausea*, trans. Lloyd Alexander (New York: New Directions, 1964), pp. 8, 135–38, 170–74, 176–78, 180–82, 234, 238.

131. Jean-Paul Sartre, *Being and Nothingness*, trans. Hazel E. Barnes (New York: Washington Square Press, 1966), pp. liv, lxxv, lxxix, 14, 17–18;. This book is henceforth called "*Being*."

132. Ibid., pp. lxxvii-lxxix, 273, 275, 371, 375, 378–79.

133. Ibid., pp. 400–402, 415, 430, 480.

134. Paul Arthur Schilpp (ed.), *The Philosophy of Jean-Paul Sartre* (La Salle, IL: Open Court, 1981), p. 40 ("The Interview" with Sartre was translated by Susan Gruenheck). This book is henceforth called "*Sartre*."

135. Jean-Paul Sartre, *Literary and Philosophical Essays*, trans. Annette Michelson (New York: Collier Books, 1962), pp. 221, 241, 243–44, 250–51. This book is henceforth called "*Essays*."

136. *Sartre*, pp. 6, 8, 28, 33–38.

137. Jean-Paul Sartre, *Existentialism and Human Emotions*, trans. Bernard Frechtman (New York: Philosophical Library, 1957), pp. 9–10. (*Note*: The main text is followed by selections from Hazel E. Barnes's translation of *Being and Nothingness*.) This book is henceforth called "*Existentialism*."

138. Ibid., pp. 13–18.

139. Ibid., pp. 18–21.

140. Ibid., pp. 21–24, 28–29.

141. Ibid., pp. 29–31.

142. Ibid., pp. 31–36, 40–46, 49.

143. Ibid., pp. 36–39.

144. Ibid., pp. 49–51.

145. Ibid., pp. 63–66 (or *Being*, pp. 694–95).

146. *Existentialism*, pp. 84–90 (*Being*, pp. 748, 751–54).

147. *Being*, pp. 57–58, 66.

148. Ibid., pp. 66–71.

149. Ibid., pp. 71–73.

150. Ibid., pp. 73–77.

151. Ibid., pp. 77–81.

152. Ibid., pp. 82–86. *See* Jean-Paul Sartre, *Anti-Semite and Jew*, trans. George J. Becker (New York: Grove Press, 1962), p. 90, for an analysis of authenticity. This work is henceforth called "*Anti-Semite and Jew*."

153. *Being*, pp. lxi, lxvii, lxxiv, 4–5, 9, 27, 30.

154. Ibid., pp. 89–91, 96–97, 101–2, 105, 107, 125–26.

155. Ibid., pp. 129–31, 143, 146–47, 150–51, 156. In *Anti-Semite and Jew* (pp. 59–60) Sartre maintains that the human condition is always "in a situation" which delimits possibilities.

156. Jean-Paul Sartre, *The Transcendence of the Ego: An Existentialist Theory of Consciousness*, trans. Forrest Williams and Robert Kirkpatrick (New York: The Noonday Press, 1957), pp. 31–32, 41, 44–45, 52, 60, 104.

157. Jean-Paul Sartre, *Essays in Existentialism*, ed. Wade Baskin (New York: Citadel Press, 1970), pp. 189–90, 198–99, 202–4, 216, 223, 240, 250, 254. (*Note*: "The Emotions: Outline of a Theory" is translated by Bernard Frechtman.)

158. Jean-Paul Sartre, *The Psychology of Imagination*, trans. Bernard Frechtman (New York: Washington Square Press, 1966), pp. 87–88, 123–24, 156, 233, 236–37. This book is henceforth called "*Imagination*."

159. Jean-Paul Sartre, *No Exit and Three Other Plays*, trans. Stuart Gilbert (*No Exit*, *The Flies*) and Lionel Abel (*Dirty Hands*, *The Respectful Prostitute*) (New York: Vintage Books, 1949), pp. 52, 61–62, 68, 86, 88–89, 91–95, 104, 108–9, 112, 116, 121–24, 126–27. This book is henceforth called "*Plays*."

160. *Between*, pp. 156, 169.

161. *Imagination*, pp. 3–8, 12–15, 17, 32.

162. *Being*, p. 6.

163. Ibid., pp. 210, 212, 265–67.

164. Jean-Paul Sartre, *Truth and Existence*, trans. Adrian van den Hoven (Chicago: The Univ. of Chicago Press, 1992), pp. 2, 4–5, 7, 10–12. This book is henceforth called "*Truth*."

165. Ibid., pp. 12–19, 21, 34.

166. Ibid., pp. 42–43, 48, 57, 61, 65, 67, 77.

167. Jean-Paul Sartre, *Search for a Method*, trans. Hazel E. Barnes (New York: Alfred A. Knopf, 1963), pp. xxxiv, 3–4, 7–8, 13–14, 21.

168. Ibid., pp. 133, 153–54.

169. *Essays*, pp. 180, 190–91, 193, 196. In *Imagination*, p. 61, Sartre distinguishes between determinism, which applies to nonconscious reality so that when a certain "phenomenon occurs such another must necessarily follow," and fatalism, which can apply to consciousness, so that a certain event ought to occur and "it is this coming event that determines the series that is to lead up to it." Since freedom applies only to consciousness, he says, its legitimate converse "is not determinism but fatalism."

170. *Being*, pp. 529, 534, 537–38, 541–43, 565, 589–90, 595, 606.

171. Ibid., pp. 677–81 (or *Existentialism*, pp. 52–56).

172. *Being*, pp. 696–704 (*Existentialism*, pp. 68–75, 77–82).

173. *Plays*, pp. 251, 253–54, 258–59, 262, 264, 266, 271, 273, 275, 278, 281.

174. Jean-Paul Sartre, *The Age of Reason*, trans. Eric Sutton (New York: Bantam Books, 1959), pp. 11, 275–76; Jean-Paul Sartre, *The Reprieve*, trans. Eric Sutton (New York: Bantam Books, 1960), pp. 280–82; and Jean-Paul Sartre, *Troubled Sleep*, trans. Gerard Hopkins (New York: Bantam Books, 1961), p. 200.

175. Jean-Paul Sartre, *What Is Literature?* trans. Bernard Frechtman (New York: Harper & Row, 1965), pp. 42–43, 265.

176. *Sartre*, p. 38.

177. *Being*, pp. 765–68 (or *Existentialism*, pp. 91–96).

178. Jean-Paul Sartre, *Notebooks for an Ethics*, trans. David Pellauer (Chicago: The Univ. of Chicago Press, 1992), pp. 3–4, 7–8, 17, 139–40, 198. This book is henceforth called "*Ethics*."

179. Ibid., pp. 431, 433, 449, 460–63, 556, 558.

180. *Plays*, pp. 133, 136, 139, 148–50, 157, 159–61, 166, 181, 199, 202, 204, 209–11, 213–14, 216, 221–25, 229–35, 240–42, 244–48.

181. *Being*, pp. 271–72, 289–92, 294, 298, 311–13, 315.

182. Ibid., pp. 317, 319–22, 326, 354–55.

183. Ibid., pp. 445, 458–59.

184. Ibid., pp. 467–69, 475–77, 483, 485, 489–90.

185. Ibid., pp. 491–94, 505, 507, 525, 689; cf. *Ethics*, p. 414.

186. *Plays*, pp. 9, 16–18, 23–31, 36–47.

187. *Sartre*, pp. 9, 12–14, 18–22, 38.

188. Jean-Paul Sartre, *Critique of Dialectical Reason 1*, ed. Jonathan Rée, trans. Alan Sheridan-Smith (London: NLB, 1976), pp. 21–23, 27, 35, 97, 113, 125, 161, 179, 191, 249n.

189. Ibid., pp. 309, 332, 393, 405, 524, 579, 635, 800.

190. *Existentialism*, pp. 22, 51.

191. *Being*, pp. 370, 693–94, 762.

192. *Ethics*, pp. 146–47, 269, 523–24.

193. *Being*, pp. 139, 379, 651–52, 660.

194. Ibid., pp. 664–70.

195. Jean-Paul Sartre, "The Wall," trans. Lloyd Alexander, in Walter Kaufmann (ed.), *Existentialism from Dostoevsky to Sartre* (New York: New American Library, 1975), pp. 292–94, 296–99.

196. *Truth*, p. 78.

197. *Ethics*, pp. 50, 201–2, 491, 493.

Bibliography

GENERAL

Copleston, Frederick, S.J. *A History of Philosophy*, Vol. VIII, Part II, IX. Garden City, NY: Image Books, 1967, 1977.

Jones, W. T. *Kant and the Nineteenth Century*, 2d ed., rev. San Diego: Harcourt Brace Jovanovich, 1975.

Jones, W. T. *The Twentieth Century to Wittgenstein and Sartre*, 2d ed., rev. New York: Harcourt Brace Jovanovich, 1975.

White, Morton. *The Age of Analysis*. New York: Mentor Books, 1955.

JAMES *Primary Sources*

Collected Essays and Reviews. London: Longmans, Green & Co., 1920.

Essays, Comments, and Reviews. Ed. Frederick H. Burkhardt, Fredson Bowers, and Ignas K. Skrupskelis. Cambridge, MA: Harvard Univ. Press, 1987.

Essays in Philosophy. Ed. Frederick H. Burkhardt, Fredson Bowers, and Ignas K. Skrupskelis. Cambridge, MA: Harvard Univ. Press, 1978.

Essays in Pragmatism. Ed. Alburey Castell. New York: Hafner Press, 1948.

Essays in Radical Empiricism and *A Pluralistic Universe*. Ed. Ralph Barton Perry. New York: E. P. Dutton & Co., 1971.

The Letters of William James, 2 vols. in 1. Ed. Henry James. Boston: Little, Brown, & Co., 1926.

Manuscript Essays and Notes. Ed. Frederick H. Burkhardt, Fredson Bowers, and Ignas K. Skrupskelis. Cambridge, MA: Harvard Univ. Press, 1988.

The Meaning of Truth. Ann Arbor: Univ. of Michigan Press, 1970.

Memories and Studies. Westport, CT: Greenwood Press, 1968.

Pragmatism. Ed. Bruce Kuklick. Indianapolis: Hackett Publishing Co., 1981.

The Principles of Psychology, 2 vols. New York: Dover Publications, 1950.

Psychology: Briefer Course. New York: Henry Holt and Co., 1910.

"The Psychology of Belief." *Mind*, XIV (July 1889), 321–52.

"Reason and Faith." *The Journal of Philosophy*, XXIV, No. 8 (April 14, 1927), 127–201.

Some Problems of Philosophy. New York: Longmans, Green & Co., 1931.

Talks to Teachers on Psychology: and to Students on Some of Life's Ideals. New York: W. W. Norton & Co., 1958.

The Varieties of Religious Experience. New York: New American Library, 1958.

The Will to Believe and Other Essays in Popular Philosophy and *Human Immortality*. New York: Dover Publications, 1956.

William James: The Essential Writings. Ed. Bruce W. Wilshire. Albany: State Univ. of New York Press, 1984.

The Writings of William James: A Comprehensive Edition. Ed. John J. McDermott. New York: Modern Library, 1968.

Writings 1878–1899. Ed. Gerald E. Myers. New York: The Library of America, 1992.

Writings 1902–1910. Ed. Bruce Kuklick. New York: The Library of America, 1987.

Secondary Sources

Dooley, Patrick Kiaran. *Pragmatism as Humanism: The Philosophy of William James*. Totowa, NJ: Littlefield, Adams & Co., 1975.

Flournoy, Th. *The Philosophy of William James*. Trans. Edwin B. Holt and William James, Jr. New York: Henry Holt and Co., 1917.

Perry, Ralph Barton. *In the Spirit of William James*. Bloomington: Indiana Univ. Press, 1958.

Perry, Ralph Barton. *The Thought and Character of William James: Briefer Edition*. Cambridge, MA: Harvard Univ. Press, 1948.

Seigfried, Charlene Haddock. *Chaos and Context: A Study in William James*. Athens: Ohio Univ. Press, 1978.

Vanden Burgt, Robert J. *The Religious Philosophy of William James*. Chicago: Nelson-Hall, 1981.

SARTRE Primary Sources

The Age of Reason. Trans. Eric Sutton. New York: Bantam Books, 1959.

Anti-Semite and Jew. Trans. George J. Becker. New York: Grove Press, 1962.

Being and Nothingness. Trans. Hazel E. Barnes. New York: Washington Square Press, 1966.

Between Existentialism and Marxism. Trans. John Mathews. New York: Morrow Quill Paperbacks, 1979.

Critique of Dialectical Reason I. Ed. Jonathan Rée. Trans. Alan Sheridan-Smith. London: NLB, 1976.

Essays in Existentialism. Ed. Wade Baskin. New York: Citadel Press, 1970.

Existentialism and Human Emotions. Trans. Bernard Frechtman and Hazel E. Barnes. New York: Philosophical Library, 1957.

Life/Situations: Essays Written and Spoken. Trans. Paul Auster and Lydia Davis. New York: Pantheon Books, 1977.

Literary and Philosophical Essays. Trans. Annette Michelson. New York: Collier Books, 1962.

Nausea. Trans. Lloyd Alexander. New York: New Directions, 1964.

No Exit and Three Other Plays. Trans. Stuart Gilbert (*No Exit*, *The Flies*) and Lionel Abel (*Dirty Hands*, *The Respectful Prostitute*). New York: Vintage Books, 1949.

Notebooks for an Ethics. Trans. David Pellauer. Chicago: The Univ. of Chicago Press, 1992.

The Philosophy of Jean-Paul Sartre. Ed. Robert Denoon Cumming. New York: Modern Library, 1966.

The Psychology of Imagination. Trans. Bernard Frechtman. New York: Washington Square Press, 1966.

The Reprieve. Trans. Eric Sutton. New York: Bantam Books, 1960.

Search for a Method. Trans. by Hazel E. Barnes. New York: Alfred A. Knopf, 1963.

The Transcendence of the Ego: An Existentialist Theory of Consciousness. Trans. Forrest Williams and Robert Kirkpatrick. New York: The Noonday Press, 1957.

Troubled Sleep. Trans. Gerard Hopkins. New York: Bantam Books, 1961.

Truth and Existence. Trans. Adrian van den Hoven. Chicago: The Univ. of Chicago Press, 1992.

"The Wall." Trans. Lloyd Alexander. In Walter Kaufmann, ed. *Existentialism from Dostoevsky to Sartre.* New York: New American Library, 1975.

What Is Literature? Trans. Bernard Frechtman. New York: Harper & Row, 1965.

The Words. Trans. Bernard Frechtman. New York: Fawcett World Library, 1966.

Secondary Sources

Cranston, Maurice. *The Quintessence of Sartrism.* New York: Harper & Row, 1971.

Danto, Arthur C. *Jean-Paul Sartre.* New York: Viking, 1975.

Desan, Wilfrid. *The Marxism of Jean-Paul Sartre.* Garden City, NY: Doubleday & Co., 1966.

Desan, Wilfrid. *The Tragic Finale.* New York: Harper & Row, 1960.

Detmer, David. *Freedom as a Value.* La Salle, IL: Open Court, 1988.

Grene, Marjorie. *Sartre.* New York: New Viewpoints, 1973.

Howells, Christina, ed. *The Cambridge Companion to Sartre.* New York: Cambridge Univ. Press, 1992.

Santoni, Ronald E. *Bad Faith, Good Faith, and Authenticity in Sartre's Early Philosophy.* Philadelphia: Temple Univ. Press, 1995.

Schilpp, Paul Arthur, ed. *The Philosophy of Jean-Paul Sartre.* La Salle, IL: Open Court, 1981.

Warnock, Mary, ed. *Sartre: A Collection of Critical Essays.* Garden City, NY: Doubleday & Co., 1971.

Postscript

« «» » » » » » » » » » » » » » » » » » »

et us conclude our study of great philosophers with a recollection of the four basic philosophical questions posed by Kant, which can conveniently structure these final observations:

1. "What can I know?"
2. "What ought I to do?"
3. "What may I hope?"
4. "What is man?"[1]

From the pre-Socratic times of ancient Greece to the present day, thinkers have attempted to answer these questions in at least a piecemeal fashion. The claim to fame of the twelve great philosophers on whom this book is focused is that they answer them in the context of comprehensive philosophical systems. The questions are quite simple in form; yet this is misleading.[2] In fact, they represent profoundly complex, yet fundamentally important, issues to which we have no final, definitive solutions. Nevertheless, let us conclude by weaving some threads together to construct the fabric of a perspective, whose warp and woof are represented by contributions from our twelve great philosophers. As this will reflect a personal point of view, it will be expressed with first-person, singular pronouns (as are Kant's first three questions).

What Can I Know?

The traditional conception of **knowledge** as justified, true belief still seems to me to be essentially correct. Without an act of intellectual commitment constituting belief by a conscious **mind**, knowledge is impossible. Second, that belief must be true in some combination of three respects—**corresponding** to reality, as was emphasized by ancient, medieval, and early modern philosophers, or **cohering** logically with other beliefs to which we are committed, as was indicated by Hegel, or **pragmatically** leading to satisfactory ways of dealing with experience, as was stressed by James. Third, the believing must be justified by some adequate reason(s) for it to count as knowing. Before Hume **rationalists** (from Plato through Leibniz) could **dogmatically** insist on the need for something like **innate** ideas to account for **universal** and **necessary** knowledge; but Hume's uncompromising critical analysis has rendered that theory less than credible. On the other hand, **empiricists** (from Aristotle through Hume himself) have difficulty providing a convincing account of how reasoning can lead to universal and necessary factual knowledge without something like innate ideas, leading us, however unwittingly and unwillingly, to **sceptical** conclusions. I think Kant is correct that knowledge requires and is limited

to the synthesizing of data of sensible experience by means of *a priori* structures of the mind. Not everything beyond this realm of knowledge must be condemned to the status of arbitrary opinion, however. There is a middle ground of rational faith determined by what James calls "**postulates** of rationality" (whose lineage can be traced back to Kant's own postulates of practical reason). These are foundational intellectual commitments for many people, which serve the heuristic function of guiding our thought and action in certain areas. As James points out, the notion that truth can be grasped by the human mind is a basic axiom of the quest for knowledge by traditional science. Human freedom is a basic axiom of **ethics** and political policy. God and an **immortal** human **soul** can be basic axioms of religious life. None of these is conclusively provable or refutable by any scientific methodology; rather, they must be judged in terms of their pragmatic value in helping us establish meaning in various dimensions of interest and endeavor. What we can objectively know is precious to us; yet these other matters of subjective, rational faith are also crucial.

What Ought I to Do?

As our thinking is properly oriented to the ideals of truth and knowledge, so our conduct should aim, in the words of the Bible, to "do that which is right and good" (*Deuteronomy* 6:18). The tricky issue considered by moral philosophers (used in a broad enough sense to include social ethicists and political theorists) is what criterion we should use to determine the right and the good. I think five mainline approaches have emerged here in our study of the great thinkers. First, there is the **virtue**-ethics approach (e.g., of Plato and Aristotle); its problems are the context-dependent selection of the qualities that are to count as virtues and the sort of persons who will serve as moral models and the consequent lack of universality of such a theory. Second, there is the **natural-law** approach (e.g., of Augustine and Aquinas), which is often rooted in **theological** assumptions regarding the divine will; its problems are that such assumptions, which can subordinate ethics to religion, are not experientially well-grounded and are doubted or rejected by so many intelligent, conscientious people. Third, there is the approach of **egoism** (e.g., Hobbes) or **relativism**

(e.g., Hume) or **subjectivism** (e.g., Sartre), whose problem is that it fails to unify us as a people and is therefore socio-politically destabilizing. Fourth, there is the approach of rational **deontology** (e.g., Kant), which is committed to discerning and doing our duty as moral agents; this is the view I favor, because of its universality for all rational beings, who are to be respected as persons, regardless of subjective preferences and likely consequences. Fifth, there is the **utilitarian**/pragmatic approach (e.g., of Mill and James); its problem is that it allows justice to be sacrificed for the sake of beneficial, desirable consequences and threatens to allow sufficiently satisfying ends to justify evil means.

What May I Hope?

In a trivial sense of the word, of course, people can hope for whatever strikes their fancy. But Kant means to ask what sorts of hope are reasonable for us as humans. Here those postulates of rationality reenter the picture. Kant seems to maintain that human experience (particularly in the area of moral responsibility) is such that we should rationally believe in God, personal immortality, and the establishment of a permanent moral order as objects of hope to which we are committed. I think this is an exaggeration and that his **moral argument** fails to support it. Nor have rationalists (like Plato and Augustine), who try to provide knock-down, drag-out arguments to justify such beliefs as knowledge, proved to be successful. James seems closer to being correct here in his observation that some people's experience is such that it is reasonable for them to believe in, hope for, and work for the sake of such ideals.

What Is Man?

Although this fourth question, unlike the previous three, does not employ any first-person, singular pronoun, in a way it is the most personal one of all, striking at the very core of our humanity. It has been the most obvious focus of this book. All ten of the topics (from "Reality" through "Fulfillment") we have studied, from the perspectives of our twelve great philosophers, have provided dimensions of theories designed to answer this question. As was indicated in the Preface to this book, I (unlike Sartre) think we do share a definable common **essence** as human beings, summarized by the phrase "personal animal." We are both physical organisms living in and biologically dependent on a material environment (i.e., animals) and beings that normally and naturally have the capacities for rational thought, social emotions, and moral freedom (i.e., persons). This synthesis can be constructively related to all twelve of our great philosophers. Empiricists (such as Aristotle, Hobbes, and James) tend to do the best job of analyzing our animal nature. Rationalists (such as Plato, Descartes, and Hegel) tend to do the best job of analyzing our capacity for rational thought. Those thinkers (such as Aquinas, Hume, and Mill) who most emphasize the values guiding our actions tend to do the best job of analyzing our capacity for social emotions. Those philosophers (such as Augustine, Kant, and Sartre) who most seriously explore the issue of **autonomous** choice tend to do the best job of analyzing our capacity for moral freedom. All twelve of these theories seem to me to be at least partially correct and helpful for answering Kant's fourth question. But, whatever my own way of putting things together, an exciting project for you to pursue is that of constructing and articulating your own perspective. Materials for critical appropriation have been provided to you by our twelve great philosophers.

Notes

1. Immanuel Kant, *Logic*, trans. Robert S. Hartman and Wolfgang Schwarz (Indianapolis: Bobbs-Merrill, 1974), p. 29.

2. Wayne P. Pomerleau, "Four Deceptively Simple Questions," *Charter* (Spring, 1986), pp. 5–13.

Appendix: LOGIC

INTRODUCTION

Logic is the systematic study of reasoning and argumentation. As in speech and writing, where we express ideas in words, combine these words to form sentences, and interrelate sentences to comprise paragraphs, so in logical reasoning we formulate concepts and combine them into *propositions*, which can be interrelated to constitute *arguments*. If our basic concepts are unclear (i.e., vague or ambiguous), that can create problems from the outset. If the propositions we use for purposes of logical reasoning are untrue, they cannot lead us to reliable conclusions. If the **inferences** we use to move from some propositions to others are *fallacious*, or faulty, the argument will be unconvincing, no matter how certainly true our **presupposed** starting points may be. So, to achieve effective reasoning, we need to relate conceptually clear, true propositions by means of logically correct inferences. We can infer propositions from other propositions in two basic ways: certainly and necessarily, in *deductive* argumentation, and with various degrees of likelihood or probability, in *inductive* argumentation. Since the purpose of any argument is to be convincing, a good argument must be convincing, while an argument is bad to the extent that it is unconvincing. To criticize an argument means to evaluate it rationally in order to determine whether, and to what extent, it is convincing (and not necessarily to tear it down or find fault with it).

Propositions

A **proposition** or statement is expressed by a declarative sentence and relates a subject term to a predicate term in such a way that the proposition as a whole can be regarded as either true or false. If we say, "The oldest living American citizen is a philosophy professor," the predicate term, "a philosophy professor," purportedly describes the subject term, "the oldest living American citizen," by means of concepts that may or may not actually apply. Thus, we can ask whether the proposition as a whole is true or false. Truth and falsehood are the (only) two possible **truth values** of a proposition in our **two-valued logical system**, although, of course, we often do not know (and sometimes need to find out) the truth value of a given proposition. Whether or not we know the truth of a particular proposition, such as the one of our example, we can *assign* a truth value of *true* (T) or *false* (F) to it, subject to rules that will subsequently be explained.

Other **multiple-valued logical systems** are also in

Logic (from the Greek *logos*, meaning reasoning).   The systematic study of reasoning and argumentation, often divided into deductive (or formal) logic vs. inductive (or informal) logic

Inference.   A process of deductive or inductive reasoning from one or more statements, called premises, to another, called the conclusion

Presupposition.   An assumption, especially of an argument

Proposition (from the Latin *propositio*, meaning what is put forward or proposed).   A statement or what is expressed by a declarative sentence relating a subject term to a predicate term in such a way that the proposition as a whole can be regarded as true or false

Truth values.   Truth or falsehood, as they apply to propositions

Two-valued logical system.   The system of (propositional) logic with two truth values

Multiple-valued logical systems.   Systems of (propositional) logic with more than two truth values

use; in three-valued logic, a third choice allows for the possibility of *uncertainty;* in more complex systems additional truth values are added, allowing for various degrees of probability. The advantages of two-valued logic, the system which we will be considering, are that it is the simplest one and also the one most widely used.

Negation, Conjunction, Disjunction

NEGATION.   If we *negate* or deny a truth value, we must assign the opposite truth value to the resulting proposition. Thus, if we assume that it is true (T) that "the oldest living American citizen is a philosophy professor," the **negation**, "The oldest living American citizen is not a philosophy professor," must be false (F). So, the negation of a true proposition (or one assumed to be true) must be false, and the negation of a false proposition must be true.

A **truth table** is a schematic device for analyzing logically related truth values in (propositional) logic. Any proposition p can be true (T) or false (F); if it is true, then its negation, not p, symbolized by $\sim p$, must be false; if the original proposition p is false, then $\sim p$ must be true. We can express this in a simple truth table as shown in Table 1.

p	$\sim p$
T	F
F	T

Table 1. The truth table for $\sim p$

CONJUNCTION.   The logical process of **conjunction** combines or joins together two propositions. In order for a conjunction as a whole to be true, both of its **conjuncts** (or propositions *conjoined* to make it up) must be true; if either of the conjuncts is false, the conjunction as a whole will be false. Throughout this Appendix we will refer to the following propositions as examples:

p: Humans are terrestrial creatures.
q: Humans are mortal animals.

r: Humans are omnipotent deities.
s: Humans are moral agents.
t: Humans are angelic beings.

If it is true that "humans are terrestrial creatures" (p) and also that "humans are mortal animals" (q), then the conjunction (symbolized by $p \wedge q$) must also be true, so that

$p \wedge q$: Humans are both terrestrial creatures and mortal animals

is true. If it is true that "humans are mortal animals" (q) but false that "humans are omnipotent deities" (r), then the conjunction

$q \wedge r$: Humans are both mortal animals and omnipotent deities

is false.

Again, remembering that every basic proposition (such as p, q, and r) can be regarded as either true or false, we can use the truth-table device to represent these relationships, setting it up so that we include every possible combination of truth values for the basic propositions involved. The truth table for two propositions contains 4 (i.e., 2^2) rows, corresponding to the 2×2 truth-value choices for each of the propositions, independent of one another.

In Table 2, the truth table for $p \wedge q$, the first of the four (horizontal) rows of truth-value combinations, is the one most of us believe applies when p and q are as previously defined. In Table 3, for $q \wedge r$, it is the second of the four truth-value combinations, which most of us believe applies when q and r are as previously given.

p	q	$p \wedge q$
T	T	T
T	F	F
F	T	F
F	F	F

Table 2. The truth table for $p \wedge q$

Negation.   The claim or assertion that a proposition is false, so that a given proposition and its negation have opposite truth values

Truth table.   A schematic device for analyzing logically related truth values in (propositional) logic

Conjunction.   The uniting of propositions, as expressed with the word "and"; in order for a logical conjunction to be true, both of its conjuncts must be true

Conjuncts.   The propositions conjoined to make up a conjunction

q	r	$q \wedge r$
T	T	T
T	F	F
F	T	F
F	F	F

Table 3. *The truth table for $q \wedge r$*

DISJUNCTION.   As we can conjoin two propositions with the conjunction "and," so we can also combine propositions using the word "or." However, in English the word "or" can be used in two different senses. Sometimes we want to say that one thing or another is the case, while leaving open the possibility that they could *both* hold; this is the **inclusive sense** of "**or**." For example, with p as previously used and with "humans are moral agents" (s), the *inclusive* form of p or s would allow that humans are terrestrial creatures, or they are moral agents, or possibly both. Thus, in the *inclusive* sense, symbolized by "$p \vee s$," there are three possibilities, as indicated by the truth value (T) in the final column of the first three rows of Table 4.

p	s	$p \vee s$
T	T	T
T	F	T
F	T	T
F	F	F

Table 4. *The truth table for $p \vee s$*

We say that $p \vee s$ is the **disjunction** of its component propositions p, s (the **disjuncts,** or the propositions that are disjoined). This is the general usage of the word "or" in logic, mathematics, and science; unless something is said to the contrary, we will be using "or" in this sense in this Appendix.

At other times, we want to say that one thing or another is the case, but not both, which is the **exclusive** sense of "**or**." For example, we could say that humans are either mortal animals (q) or omnipotent deities (r), but they cannot be both. When this *exclusive* sense of q or r is intended, it is symbolized by $q \veebar r$. The table for q or r in the exclusive sense ($q \veebar r$) is presented in Table 5.

q	r	$q \veebar r$
T	T	F
T	F	T
F	T	T
F	F	F

Table 5. *The truth table for $q \veebar r$*

Notice that Tables 4 and 5 differ in the first of their four rows, reflecting the difference between the inclusive and exclusive use of "or."

The component propositions of $q \veebar r$ (that is, in the *exclusive* sense of "or") are called **mutually exclusive alternatives**; they cannot simultaneously hold true. However, in general, in the disjunction $q \vee r$ (that is, in the *inclusive* sense of "or"), the alternatives (disjuncts q, r) might not exhaust all of the legitimate possibilities, creating what is referred to as a **false dilemma.**

Tautologies, Contradictions, and Equivalences

A **tautology** is a proposition that is true for every possible assignment of truth values to its component parts. For any proposition p, the disjunction $p \vee \sim p$ is a tautology, as is seen by truth-table analysis. In Table 6, column 3, which represents $p \vee \sim p$, contains only T's. Thus, any proposition and its negation are "exclusively joined" (in accordance with Aristotle's **law of** the **excluded middle**). For example, using the proposition s as previously given, the disjunction

---

"Or," inclusive sense.   The use of "or" in "p or q" that allows at least one of the propositions p, q to be true

Disjunction.   The uniting of propositions, as expressed with the word "or" in the inclusive sense; in order for a logical disjunction to be true, at least one of its disjuncts must be true

Disjuncts.   The propositions that are disjoined to make up a disjunction

"Or," exclusive sense.   The use of "or" in "p or q" that allows exactly one of the propositions p, q to be true

Mutually exclusive alternatives.   Two possibilities that cannot simultaneously hold true (e.g., either frail or robust); the component propositions of p or (exclusive sense) q (i.e., $p \veebar q$)

False dilemma (or **bifurcation**).   The fallacy of presuming that an either-or distinction is exhaustive (and/or mutually exclusive) when other alternatives exist

Tautology.   A proposition that is always true for every possible assignment of truth values to its component parts

Excluded middle, law or **principle of**.   A basic law of Aristotelian logic asserting the truth of the disjunction of any (significant) proposition together with its negation

$s \vee \sim s$: Either humans are moral agents or humans are not moral agents

is clearly always true.

①	②	③
p	$\sim p$	$p \vee \sim p$
T	F	T
F	T	T
	$\sim$①	①$\vee$②

Table 6. $p \vee \sim p$ *is a tautology*

A **contradiction** is a proposition that is false for every possible assignment of truth values to its component parts. For any proposition p, the conjunction $p \wedge \sim p$ is a contradiction. In Table 7, column 3, which represents $p \wedge \sim p$, contains only F's. Thus, any proposition and its negation are "mutually contradictory" (in violation of Aristotle's **law of noncontradiction**).

①	②	③
p	$\sim p$	$p \wedge \sim p$
T	F	F
F	T	F
	$\sim$①	①$\wedge$②

Table 7. $p \wedge \sim p$ *is a contradiction*

For example, the conjunction

$s \wedge \sim s$: Humans are moral agents, but (and) they are not moral agents

is obviously always false.

Two propositions p and q are said to be **equivalent**, written

$$p \equiv q$$

if their truth tables agree, row by row, for every assignment of truth values to their component parts. For any proposition p, it is easy to see, using Table 8, that

$$p \equiv p$$

(in accordance with Aristotle's **law of identity**).

p	p
T	T
F	F

Table 8. $p \equiv p$

For example, using (a variant of) proposition s, on page A–2,

Whenever a human is a moral agent, he (she) must be a moral agent

is clearly true regardless of whether or not a specific human is a moral agent.

It is also easy to see that for any propositions p and q:

$$p \vee q \equiv q \vee p$$
$$p \wedge q \equiv q \wedge p$$

For the first of these, the truth-table analysis is given in Table 9, and the second can be shown similarly (Question 6(a) on page A–15). Thus, for disjunction and conjunction the order of the disjuncts and conjuncts does not matter.

①	②	③	④
p	q	$p \vee q$	$q \vee p$
T	T	T	T
T	F	T	T
F	T	T	T
F	F	F	F
		①$\vee$②	②$\vee$①

Table 9. $p \vee q \equiv q \vee p$

Combining Several Propositions

We can combine three propositions, p, q, and r, in various ways. For example, the parentheses indicate that

$$(p \vee q) \vee r$$

is a disjunction, one of whose disjuncts is (the disjunction) $p \vee q$, whereas the parentheses indicate that

$$p \vee (q \vee r)$$

is a disjunction, one of whose disjuncts is (the disjunction) $q \vee r$. A truth table for a proposition constructed from three basic propositions contains

---

Contradiction. A proposition that is false for every possible assignment of truth values to its component parts

Noncontradiction, law or **principle of.** The Aristotelian law of thought that no proposition (or statement) and its negation (or denial) can both be true of the same thing(s) at the same time in the same respect

Equivalent propositions. Propositions whose truth tables agree, row by row, for every possible assignment of truth values to their component parts

Identity, law of. Aristotle's law which maintains that everything is what it is and cannot simultaneously be something other than what it is; for every proposition p, p is equivalent to p

8 (i.e., 2^3) rows, corresponding to the $2 \times 2 \times 2$ truth-value choices for each of the basic propositions, independent of the others. Truth-table analysis (Table 10) shows that

$$(p \vee q) \vee r \equiv p \vee (q \vee r)$$

Because $(p \vee q) \vee r$ and $p \vee (q \vee r)$ are equivalent, we can omit parentheses and write $p \vee q \vee r$ for either statement.

Similarly, the two conjunctions

$$(p \wedge q) \wedge r \text{ and } p \wedge (q \wedge r)$$

are equivalent (Question 6(b), page A–15), that is,

$$(p \wedge q) \wedge r \equiv p \wedge (q \wedge r)$$

and we write $p \wedge q \wedge r$ for either statement.

What happens when we combine conjunction with disjunction? Consider $(p \wedge q) \vee r$, in which the conjunction $p \wedge q$ is disjoined with r—as well as $p \wedge (q \vee r)$, in which p is conjoined with the disjunction $q \vee r$. Truth-table analyses (Table 11) show that

$(p \wedge q) \vee r$ and $p \wedge (q \vee r)$ are *not* equivalent—in symbols:

$$(p \wedge q) \vee r \not\equiv p \wedge (q \vee r)$$

Similarly, we can consider other propositions combined from p, q, and r, such as

$$(\sim p) \vee (q \vee r)$$

which is the disjunction of $\sim p$ with $q \vee r$, and

$$\sim(p \wedge (q \vee r))$$

which is obtained by first taking $q \vee r$, then

$$p \wedge (q \vee r)$$

and then negating this conjunction. And there can be more than three component propositions:

$$p \vee q \vee r \vee s$$
$$((\sim p) \vee q) \wedge (r \vee s \vee t)$$

etc.

①	②	③	④	⑤	⑥	⑦
p	q	r	$p \vee q$	$(p \vee q) \vee r$	$q \vee r$	$p \vee (q \vee r)$
T	T	T	T	T	T	T
T	T	F	T	T	T	T
T	F	T	T	T	T	T
T	F	F	T	T	F	T
F	T	T	T	T	T	T
F	T	F	T	T	T	T
F	F	T	F	T	T	T
F	F	F	F	F	F	F
			① ∨ ②	④ ∨ ③	② ∨ ③	① ∨ ⑥

Table 10. $(p \vee q) \vee r \equiv p \vee (q \vee r)$ *because columns ⑤ and ⑦ agree*

①	②	③	④	⑤	⑥	⑦
p	q	r	$p \wedge q$	$(p \wedge q) \vee r$	$q \vee r$	$p \wedge (q \vee r)$
T	T	T	T	T	T	T
T	T	F	T	T	T	T
T	F	T	F	T	T	T
T	F	F	F	F	F	F
F	T	T	F	T	T	F
F	T	F	F	F	T	F
F	F	T	F	T	T	F
F	F	F	F	F	F	F
			① ∧ ②	④ ∨ ③	② ∨ ③	① ∧ ⑥

Table 11. $(p \wedge q) \vee r \not\equiv p \wedge (q \vee r)$ *because columns ⑤ and ⑦ disagree in the fifth and seventh rows*

Implication and Biconditional Implication

IMPLICATION.   We sometimes want to hold that one thing or idea *logically implies* another or is a *conditional* of the other. For example,

If humans are terrestrial creatures,
|_____|
p

then they are (also) mortal animals.
|_____|
q

This is a hypothetical statement, called an **implication** or **conditional**, in which the *hypothesis* (governed by "if") is called the **antecedent**, and the *conclusion* that allegedly follows from it (governed by "then") is called the **consequent**. The symbol $\rightarrow$ (translated as "implies") is used to represent the relation of implication so that the example in this paragraph is represented as $p \rightarrow q$. What we want to rule out is the possibility of something that is true implying a falsehood. Then, by definition, $p \rightarrow q$ means that q can never be false when p is true. If the antecedent is true, the consequent must also be true; on the other hand, if the antecedent is false, the consequent can be allowed to be either true or false.

It may be helpful to think of an implication as a contract which states that if p is fulfilled by one party, then q must be fulfilled by the other party. So, if the first party fulfills her part (p is true), then the second party must fulfill his part (q is true) for the contract to be honored. On the other hand, if the first party reneges (p is false), then the second has complete freedom (q can be either true or false); the contract is not violated with either choice for q.

Table 12, the truth table for $p \rightarrow q$ is true except in the second row.

p	q	$p \rightarrow q$
T	T	T
T	F	F
F	T	T
F	F	T

Table 12. *The truth table for $p \rightarrow q$*

Here are two other statements,

$$\sim p \vee q \text{ and } \sim(p \wedge \sim q)$$

with the same truth tables as $p \rightarrow q$, as is shown in Table 13. Thus,

$$p \rightarrow q \equiv (\sim p) \vee q \equiv \sim(p \wedge \sim q)$$

When we say that one thing or idea is a **necessary condition** for another, we are asserting a kind of implication. Humans being mortal animals (q) may be a necessary condition for their being terrestrial creatures (p), so that the latter implies the former ($p \rightarrow q$). When we say that one thing or idea is a **sufficient condition** for another, we are asserting another kind of implication. Humans being terrestrial creatures (p) may be a sufficient condition for their being mortal animals (q), so that the former implies the latter ($p \rightarrow q$). Thus, with reference to an implication

$$p \rightarrow q$$

p is a sufficient condition for q

whereas

q is a necessary condition for p.

①	②	③	④	⑤	⑥	⑦	⑧
p	q	$p \rightarrow q$	$\sim p$	$(\sim p) \vee q$	$\sim q$	$p \wedge (\sim q)$	$\sim(p \wedge (\sim q))$
T	T	T	F	T	F	F	T
T	F	F	F	F	T	T	F
F	T	T	T	T	F	F	T
F	F	T	T	T	T	F	T
			$\sim$①	④ $\vee$ ②	$\sim$②	① $\wedge$ ⑥	$\sim$⑦

Table 13.
$p \rightarrow q \equiv (\sim p) \vee q \equiv \sim(p \wedge (\sim q))$

Implication (or **conditional**).   A proposition of the form, "if p, then q," which is true except when p, the antecedent, is true and q, the consequent, is false

Antecedent.   In an implication "if p, then q," the proposition p

Consequent.   In an implication "if p, then q," the proposition q

Necessary condition.   With reference to an implication, "if p, then q," q is a necessary condition for p

Sufficient condition.   With reference to an implication, "if p, then q," p is a sufficient condition for q

BICONDITIONAL IMPLICATION. When we say that one thing or idea is a **necessary and sufficient condition** for another, we are asserting a *biconditional implication* ("if and only if"). Perhaps humans being terrestrial creatures (p) may be both a necessary condition for their being mortal animals (q), so that the latter implies the former ($q \rightarrow p$), and a sufficient condition for their being mortal animals (q), so that the former implies the latter ($p \rightarrow q$). Thus, the **biconditional implication** p if and only if q (symbolized by $p \leftrightarrow q$) asserts that when p is true, q must be true and (*conversely*) when q is true, p must be true. It follows that when p is false, then q is false, and vice versa. In other words, for the biconditional implication $p \leftrightarrow q$ to be true, p and q must have the same truth values, as they do in the first and fourth rows in Table 14.

p	q	$p \leftrightarrow q$
T	T	T
T	F	F
F	T	F
F	F	T

Table 14. *The truth table for $p \leftrightarrow q$*

As was indicated, $p \leftrightarrow q$ is equivalent to the conjunction of $p \rightarrow q$ and $q \rightarrow p$, that is,

$$p \leftrightarrow q \equiv (p \rightarrow q) \wedge (q \rightarrow p)$$

as is seen in Table 15.

Contradictories, Contraries, and Converses

Propositions can be opposed to each other in various ways. When two propositions p and q are exclusively disjoined, there is a *contradiction* between them, in that one of them must be true and the other must be false; then, $p \wedge q$ is a contradiction. Such propositions are said to be **contradictories**. One example of contradictories is any proposition p together with its negation $\sim p$. For another example, we might hold that "humans are mortal animals" (q) and "humans are omnipotent deities" (r) are contradictories, assuming these were the only two possibilities. On the other hand, two propositions are **contraries** when they cannot both be true, though they could both be false. Thus, we might hold that "humans are omnipotent deities" (r) and "humans are angelic beings" (t) cannot both be true (if either of them is true, the other must be false), though they could both be false. A third sort of propositional opposition is a *converse relationship*, in which $q \rightarrow p$ is the **converse** of $p \rightarrow q$; but, unless the two propositions p and q are equivalent, the truth of one implication is no guarantee of the truth of the converse implication. For example, even if it is true that

humans are mortal animals implies they are also terrestrial creatures,

that is no guarantee that

humans are terrestrial creatures implies that they are also mortal animals.

① p	② q	③ $p \leftrightarrow q$	④ $p \rightarrow q$	⑤ $q \rightarrow p$	⑥ $(p \rightarrow q) \wedge (q \rightarrow p)$
T	T	T	T	T	T
T	F	F	F	T	F
F	T	F	T	F	F
F	F	T	T	T	T
		① ↔ ②	① → ②	② → ①	④ ∧ ⑤

Table 15. $p \leftrightarrow q \equiv (p \rightarrow q) \wedge (q \rightarrow p)$

Necessary and sufficient condition. For propositions p and q, when p is both a necessary condition for q and a sufficient condition for q; i.e., when both implications $p \rightarrow q$ and $q \rightarrow p$ are true

Biconditional implication. A proposition of the form, "p if and only if q" ($p \leftrightarrow q$), which is true when p and q have the same truth values, so that p and q are equivalent propositions

Contradictories. Two propositions, one of which must be true and the other of which must be false (i.e., it is impossible that both are true, and it is impossible that both are false)

Contraries. Two propositions such that it is impossible for both to be true, although they could both be false

Converse. With reference to an implication $p \rightarrow q$, the implication $q \rightarrow p$

(Try a truth-table analysis.) Notice that when we consider contradictories, contraries, and converses—as when we are dealing with other aspects of propositional logic (negations, conjunctions, disjunctions, and implications)—we are interested in the ways in which propositions are logically related to other propositions.

Argumentation

There is a distinction between **deductive** (or formal) reasoning and **inductive** (or informal) reasoning, depending on whether the reasoning process is designed to lead to **certain** or to merely *probable* conclusions. But in each case we are inferring one proposition, the *conclusion*, from one or more other propositions, the *premises*, which, taken together, supposedly support the conclusion.

Deductive Reasoning

An **argument** is a reasoning process that asserts that a proposition (the **premise**) or the conjunction of several such propositions implies another proposition (the **conclusion**). In deductive reasoning, an argument is said to be **valid** if whenever the premises are *all* true, the conclusion must also be true. Using P for either the single premise of an argument or for the conjunction of the premises, and C for the conclusion, an argument has the form of an implication $P \to C$, in which P is the antecedent and C is the consequent. Thus, an argument is valid if the implication $P \to C$ is a tautology because in a truth table, in any row in which *every* premise is true, the conclusion must also be true. An **invalid** argument is one that is *not* valid; in this case, $P \to C$ fails to be true for at least one assignment of truth values (one row of the truth table). In deductive reasoning an invalid argument is also called a **fallacy**.

CONJUNCTION AND DISJUNCTION. Conjunction can be used to design logical arguments. A common conjunctive argument denies a conjunction, while affirming one of the conjuncts, and concludes that the other conjunct must be false. For example:

> It is not true that humans are both mortal animals and omnipotent deities, yet they are mortal animals; therefore, they cannot be omnipotent deities.

Using our previous designations of q and r, we represent:

> $q \wedge r$: Humans are both mortal animals and omnipotent deities.

> ~$(q \wedge r)$: It is *not* true that humans are both mortal animals and omnipotent deities.

Our argument then has the form

$$(\sim(q \wedge r) \wedge q) \to \sim r$$
$$\underbrace{\qquad\qquad\qquad}_{P} \quad C$$

Truth-table analyses (Table 16) show this argument to be valid.

Deduction.   Reasoning in which the truth of all the premises of an argument supposedly necessitates the truth of its conclusion as certain, as opposed to induction

Induction.   Reasoning that takes the form of a probability argument, deriving a conclusion from the premise(s) as more or less likely, rather than as certain, as opposed to deduction

Certainty.   The assurance that a belief is wholly reliable or that a proposition is indubitably known

Argument.   A logical reasoning process designed to infer one proposition (the conclusion) from one or more other propositions (the premises), which collectively are supposed to support it

Premise.   In an argument, a proposition or statement that is used to provide support for the conclusion

Conclusion.   In an argument, a proposition that is supported by one or more other propositions (the premises)

Valid argument.   In deductive reasoning, an argument that is such that whenever the premises are all true, the conclusion must also be true

Invalid argument.   In deductive reasoning, an argument that is such that for some assignment of truth values, the premises are all true, yet the conclusion is false

Fallacy.   In deductive reasoning, an invalid argument; in inductive reasoning, used in a broader sense

Disjunction can also be used to design logical arguments. A common disjunctive argument affirms a disjunction, then denies all but one of the disjuncts, and concludes that the remaining disjunct (that has not been denied) must be true. For example:

> Humans are either omnipotent deities or moral agents; but, since they are not omnipotent deities, they must be moral agents.

Using our previous designations of *r* and *s*, we represent:

> $r \vee s$: Humans are either omnipotent deities or moral agents.
>
> ~*r*: Humans (they) are not omnipotent deities.

Our argument then has the form

$$((r \vee s) \wedge \sim r) \to s$$
$$\underset{P}{\underline{\hspace{3cm}}} \quad C$$

Truth-table analysis (Table 17) shows this argument to be valid. This common form of disjunctive argument can be called a **process-of-elimination argument**.

CONDITIONAL ARGUMENTS. There are some very common forms of **conditional** or **hypothetical arguments**, three of which are particularly important. An **affirmed antecedent argument** (*modus ponens* in Latin) asserts an implication, then affirms its antecedent as true, and concludes that the consequent must also be true. For example,

> $q \to p$: If humans are mortal animals, then they are terrestrial creatures

but (and) since

> *q*: they are mortal animals

then

> *p*: they must be terrestrial creatures.

①	②	③	④	⑤	⑥	⑦
q	*r*	$q \wedge r$	$\sim(q \wedge r)$	$\sim(q \wedge r) \wedge q$	~*r*	$(\sim(q \wedge r) \wedge q) \to \sim r$
T	T	T	F	F	F	T
T	F	F	T	T	T	T
F	T	F	T	F	F	T
F	F	F	T	F	T	T
		① ∧ ②	~③	④ ∧ ①	~②	⑤ → ⑥
				P	*C*	*P → C*

Table 16. The argument $(\sim(q \wedge r) \wedge q) \to \sim r$ is valid

①	②	③	④	⑤	⑥
r	*s*	$r \vee s$	~*r*	$(r \vee s) \wedge (\sim r)$	$((r \vee s) \wedge \sim r) \to s$
T	T	T	F	F	T
T	F	T	F	F	T
F	T	T	T	T	T
F	F	F	T	F	T
		① ∨ ②	~①	③ ∧ ④	⑤ → ②
	C			*P*	*P → C*

Table 17. The argument $((r \vee s) \wedge \sim r) \to s$ is valid

Process-of-elimination argument. An argument of the form, "if both *p* or *q* and not *p*, then *q*," i.e., $((p \vee q) \wedge \sim p) \to q$

Conditional, or **hypothethical**, **argument.** An argument involving one or more implications (conditionals)

Affirmed antecedent argument (or *modus ponens*). An argument of the form $((p \to q) \wedge p) \to q$, that asserts an implication, then affirms its antecedent as true, and concludes that the consequent must also be true

This argument is of the form

$$((q \rightarrow p) \wedge q) \rightarrow p$$
$$\underbrace{\qquad}_{P} \quad C$$

Table 18 considers this argument.

① q	② p	③ $q \rightarrow p$	④ $(q \rightarrow p) \wedge q$	⑤ $((q \rightarrow p) \wedge q) \rightarrow p$
T	T	T	T	T
T	F	F	F	T
F	T	T	F	T
F	F	T	F	T
		① → ②	③ ∧ ①	④ → ②
	C		P	$P \rightarrow C$

Table 18. *The argument* $((q \rightarrow p) \wedge q) \rightarrow p$ *is valid*

Here $P \rightarrow C$ (column 5) is a tautology (in that all of its truth values are true), so that the argument is shown to be valid.

A **denied consequent argument** (*modus tollens* in Latin) asserts an implication, then denies that its consequent is true, and concludes that its antecedent must also be false. For example:

> If humans are omnipotent deities, then they are not mortal animals. But humans are mortal animals. So they cannot be omnipotent deities.

The argument is symbolized by

$$((r \rightarrow \sim q) \wedge q) \rightarrow \sim r$$
$$\underbrace{\qquad}_{P} \quad C$$

Truth-table analysis (Table 19) shows the argument to be valid.

A **hypothetical syllogism** is a **syllogism** that infers one implication from two others. For example,

> If humans are mortal animals, then they are also terrestrial creatures. But if they are terrestrial creatures, they cannot be omnipotent deities. Therefore, if humans are mortal animals, then they cannot be omnipotent deities.

This is symbolized by

$$((q \rightarrow p) \wedge (p \rightarrow \sim r)) \rightarrow (q \rightarrow \sim r)$$
$$\underbrace{\qquad}_{P} \qquad \underbrace{\quad}_{C}$$

Truth-table analysis (Table 20) shows this argument to be valid.

There are also certain fallacious forms of arguments, two of which are notorious. The **denied antecedent argument** asserts an implication, then denies its antecedent, and (wrongly) concludes that the consequent must also be false. For example,

> If humans are omnipotent deities, then they are also moral agents. But, since they are not omnipotent deities, they cannot be moral agents.

① r	② q	③ $\sim q$	④ $r \rightarrow \sim q$	⑤ $(r \rightarrow \sim q) \wedge q$	⑥ $\sim r$	⑦ $((r \rightarrow \sim q) \wedge q) \rightarrow \sim r$
T	T	F	F	F	F	T
T	F	T	T	F	F	T
F	T	F	T	T	T	T
F	F	T	T	F	T	T
		~②	① → ③	④ ∧ ②	~①	⑤ → ⑥
				P	C	$P \rightarrow C$

Table 19. *The argument* $((r \rightarrow \sim q) \wedge q) \rightarrow \sim r$ *is valid*

Denied consequent argument (or *modus tollens*). An argument of the form $((p \rightarrow \sim q) \wedge q) \rightarrow \sim p$, that asserts an implication, then denies that its consequent is true, and concludes that its antecedent must be false

Hypothetical syllogism. A syllogism of the form $((p \rightarrow q) \wedge (q \rightarrow r)) \rightarrow (p \rightarrow r)$, that infers one implication from two others

Syllogism (from the Greek *syllogismos*, meaning a reckoning together). A deductive argument with two premises and a conclusion

Denied antecedent argument. A fallacious argument of the form $((p \rightarrow q) \wedge \sim p) \rightarrow \sim q$, that asserts an implication, then denies its antecedent, and (wrongly) concludes that the consequent must also be false

① p	② q	③ r	④ q→p	⑤ ~r	⑥ p→~r	⑦ (q→p)∧(p→~r)	⑧ q→~r	⑨ ((q→p)∧(p→~r))→(q→~r)
T	T	T	T	F	F	F	F	T
T	T	F	T	T	T	T	T	T
T	F	T	T	F	F	F	T	T
T	F	F	T	T	T	T	T	T
F	T	T	F	F	T	F	F	T
F	T	F	F	T	T	F	T	T
F	F	T	T	F	T	T	T	T
F	F	F	T	T	T	T	T	T
			②→①	~③	①→⑤	④∧⑥ P	②→⑤ C	⑦→⑧ $P→C$

Table 20. The argument $((q → p) ∧ (p → ~r)) → (q → ~r)$ is valid

① r	② s	③ r→s	④ ~r	⑤ (r→s)∧~r	⑥ ~s	⑦ ((r→s)∧~r)→~s
T	T	T	F	F	F	T
T	F	F	F	F	T	T
F	T	T	T	T	F	F
F	F	T	T	T	T	T
		①→②	~①	③∧④ P	~② C	⑤→⑥ $P→C$

Table 21. The argument $((r → s) ∧ ~r) → ~s$ is invalid

In symbols:

$$((r → s) ∧ ~r) → ~s$$
$$\underbrace{}_{P} \quad C$$

Truth-table analysis (Table 21) shows this argument to be unacceptable because it allows for a case in which both premises are true but lead to a false conclusion.

In the third row, the conjunction of the premises, column 5, is true, whereas the conclusion, column 6, is false. Thus, there is an F in the third row of column 7, indicating that the implication is not a tautology, and therefore that the argument is invalid.

Likewise, an **affirmed consequent argument** is fallacious. It asserts an implication, then affirms its consequent, and (wrongly) concludes that the antecedent must therefore also be true. (But any implication would be true when its consequent is true—even if its antecedent is false.) As an example of an affirmed consequent argument, consider:

If humans are omnipotent deities, then they are also moral agents. Well, humans are, indeed, moral agents. So they must also be omnipotent deities.

In symbols:

$$((r → s) ∧ s) → r$$
$$\underbrace{}_{P} \quad C$$

Truth-table analysis (Table 22) shows the argument to be invalid.

① r	② s	③ r→s	④ (r→s)∧s	⑤ ((r→s)∧s)→r
T	T	T	T	T
T	F	F	F	T
F	T	T	T	F
F	F	T	F	T
C		①→②	③∧② P	④→① $P→C$

Table 22. The argument $((r → s) ∧ s) → r$ is invalid

Affirmed consequent argument. A fallacious argument of the form $((p → q) ∧ q) → p$, that asserts an implication, then affirms its consequent, and (wrongly) concludes that the antecedent must also be true

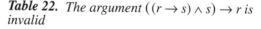

UNIVERSAL AND EXISTENTIAL PROPOSITIONS. A **universal proposition** asserts something that holds for *all* (applicable) individuals or things, that is, for *every* (applicable) individual or thing. Such propositions can be *affirmative* or *negative* in nature. Thus, "All humans are mortal animals" is a universal affirmative proposition, while "No humans are omnipotent deities" is a universal negative proposition. One single effective **counterexample** can suffice to destroy a universal proposition; so if we found even one human who was *not* a mortal animal, the affirmative universal proposition would be **refuted**. And if there were a human who *was* an omnipotent deity, the negative universal proposition would be false.

An **existential** (or **particular**) **proposition** asserts something that holds for *at least one* (applicable) individual or thing, that is, *there exists some* individual or thing. In logic, "some" means one or more.

> Some humans are moral agents

is an existential affirmative statement, whereas

> Some humans are not angelic beings

is an existential negative proposition. A single counterexample will not suffice to refute an existential statement; thus, even if there were a human who was not a moral agent, there could still be other humans who were moral agents. The universal statement,

> All humans are mortal animals

asserts a proposition about humans. We say that the **universe** to which it applies is the set of humans. Letting x vary over the universe of humans, we start with the predicate

> $q(x)$: x is a mortal animal.

Then our universal statement has the form

> for all x, $q(x)$.

The existential statement

> Some humans are mortal animals

has the form

> for some x, $q(x)$.

In general, for any "nonempty" universe (that is one that contains at least one individual) and for any predicate $q(x)$, where x varies over the universe, the implication

> for all x, $q(x) \to$ for some x, $q(x)$

is a tautology. Thus, in our example, if every human is a mortal animal, then surely there is at least one human who is a mortal animal.

Here are two equivalent statements relating negations of universal and existential propositions:

$$\sim(\text{for all } x, q(x)) \equiv \text{for some } x, \sim q(x)$$
$$\sim(\text{for some } x, q(x)) \equiv \text{for all } x, \sim q(x)$$

In the first of these, if it were not true that every human is mortal, then some human would be immortal, and conversely, if some human were immortal, it would be false that every human was mortal. (Try the second equivalence with this example in mind; see Exercise 11 on page A-15.)

An argument can be valid even though every one of its propositions is false:

> All mortal animals are humans, and all humans are omnipotent deities; therefore all mortal animals are omnipotent deities.

Since the conjunction of the premises, P, is never true, the conclusion, C, can be false here; thus, $P \to C$ is a tautology. Likewise, an argument can be invalid, even when all its existential premises are true:

> Some terrestrial creatures are mortal animals, and some mortal animals are moral agents; thus, some moral agents are terrestrial creatures.

This argument has the form

> Some A are (in) B, and some B are (in) C. Thus, some C are (in) A.

Here is a geometric refutation of arguments of this form. Let A represent the points inside the first circle, B, the points inside the second circle, and C, the

---

Universal proposition. A proposition that asserts something that holds for all (applicable) individuals or things

Counterexample. An instance that refutes a universal claim; for example, Europeans once believed that "all swans are white," until the counterexample of a black swan was discovered

Refutation. The disproof of an argument or the demonstration that a position is false or erroneous

Existential (or **particular**) **proposition.** A proposition that asserts something that holds for at least one (applicable) individual or thing

Universe. The set of individuals or things to which a proposition applies

points inside the third circle. Then surely, some *A*-points are in *B*, and some *B*-points are in *C*; but no *A*-point is in C. See the figure that follows.

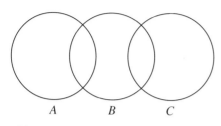

Figure A. *Some A-points are in B, and some B-points are in C; but no A-point is in C*

Sᴏᴜɴᴅ Aʀɢᴜᴍᴇɴᴛs. The most convincing sort of deductive argument (indeed, the strongest argument possible) must meet two conditions: it must be valid, and all of its premises must be true. A deductive argument which meets both of these conditions is said to be **sound**. We can try to launch a double-barreled attack on any deductive argument by attempting to show that it is invalid and also that at least one of its premises is false; if either attempt (let alone both) is successful, we have shot down the argument and shown it to be unsound. These are the two ways to refute a deductive argument.

There are certain rules of validity that a good deductive argument must obey. One of these is that it cannot contain only existential premises (this is why the last example was invalid). Another is that it must contain at least one affirmative premise. Thus, no (nontrivial) conclusion can validly follow from these two premises: "No mortal animals are omnipotent deities, and no mortal animals are angelic beings," because both propositions are negative.

Certain fallacies can vitiate deductive reasoning. For example, the **fallacy of equivocation** uses a key term in an argument in two different senses, destroying logical linkage:

> Only men are rational, but no women are men; so, no women are rational.

Although this argument may look valid, and we might accept both premises as true, it equivocates on the word "men." In the first premise it is presumably used as a (sexist) substitute for humans, while in the second it means adult male human beings. Likewise, the **fallacy of circular reasoning** can destroy the soundness of an argument:

> All terrestrial creatures are mortal animals; and, since some mortal animals are moral agents, some terrestrial creatures are moral agents. Therefore, some mortal animals must be moral agents.

Here the circularity is destructive of the argument because one of the premises used to support the conclusion is itself based on the assumption of that same conclusion. It is also **vicious** because the reasoning is sufficiently pernicious to render the entire argument worthless.

Inductive Reasoning

Inductive reasoning takes the form of a **probability argument**, deriving a conclusion from the premise(s) as more or less likely, rather than as certain. The concepts of validity and invalidity do not apply to inductive arguments, which therefore also cannot be said to be sound or unsound. Nevertheless, we do distinguish between convincing and unconvincing inductive reasoning. An inductive argument is said to be **reliable** or **strong** when its premises provide adequate evidence to

---

Sound argument.   A deductive argument that is valid and all of whose premises are true

Equivocation, fallacy of.   The logical error of using a key term in an argument in two different senses

Circular reasoning, fallacy of (or **begging the question**).   The fallacy of assuming the conclusion of an argument in its premises

Vicious circularity.   A property of argumentation whose circular reasoning is sufficiently pernicious to render the entire argument worthless

Probability argument.   Any argument (such as an inductive one) designed to establish its conclusion as more or less likely or probable, rather than as certain

Reliable (or strong) argument.   An inductive argument in which the premises provide adequate evidence to justify the conclusion to the degree of probability indicated

justify its conclusion to the degree of probability indicated; when it fails to do this, it is said to be **unreliable** or **weak**. Like deductive arguments, inductive ones require true premises; a false (or even doubtful) premise can weaken an inductive argument considerably.

The most common sort of inductive reasoning is the **generalization**. If no twentieth-century human being we have heard about so far has lived more than one hundred fifty years, it might be reasonable for us to generalize that, probably, no humans ever live more than one hundred fifty years, even though there could be some who do. A generalization can be fallacious if it is hasty (i.e., basing too sweeping a conclusion on too limited a data base) and/or unrepresentative (i.e., based on a distorted data base, as might be the case if all the humans we have ever heard about so far were sometimes sick).

One of the weakest forms of inductive reasoning, though it can still have some logical force, is an **argument from analogy**, which concludes, on the basis of comparisons we have encountered between (or among) different things, that there are similarities we have not experienced. For example, humans and chimpanzees are both mortal animals and terrestrial creatures, and in both cases are neither omnipotent deities nor angelic beings. On the basis of these similarities as well as others (for example, both are primates), we might reason that, since humans are moral agents, chimpanzees probably are as well. The **fallacy of false analogy** can arise when the similarities observed are tangential rather than **essential** and/or when crucial dissimilarities are overlooked or ignored. As with deductive reasoning, fallacies can damage inductive reasoning.

QUESTIONS

1. *Are the following propositions clear or unclear?*

   (a) *Humans are smart.*

   (b) *Most humans have at least some hair on their heads.*

   (c) *Some humans are moral agents.*

   (d) *All humans are mortal animals.*

   (e) *If humans are mortal animals, they must be terrestrial creatures.*

2. *For each of the five statements of Exercise 1 that you consider unclear, specify the concept(s) you find problematic.*

3. *For each of the five statements of Exercise 1 that you consider clear, determine whether you regard it as true or false.*

4. *Provide a truth-table analysis of each of the following propositions.*

   (a) $p \vee (\sim q \wedge p)$

   (b) $\sim(p \rightarrow q)$

   (c) $\sim(\sim p \leftrightarrow q)$

   (d) $p \wedge \sim(\sim q \rightarrow p)$

   (e) $p \leftrightarrow (p \rightarrow q)$

Unreliable (or **weak**) **argument**.   An inductive argument in which the premises do not provide sufficient evidence to justify the conclusion to the degree of probability indicated

Generalization.   An inductive inference that what is true (or false) of some observed individuals is probably also true (or false) of others that have not yet been observed

Argument from analogy.   A relatively weak inductive argument alleging similarities on the basis of comparisons previously encountered rather than on that of experience

False analogy, fallacy of.   A fallacy that can arise when similarities that are observed are tangential rather than essential and/or when crucial dissimilarities are overlooked or ignored

Essence.   The set of properties that characterize something as the type of thing it uniquely is and that is necessary for it to be that sort of thing, as opposed to its accidents

5. *Provide a truth-table analysis of each of the following propositions.*

   (a) $p \wedge (q \vee r)$

   (b) $(\sim p \wedge q) \rightarrow r$

   (c) $p \leftrightarrow ((p \rightarrow q) \wedge r)$

   (d) $(p \leftrightarrow q) \leftrightarrow ((\sim p) \leftrightarrow (\sim r))$

   (e) $((p \vee q) \wedge (\sim p) \wedge (q \rightarrow r)) \rightarrow r$

6. *Prove each of the following equivalences by truth-table analysis*

   (a) $p \wedge q \equiv q \wedge p$ *(commutativity of $\wedge$)*

   (b) $(p \wedge q) \wedge r \equiv p \wedge (q \wedge r)$ *(distributivity of $\wedge$)*

   (c) $\sim(p \wedge q) \equiv (\sim p) \vee (\sim q)$ *(DeMorgan's law)*

   (d) $\sim(p \vee q) \equiv (\sim p) \wedge (\sim q)$ *(DeMorgan's law)*

   (e) $p \rightarrow q \equiv (\sim q) \rightarrow (\sim p)$ *(law of contraposition)*

7. *Set up truth tables to prove or disprove the following arguments:*

   (a) *Humans are both terrestrial creatures (p) and moral agents (s). If humans are terrestrial creatures, they are also mortal animals (q). Consequently, humans must be mortal animals.*

   (b) *If humans are angelic beings (t), they are moral agents (s). Humans are either angelic beings or moral agents. So, humans are not moral agents.*

   (c) *Humans are either mortal animals (q) or omnipotent deities (r). Humans are not omnipotent deities. If humans are not terrestrial creatures (~p), they are not mortal animals. Therefore, humans must be terrestrial creatures.*

   (d) *If humans are omnipotent deities (r), they are not angelic beings (~t). Humans are neither angelic beings nor moral agents (~s). Thus, humans must be omnipotent deities.*

   (e) *If humans are mortal animals (q) implies that they are also terrestrial creatures (p), then humans are terrestrial creatures implies that they are also mortal animals.*

8. *Which of the following deductive arguments are valid?*

   (a) *All mortal animals are terrestrial creatures. Some mortal animals are moral agents. Consequently, some moral agents are terrestrial creatures.*

   (b) *No humans are moral agents. Some moral agents are angelic beings. Thus, some angelic beings are not humans.*

   (c) *No humans are mortal animals. Some humans are not moral agents. Therefore, some moral agents are mortal animals.*

   (d) *Some terrestrial creatures are moral agents. Some terrestrial creatures are not mortal animals. So, some moral agents are not mortal animals.*

9. *For each of the four deductive arguments of Exercise 8 that you consider invalid, say why. For each one you think valid, test the truth of the premises (with counterexamples, where possible). Which, if any, of the four arguments do you regard as sound?*

10. *Critically discuss the reliability of the following inductive arguments:*

    (a) *Since most adult Americans living today are moral agents, most adult humans living all over the planet five thousand years ago were probably moral agents.*

    (b) *Humans are like angelic beings in being moral agents who are not omnipotent deities. But, as we know, humans are also terrestrial creatures. We cannot see whether or not angelic beings are terrestrial creatures. But, since they are like humans in other ways, it is quite likely that they too are terrestrial creatures.*

11. *Prove that for any proposition $p(x)$,*

    $\sim(\text{for some } x, p(x)) \equiv \text{for all } x, \sim p(x)$

12. *Why do you suppose that logic and argumentation are considered so vitally important for philosophical purposes? What limitations do you suppose pertain to logical reasoning and argumentation?*

Bibliography

Barker, Stephen F. *The Elements of Logic*, 4th ed. New York: McGraw-Hill, 1985.

Copi, Irving M. *Introduction to Logic*, 6th ed. New York: Macmillan, 1982.

Hurley, Patrick J. *A Concise Introduction to Logic*, 4th ed. Belmont, CA: Wadsworth, 1991.

GLOSSARY

《 》 》

Absolute Spirit/Mind/Idea. The ultimate, unconditioned, uncaused, complete Reality, especially in Hegelian thought

Absurd. Loosely, contrary to reason or to the rules of logic; more precisely, for such existentialists as Sartre, lacking any ultimate rational explanation

Academician. A member of Plato's Athenian Academy, lasting from about 387 B.C. to A.D. 529; often (as in Augustine) identified with scepticism, because of the later Academy's sceptical tendency

Accident. An attribute or property of a thing that is not essential to its nature; more popularly, an unintended event

Adventitious. Coming from without, as from objects outside the mind (for Descartes); more commonly, accidental or casual

Aesthetics (from the Greek *aisthetikos*, meaning pertaining to sense perception). The branch of philosophy dealing with art and beauty; in Kant, the aesthetic examines the *a priori* conditions of sense experience

Affirmed antecedent argument (or *modus ponens*). An argument of the form $((p \rightarrow q) \wedge p) \rightarrow q$, that asserts an implication, then affirms its antecedent as true, and concludes that the consequent must also be true

Affirmed consequent argument. A fallacious argument of the form $((p \rightarrow q) \wedge q) \rightarrow p$, that asserts an implication, then affirms its consequent, and (wrongly) concludes that the antecedent must also be true

Agnosticism. The view that something, especially the existence of God, cannot be known

Alienation (from the Latin *alius*, meaning other). The sense of estrangement from or foreignness to consciousness, especially as discussed by Hegel, Marx, and existential thinkers

Altruism (from the Latin *alter*, meaning other). A selfless concern for the welfare of other people, as opposed to egoism

Analogy. A resemblance or set of similarities between different things, sometimes used as a basis for an inductive inference; some theists, like Aquinas, regard analogy as the correct way to think and speak of God

Analytic. Using or pertaining to the resolution of something complex into simpler elements (as in Descartes); an analytic judgment (since Kant) is one whose predicate term is already implicitly contained in its subject (e.g., "All bachelors are unmarried"), as opposed to a synthetic judgment

Anarchy (from the Greek *anarkhos*, meaning without a ruler). The absence of effective governmental authority, typically resulting in political disorder

Animate (from the Latin *anima*, meaning soul). Living, having a soul

Antecedent. In an implication "if p, then q," the proposition p

Anthropomorphism (from the Greek *anthropos*, meaning human being and *morphe*, meaning form). The attribution of human characteristics to something, such as God, which is nonhuman

Antinomy (from the Greek *antinomia*, meaning conflict in law). The mutual contradiction of two principles, each of which appears to be true and can be supported, especially in Kant

Antiquity. Ancient times, before the Middle Ages, including the Hellenic and Hellenistic periods—for our purposes, until the late fourth or early fifth century A.D.

Antithesis (from the Greek *antitithenai*, meaning to oppose). An idea or proposition set forth in opposition to another (as in Kant's discussion of the antinomies); in Hegelian thought, such opposition is the second phase of a dialectical process, leading to a synthesis of that antithesis and the thesis to which it is opposed

A posteriori (literally, in Latin, from the subsequent). Following and dependent on some particular sense-experience, empirical, as opposed to *a priori*

Apperception. Self-awareness, the mind's consciousness of its own inner states; in Kantian thought, it is the ego's awareness of a unity of self-consciousness

A priori (literally, in Latin, from the previous). Knowable prior to, or independently of, any particular sense experience, as opposed to *a posteriori*

Argument. A logical reasoning process designed to infer one proposition (the conclusion) from one or more other propositions (the premises), which collectively are supposed to support it; more loosely, any dispute

Argument from analogy. A relatively weak inductive argument alleging similarities on the basis of comparisons previously encountered rather than on that of experience

Aristocracy (from the Greek *aristokratia*, meaning rule of the best). A government by the superior people, favored by philosophers prior to the rise of modern representative governments

Atheism (from the Greek *atheos*, meaning godless). Disbelief in or denial of the existence of God or any gods

Atomism (from the Greek *atomos*, meaning indivisible). The view that reality is composed of tiny, indivisible physical particles; more generally, the tendency to analyze things in terms of basic, independent constituent elements

Autonomy (from the Greek *autonomos*, meaning self-legislating). Self-determination, the capacity and/or right to determine one's own views, values, and actions (in Kant, contrasted with heteronomy)

Bad faith. Self-deception, the attempts of consciousness to deny its own freedom and shirk responsibility (in Sartre)

Beatific vision (from the Latin *beatus*, meaning blessed). In Christian theology, the direct knowledge and love of God that produces happiness for the blessed in the afterlife

Biconditional implication. A proposition of the form, " *p* if and only if *q*" ($p \leftrightarrow q$), which is true when *p* and *q* have the same truth values, so that *p* and *q* are equivalent propositions

Capitalism. A socio-economic system in which private capital or wealth is used in the production and distribution of goods

Cardinal virtues (from the Latin *cardo*, meaning hinge, as if all excellence pivots on them). The most important or basic ideals of excellence—often four in number: wisdom or prudence, courage or fortitude, moderation or temperance, and justice

Cartesian circle. A problem in Descartes's philosophy, arising from his claim that the reliability of all clear and distinct ideas depends on our knowledge of God, although that knowledge, in turn, is allegedly based on our grasp of clear and distinct ideas

Categorical. Unconditional or without exception; having to do with definite concepts or structures of understanding; in Kant, a categorical imperative is unconditionally obligatory, as opposed to a hypothetical imperative, which only applies conditionally

Cause. That which explains something, especially in terms of its origin or source of change; the sufficient condition(s) of

something to be explained; Aristotle's four principles of explanation are material, formal, efficient, and final causes; Kant identifies causality as one of the twelve categories or concepts of the understanding

Certainty. The assurance that a belief is wholly reliable or that a proposition is indubitably known

Circular reasoning, fallacy of (or *begging the question*). The fallacy of assuming the conclusion of an argument in its premises

Cogito (from the Latin, *cogito, ergo sum*, meaning I think, therefore I am). Descartes's insight that I know I must mentally exist insofar as I experience any sort of thinking

Cognition (from the Latin *cognitio*, meaning learning, acquiring knowledge). The act or faculty of knowing

Coherence. A relation between experiences, beliefs, or propositions such that they are logically compatible or consistent

Communism. A socio-economic system characterized by an absence of classes and common ownership of property; in Marxist thought, this is the ideal end towards which the revolutionary struggle to overthrow capitalism is a necessary means

Compatibilism. The view (held, for example, by Hobbes, Hume, and Mill) that some human actions are free, in the sense that they do not result from external compulsion, despite the fact that all actions are causally determined

Conclusion. In an argument, a proposition that is supported by one or more other propositions (the premises)

Conditional, or *hypothetical*, *argument*. An argument involving one or more implications (conditionals)

Conjunction (from the Latin *conjunctio*, meaning a joining together or combination). The act of joining together or the fact of things being combined; in logic, this refers to the uniting of propositions, as expressed with the word "and"; in order for a logical conjunction to be true, both of its conjuncts must be true

Conjuncts. The propositions conjoined to make up a conjunction

Consequent. In an implication "if *p*, then *q*," the proposition *q*

Consequentialism. Any theory that judges morality in terms of the consequences of actions; utilitarianism is, perhaps, its most common type today

Conservatism (from the Latin *conservare*, meaning to preserve, maintain). A political ideology committed to conserving traditional values and therefore tending to maintain the existing order and to resist change (often opposed to liberalism)

Consistency. The compatibility of things, actions, beliefs, or logical propositions, such that they can coexist, or be done or held without contradiction, or be simultaneously true

Constitutive. Forming a part of, helping to make up a whole; in Kant, ideas have a constitutive (as opposed to a regulative) function when they can lead to knowledge

Contingency. That which could be otherwise (as opposed to necessity)

Contradiction (from the Latin *contradictio*, meaning a speaking against or refutation). Loosely, a denial or the act of opposing; in logic, a proposition that is false for every possible assignment of truth values to its component parts

Contradictories. Two propositions, one of which must be true and the other of which must be false (i.e., it is impossible that both are true, and it is impossible that both are false)

Contrary (from the Latin *contra*, meaning opposite or against). Loosely, what is opposed or the opposite; in logic, contraries are two propositions such that it is impossible for both to be true, although they could both be false

Converse. Loosely, a reversal of ideas or an opposite assumption; in logic, with reference to an implication $p \rightarrow q$, the implication $q \rightarrow p$

Copernican revolution. Kant's attempt to view objects of experience as needing to meet the requirements of the mind, rather than the traditional view that the ideas of the mind must meet the requirements of objects of experience (analogous to Copernicus's adopting a new model of the solar system, as having all planets moving around the Sun, to replace the old model of the Earth as stationary in the middle of the universe, with all other heavenly bodies revolving around it)

Correspondence theory. The traditional view that a belief or judgment is true if it conforms to reality, subscribed to by almost all Western philosophers before Kant; Kant's revolutionary proposal is that objects must conform to the requirements of the mind rather than the other way around; after Kant, coherence and pragmatic usefulness become alternative criteria of truth

Cosmological argument. An argument purporting to prove the existence of God as the necessary, ultimate First Cause of the universe or cosmos, whose reality (by contrast) is regarded as contingent

Cosmology. That area of inquiry that theorizes about the cosmos, or universe as an organized whole; for Kant, rational cosmology (along with rational psychology and rational theology) is one of the three branches of metaphysical speculation

Counterexample. An instance that refutes a universal claim; for example, Europeans once believed that "all swans are white," until the counterexample of a black swan was discovered

Deduction. Reasoning in which the truth of all the premises of an argument supposedly necessitates the truth of its conclusion as certain, as opposed to induction

Deism (from the Latin *Deus*, meaning God). The belief in a transcendent God who created or designed our world but does not intervene in it

Democracy (from the Greek *demokratia*, meaning rule of the common people). Government by the people, either directly (pure democracy) or through elected officials (representative democracy)

Denied antecedent argument. A fallacious argument of the form $((p \rightarrow q) \land \sim p) \rightarrow \sim q$, that asserts an implication, then denies its antecedent, and (wrongly) concludes that the consequent must also be false

Denied consequent argument (or **modus tollens**). An argument of the form $((p \rightarrow \sim q) \land q) \rightarrow \sim p$, that asserts an implication, then denies that its consequent is true, and concludes that its antecedent must be false

Deontology (from the Greek *deon*, meaning that which is obligatory, and *logos*, meaning an account). The view (e.g., of Kantians) that moral duty must be determined rationally rather than empirically and is independent of the consequences of acts, as opposed to ethical consequentialism

Design, argument from. An argument (also called teleological) for the existence of God as the Designer responsible for the combination of order and complexity characteristic of our world

Determinism. The doctrine that every event in the universe, including every human action, is causally necessitated by antecedent conditions, to the exclusion of free will

Dialectic (from the Greek *dialektikos*, meaning discourse). A process of thought, whereby one thesis, or line of inquiry, leads to its opposite, or antithesis; Plato regards dialectic as the science of first principles; Kant considers antithetical conflict an indication of metaphysical illusion, whereas Hegel sees it as an opportunity to advance rationally to a higher unity, or synthesis

Dictatorship. Autocratic government by an absolute ruler with unrestrained power

Dignity (from the Latin *dignitas*, meaning worthiness). The intrinsic worth of persons

Disjunction (from the Latin *disjunctio*, meaning a separation). The act of separating or the fact of things being separated or disjoined; in logic, this refers to the uniting of propositions, as expressed with the word "or" in the inclusive sense; in order for a logical disjunction to be true, at least one of its disjuncts must be true

Disjuncts. The propositions that are disjoined to make up a disjunction

Dogmatism (from the Greek *dogma*, meaning opinion).

Unwarranted certainty in asserting any doctrine; since Kant, the word more specifically refers to metaphysical claims not grounded in a prior critique of the cognitive powers of reason

Dualism. The view that there are two irreducible sorts of reality, often physical and spiritual, or two irreducible components of human nature, such as body and soul

Eclecticism. The selecting and combining of ideas or doctrines from diverse schools of thought

Egoism. The view that everyone does in fact (psychological egoism) and/or should in principle (ethical egoism) act ultimately to further his or her own interests, as opposed to altruism

Emotivism. The view in ethics (associated with Hume) that moral values are ultimately derived from emotions rather than from reason, as opposed to ethical rationalism

Empire (from the Latin *imperium*, meaning realm or dominion). An extensive territory, often including many nations, under the supreme authority of one person (the emperor or empress) or one sovereign state

Empiricism (from the Greek *empeiria*, meaning experience). The theory that all synthetic or existential knowledge is derived ultimately from sense experience, as opposed to rationalism

Enlightenment. An intellectual movement, especially of eighteenth-century Europe and America, advocating the ideals of reason, science, liberty, and progress

Ens realissimum (from the Latin, literally meaning the most real Being). A term Kant uses for God

Enthymeme (from the Greek *enthumeisthai*, meaning to have in mind or consider). A syllogism in which one premise, or even the conclusion, is merely implied rather than explicitly stated

Epicureanism. The view of followers of Epicurus, that the hedonistic pursuit of pleasure and avoidance of pain aims at the ultimate good

Epiphenomenalism. The view that mental events are merely by-products of physical ones rather than the results of actions of spiritual substances such as souls

Epistemology (from the Greek *episteme*, meaning knowledge, and *logos*, meaning an account). That area of philosophy dealing with the nature, conditions, and limits of human knowledge

Equivalent propositions. Propositions whose truth tables agree, row by row, for every possible assignment of truth values to their component parts

Equivocation, fallacy of. The logical error of using a key term in an argument in two different senses

Essence. The set of properties that characterize something as the type of thing it uniquely is and that is necessary for it to be that sort of thing, as opposed to its accidents

Ethics (from the Greek *ethos*, meaning custom). Moral philosophy, that area of philosophy that studies value judgments regarding "good" and "evil," "right" and "wrong," and obligation

Evil, problem of. The puzzle as to how a perfect (e.g., omnipotent, omniscient, and infinitely good) God can be compatible with the reality of evil in the world

Excluded middle, law or **principle of**. A basic law of Aristotelian logic asserting the truth of the disjunction of any (significant) proposition together with its negation (e.g., there either is or is not a one-hundred-year-old philosopher now teaching somewhere in the United States)

Exhaustive alternatives. Two possiblities that are so related that no third alternative is possible (e.g., either living or dead)

Existential (from the Latin *existere*, meaning to stand out). Having to do with what exists; existentialists relate what exists to the dynamic reality of consciousness

Existential (or **particular) proposition**. A proposition that asserts something that holds for at least one (applicable) individual or thing

Existentialism. A philosophical movement that began in the middle of the nineteenth century and became popular in the twentieth, teaching that human consciousness is individual, is free rather than being determined by some alleged common essence, and is a source of values

Extension. The essential attribute of all bodies whereby they occupy some expanse of physical space (no matter how small)

Facticity. In Sartre, the totality of facts about a person that transcend his or her freedom

Faculty. An ability, capacity, or power, as of the mind, or of the soul, or of the body

Fallacy. An error in reasoning, such that the conclusion of an argument does not logically follow from its premises; a formal fallacy renders deductive arguments invalid, while an informal fallacy is psychologically tricky because of irrelevance, ambiguity, emotional appeals, etc.

False analogy, fallacy of. A fallacy that can arise when similarities that are observed are tangential rather than essential and/or when crucial dissimilarities are overlooked or ignored

False dilemma (or bifurcation). The fallacy of presuming that an either-or distinction is exhaustive (and/or mutually exclusive) when other alternatives exist

Fideism (from the Latin *fides*, meaning faith). The view that religious truth must be accepted purely on faith rather than justified by reason

Foreknowledge. Knowledge, traditionally attributed to God, of that which is yet to be

For-itself. Sartre's term (*pour-soi*) for personal consciousness, that reality which exists as free and is radically individual and responsible, as opposed to all other reality, which he calls "in-itself" (*en-soi*); for Hegel, "for itself" refers to reality as it is determined by its relationships

Form. In Plato, an immaterial, immutable, independently existing, eternal entity, in which particular things of our world may participate, thus deriving their natures; in Aristotle, form is the essential principle in matter making it the sort of thing it is; in Kant, the *a priori* element in experience whereby the data of sensible intuition are structurally organized by the mind

Fundamental project (or **original choice**). In Sartre, a basic way of existing, freely chosen by consciousness, from which one's everyday actions and reactions stem

Generalization. An inductive inference that what is true (or false) of some observed individuals is probably also true (or false) of others that have not yet been observed

Geocentrism (from the Greek *geo*, meaning Earth, and *kentrikos*, meaning of the center). The theory of Ptolemy that our Earth is the fixed center of the universe with all other heavenly bodies, including the Sun, moving around it, as opposed to heliocentrism

Gnosticism (from the Greek *gnosis*, meaning knowledge). A movement, originating in Hellenistic times, that became popular among early Christian heretical sects, associating the material world with evil, claiming that Christ was noncorporeal, and viewing salvation as attainable through esoteric knowledge of spiritual truth rather than through ordinary faith

Good will. Generally (as in Augustine), the desire to live virtuous lives; but, more specifically (as in Kant who considers good will to be the only intrinsic, unqualified good), the will to do our duty out of a rational sense of duty

Hedonism (from the Greek *hedone*, meaning pleasure). The theory that pleasure is in fact (psychological hedonism) and/or should be in principle (ethical hedonism) our ultimate good

Heliocentrism (from the Greek *helios*, meaning Sun, and *kentrikos*, meaning of the center). The theory of Copernicus that the Sun is the center of our planetary system with the Earth revolving around it, as opposed to geocentrism

Hellenic (from the Greek *Hellen*, meaning a Greek). Pertaining to the ancient Greeks and their culture in a pure, undiluted form, prior to the death of Alexander the Great in 323 B.C., as opposed to Hellenistic

Hellenistic (from the Greek *Hellen*, meaning a Greek). Pertaining to the ancient Greeks and their culture, following the death of Alexander the Great in 323 B.C., and to Greek influences which were adopted by, and grafted onto, other cultures, such as that of Rome

Heteronomy (from the Greek *heteronomos*, meaning other law). The condition of being under the control of desires, inclinations, other people, or anything beyond one's rational will (in Kant, contrasted with *autonomy*)

Humanism. Any view (e.g., in James or Sartre) emphasizing the value and dignity of human individuals

Hylomorphism (from the Greek *hule*, meaning matter, and *morphe*, meaning form). The theory (e.g., of Aristotle and Aquinas) that everything in our world is composed of matter and form united together

Hypothesis (from the Greek *hupothesis*, meaning suggestion or supposition). An assertion that something may be the case; a proposition assumed as a basis for reasoning, argument, or action

Hypothetical argument. A valid form of inference derived from at least one hypothetical, or conditional (e.g., if-then), premise

Hypothetical syllogism. A syllogism of the form $((p \rightarrow q) \wedge (q \rightarrow r)) \rightarrow (p \rightarrow r)$ that infers one implication from two others

Idealism. The philosophical theory that reality is ultimately mental or spiritual in its nature and/or its origins (metaphysical idealism) or that we can only know minds and their ideas (epistemological idealism)

Identity. The quality of remaining the same or the condition of two things being the same; in Aristotelian logic, the law of identity maintains that everything is what it is and cannot simultaneously be something other than what it is; for every proposition p, p is equivalent to p

Immanence. Presence in something else, inherence, as opposed to transcendence; for example, the God of panentheism is immanent in the things of this world

Immortality. The unending existence of a soul or spirit, once it has begun to be

Implication (or **conditional**). That which necessarily follows from something else; in logic, a proposition of the form, "if p, then q," which is true except when p, the antecedent, is true and q, the consequent, is false

Inconsistency. A logical conflict between two statements, such that one of them must be false if the other is true

Incontinence (from the Latin *incontinens*, meaning unrestrained). A lack of moral self-restraint (identified by Aristotle with weakness of will)

Induction. Reasoning that takes the form of a probability argument, deriving a conclusion from the premise(s) as more or less likely, rather than as certain, as opposed to deduction

Inference. A process of deductive or inductive reasoning from one or more statements, called premises, to another, called the conclusion

Infinite (from the Latin *infinitus*, meaning unlimited). Unbounded, without any limits (often said of God)

In-itself. Sartre's term (*en-soi*) for all reality that is not conscious, free, and responsible for its own actions, as opposed to "for-itself" (*pour-soi*); for Hegel, "in itself" refers to reality in its immediacy, apart from any relationships

Innate (from the Latin *innatus*, meaning inborn). Inborn, not derived from sense experience; Plato and Descartes believe we have some innate ideas, whereas empiricists deny them

Interactionism. The theory (e.g., of Descartes) that physical bodies and nonphysical minds causally affect each other in human nature, despite their essential differences

Intrinsic. In itself, for its own sake, rather than as a means to something else, or instrumental; a different meaning is inherent or essential, as opposed to extrinsic or accidental

Invalid argument. In deductive reasoning, an argument that is such that for some assignment of truth values, the premises are all true, yet the conclusion is false

Knowledge. Belief that is both true and justifiably held to be true (although some philosophers criticize and deny this traditional analysis)

Laissez-faire (literally, in French, allow to do). An economic theory, associated with Adam Smith, that government should generally not interfere in the competitive activities of its citizens but should allow free enterprise; loosely, noninterference

Liberalism (from the Latin *liber*, meaning free). A political ideology committed to personal freedom and tending to promote (nonrevolutionary) progress and reform of the existing order (often opposed to conservatism)

Logic (from the Greek *logos*, meaning reasoning). The systematic study of reasoning and argumentation, often divided into deductive (or formal) logic vs. inductive (or informal) logic

Logical positivism. A twentieth-century philosophical movement that began in the 1920s and flourished until the 1950s, which holds that any empirical statement must be verifiable (or, sometimes, falsifiable), at least in principle, in order to be cognitively meaningful; this renders metaphysical (and theological) utterances literally nonsensical and reduces value (including ethical) statements to expressions of emotional preferences

Manicheanism. The teaching of Mani, a third century A.D. religious leader who tried to synthesize Christianity and Zoroastrianism, of the dualistic gnostic doctrine that

there is a God of light and goodness and an equally powerful principle of darkness and evil, which are at war in human nature

Marxism. A political and economic ideology, stemming from the ideas of Marx and Engels, calling for a revolutionary class struggle designed to overthrow the system of capitalism, move us through socialism, and achieve a communist society

Materialism. The theory (e.g., of Hobbes) that all reality is ultimately physical and that whatever we may regard as mental or spiritual is actually only an expression of some fundamentally material being

Maxim. In Kant, a subjective principle of will that can motivate action; more loosely, a general truth or rule of conduct

Mean. An intermediate point between undesirable extremes of excess and deficiency, to be determined by reason; Aristotle identifies moral virtue with such a desirable middle ground

Medieval (from the Latin *medium aevum*, meaning the middle age). Of or pertaining to the Middle Ages

Meliorism (from the Latin *melior*, meaning better). In James, the view that the world, however good or evil it may be, can become better if we freely act to help improve it

Metaphysics (from the Greek *meta*, meaning after, and *phusika*, meaning Physics; we think the word derives from the editorial placement of Aristotle's works on this subject after his writings on physics; we can think of it as "beyond the physical"). That area of philosophy that studies the nature of ultimate reality and the fundamental structures of being

Metempsychosis (or *reincarnation*) (from the Greek *meta*, meaning changed, *en*, meaning in, and *psukhe*, meaning soul). The passage of a soul, after bodily death, into a different body

Middle Ages. That period of Western history between antiquity and the Renaissance—i.e., from the late fourth or early fifth century A.D. to the end of the fourteenth century

Mind. Individual (or cosmic) consciousness; a psychological self or soul (or an intellectual aspect of the self or soul)

Mind-body problem. A philosophical puzzle as to how the physical body and the nonphysical mind are related in human nature; this problem was dramatically delineated by Descartes

Modernity (or *modernism*). That period of Western history extending from the beginning of the seventeenth century; when contrasted with contemporary times, modernity ends early in the twentieth century

Modus ponens (from the Latin *modus*, meaning manner,

and *ponens*, meaning asserting). *See* Affirmed antecedent argument

Modus tollens (from the Latin *modus*, meaning manner, and *tollens*, meaning denying). *See* Denied consequent argument

Monarchy (from the Greek *monarkhia*, meaning the rule of one). Government by a single person, such as an emperor or a queen

Monasticism. A movement in which people withdrew from the secular world to live in religious communities, under vows, such as those of obedience, chastity, and poverty

Monism (from the Greek *monos*, meaning alone or single). The view that ultimately only one type of substance or only one numerical being is real; in the first sense, Hobbes's materialism is monistic, whereas Hegel's idealism is monistic in the second sense

Monotheism (from the Greek *monos,* meaning single, and *theos*, meaning God). The belief or doctrine that one God exists, as opposed to polytheism

Moral argument. In Kant, the postulation of God as practically necessitated by our moral consciousness

Multiple-valued logical systems. Systems of (propositional) logic with more than two truth values

Mutually exclusive alternatives. Two possibilities that cannot simultaneously hold true (e.g., either frail or robust); the component propositions of *p* or (exclusive sense) *q* (i.e., $p \veebar q$)

Mystery. A doctrine, usually associated with religious truth, that defies complete rational understanding

Naturalism. The view that everything can, at least in theory, be explained in terms of natural realities, their actions, and their interrelationships, as opposed to supernaturalism

Natural law. The theory (found in ancient Stoics and commonly associated with Aquinas and scholasticism) that the nature of things (often seen as grounded in the will of God) determines an objective set of rationally intelligible principles, governing all legitimate action

Natural selection. The Darwinian principle that organisms with heritable variations that are better adapted to their environment are more likely to survive and successfully propagate

Necessary and sufficient condition. For propositions *p* and *q*, when *p* is both a necessary condition for *q* and a sufficient condition for *q*; i.e., when both implications $p \rightarrow q$ and $q \rightarrow p$ are true

Necessary condition. That without which something else could not be or occur; for example, the presence of oxygen is a necessary condition for human respiration; in logic, with reference to an implication, "if *p*, then *q*," *q* is a necessary condition for *p*

Necessity. That which could not be otherwise than it is, as opposed to contingency

Negation. Generally, a denial; in logic, the claim or assertion that a proposition is false, so that a given proposition and its negation have opposite truth values

Neoplatonism. A philosophical movement in which Plotinus was prominent, based on Platonic ideas, beginning in Alexandria in the second century A.D. and extending to at least the fifth century

Nihilation (from the Latin *nihil*, meaning nothing). In Sartre, the denial by consciousness of what is other than itself or even of its own facticity

Noema (from the Greek *noema*, meaning a thought). In phenomenology, the sense or object of an act of intentional consciousness

Noetic (from the Greek *noetikos*, meaning intellectual). Cognitive, having to do with the rational activity of intellect

Nominalism (from the Latin *nominalis*, meaning of a name). The theory (as in Hobbes) that only particulars exist and that the only universals are names, the products of human language

Noncontradiction, law or **principle of**. The Aristotelian law of thought that no proposition (or statement) and its negation (or denial) can both be true of the same thing(s) at the same time in the same respect

Noumenon (plural, **noumena**). In Kant, a rational idea, transcending all possible experience, of a thing-in-itself, as the unknowable ground of phenomenal appearances

Ockham's razor (principle of parsimony). The principle that, other things being equal, a simpler explanation is preferable to one that is more complex, that explanatory entities should not be multiplied needlessly

Oligarchy (from the Greek *oligarkhia*, meaning rule of the few). Government by a small group of people; when these people must be wealthy, it is a plutocracy

Ontological argument. An *a priori* argument purporting to deduce the necessary existence of God from the very idea of God as an infinitely perfect Being; though Kant gave it this name, the argument originated in the Middle Ages and was used by Descartes

Ontology (from the Greek *onta*, meaning really existing things, and *logos*, meaning an account). The study of being; that branch of metaphysics which speculates about the essential characteristics of Being as such, as opposed to the study of particular beings

"Or," exclusive sense. The use of "or" in "*p* or *q*" that allows exactly one of the propositions *p*, *q* to be true

"Or," inclusive sense. The use of "or" in "*p* or *q*" that allows at least one of the propositions *p*, *q* to be true

Original sin. In theology, the tendency to commit evil

supposedly innate in all humans, as inherited from Adam, the first man, who deliberately disobeyed the manifest will of God

Over-beliefs. In James, those religious beliefs a person holds over and above the core beliefs common to religions generally; for example, a Christian might subscribe to the over-belief that Jesus Christ was literally and uniquely God, while an Orthodox Jew would not

Panentheism (from the Greek *pan*, meaning all, *en*, meaning in, and *theos*, meaning God). The view that God is immanent in the world without being simply identical with the world (as in pantheism)

Pantheism (from the Greek *pan*, meaning all, and *theos*, meaning God). The view that God and the world are simply identical, with individual things being mere modifications, moments, or phenomenal appearances of God and God being absolutely immanent without transcending the world in any respect

Paradox (from the Greek *paradoxos*, meaning contrary to opinion). A seemingly absurd or self-contradictory view, often based on apparently sound reasoning from plausible assumptions (an ancient example was the saying of the Cretan Epimenides that all Cretans always lie)

Paralogism (from the Greek *paralogos*, meaning contrary to reason). In Kant, any of four fallacious arguments meant to prove something about the nature of the soul or pure ego

Pauline principle. In moral theology, the principle, associated with the apostle Paul (*Romans* 3:8), that no end, regardless how good it may be, can justify an evil means

Perfect duty. From Kant on, a moral obligation allegedly permitting no exceptions in the interest of inclinations, as opposed to an imperfect duty, which allows some discretionary choosing, for example, as to when or towards whom the duty will be fulfilled

Phenomenalism. The view (as in Hume) that we can only be aware of appearances or sense data and never of things-in-themselves; this leads some phenomenalists (like Mill) to conceive of physical objects, such as sticks and stones, as mere sets of appearances or enduring possibilities of sensation

Phenomenology. Broadly, the study of appearances providing the content for all empirical knowledge; in Hegel, it is the study of the mind by way of the hierarchy of phenomena it considers; in the twentieth century, it is a philosophical movement (from Husserl and including Sartre) which uses introspective analysis to describe in depth the various forms of intentional consciousness

Phenomenon. Generally, an object of experience; more specifically, an appearance or object of perception; in Kant, opposed to noumenon

Philosophes (literally, in French, philosophers). The eighteenth-century philosophical thinkers of the French Enlightenment, including Voltaire, Condorcet, and the editors of the great *Encyclopedia* (Diderot and d'Alembert)

Philosophy (from the Greek *philosophos*, meaning loving wisdom). The most general systematic rational inquiry; philosophers disagree about its proper definition, but the one used here is critical reflection on basic concepts, assumptions, and principles related to any areas of experience and/or reality

Physicotheology. Kant's name for that branch of philosophical theology that argues from design to prove God's existence

Platonism. The idealistic and dualistic philosophy associated with Plato, especially as it affirms the transcendent reality of eternal, ideal forms, accessible to reason alone, and regards the phenomena of the spatio-temporal, sensible world as derivative and transitory

Pluralism. The view (as in James) that reality comprises many distinct substances or kinds of substance (vs. dualism and monism)

Plutocracy (from the Greek *ploutokratia*, meaning rule of the rich). A special sort of oligarchy, in which wealthy people govern

Polis. A city-state, as in ancient Greece

Polity (from the Greek *politeia*, meaning government or constitution). Government ordained to the common good and administered by many citizens; Aristotle identifies it with the rule of the middle class and sees democracy as its perverted form

Postulate (from the Latin *postulare*, meaning to demand). An indemonstrable rational hypothesis used as a fundamental assumption of a system of thought; in Kant, freedom, God, and immortality are the three postulates of practical reason demanded by morality

Potentiality. The capacity of a thing to undergo change or become different; in Aristotle, opposed to actuality

Pragmatism (from the Greek *pragma*, meaning deed or action). A philosophical movement of the late nineteenth and twentieth centuries (beginning with Peirce and popularized by James), emphasizing the practical usefulness of ideas and beliefs as the criterion of their meaning and truth

Praxis (from the Greek *prassein*, meaning to do or practice). Practical human conduct; in Marx, it means a synthesis of theory and practice

Predeterminism. The theory that every event is necessitated according to fixed causal laws; fatalism adds to this the idea that nothing we can do will affect the outcome that is determined; the theological view of predestination identifies God's will as the original source of all predeterminism

Premise. In an argument, a proposition or statement that is used to provide support for the conclusion

Prescriptive. Having to do with what ought to be, as opposed to descriptive, which concerns what actually is

Presupposition. An assumption, especially of an argument

Prima facie (literally, in Latin, at first appearance). What initially or ordinarily appears to be the case

Principle of double effect. The view (often associated with Aquinas) that an act which produces both good and bad results can be morally permissible if such conditions as the following are met:

1. The action is not intrinsically evil.
2. The good effect and not the bad effect is intended.
3. The action causes both results (rather than either causing the other).
4. The good effect cannot be achieved without the bad.
5. The good effect provides a sufficient reason to permit the bad one.

For example, when a surgeon amputates her patient's gangrenous arm, it is permissible because:

1. There is nothing intrinsically wrong in the surgical act.
2. She intends to save his life rather than to leave him disabled.
3. The act of amputation both saves his life and leaves him disabled.
4. She cannot save his life (in those circumstances) without disabling him.
5. The good of saving his life proportionately outweighs the bad effect of leaving him disabled.

Probability argument. Any argument (such as an inductive one) designed to establish its conclusion as more or less likely or probable, rather than as certain

Process-of-elimination argument. An argument of the form, "if both *p* or *q* and not *p*, then *q*," i.e.,

$$((p \lor q) \land \sim p) \to q$$

Process thought/philosophy/theology. A contemporary theory analyzing reality in terms of dynamically changing events rather than static substances; Hegel seems to anticipate this movement

Proof. Evidence establishing a fact or an argument establishing a conclusion; often identified with a demonstration, as leading to certainty (though Hume distinguishes a proof as an argument from experience)

Proposition (from the Latin *propositio*, meaning what is put forward or proposed). A statement or what is expressed by a declarative sentence relating a subject term to a predicate term in such a way that the proposition as a whole can be regarded as true or false; an example of a proposition is provided by the sentence, "The book is on the table."

Quietism. In twentieth-century thought (e.g., both James and Sartre), a negative term for a passive lack of commitment

Rationalism. The philosophical theory that some synthetic or existential knowledge is derived from reason rather than from sense experience, as opposed to empiricism

Realism. Generally, the view that some condition or sort of entity exists independently of the human mind; commonsense realism (condemned by its critics as "naive realism") holds that perception normally grasps external objects directly or reveals them to us as they really are

Reason. Generally, the intellect, the capacity for abstract thought, logical inference, and comprehension; in Kant, reason is the intellectual faculty that engages in metaphysical speculation, as opposed to understanding, which is the intellectual faculty capable of knowledge; philosophers (such as Aristotle and Kant) distinguish between theoretical reason, which pursues knowledge, and practical reason, whose deliberations are oriented to action

Reductionism. The view that all reality and/or value can (and should) be resolved into one sort of thing; the materialist Hobbes, for example, reduces all mental activity to physical processes

Refutation. The disproof of an argument or the demonstration that a position is false or erroneous

Regulative (from the Latin *regula*, meaning a rule). Serving the heuristic function of guiding further thought and action, as opposed (in Kant) to the constitutive function of ideas that can lead to knowledge

Reincarnation. *See* Metempsychosis

Relativism. The view that truths and values vary among different individuals and/or cultures rather than being absolutely binding; thus, Protagoras the Sophist espoused relativism in proclaiming that "man is the measure of all things"

Reliable (or **strong**) **argument**. An inductive argument in which the premises provide adequate evidence to justify the conclusion to the degree of probability indicated

Renaissance (from the French *renaistre*, meaning to be born again). That period of Western Civilization, especially in fifteenth and sixteenth century Europe, marked by a "rebirth" of ideas and humanistic learning

Republic (from the Latin *respublica*, meaning public affairs or commonwealth). Any nonautocratic political order; a constitutional government, especially a democratic one

Resurrection (from the Latin *resurrectus*, meaning risen again). Returning to life after being dead

Rule utilitarianism. An ethical theory that morally evaluates actions in terms of the extent to which they conform to rules that are justified by the principle of utility, as opposed to act utilitarianism, which evaluates actions in terms of the extent to which their own consequences are justified by the principle of utility and which views rules merely as normative guidelines

Scepticism (*or **skepticism***) (from the Greek *skeptesthai*, meaning to consider or examine). The doctrine that knowledge is unobtainable, in some or even all areas of inquiry; many of the greatest philosophers (e.g., Plato, Augustine, Descartes, and Kant) try to refute scepticism

Scholasticism (from the Greek *skholastikos*, meaning learned). The educational tradition (both philosophical and theological) of medieval universities, often as influenced by Aristotle, its masters being scholastics or "schoolmen"

Self-evident. So obviously true (or false) as to require no justification (or refutation)

Social contract. An original agreement whereby individuals allegedly united to form society and to constitute the state; some philosophers (e.g., Hobbes) subscribe to this manner of justifying political obligation, whereas others (e.g., Hume and Mill) reject it

Socialism. A socio-economic system in which the society as a whole owns the means of producing and distributing goods; in Marxist theory socialism is a transitional state between the overthrow of capitalism and the achievement of the classless society of communism

Solipsism (from the Latin *solus ipse*, meaning oneself alone). The theory that all that is real is one's own mind and its states of consciousness (metaphysical solipsism) or that the only things one can know to exist are one's own mind and its states of consciousness (epistemological solipsism)

Sophists (from the Greek *sophos*, meaning wise). Itinerant teachers of ancient Greece (such as Protagoras and Gorgias), who trained young men for political life but were often regarded as eloquent charlatans, propounding relativism and scepticism; we speak of a sophism as a specious, deceptive argument and condemn sophistry, or disputation pursued merely for its own sake

Soul. Broadly, the principle of life in a living thing; more commonly, a spiritual substance that is or can be the subject of conscious thought

Sound argument. A deductive argument that is valid and all of whose premises are true

State of nature. The hypothetical condition of humans had they not entered into society by means of a social contract; Hobbes describes it graphically as a war of all against

all, in which life would be "solitary, poor, nasty, brutish, and short"; Rawls's "original position" is its analogue in contemporary theory

Stoicism (from the Greek *stoa*, meaning a portico or covered porch). An ancient (Greek and Roman) philosophical movement, emphasizing rational will, mastery of one's passions, doing one's duty, and detachment from external things over which one has no ultimate control

Subjectivism. The theory that all knowledge and/or value is relative to an individual subject's mental states or experiences, as opposed to objectivism

Sublation. In dialectical (e.g., Hegelian) philosophy, the resolution of opposites, or antitheses, into a higher unity, or synthesis; Hegel's word for it, *Aufhebung*, simultaneously means cancellation, preservation, and elevation

Substance (from the Latin *substare*, meaning to stand under). An independently existing entity, supporting, or providing the foundation for, its phenomenal appearances and properties

Sufficient condition. That which is adequate to bring about something else, so that whenever the first occurs, the second will as well; for example, a pet's being a dog is a sufficient condition for its also being a mammal; in logic, with reference to an implication, "if p, then q," p is a sufficient condition for q

Summum bonum. Literally, in Latin, the greatest good

Supersensible. In Kant, beyond the physical realm of possible sense experiences

Syllogism (from the Greek *syllogismos*, meaning a reckoning together). A deductive argument with two premises and a conclusion

Synthetic. Combining elements together to form a greater whole; a synthetic judgment (since Kant) is one whose predicate term adds new information not even implicitly contained in its subject (e.g., "All bachelors are frivolous"), as opposed to an analytic one; in dialectical reasoning (as in Hegel), synthesis is the higher unity of opposed antitheses

Tabula rasa (literally, in Latin, scraped or shaved tablet, or, more loosely, a blank slate). A metaphor for the human mind as devoid of ideas prior to sense experience, as opposed to the doctrine of innate ideas

Tautology (from the Greek *tautologos*, meaning repeating what has been said). Loosely, a repetition of the same ideas, though, perhaps, in different words (e.g., "visible to the eye"); in logic, a proposition that is always true for every possible assignment of truth values to its component parts

Teleology (from the Greek *telos*, meaning end, and *logos*, meaning an account). The study of reality as oriented towards natural ends or, in rational beings, as having purposes; Aristotle and Aquinas are teleological thinkers

Theism (from the Greek *theos*, meaning God). Belief in the existence of God or gods

Theocentrism. The view that reality is God-centered; medieval thought is distinctly theocentric, as Enlightenment thought is not

Theodicy (from the Greek *theos*, meaning God, and *dike*, meaning justice or right). The attempt to justify the goodness and justice of God in light of the reality of evil, to solve the problem of evil rationally

Theology (from the Greek *theos*, meaning God, and *logos*, meaning an account). The study of God; we can distinguish between rational theology, which is part of philosophy, and revealed theology, which is not, because the latter is based on revelation

Thesis (from the Greek *tithenai*, to put or place). An idea formulated or a proposition put forward; in Hegelian thought, this represents the first phase of a dialectical process, in which that thesis is placed in opposition to another (its antithesis), leading to a higher unity of the two (their synthesis)

Things-in-themselves. Independent realities transcending the realm of phenomenal appearances; for Kant, they are humanly unknowable, though we have (noumenal) ideas of them

Timocracy. In Plato, government by those most honored, as for courage and military prowess

Transcendence. That which is higher than or beyond the realm of natural experience, as opposed to immanence—e.g., the God of deism is transcendent; for Kantians, that which is transcendent is necessarily unknowable

Transcendental. In Kant, having to do with the *a priori* necessary conditions of organized experience (e.g., time and space), of knowledge (e.g., the concepts of the understanding), of metaphysical speculation (the ideas of pure reason), and so forth

Triadic. Threefold or pertaining to a triad, or group of three (things, properties, ideas, etc.)

Truth table. A schematic device for analyzing logically related truth values in (propositional) logic

Truth values. Truth or falsehood, as they apply to propositions

Two-valued logical system. The system of (propositional) logic with two truth values

Tyranny (from the Greek *turannos*, meaning tyrant). The rule of one who assumes absolute political power

Universal. As an adjective, pertaining to an entire class or all-encompassing rather than partial or particular; as a noun, a general concept (such as "tree") common to a number of particulars (such as pines, maples, oaks, etc.) or an abstract idea (such as justice, truth, or beauty); for Platonists, the Forms are universal entities

Universalizable. Able to be reasonably applied to all actions of a particular sort in morally similar circumstances; Kant uses universalizability as a criterion for testing whether the maxim of an action is morally justifiable

Universal proposition. A proposition that asserts something that holds for all (applicable) individuals or things

Universe. In logic, the set of individuals or things to which a proposition applies

Unreliable (or weak) argument. An inductive argument in which the premises do not provide sufficient evidence to justify the conclusion to the degree of probability indicated

Utilitarianism. The ethical theory (started by Bentham and popularized by Mill) that moral value is a function of good and bad consequences for the people who will be affected by an action; for hedonistic utilitarians (e.g., Bentham and Mill), happiness and unhappiness are measured in terms of pleasure and pain

Valid argument. In deductive reasoning, an argument that is such that whenever the premises are all true, the conclusion must also be true

Validity. Technically, the quality of a deductive argument, such that its conclusion necessarily follows from the conjunction of its premises; loosely, cogency

Vice. A morally reprehensible or evil habit or quality of character, as opposed to a virtue

Vicious circularity. A property of argumentation whose circular reasoning is sufficiently pernicious to render the entire argument worthless (e.g., "God must exist because the Bible says God exists, the Bible is the word of God, and God cannot lie")

Virtue (from the Latin *virtus*, meaning excellence or manliness). A morally excellent or good habit or quality of character, as opposed to a vice

Voluntarism (from the Latin *voluntas*, meaning will). The doctrine that will is the fundamental principle in human experience and/or in all of reality

Voluntary. Resulting from free choice rather than constrained or extrinsically determined, as opposed to both involuntary and nonvoluntary

Index

《 》 》

THE WESTERN WORLD	PHILOSOPHY	OTHER DISCIPLINES
Catherine the Great, Empress of Russia, 1762–96	*An Enquiry concerning Human Understanding*, 1748	Leonhard Euler, mathematician, 1707–83
Stamp Act, 1765	*An Enquiry concerning the Principles of Morals*, 1751	Sir Joshua Reynolds, painter, 1723–92
Partitions of Poland, 1772, 1793, 1795	*Dialogues concerning Natural Religion*, 1779	Edmund Burke, statesman, author, 1729–97
Boston Tea Party, 1773	Jean-Jacques Rousseau, 1712–78	Franz Joseph Haydn, composer, 1732–1809
American Revolutionary War, 1775–83	*The Social Contract*, 1762	James Watt, engineer, inventor, 1736–1819
Declaration of Independence, 1776	Denis Diderot, 1713–84	Edward Gibbon, historian, 1737–94
Battle of Yorktown: Colonial army defeats British, 1781	Jean Le Rond d'Alembert, 1717–83	Thomas Paine, patriot, author, 1737–1809
Articles of Confederation, 1781	Paul Dietrich d'Holbach, 1723–89	Antoine Lavoisier, chemist, 1743–94
Treaty of Paris: Thirteen Colonies recognized as independent, 1783	Adam Smith, 1723–90	Jacques Louis David, painter, 1748–1825
U.S. Constitution, 1788	Immanuel Kant, 1724–1804	Pierre Laplace, astronomer, mathematician, 1749–1827
George Washington first American President, 1789	*Critique of Pure Reason*, 1781	British Museum founded, 1753
Storming of the Bastille, 1789	*Prolegomena to Any Future Metaphysics*, 1783	Gilbert Stuart, painter, 1755–1828
Declaration of the Rights of Man and Citizen, 1789	*Grounding for the Metaphysics of Morals*, 1785	Wolfgang Amadeus Mozart, composer, 1756–91
King Louis XVI and Queen Marie Antoinette guillotined, 1793	*Critique of Practical Reason*, 1788	William Blake, poet, engraver, 1757–1827
Reign of Terror, 1793–94	*Critique of Judgment*, 1790	Robert Burns, poet, 1759–96
Maximilien Robespierre guillotined, 1794	Moses Mendelssohn, 1729–86	Mary Wollstonecraft, author, feminist, 1759–97
New French constitution protects citizens' rights and establishes a "Directory" of five leaders, 1795	Marquis de Condorcet, 1743–94	Encyclopedia Britannica, 1st edition, 1768
	William Paley, 1743–1805	Rosetta Stone discovered by Napoleon's troops, 1799
XYZ affair, 1797	Johann Gottfried von Herder, 1744–1803	
Alien and Sedition Acts, 1798	Jeremy Bentham, 1748–1832	
	An Introduction to the Principles of Morals and Legislation, 1789	
	Johann Gottlieb Fichte, 1762–1814	
	The Vocation of Man, 1800	

The Age of Ideology

Napoleon overthrows French government, 1799	Friedrich Schliermacher, 1768–1834	Johann Wolfgang von Goethe, poet, dramatist, 1749–1832
Louisiana Purchase, 1803	Georg Wilhelm Friedrich Hegel, 1770–1831	Ludwig van Beethoven, composer, 1770–1827
Lewis and Clark Expedition to the Pacific Coast, 1804–6	*Phenomenology of Spirit*, 1807	Jane Austen, novelist, 1775–1817
Napoleon, Emperor of France; Napoleonic Code, 1804	*Science of Logic*, 1812–16	Joseph Mallord William Turner, painter, 1775–1851
	Encyclopedia of the Philosophical Sciences, 1817	

THE WESTERN WORLD	PHILOSOPHY	OTHER DISCIPLINES
Napoleon invades Russia; loses half of his army, 1812	*Philosophy of Right*, 1820 *Philosophy of History*, 1832	C. F. Gauss, mathematician, astronomer, 1777–1855
U.S. renews warfare with England, 1812–14	James Mill, 1773–1836	Michael Faraday, physicist, chemist, 1791–1867
Napoleon exiled to Elba, 1814	Friedrich Wilhelm Joseph von Schelling, 1775–1854	Charles Darwin, naturalist, 1809–82
Battle of Waterloo; Napoleon permanently banished, 1815	William Hamilton, 1788–1856	Alfred Lord Tennyson, poet, 1809–92
Congress of Vienna, 1815	Arthur Schopenhauer, 1788–1860	
Monroe Doctrine, 1823	William Whewell, 1794–1866	Dinosaur bones found, 1811
Jacksonian reforms, 1829–37	Auguste Comte, 1798–1857	Charles Dickens, novelist, 1812–70
July Revolution in France, 1830	Ludwig Feuerbach, 1804–72	George Eliot, novelist, 1819–80
Reform Bill in England, 1832	John Stuart Mill, 1806–73 *A System of Logic*, 1843	Herman Melville, novelist, 1819–91
Texas annexed by U.S., 1845	*On Liberty*, 1859 *Utilitarianism*, 1861	Fyodor Dostoevsky, novelist, 1821–81
Revolutions spread through Europe, 1848	*The Subjection of Women*, 1869 *Three Essays on Religion*, 1874	Gregor Johann Mendel, botanist, monk, 1822–84
Gold found in California, 1849	Søren A. Kierkegaard, 1813–55 *Concluding Unscientific Postscript*, 1846	Heinrich Schliemann, archaeologist, 1822–90
Louis Napoleon becomes Emperor of France, 1852	Charles Bernard Renouvier, 1815–1903	Leo Tolstoy, novelist, short-story writer, 1828–1910
Crimean War, 1854–56	Karl Marx, 1818–83 *Economic and Philosophical Manuscripts of 1844*	Johannes Brahms, composer, 1833–97
Italy becomes constitutional monarchy, 1861	Friedrich Engels, 1820–95	Mark Twain, author, humorist, 1835–1910
Serfdom abolished in Russia, 1861	Herbert Spencer, 1820–1903	Peter Ilyich Tchaikovsky, composer, 1840–93
American Civil War, 1861–65	Henry Sidgwick, 1838–1900	Thomas Edison, inventor, 1847–1931
Emancipation Proclamation, 1863	Friedrich Wilhelm Nietzsche, 1844–1900	
Second Reform Bill passed in England, 1867	*Beyond Good and Evil*, 1886	
Franco-Prussian War, 1870–71		

The Age of Analysis

Dreyfus Affair, 1894–1906	Charles Sanders Peirce, 1839–1914	Henrik Ibsen, dramatist, poet, 1826–1906
Spanish-American War, 1898	William James, 1842–1910 *The Principles of Psychology*, 1890	Auguste Rodin, sculptor, 1840–1917
First airplane flight, 1903	*The Will to Believe and Other Essays in Popular Philosophy*, 1897	Claude Monet, painter, 1840–1926
Russo-Japanese War, 1904–5	*Varieties of Religious Experience*, 1902	Thomas Hardy, novelist, poet, 1840–1928
Panama Canal opens, 1914	*Pragmatism*, 1907 *The Meaning of Truth*, 1909	Pierre Auguste Renoir, painter, 1841–1919
First World War, 1914–18	William K. Clifford, 1845–79	Henry James, novelist, critic, 1843–1916
Russian Revolution, 1917	Gottlob Frege, 1848–1925	
U.S. declares war on Germany, 1917		
Peace of Versailles, 1919		
League of Nations, 1919–46		